MEDIEVAL EUROPEAN COINAGE

MEDIEVAL EUROPEAN COINAGE

WITH A CATALOGUE OF THE COINS IN THE FITZWILLIAM MUSEUM, CAMBRIDGE

1 The Early Middle Ages (5th–10th centuries), *published 1986.*
2 Germany (I). Imperial and early ducal coinage. Western Germany.
3 Germany (II). North-eastern Germany.
4 Germany (III). Central and Southern Germany.
5 France. Royal and feudal.
6 Spain and Portugal. The Kingdom of Arles. Lorraine.
7 The Low Countries, *in preparation.*
8 The British Isles (I). 924–1279.
9 The British Isles (II). 1279–1509.
10 Scandinavia. Eastern Europe. Bohemia.
11 Hungary. The Balkans. The Crusader States.
12 Italy (I). Northern Italy.
13. Italy (II). Central and Southern Italy.

Prepared under the auspices of the British Academy

MEDIEVAL EUROPEAN COINAGE

WITH A CATALOGUE OF THE COINS IN
THE FITZWILLIAM MUSEUM, CAMBRIDGE

I *The Early Middle Ages*
(5th–10th centuries)

PHILIP GRIERSON

and

MARK BLACKBURN

The right of the University of Cambridge to print and sell all manner of books was granted by Henry VIII in 1534. The University has printed and published continuously since 1584.

CAMBRIDGE UNIVERSITY PRESS

Cambridge

London New York Port Chester

Melbourne Sydney

CAMBRIDGE UNIVERSITY PRESS
Cambridge, New York, Melbourne, Madrid, Cape Town, Singapore, São Paulo

Cambridge University Press
The Edinburgh Building, Cambridge CB2 2RU, UK

Published in the United States of America by Cambridge University Press, New York

www.cambridge.org
Information on this title: www.cambridge.org/9780521260091

First published 1986
Reprinted 1991
This digitally printed first paperback version (with corrections) 2006

A catalogue record for this publication is available from the British Library

Library of Congress Cataloguing in Publication data
Grierson, Philip
Medieval European coinage.
Bibliography.
Includes index.
Contents: I. The early Middle Ages (5th–10th centuries)
1. Coins, European–History–Collected works.
2. Coins, Medieval–Europe–History–Collected works.
3. Coins, European–Catalogs. 4. Coins, Medieval–Europe–Catalogs.
5. Coinage–Europe–History–collected
works. 6. Fitzwilliam Museum–Catalogs. I. Blackburn,
M. A. S. (Mark A. S.) II. Fitzwilliam Museum.
III. Title
CJ2464.G75 1985 737.494 85-13258

ISBN-13 978-0-521-26009-1 hardback
ISBN-10 0-521-26009-4 hardback

ISBN-13 978-0-521-03177-6 paperback
ISBN-10 0-521-03177-X paperback

The research for this volume was made possible by
a generous grant from the Leverhulme Trust. The cost of the photographs was
covered by a grant from the University of Cambridge.

FOREWORD

GRAHAM POLLARD

European coins have generally been collected on a national basis, and have been catalogued, when they have been catalogued at all, on the same basis. This is as true of most public collections as it is of those in private hands. The justification of the present catalogue is that the collection of medieval European coins in the Fitzwilliam Museum is one of the most representative in existence, having largely been put together by Professor Philip Grierson, a medieval historian by profession, with the object of providing scholars in Cambridge with a good general coverage of European coins struck between the fall of the Roman Empire and the Italian Renaissance. They have been on indefinite loan to the Museum since the early 1970s and are bequeathed to it in Professor Grierson's will, but for the present he retains their formal ownership, since this gives him greater freedom in disposing of particular specimens when there are opportunities of securing better ones.

Since the Museum already possessed a substantial English, Irish and Scottish collection (*c*. 3,000 coins), Professor Grierson's share in the final total (*c*. 19,000) consists mainly of coins struck on the continent of Europe and by the Latins in the Near East. His collection originally also included Byzantine coins, but in 1955, after having been appointed to the honorary post of Advisor in Byzantine Numismatics at the Dumbarton Oaks Center of Byzantine Studies in Washington, he ceased collecting these in order to avoid the creation of a conflict of interest. Such coins as were not already in the Dumbarton Oaks collection were acquired by the Center (1956) at an independent valuation; nearly a hundred coins, half of them gold, were presented to the Fitzwilliam Museum; and the remainder have been disposed of privately over the years by gift, exchange or sale. The Western coins now in the Museum (*c*. 16,000 coins) represent the essential part of his collection.

Professor Grierson initially intended simply to leave his collection to the Museum, where they would be permanently available to students, but its range and quality make its publication highly desirable. The project of which this is the first volume is the fruit of several years of discussion and planning by the British Academy Committee responsible for the publication of the *Sylloge of the Coins of the British Isles* in consultation with Professor Grierson. It is intended that he will be responsible for the publication as a whole, but the generosity of the Leverhulme Foundation has made possible the collaboration of Mr Mark Blackburn, who has already an established reputation in the field of Anglo-Saxon numismatics, as a Research Associate. The project has thus taken shape under the auspices of the British Academy, and the work is being published by the Cambridge University Press.

The form envisaged for the Catalogue is publication in what numismatists know as Sylloge form, with all the coins illustrated and summarily described, but it is expanded with accounts of the coinage of each state or mint and extensive bibliographies. This will put each group of coins into perspective and provide a series of standard reference works that will be useful to historians and not, as Sylloge volumes tend to be, intelligible only to numismatists. Although Professor Grierson published in 1976 a general descriptive work on medieval coins (Grierson 1976a) it was necessarily limited in scope, since it had to conform to the general plan of the series of which it formed a part. The high quality of its enlarged illustrations makes it admirably suited to the study of medieval coin types, but it is far from being the comprehensive guide to medieval coinage which is one of the major desiderata of numismatic literature. The present work, when it is complete, should provide such a guide.

The plan of the work envisages a preliminary volume on the coinage of what are conventionally termed the Dark Ages, before the state pattern of the later middle ages had taken shape, and twelve volumes covering the subsequent coinages of Latin Christendom on a regional basis. Details of these will be found facing the title page of this volume. Their size is determined by the number of coins (*c.* 1,500 coins on *c.* 70 plates) to be accommodated in each, and their grouping is roughly geographical. Even the somewhat incongruous grouping in Vol. 6 of the Iberian Peninsula with Lorraine and the Kingdom of Arles has a certain justification in the relationship of these three areas to France, though it was in fact determined by the numbers of coins for the three regions making up a volume of reasonable size. Volume 1, which contains preliminary information about the project and some account of the collection as a whole, is necessarily the first to appear, but the order of publication of the others will not necessarily conform to their numbering in the series. The next one to be published will be Volume 7, on the coinage of the Low Countries.

Two aspects of the publication, the omission of the coinage of the Byzantine Empire and the inclusion of Anglo-Saxon coinage, require a few words of explanation.

The coinage of the Byzantine Empire is of course medieval in date, but it is markedly different from that of Latin Christendom. The two evolved along different lines, and save in a few localities and periods there was little contact between them. They can be regarded as distinct, capable of being studied independently of each other, and in view of several recent publications of high quality on Byzantine coins there seemed no justification in adding to them. Although the number of Byzantine coins in the Fitzwilliam Museum is unusually large, owing to substantial benefactions by C. Davies Sherborn in 1939 and by the heirs of C. J. Bunn in 1950, they are mainly copper coins, with relatively few of gold or silver, and there has never been the same policy of systematically building it up into a representative collection as there has been for that of western Europe.

The Anglo-Saxon coins included in Vol. 1 and those intended to form part of Vol. 8 may seem at first sight a pointless duplication of the Anglo-Saxon material published in the first volume of the British Sylloge in 1958. But the Museum's holdings have been expanded since that time; much research has been done on the subject in the past 25 years and the arrangement can be improved; the change in plan allows the material to be presented in a form more useful to scholars who are not numismatic specialists; and its omission would leave a work intended to provide a general survey of the coinage of Latin Christendom lacking an essential section. It is also obviously desirable to take advantage of Mr Blackburn's expertise in the field. Scholars interested in the Museum's holdings of British Celtic coins, however, will still have to consult the volume of 1958, as for the time being will those working on later Anglo-Saxon coins.

The title to this publication implies that its contents are limited to coins in the Fitzwilliam Museum, whether they are actually its property or have been deposited there on indefinite loan by the colleges and by Professor Grierson. Scholars will naturally wish to know, however, what other material is available in Cambridge, and two colleges, Corpus Christi and Queens', which have retained their collections have kindly allowed the relevant material contained in these to be included in this catalogue. The same is also the case with the Museum of the Department of Archaeology and Anthropology, whose collections include a small group of Anglo-Saxon coins used for exhibition purposes which were overlooked when the Sylloge volume was published in 1958.

CONTENTS

PLATES

MAPS

TABLES

PREFACE

This is the first to appear of a projected work in thirteen volumes on medieval European coinage. The form adopted, that of regional surveys accompanied by a detailed catalogue of the Cambridge collections, is explained in Mr Pollard's Foreword, and the plan is set out in detail in the table facing the title-page.

The credit for initiating the project largely belongs to two scholars, Christopher Brooke and Graham Pollard, who, having urged its desirability on one of us over a period of many years, applied themselves enthusiastically to enlisting the support necessary for it to be realized. We are greatly indebted to the British Academy Committee for the Sylloge of Coins of the British Isles for having taken it under its wing, seen that a detailed plan was drawn up, and secured for it Academy approval. That it has finally got off the ground is due to the generosity of the Leverhulme Foundation in providing a grant to enable the second partner to devote himself full-time to the enterprise.

Where the University is concerned our basic debt is to the Fitzwilliam Museum Syndicate for the provision of a home for the Grierson collection and a pleasant office in which to work; to the staff of the Coin Room for assistance in many ways, not least for supplying the high quality photographs necessary for the plates; to the University Treasury for a generous grant from the Chest to cover the heavy cost of these in the early volumes; and to the University Press for undertaking the publication of a dauntingly expensive work. We are grateful to the Master and Fellows of the colleges which have deposited their collections in the Coin Room for allowing us to include the medieval coins in these, and to the Master and Fellows of Corpus Christi College and Queen's College, whose collections are not on deposit, for the same kindness.

It would be invidious to list here the many scholars who have assisted one or other of us with information and advice, but we would wish to acknowledge the contributions of contemporary scholars who, without having all been necessarily consulted in its course, have nonetheless by their recent publications made a significant contribution to the work. The Vandal section owes much to Cécile Morrisson and Mike Clover, the Visigothic section to the late George Miles, the Lombard section to the late Ernesto Bernareggi, the Merovingian and Carolingian sections to Jean Lafaurie, Peter Berghaus, and Françoise Dumas, the Anglo-Saxon and Anglo-Viking sections to Christopher Blunt, the late Michael Dolley, Ian Stewart, Michael Metcalf, Stewart Lyon and Hugh Pagan. Many scholars besides these have helped us with information, or in providing photocopies of articles not accessible to us in Cambridge, or in other ways – Claude Brenot, Hélène Huvelin, Gert Hatz, Peter Ilisch, Pierre Strauss, Elizabeth Pirie.

Andrew Oddy, of the British Museum Conservation Laboratory, has kindly made available the results of the specific gravity analyses of coins in the collection made in the early 1970s and has analysed for us subsequent acquisitions. Reginald and Marjorie Piggott have prepared the maps, Patricia McCullagh and Edna Pilmer have typed drafts and redrafts of our manuscript, and Ann Johnston and Virginia Catmur have eliminated the worst of its inconsistencies and made it ready for the printer. To all of these we are most grateful.

In preparing this volume we have worked in close collaboration and are jointly responsible for it as a whole. In so far as there has been a division of labour, the first of us has been primarily responsible for Chapters 1–7 and 9, the two appendices, and the section on Collectors, Donors and Dealers, while the second prepared Chapters 8 and 10, the Catalogue, and the Plates.

PHILIP GRIERSON
MARK BLACKBURN

ABBREVIATIONS

This list includes abbreviations used in the text and in the catalogue other than those which are defined at the head of the page on which they occur. Abbreviations of periodicals are given at the beginning of the Bibliography (below, p. 339).

acq.	acquired
ANS	American Numismatic Society
AS	Anglo-Saxon
B	Belfort 1892–5, see Bibliography
bibl.	bibliography
BM	British Museum, London
BMC with suffix	The appropriate volume of the *British Museum Catalogues* as follows: *BMC AS* (Anglo-Saxon), *BMC Byz* (Byzantine), *BMC RE* (Roman Empire), *BMC Vand* (Vandals, Ostrogoths and Lombards)
BN	Bibliothèque Nationale, Paris
bt	bought
c.	*circa*
Carol.	Carolingian
CCC	Corpus Christi College, Cambridge
CG	Continental Germanic
CMH	*Cambridge Medieval History*, see Bibliography
CNI	*Corpus Nummorum Italicorum*, see Bibliography
Cohen	Cohen 1880–92, see Bibliography
coll.	collection
d.	died
DAN	*Dark Age Numismatics*, see Grierson 1979a in Bibliography
dep.	deposited, deposed
descr.	described
DO	Dumbarton Oaks Center for Byzantine Studies, Washington
DOC	*Dumbarton Oaks Catalogue*, see Bibliography
ed.	editor(s)
edn	edition
emp.	emperor, empress
Eng.	English
ex	from (used in describing coin pedigrees)

ex.	exergue
fd	found
FM	Fitzwilliam Museum
Fr.	French
g	gram(s)
G	Gariel 1883–4, see Bibliography
Germ.	German
gr.	grain(s)
illus.	illustrated
incl.	includes (d)
It.	Italian
k.	king
l.	left
LRBC	*Late Roman Bronze Coinage*, see Hill *et al.* 1960 in Bibliography
MAA	Museum of Archaeology and Anthropology, Cambridge
Merov.	Merovingian
MG	Morrison and Grunthal 1967, see Bibliography
MGH	Monumenta Germaniae Historica
MG hoard	Inventory of coin hoards in MG, pp. 339ff.
MIB	*Moneta Imperii Byzantini*, see Hahn 1973–81 in Bibliography
mm	millimetre(s)
obv.	obverse
OE	Old English
ON	Old Norse
P	Prou 1892a (*Les monnaies mérovingiennes*) or 1896a (*Les monnaies carolingiennes*), see Bibliography, as the context requires
PG	Philip Grierson collection
pl(s).	plate(s)
PLRE	*Prosopography of the Later Roman Empire*, ed. A. H. M. Jones and others (Cambridge, 1971-)
prov.	provenance
P.-V.	Procès-Verbaux
QC	Queens' College, Cambridge
r.	right
ref(s).	reference(s)
repr.	reprint(ed)
rev.	reverse
RIC	*Roman Imperial Coinage*, see Bibliography
SCBI	*Sylloge of Coins of the British Isles*
SG	specific gravity
var.	variety
w.	with
wt	weight

NOTE ON SPELLING

The spelling of proper names is a problem in all historical works that cover, as this volume does, a number of countries and a long period of time. The simplistic counsel, that one should use 'original' forms and, in the case of place-names, the current spelling in the country where the places are situated, is often impossible to follow. For early medieval times names usually survive only as Latinized forms in a wide variety of spellings, and for modern times there are countries with two or more official forms of place-names of which none corresponds to those normally used in English. We have therefore adopted the commonsense solution of using whatever form and spelling is most familiar in accepted English usage, preferring Antwerp to Antwerpen or Anvers, Louis to Ludwig or Lodovico, Odo to Eudes, Milan to Milano, though it has to be recognized that such usages can change. A century ago one would have written Lewis and Mayence instead of Louis and Mainz.

Anglo-Saxon proper names are a special problem, partly because although they are usually preserved in the vernacular they may be spelled in several different ways, partly because such diphthongs and letter combinations as *æ*, *ea*, *œ*, *cg* and *ht* have largely disappeared from modern English usage. No completely consistent solution is possible. We have in general followed the spellings of Stenton's *Anglo-Saxon England* (even if this involves both Ecgfrith and Egbert), but *Æthel-* has been retained throughout, even for Æthelstan, and some spellings consistently used on the coins (Coenwulf, Ludica) have been preferred to those of the manuscript sources.

In a few cases we have allowed ourselves liberties. There seemed no point in retaining the customary final *s*, which is not now pronounced, in Marseille*s* and Lyon*s*, when its omission gives the correct French spelling. We have followed the example of the *Cambridge Medieval History* in using Lothar and Rudolf for kings in Germany and the Middle Kingdom, Lothaire and Raoul for kings of France. We have used Dorestad instead of the modern Dutch Duurstede since it is the normal form on the coins. Cross-references are given in the index where users in other countries are likely to be confused, especially where different initial letters are involved (e.g. Ugo/Hugh).

Problems of spelling and terminology can also affect coin names. It has seemed simplest to use 'penny' for the coins with which English-speaking readers are most familiar, i.e. those struck by the Anglo-Saxons and Northmen, but 'denier' for the Carolingian *denarius* save in Italy, where it seemed unreasonable not to employ 'denaro'. The halfpenny has, in accordance with the written usage of the time, been termed an 'obol' on the Continent, but with the customary English spelling instead of Fr. *obole* or It. *obolo*.

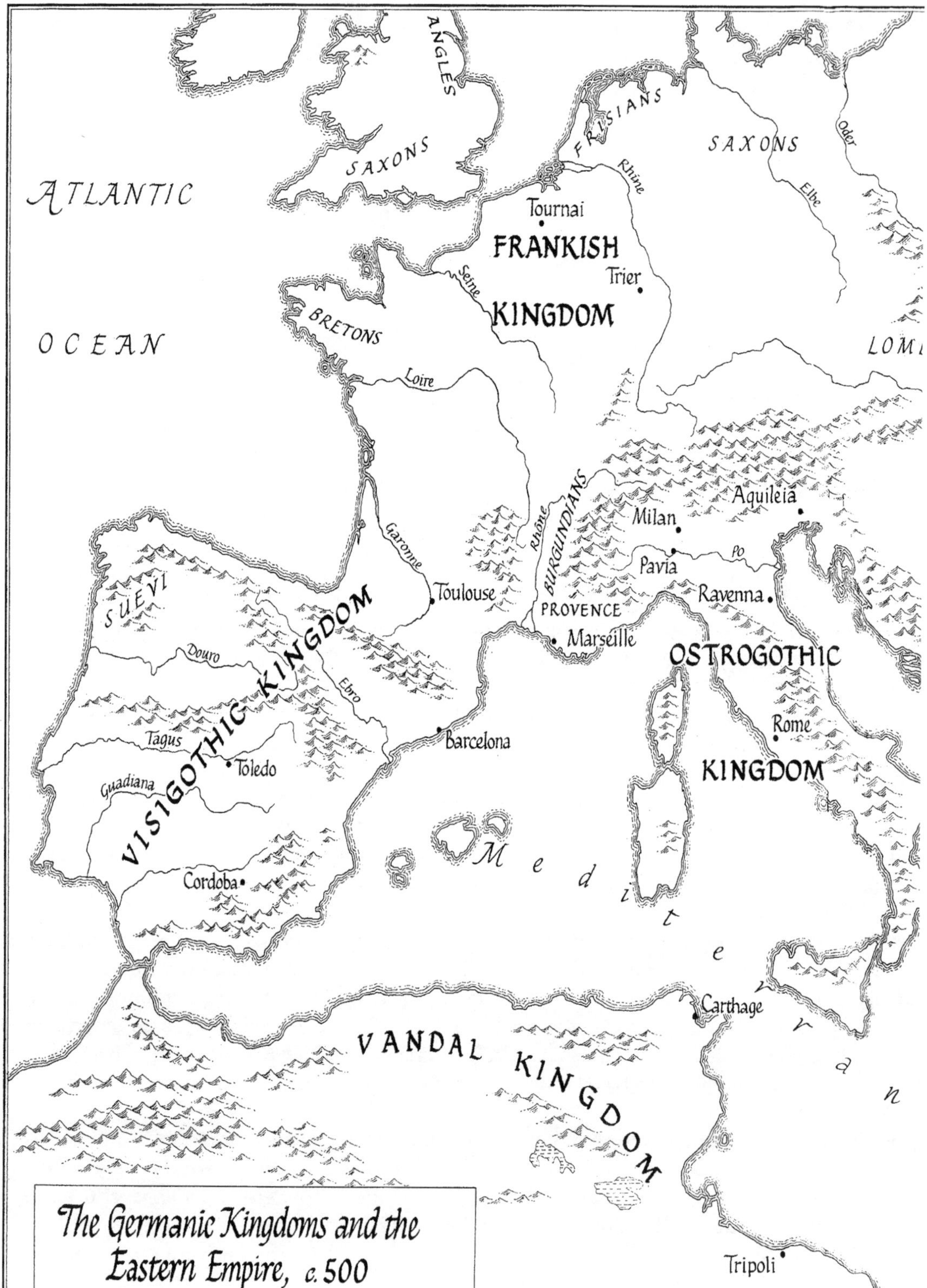

ANGLES
SAXONS
FRISIANS
SAXONS
Oder
Elbe
Rhine
ATLANTIC
OCEAN
Tournai
FRANKISH
KINGDOM
Trier
Seine
BRETONS
Loire
LOMI
BURGUNDIANS
Rhône
Aquileia
Milan
Pavia
Po
Ravenna
Garonne
Toulouse
PROVENCE
Marseille
SUEVI
VISIGOTHIC KINGDOM
Douro
Ebro
OSTROGOTHIC
KINGDOM
Rome
Tagus
Toledo
Barcelona
Guadiana
Cordoba
Mediterran
Carthage
VANDAL KINGDOM
Tripoli
The Germanic Kingdoms and the Eastern Empire, c. 500
0 100 200 300 400 500 miles
0 100 200 300 400 500 km

Oder
Vistula
Elbe
SLAVS
Dnieper
Don
Dniester
LOMBARDS
GEPIDS
Black Sea
Sirmium
Danube
THIC
me
OM
EASTERN EMPIRE
Constantinople
Thessalonica
Antioch
r a n e a n Sea
Alexandria

MERCIA
EAST ANGLES
FRISIA
Thames
Dorestad
WEST SAXONS
KENT
Quentovic
Maastricht
AUSTRAS
Meuse
ATLANTIC
Seine
NEUSTRIA
Paris
BRITTANY
Orleans
Tours
Loire
OCEAN
Chalon-sur-Saône
AQUITAINE
Loire
Lyon
Bordeaux
Rhône
Garonne
GASCONY
Arles
Marseille
SPANISH MARCH
Barcelona

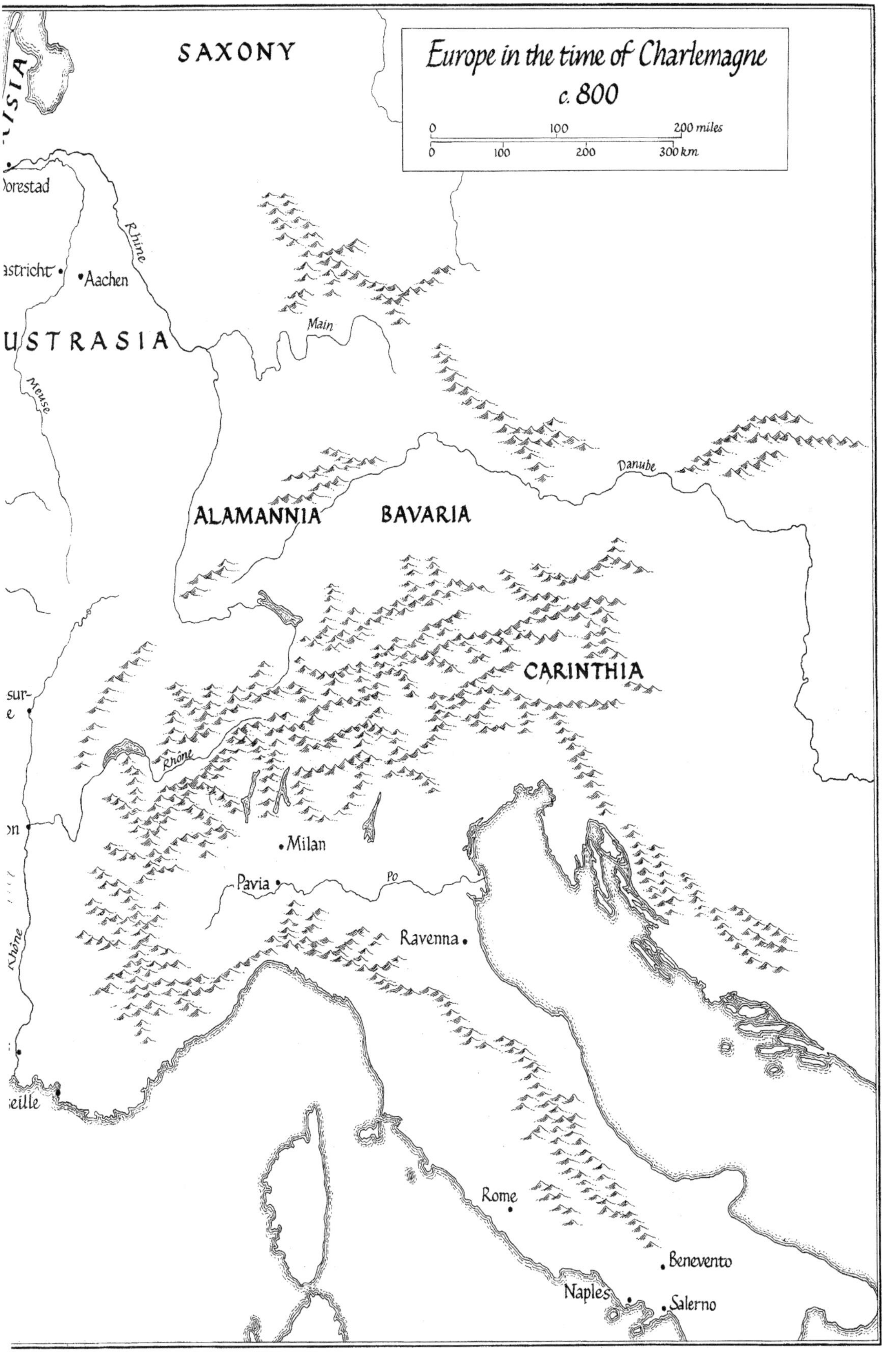

Europe in the time of Charlemagne
c. 800

1

INTRODUCTION

Literature

The only detailed descriptive work covering the coinages studied in this volume is Engel and Serrure (1891), remarkable for its day and still a standard work of reference despite being outdated in many respects. The fullest study from a monetary standpoint (Suchodolski 1982), by an author who is also an accomplished numismatist, is in Polish and consequently, apart from its many maps, tables and graphs, difficult for most readers in western Europe to use. There is a good survey of the coinages of the Germanic successor states by Le Gentilhomme (1943–4), superseding an older work by Keary (1879). Often interesting on details is Monneret (1919–21), though it has to be used with caution as the author had no direct acquaintance with the coins and was uncritical in his use of written sources. Two old works that have been unjustly neglected, partly because neither is illustrated or professedly 'numismatic', are those of Müller (1860) and Soetbeer (1862–6). Both run to the end of the Carolingian period and despite their date can still be profitably consulted, particularly that of Soetbeer, because of their authors' command of the laws, charters and other written texts and their copious citations from them.

The economic history is most fully covered by Dopsch (1927), now somewhat dated and effectively ending in the eighth century though continued by his monograph on the Carolingian period (Dopsch 1962). There are shorter but still substantial works by Latouche (1967), Doehaerd (1971), and Dhondt (1976), stimulating treatments of various aspects by Duby (1974) and Hodges (1982). The period is unevenly covered by chapters in vols. I and II of the *Cambridge Economic History of Europe* (1966[2], 1952).

The significance of the change-over from a gold to a silver coinage in the middle of the period covered by this volume has been much discussed, particularly since Pirenne in the 1920s made it one of the chief arguments in favour of his view that in all essentials the ancient world persisted to the late seventh century and ended as a consequence of Muslim expansion and not of the Germanic invasions (Pirenne 1923*, 1937). The monetary aspects of the argument figured prominently in all subsequent discussions (cf. Lopez 1943b*, Dennett 1948*, Riising 1952*, Perroy 1954*, Grierson 1960a, Cipolla 1962, Roberts 1964, Cahen 1965, Ashtor 1970, Hodges and Whitehouse 1983; the works marked with an asterisk are reprinted in Hübinger 1968b; cf. also Hübinger 1968a), and it gave rise to an equally contentious if more limited problem, that of the influence of Muslim coinage on western Europe in the eighth and succeeding centuries (Bloch 1933, Lombard 1947, Bolin 1953*, Grierson 1954a*, Himly 1955*, Duplessy 1956). On the role of coined money in the economy there has been much difference of opinion (Grierson 1959a; Metcalf 1967; cf. below, pp. 190–1, 282).

The most convenient general histories covering the period are the *Cambridge Medieval History*, vols. I–III (1911–22), and Lot, Pfister and Ganshof (1941). Works dealing with specific regions will be referred to in the appropriate sections. The most comprehensive works on the Germanic invasions, with excellent bibliographies, are Musset 1965, 1971.

(a) PEOPLES AND COINAGES (FIFTH–TENTH CENTURIES)

Medieval European coinage is customarily divided into three phases: (1) a post-Roman one dominated by derivatives of an imperial gold coin, the tremissis, (2) a late Merovingian, Carolingian and feudal one when virtually the only coins in circulation were silver pennies, and (3) a late medieval one characterized by the revived use of gold and a proliferation of 'silver' denominations ranging from pennies or their fractions in low-grade billon to silver 'groats' worth anything between 4 and 24 pence according to place and period. The coinages described in this volume are those of western Europe during the first five centuries of the middle ages, from the fall of the Roman Empire in the West, conventionally dated to the fifth century A.D., and the emergence of recognizable 'national' political units in the West in the tenth century. They thus include the whole of the tremissis coinages in gold and the first phase of the penny coinages in silver.

No precise dates can be given for either the beginning or the end of the coinages involved. The volume starts with the coins struck by the Ostrogoths, Visigoths, Vandals, Burgundians and other Germanic invaders of the Empire in the fifth century. These overlapped in both East and West with imperial issues, and some account of the latter is given later in this chapter, since they are necessary to an understanding of the Germanic coinages that first supplemented and then replaced them. They are not, however, catalogued or described in detail. Similarly, in the tenth century, when the coinages of the last Carolingian sovereigns overlapped with those of nascent feudalism, the coinages of the latter are reserved for later volumes. While in principle the volume runs to the end of the Carolingian period – 911 in Germany, 987 in France – and in England to the death of Edward the Elder in 924, a number of exceptions to these limits have been allowed. It is convenient to take the coinage of the kingdom of Italy down to the Ottonian conquest and the deposition of Berengar II (961), and that of the papacy down to the cessation of papal-imperial coinage in the 970s. In England, though the coinage of Wessex is not taken beyond 924, that of the Viking kingdom of York is continued to its downfall in 954 and the annexation of Northumbria by Eadred. The coinage of the kingdom of Burgundy (888–1032), on the other hand, has been left over to Vol. 6, since although the kingdom dates from the coronation of Rudolf I in 888 the bulk of its coinage belongs to the period from 937 onwards.

There are three main themes to the political history of the period: the establishment of the Germanic successor states, the emergence and break-up of the Carolingian Empire, and the unification of England under the house of Wessex. These will be surveyed, in such detail as seems appropriate, in the introductions to each section, but a short outline of them may be useful.

(1) *The Germanic successor states*

The Germanic world of central Europe and southern Russia was thrown into confusion in the 370s A.D. as a result of the invasion of the Huns from Central Asia. An East German people, the Visigoths, was permitted to cross the Danube by the Roman government in 376 and settle in the province of Moesia, corresponding to most of the north Balkans. The government hoped thereby to increase its own supply of mercenary soldiers, but a large national unit could not be as easily managed as the smaller bands of Germanic auxiliaries on whose services the Empire had long relied. A first Gothic revolt ended in a spectacular Gothic victory at Adrianople (378), when the Emperor Valens was killed and his army all but wiped out, and a second one, following the death of the Emperor Theodosius I in 395, resulted in the devastation of much of the Balkans and the invasion of Italy. This in turn compelled the Roman authorities in the West to transfer military resources from Gaul, thereby weakening its frontier defences and making possible a second major Germanic invasion across the Rhine in 407. The next hundred years saw the establishment of powerful states by the Vandals in Africa, the Suevi in Spain, the Visigoths in southern Gaul, the Burgundians in south-eastern Gaul and the Ostrogoths in Italy, while much of northern Gaul was occupied by petty Frankish chieftains and much of Britain by a miscellany of Jutes, Angles, Saxons and Frisians. Not all these states were to last: the Vandal and Ostrogothic kingdoms were destroyed by an imperial revival under Justinian, while the Burgundians and the Suevi fell victims to the Franks and the Visigoths respectively. But Italy was invaded and most of it was occupied by the Lombards after Justinian's death (565) and, after the unification of the Franks under Clovis (d. 511), the Visigoths were driven from all save a southernmost strip of Gaul (Narbonensis) and became instead masters of Spain.

Each of these kingdoms developed a coinage of its own, initially imitated from imperial issues but in due course developing on its own 'national' lines, and it is these coinages that form the subject of the first third of this volume. Those of the Ostrogoths and Vandals, which in both cases were short-lived, carried on the Roman tradition of using gold, silver and copper, but the other coinages were almost exclusively of gold and conformed in weight, at least initially, to the Roman tremissis. A coinage of silver deniers, however, was inaugurated in *c.* 670 in the Frankish kingdom of Neustria, and by the end of the century these had taken over completely throughout the Frankish realm, as well as in Frisia to the north and across the Channel in England.

(2) *The Carolingian Empire*

The dynasty founded by Clovis lasted with only two brief interruptions for nearly three centuries, ending with the deposition of Childeric III in 751. Since the kingdom was inherited as if it were private property it was subject to repeated partition, and despite its being periodically reunited the royal power declined from the reign of Dagobert (d. 639) onwards. But a new dynasty of Mayors of the Palace emerged in the late seventh century, took over much of the reality of royal power, recovered peripheral regions that had become independent, and in 751, in the person of Pepin the Short, assumed the crown itself. Pepin's successor Charlemagne completed his father's work, annexing the Lombard kingdom of Italy, making himself master of Bavaria and Saxony and taking the title of emperor in 800. But his empire was too large to be held together as a political unit and in due course it broke up, his line ending in Germany in 911 and in France in 987.

The typical coin of the Carolingian period was the silver denier or penny, which represented a continuation of the late Merovingian denier, although under Pepin and Charlemagne its form was changed to a broader and thinner coin much more regular in appearance and its issue was brought under royal control. The history and vicissitudes of the Carolingian silver denier form the second main theme in this volume.

(3) *The unification of England*

The third theme is the coinage of England, which followed patterns very similar to those of its neighbours on the Continent. The small, separate groups of Germanic peoples who settled in Britain during the course of the fifth century conquered little by little almost the whole country and coalesced into a number of separate kingdoms. The four main ones were Northumbria (the land extending from the Humber to the Firth of Forth in modern Scotland), Mercia (in central England, taking its name from its *march* or border with Wales), Wessex (the land of the West Saxons in the south-west up to the frontier with Cornwall) and Kent (the smallest of the kingdoms but important because of its proximity to the Continent). The minor kingdoms included East Anglia, Essex, Sussex and Lindsey. During the seventh, eighth and ninth centuries the balance of power south of the Humber shifted between the major kingdoms, till a new wave of invaders from Scandinavia, the Vikings, overwhelmed northern and eastern England, so that towards the end of the ninth century the country came to be divided into two regions, the Danelaw and the remainder dominated by Wessex. It was left to the West Saxon kings in the first half of the tenth century to conquer and annex the Danelaw, resulting in the unification of the whole country for the first time since the Roman withdrawal five centuries before.

Britain was the only Roman province in which, with the end of the Empire, the use of coinage completely lapsed. Some Continental gold coins found their way into Kent from the second quarter of the sixth century onwards, although initially their use was mainly ornamental. In the seventh century a new indigenous coinage of gold tremisses on the Frankish model was created. In the second half of the century there came a transition to silver pennies, as in the Frankish kingdom. These were initially of the small, thick module of the Merovingian denier, but they assumed the broader Carolingian fabric during the third quarter of the eighth century. In remote Northumbria an aberrant coinage of debased silver and eventually copper coins of the early thicker fabric was struck in the later eighth and ninth centuries. The production of broad silver pennies was effectively confined to south-east England and East Anglia until the last decades of the ninth century, when minting spread to other parts of Wessex, Mercia and the Danelaw. It was out of the West Saxon penny that the later coinage of England was to develop.

The right to coin

There are many features of early medieval coinage that seem strange to the historian, and sometimes anomalous even to numismatists. It is traditionally held that the right of minting is a function of sovereignty – *ius monetae ossibus principis adhaeret* – and the manufacture of coin is usually closely controlled and centralized, so that a state normally possesses only a single mint. This last condition did not obtain in the late Roman Empire, for size and poor communications made many mints necessary, but the mints were at least operated by the state and the weight, fineness and external appearance of coins were determined by it.

Such control of mint operations is found in only a few of the coinages covered by this volume. In the years immediately following their settlement in the Empire, the invaders, when they minted coins at all, minted pseudo-imperial ones, imitating either imperial coins already circulating in the lands they occupied or the current issues of imperial mints as these came to their attention. This, at least, was what occurred with the gold. Silver and bronze were being minted on only a small scale by imperial mints in the fifth century, and the new rulers had few scruples over inscribing coins in these metals with their own names or monograms. But as time passed, usually after about a century had gone by since the initial settlement, each of the Germanic peoples seems to have felt free to issue its own types in gold. The resulting coinages followed widely divergent patterns; some were centrally regulated while others were apparently issued on local initiative. In the Frankish kingdom the coins normally bear the names of moneyers and mints, and only exceptionally those of kings. In Visigothic Spain the names are those of kings and mints, never those of moneyers. The same is true of Lombard Italy, but in Tuscany there are coins with only the names or monograms of cities. Later, under the Carolingians, the coinage becomes completely royal but names of mints continue while those of moneyers are dropped. In England, where the coinage from the later eighth century is also unquestionably royal, the names of moneyers continue until the thirteenth century but those of mints only become a standard feature in the tenth.

Clearly no simple answer can be given to the question of how the *ius monetae* fared in the Germanic successor states. In none of them was it preserved in a simple and undivided form. Even in Ostrogothic Italy and Vandal Africa, where many features of the Roman state survived almost unimpaired, the right to mint seems to have been shared, how formally we do not know, with local authorities, probably out of respect for real or supposed Roman precedents. Visigothic coinage, from Leovigild onwards, is formally royal, but much can probably be attributed to local initiative. The Frankish kings of the sixth and seventh centuries probably never claimed any royal monopoly at all (below, pp. 97–8). The absence of a minting monopoly would of course not prevent rulers legislating on the coinage, for it was in the public interest to ensure that such coins as were made conformed to accepted standards of weight and fineness. But this did not mean that public authorities had to make the coins themselves.

There was, however, one limit the successor states were usually prepared to observe. Their rulers normally refrained from minting in their own names the gold solidus, the coin that seemed *par excellence* to embody the pretensions of the Roman Empire. There are, of course, exceptions. Such coins were minted by the Frankish king Theodebert in the sixth century, by Frankish rulers at Marseille from 613 onwards, and occasionally by kings or moneyers elsewhere. But there was no minting of solidi by the Visigoths after a national coinage had been created by Leovigild, and the Lombards minted solidi only at Ravenna, the chief imperial mint in Italy, during the five years between its capture by Aistulf in 751 and its relinquishment to the papacy in 756. The historian Procopius, in recording Byzantine indignation at Theodebert's presumption in doing something that (he declares) not even the Sassanian kings of Persia dared to do, makes clear the importance that the imperial authorities attached to their prerogatives in the matter (*Bell. Goth.* III.33.5–6). In detail, it is true, he is wrong. Although the normal coinage of the Sassanians consisted of silver dirhams, they struck coins in gold when they found it convenient to do so, and the Byzantine objection seems not to have been to the minting of gold as such but to the minting of gold *solidi*. The Visigothic abandonment of the solidus from Leovigild onwards was consequently not the anomaly it appears, for the pseudo-imperial solidi had, in however blundered a fashion, borne the emperor's name and so did not infringe the monopoly. The same was essentially true of the Lombards. Even the princes of Benevento, who from Grimoald

III onwards minted solidi in their own name, only began to do so after the Byzantines had ceased to mint in mainland Italy. As for Marseille, the royal solidi are differentiated from imperial ones in having a profile bust, not a facing one, and so breached the imperial monopoly in only an attenuated fashion.

(b) THE IMPERIAL COINAGE IN THE FIFTH CENTURY

Literature

The standard descriptive work of the nineteenth century on Roman imperial coinage by Cohen (1880–92) has been for the most part superseded by *RIC* (1923–), but the ninth volume of this ends in 395 and the tenth and last, intended to cover the century 395–491, has not yet appeared. One must therefore continue to use the last volume of Cohen for the Western line of emperors from Honorius (393–423) onwards, and for the Eastern emperors to use Sabatier (1862) and Tolstoi (1912–14), despite the fact that both arrange the coins of each emperor according to the alphabetical order of reverse inscriptions and the first includes many non-existent items, either the consequence of early misreadings or out-and-out forgeries. The copper coinage of the period is covered by *LRBC* (1960), though in so condensed a form as to be usable only by numismatists. There is nothing comparable for the gold and silver, though the illustrations in a British Museum volume (Carson 1981) and books by Kent (1978) and Lacam (1983) illustrate most of the numismatic types, in the two latter cases by splendid enlargements. Ulrich-Bansa's monograph on the coinage of Milan covers much more than its title suggests and makes it a guide to much of the Western coinage as a whole (Ulrich-Bansa 1949). There is no satisfactory study of the monetary system, the most useful works dealing primarily with the late fourth century and their conclusions being in many respects open to question.

The historical background is best covered by Bury (1923), Stein (1959/1949), Demougeot (1979) and Courcelle (1964), or more briefly, but still with detailed references, by Lot, Pfister and Ganshof (1941). Jones 1964, dealing with the whole period from 284 to 602, is massively documented, especially in its administrative and economic aspects.

Historical background

Theodosius I, the last emperor to be effective ruler of the entire Roman Empire, died at Milan on 17 January 395. His designated successors were his two sons Arcadius and Honorius, who had been associated co-emperors in 383 and 393 respectively. Arcadius took the East, with Constantinople as its capital, and Honorius the West, with Ravenna as the normal imperial residence from 402 onwards. During the following decades the two halves of the Empire drew further and further apart even though in form it remained a unit, with legislation issued in the names of all imperial colleagues and the officials responsible for the mints remembering from time to time that coins should be issued in the names of co-rulers in the other half of the Empire (Blanchet 1908). The list of emperors of the fifth and sixth centuries is set out in Table 1.

The history of the two halves of the Empire in the fifth century was very different. In the East, although German military leaders played a prominent role in public affairs and the Balkans suffered terribly from German ravages, the main provinces – Asia Minor, Syria, Egypt, Cyrenaica – remained subject to the rule of Constantinople. The Theodosian line formally ended

Table 1. *Emperors in the fifth and sixth centuries**

In the West	In the East
Honorius, 395–423 (tit. from 393)	Arcadius, 395–408 (tit. from 383)
Marcus (Britain), 406–7	
Gratian (Britain), 407	
Constantine III (Gaul), 407–11	Theodosius II, 408–50 (tit. from 402)
Constans (Gaul), 409–11 (Caesar from 408)	
Maximus (Spain), 409–11	
Priscus Attalus (Italy), 409–10	
Jovinus (Gaul), 411–13	
Sebastian (Gaul), 412–13	
Priscus Attalus (again, Gaul), 414–15	
Constantius III, 421	
Maximus (again, Spain), 420–2	
John, 423–5	
Valentinian III, 425–55	Marcian, 450–7
Petronius Maximus, 455	
Avitus, 455–6	
Majorian, 457–61	Leo I, 457–74
Severus III, 461–5	
Anthemius, 467–72	
Olybrius, 472	
Glycerius, 473	Leo II, 474 (tit. from 473)
Julius Nepos, 473–80	Zeno, 474–91
Romulus Augustulus, 475–6	*Basiliscus*, 475–6
	Leontius (Isauria), 484–8
	Anastasius I, 491–518
	Justin I, 518–27
	Justinian I, 527–65
	Justin II, 565–78
	Tiberius II, 578–82 (Caesar from 574)
	Maurice, 582–602

*The dates at which some emperors had the imperial title conferred on them as children are given in parentheses, as it was with these that their coinages began. The names of usurpers, and of Western emperors not recognized by Constantinople, are italicized. Coins exist of all those named in the list, save Marcus and Gratian. Names of Eastern co-augusti who never ruled independently are not included, although some had coins struck in their names (e.g. Pulcheria) or were associated on coins as junior collegues (e.g. Marcus, son of Basiliscus).

with the death of Arcadius' son Theodosius II in 450, but Theodosius' sister Pulcheria married his successor Marcian and so preserved some element of dynastic continuity to 457. Marcian, Leo I and Zeno were all experienced soldiers, while Zeno's successor Anastasius was a treasury official of proven ability. The fate of the West, in contrast, was to be one of Germanic occupation. Honorius was an incompetent nonentity, and his reign saw the abandonment of Britain, the sack of Rome in 410, the settlement of the Visigoths in Gaul, the ravaging of Gaul and Spain by mixed Germanic peoples who had broken across the Rhine frontier, and the careers of a long succession of would-be usurpers. Honorius left no son and his natural successor, his brother-in-law Constantius III whom he had reluctantly associated co-emperor in 421, had unfortunately predeceased him. Constantius' son Valentinian III was duly installed by his cousin Theodosius II after the brief interlude of a 'usurper' John (423–5), but Valentinian III's reign was no improvement upon that of Honorius. He was murdered in 455, but by that time the decline of imperial power in the West had gone too far for recovery to be possible. Most provinces were in Germanic occupation, and the imperial army itself was largely Germanic in composition. The end of the Empire in the West is traditionally dated to 476, when a Scirian officer Odovacar murdered the *Magister militum* Orestes and, after deposing Orestes' son Romulus, nicknamed Augustulus, sent a message to the Eastern emperor Zeno inviting him to accept sole rule, since with the loss of Britain and most of Gaul, Spain and Africa a separate line of emperors in the West was no longer necessary. Zeno replied that Romulus had been a usurper and that the West still had a legitimate sovereign in the person of Julius Nepos, then living in exile in Dalmatia. Odovacar agreed to accord Nepos some degree of recognition, but with his death in 480 the separate line of Western emperors came to an end.

Coinage

The traditional coinage of the Roman Empire, consisting essentially of one denomination each of gold and silver (the aureus and denarius) and four of base metal (the sestertius and dupondius of brass, and the as and quadrans of copper), had disappeared as a result of the great inflation of the third century A.D. It had been replaced in the period of the Tetrarchy by new denominations of gold, silver and bronze which were repeatedly added to or modified in the course of the fourth century. On the eve of the German invasions some degree of coherence and stability had been achieved, with three denominations of gold, two of silver and four of bronze, all of them lighter than their counterparts of the early Empire. The correct identification of the silver and bronze coins in our collections with the names mentioned in the written documents is not altogether clear, and the relationship between the denominations is uncertain and must have changed several times in the course of the century. It was in any case greatly simplified in the post-Theodosian period, when, although the gold coinage carried on unchanged, the subsidiary coinage was reduced by the middle of the fifth century to one denomination each of silver and bronze, the silver being only very occasionally struck and the copper nummus a tiny coin reckoned many thousand to the solidus.

The normal gold coinage consisted of three denominations, the solidus (or nomisma in Greek), its half the semis or semissis, and its third, the triens or tremissis. The solidus was struck 72 to the Roman pound or 6 to the ounce, so that it weighed in Roman terms 24 siliquae (or carats in Greek), the fractions in proportion. The solidus and tremissis were the coins that influenced the West, for the semissis, though important in the East from the reign of Zeno onwards, was rarely struck in the West and only one Germanic derivative, a unique semissis struck at Rome under Theoderic the Ostrogoth (below, p. 35), is known. Other gold coins, for the most part of higher values, were struck for such occasions as consular or New Year distributions. Some are multiples of the solidus, usually three- or six-solidus pieces, while others are geared to an older division of the pound into 60 units (called *aurei* by numismatists) instead of into 72. The large multiples or medallions (Gnecchi 1912; Toynbee 1944), which could be converted into splendid pieces of jewellery, were much appreciated as gifts in the Germanic world, where a high proportion of them have been found and in which they were frequently imitated. Although they had a monetary significance (Bastien 1972; Jeločnik 1967) they formed no part of the regular circulating medium. Documents and hoards alike testify to the huge quantities of precious metal in the Empire (Mickwitz 1934; Piganiol 1945; Bratianu 1938). One hoard alone, found in 1963 at Szikáncs in Hungary (Biróné Sey 1976), consisted of 1,437 solidi of Theodosius II – the original figure was presumably 1,440 or 10 Roman lb – and evidently came from the huge tributes, amounting to nearly 40,000lb of gold, paid by this emperor to the Huns over the decades 430 to 450.

The silver coin in normal use at the end of the fourth century is one called by numismatists a siliqua on the assumption that it had the value of a gold siliqua ($\frac{1}{24}$ of a solidus) as money of account. It then weighed about 2g, probably for 2.27g (i.e. 144 to the pound), but was very variable in weight. By the fifth century it was struck in small quantities and only occasionally, essentially for ceremonial purposes, and many specimens weigh little more than 1g. There were also heavier and lighter coins, miliarenses and half-siliquae, and very heavy medallions comparable to those in gold, which circulated in conjunction with stamped gold ingots (Kenner 1888; Mommsen 1888; Iliescu 1965). It is clear that the silver had nothing like the stability of the gold, and both the system of values and the denominations of the coins, despite much discussion (Kubitschek 1913; Mickwitz 1932, 1933; Adelson 1957, 1958), remain uncertain.

The absence of a substantial silver coinage in the fifth century has been regarded by some commentators (Patterson 1972) as proof of a general shortage of silver, but this was not the case. The metal existed, but was used for silver plate rather than for coin. Silver treasures of the later Empire are exceptionally abundant (cf. Kent and Painter 1977; *Archéologie* 54; Baratte 1975), and the historian Olympiodorus, the *Liber Pontificalis*, and other written records unanimously testify to the huge quantities existing in senatorial households (Allard 1907) and in the hands of the Church. The silver payments that abound in the Theodosian Code are expressed in terms of weight, and stamped silver ingots (Willers 1898; Salomonson 1961; Painter 1972; Baratte 1976, 1978), to say nothing of cut-up fragments of plate, show that it was in this way that such obligations were settled. The explanation of the lack of coin is presumably a divergence between a traditional mint price for the precious metal and that prevailing in the market, for when the mint price falls below that of the market the only silver available for turning into coin, and that only for special and limited issues, will be whatever the government has at its disposal from other sources. Such a contrast between abundant silverware and an exiguous silver coinage is one that has occurred many times in history, very notably in eighteenth-century England.

The bronze coins of the fourth century, when the full gamut of denominations was struck, consisted of four denominations, which in view of uncertainties over their nomenclature are commonly described as *Æ* 1, *Æ* 2, *Æ* 3 and *Æ* 4. The first was not minted after the 360s and the second and third virtually ceased in 395. Only the fourth survived, gradually reduced in size from a diameter of 14mm and a weight of *c.* 1.7g in 395 to about 9mm and under 1g by the second half of the fifth century. A constitution of Valentinian III (*Nov. Val.* 16.1) of 445 fixes the value of the gold solidus at 7,000/7,200 nummi ('coins'), as these copper coins, being the only ones then in circulation, had come to be called, and there is reason to believe that by the end of the fifth century it had risen to twice this figure (Grierson 1959a; cf. Adelson 1967). Even assuming that some part of the abundant small change of the late fourth century remained in circulation for some decades after 395 – hoard evidence shows that a substantial proportion failed to do so (Blanchet 1900) – it is difficult to see how the commerce of the Empire can have been in a flourishing condition with such an inadequate means of exchange, especially since in the West the circulation of these nummi seems, by the mid fifth century, to have been virtually limited to the provinces of Italy (Gnecchi 1897; Cesano 1913; Newell 1933; Lallemand 1967) and North Africa (Turcan 1972; Brenot and Morrisson 1983; and hoards cited below, p. 17). In the East they circulated more widely, and many finds, including some substantial hoards, are recorded from Egypt (Milne 1926), Syria (Seeger 1976) and the Balkans (Thompson 1954; Adelson and Kustas 1960, 1962, 1964).

Although the pattern of denominations was in principle uniform throughout the Empire, the provinces seem to have been very unevenly supplied with coin, some of them managing with virtually no silver and others with a minimum of bronze. There were between ten and twenty mints: Trier, Lyon and Arles in Gaul; Milan, Aquileia, Ravenna (after 402) and Rome in Italy; Siscia, Sirmium and Thessalonica in the Balkans; Heracleia, Constantinople, Nicomedia and Cyzicus on the shores of the Sea of Marmara; Antioch in Syria; and Alexandria in Egypt. Barcelona was briefly a mint of the Spanish usurper Maximus (Calicó 1960, Balaguer 1980), and Carthage, after over a century of inactivity, began to strike again in the 420s. Some of these limited their minting to particular metals. Trier and Milan normally struck only gold and silver, Alexandria only bronze. Gold was for much of the time minted only when the emperor was in residence there or by a travelling mint attached to his court (Kent 1956).

The mints were identified on the coins by mint letters in the field or in the exergue, either alone (e.g. TR for Trier, *Treveri*) or else combined with OB or PS, abbreviations respectively of *obryzum* and *pusulatum*, the technical terms for refined gold and silver. OB had in fact a double sense, for in Greek numerals it stood for 72, the number of solidi struck to the pound. CON or CONOB came in time to be used on all gold coins wherever they originated, for after minting in this metal during the fifth century had become virtually limited in the East to Constantinople, users came to expect its presence on all gold coins. A variant found in the West is COMOB, justifiable as the mark of a treasury official with the title *comes obryzi* but essentially a *trompe l'oeil* for CONOB. Germanic coinages, when they came into existence, were mainly influenced by the coinages of the Western mints, but solidi of Constantinople, in which the huge imperial tributes to the barbarians tended to be paid, also served as models.

The obverse type of virtually all coins was an imperial bust in military costume. The tradition of the early Empire had been one of profile busts with characterized portraiture in high relief. In the course of the fourth century the relief became much flatter and characterized portraiture was gradually abandoned, so that the same impersonal bust could be used for any number of imperial colleagues. The reason was in part a decline of classical representational art, in part a feeling that the majesty of imperial power should eclipse the features and conceal the weaknesses and deficiencies of individual rulers. A three-quarter facing bust was adopted for the solidus at Constantinople in 395 – it was a variant of one used on the last coinage of Constantius II (337–61) – though profile busts continued for the fractional gold and for the silver and bronze, as well as for solidi in the West down to the second half of the fifth century. The three-quarter facing bust, which accentuated the absence of any personal likeness, shows the emperor wearing a helmeted diadem with a circular frontal ornament; fluttering in the left field are the tails of the ribbon that secured it behind the head. He wears a breastplate and carries a spear and a shield on which is usually depicted, in rough outline, a figure on horseback stabbing downwards at a fallen enemy. The profile bust shows the emperor diademed but not helmeted, so that the details of the diadem, one of the chief insignia of imperial authority, are more clearly shown – usually it is a simple pearl-bordered band, but sometimes it is broken by large jewelled rosettes – and his armour is practically concealed by a military cloak (*paludamentum*) thrown back over his left shoulder and fastened at his right shoulder by a circular brooch (*fibula*) with three pendants. This was also an important symbol of imperial office.

Since the bulk of barbarian imitations are tremisses it is the profile bust that was normally copied on pseudo-imperial Germanic coinages. This holds good even for solidi, since in the fifth century the models for these were Western, although the three-quarter facing bust was also used, especially after the Western line of emperors had come to an end.

The reverse types of fifth-century coins show nothing like the diversity of those of the early Empire. The only pagan types to survive the adoption of Christianity as the state religion were personifications of Victory (Vermeule 1958; Bellinger and Berlincourt 1962) and of the two capital cities, Roma and Constantinopolis, which play a major role in late Roman art (Toynbee 1947, 1951). The Victory is a winged female figure traditionally shown holding a wreath and a palm or trophy and usually either facing (i.e. advancing towards the spectator) or moving to right or left (striding or running), though on semisses she is shown seated inscribing a *Vota* legend on a shield. In the fifth century a main solidus type, introduced in 422, shows her holding a long jewelled cross (Kent 1960; cf. Storch 1971, Holum 1977 and Hahn 1979a). Under Justin I the Victory of the solidus was transformed into a Christian angel, the sex of the standing figure being altered by a change in the position of the girdle (A. M. Friend in Vasiliev 1950, 421–2). Roma and Constantinopolis are normally seated figures, the cities being distinguished from each other by showing Constantinopolis with one foot placed on a ship's prow, symbolic of the naval victory won by Constantine in the Hellespont over his rival Licinius in 323. Other solidus reverse types show the emperor in military costume triumphing over a fallen enemy, standing with his foot on a human-headed serpent, or in some other fashion celebrating military achievements that in real life were usually hard to discern. For smaller coins the designs became very simple, preferred ones being a wreath sometimes containing a cross or Christogram, or on much of the silver a *Vota* formula (i.e. the word VOT(IS) accompanied by a numeral or by the word *multis*), alluding to the 'vows' taken by emperors at the quinquennial anniversary celebrations of their accessions. The last issue of Theodosius II's nummi has as reverse type an imperial monogram occupying the entire field, since the coins were now too small for the emperor's name on the obverse to be easily legible. Similar monograms were used for nummi and sometimes other low denominations of copper by most of his successors down to the end of the sixth century. This type had a strong influence on the coinages of the Germanic West.

The coin inscriptions of the fifth century are extremely uniform, and less informative than those of earlier times. References to imperial consulships and anniversaries are exceptional, and such traditional formulae as TR POT (for *tribunicia potestas*) and PONT MAX (for *pontifex maximus*, a title formally abandoned by Gratian), and even those commemorating imperial military successes (*Germanicus, Hunnicus*) which were still regularly used in public documents, disappear completely from the coinage. The normal formula on the obverse is the emperor's name preceded by DN (the title *Dominus noster*) and followed by either PF or PP (*pius felix* or *perpetuus*) AVG(*ustus*). The reverse legends refer in a general way to the type, military where the emperor is involved (e.g. *Gloria exercitus, Spes Romanorum*) and *Victoria Augustorum* to accompany a Victory type. Where *Augustorum* is abbreviated, as it normally is on solidi, the normal epigraphic convention that the number of Gs should correspond to the number of co-emperors had originally been respected, but after the first decade of the fifth century this practice, so useful for precise dating, was abandoned, and the formula is GGG or GG however many emperors there were, and even when there was only one.

(c) THE GERMANIC CONTRIBUTION

The Germanic peoples, in contrast to the Celts beyond the frontiers of the Greek and Roman worlds in the last centuries B.C., had no coinages of their own prior to their invasion of the Empire. It is true that Roman silver and gold coins had reached the Germanic world in great quantities, the silver initially either as plunder or by way of trade (Brogan 1936), the gold later through payment of mercenaries and eventually as large-scale tribute. The number of hoards from Germany east of the Rhine is enormous, and Roman coins, mainly silver but gold in the period *c.* 350 to *c.* 550, even reached Scandinavia in great quantities (Fagerlie 1967). Most of the West Germanic peoples must therefore have been familiar with Roman coins prior to their invasions, and in the late fourth century and into the fifth there was a small amount of imitation, in areas close to the frontier, of the silver siliquae of such emperors as Valentinian I and Gratian (**1.332**). It is no accident that the only Germanic law code to use silver coins (*denarii*) in the fixing of wergelds instead of gold or cattle is that of the Salian Franks (below, pp. 103–6; cf. Boone 1954 for maps of coin finds). A fair proportion of the imitations, however, were intended as ornaments (cf. Zadoks-Josephus Jitta 1959b; Nau 1966; Martin 1982).

The fact that the Germans had no coinages of their own meant that when they settled in the Empire and began to mint, they had to rely almost wholly on Roman coins as their models. These were initially the coins of the emperors on the throne when the initial settlements had taken place and who in some cases had authorized them. Imitations of solidi in the name of Honorius are attributable to the Visigoths (**1.166**) and the Suevi (**1.285**); later ones in those of Valentinian III and Severus III are probably Visigothic (**1.167–70, 174–6**). Since such coins can only be grouped on stylistic criteria and must be attributed to particular peoples on the basis of find evidence, we cannot do much with them when information on the latter is lacking or is inadequate (**1.334**, imitation of Anthemius; **1.335**, imitation of Zeno). Later solidi in the name of Anastasius, Justin I and Justinian can be distributed with varying degrees of probability between the Franks (**1.343–8**), Burgundians (**1.336**, **340**), Visigoths (**1.171**, **191–2**) and Ostrogoths (**1.112–13**, **122**), with some of the Burgundian and Ostrogothic attributions confirmed by the presence of royal monograms in the field or at the end of the reverse inscriptions. The same problems arise with the far more numerous pseudo-imperial tremisses, though fortunately the separate peoples usually displayed a liking for particular types, or modified them in easily identifiable fashions. Tremisses on which the imperial bust has a cross on the chest all belong to the Visigoths, and a peculiar distortion of the wreath-and-cross reverse type is specific to the Suevi (**1.286**ff.). Some peoples in regular communication with Constantinople seem to have tried to keep up-to-date with changes in the imperial office, though without always taking account of changes in imperial coin types (below, pp. 35–6) and often with some delay. Tremisses with the monogram of Gundomar II of Burgundy, who came to the throne in 524 and was overthrown by the Franks in 532, were all struck in the name of Justin I, who died in 527, and take no note of the accession of Justinian.

Pseudo-imperial coins in silver are exceptional, and ones in copper virtually non-existent outside Italy and North Africa, where former imperial mints simply continued to function under the Ostrogoths and Vandals respectively. The important pseudo-imperial silver coinage in Africa (**1.1–5**) was modelled on Ravennate siliquae and half-siliquae of Honorius, and the Suevi struck rare silver coins in the mid fifth century which combined the names of Honorius and their own king Rechiar (below, p. 79). The Italian silver coins of Odovacar and the Ostrogoths can indeed only be termed pseudo-imperial by stretching the ordinary meaning of the term, for despite the fact that the Ostrogothic kings neither paid taxes to Constantinople nor promulgated its legislation, they regarded themselves, at least up to 540, as imperial subjects. The absence of imitative subsidiary coinages over most of the West can only be interpreted as a symptom of the general economic decline of the area.

The degree of fidelity with which imperial coins could be imitated depended on the skills of the moneyers and die-sinkers available. Where the invaders could take over former imperial mints, as in Italy and North Africa, there was no falling-away from the standards of earlier times. In Italy, indeed, where classical traditions survived more strongly than they did in the East, there were occasional attempts in the fifth and sixth centuries at realistic portraiture, or at least the use of such realistic details as the moustache on coins of Odovacar (**1.63**) and the moustache and long hair on Theoderic's portrait medallion (*BMC Vand*, frontispiece) and the folles of Theodahad (**1.141–3**). But more often the die-sinkers had little feeling for three-dimensional representation and their linear rendering of types was either simplified or stylized, often to the point of caricature, as with the Victory on pseudo-imperial Visigothic coins of the mid sixth century. The widespread introduction of the cross as a type on Frankish coins in the seventh century must have come as a relief to many die-sinkers.

The main Germanic contribution to the coinage of the early middle ages was not therefore iconographic, nor was it made in the context of the pseudo-imperial issues; it occurred rather in the transition from these to the 'national' coinages that succeeded them. It took the form of what in the context of the emergence of medieval weight systems was a small but significant change in the standard to which the coins were struck. To this can be added the introduction of new monetary terms of Germanic origin, the shilling, the sceat (which did not last), the penny and the mark.

The invaders did not at first make any changes in the weights of the coins they imitated, despite the fact that these did not fit satisfactorily into their own weight systems, which were based on some variety of grain instead of the siliqua-carat of the Mediterranean world. The Roman pound, which is traditionally taken to have been the equivalent of 327.45g, was divided into 12 ounces of 27.29g. The ounce could be subdivided in various ways (6 solidi, 8 drachmae, 24 scripula, etc.), the lowest fraction being its 144th – the Roman weight system was strongly duodecimal – the siliqua or carat (κεράτιον) of 0.189g. This was a metric unit widely used in the Mediterranean world, and had originally corresponded to the seed (bean) of the carob tree or St John's Bread (*Ceratonia siliqua*), used in the Levant for making a kind of porridge. The exact weight at which it had become standardized varied from place to place, some 'carats' being heavier than others (Grierson 1960a, 252–4: 0.196g in Syria, 0.212g in Egypt). Ridgeway long ago showed that precise units were devised almost universally for the weighing of precious metals, which because of their high value needed to be weighed accurately, and that the measures used were obtained by averaging the weights of various types of grain (Ridgeway 1892).

The carob tree, however, was unknown in northern Europe, and while Latin Christendom in the middle ages took over for many purposes the Roman ounce and pound, these had been modified and restructured on the basis of some other kind of seed. The grains later used in Western Europe correspond to weights of about 0.05g (Paris grain 0.053g; Dutch *as* 0.049g) or 0.065g ('Troy' grain, its name taken from the Champagne fair of Troyes), i.e. standards based on the wheat grain and the barleycorn respectively. Medieval texts from the tenth century onwards describe the relationship between the three units as 1 carat = 3 barleycorns = 4 wheat grains, which is in fact very close to reality. Since the same ratios also occur in Arabic sources (Sauvaire 1882) one can assume that they have a common origin in late Roman antiquity, though the formula does not seem to occur in Isidore of Seville or the Greek or Latin metrological writers. There is no documentary evidence for these units dating back to early medieval times – weights of coins are normally expressed as fractions, such as 22 solidi (i.e. 264 coins) to the pound (below, p. 204) or 24 pennies to the ounce – but the close conformity of the weights of many early coins with widely used multiples of the units leaves one in no doubt that they did. Early sceattas, for example, generally weigh about 20 Troy grains, and where sets of coins from the same dies are available they can conform to this weight very exactly. In the Barthe hoard of Frisian silver sceattas of the late seventh century, at present in the Westfälisches Landesmuseum at Münster, the weights of 28 specimens from the same pair of dies varies between 18.1gr. and 21.5gr., apart from a defective coin of 13.9gr. and an unusually heavy one of 24.3gr.; their average is 20.0gr. (Grierson 1964, xvi–xvii). The weights of a group of 21 coins from another pair of dies varies between 18.2gr. and 20.9gr., apart from two exceptional coins of 16.8gr. and 22.5gr.; once again the average is 20.0gr. These silver coins, however, did no more than continue the weights of the gold tremisses of reduced weight that had preceded them in Gaul and England, where a similar level of accuracy obtains (below, p. 107).

The Germanic background of these weights, and the multiples used, is more evident in the

Anglo-Saxon legal codes than in those of the Continent, since the latter were drawn up in Latin and not in the vernacular. The oldest Anglo-Saxon code, that of King Æthelbert of Kent, which was written down *c.* 603 and so ante-dates the introduction of coinage, has as its monetary units the shilling (*scilling*) of 20 sceattas, terms which refer not to coins but to weights of gold. The first derives from a Germanic root meaning to cut (ON *scilja*) and implies a weight of gold cut from a ring or bar of precious metal. The second seems to have had behind it initially the notion of something very finely divided (cf. shatter, scatter) and in a pre-coinage context meant a grain of gold, though its derivative meaning of 'treasure' and the way it is used to translate a wide variety of Latin monetary terms are more familiar to students of Old English literature. (Cf. the way in which 'grain' in the singular is used both in an individual and a collective sense.) Since Anglo-Saxon gold coins when they came to be struck do in fact weigh 20 grains they can be identified with the shillings of the laws, and since cognate forms of 'shilling' exist in all other Germanic languages – the two surviving Ostrogothic charters apply it to Roman solidi – the same term was presumably used for them on the Continent. The word *sceat* has also cognate forms in other Germanic languages (Bosworth and Toller 1898, *s.v.*) and is used in the same variety of ways: *skatts* in Ulfilas translates μνᾶ ('pound') as well as δηνάριον ('penny') and ἀργύριον ('piece of silver' and 'money') in a general sense according to context, while *dinarius* is glossed as *scaz* in the so-called Keronian Glossary of the mid eighth century from St Gallen (Steinmeyer and Sievers 1879, I.112, line 33).

The two other widely used monetary terms of Germanic origin, penny and mark, do not seem to have been early in date. The first was not applied to silver coins at the time of the invasions, for Ulfilas translates the δηνάριον of the New Testament by *skatts* and never uses any word cognate to 'penny'. Its earliest appearance in England is in the laws of Ine of Wessex, of *c.* 690, and on the Continent in the Keronian Glossary of the mid eighth century already referred to (Steinmeyer and Sievers 1879, I.112, lines 33–4), the forms being *pæning* and *pfantinc* respectively. Its etymology has been much discussed (Kluge 1967, *s.v. Pfennig*; Birkhan 1971), though usually by philologists with little understanding of the numismatic context in which it first appears, but there can be no serious doubt that it shares a common root with German *Pfand*, 'pledge' or 'token', the silver coins of the late seventh century being regarded as 'tokens' in respect of the gold tremisses which had for so long been the only 'real' coins in existence.

As for *mark*, it first appears in the treaty of Wedmore between King Alfred and the Viking Guthrum of 878, though in the form of a half-mark more easily reckonable in terms of the pound, and it was not until the eleventh century that it began to be widely referred to and used in Western Europe. Its name shows that it is one of those metric or monetary terms implying the incising of a 'mark' to show that a certain number of units have been counted and one can start again, others being 'score' (for twenty) and the ancient Greek γράμμα in the sense of a small weight (from γράφω, 'scratch', 'engrave', and consequently 'write'). It was in many countries equated with two-thirds of a pound (eight ounces) and was usually somewhere between 220g and 235g, though some 'marks' were above or below this figure: two-thirds of a Roman pound would indeed have been only 218.3g. The original Germanic unit was presumably one of about this magnitude, though exactly what the figure was – it would have varied somewhat from one people to another – and how it was constructed are matters for conjecture. Possibly there was a unit of 20 'shillings', which would have weighed 26g and been easily identifiable with the Roman ounce (27.29g), and another equivalent to eight of these (i.e. a binary multiple of 2 × 2 × 2) as a mark of 208g. This is quite close to the later Scandinavian marks (Norwegian 211.3g, Swedish 212.5g, Danish 215.4g: Luschin 1926, 167–9), though below most of the medieval marks which are based on heavier ounce standards. The reason for the widespread replacement of the pound by the mark as a weight in the eleventh century was presumably the ambiguity of the term 'pound', for the monetary pound had in most places lost contact with the pound by weight, but when the mark became in turn a monetary unit of 13s 4d the old ambiguity returned.

2

THE VANDALS

Literature

Vandal coinage, largely because of its unusual types and puzzling denominations, has interested scholars since the early nineteenth century. The general pattern was established by a monograph in the mid century (Friedlaender 1849), and the Vandal series is included in two standard works on Byzantine coinage (Sabatier 1862; Hahn, *MIB* I and III (1973, 1981)). The most convenient reference works are Wroth's supplement to the BM catalogue of Byzantine coins (*BMC Vand*) and *MIB*. There is a small collection, well catalogued, at Milan (Arslan 1978). Scholars are not agreed on either the dating of the pre-regal and municipal coinages or the systems of values, so that in addition to Hahn's analysis one must consult Grierson (1959a), Morrisson (1976), and Clover (forthcoming). The separation of Vandal from imperial nummi was for long uncertain, for Wroth's 'Vandalic coinage' includes many types that are really imperial, but has now been largely solved on the evidence of coins from the Carthage excavations (Humphrey 1976) and the hoards of Le Hamma (Troussel 1950), Sidi-Aïch (Lafaurie 1960b), Tipasa III (Turcan 1961), Massafra in south Italy (Travaglini 1974), Fontana Liri near Capua (Arslan 1983), and Aïn Kelba (Morrisson 1980). The history of the Vandal kingdom is covered in the standard works on early Byzantine history by Bury (1923) and Stein (1949). There are separate monographs by Schmidt (1942) and Courtois (1955), and excellent shorter studies by Diesner (1965) and Clover (1978, 1982a).

Historical background

The kingdom set up by the Vandals in North Africa lasted almost exactly a hundred years, from the treaty with Valentinian III in 435 to its conquest by Belisarius in the winter of 533/4. Apart from its overseas possessions it corresponded essentially to modern Tunisia, with Carthage as its capital, but it extended some way westwards into Algeria and south-eastwards along the Gulf of Gabes as far as Tripoli. Mauretania to the west and Cyrenaica to the east remained technically imperial provinces, though under constant pressure from native populations whose kinglets' names are sometimes preserved in inscriptions or literary sources. The survival of imperial authority in these areas meant that their small change was easily available in Vandal Africa, a fact which explains the mixed character of coin hoards from the latter area.

The invasion of the Empire by the Vandals preceded by three decades the creation of their North African kingdom. They crossed the frozen Rhine, in company with the Alans and Suevi, on the last day of 406, and after two years of plundering and devastation in Gaul they moved in 409 into Spain. There they settled in two groups, the Asding Vandals in the north-west (Gallaecia) and the Siling Vandals in the south-east (Baetica). The Silings and their Alan neighbours were almost immediately destroyed by the Visigoths, but the retirement of the latter to Gaul made it possible for the Asding king Gunderic to absorb the remnant of the Alans, so that he and his successors assumed the title of *rex Vandalorum et Alanorum*. In 422 they moved into southern Spain, the future 'Andalusia'. But the Visigoths presented a permanent threat to their existence, and in 429, under Gunderic's brother and successor Gaiseric (428–77), the Vandals crossed into Africa at the invitation of a rebel, Count Boniface, who hoped to use them against the government of Valentinian III.

Gaiseric almost immediately asserted his independence of Boniface, and in 435 the Vandals were authorized to settle as *foederati* in Numidia (north-eastern Algeria) and parts of the adjacent provinces. In 439, apparently in a surprise attack, they captured Carthage and conquered the surrounding territory. Their new possessions were recognized by a further treaty of 442, though the precise constitutional position is disputed (Clover 1982b). Gaiseric was the most formidable Germanic ruler of the middle decades of the fifth century. He made himself master of the Balearics, Sardinia and Corsica, secured a foothold in Sicily, sacked Rome in 455, raided as far afield as the Aegean, and defeated a great imperial expedition against him in 468. His descendants (Table 2) ruled the country until March 534, when Belisarius, having captured Carthage in December 533, received the surrender of Gelimer. Surviving Vandals were enslaved or taken into the imperial service, and the Vandal kingdom came to an end.

Table 2. *Kings of the Vandals*

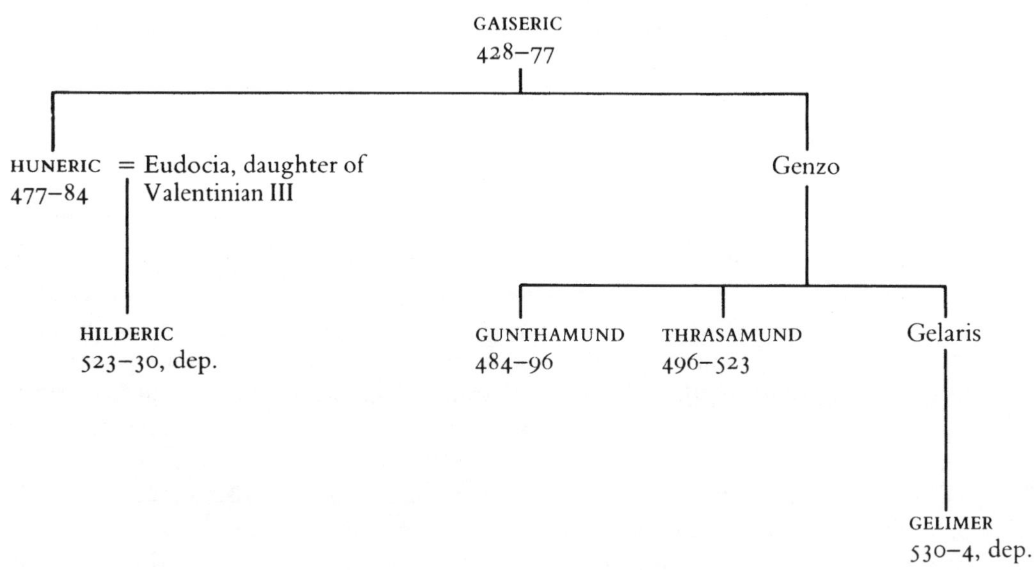

Coinage

Vandal coinage, like that of Ostrogothic Italy, is partly municipal and partly royal, with a probably substantial admixture of local and unofficially minted copper nummi. There was apparently no Vandal gold coinage: the pseudo-imperial solidi and tremisses attributed by Wroth to the Vandals are either Visigothic or Burgundian. Presumably Vandal needs in gold were satisfied by the large stocks already in the country, augmented by plunder – solidi of Constantinople predominate in hoards of the period – and by the profits of the corn and oil trade with Italy.

The 'municipal' element in the coinage consists of four denominations of copper marked XLII, XXI, XII and IIII (nummi), and the 'regal' element of three denominations of silver normally marked C, L or XXV (denarii), though there are also early pseudo-imperial silver coins, and copper nummi throughout, which are without such marks. These indications of value should make it an easy task to reconstruct the monetary system, but they have in fact been interpreted in different ways. It seems most likely, however, that the term *denarius* had recovered its original sense as a piece worth ten units or nummi, for the silver coins of the denomination normally marked DN L, i.e. 50 denarii, have under Gunthamund and in the early years of Thrasamund no mark of value in addition to the DN, and this, for a contemporary user, could scarcely have meant anything other than '500 nummi'. The 50d piece would have been a siliqua, with the 100d and 25d pieces its double and half respectively, and the solidus equal to 1,200 denarii or 12,000 nummi. The explanation of the 42 and 21 marks on the copper is that these were the closest approximations possible to units worth $\frac{1}{12}$ and $\frac{1}{24}$ of a siliqua, while the smaller copper coins marked XII and IIII were one-thousandth of a solidus and a tremissis respectively. It is true that a reckoning of the solidus at 12,000 nummi does not square with the figure of 14,400 that can be deduced (Grierson 1959a: *contra* Guey 1965, Morrisson 1976) from the *Tablettes Albertini* (Courtois *et al.* 1952), a group of commercial documents discovered in 1928, but these came from an up-country village in Algeria close to what was in the fifth century the Vandal–Imperial frontier; they could easily have retained the imperial system of reckoning, while the marks of value on the coins would represent the official reckoning in the capital.

There are two main peculiarities in the fabric of the coins, one the frequent use of abnormally thick flans smaller than the die-faces and the other die-axes approximating to 90° or 270°, presumably arising from the use of square-headed dies aligned by eye and contrasting with the normal 180° or 360° of Roman coins. Types of local inspiration are the female figure of Carthago standing in the guise of Ceres holding ears of corn – such an effigy is known from other monuments and most conspicuously from a miniature in the *Notitia dignitatum* (Clover 1978) – and two figures from the foundation legends of the city, one a standing soldier and the other the horse's head that was reputed to have been found on the site and prefigured its future military greatness (Justin 18.5: '*Ibi quoque equi caput repertum, bellicosum potentemque populum futurum significans, urbi suspicatam sedem dedit*'). Such a resort to archaic types is shared by the mint of Rome under the Ostrogoths, with its use of the head of Roma and the eagle or wolf-and-twins, and there can be little doubt that the officials of the two mints were in contact with each other, as they had been in the days of the Tetrarchy. It cannot be an accident that both at Carthage and Rome the larger denominations of copper were municipal, with no reference to Ostrogothic or Vandal sovereigns, and it is clear that the mint authorities were in each case given a free hand in the selection of their coin types.

The essential features of the coins are as follows:

Silver coins

These form three groups.

(a) Pseudo-imperial siliquae (**1.1–3**) and half-siliquae (**1.4–5**) copied from Ravennate coins of Honorius; the halves have only recently been identified and an excellent study is now available of both series (Morrisson and Schwartz 1982). They are distinguishable from original products of the Ravenna mint by their thick flans and the prevalence of 90° die-axes already alluded to.

(b) Quasi-imperial siliquae (*BMC Vand*, pl. 1.12), extremely rare and not represented here, which combine a normal imperial bust and deformed *Honorius* inscription (HONORIVS PVSAGT, without initial DN) with a novel reverse type, the standing figure of Carthago accompanied by the date ANNO IIII (or V) and the letter K. Scholars have differed as to whether they should be attributed to Gaiseric, Huneric or Gunthamund – even the revolt of Gildo, which took place in the fourth and fifth regnal years of Honorius (597/8), has been proposed (Courtois 1954) – but the most natural interpretation of the K is *Karthaginis*, a method of dating from Gaiseric's capture of Carthage on 19 October 439 which is well attested from inscriptions (Mommsen 1910; Duval 1959; Février 1966; fullest treatment in a forthcoming article by Clover). This would imply that they were struck in the two years following Gaiseric's treaty with Valentinian III in 442. The issue of dated silver coins of an original type as early as this seems at first sight unlikely, but the silver coins of the Suevic king Rechiar (below, p. 79) were also mid-century (*c.* 450), and the notion of dating could have been suggested by Theodosius II's common solidi with the inscription IMP XXXXII (=443), which with a very rare succeeding issue of 444 (with XXXXIII) represent the sole examples of regnally-dated imperial coins at this period. If this was the case, however, we would have to assume that the coins failed to gain acceptance and were replaced by the common pseudo-imperial types, which would consequently have to be dated 443–*c.* 490 instead of 439–*c.* 490 as is customarily done.

(c) Royal issues of three denominations bearing the names of the Vandal kings from Gunthamund to Gelimer (**1.6–12, 15–18, 26–7**) and usually a mark of value expressed in denarii (100d, 50d, or 25d). If, as seems likely, minting in the royal name was suggested by Odovacar's introduction of a regal silver coinage in Italy at the time of Theoderic's invasion (below, p. 28), Gunthamund's coins can be dated from *c.* 490. His 50d pieces and some of those of his successor Thrasamund lack the L for 50, as noted above. Hilderic's 50-nummus pieces (**1.21–2**) have a standing figure of Carthago instead of a mark of value. Similar coins with the name of *Iustinus* were formerly attributed to the reign of Hilderic, who was on friendly terms with Constantinople, but the designs of both bust and standing figure differ markedly from those of Hilderic's coins and the *Iustinus* ones are better regarded as Byzantine, not Vandal, and attributed to Justin II (565–78). There was a slight increase in the weights of the 50d and 25d pieces struck under Hilderic and Gelimer, perhaps to bring them into line with Athalaric's silver coins in Italy.

Municipal copper coinage

The nummus multiples were presumably struck on the authority of the magistrates of Carthage, for they lack any royal symbol. They form two classes. Class I (**1.34–42**) has on the obverse a standing figure of Carthago, holding ears of corn, in a wreath, and as reverse type an N (for *nummi*) accompanied by a mark of value (XLII, XXI, or XII), also in a wreath. The XLII multiple is common, the others are rare. Class 2 has the same denominations (**1.43–50**) but on the obverse the inscription KARTHAGO and a standing soldier, and on the reverse a horse's head and a mark of value (without N) in the exergue. The fractions are here much commoner than the 42-nummus piece and are accompanied by a lower denomination of 4 nummi (**1.51–6**) having on the obverse a bust facing left holding a palm leaf and on the reverse an N̄ with IIII below. Some scholars have thought that this coin should belong to Class I, since it has the N in addition to a mark of value, but it lacks the characteristic wreath of Class I and it is simpler to suppose that the N was dropped from the higher denominations because these had become familiar to users but was included on the 4-nummus piece because this was new. In the imperial provinces and in Ostrogothic Italy the lowest nummus multiples, in these cases pentanummia, were also late additions to the coinage system. The status of the 4-nummus piece was in fact ambiguous, for while the bust is apparently diademed there is no ruler's name. Presumably, while the municipal authorities had established their claim to the higher denominations of bronze and the nummi were 'imperial' or royal, the mint was uncertain how to treat a new denomination that fell between the two. Since it shares the anonymity of the higher denominations, however, and cannot be assigned to a specific ruler, it is best treated as forming part of Class 2.

The order of issue of the two classes seems certain, despite an absence of African hoard evidence for the larger units. Specimens of the 4-nummus piece, however, have occurred in several late hoards of nummi (e.g. Guelma, Monte Roduni, Castro dei Volsci, Sessa Aurunca) but not in early ones, and a 42-nummus piece of Class 2 was included in a group of coins brought up from the bed of the Garonne at Bordeaux which otherwise consisted entirely of Carthaginian Æ of Justinian struck in the seven years 534–41 (*RN*[4] 19 (1915), 374).

Precise dating for the whole coinage is difficult. Hahn's very late dating for both series (Class I as of the time of Hilderic, Class 2 that of Gelimer) is as unacceptable as the early one of Wroth, who made Class 2 precede Class I and attributed them to Gaiseric and Huneric respectively. It has been argued that their issue presupposes the existence of silver coins with marks of value and cannot therefore antedate *c.* 490, but this does not follow; the pseudo-imperial coins presumably belonged to the siliqua system and the numerals on the copper would have been necessary to show how they fitted into this. The fact of the larger copper denominations being non-regal is in any case best explained on the assumption of their being already in existence when the regal series began, so that kings' names came to be somewhat incongruously limited to silver coins and nummi. The large coins must, however, be subsequent to 477/8, the earliest date when the Senatorial folles of Rome with head of Roma and wolf-and-twins could have succeeded those struck in the name of Zeno (below, p. 32). One can attribute their introduction conjecturally to *c.* 480. Class I probably lasted down to the reign of Hilderic, when the taking over of the standing figure of Carthage as a type for the silver would have suggested the adoption of a different type for the bronze. Ten years (523–33) may appear too short a time to allow for the issue of coins that are today quite common, but this feature can be explained by their removal from circulation by hoarding at the time of the Byzantine conquest.

The weight system is anomalous. The variations between individual coins are so large that theoretical weights are largely guesswork, but in Class 1 the pieces of 42, 21 and 12 nummi seem to weigh respectively about 12g, 10g and 5g, while in Class 2 they are about 10g, 8g, and 4.5g, with 4-nummus pieces in good condition about 1.5g. The weights of the 21-, 12- and 4-nummus pieces are thus roughly proportional to their values, but in both classes the 42-nummus piece is only about a quarter heavier than the 21-nummus piece instead of being twice its weight. The same irregularity occurs in the coinage of Rome, with its folles and half-folles of Class 2 proportionate to each other but those of Class 3 being *c.* 10/11g and *c.* 8g respectively (below, pp. 32–3). The most likely explanation is that the Carthage mint, which had not functioned under the Principate and would not have had minting records going back to the first or second centuries A.D., was taking its cue from Rome, and that Rome for its part (below, p. 33) was reviving a feature of early imperial coinage, when the brass (orichalcum) dupondius had weighed half an ounce (13.6g) and its half, the copper as, two-fifths of an ounce (11.1g). Whether either Rome or Carthage in the late fifth century was aware that the anomaly had been justified under the Principate by the coins being slightly different in metallic composition we have no idea. It is possible, indeed, that the distinction is reproduced by these Vandal and Ostrogothic coins, and that their top denomination in each case is brass, but no analyses of their metal content are available to settle the point.

Nummi

The small change of North Africa in the fifth and early sixth centuries was provided partly by imperial issues, partly by coins of the Vandal kings from Gunthamund onwards, and partly by local imitations of either of these.

The imperial issues were of Eastern or Italian origin and had for the most part as types either, initially, a Victory or a cross in a wreath, or, from the 440s onwards, an imperial monogram. Their circulation was perhaps formally limited to Cyrenaica in the east and Mauretania in the west, but users would not have troubled to differentiate between such insignificant, badly struck coins, and North African hoards show Vandal and imperial coins in circulation together. Imperial issues do not come within the scope of this volume.

Vandal regal issues have normally on the obverse a bust and a shortened form of the ruler's name, e.g. DNRC TRSA, with as reverses under Thrasamund a Victory (**1.19–20**), and under Hilderic a cross in a wreath (**1.24–5**). Coins with a D in a wreath (**1.13–14**) are formally anonymous, but since they are not obviously 'municipal' and the numeral (500) links up with the pattern of values first made plain on the silver coinage of Gunthamund they are attributed here to this ruler. A supposed nummus of Gelimer with his monogram and a standing figure of Carthago (Regler 1954) is a nineteenth-century forgery of Cigoi (Brunetti 1966, no. 503), and the coins with a Christogram attributed to Gunthamund and Thrasamund, a monogram attributed to Thrasamund, and a cross-on-wreath attributed to Gelimer are in need of confirmation from specimens on which regal names are clearly legible. A small group with deliberately anonymous inscriptions (*Domino nostro*, etc.) has sometimes been ascribed to the early years of Gaiseric's occupation of Carthage, but was more likely minted by the rebel Count Boniface in the late 420s.

The D coins attributed to Gunthamund were preceded by anonymous quasi-imperial issues having as reverse types a rosette or a cross and four pellets in a wreath. Coins of poor fabric having as reverse types a very degenerate Victory, or a cross or Christogram in wreath (**1.31–3**), are best regarded as imitations produced to compensate for local shortages of petty cash, though die-linkages show them sometimes to have circulated quite widely. Conspicuous cases of such coins are provided by the Sidi-Aïch and Orléansville hoards from Tunisia and Algeria respectively. Of the latter we have no more than a brief notice (*RBN* 85 (1933), 172), but the former, an extraordinary accumulation of tiny coins weighing only *c.* 0.25g and with their Victory types barely scratched on the dies, has been the subject of a remarkable study (Lafaurie 1960b).

Scholars have generally assumed that these small coins, like their imperial counterparts, corresponded to the nummi mentioned in a Constitution of the Emperor Valentinian III of 445, which reckons them at 7,000 or 7,200 to the solidus (above, p. 10). Hahn has argued, however, that they are really denarii and multiples of $2\frac{1}{2}$ nummi, the nummus itself not existing as a coin at all. His reasons are partly the D used as the type of Gunthamund's coins, for this could stand for denarius, but mainly metrological, for the coins weigh about 0.7g, about half the 4-nummus piece of Class 2 (*c.* 1.5g), and far more than one-twelfth of the 12-nummus piece (*c.* 5g). Neither argument carries conviction. The best interpretation of D is 500, meaning a coin worth $\frac{1}{500}$ of a siliqua (Callu in Morrisson 1980, 242 n. 9), just as LXXII and XCVI on some early fourth-century coins had shown these to be $\frac{1}{72}$ and $\frac{1}{96}$ of a pound respectively. A copper worth $\frac{1}{25}$ of the smallest silver coin would have had to be quite large, and the lack of correspondence in weight between 42- and 21-nummus pieces shows that proportionality was not inherent in the denominational pattern. Departure from proportionality is indeed something that often occurs at the lowest level of values, since coins below a certain size are impossible to handle. It has a parallel in the contemporary coinage of Byzantium, where the pentanummia introduced by Anastasius I had to be fitted into a system with folles, half-folles and decanummia weighing respectively 16.4g, 8.2g and 4.1g, and the new coins of *c.* 2g were proportional to the higher denominations but weighed little more than twice the nummus. Here the identification of the denomination is certain, for some of the coins of Justinian bear the mark of value A, i.e. 1. The smallest denomination of the Vandals is therefore treated in this catalogue as a nummus.

3

ODOVACAR AND THE OSTROGOTHS, 476–552

(a) GENERAL FEATURES AND BACKGROUND

The earliest continuous coinage of Germanic rulers in Italy was that of the Ostrogoths, but its main features already appear under Odovacar, whose reign forms a transition between the rule of the *Magistri militum* and the more fully Germanic authority of Theoderic. The coinage of the middle ages in Italy can therefore best begin with Odovacar. It is true that he had a partial predecessor in Ricimer, *Magister militum* from 456 to 472, for copper nummi of Severus III (Cohen 18) have on their reverse a monogram that includes the letters RCME and is generally taken as referring to Ricimer (Friedlaender 1844, 5–6), who had nominated Severus emperor in 456 and is improbably alleged to have poisoned him in 465. This coinage, however, is of a quite marginal character, and a continuous regal coinage starts under Odovacar.

The coinage of Italy during the three-quarters of a century between the deposition of Romulus Augustulus (476) and the end of the Ostrogothic kingdom (552) is illustrated on Plates 3–9. It has many affinities with that of North Africa under the Vandals, but it differs profoundly from that of the Visigoths and Franks, the two other Germanic peoples who set up major kingdoms in the West, in its possession of an important subsidiary coinage in silver and copper. The silver is a 'regal' coinage in the sense that the coins normally bear the name or monogram of a king in addition to that of the reigning emperor. The copper is partly regal and partly 'municipal', struck with legends and types appropriate to the local authorities at Rome (principally) or Ravenna, and partly 'private', for official issues were supplemented by surviving bronze coins of the early Empire brought back into circulation and countermarked to give them a value as currency. The existence of an abundant silver coinage differentiates the provinces ruled by Odovacar and the Ostrogoths from those that remained in imperial hands, for in the East in this period the silver coin was vestigial and without any economic function, being apparently struck only occasionally and for ceremonial purposes. There are likewise in the East no municipal coinages, and still less anything comparable to the use of countermarked bronzes of the Principate.

Literature

The work most generally used remains *BMC Vand*, which superseded the excellent nineteenth-century monograph of Friedlaender (1844), itself the expanded version of an appendix to his monograph on Justinian (Pinder and Friedlaender 1843). The coverage in the three relevant volumes of the *CNI* (vols.

IV for Pavia, X for Ravenna, XV for Rome) is inadequate and badly presented, and the monograph of Kraus (1928), though very thorough, is uncritical. The material is covered in the standard works on Byzantine coinage, notably Sabatier (1862, I.194–211). Tolstoi (1912–14, 154–9, 207–24, 266–7, 378–410) and *MIB* (I.77–91, II.30–2, III.55–8), the last of which includes important discussions of the coinage and monetary systems. An essential article on the mints is that of Kent (1971), to which may be added Lenzi (1913) for Odovacar.

The historical background is covered in the standard works on the later Roman Empire (Bury 1923; Stein 1949) and on Italian history (Romano and Solmi 1940). Vols. III and IV of Hodgkin (1885) are fuller but necessarily old-fashioned. Recent monographs on various aspects of Ostrogothic history are Burns (1980) and Wolfram (1980), and Ensslin (1959) on Theoderic the Great. On economic life there is an important monograph by Ruggini (1961), and on art by Fuchs (1944). Geiss 1931, despite a promising title, has nothing to say about the coinage.

Historical background

Odovacar (476–93)

Odovacar – his name is variously spelled – was a mercenary of mixed Hunnic and Scirian parentage who after a military career in Gaul rose to high rank in the army in Italy in the early 470s. On 23 August 476 he was proclaimed 'king' by the troops in north Italy, and within a few days defeated and killed the *Magister militum* Orestes and deposed the latter's son, the usurping emperor Romulus Augustulus (Sept. 476). An embassy was sent by the Roman Senate at his orders to the newly restored Eastern emperor Zeno, with the message that there was no longer any need for a separate emperor in the West and that Italy would be happy to recognize Zeno. Zeno replied that there was already a legitimate Western emperor in the person of Julius Nepos, whom Orestes had deposed (28 August 475) and who was holding out in Dalmatia. Odovacar is shown by his coinage to have duly recognized Nepos, and, after Nepos' murder on 9 May 480, Zeno himself, but he in fact ruled on his own account and that of the army that had proclaimed him *rex*. His relations with Zeno deteriorated in 486/7, however, and in 488 Zeno, in order to rid the Eastern provinces of the Ostrogoths, offered Italy to their King Theoderic 'to rule in place of Odovacar until Zeno came himself'. The following year Theoderic invaded the country, defeated Odovacar on the Isonzo and again on the Adige, and occupied Milan and Pavia while Odovacar maintained himself in Ravenna. In 490 Odovacar conferred on his son Thela the rank of Caesar, which was equivalent to a repudiation of imperial suzerainty, but in August he was defeated in a third and this time decisive battle on the Adda north of Milan and the whole peninsula save Ravenna passed under Ostrogothic control. Odovacar held out in Ravenna till 493, when he surrendered in return for a promise of co-rulership (5 March). Ten days afterwards he was murdered on the pretext that he was plotting against his conqueror.

The Ostrogothic kingdom

The Ostrogoths had been one of the many groups of Germanic peoples who in the mid-fifth century were subjected to Attila. After the downfall of the Hunnic Empire in 454 they settled as *foederati* in northern Pannonia in return for a promised annual subvention of 100lb of gold, subsequently greatly increased. In the 470s and 480s, under Theoderic and various rival leaders, their depredations in the Balkans became intolerable to the Eastern emperors, with the results just described.

Theoderic, as head of a great people, was in a very different position to Odovacar, who had no more than a small personal following on which to rely. The Ostrogothic kingdom in Italy lasted for just over sixty years, from 490 to 552. The list of its kings is as follows:

Theoderic (471)	490–526	Hildebad	540–1
Athalaric	526–34	Eraric	541
(Amalasuntha	534–5)	Baduila-Totila	541–52
Theodahad	534–6	Theia	552
Witigis	536–40		

Their names are spelled very variously in our sources, since writers of different linguistic backgrounds heard and reproduced the sound of their names slightly differently, and the forms used here are those most familiar to modern readers. Baduila-Totila is a special case. He is invariably *Totila* in the literary sources, *Baduela* on the coins, and the Gothic historian Jordanes vouches for their identity: *Baduila qui etiam Totila dicebatur*. Baduila – the spellings Badu*i*la and Badu*e*la are interchangeable – was evidently his official name and Totila a familiar one used by the Goths in ordinary speech, so that it was the form that would be heard by Procopius and other imperial writers of the day.

The earlier kings were members of the Ostrogothic royal family of the Amals, the essential elements in their relationships being set out in Table 3. This shows how Theoderic tried to gain support by marriage alliances with the rulers of the other Germanic kingdoms. Later kings, from 536 onwards, without benefit of Amal connections, were chosen because of a confidence, usually misplaced, in their military skills and prospects.

The first thirty years of the Gothic period, under Theoderic (490–526) and Athalaric (526–34), represented a kind of Indian summer for imperial Italy, with the country competently and effectively administered in the emperor's name and an apparently prosperous economy. Tragedy began in 535, when Belisarius, in pursuance of Justinian's ambition of restoring 'Roman' rule in the western Mediterranean, followed up his recovery of Africa by invading Italy. Theoderic had left no sons, and his heir was his grandson, offspring of his strong-minded daughter Amalasuntha and an Ostrogothic nobleman Eutharic who had lived obscurely in Spain but claimed Amal descent. Athalaric died on 2 October 534 at the age of 17, his mother having been regent during most of his reign, and was succeeded by his kinsman Theodahad, a landowner in Tuscany mainly known for his rapacity and who was quite unfit to rule. It was his ill-treatment and eventual murder of Amalasuntha, who in according Theodahad the royal title had stipulated that she retain the reality of power, that provided the excuse for Justinian's intervention in Italy. Belisarius' capture of Naples in November 536 was followed by Theodahad's overthrow and murder by Witigis (536–40). But although Belisarius occupied Rome in December his forces were inadequate for the quick conquest he had achieved in North Africa, and it required four years of savage fighting before Witigis was by trickery induced to surrender Ravenna (May 540). Witigis died two years later in honourable captivity, and it seemed as if the Gothic kingdom should have come to an end.

Table 3. *The Ostrogothic royal house (Amals)*

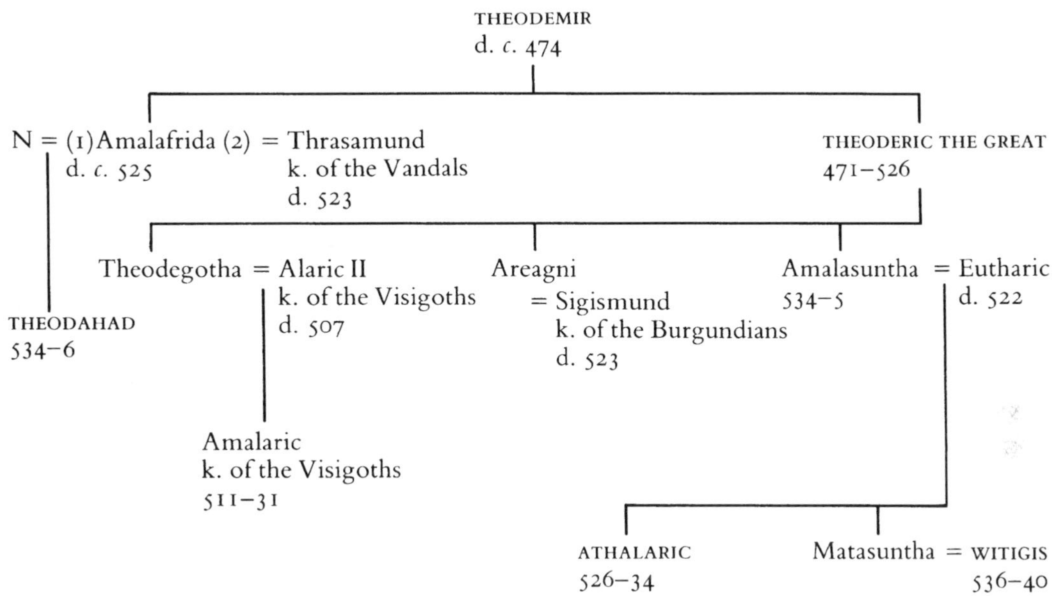

This might indeed have happened if Justinian had not recalled Belisarius to take command against Persia. The surrender of Ravenna did not carry with it that of other Gothic garrisons in north Italy. The next two kings were short-lived. Hildebad (540–1) was elected king at Verona, but was murdered within a year as a result of a private feud. He was succeeded by a Rugian adventurer Eraric (May–Sept. 541), who suffered the same fate after only six months. Only then did the Gothic luck seem to turn. The next king was Hildebad's nephew Baduila (541–52), an able soldier and popular figure who re-established his people's fortunes and recovered Rome and indeed most of the peninsula. But the Goths, although more numerous than the Vandals, had no hope of standing up to the imperial army if this were properly supplied and adequately led, as it was to be under the Armenian Narses, appointed commander-in-chief in 550.

Baduila was defeated and killed at the battle of Busta Gallorum, south of Ravenna, in June 552, and the Gothic state ended with the death of his successor Theia (Teias) on the slopes of Mons Lactuarius near Naples in September 552. Once again, however, Gothic garrisons continued to hold out in several parts of the peninsula, and Narses still had to complete its conquest and defeat a great Frankish-Alamannic invasion in 554. It was not till November 562 that Verona and Brixen, the last strongholds of importance, were captured from Goths or Franks and their city keys despatched to Justinian. The devastation of the countryside and the sufferings of the population during the long war had been appalling, and only a shadow of its former prosperity survived in the Italy of which Justinian finally became master in the last years of his reign.

(b) THE COINAGE OF ODOVACAR, 476–93

Odovacar, despite his royal title, formally ruled Italy as an imperial official (cf. Jones 1962), and during most of his reign the mints of Milan, Ravenna and Rome continued to issue coin in the name of an emperor, initially Julius Nepos (before May 480) and Zeno (474–91) during its remainder. Odovacar's own reign formally overlapped with that of Anastasius, who came to the throne in April 491 and news of whose accession would have reached Italy in May or June, but by that time Odovacar was besieged in Ravenna and is unlikely to have minted in the name of the new sovereign. At the end of his reign he issued instead, from Ravenna, silver and bronze coins with his own name and monogram. It has been suggested that they may date from *c.* 486, when his relations with Zeno began to deteriorate, but more probably they belong to the years 490–3, which explains why only Ravenna was involved.

The Italian solidi attributable to Odovacar's reign (Kent 1966) are not represented in this collection, but there are four tremisses (**1.57–60**) with a portrait and large-spiked wreath that are characteristic of Milan, which at this time practically monopolized the production of tremisses in the peninsula (Ulrich-Bansa 1949, 336ff.). The silver coins in the name of Zeno (**1.61–2**), conventionally termed half-siliquae, must belong to the same period. The style of the bust on **1.61** suggests the mint of Milan, and **1.62** has the mint-mark MD. The type of **1.61**, an eagle with wings curved upwards and a cross between the tips, corresponds to the form of the eagle that topped consular sceptres and whose appearance is known from ivory diptychs and from occasional use on coins (e.g. those of Tiberius II, 578–82). The type of **1.62**, a figure on the prow of a ship wearing a mural crown and holding staff and cornucopia, probably represents Ravenna; coins of this mint exist with RV in field. There are also coins with an eagle resembling that on **1.104–9** that must be assigned to Rome, but they are not represented here.

More interesting are the two portrait coins with Odovacar's name and/or monogram. The silver one is of extreme rarity, and the authenticity of the specimen in this collection (**1.63**) is fortunately guaranteed by its history and the circumstances of its finding being known (p. 422 below). It has on the obverse the inscription FL ODOVAC and the king's bust, bareheaded and wearing a moustache, and on the reverse the monogram of ODOVAC in a heavy wreath, with RV beneath. FL stands for *Flavius*, often assumed as an additional name in late imperial times (Mócsy 1964). Although not the earliest coin to have been struck in the name of a Germanic sovereign, since that of the Suevic king Rechiar (p. 79) preceded it by half a century, it is one of the relatively few coins of the early middle ages to show an actual portrait of a ruler. There are forgeries with a slightly different monogram; see note on **1.1452**. The copper coin is a nummus with a simplified monogram on the reverse (**1.64**). This has also been counterfeited: the two specimens in the British Museum (*BMC Vand.* pl. 5.8–9), from identical dies, are forgeries of Cigoi.

(c) COUNTERMARKED EARLY IMPERIAL BRONZE COINS

The coins described in this section, of which only about 150 are known today, formed a supplementary fractional coinage in Ostrogothic Italy and may have been used in Vandal Africa. We are fortunate that a very thorough study of them has been made (Morrisson 1983). The coins themselves, which are usually of the Flavian period, cannot have been in continuous circulation between the first and the sixth centuries; the many changes in the external appearance of the coinage during the intervening period would have made this impossible. They must rather represent casual finds of coins which were not far removed in size from those in normal use and to which a conventional value could be attached by members of the public.

The numerals on these coins, LXXXIII or XLII, are not countermarks in the usual sense of the word, since they were imposed by a series of separate chisel strokes instead of by specially prepared stamps. But they fulfilled one of the many functions for which countermarks could be used, in this case that of assigning to the coins the value of 83 or of 42 nummi. They are normally placed in either the left or right obverse field, apparently because those responsible for them wished to avoid defacing the imperial bust and thereby committing *lèse majesté*, but their roughness and irregularity points to their having been imposed by users and not by an official mint. The LXXXIII sign was reserved for sestertii (**1.65**), of which only about half a dozen specimens are known. The XLII occurs mainly on asses but is sometimes found on dupondii, which are virtually the same size as asses and would in the fifth century, when the denominations had long since vanished, have been difficult to distinguish from them even if there had been any point in doing so. They occur on sestertii only when these were unusually small in size or had been cut down (**1.90**).

Early notices of these coins, which usually did little more than publish individual specimens and speculate on their date and function, have been superseded by Cécile Morrisson's comprehensive study, based on over a hundred specimens, including those in the three principal collections at Berlin (61 specimens), Cambridge (31 specimens) and the Museo Nazionale at Rome (17 specimens). The function of the markings can be deduced from the fact that the sestertius is not valued at exactly twice the as or dupondius, i.e. not as 84 nummi but as 83, for it shows that they were intended to serve as the closest approximations possible to thirds (83 instead of $83\frac{1}{3}$) and sixths (42 instead of $41\frac{2}{3}$) of a silver unit valued at 250 nummi, i.e. of a siliqua when the solidus was reckoned at its traditional figure of 6,000 denarii, or in this case 6,000 nummi.

Scholars have differed over Africa or Italy as their place of origin. Mme Morrisson follows Friedlaender and Wroth in favouring Africa. Five specimens are known to have come from Tunisia, and the figure XLII, both as a mark of value and epigraphically in the way that the horizontal stroke of the L has been prolonged to the right and the two upright strokes of the II placed above it, corresponds to that of the folles of Carthage (though one cannot insist upon the latter feature, which is also found in inscriptions elsewhere). The size (module) of the countermarked XLII pieces is much the same as that of the commoner 42-nummus coins of Carthage, and although their weights are rather less – she works out the average of the countermarked coins as 8.67g, as against figures of 11.39g for 18 specimens of the heavier Carthage series and 9.57g for 18 of the lighter one – they fall within the right weight range, and the wide variations in the weights of individual coins show that differences in this respect did not worry users.

Mme Morrisson admits, on the other hand, the strength of the rival arguments in favour of Italy. A very high proportion of those specimens whose provenance is known or is probable were found or acquired in that country. The 17 in the Museo Nazionale were found locally, mainly in the Tiber, and 51 of the 61 specimens in the Berlin Cabinet were given to it by

Heinrich Dressel (1845–1920), who before becoming director of its classical section in 1898 had spent many years in Italy collecting inscriptions for the *Corpus Inscriptionum*. Another specimen at Berlin was bought at Padua; the one in the Livorno collection was probably found locally; one came to light in excavations at Velleia near Piacenza; one in the collection here (**1.71**) was found at Bergamo and two others (**1.77, 78**) formed part of a large hoard of fifth- and sixth-century nummi found in the early 1950s at Montelibretti in the Sabine hills outside Rome. Mme Morrisson discounts this evidence on the ground that coins tended to pass from Africa to Italy rather than in the opposite direction as a result of the sequence of Justinian's wars, and it is true that Vandal nummi and 4-nummus pieces appear in substantial numbers in Italian hoards. But large and easily recognizable coins are very different from tiny and virtually indecipherable nummi whose place of origin could scarcely be determined by users. Carthage 42- and 21-nummus pieces are not normally found in Italy. Nor, even admitting that coins from Italy become more easily available to collectors than ones from Tunisia, is it likely that this would account for such overwhelming preponderance in favour of Italian provenances, with 72 coins as against only 5. Mme Morrisson also admits that there is strong negative evidence against Africa, for apart from a single specimen in the Bardo she has seen no countermarked coins amongst the Roman coins she has examined in Tunisian museums.

This is outweighed, she believes, by the fact that a 42-nummus denomination was struck in Africa and not for Italy. This may point, however, in the opposite direction. We know from the silver coins struck after the Byzantine reconquest that a demand existed in Italy for two coin values very close to each other but useful in different ways, in this case silver coins marked PK (120 nummi) which were multiples of three folles and others marked PKE (125 nummi) which were half-siliquae. Under the Ostrogoths, however, the Roman Senate was striking coins of 40 nummi, but there were no exact fractions of the siliqua. In order to provide the latter, would it not be natural to use Roman coins of the early Empire that turned up from time to time, stamping large and heavy sestertii with LXXXIII to serve as thirds, and asses and dupondii with XLII to serve as sixths? This would explain why the vast majority of surviving specimens comes from Italy, and save us from flying in the face of the the find evidence by assigning them to Africa. Since a 42-nummus piece was used in Africa, however, it would be natural for them sometimes to be taken to that country and perhaps used there. But the balance of probability is in favour of regarding Italy as their place of origin.

The only hoard evidence for their date is the presence of two specimens in the Montelibretti hoard, which included nummi as late as Justinian's reign, though since we have no details – the owner's meticulous description of its contents has not been seen since his death in the early 1950s – we do not know if this was before or after Justinian's reconquest. The large number of late fifth-century coins of Leo I, Zeno and even Basiliscus in the hoard, however, suggests the 530s, or the 540s at latest. Two further considerations point to a relatively late date. One is that the countermarking was probably contemporary with the second, lighter issues of Senatorial folles, for coins of the earlier issue, as has been seen, were substantially heavier than the average of 8.67g ascertained by Mme Morrisson for the countermarked coins, which would not encourage users to accord them a value superior to that of the coins of 40 nummi. The other is the existence of Justinian's 120/125-nummus silver coins; since they were performing the same function of fine tuning the currency system, presumably in accordance with some popular demand, it is natural to place the two close together in time. But this does not allow us to do more than assign their use to the second quarter or perhaps to the first half of the sixth century; how much earlier they may go back we do not know.

(d) SENATORIAL AND MUNICIPAL COINAGES

The bulk of the copper coinage of Ostrogothic Italy did not, however, consist of countermarked asses but of folles and half-folles struck at Rome by the Senate. Under Odovacar and the Ostrogoths this institution enjoyed a brief Indian summer of power (Sundwall 1915, 1919; Chastagnol 1966), its prestige enhanced by the enormous wealth of the more prominent Senatorial families (Allard 1907). Amongst its new activities was a revival of the ancient Senatorial privilege of minting in bronze, so that the formula S C (*Senatus consulto*), not used since the whole coinage of the Empire had been brought under direct imperial control by Diocletian, reappeared on the coins after the lapse of nearly two centuries. The Senatorial issues began with 40-nummus pieces (folles) struck in the name of Zeno which were issued only briefly. They were followed by folles and half-folles of a purely 'Roman' character, making no reference to imperial or royal authority.

The coins in the name of Zeno alone – a unique specimen in the Hermitage of Zeno and the Caesar Leo is seemingly a coin of Zeno with the legend recut (Kent 1959, 97) – have on the obverse a bust manifestly intended as a portrait like those of the early Empire, though whether die-cutters at Rome could have had any idea of Zeno's actual appearance is a different matter. The reverse type is a Victory holding trophy and wreath advancing right, with INVICTA (or IMVICTA)ROMA as inscription, S C in the field, and the mark of value XL in the exergue. Almost all known specimens are from two pairs of obverse dies, one with a large head and the inscription IMP ZENO SEMPER AVG, the other with a smaller head and the inscription, reading outwardly and anti-clockwise, IMP ZENO FELICISSIMO SEN AVG, with IIII beneath the head. The first is extremely rare, with no more than two specimens known, but the second (**1.92**) is relatively common, with some twenty specimens recorded. The fact of so many specimens of a copper coin sharing the same dies has led some scholars to regard them as forgeries, despite the fact that some specimens have been known since the seventeenth century. The more likely explanation is a very short period of issue, as it is with the limited number of dies found in Theodahad's coinage (below, p. 38). Their unusual character may also have led to their having been preserved as souvenirs by contemporaries.

The revival of large-sized copper coins, of characterized portraiture, of an inscriptional arrangement common in Roman Republican times but not later, of a *felicissimus* title borrowed from coins of the Tetrarchy, and of SC, together with the use of a Victory type popular in the Flavian period (see **1.79–82**), all point to a deliberate excursion into archaism on the part of the Roman mint that fits in admirably with the literary interests of the Roman senators at this period. The date of the coin is disputed. Kent (1959) and Hendy (1985, pp. 488–9) both place it towards the end of Zeno's reign (*c.* 490), after Theoderic's occupation of Rome. The question depends in part on the IIII beneath the head. If it is an officina mark, like the numerals that occur on later Senatorial issues, it is irrelevant for dating purposes. But despite its resemblance to the officina marks on the later coins (see Plate 3), such a mark accompanying the imperial representation would be an anomaly, and numerals making part of the imperial inscription had in early times signified the number of times the ruler had been granted the tribunician power, or had held the consulship, or had occupied some other office. If on this coin the IIII is a regnal date, as late fifth-century practice would lead one to expect, the coin would have been struck in 477, Zeno having become emperor in February 474. In any case, the circumstances of Odovacar's instruction to the Roman Senate for sending back the imperial ornaments to Zeno and inviting him to take over the government of the West make 477 a more likely date for the coin than 490.

This coin was followed by folles and half-folles (**1.92–111**) with an obverse inscription INVICTA (or IMVICTA) ROMA and a helmeted bust of Roma, recalling that on early denarii of the Roman Republic. The reverse types, when they are not a Roman eagle, refer to the traditional origins of Rome, with Romulus and Remus suckled by a she-wolf or a fig-tree representing the *ficus ruminalis* – Rumina was the goddess of nursing mothers – beneath which, according to Livy, this scene was enacted. The reverse always includes a mark of value in Roman numerals (XL or XX) and the folles have also an officina numeral 1–5, either Roman (I–V) or Greek (A–E). There are two classes, which can be conveniently described as a heavy and a light one, though the description is not entirely accurate. Coins of the first class are all of the same type and are differentiated by weight into units and halves; coins of the second are less clearly differentiated by weight but are distinguished by types so that users would not confuse them. If the 'Zeno' coins can be treated as Class 1, the Senatorial ones are as follows:

Class 2: Heavy series

(a) Follis (**1.93–6**). Rev. type: wolf and twins, with XL above and Roman officina numeral (·IIII· being much the commonest) in the exergue.

(b) Half-follis (**1.97–9**). Same type, but XX in exergue and I or Christogram between two stars above. The stars are not supplementary ornaments or privy-marks but part of the design, occurring in earlier representations of the scene. The I or Christogram perhaps signifies the first officina, which is not recorded for the follis, but more probably is ornamental.

Class 3: Light series

(a) Follis (**1.100–9**). Rev. type: eagle, with mark of value vertically to left and normally Greek officina numeral, the fifth (E, often reversed) being the commonest, in exergue.

(b) Half-follis (**1.110–11**). Rev. type: fig-tree and two eagles, with ·XX· in exergue and no officina mark.

The weights of individual specimens of Class 2 vary over a wide range, but the folles are normally 14g/16g and the halves 7g/8g. The folles were perhaps struck 18 to the lb, which would imply a theoretical weight of 18.2g, and the weights of folles and half-folles are in the ratio of 2:1, as one would expect. The pattern of Class 3 is much stranger. The weights of individual specimens are once again very variable, with isolated folles sometimes going as high as 14g, but most are 10g/11g. The halves on the other hand sometimes go as high as 11g but are normally about 8g, well over half the follis but essentially the same weight as the half-folles of Class 2. The fact of this change in weight pattern coinciding with the change of type shows that it cannot have been an accident resulting from inadequate mint control. It must rather represent the conscious adoption of the arrangement by which, under the early Empire, dupondii had been only slightly heavier than asses instead of twice their weight. The same practice, as noted above (p. 22), was followed at Carthage.

Wroth believed that the 'light' series preceded the 'heavy' one. No hoard evidence is available, but the heavy folles correspond in weight to the 'Zeno' coins and the light ones to those of Theodahad, so the order must be the other way round. Any precise dating is difficult. Wroth supposed that the issue of both series was limited to the reigns of Theoderic and Athalaric, and Hahn has argued that Class 2 was introduced in 512, a date supported by the fact that its weight pattern coincides with that of Anastasius' large module folles, which were introduced in that year. Class 2 would have followed two *lustra* later, in 522. Against this late dating is the fact of the coinage being Senatorial in character, for by 512 there was in existence a silver coinage bearing Theoderic's name or monogram, and it is hard to imagine a newly introduced copper coinage not being equally 'royal' in character. Introduction in 512 would also leave an inexplicable gap between it and the 'Zeno' coinage, which cannot be later than 491 and may go back to 477, and the brevity of whose existence is best accounted for by its having been replaced by the first purely Senatorial type. It seems likely, therefore, that this went back to Odovacar's reign. When or why it was replaced by the second Senatorial class is impossible to say.

The purely Senatorial coinage, in any case, came to an end in 535 or 536, when it was briefly succeeded by the portrait folles of Theodahad (below, p. 38). In 537, after Belisarius' occupation of Rome, this was finally replaced by a regular imperial coinage in the name of Justinian. Meanwhile, under Athalaric, the new denomination of decanummium had been introduced, with its Roman coins (**1.132**) combining 'Roman' and royal elements, and when Rome was abandoned by the Ostrogoths a municipal coinage of decanummia was inaugurated at Ravenna between 536 and 540, when this city in turn was lost to Belisarius. Two types are known: one, not represented here, with an eagle reverse and the other with the monogram of the city in a wreath (**1.145–50**). Hahn has dated them earlier and attributed them to Rome, making them fractions of Class 2, but their Ravennate origin – the inscription FELIX RAVENNA, the mural-crowned bust of the city, the monogram on the reverse, the absence of SC – is clear (cf. Muratori 1967), and their existence explains the rarity of decanummia in the name of Witigis. The brief emergence of a second municipal coinage was presumably a consequence of the arrival at Ravenna of Roman moneyers who had fled from Rome when it was abandoned to Belisarius in December 536.

Rome was again in Ostrogothic hands under Totila, momentarily in 546–7 and more effectively between 549 and 552, but although its mint was reopened in 549 the coins then struck make no reference to the Senate (below, p. 38) and are purely royal in character.

(e) OSTROGOTHIC ROYAL COINAGE, 491–552

The royal – in part 'imperial' – coinage of the Ostrogoths supplied, with occasional overlapping, the denominations above and below the Senatorial folles and half-folles. The monetary system seems to have involved a reckoning of 12,000 nummi to the solidus, the denominations normally struck being, in gold, the solidus and tremissis, and, in silver, the half- and quarter-siliqua, the latter worth 250 and 125 nummi respectively but not bearing a mark of value, as did their counterparts in Vandal Africa and as their successors were to do after Justinian's reconquest. The copper coins were nummi and multiples of 40, 20, 10 and 5, the two higher of these being the Senatorial issues already described. These values involved the disadvantage of having a siliqua and its fractions that did not divide evenly into folles, but this was reduced, as shown above, by the countermarking of coins of the early Empire. How far the system remained stable throughout the Ostrogothic period is impossible to say. Although the two main classes of folles differ somewhat in weight, as we have seen, the change is much less considerable than the doubling of that of the Constantinopolitan copper coins in 512, and since it did not affect the half-follis it may well have involved no change in the system of reckoning.

The chief Ostrogothic mints were Rome and Ravenna, as in imperial times, with Milan also initially a mint for gold. Pavia (*Ticinum*), although the Ostrogothic capital, did not become a mint till after the loss of Ravenna to the Empire in 540. (T plus officina letter at the end of the reverse inscription on some solidi of Zeno has been erroneously interpreted as *Ticinum* by Lederer (1934), followed by Lacam (1983, II.863–80). It is really Thessalonica: see Lallemand 1964.) The mint name occurs in full on copper coins. From 504 onwards Theoderic's kingdom included *Sirmium* (Mitrovica) on the Sava in modern Yugoslavia, and some of his silver coins have been attributed to this mint, which had been of great importance in the fourth century, on grounds of provenance. Arles was in Ostrogothic hands between 509, when Theoderic annexed Provence, and 533, when Amalasuntha ceded it to the Franks, but it is not certain that it served as a mint. Correct mint attributions for coins without a mint-mark raise problems not yet satisfactorily solved. The most generally accepted attributions were for long those in the British Museum catalogue, but Wroth did not claim any special expertise in the matter – his main interests lay in the fields of classical Greek coins and British medals – and usually contented himself with reproducing the arrangement he found in the trays. These in turn went back to Count William de Salis (1825–71), who in 1859 had presented his own great collection to the Museum in return for the privilege of being allowed to arrange its Roman, Byzantine and sub-Byzantine series and who relied mainly on a remarkable but by no means infallible sense of style (Mattingly 1925). A number of his attributions have been revised by Kent (1971), but there is still a considerable element of uncertainty in the general picture.

The coinage of Ostrogothic Italy is for the most part markedly superior artistically and technically to that of Constantinople, the coins being carefully designed and struck in higher relief. There are occasional departures from normal spelling – *imvicta* instead of *invicta*, *rix* instead of *rex* – which bear out the comments made by Theoderic's great scholar-minister Cassiodorus in his *De orthographia* on the current confusion between pairs of consonants which were no longer clearly distinguished in pronunciation and the uncertain values of unstressed vowels. There are some precedents, however, in the coinage of the fifth century: one class of Theodosius II's solidi regularly has *orvis* instead of *orbis* in the legend of *gloria orbis terrarum*. One die-sinker under Theoderic always omits the second horizontal bar of the letter F (in PF), turning it into a *gamma* (e.g. **1.122–3**). The remarkable variety in monograms of the same ruler (Berges 1954) suggests that in the absence of formal models the die-sinkers must have been left very much to their own devices.

Ostrogothic gold coinage belongs mainly to the reign of Theoderic, when it was struck in the names of Anastasius and Justin I, and the reign of Athalaric, when it was continued in those of Justin I and of Justinian. It presumably continued under Theodahad and Witigis, but any coins they minted would have borne the name of Justinian and cannot be distinguished from those of Athalaric. Whether any gold coins were struck after 540 is doubtful. Wroth followed de Salis in attributing to Baduila and Theia a number of coins in the name of Anastasius, on the assumption that this ruler's name was revived for the gold as it was for the silver, but the attribution seems unsupported by evidence from finds and the coins are better placed in the category of 'uncertain Germanic imitations', presumably of Anastasius' own time.

The denominations normally minted were the solidus and tremissis. The only exceptions made part of a ceremonial coinage for long attributed to the year 500, when Theoderic celebrated his *tricennalia*, the thirtieth anniversary of his association as co-ruler by his father, with a splendid round of festivities in Rome. The coins making up this issue involved a triple solidus with his facing bust (*BMC Vand*, frontispiece; Gnecchi 1895), giving him the titles of *rex* and *princis* (i.e. *princeps*; but cf. Stückelberg 1898, Allara 1898), and a semissis showing a Victory inscribing VOT/PC (i.e. *vota principis*) on a shield supported by a winged Cupid. Only a single specimen of each, now in Rome and Leningrad respectively, is known. Almost equally rare are what appear to be the accompanying solidi, of the usual type but with either a *theta* (Theoderic's initial) or his monogram at the end of the reverse legend, and tremisses, these having a Victory running either right or left and holding a palm and wreath instead of the customary wreath and globus cruciger. The triple solidus and the semissis are mainly of iconographical interest, but the tremissis provided the model for the pseudo-imperial issues of the Burgundians and other peoples in southern Gaul and Spain (below, pp. 48, 76, 114) and so is of great numismatic consequence. It has been argued (Bernareggi 1969; *contra*, Alföldi 1978) that since Theoderic had no authority to mint gold in his own name the triple solidus must date from 526, but such a date is too late for the tremissis type, which was copied by Gundobald of Burgundy and therefore must be earlier than 516, when this ruler died. Against the date 500, however, is the fact that none of the coins has in its inscription VOT XXX (or ANNO XXX), as would be required for a tricennalian issue. The strong 'victory' element in their types and inscriptions, notably the title of *Victor gentium* accorded to Theoderic on the medallion, points rather to their having been issued in 509, after Theoderic's defeat of the Burgundians and Franks and his taking over the regency in the Visigothic kingdom on behalf of his grandson Amalaric (Grierson 1985).

The early solidi of Theoderic (**1.112–13**) continue the type of Zeno, with three-quarter facing bust on the obverse and a Victory holding a long, voided cross on the reverse. They bear, however, the name of Anastasius, and are distinguishable from the earlier Constantinopolitan solidi of this emperor by their style and by the obverse inscription usually ending PFAVG instead of PP (initially PERP) AVG as on Eastern issues. Both types were retained throughout Theoderic's reign and under Athalaric, no notice being taken of successive changes in the design of the Eastern issues – omission of the diadem tails and substitution of a fully facing bust for a three-quarter facing bust on the obverse, replacement of the voided cross of the reverse by a staff surmounted by a Christogram and eventually that of the substitution of a facing Angel for the profile Victory – so that there is normally no problem in distinguishing between Ostrogothic and imperial solidi. The coins also lack the officina letters of Constantinopolitan issues.

The distinction between particular mints in Italy is more difficult. The solidi attributed above to 509 have mint initials in the field, as solidi had often had in the fifth century, and some of Milan have a monogram of IMD at the end of the reverse legend. Coins of Rome have in the same place an A, presumably marking a 'first' officina even though there were no other officinae for the gold. Most of the coins with the name of Justin I (518–27) must have been struck prior to Theoderic's death (30 August 526), but since there are silver coins of Athalaric bearing Justin I's name a few of them, not identifiable, must have been struck under Athalaric.

The Ostrogothic tremisses were struck in the names of the same emperors as the solidi, and with the exception of the issue of 509 are all of the same type, with on the obverse a profile bust and on the reverse a facing Victory advancing right but looking backwards. The same type was struck at Constantinople, and the Italian coins are distinguished from these by their more careful design and higher, more rounded relief. No satisfactory mint attributions are possible, those to Rome being traditional. The three coins in the name of Anastasius in the collection (**1.114–16**) are necessarily of Theoderic, and the two in the name of Justinian (**1.123–4**) are of Athalaric or his immediate successors.

Ostrogothic silver consists predominantly of two denominations, conventionally called half- and quarter-siliquae, weighing about 1.4g and 0.7g respectively. The obverse type is invariably a profile imperial bust, initially and occasionally thereafter identical with that of the tremissis but normally of a design peculiar to Italy and involving a kind of collarpiece decorated with a row of large pellets. The distinction between it and the regular bust may have been intended to suggest that, despite the imperial name in the inscription, it represented the Ostrogothic king, though the mints became so accustomed to it that they continued it after the Byzantine reconquest. The reverse type is normally a royal monogram or the king's name, preceded by DN and followed by REX (or RIX), in several lines across the field. It is sometimes surrounded by the inscription INVICTA ROMA (e.g. **1.119–20**), but more often by a wreath. The traditional mint-marks RV and RM, either alone or combined with PS (for *pusulatum*, fine silver), are no longer used, so there is much uncertainty over mint attributions, but some coins of Milan are identified by the letters IMD (for MED). The formula *Invicta Roma* is sometimes followed by CM, probably standing for *Caput mundi*, an epithet often applied to Rome in the middle ages. One rare type has a Victory in the reverse field accompanied by the letters SC, something wholly anomalous on silver coins but explicable if, as seems likely, the coin in question made part of a special issue in 509. The study of Ostrogothic silver is complicated by the proliferation of forgeries, both casts or electrotypes (**1.1453–5**) and independently struck pieces.

Theoderic's silver coinage differs from that of his successors in including large units – a double siliqua (4.70g; Grierson 1960b) and a siliqua (2.52g; Kricheldorf 1958), each unique and bearing the name of Justin I – and aberrant types. One of these, a half-siliqua (**1.117**) with a monogram of IX (i.e. *Iesous Xristos*) in a wreath must be dated early in the reign, before the monogram type became general. The mint is probably Milan. The coins with *Invicta Roma* (**1.119–20**) surrounding the royal monogram normally belong to Rome, though the type was also adopted at Milan and Sirmium, coins of the latter mint being very crudely designed and rather larger in module than their Italian counterparts (Stefan 1925; Meixner 1968; but cf. Brunšmid 1924). Coins with a monogram in the wreath (**1.118, 121**) belong to Ravenna or Milan.

Under Athalaric an inscription in several lines across the field was introduced to distinguish the quarter-siliquae (**1.127–31**) from the halves (**1.125–6**), the mint being probably Ravenna. The same types continued unchanged under Theodahad (quarters: **1.139–40**), but to the early months of his 'reign', when Amalasuntha was effectively and in some measure formally ruler, are best ascribed some quarter-siliquae which combine the name of Justinian on the obverse with the monogram of Theoderic on the reverse (**1.138**). They cannot be coins of Theoderic himself, since he died before Justinian's accession, and it is customary to assign them to the reign of Witigis with a 'restored' monogram. But Witigis used his name in full on his half-siliquae, and it is difficult to believe that his monogram would not have been used on his quarter-siliquae if any such had been struck. Under Amalasuntha, on the other hand, the mints might well have hesitated to accord so open a recognition to female rule and preferred to use the monogram of her prestigious father.

The only silver coins of Witigis would thus appear to be half-siliquae, with inscription in the reverse field (**1.151–2**). But in addition to the misplaced quarters attributed to this ruler, our understanding of coinage of the late 530s was complicated in the nineteenth century by the attribution to the princess Matasuntha of silver and copper coins bearing her supposed monogram in two slightly divergent forms (*BMC Vand*, pl. 10.11–15). The silver coins of Italian fabric with one of these (*BMC Vand*, pl. 10.11) are in fact forgeries of Cigoi (see p. 332). The remainder, which are of clear African fabric, were wrongly attributed by Grierson (1959d) to the Moorish chieftain Mastinas whose activities are known to us from Procopius. They are now recognized to be regular coins of Justinian from the mint of Carthage: scholars were misled as to the interpretation of the monogram through the inclusion of the letters DM from his title (*Dominus*). The half-follis (*BMC Vand*, pl. 10.15) is also a coin of Justinian, with a monogram including DN but no M, of the mint of Ravenna.

Silver coins exist of all the later kings, though with the exception of those of Baduila (**1.153–6**) they are very rare and the interpretation of their monograms has sometimes presented problems (cf. Giannoccaro and Orlandoni 1978). On all, the imperial bust on the obverse is accompanied by the name of Anastasius or Justin I (Orlandoni 1975), although both were long since dead, because there was a natural reluctance to use the name of Justinian with whom the Ostrogoths were at war. The coinage struck in Byzantine Italy after the reconquest continued the Ostrogothic use of silver (cf. Kent 1982), with the important innovation that marks of value were for a time used as reverse types.

The copper coinage raises the same problems of mint attribution as the silver, and the following account, based largely on the two premisses that a heavy wreath normally implies the mint of Ravenna and that the *Invicta Roma* type was only adopted in the north after the loss of Rome in December 536, differs in a number of respects from those of Wroth and Hahn.

The Senate retained its monopoly of multiples up to the reign of Athalaric, who introduced both decanummia and pentanummia. His decanummia of Rome (**1.132**) make a bow to traditional Senatorial rights in having an *Invicta Roma* obverse and an SC in the reverse field, but the reverse inscription and standing-figure type claim them as royal. The Ravenna coins (**1.133–4**) retain the Roman obverse – Rome was firmly associated with copper multiples – but the identifying legend in a wreath, with no SC, shows them to be of Ravenna. Pentanummia with a V surrounded by an inscription as the reverse type were minted both at Ravenna and Rome, but on a small scale, the Ravenna issues having a *rex* in the royal title which is omitted at Rome. Neither is represented here. Others with the mark of value V in a wreath and on the obverse the name and bust of Justin or Justinian are not, as Wroth believed, coins of Theoderic (in the name of Justin I) and Athalaric (in those of both emperors), but are imperial coins of Justinian and Justin II struck after the reconquest.

Athalaric's invasion of the copper was expanded by Theodahad, who replaced the Senatorial folles of Rome by coins with his own portrait bust and with the reverse type of a Victory bearing palm and wreath copied from a Flavian prototype (**1.141–3**). Senatorial rights are recognized, however, by SC in the reverse field. The coin is one of the most remarkable struck by any Germanic ruler, and owes its existence to the fact that Theodahad, alone amongst Ostrogothic kings, spent most of his reign at Rome and not in north Italy. The brevity of its period of issue explains the frequency of die-links amongst surviving specimens, including those here. There are no corresponding half-folles. Decanummia, with an *Invicta Roma* obverse and the king's name in a wreath on the reverse, were minted only at Ravenna (**1.144**).

The only copper multiple in the name of Witigis is a rare decanummium, not represented here, with an *Invicta Roma* obverse and his name in a wreath on the reverse, but it has been suggested above that the municipal issues with *Felix Ravenna* (**1.145–50**) belong to the years 536–40. Later multiples mainly consist of decanummia of Baduila. The bulk of them, with his facing bust on the obverse and his name in a wreath on the reverse, were minted at his northern capital of Pavia (**1.157–61**), and his recovery of Rome in 549 made possible a standing-figure type like that struck at this mint under Athalaric (**1.162**). Extremely rare pentanummia were struck at Pavia and have as their obverse type a bust modelled on the municipal decanummia of Ravenna of 536–40 but with *Felix Ticinus* instead of *Felix Ravenna*.

The coin most commonly used for small transactions was the nummus – Hahn regards them as $2\frac{1}{2}$ nummus pieces – and it is at first sight an anomaly that a few appear to have been struck during Theoderic's reign. The normal type of Ostrogothic nummi is a royal monogram in a wreath, but none are known with the monogram of Theoderic, and those of Italian fabric in the name of Anastasius with a six pointed star in a wreath which may have have been struck by Theoderic are notably rare. The explanation is apparently the huge number of fifth-century nummi in circulation; they still occur in large numbers in Italian hoards buried after Justinian's reconquest (cf. Cesano 1913; Hahn 1979b). Athalaric's minting of copper, however, included nummi (**1.135–7**) as well as decanummia and pentanummia, but their 'imperial' obverses and wreaths point to their having been struck only at Ravenna. Similar coins exist for Theodahad, Witigis, Baduila and perhaps Eraric (Langlois 1849); the coins of the first two, not represented here, are attributable to Ravenna and those of Baduila to Pavia (**1.163–5**) or to Rome after 549. The last of these has on the obverse the same facing bust as the decanummium, and on the reverse a lion that continued the type of the nummi struck in Rome by Justinian prior to the Ostrogothic recapture of the city in 550.

4

THE VISIGOTHS

(a) GENERAL FEATURES AND BACKGROUND

Literature

The history of the Visigoths, from their entry into the Roman Empire (376) down to the conquest of Visigothic Spain and Narbonensis by the Arabs (711–19) falls into three well-defined periods: a 'migratory' one, from 376 to 417, the date of their settlement in south-western Gaul; a 'Gallic' one, from 417 to 507, the date of the battle of Vouillé and the conquest of nearly all Visigothic Gaul by Clovis; and a 'Spanish' one, extending over the two centuries 507–714. A study of Visigothic coinage, however, requires different divisions. The first period can be omitted entirely, for no coins can be assigned to the Visigoths before 417 and it is highly unlikely that they struck any, though their imperial protégé Attalus did. The second period, which saw a variety of pseudo-imperial issues, can stand unchanged, but the third has to be divided into two. There was initially a pseudo-imperial coinage, struck from shortly after 507 to *c.* 580, which was a continuation of, but distinct from, the pseudo-imperial coinage of 417–507, and, finally, there was the regal coinage of *c.* 580–714.

The only account of the whole of Visigothic coinage is given in two studies of Reinhart, the first dealing with its Gallic phase, that of 'the kingdom of Toulouse' (Reinhart 1938), the second with its Spanish phase, which he terms, a little misleadingly, 'the kingdom of Toledo' (Reinhart 1940). Spanish works virtually limit themselves to the Spanish phase. This is covered as a whole by Mateu y Llopis (1936), the catalogue of the Madrid collection whose publication marked the opening of several decades of rapid progress in Visigothic numismatics, and by Gil Farrés (1980), a chapter in the fourth edition of vol. III of Menéndez Pidal's immense *Historia de España* (1980). Coin finds are covered in detail by Barral (1976); cf. also Lafaurie 1971c. Material on the pseudo-imperial tremisses of the period 417–*c.* 580 is collected and discussed by Tomasini (1964), which largely but not entirely supersedes the relevant sections in Reinhart (1940). Tomasini's approach is that of an art historian, with relatively little numismatic background, while Reinhart had behind him many years of study and collecting experience made possible by long residence in Spain. There are two major hoards in the period, one from Zorita de Los Canes (Cabré Aguiló 1946; Beltrán 1953) and the other from Seville, the latter not yet adequately published (cf. Barral 1975, 1976) and in any case of less consequence. While the coinage of the Visigoths was the most important in the Iberian peninsula, there was in addition that of the Suevi in the north-west (see Chapter 6) and a meagre Byzantine coinage, between *c.* 555 and *c.* 625, in the south (Grierson 1955).

For the regal period, the nineteenth-century standard work of Heiss (1872) was superseded thirty years ago by that of Miles (1952). This is primarily based on the immense collection of the Hispanic Society of America, now on indefinite loan to the American Numismatic Society. The collection was put together in the early decades of this century by Archer M. Huntington (1871–1955), the adopted son of the railway millionaire Collis P. Huntington and a passionate admirer of all things Spanish. Unfortunately, despite the fact that he was for many years President of the ANS and its generous patron, he understood so little of the needs of scholars that he systematically destroyed the coin tickets of previous owners and with them all direct information regarding provenance.

Miles listed and classified everything that he was able to track down in public and private collections throughout the world, and since his monograph is supported by a comprehensive analysis of the coinage as a whole he left little to be gleaned by subsequent scholars. Such new coins as have come to light have usually been published singly or in small groups, apart from the catalogue of the Barcelona cabinet (Amorós 1952). Two authors have a place of their own in the literature. The immense output of Mateu y Llopis, uneven in quality but as a whole immensely important, remains scattered, but can in part be traced through his published bibliography (1972). The studies of Pio Beltrán are collected in vol. II of his *Obra completa* (1972).

The most authoritative survey of the early history of the Visigoths, down to the end of the 'kingdom of Toulouse', remains that of Schmidt (1910, I.164–304), though certain sections and topics (e.g. the circumstances of their conversion to Arianism, the nature of their settlement in Gaul) have been superseded. The period of the Visigothic kingdom in Gaul is dealt with in all works on the later Roman Empire (Bury, Stein, Demougeot, etc.). The best account of the historical and cultural background of the Visigoths in Spain is that in the fourth edition (1980) of vol. III of Menéndez Pidal's *Historia de España*. There is a convenient historical summary by R. Altamira in *CMH* vol. II (1913, ch. 6). On different aspects of the social and legal background one may consult E. A. Thompson (1966, 1969), Claude (1961a), King (1972), and several of the essays in James (1980).

Historical background

The events for which the Visigoths are remembered – their defeat of the emperor Valens at Adrianople in 378 and the sack of Rome by Alaric in 410 – took place before the Gallic phase of their history. This began in 412, when they crossed the Alps under the leadership of Alaric's brother-in-law and successor Athaulf (410–15), but their first stay in Gaul was brief. In 415 they moved into Spain, where Athaulf was murdered. It was his successor Wallia (415–18) who served the emperor Honorius by a series of campaigns against the Suevi and Vandals in Spain, and was rewarded (417) by permission to settle his people as *foederati* in western Aquitaine (*Aquitania Secunda*), including its two great cities of Bordeaux and Toulouse. The latter became their capital. When Wallia died in 418 the Goths elected as their king Theoderic I, a grandson of Alaric who for some reason had been passed over in 410. Theoderic's descendants held the throne down to 531 (see Table 4).

The Visigoths at first served the Empire with reasonable fidelity. Theoderic I lost his life as an ally of Aetius at the battle of Troyes against the Huns in 451, and in 456 Theoderic II, at the instance of Avitus, broke the power of the Suevi, who were threatening to become masters of Spain (see p. 78). But the ambitious Euric threw off all pretence at allegiance and conquered eastern Aquitaine (475), thus becoming ruler of all Gaul between the Loire and the Pyrenees, to which he also added Provence and north-eastern Spain. But although he and his followers assimilated many Roman ways, the Goths were numerically thinly spread, and being Arians and not Catholics were separated by religion from the provincial population amongst whom they lived. When Euric's successor Alaric II was defeated and killed by Clovis at the battle

Table 4. *The early Visigoths (Balts)*

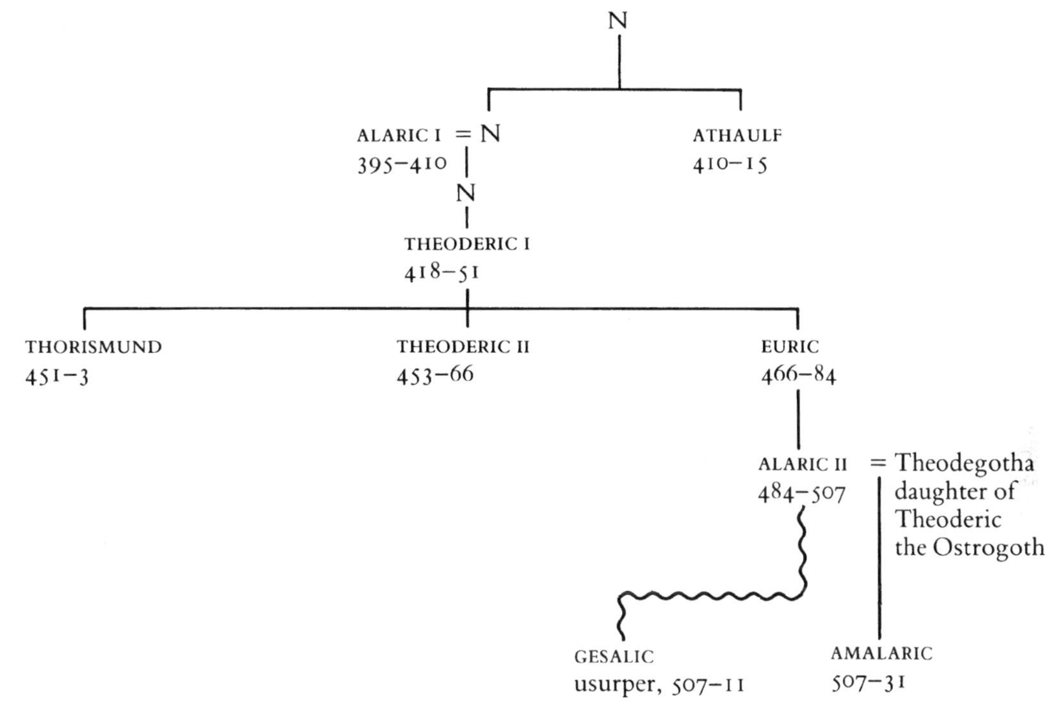

of Vouillé in 507, Visigothic power underwent a temporary collapse and the Franks extended their dominion to the Pyrenees, capturing the fabulous Gothic treasure at Toulouse on the way. But they did not reach the Mediterranean. Since Amalaric, Alaric II's only legitimate son, was not yet five years old the Visigoths elected as Alaric's successor his older but illegitimate son Gesalic. Alaric's widow, however, was a daughter of Theoderic the Ostrogoth, and he intervened in 508 on behalf of his grandson. The usurper Gesalic was first driven into taking refuge with the Vandals, and after his return was captured and put to death (511). Although Theoderic's rule proved admirable his motives were not entirely disinterested. He was determined to prevent either Franks or Burgundians gaining a foothold on the Mediterranean, so, while leaving Septimania in Visigothic hands, he annexed Provence to Italy. After his death in 526 Amalaric, who seems to have been completely unfitted to rule, was first defeated by the Franks and then murdered by one of his own followers (531). With him the Visigothic royal line of the Balts came to an end.

Alaric II's successor was Theudis (531–48), an Ostrogoth who had acted as regent during Amalaric's minority and married a wealthy Hispano-Roman provincial. He carried on the regime of Theoderic and in nearly two decades of competent rule put Visigothic royal power in Spain on a firm basis. He was murdered in 548, however, and his successor Theudegisel (548–9) sixteen months later, while Achila's reign (549–54) ended in a civil war that made possible Byzantine intervention in the Peninsula (553) and the loss to the Visigoths of much of the south. He was succeeded by Athanagild (554–67). The fortunes of the state are reflected in repeated changes of capital. Amalaric, still hopeful of a restoration of Visigothic power in Gaul, had resided at Narbonne. Theudis fell back on Barcelona. Achila moved to Mérida, on the Guadiana in south-western Spain, but as part of a campaign against the Suevi and in the hope of establishing better control over the Hispano-Roman nobility of Baetica. Athanagild, after the loss of much of the south, moved to Toledo, in the geographical centre of the Peninsula, and Toledo was to remain the Visigothic capital down to the end of the kingdom. When Athanagild died towards the end of 567 he was succeeded by Liuva I, who almost immediately associated with him his abler brother Leovigild. Liuva contented himself, apparently, with Septimania, leaving Visigothic Spain to Leovigild, and when he died in 572 Leovigild was left as sole king.

Leovigild's long reign (568–86) opened up a new era in Visigothic history. The list of his successors, down to the end of the kingdom, is given in Table 5. No genealogical table is required, for while such individual later rulers as Leovigild and Chindaswinth might through a mixture of personality, statesmanship and terrorism establish their rule for short periods, they failed to develop the central institutions of government that could carry on during minorities or overcome the obstinate particularism of the Gothic nobility. The monarchy was formally elective, and although several kings managed to secure the succession for their sons, the achievement was rarely repeated and there were no fewer than twenty kings in the space of 150 years. Even the close alliance established between Crown and Church proved a double-edged weapon. Reccared abandoned Arianism in favour of Catholicism at the start of his reign, and his successors thought to make good their lack of a semi-divine ancestry by the ecclesiastical practice of anointing. But while the Fourth Council of Toledo (633) anathematized rebels against royal authority it also laid down that the succession should be determined by election and prohibited rulers from associating their sons with them on the throne. Dynastic uncertainty and monarchical weakness, along with growing military problems arising out of the insubordination of the great magnates, go far to explain the suddenness and completeness of the Visigothic collapse after 711.

Coins are known of all the rulers, including even the short-lived Reccared II and two pretenders, Judila and Sunifred, who are not known as such from the written sources and whose identity is somewhat conjectural (Beltrán 1941). Only a few kings require special mention. Leovigild was a ruler of outstanding ability. He reconquered much of Byzantine Spain, suppressed a series of revolts that included the attempted usurpation (579–84) of his son Hermenegild, destroyed the Suevic kingdom (below, p. 78) and took over much of the Byzantine panoply of rule. Reccared abandoned Arianism for Catholicism, partly from conviction, partly because he saw the Arianism of the Goths as a bar to unity, and partly because the career of Hermenegild had shown how religious differences could be exploited to the disadvantage of the Crown. Sisebut and Swinthila between them conquered what remained of Byzantine Spain, so that Swinthila came to be regarded as the first Goth to rule the entire Peninsula, though neither he nor any of his successors succeeded in permanently subduing the Basques. Sisebut has also the less attractive distinction of being the first of a long series of Spanish sovereigns to persecute

Table 5. *Kings of the Visigoths, 567–714.*

Liuva I } brothers	567–72
Leovigild } brothers	568–86
Hermenegild, son of Leovigild, usurper 579–84	
Reccared I, son of Leovigild	586–601
Liuva II, son of Reccared I	601–3
Witteric	603–9
Gundemar	609–12
Sisebut	612–21
Reccared II, son of Sisebut	621
Swinthila	621–31
Judila (? = Geila, brother of Swinthila), pretender 631 ?	
Sisenand	631–6
Chintila	636–9
Tulga, son of Chintila	639–42
Chindaswinth	642–53
alone 642–9, with Recceswinth 649–53	
Recceswinth, son of Chindaswinth	653–72
Wamba	672–80
Erwig	680–7
Egica, son-in-law of Erwig	687–702
alone 687–95, with Wittiza 695–702	
Sunifred, pretender 692–3	
Wittiza, son of Egica	702–10(?)
Roderick	710(?)–11
Achila II, son of Wittiza (in Septimania)	711–14

The dates follow in the main those in Miles (1952, 21–42), who gives short summaries of each reign. The basis of the chronology was laid in two studies by Zeumer and Fita early in the century. The uncertainties are usually slight; e.g. Liuva I may have died in Dec. 571, not early in 572. Miles' date of *c.* 698 for Wittiza's association as king by his father has been emended to 695 on the strength of a subsequently discovered charter fragment dated to the 9th year of Egica and the 2nd of Wittiza (*J. des Savants* 1974, 220).

the Jews. Recceswinth completed the legal unification of the two peoples occupying the Peninsula by issuing the *Liber Judiciorum* (654), an amalgamation of Gothic and Roman law. Roderick, traditionally the last Visigothic king, had in 711 to meet an Arab invasion from across the Pillars of Hercules, and he and his army were destroyed in a single battle near Xeres in south-western Spain (cf. Murphy 1952). Most of the country was occupied during the next two years, save for a small area in the mountains of the north-west which retained its independence. In the extreme north-east, however, Roderick found a successor in Achila II, a son of Roderick's predecessor Wittiza, who had perhaps opposed Roderick during his lifetime and who minted after his death at Tarragona, Gerona and Narbonne (Barceló 1978). He was apparently killed in 714, when Tarragona was captured by the Arabs. Septimania must then have been briefly occupied by the Franks, for two silver deniers of Massaliote pattern but with the monogram of Narbonne occurred in the Cimiez hoard (Chabouillet 1890, pl. 6.97). The city fell to the Arabs in 719.

(b) THE VISIGOTHS IN GAUL ('KINGDOM OF TOULOUSE'), 417–507

The pseudo-imperial coinage belonging to this phase of Visigothic history consists entirely of solidi and tremisses. Since these bear no identifying letters or monograms they have to be attributed on the evidence of find-spots or, failing these, on that of statements by nineteenth-century scholars that particular coins are common in one particular part of Gaul. They can be dated only approximately. Toulouse as the Visigothic capital was presumably the main mint, but there may have been others. Claims have been made on behalf of Narbonne, where a mint existed, at least momentarily, in 414, when Athaulf was married there to Honorius' sister Placidia, for a lost solidus of Athaulf's protégé Priscus Attalus, of which we have a good eighteenth-century illustration (Kent 1974, p. 26, fig. 14), bears the mint-mark NB. But a reference to a mint there in the 460s in a poem of Sidonius Apollinaris can probably be dismissed as poetic licence, for the city was then in imperial hands and no imperial coins are known (Carson 1950). The Visigothic mint, which existed from at least the reign of Leovigild onwards, probably dates from the years after 507, when the city became for a time the Gothic capital, though the attribution to it of pseudo-imperial solidi with N at the ends of the inscription (Amardel 1898a, 1898b, 1902b) will not stand up to examination.

The models of the earlier coins were those of Western emperors, but their line came to an end in 481 and it is not certain whether minting in the name of Anastasius began before 509. The standard reference work is Reinhart 1938, though not all scholars agree with his attributions and he revised some of these himself in later works. Virtually all the main groups are illustrated on Plate 10.

The earliest solidi (**1.166**), struck between the 420s and the 440s, are imitations of Ravennate coins of Honorius (393–423). Although they have the usual mint-mark RV in the reverse field they differ from official issues of the mint in their style and lettering, notably in the absence from the GS (in the formula AAVGGG) of the tongue that distinguishes this letter from a C and which is unusually long and conspicuous on Ravennate coins at this period. Their attribution is not well documented by finds, but the Visigoths are, apart from the Suevi, the only Germanic people then likely to have been minting. The attribution was proposed by Reinhart (1938, pl. 2.2), though he later developed doubts, and is accepted by Kent (1974), who associated with the coins of Honorius some rarer ones of the same type in the names of Theodosius II and Valentinian III.

These were succeeded in the 450s by a new type, imitating coins of Ravenna with on the reverse a standing figure of the emperor with his right foot on the head of a human-headed serpent. It was struck first (**1.167–70**) in the name of Valentinian III (425–55), later in that of Severus III (461–5), the imitations of Severus substituting RA for the original RV in the reverse field (**1.174–6**). The coins differ in style from the official issues, in having the same tongueless

GS as the Honorius imitations and other characteristic features of their own. The Valentinianic solidi (Reinhart 1938, pl. 2.8–13) have a small crown above the emperor's head, the crown held by the Victory on the reverse has the form of a horseshoe, and the smooth border is replaced by a rayed one that sometimes (**1.170**) takes the form of a wreath. The most conspicuous features of the Severan series (Reinhart 1938, pl. 5.69–77), apart from the characteristic portrait, are the stylized, linear treatment of the Victory, the RA in the field, and the declining quality of the alloy, which even to the eye is sometimes inferior to those of any other coins minted in the fifth century. The meaning of the crown on the earlier coins and that of the RA on the later ones is uncertain. The reverse type was one introduced at Ravenna late in the reign of Valentinian III, after the death of Theodosius II in 450, and if it was really intended to celebrate Aetius' victory over Attila in 451 (Blanchet 1914), a crown over the emperor's head, however little justified by Valentinian's character or policy, would not be inappropriate. Its occurrence on coins from the imperial mint itself, however, is exceptional; the vast majority of coins of this very common type are without it. The RA is usually regarded as simply a blundered version of RV, and moneyers in Gaul, familiar with the AR of Arles, might well have thought it an acceptable mint-mark for Ravenna. But since they must have been familiar with RV it is difficult to see why they should have made a change. It may eventually have come to be interpreted as *Rex Alaricus* (below, pp. 46, 77).

The two coin series, with related but much rarer ones (Reinhart 1938, pl. 4.61–3) bearing the name of Majorian (457–61), and a number of others of varying styles imitating imperial solidi of Ravenna, Milan and Rome (Reinhart 1938, pls. 2–6), were attributed by Reinhart to the Visigoths. For some groups this is far from certain, but for the two represented here – they are frequent in French collections and in some cases they are known to have been found in France – this seems the best attribution. Lafaurie has argued (Lafaurie 1973b, 1980c, 1982b; Demougeot 1983) that they may have been issues of the *Magister militum* Aetius (433–54) and of his successors Aegidius (456–65) and Syagrius (465–86), the last representatives of Roman authority in Gaul. His study is based on a hoard of 15 of the Valentinianic series found in 1969 at Arçay (Cher), near Bourges, and on other find-spots recorded for the series. Those in Scandinavia and Germany aside, which are no help over localization, these tend to be in northern France and so in areas undoubtedly administered by Aetius and Aegidius. Moreover, the case in favour of the Valentinianic solidi being issues of Aetius is strengthened by the fact that some of the rare siliquae struck at Trier in the names of Theodosius II (d. 450) and Valentinian III also have a crown above the emperor's head.

The use of a crown on a particular issue, however, is likely to have resulted, at Trier as well as at Ravenna, from a general instruction to the mints, and since the silver coins minted at Trier are correctly identified by the mint-mark TRPS in the exergue it is difficult to see why Aetius, if he was indeed authorized to mint in gold, should not have used the mint-mark of Trier. The other Gallic mints, Lyon and Arles, were accustomed to identifying their solidi by LD or AR in the field, and Trier had ample precedent for doing the same with TR. This consideration, coupled with the fact that a number of the recorded find-spots are in fact from parts of France that were Visigothic from the time of Euric onwards, are arguments against Lafaurie's hypothesis, and Reinhart's attribution has therefore been retained here. It is perhaps supported by the fact that no imitative coins are known of Avitus (455–6), for this emperor was installed by Theoderic II and it would have been a matter of common courtesy to suspend any irregular Visigothic issues while he was in office.

The tremisses best attributed to the Visigoths in the fifth century are of three types. The earliest, not represented here, are in the name of Honorius, with a Victory advancing right as reverse type, and are of the same style and lettering as the solidi (Reinhart 1938, pl. 2.3–4). They are very rare, like the solidi. The second group usually bear the name of Valentinian III and have as reverse type a cross-in-wreath. Many of those illustrated by Reinhart (1938, pl. 3.29–49) seem to be regular imperial issues, but there are some that are probably Visigothic, two of which are illustrated here (**1.171–2**). They sometimes show a tendency for the outer and inner circles of the wreath-fronds to separate from one another, a feature that may have given rise to its much more extensive deformation on Suevic coins (**1.286–93**). Finally, there is a very large group (Reinhart 1938, pls. 4.59, 5.79–98, 6.111–28), bearing the names of Valentinian III, Severus III and Zeno (474–91), which has as reverse type a standing Victory holding a long, jewelled cross (**1.173**). The type was used on imperial solidi at Constantinople from 420 onwards, and its transfer to tremisses is an early example of the Visigothic propensity for employing solidus types in this way (below, p. 50). The attribution of the series to the Visigoths by Reinhart, who illustrated a large selection of them, is supported by the evidence of find-spots, of which Lafaurie has listed a long series south of the Loire and between the Garonne and the Mediterranean (*Journées numismatiques* 1974, note to no. 14). Two specimens, probably found near Béziers, were in the 1830s in the Mazel collection from which the Uzès coin here (**1.734**) derives (Mazel 1836).

The coinage of the long reign of Alaric II (484–507) is something of a problem. The Burgundian legal code of the early sixth century includes *alariciani* amongst the debased issues whose circulation is prohibited, and there can be no doubt that coins of Alaric II were in question. Since the Western line of emperors ended in 481, he must either have continued some earlier issue or minted in the names successively of Zeno and Anastasius. No base coins of the latter are known, however, nor any which would have been immediately identifiable by users as having been struck by Alaric. But it may be that his solidi were the base RA issues in the name of Libius Severus, for their poor quality is evident to the eye and RA could easily have been interpreted by users as referring to the king (Rex Alaricus). It is true that debasement already existed in Gaul well before Alaric's accession, for a constitution of Majorian of 458 refers to *solidi gallici* of poor quality whose identity has much exercised commentators (cf. Blanchet 1910; Demougeot 1983). Hoard evidence for the minting of RA coins at so late a date as Alaric's reign is in any case lacking, and the absence or rarity of Zeno/Anastasius imitations attributable to him could be in part explained by their withdrawal and melting after 507. The attribution of the baser RA solidi to the time of Alaric II nonetheless remains a plausible hypothesis.

(c) THE VISIGOTHS IN SPAIN: PSEUDO-IMPERIAL COINAGE, *c.* 509–*c.* 580

The coinage of this period consists entirely of pseudo-imperial solidi and tremisses. Copper nummi with a monogram of the letters AMR, in company with tremisses having the same

Map 1 *The main Visigothic mints*

The mints named, apart from Braga, are those represented in this collection; the number of coins from each is given in parentheses and the mints with five or more coins are in small capitals.

monogram in the field (**1.341**), were formerly attributed to Amalaric but are now recognized as belonging to the Burgundian king GUNDOMAR II (below, p. 76).

The solidi, bearing the names of successive Byzantine emperors Anastasius (491–518), Justin I (518–27), and Justinian (527–65), are very distinctive in style (**1.177**, **190–1**), and since they are found only in Spain their attribution has long been recognized. They are modelled on Constantinopolitan issues of Anastasius from 507 onwards, with a profile Victory holding a simple cross-staff surmounted by a *rho* to the left. They are thus differentiated from the solidi of the Ostrogoths, which retained the common fifth-century type of a profile Victory holding a long voided cross, and the Constantinopolitan solidi from 522 onwards, which have the profile Victory replaced by a facing angel. From the 520s onwards the staff has normally a forked base, as on

1.190–1, and the die-sinkers evidently did much as they pleased over details, sometimes replacing the emperor's shield by what was perhaps conceived of as the folds of a cloak (**1.190**) and reducing the emperor's name to a barely intelligible jumble of letters. The coins are rare, and indeed are too few to allow any satisfactory classification or mint attributions, more especially since Toledo was not yet the fixed centre of royal power that it was to become in the future.

The pseudo-imperial tremisses (**1.178–89, 192–208**) are all of what Tomasini has termed the VPW type seemingly introduced by Theoderic in 509 (above, p. 35), which have on the reverse a Victory running to the right with palm and wreath, the Victory eventually becoming deformed as the result of unintelligent copying into a strange kangaroo-like creature, with two extra 'legs' in front deriving from the skirt of the chiton, a huge sail-like wing, and a head sometimes provided with rabbit-like ears projecting upwards (**1.207–8**) or transformed into a kind of starfish design (**1.195–7**). The profile bust on the obverse is quite early provided with a large cross on the chest (**1.184**), this being one of the most distinctive features separating Visigothic pseudo-imperial tremisses from those of the Burgundians and Franks. The epaulette of the right shoulder is usually eliminated, and the design of the bust consequently takes on the appearance of three sides of a polyhedron delimited by a double line of dots above and to either side, the shape being sometimes that of a steep isosceles triangle with a V-shaped depression above at the neck (**1.195**), sometimes that of a square with a small circle at each of the upper corners (**1.192, 205**, etc.). The earliest coins, with *Anastasius* legends, must belong to the period of Theoderic, but most of the later ones, with blundered *Justinus* or *Justinianus* legends, cannot be dated with sufficient precision for ascription to the various monarchs who ruled between 526 and 568. Only the final pseudo-imperial issues can be attributed to the first years of Leovigild's reign (568–86) through their close resemblance to his earliest signed issues from *c.* 580 onwards.

The tremisses were classified by Reinhart (1940) into six groups. The earliest ones are coins of small flan (*c.* 13mm) in the name of Anastasius of a type introduced *c.* 509. The later ones, designated Groups A–E by Reinhart and struck in the names of Justin I or more usually Justinian, were attributed by him to Narbonne or Barcelona (Group A), Andalusia (B), Mérida (C) and Toledo (E), leaving a small Group D with a miscellany of different styles; all the attributions except that of Group E were treated as probable rather than certain. Tomasini (1964) attempted a much more comprehensive breakdown, lettered according to the ruler (A for Anastasius, JI for Justin I, JAN for Justinian, JII for Justin II), but while his arrangement brings together small groups of stylistically related and in some cases die-linked coins it does not greatly help towards mint attribution. This is something on which much work remains to be done, and the arrangement on Plates 10 and 11 of the relatively few specimens here does little more than group them in rough chronological order and indicate in the references where more information on related coins can be found.

The earliest coins in the name of Anastasius (**1.178–85**) and without a cross on the imperial bust, which are of the reign of Theoderic, were probably minted at Narbonne, though Tomasini allows the possibility of some being attributable to Ostrogothic Arles. Toulouse must be excluded if the coins are all Visigothic, since the city was lost to the Franks in 507, but some Frankish mints in the south may have adopted the same type. Most of the coins are of good style, apart from some deformation of the Victory, but others (e.g. **1.184–5**) show considerable deformation of the bust. For the coins in Justin I's name (**1.186–9**), usually though not always without a cross, there is the same uncertainty of attribution, those with a reverse inscription ending ·T· (**1.187**) being given by some scholars to the Frankish king Thierry I (below p. 115).

It is the much more extensive coinage in the name of Justinian (**1.192–202**), or with the imperial name so blundered that it is doubtful whether that of Justin II may not be intended (**1.203–6**), that saw the gradual enlargement of the flan of the coins and the regular presence of a cross on the imperial bust. Narbonne or Barcelona is the mint most generally favoured for most of the smaller coins, but some are given to Andalusia, an attribution which in the case of one coin here (**1.198**) is supported by the presence of a similar coin in the Seville hoard. One late coin (**1.203**) can be attributed with some confidence to Mérida, since the bust closely resembles that of Leovigild's earliest inscribed coin of this mint. At the end of the series is a group of coins of relatively large module (**1.207–8**) on which the reverse legend reads CVRRV upwards on both left and right. It is associated with obverses very different in style, one certainly of Toledo and the other probably of Mérida if one can judge by similarities to Leovigild's coins of these mints. How these two mints came to share a common die-sinker for the reverses – the Victories as well as the CVRRV legends are the same – is hard to explain. Nor is it easy to decide whether CVRRV was intended to have a meaning, for while the late date of the group suggests the possibility of some inspiration from the changes then taking place in the coinage of the Franks, *Curru* does not look like a personal name.

(d) THE VISIGOTHS IN SPAIN: REGAL COINAGE, *c.* 580–714

Visigothic regal coinage, which lasted for almost 130 years (*c.* 580–714), is one of the most immediately recognizable that exists. The coins are all of a single denomination, the tremissis – the solidus being dropped because the coins now bore the king's name instead of the emperor's (above, p. 5) – and are all of a gold that steadily declined in quality. The coins are formally royal issues – there are none bearing the names of moneyers, as with the Franks – and give the name of the mint at which they were struck. The most characteristic type, minted from 584 to 649, shows a facing bust on each side, but this was preceded by a brief transitional period exhibiting other types and followed by a much longer one with a variety of types – profile busts, pairs of busts, a facing head of Christ, a cross-on-steps, a monogram – filling the field. The designs, if striking, are always crude in workmanship, and in the final period of Visigothic coinage are barbarous in the extreme. It is one of the few medieval coin series to have been extensively counterfeited in modern times (pp. 333–4 and Plate 63).

The evolution of the coinage, and most of the varieties of type, are illustrated on Plates 12–14. The transition to the characteristic Visigothic type took place in the last years of Leovigild's reign, between 579 and 586. Miles' account (1952, 44–8) requires extensive revision. The transition was both simpler and more complex than he imagined: simpler because what he believed to be a variety of early phases are really a single phase, more complex because of the role played in it by Hermenegild, and the changes in weight and fineness as well as of type that were involved.

An essential element in the coinage change is the revolt of Leovigild's elder son Hermenegild, whom he made *consors regni* in 573 and married in 579 to a Frankish princess Ingundis, who was a Catholic. Ingundis and Leovigild's second wife Goiswintha quarrelled violently over the religious issue. The result of this domestic dispute was that Hermenegild abandoned Arianism for Catholicism and, apparently with the support of the Roman-Hispanic element in the population and the Byzantine authorities at Carthagena, rebelled against his father and assumed the title of king (579). His rebellion, which affected all southern Spain, was not suppressed till 584. Hermenegild was put to death in 585, a year after his surrender, leaving the way clear for the eventual succession of Leovigild's second son Reccared.

Sometime early in the 570s the pseudo-imperial coinage of the kingdom was brought into line with that of the Franks by the adoption of the new and slightly lighter Germanic weight standard (see p. 14) of 20 grains (1.3g) instead of the heavier Roman one of 8 siliquae (1.5g). The subsequent sequence of changes can be reconstructed without too much difficulty (Hillgarth 1961, 1966). Hermenegild took the initiative, presumably in 579 or 580, by issuing coins of the traditional Victory type but with his own name (Miles 46), thus advertising his assumption of the royal title. Leovigild replied with coins (Miles 1–8; **1.209**) bearing his own name in a variety of ways, this diversity not implying successive issues but the varying fashions in which die-sinkers at different mints interpreted what one must conjecture to have been a loosely drafted instruction to put on the coins *nominem domini nostri Leovigildi incliti regis*. Hermenegild followed up his initial issue, in which he had been simply styled *incliti regis*, with an issue having the inscription REGI A DEO VITA (Miles 47), an acclamation claiming divine sanction for his usurpation (Díaz 1960; Vives 1960).

The critical years of the revolt were 582–4. Seville was probably captured by Leovigild in 583 and Cordova in 584. In 583 Leovigild ordered the striking of a new coin type showing his profile bust and a cross-on-steps copied from that of the Byzantine solidus under Tiberius II (578–82) accompanied by the name of the mint (**1.210**). (The latter innovation may have preceded the change of type, for it is allegedly found on a coin of Toledo (Miles 27) of Class 1, but this is only known from an eighteenth-century engraving and its existence is dubious.) Evidently no precise direction was given on the form of the mint signature: usually it was simply the name alone, but on mints recovered from Hermenegild – or in the course of Leovigild's simultaneous war with the Suevi (see p. 78) – there were abbreviated and ungrammatical references to Leovigild's successes which can be reconstructed as *Emerita victoria* (Miles 38), *Cum Deo optinuit Ispali* (Miles 31) or *Cum Deo Ispali adquisita* (Miles 32), *Cum De(o) o(ptinuit) Etalica* (Miles 34; 'Italica' was an ancient town north-west of Seville), *Cum D(eo) a(dquisivit) Roda* (Miles 18; on the mint, Roda near Seville and not Rosas north of Gerona near the French frontier, see Balaguer 1983). The next year, as the civil war was ending, Leovigild changed the weight, fineness and type of the coins again. He restored the old 8-siliqua standard but reduced the fineness to 18 carats (below, p. 54), and, since the new coins had to be distinguished from the earlier ones of different weight and fineness, changed the type to one showing a royal bust on both sides (**1.211**). It has been conjectured that the second bust was intended to represent Reccared, who like his half-brother had been *consors regni* since 573, but it is more likely that the mints received a simple order to place the king's facing bust on the coins and, in default of further instruction, thought it safest to employ it on both sides. The date of the new coins is given by the use at Cordova, when the king captured it in 584, of the legend *Cordoba bis* *optinuit*, the *bis* alluding to the fact that Leovigild had captured it from Byzantium earlier in his reign (cf. Gil Farrés 1955).

The type thus created continued in its main features for over sixty years, down to the end of Chindaswinth's sole reign (649). The busts are very varied in pattern, with a good deal of regionalization and evidently much copying from mint to mint. Some varieties, especially in the north-east, have a design representing a cloak fastened with a circular fibula (e.g. **1.233**, Tarragona) but most of them have ladder-like or criss-cross patterns that are probably intended to represent a cuirass. A general feature is the absence of a crown, despite the fact that Isidore of Seville credits Leovigild with having introduced this symbol of royalty; the votive crowns bearing the names of Swinthila and Recceswinth that were found at Guarrazar in 1859 are the greatest masterpieces of surviving Visigothic art. Instead one is shown the king's long hair, falling on either side of the head to near shoulder level, this being a symbol of early Germanic monarchy. Detailed illustrations and discussion will be found in Miles (1952, 46–66), and the main variants can be seen on Plates. 12–13.

Variety in design returned with the joint reign of Chindaswinth and Recceswinth (649–53), for the use of Recceswinth's name as the reverse inscription meant that room had to be found elsewhere for that of the mint. The solution was to substitute a mint monogram for Chindaswinth's bust, while Recceswinth was given a profile bust instead of a facing one (**1.257**). (Miles 340, of the mint of Lugo, ostensibly belongs to the sole reign of Chindaswinth but clearly makes part of the same issue, the mint officials having misunderstood their instructions and failed to substitute Recceswinth's name for the LVCV PIVS of the inscription.) After Chindaswinth's death the mints were left at a loss as to what designs to use, and either continued with a profile bust and mint monogram (Seville: **1.258**) or used a profile bust and plain cross (Gerona: Miles 355), or reverted to the use of two facing busts (Cordova, Toledo: **1.259**). Subsequently they must have received instructions to use as coin types a profile bust and cross-on-steps, and these, with a mint monogram sometimes substituted for the cross-on-steps, continue to the downfall of the kingdom (Plate 14). The design of the profile bust itself varies from mint to mint, being sometimes helmeted instead of bare-headed and shown holding a cross-sceptre or with a cross in the field. It also normally shows the king with a beard, perhaps intended as a likeness, in contrast to the depersonalized beardless busts which the sixth-century coins had copied from their imperial prototypes. During the joint reign of Egica and Wittiza the standard obverse type is two profile busts facing each other with a cross-sceptre between (**1.278–83**).

An exceptional type is the facing head of Christ which from the reign of Erwig (680–7) onwards occasionally replaces the royal bust. It was used at Mérida (**1.267**) and Mentesa under Erwig and was subsequently, though only occasionally, adopted at other mints, including some in the north-east (Gerona, Tarragona) and becoming a grotesque caricature in the process. The type seems basically to have consisted of a head of Christ imposed on a cross-on-steps: the upper end of the cross is clear but its side-arms are often replaced by small semicircles representing Christ's ears, as is the case with **1.267**. Since the type first appears under Erwig (680–7) it precedes the introduction of a bust of Christ as a coin type at Constantinople by Justinian II in *c.* 692, though this likewise has a cross instead of a cross-nimbus behind the head. Both seem to reflect a theological discussion, preceding Iconoclasm and apparently provoked by the condemnation of Monthelitism by a Roman synod in 679 and by the Third Council of Constantinople in 680, as to how Christ should be represented in art, though why it should have affected a few Spanish mints is a mystery.

Obverse legends usually consist of the royal name in the nominative case followed by the royal title (*rex*, usually abbreviated to R; under Egica and Wittiza, *regis* (i.e. *reges*) usually abbreviated to RGS, RG, etc.). Only under Leovigild and Hermenegild is it, as has been noted, sometimes in the genitive and prefaced by DN. Under Chindaswinth the mint of Toledo introduced INDN, *in Dei nomine*, as a prefatory formula, and from Wamba onwards its use, variously abbreviated (INDNM, INDINMN, etc.) is normal (cf. Mateu y Llopis 1941, 1942). Under Egica it is sometimes varied to an abbreviation of *In Christi nomine* (**1.276–7**). There is little consistency in the spelling of royal names: Liuva II can be LEOVΛ, LIVVΛ, LEVΛΛ, Swinthila SVINTHVLΛ, SINTILΛ, SVINTH:L:, SVINTIIV, with variety reaching its height in complicated names like those of Chindaswinth and Recceswinth.

The epigraphy is curious and very characteristic. A is always without horizontal stroke. The letter D has sometimes the form of a *delta* and *th* in personal names is often a *theta* (e.g. CHINDΛSVINΘΛ), while an L through the die-sinker's carelessness often becomes a cross (+IVVIGI+DVS). D is sometimes used instead of B. Ligatured letters, usually only two but sometimes incorporating up to four or five, are common. A table of letter-forms and ligatures is given in Miles (1952, facing p. 148). A curious feature is the occasional replacement of letters by one, two (normally), or three pellets: e.g. SISENΛ:DVS for SISENANDVS, M⁝NTESΛ for MENTESA. The explanation cannot be a die-sinker's carelessness in failing to complete a letter he had begun, for the ends of letters were at this time made with triangular and not circular punches. Possibly they represent privy-marks of some kind, intended to identify the work of particular moneyers or distinguish between coins of different fineness, as presumably were the various sigla (pellets, stars, a flower-like object) that appear in the inscriptions or field of many of the later coins.

The reverse legends, on all save the first signed coins of Leovigild and the corresponding issue of Hermenegild, consist of a mint name accompanied by an epithet, normally PIVS or IVSTVS but occasionally VICTOR or FELIX. These do not refer to the mints, for which *pius* or *iustus* would scarcely be appropriate, but continue the royal title from the other side of the coin, so that instead of *Reccaredus rex – iustus Toleto* one has to understand *Reccaredus rex iustus – Toleto*. Under Leovigild, before the system had settled down, the reverse legends, as we have seen, sometimes commemorate his military successes. Reccared followed his father's example, celebrating victories at Mérida, Tude, Torroño, and elsewhere with such inscriptions as EMERITA VICTOR (**1.220**), VICTORIΛ IN TVDE (Miles 112) and TORNIO VICTORIΛ (Miles 111), and the practice recurs later. Under Chindaswinth and most of his successors the mint of Cordova celebrated its Roman (patrician) origin with the legend CORDOBΛ PATRICIΛ. But these are exceptional: PIVS or IVSTVS accompanied by a mint name forms the usual reverse legend.

The number of recorded mints is a little over eighty – Miles (1952, 69) gives 79, and a few further ones have since come to light – but many of them were of little importance and are represented by less than a dozen surviving specimens, sometimes even by only one or two.

Over half the known total of 3,500 surviving coins are provided by four cities: the capital Toledo in central Spain, Mérida in the south-west, and Seville and Cordova also in the south. At a substantially inferior level (100–200 coins each) there is one more mint in the south, *Eliberri* near the modern Granada, and three in the north, Saragossa, Tarragona and Narbonne, the last of these the only mint in the territory north of the Pyrenees still held by the Visigoths. In the north-west (Gallaecia) small and often unidentified mints proliferate, some probably as a consequence of gold mining still being carried on locally from Roman times. In a small collection like this the preponderance of coins from the major mints will tend to be exaggerated, since most of the mints known from only a few specimens will not appear at all. In actual fact only twelve mints are represented, four small ones (Barbi, Coimbra, Mentesa, Tucci) by only one coin each, while the 'big four' account for two-thirds of the total, fifty out of seventy-five coins.

No Visigothic mint documents have survived and nothing is known of the mint organization (cf. Barceló 1977), or how far the mints were under direct government management as distinct from being susceptible to occasional government direction. Only government intervention can explain the changes in weight and fineness of Leovigild's reign and the two conspicuous changes in type and inscription that occurred under the same ruler, to say nothing of later changes in type and inscription under Chindaswinth, Recceswinth and Egica. Only the government can have laid down that the coins should bear the names of both king and mint, and not those of moneyers as in Gaul. But it is difficult to believe that the many petty mints were in any sense 'government' creations, and one suspects that despite the general 'regal' appearance of the coinage much really depended on local initiative. It is in any case not easy to see why there were mints in some localities and not in others. The surprisingly large number in obscure or even unidentified places is a consequence of subsequent political changes in the Peninsula, for many ancient towns and villages disappeared in the aftermath of the Arab occupation or during the resettlement that followed the Reconquista from the eleventh century onwards. The modern reader may be surprised at the absence of Madrid and the virtual absence of Lisbon (Reis 1959), but both anomalies are only apparent; Madrid did not exist in antiquity – it is first mentioned in the eleventh century and its political importance dates from the late fifteenth century – and Lisbon was throughout the middle ages overshadowed by Oporto (*Portocale*), for which there are a few Visigothic coins. It is harder to understand the relative unimportance of Barcelona and Valencia, or why Carthagena, though recovered from the Byzantines in the 620s, never became a Visigothic mint at all.

The fineness of the coins changed markedly for the worse over the century and a half of their issue. The figures given in Grierson 1953b can be regarded as superseded by Oddy's figures used in this catalogue, since these were ascertained by a qualified technician using better equipment. The differences are in any case quite small, rarely exceeding 5%, and in no way change the general picture provided in the article.

Coins of Leovigild's first two classes were about 90% fine and, as has been seen, were of the light standard of 20 grains, but his third coinage reverted to the traditional tremissis standard of 8 siliquae and this was maintained for the future. The return to the Roman weight standard and its retention was presumably because the Germanic element in the Peninsula was much smaller than that in Gaul. In any case, Leovigild's readoption of the old standard was accompanied by, and was perhaps intended to conceal, a reduction in the fineness of the coins to about 75%, i.e. to 18 carats. The coins remained at this figure under Reccared, after which further reductions took place. From the mid-century onwards the coins are only about 50% gold, though the fineness differs somewhat from mint to mint; too few figures are available for easy generalization. Under Egica and Wittiza the fineness was down to 35% and the coins are pale yellow in colour as well as being deplorably designed and struck. A side-effect of the low fineness was the maintenance throughout the seventh century of high weights for individual coins, which often reach 1.5g or more, figures exceptional even at imperial mints. This feature was carried over and even exaggerated in the earliest Arab coinage of the Peninsula, where the coins were equally debased, most unusually for Muslim coins, but they customarily attain and even exceed the theoretical weight so that *thulths* (one-third dinars) of up to 1.6g or 1.7g are sometimes found.

The failure of the Visigoths to strike solidi in their regal series has been explained already (p. 5), though it is strange that it should have persisted to the end of the kingdom. A higher denomination would surely have been a convenience, and Visigothic Spain, unlike Lombard Italy, could not count on imports from contiguous Byzantine territories. The use of a facing bust and a cross-on-steps on Leovigild's Class 2 and the subsequent retention of the first of these features suggests, indeed, that the 'tremissis' might have been intended as a 'solidus', in the sense of the Germanic 'shilling', for such features characterized the solidus at Byzantium, but this is not borne out by the little written evidence available. The *Lex Visigothorum* knows the solidus and tremissis as separate denominations, as does also Isidore of Seville, and even though many of the laws are sixth century or earlier, and Isidore was an antiquarian who was copying earlier texts, they would probably have signalled a change if one had taken place.

Less explicable than the absence of a solidus is that of a subsidiary coinage in silver or copper, more especially after the Franks had introduced their silver denier in the second half of the seventh century. It is true that the denier was virtually unknown in southern Aquitaine (below, pp. 94, 145), which bordered on Spain and with which the Visigoths would have had closest relations, but the silver coinage of Provence would have been familiar in Septimania and presumably in the Spanish Mediterranean ports. The obvious explanation, and the one normally offered, is the survival and continued use of Roman coins, but such a survival is not borne out by archaeology, for Roman coins are not normally found in the excavation of indisputably Visigothic sites. The problem still awaits solution (cf. Valdeavellano 1961).

5

THE LOMBARDS

(a) GENERAL FEATURES AND BACKGROUND

The history and coinage of the Lombards in southern Italy (Benevento and Salerno) are in large measure distinct from those of the Lombards in northern Italy and Tuscany, and are dealt with separately below (pp. 66–72, 72–3).

Literature

The best collections of material are those in the British Museum and at Milan, catalogued by Wroth (*BMC Vand*) and Arslan (Arslan 1978) respectively, and in the former collection of Victor Emmanuel III; see *CNI* vols. IV (for Pavia and minor Lombard mints), V (for Milan), and XI (for Tuscan mints). Only five hoards of the later 'national' tremisses have been reported, and only of the Ossi hoard from Sardinia (Dessì 1908) and the Ilanz one from the Grisons (Jecklin 1906; Bernareggi 1977) have we good descriptions. Of two of the others, one from Landriano (15km south-east of Milan) and the other from Mezzomerico in the province of Novara, we know little more than that the first contained coins of Ratchis and Aistulf (Ruggero 1908) and the second between 50 and 100 coins of Desiderius, some in a fragmentary condition (Bernareggi 1960, 104). Of the fifth, the Biella hoard of silver coins, we know that it contained 28 tremisses of Liutprand (Cordero 1834, 226), but there are no details of what these were. The Lucchese coins illustrated by Cordero (1860, pls 1–4) suggest that a large Tuscan hoard, mainly municipal issues of Lucca but with a few of Aistulf and Desiderius, came to light in the late 1840s – it was apparently unknown to Cordero in 1834 – but was dispersed without record.

Our understanding of Lombard coinage, which for long remained in the state in which it was left by Wroth and by Sambon (1912), has been extensively revised over the past three decades by Bernareggi. After detailed surveys of the 'national' gold coinage of northern Italy (Bernareggi 1960) and Tuscany (Bernareggi 1963), of the silver coinage (Bernareggi 1965b), and the monetary references in the written sources (Bernareggi 1970), he has mapped out the coinage as a whole (Bernareggi 1971, 1983b) and offered some economic interpretations of it (Bernareggi 1976), leaving few gleanings for his successors. The fineness of the coins has been studied by Oddy (1972b). A long article by Monneret contains much that is useful and suggestive, despite its confused arrangement and frequent eccentricities (Monneret 1919, 22–9; 1920, 183–90; 1921, 191–202). The best short survey is that by Arslan in the introduction to his catalogue. For Lucca see also Massagli 1870 and Belloni 1974.

The narrative sources for the history of the Lombards are collected in a volume of the MGH entitled *Scriptores rerum Langobardicarum* (1878) and there are good editions of Lombard law (Beyerle 1962) and of the royal charters (Schiaparelli 1929–33, abbreviated below as CDL). The period is covered in the standard histories (Hartmann 1900–23, II 2; Romano and Solmi 1940), and in vols. V–VII of Hodgkin (1880–99). A break-away from the traditional political approach is provided by Wickham (1981). On problems of exchange see Bognetti 1944; Grierson 1954e; Fasoli 1958; and Tagliaferri 1964.

Historical background

The Lombards (*Langobardi*, 'Longbeards') were a West Germanic people who in the time of Tacitus had been settled on the lower Elbe but by the early sixth century had made their way across Bohemia and Lower Austria to a settlement in Pannonia (cf. Bóna 1964). Many had adopted Arianism, and from time to time they had entered imperial service, but their reputation for savagery made most of their neighbours reluctant to employ them. The Lethings, their royal family in so far as they had one, died out in the male line in 541, and a feature of subsequent Lombard history (Gasparri 1978) is the great power and independence of local leaders or dukes (*duces*: their Lombard name is unknown). Although the Lombard state was normally ruled by kings, many of whom in the seventh century were descended from or related to the Bavarian ducal family, the crown was theoretically elective and the two great duchies of Spoleto and Benevento were normally quite independent. The evidence of the coinage suggests that the same was largely true of the town authorities in Tuscany.

The Lombard invasion of Italy began in 568, or perhaps in May 569 (Bertolini 1920). Despite their relatively small numbers they had little difficulty in occupying the foothills of the Alps and the valley of the Po, but walled towns presented a greater problem. Pavia, the old Ostrogothic capital and the future capital of the Lombard state, fell to King Alboin only after a three-year siege in 571. Alboin was murdered in 572 and his successor Cleph in 574, after which there followed a ten-year interregnum since the dukes, traditionally thirty-five in number, could not agree on a successor. In 584 they elected Authari, and thenceforth the north was to be ruled by its line of kings. Meanwhile a certain Farwald had settled north-east of Rome and founded the duchy of Spoleto while Zotto and a band of followers had pushed south and, having occupied the strategically placed route-centre of Benevento, made it the capital of a great Lombard duchy that expanded from Campania to include almost the whole of southern Italy.

Lombard Italy differed from Ostrogothic Italy in that while the Ostrogoths had come as imperial representatives, and in consequence ruled the entire peninsula as a matter of right, the Lombards came as invaders and ruled no more than the area they could conquer and occupy. The disunited Italy of later medieval and modern times was one of their legacies to the future. The conquest was a slow business, for many towns held out after the surrounding countryside had been overrun, and since the Byzantines controlled the sea the occupation of coastal towns and villages was especially difficult. Even in the Po valley Cremona and Mantua held out till 603, Tuscany was not occupied till the second quarter of the seventh century – Orvieto is known to have fallen in 605, but it seems to have been exceptional – and the Ligurian coastline was not completely conquered till the 640s. Ravenna and the Exarchate did not finally fall until 751, and Rome and Naples were never captured by the Lombards at all. Although they gradually abandoned Arianism for Catholicism in the first half of the seventh century they continued to be regarded as hated enemies of Rome, and are regularly described as 'most stinking' (*foetidissimi*) and 'most wicked' (*nefandissimi*) in papal records. But the wide-spread use of Lombard personal names in Italy, and the influence of Lombard law in the peninsula, shows how deeply their influence penetrated the country.

All seventh-century kings, from 584 to 712, either belonged to the Bavarian ducal house or intermarried with it (see Table 6) but it is only from Cunincpert that their names appear

Table 6. *Kings of the Lombards, 584–712*

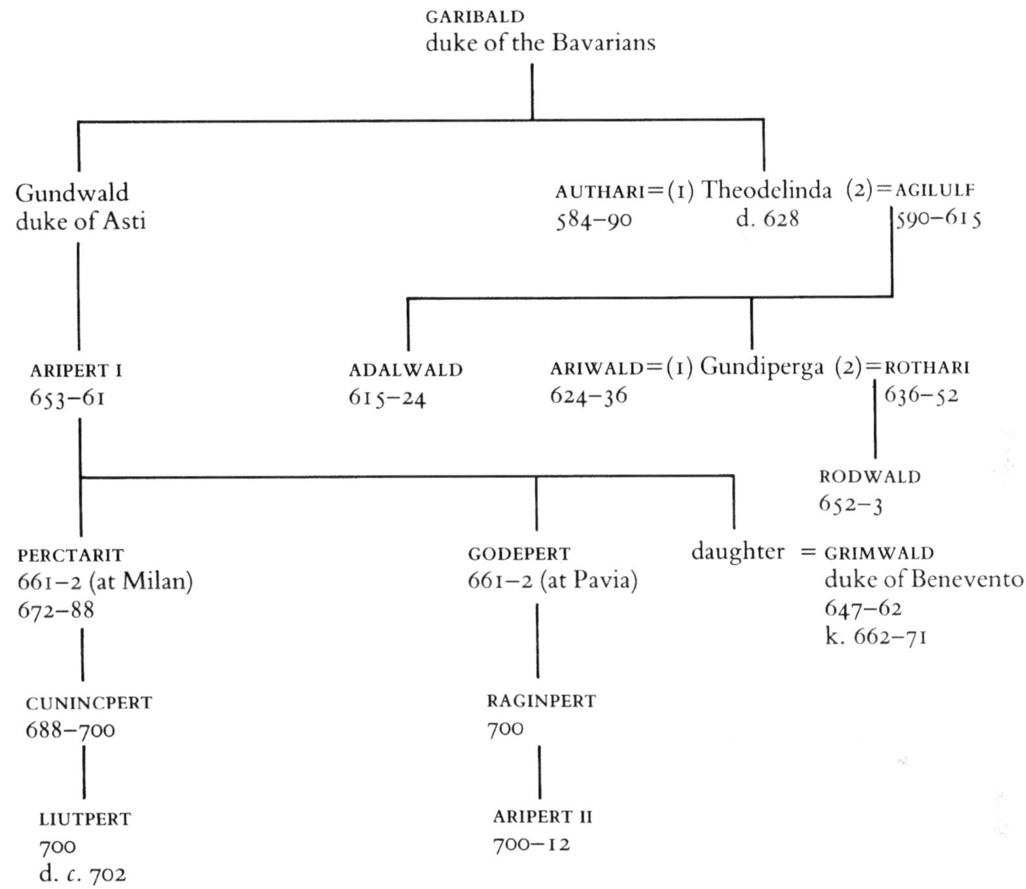

on the coins. The dynasty ended with the overthrow of the cruel and tyrannical Aripert II in 712. He was succeeded by Ansprand, a Lombard noble (perhaps duke of Milan) who had acted as regent in 700 for the infant Liutpert, son of Cunincpert, and had subsequently been living in exile in Bavaria with his son Liutprand. Ansprand died after a few months and his son Liutprand (712–44) was to prove the greatest of the Lombard kings, even establishing his authority over the dukes of Benevento and Spoleto. He was succeeded by his nephew Hildeprand (744), described as *inutilis* in the sources, who was displaced after a reign of some eight months by Duke Ratchis of Friuli (744–9). Ratchis was in turn deposed by his more energetic brother Aistulf (749–56), who captured Ravenna in 750 or 751 and threatened Rome. The result was Frankish intervention at the instance of a papacy apprehensive of being the next victim of Lombard aggression. Pepin the Short invaded Italy in 754 and again in 756, compelling Aistulf to hand over Ravenna not to the Byzantines, for whom he cared nothing, but to the papacy. Aistulf died from a hunting accident later in 756, and his successor Desiderius, a man of humble birth who had been made duke of Tuscany by Aistulf, was to be the last native king. He was attacked by Charlemagne in the autumn of 773, captured when Pavia capitulated after an eight-month siege in June 774, and despatched to die a prisoner in France. His son Adelchis, who had been his co-ruler since 759, escaped and fled to Byzantium. With Byzantine support he invaded Calabria in 788, but was totally defeated by a joint Beneventan and Frankish army and disappears from our records.

Coinage

Lombard coinage, as a result of the geographical distribution of Lombard settlements, developed along different lines in the three areas of Upper Italy, Tuscany, and the south (Benevento). The coinage of Tuscany was absorbed by that of Upper Italy in the eighth century, and indeed provided the types used under the last two kings and by Charlemagne, so its coinage is customarily grouped with that of the north under the general heading of 'Lombard coinage'. The coinage of the duchy of Benevento, geographically and politically separated from Tuscany and the north by the intervening duchies of Spoleto and Rome, is quite different in inspiration and content from the others, besides starting much later than they did and surviving much longer. It can therefore be treated separately (below, pp. 66–72 and Plates 50–1). The duchy of Spoleto, surprisingly, seems to have struck no coinage of its own, and whether it made good its lack by using Lombard coins of Tuscany or Benevento, or Byzantine coins of Rome, is still a mystery.

The development of 'Lombard coinage' (in the sense just described) followed the same general pattern as that of the other Germanic states, with the introduction of a national type preceded by a century of pseudo-imperial issues. The national coinage in its final form involves tremisses of uniform design issued in a number of different localities and bearing the names of rulers and mints, but not those of the moneyers as was customary in the Frankish kingdom. Lombard coinage has naturally its own particular features. It is much more completely one of tremisses, with no solidi at all outside Benevento. Its later silver coinage is marginal and never displaced the gold coinage, as the denier did in France. There were no early imitations of the nummus, and the only later coinage of copper, the follis struck by Aistulf, was a consequence of this ruler's occupation of the Byzantine mint of Ravenna in 751. Lombard coinage also retained the old Roman standards of weight, and to some degree of fineness, much longer than was the case elsewhere.

Lombard pseudo-imperial tremisses are of two types, one mainly copied from those of the emperor Maurice (582–602) with Victory reverse, the other copied from ones of Heraclius (610–41) and Constans II (641–68) with a cross-potent. They differ entirely in size and general appearance. The coins of the 'Victory' series have in general flans much larger than the originals, becoming still thinner and larger with the passage of time, while those of the 'cross-potent' series contract into small, thick coins, ending with pieces only 12mm in diameter as against the 20mm of the 'Victory' ones. Although on both there is a heavy annular border, this forms the actual rim on the 'cross-potent' series, while on the 'Victory' series it is set well inside it. Until recently it was assumed that the two series were successive issues: the 'Maurice' imitations were attributed to Kings Authari and Agilulf, who reigned between 584 and 615; the 'Heraclius' imitations to Kings Adalwald, Ariwald and Authari, who covered the years 615–52; and the Constans II imitations to Rodwald, Aripert I, Grimoald and Perctarit, in the three decades 652–88. Such a conclusion is quite unacceptable on numismatic grounds, since the later coins bearing the name of Cunincpert are very close in style and fabric to the Maurice imitations; they must follow up on them directly and not after an interval of over seventy years. It is now recognized that the two Lombard pseudo-imperial coinages are parallel issues, and that the 'Victory' type was struck in the north, while the 'cross-potent' one, which started a little later, represents the coinage of Tuscany and leads on to the tremisses bearing the names of Lucca and other Tuscan towns.

The absence of solidi is at first sight surprising, both because Visigoths and Franks in their pseudo-imperial phases struck them in considerable numbers and because solidi were minted by the dukes of Benevento, who even if normally independent princes were admittedly inferior in status to the Lombard kings. The explanation is probably geographical. The Lombard kings could rely on regular payments of tribute, diplomatically concealed under other names, from the Byzantine exarchs, and since such tributes would be paid in solidi the state would have an adequate supply of the higher denomination but would have to manufacture tremisses for itself. It was probably also this that so long preserved the Lombard tremissis from the weight decline that took place elsewhere (below, p. 61), for the coin would have had to maintain its relationship to the Byzantine solidus.

Lombard coinage, like that of the Visigoths and unlike that of the Franks, was formally a regal coinage. The *Edictum Rothari*, indeed, is unique amongst the early Germanic legal codes in asserting that minting could take place only with royal authorization: 'He who stamps gold or mints coin without the king's command shall have his hand cut off' (*Si quis sine iussionem regis aurum figuravit aut monetam confinxerit, manus ei incidatur*). The meaning of this clause (cap. 242) has been much discussed, partly because of the penalty, which seems to have been borrowed from Byzantine practice of the seventh century (Lopez 1943a, 450–1), partly because of uncertainty as to what is meant by *aurum figuravit*, or *signaverit* as one MS has it (Visconti 1921; Gualazzini 1961), and partly because of the problem of relating it to various coinages that seem to be non-royal or incompletely royal, notably the 'municipal' coinage of Tuscany and solitary tremisses on which the king's name is accompanied by that of a Duke Iffo or which bear the name of a moneyer (MARINVS MON). The first of these coins, however, can be dismissed as a forgery (Bernareggi 1965a, 1980), and the second, though apparently authentic (Bernareggi 1983b, 53–4, 156) is a momentary testimony to Frankish influence. As for the 'municipal' coinage of Tuscany, which was not brought under full royal control till the 740s, one suspects that the kings tolerated something they could not prevent, just as they must have done with the coinage of the dukes of Benevento. In the early days of Lombard settlement, indeed, the kings are hardly likely to have interested themselves in the coinage, and the earliest imitations were probably the result of local initiative, whether indigenous city authorities or intruding dukes, especially during the ten years 574–84 when there was no king at all. Later the kings would

Table 7. *Lombard mints*

Mint	Tuscan municipal	Aistulf 749–54	Desiderius 756–74	Charlemagne 774/81
Upper Italy				
Pavia		X	X	X
Milan			X	X
Piacenza			X	
Bergamo				X
Castelnovate			X	
Castel Seprio			X	X
Ivrea			X	
Pombia			X	
Treviso			X	
Vercelli			X	
Vicenza			X	
Ravenna		X		
Tuscany				
Lucca	X		X	X
Pisa	X	X	X	
Chiusi (?)	X			
Pistoia	X			

inevitably attempt to re-establish a royal monopoly, but the clause in Rothari's Edict of 643, in so far as it is anything more than a condemnation of counterfeiters (cf. cap. 243), is more likely to be an affirmation of royal policy than a statement of effective law.

Lombard coinage under at least the last two kings and under Charlemagne was minted at a number of separate localities, and since some mints are represented by only one or two specimens the list is probably not complete. Table 7, which includes the Tuscan municipal issues but omits Charlemagne's coin of Chur as being not truly 'Lombard' (below, p. 210) summarizes the position as it is at present known. The total of mints was much less than was the case in either Visigothic Spain or Frankish Gaul, and even when account is taken of the fact that Lombard Italy was more restricted in area than either of these, the smaller number is evidence of a more limited breakdown in Roman traditions. That the coins were actually minted in many though not necessarily all of these localities, instead of being struck at a central mint or mints and distributed locally, can be deduced from the written evidence. A diploma of 775 (CDL 278) deals with the purchase of land at Treviso *iuxta monita pupliga* by a moneyer named Lopulo; another moneyer named Grasulf was a purchaser of land in Lucca in 768 (CDL 220); and moneyers appear in the list of witnesses to charters at Piacenza in 758 (CDL 130), Milan in 765 (CDL 190), Pavia in 769 (CDL 231), and Lucca in 773 (CDL 281).

The dies, on the other hand, must have been cut at a few centres and distributed from these. Jecklin, in his description of the Ilanz hoard, noted the strong resemblance between the dies used for different mints and even the existence of some die-links between them. The number of such links has been expanded by Bernareggi, and it is clear that only a limited number of die-sinkers were at work. Since the areas involved are quite small one may presume that the dies were prepared at one or two central mints, perhaps Pavia in the north and Lucca in Tuscany. Some scholars have supposed that the coins bearing the names of such minor localities as Castel Seprio and Pombia were struck centrally, but this would run contrary to the basic purpose of local mints, that of attracting bullion, especially at frontiers, and of reducing the need to transport large quantities of cash from place to place. The explanation of minting in some tiny localities in the north-west – Castel Seprio, Castelnovate, Pombia, Vercelli – is perhaps the same as that of Visigothic mints in Gallaecia (above, p. 53), for the document known as the *Honorantie civitatis Papie* of the late tenth century shows that levies on alluvial gold found in the Pennine Alps and the upper reaches of the rivers of northern Italy made an appreciable contribution to the revenues of the Ottonian state.

Nothing is known for certain regarding the northern mints prior to Desiderius. From Cunincpert onwards there are often letters, either single or ligatured, in the field, and since the commonest of these are M (Cunincpert, Aripert II, Liutprand), S or SE (Aripert II, Liutprand), and V (Cunincpert, Liutprand) one is inclined to treat these as the initials of Milan, Castel Seprio and Vercelli. Other identifications are also possible: T for Treviso, N for Castelnovate, etc. But there are some that have no obvious equivalent (LD, H, G); a few that occur under Cunincpert are not found for Aripert II and *vice versa*; and B, the most common letter on pseudo-imperial issues of Tuscany, has no obvious mint equivalent at all. Mint identifications of the letters would consequently be hazardous, however tempting some of them may be. As for the earlier pseudo-imperial coins, we have no alternative, in view of their uniformity of style, to attributing them all to Pavia, while admitting the possibility, even the probability, that although the dies may have been made at Pavia many of the coins were struck elsewhere.

Lombard coinage underwent three well-marked weight changes. The early pseudo-imperial types were still tremisses of 8 siliquae, for although they average *c.* 1.45g, well below the theoretical weight of 1.52g, the same is true of their seventh-century Byzantine counterparts. Coins of Cunincpert and Aripert II tend to be about 1.35g instead of 1.45g, but this is more likely to be the result of casual mint practice than of a formal weight change. With Liutprand, however, there is an abrupt fall to *c.* 1.25g. This must be the tremissis (1.24g) corresponding to the 20-siliqua solidus referred to in the glosses to cap. 346 of Rothari's Edict in the Madrid and La Cava MSS, and was probably intended to bring Lombard coinage into line with the products of Byzantine mints in Italy at the time. The twelve undamaged Lombard coins in the Ossi hoard, for example, weigh between 1.17g and 1.27g, averaging 1.23g, while the five Byzantine coins of the mint of Sardinia weigh between 1.10g and 1.24g, averaging 1.20g (Dessì 1908). With Ratchis there was a further reduction to *c.* 1.05g. (His coins and those of Aistulf are too rare for averages to tell us much, but the figure is clear from the much commoner coins of Desiderius.) Various interpretations of this last standard have been put forward (Luschin 1908a, 1908b; Bernareggi 1963, 72–6), but 1.05g does not fit the barleycorn (Troy grain) pattern of

Frankish coinage (below, p. 107) and it is more reasonable to treat it as one of 20 *grani*, wheat-grains of 0.05g being the normal basis of the weight standards of later medieval Italy (Milan 0.051g, Florence 0.049g, etc.). Both under Desiderius and Charlemagne the weights of the actual coins vary quite widely, from *c.* 0.75g to *c.* 1.10g, but this is a common feature of badly debased coins (above, p. 54), as by this time Lombard tremisses had become.

Our knowledge of the fineness of Lombard tremisses depends mainly on Oddy's study of nearly a hundred coins in the British Museum and Grierson collections (Oddy 1972b). The pseudo-imperial coins of both the north and of Tuscany each seem to form two groups, one *c.* 90% fine and presumably aiming at 24 carats, the other only *c.* 80%. Cunincpert's and Aripert II's coins saw a return to a high standard (*c.* 95% fine), but the few figures available for Liutprand's reign suggest two successive reductions, the first about 70% and the second to about 50%. A similar range of figures is found for the Tuscan series with completely blundered legends, and the autonomous coins of Lucca are down to *c.* 50%. Coins of Desiderius vary between *c.* 55% and *c.* 45%, probably aiming at 50% but without much care being exercised over attaining this precise figure. Taken in conjunction with the decline in weight, the tremissis of the last days of the Lombard kingdom can have had only about a third of the gold content of its predecessor of the mid seventh century.

The general features of Lombard coinage can be easily grasped, though it has to be remembered that the tremisses are rare – the total number of specimens known probably does not exceed three hundred, as against several thousand of their Merovingian and Visigothic equivalents – and the detailed picture is bound to be somewhat modified in the future.

(b) PSEUDO-IMPERIAL, REGAL AND MUNICIPAL COINAGES

The pseudo-imperial coinage of Lombardy (568–c. 680)

The main coinage of north Italy in this period (**1.301–6**) consisted of tremisses copied from those of the emperor Maurice Tiberius (582–602) of the mint of Ravenna (*DOC* I, pl. 79.287). The coins reproduce the conspicuous annular borders and rounded lettering of their Ravennate models, these features becoming more and more exaggerated with the passage of time. The style of the coins, especially the later ones, is very distinctive, the diameter of the coins being increased from 14mm to 21mm and the consequent thinness of the flan blurring the obverse type which took its impression from the anvil die. Some of these coins have an M or a star in the field. The coin bearing the name of Aripert I (Brand sale I.91, ex Verworn (Cahn 49, 11.12.1922) 232, ex Gnecchi II (Hamburger 20.5.1902) 3956) is anomalous and has often been written off as a modern forgery (Bernareggi 1980), but it has every appearance of being authentic and presumably represents a premature move to displace the pseudo-imperial inscription by a formally royal one (DN ARIPERT REX), though we know of nothing in Aripert's eight-year reign (653–61) that would have justified such an innovation. The anomalous coin of the moneyer Marinus has already been noted (p. 59).

Prior to the Interregnum of 574–84 there are imitations (**1.294, 298–9**) of tremisses bearing the names of Justinian I (d. 565) or Justin II (565–78), whose coins between them would have formed the bulk of the circulating medium of north Italy at the date of the Lombard invasion. They are Ravennate in style but too crude to be attributed to the imperial mint, and though they occur in sites on either side of the Alps a Lombard attribution is more likely than a Bavarian one.

There are also pseudo-imperial silver coins dating to the first decades after the conquest which are best attributed to the Lombards (**1.295–7**). As with the earliest tremisses, the line between official Byzantine issues and Lombard imitations is not easy to draw save where the coins have been found on known Lombard sites and their legends and types are badly distorted (cf. Martin 1980). There are also some rare imitations of Ravennate half-siliquae of Tiberius II (578–82) which bear a monogram best attributed to the Lombard duke Farwald of Spoleto, who occupied Classis, the port of Ravenna, in or about 579 and held it for ten years (see note on no. **1.300**). Although the Byzantine mint is known to have been in the city proper and not in the port, it is easy to see why the occupation of the latter should have resulted in an exceptional issue of silver coins that have obvious affinities with those of the Ostrogoths in the early years of the century.

*The pseudo-imperial coinage of Tuscany (*c. *620–*c. *700)*

This coinage (**1.307–17**), also one of tremisses, contrasts sharply with that of the north in model, type and fabric. Instead of a Victory forming the reverse type there is a cross potent, with inscriptions showing that the models were tremisses of the emperors Heraclius (610–41) and Constans II (641–68). Because of their heavy annular border the prototypes are commonly ascribed to Ravenna, but the Tuscan origin of the copies suggests that the same feature may have occurred on Byzantine coins of Rome (cf. *DOC* II.46–7). After a phase in which the diameter of the coins became larger, expanding from 14mm to 18mm (**1.307–12**), they contract to 10–11mm (**1.313–17**), the coins in consequence becoming thicker and struck in high relief. The blundered remains of the *Constantinus* and *Victoria augustorum* inscriptions are replaced in the second half of the seventh century by a meaningless alternation of the letters V and I (VIVIVI . . .) and there are letters – B is the most common – in the field for which no explanation has been found. The dating of the coinage is conjectural, but it evidently started under Heraclius and the fineness of the later issues suggests that it ended about the turn of the century. The chief if not the sole mint was probably Lucca.

*Autonomous coinage in Tuscany (*c. *700–*c. *750)*

The municipal tremisses form two series. Both have essentially the same reverse type as the last pseudo-imperial ones, with a cross-potent and a meaningless VIVIVI inscription, but the first series replaces the profile bust and inscription of the obverse with a monogram of LVCA (**1.318**) filling the entire field and sometimes accompanied by letters or sigla (Cordero 1860, pl. 1), the second with a floral pattern and the inscription FLAVIA LVCA (**1.319**; Cordero 1860, pl. 2). There are similar coins of Pisa with FLAVIA PITA C.

The meaning of the term *Flavia* accompanying the place-name has been much discussed (Bordeaux 1908; Bernareggi 1960, 106–11; 1963, 115–20). It has an obvious parallel in the name or epithet *Flavius* which had been adopted by Odovacar (see p. 28) and the Ostrogothic kings, and is a tribute to the high esteem accorded to the Flavian emperors, more especially to Titus, in the later Roman Empire, and which according to Paul the Deacon (III.16) was conferred on Authari at his accession and retained by his successors. Whether, as applied to cities, it had any specific constitutional meaning, relating either to the status or loyalty of the towns, or signifying a formal concession of minting rights, we have no idea. It cannot have been related to the epithets on Visigothic coins, since these, although apparently accompanying the cities, really belonged with the rulers' names (above, p. 52). In Roman times it had sometimes been conceded to cities as a mark of honour; Vienna was *Flavia Vindobona*, and Spello, the ancient capital of Umbria, had its name changed to *Flavia Constans* by the emperor Constans II. But it is not impossible that, since *Luca* alone would have been too short to make a satisfactory coin inscription, *Flavia* was simply added by some ingenious mint-master to fill this out. As for the dates of these municipal coinages, their fineness suggests that they were contemporary with the reigns of Liutprand and his two successors and ended when the type was taken over by Desiderius for the whole Lombard coinage.

*Regal gold coinage (*c. *690–774)*

The regal coinage of the late seventh and the first half of the eighth century (to 756) consists mainly of tremisses (**1.320–3, 325–7**) and very light silver coins, the latter introduced under Perctarit and continued into the reign of Liutprand, the tremisses starting only with Cunincpert. Under Aistulf there was also a coinage of Byzantine types at Ravenna.

The tremisses form essentially four groups:

(1) Obverse with name and profile bust of ruler; Victory rev. (Cunincpert).
(2) Similar obverse, but St Michael reverse (Cunincpert–Liutprand).
(3) Same reverse, but facing bust or monogram on obverse (Ratchis, Aistulf, Desiderius).
(4) Star and name of ruler on obv.; cross and mint name on reverse (Aistulf, Desiderius).

Group 1, which is rare and not represented here, is, apart from the tremissis of Aripert I already mentioned, the first fully regal coinage, continuing the traditional pseudo-imperial types of the north but with the royal name and title as both obverse and reverse inscription. Various letters can occur in the field (M, N, T, V), and the decoration on the imperial bust is usually a monogram of RX. The issue can be dated between Cunincpert's accession in 688 and the introduction of Group 2 in the early 690s.

Group 2 formed the coinage of the five decades from the early 690s to the 740s, covering most of the reign of Cunincpert (688–700) and those of Aripert II (700–12) and Liutprand (712–44). Coins of the same type were probably struck during the brief reigns of Liutpert (700), Raginpert (700), Ansprand (712) and Hildeprand (744), but each of these lasted only a few weeks and no coins for them are known. The characteristic feature of the group is the winged figure of St Michael holding a cross and shield and accompanied by his name SCS MIHAHIL, usually shortened and blundered. The saint, to whom the cathedral church of Pavia was dedicated, may already have been regarded as the patron saint of the Lombard people, but for Cunincpert he had a special significance. Cunincpert's enemy Duke Alahis of Trento had sworn fealty to him in the church at Pavia, and in the battle of Cornate, at which the duke was overthrown, the archangel was reputed to have appeared in person to reproach Alahis with his perfidy. The idea of using the saint as a coin type was probably suggested by the Emperor Justinian II's introduction of the bust of Christ on Byzantine coins in the early 690s, for Cunincpert is scarcely likely to have been aware of the localized use of the latter type at a few mints in Spain (above, p. 51).

In Group 3, the reason behind the replacement of the profile bust by either a facing one or a monogram of CRVX on coins of Ratchis and Aistulf is unknown, but may have been intended to distinguish them as being of lower fineness. A great novelty resulted from Aistulf's capture of Ravenna, which took place in 751 – one of his diplomas is dated from Ravenna on 4 July of this year – for he held the city until 756, when he was compelled by the Frankish king Pepin to cede it to the papacy. Having taken over the Byzantine mint, Aistulf issued coins of Byzantine denominations – solidi, tremisses, folles – and types, showing his facing bust with a long beard and elaborate coiffure. Its features are so well marked that it is tempting to regard them as a portrait, but there are similar ones on several Lombard crosses and on the so-called helmet piece of Agilulf, so it is more likely to be a generalized representation of a Lombard king. The coins are dated by indictional letters in the field, as their Byzantine predecessors had been (*DOC* III.297–8). The only published solidi and tremisses (Brambilla 1867; Bernareggi 1968) are of indictions Z and H, i.e. 7(=753/4) and 8 (=754/5) respectively. One of the three recorded specimens of the corresponding follis is dated *Anno I*, i.e. 751/2 (Ercolani Cocchi 1983, no. 2700); the years on the others are off-flan (**1.324**) or illegible.

Aistulf's other innovation was in securing the use of his name on the coinage of the Tuscan mints of Lucca (**1.323**) and Piacenza, and probably at others still to be discovered. Since it was substituted for the meaningless VIVIVI of the obverse inscription, the royal name thus appears on the reverse, though it is more convenient in describing the coins to treat the side with the king's name as the obverse in the normal way.

The coinage of the last Lombard king Desiderius (757–74) starts like that of the end of Aistulf's reign, with St Michael coins struck in Lombardy and ones of the flower/cross type in Tuscany. But quite early the decision must have been taken to extend the Tuscan type to mints throughout the kingdom (**1.325–7**). There are consequently coins of this type for twelve mints of Desiderius, and since several further ones are known for Charlemagne the number may be increased in the future. It was thus a uniform coinage that Charlemagne found in circulation when he invaded Italy. The fineness of the coins was now finally reduced to about 50%, with individual specimens falling to 35% or even less.

Regal silver coinage (late seventh–early eighth century)

Lombard silver coins of very thin fabric (**1.328–31**; Bernareggi 1965b), their creation probably suggested by the Frankish silver deniers of the 670s, were apparently introduced under Perctarit (672–88), a monogram of the letters PER forming the reverse type and its attribution to Perctarit probable though not certain. The coins are mainly known from a hoard of about 1,600 specimens found in 1833 at Biella in Piedmont (Cordero 1834, 226–31; Promis 1858, 101–3), though discrepancies in our very unsatisfactory nineteenth-century accounts have led Bernareggi to argue that there were two hoards and not one. A further group of six specimens was discovered in

1966 during excavations in the sacristy of the church of Santa Maria di Bravone at Linguizzetta, a tiny village in eastern Corsica (Lafaurie 1967c). Initially the coins had on the obverse a crude bust filling virtually the entire field and on the reverse a monogram, with sometimes a badly delineated wreath. The busts on the earliest coins (Bernareggi 1965b, pl. 22.3, 6) resemble those of the latest tremisses in the name of Maurice and the earliest ones of Cunincpert, while the style of others (Bernareggi 1965b, pl. 22.13, 15) is closer to those of Cunincpert's later coins and those of his successors. With the passage of time the striking of the obverses became increasingly weak and was eventually abandoned, so that the coins are bracteates. The coinage must have lasted into the 720s or 730s, since the Biella hoard also contained tremisses of Liutprand, but it is unlikely to have linked up with the denarial coinage of the Frankish period. What the coins were called, or how they were related in value to the contemporary tremisses, is not known.

In addition to these silver coins a few others exist with monograms of disputed interpretation (Grierson 1956b), or with a facing bust of St Michael and a complicated cross-and-crescent-in-wreath reverse (Kos 1981). The former were wrongly attributed by Stefan to the fifth century and the Rugians settled in what is now Austria (Stefan 1957), but a satisfactory elucidation of both groups requires more evidence than is at present available. The recent quite unexpected discovery of a cumulative deposit of Byzantine silver coins of the mint of Rome, including previously unknown papal coins of the mid-eighth century (see note to **1.030**), shows that there are still serious gaps in our knowledge of this period.

(c) BENEVENTAN COINAGE

Literature

The reference work still most generally used is *BMC Vand*, but more complete lists of issues will be found in Sambon (1912), Cagiati (1916–17), and vol. XVIII of the *CNI*. Coins formerly in a large private collection are illustrated by Catemario (1953). The fullest discussion of the coinage in the light of the written evidence, mainly from the archive of the great monastery of La Cava dei Tirreni (see below, p. 72), is that of Arturo Sambon (1919). A monograph by Bertolini (1978) on representations of the cross on coins of the Iconoclastic period includes a stylistic and typological examination of the coinage prior to 774 and valuable enlargements, but its handling of the numismatic evidence is uncritical. Most of the gold coinage is badly debased, as can be seen from the long series of analyses published by Oddy (1974) which includes the coins in this collection. The history of the duchy is covered in the standard works on early medieval Italy (see p. 249), and there is a monograph by Hirsch (in Hirsch and Schipa 1968) on the duchy (to 774) and three important studies by Poupardin (1901, 1906, 1907).

Historical background

The city of Benevento (*Beneventum*) lies in Campania some 45km north-east of Naples. It is situated at the junction of the Calore (which lower down becomes the Volturno and flows through Capua to the sea) and the Sabbato, and these natural advantages made it a centre of communications, augmented when under the Romans it became the meeting-point of six roads, for it lay on the prolongation of the Via Appia beyond Capua towards Taranto and Brindisi. In early times it had been the capital of the Samnites, so that the Lombard historian Paul the Deacon calls its people Samnites and speaks of the duchy of Benevento as *ducatus Samnitorum*. It was sacked in 542 by Totila, and it was his partial destruction of its great circuit of walls that made possible its relatively easy capture by the Lombards thirty years later.

The huge duchy was essentially the creation of its first two dukes, Zotto (571–91) and the long-lived Arichis I (591–641). They conquered between them the whole of southern Italy except its two extremities, the heel (Apulia) and toe (Calabria), and the city and region of Naples, which the Byzantines were able to hold, as they held Ravenna and Rome, from the sea. The duchy and principality – Duke Arichis II abandoned the title of *dux* in favour of that of *princeps* in 774, after Charlemagne's annexation of the Lombard kingdom – never had an easy history, since it had to fight off the ambitions of the Lombard kings, the inveterate hostility of its papal neighbour (Bertolini 1952–5), and periodic revivals of Byzantine power. The end of the Lombard kingdom only replaced one enemy by the other, for the Franks always claimed to be its overlords.

The list of dukes and princes from Gisulf I, under whom an identifiable coinage began, is set out in Table 8. Only for the century 642–758 did it have a clear 'dynastic' history. Arichis I was succeeded by his son Aio (641–2), but the latter left no direct heir. He was succeeded in turn by two close friends and allies, Radoald and his brother Grimoald I, sons of Duke Gisulf II of Friuli, and Grimoald's last known descendant in the male line was a Duke Liutprand deposed by King Desiderius in 758. The dynasty, however, was continued in an attenuated form to 806, perhaps even to 817, for Arichis II is described as of 'royal and ducal descent', though the relationship is not recorded, and Grimoald IV's name coupled with his uncontested accession in 806 suggest that although he is always described as the son of an otherwise unknown Ermanrih he was somehow related to Grimoald III. But between 731 and 758 the regular succession had been repeatedly interrupted by either royal intervention or local pretenders, and after 817 no 'dynasty' lasted more than three generations at the most. Paul the Deacon comments on the almost proverbial disloyalty of the Beneventans to their rulers.

The greatest ruler of South Italy in the eighth and ninth centuries was Arichis II (Bertolini 1962). After the fall of Desiderius he assumed the use of crown and sceptre, as if heir to the Lombard state, and maintained a splendid court at Benevento (Belting 1962). Only in the last year of his life did a Frankish invasion compel him to submit to Charlemagne, and even then on terms that seem to have been left deliberately vague (Bertolini 1965). He also gave hostages for good behaviour. By ill fortune one of these was his second son Grimoald, for Grimoald unexpectedly became his father's heir through the death of an elder brother in the last weeks of Arichis' life. The pope urged Charlemagne to annex Benevento to his Lombard kingdom, but Grimoald was instead released after taking an oath of vassalage which included a promise to abandon the Lombard practice of wearing a beard and an undertaking to place Charles' name in his charters and on his coins. He adhered to these terms no longer than he had to. He dropped Charlemagne's names from his charters after 789 and by 791 was in open revolt, defeating a series of Frankish expeditions against him over the next ten years.

The next ruler, Grimoald IV, had less success, being compelled in 812 to pay Charlemagne 25,000 gold solidi and in 814 to promise an annual tribute of 7,000 solidi to the new Frankish

Table 8. *Dukes and Princes of Benevento, 689–910*

Dukes	
Gisulf I	689–706
Romoald II, son of Gisulf I	706–31
Gisulf II, son of Romoald II	731
Audelais, usurper	731
Gregory, nephew of King Liutprand	732–9
Gottschalk, usurper	739–42
Gisulf II, restored	742–51
Liutprand, son of Gisulf II	751–8
with his mother Scauniperga, 751–5	
Arichis II	758–74
Princes	
Arichis II	774–87
Grimoald III, son of Arichis II	788–806
with Charlemagne, 788–9	
Grimoald IV, son of Ermanrih	806–17
Sico	817–32
Sicard	832–9
Radelchis I	839–52
Radelgar, son of Radelchis I	851–3
Adelchis, brother of Radelgar	853–78
Louis II with Angilberga, 866–71	
Gaideris, nephew of Adelchis	878–81
Radelchis II, son of Adelchis	881–4
Aio, brother of Radelchis II	884–90
Ursus, son of Aio	890–1
(Occupation by the Byzantines, 891–4; by Guy and Lambert of Spoleto, 894–7; by Waimar of Salerno, 897)	
Peter, bishop of Benevento, regent	897
Radelchis II, restored	897–900
Atenulf of Capua	900–10

emperor, Louis the Pious. He was murdered in 817 by a conspiracy of nobles, and the reign of his successor Sico was mainly occupied by an unsuccessful attempt to add Naples to his dominions. Sico managed to hand on the throne to his son Sicard, who ruled with increasing difficulty against the pretensions of an intransigent nobility down to his murder in 839. The civil war that followed resulted in the break-up of the Beneventan state. First the treasurer Radelchis was proclaimed prince and killed his rival Adelchis, only to be faced with the competition of Sicard's younger brother Siconulf, who was proclaimed prince at Salerno. Arabs and Franks intervened on one side or the other until Louis II imposed peace on the rivals in 849. The old principality was partitioned, with Siconulf taking most of the western part (16 gastaldships) and Radelchis the rest, but with his share greatly reduced by the Muslim occupation of Bari and much of Apulia.

The reduced Benevento of Radelchis' successors was only intermittently able to maintain its independence against its neighbours. In 866 the emperor Louis II came to the aid of Benevento and other south Italian states against the Arabs of Africa, who had by then conquered most of Sicily and made substantial encroachments on the mainland. Since he regarded himself as sovereign of the whole peninsula he occupied Benevento (866–71) and took over its mint for the striking of silver denari, some in association with Adelchis but most of them in his own name or in that of the empress Angilberga. Only two types refer in their legends to Benevento, but all are of the same weight and fabric – they differ completely from Louis' northern coinage – and they must all have been minted either at Benevento or by Beneventan moneyers accompanying Louis' army and in his service. The role of Angilberga is explained by the exceptional position she enjoyed in Louis' affections and the prominent role accorded to her as *consors imperii* in public affairs (Odegaard 1951; Delogu 1964). The coinage ended in 871, when Louis and Angilberga were made prisoners by Adelchis and only released after taking an oath, promptly violated, to leave south Italy and not return.

Two decades later Benevento again lost its independence. Aio was succeeded in 890 by his ten-year-old son Ursus, who was deposed a year later by the *protospatharius* Simbaticus, envoy of the emperor Leo VI in Italy, and Benevento was annexed by Byzantium (Gay 1904). In 894 the Greeks were expelled by Guy of Spoleto, after whose death (Dec. 894) the principality was first occupied by Waimar of Salerno and then recovered by Radelchis II (897–900). It continued as an independent state down to 1051, when Pandulf III and his son Landulf VI were overthrown by malcontents and the city submitted to Pope Leo IX. They recovered the city in 1054, after Leo's death, but by that time most of the principality had been occupied by the Normans and Benevento itself was finally annexed by the papacy in 1077. By then its coinage had long since come to an end.

Coinage

The identifiable coinage of Benevento started in the late seventh century with pseudo-imperial solidi and tremisses attributable to Gisulf I. These have the letter G in the field (**1.1086**), and the attribution to the dukes of earlier coins of south Italian fabric without any distinguishing letter (**1.1085**) is conjectural. From Gisulf onwards the sequences of coins, of steadily decreasing fineness and attributable to individual rulers through initials or other symbols in the field, is unbroken. Arichis II marked his assumption of the title of prince in 774 by changing the obverse inscription and the form of the bust on his coins, but he still identified these only by his initial in the field. Grimoald III was the first to use his full name, initially with no title and in association with that of Charlemagne but later alone and styling himself *princeps*, so that from his reign onwards one can speak of a 'national' coinage. He also introduced a silver denaro to supplement his denominations of gold. Grimoald IV dropped the use of this metal, apparently thinking that if the Franks needed no gold coinage he could also do without one, but its use was revived by Sico and continued to Radelchis I. Silver denari continued to be struck to the end of the ninth century, and perhaps a little beyond; the types are often original and in any case unrelated to the Carolingian denari of the north. An exceptional group of issues was that of Louis II and his wife Angilberga already mentioned. Coins have been attributed to all the rulers listed in Table 8 save Radelgar (851–3), who was only a child and whose reign was brief, but a number of the attributions are uncertain.

The obverse type of both the solidus and tremissis is a facing bust copied from that of Byzantine coins, but probably assumed by most users to represent the Beneventan ruler and not the emperor. A conspicuous feature, particularly on the later issues, is a rough beard, which was an adjunct of the long hair whose retention by the princes was interpreted as a mark of their Byzantine predilections. The matter became the subject of altercation between themselves and the Franks, who repeatedly made it a condition of peace terms that the Beneventan dukes should submit to being shaven *more Francorum*.

There are five forms of bust. The first two, one showing the emperor in armour and holding a spear (cf. **1.1085**) and the other with him wearing a loros and holding a cross potent and a globus surmounted by a similar cross (**1.1086**), are limited to the reign of Gisulf I and are copied from the coins of Tiberius III (698–705) and Justinian II restored (705) respectively. The third, showing the emperor holding a globus cruciger (**1.1087–91**), goes back to that of the early years of Justinian II (685–*c.* 692) and was used continuously from Romoald II's accession (706) to the middle of Gottschalk's reign (*c.* 740?). The inscription shows the model to have been a coin of Justinian II, and the type was probably chosen because of its familiarity through its having been used by many emperors during the seventh century.

The fourth type of bust (**1.1092–3**) shows the emperor holding in his left hand an akakia, a small scroll-like object which was an important symbol of rule in Byzantium, in addition to the globus cruciger in his right. It was probably copied from Roman solidi of Leo III (717–41), though in this particular form it had been introduced by one of Leo's predecessors, Anastasius II (713–15). Its introduction is hard to explain, but it is possible that the news of Leo III's death in 741 caused the Beneventan die-sinkers to give some attention to a design they had been content to copy mechanically almost without change for nearly three decades.

The fifth type of bust (**1.1094–7**), introduced under Arichis II, saw the abandonment of the akakia and a reversion to a cloaked figure with globus cruciger rather simpler in design than that used earlier in the century. Its introduction accompanies the replacement of a blundered pseudo-imperial legend by the odd *Dns Victoria*, probably alluding to Arichis' signal victory over the Neapolitans in 765 and arising from a mishandled instruction to the moneyers to celebrate this in the coin inscription. Under Grimoald III the same type was formally retained, but the folds of the cloak are differently arranged (**1.1098–9, 1101**). This type lasted to the end of gold coinage in Benevento (**1.1103–4, 1108–10**).

Grimoald III was the first to place his full name on the coins, but the initials in the field that sufficed for his predecessors usually create no problems. There was only one duke in the period with the initial R (Romoald II) or L (Liutprand), while G and A with early types of bust can only be Gisulf I and Audelais respectively. But there is some uncertainty over the coins of the two decades 731–51, with G, DG, G and a monogram of ΘV, or a glove in the field, for there were three dukes of the period with the initial G, one of them with two separate reigns. The attributions of the two coins here with G (**1.1089–90**) and the one with DG (**1.1091**) to Gregory and Gottschalk respectively are customary, but may have to be revised in the future.

The normal reverse type of the gold coins is a cross-potent, either on steps (solidus) or a flat base (tremissis). These had been the standard reverses of the corresponding denominations at Byzantium during almost the whole of the seventh century, and the familiarity explains both their introduction and their long continuance. The only exception to these types is the facing figure of St Michael (**1.1103**), copied from the facing angel of Byzantine solidi of the sixth century, which appears on solidi of Sico after his revival of a gold coinage. The archangel was already a national symbol of the Lombards, and the famous shrine of St Michael at Monte Gargano, on the Adriatic coast, lay in Beneventan territory. The type, however, only gave plastic form to the inscription *Archangelus Michael* introduced on the denaro by Sico's predecessor Grimoald IV, and the circumstances of its adoption are unknown. It may be that Grimoald, who besides being treasurer before his accession was a highly successful general, had commended himself to St Michael prior to his victory over the Franks on the river Trigno in 806, as Cunincpert had done on a similar occasion (above p. 64).

Beneventan silver coins resemble in general those of the Franks and the papacy, though the details are different. The obverse type is usually a monogram and the reverse some variety of cross, either a simple equal-armed one, or one having what appear to be rays in each quarter, or a cross-on-steps borrowed from the solidus. A novel type is a flower design which seems to represent an ear of corn between two ivy leaves, the latter either erect (**1.1102**) or curled over. Its significance is unknown. There are occasionally symbols in the field, usually pellets or triangles but occasionally an *alpha* and *omega* or an object that looks like a monstrance. Some may be only decorative, but others may mark the products of individual moneyers or coins of particular fineness.

In weight and fineness the Beneventan gold coins are much inferior to their Byzantine models, or at least to those of the capital. Their initial weight (*c.* 700/730) is about 4.15g for the solidus, 1.36g for the tremissis, but under Romoald II's successors the solidus rarely attains 4.0g, and weighs about 3.9g for the rest of the eighth century, with the tremissis in proportion. In the first half of the ninth century the solidus fell to a fairly steady 3.75g, though the British Museum specimen of Radelchis is 4.44g. Eccentrically high weights are an occasional phenomenon in badly debased coin series (see pp. 54, 62).

What these weights were intended to represent is difficult to say. Sambon and other scholars (cf. Sambon 1902) have postulated a light solidus struck 84 to the lb instead of 72, implying a weight of 3.78g, but the only documentary evidence for such a coin is a passage of doubtful interpretation in the Theodosian Code and it is difficult to see the relevance of this to late seventh- and early eighth-century Italy. The initial weight of *c.* 4.15g corresponds to that of the contemporary Byzantine solidi of Sicily (*DOC* II. 16–17), representing 79 or 80 solidi to the lb, so that its Beneventan counterpart may represent no more than an alignment with a current and widely accepted coin, but 3.9g suggests the abandonment of the carat weight system altogether in favour of that of the grain (barleycorn) of 0.065g (see p. 14), making the tremissis a coin of 20gr. and the solidus one of 60gr. The final fall to 3.75g, made after the introduction of silver coins, perhaps indicates some adjustment to the units used for these, whatever they may have been. (The later Neapolitan *acino* or grain was 0.044g, appreciably lighter than the wheatgrain of *c.* 0.05g elsewhere.) The possibilities are too numerous for any certain conclusion.

Beneventan gold coins are all of base metal, the later ones very pale in colour. Sambon's figures for fineness (Sambon 1919, xiv), presumably based on the touchstone, are all somewhat high, and it is possible that while Oddy's figures (Oddy 1974) are more accurate in terms of percentages they are too low when reckoned in terms of carats, since he treated Constantinopolitan solidi as only about 90% fine though taken by contemporaries as of 24 carats. The earliest coins contain about 75% gold, but under Gregory the fineness was reduced to about 60%, a figure at which it remained fairly stable for some forty years (732–*c.* 770), though single issues seem to have been no more than 50% to 55%. Arichis II's latest coins fell to 50%, Grimoald III's later issues to 40%, and Sico's and Sicard's to 35%; the only available figure for Radelchis' is 25%. Such figures presumably reflect the political and economic difficulties of the Beneventan state in the first half of the ninth century, when it was under pressure from its Carolingian, Byzantine and Muslim neighbours. Later times, which idealized the period of Arichis II as a golden age, treated his coinage as one to be emulated rather than deplored.

Beneventan silver coins seem to be of two weight standards, falling from *c.* 1.4g under Grimoald III and IV to *c.* 1.3g under Sico and his successors. A document of 816, equating 4 tremisses 4 denari with one half of three solidi, shows that 6 denari were reckoned to the tremissis (Sambon 1902). This is about what one would expect, for the tremissis at this time contained about 0.5g of gold, and if one assumes a gold:silver ratio of 1:12, silver coins worth one-sixth of a tremissis should weigh 1.0g if of pure silver, or a little more if they were not.

(d) SALERNITAN COINAGE

Literature

The early coinage is covered by vol. XVIII of the *CNI* (1939), in the Sambons' *Repertorio* (Sambon 1912) and *Recueil* (Sambon 1919), and in the monographs of Cagiati (1925) and Cappelli (1972). The tenth- and eleventh-century coin attributions given in these works require extensive revision (Grierson 1956a, 1972), but this is not the case for the coins within the time-span covered by this volume. Most of what we know about coin names and monetary circulation comes from the eight volumes (to 1065) of the *Codex diplomaticus Cavensis* (Morcaldi *et al.* 1873–83), a vast collection of documents from the monastery of La Cava dei Tirreni north of Salerno, but the Byzantine emperors by whose regnal years they are dated were not always correctly identified by the editors and the chronology is sometimes astray by as much as two centuries. The most detailed history of the principality is by Schipa (1887), reprinted in Hirsch and Schipa 1968, to which should be added Delogu 1977.

Historical background

The city of Salerno, 100km south of Benevento on the gulf of the same name, first became important under Arichis II and Grimoald III of Benevento, who fortified it and found it in many ways a more satisfactory place of residence than their traditional capital. Siconulf established himself there in 839, after the murder of his brother Prince Sicard of Benevento, and in 849 the principality of Benevento was partitioned between himself and Radelchis (above, p. 68). The early years of the principality were ones of great difficulty. Siconulf died almost immediately (December 849), and there followed some years of almost continuous civil war. It was not until 861 that Waifer (Guaiferio) established a dynasty that was to reign almost uninterruptedly for over a hundred years. Siconulf's share of the old principality of Benevento included all the Tyrrhenian coastland from Nola (north of Salerno) southwards across Lucania into northern Calabria (Cassano, Cosenza), but most of these southern lands were lost to the Byzantines later in the century and the coastal settlements were exposed to Arab raids, so that the principality was often limited to Salerno and the surrounding region. Nonetheless it remained an independent and usually prosperous state for over two centuries, until in 1077 it succumbed to the Norman adventurer Robert Guiscard and became the capital of his duchy of Apulia.

Coinage

The coinage of the principality falls into two phases, the first in the ninth century, between *c.* 840 and *c.* 900, and the second in the eleventh, from its early decades to 1077, though there is no break between the end of the latter and Guiscard's subsequent coinage in Salerno as duke of Apulia. Almost nothing can be attributed to the intervening century. The archives of La Cava show the widespread use of Byzantine gold, supplemented from the early tenth century onwards by Cufic quarter-dinars (taris) minted by the Arab rulers of Sicily, and of Byzantine folles.

The later coinage of Salerno will be dealt with in Vol. 13. That of the ninth century follows the same pattern as that of Benevento, with Siconulf (839–49) striking solidi (**1.1120**) and denari (**1.1121**), his successors denari only. Siconulf never abandoned the title of prince of Benevento, which appears in full on his denari (PRINCE BENEBENTI). The denari, with the exception of those of Siconulf and Waifer (861–80), are of great rarity, most of them either unique or known in two or three specimens only, and apart from the specimen of Siconulf are not represented here. The usual types are a monogram and a cross-potent-on-steps, with triangles, globules, or other privy-marks in the field. They weigh *c.* 1.2g, the later ones being lighter and perhaps of baser metal. In the 870s they were rated at 16 to the notional gold tremissis, but the Frankish reckoning in terms of solidi of 12 deniers was also widely used. The coinage ended under Waifer's son Waimar I (880–901).

6

MINOR GERMANIC PEOPLES

(a) THE BURGUNDIANS

Literature

An article by Ponton d'Amécourt remains the most complete survey of the coins with royal monograms (Amécourt 1866a), though it omits the solidi of Sigismund with S at the end of the reverse inscription and the tremisses of Gundomar. It has also to be read in the light of the hoard evidence, itself not very satisfactorily preserved (Lafaurie 1964a). The coins are included in Belfort's work on Merovingian coins (Belfort 1892–5), but not in that of Prou (1892a); the tremisses are covered by Tomasini (1964). There are separate studies on Burgundian minting at Lyon (Lafaurie 1972b), on the unusual legends of the silver coins (Tricou 1965), and on the early coins without monograms and the interpretation of the coin references in the *Lex Burgundionum* (cf. Lafaurie 1976d; Oddy 1980). Burgundian history is covered in the standard works on early Byzantine history (Bury 1923; Stein 1949) and on the Germanic invasions, but there is only one full monograph (Jahn 1874). References to individual kings are collected in *PLRE*, *s.v.*

Historical background

The Burgundians, despite their small numbers, left a much more permanent mark on the face of Gaul than did the Visigoths. In the early fifth century they were an East Germanic people settled on the upper Rhine, where subsequent tradition, as embodied in the *Nibelungenlied*, gave Worms as their capital. In 436 they were almost annihilated by a Hunnic attack instigated by Aetius, who a few years later (443) transferred the remnant southwards to the region of the Jura. There they formed a petty state in the region of Geneva, recognizing imperial suzerainty and usually on good terms with successive emperors. As imperial authority crumbled in the 460s they were able to expand, till eventually their kingdom included the important cities of Lyon and Vienne and extended from Chalon-sur-Saône in the north to Avignon and the Durance in the south.

The chronology of the early Burgundian kings and even their order of rule are uncertain. In *c.* 480 it seems that the kingdom was divided between the four sons of Gundioc, with Gundobald reigning at Lyon, Godegisel at Besançon, Chilperic II at Geneva, and Gundomar I at Vienne. By 493 Chilperic and Gundomar had disappeared, and in that year Gundobald, who had for a time been *Magister militum* in the West and was by far the ablest member of his house, defeated a Frankish invasion under Clovis and put to death his remaining brother, who had sided with the enemy and was by then ruling at Vienne. When Gundobald died in 516 he was succeeded by his eldest son Sigismund, and Sigismund in turn (524) by a younger son Gundomar II. But the numerical feebleness of the Burgundians, aided by the feuds and follies of their kings, led to the kingdom's being conquered and partitioned by the Franks in 532/4.

Coinage

The origins of Burgundian coinage are obscure, and only coins of the last three kings, Gundobald, Sigismund and Gundomar II, are easy to recognize. They have close analogies with those of their Ostrogothic contemporaries, since they minted gold in the names of the reigning emperors and silver and copper in their own. But their tremisses differed in type from contemporary imperial issues; they went further than the Ostrogoths in their conspicuous placing of initials or monograms in the field of their gold but less far in that they never used their full names, only their monograms, on silver and copper; and they minted no large bronze. The fact of their striking silver and copper coins suggests that commerce in the Rhône valley was still of importance, but the absence of multiples of the nummus similar to those of Italy and North Africa suggests equally that its importance was not very great.

Early pseudo-imperial issues

One would expect the pseudo-imperial issues with regal monograms to have been preceded by ones without them. The *Lex Burgundionum*, in forbidding the circulation of *valentiniani* and *genavenses* (see below), seems to imply the existence of Burgundian coins earlier than those bearing Gundobald's monogram, for the banned coins were presumably ones issued by his brothers at Valence and Geneva respectively, but the law does not say how they were to be recognized.

The British Museum catalogue assigns two groups of gold coins to the Vandals which certainly do not belong to this people, and which may well be Burgundian. The earlier group consists of imitation solidi and tremisses of Valentinian III (*BMC Vand*, pl. 1, 1–2) which by the style of their busts seem to be related to the second group (*BMC Vand*, pl. 2, 7–8), tremisses bearing the name of Anastasius, and these in turn are stylistically related to coins bearing the monogram of Gundobald. Without evidence of find-spots, however, their Burgundian origin cannot be pressed, and we are forced to begin the Burgundian series with coins of Gundobald.

Gundobald (c. *473–516*)

The last three decades of Gundobald's reign coincided with that of the Eastern emperor Anastasius (491–518), and all his identifiable gold coins bear this ruler's name. The solidi have on the reverse a profile Victory holding a voided cross and a monogram of the letters GVB in the left field (**1.336**). Although this type of reverse was struck by the Ostrogoths as well as in the East, the Burgundian model probably came directly from Constantinople, for it has preserved an officina letter not found on the Italian issues. We do in fact know that Gundobald maintained close diplomatic relations with Anastasius, not altogether to the pleasure of the Ostrogoths. His main series of tremisses, while they have the same monogram in the reverse field, have for type a Victory advancing to the right (**I.337–8**) bearing palm and wreath, which was also used by the Visigoths and the Franks in southern Gaul (pp. 48, 114) and was modelled on the exceptional Ostrogothic issue that apparently commemorated Theoderic's defeat of the Burgundians and Franks in 508/9 (above, p. 35). This implies that the coinage dates from the last years of Gundobald's reign. It may seem strange that it should have been modelled on that of a victorious enemy, but it seems clear that Theoderic carried out a major recoinage in Spain and Narbonensis, to rid the country of the debased issues of Alaric II, and the Burgundians would have been anxious to profit by the good reputation of the new coinage.

Gundobald's rare silver coins are of two denominations and types. The smaller (*c.* 0.3g) has on the obverse Anastasius' name and bust, and on the reverse the monogram of Gundobald with a cross above. The larger (*c.* 1.45g) is more independent, having a large monogram of GVB in the field surrounded by the inscription PAX ET ABVNDANTIA, and on the reverse a Victory like that of the tremissis, with L D in the field. The copper nummus (*c.* 0.07g) has on the obverse a bust to the right, with no inscription, and on the reverse the usual monogram with L D beneath (**I.339**). The L D stands for Lyon (*Lugdunum*), and it is probable that this was the mint of all the coins, though the terminal letters of the obverse or reverse inscriptions on the gold, which in some cases are no more than the officina letters of the coins used as models but more often are simply blundered or miscopying, have been construed in the past as the marks of other mints.

Sigismund (516–24)

Solidi and tremisses of the same type were struck by this ruler, presumably at Lyon, with the name of Anastasius and a complex monogram including all the letters of the name SIGISMVNDVS. There is also a silver coin with this monogram, and the name of Anastasius, in the local museum at Auxerre.

Gold coins bearing the name of Justin I of very distinctive style – without monograms but with instead an S at the end of the reverse inscription on the solidus (**I.340**) and one preceding the reverse inscription on the tremissis – can also be attributed to Sigismund. They are apparently known only from a single hoard, found in 1845 at Gourdon, near Chalon-sur-Saône, which contained in addition other coins of Gundobald and Sigismund and pieces of gold and silver plate (Lafaurie 1958b). The solidi, of which there were at least twenty in the hoard, were uncirculated and all from the same pair of dies. Since they have never been found elsewhere, they presumably represent a small local issue, perhaps of Chalon-sur-Saône, which was to be a major mint in Merovingian times.

Gundomar II (524–32)

No solidi of Gundomar are known. The majority of his tremisses are of the usual type, but are struck in the name of Justin I (518–27) and have a monogram of MAR in the field (**I.341**) as do his nummi. This final syllable of the king's name was probably a form in common use at the time, for personal names were often shortened in this fashion in the Germanic world. The coins were formerly attributed to the Visigothic king Amalaric, but their Burgundian style is evident and their attribution not in doubt. The mint was probably Lyon.

There are in addition tremisses with the name of Justinian, with a G in the left field of the reverse and a star in the right, which are of Burgundian style and presumably belong to Gundomar II although to some mint other than Lyon. This may have been Chalon-sur-Saône, but Geneva is also possible, with the G doubling as an initial of the name of the mint.

The Burgundians are unusual amongst the Germanic peoples in that their legal code, the *Lex Burgundionum*, called in later French tradition the *Loi Gombette* from the name of the king who promulgated it *c.* 500, takes notice of the coinage, for it orders that all solidi shall circulate freely whatever their weight apart from four types (*valentiani*, *genavenses*, Gothic coins which from the accession of Alaric II have been debased, and *ardaricani*), the clause running *De monetis solidorum praecipimus custodire ut omne aurum, quodcumque pensaverit, accipiatur, praeter quatuor monetas, valentiani, genavensis, et gothium, qui a tempore Alarici regis adaerati sunt, et ardaricanos.* A variant of *valentiani* found in some manuscripts is *valentiniani*, with the possibility of an allusion to the very debased Suevic tremisses bearing the name of Valentinian III, but coins from a remote corner of Spain are unlikely to have troubled the Burgundians, and coins of Valence, in company with those of Geneva, are more probably meant. The other coins are those of Alaric II (484–507), king of the Visigoths, which it has been suggested (p. 45) may be the Gaulish solidi with RA in the field, but no satisfactory explanation of *ardaricani* has been put forward. An attempt has been made (Oddy 1980) to distinguish the *genavenses* from other Burgundian coins by their fineness, but the wording of the clause implies that only the Gothic coins were debased, and the others were presumably banned for political reasons.

(b) THE SUEVI

Literature

The standard nineteenth-century studies (Allen and Teixeira 1865; Heiss 1891) were superseded in 1937 by one written by an Austrian engineer who had settled in Spain (Reinhart 1937a; also Reinhart 1942 for a Spanish résumé with some fresh material). Suevic coins are usually included in such museum catalogues of Visigothic coins as exist, but the few in the British Museum have been published separately (Barceló 1974). The find-spots of Suevic coins have been listed with those of the Visigoths (Barral 1976). The little that is known of the history of the Suevi will be found in the standard works on the Germanic invasions and in vol. III of the fourth edition of Menéndez Pidal's history of Spain (Menéndez Pidal 1980). There are in addition two monographs, Beninger 1940 and Reinhart 1952. There is some uncertainty over the dates of the kings; the list below is based on the *PLRE*.

Historical background

The generic term *Suevi* covered a group of West Germanic peoples of whom the most important were the Alamanni, who settled in south-western Germany (Swabia), and the Quadi, who joined the Vandal invasion of Gaul in 406, crossed the Pyrenees in their company in 409, and in 411 were authorized to settle as *foederati* in the western half of Gallaecia (north-western Spain). In 419 they expanded into eastern Gallaecia, which had been first occupied and then abandoned by the Asding Vandals (see p. 18), and in the 430s their king Hermeric constituted a virtually independent state around Braga (*Bracara*) in what is now northern Portugal. His successors

Table 9. *Kings of the Suevi.*

Hermeric, 419–38, abd.	. . . .
Rechila, 438–48 (Aug.)	Ariomir, 558/9–561 ?
*Rechiar, 438–55 (Dec.)	Theodemir, 561/6–70
Maldras, 456–60 } rivals	Miro, 570–83
Rechimund, 459–61 } rivals	Eboric, 583–4
Frumarius, 460–5	*Audeca, 584–5, dep.
Remismund, 465–9	Malaric, 585 (usurper)

Rechila and Rechiar, profiting by the Vandal passage into Africa, seized Mérida (439) and Seville (441) and parts of Carthaginensis. For a time it looked as if the Suevi, despite their small numbers, were to become masters of the whole Peninsula.

Rechiar's reign, however, marked the high point of Suevic fortunes. An attempt to expand into Tarraconensis brought him into conflict with the Visigothic king Theoderic. Braga was sacked, Rechiar captured and put to death (Dec. 455), and the kingdom reduced to warring factions within its original boundaries in Gallaecia. It soon after disappears from our written sources for nearly a century: we know nothing of it, not even the names of its kings, between the death of Remismund in 469 and the mid sixth century. It then again re-emerges into the light of history – a succession of five kings are known – until in 585 it was conquered by Leovigild and incorporated as a sixth province in the Gothic state. A revolt under a usurper Malaric came to nothing. Its known kings are listed in Table 9 with an asterisk against the names of the two who appear on the coins.

Coinage

It has been unkindly said that the course of history would not have been changed one *iota* if the Suevi in Spain had never existed, but their coinage is of some consequence. Rechiar was the first Germanic ruler to mint coins bearing his own name, and for a period of over a century the Suevi issued a coinage of gold, mainly pseudo-imperial tremisses, probably from locally produced supplies of the precious metal. The Gallaecian mines had been important in Roman times and there is no reason to suppose that they were exhausted.

Suevic coinage is mainly one of tremisses, but there are rare solidi and still rarer silver coins. The solidi are imitated from those of Honorius (393–423) of the mint of Milan and are identifiable only by style and provenance (Reinhart 1937a, 1944; Beltrán 1957; Guadan 1958). Most of them have inscriptions much more blundered than the one in this collection (**1.285**). The siliqua has a normal obverse of one of Honorius but as reverse type a cross between the letters BR (for *Bracara*) in a wreath surrounded by the inscription IVSSV RICHIARI REGES. For over a century the authenticity of what was then the one known specimen, acquired by the Bibliothèque Nationale at the Gosselin sale in 1864, was widely doubted, but in 1940 it was confirmed by the finding of a fragmentary specimen during excavations at a locality not far from Braga itself.

Honorius' name was used on the solidi and the siliqua because his coins were in current circulation at the date of the Suevic settlement, which had taken place with his authorization.

The tremisses were copied ultimately from those of Valentinian III (425–55), with obverse inscription DN PLA(*cidius*) VALENTINIANVS PF AVG and a cross (with CONOB beneath) as reverse type, but presumably by way of the imitations of the Visigoths (above, p. 46). The earliest issues, attributable to the 430s or 440s, are similar to the Visigothic imitations and only distinguishable from these when the style of the bust can be matched with that of an issue that is indisputably Suevic (cf. Metcalf and Schweizer 1970, pl. 1.1–2). The latter are recognizable by their startlingly distorted reverse, the wreath having become a double circle of hatchings or dots provided with two lateral outer segments extending almost to the edge of the coin. They form two groups, one with a normal imperial bust (**1.286–7**) and the other with a bust and a spear-head breaking the inscription (**1.288–90**). The spear-head was presumably envisaged as part of the imperial equipment, though no shaft is shown and no such feature occurs on official issues of Valentinian III. The detail was probably borrowed from the emperor-with-spear type characteristic of Eastern solidi and used with growing frequency in the West from the 470s onwards. It is true that some tremisses of Majorian (457–61) show the emperor with a spear, but it is held quite differently in front of his body.

These pseudo-imperial tremisses must have been struck at several mints, for there is much variation in the style of the bust. The blundering of the inscriptions, with their reversed and distorted letters, also takes many forms. There is indeed no good reason to suppose that it was all in any sense a 'royal' coinage and not one simply issued by local authorities. No precise dating is possible in the absence of hoards, though coins of relatively good style are likely to be of the mid or late fifth century. The later coins are badly debased, and even coins of good style are not necessarily of pure gold. Analyses of specimens at Oxford (Metcalf and Schweizer 1970) and of some of those in this collection give gold percentages ranging from 90% downwards to 60%. Graffiti on the surfaces of some specimens may have been intended to identify coins of good or bad quality, but their exact interpretation is uncertain (Barral 1980).

In the last years of the kingdom the hopelessly corrupt Valentinianic inscriptions on the coins were replaced by some form of 'national' one, a change presumably suggested by the appearance of 'national' features on Visigothic and Frankish coins in the 570s and 580s. Symbols or letters also begin to appear in the field. Many of the inscriptions are no better than gibberish and have defied interpretation (**1.291–2**), while the identification of the letters in the field as the initials of particular mints (Mateu y Llopis 1942) are only occasionally convincing. Of inscriptions that are legible, that of one coin, formerly in the Madrid collection but lost since 1936, contains the elements ODIACCA REIGES, best interpreted as referring to the last Suevic king, whose name appears in the Latin sources as *Audacer* (Grierson 1962a). The majority contain elements which can be construed as place-names (Reinhart 1941; Mateu y Llopis 1942; Beltran 1958a), normally accompanied by *munita* (i.e. *moneta*, 'mint') and sometimes by *Latina* as well, either referring to the municipal ('Latin') origin of the coins or more probably arising from an unintelligent reproduction of the wording of an instruction to the moneyers to place on the coins the *Latin* name of the *mint*. About half a dozen names have been identified with some degree of assurance. The only coin of the group in this collection (**1.293**) is one of León (*Legio*) with the inscription LEIOIA COTIS MVNITA, perhaps indicating that it was struck after the Visigothic conquest and before a new type was introduced. Reinhart had indeed initially attributed to the Suevi a number of coins of 'Victory' type (Reinhart 1937a, nos. 79–85), but later came to believe that they were Visigothic, although it has been suggested (Beltran 1958a) that the blundered inscription on one (Reinhart 1937a, no. 82) contains the elements of MIR RX and refers to one of the last Suevic kings.

7

THE FRANKS AND FRISIANS IN THE MEROVINGIAN PERIOD

(A) GENERAL FEATURES

Literature

The two standard works of reference, both going back to the 1890s, are Maurice Prou's catalogue of the Merovingian coins in the Paris Cabinet des Médailles (Prou 1892a) and Auguste de Belfort's five-volume *Description générale des monnaies mérovingiennes* (Belfort 1892–5).

Prou's catalogue is an outstanding work of scholarship. It was made possible by the fact that he could draw on a half-century of intensive study by a succession of able numismatists, beginning with Cartier and continuing through Lenormant, Longpérier, Duchalais, Deloche, Charles Robert and above all Ponton d'Amécourt, who had published an enormous mass of material and largely made sense of a coinage of exceptional diversity and difficulty. The national collection, already one of great importance by the mid-century, had been nearly doubled in size in 1889, when a special grant of 180,000 francs enabled it to acquire 1,131 Merovingian coins from the collection of Vicomte Gustave de Ponton d'Amécourt (1825–88), who had died the previous year. This fabulous collection, which for over thirty years had formed the basis of its owner's many publications as well as being put freely at the disposal of interested scholars, had already included over 800 tremisses by 1863, when a single acquisition had enlarged it by 443 more coins. It had reached a total of nearly 2,000 at the date of Amécourt's death, and even after the Cabinet de France had made its choice enough remained for the greatest sale of Merovingian coins that has ever taken place (Rollin & Feuardent 9.6.1890). As a preliminary to his catalogue Prou published an inventory of the Cabinet's acquisition (Prou 1890), and he had in addition begun to clear the ground with half a dozen important articles published between 1884 and 1891. His catalogue includes the hundreds of silver deniers from the Cimiez hoard presented in 1887 by Arnold Morel-Fatio (below, p. 142), though it is customary for reference purposes to use Morel-Fatio's own listing of these, published by the director of the Cabinet in accordance with the donor's wishes (Chabouillet 1890), in preference to Prou's numbering.

Prou's catalogue is in any case not altogether easy to use, even with the help of a subsequent tabular analysis by Farcinet (1893). Merovingian coinage cannot be arranged chronologically, as can that of the Visigoths and as the historian would wish, since coins bearing royal names are relatively few and the others can be dated only very roughly. From *c.* 570 onwards, however, the bulk of the coins bear the names of local mints, and a geographical arrangement is possible. Prou followed a tradition that went back to Longpérier's catalogue of the Rousseau collection (Longpérier 1847) and grouped them on the basis of the administrative divisions of the late Roman Empire. Quite apart from the fact that not every scholar carries in his head the sequence and territorial layout of *Lugdunensis I–IV, Belgica I–II, Germania I–II*, and so on, these bore no relationship to the political divisions of the *regnum Francorum* when the coins were being struck and only a very partial relationship to the typological or stylistic groupings suggested by the coins themselves. It would also have been an improvement if the silver coins had been made a separate section, since they are chronologically distinct from the gold. Finally, although the coins are generously illustrated on 36 plates (nearly 1,200 coins), there are often no illustrations of the large number of those still unidentified, where they would have been particularly useful to later scholars.

Belfort's work is quite different in character and arrangement from that of Prou. He was himself a collector of Roman coins, not a specialist in the Merovingian series, but he had been a close friend of Amécourt and was persuaded by the latter's son to take over and publish what was in effect the card index of information of coins and mints which his father had accumulated during thirty years of study. The entries are in alphabetical order of the names of mints in their Latin forms as known from the written sources or inscribed on the coins and decipherable with varying degrees of certainty, an arrangement making for easy reference but obscuring the numismatic relationships. The coins classified under mints fill the first three volumes, leaving the pseudo-imperial issues and other coins of 'ateliers indéterminés', including a few royal series, to vol. IV. Vol. V contains an extremely detailed index of the legends and a concordance with the numbers in Prou's catalogue, which appeared while Belfort's work was in progress. The *fichier* had never been systematically revised by its original compiler and there is inevitably a certain amount of duplication, the same coin sometimes appearing more than once with different readings or mint attributions, but the precision and general reliability of the text combine with the high quality of the line illustrations to make the work as a whole a wonderful tool of research.

No other collection of Merovingian coins bears comparison with that of Paris, or can ever conceivably do so. Supplements to Prou's catalogue were published by Prou (1896b) and Dieudonné (1908). But there is no systematic listing of the exceptionally rich and important acquisitions associated with the years of M. Lafaurie's membership of the staff (1944–76), especially those subsequent to the great MMAG Basel sale of 8.12.1949, though many of them provided material for his own numerous publications. French provincial collections usually contain from two or three to up to fifty Merovingian coins, and are often of importance because of local finds. The opportunity has been taken by M. Lafaurie to catalogue and discuss them on the occasion of the annual 'journées provinciales' of the Société française de numismatique. The most important, with the date of the catalogues, are Autun (Musée Rolin) 1977, Montpellier (Société archéologique) 1974, Perpignan (Collection Puig) 1979, Rouen (Musée Départemental des Antiquités) 1978, and Saint-Omer (Musée) 1983. The sixty or so Merovingian coins at Lyon have not been catalogued. Marseille, which had an important collection in the last century, lost the bulk of its gold coins in a great theft in 1902 (cf. *RN* 1902, 468–79).

The chief collections outside France are those in Berlin and Brussels; there is a detailed and fully illustrated catalogue of the latter (Vanhoudt 1982). There are many silver coins, mainly from finds in the Netherlands, at The Hague, and although there is no systematic catalogue many of them have in fact been published in various contexts. Other public collections of consequence are in the British Museum (Prou 1888b, rarities in the 'national' (gold) series; the Sutton Hoo coins in Kent 1975), the Ashmolean Museum at Oxford (Crondall coins in Sutherland 1948, some others in Metcalf and Hamblin 1968), Copenhagen (Thomsen 1873–6, nos. 1118ff.), and the American Numismatic Society (Dickie and Parrott 1950). Nineteenth-century sale catalogues were not usually illustrated – this was true even of the Amécourt sale – and the material in them was picked up in the standard works. The most notable sales in the present century were those of the Bais hoard (Hamburger 19.10.1928; see below, p. 141) and the Merovingian coins in the Fürstenberg collection (A. E. Cahn Cat. 79, 14.12.1932, mainly ex de Saulcy), the Lord Grantley collection (Parts I and II, Glendining 29.11.1943 and 27.1.1944; see below, pp. 396–7), and the unidentified collection in MMAG Basel sale VIII (8.12.1949; see below, p. 402, *s.v.* 'Collection mérovingienne'), but there were significant Merovingian series in other sales of French coins: Hauët (Serrure 24.2.1908), Récamier (Bourgey 2.3.1925, esp. coins of Lyon), Ducrocq (M. Ratto 26.3.1926),

Bordeaux (Part I, Feuardent 26.4.1926), Motte (Bourgey 11.12.1951; Merovingian coins described in Rolland 1932), and Théry (Part I, Vinchon 22.10.1963).

Comprehensive surveys of Merovingian coins will be found in the first volumes of the manuals of Engel and Serrure (1891) and Blanchet (1912). Both are inevitably out of date, but their carefully compiled lists of mints and moneyers, superseding earlier ones drawn up by Cartier and Barthélemy, remain of value. Although Serrure wrote before Blanchet, and indeed before the publication of Prou's catalogue, his account is often superior. Merovingian coins were one of his special interests; he had studied under Charles Robert and as both dealer and scholar had an unrivalled knowledge of the material on the market and in the private collections of the time.

With Prou's retirement from the Cabinet des Médailles in 1899 – he took up the chair of diplomatic at the École des Chartes left vacant by the premature death of his master Arthur Giry, and most of his later work is that of a professional *chartiste* – the subject went into a temporary eclipse from which it only emerged in the 1930s, after Pierre Le Gentilhomme entered the Cabinet in 1932. The Merovingian series became one of his main interests, and the sections on it in the course of four lectures he gave to the Collège de France in 1942 form the best introduction to the subject that exists (Le Gentilhomme 1943–4). After his death in 1947 at the age of 37 his mantle was taken up by his pupil Jean Lafaurie, whose understanding of the coinage and immense scholarly output (bibl. in *Lafaurie* 1980a) have dominated the field for the past forty years. Most notable has been his patient reconstruction of nineteenth-century hoards, inadequately described at the time and usually now dispersed, so that virtually our entire picture of the chronology of the coinage, which had baffled nineteenth-century scholars, is due to him.

The best recent history of the Merovingian period is Tessier 1964, which despite the limitation suggested by its title (*Le baptême de Clovis*) is in fact a history of Gaul from 481 to 687. It has a particularly good bibliography. A more precisely documented record will be found in Lot, Pfister and Ganshof 1941. The complex sequence of territorial partitions is carefully worked out by Ewig 1952 (to 613) and 1953 (from 613 to 714), with Longnon 1878 as still the standard work on the geography of sixth-century Gaul and Longnon 1885 providing the best maps. The only detailed bibliography of the coinage (Amécourt 1866b) is now over a hundred years old.

Registers of Merovingian mints were compiled in the nineteenth century by a succession of scholars from Cartier to Barthélemy, but even the most complete (Engel and Serrure 1891, I.118–49; Blanchet 1912, 249–334) are now in need of revision, expansion and occasional excision. The multiplicity of mints and the problem of identifying the smaller ones means that place-name studies are of particular importance. It may seem invidious to choose between the standard works of Longnon, Dauzat and Vincent on the subject, but the general surveys by the last of the place-names of France (Vincent 1937) and Belgium (Vincent 1927) are perhaps the most useful, though for Belgium, the Netherlands, Luxemburg and the adjacent parts of south-western Germany and northern France the most detailed work is now Gysseling 1960. A remarkable study by H. Leclercq on French place-names in the *Dictionnaire d'archéologie chrétienne et de liturgie* IX.1 (Paris, 1930), cols. 656–984, *s.v.* 'Lieu (noms de)' includes (cols. 741ff.) a detailed list of those attested for the Merovingian and earlier periods, with a very full bibliography. The monumental *Dictionnaire toponomique de la France* (Paris, 1861–) is a wonderful reference work for the 34 départements it covers, but these are only a third of those that exist and since no volume has appeared since 1954 the work must be regarded as having ceased publication.

(a) HISTORICAL BACKGROUND

The Franks were a West German people who are first heard of as settled in the lower Rhineland in the fourth century A.D. They were *foederati* of the Romans, and carried out their duties with reasonable fidelity in the great campaigns of the fifth century. In the mid fifth century they were settled mainly in what is now Belgium and northern France and parts of western Germany, where their name still survives in the middle Rhineland and the valley of the Main as Franconia (Germ. *Franken*). Like other West German peoples they did not form a single political unit, but were ruled by a number of kinglets from such centres as Tournai and Cologne.

The role of the Franks in the history of Western Europe was due essentially to the genius of Clovis (481–511), descendant of a perhaps legendary Merovech who gave his name to the dynasty. Clovis started his career in 481 as a petty ruler of a small group of Salian Franks around Tournai on the modern Franco-Belgian frontier. He ended in 511 as sole ruler of a huge area extending from Thuringia to the Atlantic and from the Low Countries to the Alps after a thirty-year reign distinguished by violence, intelligence and a total lack of scruple admiringly recorded by Gregory of Tours. He destroyed the last Roman outpost in Gaul, the so-called kingdom of Syagrius (above, p. 45); he eliminated the other kings of the Salians and Ripuarians and made himself sole king of the Franks; he conquered the Alamanni in what is now Swabia and extended his kingdom south-eastwards as far as the Alps; he defeated the Visigoths at Vouillé and annexed the whole of Aquitaine, though he failed to capture Narbonne or reach the Mediterranean (above, p. 41); and by adopting Catholicism instead of Arian Christianity he formed close links with the Church, the major institution that had survived the collapse of the Roman Empire in the West. He had essentially made a West German people behave as if it were an East German one, and by having a West German base on which they could draw the Franks were able as a political entity to survive their occupation of large areas in which they were completely outnumbered by Latin-speaking provincials.

The Frankish kingdom survived, however, despite its own defects. The Franks had little idea of the state as a public institution, and the *regnum Francorum*, while remaining a family inheritance, was inherited according to the rules of private law, divided on each occasion between the sons or nearest male relatives of the deceased. Clovis I left four sons, and the four kingdoms which they received are usually known by the names of their capitals (Metz, Soissons, Orléans and Paris) since the 'kingdoms' consisted of regions dispersed through the *regnum* that were mainly conceived of as sources of revenue without being necessarily self-contained units. The genealogy of Clovis' immediate descendants (Table 10) shows how three of the lines died out

---

Note. Table 10 is based on that in Tessier 1964, 369, but has been simplified by the omission of alternative dates which are without importance save for the specialist. Some of those given here, like that of the death of Childeric I, are arrived at by subtraction – Gregory of Tours says that Clovis, who died on 27 November 511, reigned for thirty years – and may be a year out (482 or even 483); for others, like that of Dagobert I, we know the month and day (19 January) but are uncertain of the year (638 or 639). The list does not include Chlotar's I's son *Chramn, who rebelled against his father and was killed in 558, though a coin of his exists (see p. 91), or Gondovald, who also claimed to be Chlotar I's son (see p. 130), or **Childebertus adoptivus* (below, p. 88), the son of Grimoald who was intruded as king in Austrasia by his father and ruled 656–62. Many modern authors take no account of the brief 'reigns' of Sigebert II (613) and Clovis III (675), so that Sigebert III (639–56) and Clovis IV (690–5) become Sigebert II and Clovis III respectively.

Rulers whose names are marked by an asterisk are those for whom coins are known.

Table 10. *Kings of the Franks (Merovingians), 458–751*

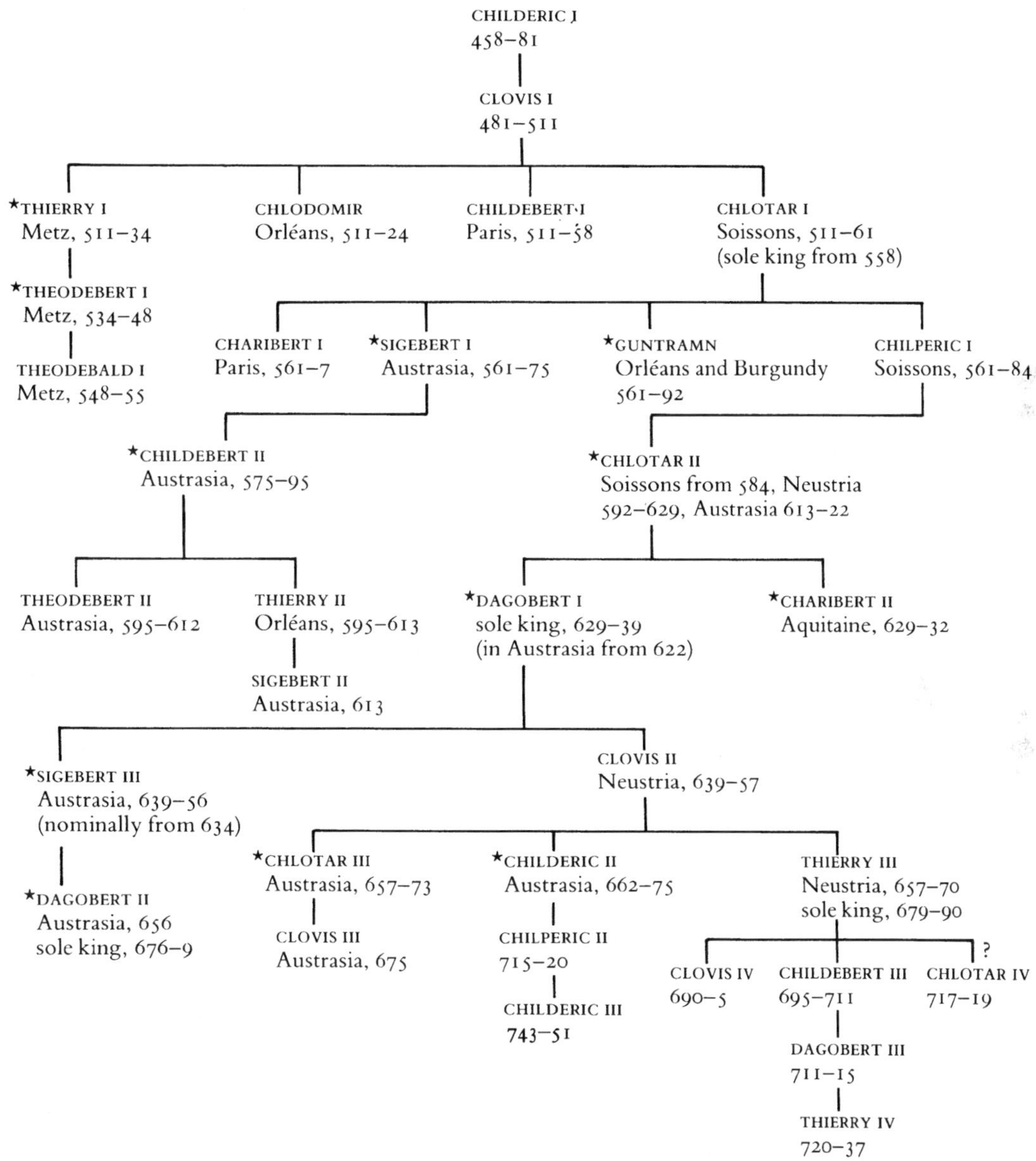

The last rulers, from 679 onwards, were sole kings apart from the puppet ruler Chlotar IV (717–19) set up by Charles Martel as a rival to Chilperic II.

during the lifetime of Clovis' longest-lived son Chlotar I, who was consequently able to reunite the kingdom in his own hands in 558. By his time the kingdom was even larger than it had been at Clovis' death, for the vigour of the Franks and the ambitions of its rulers were still unexhausted. Thuringia was conquered by Thierry in the early 530s; the kingdom of the Burgundians was destroyed in 534 (above, p. 75); Provence was acquired from the Ostrogoths in 537; and much of North Italy was occupied by Theodebert I in the early 540s, though the last was not retained and it was recovered by Justinian's armies in the 560s.

Chlotar I, like his father, had four sons to be provided for, and the kingdom was once again divided when he died in 561. One of the kings, Charibert I (Paris, 561–7), ruled only briefly, but the others were destined for longer reigns that saw the transition from a pseudo-imperial coinage to a fully 'national' Frankish one. The next half-century is the period of Frankish history that is best remembered, for it was then that the one great Frankish historian, Gregory of Tours (bishop 573–94), was writing from personal knowledge. The 'kingdoms' were now beginning to have a certain degree of territorial coherence – it is in Gregory that we first hear of Austrasia, the 'eastern' realm, in contrast to Neustria, the 'new' realm that had been acquired by Clovis between the Oise and the Loire – but the vigour and violence of Clovis' descendants was now directed against each other instead of against external enemies, and the dynastic history of the period, exacerbated by the feud between Fredegund (d. 597), mistress and later wife of Chilperic I, and Brunhild (d. 613), wife and subsequently widow of Sigebert I, was as complicated as it was savage.

In 613 Chlotar II (584–629) was left the only legitimate survivor in the male line amongst Clovis' descendants and again united the whole *regnum*. The last years of his reign and that of his son Dagobert I (629–39) represent the high point of the Merovingian dynasty. Dagobert was indeed the last Merovingian king who can be said in any real sense to have 'ruled' the entire kingdom, for although his grandson Childeric II of Austrasia was still an active sovereign his control of Neustria lasted for only two years (673–5). From 679 onwards, it is true, there was technically only one king at a time, but by that date they reigned rather than ruled. For it was also under Chlotar II and Dagobert that the palace official (*maior domus*) is first encountered whose line was eventually to displace that of the Merovingians. Arnulf, an Austrasian nobleman who as *domesticus et consiliarius regis* assisted in securing the accession of the Neustrian Chlotar's succession in Austrasia in 613 and was made bishop of Metz in 614, was one of the chief advisers to the young Dagobert when he was made sub-king of Austrasia in 622. His son Ansegiselus married Begga, the daughter of another great magnate, Pepin I, traditionally called 'of Landen', and it was their son Pepin II 'of Herstal' who founded the fortunes of what was to become in due course the Carolingian dynasty.

The chronology and succession of rulers between 634 and 679 unfortunately requires some discussion, since the revision to which it has been subjected by modern scholars has drastically altered our picture of the final stages of Merovingian gold coinage. The dates of the kings, and with them the establishment of the boundaries between the various kingdoms, are very difficult to establish, since they involve linking up the figures in regnal lists and the dating clauses of charters with vaguely dated events in official histories and hagiographical records. The basis of our knowledge was laid by a magisterial article by Krusch in 1882, to which a long series

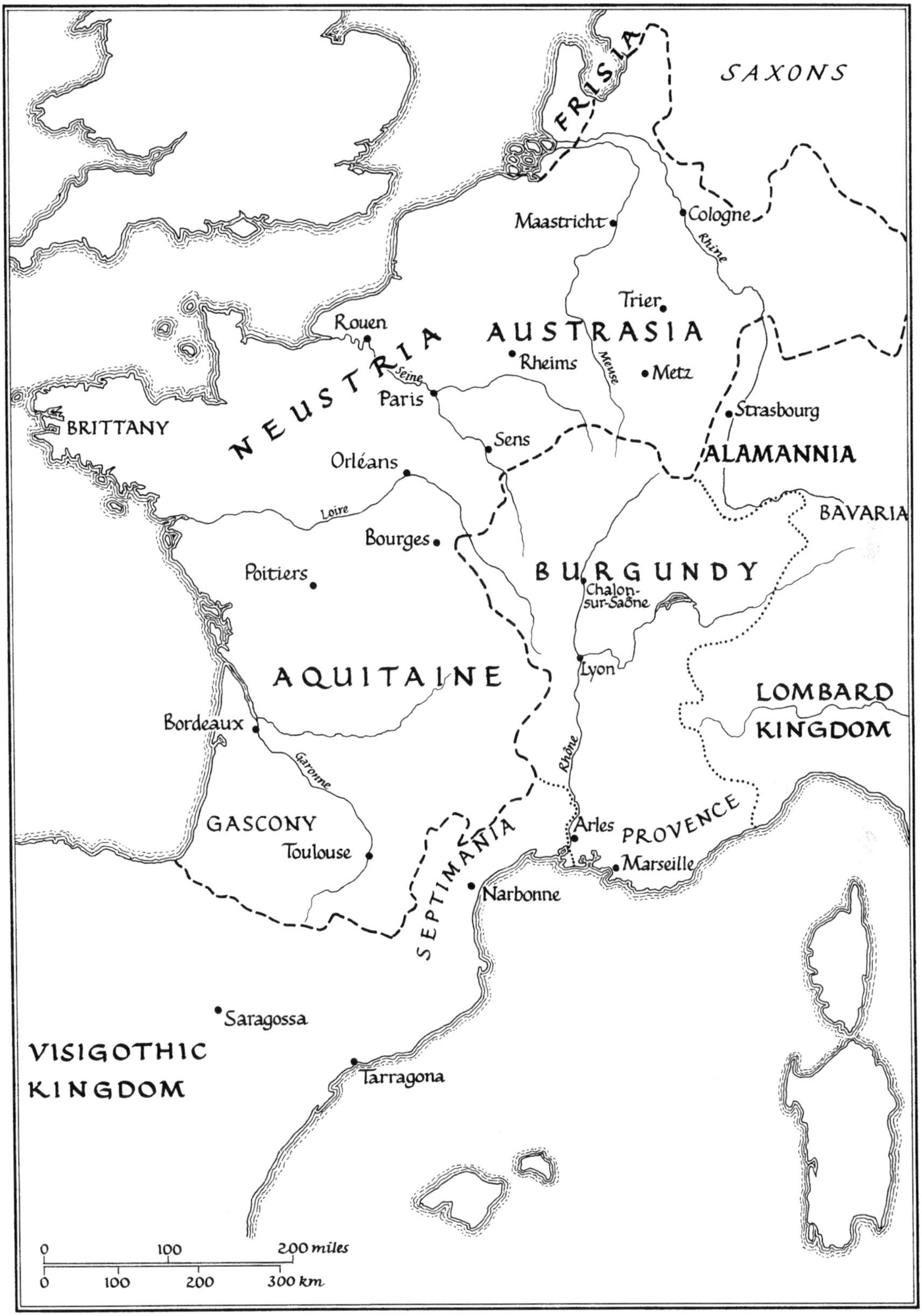

Map 2 *The Frankish kingdom, c. 600*

of subsequent scholars – Havet, Vacandard, Levillain, and most recently Dupraz – contributed new precisions or corrections, two at least of great consequence to the numismatist. What follows is mainly based on Dupraz 1952, though some dates are still debated, even that of the death of Dagobert (19 January 638 or 639).

The basic territorial division is that between Austrasia and Neustria. Dagobert's son Sigebert III (638/9–56) was created king of Austrasia in late 633 or early 634, partly as a sop to Austrasian *amour propre* and partly because a separate centre of government was required for the defence of Austrasia against the Saxons. After Dagobert's death Sigebert added Burgundy and Provence to his dominions, and most of the coins that bear his name were in fact struck at Marseille. From 642 onwards to his death in 656 he reigned in the shadow of his Mayor of the Palace, Grimoald, the eldest son of Pepin I, who, since the office was not yet accepted as hereditary, had after a struggle eliminated a rival occupant. Having for long been childless, Sigebert adopted Grimoald's son and gave him the royal name of Childebert. Subsequently he had a son of his own, the future Dagobert II.

When Sigebert died, Grimoald set aside Dagobert and installed his own son as king, a usurpation which came to an abrupt end when a Neustrian conspiracy led to the seizure and death of them both. It was formerly supposed, on the authority of a royal list, that the reign of *Childebertus adoptivus* lasted only a year, but there is good reason to believe that it really lasted only just short of seven years, from 656 to 662. This revision of Austrasian royal chronology means that gold coins of Marseille in the name of *Childebertus*, formerly awkwardly attributed to Childebert III in the early eighth century, can be transferred to the 'adopted Childebert', with the consequence that the minting of Frankish gold ended nearly half a century earlier than had been formerly supposed.

The overthrow of Grimoald and his son inaugurated two decades of Neustrian predominance, the kings being less important than the successive Mayors of the Palace. Of these the most important was Ebroin, though he had to fight for power against the Burgundian Leodegar, more familiar to posterity as St Leger, bishop of Autun, who was captured and put to death in 677(?). Ebroin himself was murdered in 683 or perhaps earlier (680?), and a quarrel between rival Neustrian Mayors made possible the intervention of Pepin II, a nephew of Grimoald and Mayor of Austrasia, and the total defeat of a Neustrian army at Tertry near Saint-Quentin.

It was now the turn of Austrasia and the Arnulfings, though these had their own dynastic crises to overcome. Pepin's 'reign' lasted from 687 to 714, but his two legitimate sons Drogo and Grimoald predeceased him, and on his death the office of Mayor passed to Grimoald's infant son Theudoald under the regency of Pepin's widow Plectrudis. A Neustrian revival and five years of civil war followed, until Charles Martel, an illegitimate son of Pepin, disposed of his Neustrian rival Raginfred and compelled Plectrudis to hand over Pepin's treasure and abandon the cause of her grandson. Charles ruled from 719 to 740, and when he died his legitimate sons Pepin 'the Short' (Mayor 740–51) and Carloman (740–7) divided the office of Mayor, only to be faced with the challenge of Charles' illegitimate son Grifo, who gave Pepin trouble off and on for a decade. It was Pepin's good fortune that Carloman abdicated for motives of religion in 747, for although he left two young sons Pepin was able to set them aside, thus becoming sole Mayor in preparation to becoming king. By this time the Merovingian 'kings' were sovereigns in no more than name, the *rois fainéants* of tradition. Charles Martel indeed let the crown lapse completely in 737, on the death of Thierry IV, and his sons restored it only in 743, in the person of Thierry's distant cousin Childeric III, in the belief that it would strengthen their hand against Grifo and other rebels. Childeric was deposed in 751 and Pepin, Charles Martel's son and a great-great-grandson of Pepin of Landen and St Arnulf of Metz, became at last king in his place.

The long period of disputed successions and attendant struggles for power amongst the great magnates that had followed Dagobert's death saw the effective emancipation from Frankish control of most of the peripheral parts of the state. Brittany, Frisia and Bavaria had always been more or less independent and these were now followed by Aquitaine and Alamannia under their dukes, by Provence under its patricians, and even by Burgundy under a succession of great magnates. The reigns of Pepin II, Charles Martel, and Pepin the Short were largely filled with attempts to recover these areas and to control and avenge Saxon raids into Franconia and the Rhineland.

The most important of the lost duchies, from the standpoint of Pepin II and his two successors, were probably the three German ones, where it was the Mayors' support for Christian missions, a support that was at least in part politically motivated, that brought the Frankish rulers into close touch with the papacy. The most urgent problems were in Frisia. In the late 670s, when the Northumbrian Wilfrid passed through the country on his way to Rome, much of it was completely independent under a 'king' named Aldgisl. Ten years later Pepin had conquered southern Frisia, including Dorestad, from another 'king', Radbod, and in 695 Willibrord was able to set up his mission at Utrecht under Frankish protection. After Pepin's death in 714 Radbod recovered his independence, expelled Willibrord, and in 716 felt strong enough to raid Cologne. Even before Radbod died in 719, however, Charles Martel managed to re-establish Frankish control in the south; Willibrord was restored to his see in the 720s and a great military expedition in 734 resulted in the conquest of central Frisia, though complete mastery of the country was not achieved till the reign of Charlemagne.

It was much the same in Alamannia and Bavaria. In the late seventh century Duke Gottfried of Alamannia claimed that he owed allegiance to the king of the Franks, not to Mayors of the Palace, and it required a series of campaigns between 709 and 712 to bring his successor Willehari to heel. In 730 Duke Lantfrid was deposed by Charles Martel and Alamannia incorporated into the kingdom, but when Charles died Lantfrid's brother Theutbold proclaimed himself duke and the country was only reconquered after more fighting (744–6). Bavaria for its part had always been virtually independent under its Agilolfing dynasty, which had close relations with the Lombards in Italy and had always been able to fall back on them for support. Charles Martel reduced its duke Hucbert to some sort of obedience in the 720s but left the duchy in existence, so that when Hucbert died in 739 he was succeeded by a relation, Odilo. The latter revolted after Charles' death on the usual pretext of there being no Frankish king, but even after Pepin had brought him to terms the duchy was allowed to continue, and indeed survived to 788.

The three 'French' regions that were the counterparts to these were Burgundy, Provence and Aquitaine. Burgundy was the most easily dealt with, since it was no longer a political unit and the Frankish mayors had merely to bring a turbulent nobility to heel. During the first decade of the eighth century it was dominated by a warlike prelate, Savary of Auxerre, who is represented in the *Gesta* of his see as having conquered the Orléanais, Nivernais, Tonnerrois, Avallonais and the county of Troyes, and who met his death in the aftermath of a military expedition against Lyon (715?). His successor Ainmar, described as *vocatus episcopus* and so presumably never consecrated, was eventually imprisoned by Charles Martel at Bastogne and killed after escaping (731?), but Burgundy remained a source of trouble throughout the 730s. Provence for its part had become virtually independent under its patricians (below, pp. 142–3), and Charles Martel's attempts to subjugate it in the 720s and 730s were complicated by Arab and even Lombard intervention, so that Frankish control had not been fully reasserted before he died.

The remaining region, Aquitaine, was the equivalent of Bavaria in putting up the longest and strongest resistance to absorption. In the third quarter of the seventh century it had become independent under its duke Lupus (d. 676?). His successors over the years expanded his rather small 'duchy' (below, p. 94) to something like the traditional frontiers, but the desperate paucity of written sources leaves the details of its history largely unknown. In the early 730s its duke was Eudes (Odo). Charles led two indecisive expeditions against him in 731, but the Arab invasion that culminated in the battle of Poitiers (732) allowed him to intervene in force, and much more successfully. In 736, however, he had to accept the succession of Eudes' son Hunald whom he had earlier envisaged setting aside, and the independence of Aquitaine was in the end only broken by a series of annual expeditions between 760 and 768 by Pepin the Short that wrought untold devastation in the province. Its last duke, Waifar, was killed in 768, but even after Pepin's death there was a last uprising under Hunald – a namesake and presumably a relative of the earlier Hunald (d. 756) – which was suppressed by Charlemagne in the first year of his reign (769).

(b) PHASES OF THE COINAGE

Frankish coinage of the Merovingian period can be divided into three well-marked phases. The first (*c.* 500–?587) is mainly one of pseudo-imperial gold solidi and of tremisses with Victory as a reverse type. The second (?587–*c.* 670) is a 'national' coinage of tremisses of slightly reduced weight which normally bear the names of mints and moneyers and have as reverse type some form of cross. The third (*c.* 670 onwards) is one of silver deniers. In both the first and the second there are aberrant elements. In the first there are some royal issues in gold, silver and bronze and some transitional issues towards its close, together with a continuation of the meagre issues of tiny silver coins (*argentei minuti*) that had begun in the period before Clovis and are essentially pre-Merovingian in character. In the second there are a few solidi, some varieties of reverse type in the tremisses, and a remarkable quasi-imperial coinage in Provence of solidi and tremisses. In all three phases the coinage is essentially non-royal in character. Central control over it seems to have been minimal, and coins bearing royal names form only a minute proportion of those that were struck. The most marked characteristic of its 'national' phase is indeed its being a coinage of local mints and moneyers, and although these features are not so evident in the first phase and the names of moneyers and mints are absent from many deniers in the third, the same kind of monetary organization, or the same lack of it, seems to have existed throughout.

Certain aspects of the coinage are best discussed in the separate context of each phase: the internal chronology, the regional features of the coins, the evolution of types and inscriptions. But five topics may conveniently be examined in the context of the coinage as a whole. They are the overall chronology of the three phases, the organization of minting, the metrology and fineness of the coins, their denominations and values, and finally their classification.

The expansion of the Frankish kingdom during the reigns of Clovis and his sons meant inevitably that Frankish pseudo-imperial coinages had several different initial dates. Coinages in the purely Frankish area in the north do not seem to have begun earlier than *c.* 500; those in Aquitaine and Burgundy-Provence are necessarily post-507 or post-534, though each had earlier pseudo-imperial Visigothic and Burgundian coinages behind them. At the other end, the Victory types that characterize the pseudo-imperial coinage continued in many mints beyond *c.* 570, and there seems reason to suppose that they were not formally abolished till 587, but between these dates other types were beginning to appear and the names of kings, moneyers or mints were starting to replace the traditional blundered imperial legends.

The effective transition to the 'national' coinage began in the late 560s or early 570s, though it had a precedent in 557/8. The main date can be inferred from the fact that while there are no regular issues of Chlotar I, who died in 561, there are coins of Sigebert I of Austrasia (561–75) minted at Toul (B 4484 = P 978, and probably B 4485) and Rheims (B 3759 = P 1028), as there are also coins of his longer-lived brother Guntramn of Burgundy (561–92). The transition therefore began before 575. It is tempting to say that it began after 567, since no coins are known bearing the name of Charibert I of Paris, who died in that year, but since there are equally none of Chilperic I, who lived till 584, it is clear that there are either gaps in our evidence or that minting in the name of one king did not entail minting in those of his brothers. There was in any case a precedent from before 561, for a unique coin exists (B 5492 = 5493 = P 34) with the two names of Childebert I (d. 558) and Chramn which must belong to 557/8, when Childebert gave support to his nephew Chramn, an apparently illegitimate son of Chlotar I who revolted against his father but was captured, strangled and burned with his family (Greg. Tur. *Hist. Franc.* IV. 13). Although neither name is accompanied on the coin by the title of *rex*, Frankish custom would have made it impossible for a family name like that of Childebert to have been used outside the royal house, and if Hermenegild in Spain was alive to the possibility of using a coin legend as propaganda, so might an earlier pretender in Gaul. (The coin was presumably issued by Chramn and not by Childebert even though his name appears on the reverse.) But it is equally clear that the initiative was not immediately followed up, and that the transition to a new coinage began some years later.

It is more difficult to determine exactly what the initial changes were, how they were brought about, and over what area. For the parallel changes in Spain one can infer the sequence of events with some assurance (above, p. 50): a royal order to place the king's name on the coins, but with no references to a change of type or weight; a subsequent order for a new type (profile bust and cross) and the addition of the mint name; and a final one introducing a new type (facing busts) and altering the weight and fineness. In France, with no single central authority, the pattern must necessarily have been more complicated. Although types and even a common pattern of legends could sometimes be extended over great distances by simple copying, it is impossible to believe that the typical mint-and-moneyer coinages came into general production in this way. The final stage must have involved some agreed directive to moneyers prescribing as types a bust and cross and as legends the names of mint and moneyer, together with a general reduction in the weight from 8 siliquae (1.5g) to 20 grains (1.3g). It will be argued below that this can best be dated to 587. But the earlier changes display much less uniformity. Some mints made substantial changes in type, others only small ones; some introduced a royal name, but more did not; some substituted the name of a moneyer or a mint for part of a pseudo-imperial inscription instead of dropping this completely (cf. ELA on **1.362**). One of the three coins of Sigebert cited above has only a royal name and that of a mint (SIGEBERTVS REX and TVLLO), the second has a royal name and a moneyer's (SIGEBERTVS REX and MANOBIO), and the third has the names of king, moneyer and mint (DN SIGEBERTVS REX and DACCI REMVS CIVVT). Sometimes there was a reduction in weight, but sometimes not.

It seems clear that unlike the change attributed here to 587, which created something approaching a uniform coinage throughout the kingdom, the earlier ones did not affect the whole of the *regnum* but only parts of it. What probably happened was that one of the kings instructed the moneyers in his kingdom to differentiate newly struck coins from those already in circulation but without saying how this should be done. The moneyers adopted various devices, some of them changing the types and others the legends so as to indicate where and by whom the coins were struck. The resulting changes would be taken up sporadically elsewhere. The most likely ruler to have attempted such innovations is the cruel but imaginative Chilperic I of Soissons, described unflatteringly by Gregory of Tours as 'the Nero and Herod of our time' and famous for his attempts to innovate in theological matters and to enforce on schools the use of four new letters he had added to the alphabet (Greg. Tur. *Hist. Franc.* V. 44). But some of his activities were more serious, notably his order to have city walls put into a proper state of repair and his reconstruction of the circuses at Paris and Soissons so that he could offer spectacles to his subjects (*ibid.* V. 11). He is exactly the kind of ruler to have thought of making changes in the coinage, and although these cannot be associated with his original kingdom in the north, between Soissons and the Channel, his share of his brother Charibert's kingdom in 567 gave him western Neustria and most of western Aquitaine (cf. Greg. Tur. *Hist. Franc.* IX. 20), an area that included three of the mints (Agen, Comminges, Oloron) with novel types that made part of the Canterbury hoard and were probably all struck in the 570s. As for the occasion, one suspects that it would have been the introduction of the weight reduction discussed below (p. 107), for some change in the external appearance of the coins would have been required if users were to differentiate between the new, lighter coins and the older, heavier ones.

This inchoate period of minting ended with the introduction of a relatively uniform coinage involving a bust and a cross. This can be dated with certainty to after 579, for the substitution of crosses for Victories as coin types must have followed the similar change at Constantinople, where it was the main feature of the coinage of Tiberius II, who became sole emperor in September 578. It was taken up by Leovigild in Spain, though only briefly, probably in 583 (above, p. 50), and it provided the model for the new type introduced at Marseille in the name of successive Byzantine emperors (below, pp. 129–30). It was presumably the success of this coinage that resulted in its being generalized throughout the Frankish kingdom, but the political events of the 580s make it unlikely that this could have happened earlier than 587.

The reason is that in the early 580s there was no occasion on which the heirs of Chlotar I were on sufficiently good terms with each other for a pact on such matters to be conceivable. The savage vendetta between the rulers of Austrasia and Neustria, provoked by Chilperic's murder of his Spanish queen Goiswintha, sister of Sigebert's wife Brunhild, had just begun. The years 582–5 were largely filled by the attempt of the pretender Gondovald, who claimed to be a son of Chlotar I overlooked in the partition of 561, to secure a kingdom for himself. This in turn overlapped the succession problems created in 584 by the murder of Chilperic I, an event exceptional only in its having been committed by a private enemy and not by a relative. It was not till 587 that an attempt on the life of Childebert II and difficulties in the position of the childless Guntramn resulted in a moment of unwonted harmony in the Frankish world. In November 587 Childebert II and Guntramn, who was both king of Burgundy and was also attempting to act as a regent for his infant nephew Chlotar II, met at Andelot (dép. Haute-Marne), near Chaumont on the borders of their respective kingdoms, and concluded an elaborate pact revising the current territorial divisions, making arrangements for the succession, and undertaking to remain on good terms in the future. Gregory of Tours, who shortly afterwards visited Guntramn on diplomatic business, obtained a copy of the document (Greg. Tur. *Hist. Franc.* IX. 20). It is entirely preoccupied with affairs of state and does not refer to the coinage, but there seems a strong probability that it was at Andelot either that the new coinage was introduced or that, having been introduced shortly before in one of the kingdoms, it was by mutual agreement generalized on that occasion throughout the *regnum Francorum*.

The date at which, nearly a century later, the gold coinage was replaced by one of silver can be determined within fairly narrow limits. Most tremisses, bearing the names only of mints and moneyers, are unhelpful, but there was a meagre royal coinage. The abandonment of the traditional early eighth-century dating for the end of the gold coinage has already been mentioned (p. 88), and the last gold coins of Marseille are not tremisses and solidi of Childebert III (695–711) but tremisses of anomalous type (below, p. 131) struck in the 670s by Clovis III (675) and Dagobert II (restored 676–9). Elsewhere gold coins have been attributed to the same Dagobert II and to Clovis IV (690–5) and Dagobert III (711–15). The first of these coins (B 1848 = P 64), with the name of the moneyer Donatus, is now universally assigned to Dagobert I. The second (B 5503 = P 71), with the obverse legend CHLODOVIO RIX and the name of the moneyer Eborino, was still doubtfully attributed to Clovis IV by Prou but is better given to the short reign in 675 of Clovis III. The third (B 5498 = B 5501 = P 69), with the name of the moneyer Waldebertus, is again one of Dagobert I. There is in fact no evidence for the minting of gold anywhere in the Frankish kingdom later than the 670s.

The introduction of silver was attributed by Prou (1892a, cix) to the reign of Charibert II of Aquitaine (629–32) since a denier exists (B 5499 = P 65) with a legend read as CARIBERT and an undeciphered monogram. It is now agreed that the name was misread and is really that of a moneyer BERTCARI. Lafaurie in a series of recent publications has proposed *c.* 670 or 660/670 (Lafaurie 1969a, 121; 1970, 118). It is true that the earliest name of a bishop that can be read and dated (674–684/688) with any confidence is that of Lambert on a denier of some abbey in the diocese of Lyon (B 1843 = P 97: LAMBERTVS IPS), for although others may well be earlier we lack the written sources to date them properly. But the names of two secular rulers go back to the preceding decade. One, the only occurrence of a royal name on a denier (B 6463; Lafaurie 1965b) is that on a coin of Childeric II of Austrasia (662–75), and since this was struck at Tours it must date from 673–5, between his acquisition of Neustria and his own death. Almost contemporary with it are two deniers (B 3460 = P 993; Bais 99 in Lafaurie 1981d, xxii–xxiii, 44–5) bearing in very conspicuous fashion the legend EBROINVS, certainly the great Neustrian Mayor of the Palace of this name, who held office for two periods, from the early 660s to 673 and again from 675 to 680 or 683, the exact year of his murder by a disgruntled retainer being uncertain. Deniers were in normal circulation in the Paris region by 682, when a charter of Saint-Germain-des-Prés includes a sale of property for 30 *solidos in argento* (Guérard 1844, II. 341–2).

A good case can in fact be made out for attributing the monetary revolution to Ebroin himself. It has usually been taken for granted that the silver denier came into existence, in some fashion not fully explained, without the formal intervention of any political authority. Such a view is not easy to accept. Even in the Frankish kingdom, where local and effectively private minting predominated, there would have had to be some legal provisions stating how many deniers creditors should receive in settlement of a debt contracted in gold solidi and tremisses; injured parties would want to know the official rates at which the compensations of the old legal code were to be translated into new coins. The denier was not a debased tremissis whose nominal value was known and whose actual value could be settled by discussion or arbitration. It was something the valuation of which would have to be determined by law, and until it had been given an official existence and a value moneyers would certainly not think of introducing it. Only a Frankish king or his representative, a Mayor of the Palace, would have been in a position to do such a thing.

There was in the 660s and 670s no single political authority in France, any more than there had been when the reduced tremissis had been introduced a hundred years before, but the denier did not necessarily come into existence everywhere at the same time. In one part of the kingdom, indeed, the duchy of Aquitaine during its earliest phase, it never came into existence at all. It was in the third quarter of the seventh century that Aquitaine became a virtually independent political entity, first under Felix, 'patrician of the city of Toulouse', then under a certain Lupus described indifferently as duke or prince (Rouche 1979, 97ff.), and then under their unnamed successors, for written sources for the history of Aquitaine over a period of nearly a century are almost completely lacking. But while the north and north-east – Poitou, Berry, Limousin, Auvergne – remained attached to Neustria under Ebroin's jurisdiction and had an abundant silver coinage, in the remainder of Aquitaine it is totally lacking (map in Rouche 1979, 303) save at Bordeaux, whose total output is represented by only two coins from the same pair of dies (B 1098; P 2171, both from the Plassac hoard), and Narbonne, which was not formally part of Aquitaine at all and which in any case minted only briefly in silver, under the influence of Marseille, between 714 and 719 (below, p. 143).

It was in Neustria, however, that the connection of the denier with the tremissis was closest, with coins giving the names of mints and moneyers just as before. And it was apparently from

Neustria that the use of the denier spread to Austrasia, Burgundy and Provence, first as Ebroin extended his authority and then after the *regnum* came together under Pepin of Herstal as a consequence of the battle of Tertry (687). In Provence, however, it did so with a difference, for the gold coins of Marseille struck in the names of Frankish kings were succeeded by deniers bearing the names or monograms of patricians and of a different weight standard to that employed elsewhere. Since the spread of the silver denier is traditionally so closely bound up with the Arnulfing/Carolingian dynasty it must seem a paradox to assign its origins to Ebroin, representative of the rival mayoralty of Neustria, but despite the absence of written evidence the early history of the coinage suggests that this was the case.

This is not the place to discuss the roles, economic and other, of Merovingian coinage. In the earlier period, the continued minting of small change in the Rhône valley is evidence for the local survival of small-scale retail trade to the middle of the sixth century, though the region notably failed to follow the example of North Africa, Italy and the eastern Mediterranean in their revival of large denominations of copper. The limitations of the coinage elsewhere to gold implies a much more restricted commercial life. The kings had certainly a passionate interest in money, despite their limited minting of it themselves. The amassing of the royal treasure, not for public expenditure as in Roman times but primarily for distribution to enhance the king's prestige and secure the loyalty of his followers (cf. Grierson 1959b) and secondarily for the payment of services and the purchase of luxuries, was one of the chief activities of the crown (Doehaerd 1949). The fate of the royal treasure on the death of each monarch is regularly noted by Gregory of Tours.

Gold coinage was of course accessible to a wider public, though in view of its high purchasing power the functions it could perform must have been quite limited. Sums of solidi appear in the few surviving Merovingian wills, and other sources show coin being used for the purchase of landed estates, of slaves, and of luxury imports (Kloss 1929, extremely well documented; Claude 1961b) as well as for bribes and for settlements of the compensations that make up the bulk of the *Leges barbarorum*. Tolls seem to have been normally assessed in coin even if sometimes paid in kind, and the distribution of Merovingian coins far from their places of origin can often be associated with trade routes and the needs of merchants (Werner 1961; Lafaurie 1961). But if major fairs already existed in the early seventh century, like that of Saint-Denis which was founded by Dagobert, the proliferation of local markets and of petty commerce involving the use of silver deniers belongs to the last phase of the Merovingian period.

It is here, most probably, that the real cause of the transition from gold to silver must be sought. Some scholars have preferred to see in it the result of a gradual diminution in the stock of gold available in the West. Gold was supposedly exported on a substantial scale to the Byzantine and Muslim worlds in exchange for articles of luxury; it was also removed from circulation through thesaurization by the Church; and of course some would disappear through a natural process of wear and tear. Such gold could not be replaced, for Western Christendom had little to export and had no domestic sources of gold of any consequence. A silver coinage was introduced to make up the deficiency.

This reasoning fails to take account of the fact that the economic niche filled by the silver must have been quite different from that of the gold. The new denier was worth only a fraction of the old tremissis. When a local shortage of gold and a corresponding affluence of silver in the second half of the fifteenth century resulted in the introduction of new silver denominations, these were heavy coins, testoni of *c.* 8g and guldengroschen (later talers) of *c.* 28g. They were intended to have the value of a gold florin and a pound in money of account respectively, replacing in the first case a gold coin and in the second giving material form to an even more valuable currency unit. In the seventh century it would have been quite possible technically to have done the same, and replaced the gold coins by heavy silver ones of the same value. It was not done, however, and the obvious explanation is that the new coins of much lower value were expected to fulfil a different function. Although the close association of market, toll and mint (*mercatum, teloneum et moneta*) is most characteristic of tenth- and eleventh-century German charters, there seems good reason to suppose that the association of markets and the minting of silver deniers went back to the last decades of the seventh century.

The source of the precious metal used for late Merovingian silver coinage is something of a problem. The only important mines in the kingdom, those at Melle in Poitou, seem to date mainly from the Carolingian period (below, pp. 235–6), though this may be in part an illusion resulting from their product being used by the mint of Poitiers instead of being, as in Carolingian times, turned into coin at Melle itself. The development of central European mining also lay in the future, and was in any case confined to areas that lay beyond the eastern frontiers of the Frankish kingdom. It has been argued that some came from the Muslim world, either directly in exchange for gold (cf. Grierson 1960a) or by way of Scandinavia, but the first type of transaction, if it took place at all, would have been of marginal importance and the second, whose reality is equally open to doubt, would have been a Carolingian and not a Merovingian phenomenon.

The most probable source, though not one of a kind that economists always find it easy to accept, is that a shift in the equilibrium that always exists between silver plate and silver coin was in process, and the bullion was supplied by the wealth of the Church. The late Roman Empire, *pace* Patterson 1972 (above, p. 9), was extremely well supplied with silver, but preferred to use it for plate instead of for coin. From the fourth century onwards this plate had tended to move out of Senatorial possession into that of the Church, sometimes through straightforward gifts and legacies from laymen but often as a result of wealthy senators and landed proprietors, men like Sidonius Apollinaris, St Remigius and St Didier (Desiderius) of Auxerre, themselves becoming bishops and leaving their wealth to the local churches they had ruled. In the case of St Didier a detailed account of the legacy, with summary descriptions of each object and its weight, has survived (Adhémar 1934), though the objects themselves disappeared when Auxerre was plundered in 1567 during the Wars of Religion. The descriptions show it to have been a great family hoard of late Roman silverware, ranging in importance from silver gilt missoria each weighing forty or fifty Roman pounds to a dozen spoons weighing a total of 3lb 2oz, the silver objects received by the cathedral totalling 420lb 7oz, i.e. about 140kg, and those going to the abbey of Saint-Germain just over 120lb (40kg). The private plate of a wealthy family, furthermore, would not include the still heavier silver objects – ciboria (altar coverings), massive silver grilles and candelabra, and so forth – with which many churches were decorated. The ciborium of St John Lateran, presented by Valentinian III to replace that plundered by the Visigoths, was reckoned to weigh 2,000 Roman lb (*Vita Xysti III*, cap. 4, in the *Liber Pontificalis*), a figure that seems incredible until we remember that when the French plundered the churches of Malta in 1798 the Mint received 6,570 *livres* of silver (over three tons) from the Conventual Church of St John alone (Denaro 1955).

The wealth of the seventh-century Frankish Church in precious metal must have been huge, though it was no doubt inferior to that of the churches of Rome and many of those in the lands still ruled by Byzantium. Apart from the case of Auxerre, however, little is known of it in detail, as indeed remains true of the Carolingian period despite the detailed *descriptiones* we know to have been drawn up then on royal instructions (Lesne 1910–43, III. 1ff., 155ff.). Auxerre was also exceptional in keeping its treasure until the sixteenth century, for the secular (not to say military) interests of many churchmen in the late Merovingian period and the needs of Pepin and his successors resulted in a very extensive secularization of Church property. This has traditionally been ascribed to Charles Martel (Lesne 1910–43, II:1.1ff.), but St Boniface, writing in 742, refers to its having begun sixty or seventy years earlier (*non minus quam per sexaginta vel septuaginta annos*). It has usually been studied in its social aspects, for the taking over by laymen of the Church's landed estates is generally accepted as having made possible the creation of the costly cavalry arm of the Carolingian period, but it seems safe to assume that the same process must have brought huge quantities of silver back into circulation. It also explains why ecclesiastical institutions struck far more silver deniers than they ever had gold tremisses.

(c) MINTING ORGANIZATION

The monetary organization of the Franks has to be approached by way of the period of 'national' gold coinage, *c.* 580–*c.* 670, for the earlier pseudo-imperial coinage is effectively anonymous and, while the later denarial period probably continued the main features of its predecessor, it did so only in a somewhat degenerate and perhaps, owing to the emergence of local markets, rather different form. In the middle period the bulk of the coinage is more or less uniform in weight and fineness, and there is a great predominance of coins having as types a bust and a cross, though there is much variety in detail and a few isolated types, even groups of types, quite different from the norm. The coins were struck by named moneyers (*monetarii*), and professedly at a greater number of localities. Who were the moneyers, was this great dispersion of minting real, and if it was, how is it to be explained? As a preliminary, what was the role of the state?

The answer to the last question must be that it seems to have been very small. This is what we would expect. The successors of Clovis may have done their best to maintain many aspects of late Roman administration, particularly those which offered them financial advantages, although the fact that such documents as we possess were drawn up by clerics and in Latin means that their authors were forced to employ a technical vocabulary that must often have had as little connection with real life as the Cabinets and legal officers of the Sandwich Islands in the mid nineteenth century had with their similarly entitled counterparts in Europe. The fashion in which the *regnum Francorum* was constantly divided and redivided, and the territorial incoherence of the partitions, show that the Franks, of all the major settlers in the Empire, had the feeblest idea of the State. They never, certainly, claimed any monopoly of minting, and the Salic Law, unlike the laws of the Burgundians, Visigoths and Lombards, contains no clauses condemning those guilty of false coining or of minting without royal authorization.

The indifference of the Frankish kings to the exercise of minting by their subjects can be most clearly demonstrated in respect of the Church, particularly from the second half of the seventh century onwards. Coins were then being struck in the names of a number of bishoprics and abbeys, but although many charters to these exist, meticulously listing their estates and privileges and setting out the nature and limitations of their exemptions from taxes or tolls, there is not a single one conferring the grant of *moneta* or complaining about its exercise. The only explanation must be that the kings laid no claim to a monopoly of minting themselves or sought to impede their subjects from striking coin. There would obviously be some limitations. The coins themselves point to the existence of administrative provisions being occasionally issued on the general conditions of minting, changing the weight of the coins in the second half of the sixth century and the metal in the second half of the seventh, ordering that the coins should bear the names of mint and moneyer, perhaps even indicating in broad terms the designs (above, pp. 92–3). But any such prescriptions must clearly have admitted of exceptions, for they did not prevent the subsequent introduction of different designs or the omission in some series of moneyers' and mint names, and the mixed character of hoards suggests that little or no attempt was made to lay down what the fineness of the coins should be (below, p. 109).

Who were the *monetarii*? The term is a Roman one, and in the later Roman Empire was applied to members of the *collegia monetalis*, one of the great manufacturing corporations that made a wide variety of objects – arms, armour, clothing, even soap – for the imperial government and came under the jurisdiction of the Count of the Sacred Largesses (Jones 1964, II 427–8, 435–7, and refs. in III 113–15; Lopez 1953). They were partly slaves, partly freedmen, and often persons of consequence and wealth; a Ravennate *monetarius* in the sixth century has the relatively distinguished title of *vir clarissimus*. The names of hundreds of *monetarii* of the Merovingian period are known from the coins, though references to them in the written sources are rare. Gregory of Tours has a story about a Parisian *monetarius urbis* who built a chapel in honour of St Crescentia in gratitude for his recovery from an illness (*De glor. confessorum*, cap. 105), and the author of the life of St Yrier of Limoges formerly attributed to Gregory mentions a lady named Ricovera who was the wife of a *monetarius* at Tours (*Vita S. Aridii*, cap. 33, in MGH, *Script. rer. Merov.* III 591). Nineteenth-century scholars, notably Ponton d'Amécourt, ransacked the chronicles to find the names of prominent persons who could be identified with the *monetarii* of the coins, but these identifications, which played havoc with attempts to establish the chronology of the coinage, are now universally rejected. It has even been doubted (Longuet 1939) if Abbo, the experienced goldsmith (*faber aurifex probatissimus*) who was in charge of the public mint at Limoges (*qui . . . in urbe Lemovicina publicam fiscalis monetae officinam gerebat: Vita S. Eligii* I. 3) and to whom Eligius was apprenticed, was technically a *monetarius*, for he is not given this title, no Limoges coins struck in his name are known, and although an Abbo was a moneyer at Chalon the identification of the two is no more than an assumption of Ponton d'Amécourt, who worked out his supposed career in some detail

(Amécourt 1868b, 1882). Eligius was indeed a *monetarius*, as we know from the coins (detailed study by Lafaurie 1977a), but it was his reputation as an accomplished goldsmith that brought him into the service of Chlotar II (*Vita* I.5; on this side of his activities see Lusuardi Siena 1973; Vierck 1974) and the only written reference to his connection with the *publica moneta* is not easy to interpret (*multos ex publica moneta misit solidos: Vita S. Eligii* II.78).

The varying views on the *monetarii* held by scholars from the seventeenth century onwards are brought together in Dieudonné 1942, an article written to clear the author's own mind on the subject. These views were determined in part by the social and political background of the period in which each scholar was writing and in part by his personal training and experience. The moneyers were regarded as royal officials or tax farmers in the age of Louis XIV; they were private entrepreneurs to scholars imbued with the spirit of early capitalism; or members of the financial bureaucracy for Charles Robert, a high-ranking civil servant under the Second Empire. Some proposed identifications can at once be discarded. The moneyers, with the exception of St Eligius, who owed his distinction to other qualities, were not normally royal officials of consequence, for they do not figure amongst the witnesses to charters or in the pages of the chronicles of the day. At the other extreme they were not normally die-cutters, though presumably those trained as goldsmiths would have been qualified to act as such. Longuet (1939) illustrated coins from two mints in southern Normandy and one from a mint two hundred kilometres away in Touraine for which the dies were evidently cut by the same hand (cf. **1.434–5**, though here the mints are contiguous), and Bauer (1951) equally showed how a single die-cutter, whom he characterized as the 'Master of Huy' because only for this mint (on the Meuse in Belgium) is there a solidus (P 1199), must have been responsible for dies used in some eighteen mints and as many moneyers in the north and north-east scattered over an area extending from Cologne as far afield as Strasbourg and Soissons (list augmented by Lafaurie in *BSFN* 1951, 106). Nor can they have been landed proprietors: the names of many places in France go back to those of their owners in Merovingian times, and the place- and personal names on the coins are never the same. It has been widely held that the moneyers' names were intended as guarantees of the weight and fineness of the coins, but in the countryside the names of landed proprietors would surely have done this better.

This local minting suggests a possible solution. That the coins were actually struck at the localities named on them, despite the apparent unimportance of many of the places, was convincingly argued by Prou (1888c), despite occasional die-links between coins from different mints, for it is the only possible interpretation of such words as FIT, FIET (for *fitur*) that appear on many (below p. 120). But while such places as Chalon and Limoges could well support several moneyers and have had a substantial mint output, it is impossible to believe that the smaller localities could have had resident moneyers, or even resident goldsmiths who could turn their hands to minting when required, or that they minted systematically and regularly over long periods of time. The picture becomes different, however, if we cease to think of such places as Charly (Aisne) or Vendières (Aisne) simply as villages and remember instead that they would have normally been also the residence of some large landed proprietor, the equivalent of the lord of the manor of later times, and that the coins would have been struck on his behalf rather than that of the villagers. He might have had in his household a skilled goldsmith of the kind that royal bailiffs (*iudices*) are enjoined to have in each *caput fisci* by chapter 45 of the *Capitulare de villis* of Carolingian times (*Capitularia* I.87: *Ut unusquisque iudex in suo ministerio bonos habeat artifices, id est fabros, ferrarios et aurifices et argentarios*), but more often, if he needed to turn plate or jewellery into coin or even for reasons of vanity wished to do some minting, he would have had to obtain the services of a moneyer from elsewhere. He might even succumb to the blandishments of a wandering moneyer looking for work, just as itinerant goldsmiths, with a small stock in trade of tools and patterns, must often have persuaded persons of wealth to allow them to refashion their old jewellery and plate. Such minting would be only occasional and haphazard, just as was the functioning of many small mints in feudal times and just as the maintenance of an orchestra or a chemical laboratory in a princely household was to be in the eighteenth century. Minting in the countryside would ultimately depend on the whims and resources of great proprietors, even if in towns it was normally sustained on a more regular basis.

Moneyers would, on this hypothesis, have been persons of some means, often though not necessarily goldsmiths – they would need some source of livelihood when no minting was being done – and would normally have been resident in the small towns of Frankish Gaul although available for work elsewhere. That the title was sometimes hereditary, as it had been in Roman times and was to be later (Lopez 1949), was noted by Maxe-Werly (1867), who pointed out that the recurrence of particular elements (*Fil-*, *Theud-*) in personal names of moneyers at Rheims (Filamarius, Filacharius) and Metz (Theudelenus, Theudegiselus) fits in with what we know of the way in which these were inherited at the time. In some places, notably at Chalon but occasionally at Lyon and a few other mints, we find associations between moneyers (**1.396–7**, *Baudomere et Rignoaldo m*; **1.399**, *Wintrio et Duccio*), and Ponton d'Amécourt may have been right in some of the migrations of moneyers from place to place that he postulated, notably from Chalon to Limoges. It was certainly the case for Madelinus, who struck coins of the same type and style at Maastricht and Dorestad (below, p. 137), and Longuet's criticism of some of Ponton d'Amécourt's assumed migrations of moneyers from Chalon to Limoges goes too far, for it is largely based on the dissimilarities between the coins, and on his own showing this could be expected if they had used different die-cutters. Usually the moneyers would simply have worked *in* particular places and we are only employing a convenient shorthand when we speak of, say, 'the mint of Dorestad', though in larger towns they may have been employed by some municipal authority – Gregory of Tours' phrase *monetarius urbis* implies something more than a moneyer working 'in' Paris – or by a local bishop or abbot. They would also naturally be called on to supervise the melting down of the coin collected in taxes, as the *Vita S. Eligii* I.15 depicts a *monetarius* doing in company with a royal *domesticus* in an unnamed *moneta publica*, in accordance with imperial practice since the late fourth century (novel of Valentinian I in *Cod. Theod.* 12.6, 12, 13), though even apart from the accompanying miracle there are grounds for doubting whether this was very generally done (below, p. 128–9).

Coins struck in the names of moneyers and mints do not exhaust the coinage of the middle Merovingian period. There are also coins struck in the names of the Frankish kings, or on behalf of churches or monasteries with such legends as *racio eclisie* or *racio baselici* or *racio S. Martini*, or for royal domains with *racio fisci* or *racio domni* (cf. Prou 1892a, li–lxi), and for the complex of court institutions that formed the Palace (*Palati moneta, in Palacio fit, in Scola fit, Escolare,* etc.; cf. Amécourt 1885 and Prou 1892a, xlviii–lii). For all of these issues moneyers would be employed, their names being sometimes present on the coins and sometimes not. But in essence this coinage was 'private', just as was that of the moneyers. The distinction made by nineteenth-century scholars between royal coinage, ecclesiastical coinage and the coinage of the moneyers is artificial and indeed quite meaningless.

How is the position before the period that has been discussed to be envisaged? We have no idea of the number of moneyers employed at Trier and Lyon, the two major mints of late Roman Gaul, or at the less important mint of Arles, but it must have run to several hundred. Not all such 'moneyers' would be equally competent, either to practise minting themselves of to teach their profession to others. Die-cutters, smelters and metal refiners would have acquired specialist skills quite different from those of the clerical staff on the one hand and those of the hammer-men who did the actual striking on the other. Cassiodorus, after Theoderic's assumption of power in Spain, writes (*Variae* V.39) of the need to recall to their public duties the moneyers who had abandoned them and taken work with private persons, presumably striking on behalf of these some proportion of the coins that we class as pseudo-imperial. The same must have occurred on an even larger scale in Gaul. With the widespread breakdown of government the old mints, deprived of regular consignments of bullion and no longer having to supply coin to Roman armies and overstaffed and complex bureaucracies, could not have continued to offer regular employment. Many moneyers must have had to take service with the various Frankish kings, some of whom ruled in parts of Gaul where there had been no mint previously, or they found work with municipal authorities or great local magnates, or perhaps more and more, as time went by, they set up in business on their own behalf. Only in the last decades of the period of pseudo-imperial coins do names begin to appear, sometimes as at Vienne and Lyon accompanied by survivals of traditional mint terminology in such coin inscriptions as *De officina Laurenti* (P 1303) and *De officina Maret . . .* (P 37–8).

As new generations had to learn the art of minting, or sometimes discover it for themselves, and many moneyers necessarily worked in isolation or in small groups no longer subject to the discipline of a well-established mint, there was a general decline in skill. A notable feature of the later moneyers' coinage is the large size of the irregularly arranged and crudely cut letters in the inscriptions, and the way in which the upper parts of these are often off-flan, in contrast to the small, neat lettering of late Roman coins well inside a raised and clearly marked border. The die-faces were being made too large for the flans, and the flans themselves were no longer being cut out as roundels from thin sheets of hammered gold; they are instead cast globules of metal which, when struck, failed to expand outwards as far as the circumference of the corresponding die-faces. The phenomenon may in part be due to the fact that the dies were being made by itinerant artisans no longer themselves working in mints and fully conversant with the moneyers' needs, but in part it was due to a general decline in standards outside the few regular mints that survived. The decline was only occasionally relieved by the emergence of artists of real talent, men such as the 'Master of Huy' (above, p. 99) with his inspired copies of the bust on a coin of the fourth-century emperor Magnentius (below, p. 118) and the man responsible for the dies used for the coinage of Banassac in the time of Charibert of Aquitaine (**1.424**).

(d) DENOMINATIONS AND VALUES

The denominations of Frankish coinage in the Merovingian period, apart from the early *minuti argentei* and the silver and copper coins of Provence and Burgundy, offer at first glance no problems of identification, for there were on the surface only three denominations, the solidus, the tremissis, and from *c.* 670 onwards the silver denarius. We only know their Latin names, two of which (sou, denier) carried on into French. The old name of the solidus continued, though literary sources like Gregory of Tours often preferred the more classical *aureus*. The triens or tremisses continued to be called by either of these names: Gregory prefers triens – he spells it *trians* or *treans* – but tremissis occurs in other texts from the sixth to the eighth century, with even a German form *dremise*. French scholars since the nineteenth century have usually called the coin a triens, but they treat the word indifferently as singular or plural and ignore the correct Latin plural *trientes*. British scholars, influenced perhaps by the existence of the OE word *thrymsa* (below, p. 157), have usually preferred tremissis, which is the term used in this volume.

The silver coin was called a *denarius*. This is the regular word in written documents, and is actually used in the inscriptions on early coins of two moneyers, Ragnoald at Lyon and Maurinus at Orléans (*Lugduno dinarios, dinario Aurelia(n)i*: B 2532=P 96; B 542, incorrectly described: both illus. in Lafaurie 1967e, 47, fig. 4), so that literate users should be in no doubt as to what they were handling. Presumably, since Frankish was a Germanic language, their name in the vernacular was some word cognate to 'penny', but no text survives to record its precise form. *Denarius* gave rise to the later French *denier*, the word generally used here to describe the late Merovingian silver coins. The term *saiga* (cf. Schröder 1904; texts collected in Soetbeer 1862, 356–9), which was applied to the coins by some nineteenth-century scholars, is best avoided. Although it did come to be used in places for the silver penny, as is explained in Charlemagne's revised version of the *Lex Alamannorum*, its use was limited to southern Germany (Alamannia, Bavaria), and there is no evidence for its having occurred in Frankish. It is probably derived from a word meaning seed (cf. modern Germ. *säen*, 'to sow'), thus linking up with other metrological terms applied to small weights of gold.

This simplified picture, however, does not cover all the facts. The first complication is the existence and indeed the predominance after the 580s of a lighter solidus and a lighter tremissis, weighing respectively 3.9g and 1.3g instead of 4.5g and 1.5g. The second complication is the double weight pattern of the denier, for there are coins of both 1.3g and 1.1g. The third is the double valuation of the denarius in terms of the solidus, for in the Salic Law 40 denarii make a solidus and from the late Merovingian period onwards the solidus is normally reckoned at 12 denarii, though there is an exception in southern Germany in the Bavarian 'long shilling' of 30 pennies with a corresponding pound of eight shillings.

The first two of these will be dealt with in the context of the coins themselves. The reduction in the weight of the solidus and tremissis, which took place in the late sixth century, is best explained as resulting from the replacement of a Roman by a Germanic weight pattern (above, p. 14–15). The two weights of the late Merovingian denier seem likewise to have been due to the simultaneous use of Germanic and Roman standards (below, p. 108). But the double reckoning of the solidus in terms of denarii has given rise to a vast literature that requires notice here, for it raises problems of great importance to scholars in several fields. On it largely depends the dating of the *Lex Salica*, or more exactly that of the earliest of the several codes of varying length that are collectively known by this term.

The problem can be stated briefly. The normal formula for the compensations in the law code is *N denarii, qui valuit N÷40 solidi*, the sums being always stated first in denarii and the ratio 1:40 being invariable. For example, Title II, *De furtis porcarum*, on the theft of pigs of varying ages and quality, begins, in rough translation, 'If any one shall steal a sucking pig, and it is proved against him, he shall be fined 120 denarii, which makes three solidi.' In contrast to this is the value of 12 denarii attributed to the solidus in the late Merovingian and Carolingian periods (below, p. 106). The ambiguity was a source of trouble as late as the reign of Charlemagne. A person who had lent money in terms of the solidi of the day, for example, might conceivably claim to be repaid at the ancient reckoning of 40 denarii instead of the current one of 12. Cap. 41 of the acts of the Council of Rheims of 813 petitioned the emperor to have the 40-denarius reckoning formally abolished, as indeed (it claimed) Pepin had ordered in an edict now lost, since it was a source of much perjury and false witness (MGH, *Concilia aevi Karolini* I. 257), and Archbishop Hincmar prefaces the text of the will of St Rémi in his revised *Vita S. Remigii* with a reminder to readers that the solidi it refers to were worth 40 deniers and were not the less valuable units of their own day (MGH, *Script. rer. Merov*. III. 336). The matter is complicated by the differing ratios obtaining in other Germanic codes. That of the Ripuarian Franks, i.e. the Franks living along the banks (*ripa*) of the Rhine in contrast to the 'Salian' branch to which Clovis belonged, gave the solidus a value of 12 denarii. In Charlemagne's day the West Frisians between the Sincfal and the Fli equated their traditional solidus with two and a half of the new deniers, the East Frisians between the Weser and the Lauwers at two, and the inhabitants of Middle Frisia between the Lauwers and the Fli at three (*Lex Frisionum, Additio* III. 73, 78 in Eckhardt 1982, 96 and 98).

What was this *denarius* worth $\frac{1}{40}$ of a solidus? We cannot expect to discover this without knowing when the compensations were first formulated. The *Lex Salica*, unlike the Visigothic and Burgundian codes, has no formal prologue recording the date and circumstances of its promulgation. It has customarily been attributed to the reign of Clovis, and specifically, to the last three or four years thereof, since a passage in it implies the extension of Frankish power south of the Loire (Brunner 1906, 434–40). But in a series of articles early in this century Benno Hilliger argued that the code could not be earlier than Chlotar II since the compositions in it are all based on the denarius, which he took to be the late Merovingian denier and dated back to this reign (Hilliger 1903, 1907; *contra*, Brunner 1908). The argument is fallacious, for the Merovingian denier dates from *c*. 670 and not from the beginning of the seventh century, and a massive study by Luschin von Ebengreuth (1910a), admirably summarized by Prou 1910, seemed to leave little further to be said.

French numismatists, however, more concerned with the monetary units involved than with the date of the *Lex Salica*, continued to discuss the identity of the *denarius* and the origins of the sou of 12 deniers, with variants on solutions already proposed by Prou (1892a, i–xiii) and Babelon (1901). There was a sudden crop of articles and notes in the 1920s by Dieudonné (1920b, 1923, 1926), supplemented by Naville (1922) and Tourneur (1923), though Dieudonné, influenced by Le Gentilhomme 1940b, subsequently changed his mind on some points of substance (Dieudonné 1939, 1943). In 1947 the issue figured conspicuously in the absurd attempt of Simon Stein to demonstrate that the *Lex Salica* was a ninth-century forgery of Archbishop Hincmar of Rheims (Stein 1947, esp. pp. 407–9; demolished by Wallace-Hadrill 1952, amongst others). Karl August Eckhardt, who was responsible for what are now the standard editions of most of the *Germanenrechte* and of the only satisfactory edition of the Salic code, did his best to master the literature (Eckhardt 1951, esp. the bibliography on p. 16 n. 66), but his final conclusions, as set out in the introduction to his edition of the *Pactus legis Salicae* (Eckhardt 1954, 189–92), did not satisfy all numismatists. The matter remains an open one, and the argument that follows develops the point of view expressed by Grierson very briefly in Wallace-Hadrill 1952, 112 n. 1.

The reduction in the weight of the solidus and tremissis, which has played a prominent role in the discussion, may be dismissed as irrelevant. It occurred in the second half of the sixth century, and while it apparently resulted from the adoption of a Germanic weight standard, it was not in Germanic units that the compensations of the Salic Law were formulated. The basic term is denarius, with solidus as a supplementary gloss, and not words cognate with the *sceat* and *scillinc* of Kentish law (below, p. 157). Since the authors of the code were perfectly capable of using Germanic terms when they wished – and frequently, to the confusion of commentators, did so – one can only assume that the penalties were traditionally reckoned in terms of Roman silver coins, which would have been appropriate to a West German people settled on the Roman frontier and also more available to small farmers than much more valuable solidi. But when the laws were committed to writing, silver 'denarii' were no longer current, and there was no alternative to giving their equivalences in solidi. The relative values would have taken account of the market ratio between gold and silver and could fortunately be rounded off at the convenient figure of 40, i.e. two score, the phrase *tanti denarii qui valuit tanti solidi* being repeated each time because of the formalism that pervades all early legal codes.

If the code cannot be earlier than 507, or later than 511 because of the division of the kingdom after Clovis' death, the solidi must have been the standard imperial solidi of the day, whether imperial originals or Germanic imitations, i.e. coins of a theoretical 24 siliquae or 4.55g. They would have been the same kind of solidi as made up the Vedrin hoard (below, p. 113) and of which a hundred, or perhaps rather more, were found in the tomb of Childeric (Chiflet 1655, 251–6; Dumas 1975), though the mixed character of these, involving over half a dozen fifth-century emperors of whom two were usurpers, makes it unlikely that they represent an imperial gift from Constantinople as has been suggested (Werner 1971). They will not have been the solidi of 3.9g, i.e. of 60 grains, which did not yet exist, or the *solidi gallici* of the fifth century, which were inferior to official issues in fineness, not in weight.

Solidi of 4.55g, at a value ratio of 1:40, imply that the denarii of the Salic Law would have been silver coins equivalent to about 0.11g of gold. One of the gold:silver ratios we have for the fifth century, a constitution of 422 (*Cod. Theod.* 8.4.27) allowing *primipilares* to substitute four solidi for each pound of silver due in fees to higher officials, is of a limited and concessionary nature – this is implied by the provision that the *primipilares* can pay in silver if they are feeling generous – and the ratio of 1:18 it implies can be neglected. What was evidently closer to the normal ratio is the general provision of a constitution of 397 (*Cod. Theod.* 13.2.1) allowing anyone owing silver to the treasury to pay in gold at the rate of 5 solidi a pound, i.e. at a ratio of 1:14.4, but implying that such a rate is favourable and the silver is really worth a little more. If we assume a ratio of 1:14, we would expect the denarius of the Salic Law to be a silver coin of about 1.5g. This enables us to exclude two possibilities, the denarii of the early Empire and the minuscule silver coins of the late fifth and early sixth centuries which are mainly known to us as grave goods in Frankish tombs.

Republican and early Imperial denarii have played a role in the discussion partly because of Tacitus' tribute to their popularity amongst the Germans (*Germ.* 5), partly because of the scale on which they have been found in hoards beyond the Rhine (above, p. 12), but mainly because of the presence of some two hundred in Childeric's tomb. Chiflet (1655, 270) gives a list of 42 that he had actually seen, ranging from the late Republic to Constantius II but concentrated in the later second century (Hadrian to Commodus); four of them, which he illustrates, had been pierced for use as jewellery. They differ completely in date from the gold solidi of the tomb, which are coins current in Childeric's own day, and must represent a hoard, or part of a hoard, that had chanced to fall into the king's hand. Chiflet does not give the weights, but denarii of Antoninus Pius and Marcus Aurelius in good condition weigh *c.* 3.6g, having probably been struck 90 to the lb, and even allowing for the fact that the denarii reaching Germany would often have been very worn the discrepancy between this weight and 1.5g is far too great for such coins to have been the denarii of the Salic Law. (The solitary second-century denarius in the late fifth-century Vedrin hoard of solidi, though badly mutilated, still weighed 2.86g.) Coins of this kind would normally have been used as sources of bullion or as jewellery, like four of Childeric's coins, and not as currency.

If early imperial denarii were too heavy, however, the *minuti argentei* of Frankish tombs are too light. Their weight varied between *c.* 0.15g and *c.* 0.4g (below, p. 111), and by no stretch of the imagination could they have ever been reckoned 40 to the solidus. They were, in any case, 'current' after a fashion in Clovis' time, and if they had really been the denarii of the Salic Law the glosses *qui valuit tanti solidi* would have been superfluous.

The coins in question must in fact have been the 'siliquae' of Honorius (393–423) and his successors, which were reduced in weight shortly after the death of Theodosius I in 395. The siliquae of the preceding decades had been coins of *c.* 1.9g, though since they were struck *al marco* and not *al pezzo* their weights commonly vary between 1.8g and 2.1g. Under Honorius, and perhaps in 397, the weight was reduced to *c.* 1.5g (*RIC* IX. xxviii), and the resulting quite common coins would have been those which the Franks found circulating in northern Gaul as they began to expand from their initial settlements in the lower Rhineland and Toxandria during the political vacuum that followed the breakdown of the Rhine frontier in 407. What the silver coins were termed by the Roman provincials we do not know – *siliqua* states simply what modern numismatists have believed their value to have been – and it may well have been denarius. In any case a Germanic people, familiar with this as the traditional name of Roman silver coins, would have found it a natural term to use. Moreover, this early phase of expansion is that in which the penalties of the laws would have been formulated as precisely as possible before they were forgotten. A century later, when after the much wider expansion under Clovis the laws came to be written down, it was found necessary to adapt the penalties to a society that no longer knew silver 'denarii', and substitute gold solidi instead.

This still leaves undetermined the origins of the solidus of 12 denarii. The earliest formal statement of this reckoning that can be dated with certainty is in the circular of the Mayor of the Palace Carloman of 1 March 743 sending out the acts of the Council of Estinnes (*Liftinas*), for a clause prescribing the tax of a solidus per *casata* for the benefit of the Church glosses the word *solidus* with the phrase *id est duodecim denarii* (MGH, *Concilia* I.7, cap. 2) lest recipients should think that the 40-denarius unit was intended. A total of *cautiones* expressed in solidi and denarii in a Le Mans document of 721, however, as Ferdinand Lot pointed out, only works out correctly for solidi of 12 denarii (Lot 1921, 122–3, 128–9). It is also possible that the well-known passage in the Ripuarian Law (cap. 40.12 in MGH, *Leges* III.2 (1954), 95; cf. pp. 150–1) which sets out how payments stated in solidi could be settled in cattle or other goods and ends with valuing the solidus at 12 denarii (*quod si cum argento solvere contigerit, pro solido duodecim denarios, sicut antiquitus est constitutum*) may be still earlier, but it has a Carolingian flavour about it and may be later. The texts of 721 and 743 are clear, however, and since the weight of the denier had not changed it is reasonable to assume that this was the value of the late Merovingian denier from the first.

When it came into existence, however, the new denier would have to be related to the current tremissis, and here there would seem to be two possibilities. One is that the debasement of the tremissis had gone so far that the gold content of three of them, i.e. of a notional solidus, was worth only twelve of the new silver coins. The other is that since gold solidi were virtually never struck except at Marseille, the word 'solidus', as that of the basic denomination in normal use, had come to be applied to the tremissis, and so that this coin, either debased or pure, was worth 12 deniers. Such a change in terminology from, say, the reign of Dagobert onwards was envisaged as a possibility by Amécourt (1883a, 11 n. 1), and Grierson was for long of the same opinion. In its favour was the situation in England, where the Germanic term *scillinc* for the basic monetary unit seems to have been applied to the 20-grain gold coin of tremissis size from the first (below, p. 157).

But it would have been more natural to relate the denier to the current solidus, and the revised version of the Alamannic Law (MGH, *Leges Germ.* VI.1; 2nd edn, 1966), which by its references to Duke Lantfrid (712–30) and King Chlotar IV (717–19) can be dated to 717/719, shows in its compensations that the distinction between solidus and tremissis was still maintained in the early eighth century in at least one part of the Frankish kingdom. The fineness of tremisses, furthermore, had fallen by the 660s to between 30% and 40% (Kent 1972a). If we assume a figure of one-third, the gold content of the notional solidus would have been about 1.3g and a silver denier of the same weight would have had the value of about its twelfth. It is true that the gold:silver ratio may not have been precisely 1:12 – this figure is only attested two hundred years later in clause 24 of the Edict of Pîtres of 864 (MGH, *Capitularia*, II. 320) –

but it is likely to have been of the same order. The much lower values of the solidus in the *Lex Frisonum* (cf. Scholten 1945; Siems 1980, 222–65) would have reflected the much poorer content of the debased tremissis in Frisia, just as the four- and five-penny shillings of the Mercians and West Saxons did that of the final stages of the debasement of the English thrymsa (below, p. 157).

(e) METROLOGY AND FINENESS

The initial weights of the basic Frankish denominations, the solidus and tremissis, were as they had been in late Roman times: 24 and 8 siliquae respectively in the units used at the time, or in modern terms 4.55g and 1.52g if one assumes the correctness of the traditional equivalent of the Roman pound as 327.45g. These figures, or ones approximating to them, are the weights of the early pseudo-imperial solidi and tremisses in good condition, and the solidi and tremisses of Theodebert I. The weights are usually a little less in practice, partly through wear and partly through irregularities in minting, but not more so than is the case with regular imperial issues.

Later Merovingian tremisses of the 'national' period, however, weigh a little under 1.3g, and the much rarer solidi about 3.9g. These figures are too much below the traditional weights to be accidental, and it is clear that an intentional weight reduction has been made. The change is best interpreted (above, p. 14) as the substitution of a Germanic standard based on the (Troy) grain or barleycorn of 0.065g, the new coins having a theoretical weight of 20 grains. Many coins in practice fell below this figure, but it could be very closely attained. Translating the published grams into grains, only 6 of the 37 Frankish coins in the Sutton Hoo hoard fall below 19gr. and only one rises above 21gr.; the average is 19.6gr. In the Crondall hoard only two of the 25 Frankish coins fall below 19gr. and none rises above 20.2gr.; the average is 19.6gr., only just short of the 20.0gr. of the Anglo-Saxon coins in the hoard. Although the figure of 20gr. is attested by no Frankish text comparable to the passages in the Kentish code of Æthelbert (below, p. 157) showing the Germanic shilling as weighing 20 sceattas (grains), there seems every reason to take the same adjustment as the explanation of the weight change in the two countries.

The new coins were assumed not to require explanation to most of the population, but at Marseille, and in many Provençal, Burgundian and other mints under its influence in the southern and eastern parts of the kingdom, it was thought best to record it for literate users, partly because the coins would be used by foreigners and partly because more heavily Romanized areas, with their traditional Mediterranean background, were less familiar with Germanic weight standards and preferred the siliqua-carat to which they were accustomed. A reduced solidus of 60 grains instead of 24 siliquae would weigh between 21 and 20 siliquae, so that Provençal solidi are marked XXI or XX, usually the former. A reduced tremissis of 20 grains would fall between 6 and 7 siliquae but be much closer to 7, so VII is regularly marked on the coins. No explanation for the figures is usually offered, but some moneyers at mints in Burgundy – Chalon-sur-Saône, Autun, Mâcon, Besançon and Moutiers-en-Tarantaise – added the phrase DE SELEGAS or variant in the inscription (**1.395**: VESVNCIONE DE SELEQVS), and this, as Deloche (1880) pointed out, is to be read with the VII in the field as a statement of weight of the coin, warning literate users that it was no longer the traditional tremissis of 8 siliquae.

The same duality of weight occurred in the silver coins, but in this case with the Roman element lighter than the Germanic one. Twenty-five years ago Lafaurie published an illuminating graph of weights in which, superimposed on each other, were shown the weights of all deniers in the Cabinet des Médailles, the deniers of the Bais hoard, and the deniers of Pepin and Charlemagne prior to the reform of 793/4 (Lafaurie 1961, 259). The first two of these showed two peaks, one in the weight interval 1.0g/1.1g and the other in the interval 1.1g/1.2g (all deniers) or 1.2g/1.3g (Bais only). It was clear even then that the pattern was distorted by the huge number of Provençal coins from the Cimiez hoard in the BN, and Lafaurie subsequently both corrected the figures – not all early weighings were reliable – and refined their analysis, the coins in the various hoards being shown separately, though the first graph has by no means lost its value (Lafaurie 1981d, xxv–xxxvii). It is clear that deniers of two different weights were in circulation, largely in different parts of the country, one group of coins weighing *c.* 1.1g and the other weighing *c.* 1.3g.

Lafaurie has tended to interpret these in terms of their relationship to the Roman pound, but it is more likely that they resulted from the same Germanic/Roman duality as was the case with the gold. The coins of a theoretical 1.3g were of the same weight as the reduced tremissis, i.e. 20 grains, and it is this weight, as one would expect, that predominated in Neustria and Austrasia and is the original weight of the Frisian and English sceat (below, pp. 150ff). The lighter weight, which predominated in Provence, is meaningless in terms of grains but is very close to that of the Roman scruple (*scripulum*) of 6 siliquae, or 1.14g, and may have represented that figure. When by the capitulary of Vernon in 754/5 Pepin laid down that not more than 22 solidi, i.e. 264 coins, should be struck to the pound (below, p. 204), and thus established the standard of the pre-reform deniers of Pepin and Charlemagne, he was in effect abolishing the light Roman/Provençal standard, for 264 coins to the Roman lb of 327.45g would give a coin of 1.24g, effectively the same as one of 20 grains.

With regard to fineness, much information has become available in recent years. For the gold, Metcalf at Oxford, in association with various specialists, published a series of figures mainly based on milliprobe analysis for material in the Ashmolean or made available there (Hawkes *et al.* 1966; Metcalf *et al.* 1968; Merrick and Metcalf 1969; Metcalf and Schweizer 1970). Kent, in connection with his study of the Sutton Hoo coins, set in motion a far-reaching project for analysing hundreds of coins by the specific gravity and other methods in the hope that changing standards in fineness might provide an objective basis for dating. The work was carried out by Oddy and a number of colleagues in Britain and the United States. Their published figures cover nearly a hundred coins in the British Museum, almost half of them from Sutton Hoo (Oddy *et al.* 1972), together with those for the coins in three Low Country hoards (Velsen, Escharen and Nietap) and in the English Crondall hoard (Oddy 1972a). Oddy at the same time ascertained the finenesses of the coins in the Grierson collection, which were deposited in the British Museum for the purpose. The results, though used by Kent, were not published in detail by him and are made available in the text of the catalogue here for the first time. A number of further figures, mainly from material in Paris, are provided in Stahl 1982 for the extensive series of CA coins he was studying, though since he is not an expert and used less sophisticated apparatus the results, as he admits (p. 16), are likely to be less reliable than those of Oddy.

Apart from the general statement that there was over the years an evident general decline in the fineness of Merovingian gold, first in the period of the pseudo-imperial coinage and subsequently in that of the national coinage, it is difficult to know how best to interpret these figures or whether, in detail, any precise interpretation of them is possible at all. Metcalf initially proposed to fit them into a pattern of systematic reductions in fineness by one-sevenths, i.e. through a 'reduced' tremissis of 7 siliquae having successively one, two, three . . . of its notional siliquae replaced by silver (Metcalf *et al.* 1968). This view was accepted by Bendixen (1974, 88–9), but it assumes a degree of central control which is highly unlikely, involves a fraction that does not look probable, and is based on figures that were too few to begin with and of which some seem to be dubious, for while the footnotes to the tables in Oddy 1972a, 117–18, show that in the six cases of Crondall coins analysed by both milliprobe and specific gravity methods three agree quite closely (58/62%, 62/64%, 71/75%), for one there is only a moderate agreement (74/80%) and for two, Quentovic coins of Dutta, the discrepancy is wide (71/59%, 71/57%). Kent's study of a much larger number of figures, in an attempt to relate the finenesses of Sutton Hoo to those of coins bearing royal names and therefore roughly datable, was sharply criticized by Brown (1981), who showed that while the Sutton Hoo date remained acceptable the grouping of the figures was arbitrary and their statistical treatment often quite misleading.

Even if the detailed figures for the BN material ascertained by Kent were available we might well not be much the wiser. The varying quality of the gold content of coins in a single hoard shows that users were prepared to accept as currency whatever came their way. Nominally the coins must all have had the same 'value', and probably users would be satisfied by eliminating any that were plainly false, like the tremissis of plated copper that formerly made part of the Crondall hoard (Grierson 1970). If they disliked the colour of some they could presumably resort to the touchstone, an object sometimes included amongst Frankish grave goods (Werner 1954), and insist on being allowed a discount. Even if the kings sometimes tried to establish a standard, for which there is no evidence, one has the impression that the moneyers melted down what gold came their way without any attempt to ascertain its alloy or to purify it before turning it into coin. This was, after all, something that would have been beyond the capacity or resources of an ordinary goldsmith, even if a large mint like Chalon or Limoges would have been able to undertake it, as indeed we are given to believe they sometimes did (above, p. 100, but cf. p. 128). Decline in quality would not be uniform, but would be a natural consequence of repeated meltings and remeltings, especially since jewellery and pieces of plate would often have gone into a 'melt'. Gregory of Tours (*Hist. Franc.* VII. 24) tells how a bishop of Poitiers had a gold chalice melted down and turned into coin (*in numisma redactum*) when he needed to buy off a plundering expedition, and the interchangeability between plate, jewellery and coin is a phenomenon in all societies. Pieces of plate that were supposedly of gold, however, would often have been of silver gilt, and the mounts of jewellery are often of inferior fineness.

The same picture obtains for the silver, though since virtually no deniers exist with royal names we lack a comparable basis for establishing their chronology. The evidence for the main Merovingian series is virtually limited to that published by Metcalf (1983a) for the material in this collection. It is repeated in summary form (i.e. figures for silver content, ignoring those for such minor constituents as tin and bismuth) in the text of the catalogue. Some mints were clearly able to maintain a high quality of silver of 90% or over, not far removed from the argent-le-roi and sterling silver of later times, but in other mints the silver was poor and even in 'good' mints poor quality coins do occur. Coins of Marseille of the same type and sometimes even struck by the same dies can have figures as disparate as 93% and 65% (**1.559–60**), or 82% and 54% (**1.567–8**). One cannot assume any formal change in the alloy, or even any intentional dishonesty on the part of the moneyers. The more likely explanation, once again, is that moneyers normally melted down whatever silver came their way, with no more than a rough estimation of quality, and turned it into coin, and that users, as is clear from the hoards, did not differentiate between their quality. The same was to occur in the Carolingian period, where despite frequent legal prescriptions for the use of pure silver, the coins in the Bourgneuf hoard, which were chemically analysed in the 1890s by the French mint (below, p. 194), show equally extraordinary variations in fineness.

(f) CLASSIFICATION

The chaotic and highly localized character of Merovingian coinage makes a wholly satisfactory arrangement of it impossible. The objections to Prou's reliance on Roman administrative divisions have been noted already, and even with the help of the subsequent analysis by Farcinet (above, p. 81) one cannot obtain any clear picture of the coinage from his catalogue. An alphabetical arrangement like that of Belfort is useful for reference, but it makes neither historical nor numismatic sense and runs up against the many problems created by semi-legible inscriptions and uncertainties over mint attributions. Ponton d'Amécourt once suggested (*ASFN* 1875, 68–70) the use of the regions enumerated in a charter of Dagobert III (711–15) to Bishop Rigobert of Rheims. In this the estates of the see, other than those held locally, are described as being situated in Austrasia, Neustria, Burgundy, the region of Marseille (*in partibus Massiliae*), Auvergne (*Arvernio*), Rouergue (or ?the Rhône valley: *Rodonico*), Gévaudan (*Gavilitano*), Touraine or Poitou (*Turonico seu Pictavico*), Limousin (*Lemovico*), or elsewhere, the latter perhaps including Gascony (*Wasconia*), an uncomfortable frontier region with which the bishop was to become better acquainted when he was deposed and exiled there by Charles Martel. Although such an arrangement leaves some gaps, it would correspond in some measure to the stylistic grouping of the coins.

A smaller collection like this, however, can follow a broad regional arrangement without fear of confusion, especially if the silver is kept separate from the gold, as on chronological grounds it clearly should be. The coins on Plates 20–30 are therefore arranged under the broad headings of Burgundy and Provence, Aquitaine, Neustria, Austrasia and Frisia, and within these in alphabetical order of mints according to their modern spellings. Unidentified mints, where legible, are listed under their Latin forms in whatever region they seem on stylistic or other grounds to belong, and the same is done for coins with still undeciphered inscriptions. Unattributed coins of uncertain regional groupings are put at the end, and the consequent layout may be summarized as in the table opposite.

Discrepancies in the grouping of the gold and silver are in part a consequence of changes in the geographical density of mints and mint output, but in the main reflect the uneven represen-

<table>
<tr><th>Region</th><th>Gold
nos.</th><th>Silver
nos.</th></tr>
<tr><td>Burgundy and Provence</td><td>392–420</td><td>539–78</td></tr>
<tr><td>Aquitaine</td><td>421–50</td><td>579–95</td></tr>
<tr><td>Neustria</td><td>451–88</td><td rowspan="2">} 596–613</td></tr>
<tr><td>Austrasia</td><td rowspan="2">} 489–522</td></tr>
<tr><td>Frisia</td><td>633–64</td></tr>
<tr><td>Uncertain</td><td>523–38</td><td>614–32</td></tr>
</table>

tation of mints in the collection. This likewise explains the incongruous linking of such regions as Burgundy and Provence, and of Austrasia and Neustria, which in a larger collection could be advantageously kept separate. Inadequacies in coverage are inevitable in a coinage like that of the Merovingian period. Many mints are known only from one to five coins and must consequently be unrepresented in any individual collection, and even some important mints are by chance represented here by only one or two coins, or even by none at all.

The earlier pseudo-imperial tremisses on Plates 18 and 19 are arranged roughly under the names of emperors when these can be deciphered, and are consequently in rough chronological order, but on many the legends are totally blundered and the coins are grouped according to style. A few Merovingian coins from southern Gaul are probably mixed in with the earlier pseudo-imperial 'Visigothic' issues on Plates 10 and 11.

B. PSEUDO-IMPERIAL AND OTHER COINAGES, *c.* 500–570/580

(a) GENERAL FEATURES

The coinage of Frankish Gaul during this period consisted mainly of pseudo-imperial solidi and tremisses of normal weight, copied in part from Ostrogothic models but bearing the names, increasingly blundered by the passage of time, of Byzantine emperors. They are described in the next section (b). There were also limited royal coinages, partly carrying on from those of the Burgundians and Ostrogoths and limited to Burgundy and Provence, partly arising from the personal vanity of Theodebert I (534–48) and struck in the aftermath of his invasion of Italy in the 540s. They are described in section (c). There was also a marginal coinage of what are best called *minuti argentei*, very light and fragile silver coins varying in weight from about 0.15g to 0.4g which have been discovered in Frankish graves scattered over a wide area but for the most part in the region between the Seine and the Rhine. Since virtually every known specimen has come to light in the course of excavations they are not represented in this collection, but account must be taken of their existence.

The normal obverse type of the coins is a profile imperial bust and the reverse type some derivative of a seated Roma, though there are such variants as a standing soldier with a spear or a figure carrying a cross. They are in any case figural types going back to late Roman models, making them quite distinct from the sixth-century Frankish coins of Provence with monograms which derived their inspiration from coins of the Ostrogoths (below, pp. 115–16). It is often difficult to distinguish 'Roman' originals (cf. Cahn 1938; Grierson 1983b), minted initially at Trier and subsequently in the so-called 'kingdom of Syagrius', from Germanic and mainly Frankish imitations. Many of those with the names of Western emperors of the second half of the fifth century down to Anastasius, and even to Justinian in the mid sixth century, have relatively correct legends, while others have no more than jumbled letters or series of meaningless strokes.

These early silver coins were initially studied by Cumont and Prou on the basis of coins found at Eprave near Dinant in Belgium and at Ville Dommange near Rheims in France (Cumont 1890, 1893; Prou 1891). A comprehensive and masterly survey, with a bibliography and a map of finds, was provided by Lafaurie as a background to his description of a specimen found in 1961 at Fleury-sur-Orne in Normandy (Lafaurie 1964b; the map of finds on p. 211 is now superseded by that in Lafaurie 1971d, 187), and further discoveries of varying importance have come to light since he wrote. One may mention particularly those at Ouerre (dép. Eure-et-Loir) near Chartres (Lafaurie 1966b), Hérouvillette (Calvados) in Normandy (Lafaurie 1971d), Genainville (Val-d'Oise) north-west of Paris (Mitard 1978), and Vron (Somme) and Houdain (Nord) near Lille (Dhénin 1980b; cf. Dhénin 1970), as well as Lafaurie's re-examination of those found by the abbé Cochet at Envermeu (Seine-Maritime) in Normandy in the last century (Lafaurie 1978d).

Although most of these coins have been pierced for use as jewellery this can be ascribed to their having been found as grave goods, and there is no doubt that many of them must have been made, either officially or unofficially, as small change. It is possible, however, that they were made specifically for distributions to the poor, as seems to have been the main function of the tiny half-siliquae of the early fifth century and was to be that of some coins of unusually low denominations in late medieval times, when their function was signalled by their being known collectively as *moneta pauperum*, a phrase sometimes used in their inscriptions. A tenth-century text that is shown by its context to be a copy of a sixth- or seventh-century one listing the office-holders of the Merovingian court (Conrat 1908, esp. pp. 248–9; cf. Wallace-Hadrill 1962, 217–18) alludes to the way in which, in the royal presence, the treasurer (*consul*) responsible for the royal gifts would scatter tiny silver coins (*minutos argenteos*) to be scrabbled for by the poor under the benevolent smile of the sovereign (*Interdum consul coram rege minutos argenteos super planam terram spargit, ut certatim pauperes propriis et velocissimis manibus sibi, ut valuerint, rapiant, ut letus rex aspiciat subridens*). Such 'coins' could serve as money: Gregory of Tours has a tale (*De virtut. S. Martini* I.31) of a dishonest cleric pretending to have received in alms an *argenteus* when he had really received a *trians*, and another (*In glor. confessorum*, cap. 110) of a dishonest entrepreneur buying wine for a *trians* and retailing it for *argentei* after diluting it with water on such a scale that he soon made a profit of 100 solidi. Unless these are merely pious anecdotes repeated from one source to another, they are events that must have occurred during Gregory's youth, for no silver coins remained in circulation in Gaul in the 570s and 580s, at the time that he was writing.

(b) PSEUDO-IMPERIAL SOLIDI AND TREMISSES

The Franks seem to have struck no solidi of their own prior to *c*. 500, or perhaps even during the lifetime of Clovis. This is the only conclusion to be drawn from the contents of the Vedrin hoard of solidi of Leo I and Zeno, buried in the early 490s, for Vedrin lies just outside Namur and in territory well settled by the Franks (Lallemand 1965). The hundred or so solidi found in 1653 in the tomb of Clovis' father Childeric at Tournai were likewise all imperial, for although virtually all were lost in the great Paris theft of 1831 we have sufficiently good illustrations of the twelve different types that were represented to be able to judge (Chiflet 1655, 252; Werner 1971; Dumas 1975). That pseudo-imperial Frankish solidi only started with coins of Anastasius can also be inferred from the contents of the small hoard found in 1807 at Houdain-lez-Bavai (dép. Nord) south-east of Tournai in the heart of Clovis' kingdom and buried either shortly before or after his death. Five of the seven gold coins it contained (Gricourt 1960) appear to have been normal imperial solidi and the only imitations were two of Anastasius closely resembling **1.343**.

By the 520s, however, there was an abundant Frankish coinage of pseudo-imperial solidi. The main evidence for this comes from the contents of the Chinon hoard of 81 solidi. These consisted of a very worn one of Zeno, of which no details are available and which was probably a regular issue, and 80 imitations, 70 struck in the names of Anastasius and 10 in that of Justin I (Robert 1882a; cf. Grierson 1975). Two were Ostrogothic and a few were Burgundian, with the monograms of Gundobald (d. 516) and Sigismund (516–24), but the rest were imitations that from the location of the hoard – Chinon (dép. Indre-et-Loire) is in central France, south-west of Tours – can only have been Frankish. In 1882 Robert published 37 of them that had been acquired by Gariel, with indications of the identities of the others. The legends are blundered in various ways and they clearly came from more than one mint, though they have about them a strong family likeness and are quite different from pseudo-imperial Visigothic and Burgundian coins. Many have letters in the field (e.g. H, A, AL, M) which probably stood for mints (eg. L for *Lugdunum*, Laon), since this had been Roman practice and seems to have occurred on some of Theodebert's solidi (below, p. 117), or in some other way identified issues; moneyers' initials are scarcely possible at so early a date. Gariel gave a few of his coins to the museum of Auxerre but most were dispersed as lots 299–329 in the sale of his collection (Hoffman 27.4.1885); presumably the others that he had not acquired had already gone to other collectors. One of the coins here (**1.347**) is certainly from the hoard, for it is shown on Robert's plate.

The other Anastasius imitations (**1.343–6**, **1.348**) are all stylistically related to ones in the Chinon hoard or to ones from isolated finds in former Frankish territory; **1.343**, for example, resembles the Houdain coins, a Chinon coin, and one found in a grave at Hordain south of Lille (Dhénin 1980b), though a systematic study of these has yet to be made. A later hoard discovered at Viviers in 1926 apparently dated from the mid 530s, after the downfall of the Burgundian kingdom, but most of it was dispersed and our accounts of it are very inadequate. It was in any case more Burgundian than Frankish in composition (Vassy 1928; also the partially independent notes of Blanchet in *RN* 1929, 110–11, and *RN* 1932, 116). A hoard found in 1804 at *Alesia*, i.e. Alise-Sainte-Reine (dép. Côte-d'Or), which contained coins of Theodebert I and so must be later than 534, can be partially constructed from contemporary accounts and the registers of the Cabinet des Médailles, which acquired over seventy coins from it (Testart 1907; Lafaurie 1983d, superseding Lafaurie 1959, 1966a). It consisted of some 350 solidi and tremisses, the latter predominating in the proportion of eight to one, together with a number of other gold and silver objects.

Pseudo-imperial tremisses did in fact form the main coinage of sixth-century Gaul, and the sequence of the four emperors in whose names the Frankish ones were issued – Anastasius I (491–518), Justin I (518–27), Justinian (527–65) and Justin II (565–78) – gives a rough chronological framework for the coinage, though we cannot assume too close a correspondence with changes of ruler at Constantinople. It is in any case not always easy to distinguish a badly blundered IVSTINVS from an equally badly blundered IVSTINIANVS, the clue being often the break in the legend above the emperor's head. On imperial issues these are IVS–TINVS and IVSTI–NIANVS, with the position of the T often more revealing than the presence or absence of a badly formed A. The occurrence of Justin's name twice in the series is a minor problem, for blundering was much worse in the 570s than it had been in the 520s and the later coins can easily be distinguished. Some coins, of course, have no recognizable traces of an imperial name at all. On Plate 19 three coins (**1.385–7**) have been added to the series that are certainly later than Justin II, but they may not be Frankish at all.

If the chronology is reasonably clear, however, the same is not true of localization. There are basically two reverse types, a facing Victory – more precisely, a Victory advancing towards the spectator and looking left – holding a wreath and globus cruciger, and a profile Victory – more precisely, a Victory advancing right – holding a palm (or trophy) and a wreath. Tomasini (1964) in his study of the latter type characterized them as the VPW ('Victory with palm and wreath') and VGC ('Victory with globe and cross') types, and these convenient acronyms will be employed here. The VGC type was characteristic of Ostrogothic Italy and it was mainly adopted in the mints of Austrasia and Neustria, i.e. all the northern half of the Frankish kingdom. The VPW type started as a very restricted special issue in Italy and was adopted by Theoderic for the Visigothic kingdom when he took this over in 509 (above, p. 35). From there it spread to neighbouring Frankish Aquitaine and was adopted by Gundobald for the Burgundian kingdom, where it continued to dominate after Burgundy's conquest by the Franks in the 530s.

A regional classification must be based primarily on the find evidence, coupled with the identification of particular groups with stylistic features which are continued in later series on which mint names occur. The find evidence is patchy. One very important hoard of the 560s found in the 1930s at Monneren (dép. Moselle), north-east of Metz, and consisting mainly of VGC issues, is known only through a plate of casts published by Reinhart (1939a), for nothing has since been heard of the coins and they are generally believed to have been lost in the War. The Velsen hoard of about the same date (Chijs 1866, 353–60 and pls. 22–3; Lafaurie and Zadoks-Jitta 1958; Oddy 1972a) comes from the province of Noord Holland, west of Amsterdam, so that although its contents are important they throw no light on the place of origin of the coins. The Alesia hoard just noted of 1804 is essentially one of VPW imitations of both the Aquitanian ('Visigothic') and Burgundian varieties. For France there is also much casual information about single finds and smaller groups, but it has yet to be brought together and systematically studied in the way that the German material was brought together by Werner (1935). Find evidence can in any case be sometimes misleading. The plates in Chijs 1866, which for the most part illustrate coins found in the Netherlands, include many tremisses which other evidence shows to have been minted in Burgundy, but which reached the Low Countries because Burgundy lay on the main route connecting the lower Rhineland with the Mediterranean.

The collection here is too small to justify any systematic attempt at a regional classification. The majority of the VPW coins from southern Gaul have been included with the Visigothic series on Plates 10 and 11, since no satisfactory criteria have yet been proposed for distinguishing Frankish from early Visigothic issues and it seemed therefore desirable to keep them all together for the convenience of students. The only exceptions are **1.349–50**, **360–1**, **383** which are unlike any that are clearly Visigothic and are best treated as Frankish. A coin that must have been struck in Burgundy after the Frankish conquest (**1.342**) has also been put at the end of the Burgundian series to show the continuity of style.

The majority of the tremisses (**1.351**ff.) on Plates 18 and 19 are consequently of the VGC type, and range from coins of very good style and fabric to ones on which the designs are no more than caricatures and the inscriptions completely meaningless. A number (e.g. **1.366**) display what Amécourt (1877a) described as the 'boucle perdue' type of bust, with the tails of the diadem detached from the head and forming a separate loop in the field, and are attributable to a long series of Austrasian and Burgundian mints. Many show a tendency for the Victory to be reversed from right to left (**1.366–8**), the bust being sometimes reversed as well (**1.368**). A Victory with peculiar dotted wings (**1.378–80**) seems to be characteristic of the upper Rhineland and Alamannia (Reinhart 1939a, with excellent illustrations); specimens were found in a tomb at Munningen in Bavaria (Cahn 1930) as well as in other graves studied by Werner (1935). The notes on individual coins suggest parallels from other sources and possible localizations.

A few pseudo-imperial tremisses have letters in the field or at the end of the inscriptions which have been interpreted as references to rulers or mints. Lenormant (1848–54) proposed to treat an initial reversed C and a terminal C in the obverse legends as a *marque chlodovienne*, the initial of Clovis and three of his sons. This view has been rejected by all subsequent scholars, but Lafaurie (1968a) adheres to the view that a terminal ·T·, i.e. a T conspicuously picked out by a pellet on either side, stands for *Theodericus* and that such coins should be attributed to Thierry I (511–34). Although there are a few cases in other series where a similar interpretation is certain – a terminal *theta* or monogram on rare solidi of Theoderic the Ostrogoth (above, p. 35), the terminal S interpreted as the initial of Sigismund of Burgundy (above, p. 76; **1.340**) – the attribution is not wholly convincing, and the specimen in the collection here (**1.187**) has been left amongst the anonymous issues.

(c) ROYAL ISSUES

In addition to the pseudo-imperial Frankish series of the first two-thirds of the sixth century there are two royal ones, distinct from each other though having one ruler in common, each localized and resulting from special circumstances. The first consisted only of silver and copper coins in Burgundy and Provence that succeeded the coinages of the Ostrogoths in Provence and of the Burgundians further north. The second are the gold coins of Theodebert I (534–48), famous because their solidi, in the eyes of at least some Byzantines, infringed the imperial monopoly of striking coins of this denomination.

The first series is represented here by two bronze nummi, one (**1.391**) of Childebert I king of Paris (511–58), and the other (**1.388**) of his brother Thierry I of Metz (511–34). They acquired part of the Burgundian kingdom in 523/4, and Childebert divided the rest of it with Thierry's son Theodebert after the defeat and death of Gundomar II in 534 (above, p. 75). The coinage as a whole consists of small silver and bronze coins struck in the names or with the monograms of Childebert and of two or possibly three successive kings of Austrasia, Thierry I (511–34), Theodebert I (534–48) and Theodebald (548–55), the reading of the monogram of the third not being certain. The attribution of a further monogram to Guntramn, who succeeded his father Chlotar I in Burgundy and Provence in 561, must be regarded as doubtful, since it is not likely that the coinage lasted so long. Some of the coins are identified by the royal names in full (TEVDERICI, REX HELDEBERT, etc.), others only by their monograms, the reverse types being normally a cross or Christogram. There are also anonymous coins having as types only a Christogram and a cross, and others with monograms of uncertain interpretation. Since the coins are bronze, one cannot exclude the possibility of these being the names of local governors or other officials, not of kings at all. They are mainly known from excavations carried out at Marseille in the 1840s for the creation of the port of La Golette and subsequent more scientific ones over the past two decades (Lagoy 1843, 1856; Brenot 1980), though a few are known from other neighbouring sites, notably Saint-Rémy and Saint-Blaise (Rolland 1961; Lafaurie 1983a), and the mint is generally taken to be Marseille (Lafaurie 1973d). Mints of the small silver coins include Chalon-sur-Saône (CABILONNV) and Arles or perhaps Clermont (AR).

The other group of regal issues in this period is that struck in the name of Theodebert of Metz (534–48), represented here by a solidus (**1.389**) in the Lewis collection at Corpus Christi College that formerly made part of the Gariel collection. Some thirty-five solidi are known and nearly fifty tremisses (Lafaurie 1983d, 118), the extreme rarity of the coins on the market arising from their obvious historical interest, so that virtually all are now in museums. The solidi are normally of the regular imperial type of the fifth and early sixth centuries, with an armoured bust on the obverse and a Victory holding a long cross on the reverse, the obverse legends being some variant of DN THEODEBERTVS REX or VICTOR and the reverse the VICTORIA AVCC of imperial issues, but there are many variants. The most remarkable is a unique piece found in Belgium in the mid nineteenth century and now in the Cabinet des Médailles in Paris which has DN THEODEBERTVS VICTOR on the obverse and as reverse type a Victory trampling on a fallen enemy, an amalgam of the customary Victory with a common Western imperial type of the fifth century (Callu 1980). The tremisses normally have a Victory running right with palm and cross, and both solidi and tremisses usually have a letter or letters in the field.

There is no modern study that brings together the whole of the material, though a considerable literature on the subject exists. This is due in part to their exceptional character – nothing similar was struck by either of Theodebert's uncles Chlotar I or Childebert I, despite the fact that they controlled between them well over half the *regnum Francorum* – and in part to the fact that their existence is noted in the famous passage of Procopius, in which, reflecting on the Gothic recovery of Italy after the recall of Belisarius, he observed that Germanic peoples now occupied all the West, including Provence, where their kings could preside over chariot races at Arles and did not even scruple to strike gold coins bearing their own effigy and name (*Bell. Goth.* III.33.5–6). Their uniqueness and their abundance, however, are both explicable (Deloche 1886c). It was Theodebert and not his uncles who led the great Frankish invasion of Italy in 539 and despite serious reverses had subsequently succeeded in annexing much of the north with the revenues that went with it, while even earlier he had had a half-share of the 50,000 solidi that Theodahad had paid Childebert in 536, ostensibly as compensation for the murder of their cousin Amalasuntha (Greg. Tur. *Hist. Franc.* III.31). Theodebert had great resources in gold, and his successes were such as to go to the head of any ruler of the time.

What is less clear is where the coins were minted. The letters in the field, which are not always easy to decipher, are usually taken to represent mints: LAV C is Laon (*Lugdunum Clavatum*), COL V is Cologne (*Colunia* rather than the obsolete *Colonia Ubiorum*), M is Mainz (*Moguntiacum*) or more probably Metz (*Mediomatricum*: **1.389**), BO is Bonn (*Bona*), RE is Rheims (*Remis*), and so on, though other scholars have argued for a central mint at Metz (Deloche 1886c, 1888, 1890b; *contra* Robert 1887). The style of the solidi has even suggested to some scholars an Italian origin for the coins, with BO for Bologna (*Bononia*), or at least an Italian one for the die-sinkers (Prou 1892a, xxxii), but they do not in fact resemble Ostrogothic coins and indeed none seems to have been found in Italy. The style and type of the Victory on the tremisses points to a region influenced by the Burgundian coinage of Lyon and Chalon-sur-Saône, and the stylistic uniformity of the solidi, linked with the variety of letters in the field, suggests a single die-sinker working for an itinerant court and producing dies with mint-marks to match the royal residence of the moment, with perhaps a concentration of these in the Rhineland (Cologne, Bonn, Mainz) and central Austrasia (Metz, Verdun, Toul, Rheims). The minting may in any case have been quite a brief phenomenon – the three surviving solidi of Cologne, at Paris, Berlin, and London, were all struck by the same pair of dies (Hävernick 1935, 15, no. 4) – and the coinage was not continued by Theodebert's feeble son and successor Theodebald despite his having been sent much treasure from the eventually abortive Franco-Alamannic invasion of Italy in 553/4.

C. 'NATIONAL' GOLD COINAGE, *c.* 570/580–*c.* 670

(a) GENERAL FEATURES

The second phase of Frankish coinage, which lasted almost exactly a century, is essentially one of gold tremisses of reduced weight (1.3g), usually with some variety of cross as reverse type and as legends the name of the mint where the coin was struck and that of the moneyer responsible for it. This is, of course, an oversimplification. Solidi were still sometimes minted, and indeed formed part of the regular coinage at Marseille. There are coins bearing royal names and omitting those of the moneyer or mint. There are designs other than the cross. There are ecclesiastical coins without moneyers' names. There was in Provence, between *c.* 580 and 613, a reversion to minting in the names of the contemporary emperors at Byzantium. But these reservations do not seriously affect the fact that the Frankish 'national' coinage, from *c.* 570/80 to *c.* 670, was essentially one of reduced tremisses that have as types a bust and a cross and as inscription the names of mint and moneyer, the number of recorded mints usually being put at about 800 and the names of moneyers at over 1,500.

Some aspects of the coinage in this period have been discussed already: its limiting dates (pp. 90–5), the role of the moneyers (pp. 97–102), the metrology and fineness of the coins (pp. 107–10). Others can only be described on a regional basis. This section will be limited to the types, the inscriptions and the internal chronology of the coinage, with summaries of the main hoards on which the latter is based.

Types

The obverse type in this phase of Frankish coinage is almost invariably a profile bust turned to the right (or rarely a profile head cut off sharply at the neck) that derives from the traditional profile bust of the late Roman tremissis. It is occasionally turned to the left, but this probably originated as a die-sinker's error. In contrast to Visigothic Spain a facing bust is quite exceptional, though it occurs on one group of coins at Chalon and was taken up by the moneyer Arnoaldus at Paris (**1.469**) in the mid seventh century, as well as occurring sporadically elsewhere. It was ingeniously argued by Longuet (1930) that the curiously hirsute bust on the Paris coins was inspired by a facing Victory, for the long hair hanging down either side of the face resembles the trailing wings of a Victory, but this seems unlikely. How the bust was interpreted by users we have no idea. Probably they took it for a Frankish king despite its anonymity.

The varieties of profile bust are analysed at length in Engel and Serrure (1891, 151–62), and there is no need to reproduce their account here. The variations very largely came about as separate die-cutters, or schools of die-cutters, exaggerated and schematized different elements in the traditional design – the epaulette on the right shoulder, the folds of the chlamys, the neckline, the diadem, the treatment of the hair. It is possible to distinguish strongly marked regional schools, centring in the south on Marseille and in the north on Trier (cf. Yvon 1953) with others at Chalon-sur-Saône, Limoges and elsewhere. The bust in some places becomes square or trapezoidal, in others it is a simple curved mound. The detailed examination of these variants was indispensable to Amécourt and others in their study of the regional classification of Merovingian coinage, and can help in dating as well.

Occasionally, independently of the gradual evolution of a long accepted design, a die-cutter would take some ancient coin as a model and make a fresh start. The most conspicuous case is the one studied by Bauer and commented on by Lafaurie (above, p. 99) where the design is based on an immediately recognizable coin of the fourth-century usurper Magnentius (350–3), but such direct recourse to antiquity was not unique. Some coins of the moneyer Thrasemundus at Maastricht (B 4436) copy the helmeted bust of small bronze coins of Crispus or one of his contemporaries. A few die-cutters even took Visigothic coins as their models.

During the transitional period (*c.* 570–87) prior to the emergence of a fully 'national' Frankish coinage the transitional facing or profile Victory of the pseudo-imperial coinage was in general retained as the reverse type, for there are facing-Victory coins of Guntramn of Burgundy (561–

92) struck at an unspecified mint (B 5490), and ones of Sigebert I of Austrasia (561–75) with a profile Victory minted at Toul (B 4484) and by a moneyer named Manobio probably at Trier (B 4485). The same preference was maintained at a few other mints; there are well-designed Victories at Angers (B 159; **1.451**) and badly-designed ones at Nantes (B 3092–3100; **1.459**). It was only after 587 that Victory types were universally abandoned in favour of ones involving some variety of cross.

The 'cross' types, as noted already, came originally from Constantinople. The basic reason for their introduction was presumably the need to provide users with a simple way of distinguishing the new 'reduced' tremisses from their heavier predecessors, though religious and technical considerations – a cross was easier to design than a Victory – no doubt played their part. Though the immediate model was provided by the tremissis of Tiberius II there was probably some subsequent influence of the cross-in-wreath type of the fifth century (above, p. 11), since it seems to have suggested the cross in a pseudo-wreath or a circle of pellets that was adopted in many mints in the seventh century (below, p. 133).

Plates 20–5 show the variety of crosses that occur. The two basic designs are the so-called Greek cross with arms of equal length and the Latin cross with a longer upright beneath the intersection. Sometimes the cross was provided with a base, for the most part some locally devised variant of the standard Byzantine globus or horizontal line, and the details are often helpful in determining the region where coins with indecipherable legends originated. There are two forms very characteristic of Frankish coinage that have no counterparts in the variety of heraldic crosses that proliferated in the West from the twelfth century onwards. One is the so-called cross chrismée, which instead of the simplified form of Byzantine Christogram with a cross surmounted by a P, i.e. the Greek letter *rho* (as on **1.295–7**), has instead a Latin R at the top (e.g. **1.393**). The other is the much more widespread cross ancrée, though what looks like an inverted anchor at the top is really a cross with the R doubled for reasons of symmetry. It has been argued (Prou 1892a) that it is really an *omega*, for an *alpha* is sometimes found at the base (e.g. B 3341–2 = P 708–9), and that it represents an attempt to amalgamate these symbols of the Godhead (*Apocalypse* I.8) with the cross instead of suspending them from its arms, but in the West the *omega* is normally ω, not Ω, and the combination cited by Prou proves only that Eligius had noted the possible symbolism, not that the cross ancrée originated in this way. The cross ancrée in any case has many variant forms, the upper arches being sometimes strongly looped and at others nearly flat, and it is found in all parts of the kingdom save Provence, where the simpler cross-on-globe preferred at Marseille predominated. How the cross chrismée started one can only conjecture, but one may suspect that some supplementary phrase in a mint instruction (e.g. *crux nostri salvationis signum*) may have suggested to a die-sinker that a design more elaborate than a simple cross was required.

Often the crosses are accompanied by letters in the field, two of them being very widely used. One is VII, indicating the reduction in the weight of the coin to the equivalent of 7 siliquae, which occurs most frequently in Provence but extended up the Saône valley and across Burgundy into the Rhineland (**1.507–8**). The other is CA, which initially stood for the mint of Chalon-sur-Saône (*Cabillonum*; **1.396–401**) but because of the importance of this mint and the reputation of its coins came to be widely copied elsewhere (Stahl 1982). Other letters can also signify mints: MA for Marseille (**1.403–9**), SE perhaps for Sisteron (*Segestum*; **1.415**), and LEMO in all quarters of a cross for Limoges (*Lemovicum*; B 2139). The CG which occurs on coins of a number of mints in Burgundy and Aquitaine, notably in the Pyrenees (**1.434**: Saint-Bertrand-de-Comminges), may be the immobilized CG of a Lyon coin (P 86) with LV in the obverse field and CG in the reverse (i.e. *Lucgdunum*), but since it is normally accompanied by VII it more probably stands for *celegas*, i.e. *seliquas*. But the symbols in the field might be no more than pellets or stars presumably simply decorative in character and a survival from Roman times (Amécourt 1877b).

Apart from the cross there are only a few reverse designs on Merovingian gold coins. Most seem to be original, though a unique tremissis of Toulouse has a reverse copying the wolf-and-twins of a late Roman coin (Lafaurie 1969d). Animal designs are for the most part of birds or monsters (Lafaurie 1974b) – one of the Escharen coins has a kind of dragon looking backwards (**1.515–16**) – but these are commoner on the deniers and sceattas than on the gold (below, p. 139). The chalice on coins of Javols-Banassac (**1.420–30A**) is a play on the name of the mint (below, p. 133). A few mints, almost exclusively in Aquitaine, used mint initials or monograms instead of either cross or design, notably Clermont-Ferrand, Brioude and Rodez (below, p. 133). Ecclesiastical mints sometimes showed the standing figure of a saint, or of two saints, usually holding one or two crosses and not always easy to identify (cf. **1.532**), and a coin of Rouen has what appears to be some kind of monstrance (**1.475**). A type of particular interest shows a moneyer at work (Lafaurie 1964c). Most of the aberrant designs occur on the early transitional coins between the pseudo-imperial and the 'national' series, antedating the general instruction on the use of a cross, but others like those of Banassac and Rodez were introduced in the 620s, so presumably the presence of a cross, though customary, was not regarded – or had come not to be regarded – as obligatory.

Inscriptions

Apart from the exceptional coins with a royal name, usually followed by *rex* and accompanied by the name of either a mint or a moneyer, or very occasionally by both (**1.414**), the inscriptions in this phase of Frankish coinage normally do no more than record that a coin was made at a certain place by a particular moneyer. The operative FIT, FIET, FITVR (for *fitur*, 'is made'; cf. Prou 1909, 18–20) is often but not invariably present. There may be no room for more than the place- and personal names, the personal name being sometimes followed by M, MON, MONET, MVNET, or some other abbreviation for *monetarius* and the place-name by *vicus*, or VICO in the ablative, a term which in the seventh century was applied to any small town or village, or to the quarter of a 'city'. *Civitas* (CIVI, CIVE, etc.) was reserved for places that had once been Roman administrative centres and in the Frankish period were all episcopal sees.

Many of the place-names offer no problems of identification. They are those of Roman times and in such cases usually continue in vernacular forms today. The minor ones are often difficult, the more so since they are often only partially legible and it is not clear where they begin or end. Later medieval charters provide clues to many of them, and enable us to reconstruct their history (cf. Deloche 1879). A special problem is created by places which, either because of their general character (*loco sancto*, *Wiccus*, *Sancti Martini*) or because of their ambiguity, can occur in several parts of the *regnum*. Is TRAIECTO Maastricht or Utrecht, WICCVS Quentovic or Wijk-bij-Duurstede, PALATIOLO Palaiseau near Paris or Pfalzel in the lower Rhineland? The evidence of find-spots sometimes combines with that of typological and stylistic affinities to provide satisfactory solutions to such ambiguities, but uncertainties over many small localities still remain.

The second element in the normal inscription consisted of a moneyer's name, the presence of which was almost universal save at Marseille. The names are indifferently Germanic or Roman; a few are Jewish (e.g. **1.402**: Joseph), but since these are also Biblical their holders were not necessarily Jewish by race or religion. The Germanic names were practically ignored in the great lexicon of Förstemann (1900) but are now proving of great interest to philologists concerned with the reconstruction of the phonetics of the language spoken in the sixth and seventh centuries. For this the numismatic evidence, despite the many problems of dating and decipherment, was extensively used in what was for long the classic study of Frankish in Merovingian times (Arbois de Jubainville 1900), but it is now in process of re-examination by modern scholars (Felder 1970, 1978, 1980a; Wells 1972). (It is, on the other hand, ignored in Morlet 1968–72, the standard work on personal names in France between the sixth and the twelfth century and one essential for tracing names in charters and other documents.) Moneyers' names found on the coins frequently end in *-o*, which is best construed as the ablative case of a personal name ending *-us*, i.e. as indicating a coin struck 'by' a particular moneyer, but it can also be a nominative, and we have to rely on the occurrence of identical or parallel forms in charters or other written sources to determine their identity.

There are a number of cases where two or more personal names that have the same radical occur in a particular mint, and in view of the regularity with which some element in Frankish personal names was hereditary it is likely that such moneyers were members of the same families (above, p. 100). Occasionally the same names occur on both tremisses and deniers. At the important mint of Chalon there are three (Inportunus (**1.539**), Abbo and Mummolus), and the time intervals involved makes it likely that they are relations and not the same individuals, though some of those on the silver may be no more than immobilizations.

The few inscriptions that are neither personal names nor place-names have all been discussed already. One is the group associated with such formulae as *In palacio fit*, *Palati mo(neta)*, *In scola fit*, *E scola re(gis)*, *Racio domni* that indicates minting in the palace (above, pp. 100–1). Related to this is the formula *Racio ecclesiae*, or *racio* followed immediately by the name of the saint to which the particular church responsible for the coin was dedicated. Quite different is the explanatory inscription DE SELEQVAS VII or variant used at a few mints to warn users of the reduced weight of the new tremissis of the late sixth century (above, p. 107). The unusually precise identification of his workshop (*officina*) by the early Vienne moneyer who used the formula *De officina Laurenti* (above, p. 101) represented a refinement not thought necessary by his successors or by moneyers elsewhere.

The inscriptions on the coins are naturally in Latin, and exhibit the changes in spelling and syntax which also affect the written documents and were a feature of the transition from Low Latin to French (Prou 1909; Breillat 1935), without benefit of the return to classical orthography that was to be a feature of the Carolingian Renaissance. Their narrow range of content, however, renders them of limited interest to the linguist who is not a phonologist or has no specific interest in personal and place-names.

Chronology

The only coins that can be dated directly by their inscriptions are those that include the names of kings or, for Provençal quasi-imperial coins up to 613, the names of Byzantine emperors. These can be used for dating other coins found with them in hoards or related to them in type, though since the number of Merovingian personal names was limited and the names are repeated one has to be certain which Dagobert or Chlotar is intended. The identifications in the older literature are not always correct, and there is always the possibility of names being immobilized on so disorganized a coinage. The declining fineness of the coins is also a guide to dating, even if it is not one that can be applied with the degree of precision that some scholars have supposed (above, p. 109).

In default of more exact criteria we have to fall back on the evidence of hoards. Stray finds of Merovingian coins are relatively common, and extremely important for the study of circulation patterns and for the identification of mints, but they do not help over chronology. Ponton d'Amécourt was of the opinion that such stray finds had supplied the majority of coins known in his day but this is scarcely possible; there must have been hoards antedating the beginnings of scientific numismatic study in the nineteenth century of which we know nothing. Even in the past century hoards continued to be dispersed before any proper description of them could be made, and there was at least one that was in large part melted down. But we have details of fourteen hoards of varying sizes, some of them available for study directly but most of them reconstructed with varying degrees of certainty by Le Gentilhomme or Lafaurie. Two (Canterbury and Faversham) belong to the transitional coinage of the 570s and 580s and another (Escharen) can be dated to *c.* 600/610, but most of them belong to the five decades between *c.* 620 and *c.* 670. They can be summarized as follows, in approximate chronological order:

Canterbury, St Martin's (Roach Smith 1845; Grierson 1952c; *SCBI* Merseyside Museums 5–10; Hawkes *et al.* 1966 for metal analyses).

This small group of five or six tremisses and one solidus, all mounted, is not a monetary hoard in the usual sense of the term, but a group of grave goods found 'some years' before 1844 in or near the churchyard of St Martin's Canterbury (on the location see Rigold 1975, 655) and no doubt from the burial ground of the pre-Augustinian Christian community there. It is now preserved in the Merseyside Museums, Liverpool. One coin is an Italian tremissis of Justin II, another is the famous 'medalet' of Bishop Liudhard (below, p. 160), another is a Germanic tremissis of uncertain localization, and three – possibly four – are Merovingian coins, each unique, with names of moneyers and mints. One is a solidus struck by Leudulf at *Ivegio vico*, two are tremisses of Nonnitus and Leonardus struck at the southern French mints of Saint-Bertrand-de-Comminges and Agen respectively, and a third, whose attribution to the group is conjectural since it is separate from the others and in the Bibliothèque Nationale, is one struck by Launebo at Oloron. Their interest is that they all belong to the brief phase in Frankish coinage between the introduction of mint and moneyer's names and the generalization of types involving a cross, for all have pictorial types: a nimbate figure on horseback, two standing figures, a modified Victory. A date of *c.* 580/590 fits in well with the medalet of Liudhard, who came to England as Queen Bertha's

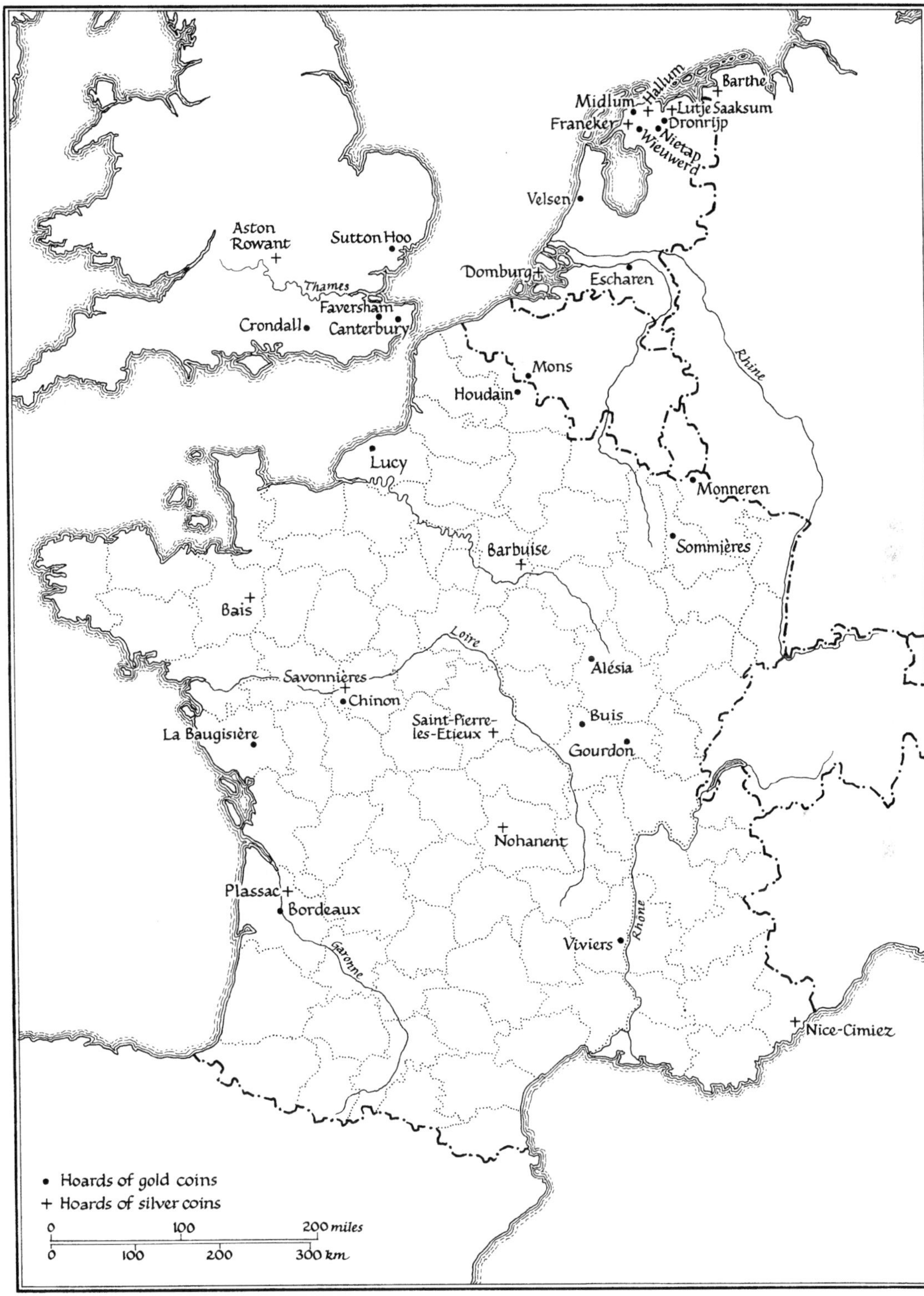

Map 3 *Frankish and Frisian coin hoards*
The dotted lines represent current administrative boundaries, since these may be helpful in identifying the find-spots on modern maps.

chaplain sometime in the late 570s or 580s. Since they were used as ornaments the burial date could have been somewhat later than the original assembly of the group. This may account for the additional wear on the coin from Comminges and its baser and different style of loop which, like the intaglio pendant, is only otherwise known in a seventh-century context and prompted the suggestion that the hoard may have come from two separate graves (Hawkes *et al.* 1966, 105–6). However, it is unlikely that two presumably adjacent graves, one substantially later than the other, should each have contained unique coins of about the same date (*c.* 570/580).

Faversham (Rigold 1975, 655, 668–71).

Another Kentish grave find consisting of six mounted tremisses from King's Field cemetery, Faversham, was turned up in about 1880 and passed, via the Franks collection, to the British Museum's Department of Medieval and Later Antiquities. It was recently reconstituted by Mrs L. Webster and summarily, though efficiently, published by Rigold before his death. Three coins of Marseille, Arles and Uzès belong to the quasi-imperial Provençal coinage (below, pp. 129–30), and, since their types derived from the imperial issues of Tiberius II and Maurice, they need be dated no later than *c.* 590. A fourth coin, of Agen, is overstruck on a Provençal coin of similar type and is not much later. The last two are from the Neustrian mints of Campbon near Nantes, with a long cross between two standing figures and an early cross-in-wreath reverse, and Lisieux in Normandy. The coins were probably brought together in the 590s, although again a slighly later date of burial is possible.

Escharen (Wilde and Dompierre de Chaufepie 1898; Lafaurie 1960a; Oddy 1972a for metal analyses).

A hoard of 66 solidi and tremisses found in 1897 at a locality south-west of Nijmegen, close to the left bank of the Maas, in the modern Dutch province of Noord-Brabant. Over half were acquired by The Hague, ten are at Brussels, and the rest are in various collections, including four here (**1.491**, **501**, **515–16**). The coins form two main groups, one local and the other from Provençal mints, with a few older coins and a scatter from mints throughout the kingdom. The date can be fixed as *c.* 600/610, preceding Chlotar II's acquisition of Provence in 613 and the appearance of many of the coin types most characteristic of the second phase of Frankish coinage.

Wieuwerd (Jansen 1866; Lafaurie *et al.* 1961).

This pot-hoard of 39 pieces of gold jewellery and coin ornaments was found in 1866 in a mound near Wieuwerd, south-west of Leeuwarden in the province of Friesland. It is now, almost complete, in the Museum of Antiquities at Leyden. The coins, most with attached loops but seven with very elaborate mounts, are mainly solidi, either Byzantine or of Marseille, some quasi-imperial but the majority of Chlotar II. There are also some mounted tremisses, one Visigothic and the rest Frankish. The coins used must have been collected *c.* 620, the latest ones being two solidi of Heraclius' Class IIa datable to 613/616, the tremissis of Sisebut (612–21), and the Marseille coins of Chlotar II, which were struck from 613 onwards. The formation of the hoard about 620 dates both the coinage of the moneyer Ansoaldus of Maastricht and the changes in the design of Chlotar's Massaliote coinage, but the hoard would have been more useful for dating if it had included coins of a greater variety of mints bearing the names of moneyers. Since the coins had been turned into jewellery the date of burial may have been nearer the middle of the century.

Sutton Hoo (Kent 1975, superseding earlier descriptions; Oddy *et al.* 1972 for metal analyses).

This was a hoard of 37 Merovingian coins, 3 blanks, and 2 small gold ingots which made part of the rich grave goods found in 1939 in the ship burial mound at Sutton Hoo, near the Suffolk coast in East Anglia. Although there were in it no regal coins later than one of Theodebert II (595–612) and it included five other coins of the same period or earlier, the initial tendency was to date the hoard to about the middle of the seventh century (Le Gentilhomme 1940b, 144–5; Grierson 1952a). The current view, based partly on a study of the fineness of the coins (above, p. 108–9), is to ascribe it to the 620s and regard it as supporting the view that the burial is that of King Rædwald of the East Angles, who died in 625. It has been argued (Grierson 1970, 1974c) that the three blanks were added to the 37 coins to make up a total of 40, and serve as a kind of grandiose Charon's obol for the 40 rowers of the great ship, but not all scholars accept this view.

Dronrijp (Dirks 1887; Boeles 1947; 1951, 309–10 and *passim*).

This was a pot-hoard of 28 coins, 3 blanks, a large gold ingot (45.5g), and fragments of a purse found in 1876 at Dronrijp, a village 9km west of Leeuwarden. Most of the coins were local issues, very barbarous in design, that were later classed by Boeles as 'Dronrijp types A–D' (below, p. 137). Merovingian issues were relatively few, but included a Maastricht coin of Ansoald, two of Huy, a number of Mainz and the neighbourhood, and two from Orléans and Ruan. The hoard was acquired *en bloc* for the Frisian Museum at Leeuwarden.

Dating is rendered uncertain by the existence of 'another' hoard, Dronrijp II, also alleged to have been found in 1876. It was acquired by a local collector, Mr Bloembergen Santée, and in 1877 passed to Mr Loexma Ypey of Leeuwarden. Dirks knew of it but doubted if the coins came from the same hoard, but Boeles, who tried to reconstruct it in the first edition (1927) of his *Friesland tot de elfde eeuw*, thought they did. He later developed his account (Boeles 1947; 1951, 309–10), but while there is (if he is correct) considerable overlap between the two hoards, Dronrijp II allegedly contained two Madelinus coins of Dorestad, while there was none in Dronrijp I. This would date the hoard to at least the 630s, rather than the late 620s. But the village that once occupied the *terp* of Dronrijp may well have had more than one rich inhabitant, and two independent hoards are not impossible. The hoard as described by Dirks would belong to the 620s.

Lucy (Cochet 1852; Lafaurie 1978e).

This is not a normal monetary hoard, but a group of five tremisses found together on 22 September 1851 by the abbé Cochet in a tomb he was excavating at Lucy (dép. Seine-Maritime), a village in the valley of the Eaulne a few miles inland from Dieppe. Four of the coins are in the museum at Rouen and one in that of Le Havre. The types and names of moneyers led Lafaurie, in republishing the find, to date it *c.* 625/30.

Nietap (Boeles 1947; 1951, 309ff.; Pol 1977).

A hoard of over 40 coins mainly found in 1900 and 1901 at Nietap in the northern Netherlands, on the boundary between the provinces of Groningen and Drenthe. Boeles thought there might have been two hoards and described them as such, but it is more likely that there was an original hoard of 1900 that was scattered by the breaking of the container, so Boeles' list of contents can be amplified and revised (Pol 1977). His studies remain important, however, since in them he established the nomenclature of Dronrijp types A–D, and his plate of coins is also the better of the two. Pol describes 34 coins and two blanks, and dates the hoard 630/635. Its main contents are 8 Maastricht tremisses and derivatives and 14 Dronrijp type coins, with a few other Merovingian coins and Frisian imitations. There is a substantial overlap with the Dronrijp hoard, a little with the Mons hoard. The presence of only two Maastricht moneyers, Ansoaldus and Thrasemund, and the absence of any coins of Madelinus or of Dorestad suggests the slightly earlier date of *c.* 630.

Mons (known from some confusing and inadequate references by Lelewel in *RN* 1836, 323–5, and *RBN* 1(1841–3), 115–16, and by the presence of some coins from it in the J. B. Leclercqz sale catalogue, Brussels, 2 April 1839, which Lelewel compiled).

A small hoard of some 20 coins found in 1820 which included about five Byzantine coins or imitations of Phocas and Heraclius, two tremisses of Swinthila (626–31), one coin each of Soissons (Elafius) and Rodez (Vendemius), and twelve coins of local or Frisian origin, four of them Maastricht derivatives (as **1.497**) and eight of the type usually now called Dronrijp D (as **1.519–20**). The Swinthila coins put the deposit after 630 and the Dronrijp group is probably not later.

La Baugisière (Fillon 1845; Fillon and Rochebrune 1865; Le Gentilhomme 1938b, 136–8, 152–3).

This huge hoard was found in or about 1810 at La Baugisière (dép. Vendée, comm. Saint-Michel-le-Clercq), close to Fontenay-le-Comte. Many of the coins – allegedly over 3,000 – were melted down, but 50 reached the Cabinet des Médailles in 1811 and Benjamin Fillon, who remembered having seen them as a child hawked round at five francs apiece, was able to collect much scattered information about them thirty years later. Le Gentilhomme was prevented by the Second World War and his premature death in 1947 from publishing the detailed reconstruction he promised, but in the article cited he lists such mints and moneyers as he could identify and provides a map of the mints. The only royal coin noted was a Marseille tremissis of Sigebert III (634–56), so the date of burial was after 634, and the general composition suggests some time in the late 630s.

Buis (Le Gentilhomme 1938b; Lafaurie 1977b).

This large hoard came to light at Buis (dép. Saône-et-Loire, comm. Chissey-en-Morvan), north-west of Autun, in or about 1855. Although the coins were gradually dispersed, a local antiquary, M. de Charmasse, who saw between 300 and 400 of them, was able to draw up a list of 55 types and varieties, reproducing the legends on each and sketching the form of the crosses that formed their reverse types. Le Gentilhomme reproduced this list, which reached the Cabinet des Médailles with the papers of Barthélemy, and added one further coin and a few supplementary details about the hoard from contemporary numismatists. From a number of supplementary sources, Lafaurie (1977b) has been able to increase the number of coins recorded from 56 to 75, but only in a very few cases can the specimens be identified today; one is in this collection (**1.419**). Although the hoard contained no royal coins later than a Marseille tremissis of Chlotar II (d. 629), its sequence of moneyers of Chalon-sur-Saône points to a date of burial in the 640s. It may indeed have occurred in September 641, when the patrician Willibad fell victim to a complicated intrigue described at length by Fredegarius, for his murder near Autun was followed by a great plundering and scattering of treasure. The hoard is mainly important for the coinage of Burgundy.

Crondall (Akerman 1844; Lefroy 1870; Amécourt 1872; Sutherland 1948).

This hoard of 100 gold coins, with two jewelled ornaments and rings, was found in 1828 at Crondall in Hampshire, on the Surrey border, in southern England. It is usually thought of as an Anglo-Saxon hoard (below, pp. 161–2), since two-thirds of its contents are English, but it includes 24 distinctively Merovingian or Frisian coins, together with a few of uncertain attribution. The coins are all in the Ashmolean Museum at Oxford, having been acquired at the second Grantley sale in 1944; Lord Grantley himself had bought them in 1895 from the estate of the Lefroy family which had owned them since their discovery. The standard account is that of Sutherland 1948, though it omits one Merovingian coin that had become separated while in Lord Grantley's possession; fortunately it was identifiable from Akerman's and Lefroy's plates and is now at Oxford with the others (Grierson 1953d). The hoard, which was apparently in a purse though no trace of one was found, has been construed as a single payment, perhaps a wergeld, of one hundred Anglo-Saxon shillings, for this total was made up by the addition of several blanks or amateur strikings of appropriate weight to the coins the original owner possessed or borrowed, while a Byzantine tremissis that had once formed part of a necklace was also substituted for a plated forgery in it (Grierson 1970). Over a quarter of the 24 Frankish coins in the hoard are from the mint of Quentovic, the main Channel port and the one closest to southern England (below, pp. 134–5), and there is one from the neighbouring mint of Amiens, but there is also a group from the Meuse valley and the lower Rhineland that must have reached England by a different route. Sutherland no. 86 (pl. 5.3), not identified by the author, has to be added to the Rhineland group, as it is a coin of Cologne. The finenesses of the coins are given by Oddy 1972a. Opinions on the date of the burial have varied over several decades in the mid seventh century, for it contains no closely datable coins, but it is now generally put at *c.* 650 or a little earlier (Kent 1975; Rigold 1975, 659).

Sommières or **Saint-Aubin** (Maxe-Werly 1890).

A hoard of 28 coins found in 1840 at a locality named Sommières in the commune of Saint-Aubin-sur-Aire (Meuse), south-east of Bar-le-Duc. A local government official acquired 22 of them, and after his death they were bought by the museum at Bar-le-Duc; five were acquired by a local collector; on only one is no information available. The hoard is very mixed, with only a few coins of local mints (Verdun, Moyenvic, Dieuze), and cannot be dated precisely. It included three royal issues, one of Charibert of Aquitaine and two of Dagobert I (not of Dagobert II, as Maxe-Werly thought for one of them), so the date of burial must be somewhere in the four decades 630/670, but it is difficult to be more precise. The absence of any demonstrably early coins suggest the 650s or 660s.

Bordeaux (Le Gentilhomme 1936; Lafaurie 1952b; 1963b, 309–13).

A hoard found in November 1803 of over 184 Merovingian and Visigothic coins, 182 of which were acquired for the BN in May 1804. What purported to be a list of them was drawn up some years later and served as the basis for Le Gentilhomme's tentative reconstruction of its contents, which he dated to the mid 670s on the ground that they apparently ended with coins of King Wamba (672–80). Miles (1952, 165) subsequently pointed out that the listing could not be correct, as it included three 'modern' forgeries, and Lafaurie concluded that it did not refer to the hoard at all. While a number of coins in the BN whose provenance is not otherwise accounted for may well come from the hoard, one cannot be certain of this in any particular case. In his final reconstruction Lafaurie (1963b, 309–13) listed 155 Merovingian and 18 Visigothic coins and accepted *c.* 700/705 as the date of burial on the ground of its having included Visigothic coins down to the joint reign of Egica and Wittiza (698–702). The datable Merovingian coins in it, however, end with Massiliote issues of Childeric II (d. 675, but may have ceased minting earlier), and since there is a concentration of coins of Recceswinth (653–72) one must assume its having been put together in the 670s. If it did indeed contain still later Visigothic coins one may suppose that, like the Ilanz hoard of Lombard and early Carolingian tremisses buried in the period of the silver denier (below, p. 210), it represented some kind of family treasure put together well before its final date of burial. But the details of the Visigothic content are doubtful, and Le Gentilhomme's original date for the burial of *c.* 675 seems more likely.

With the evidence of fourteen hoards in a period of about a century one might hope to be able to work out a more precise chronology than has in fact proved possible. There are several obvious difficulties. One is the gap of over two decades between Escharen and the hoards attributed to the 620s; we remain very ignorant for the first two decades of the seventh century. Another is the diversity of the coinage, so that there is less overlapping of mints and moneyers and fewer die-linkages than might have been hoped. Yet another is the fact that the contents of the main French hoards – La Baugisière, Buis, Bordeaux – are only known imperfectly, while the foreign hoards from England and the Low Countries whose recording leaves nothing to be desired are not necessarily either typical or informative. Scholars have succeeded in establishing the sequence of moneyers in many mints, but the activity of moneyers must often have overlapped and it is impossible to estimate how long they might have remained active. Only in the case of Eligius, who became a bishop in 641 and presumably stopped minting in that year, can a firm date be proposed. Many Merovingian gold coins can be dated within a decade or so, but in certain cases it remains hard to say if a particular coin was minted in the 630s or the 640s – or even in the 650s. The chronology of Merovingian gold coinage is a jig-saw puzzle still in process of being worked out.

(b) ROYAL COINAGES

Royal coins, in the sense of coins bearing the name of a Frankish sovereign, are rare save for (1) those of Marseille, where they were minted by a series of kings from Chlotar II to Dagobert II (second reign 676–9), i.e. from 613 to the late 670s; and (2) those of the short-reigned Charibert of Aquitaine (629–32) struck at Banassac, which probably for the most part come from some single hoard of which no particulars are recorded. Coins exist, however, for virtually all sovereigns between *c.*570 and *c.* 670 (see those marked with an asterisk in Table 10), though apart from Dagobert and Sigebert III the number of specimens known for any single king can almost be counted on the fingers of one hand.

Apart from the Marseille coinage, which is discussed below, the royal coins normally bear the king's name and that of either a moneyer or a mint, there being no room for both. There are a few exceptions, e.g. one of Dagobert struck by the moneyer Romanus at the mint of Saint-Maurice d'Agaune (**1.414**). Even when the mint name is absent the place of striking can often be surmised, either because of the known affiliations of the moneyer responsible or because of local peculiarities of style. The types normally conform to regional patterns and are consequently very diverse. Both Prou and Belfort class regal coins under their mints, with the exception of those for which no mint could be suggested with confidence (P 32–71; B5449–5507, 5880–6), so that they are scattered through their volumes and one must have recourse to the surveys in Engel and Serrure (1891–1905, I.69–86) or Blanchet (1912, 196–205) to get a picture of the coinage as a whole.

In view of the small numbers in this collection there would be no point in describing the coinage in detail, but it is worth emphasizing its marginal character. Why were the coins struck? How was production organized?

The marginal character of the coinage is very evident from the hoards. There were three royal coins in the Sommières hoard and some perhaps in that of Bordeaux, but there were none at all in those of Canterbury, Escharen, Mons, Dronrijp, Nietap or Crondall, and only one in Sutton Hoo. If there were eleven coins of Chlotar II in that of Wieuwerd, they were all of Marseille and mainly solidi, their presence being explained by the fact that their proprietor wanted them for transformation into jewellery and the quasi-imperial and royal issues of Marseille would be virtually the only source of solidi other than Byzantine imports. The same is true of the four solidi of Marseille and Arles – three quasi-imperial and one of Chlotar II – on a necklace from a grave at Sarre in Kent (Roach Smith 1860; Rigold 1975, 655, 668). Such a level of rarity makes one hesitate over accepting, as evidence of a general practice, the story in the *Vita S. Eligii* (above, p. 100) of the regular melting down of coin received in taxes and its transmission in ingot form to the treasury. If this was really still being done, royal coin should be both more abundant and of better quality. It is more likely that taxes normally reached the treasury in the form of locally produced coin, and in so far as the gold was not required by the court goldsmiths to be turned into jewellery or plate it was in the same form that it was distributed again. The meagre royal issues would presumably result from the fact that old jewellery and plate was not always wanted, and kings sometimes needed extra coin. The court goldsmiths could sometimes turn it into coin themselves, especially if like St Eligius they had been trained as moneyers, but in most cases a local moneyer would be brought in to do what was required. No regular 'royal mint' or 'royal mints' existed. Although some of the royal coins are from such places as Paris and Limoges where the kings are known to have resided frequently, many are from small localities where the king by chance may have spent a few days on one of his progresses, while many important places are totally absent from the list. Royal minting was evidently a matter of chance.

To this rule Marseille is an exception. Its coinage existed quite independent of any aulic context – few Frankish sovereigns appear ever to have visited the city – and is doubly unique in its systematic retention of the solidus as part of the regular currency and in the almost total absence from its coins of the names of moneyers. These peculiarities can be understood only in the light of the quasi-imperial coinage that preceded it and which was issued over the few decades between *c.* 580 and 613. The hundred or so known specimens of this latter coinage have been meticulously catalogued (Rigold 1954), though there are only two in this collection (**1.403–4**, but cf. **1.415**, **418**). 'Quasi-imperial' is a better term for it than pseudo-imperial, for although struck in the names of successive Byzantine emperors the coins are not imitations of imperial issues, differing most conspicuously in the use of profile instead of facing busts on the solidi, in the details of the crosses that formed the reverse types, and in the normal presence of mint letters and marks of value in the field.

The coins consist of solidi and tremisses with on the obverse an imperial bust, facing or (more frequently) profile on the solidi and always profile on the tremisses, and on the reverse a cross-on-base above a globe beside which are letters indicating the mint and the value in siliquae (XX or XXI on solidi, VII on tremisses). From some date in Maurice's reign the reverse type is separated from the inscription by a pseudo-wreath or a circle of dots. The emperors whose names occur are Justin II (565–78), Tiberius II (578–82), Maurice (582–602), Phocas (602–10), and Heraclius (610–41), though since the 'Heraclius' coins are followed by ones of identical type in the name of Chlotar II, who took over Provence in or soon after his conquest of Austrasia in 613, they must have ended quite early in Heraclius' reign. The mints involved are Marseille (MA), Arles (AR), Uzès (VC, *Ucetia*), and Viviers (VIVA, *Vivaria*), though there are a few irregular and imitative issues from further afield. The significance of the letters XXI, XX and VII, signifying approximations in siliquae to weights of 60 and 20 grains, has already been explained (above, p. 107). The inscriptions are of the regular imperial pattern, though often slightly blundered.

The earliest name to be found on the coins is that of Justin II, and Rigold dated them to the last years (*c.* 575–8) of his reign, but it is impossible to place them so early, for Justin II's Constantinopolitan and Italian tremisses have a Victory reverse type. The cross-potent-on-globe is copied from the semissis type of Tiberius II. They must thus be dated after 578, or effectively from *c.* 580 onwards, with probably a time-lag of a year or so in keeping up with changes of ruler at Constantinople and, at the start, the use of the name of an emperor who was already dead.

It was suggested in the eighteenth century that this coinage provided evidence for a temporary imperial restoration in southern Gaul connected with the revolt of the pretender Gondovald (Bonamy 1746; Deloche 1883a; revived by Goubert 1942 but tacitly abandoned in Goubert 1955). This theory was demolished by Robert (1883, and cf. Blancard 1884–5), who pointed out that the localities involved are not those in which Gondovald is known to have received support and that the coinage was struck over a period much longer than the pretender's brief public career. It is in any case clear, from Gregory of Tours and other sources, that no 'imperial restoration' occurred in Provence at this time; Provence was in Frankish hands throughout. Another suggestion (Grierson 1959c), that the coins were minted by the managers of the great papal estates in Provence, has commended itself to nobody, despite some circumstantial evidence in its favour and a reference, in two of Gregory the Great's letters, to the unacceptability of *solidi Gallicani* in what remained of imperial Italy.

Possibly the true reason was the ambiguous position of Marseille *vis-à-vis* the Frankish kings, who had little interest in theoretical considerations of sovereignty but a great deal in practical sources of revenue. Authority over Marseille, particularly important because of the tolls that still could be extracted from what remained of Mediterranean commerce (Ganshof 1960), was in the second half of the sixth century normally divided between several kings with the right to a share in its revenues. There were no problems as long as the pseudo-imperial coinages dominated the scene, but after the 570s the minting of coins in the name of one of the competing rulers would only offend his colleagues, while the use of moneyers' name would have run contrary to the traditions of one of the most profoundly Romanized parts of Gaul. It therefore might well have seemed to the patricians of Provence, or to whatever other local authority controlled the mint, that the best solution was to mint in the name of the reigning emperor at Constantinople, though since these emperors still interested themselves in the politics of the western Mediterranean it must have meant walking a tightrope over loyalties (cf. Goffart 1957). The reunification of the kingdom by Chlotar II in 613 brought the divided control of Marseille to an end, and from then onwards the gold coinage of the city was royal and not quasi-imperial in character.

The coins of Marseille (**1.405–9**; cf. also **1.1473**) with royal names (B 2465–2584; P 1380–1426; Manteyer 1942, 639–55; Felder 1980b; Lafaurie 1981c) are solidi and tremisses of decreasingly fine gold bearing the names of Chlotar II (613–29), Dagobert I (629–39), Sigebert III (639–56), Dagobert II (656), *Childebertus adoptivus* (656?–662), Childeric II (662–75), Clovis III (675), Dagobert II (restored 676–9). Coins formerly ascribed to Childebert III (694/5–711) and Dagobert III (711–15) are really of *Childebertus* and Dagobert II. The inscriptions are often blundered and the letters deformed. Under Sigebert III and later there are often one or more letters (C, EL, B, A, etc.) in front of the king's bust on the obverse, the EL usually being taken to represent Eligius and the others identified by Manteyer (1942, 654–5) as the initials of patricians or other royal officials known from the texts. A curious type of Childeric II, known for both solidus (**1.409**) and tremissis, shows the royal bust under a kind of portico whose significance is unknown. The tremisses of Dagobert II and Clovis III mark a break with tradition, for their reverse type is a cross-potent-on-steps copied from the contemporary Byzantine solidus instead of the cross-on-base-and-globe used under their predecessors. The change may possibly be a consequence of a breach in continuity, the minting of gold having been suspended late in Childeric II's reign (*c.* 670?) and then revived only briefly in the late 670s under Clovis III and Dagobert II (restored).

Just as Marseille in the period of quasi-imperial coinage had had its derivatives at other mints in Provence, so there are coins of Chlotar II and his successors from Arles, Viviers, and other mints in the south. Elsewhere in France royal minting was meagre. The royal coinages of the final stages of the pseudo-imperial period have been noted already (above, p. 91). Of most of the kings who ruled between 585 and 670 a few coins are known, almost always with a mint name and sometimes with that of a moneyer also. The most extraordinary piece is a medallion – a sesqui-solidus if one allows about a gram for the part of the mount still attached to it – which was struck on behalf of Dagobert I by the moneyer Ansoindus at Limoges and gives him the title DOMNVS DAGOBERTHVS REX FRANCORVM. Found in Surrey in the mid nineteenth century and eventually acquired by the French national collection (P 1934), it is generally assumed to have been a royal gift from Dagobert to some English king, for the old imperial tradition of medallions as suitable presents for foreign potentates would still have been remembered in France (Deloche 1879). The only royal coins in this collection are one struck at Saint-Maurice d'Agaune by the moneyer Romanus on behalf of Dagobert I (**1.414**), presumably on the occasion of some visit by the king to this famous shrine; one of the brief reign (629–32) of Charibert of Aquitaine struck at Banassac (**1.424**); and one of Clovis II (639–57) struck by the moneyer Dendus, probably at Marcilly-en-Gault near Blois (**1.437**). Lafaurie's account of this coin is expanded into a survey of Clovis II's whole coinage (Lafaurie 1971e). A tremissis of Metz (**1.1474**) in the name of Chulderic, though acquired as authentic, is a modern forgery.

(c) BURGUNDY AND PROVENCE

The coinage of Burgundy was dominated by that of Chalon-sur-Saône, which enjoyed a position of commercial and strategic importance on the west bank of the Saône and was the effective capital of the kingdom of Burgundy under Guntramn and his successors. Mint output was exceptionally large, and its peculiar feature of linked names of moneyers, something rarely found elsewhere, suggests a demand for coinage that could only be satisfied by entrepreneurs agreeing to pool their resources. The characteristic reverse type, a cross, sometimes chrismée or on a step or steps, flanked by the letters CA (for *Cabillonum*), was influential as a model and was copied very widely elsewhere, notably in Austrasia where the coins arrived by way of trade. Ponton d'Amécourt's monograph (Amécourt 1873) still retains its importance for the richness of its documentation – it illustrates over 130 coins – and for its broad classification of phases and types. Its chronology was drastically revised, however, by Le Gentilhomme in an appendix to his reconstruction of the Buis hoard (Le Gentilhomme 1938b), for Amécourt's attribution of coins of Chlotar II to Chlotar I resulted in the series as a whole being dated some forty years too early. The coinage is reasonably well represented here (**1.396–401**, with the attribution of

1.398 uncertain) and including four with names of associated moneyers but without any of Amécourt's Group 5, which has a facing bust on the obverse.

The three other Burgundian mints – of Autun (**1.393–4**), Mâcon (**1.402**) and Troyes (**1.416–17**) – were of less importance. Autun took its name (*Augustodunun*) from Augustus, who magnificently reconstructed it as a replacement for Bibracte as the capital of Roman Gaul, but in Merovingian times it was of much less account than Chalon. Its coinage is largely modelled on that of this city, with AG in the field instead of CA and usually a cross chrismée for type, though unlike Chalon there is usually no wreath inside the legend. A peculiar feature is the occasional occurrence of two overlapping busts instead of a single one as the obverse type. Prou, whose catalogue of the coins of Autun (Prou 1888a) requires little revision, suggested that it originated in a double striking, but it is used by several moneyers and was more likely copied from some Roman coin. It inspired numismatists from Chiflet and Leblanc onwards into remarkable flights of fancy, the figures being identified with such personages as Sigebert and Brunhild (Chiflet 1655) or Guntramn and Childebert II (Lelewel 1835). The coin of Besançon here (**1.395**) is interesting because of the specific reference to siliquae in its legend (above, p. 107). A notable feature consists of the coins from Alpine mints: Saint-Maurice d'Agaune (**1.414**) in the Valais with its great shrine (cf. Besson 1910); Moutiers-en-Tarentaise (**1.411–13**), in the upper reaches of the Isère; Albens in Savoy (**1.392**); and, further south, Sisteron (**1.415**), at the junction of the Durance and the Buëch. A serious gap is Lyon, whose coins resemble those of Chalon but have LV beside the cross. They are much less abundant, however, and Lyon seems to have been less important in the seventh century than it had been in the sixth.

The coinage of Provence is essentially that of Marseille, which has been described already (pp. 129–31), and the few neighbouring mints, effectively Arles, Uzès, and Viviers, which minted coins of the same type. Of these, Viviers is the only one represented here (**1.418**).

(d) AQUITAINE

Aquitaine in the middle Merovingian period was rarely a political unit (Rouche 1979) and it is difficult to determine how the repeated partitions to which it was subjected may have affected its coinage save during the brief period of Charibert. The coins in this collection (**1.421–50**) come almost exclusively from Gévaudan and Rouergue and not from the centre and west of the province. Two important mints, Limoges (Lafaurie 1975b, 1975c), remarkable for the existence of several solidi and for its association with the goldsmith Abbo who taught St Eligius his trade (above, p. 98), and Brioude are not represented at all, and for Bordeaux, Clermont-Ferrand (*Arvernis*) and Toulouse there are only single coins (**1.431**, **433**, **448**), though for each city a number of moneyers are known – nearly twenty for Bordeaux – and their mints were all of considerable importance (Bordeaux: Jullian 1890 and Lafaurie 1963b; Clermont-Ferrand: Lafaurie 1972d). The coins of the Pyreneean mints of Saint-Bertrand-de-Comminges (**1.434**) and Foix (**1.435**) are noteworthy because their identical busts show them to have shared the services of a single die-sinker. Comminges (*Convena*), an important site in Roman times, was occupied in 585 by Gondovald (above, p. 130) and according to Gregory of Tours (VII. 38) was totally destroyed by the army of Guntramn after an epic siege. The coin here, however, is one of a number that are certainly later in date and the destruction cannot have been as complete as reported. The town takes its modern name from St Bertrand, an early twelfth-century bishop (d. *c.* 1125) who founded the magnificent cathedral that dominates the town today.

Two-thirds of the Aquitanian coins here are of Javols-Banassac and Rodez. These series are remarkable because of their unusual types – chalice or monogram instead of cross – and because neither place seems to warrant the large mint output indicated by the number of moneyers involved, as well as by the relative abundance of the coins and their wide dispersion (Amécourt 1883a; Lafaurie 1973e, with map of finds on p. 129).

Banassac (*Bannaciacum*) is a small village close to Mende, capital of the département of Lozère, in the Gévaudan (*civitas Gabalitorum*), a region that takes its name from a Gaulish tribe and has given its name to the modern Javols, also close to Mende. Rodez (*Rutenis*) is the capital of the département of Aveyron and was the centre of the ancient *civitas Rutenorum*, the modern Rouergue. Banassac had been an important pottery centre in Gaulish times and up to the second century A.D., but apart from their coinage neither Banassac nor Rodez were of any consequence in Merovingian or later times. Their emergence as mints was a consequence of Dagobert's creation of a sub-kingdom of Aquitaine for his short-lived and simple-minded son Charibert II (629–32), though why mints should have been located in these particular spots, rather than at Toulouse or Bordeaux, has so far defied explanation.

Belfort and other scholars have given the coins with a *Gabali* legend alone, without BAN, to Javols, but the family resemblance of the whole coinage is so close that it seems best to assign them all to Banassac, as has been done here. Charibert's name appears on only a few of the coins of Banassac (**1.424**) and on none of Rodez, but it serves to date the whole group to the 620s and 630s, and it may have been the problem of finding room for the name of a king as well as of a moneyer that suggested the replacement of the customary cross by the name of the mint in monogrammatic form, more especially since there were precedents in the AR used at neighbouring Clermont-Ferrand (**1.433**) and related mints (**1.436**) and the BR of Brioude. The further substitution of a chalice for a monogram at Javols-Banassac had probably nothing to do with the ancient industry of the locality – there is no evidence for the survival of this beyond the second century A.D. – but is rather a play on the word *gabali* since this was close to a Celtic word for a cup which carried on into Old Fr. as *gobelet* and was eventually borrowed into English as *goblet*.

The only other Aquitanian coins here requiring notice are **1.438** of Neuvic-d'Ussel and **1.439** of Rodez, both of which have a dotted inner circle round the inscription. It has been suggested (Lafaurie 1981a) that this was adopted at a number of mints under Charibert II as a mark of Aquitanian individuality, and, although it is difficult to envisage its resulting from a specific mint instruction, the pattern of the twenty or so mints involved corresponds with one exception to those in Charibert's kingdom and covers too large an area, from Bourges in the north to Foix in the south, to be easily explicable as the result of copying between mints.

(e) NEUSTRIA

The concept of 'Neustria' probably went back to the days of Clovis and referred to the 'new' territories annexed during the first two decades of his reign prior to his attacks on the Alamanni and the Visigoths, though the term is not attested before the third quarter of the sixth century.

It had no very well-defined boundaries, but comprised roughly all north-western France between the Loire and the Channel, with the exception of Brittany, which was effectively independent; it also included western Belgium between the Scheldt and the sea. It had a large number of mints, many of them in familiar localities – Angers, Nantes, Blois, Orléans, Paris, Rouen – but many more at places of only secondary importance, and a few at ones that have disappeared. No fewer than 22 are represented in the collection here. The dominant reverse type was the cross ancrée, which occurs on over half the 38 Neustrian coins in this collection (**1.451–88**), and certain obverse types, notably the curiously deformed Orléans bust, dominated mints in the neighbourhood. The most important mint was Paris, one of the chief cities of Roman Gaul and a traditional Frankish royal residence, although like Marseille it was often held jointly by two or more kings.

The only substantial study of a Neustrian mint is one by Ponton d'Amécourt on the coins of Le Mans and its region (Amécourt 1881–3). The mint itself is not represented here, but CE (for *Cenomannicum*), used at a number of neighbouring mints, occurs at Corbon, the only known coin of which, with a pedigree going back to Lecointre-Dupont in the 1840s, is in the collection (**1.454**). For the coinage of Paris a tentative chronology has been proposed by Lafaurie (1981f), and there is naturally much regarding its coins in his study of St Eligius (above, p. 99). Once again we have no coins of Eligius, but a derivative from Moussy (**1.458**) has the characteristic EL in the field. Amiens, a moderately important mint – the sequence of its moneyers has been worked out by Lafaurie 1969b – is not represented. There are three coins of Orléans (**1.461–3**) or the neighbourhood, each with its characteristic bust, but despite the abundance of coins of this mint we lack a comprehensive study. Noteworthy types are those of two early coins, a profile standing Victory with a cross on a coin of Angers (**1.451**) and a derivative and crude Visigothic Victory (**1.459–60**; cf. Lafaurie 1973c) at Nantes, a port linked on the one hand with Spain and on the other with the Netherlands, for there was an early coin of Nantes in the Velsen hoard. One of the two coins of Rouen (**1.475**) has an unexplained type, but the mint seems to have been relatively unimportant, perhaps because in the 620s the town was in process of being replaced as a port by Quentovic.

This was a place situated near Etaples at the mouth of the Canche, though the actual site has not been found. On Merovingian coins it is simply *Wiccus*, the fuller name only appearing (as *Quentovicus* or variant) on Carolingian coins (**1.749, 886–8**) when it was thought necessary to distinguish it from other *vici* elsewhere. Because of the ambiguity of *Wiccus* some nineteenth-century scholars proposed to identify it with Wijk-bij-Duurstede, or even Wijk-lez-Maastricht (Alvin 1914), but even apart from the evidence of local finds the legends on some coins identify it precisely as VVIC IN PONTIO, Wic-en-Ponthieu. The Roman word *vicus* had meant simply a village, but as adopted into the Germanic languages it was thought to mean pre-eminently a trading centre and it became an element in place-names all over northern Europe that were often though not invariably connected with mints (Jesse 1955), to say nothing of serving in a roundabout fashion as the root of 'Viking'. Quentovic is not mentioned by Gregory of Tours, and it was apparently not till the early seventh century that it came to replace Boulogne, which had been the main cross-Channel port in Roman times but had apparently become unusable because of the silting-up of the Liane estuary. From the seventh to the ninth century Quentovic enjoyed a practical monopoly of communications with southern England (Fengler 1907; Dhondt 1962), till in the tenth century, repeatedly sacked by the Vikings and in its turn rendered unusable by the silting-up of the river on which it stood, it was replaced by Wissant, which ultimately, in the twelfth century, gave way to Calais (cf. Grierson 1941, 73–81). The coins of Quentovic, a mint well represented here (**1.471–4**), reached southern England in some quantity in the mid seventh century; there were seven at Crondall, over a quarter of the Frankish coins in the hoard, and one of its moneyers, Anglus (ANGLO MONET), was presumably an Anglo-Saxon, at least in his origins.

(f) AUSTRASIA AND FRISIA

Austrasia corresponded roughly to the area between Frisia and the Alps, comprising not only the former *Germania Inferior* and *Belgica Prima* (Trier, Metz, Toul, etc.) but also the bulk of *Germania Secunda* and the eastern part (Rheims, Chalons-sur-Marne) of *Belgica Secunda*. The southern part, from Alsace to the Alps, often formed part of the kingdom of Burgundy and much of its coinage has closer affinities with that of Burgundy than with that of the rest of Austrasia. The kings of Austrasia also normally reigned over large detached areas in Aquitaine and even Provence, but the coins struck in these, even when they bore the names of Austrasian kings, belonged to the coinages of the regions in which they were situated.

Frisia, as defined in the *Lex Frisionum*, was an area extending from the Zwin or Sincfal, the estuary on which Bruges was situated and which is now silted up, to the mouth of the Elbe, so that it included the whole coastline of the Netherlands and virtually all that of north-western Germany. It was thus much larger than the modern Dutch province of Friesland. Its southern frontier, however, was very vaguely defined and fluctuated considerably, while the whole geography of the country, and in particular the pattern of islands and rivers, was very different from that which obtains today. A population that had originally been settled mainly on the dunes, or on the artificial mounds (*terpen*) on which many of the villages were constructed, and had devoted itself mainly to agriculture and fishing, had added trade to these traditional activities, so that by the seventh century most of the trade in the North Sea was in its hands (Jellema 1955; Lebecq 1983). The political history of the country can be reconstructed only in patches, as it is only occasionally mentioned in Frankish annals and lives of saints (cf. Fockema 1949; Halbertsma 1966; Lebecq 1978), but its overseas connections were far-reaching. Trade with Scandinavia provides the best explanation of the number of Constantinopolitan solidi of Leo I and other emperors occurring in the Midlum hoard (Boeles 1951, 503–4, nos. 13ff; Zadoks-Josephus Jitta 1960), and maritime connections down the Atlantic coast are indicated by the presence of a coin of Nantes in the Velsen hoard and of Visigothic coins in those of Mons and Wieuwerd (above, pp. 124–6). The wealth of the country in the mid seventh century is vividly displayed by the number of gold coins mounted as jewellery in the latter hoard.

The three major mints in Austrasia proper were Rheims, Metz and Maastricht, but there were a great number of important secondary ones, mainly in the Meuse valley south of Metz, where there were important salt-pans and a salt industry had flourished from very early times, as many place-names (Marsal, Château-Salins, etc.) bear witness. Huy was also a major mint on the lower Meuse. The coinage of Austrasia has not been studied as a unit, but the Metz–Verdun–Toul region was of special interest in the nineteenth century to two numismatists, Charles Robert and Louis Maxe-Werly, who produced a series of studies either on the region as a whole (Robert 1852, with supplements Robert 1863b, 1867, 1882b) or on particular mints (Robert 1868 on Toul; Maxe-Werly 1862, 1867, 1888–9 on Rheims), to which may be added Heidrich 1974. More recently, for Metz, there is a comprehensive study by Stahl 1982, though the methodology is often debatable, and for Dinant, Meert 1960. For the middle Rhineland there is an old study by Senckler 1850 and a modern one by Diepenbach 1950, and for the upper Rhineland and Switzerland, Wielandt 1939a, 1939b, 1941, Roehrich 1944, and Geiger 1979a, 1979b. For Frisia there is a comprehensive study by Boeles 1951 (gold: pp. 258–317, silver: pp. 359–81, and finds meticulously analysed on pp. 520–74; cf. also Pol 1978) with a valuable essay by Zadoks-Josephus Jitta 1959b and surveys of Merovingian finds in the region by Lafaurie 1975d and Ypey 1959. For the economic background there is Boeles 1954.

The Austrasian and Frisian coins on Plates 24–5 include a few groups linked by resemblances in style and fabric, but the areas and period involved are so large that variety is inevitable and many important mints, including Rheims, are unrepresented. Of Metz there is only a contemporary (?) forgery (**1.1474**), and of Maastricht there is only a single coin (**1.496**) with a blundered moneyer's name. The bust is of the group studied in Bauer 1951 (above, pp. 99, 101–2), but the coin is struck from badly worn dies and the resemblance to the others hard to discern. The normal types in the area are a bust and cross, with often a close reliance on models from Marseille (map in Vercauteren 1934a, 449) and from Chalon-sur-Saône (Stahl 1976, 1982), but in some parts there are crosses, or derivatives of crosses, on both sides. A less important Austrasian group, not represented here, has as obverse type a kind of eight-rayed cross instead of a bust (Lafaurie 1980b). The proportion of coins from unidentified and perhaps intentionally unidentifiable mints is very high, many coins being without legends or having only a few letters or strokes devoid of specific meaning. The proliferation of what even in a Merovingian context can only be regarded as irregular mints is a feature of both Austrasia and Frisia.

The earliest coin, which goes back to the transitional period and comes from the Escharen hoard, is one of Cologne (**1.491**). A number exist from the same roughly made and damaged dies (Hävernick 1935, no. 7; Yvon 1953), and it is interesting as being one of the class where a mint name replaces part of a pseudo-imperial inscription (cf. above, p. 92), for COLONIA takes the place of the letters DNIVSTINI and the whole, on better preserved specimens, reads COLONIA–ANVSPPAVC. The reverse legend is meaningless and the virtually indistinguishable type represents a Victory standing left and holding a cross. The bust is of the same group to which a slightly later coin of Binson (**1.489**) belongs. Also from the lower Rhineland is a coin of Zülpich (**1.503**) with a legible inscription, but for the Mainz region and the middle Rhineland there are only coins of very rough fabric and somewhat uncertain attribution (**1.508ff.**; cf. Diepenbach 1950). For the Moselle valley there is a coin of Dieuze (**1.492**; cf. also **1.504**).

Maastricht and Frisia are better represented. Maastricht had been an important passage (*traiectum*) across the Maas in Roman times and was in the seventh century the seat of the bishops of Tongres, who only later moved to Liège. It may have been already a royal *palatium*, as it certainly was later, for some coins of the moneyer Godofredus (B 4431) have TRIECTO followed by PA (Picqué 1888). It was the major mint in the area, and the names of an impressive succession of moneyers appear on the coins. Dutch scholars, from the early eighteenth century onwards (Serrure 1882), were inclined to attribute coins with TRIECTO to Utrecht, and Ponton d'Amécourt tried to divide them between the two mints, but Belfort's publication of his arrangement provoked a brief flurry of controversy (Cumont 1894; Belfort 1894) which left Maastricht in possession of the entire series. Frisia had been virtually independent during the sixth century, the most striking tribute to this being a coin of which there were two specimens in the Escharen hoard (Lafaurie 1960a, nos. 43–4), bearing the name of the region itself and an otherwise unknown kinglet Audulfus who took over for himself the *Victoria* formula on the reverse of Provençal quasi-imperial coins (above, p. 129) in the same way as Chlotar II was to do after 613 (AVDVLFVS FRISIA and VICTVRIA AVDVLFO: cf. Grierson 1974a). It is one of a large group of Provençal derivatives with cross-on-globe reverse in the hoard which, with the Provençal coins themselves in it, testify to the close trading connections between Frisia and Provence. Another of this type here is **1.501**, a tremissis of Tiel or Nijmegen identified by a blundered NIOMAGO. Yet another early Frisian group (**1.515–16**) has as an obverse type, first explained by Lafaurie, a quadruped looking backwards, such as occasionally appears on Celtic coins. The reverse, however, is no more than a cross and a series of strokes instead of an inscription, so the coins, of which there were at Escharen fourteen specimens from the same clumsily made dies, are evidently a local product.

Under Dagobert the southern part of Frisia was briefly re-annexed by the Franks. The area involved included Dorestad, situated at the junction of the Lek and the lower Rhine (Kromme Rijn) and destined, from the early seventh to the late tenth century, to be one of the major trading ports in the Frankish kingdom and during much of that time a major mint. Coins from it began to come to light in the 1830s, when neighbouring Frankish cemeteries were being exploited by the local villagers as a source of bone manure (Serrure 1885), and although the site of the seventh-century port has not yet been located its Carolingian successor has yielded rich rewards to the archaeologists (Holwerda 1930; Van Es 1969; Van Es *et al.* 1980). Two Maastricht moneyers, Rimoaldus and much more importantly Madelinus, set themselves up at Dorestad, striking virtually identical coins in the two places (Zadoks-Josephus Jitta 1961). The Dorestad coins of Madelinus (**1.493**) served as a model for what are usually described as Frisian imitations (**1.494–5**), on the assumption that they were struck further north and probably after the Frisian recovery of Dorestad, but some may be no more than products of Madelinus' own workshop when it lost the services of a good die-sinker and had to fall back on its own resources. They are a little larger than their models, with type and inscriptions carelessly rendered. Deniers of the same design are also known (**1.633**, and below, p. 151). In the middle decades of the century many other imitative coins were struck in Frisia, known mainly from the Nietap and Dronrijp hoards and with the main type characterized by Boeles as Dronrijp types A–D (**1.517–21**; see Boeles 1947). One feature of this group, apart from the strangely deformed bust, is the LV in the reverse field flanking the cross which led some scholars to attribute them to the mint of Leyden (*Lugdunum Batavorum*), or even to Lyon in Gaul, but they are more likely a distorted and immobilized VII and exactly where the coins were minted is unknown. A more elegant Maastricht imitation is **1.497** with obverse legend +TFIC CTOS blundered from

+TRAIECTO F(*it*). About a dozen specimens, all from the same dies, are known, and since there were four in the Mons hoard they must be earlier in date than the others and probably originated from some locality in Belgium itself.

D. SILVER COINAGE, *c.* 670–*c.* 750

(a) GENERAL FEATURES

The silver deniers of the final Merovingian period owed nothing to the two earlier silver series (above, pp. 111–12, 116) from which they were widely separated in time. Many of their features have been discussed already: the date and circumstances of their introduction (pp. 93–5), their nomenclature and value (pp. 102–7) their weight and fineness (pp. 108–10), and the significance of the displacement of a gold coinage by a silver one (pp. 95–7). It remains to say something of the literature, their types and inscriptions, and their dating.

Literature

The short accounts in Prou 1892a, cv–cxv, and Blanchet 1912, 244–7, are in most respects superseded by Lafaurie's introductions to his reconstructions of the Savonnières, Saint-Pierre-les-Etieux, and other hoards (Lafaurie 1963a, 1969a) and to his reprint of Prou and Bougenot's account of the Bais hoard (Lafaurie 1981d). For the coinage of Provence the basic account is that of Morel-Fatio (in Chabouillet 1890). For that of Frisia, not always easy to distinguish from that of Francia on the one hand and that of England on the other, there is a short, clear survey by Op den Velde 1982, with a good bibliography. Only the 'porcupine' type is the subject of a systematic modern study (Metcalf 1966a). The material collected by Chijs (1866) and the studies of Dirks (1870), Boeles (1951), and Hill (1954) remain important. Our knowledge depends largely on the prolific finds from the Low Countries which are listed in Op den Velde *et al.* 1984, with good maps, especially the many single-finds from Domburg in the island of Walcheren (Rethaan Macaré 1838, 1856; De Man 1899, 1907, 1925) and hoards such as Hallum (De Haan 1866), Franeker (Dirks 1870) and Lutje-Saaksum (Hill 1955; Hill and Sharples 1974). To these must be added finds and hoards from France, England (below, p. 185), northern Germany (Berghaus 1958; Hatz 1959, 1983; Hill 1977b; Metcalf 1969b), Denmark (Bendixen 1981, 1984) and the Rhineland (Zedelius 1980). The circulation of sceattas on the Continent is discussed in Callmer 1984. The penetration of Frisian and Anglo-Saxon coins into Frankish Gaul was discussed by Le Gentilhomme (1938a). The metallic compositions of a substantial number of Merovingian and Frisian silver coins, many of them from this collection, are published in Metcalf and Hamblin 1968 and Metcalf 1983a.

Types and inscriptions

The Frankish denier started as an independent denomination and not as a debased tremissis, but the designs of the earliest ones, with a bust and some form of cross accompanied by the names of moneyer and mint, were not very different from those of the coins they were replacing. The deniers became generally smaller and thicker, and they were often irregularly shaped as, for example, at Marseille. A bust remained the dominant obverse type, though geometric and epigraphic designs were also used. At some mints a cross was retained for the reverse, notably in the Poitiers region (**1.593–5**) and a cross ancrée at Paris (**1.597–604**), but letters, monograms or more striking geometric types were commonly employed. There are a few naturalistic designs of some quality, such as the figure of a nimbate Christ on an ass (**1.590**) or two standing figures on coins of Le Mans, while at some mints animal designs were favoured (Lafaurie 1974b). Some of the later issues have types that link up with those of Carolingian coins of the third quarter of the eighth century (Amécourt 1868c). In Frisia, as in England, the coins occasionally drew on standard themes of Germanic art such as a beast looking backwards (**1.664**), but more often they copied and developed the designs of Anglo-Saxon or Merovingian issues.

The majority of Merovingian deniers bear some form of legend, in contrast to the mainly uninscribed issues of the Frisians and Anglo-Saxons. However, coins from the more northerly mints sometimes have only a few letters or an indecipherable monogram forming the design or are uninscribed, and they often cannot be distinguished from imitations and derivatives struck by the Frisians. In general, there is a greater proportion of coins that cannot be attributed to mints in the silver coinage than in the gold that had preceded it, either because their legends are less informative or less literate, or because they are more crudely produced with part of the inscription off the flan.

A notable difference from the gold coinage is the virtual disappearance of royal names. The only denier with the name of a king is one of Childeric II (662–75) (Lafaurie 1965b). This can only in part be a consequence of the eclipse of the monarchy in this period, for the kings' names are not replaced by those of Mayors of the Palace. There are indeed two early silver coins of the 670s or early 680s with the name of Ebroin (B 3460 = P 798, and one from the Bais hoard: Prou and Bougenot 1907, no. 99), but there are none of any of his Austrasian successors, Pepin II, Charles Martel, or Pepin the Short before he became king. The fact is surprising, as such coins would at least have been suited to the distribution of alms, and although official moneyers have often been reluctant to mint in metals less noble than those to which they were accustomed, it is hard to credit those of the seventh century with such prejudices. At Marseille, where the tradition of placing the king's name on the gold coinage had been strongest, the name or monogram of successive patricians of Provence is found on most coins until at least the second decade of the eighth century.

As in the gold coinage, the standard legend names both the mint and the moneyer, but some give only the mint, notably Paris (**1.598**), or the moneyer (**1.616**), while others are blundered beyond recognition (e.g. **1.579–90**). There appears to have been a considerable extension of ecclesiastical minting, first commented on by Fillon, though this has not yet been systematically studied. Coins are known for more bishoprics and monasteries than had been the case earlier, and the names of bishops and abbots, or what are believed to be their monograms, appear on some of them, although it is probable that the number of such names has been exaggerated, and that some of the single syllables which have been expanded to fit in with the names in episcopal lists are not to be construed in this way at all. Most of the ecclesiastical issues name only the see or monastery that produced them (**1.541**, Lyon; **1.608**, St Martin of Tours), though occasionally even that is omitted and they have only a formula such as *Racio ecclesie* (**1.591–2, 614–15**). The reason for this increase, as already suggested, may be that the silver for the new coinage came in large measure from the treasures of the Church, but it probably also reflects the growing use of coined money in the internal economy of ecclesiastical estates.

The only inscriptions on Frisian coins are those copied either from earlier issues (**1.633**, copying tremisses of Dorestad) or from contemporary Merovingian or Anglo-Saxon coins (**1.639–45**, copying English runic coins). One exception is a variety of the 'porcupine' type which has the letters VIC or VICO on the reverse (**1.650–1**), possibly standing for *vicus*.

Chronology

There are few external aids for dating the coins. Save for the unique coin of Childeric II and the two of Ebroin, we cannot tie the coins into the established chronologies of the kings and the Mayors of the Palace. The few named bishops who can reasonably be identified with persons recorded in written sources belong mostly to the last quarter of the seventh century and we rarely have more than an isolated date for them through their appearance as present at Church Councils or as recipients, grantors or witnesses of charters (Lafaurie 1969a, 115–22; Lafaurie 1974a, 44–5). The largest group of coins that can be independently dated are those of Marseille with the names of patricians of Provence, but even here the dates of these are inadequately recorded (below, pp. 142–3).

As with the gold coinage we have to rely mainly on the comparative evidence of hoards, the contents of which are very largely known through meticulous reconstructions by Lafaurie, three of them in a single fundamental article (Lafaurie 1969a). The French hoards can be considered apart from the English and Low Country ones since, although Frankish deniers merge into Frisian sceattas and these again into English ones, Frankish deniers themselves are rarely found outside their country of origin (Lafaurie 1981d, ii–iv). These hoards are, however, important for arranging and dating the Anglo-Saxon and Frisian coinages and are considered further in the next chapter. The six principal hoards of Merovingian deniers – Saint-Pierre-les-Etieux, Plassac, Nohanent, Bais, Cimiez and Savonnières – are described briefly below in the order of their deposit as worked out by Lafaurie from the development of coin types, sequences of moneyers, considerations of fabric, etc. While commenting on the difficulty of ascribing dates to them, he has suggested that all six hoards were deposited in the 730s and 740s, with the last possibly *c.* 750–1 (Lafaurie 1969a, 148–50; 1974a, 33; 1981d, xxv). However, these seem too late and a revised dating, discussed in Blackburn 1984, attributing all but the Savonnières hoard to the first two decades of the eighth century, will be considered below. (See also Map 3, p. 123 above.)

Saint-Pierre-les-Etieux (Buhot 1884; Lafaurie 1969a).

A pot-hoard of rather more than 100 deniers and one tremissis (of Banassac) found in February 1882 at Saint-Pierre-les-Etieux in Berry, on the road between Charenton and Le Creuset, so that Belfort in his *Description* (1892–5) styles it the Creuset hoard. An account of 61 coins that he had been able to examine was published almost immediately by A. Buhot de Kersers, a local antiquary and numismatist (Buhot 1884); nearly thirty more are known from Barthélemy's drawings of tinfoil impressions made for Maxe-Werly that are now in the museum at Bar-le-Duc; and a few others were located by Lafaurie while working on his description of the hoard. Two-thirds of the coins are now in either the Cabinet des Médailles (24) or the local museum at Bourges (30); the rest are scattered, three being in this collection (**1.542, 596, 599**). A fifth of the coins in the hoard were struck at Bourges or in the neighbourhood; the rest are from a variety of scattered mints, with significant numbers from Paris and its region (11), Chalon (8) and Provence (8), with eleven sceattas of Series BII, C, D and early E. None of the coins names individuals who can be independently dated. Lafaurie dates this hoard and the next, Plassac, *c.* 730–5 and has suggested a possible association with the campaigns of Charles Martel in Aquitaine and against the Arabs.

Plassac (La Grange 1851; Lafaurie 1963a).

A hoard of 170 deniers found at Plassac, near Bordeaux, was acquired by the Marquis de La Grange in 1850. Its contents have to be reconstructed from the 77 identifiable specimens which he listed (La Grange 1851) and from the sale catalogue of his collection (Rollin & Feuardent 19.2.1877), though since the latter included Merovingian coins from other sources it must be used with caution. Lafaurie's final listing runs to 173 coins plus four hammered silver fragments, and not all the coins can be traced or even identified. Nearly half the coins (79) are now in the Cabinet des Médailles; six (**1.586**, **589**, **594**, **615**, **618–19**) are in this collection. Over a third of the hoard consisted of coins of Poitiers or Bourges and their respective neighbourhoods, and nearly as many are from unidentifiable mints. There were twelve sceattas of Series B and D and possibly an early variety of the Frisian 'Star' type (cf. **1.638**). Again there are no coins that can be independently dated.

Nohanent (Lafaurie 1969a; supplement *BSFN* 27 (1972), 230).

This small hoard of 35+ deniers was found at Nohanent, on the outskirts of Clermont-Ferrand, in 1877, but its existence was unknown to scholars prior to 1956. In that year the Cabinet des Médailles acquired a small collection of Merovingian coins formed in the nineteenth century by Augustin Chassaing, a judge at Le Puy, and with it three letters of 1877 from the collector-dealer G. Grange of Clermont-Ferrand referring to it. M. Grange had available 35 coins, not the complete hoard, and he sent wax impressions of a number of those he had to Chassaing, with descriptions of others. Chassaing bought only two, but the letters and impressions allowed Lafaurie to recognize a number now dispersed in various collections, including two here (**1.540**, **576**). The only coin with a personal name which can be recognized is one of Nordobertus, bishop of Clermont-Ferrand in the early eighth century (after 701), prior to Bubus and Procolus whose coins were present in the Cimiez hoard (Lafaurie 1969a, 215–16).

Bais (Durocher 1905–6; Prou and Bougenot 1907; Hamburger sale, 19.10.1928; Lafaurie 1981d).

A pot-hoard of 407 silver coins, with two rings and some ingots and cut-up silver fragments, that was found in 1904 by a farmer at Bais, some 40km south-east of Rennes on the former Breton frontier. Some 18 or 19 coins were acquired by a local collector, who published 15 of them (Durocher 1905–6); a few were bought by other collectors, not all of which could subsequently be traced; but the great majority (358) were bought directly from the finder by the collector S. Bougenot. A careful description of these, and of all others on which information was available, was published in 1907 by Prou and Bougenot, whose description and plates were used by Hamburger as the basis of a sale catalogue when the Bougenot share was sold in Frankfurt-am-Main in 1928. The coins are now widely dispersed and many are untraceable. The original Prou–Bougenot description was reprinted by Lafaurie in 1981 with a lengthy introduction (74 pp.) revising a few of Prou's attributions but in the main devoted to discussing the find in the general context of Merovingian silver coinage.

A feature of the hoard is the very wide variety of mints represented in it, which led Prou to suggest that it was a moneyer's accumulation for remelting, as this would also account for the ingots, silver fragments and rings. A large proportion of the coins are from the Bourges–Poitiers region, though mints in the Seine and Loire valleys were also well represented. There were 29 sceattas of Series A, B, D and E. A few coins are very early: there is one (no. 99) of Ebroin (d. 680 or 683), and Prou noted that a denier of Sens (no. 62) has a bust that is virtually identical with that on an Orléans tremissis of Clovis II (639–57). A number of other coins have been tentatively attributed to particular bishops of the late seventh century (Lafaurie 1981d, xxiii–xxiv, lv), though most of the attributions are rather uncertain. Lafaurie dates the hoard *c.* 735–40.

Cimiez (Chabouillet 1890, publishing Morel-Fatio's report of the hoard, abbreviated as 'MF' below).

This huge hoard of over 2,000 deniers came to light *c.* 1850. Accounts of the finding vary slightly, with Vence and Grasse, both in the neighbourhood, as rivals to Cimiez, but the latter seems to have the better claim. Since Cimiez is a suburb of Nice, Lafaurie prefers to write of the Nice-Cimiez hoard. The two major parcels from it consisted of 380 coins acquired by a merchant at Vence in November 1851 and 1,914 coins bought at Nice in 1856 by Arnold Morel-Fatio, a Swiss banker domiciled in Paris and a distinguished numismatist. The Vence parcel began to come on the market at once; Fillon was able in 1853 to describe and illustrate a large selection that had been acquired by the Lyon collector Henri Morin (Fillon 1853, 95–111), and Carpentin, a Marseille scholar, when publishing a further group in 1864, first recognized the true identity of Nemfidius (Carpentin 1864). Morel-Fatio disposed of duplicates during his lifetime but presented the core of the collection (497 coins) to the Cabinet des Médailles in 1887, together with a detailed description of 1,920 coins, which was published with admirable promptitude by the director of the Cabinet (Chabouillet 1890; cf. Lafaurie 1981d, xii–xiii). They were subsequently studied by Manteyer (1942, 656–67), but most of his conclusions must be dismissed as fanciful, despite the acceptance of many of them by Lafaurie (1963a, 73; 1969a, 118ff.).

Most of the deniers in the hoard bear the name or monogram of some patrician of Provence, which enables us to date its deposit fairly precisely, and this makes the hoard crucial for the chronology not only of the Frankish coinage, but of the Frisian and Anglo-Saxon coinages as well (Blackburn 1984, 170–4). The successive issues of Marseille and their dates are discussed in Section (b) below (pp. 147–9). Of the 1,500 or so coins of Marseille in the hoard, a handful were of the very earliest types attributed to the 680s. There were 6 coins in the name of Antenor and 67+ of Ansedert, who are not recorded in written sources but were presumably patricians in the late seventh century. The overwhelming majority of the coins (1,189+) bear the name or monogram of Nemfidius, whom we know to have held office during the later years of Pepin of Herstal (687–714), and there was a smaller number (102+) of his successor, another Antenor, who was patrician at the time of Pepin's death. The only other significant group was 153+ coins with a large M (for *Massilia*) and a cruciform monogram, apparently with the letters OCΛC, but which was probably copied from a coin of Nemfidius. There are many die-links and die-duplicates among the coins of Nemfidius, the second Antenor, and the OCΛC group; the latter two in particular were struck from very few dies and their issue can have been only brief.

These are the only identifications with patricians that can be made with any degree of confidence, and the further ones proposed by Morel-Fatio or Manteyer and hesitantly accepted by Lafaurie will not stand up to examination. The names of two later patricians are known, Metrano (*c.* 720?) and Abbo (d. 739, but no longer in office), while we hear of the rebellion of a *dux* Maurontus in 737. Morel-Fatio (Chabouillet 1890, 31) believed that the deniers with the name of *Massilia* alone, or with a large M and no name of patrician, belonged to the period between Antenor and his successor Metrano or perhaps to Metrano himself, the M identifying both mint and patrician. This would date the hoard to *c.* 730. Fillon (1853, 102) put it about a decade later (*c.* 740), since he regarded the coins without moneyer's names as typical of the period of Charles Martel. An obvious possibility would be its burial on the occasion of either Charles' expedition of 736 or his far more destructive one of 737, when he was provoked by the rebellion of the *dux* Maurontus and his alliance with the Saracens in the Narbonensis into ravaging southern Provence, burning the 'most famous' cities of Nîmes, Agde and Béziers and destroying their walls and the surrounding countryside. Le Gentilhomme in fact suggested 737 on the ground that in this year Cimiez was destroyed by the Lombards (Le Gentilhomme 1938a, 28), but this event seems to be fiction: Paul the Deacon, our only authority for Liutprand's plans for assisting Charles Martel against the Saracens in this year, mentions no such incident. Manteyer argued for an even later date by identifying the letters on the coins with several magnates posterior to Antenor: a few coins with M alone as being ones of Metrano, two with a large A or MA monogram to which are attached B, R and two Os (MF 91) with the patrician Abbo, those with M and OCAC, which he reconstructed as a monogram of MAVOS, with the *dux* Maurontus, and seven coins with KAP and PAS (MF 119–21), interpreted as KA(*rlus*) P(*rovinciae*) PA(*triciu*)S, with Charles Martel during the short period before his death in 741 when he might have assumed the title of patrician.

These interpretations are unacceptable on numismatic grounds, for they imply that a hoard of the 740s consisted overwhelmingly of coins minted between *c.* 700 and *c.* 715 that are closely die-linked. A hoard of over 2,000 coins buried near Marseille as late as that would also have contained more coins of the subsequent 'officials' enumerated above. A more reasonable dating would be near *c.* 715/20, closer to Nemfidius' own time, the more so since such other coins in the hoard as are datable all belong to the first two decades of the eighth century. There were coins of Bubus and Procolus, bishops of Clermont-Ferrand after Nordbertus, whose coinage was represented in the Nohanent hoard. There were also two deniers of Narbonne of the Marseille pattern that have as their reverse type the letters NARB attached to the arms of a cross with O in the centre (MF 106, pl. 6.97), which must have been struck between 714, when Visigothic rule in the Narbonensis ended, and 719, when it was overrun by the Arabs (above, p. 44). The attribution of coins reading RAN(E) and PAL to two bishops of Nîmes, Ranemir (*c.* 673) and Palladius (supposedly *c.* 737), cannot be sustained (below, p. 149), while others given by Lafaurie to Austrobertus, a bishop of Vienne in the 730s, depend for their identification upon a monogram which has been variously interpreted and their attribution is quite uncertain.

Savonnières (Lafaurie 1963a).

The latest of the six hoards consisted of 45 deniers found in an earthenware pot at Savonnières, near Tours, in 1865. They were quickly dispersed, but eight were acquired by Ponton d'Amécourt, who noted the locality of the hoard in his study of the Merovingian coinage of Touraine (Amécourt 1868a), and 35 are known from the collection of drawings given by Barthélemy to the Cabinet des Médailles (Prou 1893). Lafaurie was consequently able to reconstruct almost the entire hoard (39 coins) and indicate the present whereabouts of many coins, one of them being in this collection (**1.608**). The contents were strongly localized, 30 of the coins being of the abbey of St Martin of Tours or of the cathedral (in the name of St Maurice) and the rest of Chinon, Châteaudun, probably Savonnières and an uncertain mint or mints with a pentalpha as type. There were no sceattas in the hoard. The coins are struck on a lighter standard than those in the earlier hoards and their larger, squarer flans reflect a change in mint technique, which perhaps foreshadows those of the earliest deniers of Pepin. The coins of Tours are evidently later in date than the few in the Saint-Pierre-les-Etieux, Plassac and Bais hoards. Savonnières presumably also post-dates Cimiez and thus belongs to the period *c.* 720–55, though since there were no mints common to both hoards we are unable to date it with any certainty. Lafaurie would put the hoard very late, *c.* 742–5 or even *c.* 750–1.

The redating of the Cimiez hoard to *c.* 720 implies still earlier dates for the hoards from Saint-Pierre-les-Etieux, Plassac, Nohanent and Bais, but this is quite consistent with their compositions. As we have seen, the only independently dated coins in them belong to the late seventh or early eighth century. Although these hoards were all found far from Provence, such coins of Marseille as they contain pre-date those of Nemfidius (Table 11) which would be hard to explain unless they had been deposited fairly early in the eighth century before his coins had had time to be disseminated widely. Having regard to the Anglo-Saxon and Frisian coins in these hoards, which belong to the Primary and Intermediate phases (below, pp. 164–8), the following revised dates of deposit are proposed:

Saint-Pierre-les Etieux (1882), *c.* 700/705
Plassac (1850), *c.* 705
Nohanent (1877), *c.* 705/710
Bais (1904), *c.* 710
Cimiez (1851), *c.* 720
Savonnières (1865), *c.* 740?

It follows that our knowledge of the Merovingian silver coinage is more limited than has hitherto been appreciated. With all the major hoards deposited during the first two decades of the eighth century and that from Savonnières being small and very localized, we are dependent for our knowledge of the final 35 years of the coinage on isolated finds. These are of course difficult to date and they appear to be rather less common than is the case for the isolated finds of sceattas in England or Frisia, though there is as yet no systematic publication of them. Even for the late seventh and early eighth century, there are areas of France, notably the north-east, that are greatly under-represented in the hoards, and there must be many coin types and mints of which we have little or no knowledge.

Table 11. *Coins of Marseille in the hoards from Saint-Pierre-les-Etieux, Plassac, Nohanent, Bais and Cimiez. (For the types, see pp. 147–8 below.)*

	Saint-Pierre-les-Etieux	Plassac	Nohanent	Bais	Cimiez
M/hatched reverse	2	—	—	3	3
Early portrait/cross-on-base	2	—	1	3	3
Antenor I	—	—	—	—	6
Anserdert	—	—	—	—	67
Nemfidius (*c.* 700)	—	—	—	—	1,189
Antenor II (*c.* 714)	—	—	—	—	102
OCAC	—	—	—	—	153
Other	1	—	—	2	19
Total	5	—	1	8	1,542

Classification

The Merovingian and Frisian deniers in this collection are catalogued and illustrated on Plates 26–30. They are classified on a roughly regional basis, but with the exceptions of the coins of Provence and Frisia there would be no point in discussing them in the same fashion as was done for the gold. Coins of Provence are common because of the Cimiez hoard and those of Frisia because of their wide dispersal in hoards and single finds in the Low Countries and England, so that in both cases the material exists for establishing an approximate chronology and discerning the pattern of local minting. For mints elsewhere our material is much slighter, and only for a few mints can one establish credible sequences of issues. The following notes are limited to the regions outside Provence and Frisia.

The only deniers of Burgundy in the collection are two of Chalon-sur-Saône (**1.539–40**), the second one being from the Nohanent hoard, and one of a bishop of Lyon (**1.541**), its identity clear from $\overline{\text{LV}}$ on the obverse and a cross with what seem to be the letters EPS on the reverse. One of the Chalon coins has the name of the moneyer Inportunus, which is also found on the gold and may represent an immobilization of the legend. A denier attributed by Ponton d'Amécourt to Chalon in his monograph on the coins of this mint (Amécourt 1873, pl. 5.150–1) but which is unlike other coins of Chalon in fabric and type, belongs rather, on the evidence of the very inadequately published hoard of Barbuise, to some mint in the neighbourhood of Rheims (**1.607**, and note on this coin).

There is, as noted already (p. 94), no silver coinage for southern and western Aquitaine, and the coins here come from the north (Poitou, Berry) or from the Limousin, which in Ebroin's time still formed part of the kingdom of Neustria. The Bourges group (**1.579–90**) is characterized by reverse types normally consisting of a cross formed from four or five large globules in a circle of similar globules. They were formerly attributed to Poitiers, but are now given to Bourges on the evidence of the Saint-Pierre-les-Etieux hoard, though few specimens have a legible name of mint or moneyer. Some of them have as obverse type a head wearing a radiate crown and a diadem on which the knot behind has been doubled to form two loops, giving with the diadem the incongruous aspect of a pair of scissors. The series is unusually well represented here as a result of Lord Grantley's purchase of several coins going back to the Plassac and Saint-Pierre-les-Etieux hoards. There are a few typological linkages with other series: **1.589** has a reverse of a 'standard' pattern copied from some Frisian or English coin, and **1.590**, one of those with a legible mint name (*Cornacus*, probably Gournay, some 66km south-west of Bourges), has the unusual type of Christ seated on an ass, representing the entry into Jerusalem. It has usually been described as a mounted horseman, but the nimbus containing a cross provides a clear identification.

The other two groups, those of Poitiers and Limoges, are smaller. Two of the Poitiers coins (**1.593–4**) bear the names of both mint and moneyer. The third coin is linked to **1.594** in that the cross has two pellets at the end of each arm, but its blundered legends and poor metal show it to be a contemporary imitation. The two coins attributed to the church of Limoges (**1.591–2**), both of the moneyer Theodoald, have as obverse type a large ER, i.e. *Ecclesiae racio*, but the mint is conjectural (cf. Lafaurie 1969a, 170, note to no. 54). Prou originally attributed coins with ER on the obverse to Paris (P 822–8), but the relatively large number of specimens known seems to indicate a more important mint, and in his account of the Bais hoard he settled for Limoges itself (Prou and Bougenot 1907, 57–60). The reverses are related to those of coins that can be linked up as being from Limoges (Bais nos. 133 and 138), and ER does occur on other coins of the Limousin. Lafaurie (1969a, 196, note to no. 75) suggested for these coins Neuvic d'Ussel (Corrèze: see **1.438**) in the *civitas Lemovicum*, since a very similar piece with a different moneyer's name has the legend *Novovico*.

It has been suggested above (pp. 94–5) that it was in the kingdom of Neustria that the silver denier was originally introduced. The chief mints, so far as one can judge from surviving coins, were Amiens (cf. Lafaurie 1969b), Rouen (cf. Lafaurie 1978c), Paris (cf. Lafaurie 1981f) and St Martin of Tours, though there are a few others, like Le Mans and Angers, with identifiable mint names. But some prolific mints of the earlier period, and most notably Quentovic, seem to have disappeared entirely. It is possible that cross-Channel trade was at this time undergoing a period of eclipse, for there are equally no silver coins that can be attributed with certainty to its Frisian counterpart Dorestad (but cf. below, p. 153), though both revived in the Carolingian period. As for Austrasia, which probably adopted a silver coinage after Childeric II became sole king in 673, the main silver mints seem to have been Rheims, Metz and various Rhineland towns.

In both Neustria and Austrasia new mints were probably opened, but the virtual anonymity of so much of the silver coinage makes it impossible to identify them with certainty. Only a few mints carried on the full mint-and-moneyer identifications of the earlier coinage, and that only for a period. **1.597–8** bear the name of Paris and that of a moneyer, but the moneyer's name is blundered and illegible; subsequently there is only a mint name (PARISIVS), and eventually we have coins which can be attributed to Paris or its neighbourhood only by their use of types, notably the cross ancrée with vertical attachments suspended from the ends of its cross-arms, which had previously been much used at the mint. Other mints have equally characteristic types – a rosette at Amiens, a central S or a monogram with an S across the N that formed its central element at St Martin of Tours (cf. **1.608–10**) – but these are not the only types employed at each mint and were in any case copied in the neighbourhood. **1.608** is a coin of St Martin of Tours with names of both mint and moneyer (SCI MARTINI, VINCTER), and Vincter is only one of several moneyers known for the mint in the denarial period. **1.613**, a coin of Void on the Moselle, has also the name of both mint and moneyer but is not typical of the denarial coinage of the region – it is struck from tremissis dies – and other north-eastern mints tend to be identified by initials (RM for *Remis*, Rheims (**1.604–6**); ME ligatured for *Mettis*, Metz (**1.596**)). The two letters alone are uninformative by themselves but the identification is confirmed by the finding of specimens in the neighbourhood. There are coins with *Racio ecclesie* (**1.615**) or a moneyer's name (**1.616**, Apalsar) whose mints are undetermined. But the general tendency is for the emergence of essentially anepigraphic types, or types accompanied by quite meaningless inscriptions. The mints of such coins might be known locally, but could not be recognized by users further afield.

(b) PROVENCE

The deniers of Provence (**1.542–78**) are proportionately the most numerous in the Merovingian series, both here and in other collections, as a consequence of the distorting effect of the Cimiez hoard. Most can be attributed to Marseille, confirmed in many cases by the legend *Massilia* or a large M in the field, and although attempts have been made to identify others with mints at Arles, Nîmes and Vienne these are at best doubtful and at worst demonstrably wrong. The practice of placing the king's name on the coins of Marseille ceased with the introduction of the denier, but the tradition of naming the governing authority was continued in the silver coinage by the inclusion of the name of the chief official of the region, the patrician of Provence. The earliest coins of Marseille, with a diademed bust and a cross-on-base, are related in design to the gold coinage, but the introduction of a variety of new types and a marked change of fabric towards the end of the seventh century set this series apart. Although the die-cutting was usually literate and at times quite skilled, coin production, on small, thick and irregularly shaped flans, was somewhat crude. The lack of efficient mint control is also reflected in the wide variation of weights, even among die-duplicates, from *c.* 1.25g to under 1.00g, and of finenesses, from *c.* 90% to *c.* 60% silver.

The chronology of the coinage depends largely on that of the patricians of Provence, and this, despite the work of two excellent scholars (Kiener 1900, 254, 264–5; Buchner 1933, 98–100) on the history of Provence at this period, remains obscure. The patricians Nemfidius and Antenor are known not from contemporary documents but from ones of Charlemagne's time that are not easy to follow and give no dates. The most important is a legal record of 780 reconstructing the history of some property which the *patricius* Nemfidius had given to the abbey of St Victor at Marseille somewhere about the start of the century. After Nemfidius' death his successor the patrician Antenor had seized the property and caused such records of the transactions as he could find to be burned. One charter was saved by Nemfidius' widow Adeltrudis, who with her three unnamed sons confirmed the gift. Antenor subsequently took advantage of the *rixas vel contentiones que in Provincia fuerunt* to seize the property again, and his successors Metrano, *qui fuit patricius in Provincia*, and subsequently Abbo, held it in benefice. Abbo's will, dated 739, has survived, but does not style him patrician, probably because he had lost his post in 736, when Charles Martel occupied Provence as far as Marseille and Arles and 'set up his judges' (*usque Massiliensem urbem vel Arelatum suis iudicibus constituit*), thus abolishing the old patriciate, which is not heard of again (Zöllner 1970, 94). Kiener suggests that Abbo became patrician at some date after 726, when we hear of him as *rector* of Maurienne and Susa. Metrano would then have been in office *c.* 720 and Antenor at the time of Pepin's death (714), for another document of Charlemagne's reign refers to his activity *quando Provincia revellavit* [sic] *contra bisavio vestro Pipino* (Buchner 1933, 98) and the *rixas vel contentiones* were probably those that broke out in 714. For Nemfidius no closer date can be suggested than *c.* 700/710.

The basic sequence of issues at Marseille seems to have been (a) a *Massilia* series without personal names, (b) an *Antenor* series with his name in full, (c) an *Ansedert* series with name in full, (d) the *Nemfidius* series with name in full or monogram, (e) a second *Antenor* series with monogram, and (f) an unattributed series with OCAC in the arms of a cross. There are also miscellaneous coins of Massiliote fabric, some of disputed mint attribution. The abbreviation 'MF' in the paragraphs that follow refers to Morel-Fatio's numbering in Chabouillet 1890.

(a) *Massilia* series, not represented here, has on one side a bust and on the other a cross-on-base and the legend *Massilia* (MF 73–5, pl. 2.21–3). There were only three in the Cimiez hoard, and there was one in Saint-Pierre-les-Etieux and in Nohanent. They appear to lead the silver coinage and can probably be dated to the 680s. A few coins of the same type and similar style in the Saint-Pierre-les-Etieux and Bais hoards replace *Massilia* by '*Ebalgo*' or '*Audevert*', but as each is known only from a single die one hesitates to identify them as names of moneyers or patricians. 'Audevert' may be a corruption of Ansedert, though the coin appears to be much earlier than any of his others. Other types, with *Massilia* around a simple cross or a large M or MA (MF 76–85, pl. 2.24–31), of which there were thirteen in Cimiez, may be of a slightly later date.

(b) First *Antenor* series, of the same bust/cross-on-base type as the last, but of a somewhat developed style and with the legend *Antenor* (MF 1–5, pl. 1.17–20). They are recorded only from the Cimiez hoard, in which there were six, but none is present here. The person named cannot be the patrician Antenor of the written sources since he was Nemfidius' successor and his coins are of quite different design and fabric. Whether the earlier Antenor was a patrician of whom we have no record, or a simple moneyer, we do not know for certain, but as the Marseille tradition was one of a public coinage struck successively in the names of emperors, kings, and patricians, and not one of moneyers, it is more likely that he was a patrician.

(c) *Ansedert* series (**1.543–6**). These are of a greater variety of types, all with Ansedert's name spelled out and sometimes a large M or monogram of MA in the field of the obverse and reverse to identify the mint (MF 6–24, pl. 1. 1–16). These coins are struck on smaller, more irregularly-shaped flans, which also characterize subsequent issues of Marseille. There were 67+ in the Cimiez hoard. Ansedert's name does not appear in the written sources, but he was probably the patrician who immediately preceded Nemfidius, and the coins belong to the 690s or early 700s.

(d) *Nemfidius* series (**1.547–66**). These are by far the commonest of the Massiliote deniers, with some 1,200 in the hoard and 20 in this collection. They are of various types, with the earlier coins resembling those of Ansedert and Antenor in having Nemfidius' name spelled out in full and the later ones having as obverse type a crude bust, usually accompanied by a cross, and on the reverse a monogram of the chief letters of Nemfidius' name (MF 25–72, pls. 2–5.42–88; variations tabulated on pl. 4). Although Nemfidius is given no title, it is reasonable to identify him with the patrician and thus date them *c.* 700/710.

(e) Second *Antenor* series (**1.567–9**). These have on the obverse ANT in monogram and on the reverse SM or a monogram of AR or ARD (MF 109–11, pl. 7.119–21). There were 102+ in the hoard, many of them die-duplicates, and it seems reasonable to attribute them to the patrician Antenor who succeeded Nemfidius and who may have been either the earlier Antenor restored or a relation, perhaps a son. It has been suggested that the AR(D) indicates the mint of Arles, leaving coins with SM for Marseille, but this is unlikely since there are die-links between them (**1.567–8** with ARD and **1.569** with SM are struck from the same obverse die) and the fabric and appearance of the coins is purely Massiliote. The coinage was struck from relatively few dies and would appear to have been only brief.

(f) *OCAC* series (**1.572–5**). These have on the obverse a large M surmounted by a cross for *Massilia* and on the reverse a cross with crude letters in the angles. Morel-Fatio read them as OCΛC or OCΛ (MF 86–9, pl. 2.32–5), but they are probably no more than very degenerate and retrograde copies of the NFDS cruciform monogram found on coins of Nemfidius (**1.555**; MF 52–5, pls. 3–4.65–8). Manteyer's attempt to read in it the name of *dux* Maurontus must be regarded as fanciful (above, p. 142). This is one of the latest groups in the Cimiez hoard, for the 153 specimens in it are struck from only a handful of dies, and it may have been struck during a period of unrest after Nemfidius' death.

One coin in the hoard with the same obverse design has a cross-crosslet over saltire reverse apparently derived from an Anglo-Saxon sceat of Series W (below, p. 170). Two others with the same reverse design have a clear though problematic obverse, with a monogram of MA similar to that on coins of Ansedert, but which may also double as a letter A in the name (?) formed by the letters in the field, ROBO. Manteyer identified it as the patrician Abbo, but the letters do not fit and he would be too late. We cannot offer a satisfactory interpretation.

The hoard also contained some fourteen coins reading RAN or RANE (**1.570**; MF 98–100, pl. 6.94–6) and sixteen of similar type reading PAL (**1.571**; MF 101–5, pl. 6.89–93). Morel-Fatio suggested, without much show of conviction, that they might have been struck by two eighth-century bishops of Nîmes. Ranemir in fact became bishop in 673 (Duchesne 1907–15, I.312), but he was an intruder and had ceased to be bishop *c.* 680. Palladius' name is known only from a (lost) episcopal list, and Duchesne considered him an accidental duplication of a sixth-century bishop Pelagius. With one bishop the wrong date and the other probably non-existent, the attribution to Nîmes, though endorsed by Manteyer (1942, 662–4), who discussed their metrology at some length, and by Lafaurie (1981d, xviii), falls to the ground. The coins are of Massiliote fabric, and the style of busts suggests that they are contemporary with coins of Nemfidius, but their mint remains uncertain.

Two other groups of coins have been attributed to Marseille or the region, but if so they are of such different fabric and design to those just described that they must be the product of a separate mint. The first and the earlier of the two issues has a large M on the obverse and crude hatching on the reverse (**1.542**). There were three in the Cimiez and Bais hoards and two in those of Saint-Pierre-les-Etieux and Nohanent, which is similar to the distribution of the early bust/cross-on-base coins. An attribution to Marseille is supported by an isolated find from Saint-Rémy-de-Provence (Lafaurie 1969a, 175), though it cannot be regarded as certain. The second type has on one side a bust with a cross before it and on the other a distorted cross ancrée with VII in the field. On the earliest coins, present in the Saint-Pierre-les-Etieux and Nohanent hoards (**1.576**, from the latter), the bust is fairly well formed with hair flowing down behind the neck, but later it becomes grotesquely deformed (**1.577–8**) under the influence of Frisian 'porcupine' sceattas. There were 22 specimens of this later type in the Cimiez hoard (MF 107, pls. 6–7.106–17). The suggestion that they were the prototype for the 'porcupine' design is contradicted by the evidence of the French finds which show that the 'porcupine' type was already fully developed when the earliest VII coins were being used. Fillon (1853, 91) attributed the type to Mainz without giving any good reason, while Prou (1896a) and Le Gentilhomme (1938a) rejected them altogether from the Merovingian series. However, Morel-Fatio's suggestion that they are Provençal has been adopted by Lafaurie (1969a, 175) and seems preferable in view of the number in the Cimiez hoard and the use of VII regularly found on tremisses of the region, even if his typological parallels with the early Carolingian coins of Marseille are unconvincing.

(c) FRISIA

The silver coinage of what has been termed Greater Frisia consists of several distinct series of uninscribed coins which, like their English counterparts, are generally known as 'sceattas' (below, p. 157). Imitations of Merovingian and English coins also occur in finds from the Low Countries and were probably produced locally. No clear distinction can be drawn between the North Frankish and Frisian coinages as the former were also sometimes uninscribed and most of the issues can be attributed to only an approximate period and region. Moreover, the Frisian/Frankish border was pushed progressively northwards during the eighth century. Pepin of Herstal had extended it to the Rhine in 690–5, Charles Martel took the lands immediately to the north, including modern Gelderland, in 719, and central Frisia, with modern Friesland, in 734, while north-eastern Frisia was conquered by Charlemagne between 770 and 800. Thus some of the coins described in this section may have been struck under Frankish rule.

Frisian sceattas are found extensively in France and England, and Frankish and Anglo-Saxon coins are in turn found in the Low Countries, although in much smaller numbers. This overlap in circulation has made it difficult to distinguish Frisian sceattas from English ones. The attribution of some of the major series has changed even very recently, while for certain minor types there is insufficient evidence to identify their origin. The chronology of the earlier Frisian sceattas is based on their occurrence in French and English hoards and it is therefore affected by the revised dating proposed below (pp. 184–9).

The change from a gold to silver currency probably followed closely that of the Franks and Anglo-Saxons in the late 660s or 670s. The first silver coins continued the design of the gold 'Madelinus' issue. Towards the end of the seventh century the 'porcupine' and Continental Runic types were introduced and there seems to have been a dramatic increase in coin production, following a similar expansion in England. Most of the Frisian sceattas found in France and England belong to the first one or two decades of the eighth century, reflecting a boom in Frisian trade. The recent suggestion that this was a period of recession in Frisia (Op den Velde *et al.* 1984, 136) was based on the view that the early varieties of the 'porcupine' type are English, but it is more likely that they were struck in Frisia (below, p. 153). The later coins of 'porcupine', Woden/monster, Interlace and Star types rarely occur in French and English hoards and more detailed work is required before they can be satisfactorily arranged and dated. These coinages probably came to an end with the introduction of Pepin's broader penny at Dorestad, derivatives of which may have been produced further north in Frisia.

Despite the coins' anonymity and their apparent diversity of design, particularly among those of the 'porcupine' type, the general standard of technical production was very high. The weights were often closely controlled and the dies aligned in regular 90° positions as on most English sceattas (Hill 1977a). Such metal analyses of Frisian coins as have been made (Metcalf and Hamblin 1968; Geiger 1980; **1.633–64**) indicate that the earliest 'porcupine' and Continental Runic coins are of as good silver as their English counterparts, *c.* 90% or more. Many of the later issues are of surprisingly good silver (80% or more) compared with the English coinage which became very base, although the Woden/monster and Interlace issues fell to less than 50% silver, and insufficient analyses are available to show the pattern of finenesses in detail. A number of sceattas from Frisian and Danish finds have a thin scratch across their face. This may have been a local practice for testing the silver, but no systematic study of it has been made.

The principal Frisian hoards of this period are:

Escharen (1980), on the Lower Rhine. Nine coins of the Continental Runic type, including four mules with a 'porcupine' obverse (*BMC AS* type 10). Deposit *c.* 710. (Op den Velde *et al.* 1984, 140)

Hallum (1866), 15km north of Leeuwarden. About 225 coins, mainly of Woden/monster type (173), but with 13 'porcupines' ('plumed bird' and Classes A, C and various derivatives), 24 Star-of-David and 2 Interlace coins. The Anglo-Saxon types suggest a date of deposit *c.* 720. (Dirks 1870; Op den Velde *et al.* 1984, 141)

Föhr (1976), North Frisian Islands. 77 coins mainly 'porcupines' (including 'plumed bird'), some Star-of-David, English Series J, and Frankish coins including one said to read MILO. (Unpublished, see Hatz 1983, 206 and 214; Bendixen 1984, 152)

Franeker (1868), near Leeuwarden. About 400 coins, *c.* 360 'porcupines' (Classes E, F and B), 36 Star, 1 Interlace and 6 Frankish. (Dirks 1870; Op den Velde *et al.* 1984, 120 and 141)

Dorestad (1846). 8 coins: 6 'porcupines' (Classes E and F) and 2 Interlace. (Op den Velde *et al.* 1984, 142)

Terwispel (1863), in Friesland near Oldeboorn. 161 coins, all of Woden/monster type. (Dirks 1863, 1870; Op den Velde *et al.* 1984, 142)

Lutje-Saaksum (1917), north of Groningen. 27 coins, all 'porcupines' (mostly derivatives, but including Class G). (Hill 1955 as two hoards; Hill and Sharples 1974)

Barthe (1838), near Oldenburg, West Germany. About 750 coins, all 'porcupines' (mostly derivatives, but including Classes A, G and 'plumed bird'). (Unpublished, see Berghaus 1958; Hill 1977b)

'Franceschi' hoard, purchased before 1966 by M. Franceschi, Brussels. 35 coins, all 'porcupines' (derivative types), possibly a parcel from the Barthe or Lutje-Saaksum hoards. (Metcalf 1969b)

The principal series of Frisian sceattas are:

(i) 'Madelinus' type

The gold coinage of the Dorestad moneyer Madelinus, which became increasingly stylized in the mid seventh century (**1.493–5**), was also struck in silver (**1.633**), although specimens are very rare. The legends are further degraded and the bust more stylized. They presumably represent a continuation from the gold coinage in the last quarter of the seventh century, which would explain their absence from the later English, French and Frisian hoards.

There were four in the small hoard from Wittnauer Horn in Switzerland (Geiger 1980), together with one Frankish coin attributed to Yzeures-sur-Creuse and three Interlace coins similar to that in the Franeker hoard. The dating of this find is problematic for the Interlace coins seem to be considerably later than the 'Madelinus' group and were perhaps added to an earlier accumulation of coins. Three of the 'Madelinus' coins have finenesses ranging from 77 to 94% silver and the fourth, which may be an imitation, has 64% silver. The only other find provenance for this issue is a pair of die-duplicates found in excavations at Danekirk in Denmark (Bendixen 1981, 99). These coins were not necessarily struck at Dorestad since the type had for long been an immobilization.

(ii) Interlace type

This type, somtimes known as the 'Maastricht' type after an erroneous nineteenth-century attribution, has a stylized left-facing bust on the obverse and an interlace and pellet design on the reverse (**1.634–5**). A similar interlace design occurs on coins of Pepin and Charlemagne without mint name (MG 33 and 230), and they presumably come from the same region and possibly the same mint as the sceattas (Amécourt 1868c). A Lower Rhineland origin is suggested by the find distribution (Zedelius 1980; Op den Velde *et al.* 1984, 132 and 138), and they are particularly plentiful at Dorestad, though the Carolingian interlace coins cannot have been struck there. Apart from the Wittnauer Horn find referred to above, they have occurred in three Frisian hoards dating from *c.* 720 onwards: Hallum, Föhr and Franeker. We cannot be sure when the type was first introduced, but their recorded finenesses, ranging from 35% to 86% silver (Metcalf and Hamblin 1968, 35; Geiger 1980, 56; **1.634–5**), their absence from English and French hoards of the early eighth century and their scarcity among English single-finds (only one recorded) would be consistent with a dating of *c.* 710–50 for the issue.

(iii) Star-of-David type

This type was attributed by de Coster, Amécourt and others to Herstal, 5km below Liège on the Meuse, the star device being interpreted as a play on the eighth-century name *Aristalium.* It is broadly contemporary with the Interlace type and has a similar find distribution, including the same three Frisian hoards, though since the Star type was much more plentiful in the Hallum and Franeker hoards it may have had a more northerly origin. Two specimens which have been analysed (**1.636–7**) are both *c.* 80% silver, but others have a more base appearance. The type was not present in the English and French hoards of the early eighth century other than the Cimiez hoard; it has been suggested that coins with two intersecting As in the Plassac hoard (**1.638**) may have been its forerunner (Lafaurie 1969a, 208), though this is doubtful especially as none is recorded from Frisia.

(iv) Continental Runic (Rigold Series D)

The obverse design of this type (**1.639–45**) is a direct copy of the English coins of Series C which were struck in Kent or East Anglia from *c.* 700 (below, p. 175). The original runic inscription *æpa* or *epa* is sometimes preserved in a recognizable form, but it is often entirely blundered. The bust on some is so degenerate that it is just a series of vs (representing the crown) and pellets (cf. **1.645**). The reverse design is quite different from the English one in having a bold cross with a pellet in each quarter and a variety of meaningless letter-like forms around it, usually with + at the top and o at the bottom. Two related varieties mule it with the designs of the 'porcupine' issue, either as two obverses (*BMC AS* type 10) or as two reverses (*BMC AS* type 8). These are commonly found with regular Continental Runic coins, although to judge from their style they are probably the product of another mint.

The type cannot have been introduced before *c.* 700 and it enjoyed a short but extremely prolific life. It was present in all the French and English hoards of the early eighth century. By the time the Aston Rowant hoard was deposited *c.* 710 it had undergone virtually its full development and suffered a dramatic fall in weight standard from *c.* 1.25g to *c.* 0.70g. It was the largest element in this hoard (179 out of 324 coins) and it is also common among single-finds in England, yet a Continental origin seems assured. More than 200 have been found on Domburg beach, including many close parallels with coins from Aston Rowant, and they are prominent in the small groups of coins from Escharen, Domnelen and La Panne. There are a number of isolated finds from the Lower Rhine, including Dorestad, but very few from central or northern Frisia. An origin south or west of the Rhine might be inferred from this pattern – Domburg or Quentovic have been suggested (Metcalf 1984c) – but we should not rule out a Rhineland site such as Dorestad, for their somewhat lower representation in the finds there compared with Domburg may reflect a chronological difference in the layers that have been uncovered. The issue seems to have ended sharply *c.* 710/720 perhaps as a result of the pressures which led to the fall in weight. There is no indication that their fineness suffered a significant decline from its original standard of *c.* 90% or more.

(v) 'Porcupine' type (Rigold Series E)

The name 'porcupine' has been coined for the strange obverse design of this type which has so far defied a satisfactory explanation. It probably derives from a long-haired bust, but most of the specific prototypes that have been suggested post-date the earliest 'porcupine' coins and are either unrelated or in some cases have themselves been influenced by the 'porcupine' design (e.g. the Massiliote VII coins, above, p. 149). The reverse copies the square standard design of the Anglo-Saxons, first developed from Roman models in the pale gold coins of Pada and repeated in the early silver coins of Series A and C from which the 'porcupine' reverse probably derives.

They are the most abundant type of sceat, for several thousand specimens have survived in hoards and single-finds from the Low Countries, western Germany, France, and England. Metcalf (1966a) has proposed a classification into nine principal classes ('VOIC' or 'VICO', 'plumed bird', and Classes A–G), but these account for less than half the coins of this type. The remainder either fall between two or more classes or do not resemble any, and these have been termed secondary derivatives (Metcalf 1969b) although they are not necessarily later in date.

One of the earliest varieties has the letters VOIC or VICO in the centre of the reverse (**1.650–1**), possibly the ablative of *vicus*. Another early type has a 'plumed bird' (**1.653–5**) which is probably a development of the 'porcupine' design rather than its prototype. This variety seems to have been struck over a fairly long period, there are several distinct reverse designs and it appears to have been the subject of imitation. The 'VICO' and 'plumed bird' varieties, as well as Classes D and G (**1.646–9**), were present in most early eighth-century French and English finds and should probably be dated 690/700–*c.* 710 (below, pp. 187–8). The later varieties of 'porcupine' are much less common in England, and this led to the suggestion that the early varieties were in fact English (Metcalf 1966a). However the fact that they also occur in significant numbers in French hoards in company with the equally prolific Continental Runic coins implies a similar date and origin for them both. Metcalf (1984a, 32) now also prefers a Frisian origin for these varieties on the ground that their find distribution in England is not localized and they do not fit into the English series happily. There remain some derivatives which must be English: the 'Æthilired' type, Series T and probably the 'VER' group (**1.690A**) and its associates (below, p. 176).

The remaining varieties – Classes A and C (**1.656–9**) present in the Hallum hoard, Classes B, E and F (**1.660–1**) in the Franeker hoard and the unclassified types (**1.662–3**) in the Barthe, Lutje-Saaksum and 'Franceschi' hoards – appear to be later in date, but one suspects that they were struck over a more limited period than their quantity and variety might imply. Few of the Continental finds have been illustrated photographically and more detailed work on the styles, dies and weights is required before we can gain a proper understanding of their chronology and places of origin.

To judge from its Anglo-Saxon element, the Hallum hoard was deposited at much the same time as the Cimiez hoard, *c.* 720. Both contain a few coins of the earlier varieties and of Classes A and C, together with a number of derivatives or imitations which have parallels in the Barthe and Lutje-Saaksum hoards. The Franeker hoard appears to be a little later and has a very different composition, for although it contains a few coins of Class A and derivative types, the great majority are of three distinct and independent varieties, Classes B, E and F. It is not clear to what extent the differences in composition are geographical rather than chronological. Admittedly Franeker is not far from Hallum, but derivatives of Classes E and F in the Hallum and Cimiez hoards suggest that there is not a great difference in date. The suggestion that coins of Classes E and F, which are struck on slightly larger flans, might be contemporary with coins of Charlemagne (Lafaurie 1961, 266) is most improbable.

The derivative types display a great variety of design, but in other respects they reflect careful management, with finenesses of *c.* 70 to 85% silver (Metcalf and Hamblin 1968, 37), well-controlled weights (Grierson 1961, 354) and regular die-axes. Die-links between the Lutje-Saaksum and Barthe hoards (Hill 1955) and analogies with coins in the Hallum and Cimiez hoards suggest that this was a parallel coinage possibly from eastern Frisia (Metcalf 1969b, 103–4).

(vi) Woden/monster (Rigold Series X)

The Woden/monster type is so called after its facing bust with radiating hair, moustache and beard on the obverse and a mythical beast on the reverse, usually with its body facing right but looking over its back. The type dominated the find from Hallum and was apparently present in the Cimiez hoard, so that it was already in issue by *c.* 720 and it may have been struck over a long period. Recorded finenesses mostly fall in the range *c.* 90%–*c.* 35% silver (Metcalf and Hamblin 1968, 33–4), but some are virtually pure copper (Callmer 1984). The 161 coins in the Terwispel hoard, all of this type, appear crude in execution and very base, although they were heavily corroded when found and have been roughly filed, obliterating much of their design. The type was copied on early ninth-century Scandinavian coins probably struck at Hedeby, but this need not imply, as some scholars have suggested, that sceattas remained in circulation there until *c.* 800.

Woden/monster coins have been found in the Lower Rhineland, in Frisia, a few in England, and in Denmark where they dominate the single-finds. It was generally thought that they come from central or northern Frisia in view of their prominence in the Hallum and Terwispel hoards, but Metcalf (1984c) has suggested that they may be a Danish coinage. The evidence for their origin is, however, indecisive.

A few coins of particularly fine style and good silver appear to be English and may even be the prototype for the main Continental issue. There are also English derivatives combining the Woden obverse with various designs: two standing figures, an annulet-cross, etc.

8

THE ANGLO-SAXONS: SIXTH–MID EIGHTH CENTURIES

(a) BACKGROUND

Literature

This chapter covers the early gold coinage and the first phase of silver coinage in Anglo-Saxon England. The gold coinage was the subject of an excellent monograph by Sutherland (1948), whose principal purpose was to publish the Crondall hoard but who in fact surveyed the whole field and included a corpus of the coins then known. Stewart has summarized subsequent work, mainly concerned with the dating of the series, and listed a few additions to the corpus (Stewart 1978). The occurrence in England of Continental gold coins of the sixth and seventh centuries is considered in Kent 1975 and Rigold 1975, the latter including a list of known single-finds and hoards.

The literature on the more abundant silver coinage is necessarily larger and more complex. Much of the early analysis by Philip Hill (1950, 1951, 1952) and others relied on stylistic associations and assumed progressions which are now seen to be unsound. Rigold 1960 marked a breakthrough in arrangement and chronology, distinguishing a Primary and Secondary phase of the coinage, and later an Intermediate phase as well. His subsequent arrangement into some 26 distinct series (Rigold 1977a and Table 12 below, pp. 174–83) has been widely adopted. The single-finds and smaller hoards have been well documented (listed in Rigold and Metcalf 1984) but the publication of the only major English hoard of this period, Aston Rowant 1971–74, is badly needed. Metcalf has published a number of studies of individual types, references to which will be found below, and has commented on their distribution patterns (Metcalf 1974a; 1977; and 1984a). He has also published a large number of metal analyses. There is no modern comprehensive account of this coinage, which is currently a field of active research as is reflected in the papers to a recent Oxford symposium (Hill and Metcalf 1984). These include a general survey (Stewart 1984), a discussion of the chronology (Blackburn 1984) and a die-study of the Northumbrian issues (Booth 1984).

For references to general numismatic and historical works on the Anglo-Saxons, see Chapter 10.

Historical background

The settlement in England of the West German peoples traditionally grouped together as the Angles, Saxons, Jutes and Frisians was quite different in character to that of the other Germanic migrations described in preceding chapters. Their numbers were smaller, and although each small contingent in the invasion period must have had its own leader there were no equivalents in England of Alaric or Theoderic, or even Clovis. Under pressure from the barbarians elsewhere in the Empire, the Roman legions had withdrawn from Britain in the first years of the fifth century, and the Romano-British communities which remained came under increasing pressure from the Picts in Scotland, the Scots in Ireland and raiders from the Continent. The loss of security led to a rapid breakdown of society, and from the mid-fifth century small groups of newcomers were able to establish themselves in the south-east and east of the island without great difficulty. It took two centuries of struggle, however, before they mastered the whole of 'England'. During the sixth century they coalesced into a number of separate kingdoms, some of them substantial territorial units – Mercia, East Anglia and Wessex south of the Humber, Deira and Bernicia north of it. Others such as Kent, Sussex, Middlesex, Essex and Lindsey were rather smaller, though Kent ranked as a political heavyweight because of its good harbours and close connections with the Continent.

The most important event in the history of seventh-century England was its progressive conversion to Christianity, partly through the influence in the north and west of Celtic missionaries from Ireland, but mainly through that of missionaries from Rome in the remainder of the country. The circumstances of Augustine's mission to Kent in 597 resulted in Canterbury becoming the primatial see in the newly founded English Church, though its claims to primacy were always to be offset by the near equal position attained by York in Northumbria, the great northern kingdom formed by the union of Deira and Bernicia that extended into the Scottish lowlands as far as the Clyde. With Christianity came the use of Latin for many purposes, though the vernacular was a written language in England much earlier than its equivalents in the other Germanic states. Bede, the great Northumbrian scholar of the early eighth century, writing his history of the establishment of the Church in England and the conversion of the country, weaves into his tapestry a picture of the political evolution of the country. Kent is depicted as the most powerful kingdom south of the Humber in the days of Æthelbert, the king of Kent who received St Augustine, though one suspects that Bede's opinion of him was coloured by the role he played in the establishment of Christianity. Later in the seventh century, Rædwald of East Anglia and Penda of Mercia were in turn the strongest rulers south of the Humber, although Northumbria continued to enjoy considerable influence beyond its borders. At the beginning of the eighth century authority in England was again fragmented, but by the end of it Mercia, under Æthelbald and then Offa, had emerged as the pre-eminent power and was on the verge of dominating the whole of England.

(b) GENERAL FEATURES OF THE COINAGE

Britain was the only province of the Roman Empire where the barbarian invasions brought a complete end to coin production and monetary circulation for almost two centuries. The last decades of Roman rule saw the burial of copper coins on a huge scale, and clipped silver 'siliquae', the clipping apparently resulting from the growing shortage of metal, are a feature of early fifth-century hoards. Scholars no longer accept the view, once widely held (Hill 1949), that the copies of late Roman bronze coins traditionally known to archaeologists as 'barbarous radiates' and the tiny *minimi* or *minimissimi* remained in continuous use until the end of the sixth century and even influenced the designs of the earliest silver sceattas. Archaeological evidence shows that these were largely contemporary with their models, and their use cannot be traced beyond the late fourth century (Kent 1961, 5–7).

The Anglo-Saxons learnt the use of coinage from their Continental neighbours and this is reflected in the monetary system which they adopted. Their first use for foreign coin was during the sixth century as ornaments mounted in jewellery. By the early seventh century Continental coins began to play some monetary role, although for several decades this must have been very limited, and the same is true of the earliest coins struck by the Anglo-Saxons themselves. These were primarily gold tremisses or shillings of reduced weight (*c.* 20gr.) similar to the Merovingian, with only a limited minting of solidi for ornamental or ceremonial purposes. There appear to have been several mints or ateliers operating, but the output of each was very small. Although the coinage grew in the third quarter of the century, it was still tiny in comparison with that of the Franks. As in Gaul, the gold standard fell progressively until *c.* 675, when the by then very pale gold shillings were abandoned in favour of a coinage of silver pennies of similar module and weight to the Merovingian denier. The last quarter of the seventh century saw a dramatic increase in the scale and use of coinage. Minting and circulation, which in the gold and early silver phases had been limited essentially to south-east England, i.e. Kent and the lower Thames valley, expanded in the early eighth century into East Anglia, Wessex, southern and eastern Mercia and Northumbria. At the same time there was a brief influx of coin from Frisia and the lower Rhineland. However, a rapid debasement followed, and by the mid eighth century the striking and use of coins seems virtually to have ceased. Coinage was restored in the third quarter of the century, in the form of the broader and thinner pennies of Offa and his contemporaries, innovations again inspired by developments in the coinage of the Franks.

The terms 'thrymsa' and 'sceat' (pl. 'sceattas', the *sc* pronounced *sh* as in 'shatter') have been used since the seventeenth century to describe the early Anglo-Saxon gold and silver coins respectively. 'Thrymsa', derived from the Latin *tremissis*, is used in later Old English sources to refer both to coins, although not specifically gold coins, and to the sum of four pennies, i.e. a third of a shilling. It may have been used earlier, but the more usual term for the coin was presumably that found in the seventh-century laws, i.e. shilling (OE *scillinc*). The term 'sceat' is a modern misnomer based on a misunderstanding of the laws of Æthelbert of Kent where it is used, but to refer to a weight of gold equivalent to one-twentieth of a shilling (Grierson 1961). These laws belong to the early seventh century, more than sixty years before the appearance of the silver coinage. To contemporaries the silver coins, when they came to be introduced, were known as pennies (OE *pening*, pl. *penegas*; on the meaning of the word see above, p. 15), and are first mentioned in the laws of Ine of Wessex (promulgated 688–94), the old shilling being equated with five pennies in Wessex (Ælfric, *Grammar* 50) and four in Mercia (cf. Liebermann 1903–16, II.640–1). In Kent it was probably twelve pence from the first, since the laws of Æthelbert had been drawn up at a date when the shilling was of high quality gold, and the same is probably true of south-east England generally. Though the only pre-Conquest documentary evidence for this figure is by chance from East Anglia (*Liber Eliensis*, cap. 11a, 25, etc.; cf. Whitelock in Blake 1962, xvii n.1), there is other literary evidence for it, e.g.

the OE version of *Exodus* 21.10 (freely varied from the Vulgate) and Egbert's *Penitential* IV.60 (Thorpe 1840, II.222–3). Since the same value held good in France, though it had come about in a different way (above, p. 106), it was generalized by the Normans and the old four-penny and five-penny values disappeared.

Several of the gold and early silver issues copy Merovingian designs; one of the earliest coins was indeed apparently produced in Canterbury by a Frankish moneyer. Imperial prototypes were also popular, but whereas in France these were coins of fifth-century Rome which continued to circulate or of sixth-century Byzantium which were imported, such coins were not currently available in England and the models employed by the Anglo-Saxons were usually fourth-century, having presumably been discovered in hoards or other finds. In the eighth century native designs flourished, often drawn from a common stock of Germanic mythical motifs. There are a variety of animal types – beasts, birds, wolves – standing or seated figures, profile and facing busts holding a cross, cup, or falcon, and some purely geometric designs.

As in the Merovingian series, there are very few coins bearing royal names struck south of the Humber before the mid eighth century, the only exception being an early gold issue in the name of Eadbald of Kent (616–40). Northumbria, by contrast, was for a time the only kingdom in northern Europe issuing an overtly regal coinage. It was initiated by the remarkable King Aldfrith in about 700, and the form was copied in the 750s or 760s by Beonna of East Anglia.

The majority of the silver and some of the gold coins are uninscribed other than with pseudo-legends copied from the designs or prototypes. Where they do have intelligible inscriptions these are either mint names or personal names, though the Frankish practice of including the name of both the moneyer and the mint was not adopted. Canterbury is mentioned on only one early seventh-century coin, but London is found on three gold issues of the 630s or 640s and on some silver coins of the 720s or 730s. An ornamental piece of the late sixth century has the name of Bishop Liudhard. Other names are thought to be those of moneyers or private individuals sponsoring the issue, although only two are specifically described as such, EVSEBII MONITA and WITMEN MONITA; a third, ABBONI MANET, is probably copied directly from a Merovingian coin. These names, many of them in runes, include Aniwulufu (Eanwulf?), Ean . . . and Pada on the gold coinages, and Æpa, Æthilired, Ver . . ., Spi, Wigred, Tilbert, Efe, Werferth and Wilred on the silver coinages. There are also a number of unidentified words or inscriptions on the coins, *skanomodu*, *benu/tigo* or *benu/tid*, *delaiona*, LEV, LELVS, MONITA SCORVM. The use of runes starts with the coins of the south-east in the late sixth century and continues there until the end of the seventh century. They are common on coins of East Anglia throughout the eighth century and occur occasionally on the Northumbrian coinage of the first half of the ninth century. This pattern accords well with the survival of other runic inscribed objects (Page 1973).

Who was responsible for the coinage? As with the Merovingian series, it is far from easy to define the nature of the issuers and the degree of official regulation. In most periods reasonably consistent standards of weight and fineness were maintained and although there is a great variety of types it is evident that the majority of coins were struck by a limited number of mints to specific designs, with a number of small, often imitative issues making up the rest. This implies that there was some regulation of the currency at least in the principal minting areas of Kent and the Thames valley.

Whether the coinages south of the Humber may be regarded as royal issues is doubtful. The absence of royal names contrasts markedly with the coinage of Northumbria. Certain designs on the later silver coins have been seen, in particular by Metcalf (1972a, 1977), as representing kings – figures or busts wearing diadems or headgear interpreted as the royal *cynehelm*, seated on a throne or standing and often holding one or two crosses or a falcon – but these are susceptible to other interpretations, and even if they were intended to depict royalty they could have been part of the general stock of popular iconographic designs. In the formative phase of the gold and earlier silver issues there is not even this hint of royal participation, but we do find a number of personal names. Three are of particular importance, Witmen, Pada and Æpa, for their coinages represent a significant proportion of the output of south-east England and they may each in their time have been the sole or major issuer in Kent.

It is difficult to avoid the conclusion that these men were operating with a considerable degree of autonomy. The same may be true of other issues of the period, though minting in London, where coins were either mint-signed or uninscribed, could have been organized on a different basis. The East Anglian coinage in the later silver phase also records the names of several moneyers. The role of moneyers in south-east England must still have been of importance at the end of the sceat period in view of the prominence they were given in the new broader flan coinage. We do not know exactly when the coinage was brought under royal control, but the process probably occurred in several stages of increasing regulation, which may have begun during the sceat phase and continued down to the end of the eighth century and even beyond.

In considering the early Anglo-Saxon coinage it should be borne in mind how rare the gold coins are: fewer than 125 are known, and there is only one recorded hoard in which they have occurred, that from Crondall in Hampshire. In contrast we have several thousand sceattas from some 25 English and Continental hoards or grave groups and from many excavations or chance finds. These hoards are discussed below in connection with the chronology of the silver coinage.

(c) EARLY GOLD COINAGE

The development of the Anglo-Saxon gold coinage can only be understood against the background of the imported Continental coins and the uses to which they were put. Very few coins struck during the century following the Roman abandonment of Britain have been found in England (cf. **1.334**), but from the 530s or 540s they seem to have begun arriving in small but appreciable numbers. Merovingian coins predominate in English finds of the sixth and the first half of the seventh centuries (cf. **1.373**, **411**, **437**, **465**, **490**), but there are also some imperial, Lombardic, Visigothic and other Germanic pieces (cf. **1.313**). The earliest hoard, found in 1848 at Kingston-on-Thames, probably dates from the second quarter of the sixth century, for although we only have a very summary account it is said to have contained at least ten tremisses in the name of Justin I (518–27), probably Frankish or Burgundian derivatives (Rigold 1975, 665). Initially these coin-finds seem to be concentrated mainly in East Kent and the lower Thames valley, and only in the seventh century do they occur in significant numbers outside this area, spreading further up the Thames valley and around the east coast of England. That the finds are relatively plentiful – there are over a hundred Continental coins known from single-finds and grave groups, more than twice as many as the recorded finds of Offa – is due in large measure to the pagan and early Christian burial practice of including personal property in the grave. Many of the coins had been used as jewellery and were mounted or pierced for suspension. Three grave finds from Kent of the late sixth or early seventh century, from St Martin's at Canterbury and from Faversham and Sarre (above, pp. 122–4 and 128), consisted entirely of looped coins. After *c.* 625 the proportion of mounted coins is much smaller, due partly to wider acceptance of coin for monetary purposes and partly to changes in funerary practice.

The introduction of a domestic coinage in England did not bring the import of Frankish coins to an end. The Sutton Hoo hoard from East Anglia, which has already been described (p. 124–5), consisted entirely of Frankish coins, despite the fact that it dates from the 620s and is therefore later than the earliest Kentish coins, though it is possible that the hoard was put together on the Continent. Even in the mid century, when coinage in the country was well established, a quarter of the coins in the Crondall hoard (above, p. 126–7 and next paragraphs) were still Frankish. But as domestic output grew in volume during the second half of the century the demand for foreign coin lessened, and silver Merovingian coins are rarely found in England (but see **1.625** from Reculver). Frisian coins of the early eighth century, on the other hand, occur in significant numbers, as do English coins of the same period in Frisia, in both cases reflecting a flourishing Anglo-Frisian trade (above, p. 150).

The first Anglo-Saxon coin-like objects date from the late sixth century and were probably intended for ornamental use. The St Martin's grave find included a large looped 'tremissis' with the name of Liudhard, LEVDARDVS EPS (Sutherland 1948, pl. 1.1; *SCBI* Merseyside 6), the Frankish bishop whom we know from Bede accompanied Queen Bertha to Kent as her chaplain when she married King Æthelbert probably in the late 570s or early 580s (Brooks 1984, 6; Wood 1983, 15–16). A solidus, probably English and of much the same period, is copied from a coin of Honorius, but with the word *skanomodu* in runes inserted into the legend (Sutherland 1948, pl. 2.1; Berghaus and Schneider 1967). It had been looped for suspension, as had four of the five recorded seventh-century solidi, and all were probably made as jewellery from the first. These also copy recognizable fourth-century models – an obverse from a coin of Helena (Sutherland 1948, pl. 1.28), a reverse with two emperors taken from a coin of the time of Gratian (Sutherland 1948, pl. 1.29) – though one type of which four specimens are known link a fourth-century obverse with the cross-on-steps design of a contemporary Byzantine solidus (**1.665**).

A late sixth-century tremissis of Corneillan in south-west France was the model for what is arguably the earliest English 'coin', found at Folkestone in Kent, but today known only from an eighteenth-century drawing and from eighteenth- or nineteenth-century forgeries (see note on **1.1479**). Like the *skanomodu* solidus, it seems to have a runic word inserted into the legend, in this case a personal name *aniwulufu* (i.e. Eanwulf), possibly a moneyer, though we really do not know. Another coin, but of quite different character, bears the name of a moneyer Eusebius (EVSEBII MONITA) at Canterbury (DOROVERNIS CIVITAS) (Sutherland 1948, pl. 1.2). It is of Frankish workmanship, similar in style and epigraphy to certain coins of Theodebert

II (595–612) (Belfort 344ff.) and was presumably struck by a visiting Frankish moneyer in the early seventh century. This is the only early English coin to carry the names of both the mint and moneyer, and Canterbury is not named again on the coins for two hundred years. Stewart (1978, 150) has suggested that two crude imitations of Victory tremisses might be English coins of this same period – one has an English find provenance and is 85% fine, slightly less than the Liudhard and *skanomodu* pieces – but a Continental origin seems more likely.

Despite the flourishing exchange of luxury goods between Kent and the Continent and the reputation of the Kentish court abroad, the initial attempt to introduce a coinage during Æthelbert's reign seems to have been a failure. The absence of indigenous coins from the Sutton Hoo hoard, even if we assume that it was assembled in East Anglia which is not certain, does not necessarily mean that none was to be found in Kent or the Thames valley in the 620s – it was not until the end of the century that coin flowed freely from the South-East to East Anglia – although we know that Rædwald himself had contact with Æthelbert's court, where he was baptized. But the earliest coins in the Crondall hoard, which provided most of the surviving Anglo-Saxon gold coins, probably belong no earlier than *c.* 630. There is only one group of coins absent from Crondall which might belong to an earlier period, as they are of finer gold (63–73%) than most coins in the hoard. They have a crude portrait and a cross-on-steps design, with a runic inscription *benu :tigo* or *benu : + :tid* on four specimens and TARE. . ./BER. . . on a fifth of different style (Sutherland 1948, pl. 1, 23–7; Page 1973, 123; *SCBI* Mack 307, but the last may be Merovingian). Only two of the five pieces have known find provenances (Dorchester, Oxon. and Eastleach Turville, Glos.) and it has been suggested that they were struck in the Thames valley (Rigold 1975, 663) which may account for their absence from the Crondall hoard. In any event they must have been a small issue as four of the five specimens are die-linked.

Not until the 630s and 640s was coin production sustained in England, and it is this phase which is represented in the Crondall hoard from Hampshire, now dated *c.* 650 or a little earlier (Kent 1975; Rigold 1975, 659). The 69 Anglo-Saxon coins in the hoard were of ten distinct types, apparently the products of several 'mints' or workshops, although each was struck from a small number of dies. The heavy degree of die-linkage in the hoard – only nine of the 69 coins do *not* die-link with others in the hoard – suggests that it was drawn from a limited stock which had seen little circulation, and one might infer that the hoard was likely to be very unrepresentative of the coinage generally. But this does not seem to be the case, for of the fourteen contemporary coins found elsewhere – probably all isolated finds – no less than eleven die-link with coins in the hoard. It would appear that the coinage before *c.* 650 was indeed very small and used by a limited group of people for special purposes or transactions. This is in marked contrast to the later gold coinage where the finds are more plentiful and there are few die-links between them.

One of the earliest coins in the hoard bears the name of Æthelbert's son, Eadbald of Kent (616–40), who may have been responsible for promoting the new phase of coinage. The obverse has the legend AVDVARLD REGES, which can be compared with contemporary renderings of his name in Latin as *Adulualdi* and *Audubaldi* (Bede II.8, 10, 11). The reverse legend of the Crondall coin is somewhat blundered, but a second specimen from the same obverse die has a reverse legend which includes the name LONDENVS (Sutherland 1948, 52–3 and pl. 4.22–3).

This is the first of three types which can be attributed to London and it is important for showing Eadbald's authority in the city which was formally part of the kingdom of Essex. The Crondall coin is 69% gold, one of the finest in the hoard. The coins leave one in no doubt of the importance of London, which Bede a century later describes as 'an emporium of many nations', though a paucity of archaeological evidence from the early and middle Saxon period has led some to question its significance. Biddle (1984) has suggested that the site of London before the Viking invasions should be sought to the west of the Roman city, along the present Fleet Street and the Strand.

The same reverse design, a Latin cross on a small globule, is repeated on the second type attributable to London (Sutherland 1948, pl. 3.1–7). This has a facing bust with a hatched border and an inscription LONDINIV around the upper part of the reverse. There are ten specimens known, all from the Crondall hoard and struck from one obverse and three reverse dies. They all have the same 90° die-axis and closely regulated weights. The third type has elements of the same design, a hatched border on the obverse and a plain cross on the reverse, but the portrait is in profile and the reverse inscription, a very blundered form of *Londinium*, has an initial cross and fills the entire border. The composition is sufficiently different to suggest that these coins may go back to another literate London prototype, and they may have been produced at a different workshop since their weights and die-axes show much greater variation. The finenesses of these two groups is similar (60–70%), and rather higher than those of the 'Kentish' groups described below. There are single-finds of this third London type from Dover (Kent), Warminster (Wilts.) and a plated forgery from Kilmaurs (Ayrshire, Scotland).

None of the other Crondall gold coins has a recognizable mint-name, but there is sufficient variety among them to suggest that they were produced at more than one workshop. The largest group bears the name of a moneyer Witmen, WITMEN MONITA (Sutherland 1948, pl. 3.20–32; pl. 4.1–14). Such a title is not found again until the ninth century. One literate specimen from finely cut dies leads the series, but the portrait soon became stylized, the legends blundered, the fineness reduced from 61–70% to 43–62%, and the size of the flan, though not the weight, also reduced. The distribution of single-finds suggests a Kentish origin for this group: two from near Canterbury, one each from near Sittingbourne in Kent and Blackfriars, London.

Another group appears to include the personal-name element *Ean-* in an otherwise indecipherable legend. There were four specimens in the Crondall hoard, all from the same pair of dies but in different stages of recutting (Sutherland 1948, pl. 4.24–7). A fifth specimen was found in or near the Isle of Thanet, Kent.

Other Crondall types imitate Merovingian or Roman designs. One with the legend ABBONI MANET, if it is indeed English, is probably inspired by coins of the prolific late sixth-century moneyer Abbo of Chalon, rather than being the work of a true Frankish moneyer (Sutherland 1948, pl. 1.3–4). Other types imitate the 'cross-on-steps' and the 'cross ancrée' designs, and some copy coins of Limoges including the mint-signature LEMC (Sutherland 1948, pl. 1.5–7, 13–14, 18–22, and 8–12). Only one group in Crondall derives from a Roman prototype, a fourth-century copper coin of Licinius I (*RIC* VII, 259.224, etc.), most carefully copied and of exceptionally good workmanship (Sutherland 1948, pl. 2.6–15).

During the third quarter of the seventh century the scale of the coinage increased, as presumably its use became more general. The fineness of the coins continued to fall from about 50% gold to 15% or even less. One group (**1.666**) not represented in the Crondall hoard has an average fineness of around 50% gold. It is related in elements of its design to the '*Witmen*' series – the portraiture on one specimen is so similar to that of the '*Witmen*' coins that it appears to be the work of the same die-cutter. The legends are variations on the seemingly meaningless word 'Wuneetton', apparently a corruption of *Witmen moneta*. The group would thus appear to be a continuation of the '*Witmen*' coinage, immediately post-dating Crondall, although the possibility that they derive from a different literate prototype cannot be excluded.

Another group absent from Crondall but of comparable fineness may have been struck at York (**1.1480**, an electrotype). The obverse has an oval face (?) flanked by crosses over a lattice design, possibly derived from the camp-gate reverse of some late Roman bronze coin. The legend on the reverse is meaningless. Three die-duplicates appear to have been found at York, probably together, in the 1840s (Sutherland 1948, pl. 4.18–20). Another specimen, which inspired an elaborate forgery (**1.1481**, see note on coin), must have been known in the eighteenth century, and this could be the coin recently acquired by the British Museum (Sotheby 9.10.1979, lot 119).

The largest series of pale gold coins (**1.667**) imitates a fourth-century solidus with the reverse type of two enthroned emperors and a Victory between them. There are 22 specimens known, struck from 17 obverse and 21 reverse dies, suggesting a substantial coinage. The recorded finenesses fall in the range *c.* 40–20% gold, though one coin (*BMC AS* I, 3.9), looks much baser, and, if it is authentic, may represent a deliberate, early striking in silver. These coins were probably struck during the 650s or 660s in Kent; the three recorded English find-spots are all in this county (Reculver, Lymne, and Hollingbourne?), and some elements of the design are taken up on the early Kentish silver coins of Series A. A Merovingian coin of the moneyer Baudulf (B 5447) with the same reverse type, and probably inspired by this issue, was present in the Bordeaux hoard deposited *c.* 675 (Le Gentilhomme 1936; Rigold 1975, 660; Stewart 1978, 152 n. 57).

Contemporary with this issue are two small groups also inspired by Roman prototypes; both have finenesses of *c.* 30%. One, known from a unique coin found at St Albans, Hertfordshire (Sutherland 1948, pl. 2, 5), copies coins of Crispus, but has a runic legend, *delaiona* retrograde (Page 1973, 122). The second group has a clasped hands reverse similar to that of the third-century *Concordia* type of Carausius (Sutherland 1948, pl. 2.2–3). Two of the three known specimens have Kentish find-spots (Faversham and Strood?), and the form of bust was to influence the silver coins of Series A. Like the Two Emperors type, this group was probably struck in Kent.

Two series span the transition from pale gold to silver. The first encompasses a variety of obverse and reverse designs, most of which incorporate in the reverse the personal name *pada* in runes, either on a modified Roman standard (**1.668**) or inserted into the legend (**1.669**). The former association of 'Pada' with King Peada of Mercia (d. 656) is unacceptable since the coinage is unlikely to have started so early and certainly continued into the 670s. The name is now thought to represent a moneyer. Eleven specimens in pale gold are known, the best being 30%

fine, and about 20 supposedly in silver (Rigold 1960, 31–2; 1966, 5). There is greater variety of design in the gold coinage and no die-links have been recorded. Thus despite its relative scarcity it may have been more protracted than the silver coinage. The find distributions of both phases are predominantly Kentish, and their designs influenced the silver coins of Series A, which may have been produced at the same mint, probably situated in East Kent.

The other transitional group (**1.670–1**) also bears the name of a moneyer, VANIMVNDVS MONE in its most literate form, but this is copied from the reverse of a pale gold tremissis of the moneyer Warimundus from the Austrasian mint *Matrico* (?Mairy, Meurthe-et-Moselle, Prou 1892a, 917; see Rigold 1966, 2). Two reverse designs are employed, the first, a typical Merovingian cross-on-base with CA in the field, is replaced by a simple cross in a border, but both share the same obverse with a helmeted bust derived from a fourth-century prototype. None of the earlier coins has been analysed, but those with the later reverse have less than 10% gold and some appear to be only silver. Most of the 15 recorded specimens come from Continental collections, a number, like the two here, from that of Sivard de Beaulieu (d. 1826) who appears to have had access to a significant hoard of the late seventh century. One has an English find provenance (Colchester, Essex) and another was acquired by William Hunter in the eighteenth century (*SCBI* Glasgow 77) and is likely to be an English find. An English attribution, argued most persuasively by Rigold, is justified by the use of a fourth-century model for the obverse, the treatment of the design, particularly in the use of annulets, the low gold content of the coins fading into silver, which was unknown in Francia, and by the perpetuation of the same blundered reverse legend on silver coins of Series B. The 'Vanimundus' and the Series B coins seem to be successive products of one mint, which the finds suggest was probably located in Essex, arguably at London, rather than in Kent (below, p. 165).

(d) EARLY SILVER PENNIES OR 'SCEATTAS'

The first silver pennies were struck on small thick flans, of similar diameter to the gold shillings and to the contemporary Merovingian deniers. These continued to be used until the third quarter of the eighth century when they were superseded by a broader thinner flan which was to serve throughout the rest of the Middle Ages. The coinage displays a perplexing variety of designs and combinations – 109 different types, mostly uninscribed, have been distinguished in *BMC AS*, Hill 1953 and Stewart 1984 – but these have been grouped by Rigold (1977a) into 26 series, divided between three phases, Primary, Intermediate and Secondary, and this is now accepted as the standard classification for the coinage. The old *BMC* classification, as extended, is still useful for defining specific types. The principal types of each series are described and illustrated in Table 12 on pp. 174–83 below.

Primary phase

The earliest silver coins continue the designs of the pale gold coins of the Pada (Pa) and 'Vanimundus' (Va) series, and they are often indistinguishable save by scientific analysis. A few coins of the Primary Series A and B and possibly Series F have significant gold contents (5–10%), suggesting the occasional use of bullion derived in part from later gold coins. No mixed hoards or grave finds containing both pale gold and early silver coins have been found in England, but some pale gold coins of Pada which had been taken to the Continent remained in circulation for many years (cf. Cimiez hoard dep. *c.* 720). The progressive debasement of the gold shilling was presumably accompanied by inflation, and this may account for the difference between the freeman's wergeld of 100 shillings in an early seventh-century Kentish law and its counterpart in later West Saxon and Mercian laws of 200 shillings (Whitelock 1979, 52–3). We cannot be sure at what stage the silver coins were revalued and renamed 'pennies', but the term was sufficiently well established to justify legislative use by at least the early 690s (above, p. 15). Rigold has suggested that the redesignation may have accompanied the introduction of Series A and B (Rigold 1960, 16–17), which appear to be the respective successors of the Pada and 'Vanimundus' series. Something prompted radical changes of design in both series, and the absence of Pada and 'Vanimundus' coins from the Hougham and Milton Regis hoards and the smaller groups from graves in Kent suggests that they were effectively driven out of circulation, if not formally recoined, by Series A and B (for the finds see Table 13, p. 185, below).

The designs of Series A are a montage of elements taken from earlier Kentish gold coins: the bust from the *Concordia* type, the A behind the head from the Two Emperors type, the obverse legend and the reverse design from different Pada types. The find distribution is essentially from East Kent and the Thames valley, and a Kentish origin is most likely. In contrast the designs of Series B are novel to the Anglo-Saxon coinage; the basic type, like that of the 'Vanimundus' coins, is Merovingian, but the serpent-headed torque and the bird (the Holy Dove?) on top of the cross are innovations. However, the legends continue to reproduce blundered forms found on the last 'Vanimundus' coins. Rigold gave Series B to Kent since the large majority have come from hoards and other finds there in which they enjoy roughly equal representation with coins of Series A. However, Metcalf's more recent suggestion that both the 'Vanimundus' series and Series B may be East Saxon seems preferable (Metcalf 1976a, 12–13; 1984a, 28). The only recorded 'Vanimundus' find from this country is from Colchester, while a group of three early and very rare Bx coins (*BMC AS* 26) were found at Mucking and another at Cranham, all in Essex. The find distribution of BI coins is also slightly wider than that of the contemporary Series A. London is an obvious candidate for the mint in view of its importance in the earlier gold and later silver coinages, but no firm attribution can be proposed on the evidence currently available.

The preliminary issues of both these series (Rigold's varieties A1 and Bx), like those of Series Pa and Va, are very rare, yet the paucity of die-links suggests that they were not insubstantial (Rigold 1977b). However, our knowledge of the later varieties is more detailed than for any other series thanks to the discovery of the Hougham hoard, with some 300 coins, and six smaller finds from graves in Kent and Essex. The practice of placing groups of coins in graves as token grave goods died out at the beginning of the eighth century, the find from Garton-on-the-Wolds, Yorkshire, of *c.* 725 being a late survivor. For the later period there is one large English hoard from Aston Rowant in Oxfordshire and six smaller ones, but the majority of Intermediate and Secondary coins derive from single-finds. The occurrence of Series A, BI, BII and C together in a sequence of early hoards encouraged Rigold to deduce their relative chronology: A1 and Bx were followed by A2 and BIA (represented in the Hougham hoard), and thence by A3,

BIB and BIC (present in the grave-finds from Milton Regis, Finglesham, Broadstairs and Barham). Series A then ceased, but variety BII continued and is first found in the Southend grave-hoard in conjunction with a new series, C.

Series C has similar designs to A3 but with the name 'æpa', 'apæ' or 'epa', assumed to be that of a moneyer, inserted in runes into the TIC inscription, leaving only the initial T surviving. Series C must have spread over a considerable number of years since the early coins (Rigold's R1a and R1b; Rigold 1960, 17) were used as a prototype for the Continental Runic series (Series D), which underwent considerable stylistic development and a dramatic fall in weight standard before the deposit of the Aston Rowant hoard in which it constituted the major element. Early coins of Series C were absent from the hoard, but the later varieties (R1x and R1y) were well represented and seem to have been fairly recent additions. In the Secondary phase this design was perpetuated in an increasingly stylized form in Series R, which the find distribution shows to be undoubtedly East Anglian.

The origin of Series C is not so clear-cut. Rigold regarded it as a Kentish successor of Series A, while Metcalf gives it to East Anglia. The distribution of Series C, which has been found in Kent, East Anglia, the Midlands and Yorkshire, is wider than that of the more prolific Series R of which few specimens have occurred outside East Anglia and the East Midlands. The attribution of Series C to Kent implies the use of runes there in the early eighth century, but the Pada coinage represents a precedent from one generation earlier, and there is evidence from inscribed artifacts for their use there in the seventh century (Page 1973, 18–37). The attribution to East Anglia would allow an early introduction of minting there, which is no objection in itself, but at a time when production at the major and perhaps only mint in Kent would have ceased. There is no direct stylistic link between Series A and Series C, nor between early and late Series C, or late Series C and Series R. It seems right therefore to keep an open mind as to whether the early coins of Series C, and possibly also the later coins of that series, were the successors of Series A in Kent, parallel with the late Primary and Intermediate BII coins. Series R would then represent an East Anglian copying of the earlier Kentish series, often reproducing the name of a Kentish moneyer 'epa'.

The first silver coins in Northumbria belong to the end of the Primary phase and are remarkable for bearing the name of King Aldfrith (685–704), who was renowned for his learning and his patronage of scholarship. On the obverse they have + ALdFRIdVS and on the reverse a beast walking left, a design which recurs on the later Northumbrian coinage. The alternative attribution to the late eighth-century king, Ealdfrith of Lindsey (Lyon 1956, 229), must be rejected, for their high weight and fineness is consistent with a date in the Primary phase, but not in the late eighth century, and Dr Metcalf has informed us of a specimen recently found at Southampton stratified in an early eighth-century context. Only seven specimens are known with some die-linking between them, so it was not a large coinage (Booth 1984, 97). The coins formerly attributed to Egfrith of Northumbria (670–85) have been shown to be modern forgeries (Pirie 1982, 3–4).

It has been suggested that Series F may also have an origin in the Primary phase and possibly in Wessex (Metcalf 1978, 15). The design is fundamentally Merovingian – the bust probably copies deniers of Paris – and it has often been regarded as Continental. However, the reverse also shows influences from Series A and B, and one of the few specimens that have been analysed apparently has a significant gold content (**1.687**), comparable to some coins of A2 and BIA. The Aston Rowant hoard contained at least fifteen specimens and three single-finds are recorded from London, Dorset and Yorkshire, while a number of others, early acquisitions of the British Museum and the Hunterian Museum, are presumed to be English finds. The series appears to be English, though the location of its mint remains uncertain. A western origin might explain its absence from the Kentish hoards if it is indeed a Primary series. However, the substantial number present in the Aston Rowant hoard suggests that much of the issue is Intermediate, but without a full publication of the hoard it is difficult to judge to what extent the series might have extended back into the Primary phase.

The Primary phase saw the establishment of a well-produced and well-regulated coinage at two centres, in Kent (at Canterbury?) and probably in Essex (at London?), and possibly at a third in Wessex or southern Mercia. The circulation of the coins from the two main mints was essentially limited to Kent, Essex and the lower Thames valley. A number passed to the Continent and have been found at Domburg and in certain French hoards, but little or no coin appears to have come from the Continent to England in this period.

Intermediate phase

Towards the end of the Primary phase, Series A was probably replaced by Series C with the addition of a moneyer's name, and variety BI was succeeded by BII; in both cases the dies were of cruder workmanship than their predecessors. These types continued into the Intermediate phase which is marked by (a) an expansion of the area of circulation into East Anglia, the East Midlands and up the Thames valley, and (b) an influx of coin from the Continent, principally the Lower Rhine and Friesland.

The Aston Rowant hoard provides a valuable indication of the range of coinage in southern England during the Intermediate phase, although the proportions of the various types may not have been typical of the currency of any region. The 324 coins comprised 4 of Series A, 26 of Series B (including a derivative), 46 of Series C, 179 of Series D, 61 of Series E, and 8 Merovingian coins (*Coin Hoards* 1 (1975), 87). The report of the first of the two parcels to be declared included 15 coins of Series F (Kent 1972b, one illustrated), and these are presumably subsumed in another category in the later listing. The hoard was probably deposited *c.* 710, and already the older Primary coins of Series A and BI were scarce and early coins of Series C were absent. The later coins of Series BII, C and F were more numerous, but together the English series account for only a quarter of the coins in the hoard. The remaining three-quarters are virtually all of the Continental Runic type (Series D, including both *BMC AS* 2c and 8) or the 'porcupine' type (Series E). The 'porcupines' were of the varieties that most commonly occur as single-finds in England: 'plumed bird', 'VICO' and classes D and G (Metcalf 1966a). Metcalf argued that these were English varieties, but it is more probable, as he now suggests (Metcalf 1984a), that they are Frisian and were struck during the first decade of the eighth century when Anglo-Frisian trade appears to have been at its height (above, p. 153). A handful of coins in the hoard are derivatives combining features of Series C and E and may be English (Blackburn and Bonser 1984a). The number of coins of Series D is unduly large compared with the other series and their relative proportions among single-finds. This suggests that part of the hoard represents a parcel of coins from the Continent which had been kept together, and that it does not fairly reflect the composition of the currency of southern Mercia.

Coins of the Continental Series D and E also occur in substantial numbers among English single-finds. Those of Series D are found mostly in the Thames valley, the south Midlands and East Kent, while coins of Series E, which are more numerous, are also found in the Severn valley, along the coast of Hampshire and Dorset, and in East Anglia, Lincolnshire and Yorkshire. They appear to have entered England mainly by way of Kent and the Thames estuary, and to have been distributed in the general movement of coin away from the South East. Most of them are of varieties represented in the Aston Rowant hoard and must have arrived during a very limited period, perhaps no more than a decade. A smaller proportion of the Series E coins are of other (later) varieties, and some coins of Series X ('Woden/monster' type) from Northern Frisia or Denmark arrived during the Secondary phase.

The earlier Primary coins were struck on a weight standard similar to that of the late gold coinage, *c.* 1.25–1.30g (*c.* 19–20gr.) and presumably intended to be 20 grains. The coins of varieties A2 and BIA in particular, which are sufficiently plentiful to study statistically, reveal that the weights of individual coins were carefully regulated. After the deposit of the Hougham hoard the weight standard fell and most late Primary and Intermediate coins lie between 1.10g and 1.25g (*c.* 17–19½gr.), although some weigh as much as 1.30g (20gr.) or as little as 1.00g (15½gr.). In England there was no counterpart to the dramatic fall which occurred in Series D on the Continent. The Primary and Intermediate series maintained a good standard of silver (*c.* 90–95%). Higher traces of gold are found in the earlier coins and those from Frisia, and the later English (Primary and Intermediate) coins often have slightly more tin, presumably reflecting differences in the source of metal and not deliberate adulteration.

Secondary phase

The Secondary phase saw a further expansion in the area of circulation into central Wessex, East Anglia (previously restricted to the coast), southern and western Mercia and Northumbria. The only parts of England from which there are few if any finds, besides the virtually uninhabited Fenlands, the Pennines and the Weald of Kent and Sussex, are the south-west and the north-west. Single-finds from this period are probably more plentiful than from any other in England until the twelfth century. Some coins come from graves, but the majority represent casual losses from circulation (Hinton 1986). The early Saxon port of Southampton (*Hamwic*) has produced more than 200 early pennies from excavations and chance finds; most of these belong to the Secondary phase and have been found along street frontages or in rubbish pits, having been gathered up with refuse from floors and streets. Significant numbers have also been found at sites in East Kent (Richborough, Reculver and Canterbury), East Anglia (Barham, Burrow Hill, Lakenheath and an unidentified site near Cambridge), Lincolnshire (near Grimsby) and Yorkshire (North Ferriby, Whitby, York and Sancton), and from the vicinity of several Iron Age hill forts (Hod Hill in Dorset, St Catherine's Hill near Winchester, and Walbury Camp in Berkshire). Such concentrations of finds at particular sites are not repeated in the later Anglo-Saxon period. This abundance of finds and the scarcity of die-links among the surviving material suggests that the coinage had grown considerably and that its function was primarily commercial.

There was also an extension and consolidation of regional minting in the Secondary phase, which can be seen most clearly in East Anglia, Northumbria and Wessex, where the various series enjoyed a largely local circulation. An East Anglian mint may have been established in the late Primary or Intermediate phase with Series C (above, p. 166), but the later runic Series R, which copies the designs of Series C, has an unequivocal East Anglian distribution. It was an extensive series, produced throughout the Secondary phase, possibly from the same mint that was later to strike the regal East Anglian and Mercian coinages. Series Q may also be East Anglian, and if so it was the product of a separate centre. In Northumbria, there appears to have been an interval after the brief coinage of Aldfrith when no coins were struck. The regal coinage was resumed by Eadbert (737–58) in the later Secondary phase, and although there are a number of imitations which may have a north-eastern origin, there is no substantive coinage which might obviously fill this interval.

The coinage attributed to Southampton (Series H) has been found there in large numbers, and single-finds have been made in other parts of south Wessex but virtually none elsewhere. It appears to have commenced in the mid-Secondary phase and to have lasted for some years; the scale of loss at *Hamwic* – assuming that it does not represent rejection – implies a fairly long period of circulation. However, the recent speculation that it lasted well into the second half of the eighth century (Andrews and Metcalf 1984) is not compelling. After this issue minting was not sustained in Wessex and there were only occasional small prestige issues until the end of the ninth century when Winchester became one of Alfred's most substantial mints.

Metcalf has suggested that local coinages were also produced in southern Mercia (Series J, and varieties of Series U and K), in the region of the 'Hwicce' in western Mercia (a variety of Series K and L), in Sussex (Series G), in West Kent (Series W), in Essex (Series S), in Middle Anglia (Series T) and in Lindsey (Series Q). However, for some of these the number of finds is very small, and in each case the distribution pattern is less distinct than for the three areas described above, partly because of the more rapid mixing of coin between central and south-east England. The evidence of the coin finds is thus to some extent ambiguous, and Metcalf's interpretation of them is coloured by his view that they were regal issues and that many of their designs had political significance (above, pp. 158–9). Many of the designs on Secondary coins are drawn from familiar elements of contemporary Anglo-Saxon art, rather than from other coins as they had been previously (Morehart 1984), and a much greater variety of types and combinations is found.

Series G, J, R, U and possibly W were probably the earliest Secondary series. They were struck in silver almost as fine as that of the Primary and Intermediate coins, and their weights are only slightly lower, mostly lying in the range 1.0–1.2g (*c.* 15½–18½gr.). They were present in the hoards from Hallum, Cimiez and Föhr, and in the Garton-on-the-Wolds grave-find.

Series J initially followed the diademed head/bird-on-cross design of Series B (**1.694–5**), but it later adopted an obverse with two similar diademed heads confronting and a reverse with an array of four flying birds (**1.696**) both designs being known from contemporary metalwork (Morehart 1970; Nau 1982). The series has a wide distribution, comparable in many respects with that of Series E, but Metcalf has pointed to the presence of several finds in the Oxford region and their absence from the West Midlands as support for his view that they were struck in southern Mercia (Metcalf 1972a, 59–61). Further finds may help to confirm or alter this pattern – as for example a recent find from near Cambridge (Blackburn and Sorenson 1984) – and it may be necessary to reconsider Rigold's original proposal that they come from the same mint as Series B (London?), their wider distribution being due to the rapidly expanding circulation in the early Secondary phase.

Series G has a diademed bust with a cross before the face, also found later on some varieties of Series J, K, L, O and Q, while on the reverse it has a standard, a further indication of its early date since this design is not found on other Secondary coins, apart from the immobilized Series R of East Anglia. There are a few finds from Sussex to support Metcalf's tentative attribution to Selsey (Metcalf 1972a, 65), but they have also been found elsewhere in England and on the Continent, including a number of apparent imitations. This would suggest that they came from a site participating in foreign trade.

Series U is one of the fundamental Secondary series which was to influence the designs of many others. The obverse shows a figure holding two long crosses standing on a curved surface (**1.718**). The figure is wearing some headgear, which it has been suggested could be a royal *cynehelm* (Metcalf 1976b, 69). It is not clear whether the design was first adopted in Series U or W, but a figure recurs frequently in later issues (Series K, L, N, O and insular varieties of X), shown either standing or seated and holding one or two crosses or a falcon; on some there are two standing figures. A unique type of Series U has an archer kneeling before a tree for which Morehart (1984) has found parallels in contemporary sculpture, and although the archer has ties behind the head as if from a diadem she has shown that it is unlikely to represent an important personage since the bow and arrow was not then a prestigious weapon. The principal reverse type of Series U, a bird in a branch pecking berries, is a very common motif in Anglo-Saxon art, and is also found in Series H and Q. Two stylistic groups within the series have been discerned, one of which has been attributed to East Kent and the upper Thames (Metcalf 1972a and 1984a, 36). It appears to have been succeeded by Series K, and two minor types (*BMC* 23a and 23e) which Rigold included in Series U are somewhat later.

Series W has a standing or a half-length bust looking left and holding two crosses. The reverse design is a cross-crosslet over a saltire, sometimes with an annulet at the centre. Only about ten coins of this Series are known and they fall into several distinctive groups (Blackburn and Bonser 1984b, 235–6). This type with a half-length bust and grotesque face appears to be the earlier. Their weights (1.01–1.26g) and an analysis of one coin with a half-length bust (91% silver; $1\frac{1}{2}$% gold) suggest that they were struck no later than the early Secondary phase, and they could well be Primary or Intermediate. Four specimens with standing figures come from French finds (Prou 1892a, nos. 1615–18), two of them from the Cimiez hoard, and their distinctive style suggests that they may be Merovingian, possibly struck at Marseille since four other coins in the Cimiez hoard of the Marseille mint have very similar reverse designs. If they are indeed Frankish, rather than English imports, it is probable that the Marseille mint copied the design of Series W rather than *vice versa* as the four related coins appear to have been among the latest in the hoard, contemporary with early or mid-Secondary sceattas. English finds are from Kent (2), Southampton, Dorset and Lincolnshire, implying a south-eastern origin with coastal distribution from there; the suggested West Kent attribution (Metcalf 1984a, 44) is a possibility.

The mid-Secondary phase saw the introduction of a number of new types, represented in the hoards from Hallum, Cimiez, and the Garton-on-the-Wolds grave-find, and showing a general decline in fineness to *c.* 60–80% silver. These are Series K, H, N, T and Z, and probably M, O and V for which there is no hoard provenance. Series K may be the successor to Series U, reflecting a similar high standard of die-cutting and novelty of design. Metcalf has distinguished two styles within it, which he regards as the work of the same Kentish and Mercian die-cutters of Series U (Metcalf 1984a, 38), while others are in the style which Metcalf attributes to Hwiccia (Metcalf 1984a, 36; Biddle *et al.* 1986, n. 24). The principal obverse design shows a bust, with diadem ties in a loose knot behind the head, usually turned to the left but occasionally facing. There are a variety of reverse designs, most of which incorporate a wolf. On some coins it is lying on its back with its hind legs and tail following the border, but subsequently the front and then the hind legs disappear leaving a wolf-headed serpent (**1.697–8**), which may itself be enclosed in a torque with a tiny head (**1.699**). Another, possibly earlier, reverse of Series K shows a hound looking backwards and standing in front of a tree, which has parallels in other contemporary art (Morehart 1984, 183). Similar animals were popular subjects for coin designs – standing beasts appear on Series M, N, O, Q, X, Y and Z, and a whorl of wolves' heads on Series H, S and U – though as common themes in Germanic art they are not necessarily related to one another.

The coins of Series H, minted in or near Southampton, are difficult to place chronologically. The Southampton (Kingsland) hoard contained only coins of this series and is no aid to dating. We are not even sure of the correct sequence of the three types. The series is presumably headed by type 39 or type 49, which both use a bird design apparently influenced by Series U (**1.691–3**). This would suggest a mid-Secondary origin which would accord with their finenesses (60–80% silver), although the weights (*c.* 0.9–1.0g) are somewhat lower than other coins of this period. Type 48 derives its design, a whorl of wolves' heads, from the later type 23e (assigned to Series U) and its absence from the Southampton (Kingsland) hoard could imply that it is the latest of the three types, though it may be contemporary and come from another mint in the locality (Metcalf 1984a, 37). The series is a large one and it probably continued into the late Secondary phase, maintaining similar standards of weight and fineness throughout.

Series M, N, V and Z are self-contained and distinctive issues. Series N shows two standing figures with one or more crosses (**1.704–6**), and this design is also reproduced on some (English?) varieties of Series X (*BMC* type 30) of much the same date. Series V is unusual in the Secondary phase in that its obverse copies the design of a fourth-century Constantinian coin depicting the wolf and twins. This design is again used at the end of the eighth century by Æthelberht of East Anglia, but the southerly distribution precludes an East Anglian origin for Series V. Series Z with a large facing bust and long-legged beast may have been copied from an Ancient British bronze coin of Cunobelin, but its place of origin is uncertain.

Series T is one of the few inscribed Secondary series. It combines a diademed bust with a 'porcupine' design. Most of the inscriptions are enigmatic – LEV (**1.717**), LELVS, TΛΛVM, MONITΛSCORVM, etc. – but some have Ɛ LVNDONIM. Two specimens with this reading are known (Hill 1953, 103), and one is from the Hallum hoard, which suggests that they are earlier than the similarly inscribed coins of Series L. The use of the 'porcupine' design and the fineness of one 'LEV' coin which has been analysed (60–74% silver) reinforce the view that Series T belongs relatively early in the Secondary phase. The type may have been struck at more than one mint; some are presumably from London, but the few finds of coins with other legends suggest that they could come from a mint in the East Midlands (Metcalf 1984a, 39–40).

The coins of *BMC* types 23a and 23e (assigned by Rigold to Series U, but attributed by Metcalf to a new Series P) are problematic. Their poor silver (30–40%) and light weights would suggest a relatively late date, and their designs – a standing figure (with square shoulders) combined with either a standing beast or a whorl of wolves' heads – would sit well beside late coins of Series K and coins of Series L, with which they occurred in the London B hoard. Such a dating would be consistent with the wolf-whorl design having been copied in Series S and H. However, the alleged presence of a specimen of type 23e in the Cimiez hoard would indicate an earlier date, in the mid-Secondary phase, which in turn would imply a dramatic decline in fineness at its mint of origin in the south-east. While it is quite likely that at times different standards ruled at different mints, as for example in Series H where a relatively high standard seems to have been maintained throughout, it is possible that types 23a and 23e are later and that the Cimiez provenance is an error resulting from a confusion in the Morel-Fatio collection.

The late Secondary phase saw further debasement, reducing the fineness at some mints to as little as 20%, and a further reduction in weight standards to 0.8–1.0g ($12\frac{1}{2}$–15gr.) or even less. The reductions may not have been as great at all mints. To this period probably belong the later coins of Series H, K and R and the new Series L, Q, S, Y (in the name of Eadbert) and the coinage of Beonna. The five later hoards from East Anglia, London and Southampton (Table 13) contain only coins from their own localities and cannot provide a relative dating between the regions so that one is forced back on other less reliable criteria.

In the south-east, as the 'knot-bust' issues of Series K were drawing to a close, new types with a diademed bust (Series L) were introduced, some with a London mint-signature, *(De) Lundonia* or a blundering of it (**1.700–1**). The coins of Series L are notably base, many falling to below 30% silver. They have a wide distribution, principally in the Thames valley, East Anglia and the Midlands, but with few in Kent or Wessex, possibly because finer standards prevailed there. As in earlier phases, it is hard to identify the Kentish issues with any certainty thanks to the rapid dispersal of coin to other parts of England. Possible candidates include *BMC* 23a and e (Series U), later issues of Series K and O, and perhaps Series S, although its distribution is mainly north of the Thames, or some of the uninscribed varieties of Series L.

A particular base and blundered variety of Series L dominates the few finds from West Mercia, and Metcalf has suggested that it may have been a local 'Hwiccian' issue, possibly struck at Worcester (Metcalf 1976b; 1984a, 38). However, several specimens have been found in London and one near Cambridge (**1.701**), and it is possible that they were produced in the London area, the West Mercian finds deriving from one or more large payments made to that region.

The coins of Series Q with a walking beast and a bird, or occasionally a bust or standing figure, can be divided into two distinctive groups. One is in an angular style engraved in simple lines, while the other has more rounded or modelled subjects. It is not clear whether the division is chronological or geographical. The angular variety is arguably East or Middle Anglian, although the find distribution is slightly wider than that of Series R which it occasionally copies (**1.707**). The rounded variety is probably not Northumbrian, despite the similarity with the beasts on the coinages of Aldfrith and Eadberht. There are two finds from York and one from Whitby, but in other respects the distribution is similar to that of the angular variety and they probably belong to the same region. The suggestion that they come from Lindsey (Metcalf 1984b, 200–2) is conjectural, none having been found there. The angular variety belongs to the mid or late Secondary phase; it occurred in the hoard from near Cambridge and one specimen analysed had *c.* 50% silver.

In Northumbria, the tradition of a regal coinage was revived by Eadbert (738–58). His coins (Series Y) maintained a slightly heavier weight than was current in the south (0.90–1.10g) and a considerably higher silver standard (50–90%). There is one basic design with the king's name EADBERhTVS, EOTBEREhTVS or EOTBERHTVS around a small cross and on the other side a walking beast, similar to but not the same as that on the coins of Aldfrith. The dies fall into several distinct groups, distinguished by the form of the king's name and the obverse cross, and the direction of the beast and any additional symbols in the field. Booth (1984) has divided the coinage into seven classes (A–G) which he suggests represent deliberate variations intended to differentiate the products of different moneyers (or even mints), or of different periods, although he has been unable to propose a chronological sequence. A second series of coins combines the name of Eadbert with that of his brother Ecgbert (*c.* 732–66), who is shown as a standing figure holding a cross and a crozier, or two crosses. This issue established a precedent for the archiepiscopal coinages that were to follow at York until the Viking conquest in 867 and at Canterbury until 923. Eadbert's coinage was substantial and may have extended over most of his reign. Booth has recorded 99 coins of the regal issue and 28 of the archiepiscopal issue, with little die-linking between specimens. His die-study shows that the side with the king's name was the upper (i.e. reverse) die and that with the beast or archbishop was the lower die, no doubt because it was more difficult to make and would have lasted longer. Only when the moneyer's name occurred on the coins was it necessary for this to be on the reverse die, so that the moneyer could lock it up when not in use. Eadbert's coinage enjoyed a largely Northumbrian circulation, with just the odd specimen having been found in north Lindsey and Norfolk, and across the North Sea at Dorestad and in Norway.

In East Anglia, Series R continued to flourish, although the coins were very base and light. The bust became extremely stylized, but some new geometric reverse designs were introduced and among the most base coins the names of two new moneyers appear, Tilbert (**1.713**) and Wigræd (**1.714–15**). The first coinage in the name of an East Anglian king, Beonna, was struck on the small sceatta module *c.* 760 (see Chapter 10). The Middle Harling hoard shows that late coins of Series R continued to circulate alongside those of Beonna, but it is not clear whether there was continuity of minting between the two issues.

Table 12. *The principal series of sceattas*

Abbreviations: *BMC* = *BMC AS* 1; Brooke = Brooke 1950; HM&M = Hawkes *et al.* 1966; MM&H = Metcalf *et al.* 1968; North = North 1980.

Series	Illustrations (*BMC* no.)	References	Comments
Transitional pale gold/silver c. *670–80?*			
Pa	 (PIA) (PIII)	*BMC* 23.1–3 (as Peada of Mercia); Brooke 1–4; North 31–2, 151–4	'Pada' inscribed in runes on rev. of all but one type. Based on a variety of 4th-c. models. Probably Kentish. Hoards: Cimiez. Single-finds: East Kent, lower Thames and Continent. For classification and corpus, see Rigold 1960, 31–2; Rigold 1966, 5. Finenesses range from *c.* 30% gold to good silver (HM&M F.2, O.13–14; **1.668–9**); two mounted coins from Dover are said to be only 86% and 66% silver (Rigold 1960, 53).
Va		*BMC* -; Brooke -; North-; Belfort 1892–5, 3300–7; Prou 1892a, 2730–1	'Vanimundus Mone' or degeneration on obv., copied from a Merovingian coin. This legend is perpetuated in Series B. Metcalf (1976a, 12–13) has suggested an Essex origin. Distribution: one from Colchester (Essex), many from Continent, possibly from an early 19th-c. hoard. For classification and corpus, see Rigold 1960, 33 (additional specimens HM&M, O.16–17 and Vanhoudt 1982, no. 215). Finenesses range from *c.* 10% gold to silver (HM&M O.15–17; MM&H Ca.1; Oddy 1978, SG498; **1.670–1**).
Primary and Intermediate series c. *680–710*			
A	 2a (A3)	*BMC* 2a; Brooke 5; North 40	Elements of design derived from Two Emperors, *Concordia*, and Pada thrymsas. Probably Kentish. Distribution: primarily East Kent and Thames valley. For classification into three groups, see Rigold 1960, 34. This series belongs early in the Primary phase. The first two groups (A1, A2) were struck to the full thrymsa standard *c.* 1.27g, A3 was on a lower standard (less than 1.20g). Present with Series BI in Kentish hoards and grave finds. Finenesses: *c.* 95% silver, one

A2 coin had 6–7% gold (HM&M F.3–4; Rigold 1960, 53, no. 9489; Metcalf 1978, O.185–9).

B

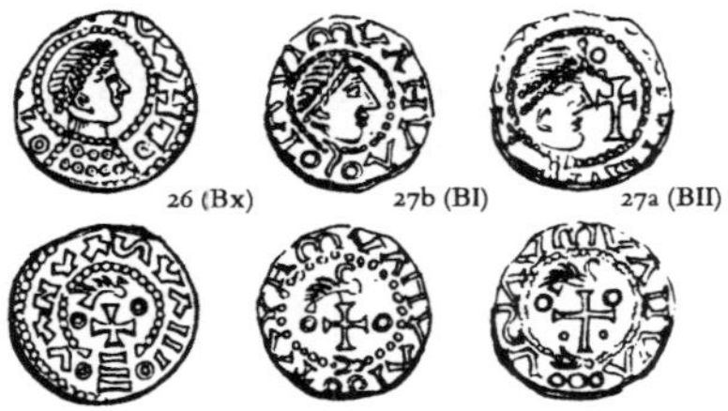

26 (Bx) 27b (BI) 27a (BII)

BMC 26, 27a–b, 29; Brooke 11; North 124–9

'Bird-on-cross' type. Legend derived from degraded 'Vanimundus' of Series Va. Annulets and crosses in field and in legends consciously varied, apparently to distinguish the dies. For detailed classification and die-analysis, see Rigold 1960 and 1966. Bx and BI are contemporary with Series A, BII is later Primary and Intermediate, and BIII is Secondary (= Series J). Rigold regarded the series as Kentish, but Metcalf's (1984a, 28) proposed East Saxon origin (? at London) is preferable. However his attribution of BII to Frisia (Metcalf 1966b, 33) seems unnecessary and has not been pressed by him. Distribution: early Bx coins in Essex; BI coins mostly from Kentish hoards; BII has the wider distribution, Kent, East Anglia and the East Midlands, which might be expected of an Intermediate series. Fineness: *c.* 90–95% silver (HM&M F.5–10; Rigold 1960, 53 nos. 9487–8; Metcalf 1978, O.190–5, M.7).

C

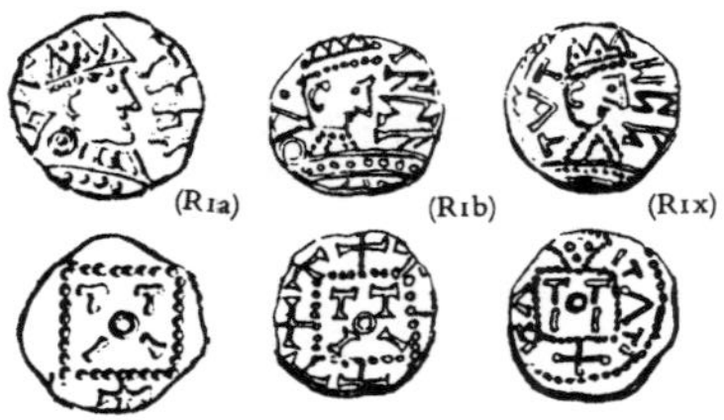

(R1a) (R1b) (R1x)

BMC 2 'runic' (some), 2b (some); Brooke 6 (some); North 157–61, 164–6 (some)

Design similar to Series A, but with T æpa, T apæ or T epa (the second element, a moneyer's name?, in runes). Early coins (R1a–b) are late Primary, found in the Southend and Birchington grave-hoards, and as single-finds in Bucks. and Yorks. Later coins (R1x–z) are Intermediate, with distribution: Kent coast, East Anglia, the Midlands and Yorks., and in Aston Rowant hoard. Metcalf (1984a, 37) attributes them to East Anglia, but it is possible that they are the successors to the Kentish Series A (above, p. 166). Classification is that of Rigold 1960, 17. Fineness: 11 early coins fall in range 92–97% silver; no later coins have been analysed (Rigold 1960, 53 nos. 9490–4; Metcalf 1978, O.66–71).

Table 12 (*cont.*)

Series	Illustrations (*BMC* no.)	References	Comments
D	 2c, 2c, 8	*BMC* 2c, 8, 50; Brooke 9; North 50, 168–9, 172	'Continental runic' type. Obv. of *BMC* 2c is copied from early Series C, but æpa inscription is blundered on most. A short but very extensive issue of the late Primary/Intermediate phase. Probably struck in the Lower Rhine region (above, pp. 152–3). Large numbers were brought to England; 179 in the Aston Rowant hoard and single-finds in the south, the Midlands, East Anglia, Lincs. and Yorks.
E	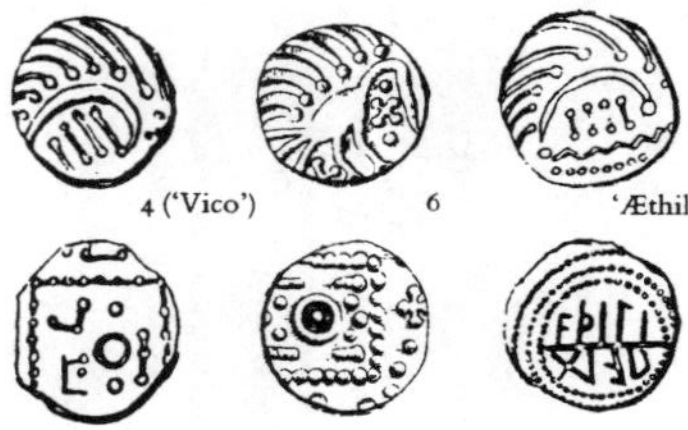 4 ('Vico'), 6, 'Æthilired'	*BMC* 4–6, 'Mercia: *Æthelred*'; Brooke 7–8; North 45–9, 155–6	'Porcupine' type. The great majority are probably Frisian (above, p. 153). A large series struck over many years and with wide variations in design. The principal types have been classified by Metcalf (1966a), but many fall outside his classification. Those found in England (widely distributed) are mostly Intermediate in date. There are a number of Intermediate or early Secondary derivatives, apparently of English origin. Some reading 'æthiliræd' were formerly attributed to Æthelred of Mercia (674–704), but although this might just be feasible chronologically, the recorded find-spots are south of the Thames and it is preferable to regard him as a moneyer. Another substantial group has a bust derived from Series A or C with hair developed from Series E; some have inscriptions 'VER', probably a personal name (**1.690A**; Blackburn and Bonser 1984a, one has *c.* 95% silver). The 'porcupine' design also occurs in Series T (*q.v.*).
F	 24b	*BMC* 24a–b; Brooke 10; North 61–2	'Cross-on-steps' type. The design is basically Frankish, with influence from Series A and B. There were at least 15 in the Aston Rowant hoard (Kent 1972b, but not listed in *Coin Hoards* 1 (1975), no. 347), and single-finds from Dorset,

London and Yorks. Metcalf (1978, 15) has argued for a Wessex attribution in the Primary phase, though most appear to be of Intermediate date. Only the four coins in this collection have been analysed (**1.687–90**), three with 92–93% silver and one with *c.* 10% gold.

See also Series W and Y

Secondary Series c. *710–50(?)*

G

3a

BMC 3a; Brooke -; North 43

Early Secondary. Hoards: Hallum, Cimiez, Garton, and Föhr. Some of the Continental finds are imitations. Single-finds: Sussex, Essex, Southampton, Northampton and Yorks. Metcalf (1972a, 65 and 1984a, 39) has suggested a South Saxon origin (?Selsey). Fineness: two coins of correct style have *c.* 90% silver; three imitations range from *c.* 20% to 60% silver (Metcalf and Hamblin 1968, O.124–5; Metcalf 1978, M.8, O.201–2).

H

48 49

BMC 39, 48–9; Brooke 25; North 96, 102–4

'*Hamwih*' (Southampton) series. Mid/late Secondary. The reverses copy designs of succeeding types of Series U, 'bird-and-branch' and 'whorl-of-wolves' heads'. Found in large numbers in excavations at Southampton and in Southampton (Kingsland) hoard; other finds are mainly from Hampshire, Sussex and Dorset. Blunt (1954) first proposed a Southampton attribution for types 39 and 49, which has been supported by subsequent finds (Addyman and Hill 1968). Metcalf has aired the possibility of another West Saxon mint for types 39 and 48 (Metcalf and Stós-Gale 1982, 145). A detailed analysis and corpus of Series H coins is to be included in Metcalf's publication of the Southampton excavation finds. Fineness in all types variable *c.* 60% to 80% silver (Metcalf 1978, Ca.6, O.60, O.203–4; Metcalf and Stós-Gale 1982, S.1–12, M.16).

Table 12 (*cont.*)

Series	Illustrations (*BMC* no.)	References	Comments
J		*BMC* 27b (some), 36–7, 60, 72; Brooke 11, 13; North 126–9, 134–5, 141	A late phase of the 'bird-on-cross' type (Rigold BIII), and its apparent successor with confronting heads and an array of four flying birds (*BMC* 37). Other types included in the series may be mules or derivatives. Early Secondary. Hoards: Hallum, Cimiez, Garton, and Föhr. Single-finds (wide distribution): S. and E. Midlands, East Anglia, Kent, Southampton and Yorks. (cf. distribution of Series E). Fineness 82–92% silver, but some contemporary imitations show much less (Metcalf 1978, 16, revising earlier analyses; Metcalf and Stós-Gale 1982, S.13, an imitation). Metcalf (1966b and 1972a) attributes them to southern Mercia (Abingdon?), but Rigold (1966) preferred a Kentish or Middle Anglian attribution. It is possible that they come from the same mint as Series B (London?).
K		*BMC* 20, 32a, 33, 42, 52, 75; Brooke 17, 21, 35; North 74, 86–9, 93–4, 100–1, 105, 123	'Wolf' types. Mid/late Secondary, successor to Series U. Hoards: Garton and London B. Single-finds (wide distribution): C. and S. England. Metcalf and Walker (1967) have distinguished two principal styles, which have been attributed to mints at Canterbury and (?) Abingdon, and a third which M. associates with Hwiccia (Metcalf 1984a, 36–38). Finenesses: types 20, 42 and 52 have shown *c.* 65–85% silver; types 32a and 33 have shown *c.* 40–60% silver (MM&H O.47–8, O.62–5; Metcalf 1978, O.206 bis-7; Metcalf and Stós-Gale 1982, M.17).
L		*BMC* 12–19; Brooke 14–17; North 63–73	'London' types with (D)E LVNDONIA inscription, often blundered, and related types. Late Secondary; for an earlier issue with this inscription see Series T. Hoards: London B and C. Single-finds (wide distribution): Thames valley, East Anglia, Sussex, Hampshire, Kent, S. and W. Midlands, Lincs. and Yorks. Metcalf has identified one group with degraded legends which is found mainly in West Mercia ('Hwiccia')

and he suggests may be a local issue (Metcalf 1976b), but it has also been found at London and near Cambridge. Finenesses of the main series range from *c.* 20 to 50% silver; the 'Hwiccian' group even less (Metcalf 1978, O.49, O.52–5, O.208, M.9).

Series	Coins	References	Description
M		*BMC* 45, 62; Brooke –; North 122, 142–3	Hound and spiral branch. Mid-Secondary? Single-finds (few): Kent, Thames valley and Southampton. Finenesses: *c.* 50–75%; the unique coin of type 62 (with a wolf-mask) is *c.* 40% silver (Metcalf 1978, M.10, O.209–11).
N		*BMC* 41; Brooke 32; North 97–9	The figures are either confronting one another (type 41a) or facing (type 41b). Mid-Secondary. Hoards: Cimiez, and a related coin with two figures and a cross, but a 'porcupine' rev. was present in Hallum. Single-finds: Kent, Midlands, Thames valley, Southampton and Wilts. Metcalf (1974b) has distinguished two principal styles, which may be successive or possibly products of separate mints. No analyses.
O		*BMC* 21, 38, 40, 57; Brooke 28; North 95, 111, 113–14	The animal in types 40 and 57 is similar to that in Series N, but simpler and lacks forelegs. Type 21 is a mule of obverse types 40 and 57. The bird-in-torque of type 38 was copied on the Continent (**1.631**). Mid/late Secondary. Single-finds: Kent, East Anglia and Thames valley. Fineness: two specimens *c.* 50–60% silver (Metcalf 1978, O.50, O.212).
Q		*BMC* 35, 44, 64, 65, 71, 73; Brooke 33; North 133, 136–8	The principal type (*BMC* 44) has bird (derived from Series U) and a walking beast. Others combine one or other of these with designs from other series; bust and cross, standing figure, bust and runic 'epa', etc. There are two distinct series, one with smooth lines and rounded animals and the other more angular with pellets and a cross or crosses in field of the bird design (Metcalf 1972a, 56–7; Rigold 1977a, 25). The

Table 12 (*cont.*)

Series	Illustrations (*BMC* no.)	References	Comments
			latter is East or Middle Anglian (it occurred in the Cambridge hoard and is muled with designs of Series R), the former group is probably the same, and despite associations it is unlikely to be Northumbrian. Metcalf (1984b, 200–2) tentatively attributes the series to Lindsey. Mid/late Secondary. Fineness of one specimen analysed of the angular type is *c.* 50% silver (MM&H O.79).
R	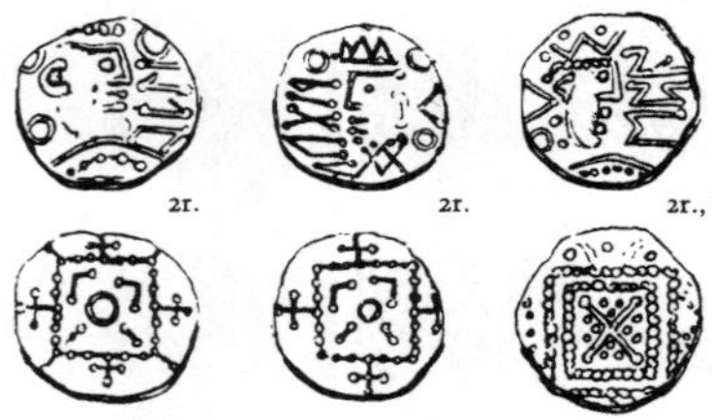 2r. 2r. 2r., var.	*BMC* 2 'runic' (some), 51, 56, 70; Brooke 6 (some); North 157–61, 164–6 (some)	Similar to Series C, but composition cruder and more stylized, lighter weight and more debased. Many of the legends repeat the name 'epa' etc. from Series C, but some have the names 'spi', 'wigræd' or 'wigrd', and 'tilberlt'. Some later coins have geometric reverses which lead into Beonna's coinage. The series was probably struck throughout the Secondary phase. Hoards: Cambridge and Middle Harling. Single-finds: East Anglia and E. Midlands. Finenesses: analyses of many specimens have shown that they range from *c.* 90% silver (early 'epa') to *c.* 20% silver ('wigræd' and 'tilberlt'); coins of 'spi' have not yet been analysed, but they appear to be of relatively good silver (MM&H pp. 29–31; Metcalf 1978, 17–18; O.78 is probably a coin of 'tilberlt').
S	 47	*BMC* 47; Brooke 23; North 121	Female centaur ('sphinx') and a whorl of four wolves' heads, their tongues meeting in the centre. Late Secondary. Single-finds (few): London, Herts., Beds., Essex and Kent. Metcalf (1976a, 11–13) has suggested that the centaur is derived from a coin of Cunobelin and has tentatively proposed an East Saxon attribution for Series S; but coins of Cunobelin are found widely in S. England, and Morehart (1984, 190 n. 53) has pointed to sculptural parallels for the design. However, the find distribution points to an origin north of the Thames. Fineness: one variety has *c.* 50% silver (Metcalf 1978, M.13).

T

BMC 9, '12/5' (Hill 1953, 103); Brooke 7 (some); North 80

A diademed bust with various inscriptions combined with a 'porcupine' design. Early/mid Secondary. Type '12/5', reading (D)E LVNDONIM was in the Hallum hoard and is apparently a precursor of Series L. Others have enigmatic inscriptions +LEV (type 9), +LELVS, TΛΛVM+ (Domburg find), MONITΛSCORVM+. Single-finds: several from the E. Midlands and one each from London and Kent. Fineness: one +LEV coin, 60–74% silver (MM&H O.45). Metcalf (1984a, 39–40) has suggested that type 9 may have been struck in the E. Midlands (? at Stamford). Type '12/5' was not allocated a place in Rigold's original scheme, the inference being that it is an imitative mule, but its presence in the Hallum hoard suggests that it ante-dates its putative prototype (type 12).

U

BMC 23a–e, 63, 76; Brooke 22; North 81–5, 112

The two principal types of this series – a standing figure on a curved surface, with a 'bird-and-branch' (type 23b–d) and later, with a whorl of three wolves' heads (type 23e) – were copied and modified in other series (H, L, Q, S). Metcalf (1972a and 1977) has distinguished two stylistic groups which he attributes to mints at Canterbury and (?) Abingdon (Metcalf 1984a, 36, 38). He also suggests that Series U was succeeded by Series K at these mints. Types 23b–d are early Secondary; types 23a and 23e appear to be later (although type 23e was reputedly present in the Cimiez hoard, see p. 172). Single-finds (wide distribution): S., C. and E. England. Fineness: type 23b, *c.* 65–90% silver; type 23e, *c.* 30–40% silver; a unique coin with a kneeling archer (Metcalf 1983b; Morehart 1984) has *c.* 70% silver (Metcalf 1978, 18; Metcalf and Stós-Gale 1982, S.14–15).

Table 12 (*cont.*)

Series	Illustrations (*BMC* no.)	References	Comments
V	 7	*BMC* 7; Brooke 20; North 122	She-wolf and twins/bird-in-vine. Mid Secondary? Single-finds: Kent (4), Southampton, and Reading, suggesting a Kentish origin (Metcalf 1984a, 45). Fineness: *c.* 55–75% silver (MM&H O.46 bis; Metcalf 1978, O.46).
W	 54	*BMC* 54; Brooke -; North 148	Intermediate or early Secondary? Hoard: Cimiez. Single-finds: Kent (2), Southampton, Dorset and Lincs. For a corpus, see Blackburn and Bonser 1984b. One specimen has been analysed with 91% silver and 1.5% gold (Metcalf and Stós-Gale 1982, S16). S. Eastern origin is likely; Metcalf (1984a, 44) has suggested West Kent.
X	 31 30b	*BMC* 30a–b; 31 Brooke 27; North 116–17, 170–1	'Woden/monster' type. Frisian or Danish; late Intermediate/Secondary phase (above, p. 154). Some English variants also use this design (e.g. type 30a–b), one of which has *c.* 90% silver (Metcalf and Stós-Gale 1982, S.17).
Y	 Aldfrith Eadbert Egbert	*BMC* pp. 140–1, 139, 189; Brooke p. 10; North 176–8, 192	Regal coinage of Northumbria. Presumably struck at York. Late Primary coinage of Aldfrith (685–704); fine silver (*c.* 93%; information Archibald and Cowell). Late Secondary coinage of Eadbert (737–58) and Archbishop Egbert (732/4–66). Fineness variable: 50–75% silver, but considerably better than most of the southern issues (MM&H pp. 50–2). For a corpus and die-analysis, see Booth 1984.

Type	References	Notes
Z 	*BMC* 59, 66; Brooke –; North 119?, 145–6	Early/mid Secondary. Hoard: Cimiez. Single-finds: London and Carlisle. Metcalf (1976a, 12) has suggested that the type is copied from a coin of Cunobelin (Mack 223) and that the issue may be East Saxon; but coins of Cunobelin are found widely in S. England, and it is doubtful that the inscription CVN would have been understood in the eighth century. Fineness: one specimen has 65–75% silver (MM&H Ca.5).
Beonna 	*BMC* p. 83; Brooke p. 11 (as Northumbrian); North 430	Regal coinage of Beonna of East Anglia (749–758f.). Three moneyers are recorded: Efe, Werferth and Wilred. One type has an interlace design with no moneyer's name. Hoard: Middle Harling. Single-finds: East Anglia. Struck on slightly larger flans than the other sceattas, attempting to restore the fineness and weight. See p. 278 below and Pagan 1968, which will be superseded by Miss Archibald's forthcoming report of the Middle Harling hoard. Three coins from this hoard are in the collection (**1.1121A–C**).

(e) CHRONOLOGY OF THE SCEATTAS

The relative chronology of the later gold and early silver coinages outlined above is based primarily on the evidence of some 25 hoards and groups of coins from graves, from both England and the Continent (see Table 13). Many of them are small or contain only a few Anglo-Saxon coins among a greater number of Continental ones, and by no means all the known types are represented in them. Where hoard evidence is lacking some use can be made of weights, finenesses and associations of type, although all of these involve conjecture when applied to chronology and must be treated with caution, especially since there are indications that different weights and alloy standards may have applied from mint to mint (above, p. 182). We are fortunate in having a large number of metal analyses which are useful, but for many issues more are required to confirm patterns and highlight anomalous results.

In the Primary and Intermediate phases we are relatively well informed since the hoards are more plentiful and detailed studies by Rigold and Metcalf have provided classifications for the major series. In the Secondary phase we are less fortunate. Hoards are fewer and smaller and come mostly from the fringes of the circulation area, and less work has been done to distinguish substantive types from derivatives and imitations. For many of the Secondary series there is still considerable uncertainty about their position in the sequence of types and their duration. The relative chronology indicated in Table 14 must therefore be regarded as tentative, pending more detailed research on individual issues.

To place an absolute chronology on these coinages is even more difficult, for there are very few points at which one can date them from independent evidence. Rigold (1960, 22–9) considered that the transition from gold to silver occurred *c.* 685, that the Primary series A and B commenced *c.* 695, and that the Secondary phase ran from *c.* 725. He regarded the Primary coinage as the great achievement of King Wihtred of Kent (690–725) and suggested that it commenced immediately after the payment by the people of Kent in 694 of a large wergeld in compensation for the killing of Mul, a member of the West Saxon royal house. This chronology assumed that the Crondall hoard was deposited *c.* 670, but, with the redating of the Merovingian series suggested by Lafaurie and subsequently supported by Kent's investigations in connection with the Sutton Hoo hoard, a revised date of *c.* 640/650 has been generally accepted (above, p. 127). To take account of this, Rigold was inclined to stretch the post-Crondall gold coinage over a longer period and move the transition to silver back only five years to *c.* 680 (Rigold 1966 and 1975). He attributed the initial Bx coinage to the early 690s (Rigold 1977b), but otherwise left the chronology of the silver coinage much as before. In 1961 Kent also placed the inauguration of the silver coinage *c.* 680–90, but suggested that it had expired by 750, resulting in a period of perhaps two decades of coinlessness in southern England before the introduction of the broad penny (Kent 1961, 12). More recent comments suggest that he now inclines to an earlier chronology; he has proposed a date as early as *c.* 655–60 for a pale gold shilling of Pada (Hawkes *et al.* 1966, 116), and his date of *c.* 710–15 for that Aston Rowant hoard (Kent 1972b) implies a rather earlier end for the Primary phase than Rigold would have allowed. Metcalf has also inclined to an earlier dating for the pale gold and earliest silver issues, but he has broadly followed Rigold for the later ones, adopting Kent's idea of a collapse of the currency in the 740s (Metcalf 1974a, 208–10, 215).

Table 13. *English and Continental hoards containing Anglo-Saxon sceattas*

	ENGLISH	FRANKISH	FRISIAN
680			
	Mucking (Bx)		
690	Hougham (A2, BIA) Milton Regis (A2-3, BIA-C) Finglesham (A2-3, BIB-C) Broadstairs (A2-3, BIB-C) Barham (A3, BIB-C)		
	Southend (A3, BII, C(R1a-b)		
700	Birchington (BII, C(R1b), D)		
		Saint-Pierre-les-Etieux (BII, C(R1a), D, E) Plassac (BI, D, Star?)	
710	Aston Rowant (A, B, C(R1x-y), D, E, F)	Nohanent (B, D, E) Bais (A, BI-II, D, E)	Escharen 1980 (D, D/E)
720		Cimiez (Pa, A, D, E, G, J, N, U (23e)?, W, X, Z, Star)	Hallum (E, E/N, G, J, N var., T, X, Star, Interlace) ?Föhr (E, G, J, Star)
	Garton-on-the-Wolds (G, J, K, R)		
730	?Southampton, Kingsland (H)		
	?Cambridge (Q, R)		
	London B (K, L, U(23e))		
740	London C (L)		
750			
760	Middle Harling (L, R, Beonna)		

The English hoards are described in Rigold and Metcalf 1984. The 'London A' hoard, included in the first edition of their checklist, has been omitted as Metcalf now regards it as an accumulation of single-finds. The contents of the 'Southampton A' hoard are uncertain, and it has been omitted from the table. The Frankish hoards are described on pp. 140–3 above and those from the Low Countries on pp. 150–1.

The Anglo-Saxon and Frisian contents of each hoard are indicated in parentheses.

Rigold based his chronology on a range of historical events and on a number of Continental hoards, but from among the points he considered there are five dates on which he placed most reliance: (a) the deposit of the Crondall hoard, (b) the reign of Wihtred of Kent and the wergeld of Mul, (c) Æthelbald's lordship over London from shortly before 732, and the deposits of (d) the Hallum and (e) the Cimiez hoards. Whether one takes Kent's date of *c.* 640/645 for Crondall or Rigold's *c.* 650 makes little difference to the later coinages. Wihtred's long and successful reign provides a possible context for the early development of the silver coinage, but imposes no real constraints on the dating if other evidence points in a different direction. As often as not, coinages respond to commercial and social rather than political factors, and developments on the Continent are likely to have had a profound influence. The silver denier was probably introduced in Neustria in the late 660s, and was rapidly adopted elsewhere. But Continental parallels, like the reign of Wihtred, although pertinent to the interpretation of the coinage, are not necessarily a secure basis for dating.

Rigold saw the payment of the large wergeld for Mul as exhausting the currency of the Pa and Va issues, and the new political climate which followed as providing an incentive for the inauguration of Series A and B. Metcalf has questioned whether this would have had such a significant effect on the currency (Metcalf 1974a, 208 n. 16; and see Blackburn 1984, 169 n. 19). In any event the historical association is too uncertain to form a basis for dating. The change from gold to silver had on Rigold's admission taken place at least a decade earlier, and it is not clear why a heavy payment such as this should have prompted a change of coin type. It is more likely to have caused a weight reduction such as that observed after the deposit of the Hougham hoard.

The watershed between the Primary/Intermediate and the Secondary phase Rigold put *c.* 725–30, and he suggested that the coins of *BMC* type 12 with *(De) Lundonia* were issued by Æthelbald of Mercia (716–57) in the early 730s to mark his acquisition of administrative authority over London which he infers occurred *c.* 731 (Rigold 1960, 24). This type was not present, however, in the Hallum or Cimiez hoards, and Metcalf has pointed out that, if debasement is any guide to chronology, it cannot belong to the beginning of the Secondary phase (Metcalf 1978, 16). He suggests that either the historical interpretation should be modified or the end of the Primary phase should be moved back perhaps as much as a decade or more. The revised chronology proposed below places type 12 in the 730s and would permit an association with Æthelbald's growing authority there, although there must be considerable doubt as to whether this was its purpose, especially since the rare coins of Series T with a similar inscription appear to belong a decade earlier.

The Continental hoards are important for dating the silver coinages, Continental and English. Rigold accepted the traditional dates of 734 for Hallum and 737 for Cimiez, and in this he was following other distinguished scholars, including Le Gentilhomme and Lafaurie. These were the dates proposed in the original hoard reports by Dirks (1870, 285–6) and Morel-Fatio (Chabouillet 1890, 2–3), and both depended largely on supposed associations with particular campaigns, that of Charles Martel in Friesland in 734 and that of the Lombards in Provence in 737. Neither of these suggested historical contexts is so compelling that it can override the internal numismatic evidence which points to earlier dates for both hoards. It has been argued above (pp. 142–4), mainly on the evidence of the coins of the patricians of Provence, that the Cimiez hoard should be dated *c.* 720 and that the French hoards of Saint-Pierre-les-Etieux, Plassac, Nohanent and Bais, containing Primary and Intermediate sceattas, belong to the first decade of the eighth century rather than the 730s and 740s as had previously been supposed. The Aston Rowant hoard is contemporary with this latter group and that from Hallum appears to be slightly earlier than Cimiez.

The implications for the chronologies of the Anglo-Saxon and Frisian coinages are considerable. It is necessary to put back by some ten or fifteen years the beginning of the Secondary phase, for the Cimiez hoard contained early and mid Secondary types. This in turn implies rather earlier dates for the Primary and Intermediate phases. Taking the Crondall hoard (*c.* 640/650) and the Cimiez hoard (*c.* 720) as two reasonably firm dates, we may distribute the various phases of the coinages around them, based on their size and complexity and changes in the composition of the currency as reflected in the hoards, although the periods to be given to each is largely a matter of guesswork. Unfortunately we lack hoards which might show to what extent the post-Crondall London and Witmen derivatives, the 'Two Emperors' type, and the *Pada* and 'Vanimundus' gold coins formed separate phases of currency, although we may infer from their differing finenesses that they are likely to have done so. In the Primary silver phase sufficient time must be allowed for the sweeping away of the Pa and Va series and the earliest types of Series A and B before the collection of the Hougham hoard. The A2 and B I A coins which this contained had in turn largely disappeared from circulation by the time the Barham and Southend finds were put down. In the Intermediate phase, between Southend and Aston Rowant we must allow for the development of the extensive Continental Runic (Series D) coinage and its drastic fall in weight, while balancing against this the relatively small number of English coins of the Intermediate phase, if, as seems right, Metcalf's latest suggestion that the majority of the 'porcupines' (Series E) found in this country are Frisian is accepted (above, p. 153). And how long did the early Secondary phase last before the deposit of the Cimiez hoard? However one arranges the silver coinage, the schedule looks extremely tight.

The change from gold to silver must be put back firmly into the 670s and possibly even earlier. It is not necessary to assume that the Anglo-Saxons were following the Merovingians in adopting a silver coinage, but historically it is probable and the continued flow of Pa and Va coins, gold and silver, to the Continent suggests that the currencies were never far out of line. We would tentatively suggest that the Primary phase (including the silver coins of Series Pa and Va) occupied the last quarter of the seventh century and the Intermediate phase the first decade of the eighth, with any movement from this likely to take them earlier, not later.

The arrangement of the coinage struck in the 40 or 50 years between the deposit of the Cimiez hoard and the introduction of the broad penny poses a different problem. The new broad pennies began to be struck in south-eastern England in the 760s or at the latest in the 770s. There are far fewer sceattas and sceat-types to be attributed to the middle decades of the century than to earlier phases. The period also saw dramatic debasement and a decline in weight standard. Already during the second quarter of the eighth century output must have fallen to a very low level and may even have ceased at many mints. Series L seems to have been more extended than most, with a long run of very debased coins, but it is impossible to judge how long it

Table 14. *A chronology for the sceattas*

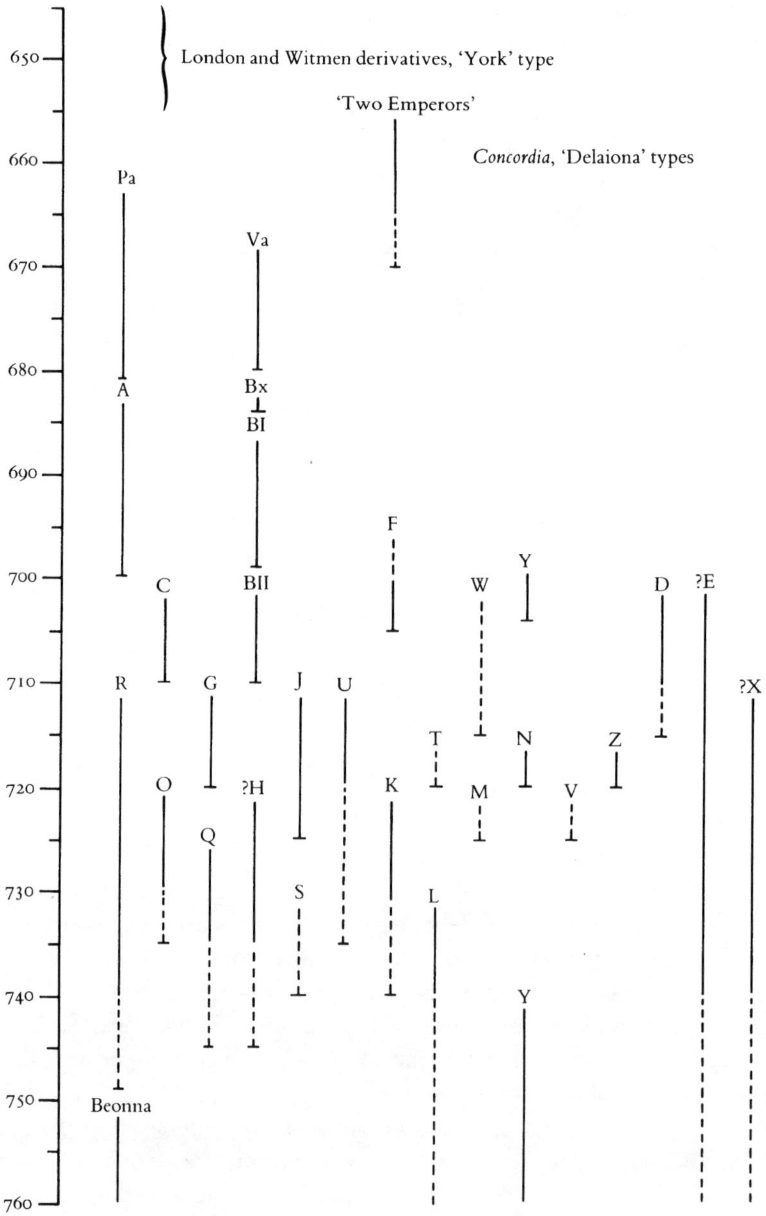

may have lasted. At York, Eadbert restored the standard of the Northumbrian coinage probably in the early 740s, and created a good currency which continued until the end of the century. In East Anglia, Series R became very debased, but the survival of a certain number of sceattas alongside the coins of Beonna in the Middle Harling hoard suggests that the use (if not the minting) of coins persisted without a break, at least in that region of England. The tentative chronology outlined here is reflected in Tables 13 and 14.

9

THE CAROLINGIANS

(a) GENERAL FEATURES

Literature

The basic surveys of Carolingian coinage are those of Gariel (1883–4), Prou (1896a), and Morrison and Grunthal (1967). Prou's work, a catalogue of the coins in the Bibliothèque Nationale with a comprehensive introduction, is excellent; a selective supplement was published by Dieudonné (1915). Gariel's work is more complete than that of Prou but is very uneven, in part because its author died in 1884 and his second volume, in which the coinage is systematically described, was never revised, in part because he was no historian and had little stylistic sense, so that his ruler- and mint-attributions are in frequent need of correction. Morrison and Grunthal is not in this respect an improvement, for a high proportion of their attributions are inadequate or incorrect; see reviews by Grierson and Lafaurie respectively in *NC* 1969, 346–50, and *RN* 1967, 291–5. It is chiefly valuable for its illustrations, especially of coins in the Berlin collection, which explains why, in the text that follows, Morrison and Grunthal references (MG) are generally preferred to Prou (P) or Gariel (G). A fourth work covering the whole coinage (Frère 1977b, with supplement Frère 1980) is essentially derivative, with no systematic revision of the conclusions or attributions of its predecessors, but it has useful maps and excellent plates of coins from mints situated in modern Belgium. The only important collection apart from that of the BN to have been catalogued is that in the British Museum (Dolley and Morrison 1966), but the catalogue shares many of the defects of Morrison and Grunthal (see Grierson's review in *NCirc* 1968, 81–2). Useful discussions of the coinage can be found in the nineteenth-century works of Müller (1860) and Soetbeer (1862–6). The only analytical bibliography (Colin 1868) is over a century old.

Morrison and Grunthal 1967 includes a list and analysis of Carolingian coin hoards, but the dates assigned to these are unreliable and there are many inaccuracies and some gaps, so that despite its usefulness for reference purposes it is essential to check its sources. Vol. I of Gariel (1883) reproduced *in extenso* all hoard descriptions and illustrations known prior to 1880. Hoards ante-dating 800 are admirably covered by Völckers (1965), Low Country hoards by Boeles (1915), and those from the British Isles by Dolley and Morrison (1963; Dolley 1965b), but for the Low Countries much new material has come to light since Boeles wrote. Finds in north-western Germany have been published by Berghaus (1973) and those in Denmark by Galster (1959), to which must be added the immensely important finds from Hedeby and Krinkberg (Nöbbe 1936a, 1936b) and the Norwegian find of Hon (Holst 1931, 1951; Skaare 1966). The role of coined money in the economy is difficult to assess, so that the most divergent views have been expressed (Gaettens 1955; Dopsch 1930; Grierson 1959b; Metcalf 1967). Germany is something of a special problem (Hävernick 1947, 1961; Hess 1962), and while some scholars have taken it for granted that coins were distributed almost exclusively by trade (Vercauteren 1934, 1960; Metcalf 1967, 1981), others have envisaged different possibilities (Morrison 1963; Grierson 1981).

A few auction sale catalogues are of importance, notably those of the collectors Ernest Gariel (Hoffmann 27.4.1885), Henri Meyer ('Vente H. M.', Rollin & Feuardent 26.5.1902), and Henry Grunthal (in MMAG Auct. 39, 9.5.1969), to which must be added the coins of the Pilligerheck hoard in Kress Auct. 140 (7.8.1967). The first and second of these sales involved general collections of French coins, with exceptionally good Carolingian series. Only a few coins in the Gariel sale were illustrated, since it was assumed that the illustrations in the owner's own monograph on the series would serve instead. Many of the coins were acquired by the French collector Ferrari de la Renotière and eventually resold in 1910 to the Berlin cabinet, the sudden expansion of whose Carolingian holdings from 700 to over 1500 coins was celebrated in a lengthy descriptive article (Menadier 1911), though the coins are best accessible to scholars, and that only partially, in the plates of Morrison and Grunthal. The Meyer and Grunthal catalogues are copiously illustrated, though the quality of the Meyer illustrations is poor. The Meyer collection, that of a wealthy Alsatian industrialist domiciled in Paris, was put together over the years 1865–1900. The Grunthal collection was that of an American numismatist of German origin who had studied at Berlin and who, during the years he worked on the staff of the Museum of the American Numismatic Society (1953–73), transformed the Carolingian collection there from one of no consequence into one of the most important in existence (Grunthal 1958). The Pilligerheck coins, which are of the late 830s and early 840s and very fully illustrated, were withdrawn from the Kress sale because of treasure trove problems.

The fullest account of the political background of the Carolingian period is provided in the series of monographs published under the general title of *Jahrbücher des fränkischen Reiches* (Leipzig, 1869–), though the earlier volumes are out-of-date and only those on Louis the Pious (Simson 1874–6) and the East German kingdom (with Lotharingia) from 841 (Dümmler 1887–8) retain their value. A projected French counterpart covers no more than the period 877–987 (below, p. 243). The most convenient, well-documented surveys are the relevant sections of Lot, Pfister and Ganshof (1941) and a book by McKitterick (1983).

Carolingian charters and legislation relating to coinage were collected by Barthélemy in the first volume of Gariel (1883). Although the texts themselves are usually reliable the dating of the capitularies is frequently incorrect, and they cannot be safely cited without reference to the *Capitularia regum Francorum* of Boretius and Krause (MGH *Capitularia*). The difficulty is that most of the documents are themselves undated, and one can only determine when they were issued from a comparative study of their contents and occasional references in contemporary annals. Boretius' dating has in turn undergone some revision (De Clercq 1936). Better editions of the charters than those used by Barthélemy are also, save for the reign of Louis the Pious, now available.

Historical background

Since the Carolingian 'empire' existed in a recognizable form for nearly two centuries and included all western Europe except the British Isles and most of Spain, its history is one of great complexity. The student's difficulties are increased by the fact that members of the dynasty, like the Merovingians before them, had a very limited repertory of personal names, and even with the help of the nicknames by which they are usually known it is sometimes hard to keep in mind the distinction between two or three contemporary rulers each named Charles or Louis.

The situation would be simplified if scholars could agree to call those who ruled primarily in Germany Karl and Ludwig and those in France Charles and Louis – or in Italy Carlo and Lodovico – but the current terminology is too widely accepted to be dispensed with. The example of the *CMH* has been followed, however, in spelling tenth-century West Frankish rulers as in French, so that *Rodulfus* and *Lotharius* are 'Raoul' and 'Lothaire' instead of Rudolf (e.g. of Burgundy and Italy) and Lothar (in the Middle Kingdom).

The dynasty takes its name not from Charlemagne himself but from his grandfather Charles Martel, who was never more than Mayor of the Palace. His son Pepin the Short (741–68) exchanged the title of Mayor for that of king (751), and the successes of his long reign – the reconquest of Aquitaine, expeditions against the Saxons and Lombards – set the pattern for the much greater achievements of his son Charles the Great or Charlemagne (768–814). Charles conquered and annexed the Lombard kingdom, adding the title of *rex Langobardorum* to those of *rex Francorum* and of *patricius Romanorum*, which he had received as a child from Pope Stephen III. He made himself master of Germany, deposing the last duke of Bavaria and in thirty years of warfare conquering the land between the Lower Rhine and the Elbe which was the 'Saxony' of the time. In 800, at Rome, he received from Leo III the imperial title. He proved an effective and innovative legislator and administrator; subsequent tradition did not go astray in regarding him as one of the greatest rulers in European history.

The Carolingians, however, had inherited from the Merovingians the custom of partitioning the kingdom as if it were private property on the death of each ruler. Charlemagne had three legitimate sons, two of whom, Pepin and Louis, received sub-kingdoms in their father's lifetime, but Pepin and the eldest son Charles predeceased him and Louis was left to become sole ruler on Charlemagne's death in 814. Louis the Pious in turn created sub-kingdoms for his three sons by his first wife, and all might have gone well if it had not been for his second marriage and the birth of a fourth son, Charles, later known as the Bald, for Charles had by Frankish custom as much right as his brothers to a share in the inheritance.

Louis' efforts to find a kingdom for Charles, coupled with the ambition of the eldest son Lothar to make a reality of the imperial office and the determination of his two brothers to prevent him doing so, resulted in a decade of rebellion and civil war that ended, three years after Louis' death, in the partition of the empire in 843. The eastern third became the share of Louis the German and, repeatedly divided between sons and reunited when they died without male heirs, continued in the hands of Louis' descendants till the death of Louis the Child in 911. The western third was the portion of Charles the Bald, though he had to fight for the Aquitanian half of it against Pepin II, son of his brother Pepin I who had died in 838. Charles' descendants continued to rule it, though not continuously, down to 987. The central third, the share of the eldest son Lothar I, which is called by modern historians the Middle Kingdom, consisted of a wide strip of land extending from Frisia in the north to Provence in the south and extending beyond the Alps to include the kingdom of Italy. It was divided up in 855 between Lothar's three sons and in the end was either annexed by its French or German neighbours or gave rise to the later kingdoms of Arles (Burgundy–Provence) and Italy.

This complex succession of rulers and their relationships is set out in the accompanying genealogical table (Table 15), continued by others on pp. 221, 226 and 244. They are, of course, no

Table 15. *The early Carolingians, 719–840*

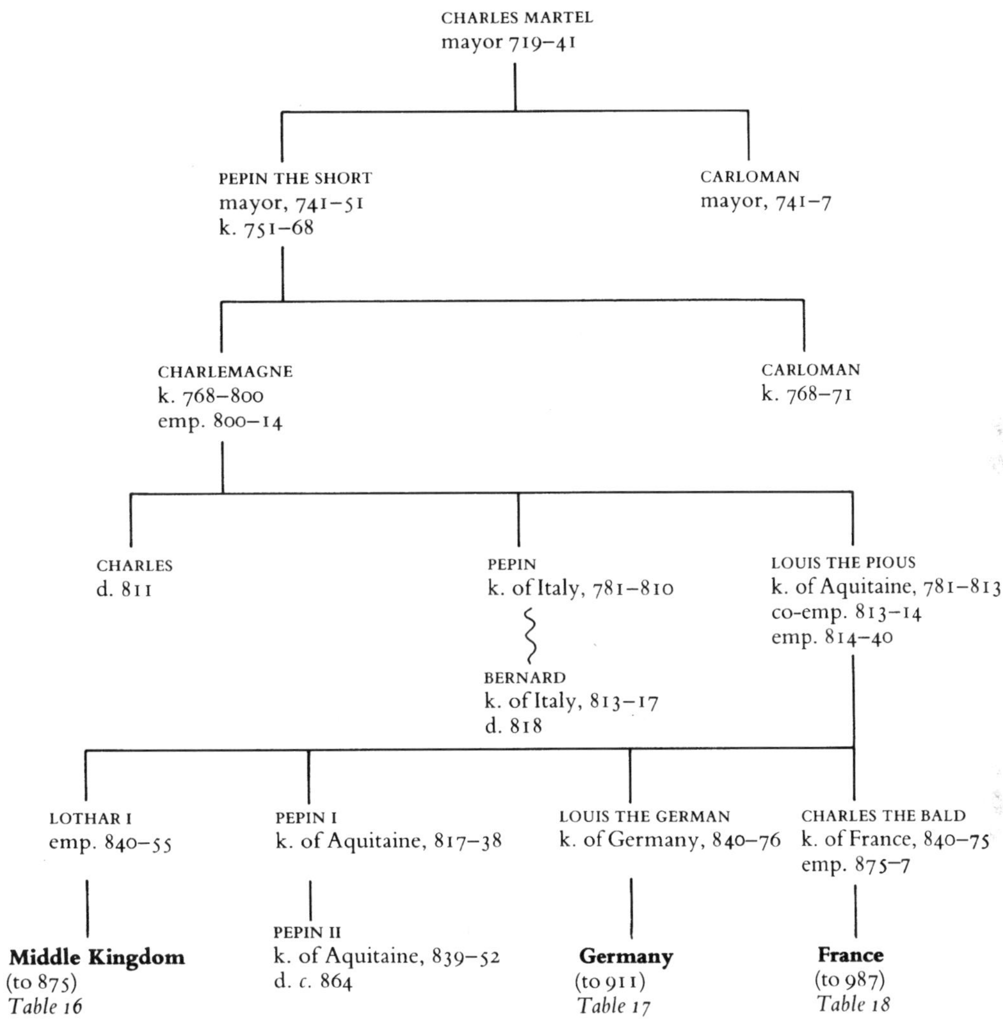

Note. Louis the Pious' sons Pepin and Louis had the title of king from 817 onwards, Charles that of king from 839, and Lothar that of emperor from 817. The three elder boys, once they came of age, had much real power as well as the titles of king or emperor, but since none of them minted during their father's lifetime the accession dates of Louis' surviving sons have been given as 840.

more than the framework for the political history; more important to the historian are other themes: the disintegration of royal authority and the advance of feudalism; the invasions of the Vikings and subsequently those of the Magyars and Saracens; the problem of establishing a *modus vivendi* with the papacy; the Carolingian Renaissance of letters. But since coins are struck on behalf of sovereigns and bear their names, it is this aspect of the political history that is most relevant here.

Coinage

Carolingian coinage is essentially one of silver pennies weighing 32 wheat grains, or *c.* 1.75g in modern units. Individual specimens vary in weight a good deal, since the coins were struck *al marco* and not *al pezzo*, so that well-preserved coins can sometimes fall below 1.6g or exceed 1.8g. Some scholars have postulated a temporary weight increase under Louis the Pious, and his coins are sometimes unusually heavy (e.g. **1.782** and **1.783**, 1.83g and 1.97g respectively), but a general weight change seems unlikely (below, pp. 215–16). The earliest coins of Pepin, Carloman and Charlemagne were substantially lighter (*c.* 1.3g) and geared to a different weight system (below, p. 204), and in the later ninth century there was some irregular decline in weight (pp. 235), but the high level of stability maintained over so long a period is remarkable. The fineness, on the other hand, despite references in the capitularies to the requirement of purity, is in fact very variable, and this not only in the later stages of the coinage. Analyses carried out in 1898 by the Monnaie de Paris (Prou 1898) of eight deniers in the Bourgneuf hoard of *c.* 877 showed that while two coins were over 90% silver (94%, 91%) and two others not far short of this (87%, 81%), four were below 50% (46%, 46%, 44%, 42%). Two others in the slightly earlier Fontaines hoard analysed at the same time gave figures of 93% and 46%, in both cases almost as if the coins of inferior fineness were intended as obols, though there is no external way users could have distinguished the coins of good quality from those of bad. One has the impression that many moneyers turned into coin whatever silver came their way without any attempt to purify it first, something indeed which they may not always have been technically capable of doing.

Carolingian deniers were about 20mm in diameter, though the earlier transitional issues were smaller (*c.* 14–17mm), and in north Italy, in the last decades of the ninth century, there was a curious development of gigantism, with the diameter of the coins expanding to *c.* 33mm. Since there was no corresponding increase in weight the coins consequently became so thin that the design and inscription on each face partly obliterated that of the other (pp. 251–2). Obols (half-deniers) were confined to a few periods and regions, and in large parts of the Empire, notably in Italy, were never struck at all. Gold coins were issued only by Charlemagne and Louis the Pious, and apart from Charlemagne's early tremisses on the Lombard pattern, which were struck for Italy only, they formed an insignificant element in the circulating medium. Silver multiples were never issued at all.

The silver denier was not a Carolingian innovation. It had, as we have seen, been the predominant coin of Neustria and Provence since *c.* 670 and the sole coin struck in the Frankish kingdom and in Frisia since about 680. But under the Merovingians it had represented a completely unorganized coinage, struck in a great number of places and to all appearances independent of any central control. Pepin and his son Charlemagne re-established a state monopoly of minting as it had existed in the Roman world, and imposed uniformity in weight and design. This high degree of royal control, it is true, did not last for long. In the second half of the ninth century it became increasingly ineffective, and in the first half of the tenth a small number of feudatories even began to mint in their own names. But from the reign of Charlemagne to the early tenth century the coinages of the various parts of the empire were uniformly struck in the names of the rulers of its various parts or, in exceptional cases, in those of their consorts: Angilberga, wife of the emperor Louis II (p. 69); Emma, wife of Lothaire of France (p. 248).

The right to mint was limited to the kings who at any given moment exercised supreme authority. It was not enjoyed by the many sub-kings who were set up during their parents' lifetimes to spread the administrative burden and ensure that intended successors acquired some experience in government (Eiten 1907). The only exception to this rule occurred near the beginning of the period, before the system had fully taken shape, for there are a few, exceedingly rare, coins struck by Charlemagne in the name of his infant son Louis when the child was taken on a royal progress through his sub-kingdom of Aquitaine in 781 (below, p. 207). This coinage was not continued. Subsequent deniers from Aquitanian mints all bear the name of Charlemagne, and there are no coins of Charlemagne's second son Pepin, who was king of Italy from 781 to 810, or of Pepin's son Bernard, who succeeded his father in Italy and was king from 813 to 817. The same arrangement was continued under Louis the Pious, and the attempts by scholars to distinguish between coins of Pepin I and Pepin II of Aquitaine form a pointless exercise, for Pepin I, who died in 838, before his father, would never have minted at all. It was apparently assumed by some mints in 840 that this arrangement would continue, and minting rights be confined to the emperor Lothar, for a few coins were briefly struck by some mints ('Aquitaine', Bordeaux, Tours, Troyes) quite remote from the area that subsequently formed his share of the inheritance. But Lothar's endeavour in the 840s to make a reality of the imperial office and reduce his brothers to the rank of sub-kings proved unsuccessful. While the title of *augustus* remained one of great prestige and was much coveted by ambitious sovereigns in the future, it carried with it no jurisdictional rights, in minting or in anything else. The reality of power lay with the separate kings.

In addition to the main series of Carolingian coins there were peripheral issues in Italy, at Benevento, Rome and Venice, which are only semi-royal, since they were minted in places where the rulers had some claim to suzerainty but not full sovereignty. Carolingian intrusions into Beneventan coinage were very brief, and limited to the two periods 788–*c.* 790 and 866–71. The first occasion arose when Arichis II of Benevento died in 788, for his second son Grimoald III, who had unexpectedly become his heir through the death of an elder brother a few weeks previously, was a hostage at Charlemagne's court and secured his release only in return for an undertaking, quickly broken, to employ the king's name or monogram in his charters and on his coins (above, p. 67). On the second occasion the emperor Louis II had been able to seize Benevento in the course of the Arab war, and minted not as suzerain but in full sovereignty. At Rome, however, Charlemagne had better fortune than at Benevento. When he was crowned emperor in 800 he assumed that his new dignity gave him suzerainty over Rome, and thenceforward, down to the 970s, all coins struck by the popes bore the emperor's name or monogram except during an imperial vacancy and sometimes even then (below pp. 259–66).

The position at Venice was less clear-cut, for the Carolingians never managed to establish any real degree of control over the city and their relations with it were regulated by a series of agreements of which the earliest ones have not survived. The city was in fact self-governing under its own doges (*duces*), though there were political and commercial advantages in continuing to claim that it formed part of the Byzantine Empire. Its proximity to the Italian mainland equally made it incumbent to recognize whoever ruled in north Italy and to strike coins acceptable on the mainland. There are consequently coins of Louis the Pious (**1.789**) and Lothar I with the mint-signature of Venice, and ones attributable to the 830s with inscriptions that invoke divine protection for an unnamed emperor or emperors, a prudent neutrality between East and West being thus maintained (below, p. 217). From the late ninth century onwards, and perhaps from 855, there are also coins in the names of emperors or Italian kings which, despite their having a *Christiana religio* inscription instead of a proper mint-signature, there is good reason to ascribe to Venice. At no time in this period, however, was imperial sovereignty over Venice a reality, and it is no more than a matter of convenience that the coins are catalogued here under the rulers whose names they bear.

Although Charlemagne had re-established the royal monopoly of coinage, coins continued to be struck at a large number of mints. There are, taking the Carolingian period as a whole, over 150 whose names appear in an identifiable form on the coinage, and there are at least 50 more amongst the unidentified deniers of the period 751–93. They were very unequally distributed, and although the counts were the officials nominally in charge of them (Lafaurie 1978b) there was at no time a mint for every count in the Empire. Nine-tenths of them were situated between the Loire and the Rhine, in the broad region of northern and eastern France, the Low Countries and western Germany where the strength of the Carolingian dynasty lay. Germany east of the Rhine had practically no mints at all: Regensburg under Louis the Pious and occasionally later, Würzburg under Louis the Child. Aquitaine and Provence had few mints, though some of those in Aquitaine were extremely active. In Italy there were only four mints of importance: Milan in 'Austrasia', Treviso or later Venice in 'Neustria', a third, Pavia, connected with the central administration of the Palace, and the fourth the papal-imperial mint at Rome. One would have expected a mint in Tuscany, but Rome seems to have virtually taken the place of Lucca, so important in the Lombard period.

The number of Italian mints changed very little after the reform of 781, but elsewhere the figures were very variable. The coinage of Pepin and the early years of Charlemagne was being struck in at least 100 mints, many of them in small, apparently unimportant localities and under conditions which represent a survival from those of the Merovingian period. Fewer than 40 mints are known for coins of Charlemagne's Class 3 and only about ten for his Class 4. Although neither list is likely to be complete, the reduction was undoubtedly the result of royal policy. A capitulary of Thionville *de falsis monetis* in 805 directed that minting should be limited to the royal *palatium* 'unless we have ordained otherwise', and another of Nijmegen in 808 ordered that coins should only be struck 'in our palace' (*nisi ad curtem*). Although, as was the case with much Carolingian legislation, these provisions were never put into effect, they are evidence of royal policy, for a high number of mints were thought to make counterfeiting too easy. Some 40 mints accounted for the coins of Louis the Pious' Class 2, and about the same number were active in the reign of Lothar I and the early years of Charles the Bald. With the recoinage of 864 and the introduction of Charles' *Gratia Dei rex* ('GDR') type (below, p. 233) to facilitate the payment of Danegeld a vast expansion occurred, with over 130 mints in operation. This was, however, no more than a short-lived reaction to deal with an emergency, and by the end of the ninth century the total was down to about 50.

The contrast between the large number of mints whose names appear on the GDR coinage and the figure of only nine and the Palace enumerated in the capitulary of Pîtres that inaugurated it, coupled with the existence of occasional die-links between coins bearing different mint names, has led Lafaurie to argue (Lafaurie 1968c; 1976c, 67–8) that the true number of mints was quite small, being limited to a few regional ones working as 'véritables usines' on behalf of the much larger number whose names are inscribed on the coins. Against this both practical and administrative objections can be urged (Grierson 1981, 43–5). Local minting would have been needed if private persons were to obtain new coins in exchange for old ones, since there is good reason to believe that the mints did not have large reserve stocks, and the responsibility of the counts for the good quality of the coins, a matter often insisted upon in capitularies, would have required that minting should take place actually under their jurisdiction. Die-links between mints can in part be explained by the disorders of the time, for the Viking invasions must have led to the frequent migration of moneyers, as it did of monks and no doubt many others, from one place to another. Individual moneyers may also have sometimes changed their place of work – as we know to have sometimes occurred in Anglo-Saxon England, where the moneyers' names were inscribed on coins, as they were not in France – or have been in charge of more than one mint.

Most of the mints whose names occur on the coins from 794 onwards are easy to identify, despite occasional inversions of letters, misspellings, and the insertion of initial aspirates which are not always appropriate (e.g. HBLESIANIS, HTVRONES), but over some (e.g. *Curtisasoniensis*, *Sennes*) there has been debate and a few (e.g. *Alaboteshaim*, *Aldunheim*) still remain uncertain. What determined the choice of localities is far from clear. Minting was not closely associated with the royal household or the court, despite legislation to this effect. Although Charlemagne spent most of the last two decades of his life at Aachen there are no coins of his professing to have been minted there, and there are none from such favourite royal residences of Charles the Bald as Verberie, Quierzy, or Ponthion. While coins exist with the inscription *Palatina moneta* (Lafaurie 1976c), they form only a small minority of those that were struck, and it is clear that the practice of melting down and reminting such coins as were collected in taxes or tolls did not obtain. The mint of Melle undoubtedly owed its importance to its silver mines, and Quentovic and Dorestad, situated at the mouth of the Canche and on a branch of the lower Rhine respectively, to their being commercial centres. But the few other mints whose trading activities justified their using the epithet of *portus* did not strike on any extensive scale (Tournai, Valenciennes, Maastricht). Abbeys could expect substantial cash incomes which they would wish to turn into coin, but there are few monastic mints. A number of mints were situated in episcopal towns, but a quite secondary role was played by such places as Cologne and Liège, which seem for long periods to have issued no coin at all despite their ecclesiastical and commercial importance. Many of the mints opened in connection with the payment of Danegeld were situated in small towns or hamlets which can have had no more than a few hundred inhabitants at the most.

Apart from coins with *Christiana religio*, which deliberately avoided any reference to a mint, there are two mint inscriptions, *Palatina moneta* and *Aquitania*, which seem to be deliberately ambiguous. It is usually assumed that *Palatina moneta* could cover many localities, the mint operating as part of an ambulatory royal household that moved from one royal palace to another. It must be doubted if this was really so, for there are no *Palatina moneta* coins of, e.g. Pepin II of Aquitaine, or of Charles the Bald as emperor, or of Charles the Fat, or of any of the Carolingians after Charles the Simple. The fact that it was used by both Lothar I and Charles the Bald, however, shows that more than one locality must have been involved, however uncertain their identity may be. As for *Aquitania*, it is possible that it always meant Bordeaux.

Many mint names, at one time or another, are accompanied by qualifications referring to their status. The basic reason behind them was to fill up space where a mint name was inconveniently short – *Aginno* (Agen, in south-west France) was expanded to *Agin civit* under Charlemagne, coins with the two forms being die-linked – but where they are common, notably on Charles the Bald's GDR coinage, they were probably intended to underline the character of the mint. *Civitas*, often abbreviated to *civis* or *ci*, is much the commonest, no doubt because the *civitas* represented the basic territorial unit of late Roman times and had survived in the organization of the Church, so that each *civitas* was the seat of a bishop and, in the Carolingian period, of a royally appointed *comes*. *Castrum* and *castellum*, implying a fortified settlement and used interchangeably, are also common. *Vicus*, so frequently found on Merovingian coins, had by the ninth century fallen out of fashion and occurs at only a few mints in Belgium and north-eastern France. *Palatium* and *fiscus*, the latter a technical term for a royal estate, are both exceptional, *fiscus* being also limited to Belgium and the north-east (Vannérus 1948). *Moneta*, variously abbreviated, is fairly common, though one would have thought scarcely necessary. The others – *portus* (a trading settlement), *urbs*, *monasterium* or *cella*, *villa* (a large estate) – are rare, with *urbs*, *cella* and *villa* each used only once. *Flavia*, continued on Charlemagne's Italian tremisses from those of the Lombard period, presumably retained its previous meaning, whatever this may have been (above, p. 63–4). Mint names are indifferently in the nominative or accusative case, rarely in the dative or ablative. Occasionally some preposition is used to signify that a coin was struck 'in' or 'at' the place in question, the words being sometimes aspirated (HIN for IN, etc.). *Ad* and *de* are each used only once (HAD TVREGVM, 'at' Zurich; DE FISCO CVRINIO, 'of' the fisc of Curinge), but *in* was popular in the Meuse region (IN VICO NAMVCO, IN PORTO TRIECTO, etc.). *Ex* occurs only once, in the formula EX METALLO NOVO, signifying that the coin was made either 'from' newly mined metal or from a newly opened mine.

The types used on Carolingian coins are very limited in number, and tend to be epigraphical rather than pictorial in character. In the transitional period between 751 and 793 the coins retain a number of vestigial elements from the Merovingian period (Amécourt 1868c, 306–25), such as an interlace design on coins formerly attributed to Maastricht (see note on **1.634–5**) or a standing figure with two crosses at Chartres. But from 771 onwards the obverse type was determined, in a fairly precise fashion, by the central authority, and from 793 the types of reverses as well. Four types thenceforward dominated the coinage: a monogram, a cross, a temple, or an inscription in one or more lines across the field. A bust was used only occasionally, and other types scarcely at all.

Monogram

Charlemagne's monogram, in the form used to validate his diplomas, was used in the period before 793 on coins of Treviso, and in 793/4 became the main obverse type of the coinage. It was quite literally the royal 'signature': the four letters KRLS would be drawn by a scribe at the bottom of a charter, and the king turned them into a monogram by linking them with four strokes forming a lozenge (for O) and inserting a chevron to link up with this as an A. At Ravenna the monogram took a different form, that of Charles' name in Greek. The use of a monogram was dropped under Louis the Pious, but Charles the Bald revived that of his grandfather, and a *Ludovicus* monogram occupying the entire field was used on some rare deniers of Louis the German. Under later rulers monograms are common, those of Odo sometimes incorporating the title REX and one of Raoul being an ingenious modification of the *Karolus* monogram with an R replacing the K, so that the difference is only apparent on careful examination. In the later ninth century the *Karolus* monogram was sometimes used as an accepted obverse type even when the inscription shows the coin to have been issued by Louis of Saxony or Odo of France. The monogram is normally spelled with a K, but on the Italian coins of Charlemagne a C was preferred, and this occasionally appears later, though more through the K being badly formed than by the intentional substitution of another letter. In a number of mints, during the GDR coinage, it has regularly the form of an H as a result of the sloping strokes of the K being placed vertically one above the other. The thinner strokes in the central lozenge, intended to add to it a chevroned A, are often omitted. Monograms are also regularly used on papal-imperial coins (below, pp. 264). Some of the letters of the king's name or title placed in the field are used from time to time, and can be regarded as the equivalent of a monogram. They dominate the coinage of Pepin and that of Charlemagne's reign before 793, and they subsequently remained popular in Aquitaine, with Louis the Pious' name in two lines (LVDO/VVIC) on his obols (**1.177–8**), with CA/RL or LV/DO on some coins of Toulouse of the mid ninth century (**1.922, 966**), and with IV (for LV) on coins as late as the reign of Louis IV.

Cross

An equal-armed cross, with the ends of the arms usually pattée, is by far the commonest reverse type, being a kind of religious counterpart to the royal monogram of the obverse. It is essentially a continuation of a Merovingian type. On some issues it is accompanied by four pellets, one in each quarter. Occasional variants occur, such as crescents instead of pellets or eight pellets instead of four, or two annulets instead of pellets. A cross-on-steps occurs on rare deniers of Charlemagne of Mainz (**1.742**) and *Sennes* (MG 94). On north Italian coins of the first half of the tenth century a *chi-rho* monogram (Christogram) was substituted for the cross at Pavia and Milan (**1.1017, 1019, 1021–2**).

Temple

A tetrastyle temple, with a triangular gable and a cross in the interior, was a new type introduced on Charlemagne's last coinage, that having his portrait on the obverse. It was usually but not always accompanied by the inscription *Christiana religio* (Völckers 1952). While deriving iconographically from the temples often shown on Roman coins, with a cross substituted for a cult image (Fallon 1958), it was clearly intended to have a special Christian significance. A phrase used by Einhard in describing Charlemagne's buildings at Aachen suggests that it was intended to represent the portico of the royal chapel (Grierson 1976b, 628–30).

The temple was continued on much of Louis the Pious' first coinage, dropped from his second coinage, and revived again for his third coinage, when it was moved to the obverse and became the main type of the coin. It was in this form that it enjoyed its greatest success, being struck throughout the whole Empire and treated as the imperial type *par excellence*. It was carried on by Lothar I and Charles the Bald, though in many places with mint names substituted for the *Christiana religio* legend. In Italy it was used by Louis II and his successors without interruption right into the tenth century. It enjoyed a particular success in the Low Countries, and gave rise in tenth-century Germany to one of the most widespread of Ottonian types, the so-called *Holzkirche* ('wooden church'). Many Swiss mints (e.g. Lausanne, Geneva) were still striking coins of the temple type as late as the twelfth century. At Saint-Maurice-d'Agaune even the name of Louis the Pious was still on the coins in the early fourteenth century.

Inscription in one or more lines

Some of the transitional coins of the period 751–93 had mint names in two lines across the field, and Charles used CARO/LVS in two lines as the regular obverse type for coins of his Class 2, the AR ligatured. The mint name across the field was revived in a more regular form for Louis the Pious' Class 2. Later it recurs from time to time, sometimes with a cross between the lines or with crosses above and below or, in tenth-century Italy, replacing the temple as the central type and with a royal name around it.

Other types are of more occasional use. A *bust* occurs rarely and almost invariably in profile, the only facing bust being that on a unique tremissis of Charlemagne of doubtful authenticity struck at Lucca. The fact is of considerable significance, for facing busts were at this time the only type used at Byzantium, whence they were borrowed by the dukes of Benevento and the popes. It is clear that Charlemagne, in introducing a bust on his last coinage, that on which he finally assumed the imperial title, was deliberately looking back to Roman models and not to contemporary Byzantium. A bust was continued on the first coinage of Louis the Pious, and on his gold as well. There are also rare coins with busts struck by Lothar I, Charles the Bald, and Pepin II, perhaps because at some mints in the 840s it was thought appropriate to start a new reign with such a type. The only later use of a bust, however, was on deniers of Louis IV of the mint of Chinon. The quality of the work under Charlemagne's successors shows very clearly that portraiture was beyond the powers of most die-sinkers of the period.

Other unusual types were a gateway, a ship, coining implements and a wreath. A *gateway* was introduced as an alternative to the temple in some cities of Roman foundation (**1.748**) for Charlemagne's last coinage and continued at a few mints, notably at Orléans, into the middle years of the ninth century (**1.835–7**). A *ship* was likewise an alternative to the temple and was introduced at Quentovic (**1.749**) and Dorestad on Charlemagne's portrait coinage and continued on the first coinage of Louis the Pious at the same mints (**1.757**). *Coining implements* in the form of an upper and lower coin-die, with a pair of hammmers, was used on some coins of Charlemagne's Class 4 with the inscription METAL(*lum*) GERMAN(*icum*), and on Louis the Pious' portrait coins of the mint of Melle (**1.758**). A *wreath* enclosing a cross, copied from the design of a late Roman tremissis, is the reverse type of Louis the Pious' gold solidus (**1.750**ff).

The inscriptions on Carolingian coins are not much more varied than the types, though they play a more prominent role than they had done on Merovingian coinage. They are in much larger letters, both absolutely and in proportion to the size of the coins, and were evidently intended to be legible to users. They normally consist of a royal name and title on one side of the coin, and the name of a mint on the other. Alternatives are religious phrases, either of a general character (e.g. *Christiana religio*) or referring to the ruler (e.g. *Gratia Dei rex*), or the personal names of moneyers or other officials. The inscriptions used in the transitional period retain the brevity of those on the coins of the late Merovingian period, so that their meaning is often obscure.

From the introduction of Charlemagne's Class 3 onwards the inscriptions normally start with a cross, though one not necessarily placed at the top of the coin. When a monogram is the type, indeed, the cross is frequently placed to the left, i.e., at 9 o'clock in relation to the type, since this is where one would most naturally start to read an inscription. The authors of the *Sylloge* volume of Carolingian coins in the British Museum, being accustomed to the placing of the initial cross at the top on Anglo-Saxon coins, failed to take account of this, and illustrated the coins so that the cross is always at 12 o'clock. The monogram is in consequence, so to speak, flat on its face. On coins of Charlemagne's Class 4 the initial cross is normally placed beneath the city gate or ship, so that the inscriptions start at bottom left, i.e. at 7 o'clock. The careful positioning of the cross that breaks the legend METxVLLO (below, p. 238), so that it always occurs in the same place in relation to the monogram, shows that the die-sinkers sometimes received precise instructions on such details.

Royal names are inscribed in full (CARLVS, HLVDOVVICVS, PIPINVS, etc.) save where, as we have seen, they are abbreviated to form the type (PIPI, CA/RL). Titles, which are normally present, are either REX FR(*ancorum*) or simply REX, or IMP(*erator*) in the case of emperors, or some abbreviated form of these. Some of Pepin II of Aquitaine's coins style him REX EQ(*uitanio-rum*). One rare coin of Pepin the Short gives him the title DOM(*inus*), and the old Roman formula DN (for *Dominus noster*), used on early Italian tremisses of Charlemagne, is taken over for some of the Italian and Provençal portrait deniers of Charlemagne and Louis the Pious. IMP is sometimes extended by AVG(*ustus*) on imperial coins of Charlemagne, Louis the Pious, and Lothar, and both terms, either abbreviated or in full, are used by later emperors, particularly in Italy. *Pius* is used as an epithet on a Laon coin of Charles the Bald (MG 792) and by some rulers in Germany and Italy from the 890s onwards (e.g. **1.830–1**, **1021–4**), in the last case perhaps in imitation of Byzantium, for its Greek equivalent (*eusebes*) appears on silver miliaresia of their contemporary Leo VI (886–911). A rare issue of Charlemagne's deniers of the mint of Ravenna of Class 3 gives him his Italian titles as well, CARLVS REX FR(*ancorum*) ET LANG(*obardorum*) AC PAT(*ricius*) ROM(*anorum*), and these titles reappear updated on Italian and Provençal coins of his Class 4: D(*ominus*) N(*oster*) KARLVS IMP(*erator*) AVG(*ustus*) REX F(*rancorum*) ET L(*angobardorum*). Two titles found on much of the later coinage are GRATIA D-I REX, introduced on Charles the Bald's coinage in 864, and MISERICORDIA D-I REX, introduced by Louis III. The abbreviation of DEI to D-I may appear strange, as there would usually be room for an E, but since early Christian times there had been a traditional preference for abbreviating *nomina sacra* instead of reproducing them in full.

The spelling of personal names, even apart from manifest errors, is erratic. Thus we find CARLVS, KARLVS, CAROLVS, HCAROLVS, and HLVDOVVICVS, LVDOVVICVS, LVDOICVS, LODOVVICVS, etc. Some of these represent the vagaries of particular mints or die-sinkers, but others must have been directed centrally: e.g. the consistent replacement of the CARO/LVS of Class 2 deniers of Charlemagne by the CARLVS of his Class 3. Such spellings as HCAROLVS and HCARLOMANNVS, though widely diffused, are anomalous, for no aspirate before the *k*-sound is possible, but were due to an unintelligent carrying over of the initial H in *Hludovicus* and *Hlotharius*, where it has a proper role. The same sometimes occurs in place-names (above, p. 197).

Other personal names are rare, being practically limited to coins of the early transitional period. As with royal names of this period they are normally short, either because they represent abbreviated forms or because the names themselves had only a few letters. The identity of the persons involved is debatable; some may simply be moneyers, but MILO was probably a count of Narbonne and RODLAN, more doubtfully, Count Roland, of epic fame (below, p. 207). A monogrammatic FR which occurs on deniers of Corbie of the 880s has been identified with an Abbot Franco who is attested in 901. In the tenth century, with the growth of local influence over the coinage, the initials of bishops or other private persons begin to appear in the field, and ultimately the names of dukes or counts replace those of sovereigns in the legends.

The *Christiana religio* formula was introduced on Charlemagne's last coinage, in association with the 'temple' type, but its immediate use, both on these coins and those of the first issue of Louis the Pious, was relatively restricted. On Louis' third coinage it was used in all mints without exception and thereafter remained in constant use, notably in the Middle Kingdom and in Italy. The intention behind it was an affirmation of the close dependence of the Empire on the Christian faith. The opening letters are invariably Greek (XP not CHR), the Greek connection being underlined in its original spelling with a *sigma* (XPICTIANA) on coins of Charlemagne, this being replaced by a Latin S (XPISTIANA) on a few of those of Charlemagne and on all later ones.

The lettering of Carolingian coin inscriptions, after the early transitional period, presents few problems of decipherment. The letter A is usually unbarred in inscriptions, but has a chevron when forming part of a monogram. B can also have the form b or ϴ. C and G are sometimes interchanged or reversed, D has the form Δ on coins of Saint-Denis, presumably a tribute to the saint's Greek nationality, and E and I can be interchanged (e.g. MONITA for MONETA). O has often the form of a lozenge ◇, particularly in the north-west and at certain mints (Le

Mans, Blois). T can have a cursive form resembling a P written backwards and not very different from a Q. The ligaturing of some letter combinations is frequent: MP for IMP, HL for HL and TH for TH in *Hlotharius*. Errors that are at first sight surprising (e.g. CIXI for CIVI on some coins of Dax) can sometimes be explained by the way in which the letters were formed. In this case the letters V and X are unlike phonetically and are usually made quite differently, a V by two sloping strokes joined by a triangular punch at the bottom, an X either by two intersecting strokes or by four triangular punches pointing inwards. But V is sometimes made by two intersecting strokes crossing each other near the bottom, and its transformation into an X would be easily accomplished by another die-sinker, in copying this, raising the point of the intersection, probably because he did not understand the inscription (CIVI ACVIS) and thought an X was intended in the first place. An increasing use was indeed made, as time went on, of circular and triangular punches for forming the details of the letters and monograms, though since the punches were small the letters usually remain legible. They are thus very different from those of much French coinage in the eleventh century, where it is often not clear to which letter a particular punch-mark belongs.

The standard of literacy displayed is unpredictable. Some mints retain accurate inscriptions throughout, with nothing worse than the occasional reversal of a letter from left to right or the placing of it upside down. In others the deformation of personal and place-names is common. Such blunderings are not necessarily confined to immobilized coinages much later than the original issues. The Lauzès hoard (Béchade 1906), buried *c.* 840 and thus virtually contemporary with the original issues of Louis the Pious' temple type, included coins with such forms as +PIANA REIICIO and +PISTIANA RELGIO, to say nothing of ODOVVISVS for HLVDOVVICVS. Blundered forms themselves were easily immobilized; LOTARIVS is normally rendered IOTAMVS on coins of Dorestad. Lothar's name, indeed, especially on coins of the Low Country mints of Dorestad, Maastricht and Huy, is amongst the most grotesquely blundered in the whole Carolingian series. Such blunderings, especially when carried to the point of rendering a mint name completely illegible, may often be attributed to contemporary counterfeiters, whose activities are frequently referred to in Carolingian legislation, or to the Viking invaders, but the fact of their being particularly prevalent in such large mints as Melle and Toulouse suggests that a contributing factor was the difficulty of procuring sufficient trained personnel.

(b) PEPIN THE SHORT, 751–68

Literature

Pepin's coinage is covered in the standard works on Carolingian coinage (above, p. 190–1), and has been dealt with, in a rather general fashion, by Lafaurie (1974a). Much of our knowledge comes from a single hoard found at Imphy (MG hoards 1), near Nevers in the upper Loire valley, which was buried early in Charlemagne's reign (*c.* 775) and contained 45 coins of Pepin, about a third of those known to exist (Longpérier 1858; Völckers 1965, no. 1). The history of the reign is covered in the standard works, to which may be added Riché 1974.

Historical background

Pepin the Short succeeded Charles Martel in 741 as joint Mayor of the Palace with his brother Carloman. The latter abdicated in 747, and in 751 Pepin deposed Childeric III, the last Merovingian sovereign, and had himself elected king and consecrated by St Boniface. The change of dynasty was reinforced by a further consecration in 753 at the hands of Pope Stephen III, who had come to France to seek Pepin's help against the Lombards.

Pepin's seventeen-year reign as king firmly established the new dynasty. He conquered Septimania from the Arabs in the 750s – its capital Narbonne fell in 759 – and in a series of brutal campaigns between 760 and 768 he destroyed the duchy of Aquitaine and annexed the whole of Gaul south of the Loire. He twice invaded Italy and compelled Aistulf to hand over Ravenna and his other conquests to the papacy (above, pp. 57–8). By the end of his reign he had effectively established the Frankish frontiers as they had been two and a half centuries earlier in the days of Clovis. He compelled the duke of Bavaria to do homage to him, and began the series of Saxon campaigns which under Charlemagne were to end with the annexation of all Germany between the Rhine and the Elbe.

Coinage

It was probably a wish to affirm his new royal authority that led Pepin to legislate on the coinage, a clause in a capitulary of 754/5 providing that not more than 22 solidi (i.e. 264 deniers) should be struck to the pound by weight. On the assumption that the pound in use corresponded more or less to that of Rome the resulting coins should have weighed about 1.24g, which corresponds fairly well to the average of existing coins in good condition. The measure was evidently intended to drive out of circulation the lighter group of Merovingian silver coins of *c.* 1.1g (above, p. 108). It had probably been preceded by an order that all coins should bear some recognition of Pepin's new position, although no precise instructions as to the form it should take were laid down. One may conjecture some formula like *nomen Pippini regis aut monogramma eius*, as this would account for the *n* (resembling a Greek *pi*) that sometimes precedes Pepin's name, as on **1.719**, and the varying use of RP, RF, PIPI, etc. The preferred form seems to have been initially RP (for *rex Pippinus*) and later RF (for *rex Francorum*), although some mints retained RP to the end of the reign. It was presumably the requirement of an explicit royal legend that resulted in the marked change in the external appearance of the coins, which are now appreciably thinner and broader (*c.* 14–16mm), as well as being more completely circular, than their Merovingian predecessors. The reverse types are extremely varied, ranging from human figures and geometrical designs to a few letters, and the details were evidently left to the die-sinkers' ingenuity, with no requirement that any indication of mint should be rendered in identifiable fashion. Some forty different types are known and more will no doubt come to light, but most of them exist in only one or two specimens which are now in public collections. There are only two in the collections here (**1.719, 720**), and the authenticity of the second cannot be guaranteed.

(c) CHARLES THE GREAT (CHARLEMAGNE), 768–814

Literature

The most complete listing of Charlemagne's coins, apart from the gold tremisses which are simply omitted, will be found in Morrison–Grunthal (1967). The older works on Carolingian coinage by Gariel and Prou, and the sections in the manuals of Engel and Serrure and of Blanchet, require extensive revision, partly because all save Blanchet were written before the discovery of the Ilanz hoard and partly because the distinction between the coinages of Charlemagne, Charles the Bald, and Charles the Simple had not yet been satisfactorily worked out despite a considerable literature on the subject (below, p. 209). There is no satisfactory monograph, since that of Cerexhe (1886–7) was without scientific pretensions and is now completely superseded and Grierson's essay (1965b), though essential for the chronology and the general pattern of the coinage, does not enter into details of the mints. A publication of the contents of all relevant hoards, undertaken in the hope of establishing criteria for identifying Charlemagne's coins, is provided by Völckers (1965), though there is one important hoard to be added to his list, that found at Breuvery in 1912 (Schmit 1920; Metcalf 1968) and there are important subsequent discussions of the Ilanz hoard by Bernareggi (see below, p. 210) and of the Sarzana hoard by Lafaurie (1972a).

Historical background

Pepin, some weeks before his death, divided his kingdom according to Frankish custom between his two sons Carloman and Charles. The frontiers are not known for certain, but Carloman seems to have received most of the southern and eastern regions (Septimania, Provence, Burgundy, Alamannia), while both had shares of Austrasia, Neustria and Aquitaine. Carloman died in 771, whereupon his brother set aside his two sons and annexed his kingdom.

Charles' reign was one of outstanding military achievement. He changed his father's policy of limited intervention in Italy at papal request into one of outright conquest. He invaded the country in 773 and in 774, after capturing and deposing the Lombard king Desiderius, he assumed the title of *rex Langobardorum*. In 787 he deposed Tassilo, the last Agilolfing duke of Bavaria, on a charge of treason and incorporated the duchy in his kingdom, and in thirty years of warfare, between 773 and 802, he subdued the independent Saxons and enforced their adoption of Christianity as the only way of guaranteeing their future loyalty. In a series of campaigns in the 790s he destroyed the Avar state in what is now Hungary, and established a well-fortified frontier against the Slavs. In northern Spain he extended the Frankish frontier across the Pyrenees, incorporating in his kingdom the area extending from the Basque country to Catalonia which was later to be known as the 'march' of Spain. He was crowned emperor by Pope Leo III on Christmas Day 800, and by a mixture of war and diplomatic activity extracted a formal recognition of his imperial title of emperor – though not that of *basileus Romaion*, 'emperor of the Romans' – from the Eastern emperor Michael I in 812.

Charlemagne's military successes were due more to the resources at his command and his energy and persistence in the pursuit of his aims than to any purely military talents, for he seems to have been at best a mediocre general. But he was a born administrator, legislator, and reformer, and the mass of legislative and administrative provisions that dates from his reign bears eloquent testimony to the restless energy and determination that he devoted to every aspect of government. But he could not do everything. Although he never abandoned supreme power, he recognized very early that the outlying parts of his empire would have to be hived off as appanages for his children. In 781 Pope Adrian I crowned his younger sons Pepin and Louis kings, and, although both were still too young to rule, Pepin was placed in nominal charge of Italy and Louis of Aquitaine. In 806, in a document known as the *Divisio regnorum*, Charlemagne drew up detailed arrangements for the succession. Pepin's kingdom was to be enlarged by the addition of Alamannia and southern Bavaria; Louis' kingdom was to be expanded so as to include all southern Gaul; the eldest boy, Charles, who had not had a separate kingdom but played a prominent role in his father's military campaigns, was to have all the rest, effectively the whole empire north of the Loire, the Doubs, and the Danube. No mention was made of the imperial office, for this could not be disposed of by will and Charlemagne had not yet obtained the recognition from Byzantium that was in theory necessary to make his position fully legitimate. In any case, since Pepin died in July 810 and Charles in December 811 the provisions of the *Divisio* never came into effect. Louis was recognized as sole heir, apart from a sub-kingdom in Italy created for Pepin's son Bernard, in September 813, and, since Byzantine recognition had now arrived, promptly co-opted emperor. Four months later, on 28 January 814, Charlemagne died.

Coinage

Charlemagne's coinage is basically one of silver deniers – as far as is known he did not strike half-deniers (obols) – apart from the local issue of gold tremisses in Italy for a few years (774–81) after its conquest.

He made the coinage fully royal, bringing to an end the few anomalous types on which personal names still survived; he extended the use of the silver denier to Italy; and he changed the designs of the coins three times, establishing a uniform obverse type in 771, uniform obverse and reverse types on larger flans in 793/4, and introducing coins having his bust as their obverse type in 812. The first two of these changes illustrate the steady growth in order and system that characterized his administration in general, while the third celebrated his recognition as emperor by reviving one of the most distinctive features of Roman imperial coinage. In 793/4 the weight of the coins was also increased by about a quarter, from *c.* 1.3g to *c.* 1.7g. Economic explanations for this change have been put forward, such as a desire to stabilize prices in a situation where the price of silver was falling (Doehaerd 1952), perhaps in response to an expansion of mining output in the Muslim world (Bolin 1953). It is more likely, however, that they formed simply a belated element in a general reform of weights and measures which began with the *Admonitio generalis* of 789 (Grierson 1965b, 528–30). This would have involved a change in the fundamental weight unit from the Troy or barley grain (0.65g) to the Paris or wheat grain (0.52g), the old denier being the equivalent of 20 barleycorns and the new one 32 wheat grains. From Italian records of the decades following the change it appears that, at least in some regions, 12 of the old deniers were treated as 9 of the new (Capobianchi 1892, 82ff.).

Specimens of each of the types of denier issued during the reign are shown on Plates 33–4. The regular issues may be summarized as follows:

Class 1, 768–71 (**1.721**)
These are deniers continuing the general pattern of Pepin's coins, weighing *c.* 1.3g and with no attempt to regularize the designs of either obverse or reverse. Carloman's coins are distinguished from those of Charles by the presence of an M in the royal name or monogram, i.e. CAR/LOM or a monogram of the letters CARLM. The coins of both sovereigns of the class are of extreme rarity, and it is represented in this collection by only a single specimen of Charles of the mint of Chartres.

Class 2, 771–93/4 (**1.722–33**)
These coins weigh the same as those of Class 1, and apart from a few struck on behalf of Charles' son Louis, occur in Charles' name only. Their introduction can best be attributed to 771, when Charles became sole ruler, and it would have been natural to call attention to the fact by ensuring that only a single version of his name appeared on his coins. This takes the form of CARO/LVS in two lines, the AR ligatured. The reverse types remain unregulated, and a number of mints – there were at least 100 – cannot be identified with certainty, since the few letters making up their types have either no obvious connection with any specific locality or are open to several possible interpretations. Many of the mints are known from only one or two specimens, now for the most part in public collections. Although much commoner than coins of Class 1, since they were struck over two decades, coins of Class 2 must nonetheless be accounted very rare.

A few coins of Class 2 have on their reverses the names of individuals (*Gervasi*, *Odalricus*, etc.) who are generally assumed to represent great magnates and not simple moneyers (Barthélemy 1877, 526ff., against Longpérier 1858). One of them, RODLAN(*dus*), is generally identified with the Count Roland of epic fame (Stiennon 1960; *contra*, Aebischer 1965, 881–901). Also contemporary with coins of Classes 1 and 2 are ones of Narbonne bearing the name of its Count Milo, whose existence is known from documents (Amardel 1901; *contra*, Aebischer 1965, 888–93). The specimen in this collection (**1.1497**) was acquired as authentic, allegedly forming part of a hoard in which several dies were represented, but the fabric is unsatisfactory and it should probably be regarded as false. Narbonne was the capital of the old Gothic province of Septimania, and the king's representative there might well have retained a sufficient degree of independence to mint without reference to his master. An earlier denier of Milo had borne the name of Pepin.

An exceptional element in this class is formed by a small group of coins usually having on the obverse HLV/DVV (or II) in two lines across the field (Lafaurie 1955). They are from four mints, Bourges, Saint-Etienne of Bourges, Clermont and Limoges (Lafaurie 1967a, with CHLO/DVICS), and their extreme rarity (about six specimens known), coupled with the situation of their mints, points to their having been an exceptional issue struck in 781 on the occasion of the parade of Charles' two-year-old son Louis through Aquitaine, of which he had just been appointed king.

Coins of Class 2 were initially struck in the Frankish kingdom only. When Charles took over the Lombard kingdom in 773/4 he at first continued the coinage of debased gold tremisses to which people were accustomed, but in his own name instead of that of Desiderius (below, p. 210). A phrase in the capitulary of Mantua, best dated to Charles' visit to Italy in 781, shows that it was in this year that they were replaced by silver denari[1] on the Frankish model. They are of a broad, thin fabric very different from the coins struck in France, with pointed serifs at the ends of letters. The obverse type is the standard CARO/LVS save at Treviso, where, perhaps through some misunderstanding of instructions, a *Karolus* monogram is used instead (**1.1498**). The initial reverse type was R F, as used in some French mints, but accompanied by a monogram usually identifiable as a mint name (**1.733**). Subsequently, at least in a few cases, this was replaced by a mint name (MEDIOL', PAPIA) in the field. The moneyers at Lucca devised elaborately decorated designs based on those of some contemporary Anglo-Saxon coins that had fallen into their hands but with LUCA replacing the OF ℞ M in the quarters of the elaborate cross design of the English models (Monneret 1921, 204–9; Blunt 1948b). The use of these is not hard to explain, for Lucca lay on the main pilgrim route to Rome and seems to have had a small English colony. An Anglo-Saxon lady purchased land at Lucca for founding a church in 782.

*Class 3, 793/4–812 (**1.735–47**)*

The heavier *novus denarius* of this class has on one face the monogram of KAROLVS (above, p. 199), though because of its small size it often lacks the central V (completing the chevroned letter A) within the central lozenge. On the other face there is a cross. The inscriptions are CARLVSREXFR and a mint name, the latter being usually but not always on the same side as the cross. The quarters of the cross are normally void, but sometimes there is in each a pellet or crescent (**1.740**). Some coins of Mainz and Sens replace the cross with a P, perhaps for *prima*, Mainz being the primatial see of Germany and Sens sometimes claiming the primacy of Gaul. Mainz can also have a cross-on-steps (**1.742**). The general design of the class, with circular inscriptions in large letters surrounding a cross, monogram, or other simple design, goes back to the tremissis coinage of the late Lombard kingdom (**1.323**), but a more immediate model would have been provided by coins of the kings of Kent (**1.1122**), with the king's name surrounding an RX monogram, which would have been familiar to influential circles at Charles' court.

Coins of Class 3 were struck also in Italy, mainly at Milan (**1.743**), Pavia (**1.744–5**) and Treviso (**1.746–7**) in the north but with very rare issues at Lucca (MG 223) and Pisa (MG 224; Panvini 1976, 209–14) in Tuscany. At Ravenna, the ancient capital of the Byzantine exarchate, Charles' monogram in Greek was used (M. Thompson 1966) and the inscription gives him the titles of king of the Lombards and patrician of the Romans (above, p. 202; note on **1.1499**).

Class 3 was probably introduced in the winter of 793/4 and ended in 812. The initial date is determined by an allusion to *novi denarii* in a clause of the Council of Frankfurt in May 794, and Charles' preoccupation with the Avar war over the years 790 to 793 makes it unlikely that he could have carried through such a major currency change before the end of 793 (Grierson 1965b, 507–11), though Suchodolski would prefer 790 (Suchodolski 1981b, following Grierson 1954b). It certainly continued for some time after Charles' imperial coronation on Christmas

[1] See p. xxi for this spelling when referring to coins minted in Italy.

Day 800 and may have ended in 808, when in a capitulary of Nijmegen Charles ordered that minting should be restricted to the Palace 'unless we direct otherwise' (Grierson 1965b, 524–7). But there are no known coins of Charlemagne with the inscription *Palatina moneta*, and it would seem that this clause, like much Carolingian legislation, was never put into practice. The extreme rarity of coins of Class 4 suggests in fact that Class 3 continued down to Easter 812, when Charles' imperial title was formally recognized by a Byzantine embassy in the Palace chapel at Aachen.

There was in the nineteenth century much confusion as to whether coins of this type should be assigned to Charlemagne, to Charles the Bald, or to Charles the Simple. In his catalogue of the Rousseau collection, Adrien de Longpérier, one of the most eminent French numismatists of the day, refused to attribute any to Charlemagne and maintained that they were all of Charles the Bald (Longpérier 1847, 151–2). The contrary was argued by Louis de Coster on the ground that Dorestad, where many specimens of this type had been found, never formed part of Charles the Bald's kingdom (De Coster 1852). A long controversy followed, Coster following up his original article by two more, Cartier and other scholars intervening in his support, Fillon starting as an adherent of Longpérier but subsequently announcing his conversion, and Longpérier dismissing the Dorestad coins as forgeries and obstinately maintaining his own opinion (refs. in Engel and Serrure 1889, II. 122, note to no. 4178). It is now recognized that Longpérier was quite wrong, and that most coins of this type belong to Charlemagne: it was indeed to establish this beyond all possible doubt that Völckers undertook his study of the early hoards (above, p. 205). It is the case for all coins from Italian mints, since Charles the Bald never ruled Italy as king, and with a few rare exceptions (see **1.909**) for all those minted in France north of the Loire, for when Charles the Bald reintroduced the monogram in 864 he did so with a *Gratia Dei rex* inscription, not a *Carlus rex Fr* one. But hoard evidence shows that coins from Aquitanian mints, where Charlemagne's type was revived in or soon after 840, can belong to either sovereign. Sometimes, as apparently at Toulouse, a different form of mint-signature, in this case the presence or absence of CIVI, allows us to distinguish between the coins of the two rulers (Pierfitte 1933), but at Melle and some other mints there seems to be no difference at all and we have to leave the matter open (see introductory note to **1.923–33** on Plate 42). The design and lettering of the coins are so simple that stylistic arguments can rarely be convincingly used.

Class 4, 812–14 (**1.748–9**)

Portrait deniers with a laureate bust of Roman type, having on the reverse either a tetrastyle temple (with inscription XPICTIANA RELIGIO), a city gate (Arles, Rouen, Trier), a ship (Dorestad, Quentovic), or coining-implements (Melle, with METALL GERMAN; for the mint, below, p. 236). These coins are of extreme rarity, since a *renovatio monetae* early in Louis the Pious' reign removed most of them from circulation, and more varieties and mints probably remain to be discovered. About thirty specimens have been recorded, two of them, of Arles and Quentovic, being in this collection (**1.748, 749**). The imperial character of the issue is evident both from the portraiture – there seems to have been a serious attempt at a personal likeness

– and the substitution of IMP(*erator*) AVG(*ustus*) for REX FR (*rex Francorum*), with at some mints an initial DN (for *Dominus noster*) as well. They have been discussed at length by Grierson (1965b, 518–24, with enlargements of the portraits) and Lafaurie (1978a).

In addition to the above series, which form the main coinages of the reign, there are also the following:

(1) The Italian tremisses of base gold (fineness *c.* 10 carats) struck in Charlemagne's name between 773 and 781, and known mainly from the forty specimens that made part of a hoard found in 1904 at Ilanz, on the Lukmanier Pass north-west of Bellinzona. The coins, which are preserved in the Rhätisches Museum at Chur, were published at the time by Jecklin (1906) and commented on by other scholars (Bordeaux 1907; Luschin 1908a, b) but so far as the tremisses are concerned Jecklin's account is now superseded by two studies of Bernareggi (1977, 1983a) which correct a number of obscurities and errors in Jecklin's hoard description. The hoard was buried *c.* 795, for while the great bulk of its contents ante-date 794, and so far as the gold is concerned are earlier than 781 – the 40 tremisses of Desiderius and the 40 of Charles evidently formed some kind of family hoard – there were two examples of Charles' reformed denier introduced in 793/4. Jecklin's initial attribution of the hoard to the 770s took no account of the date of the later of the two Arabic dirhams that it contained (A.H. 173 = A.D. 789–90), the situation being still further confused when Karabacek read the date on the coin as 193 (= A.D. 808/9), the words for 'seven' and 'nine' in Cufic script being very similar (Grierson 1953a).

The tremisses are essentially of the same type as those of Desiderius (**1.323**) and are mainly from Milan and Bergamo, with one each from Pavia, Castel Seprio, Chur and Lucca. There seems a good case for supposing that the coin of Chur (with the title RXF) and those of Milan without any regal title were struck before the fall of Pavia and the capture of Desiderius, and the coin of Pavia (which also lacks the regal title) just after this event, after which the mint of Pavia, too closely associated perhaps with the preceding regime, was temporarily closed. The coin of Chur is anomalous in giving Charlemagne his Frankish title and having CIVI in the field; the explanation is probably that Chur, though not technically part of the Lombard kingdom, was sufficiently closely associated with it for its mint to find it more natural to strike gold tremisses than silver deniers (Simonett 1978).

About ten other gold tremisses of Charlemagne are known in addition to those in the Ilanz hoard, the most interesting being one of Pisa or Pistoia (*Flavia Pitac*: *CNI* IV, pl. 18.4) and another of Lucca with a facing bust of the king (*ibid.*, pl. 4.14). There is none in this collection.

(2) Denari struck at Rome by Pope Leo III from 800 onwards bearing Charles' name and the monogram of IMPA (for *imperator*); see p. 262 below.

(3) Gold and silver coins of Grimoald III of Benevento struck between 788 and *c.* 790 which bear Charlemagne's name or monogram in recognition of his overlordship (p. 67 below; **1.1098**).

(4) Several types of gold 'solidi' bearing Charles' name in some form or other and the mint-signatures of Uzès, *Aurodis*, or Dorestad. Since these all appear to be ceremonial coins, not intended as part of the normal circulating medium, their discussion has been relegated to Appendix 1 (p. 328; see also the note on the solidus of Uzès (**1.734**) in this collection).

(d) LOUIS THE PIOUS, 814–40

Literature

There are no studies specially devoted to Louis' coinage, which is covered by the general literature (above, pp. 190–1). No hoards buried during the period of his first (portrait) coinage have survived.

The majority of known specimens of his second coinage, with mint name across field, come from the two large hoards, amounting between them to over 1,000 coins, of Veuillin (MG hoard 15; Gariel I.60–4, but better Bompois 1871) and Belvézet (MG hoard 14; Gariel I.65–8, from Saulcy 1837a). The latter, with three temple-type coins as against nearly 250 of Louis' Class 2, must have been buried just after the introduction of Class 3. For this many hoards are known, since it was struck over a longer period and in more troubled times, but the descriptions are usually inadequate for scholarly purposes. The most important ones for which good descriptions are available, and which were either buried during Louis' lifetime or sufficiently soon after his death to contain large numbers of his Class 3, are almost all from the Netherlands: Achlum (MG hoard 29; Boeles 1915, 30ff.), Dorestad 1972 II (Van Gelder 1980), Ide (MG hoard 52; Van Gelder 1965), Oudwoude (MG hoard 48; Wigersma 1902), with Roermond not yet satisfactorily described at the time of writing (summary by Van Gelder 1969). Much of the material from Pilligerheck is available in usable form (below, p. 217), and there are good if inadequately illustrated descriptions of the Belgian hoard of Zelzate (MG hoard 51; Naster 1950) and the French hoards of Chaumoux-Marcilly (MG hoard 54; Chenu 1932) and Lauzès (MG hoard 42; Béchade 1906). The important Swiss hoard from Hermenches (MG hoard 22; Gruaz 1922; Martin 1966) still lacks a proper description, but since it is preserved almost intact in the museum of Lausanne one will no doubt be eventually forthcoming.

Historical background

Louis was crowned king in 781 at the age of two by Pope Adrian I, and given Aquitaine as an appanage. He was created co-emperor in September 813, and succeeded Charlemagne on the latter's death four months later (28 January 814).

The dynastic history of Louis' reign is highly confused, since he was scarcely on the throne before he began to plan his succession. In 817 he created his eldest son Lothar I co-emperor and his younger sons Pepin and Louis kings, and by a document known as the *Ordinatio imperii* assigned Aquitaine to Pepin and southern Germany to Louis. It was at the same time made clear that the appanages were to be personal and not hereditary and that the two younger brothers were to be subject to Lothar, who would inherit the greater part of the empire. Louis' nephew Bernard of Italy (above, p. 206), alarmed at going unmentioned in the *Ordinatio* and fearing it portended his exclusion from the succession, promptly rebelled (817), but was compelled to surrender, condemned to death, blinded instead, and died in consequence (18 April 818).

All might have gone well if Louis had not in 819 contracted a second marriage to Judith (see Table 16, p. 221), daughter of Count Welf, one of the great magnates of Swabia, for the birth of their son Charles in 823 made the creation of a further appanage necessary. In 829 Louis announced that the boy's share was to be an area corresponding to modern Alsace and parts of neighbouring Swabia and Burgundy. Such a share, which would have been at the expense of Lothar's portion, was not in formal breach of the provisions of 817, but Lothar and a strong imperialist party believed that Louis' feeble government was weakening the state, while Pepin and Louis feared that, in view of Judith's influence over her husband, Charles' portion might grow in the future at their expense. Civil war broke out in 830 and continued intermittently, against a background of increasingly savage Viking attacks and a spectacular decline in royal power and prestige, for the next decade. One partition scheme followed another, each accompanied by the disgrace of a party at court or the dispossession of some group of magnates, each one in turn breaking down as a result of the duplicity and mutual distrust of the three elder brothers. The unhappy Louis was deserted by his followers in the summer of 833 and deposed (October), recovering his throne only after four months of humiliation at the hands of Lothar. When Pepin of Aquitaine died in December 838 his share was transferred to Charles, but he left a son Pepin (II) prepared to contest the succession.

Louis' death on 20 June 840 was followed by a renewed outbreak of civil war, with Lothar hopeful of making a reality of the imperial title, Louis (the German) firmly entrenched east of the Rhine and determined to defend his independence, and Charles and Pepin on the point of taking up arms over their rival claims to Aquitaine. Lothar and Pepin were natural allies against Louis and Charles, but the indecisive and bloody battle of Fontenoy in June 841 made it clear that Lothar could not raise enough support to master his brothers. On 14 February 842, by the Oath of Strasbourg, Louis and Charles swore to remain allies until Lothar came to terms, and a commission was in due course set up to partition the empire between them. By the Treaty of Verdun (August 843) each of Louis' surviving sons received an enlarged version of what he already had, with Louis taking all Germany east of the Rhine, Charles an area corresponding to most of western, northern and southern France, and Lothar the central portion running from Frisia in the north to the Beneventan frontier in the south and including the two imperial capitals, Aachen and Rome. The claims of Pepin were ignored.

Coinage

The political complications of Louis' reign are not reflected in its coinage. There are, it is true, a number of deniers bearing the names of Lothar, Charles or Pepin which do not fit into the regular pattern of the coinage after 840, either because of their unexpected types (e.g. bust, mint-signature in field), incongruous mints (e.g. coins of Bordeaux in the name of Lothar), or eccentric legends (e.g. Lothar I as REX AVG instead of IMP AVG). Scholars have in the past assigned them to various dates in Louis' reign, and in the case of Lothar have been able to cite the statement of a contemporary pamphlet, the *Epitaphium Arsenii* of Paschasius Radpert, to the effect that Lothar was made Louis' equal *in omni potestate et honore, in omni conscriptione et nomismate*. But such early datings are not borne out by hoards. None of these that were clearly buried during Louis' reign and of which reliable accounts are available – Belvézet, Veuillin, Angers, Dorestad 1845/6, Hermenches – despite their size and often varied composition, contain any coins of either Lothar or Pepin, or indeed any that cannot be attributed to Louis or his father. In some cases the rulers whose names occur on the 'irregular' coins were not yet kings when the comparable types of Louis were being issued; Charles the Bald, indeed, was not even born when Louis was minting his portrait coins or those with a mint name in the field. The balance of probability points to the 'irregular' coins dating from after 840, the choice of type resulting from inadequate instructions being received by a mint. Further study may reverse this verdict, for the fact is in itself surprising: one might have expected Louis to strike brief accession issues for his sons, comparable to his own Aquitanian accession coins of 781, and Lothar to have minted at least during the few months of 833/4 after he had secured his father's deposition and could regard himself as sole emperor. If such issues can ever be identified, however, they will have been of a token and ceremonial character and involve no change in the overall coinage pattern of Louis' reign.

The bulk of this coinage consists of deniers and obols – the last are a novelty – struck between 814 and 840. There were in addition (a) the very rare light deniers corresponding in weight and type to Charlemagne's coins of Class 2 but in Louis' name, which were struck in 781 and have already been noted (above, p. 207); (b) a coinage of gold solidi which belongs to the early years of the reign and is described in Appendix 1 (pp. 329–30); and (c) papal-imperial denari struck at Rome (below, p. 260).

The regular deniers all give Louis his full imperial title (HLVDOVVICVS IMP) and form three main classes, characterized by (1) a bust as obverse type, (2) the mint name in the field, and (3) a temple surrounded by a *Christiana religio* legend. There are in addition some rare deniers with either (a) a temple and mint-signature or (b) a cross on both sides of the coin, with the king's name on one side and that of the mint on the other. The first of these are either forgeries or coins that date from the years after Louis' death, when the temple type was continued in the Low Countries (below, p. 217). The second probably represents a variety of Class 2 resulting from an ambiguity in the instructions sent to the mints (below, p. 215).

Louis' regular issues of deniers were as follows:

Class 1. With bust, 814–19 (**1.757–61**)

This continued the types of Charlemagne's Class 4 and lasted down to 819, when a capitulary (MGH, *Capitularia* I.290) includes a rubric *De nova moneta* which can only refer to Class 2. Specimens are rare, as a result of its efficient replacement by the next class, but less so than the portrait coins of Charles. Nine named mints are recorded for the Frankish kingdom and three for Italy, but Treviso is known from a unique specimen and several other mints from only two or three, so that more may well be discovered. The commonest type is a gateway (Arles, Orléans (**1.759**), Sens, Strasbourg, Toulouse, Tours; Pavia, Treviso), but there is a temple for Milan, a ship for Dorestad (**1.757**) and Quentovic and coining implements for Melle (**1.758**). The style of the imperial bust is usually good, but at Melle and Toulouse it degenerates into a caricature. There are also coins with a tetrastyle temple and *Christiana religio* inscription, the first word being spelled with an S (XPISTIANA) and not with a C (Greek *sigma*) as under Charlemagne. Obols are known for three mints, Melle, Toulouse and Tours.

Class 2. With mint name in field, 819–22 (**1.763–90**)

These very distinctive deniers are relatively common, since over a thousand specimens were

FRISIA
SAXONY
Dorestad
Cologne
Rhine
EAST FRANCIA
Main
Mainz
Quentovic
Meuse
Cambrai
Trier
Moselle
Rouen
Rheims
Verdun
Metz
Regensburg
WEST FRANCIA
Meaux
Paris
Seine
Danube
Strasbourg
BRITTANY
Rennes
Sens
ALAMANNIA
Orléans
Nantes
Loire
Tours
Besançon
BAVARIA
Bourges
BURGUNDY
Melle
Chalon-sur-Saône
Chur
AQUITAINE
LOMBARDY
Treviso
Lyon
Milan
Vienne
Pavia
Venice
Bordeaux
Dordogne
Po
Rhône
STATES OF THE CHURCH
Garonne
Lucca
PROVENCE
TUSCANY
Dax
Toulouse
Arles
Marseille
SEPTIMANIA
Narbonne
SPANISH MARCH
Roda
Ampurias
Rome
NAVARRE
Barcelona
SPAIN
0 100 200 miles
0 100 200 300 km

found in the Veuillin and Belvézet hoards (MG hoards 14 and 15), though the products of one mint (Venice) accounted for a fifth of them. Some forty mints are known for the Frankish kingdom, but no more than six for Italy and four for Germany, only one of the latter group being identifiable with certainty (Regensburg, REGA/NESB/VRG). The terminal date of the issue is known from a capitulary (MGH, *Capitularia* I.306) probably dating from 825 – it cannot be later than 827 – which refers to a coin withdrawal ordered three years previously though not very effectively carried out. It has been argued (Lafaurie 1983c, 141, and elsewhere) that it continued down to 829, since a Worms capitulary of that year included a clause reminding counts and others of their obligation to ensure the acceptance of 'good' deniers *quos populus non vult recipere* (MGH, *Capitularia* II.15–16), but there is no implication that the deniers are a new issue and the clause is more probably concerned with the problem of extending the use of coined money in Germany east of the Rhine (but cf. Suchodolski 1983).

What is best regarded as a variety of this class consists of very rare deniers of Louis with the same obverse as the others but on the reverse the mint name around a cross instead of in the field. They are known for the mints of Melle (**1.762**) and Toulouse (MG 419), and the existence of obols of this type for 'Aquitaine' and Bourges suggests that deniers of these mints may yet be found. The presence of two specimens of Melle in the Veuillin hoard shows that the type dates from early in Louis' reign. Its most likely explanation is an initial misunderstanding of a mint instruction prescribing the type, perhaps the ambiguity of some phrase like *nomen nostrum habeatur in gyro et in medio crux, in altera parte nomen civitatis*, a mistake subsequently corrected by the issue of normal types with METALLVM or TOLO/SACIVI/TAS across the field. The mint of Cologne made something like the same error when it inserted a large cross between the two lines of the inscription (MG 341).

Obols exist for Class 2 as they do for Class 1. They are recorded for fourteen mints, and more may yet come to light. Half of the mints, instead of placing the mint name across the field, did this for the emperor's name (LVDO/VVIC). Since the imperial title is absent it has sometimes been supposed that these obols were struck before 813, but since several of the mints involved are not in Aquitaine (e.g. Quentovic, Rheims) this is impossible. Obols corresponding to the variety with a cross on both obverse and reverse exist for Melle (MG 401–5), 'Aquitaine' (MG 392) and Bourges (MG 509=411, rev. blurred through double striking).

It was noted by Bompois, in publishing the Veuillin hoard (Bompois 1871), that the weights of the coins in this find sometimes reached 1.8g, and the idea that Louis' Class 2 was struck to a higher weight standard than that of Charlemagne's later coins is expressed graphically in Morrison and Grunthal 1967 (p. 41) and has been accepted by Suchodolski, Lafaurie and others. It seems open to question. A frequency table of the weights of surviving specimens of this class does indeed point to a median weight of 1.8g or a little over instead of *c.* 1.7g. It is possible, however, that the contents of the Veuillin and Belvézet hoards which provide virtually all our

---

Map 4 *The mints of Louis the Pious*

Three Rhineland mints of Louis' second coinage, *Alaboteshaim*, *Aldunheim* and *Stottenburc*, are omitted, since their precise location is uncertain. Coins were also minted in the name of the Palace and *Aquitania*. The dotted lines indicate the boundaries of the kingdoms of Charles the Bald (West Francia), Lothar I (the Middle Kingdom) and Louis the German (East Francia) as established by the Treaty of Verdun (843).

material are not random samples, but accumulations of heavier coins picked out by their original owners. Bompois noted that the 195 Venetian coins in the Veuillin hoard, although unworn, were in general much lighter than the others, which is what one would have expected of a group external to the main contents of the hoard and to which this process of *triage* would not have been applied. One has to balance the possibility of the evidence of the Veuillin and Belvézet hoards being distorted in this way against the improbability of the government having ordered an otherwise inexplicable and quite temporary weight change.

Class 3. Temple type with 'Christiana religio' inscription, 822–40 (**1.791–810**)

This coinage, of both deniers and obols, has the same obverse type as Class 2 but reverts to some of the coins of Class 1 for its temple and *Christiana religio* reverse. Type and inscription accorded with Louis' strongly religious cast of mind, and the elimination of mint names represented an affirmation of imperial authority. Henceforward there would be an absolutely uniform coinage circulating throughout the Empire, with no reference to specific localities. Such mint anonymity must have rendered the proper control of the coinage more difficult, however, which presumably explains why it was virtually abandoned after 840. Coins of Louis' Class 3 are by far the commonest of all Carolingian coins, having been minted in so many localities over a relatively long period of time.

The attribution of coins of the temple type with a *Hlvdowicvs Imp* inscription involves three problems: (a) the separation of Louis' coins from those of later emperors of the same name, (b) the separation of his coins from immobilizations of the mid ninth century, and (c) the mint attributions of Louis' own coins.

The first difficulty affects only north Italy, where the same type was used for coins of Louis II (855–75) and Louis III the Blind (900–1), but coins of Louis II are in general of larger flan and those of both are quite different in fabric from Louis the Pious' coins (below, p. 252). The second problem is less serious than is usually supposed, for while the Muizen and Zelzate hoards (Roosens 1950; Naster 1950) show that this type of coin still dominated the monetary circulation of the Low Countries as late as the 870s, so that they can fairly assume a continuation of the type after 840, hoards of the second half of the ninth century from other parts of the Empire usually contain few if any of the type and show the phenomenon to be a local one. One is, in any case, perhaps too ready to write off as later imitations coins that are really of Louis' own time, for all substantial Carolingian issues include many coins with blundered inscriptions owing to the difficulty of securing competent die-sinkers. There is, however, one special case of the perpetuation of Louis the Pious' temple type, that of the coinage of the abbey of Saint-Maurice-d'Agaune in western Switzerland, where such coins were being struck from at least the eleventh to the early fourteenth century (Morel-Fatio 1871; Ladé 1890). The deniers of this mint are, at least in their later stages, much lighter than their Carolingian prototypes, weighing *c.* 1.2g instead of *c.* 1.7g, and are different from these in style and fabric; the later ones also spell Louis' name without the aspirate (LVDOVVICVS). The few in the collection here will be published in Vol. 6.

The third problem remains a real one, and since the anonymity of the *Christiana religio* coins was clearly intended to conceal their precise mints it is not surprising that attempts by modern scholars to localize these have made little progress. Prou did no more than make a rough distinction between the coins on which the temple is relatively tall and narrow (P 987–1001) and those on which it is squat and dumpy (P 1002–41; some of these are immobilizations with blundered inscriptions). The coins vary in the form of the temple columns (simple or bossed), in the shape of the crosses within the temple and in the obverse field, in the letter-forms and the ways in which the letters of Louis' title IMP can be ligatured, and in the occasional presence of groups of pellets, or of a crescent or a V-shaped design, beneath or beside the temple. These have been carefully noted in only a few hoard descriptions, notably in those of the Ide and Zelzate hoards (Van Gelder 1965; Naster 1950), and in the text of the auction catalogue in which a large part of the Pilligerheck hoard was offered for sale (Karl Kress Cat. 140, 7.8.1967; cf. also Lafaurie 1969c), but their systematic study has still to be undertaken. A few varieties can be localized by the occurrence of the same details on earlier issues of Louis himself or later ones of Charles the Bald or Lothar I. Two coins below are attributed on such grounds, one to Milan (**1.791**), with pellets between or inside letters as privy-marks, a feature peculiar to this mint and found on coins of Louis I's Classes 1 and 2 (**1.787**), and the other tentatively to Pavia (**1.792**), based on its Italianate lettering and form of cross.

An apparent variety of Class 3 consists of coins with a mint name instead of *Christiana religio*, but these do not really belong to Louis' reign. They have been recorded for only three mints, Milan (MG 450), Dorestad (MG 337) and Maastricht (MG —). The only known specimen of the first, now at Berlin, is a nineteenth-century forgery. The authenticity of the others is guaranteed by the presence of a single specimen of each in the Pilligerheck hoard and one of Dorestad (with DORESTATVS MON) in the Ide hoard (Van Gelder 1965, 247). But Van Gelder, in publishing the latter, noted the similarity of its fabric to that of Lothar's coins with IOTAMVS (**1.819**) and attributed it to some unofficial Frisian mint in the 840s or 850s. Although it is conceivable that Louis, just before his death in 840, might have decided to restore the use of mint-signatures and sent out instructions to this effect, the fact that the only mints for which such are known come from an area in which immobilization and imitation were common makes it more likely that the coins are derivatives of the kind envisaged by Van Gelder.

Another variant of Class 3 consists of the Venetian coins in which the emperor's name is replaced by the ambiguous inscription + DS CVSERVA ROMA NP (*Deus conserva Romanorum imperium*, 'God preserve the Empire of the Romans') and the *Christiana religio* one by + XPE SALVA VENECIAS ('O God, preserve Venice'). The Hermenches hoard from western Switzerland (Gruaz 1922; Martin 1966), which contained two specimens amongst nearly three hundred of the normal coins of Class 3, dates them towards the end of Louis the Pious' reign. How it came about that Venice, which was still formally part of the Byzantine Empire, minted Western-type silver denari in the names of Carolingian sovereigns from Louis' Class 2 onwards is something of a mystery (Papadopoli 1893, 1ff.), but the city's hinterland made use of such coins and Venice was sufficiently remote from Byzantium to be able to act in most respects on its own. The ambiguous legend on the coins of Class 3 presumably marks an attempt not to commit itself to one empire or the other, but under Lothar I there was a return to the name of a Western ruler.

(e) AQUITAINE

Aquitaine, when used as a geographical term in the Carolingian period, corresponded roughly to France south of the Loire, including Gascony and sometimes even Narbonensis, between the Pyrenees and the Garonne and lower Rhône delta respectively (Auzias 1937). In the later Merovingian period, as has been seen (pp. 90, 94), it had become virtually independent under its own dukes, so that it had to be conquered and forcibly re-annexed to the Frankish realm by a series of annual campaigns in the last years of Pepin's life (760–8). Its relatively minor role in the Carolingian period was in part a consequence of the devastation which these repeated campaigns entailed. More important, however, was the fact that the centre of Carolingian power had moved to the north and east, while Provence, as a result of Muslim mastery of the western Mediterranean, was in full decline. Its chief centres were Toulouse, its political capital, and Bourges, which in effect, though not formally, was its religious centre. Both, from the minting point of view, were eclipsed by the village of Melle in Poitou which had important silver mines in its vicinity, but their coin output was from time to time quite considerable.

Charlemagne's accession in 768 was followed by a fresh rebellion in Aquitaine, which was quickly repressed. In 781 the region was conferred as an appanage on his son Louis, who had been crowned king by the pope, though since he was only two years old it had to be administered on his behalf by two Frankish regents until he came of age. This arrangement was intended as no more than a sop to local feeling, and Aquitaine continued for most purposes to be treated as a part of Charles' dominions. The only coins struck specifically for Louis as king are the rare deniers of 781 referred to already (p. 207). Obols with either his name or the legend AQVITANIA in two lines have sometimes been attributed to the period before 814, since they do not give him the imperial title, but this was because of lack of space on the coins and there is no reason to separate them from his imperial deniers of Class 2. A few rare obols that include a *royal* title (LVDOVICVS R or RE) have been ascribed (Duplessy 1978d) to 853 or 854 and the invasion of Aquitaine by Louis the Young, son of Louis the German, but it seems more likely that the inscription is a die-sinker's error.

In 817 the sub-kingdom was revived for Louis the Pious' second son Pepin I, who died before his father on 13 December 838. Pepin had a more complete apparatus of government at his disposal than his father had had, including a regular chancery (Levillain 1926), and scholars have long discussed how his coins should be distinguished from those of his son Pepin II. The exercise must be regarded as a waste of effort, for there is no reason to suppose that any of Louis' sons exercised minting rights during his lifetime (above, p. 213; Duplessy 1978a). After Louis' death a few Aquitanian mints struck coins in the name of the emperor Lothar, apparently on the assumption that the new emperor would exercise the same monopoly of minting as his father had done (above, p. 195).

Pepin I left a son of the same name as himself, but Louis set aside his claims in favour of Charles the Bald. Pepin II, however, was proclaimed king by a faction in Aquitaine, and was effectively ruler of part of the country from 839 to 852. His minting is unlikely to have begun before Louis' death, and his subsequent coinage (**1.811–17**) has to be fitted into a pattern dictated by his shifting relations with Charles the Bald and the varying loyalties of the magnates. Probably most of the coins date from between 845, when he was recognized by Charles at the treaty of Saint-Benoît-sur-Loire, and 848, when Charles was crowned at Limoges and occupied the whole of the north. Pepin still held most of the south and south-west, however, and minting in his name could have continued at Toulouse to 849 and at *Aquitania* till 852, when he was betrayed to Charles by Duke Sancho of Gascony, tonsured, and relegated to the monastery of Saint-Médard of Soissons. Although he escaped in 854, his subsequent career (854–64) was that of a brigand adventurer, sometimes in alliance with the Northmen, rather than of a king, and any resumption of minting on his part is unlikely. In 864 he again fell in Charles' hands, and apparently died soon afterwards in prison.

Some of Pepin's II's coins, attributable to 840 or 841 and of great rarity, have his bust (Bourges, 'Aquitaine'), a type going back to Louis the Pious' coinage of Class I, but most are later and bear his monogram (Melle, Poitiers, Toulouse: **1.814–17**). The temple, carried on from Louis the Pious' last type, occurs only at Dax (AQVIS VRBI) and on coins with AQVITANIORVM (**1.811**) or XPISTIANA RELIGIO. His obols of Cahors and 'Aquitaine' (**1.812–13**) have an inscription in two lines or three (EQVI/TANI/ORVM). At Limoges there is a cross on both sides. The king is sometimes styled simply *rex*, but this can be followed by AQ (or EQ), for *Aquitaniorum*. The commoner types are found mixed in hoards with coins of Charles the Bald, and a careful analysis of the material should make possible a better chronology than we presently have. The mint of Melle may for a time have been exploited in common by the two sovereigns, for there is some reason to think that the treaty of 845 created a joint jurisdiction over Poitou.

Aquitaine formed a separate kingdom on two other occasions during Charles the Bald's reign, for his second son Charles the Young was king from 855 to 863 and his eldest son and eventual successor Louis the Stammerer was king from 867 onwards. For neither reign is a coinage likely. Charles the Young was barely eight years old at his accession and only fifteen when he was deposed and taken into custody by his father, who found him too easily exploited by factious magnates. He was never reinstated, for he was terribly injured in a mock combat in 864 and died two years later. Louis was of maturer years, but Charles suspected his loyalty and good sense and surrounded his rule with elaborate limitations and safeguards. Only for Toulouse are there coins with an anomalous LV/DO in the field that could conceivably have been struck by Louis the Stammerer as king of Aquitaine, but in default of positive evidence it seems best to assume that like his predecessors he had no right of coinage; the specimen here (**1.966**) has therefore been attributed to his reign as king of the West Franks. Charles the Bald's own coinage in Aquitaine remained distinct in type from that of his more northern territories, notably in its failure to adopt the GDR type introduced by the Edict of Pîtres in 864 (below, p. 232).

(f) THE MIDDLE KINGDOM (LOTHARINGIA, ITALY TO 855, PROVENCE)

Literature

Since the coinages of the Middle Kingdom do not form an entity after 855, there is no specialized literature on them as a whole. Frère (1977b, 1980) is especially useful on the coinage of Lotharingia, and there are good articles on the Dorestad mint (Van Gelder 1961) and bringing together the coins of Trier (Bordeaux 1893). There are also descriptions of several important Low Country hoards of the 840s and 850s (Midlaren and Wagenborgen: MG hoards 54–5), though of two others, Pilligerheck (MG hoards 53: Lafaurie 1969c; Kress Catalogue 140, 7.8.1967) and Roermond (Van Gelder 1969) we have only interim accounts. The history of the Middle Kingdom is well covered, with admirable monographs on Lotharingia (Parisot 1899), Provence (Poupardin 1901) and Burgundy (Poupardin 1907), and on the 'international' relations of the period 843–77 (Calmette 1901).

Historical background

The Middle Kingdom, as historians are accustomed to term it, existed in its original form for only fifteen years, but it left a permanent mark on European history. Lothar I's share of his father's empire gave rise to a group of states which on the one hand each acquired a considerable degree of political coherence, and on the other, because of their geographical situation, could never remain for long politically independent. Their fate was to be alternately either annexed by whichever of their neighbours happened to be the stronger or, when neither of these had an obvious advantage, partitioned between them.

The relationship of the rulers involved is shown in Table 16. Lothar I, Louis the Pious' eldest son, inherited the imperial office and a strip of territory that corresponded roughly to modern Holland and Belgium, Germany west of the Rhine, much of eastern France from the Belgian frontier to the Mediterranean, all western Switzerland, and north and central Italy as far south as the frontier with the principality of Benevento. Such a combination of languages and nationalities was less incongruous to contemporaries than it seems to us, for the bonds of social cohesion and loyalty were personal or regional, and the importance of linguistic differences, though recognized in the Oath of Strasbourg (842), was reduced by the general use of Latin in the administration and by the Frankish origin of the bulk of the ruling class throughout the Empire. Nonetheless, for obvious geographical reasons, Italy could not easily be ruled by a sovereign whose main interests lay north of the Alps. Lothar never visited the country after 840 and formally handed it over to the eldest son Louis II in 844, retaining for himself all lands north of the Mediterranean and the Alps.

When Lothar I died on 29 September 855 his empire was divided up between his three sons. Louis' share was Italy and the imperial office, for he had been co-emperor since April 850. Lothar II inherited the northernmost section, from the North Sea and Frisia as far south as the Jura, and Charles, the youngest son, the Rhône valley and Provence. When Charles, an unhappy epileptic, died childless in 869 his kingdom was divided without too much difficulty between Lothar II, who took the north, and Louis II, who took Provence and some adjacent *civitates*. Lothar II's succession raised more problems, for Louis II, his natural heir in default of legitimate progeny, was too remote to make good his claims against Lothar's uncles, Louis the German and Charles the Bald, who had every intention of annexing his kingdom for themselves. When Lothar II died in 869, Charles the Bald tried to seize the whole inheritance, which after thirty years of rule by two sovereigns of the same name was already coming to be known as Lotharingia (Lorraine), but he eventually had to agree to the partition of Meerssen with his brother Louis the German in August 870 (below, p. 226). The emperor Louis II protested at this ignoring

Table 16. *Rulers of the Middle Kingdom*

This table, which shows the relationships between the principal rulers of the Middle Kingdom, has to be supplemented with Tables 15 and 17–18 for the kings of Germany and France.

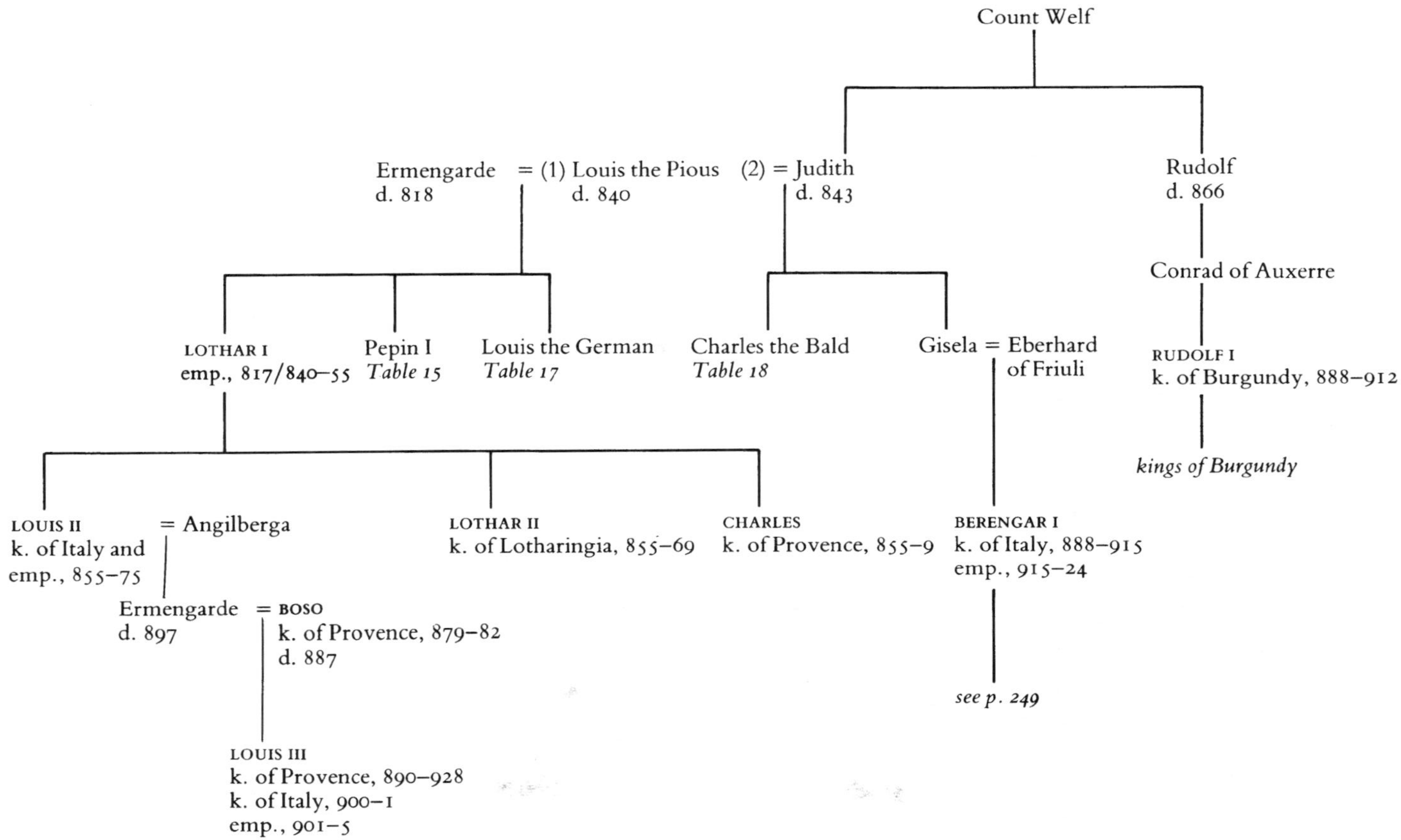

of his own claim to be his brother's legitimate heir, but he did so in vain, and when he himself died in 875 his kingdom and the imperial office were also annexed by Charles the Bald.

The arrangements concluded at Meerssen did not last, for the possession of Lotharingia, where royal domains (*fisci*) were exceptionally numerous and which had sentimental attractions as the homeland of the dynasty, was too desirable for it not to be fought over whenever opportunity offered. When Louis the German died in 876 Charles tried to seize his share, but was foiled by Louis' son Louis of Saxony. When Louis the Stammerer died in 879 it was Louis of Saxony's turn, and in 880 he compelled Louis the Stammerer's two sons, Louis III and Carloman, to abandon their claims to him. Lotharingia, thus reunited, remained a German possession from 880 to 911, ruled in turn by Louis of Saxony, Charles the Fat, Arnulf, Zwentibold, and Louis the Child (below, pp. 226–8). But when Louis the Child died in 911 and was succeeded by Conrad of Franconia as king of Germany, the French king Charles the Simple was able to take advantage of local sentiment in favour of the Carolingians and annex it to France. After Charles' deposition in 922, however, this factor no longer operated, and Henry the Fowler re-annexed Lotharingia to Germany (925). Thenceforward, despite repeated French attempts to recover it, it formed an integral part of the German kingdom.

Meanwhile Burgundy, Provence and Italy had gone their own ways. Boso, son-in-law of the emperor Louis II and brother-in-law of Charles the Bald (see Table 16), tried to establish himself as king in Burgundy and Provence after the death of Louis the Stammerer in 879, but he was overthrown in 882 and his kingdom partitioned between Charles the Fat and Carloman of France. The deposition of Charles the Fat in 887 was followed by a more decisive break with the past. First, a new kingdom of Burgundy was created by Rudolf, a member of the great Welf family to which Judith, the second wife of Louis the Pious, had belonged. He was elected king at Saint-Maurice-d'Agaune in January 888. Immediately afterwards, in February 888, the Marquess Berengar of Friuli, whose mother Gisela was a daughter of Louis the Pious, had himself elected king of Italy. Finally, in 890, Boso's son Louis, later nicknamed 'the Blind', was elected king at Valence and quickly reconstituted his father's kingdom in Provence.

The histories of these three kingdoms were closely interconnected. The separate kingdom of Provence had only a brief existence (888–933), for Louis died without legitimate heirs in 928 and in 933 Count Hugh of Arles, who was effective ruler but without the royal title, ceded it to Rudolf II of Burgundy in exchange for Rudolf's claims in Italy. The latter kingdom retained its political unity but was subject to repeated German, Provençal and Burgundian invasions, since the country was desirable both in itself and as providing a stepping stone to the still coveted imperial crown (below, p. 250). Eventually it fell to Germany, being annexed by Otto the Great in 951 and brought under his effective rule in 962. The same fate eventually befell the kingdom of Burgundy–Provence in the 1030s, for Rudolf I's great-grandson Rudolf III died without direct heirs in 1032 and Conrad II of Germany, after a brief contest, secured the crown (2 February 1033). All the lands of the Carolingian 'Middle Kingdom' were thus in the end acquired by Germany, the more powerful of its two neighbours.

Coinage

Lothar I and Charles the Fat were the only rulers in a position to mint throughout the entire area of the Middle Kingdom. Lothar I's coinage can be considered as a unit, but after 855 the coinages can best be studied individually under the separate headings of Lotharingia, Provence, Burgundy and Italy. The last of these, however, the most important and the best represented here, is so complicated that it requires a separate section to itself (pp. 249–59, Plates 46–7), and the coinage of Burgundy will not be included in this volume at all. Although the kingdom formally lasted from 888 to 1032, its coins belong mainly to the two long reigns of Conrad III (937–93) and Rudolf III (993–1032) and are subsequent to the general date at which this volume closes. They are therefore better held over for the section on the kingdom of Arles in Vol. 6. Coins struck south of the Alps by Rudolf II of Burgundy and Hugh of Arles, however, form part of the coinage of Italy (below, pp. 257–8).

Lothar I (840–55)

Hoard evidence suggests that none of Lothar's coins was minted during his father's reign (above, p. 211), and the three types that occur ((a) with bust and temple, (b) with temple and either mint name or *Christiana religio* inscription, and (c) with cross and mint name across the field), do not seem to follow in chronological order. Nor can they have resulted from precise mint instructions, for the diversity in the spelling of Lothar's name and the choice of titles (*Hlotharius, Hlutharius, Lotharius*; *Imp, Imperat, Imp aug, Agus* or *Agustus*, even *Rex imp*) contrasts sharply with the uniformity in those of his father's coinage and that of his brother Charles. In the latter case, it is true, there may equally have been no proper mint instructions, but there was always the model of Charlemagne's coins to fall back on, while Lothar had no homonymous predecessor. Thirteen mints are recorded, and the list is probably not complete, as coins of two of them, Namur and Dinant, first came to light in the Roermond hoard of 1968 (Van Gelder 1969). There are in addition the coins with *Christiana religio* and *Palatina moneta* legends. Some mints struck coins of both temple and mint-name-in-field type, but in what order is unknown.

Coins of Dorestad with Lothar's name correctly spelled (HLOTHARIVS) and of good fabric are relatively rare (**1.818**). The vast majority have the obverse inscription corrupted to IOTAMVS – the I is an inverted L and the M a ligaturing of R and I – and are of much rougher workmanship (**1.819**). A corrupt inscription of this kind is not necessarily proof of imitation, as one knows from the common twelfth-century Cologne coins of Archbishop Philip of Heinsberg on which his name is regularly transformed into HITARC from PHI + ARC... (Hävernick 1935, nos. 503ff.), but in this case the contrast in workmanship suggests that the coins with the IOTAMVS legend, which is also sometimes found on coins of 'Mainz' and 'Huy' (De Jonghe, 1897), were not minted at Dorestad, but are contemporary or slightly later Frisian or Viking imitations (Van Gelder 1961). This is indeed suggested by what is known of the history of Dorestad during these years between 834, when its great built-up area of wooden houses and wharves (Holwerda 1930; Van Es 1969; Van Es *et al.* 1980) was first attacked by the Northmen, and 863, when it was sacked by a Danish band (*depopulato emporio quod Dorestatus dicitur*) on its way to Neuss and Cologne and is mentioned by the *Annales Bertiniani* for the last time. Between these dates it was repeatedly plundered or burnt or held to ransom – in each of the three years 835–7, in 847, and in 858 – besides being ceded to Roric in 850 and held by him and Godfrey for five years. It is not surprising that coins bearing the name of the town should have been struck elsewhere. *Christiana religio* imitations in the name of Louis were also being minted during Lothar I's reign (above, p. 217), and it may well be that many of the imitative gold solidi belong to this period (pp. 329–30).

Lothar I's Italian coins all have the mint name across the field, coins of Treviso (MG 559) and Venice (MG 560) being rare but those of Milan (**1.821**) and Pavia (**1.822**) fairly common. The coinage was better organized than in Lotharingia, the emperor's name being consistently spelled HLOTHARIVS (with HL, TH and IMP usually ligatured) and followed by IMP or IMP AV according to the mint. Most coins of Milan continue the use of pellets as privy-marks (above, p. 217), but these are occasionally absent, as on **1.821** here, and since they do not appear on later coinage the practice was presumably abandoned late in the reign. The situation in Burgundy and Provence is obscure, for no coins of Lothar are known for any of the traditional mints in these regions – Besançon, Lyon, Vienne, Arles, Marseille. Possibly, in default of any instructions, the mints, or some of them, continued striking *Christiana religio* coins in the name of Louis the Pious, which would help to explain why this type was revived later in the Jura region and the Valais (above, p. 216). The existence of deniers struck in Lothar's name at Bordeaux (MG 555), Tours (MG 553), Troyes (MG 535–40), and of obols of 'Aquitaine' (MG 554), probably resulted from the assumption by these mints that, as under Louis the Pious, all coinage would be 'imperial' and not struck in the name of the regional kings.

Lotharingia (855–925)

The reign of Lothar II (855–69), who gave his name to Lotharingia, was an unhappy one, with the Northmen raiding Frisia and Lotharingia and the king preoccupied by his attempts to secure the succession for his illegitimate son Hugh and thus foil his uncles' plans to divide his inheritance between themselves. His coins, which with the disappearance of Dorestad are rare and not represented here, differ from those of his father in using the title *rex* instead of *imperator* or *augustus* and were struck at many fewer mints. The temple type was struck at Metz and Verdun, and at whatever mint or mints was producing coins with the *Christiana religio* legend, while the mint-name-in-field type was struck at Strasbourg and Metz.

After the Partition of Meerssen (870) Charles the Bald and Louis the German minted in Lotharingia, opening new mints or reviving old ones for the purpose, but they did so on only a small scale and more perhaps to signal their annexations than with any economic purpose in mind. Charles the Bald, who paid Lotharingia the compliment of treating it as a distinct kingdom, having himself crowned at Metz and starting a new series of regnal years from that date, even minted in 869/70 in some localities which he had subsequently to relinquish to Louis the German (below, p. 227). Louis the Stammerer presumably minted in Lotharingia in 877–9, but his coins cannot be distinguished from those of his namesake Louis of Saxony, who inherited his father's share of Lotharingia in 876 and acquired the rest of it after Louis the Stammerer's death in 879. His coins and those of his successors down to 911 can best be regarded as part of their coinage as kings of Germany (below, p. 227–8), since save under Zwentibold Lotharingia had no formal existence as a political entity during these years. When Charles the Simple acquired Lotharingia in 911 he continued to mint at Cologne (**1.999**), Metz, Toul and Strasbourg (**1.1000**), as Louis the Child had done.

The small volume of Lotharingian coinage under Lothar I's successors is not difficult to understand. The country was during the middle years of the century subject to constant Viking inroads, the island of Walcheren even being handed over to the Danish leader Harold in 843 for much the same reason as Rollo was to receive Normandy from Charles the Simple in 911, in the hope that its Viking ruler would protect the interior against further raids by his compatriots. Harold's nephew Roric was given Dorestad *et alios comitatus* in return for an oath of allegiance in 850. A half-century of terror was ended by Arnulf's great victory over the Northmen on the Dyle near Louvain in 891. Hoards and site finds in the Low Countries of the end of the ninth and the early tenth century show a substantial local circulation of south German and even Italian coins, which no doubt reached the country by way of trade through the Rhineland (Boeles 1915), but the main beneficiary of the ending of the Viking invasions in the region was Cologne. This quite suddenly emerged as an important mint at the very beginning of the tenth century and acquired a pre-eminence it was never to lose.

Provence (855–928)

The numismatic history of the southern part of the Middle Kingdom in the second half of the ninth century is perplexing, for apart from some rare coins of Arles and Uzès (Dumas and Temple 1974a) there are no coins that can be attributed with any confidence to Charles of Provence (855–9) and there seem to have been long gaps in minting activity at the traditional mints of Lyon, Vienne and Arles. The Lyonnais was acquired by Charles the Bald after Lothar II's death in 869 and rare coins of the GDR type were struck (MG 1038). Marseille, which had been for over two centuries the southern counterpart of Dorestad, disappears completely and perhaps not surprisingly, for after the Arab conquest of Sicily Provence was as exposed to Arab attacks as the northern coastline was to those of the Vikings (Ganshof 1938).

The coinage of the later kingdom of Provence is meagre. Boso's rare coins consist of deniers and obols struck at Vienne (MG 1262–3) and deniers, known only from a single specimen in the museum of the Société archéologique de Montpellier, struck at Arles (MG -; Bonnet 1909). The obverses have the inscription BOSO GRACIA DEI, with REX across the field; the reverses have VIENNA CIVIS and a cross or ARELA CIVIS and a *Karolus* monogram. At the end of the century, as at Cologne and Mainz, there was some revival of activity. A southern expedition of Carloman of France produced the deniers of the Avignon hoard (MG hoard 68) struck at Arles (MG 1207ff.) and at Substantion (**1.968**), a locality in the neighbourhood of Montpellier which was the residence of the bishops of Maguelonne down to the twelfth century. Of Louis III (890–928) there are also coins of Arles (MG 1652–4) and Vienne (MG 1572–3), as well as his north Italian issues of 900–2 (below, p. 256) and the papal-imperial coins in which his name is associated with those of Benedict IV (**1.1066–8**) and Christopher between 900 and 904.

(g) THE EAST FRANKISH KINGDOM (GERMANY), 840–911

Germany was in the Carolingian period still unused to coined money, and is represented in this collection by only six coins of the last two kings of the dynasty, all of them minted in localities on the west bank of the Rhine. In the reign of Louis the Pious, coins of his second type were minted at Regensburg on the Danube, the capital of Bavaria and an important commercial centre, and it is possible that three unidentified mints of the same coinage with German names, *Alaboteshaim*, *Aldunheim* and *Stottenburc*, may have been situated in Germany proper east

Table 17. *Kings of Germany, 840–911*

LOUIS THE GERMAN
817/840–876

- CARLOMAN
  k. of Bavaria 876–80
  k. of Italy 877–9
  - (illegitimate) ARNULF OF CARINTHIA
    k. of Germany 887–99
    k. of Italy 894–6
    emp. 896–9
    - (illegitimate) ZWENTIBOLD
      k. of Lotharingia
      895–900
    - LOUIS THE CHILD
      899–911
- LOUIS THE YOUNG
  k. of Saxony
  876–82
- CHARLES THE FAT
  k. of Swabia, 876–87
  k. of Italy, 879–81;
  emp. 881–7
  dep. 887;
  d. 888

of the Rhine. There is written evidence for a minting concession to the abbey of Corvey in Saxony in 833 and one to the bishopric of Hamburg at some unspecified date (Jesse 1921), in the former case specifically in the hope of stimulating trade, but the coins would have been of the anonymous temple series and, if ever really minted, cannot now be identified.

The eastern part of the Empire formed in 840 the share of Louis the Pious' third son, Louis the German, who had already ruled Bavaria since 817. It remained in the hands of his descendants down to 911, when his family died out in the male line (see Table 17). The few known coins of these rulers prior to Arnulf are almost all of Lotharingian or Italian mints, since much of Lotharingia was in the hands of one or other ruler from 870 onwards and three of them were for a time in possession of Italy. Their coinages may be summarized as follows:

Louis the German (Germany, 840–76; half Lotharingia, 870–76)

Louis' earliest coinage was confined to rare pennies struck at Mainz (MG 594), a locality expressly assigned to him by the Treaty of Verdun. They are of an unusual type, with a monogram of *Hludovvicus rex* filling the entire obverse field. In 870 he acquired half of Lotharingia under the terms of the Treaty of Meerssen. Since this area or parts of it was ruled during the next half-century by three German kings named Louis (himself, Louis the Young, Louis the Child) and two French ones (Louis the Stammerer, Louis III) there has been much confusion over the correct attribution of Lotharingian coins inscribed *(H)ludovvicus rex*. Those combining a *Hludovvicus* inscription with a *Karolus* monogram and struck at the palace mint and at Huy, Maastricht, and Visé certainly belong to Louis the German. The linkage probably derives not from the existence of a joint coinage with Charles the Bald, as some scholars have thought, but from the continued use, in default of instructions to the contrary, of the monogrammatic types introduced at those mints by Charles in 869 (below p. 233).

Louis the Young (Saxony and part of Lotharingia, 876–82)
Coins of Metz (MG 1241) and neighbouring Marsal (MG 1243) could be of either Louis the Young or his father, but the spelling LVDOVVICVS (without initial H) favours the former.

Carloman (Bavaria, 876–80; Italy, 877–9)
No Bavarian coins of Carloman are known, but he minted large deniers of temple type at Milan and Pavia (**1.1010–11**; see p. 253).

Charles the Fat (Swabia from 876; Bavaria from 880; Saxony and Lotharingia from 882; France from 884; Italy from 879 and the title of emperor from 881; dep. 887)
No Swabian or Bavarian coins are known, but Charles minted as emperor in several Lotharingian mints as well as at Milan and Pavia (**1.1012**; see p. 253). The problem of separating French coins from those of Charles the Bald as emperor is discussed below (pp. 233, 235). It is probable that the only ones of Charles the Fat are those from Lotharingian and Provençal mints, all of which use his title alone, without his name, in their inscriptions.

Arnulf of Carinthia (Germany, 887–99; Italy, 894–6; titular emperor from 896)
Arnulf was the first German ruler to mint on a substantial scale, and that only at Mainz (MG 1533; **1.826–7**), where he seems to have introduced a new weight standard, his coins rising to 1.8g or even 1.9g, despite their slovenly fabric and often blundered inscriptions. They are of the temple type (with MOGONCIA CIVIT) and spell the king's name ARNOLDVS, a recognized alternative at the time. His coins of Regensburg in Germany (MG 1534) and Toul in Lotharingia (P 136) are each known in only a single specimen, but skilful modern counterfeits exist of the Toul coin (MG 1535, as genuine; **1.1504**) by the Italian forger Tardani (Grierson, 1958, 314, no. 10).

Zwentibold (Lotharingia, 895–900)
This ruler owes his surprising name to his having had as godfather a Moravian prince named Sviatopluk. He minted at Cambrai (MG 1544) and Trier (MG 1547), though only a single coin of each mint is known. A further coin in the museum at Epinal, supposedly struck by Zwentibold at Saint-Dié (Laurent 1851, no. 1), is in reality of the eleventh century, and though the mint is correctly read the attribution is doubtful (Maxe-Werly 1879, 255–65; Dannenberg 1894, 543). After Zwentibold's assassination in 900 Lotharingia passed to the kingdom of Louis the Child.

Louis the Child (Germany, 899–911; Lotharingia from 900)

Louis the Child's relatively abundant coins have as types a mint name either across the field or around a temple; on coins of Trier there is a small temple in the centre and the mint name, TR/EV ER/IS, is arranged in three lines. His coins are distinguished from those of earlier rulers of the same name partly by hoard evidence but mainly through their resemblances to coins of his predecessor Arnulf or of Charles the Simple, who succeeded him in Lotharingia. His coins of Cologne (MG 1557–61: **1.828**), Mainz (MG 1546–8: **1.829**), and Strasbourg (MG 1550–6: **1.830–1**) are relatively common. Those of Basel (MG –; Wielandt 1971, no. 2; Schärli 1983), Trier (MG 1566), Würzburg (MG 1549) and Zurich (MG 596, as Louis the German and uncertain mint) are extremely rare, only one or two specimens of each mint being known. The existence of coins of Basel is puzzling, for one would have expected this city to have made part of the kingdom of Burgundy, as it did later, and it has consequently been argued that the R above and S below BASILEA on the reverse stand for *Rodulfus*, making the coins ones of Rudolf I of Burgundy. But the close parallel between them and coins of Strasbourg which have the initial and final letters of episcopal names above and below the mint name (O–S for *Otbertus*, G–S for *Gotfridus*, R–S for *Richwinus*) makes it virtually certain that the R is the initial of a bishop of Basel whose name does not happen to appear in the written sources (Schärli 1983). Louis also minted at Constance, but the only known coin, from the Cuerdale hoard (Dolley and Morrison 1966, no. 270a), lacks his name, since dies with CONSTANCIA CIV (around cross and pellets) and XPISTIANA RELIGIO (around a temple) were inadvertently used together.

Louis died in 911 at the age of only 18. Duke Conrad of Franconia was elected his successor by a majority of the German magnates, but those of Lotharingia, where Carolingian associations were strong, accepted the rule of Charles the Simple down to 925, when Henry the Fowler recovered it for Germany. Charles' coins of Cologne and Strasbourg are noted later (p. 247; **1.999–1000**). Those of Conrad and Henry the Fowler, and of their successors as kings of Germany, will be dealt with in Vol. 2.

(h) CHARLES THE BALD, 840–77

Literature

Charles the Bald's coins are covered in the standard works (above, p. 190). An essential article by Manfred Van Rey (1972) deals comprehensively with the mints, in particular with their geographical distribution and status, and provides lists and maps of coin hoards. Although it can be faulted on points of detail (e.g., the mint of Courtrai is probably a fiction, the problem of separating Charles the Bald's own GDR coins from later immobilizations is underrated), it provides the most detailed and reliable guide to the coinage of the reign. The title of a paper given by Metcalf (1981) at a colloquium on the reign, 'A sketch of the currency in the time of Charles the Bald', may mislead, for it is basically a study of coin circulation in the light of several important hoards. It follows the essentially economic interpretation for these put forward by Vercauteren in his analysis of the Glizy hoard (Vercauteren 1934b), while Grierson has preferred to relate the majority of them to the disorder created by the Viking invasions (Grierson 1981). Two of the early period require special mention, one from Eekeren near Antwerp (De Coster 1862) because it was overlooked by Morrison and Grunthal (1967) and has remained unknown to most French scholars, and the second from Roermond. This is the largest Carolingian hoard ever to have come to light in the Low Countries, though only a bare summary of its contents is available at the time of writing (Van Gelder 1969). An important hoard of GDR coins found at Cosne-sur-Loire in 1931 was published by Lafaurie (1975a), and the same author's brief account of two GDR deniers found *c.* 1967 at Clairoix near Compiègne contains important observations of the possibility of 'central' minting and of variations in the form of the *Karolus* monogram (Lafaurie 1973a).

Historical background

Charles, the only son of Louis by his second marriage, was born on 13 June 823. Various projects for his future share in the Frankish kingdom were announced by his father in 829, 831 and 835, but only in September 838, after he had attained his majority, was he formally crowned and placed in charge of an enlarged 'duchy' of Maine which included all Neustria between the lower Loire and the lower Seine. In 839 he was given Aquitaine as well, and was in process of trying to take it over, against the resistance of Pepin II and his supporters, when Louis died (20 June 840). Between that date and the Treaty of Verdun (August 843) Charles' fortunes fluctuated greatly, but he managed throughout to maintain some hold on Neustria and the treaty assigned him most of the western part of the Empire. Pepin held out in Aquitaine, however, and in 845, by the Treaty of Saint-Benoît-sur-Loire, Charles had to recognize his position. Aquitaine remained a problem throughout the reign, for even after Pepin himself was deposed in 848 Charles had to hive it off as a sub-kingdom, first to his son Charles of Aquitaine (855–63) and later (867) to the future Louis the Stammerer (above, p. 219).

The selfish ambitions of Louis' sons, blindly pursued in the face of the growing indiscipline of the Frankish magnates and constant Viking attacks, dominated the political history of the middle decades of the century. Lothar still had hopes of exploiting the imperial title, either directly or through the agency of his uncle Bishop Drogo of Metz, whom he had appointed papal vicar. Louis sent one of his sons to invade France in 854, and came himself in force in 858, when only the loyalty of the French bishops saved Charles' throne. The two brothers then came together in order to prevent the marriage of their nephew Lothar II to his mistress Waldrada, for he had no sons by Queen Theutberga and if he died childless they proposed to ignore his brother and divide his kingdom between them. In 867 they agreed on their respective shares, but when Lothar died in August 869 Louis was gravely ill and Charles, in violation of their accord, tried to seize the whole of Lotharingia for himself. Louis' recovery forced him to come to terms, but the Treaty of Meerssen (8 August 870) still left him with a substantial accession of territory. A further attempt at eastern expansion, when Louis the German himself died in 876, was foiled by the dead man's heirs. By that time, however, he had acquired Italy, where his insatiable ambition, encouraged by Pope John VIII, caused him to intervene after Louis II died in 875. He was crowned emperor at Rome on 25 December 875 and accepted as King of Italy at Pavia the following February. But his Italian ambitions proved his undoing. A revolt in France broke after his return to Italy in the summer of 877, and he died on the way back, at the foot of the Mont Cenis pass, on 6 October 877.

Charles was the longest lived of Louis the Pious' four sons, and the number of his coins that survive, and no doubt the number that were originally issued, far exceeds that of all his brothers and nephews combined. The reason was partly that he ruled that part of the Empire in which the use of coined money was most firmly entrenched, partly because of the enormous ransoms he had to pay to the Northmen from 845 onwards, more especially in 845, 861/2 and 866. The huge multiplication of mints that took place half-way through his reign, and the volume of coinage which they issued, has to be seen against the background of these payments. His reign was one of great unhappiness for his subjects. Wide areas of the countryside were repeatedly devastated during civil wars or invasions; towns and villages were burnt and their inhabitants killed or carried off into slavery. Immense sums had to be raised to ransom captives or buy off the Northmen, while a shiftless monarch wasted his energies and resources in ambitious plans of political expansion at the expense of his relations.

Charles the Bald's meagre north Italian coinage and his papal-imperial coins of 876/7 are noted on pp. 253, 259. The confusion between some of his Frankish coins and those of Charlemagne has already been alluded to (p. 209), and the problem of distinguishing them from those of Charles the Simple, or rather from the posthumous immobilizations of his GDR coinage, will be dealt with later (p. 246). The great bulk of his surviving coins are of the issue that started in 864, characterized by a *Karolus* monogram and the inscription GRATIA D–I REX (above, p. 202). It has traditionally been styled 'the type of the Edict of Pîtres', since it was introduced under the terms of this edict, but Lafaurie has pointed out that the design deviates somewhat from the norms there prescribed and prefers to call it the 'GDR type', which term will be employed here. Prior to 864 the main types are either ones with a temple (Class 1e below) or with a monogram and cross (Class 1d). The second of these continued in most Aquitanian mints to the end of the reign. There are in addition, at the very start of the reign, three exceptional types used at only a few mints: a cross and the mint name across the field (Class 1a), a bust and the mint name similarly placed (Class 1b), and a cross and a gateway (Class 1c). In 876–7, from the very end of the reign and a relatively small number of mints, there are also coins giving Charles the imperial title.

Coinage of 840–64 (and later in Aquitaine)

Although Charles had received the royal title and a small appanage in 838, the regnal dating of his charters is reckoned from his father's death and he is not likely to have minted before 840. Since the types struck over the years 840–64 did not succeed each other in chronological order, it seems best to make them a single class. They have, indeed, one element in common, the normal use of a mint name in the inscriptions. It seems to have been widely felt in 840 that the replacement on the coins of Louis' name by that of one or other of his sons should be accompanied by a revival of mint names, but the variety of types that were used in each kingdom shows that the mints cannot have been acting on any precise instructions. A few mints, indeed, made no change at all, retaining the temple type and the *Christiana religio* legend. Most retained the temple but substituted a mint name for *Christiana religio*; a few reverted to earlier patterns, such as the mint-name-in-field of Louis the Pious' Class 2 or the mint name and monogram of Charlemagne's Class 3. There was naturally some regional grouping, with mints waiting to see how a neighbour was acting and then copying it, and in some cases a local type was in due course abandoned in favour of the temple type that was most generally used. In the following classification the short-lived groups which were limited to the early 840s are placed first, leaving till later the more durable types which likewise started in the early 840s but continued till 864 or in some cases even later.

Class 1a. Cross/mint name in field

The main group of these coins comes from the three neighbouring mints of Paris (**1.833**), Meaux (**1.832**) and Sens (MG 1415–16). Their obverse legend is CARLVS REX (without FR). They were attributed to Charles the Simple (by Gariel, and in the case of Sens by Morrison and Grunthal) or to Charlemagne (by De Coster and by Engel and Serrure), but hoard evidence (Pilligerheck, Wagenborgen) shows them to date from the very beginning of the reign of Charles the Bald. They cannot have been struck before 840, since all the places concerned lie outside Charles' 'duchy' of Maine, and they probably belong to 840 itself. One of the mints, probably Paris, must have decided to revive the similar type of Louis the Pious, and the others copied it.

There are two other groups of coins of Charles the Bald with the mint name in the field, one from Aquitaine and the other from the Spanish March. The first consists of the coins of Melle discussed below (pp. 237–8), and the obols with CARLVS REX and a cross and AQVI/TANIA in two lines across the field (**1.834**). There are similar coins of Pepin II (**1.812–13**), and Charles' coins presumably continued these after Charles took over Aquitaine in 848. The other group consists of obols of Barcelona with CARLVS REX F and BARC/NONA (Crusafont 1980; 1982, 162, no. 7). They were probably struck in the 840s, but cannot be dated precisely.

Class 1b. Bust/mint name in field

This type, known only for Bourges (MG 1068–9), has no FR in its obverse legend and can be dated with confidence to 840/1. Charles had arranged a meeting with Pepin at Bourges in the summer of 840, and was there in July, but Pepin did not come and in August Charles had to leave the city and take refuge north of the Seine. He was back in January 841, but Pepin had reoccupied northern Aquitaine, where the bishop of Bourges was one of his warmest supporters, during the interval. Since a coin with a virtually identical bust exists for Pepin II (MG 609), it is natural to attribute this to the autumn of 840 and assume that Charles' derivative type, with an obverse copied from Pepin's and a reverse from that of the Paris–Meaux–Sens group, belongs to the winter of 840/1.

Class 1c. Cross/gateway

This is known only for the mints of Orléans (**1.835–7**) and Chartres (MG 931); at Orléans it represented a return of the gateway type used on the portrait coins of that mint under Charlemagne and Louis the Pious, and at Chartres a copy of this. The coins of Orléans are common, and are dated by their occurrence in most of the hoards of the early 840s. They presumably continued to 864, and although then replaced by GDR coins the gateway type was to remain very typical of the mint in the early feudal period.

Class 1d. Monogram/cross

This is a return to Charlemagne's Class 3, and since it is known for about twenty mints it is in a different category to those already discussed. The obverse inscription is often simply *Carlus rex*, without FR(*ancorum*), and only where this is so can we be certain, without hoard evidence, that the coins are ones of Charles the Bald and not of Charlemagne. Coins of this class fall into two groups: those of mints where it formed the main coinage of 840–64 and was then replaced by the GDR coinage, and those of mints where it formed the main (and generally the sole) type struck throughout the reign. The mints of the first group are mainly in Neustria and Burgundy, the type in a few cases following on from coins of Classes 1a–1c. Why mints such as Beauvais (**1.909**), Noyon (MG 802–3), Compiègne (MG 788–9) and Chelles (MG 856) should have adopted this type instead of the temple type that predominated in their parts of the kingdom is difficult to explain. The second group is mainly composed of mints in Aquitaine (Bourges, Melle, Clermont, Toulouse, Agen and Dax), where the GDR type was never introduced, though occasionally there were other types in the later years of the reign (below, p. 242).

Class 1e. Temple type

This type continued the final one of Louis the Pious, but with a mint name normally substituted for *Christiana religio*. The obverse has *Carlus rex Fr* around a cross with a pellet in each quarter, though there are variants: *Carolus* for *Carlus*, *Fr* omitted, sometimes no pellets in the quarters. Laon has legends of its own: *Carolus rex pius* (MG 792) or *Karolus gratia Dei rex* (MG 793), while some coins of Sens have *Tempus Carlus rex* (MG 982). In addition to the anonymous mints using the *Christiana religio* legend (**1.846–9**) there were eleven named ones, four of which are represented here (**1.842–5**).

The class was probably being minted in some places from 840 onwards but in the main must date from 843, when Charles' possession of the territories in which the mints were situated received legal sanction by the Treaty of Verdun. Those struck at Bourges must postdate 848, since prior to that year the city had formed part of the kingdom of Pepin II.

Class 2. GDR *type (864–77)*

The temple type was succeeded by the GDR one – i.e. with legend *Gratia D(e)i rex* and a monogram – which came into existence as a result of the Edict of Pîtres (25 June 864). This edict (MGH, *Capitularia* II.314–18; cf. Grierson 1981) included 17 sections (capp. 8–24) dealing with monetary matters, and prescribed the introduction of a new type of denier reviving the monogrammatic type of Charlemagne's reformed coins with on one side the royal name and monogram and on the other the mint name and a cross (cap. 11: *Ut in denariis novae nostrae monetae ex una parte nomen nostrum habeatur in gyro, et in medio nostri nominis monogramma; ex altera vero parte nomen civitatis et in medio crux habeatur*). The new coins (cap. 12) were to be struck, according to ancient custom (*sequentes consuetudinem predecessorum nostrorum*), only at the Palace and at nine named mints (*ut in nullo loco alio in omni regno nostro moneta fiat nisi in palatio nostro et in Quentovico, ac Rotomago (quae moneta ad Quentovicum ex antiqua consuetudine pertinet) et in Remis et in Senonis et in Parisio et in Aurelianis et in Cavillonno et in Metullo et in Narbona*) and were to be the only coin that would remain legal tender (cap. 10) after the following Martinmas (11 November).

The main object of the reform was to rid the circulating medium, already much reduced in volume as a result of the Danegeld payments of 845, 860/1 and 862, of the many counterfeits in circulation (Lafaurie 1981e, 1983c), and it was presumably this consideration that led to a change in the design, perhaps authorized only verbally, since the substitution of the GDR inscription for Charles' name would differentiate the new coins from the products of mints striking coins of Class 1d. The limitation of coining to ten mints was likewise abandoned, and the GDR coins came to be struck, during the period 864–76, while Charles had still only the title of king, at over 110 mints. About 30 of these must date from after the annexation of much of Lotharingia in 869, but the others ante-date this event. The multiplication of mints was no doubt partly intended to facilitate the recoinage – a charter of 22 November 864 granted Bishop Erchenraus of Châlons-sur-Marne the privilege of having a mint in his episcopal city with precisely this in mind – but is better explained by the need to provide the money required for the Danegeld of 866, which we know to have been comprehensive in its incidence and to have been levied on all classes of the population.

Some problems of attribution are raised by coins struck in Lotharingia after 869. Lothar II died in Italy on 8 August, and the news reached Charles a fortnight later. With a promise of local support he resolved to ignore the partition arrangements he had made with his brother Louis the German, and had himself crowned at Metz on 9 September. Louis naturally protested, and after several months of negotiations the brothers met on 9 August 870 at Meerssen, near Maastricht, and Lotharingia was partitioned, Charles abandoning the eastern half of the kingdom but retaining, roughly, everything west of the Meuse, the Ourthe and the Moselle.

The result of the extension of Charles' territory in 869 was the opening of a further thirty mints striking the GDR type. Half a dozen of these, however, were in localities ceded to Louis in 870. This change of allegiance resulted in the minting of a number of anomalous coins with a *Hludovvicus rex* inscription but a *Karolus* monogram (above, p. 227). Charles' Lotharingian coins are scarce and contrast with the general commonness of his GDR coinage; not a single specimen is included amongst the 60 GDR coins attributed to Charles the Bald as king in the present catalogue. For the mints of the GDR coinage, see Map 5, p. 234 below.

Class 3. Imperial coinage (876–7)

Frankish coins giving Charles the imperial title might be expected for the eighteen months between his return to France in March 876 and the arrival of the news of his death in October 877. They are in fact known for only thirteen mints, to which coins with the *Christiana religio* legend must be added. Several of the mints are known in only one or two specimens, and only the products of the mints of Nevers (**1.919–21**) and Bourges (**1.913–18**) are common. Other mints must have either been inactive during this period or continued the coinage of Class 2 without change. Evidently no general instruction was sent out to the mints, for the form taken by the imperial inscriptions is very varied, though there are regional groupings that show how one mint sometimes copied another. The precise mints that did strike imperial issues conform to no intelligible pattern. One might have expected them to relate to Charles' own movements during 876/7, but this is not the case.

Scholars have generally thought it to be impossible to distinguish coins of Charles the Bald as emperor from those of Charles the Fat (885–7) save in the case of such mints as Metz which

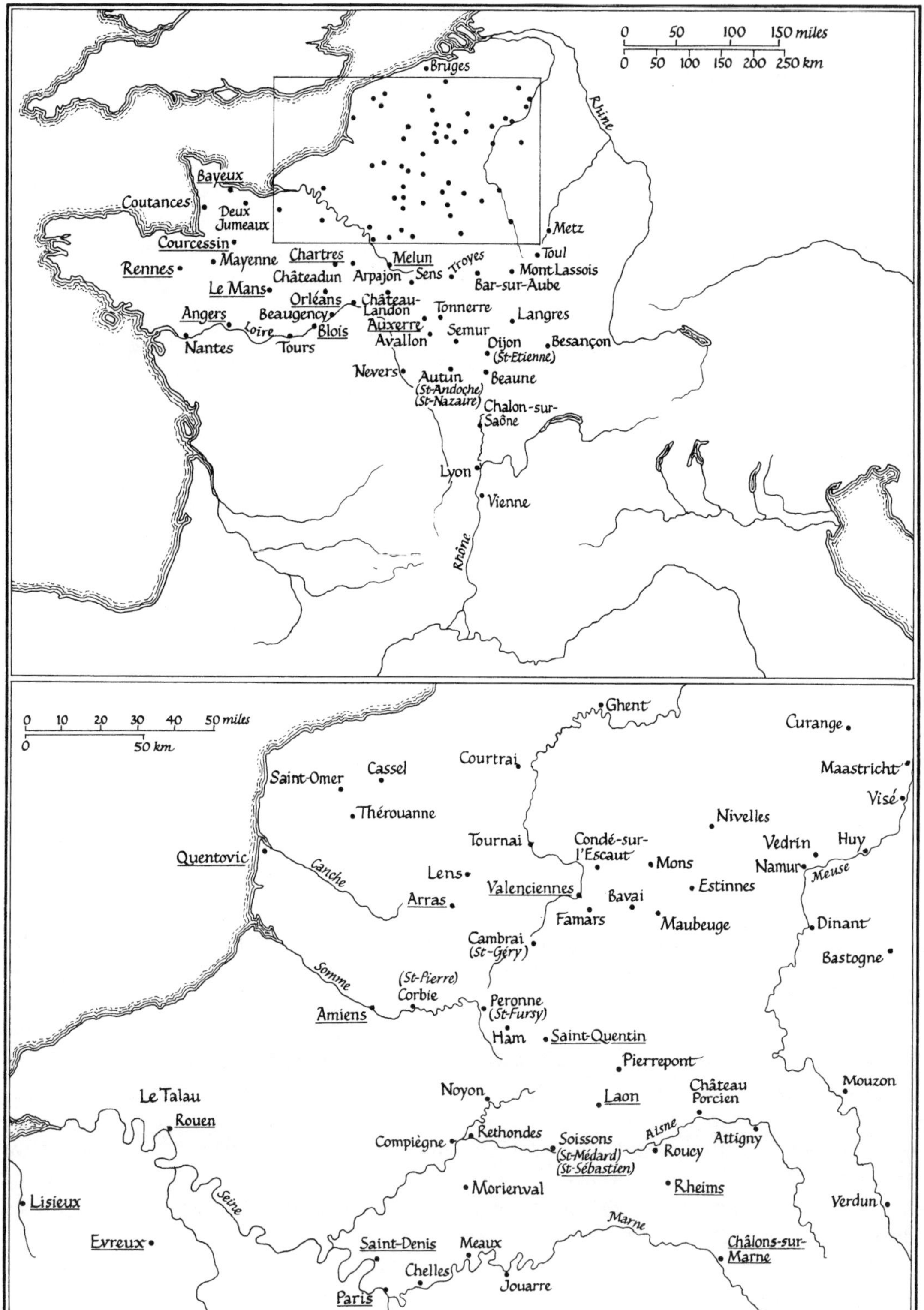

0 50 100 150 miles
0 50 100 150 200 250 km
Bruges
Rhine
Bayeux
Coutances
Deux Jumeaux
Metz
Courcessin
Toul
Rennes
Mayenne
Chartres
Melun
Troyes
Mont Lassois
Châteadun
Arpajon
Sens
Bar-sur-Aube
Le Mans
Orléans
Château-Landon
Tonnerre
Langres
Angers
Beaugency
Auxerre
Loire
Blois
Semur
Nantes
Tours
Avallon
Dijon
(St-Etienne)
Besançon
Nevers
Autun
(St-Andoche)
(St-Nazaire)
Beaune
Chalon-sur-Saône
Lyon
Vienne
Rhône
0 10 20 30 40 50 miles
0 50 km
Ghent
Curange
Courtrai
Maastricht
Saint-Omer
Cassel
Visé
Thérouanne
Nivelles
Tournai
Condé-sur-l'Escaut
Vedrin
Huy
Quentovic
Mons
Namur
Canche
Lens
Meuse
Valenciennes
Estinnes
Arras
Bavai
Famars
Maubeuge
Dinant
Cambrai
(St-Géry)
Bastogne
Somme
(St-Pierre)
Corbie
Peronne
(St-Fursy)
Amiens
Ham
Saint-Quentin
Pierrepont
Château Porcien
Mouzon
Noyon
Le Talau
Laon
Rouen
Aisne
Rethondes
Soissons
(St-Médard)
(St-Sébastien)
Attigny
Compiègne
Roucy
Morienval
Rheims
Lisieux
Verdun
Seine
Marne
Evreux
Saint-Denis
Meaux
Châlons-sur-Marne
Chelles
Jouarre
Paris

never formed part of Charles the Bald's kingdom. Lafaurie, in his account of the Rennes hoard (Lafaurie 1965a) attributed a group of coins from Bourges and Arles to Charles the Fat because of their low weights, but these average only 1.36g, with 1.59g as the weight of the heaviest coin, figures well below the level to be expected of either monarch. The close die-linking of the coins, in a hoard that dates from *c.* 920, shows that they must in fact be later imitations.

There are a few hoards, however, which are shown by their contents to have been buried before Charles the Fat's accession, and using these as a basis it is possible to determine the local use of particular forms of inscription, e.g. *Karlus inper. aug.* at Arles, Nîmes, Uzès and Béziers, and thus to identify groups of mints as having struck coin under Charles the Bald even when there is positive hoard evidence for dating in the case of only one or two of them. A detailed study of these relationships shows that Charles the Fat minted only in Lotharingia, of which he was king from 882 onwards, and there only at Maastricht, Metz, Verdun and perhaps Saint-Géry of Cambrai, but never in West Francia. This is perhaps to be expected, for in West Frankish eyes he was a foreign ruler, accepted only grudgingly in default of an alternative, and his own intervention in West Frankish affairs, his attempt to relieve the siege of Paris by the Northmen in 886, was an ignominious failure.

(i) THE CAROLINGIAN COINAGE OF 'MELLE'

Coins of Melle bearing the name of Charles (CARLVS REX FR) rank with the *Christiana religio* series of Louis the Pious as one of the two commonest types of Carolingian coins, despite their having been struck at only a few mints in Poitou instead of at a huge number throughout the Empire. They owe this pre-eminence to the silver mines which made an otherwise unimportant *vicus* one of the chief mints of the period. Unfortunately the vast majority of the coins are of a single type that was struck with only a few brief interruptions over nearly a century and a half, so that individual coins can rarely be dated with any precision. Even an iron upper die, with + CARLVS REX FR round a cross, which was found during excavations at Melle itself and is now in the archaeological museum at Niort (Breuillac 1909), cannot be satisfactorily dated. The following pages attempt to put the coinage into perspective.

The coins, whether struck at Melle itself or at some neighbouring locality, all bear in one form or other the mint name of Melle (Deux-Sèvres, arr. Niort), a small town in central Poitou 20km south-east of Niort. It is built partly on the bank of the River Béronne and partly on the slopes of a steep hill containing argentiferous lead mines which were worked from Roman times until at least the end of the twelfth century and were particularly productive in the Carolingian period (Traver 1938). Its original Latin name was apparently *Medolum* – it appears as *Medolo vico* on Merovingian gold and silver coins (B 2883–4; Prou and Bougenot 1907,

---

Map 5 *The mints of the GDR coinage of Charles the Bald*

Mints represented in this collection are underlined. There are also GDR coins of the Palace (PALATINA MONETA) for which no specific mints can be indicated, as well as a few with more or less clear place-names for which no satisfactory identifications have yet been proposed.

no. 208, Bais hoard) – but since *metallum*, the Latin word for a quarry, was also used for 'mine' (whence 'metal' in English and other languages) the two were easily confused and *Metalo*, *Metalu* or *Metullo* are used from time to time (B 2878–82).

Documentary evidence for silver mining in Merovingian times is lacking. Dagobert's alleged grant of 8,000lb of lead *ex Metallo* to cover the roof of the abbey church of Saint-Denis is of doubtful authority, for the *Gesta Dagoberti*, our only source for the grant, was composed at Saint-Denis in the fourth decade of the ninth century and often reflects conditions of the writer's own day and not those of two hundred years earlier. Certainly little silver was minted in Merovingian times at Melle itself – only a single denier, that in the Bais hoard, is known – but Melle may well have been the source of the silver used at Poitiers, whose output of deniers in the late seventh and early eighth century was very large indeed (B 3594ff.). A table in Lafaurie's revised catalogue of the Bais hoard (Lafaurie 1981d, xvi–xx) shows that in 1892 the number of Poitiers deniers in the Bibliothèque Nationale (46) was only exceeded by those of Marseille (220) and Paris (55), while there were no silver coins of Melle at all.

Under the Carolingians this situation was apparently reversed, with Melle becoming one of the chief mints of the Empire and the name of Poitiers virtually disappearing from the coinage (Richard 1893). The only coins with a *Pectavo* legend are rare deniers and obols – the latter perhaps not all authentic – of Pepin II of Aquitaine (MG 605 [=P 677], 605a; Prieur 1927), probably struck because Melle was in the hands of Charles the Bald at the time, and a coin with the mint-signatures of both Poitiers and Melle which is described below. Its supersession was apparently a consequence of the discovery of new veins of silver at Melle, commemorated by such coin inscriptions as *Ex metallo novo* and *Metall German*, in the first years of the ninth century, though the relative commonness of coins of Charlemagne's early type with *Medolus* or *Metolus* (**1.727–8**) show its importance even earlier. The form *Medolus* disappeared in the ninth century. MSS of the *Annales Bertiniani* refer to the place as *Metallum* or *Metullum* in 848, and it is *Metullum* in the Edict of Pîtres (864). These are the forms that were to prevail in the future.

Unfortunately their regular use is accompanied by a major problem, that of identifying the rulers responsible for most of the coins. Although Melle was specifically mentioned in the Edict of Pîtres, the GDR inscription was never used there, no doubt because the place was regarded as normally forming part of the kingdom of Aquitaine, where the GDR formula was not adopted. Coins of a single type, with a monogram and a cross with *Carlus rex Fr* and *Metullo* (or variants) as inscriptions, were struck by Charlemagne, Charles the Bald and Charles the Simple, to say nothing of being immobilized during much of the intervening periods and thereafter to the middle of the tenth century. Although individual specimens can be described as 'early' or 'late' on the evidence of style, issues of Charles the Bald's early years cannot be satisfactorily distinguished from those of Charlemagne nor those of his later years, presumably continued during the 880s and 890s, from those of Charles the Simple and immobilized under his immediate successors. It is for this reason that all ninth- and early tenth-century coins with the mint-signature of Melle in this collection, apart from those of Louis the Pious and Pepin II (**1.758**, **762, 774–8, 814–15**), have been grouped together on Plates 42–3. Other types, not represented in the collection, are all extremely rare. The full sequence, omitting the *Medolus* coins of Charlemagne's early years, is as follows:

CHARLEMAGNE. *Class 3 (794–812). Monogram and cross.*

1 (a) With METVLLO, MG 172.

Attributable to Charlemagne because of specimens in early hoards: Biebrich *c.* 800 (MG hoard 11), Steckborn *c.* 800 (MG hoard 278), Ibersheim *c.* 810 (MG hoard 13), Bondeno *c.* 810 (MG hoard 12), Dorestad *c.* 820 (MG hoard 18), Belvezet *c.* 825 (MG hoard 14).

2 (b) With EX METALLO NOVO (or variant), MG 309–12.

Attributable to Charlemagne on the basis of a specimen in the Ibersheim hoard of *c.* 810 (MG hoard 13).

Class 4 (812–14). Bust and minting implements.

3 (a) With METALL GERMAN, MG 313.

Customarily ascribed to some mint in Germany, but the use of the same reverse type at Melle under Louis the Pious suggests that coins were struck at this mint and *german(um)* was meant to refer to 'genuine', newly mined metal.

LOUIS THE PIOUS. *Class 1 (814–19). Portrait and minting implements.*

4 With METALLVM, MG 396; obol: MG 397.

Class 2 (819–22). Mint name in field.

5 With META/LLUM, MG 398–400, 406. The corresponding obol has Louis' name instead of *Metallum* across the field, either in one line (MG 395: LVDOIC) or two (MG 393–4: LVDO/VVIC).

There are in addition the anomalous, rare deniers (MG 407; **1.762**) with Louis' name (+ HLVDOVVICVS IMP) and + METALLVM each round a cross. It has been suggested above (p. 215) that these were struck in 819.

Presumably coins of Louis' Class 3 were struck at Melle, but they cannot be specifically identified.

CHARLES THE BALD. *Class 1 (840). Temple type.*

6 With METVLLO, MG 1059.

The only recorded specimen of this coin, which has the obverse inscription CARLVS REX FRANCO around the temple, was acquired by Lecointre at Strasbourg in *c.* 1850 and published by Fillon 1856, 40–1, from where Gariel's reference and illustration are taken (Gariel II.195, no. 8; pl. 21.8), though he wrongly states that Fillon attributed it to Charles the Simple. It does not occur in any of the 'Pepin' hoards, and must represent a very brief issue. Probably it was struck in the early months of 840, since it is an adaptation of Louis the Pious' last type.

Class 2 (840–5?). Mint name in field.

7 With META/LLVM, MG 1056; obol: MG 1057.

This was known in the mid nineteenth century by three specimens only: a denier in the Rondier (ex Briquet) collection at Melle (cited by Lecointre-Dupont 1840b), another found in 1860 at Saint-Maixent and acquired by Richard (Rondier 1863), and an obol in the Rondier collection. The Brioux hoard of 1878 brought to light 70 deniers of this type and 2 obols, mixed with Melle deniers and obols of Pepin II and deniers of Charles the Bald of the types numbered 9 and 10 below. The presence of the latter types dates the hoard to *c.* 850, after Pepin's downfall in 848.

PEPIN II OF AQUITAINE (845?–48).

8 With METVLLO, MG 606 (with PIPINVS REX EQ), 607 (no EQ); obol: MG 608.
The dating of Pepin's coins is discussed above, p. 219.

CHARLES THE BALD (848–77)

9 With METVLLO, MG 1063; obol: MG 1060.
Hoard evidence for attribution to Charles the Bald is too plentiful to require citation.

10 With METXVLLO, MG 1064; obol: MG 1061.
That this type, with an intrusive X in the inscription (denier) or the field (obol), had already started quite early in Charles the Bald's reign is shown by the presence of specimens in the Brioux hoard (MG hoard 32), datable to *c.* 850 by the high proportion of coins of Pepin that it contains.

The innovation of no. 10, with an X breaking the inscription between the T and the V, or, on the obol, placed in the third 'quarter' of the monogram, is something of a problem. The letter is carefully positioned, coming normally in the bottom left of the inscription and occupying a corresponding position on the obols, so that someone requiring to check whether a cross was present or not would know exactly where to look. The die-cutters had clearly been instructed not merely to insert a cross but where to place it. Why was this done?

Lecointre-Dupont suggested that the letter might have been intended to distinguish feudal from royal issues, and has been followed in this by most later scholars. It is, however, unlikely, for Carolingian counts were more concerned to conceal their usurpations than to advertise them. An alternative and perhaps more probable explanation is that it was intended to show that coins so marked were not struck at Melle but elsewhere, probably for the most part at Poitiers. The existence of a mint at Melle, a mere *vicus* with no pretensions to secular or ecclesiastical importance, was in itself anomalous, and it would be natural for counts of Poitou to prefer minting at the centre of their *pagus*, while retaining a coin inscription already well established and known as a mark of good silver. There are no stylistic differences between coins without an X and those on which one is present, but one would not expect this: the mints were not far apart and the same die-sinkers would work for both. Certainly in the eleventh century the MET/ALO inscription, the only one then used by the counts of Poitou, covered coins being struck at Poitiers, at Niort 20km from Melle, and at Saint-Jean d'Angely in the south-west of the county, for the profits of minting at the two latter places were granted to Cluny early in the century, and a tithe of the profits at Poitiers itself was bestowed on the monks of Saint-Nicolas, a priory founded by the countess Agnes in the late 1040s (Bisson 1979, 45, 48).

There is, it is true, no documentary evidence that minting in these localities had started as early as the ninth century, but there is an important piece of corroborative numismatic evidence for X indicating the mint at Poitiers. The Bonnevaux hoard of the 880s (MG hoard

70) contained three deniers without any royal name but with on one side + METXVLLO round a *Karolus* monogram and on the other + PICTAVI CIV round a cross (Gariel I.125, no. 11; MG p. 364). They must represent an accidental muling of dies not meant to be used together. The most reasonable explanation of the two being available at the same mint is that after Charles the Bald had come fully into possession of Poitou it was decided to resume minting at Poitiers, and dies with *Pictavi civi* were prepared. Subsequently it was thought preferable to take advantage of the reputation of the *Metullo* coinage, but this was varied to *Metxullo* to distinguish the coins struck at Poitiers from those struck at Melle itself. It was the accidental linking of some of these with *Pictavi civi* ones that provides the essential clue to what had taken place.

CARLOMAN (882–4)

11 With CARLOMAN RE (or RX) and METXVLLO, MG 1199–1200.

This extremely rare denier, of which there was a specimen in the Bonnevaux hoard, breaks the sequence of the *Carlus rex Fr* series, and is presumably to be explained by a wish to indicate which mints had fallen to Carloman's share after the partition of the West Frankish kingdom between him and his brother early in 880.

CHARLES THE SIMPLE (897–922)

12–13 As nos. 9 and 10 of Charles the Bald.

The occurrence of hundreds of both these types in the Cuerdale hoard of *c.* 905 (MG hoard 98) shows them still being struck during the reign of Charles the Simple. But the presence of over 5,000 specimens in the Bonnevaux hoard (MG hoard 70) of the 880s is proof of their being minted in quantity before his accession and they are clearly better treated as immobilizations of Charles the Bald's coins and not specifically attributed to Charles the Simple. The type presumably continued to be struck after the latter's overthrow and imprisonment (923), but there is virtually no hoard evidence for the period.

This traditional type of Melle was replaced in the mid tenth century, at a time when minting there had entirely escaped royal control and was in the hands of the counts of Poitou, by one retaining on the obverse a cross and CARLVS REX FR (or variant) but having a reverse never actually used in Carolingian times, the legend MET/ALO in large letters across the field. It is the sole Poitevin type represented in hoards of the eleventh and most of the twelfth century; only in the last decade of the latter do these begin to be mixed with the new types struck by Richard Coeur-de-Lion. In the Fécamp hoard of *c.* 980 the coins are already entirely of the MET/ALO type (nos. 8381–8421), and a hoard some thirty years earlier, found at Javarzai near Niort in 1837 (Lecointre-Dupont 1840b, 50–1), shows this type already in normal use, with 222 *Metalo* deniers as against a single *Metxullo* one. There was a specimen of the *Metalo* type in the small Port St Mary (Ballaqueeny) hoard of 1873/4, from the Isle of Man, which since it contained coins of Eadwig (955–9) but none of Eadgar (959–75) was presumably buried in the late 950s (Dolley and Morrison 1962). This is the closest dating that we have. Mme Dumas conjectures (1971, 242 n. 3) that the new type may have been introduced by Hugh the Great, the redoubtable Duke of the Franks, whom charter evidence shows to have briefly made himself master of Poitou in 938, perhaps even in 937 (Auzias 1937, 481–92), to the detriment of its rightful possessor, the youthful William Towhead (934–63).

Why was the change made? One does not abandon a familiar coin type without good reason, for acceptability and familiarity are bound up with each other. The usual explanation for a change, that it marks the replacement of one ruler by another, cannot apply here, since both types perpetuate the name of a Carolingian ruler long since dead. Obvious possibilities are that it marked a change in value, by a diminution – or increase – in weight or fineness, or that it was intended to bring the coinage of Poitou into line with that of one of its neighbours. There is no reason to believe that the first was the case, but the second, if Hugh the Great was in fact responsible, is a possibility, for the coins struck by Hugh the Great at Paris in the name of King Raoul (923–36) and immobilized thereafter (MG 582–5) have as their type the mint name PARISI/CIVITA in two lines across the field, with a cross above and below. The resemblance is admittedly not close, for the Paris coins are of much neater and more regular workmanship, but an instruction to the Poitevin moneyers to place the mint name across the field in two lines could well have resulted in MET/ALO, and seven of the *Metalo* coins in the Fécamp hoard do in fact have a cross above and below, like the Paris coins. Those in the Javarzai hoard, however, do not, and neither does the specimen from Port St Mary, so one cannot make too much of this detail. For our purposes it is sufficient to note that the coinages illustrated on Plates 42–3 came to an end in the mid tenth century, though it is unlikely that any of the specimens there represented are quite so late.

(j) WEST FRANKISH COINAGE, 877–97

Historical background

The two decades that followed Charles the Bald's death in 877 were decisive for the fortunes of the Carolingians in France. A series of short reigns both east and west of the Rhine ended with the formal reunification of the entire Carolingian Empire in the hands of the one totally worthless member of the dynasty, Charles the Fat. His deposition in the winter of 887 was followed by the succession in France of a non-Carolingian, Odo, or Eudes in modern French, who reigned for ten years. The dynastic history was played out against a background of Viking raids on the largest possible scale, involving the devastation of much of northern France. The period divides into two exactly equal halves. The first (877–87) is that of the successive reigns of Charles the Bald's son, grandsons, and nephew. The second (887–97) is that of the reign of Odo, but Odo's position was contested from 893 onwards by supporters of Charles the Simple, another grandson of Charles the Bald, in whose person the Carolingian dynasty was eventually to be restored.

The succession to Charles the Bald posed no serious problem. The king was not on good terms with his son Louis the Stammerer, and the capitulary of Quierzy, drawn up in June 877 on the eve of his departure for Italy, included several provisions intended to prevent Louis, who was to act as regent, from abusing his powers. But Louis was the only legitimate heir and had already had some political experience as sub-king of Aquitaine, so when Charles died he had little difficulty in securing the throne. He died on 10 April 879, after a reign of less than two years, leaving two sons, Louis III and Carloman. A group of discontented magnates offered the crown to Louis of Saxony (see Table 17), but when it became clear to Louis that he would receive only limited support he allowed himself to be bought off by the cession of Charles the Bald's share of Lotharingia. In the autumn of 879 the two boys partitioned the West Frankish kingdom between them, Louis taking the north (*Francia* and Neustria) and Carloman Burgundy and Aquitaine.

Louis' reign was brief, for he was killed in an accident on 5 August 882, and Carloman, who took over his share of the kingdom, died two years later, on 12 December 884. They had by this time a half-brother, Charles, later to be unflatteringly known as 'the Simple', born on 17 September 879 after his father's death. In view of the peril from the Northmen, the accession of a five-year-old boy was unthinkable, more especially since the legitimacy of his father's second marriage was contested and there were many who regarded Charles as a bastard. After some delay the crown was offered to Charles the Fat, the last surviving son of Louis the German (June 885). A worse choice could hardly have been made. Charles' attempt to relieve Paris, besieged by the Northmen, was an ignominious failure, the besiegers being eventually bought off by an authorization to pillage Burgundy, and his overthrow by his nephew Arnulf of Carinthia in the early winter of 887 left the West Frankish throne again vacant. Odo, son of Robert the Strong, one of the great magnates of Charles the Bald's time and himself the hero of the siege of Paris, was elected by a large group of nobles in the last week of 887 and crowned on 29 February 888.

But Odo had his own complement of enemies, led by Archbishop Fulk of Rheims. Fulk's first candidate was Guy of Spoleto (below, p. 253), but Guy had lived too long in Italy and preferred a career in that country. His second candidate was Charles, now in his early teens, and the boy was crowned at Rheims on 23 January 893. Support for the pretender, however, was limited to the north and north-east of the kingdom, while Neustria remained loyal to Odo, as in general did Aquitaine, though its magnates were in practice indifferent to the claims of either. Desultory fighting between the rivals ensued, with Odo steadily gaining the advantage, till in 895 Charles was driven humbly to beg for peace and 'a share of the kingdom, whatever it might please Odo to grant him'. A plan to cede him the northern *pagi* (Rheims, Laon, Vermandois, Artois), where his support was concentrated, came to nothing, and in the end (897) he had to content himself not with a petty kingdom but with the easily defensible fortress-rock of Laon as a *locus refugii*. Odo himself, however, was by this time seriously ill, and when he died on 1 January 898 he designated Charles as his successor and instructed his followers to swear allegiance to him.

Coinage

The coinage of the two decades consists almost entirely of monogram/cross types, without any revival of the other types – bust, mint-signature-in-field, temple – used earlier in the century.

It involves several problems which, despite the plethora of hoard evidence attributable to the Viking invasions, have not yet been satisfactorily settled.

The separation of the coins of Charles the Fat from those of Charles the Bald as emperor seems to be fairly clear (above, p. 235), but how is one to distinguish coins struck during the reign of Louis the Stammerer (877–9) from those of the reign of Louis III (879–82)? Odo's coins ought to be easily identifiable, since he was the only Frankish ruler of this name, but in the tenth century, some of Raoul's moneyers devised for their master a monogram almost identical with that of Odo, which in any case was later immobilized at several Aquitanian mints (Limoges, Mâcon). It is possible that coins were struck at a few mints in the name of Charles the Simple before 897, though the bulk of his coinage is undoubtedly subsequent to this year. A complication is the evident immobilization of Charles the Bald's monogram at such common and prolific mints as Angers and Bourges, for this is the only explanation for the absence of coins of Louis II or III from them.

It is, one may suggest, this phenomenon that provides a key to the 'separation' between coins of the two Louis. Although Carloman became king of all France on Louis III's death and was its sole ruler for nearly two and a half years (Aug. 882–Dec. 884), it is a striking fact that his mints are limited to that part of France which he acquired in 882, just as the mints of 'Louis' are all in those regions that formed Louis III's share in the same partition. There are, further, with the exceptions of some deniers of Toulouse of irregular type, no coins of 'Louis' from any mint that had belonged to Louis II but not to Louis III. It seems reasonable to infer that no general mint instruction for a change in type or legend was issued on the accession of Louis II in 877, so that those mints which were then active would have continued to strike the GDR type of Charles the Bald, royal or imperial according to the mint, without any change. The same would have continued after the joint accession of Louis III and Carloman in April 879, and it would only have been the subsequent division of the kingdom between them in the autumn that resulted in mints receiving new instructions regarding the coinage.

The view here taken is therefore that no coins of normal type bearing the name of Louis were minted in the reign of Louis II, and that the only one of such type in this collection (**1.967**) belongs to Louis III. There is, however, a denier of Toulouse (**1.966**), with the legend *Ludovicus rex* and LV/DO in the field, which has a parallel in an imperial coin of Charles the Bald of the same mint with *Carlus imp. r.* and CA/RL (**1.922**). It is conceivable that it was struck by Louis II while still only king of Aquitaine (above, p. 219), but the very limited powers conferred on Louis by his father make this unlikely. It seems preferable to treat it as the only real issue of Louis II and as resulting not from any general mint instruction but from the initiative of local moneyers, anxious in 877 to update their coinage. This leaves the reigns of Louis III and Carloman represented in this collection by a single coin each, one of Tours (**1.967**) and the other of Substantion (**1.968**), out of the ten or so mints known for each ruler. The coin of Tours has the obverse inscription *Misericordia D(e)i rex* instead of the old GDR formula, the reason for the change, found at a number of mints that evidently copied each other, being unknown. Substantion, a now abandoned site near Montpellier, is a strange locality for a mint and does not occur again, but it was in later times a residence of the counts of Melgueil and Carloman may have spent some time there during the joint campaign of the brothers against

Boso in 880. Carloman's deniers of the mints of Arles and Substantion are common, since several hundred were found in the Avignon hoard of 1822, but otherwise his coins and those of Louis III are rare and were probably minted on only a small scale.

This is not the case for the coins of Odo, which were struck at nearly thirty mints, the products of some of which being extremely common (**1.976–89**). This may be partly a consequence of his reign having lasted longer than those of his four predecessors, but it is also likely that as a non-Carolingian he would have been anxious to secure explicit recognition of his authority as widely as possible. Any mint instruction, however, must have been couched in very general terms, without specifying details of type or inscription, for the arrangement of the letters of his name in the field – it was too short to lend itself to monogrammatic treatment unless joined up with REX, as at Blois and Tours (**1.980–7**) – are very variously arranged. Some mints even retained a *Karolus* monogram as their type while having Odo's name in the inscription. The OD/DO in two lines used at Toulouse (**1.988–9**) was obviously suggested by the CA/RL and LV/DO of recent issues of that mint. The three letters ODO were often thought to be insufficient and are augmented by a cross, and the king's name is sometimes spelled HODO. The retention of the H in the Blois–Tours monogram is in any case explicable by a desire to make this resemble the *Ludovicus rex* monogram used at the same two mints under Louis III, a resemblance increased by the retention of the *Misericordia D(e)i rex* formula in the inscription.

(k) WEST FRANKISH COINAGE, 897–987

Literature

There are no special studies covering the coinage of the last hundred years of Carolingian rule, but that of Raoul has been intensively dealt with (see below) and there are two general surveys of the transition from the Carolingian to the Capetian period (Lafaurie 1970, Dumas 1973). Much new light was thrown on the coinage of the third quarter of the tenth century by the finding in 1963 of the huge Fécamp (Normandy) hoard, which dates from the mid 980s (Dumas 1971; on the date, Pagan 1973b). There is no comprehensive general work on the history of the period, but there is a good summary with an excellent bibliography by K. F. Werner in Schieder 1976 (I.731ff.), and all the reigns are covered in the series of detailed monographs that made part of a projected *Annales de l'histoire de France à l'époque carolingienne* that was planned in the late nineteenth century: Odo (Favre 1893), Charles the Simple (Eckel 1899), Robert I and Raoul (Lauer 1910), Louis IV (Lauer 1900) and the last Carolingians (Lot 1891).

Historical background

Only two of the six kings who reigned in France between 897 and 987 were not of the Carolingian house, but once the tradition of Carolingian rule had been breached in 888 the throne might be considered open to the ambitions of any powerful but disaffected subject. Although it would be a mistake to see Carolingians and Robertians competing for the crown over the whole period 887–987, the great magnates had in the last decades of the ninth century become so independent that they were bound to resent attempts on the part of successive rulers to reassert their authority, and it was the Robertians who mainly profited from this attitude.

Table 18. *West Frankish kings, 877–987*

(a) CAROLINGIANS

- CHARLES THE BALD, k. of France, 839/840–75, emp., 875–7, *see Table 15*
  - LOUIS II THE STAMMERER, k. of Aquitaine, 867–77, k. of France, 877–9
    - LOUIS III, k. 879–82
    - CARLOMAN, k. 882–4
    - CHARLES THE SIMPLE, k. (893) 897–922, d. 929
      - LOUIS IV D'OUTREMER, k. 936–54
        - LOTHAIRE, k. 954–86
          - LOUIS V, k. 986–7
        - Charles of Lorraine, d. 992/5
  - CHARLES THE YOUNG, k. of Aquitaine, 855–63, d. 866

(b) ROBERTIANS (later CAPETIANS)

- Robert the Strong, duke of the Franks, d. 866
  - ODO (Eudes), k. 888–97
  - ROBERT I, k. 922–3
    - Hugh the Great, duke of the Franks, 923–56
      - HUGH CAPET, duke of the Franks, 956–87, k. 987–96
        - *later kings of France*
    - Emma = RAOUL, duke of Burgundy, k. 923–36

The Carolingian and Robertian successions are set out in Table 18. Charles the Simple (897–922) had two obvious achievements to his credit, the creation of the duchy of Normandy by the treaty of Saint-Clair-sur-Epte in the autumn of 911, which ended the worst phase of the Northmen invasions, and the annexation of Lotharingia a few months later, after the death of Louis the Child (above, p. 224). But power had passed irrevocably into the hands of the great magnates, the most prominent amongst whom were the counts of Flanders and Vermandois and the dukes of Normandy, of the Franks, and of Burgundy. The concentration of Charles' interests in Lorraine, where the royal domain was especially rich, and his reliance on an allegedly low-born favourite named Hagano led to a crisis in the early 920s. Odo's surviving brother Robert was elected king (29 June 922) by a party amongst the magnates. When Robert was killed in a sudden attack by Charles a year later (15 June 923) he was succeeded by his brother-in-law Raoul, count of Autun and duke of Burgundy. Raoul's reign, however, was little more than a prolonged struggle against rivals, of whom the most dangerous was the ambitious and unscrupulous Herbert of Vermandois, into whose hands Charles had fallen in late 923 and who tried to restore him as a puppet ruler in 927–8.

When Raoul died in 936, however, without leaving a male heir, the magnates were unable to agree on a successor from amongst themselves. Charles had died, still a prisoner, in 929, so his son Louis, who had been brought up in exile at the English court – his mother Otgiva (Eadgifu) was a half-sister of Æthelstan – was recalled 'from overseas' and elected king. He reigned for nearly two decades (936–54), but despite his ambitions and very considerable abilities the Crown was now too weak to maintain itself against the magnates.

The king's problem was by this time partly administrative – the counts were no longer royal nominees, but magnates who expected to pass their offices on to their sons and be able to acquire others by marriage – and partly one of poverty, for the royal domain had been greatly diminished by grant or usurpation during the short reigns, disputed successions and other troubles of the last decades of the ninth century and of the 920s and 930s. One obvious remedy was for the Crown to annex for itself one or more of the great fiefs when opportunity presented, but any such attempt was bound to result in a coalition of magnates to prevent it. Louis began by shaking off the tutelage of Hugh the Great, the head of the Robertian family, who had succeeded the ageing Herbert of Vermandois as the most powerful magnate in northern France, but his attempt to take advantage of the civil wars that followed the accession of Otto I (936) in Germany by seizing Lotharingia resulted in such a coalition and the defeat of the project. The same happened when he intervened in Normandy after the murder of its second duke, William Longsword, in 943, though in the end, thanks to the intervention of Otto on his behalf, he managed to reassert his authority and even bring Hugh the Great to heel (950). At one time, however, he had been Hugh's prisoner and in danger of sharing the same fate as Charles the Simple.

Louis' son Lothaire (954–86) was only 13 at the time of his accession and the regency fell to Hugh the Great. When the latter died in 956, leaving only children under age, the regency was taken over by Archbishop Bruno of Cologne, brother of Otto I and duke of Lotharingia, who was able to protect Louis' interests and keep his ambitions in check. After the death of Otto in 973, however, Lothaire's reign became a series of unprincipled and futile attempts to seize Lotharingia or Alsace. In the course of these he alienated Hugh the Great's son and heir, Hugh Capet, and Adalbero the powerful archbishop of Rheims, who was a Lotharingian by birth and a warm admirer of the Ottos. Lothaire died prematurely in 986 and was succeeded by his son Louis V, associated on the throne since 979 and a bitter enemy of Adalbero, whose deposition he tried to secure. When Louis in turn died in 987, leaving as representative of his house his unpopular uncle Charles, who had entered Ottonian service and was duke of Lower Lotharingia, Adalbero and Hugh decided to have done with the relatively powerless Carolingians once for all. Hugh was elected king at Noyon on 1 June 987 and crowned by Adalbero a month later. The circumstances were in part accidental, but they were also a recognition of the fact that Hugh was by far the most powerful magnate in France and that, the Carolingians having failed to achieve mastery by adding one of the great principalities to what remained of the royal domain, the only solution for the problems of government was for the head of one of the great principalities to take over the crown and what remained of the royal domain for himself.

Coinage

Coins are known of all but one of the kings of this period, and even, unusually for the Carolingian period, of one queen. There seem to be none of Robert, for the monogram on some of those formerly attributed to him is now recognized as a misreading of that of Raoul and others are simply forgeries. The attributions and dating of a high proportion of the coins of the period are, however, very uncertain. Even when coins with the name or monogram of Charles the Simple are attributable on hoard evidence to his reign they were in some mints not really 'his', but immobilized types of Charles the Bald being struck before Charles the Simple's accession as well as after his downfall. While the minting of coins with the monograms or names of Raoul and Lothaire cannot have started before 923 and 954 respectively, they certainly did not end with the deaths of these rulers, being either continued under their immediate successors or revived later.

It is in any case only by convention that many of the coins are classed as 'royal'; they were really coins of the great feudatories, who issued them in the king's name but to their own profit in what were effectively their own mints. It is indeed significant that there are no abundant royal coinages at Laon and other places known to have formed part of the royal domain and which represented the last strongholds of the dynasty, the explanation being presumably that the kings now lacked the resources that would permit them to mint extensively on their own behalf.

A few of the great feudatories were indeed from the 920s and 930s openly assuming the right of minting; there are deniers (Lafaurie 1970, Dumas 1973) with the names of the duke of Normandy William Longsword (*c.* 930–43) minted at Rouen, of Hugh the Great (923–56) minted at Senlis, of William the Young of Auvergne (918–26) minted at Brioude, just as there are later of William Longsword's successor Richard I (943–96) minted at Rouen, of Hugh the Great's successor Hugh Capet (duke 956–87) minted at Paris and Saint-Denis, and of Thibaut the Tricker, count of Blois and Chartres (943–75/8), at Chartres and Beaugency. Those of William of Auvergne, indeed, with the inscription VLELMO COMES and datable to the 920s by the Rennes hoard (Lafaurie 1965a) and by the grave-finds in Hungary which they reached as a result of the great Magyar invasions which began to afflict France from 917 onwards, are customarily regarded as the earliest feudal coins in France bearing the names of those who issued them. This was a real novelty, for since with few exceptions feudal coinage in France arose by usurpation and not by grant (Volz 1971), usurpers preferred to conceal the fact by minting anonymously (e.g. at Auxerre) or in the name or with the monogram of a Carolingian monarch who might or might not be the one actually on the throne. Ecclesiastical mints could sometimes behave more openly (Barthélemy 1851; Kaiser 1976a), though not all supposed concessions are genuine (Kaiser 1976b). Abbots Angilbert and Fulco of Corbie put their initials on deniers as early as the 880s (Castellane 1916; Lafaurie 1970, 133) and St Martin of Tours was in 919 granted the right of having its own coin type, this being a head of St Martin modelled on that of a coin or medallion of Constantine the Great. Our knowledge of the earliest feudal coinages is complicated by the existence of modern forgeries, the most dangerous being those of Farrigault in the present century (e.g. deniers of Etampes and Beaugency of Hugh the Great) but others, much cruder, go back to at least the 1830s (e.g. some of the deniers of Rouen of William Longsword).

Coins of Charles the Simple (**1.990–1000**) are for the most part of the same types as those of Charles the Bald, though there are exceptions, as with the deniers of Paris with mint-signatures in the field (**1.996–7**). They were struck at far fewer mints, for many of those created in the 860s in connection with payments to the Northmen (above, p. 233) had been only temporary in character. Coins struck at Cologne (**1.999**) and Strasbourg (**1.1000**) after the annexation of Lotharingia in 911 raise no problem of attribution, as Charles the Bald did not mint at either place and in type and fabric they are identical with ones of Louis the Child. But for French mints the distinction between coins of the two rulers is often difficult to make, since although coins of Charles the Simple tend to be rougher in fabric and lower in weight, such criteria are not always easy to apply to single coins without any hoard affiliations. Nor, even where hoard evidence is available, does it always help, for scholars have sometimes differed as to whether mixed hoards are of Charles the Bald and Odo, or of Odo and Charles the Simple. A reliable guide to the issues of many mints is fortunately provided by the great Cuerdale hoard from Lancashire (Hawkins 1843), which is very closely datable by its English (and Italian) contents to *c.* 905 (Dolley and Morrison 1963, 80), for although Hawkins, in first publishing it, tended to follow Fougères and Conbrouse, the only authority available in 1843, in ascribing most of the *Karolus* coins in it to Charles the Bald, it is now recognized that in view of the date of the hoard they must virtually all be of Charles the Simple. The hoard is in any case important in showing that coins of some mints, notably Limoges and Melle, are of a workmanship that would otherwise tempt scholars into dating them much later and treating them as feudal and not royal issues.

Coins of Charles the Simple's successors are for the most part relatively rare, since they were struck at fewer mints and on a much smaller scale. Hoards in any case are less numerous, since the invasions of the Northmen had effectively come to an end and those of the Magyars, though appalling to populations immediately in their path, were more quickly over and affected smaller areas of the countryside. The coinage is under-represented in this collection, with only two coins of Raoul, one of Louis IV, and two of Lothaire, while of Louis V there is none.

The coins of Raoul (923–36) have basically a *Rodulfus* monogram (**1.1001–2**) closely and no doubt deliberately resembling the *Karolus* one, with an R replacing the K and including an F, but it is often so badly formed that confusion between the two monograms is easy and coins have sometimes been attributed to the wrong rulers, with unfortunate consequences where hoard descriptions are involved. An alternative monogram modelled on that of Odo (**1.1003**) adds to the confusion, and hoard evidence shows that at some mints these monograms continued to be used long after Raoul's death. Our knowledge of the coinage has been greatly extended in recent years, with the discovery by Duplessy and others of a whole series of new types or mints; the material has been brought together in a magisterial study of Dumas (1980; add Dumas 1981 and Wit 1980). Virtually all Raoul's mints are situated north of the Loire, with only three in Aquitaine (Bourges, Angoulême and Le Puy), and none at all north-west of Beauvais or west of Chartres and Châteaudun. His supposed coins of Courcessin have either a misread *Karolus* monogram – this is the case with MG 1590 – or are modern forgeries (**1.1508**).

For Lothaire's long reign of over thirty years (954–86) one would expect a fairly abundant coinage, but in fact it is both exiguous and difficult to distinguish from the feudal issues of the time and later. Two of the great magnates, Herbert III of Vermandois (d. 995) and Archbishop Adalbero of Rheims (969–89), who was in due course to preside over the change of dynasty, minted jointly with the king, putting their names openly on the coins, and of the fifteen or so mints on which Lothaire's name occurs and of which some coins at least go back to his reign, fewer than half can be regarded as part of the royal domain.

The coin types, like the spelling of the king's name (*Lotarius* at Chalon, *Loterius* at Bourges, *Lotharius* at Arras, etc.) are extremely varied, and are evidence of a lack of central control. One mint will use a *Karolus* monogram, another a temple or a legend in two lines; at Chalon there is a large B for *Burgundia* (MG 1163), at Mâcon a small cross and four annulets deriving from the *Odo* monogram (MG 1164–5), at Rheims (MG 1660) and Soissons (MG 1668) REX across the field, at Laon a floral pattern (Gendre and Dhénin 1974). It was in Lothaire's reign that a royal bust made its reappearance at a number of Neustrian mints, though not at ones where it had been used under Charlemagne and Louis the Pious, the new type being that which was to give rise to the 'tête-blèso-chartraine' of the feudal period: Blois, Vendôme, Chinon (Dumas and La Perrière 1977), Chartres, etc. At Bourges the *Karolus* monogram (MG 1666–71) was replaced in the eleventh century by a temple (MG 1672–7), but with the inscription LOTERIVS REX left unchanged. These coins are commonly, though wrongly, attributed to Lothaire's reign, but in view of their date the three specimens in this collection will be catalogued in due course as feudal issues.

Lothaire's coins are exceptional in including a group, known from 8 specimens in the Fécamp hoard (Dumas 1971, nos. 8544–51), which have as their reverse legend a blundered version of the name of his queen (ENMA PEIONA, for *Emma regina*) instead of that of a mint (Dumas 1976). They were presumably struck at some locality where the queen had received the profits of the local mint as part of her dowry, and the style suggests a Burgundian mint, perhaps Dijon.

Louis V's only true coinage is that of Rheims, the type being a revival of one of Louis IV with a double circle of inscription, LVDOC inside and a blundered version of *Gratia d–i rex* outside. Coins in his name of Saintes (STCNAS) and Bordeaux (LODOICVS without *rex*, and a type derived from the Odo monogram) are feudal in character, for although the dating clauses of charters show that Louis' kingship was formally recognized as far south as the Pyrenees, royal authority there was non-existent.

(I) THE KINGDOM OF ITALY, 855–961

Literature

The coinage of Carolingian Italy in this period is included in Gariel (1883–4), but his ruler and mint attributions are often incorrect. Since much of it was issued by rulers who were not of Carolingian descent or were so only in the female lines its representation in Prou (1896a) and Morrison and Grunthal (1967) is haphazard. Apart from coins bearing the mint-signature of Pavia or Verona, most of it is illustrated in *CNI* V (*Milano*), since virtually all of the coins have been traditionally (though wrongly) attributed to Milan. How to distinguish between the products of Milan and those of Pavia in the 890s was explained some years ago (Grierson 1978), and a detailed study of mint and regnal attributions over the whole period is forthcoming. The clearest summaries of the complicated history of the period are provided by a monograph of Fasoli (1962), the final chapters of Romano and Solmi (1940) and the opening ones of Mor (1952), and chapters 2, 3 and 7 of vol. III of the *CMH* by Poupardin and Previté-Orton. A more modern discussion of the background will be found in Wickham (1981). The role of Frankish immigrants and of the great families is studied in Hofmeister 1906, Tellenbach 1957 and Hlawitschka 1960.

Historical background

Louis II had inherited the imperial title, but was effectively king of no more than Italy and was mainly preoccupied with Italian affairs. His death in 875 without male heirs was followed by three-quarters of a century of virtual chaos. No individual emerged amongst the feudal nobility strong enough to take over effective government for any period of time; Liutprand indeed credits the magnates with a fixed policy of electing rival rulers who could be played off against each other and thus kept from exercising real power. The pattern was complicated by the recurrent intervention of French, German or Provençal monarchs or magnates whose main interests lay elsewhere but who were hopeful of obtaining the titles of king of Italy or emperor and drawing on the country's wealth.

In Italy itself the two main families to emerge were those of Friuli-Ivrea and Spoleto, both of Frankish origin and the first able to claim Carolingian descent through the marriage of its founder, Marquess Eberhard of Friuli (d. *c.* 864), to Gisela, daughter of Louis the Pious. The period of Spoletan ascendancy was brief and confined to the years 888–98, when Marquess Guy or Guido and his son Lambert were in succession kings and emperors. Guy's rival was Eberhard's long-lived son Berengar I, who entitled himself king from 888 to 915 and emperor from 915 to his death in 924 (Arnaldi 1967). He had no sons, but his daughter Gisela married Adalbert, Marquess of Ivrea in north-western Italy, and their son Berengar II became king in 950.

Intervention from outside, encouraged by a papacy in desperate need of military aid against the Saracens, began immediately on the death of Louis II. Italy was formally ruled in turn by Charles the Bald of France (875–7), Carloman of Bavaria (877–9), and Charles the Fat of Germany (879–87), but the main concerns of each sovereign lay north of the Alps. Arnulf of Carinthia (nominally 894–9) and Louis (III) of Provence (900–5) were no more than rivals to local rulers, though Louis might well have transferred the centre of his power to Italy but for his blinding in 905. From 905 to *c.* 920 Berengar I ruled virtually without a rival, but in the 920s another phase of transalpine intervention began, under King Rudolf II of Burgundy and Hugh, count of Arles, who in the end, being not himself fully sovereign in Provence, moved permanently to Italy. He managed to hold on to power after a fashion until 947 and was succeeded by his son Lothaire, but the latter died in 950. Berengar II, who had been effectively regent since 945, was then elected king (December 950) in company with his son Adalbert, but in September 951 Otto I of Saxony invaded the country and compelled them to become his vassals. After a further decade of virtual anarchy Otto returned (August 961) and this time, after his imperial coronation at Rome on 2 February 962, he deposed and eventually captured Berengar and drove Adalbert into exile. From 962 onwards the *regnum Italicum*, as it was now regularly called, formed a part of the Holy Roman Empire.

The extraordinary complications of these struggles for power mean that the nominal dates for the 'reigns' of the contestants signify very little. 'Effective reigns', in the sense of the periods when the various parties exercised physical control of the Po valley and the north-east in which the mints were situated, are far more important. An attempt to disentangle the chronology will be made below, in the context of the coinage. The various rulers were in any case trying to govern a country in which local power, exercised in part by feudal magnates, in part by bishops and municipal authorities, was steadily encroaching on royal power. Saracen raids were a constant menace on the southern frontier and in the north-west, where there was a substantial Muslim settlement at *Fraxinetum* on the coast of Provence. From 899 onwards the kingdom was exposed to terribly destructive Magyar raids (Fasoli 1945) which on one occasion covered the whole length of the peninsula and reached Otranto in the extreme south. The popes represented a political factor that had also to be taken into account, since although they had no formal say in the affairs of the kingdom they were closely allied with the nobility of Spoleto and Tuscany and could give or withhold the imperial crown.

Coinage

The coinage of Carolingian Italy consisted entirely of denari, the absence of obols perhaps reflecting a general level of prices higher than in France. From 855 to 902 the coins were all of the 'temple' type, with a cross and four pellets on the obverse and a tetrastyle temple on the reverse, the legends being the ruler's name followed by his title (*rex* or *imperator*, usually abbreviated) and XPISTIANA RELIGIO. There is thus no formal indication of where the coins were struck. In the 890s some coins of Milan and Pavia bear a mint name, either replacing *Christiana religio* or substituting MEDI or PAPI for the columns and central cross of the temple design. After 902 the temple is replaced by the mint name in the field sometimes accompanied by C (for *civitas*) and the cross by a Christogram or regal monogram. The mint of Venice persisted with

Table 19. *The* Regnum Italicum, *855–973*

Kings or emperors	Nominal reign	Probable minting period
Louis II (sole emperor)	855–75	855–75
Charles the Bald (emperor)	875–7	876–7
Carloman of Bavaria (king)	877–9	877–9
Charles the Fat (king)	879–81	879–81
(emperor)	881–7	881–7
Berengar I of Friuli (king)	888–915	888–9 (first period)
Guy of Spoleto (king)	889–91	889–91
(emperor)	891–4	891–4
Arnulf of Carinthia (king)	894–6	894, 895–6
(emperor)	896–9	896
Lambert (emperor, alone from 894)	892–8	894–5, 896–8
Berengar I (king, restored)	—	898–900 (second period)
Louis III the Blind (king)	900–1	900–1
(emperor)	901–28	901–2
Berengar I (king, again restored)	—	902–15 (third period)
(emperor)	915–24	915–24
Rudolf II of Burgundy (king)	923–33	923, 924–6
Hugh of Arles (king)		
(alone)	926–31	926–31
(with Lothaire II)	931–47	931–47
Lothaire (king, alone)	947–50	947–50
Berengar II (king, rival from 945)	945–50	
(with Adalbert)	950–63	950–61
Otto I (king)	951–62	951–62
(emperor)	962–73	962–73

Christiana religio coins down to the middle of the tenth century, the formula being much blundered and simplified, e.g. to PIITΛNCIO.

The most obvious feature of the denari between *c.* 860 and 896 is the increase of their module from *c.* 24mm to *c.* 34mm, after which they were again reduced to *c.* 22mm. Over the next half-century they tended to contract, the external diameter sometimes falling to *c.* 19mm and that of the die face to *c.* 14mm, so that there are broad, plain outer borders on the coins. Since the increase in module was not accompanied by an increase in weight the coins of the 880s and 890s became exceedingly thin, the details of the design and lettering on one face appearing incuse on the other thus blurring the general features of its type and rendering letter-forms difficult to decipher. There is usually a conspicuous circular ring surrounding the legend, and the outside borders are somewhat turned up. Italian scholars are accustomed to describe such coins as *scodellati* (from *scodella*, 'saucer'). The fabric is to some extent a reversion to that of the Lombard gold coins of the seventh/eighth centuries (above, pp. 58, 62), but in a greatly exaggerated form. A broad flan might have been suggested by that of the contemporary Byzantine silver miliaresion, though since this was a heavier and thicker coin the fabric is quite different, but the absence of *scodellati* at Benevento, even when the mint was occupied by Louis II, tells against this explanation, for Byzantine influence was normally much stronger in the south than in the north.

Our knowledge of the chronology and mints of these coins depends mainly on hoard evidence, which is virtually limited to the 890s and the early decades of the tenth century. The most useful hoards for the study of the large denari are one of over 250 coins buried in *c.* 892 which was discovered at Pavia in 1934 and about which information in a summary form is available (Cremaschi 1955; Grierson 1978), and another of 63 coins, buried in March or April 894, which was discovered at Briosco, north of Milan, in 1837 and of which a partial description exists (Bergmann 1838; Deschamps 1839). For the smaller denari after 896 the most important sources of information are a hoard found at Wiesendangen near Zurich in 1842 (Hahn 1922), the Italian coins in the Cuerdale hoard of 1840, which dates from *c.* 905 (Hawkins 1843; cf. Dolley and Morrison 1963, 80–1) and the many small funerary deposits of the first half of the tenth century from Hungary (Huszár 1955; Gedai 1972).

The problem of identifying the mints responsible for the *Christiana religio* coins has now been largely solved (Grierson 1978). The anonymous coins of the 890s can be divided up according to the appearance of the central cross and certain differences in letter-forms which are also present on the rare mint-signed issues of Milan and Pavia of the 890s and the much commoner coinages of these two mints after 902 (**1.1017**, **1019**). Coins of Milan have one or more arms of the cross ending in a spike and have barred As and normal Bs (**1.1016**), while those of Pavia have flat, slightly splayed ends to the arms of the cross, unbarred As, and Bs in the form of a barred D (**1.1014–15**). Mint attributions for the 870s and 880s, when the differentiation in the form of the cross had not yet developed, depend partly on the use of barred or unbarred As and partly on the spelling of the rulers' names, coins of Milan having an initial aspirate (*HCarolus*, *HCarlemannus*) and those of Pavia not. After 902 the anonymous *Christiana religio* type persisted at a mint that must be identified with Venice (**1.1018**, **1020**), since its characteristic broad and slightly concave border and degenerate temple type is continued on mid tenth-century coins with the mint name VENECI/A replacing the temple columns (the A beneath). Some irregular coins which do not fit into this pattern can be attributed to the mints of Verona and Modena, whose existence at this time is known from documents.

The sequence of rulers' effective reigns and of their coins, omitting the papal-imperial issues of Rome (pp. 260–1) and the Beneventan issues of Louis II (p. 69), is as follows:

Louis II (king, 844–50; co-emperor, 850–5; sole emperor, 855–75)

Louis II's coins date from 855, when his father's death left him sole emperor. They are of the same type as the final issue of Louis the Pious, the earliest ones being only a little larger than those of his grandfather but of rougher fabric and with badly formed letters (**1.1007**). Later ones are of larger module, 24mm as against 21mm, with broader outer borders (**1.1008**). They should probably be distributed between the three mints active under Lothaire I, Milan,

Pavia and Venice, with coins of Milan having, in contrast to those of Pavia, a barred A and a tendency of the L in *religio* to become an I, but it is not clear what coins should be assigned to Venice.

Charles the Bald (emperor, 875–7)

Charles the Bald's coins (with HCAROLVS IMPER or variant) are of the same size and fabric as those of Louis II, and were probably struck at the same mints (**1.1009**).

Carloman of Bavaria (king, 877–9)

Carloman was elected king of Pavia in October 877 and ruled till the summer of 879, when he fell incurably ill – he died on 22 March 880 – and his brothers Louis (of Saxony) and Charles (of Swabia) divided his dominions between them, Charles taking Italy, apparently with the assent of the dying monarch.

Carloman's denari are of larger module than those of his two predecessors (*c.* 27mm). Under him the features that differentiate the products of the various mints are much clearer. Coins with his name in the form CARLOMAN REX (barred A, S on rev. normal) are probably of Milan (**1.1010**), and those with HCARLEMANNVS RE (unbarred A, S in form of a reversed Z) are of Pavia (**1.1011**), but there are also coins with HCARLOMAN REX (barred A, normal S) and CARLEMANNVS RE (unbarred A, S as reversed Z) whose mint attributions are unclear.

Charles the Fat (king, 879–81; emperor, 881–7)

Charles was briefly king (Oct. 879–12 Feb. 881), but despite his having spent the two winters of 879/80 and 880/1 in Italy he does not seem to have minted with the title of *rex*. His imperial denari are larger than those of Carloman (*c.* 30mm), the details of the lettering being by now often difficult to make out, and they have a broad outer border of 3 or 4mm. Only two types, in almost equal numbers, were represented in the Pavia hoard, one with KAROLVS IMP (barred A, normal S: **1.1012**) of Milan, the other with HCAROLVS IMPER (unbarred A, S in the form of a reversed Z becoming an I) of Pavia. Probably varieties attributable to the other mints will come to light.

Berengar of Friuli (king, 888–915; emperor, 915–24)

(a) *First minting period* (early 888–Feb. 889)

The chief competitors for power after the deposition of Charles the Fat (October 887) were Berengar of Friuli and Guy of Spoleto. Since Guy was absent in France, where he had hopes of obtaining the French crown, Berengar was elected king early in 888 and secured some kind of recognition from Arnulf of Germany. Later in the year Guy, disappointed of his French hopes, returned to Italy and was in turn elected king in February 889. Berengar took refuge in his margraviate of Friuli, refusing to recognize his rival.

Berengar's coins of this period are large denari, dated by their presence in the Pavia hoard of *c.* 892, with his name and the title *rex*. They form three groups, a Milanese one (with spiked cross-arms, barred As, and normal Bs and Ss), a Pavese one (with flat-ended cross-arms, unbarred A, barred D for B, D for P, and an S often becoming I, so that XDIITIΛNΛ does duty for

XPISTIANA: **1.1013**), and a third one with Berengar's name spelled BERNE (or I)KARIVS and pointed cross-arms, A or Λ, and B and S correct. The last group can plausibly be attributed to Verona, which became Berengar's capital after his loss of Lombardy. It is probable, indeed, that it was only after 889 that the mint of Verona was opened and the coins struck from that date onwards.

Guy of Spoleto (king, 889–91; emperor, 891–4)
Guy was crowned king in February 889 and emperor on 21 February 891. He lost Milan and Pavia to Arnulf of Germany for between two and three months early in 894 (January–March), but recovered them in March and held them till his death the following December.

Since Guy's name was short and he had some need to assert his legitimacy against Berengar, a *gracia Dei* formula was added in the legend to his royal title (VVIDO GRACIA DI RE). His Milanese and Pavese (**1.1014**) issues exhibit the same features as do those of Berengar. The Pavia hoard contains a few anomalous coins, including some with VVITO instead of VVIDO and other peculiarities of lettering, but since these do not carry over into Guy's imperial coinage – this drops *gracia Dei* in order to include more letters of *imperator* – they are better regarded as arising out of the usual teething troubles created by the initiation of a new coinage than as products of a third mint.

Arnulf of Carinthia (king, 894–6; emperor, 896–9)
(a) *First minting period* (March 894)
Arnulf, an illegitimate son of Carloman of Bavaria (above, p. 226), became king of Germany on the deposition of Charles the Fat and was accorded a position of somewhat undefined supremacy by Odo of France and Berengar of Italy. He came briefly to Lombardy in January 894, and after capturing Bergamo received the submission of Milan and Pavia. The dating of later diplomas shows that he was crowned king at Pavia in early March, but towards the end of the month, for reasons unknown, he returned to Germany.

Arnulf's Italian coins as king, as revealed to us by the Briosco hoard, are all of the temple type but have two varieties of legend: (a) HARNOLFVS REX and XPISTIANA RELIGIO, and (b) ARNVLFVS PIVS REX and BERENGARIVS REX, with MEDI replacing the columns of the temple and central cross. A third variety, with ARNOLFVS PIVS REX and MEDIOLANVM CIVIS, is probably no more than a forgery of Cigoi (p. 332), for no specimens occurred in the Briosco hoard or in any of the Low Country hoards of this period containing large-module denari, and dies for both obverse and reverse are amongst those of Cigoi in the Museo Nazionale at Rome (Grierson 1958, 314, no. 11).

Since there were several specimens of (b) in the Briosco hoard of March 894, and apparently only one of (a), it is natural to ascribe (a) to March 894 and (b) to the three months of Arnulf's second visit to Italy in the winter of 895/6. The specimen of (a) at Vienna (from Briosco) has the characteristic features of the mint of Milan, but the coins were probably struck at Pavia as well.

Guy, restored (March–December 894)
Coins of this period cannot be distinguished from Guy's imperial issues of Feb. 891–Jan. 894.

Lambert (co-emperor, 892–4; sole emperor, 894–8)
Guy's son Lambert was created co-emperor on 30 April 892 and succeeded his father as sole emperor in December 894. In November 895 he had to abandon Lombardy in face of Arnulf's second invasion, but recovered it the following summer and reached an agreement with Berengar whereby the latter was to continue his rule unmolested in the north-east. Lambert was killed in a hunting accident on 15 October 898.
(a) *First minting period* (Dec. 894–Nov. 895)
The coins of this period are Lambert's large-module denari. The identification of their mints presents no problem, as they reproduce the customary Milan/Pavia features of preceding reigns (Pavia: **1.1015**).

Arnulf of Carinthia (king, 894–6; emperor, 896–9)
(b) *Second minting period* (Dec. 895–Feb. 896 as king; March 896 as emperor)
Arnulf left Germany in October 895 and arrived at Pavia, in company this time with Berengar, on 1 December. In January 896 he left for Rome, where he was crowned emperor on 22 February. In March he attacked Spoleto, which was defended by Guy's formidable widow Ageltrude on behalf of her son, but he was struck down by paralysis, forced to abandon the siege, and returned reluctantly to Germany, where he died after a long period of suffering on 8 December 899.

The 'royal' coinage of Arnulf's second visit was that struck in association with Berengar, as noted already. The authenticity of at least some Milanese specimens is guaranteed by their presence in the Briosco and Odoorn hoards, but a supposed parallel Pavese coinage, with PAPI instead of MEDI replacing the columns of the temple, while in itself probable, has no hoard evidence behind it and the authenticity of the few recorded specimens must be regarded as doubtful. The 'royal' coinage was followed by an imperial one without Berengar's name which must be dated to March 896. It is known from a unique specimen (ARNVLFVS IMPER), exhibiting the usual features of the Milanese mint, which was in the Briosco hoard and is now at Vienna (Grierson 1978). No Pavese equivalent is known.

Lambert (emperor, 894–8)
(b) *Second minting period* (April 896–October 898)
The coins struck by Lambert when he reoccupied north Italy after Arnulf's return to Germany are completely different from those of 894–5, for it is to 896–8 that his small-flan denari must be assigned. Coins are known with the characteristic features of Milan and Pavia. The reasons for the change in fabric, apart from its manifest convenience, are unknown, for the staffs of the two mints, or at least their die-sinkers, were still clearly the same. Possibly the silver pennies that Arnulf must have brought with him from Germany had reminded the mints or the public of the greater practicality of more normal-sized coins.

Berengar I (king, 898–915)

(b) *Second minting period* (898–900)

Lambert's unexpected death left Berengar without competitors. But he failed completely to deal with the terrible Magyar invasion of 899, and in 900 a new rival appeared in the shape of Louis of Provence, who on 11 October occupied Pavia and was crowned king, leaving Berengar once again to retire to the north-east.

Berengar's second minting period in Lombardy thus lasted two years, from October 898 to October 900. His Milanese (**1.1016**) and Pavese coins are of the same type as the small-module denari of Lambert, *c.* 24mm in diameter, and bear the inscription BERENGARIVS REX (or R). It was presumably at the same time that this module was adopted for his mint at Verona, for there are small as well as large coins spelling his name BERE(or I)NKARIVS. The five surviving coins from the Wiesendangen hoard are all of this type (Hahn 1922), as is only natural, for Verona lay at the foot of the Brenner Pass and Italian coins found near Zurich would probably have come by that route.

Louis the Blind (king, 900–1; emperor 901–28, but effectively only 901–2)

The Italian kingdom was a natural object of ambition to Louis, since his mother Ermengarde, wife of King Boso (above, p. 221), was a daughter of Louis II, the last effective ruler of the peninsula. His coronation as king at Pavia on 11 October 900 was followed four months later at Rome by that as emperor (15 or 22 February 901). He spent the following sixteen months in Italy, mainly at Pavia, till in June or July 901 he was expelled by Berengar, taking an oath never to return. He did return in May 905 and met with much initial success, even occupying Verona, but on 11 July he was seized in a popular rising on Berengar's behalf, blinded, and sent home for good. He died in Provence on 5 June 928.

Louis was therefore in a position to mint as king for four months in 900/1 and as emperor for sixteen months in 901/2. A resumption of minting in 905 is unlikely, for virtually no coins of Louis occur in Hungarian grave-finds, as one would expect them to have done if any had been struck in 905. His second visit was in any case a very brief one. Coins of 900–2 were first identified and studied by Gaettens (1932) and Laffranchi (1933). A rare coin with the legend HLVDOVVICVS REX, which could only belong to Louis III since neither of the earlier Louis minted as king in Italy, served to identify two specimens of Louis III's imperial issues, with which they are identical in fabric and lettering. The arguments of both scholars are confirmed by the presence of a number of specimens in the Cuerdale hoard of *c.* 905, and in fact the coins are less rare than appeared to be the case fifty years ago. Specimens with the usual features of both Milan and Pavia are known, and there are coins with a mixture of letter-forms which should perhaps be attributed to Modena.

Berengar (king, 888–915; emperor, 915–24)

(c) *Third minting period* (902–15 as king, 915–24 as emperor)

For nearly two decades, from the summer of 902 onwards, Berengar's position seemed secure, though he proved markedly ineffective at dealing with the problems of the peninsula. In 915 he was crowned emperor by Pope John X. In *c.* 920 he had to face an invasion by his neighbour

Hugh of Arles, regent of Provence for Louis the Blind, and in 923 a group of discontented subjects invited the intervention of Rudolf II of Burgundy. Berengar was defeated at Piacenza on 17 July 923 and, as so often before, retired to Verona and the north-east, but Rudolf's position was threatened by the ambitious Hugh and before the end of the year he returned to Burgundy. Berengar reoccupied Lombardy, but his recovery of power was brief, for he was murdered on 7 April 924 by his stepson in a family quarrel.

Berengar's third minting period at Milan and Pavia falls therefore into two phases, 902–15 as king, 915–24 as emperor, though there were a few months in 923/4 during which he lost control of these mints. It was presumably in 902, to emphasize his recovery of Milan and Pavia, that he abandoned the traditional type of cross and temple and the coins began again to record where they were struck. The cross was replaced by a Christogram and the temple by the mint name in three lines, PΛ/PIΛ/CI (**1.1019**) or MEDI/C/OLA (**1.1017**), the C or CI standing for *civitas*. The inscriptions are *Berengarius rex*, or *Berengarius imp* after 915, and the reverse inscription a blundered and simplified version of *Christiana religio*. The ends of the cross-arms of the Christogram are pointed or flat according to whether the coins were struck at Milan or Pavia, and the customary differences in letter-forms are maintained. There are no similar coins with a *Bernekarius* inscription, and it is possible that with Berengar's recovery of Milan and Pavia the mint of Verona was closed; it may indeed have been so in 898. It is true that *monetarii* appear as witnesses in Verona charters of 911 and 913, but it is not clear that it was at Verona that they held office. There are, on the other hand, many temple-type coins with *Berengarius rex* or *imp* having pointed cross-arms and a broad outer border which must be ascribed to Venice (**1.1018**, **1020**). The retention of the traditional type is to be explained by the fact that although Venice, as a matter of policy and courtesy, placed the emperor's name on the coins, its mint was not under his control and would not be bound by whatever directions regarding type and use of mint-signatures that he might choose to give to his own mints.

Rudolf II of Burgundy (king, 924–6)

The news of Berengar's death brought Rudolf back to Italy, where we find him at Pavia on 18 August 924. For two years he maintained himself with ever-increasing difficulty against Hugh of Arles. In the summer of 926 he abandoned the struggle and retired to Burgundy, formally abandoning his Italian claims to Hugh in 933. He died in 937.

Rudolf may have been minting in the second half of 923, but the bulk of his Italian coinage must belong to 924–6. His coins of Pavia (**1.1023**) and Milan (**1.1021–2**) are of the same types as those of Berengar's final issue, but have as obverse inscription RODVLFO PIVS REX. The letters are very badly formed, each stroke being reduced to a single thick bar, and the diameter of the coins is 21mm or less. In 925 he concluded with Venice a *pactum* that included a formal grant of minting rights (*simulque eis numorum monetam concedimus, secundum quod eorum provincie duces a priscis temporibus consueta more habuerunt*), but the Venetians do not seem to have taken his kingship seriously and there are no *Christiana religio* coins in his name.

Hugh of Arles (sole king, 926–31; with Lothaire, 931–47)

Hugh was crowned king of Italy at Pavia in 926 and reigned with some degree of success for over twenty years. He associated with him as king his son Lothaire, whose position he consolidated by marrying him to Adelaide, daughter of Rudolf II of Burgundy and reputedly the most beautiful woman in Italy. He maintained himself in power by a complex network of marriage alliances and by reliance on relatives imported from France, a policy that did not endear him to his Italian subjects. He failed in both of his major ambitions, for he never managed to incorporate Rome in his dominions or to acquire the imperial title. Early in the 940s his power began to disintegrate, largely to the profit of Berengar I's grandson, the Marquess Berengar of Ivrea, who in a *coup d'état* in April 945 managed to take over effective government of the country. From 945 to 947 Hugh continued to reign as a figurehead, but in April 947 he was allowed to return to Provence, where he died a year later (10 April 948).

Hugh of Arles' coins of Milan and Pavia form the two series one would expect. The reverse, with a truncated *Christiana religio* inscription around the mint-signature in the field, remained as before. The obverses have +HVGO PIVS REX or, after 931, +VGO LOTHARIVS around a crudely formed monogram of HVGO (**1.1025–6**). At Venice the traditional *Christiana religio* coinage continued, with an almost illegible legend blundered from VGO PIVS REX (**1.1024**), no attempt being made to recognize Lothaire's association in 931. Verona, however, after issuing anonymous coins, presumably in the 920s, with +HI XPI NOMINE (*In Christi nomine*) and a cross and VERONA in the form of a cross in the field (*CNI* VI, 251.1), struck rare coins of Hugh and Lothaire in the 930s and 940s. They have the same reverse as the coin just described but, on the obverse, +HVGO LOTHARIO IX around REX across the field.

Lothaire (sole king, 947–50)

Lothaire's sole reign was brief, for he died on 22 November 950. His coins of Milan, Pavia (**1.1027–8**) and Verona continue the same types as those of his joint reign with his father, but with a different monogram in the case of Milan and Pavia. There are no coins of his attributable to Venice.

Berengar II, with Adalbert (kings, 950–63; deposed)

Lothaire's death made possible the succession of Berengar II, who was elected at Pavia on 15 December 950 and immediately associated with himself his son Adalbert. In order to consolidate his position he attempted to marry the latter to Adelaide, Lothaire's widow, and on her refusal had her thrown into prison. This provided the occasion for a new intervention from beyond the Alps. Otto I of Germany crossed the Brenner, assumed the title of king of Italy at Pavia (23 September 951), and married Adelaide, but he had almost immediately to recross the Alps. Berengar made peace overtures, and in August 952, in a diet at Augsburg, did homage to Otto in return for the government of Italy without the title of king. According to the almost unanimous testimony of chroniclers he was notorious for his greed and lack of scruple, and proved one of the worst rulers of his age. On Otto I's second Italian expedition (August 961) he was blockaded in the fortress of San Leo, south-west of San Marino in the Apennines, but he was finally compelled to surrender (December 963) and died a captive in Germany (August 966). Adalbert himself died an exile in Burgundy in the 970s.

The coins of Berengar II and Adalbert are reasonably common, and despite Berengar's undertaking in 952 to abandon the royal title they must have been struck over the whole decade

950–61. The denari of Milan and Pavia, which are not represented here, include the names of both father and son, but those of Verona (**1.1029**) were struck in Berengar's name alone.

(m) PAPAL AND PAPAL-IMPERIAL COINS, *c.* 735–*c.* 980

Literature

The papal and papal-imperial coins of the eighth to tenth centuries are traditionally termed *antiquiores*, since they are separated by over three centuries from the main papal series that started under Boniface VIII (1294–1303). The earlier works on them, by Leblanc, Vignoli, Scilla, Muratori, Fioravanti, and other scholars of the late seventeenth and eighteenth centuries, are today only of value when they describe coins that no longer exist or cannot now be traced. Their modern study begins, and apart from modifications on points of detail virtually ends, with a monograph of Promis (1858), though there is one important later study of their constitutional status (Pflugk-Harttung 1904). The two main collections of material are those in the Vatican and in the former king of Italy's collection, now in the Museo Nazionale delle Terme at Rome, the former published in vol. I of Serafini's splendid catalogue (Serafini 1910; there is some supplementary material in vol. IV) and the second included in vol. XV of the *CNI*. The more recent listing of early papal coins, that in vol. I of Muntoni (1972), marks no serious advance on these. The study of the series is not facilitated by the existence of numerous forgeries: see Appendix 2 and **1.1510–29** with accompanying notes. The total number of genuine coins known to exist is not far short of a thousand.

There is a vast literature on the emergence of a papal state in the eighth century and the subsequent attempts to arrive at satisfactory constitutional arrangements between the popes and the kings of Italy, who normally were also crowned emperors and as such had ill-defined claims to sovereignty over Rome. The authoritative work on the origins of the Papal State was for long that of Duchesne (1904), whose author had produced a monumental edition of the *Liber Pontificalis*, the collection of often contemporary papal biographies which is our main authority for papal history in the period (Duchesne 1886–92). Of more recent works the most useful are vols. IX and X of the multi-volume *Storia di Roma* (Bertolini 1941; Brezzi 1947) and, in English, Llewellyn 1971 and the early chapters of Partner 1972 for the history of the Papal State, Ullmann 1970 for the constitutional background. Fully documented biographies of the popes are available in vols. I–IV of Mann 1902.

Historical background

The papal States (*Patrimonium Petri*) extended across the Italian peninsula, separating Frankish Italy proper from the old Lombard duchies of Spoleto and Benevento. They consisted essentially of two blocks of territory, linked to each other by a narrow corridor following the Tiber valley with Perugia at its centre. On the Adriatic coast were the Romagna and the Pentapolis, extending from the mouth of the Po southwards to Ancona. On the Tyrrhenian coast the area extended from Civitavecchia as far south as Terracina.

The state came into existence in the second half of the eighth century, and had a double origin. In the Tyrrhenian area, centred on Rome itself, the popes, with the immense prestige of their office and their great wealth, had little by little come to supplant the dukes appointed by Constantinople. Although the exact steps by which they took over the government of Rome and its surrounding territory cannot be precisely traced or dated, formal recognition of Byzantine authority does not seem to have continued beyond 781, when the emperor's regnal years ceased to be used for dating papal documents and the minting of imperial coins in the mint of Rome had already come to an end (*DOC* III.90–1). The area centred on Ravenna, on the other hand,

Table 20. *Popes of the* Antiquiores *period*

What may be regarded as the 'authorized' list of popes is one carefully revised by Angelo Mercati, Prefect of the Vatican Library, and published in the *Annuario Pontificio* in 1947. It is available in English, with Mercati's introductory essay, in *Medieval Studies* 9 (Toronto, 1947), 71–80. There has always been some confusion in the numbering, either because of uncertainty as to which names should be omitted as being those of antipopes or for other reasons. The following list covers the period of the *antiquiores* and indicates for which popes coins are known. An asterisk means that these are represented by genuine coins in the collection, a dagger that they are represented by forgeries. A number of the earliest coins are cited from the Tiber hoard (see note to **1.1030**), which is unpublished at the time of writing but whose contents have been kindly communicated to us by Mr M. D. O'Hara.

Gregory III, 731–41	Minted with Emp. Leo III: **1.1030★**; also *exagia*.
Zachary, 741–51	Minted with Emp. Constantine V (Tiber hoard); also *exagia*: **1.1513†**.
Stephen (II), 752	Died before being crowned, so often omitted.
Stephen II (III), 752–7	Minted with Emp. Constantine V (Tiber hoard).
Paul I, 757–67	Minted with Emp. Constantine V (Tiber hoard). A forgery of Cigoi also exists.
Constantine (II), 767–8	Antipope. No coins known.
Stephen III (IV), 768–72	Minted with Emp. Constantine V (Tiber hoard).
Adrian I, 772–95	Minted alone: **1.1031–2★**.
Leo III, 795–816	Minted alone: **1.1033★**, with Charlemagne: **1.1514†**, and with Louis I the Pious.
Stephen IV (V), 816–17	Minted with Louis I.
Paschal I, 817–24	Minted with Louis I.
Eugenius II, 824–7	Minted with Louis I.
Valentine, 827	Minted with Louis I.
Gregory IV, 827–44	Minted with Louis I (827–40): **1.1034–8★**, with Lothar I (840–4): **1.1039**.
Sergius II, 844–7	Minted with Lothar I: **1.1040–1★**.
Leo IV, 847–55	Minted with Lothar I: **1.1042–5★**.
Benedict III, 855–8	Minted with Lothar I (855), with Louis II (855–8): **1.1046–7★**.
Anastasius, 855	Antipope. No coins.
Nicholas I, 858–67	Minted with Louis II: **1.1048–9★**; **1.1515–16†**.
Adrian II, 867–72	Minted with Louis II: **1.1050–1★**.
John VIII, 872–82	Minted with Louis II (872–5): **1.1052★**, with Charles the Bald (875–7) and Charles the Fat (881–2): **1.1053★**; also at Capua: **1.1510–11†**.
Marinus I, 882–4	Minted with Charles the Fat.
Adrian III, 884–5	Minted with Charles the Fat: **1.1517†**.
Stephen V (VI), 885–91	Minted with Charles the Fat (885–8): **1.1054–6★**, alone (888–91), with Guy of Spoleto (891).

Table 20 (*cont.*)

Formosus, 891–6	Minted with Guy of Spoleto (891–4): **1.1057–9★**, with Arnulf of Carinthia (894–6)
Boniface VI, 896	No coins known (pope 10–26 April).
Stephen VI (VII), 896–7	Minted with Arnulf (896): **1.1060–1★**, **1.1518–19†**; with Lambert (897).
Romanus, 897	Minted with Lambert: **1.1062★**.
Theodore II, 897	Minted with Lambert.
John IX, 898–900	Minted with Lambert (898 and later): **1.1063–4★**, **1.1520†**.
Benedict IV, 900–3	Minted alone (900–1): **1.1065★**, with Louis III (901–3): **1.1066–8★**.
Leo V, 903	No coins known (pope July–September).
Christopher, 903–4	Antipope. Only forgeries known: **1.1521†**.
Sergius III, 904–11	Minted with Louis III (904–5), alone (905–11): **1.1069–71★**.
Anastasius III, 911–13	Minted alone.
Lando, 913–14	No coins known (pope July 913–February 914).
John X, 914–28	Minted alone (914–15): **1.1522†**, with Berengar I (915–24 or to 928?): **1.1072–4★**.
Leo VI 928	No coins known (pope May–December).
Stephen VII (VIII), 928–31	Minted alone.
John XI, 931–5	Minted alone (931–2), with Alberic (932?): **1.1523–4†**.
Alberic	*Senator* and *Princeps Romanorum*. Minted alone (932–54): **1.1076–7★**, **1.1525†**, as well as with popes as indicated.
Leo VII, 936–9	Minted with Alberic (936?): **1.1075★.**
Stephen VIII (IX), 939–42	No coins known.
Marinus II, 942–6	Minted with Alberic (942?).
Agapitus II, 946–55	Minted with Alberic (946?), alone (954–5).
John XII, 955–63	Minted alone (955–62), with Otto I (962–3): **1.1078★**; forgery in the name of Octavian: **1.1526†**.
Leo VIII, 963–5	Sometimes regarded as antipope, on the ground that the deposition of John XII was illegal. Minted with Otto I.
Benedict V, 964	Usurper. Minted with Otto I? (the coins may be of Benedict VI).
John XIII, 965–72	Minted with Otto I: **1.1079–81★**; **1.1527†**.
Benedict VI, 973–4	Perhaps minted with Otto I (d. 7.5.973) and with Otto II.
Boniface VII, 974	Antipope. No coins known.
Benedict VII, 974–83	Minted with Otto II: **1.1082–4★**.
John XIV, 983–4	No coins known for certain, and probably did not mint.
Boniface VII, restored 984–5	Antipope. Probably did not mint.
John XV, 985–96	Did not mint.

1.1528 and **1.1529** are forgeries in the names of Leo IX and Henry III (1049–54) and of Paschal II (1099–1118) respectively.

was conquered from Byzantium by the Lombards in 751 (above, p. 57), and when the Lombard king Aistulf was compelled to resign it to Pepin in 756 the Frankish king, instead of returning it to Byzantium, handed it over to Pope Stephen II.

The exercise of sovereignty presented the popes with problems that offered no easy solution, for they were not powerful enough to deal with local enemies – this was apparent in the disputed election that followed the death of Paul I in 767 – or more distant ones. When Charlemagne visited Rome at Easter 774 he therefore promised Adrian I a much vaster state, comprising all Italy south of a line drawn from Luni in the west to Venice in the north-east. This would have left the popes strong enough to stand up against the Lombards, the Byzantines, and their Spoletan and Beneventan neighbours and not require repeated Frankish intervention in the peninsula. Two months later, however, Charlemagne's plans were changed, for after the capitulation of Pavia he made himself king of the Lombards. Since he now saw no need to create a strong papal state he did nothing either to implement his undertaking or, apparently, to explain to Pope Adrian why he was not doing so. Some years of acrimonious correspondence ensued, till Charles on his second visit to Rome in 781 straightened out matters. The popes were left with a papal state much smaller than that envisaged in the donation of 774 but which corresponded more or less to that described at the opening of this section. Sovereignty over it seems to have remained a little uncertain, for while Adrian I, and after him Leo III, were able to mint at Rome without reference to Charles, Charles for his part minted at Ravenna, at least after 794, without reference to the pope (above, p. 202 and note on **1.1499**).

Charlemagne's coronation on Christmas Day 800 partly solved the constitutional issue. Our best testimony to this is in fact the coinage of Rome (Grierson 1952b). Minting, an essential mark of sovereignty, remained in papal hands, but the coins of the papal mint were struck in the names of both emperor and pope. This arrangement lasted for over a century and a half, despite the many fluctuations in the position of the popes. Their problem was that they were more venerated outside Rome than inside it, where their independence was threatened by the local aristocracy. They had in addition to take account of Saracen attacks and, from the late ninth century onwards, of a revival of Byzantine power. Emperors beyond the Alps could give them help only in emergencies, not in a continuous fashion, while emperors whose power base was in Italy were too close for comfort. In the early tenth century the decline of imperial power paved the way for what the great sixteenth-century Church historian Cardinal Baronius bluntly termed a pornocracy, when Rome was ruled in turn by the lovers, husbands or sons of two remarkable women, Theodora and Marozia. Only the eventual intervention of the Ottonian emperors saved it from becoming no more than a petty Italian lordship.

Coinage

The Papal States were thus an anomalous element in the Carolingian Empire, and in the Ottonian Empire after it, for with papal claims to sovereignty went a coinage. The continuous history of this lasted almost exactly two centuries, from Adrian I (772–95) to Benedict VII (974–83). Prior to Adrian's time there are copper 'coins' of Popes Gregory III (731–41) and Zachary (741–51), but where these are not forgeries they seem rather to be coin weights (*exagia*) for weighing solidi and tremisses. They are discussed in the note to **1.1513**. There was also an approach to a silver coinage with an imperial bust on one side and a series of papal monograms or initials on the other (see note to **1.1030**). At the other end, the only coins ostensibly later than those of Benedict VII and Otto, denari of Leo IX (1049–54) and Henry III and a silver bracteate of Pope Paschal II (1099–1118), are forgeries, the first group being the work of the early twentieth-century forger Tardani and the latter going back to the eighteenth century (see notes to **1.1528** and **1529**). The normal practice, from 800 onwards, was for the coins to be struck with the names or monograms of both pope and emperor. After an emperor's death the pope would continue to use his name on the coins until a new one was crowned, though when a pope was elected during an imperial vacancy he would start minting in his name alone. The only anomaly in the series was provided by the Senator Alberic, Marozia's son, who minted in his name alone, something no emperor ever attempted to do at Rome.

The coinage is entirely one of silver denari: no gold was ever struck, nor are there obols. The abandonment of gold in favour of silver was a consequence of the close political and economic ties between the papacy and the Frankish and Anglo-Saxon worlds. The princes of Benevento, in contrast, remained more closely linked with Byzantium and continued to mint gold coins for seventy years after their issue had ceased at Rome. The weights of the Roman denari, however, seem to have conformed only for a time to those of the Frankish kingdom, though precise comparisons are rendered difficult by the rarity of the coins, by the poor state of many specimens, by their having been struck *al marco* with a consequent wide weight span, and by the existence of many forgeries.

The earliest coins, with a GREO monogram, weigh *c.* 0.35g and are probably double siliquae (0.189g) by weight, though it is unclear how they were related in value to the debased solidi and tremisses then being struck by the Roman mint. Pope Adrian's earliest silver coins of the late 770s (see note to **1.1031**), are likewise Roman in their weight pattern, for at *c.* 1.15g they probably represent a scruple (*scripulum*) of 1.14g. Coins of his Class 2, and those of Leo III's Class 1, i.e. the coinage of the two decades 781–800, weigh *c.* 1.3g, thus conforming to the light Frankish denier introduced into Italy in 781. In 800, with the start of the papal-imperial series, the 'new' Frankish standard of *c.* 1.75g was adopted. A document of the great abbey of Farfa, which lay in the Papal States north of Rome, shows that in 816 nine new denari of the *moneta S. Petri* were the equivalent of twelve of the old denari (Capobianchi 1900, 57), which is what the weight change involved would lead us to expect.

The link between Frankish and papal coinage lasted only some forty years. The earliest denari of Gregory IV (828–44) remain of good weight, but his later ones are very irregular and those of his successors rarely reach 1.6g, the average being about 1.3g and individual specimens in good condition being sometimes not above 1.0g. It seems likely that at some moment after Louis the Pious' death, with Italy becoming a kingdom more and more distinct from the rest of the Frankish dominions, the papal mint abandoned the Frankish 16oz pound in favour of the old 12oz one and made the denaro $\frac{1}{240}$ of this, i.e. a nominal 1.36g. This new weight standard lasted for a century. Alberic (932–54) then apparently reverted to the Frankish standard, for from his reign to the end of papal minting the coins normally exceed 1.35g in weight and often reach 1.7g. The reason was perhaps a wish to align them with the coinage of Lucca. This underwent a marked revival in the 930s under the marquesses of Tuscany, and the city became under the Ottonians one of the main mints of Italy.

The great majority of *antiquiores* resemble in their size and general appearance those of the Frankish kingdom of Italy and its Ottonian successor. This is not true of papal coins struck prior to 800, or of those of the two decades after 877 and prior to the revival of the Empire in 962. The earliest papal coins still display many Byzantine features. In the last quarter of the ninth century they failed to follow the example of north Italian mints in the introduction of large-module half-bracteates, nor do their tenth-century coins exhibit anything comparable to the turned-up edges of *scodellati*. Under Alberic there was a belated introduction of thin coins of rather large module (*c.* 25mm), and when this brief aberration ended the coins were made smaller (*c.* 18mm) and thicker than they had been in the ninth century. In this they were only conforming to the general pattern of Italian coins in the Ottonian period.

Since papal coins had to include the names or monograms of two co-rulers, the usual Frankish pattern of a monogram on one face and a cross on the other could not be taken over unchanged. The normal obverse inscription was + SCS PETRVS and the type a monogram containing the chief letters of the pope's name and sometimes including a cross or the letters PA (for *papa*). The reverse balances this with the emperor's name and in the field a monogram of IMP or IMPA or, if IMP(*erator*) makes part of the inscription, a monogram of PIVS or ROMA(*nus*), the latter having several variant forms. The monogram is sometimes replaced by the equivalent letters in several lines across the field (e.g. PP/GRE/II or RO/MA) or by some other inscription (e.g. FI/ERI/IV(*ssit*)). The monograms are in general easy to decipher (cf. Pflugk-Harttung 1903), but at least one has defied identification, perhaps because it is that of the otherwise unrecorded name of a pope who changed his name on his election (see note on **1.1056**).

An obviously suitable type for a papal coin was a bust of St Peter. This was used on coins struck by Leo III before 800 (**1.1033**), and the type was revived by John VIII (**1.1053**), after which it is common, being used on nearly a third of the issues between then and the end of papal coinage a century later. In a few cases it is not easy to say if the bust, whether mitred or not, represents St Peter or the reigning pope (see **1.1072**). Since the popes of the period were accustomed to identify their authority with that of the Prince of the Apostles and sometimes used his name in the first person when addressing correspondents, it is possible that neither they nor contemporary users would have made much distinction between them. In a few instances – Adrian I (**1.1031–2**), Benedict VI or VII (**1.1082–3**) – the inscriptions make it clear that the effigy is that of the pope (cf. Ladner, 1935, 1941). Other types are rare: a church under John X, a hand flanked by the letters R O (i.e. a rebus for *Romanus*) under Benedict IV and Louis III (**1.1068**), a hand alone under John XIII and Otto I, a plant under Boniface VI and Otto II. The meaning of the last is obscure, as is that of the rosette which is sometimes prominent in inscriptions and types from the 870s onwards.

Two types of particular interest, not represented in this collection, are found on coins of John XI (931–5), for the details of a flower pattern and church on the reverses of these show them to have been inspired by rare Anglo-Saxon coins of Edward the Elder (899–924) and Æthelstan (924–39) respectively (Blunt 1948b). Anglo-Saxon coins reached Rome in substantial numbers (Blunt 1986), either as official offerings of Peter's Pence or as pilgrims' gifts, though by chance neither of these flower types is represented in the large hoard (Rossi 1884) of 830 Anglo-Saxon coins of the period that was found in 1883 during the excavation of the house of the Vestals at Rome and was buried during the pontificate of Marinus II (942–6).

The practice of minting in the joint names of pope and emperor broke down in the 920s for nearly four decades, since there was a gap in the sequence of emperors between Berengar I, who died in 924, and Otto I, who became emperor only in 962. This gap coincided with the seizure of Rome by a powerful local magnate, Alberic II of Spoleto, son of Marozia, who drove out Hugh of Arles in 932, took control of Rome with the titles of *Senator* and *Princeps Romanorum*, held the city for two decades down to his death in 954 (Sickel 1902; Arnaldi 1957), and in dying was able to leave it to his son Octavian, who ruled it first under the same titles as his father and subsequently, as John XII (955–63), with that of pope.

Alberic is variously judged by chroniclers of the time, though they agree on the effectiveness of his authority. Benedict of S. Andrea, for whom he was a *gloriosus princeps* characterized by his handsome presence and 'old-time worth' (*grandevus virtus eius*), admits to his formidable character and the way in which 'his yoke lay heavily on the Romans and on the holy Apostolic See' (*erat enim terribilis nimis et aggrabatum est iugum super Romanos et in Sancte Sedis apostolice*). For Liutprand, a less well-disposed contemporary, he is *impiisimus Albericus*, a usurper and tyrant who treated the pope as a domestic servant at his beck and call (*dominumque apostolicum quasi servum proprium in conclavi teneret*). The truth of these strictures is very evident from his coinage. The pope at the time of his accession was John XI (931–5), who prior to 932 had minted in his own name. Alberic promptly took control of the mint, and while leaving John's name and monogram on the obverse of the coins made plain the source of authority by placing his own name, followed by FIERI IV(*ssit*) in the field, on the other (see **1.1523**, forgery). Coins of subsequent popes in association with the Senator are exceedingly rare: two fragments of those of Leo VII (935–9: see note on **1.1075**), *unica* of those of John XI (931–5), Marinus II (942–6) and Agapitus II (946–55), and none at all of Alberic in association with Stephen VIII (939–42), though specimens may yet come to light. In contrast to these are the relatively common coins with the name and title of Alberic (ALBRICVS PRIN) and a monogram in the field containing the letters PAC–VS (**1.1076–7**). The monogram has been read by some scholars as *Agapitus*, making the coins a joint issue of Senator and pope, but either *patricius* or *pacificus* is more likely (see note to **1.1076**), leaving the coins to Alberic alone. It seems clear these formed the main issue of the whole period 932–54; the rare papal-senatorial coins were no more than complimentary issues struck in the name of each pope on his accession.

The date and circumstances in which the issue of the *antiquiores* came to an end are both unknown. The latest coins are those in the names of Otto (II) and a Pope Benedict. There were three popes of this name in a very short period: Benedict V (964–6), Benedict VI (973–4) and Benedict VII (974–83). No satisfactory distinction can be made between the coinages of the three, but the first two pontificates were short and some at least of the five types known must belong to the nine years of Benedict VII. The relations between this pope and Otto II were exceptionally friendly, and there seems to be nothing in the political history of the period that could have led either of them to close the mint of Rome.

Benedict VII's successor John XIV was nominated by Otto II in late November or early December 983. He reigned for only four months, since Otto's death on 7 December 983 left him without a protector. In April 984, after a *coup d'état* by a certain Boniface (VII) who had been briefly antipope in 974, he was overthrown and locked up in Castel S. Angelo, where he died, reputedly murdered, on 20 August. Coins have been ascribed to him, but very doubtfully. There are certainly none of either Boniface VII's second pontificate (984–5) or that of John XV (985–96), for these coincided with an imperial vacancy and there are no coins of this period in the name of a pope alone. Nor are there any of Crescentius *de Nomentana*, who exercised a virtual dictatorship over Rome during the pontificates of John XV (985–96) and Gregory V (996–9) comparable to that of Alberic earlier in the century and who might have been expected to emulate his predecessor in issuing coin.

Minting at Rome therefore stopped some time during the pontificate of Benedict VII, and at latest by the winter of 983/4. A formal imperial prohibition by Otto II may be ruled out. The popes minted by ancient custom, not imperial concession. If they had simply been prevented from minting by Otto II, they would surely have seized the opportunity to reopen the mint during the thirteen years between Otto II's death in 983 and Otto III's coronation in 996 or after the eclipse of imperial authority in Italy that followed Otto III's own death in 1002.

The explanation, in fact, was probably economic rather than political. Denari of the imperial mints in Italy – Pavia, Milan and Verona in the north, Lucca in Tuscany – had become by the second half of the tenth century so generally acceptable that their papal counterparts could not compete with them. The position of Rome can be compared with that of Ravenna and Aquileia. The archbishops of both were granted minting rights in this period, Ravenna by Pope Gregory V in 998 and Aquileia by Conrad II in 1028, but neither grant came to anything. No use at all seems to have been made of the first, and the coinage of Poppo of Aquileia is known only from a single specimen found in Poland in 1878. The papal coinage of Rome was thus not the only one in Italy unable to compete with the output of the imperial mints, though it still remains surprising that the popes, usually so jealous of their privileges and solicitous in the maintenance of ancient traditions, should not have continued to mint on a token basis, at least for ceremonial purposes.

10

THE ANGLO-SAXONS AND VIKINGS: EIGHTH – TENTH CENTURIES

(a) GENERAL FEATURES

Literature

There is no comprehensive survey of Anglo-Saxon coinage. Those of Lindsay 1842, Hawkins 1887, *BMC AS* and to some extent Brooke 1950 are now outdated, and Sutherland 1973 deals only briefly with the period. The most useful general account will be found in the booklets of Dolley 1964 and 1965a, although limited in information by their size. A number of excellent papers survey particular coinages or periods and are referred to in the relevant sections below.

The type catalogue by North (vol. I, 1980) takes account of recent literature and is useful for quick identification and reference. The British Museum collection was published in 1887–93 (*BMC AS*) with additions in Brooke 1922–5; the provenances of the coins, omitted in the main catalogue, are given in Dolley and Strudwick 1955. Other important collections have been published in the *Sylloge of Coins of the British Isles*; particularly relevant to this period are vols. 1 (Fitzwilliam Museum), 2 (Hunterian Museum, Glasgow), 4 (National Museum, Copenhagen part 1), 9 (Ashmolean Museum, Oxford), 20 (R. P. Mack collection) and 26 (East Anglian Museums, including the Morley St Peter hoard). A number of auction catalogues have outstanding material, most notably Montagu parts I and V (Sotheby 18.11.1895 and 16.11.1897), Carlyon-Britton parts I–III (Sotheby 17.11.1913, 20.11.1916 and 11.11.1918) and Lockett, parts I, VII and X (Glendining 6.6.1955, 4.11.1958 and 26.4.1960). Most of the earlier Anglo-Saxon coins in the Lockett collection are illustrated in the catalogues, but a complete photographic record of the English, Irish and Scottish coins in the collection was made by the British Numismatic Society, copies of which were available for purchase. Lockett's own manuscript catalogues of the collection, which often give fuller provenances, are the property of the British Numismatic Society but are deposited in the Coin Room at the British Museum.

On the hoards, Thompson 1956 provides a detailed though often inaccurate listing. Subsequent emendations are summarized by Dolley in his 'check-list' of hoards (Dolley 1966, 47–54), to be further updated in Blackburn and Pagan 1986.

The most authoritative historical work is Stenton 1971. Shorter surveys include Hunter-Blair 1977, Brooke 1963, and Fisher 1973. On the Viking communities in Britain see Smyth 1975–9 and Loyn 1977. On the social, economic and administrative aspects see Loyn 1968 and 1984, and for the church of Canterbury, Brooks 1984. The *Anglo-Saxon Chronicle* and other significant documents can conveniently be consulted in translation in Whitelock 1979 and for the reign of Alfred in Keynes and Lapidge 1983, both with critical introductions and references to the best editions of the texts. There are few documents that relate directly to the coinage. The essential guide to the charters, most of which are collected in Birch 1885–93, is Sawyer 1968; writs are collected in Harmer 1952 and wills in Whitelock 1930. Powicke and Fryde 1961 is useful for its lists of regal and episcopal dates, although some of the latter have been revised in O'Donovan 1972–3. Hill 1981 provides stimulating maps and diagrams.

Historical background

This chapter covers the two and a half centuries from the introduction of the broader 'penny' coinage until shortly before the first unification of England, i.e. from the reign of Offa (757–96) to that of Edward the Elder (899–924), but the Anglo-Viking coinages, which continued intermittently beyond 924, are taken to their final conclusion in 954. It thus encompasses the coinages of five kingdoms and several regions of Viking settlement, together with those of a few archbishops of York and Canterbury and perhaps bishops of London and Rochester. It has until recently been customary to arrange it under rulers – coins of the kings of Kent, of Mercia, and so on – but so interrelated are the coinages, successively ousting one another from a limited number of mints or forming groups characterized by identical or virtually identical types, that they cannot satisfactorily be considered in isolation. In this they reflect the history of the period generally.

The first century of the coinage (*c.* 770–*c.* 870) can be divided broadly into two phases. Until *c.* 825 Mercia was the dominant power in England south of the Humber, and save for some brief interludes it largely controlled the mints in that area. It absorbed the weakest kingdoms such as Middle Anglia and Lindsey, while others, East Anglia, Kent, Essex and Sussex, became subservient to it; only Wessex remained independent. But the first half of the ninth century saw a decline in Mercian power, especially after its defeat by Wessex at the battle of *Ellendun* in 825. Within a short time Mercia had lost control of Kent and East Anglia, but its fortunes reached their lowest ebb in 829, when Egbert of Wessex 'conquered the kingdom of the Mercians and everything south of the Humber' and had coins struck at London bearing the title *Rex M(erciorum)* (**1.1166**). Mercian independence was restored in the following year, but Egbert was left in control of Kent (with the important mint of Canterbury), Sussex and Essex (which did not include London at this date), while East Anglia remained under the control of local kings. Northumbria, separate and remote from the politics of southern England, was independent throughout.

Viking raids on Britain began in the last decade of the eighth century. They became more intense in the 830s and 840s and again in the 860s, resulting in the conquest of York in 866/7 and East Anglia in 869. In 874 the Vikings defeated the Mercian king and settled much of eastern Mercia, as well as Northumbria and East Anglia. This region, known as the Danelaw, became deeply impressed with Scandinavian culture and institutions, and the towns of York and Lincoln assumed a new commercial impetus.

Wessex was the only English kingdom to survive these wars, and Alfred the Great (871–99) was accepted as ruler of all England outside the Danelaw. He regained London in 886 and entered into a treaty with the Danes in East Anglia. His son Edward the Elder inflicted a major though

Table 21. *Kings and archbishops in England*, c. *760–924*

MERCIA	WESSEX	KENT/S.E. ENGLAND
Offa (757–96)	*Cynewulf (757–86)*	Heabert (*c.* 765)
Ecgfrith (sub-king) 787–96: king 796)	Beorhtric (786–802)	Egbert (*c.* 765–*c.* 780 or later)
Coenwulf (796–821)	Egbert (802–39)	*Ealhmund* (*c.* 784)
Ceolwulf I (821–3)	Æthelwulf (839–58)	Eadbert Praen (796–8)
Beornwulf (823–6)	*Æthelbald* (sub-king 855–8; king 858–60)	Cuthred (798–807)
Ludica (826–7)	Æthelbert (860–5)	Baldred (expelled 825)
Wiglaf (827–9 and 830–*c.* 840)	Æthelred I (865–71)	Æthelwulf (sub-king 825–39)
Berhtwulf (840–52)	Alfred (871–99)	*Æthelstan* (sub-king 839–*c.* 851)
Burgred (852–74)	Edward the Elder (899–924)	Æthelbert (sub-king 855–8; king 858–65)
Ceolwulf II (874–*c.* 880)		

NORTHUMBRIA	VIKINGS OF YORK	EAST ANGLIA
Eadbert (738–58)	*Halfdan I* (876–7)	Beonna (749–57 or later)
Oswulf (758)	Guthfrith (*c.* 883–95)	*Æthelred*
Æthelwald 'Moll' (759–65)	Siefred (895–*c.* 901?)	Æthelbert (d. 794)
Alchred (765–74)	Cnut (*c.* 900–*c.* 902)	Eadwald (*c.* 796–800?)
Æthelred I (774–9)	Æthelwold (900)	Æthelstan (*c.* 825–*c.* 845)
Ælfwald I (779–88)	*Halfdan II* (*c.* 902–10)	Æthelweard (*c.* 845–55)
Osred (788–90)	*Eowils* (d. 910)	Edmund (855–69)
Æthelred I (790–6)	Ragnald (*c.* 914?, *c.* 919–21)	
Osbald (796)	Sihtric Caoch (921–7)	**VIKINGS OF EAST ANGLIA**
Eardwulf (796–*c.* 808 and *c.* 808–10?)	*Guthfrith* (927)	Guthrum (Æthelstan) (880–90)
Ælfwald II (*c.* 808?)	Anlaf Guthfrithsson (939–41)	*Eohric* (d. 902)
Eanred (*c.* 810–*c.* 840)	Anlaf Sihtricsson (941–3, 949–52)	
Æthelred II (*c.* 840–*c.* 844)	Sihtric (*c.* 942)	**ARCHBISHOPS OF CANTERBURY**
Redwulf (*c.* 844)	Ragnald Guthfrithsson (943–4)	
Æthelred II (*c.* 844–*c.* 848)	Eric Bloodaxe (948, 952–4)	*Breguwine* (761–4)
Osbert (848/850–67)	**ARCHBISHOPS OF YORK**	Jaenberht (765–92)
Ælla (d. 867)	Egbert (*c.* 732–66)	Æthelheard (793–805)
There followed a series of nominal English kings appointed by the Vikings.	*Æthelbert* (767–80)	Wulfred (805–32)
	Eanbald I (780–96)	*Feolgild* (832)
	Eanbald II (796–830s?)	Ceolnoth (833–70)
	Wulfsige	Æthelred (870–88)
	Wigmund (*c.* 837–*c.* 854)	Plegmund (890–923)
	Wulfhere (*c.* 854–900?)	

Note: Those with names in italics are not known to have struck coins. Some of the traditional dates for the kings of Northumbria and the archbishops of York are at variance with the numismatic evidence (below pp. 301–3).

not final defeat on the Northumbrian Vikings in 910 at Tettenhall (Staffs.), and by the end of his reign East Anglia and the Danish Midlands had been reconquered. In 927 the people of York submitted to Æthelstan (924–39), who on charters and coins claimed with some justification to be 'king of the whole of Britain' (*rex totius Britanniae*). But on his death the Norsemen of Dublin seized the opportunity to return to York, and they were not finally ousted until 954.

Coinage

The penny was virtually the sole denomination in mid and late Anglo-Saxon coinage. A small number of round halfpennies were struck in the late ninth and tenth centuries, apparently introduced as part of Alfred's currency reform in the 880s. The view that they were third-pennies (Grierson 1957) must be abandoned, despite the occurrence of this fraction in the laws, for the coins in the name of Alfred on which the argument was mainly based are in fact light-weight Viking imitations (Dolley and Blunt 1961, 89) and the few tenth-century specimens are too heavy to be thirds (Blunt 1962b). (Grierson's article retains its value, however, for its illustrations and its reconstruction of the Stamford hoard.) Halfpennies were also produced by cutting pennies in two with a chisel from at least the mid ninth century onwards, although they are rare until Eadgar's reform of *c.* 973 after which cut farthings are also often found (on the technique of cutting, see Northover in Biddle *et al.* 1986). Thereafter, except for a unique issue of round halfpennies under Henry I, this was the only way in which fractions of the penny were made until Edward I revived round halfpennies and introduced round farthings in 1279. The only coins of higher value were gold *mancuses* – the word came from Arabic – which had a value of 30 pence, and these were struck only occasionally and for eleemosynary purposes (below, pp. 327, 330). The same is expressly proclaimed by the inscription ELIMO– on some heavy silver coin-like objects of Alfred, though their weight (*c.* 160gr./10.5g) suggests that they were ⅓ oz pieces and not simple multiples of the penny.

The weight of the penny itself underwent three major changes during the eighth and ninth centuries (Lyon 1969, 212–14). With the introduction of the broader penny fabric in the 760s or 770s the weight was restored to that of the earliest Primary series of sceattas, with a median of *c.* 18gr. (1.17g) apparently representing a theoretical standard of 20gr. (1.30g). Towards the end of Offa's reign, probably in 792, the weight was increased, resulting in a median of *c.* 21gr. (1.36g), which may represent a theoretical weight of 22½gr. (1.46g). A similar standard was adopted by the independent East Anglian kings and in the Viking coinages of the late ninth century; it was adhered to with varying degrees of accuracy at the Kentish and London mints, although in the mid ninth century, when there was also some debasement, the median weight declined slightly. In the 880s Alfred raised the weight standard, and the later coins of Alfred and those of Edward the Elder and Æthelstan have a median of *c.* 24gr. (1.56g), although the weight again declined in the third quarter of the tenth century. In Northumbria, the weights of the small thick module coins, which continued to be struck during the second half of the eighth century and again for some forty years in the mid ninth century, remained broadly unchanged, with a median of around 18gr. (1.17g) but with individual coins often well above or below this figure. The 1.75g standard of Charlemagne's reformed coinage of 793/4 was nowhere adopted in England, since it was based on a lighter grain (above, p. 206) and resulted in a denier equivalent to about 27 English grains.

By the mid eighth century the silver coins of southern England had become extremely base, less than 20% silver at some mints. In Northumbria, the coins of Eadberht (738–58) are about 50–75% silver, a standard which was broadly maintained under his immediate successors, but in the second quarter of the ninth century, when minting resumed in the north after a break of 20–30 years, the quality of the coins declined sharply, becoming merely brass in their later stages. For southern coinage there is little information on late eighth- and early ninth-century pennies, but what there is suggests a high standard of 95% silver or more (Metcalf 1972b, 408). During the second and third quarters of the ninth century some debasement is apparent, and the fineness may have been deliberately manipulated in the course of some issues (see pp. 307–9 below), while towards the end of the Lunette type, in the early 870s at the height of the Viking wars, the standard fell to 20% or less. Within a few years Alfred was able to restore the coinage to more than 90% silver, a fineness maintained for English and Viking coins alike in the late ninth and early tenth centuries.

With the introduction of the broader penny *c.* 770 the coinage of southern England became for the first time specifically royal in character, as had the coinage of the Franks a few years earlier (above, p. 195). Most coins bear the name of a king, normally in a circular inscription, with the title *rex* and often the name or initial of the appropriate kingdom or people, *Merciorum*, *Saxoniorum* or *Saxoniorum Occidentalium*, *Cantiorum*, and *Anglorum* (for England or, on the East Anglian coins, for Anglia). *Rex* $\bar{H}$ (for *Hrofesceastre*?) is found on some Rochester coins of Baldred. On the reverse they normally bear the name of the moneyer, and only very occasionally the mint. In this respect they differ from the earlier gold and silver coinages which were for the most part uninscribed. To what extent this represents a change in the organization of the currency it is hard to say (see p. 159 above). An exceptional issue bears the name of Offa's queen, Cynethryth.

The Anglo-Saxons occasionally followed the Carolingian practice of granting their heirs a sub-kingdom to rule during their life, but few of them were allowed to strike coins. Cuthred was an exception, for between *c.* 800 and 807 he issued coins at Canterbury as sub-king of Kent, probably to the exclusion of his brother, Coenwulf of Mercia. Æthelwulf may also have struck coins as sub-king of Kent during his father's lifetime (below, p. 291), though they more probably belong after his accession to the West Saxon kingdom. No coins are known for Ecgfrith as sub-king of Mercia, for Æthelstan or Æthelbert as sub-kings of Kent or for Æthelbald as sub-king of Wessex. Similarly, in the tenth century, Edgar apparently did not strike any coins as king of the Mercians and Northumbrians during Edwig's reign (955–9).

During most of the medieval period the archbishops of Canterbury and York, and from time to time other prelates, enjoyed limited rights of striking coin or participating in the profits of minting (Blunt 1960). From the eighth until the early tenth century, many ecclesiastical coins bore the name of the prelate or were differentiated from the regal coinage by their design. Thereafter, until the fourteenth century, they were usually indistinguishable from the regal coins.

The earliest recognizable ecclesiastical coins are those of Archbishop Egbert of York with

King Eadbert (738–58). Later in the eighth century, Archbishops Jaenberht and Æthelheard of Canterbury and Bishop Eadberht of London followed this Northumbrian precedent, placing the king's name on the obverse and their own on the reverse – the position of the dies is indicated by an obverse die-link between Offa's and Jaenberht's coinages (Blunt 1958). The coins of Archbishop Wulfred (805–32) omit any reference to royal authority, and his skilful diplomacy avoided choosing between Coenwulf of Mercia and Cuthred of Kent, for both of whom the Canterbury mint had issued coins, while at the same time promoting the independence of the Church. Wulfred's earliest coins have the mint name, *Doroverniae civitatis*, on the reverse, but thereafter they have the moneyer's name. The same formula with a moneyer's name was employed by subsequent archbishops of Canterbury and York.

The bishop of London appears to have exercised minting rights for only a brief period during the 780s. The only episcopal coins of Rochester which have been distinguished belong to Bishop Beornmod (803/5–842/4), although none bears his name. Their attribution depends on the replacement of the moneyer's name with that of either St Andrew (the dedicatee of the minster at Rochester), or the mint (*Dorobrebia*), or the kingdom (*Saxoniorum Occidentalium*). The bishop's right to employ one moneyer is recorded again in a law code of Æthelstan (924–39), but we do not know how long it continued thereafter. There were no coins struck in the name of the archbishops of York after 867 or of Canterbury after 923, but the same code records rights at the Canterbury mint of the archbishop to two moneyers and of the abbot of St Augustine's to one moneyer. The substantial coinage invoking the name of St Peter struck by the Vikings at York in the early tenth century is probably not an ecclesiastical issue. At some stage, presumably later in the tenth century, minting rights were restored to the archbishops of York and maintained until the sixteenth century (Brooke 1950, 152–3).

The designs of the earlier ecclesiastical coinages were related to the regal coinage; they followed the current trend for either portrait or non-portrait issues and often adopted similar geometric designs. However, some followed papal prototypes, such as the three-line design used by Jaenberht and Bishop Eadberht and the facing tonsured bust used by Wulfred and Ceolnoth.

Few coins of this period bear the name of the mint. London (*Lundonia*), which was named on the early gold and silver coinages, is found on two special issues, one marking Egbert's conquest of the Mercians in 829–30 and the other Alfred's recapture of the city in 886. Canterbury (*Dorovernia* or *Dorobernia*: V and B were interchangeable) is specifically named on some coins of Ceolwulf I and on some of the archbishops Wulfred and Ceolnoth, and Rochester (*Dorobrebia*) is also found on some of Ceolwulf I's coins. Other issues have the ambiguous form DORO or DOROB which could stand for either city and in Æthelwulf's coinage it probably served for both; on Egbert's and Alfred's coins it is thought to refer only to Canterbury. At the end of the ninth and the beginning of the tenth century other mint names occur; on Alfred's last coinage – Exeter (EXA), Gloucester (GLEAWA), Oxford (OHSNAFORDA), and Winchester (WIN) – on Edward the Elder's – Bath (BAÐ) – and in the Viking coinages – York (EBRAICE or EBORACE) and Lincoln (LINCOLLA or LINCOIA).

Although the great majority of coins are silent as to their place of origin, many of them can be attributed to specific mints with varying degrees of confidence. Coins of the archbishops of Canterbury can be assumed to have been struck at Canterbury and those of the kings of Kent and of East Anglia presumably emanate from mints in the kingdoms. The moneyers of these issues can thus be localized, and their products for other rulers associated with the same mints. For other moneyers one may be able to suggest attributions based on similarities of type or die-cutting style, although such arguments must be used with caution for types may have been standardized at several mints and dies distributed from one main centre. Thus, while we have evidence for only four or five mints operating in the south before the end of the ninth century, it is possible that there were others of which we are unaware. Table 22 shows the recognized activity of the mints *c.* 750–900 and the changing political control of each.

The Northumbrian coinage, with its small module and base metal, remained entirely separate and distinct from those in the south. The regal and ecclesiastical coins are thought all to have been struck at York, although it is possible that some were struck elsewhere. The 'styca' coinage appears to have ceased with the Viking occupation of York in 867, and minting was not resumed until the 890s when the Vikings struck broad-flan pennies of fine silver.

In the south there was probably in most places a break in minting between the sceattas and the broad-flan pennies. In East Anglia minting may have been interrupted in the mid eighth century, but Beonna had resumed striking a reformed sceat coinage in his own name before Offa took control of the mint and one of Beonna's moneyers continues into the broad-flan series. The mint remained active until the Viking conquest of East Anglia in 869, striking primarily for the Mercian kings until 827, with two or three brief interruptions by local rulers, and thereafter for the independent kings of East Anglia. The sequence of moneyers suggests that the same mint was operating from Beonna until the Viking conquest, and indications suggest that no more than one mint was involved. Its location is uncertain, but recent commentators have preferred a southerly site, perhaps Ipswich (Pagan 1982a, 49; Archibald 1983). There was a break of some twenty years before the Vikings of East Anglia commenced striking coins, and Norwich is a strong candidate for at least part of the series which followed.

The majority of the southern coins appear to have been produced at three mints: Canterbury, Rochester and London. Canterbury operated more or less continuously throughout the period. It was probably the mint which initiated the broad-flan coinage in the 760s or early 770s and, save for brief interludes when local rulers seized control, it was dominated by the Mercian kings until *c.* 823. It then passed via a Kentish usurper into the hands of the kings of Wessex and it remained their principal mint until the end of the ninth century. Rochester is first identified as a mint *c.* 810, although it may have been active earlier. Its fortunes followed closely those of Canterbury and its products can be traced until the mid 850s, after which we do not know whether the mint was closed or continued to operate with dies sent from Canterbury. It is next recorded from a single mint-signed coin of Æthelstan (924–39), although its prominence in a law code of the same reign in which it is accorded three moneyers, including one for the bishop, suggests that it was a mint in the later ninth and early tenth century.

The products of the London mint are more difficult to identify. Several groups of coins struck for Mercian kings and with no specific associations with Kent or East Anglia have plausibly been attributed to a mint in Mercia, which it is reasonably assumed was at London (Blunt, Lyon and Stewart 1963, 30–6). However, the definition of the group, particularly under Offa,

Table 22. *Mint control and activity in England*, c. *750–900*

	CANTERBURY	ROCHESTER	LONDON	EAST ANGLIAN MINT	SOUTHAMPTON/ WINCHESTER	YORK
750	'sceattas'?		'sceattas'?	'sceattas'?	'sceattas'?	Northumbrian ('sceattas')
c. 760				E Anglian		
c. 770	Kentish?		Mercian	Mercian		
	Mercian					
c. 792				E Anglian		
794?				Mercian		
796	Kentish			E Anglian		
798	Mercian			Mercian		
c. 800	Kentish				West Saxon	
807	Mercian					
c. 810		Mercian				
c. 822	Anonymous					
c. 823	Kentish	Kentish				
825	West Saxon	West Saxon				
827			Mercian	E Anglian		
829			West Saxon			
830			Mercian?		West Saxon	Northumbrian ('stycas')
c. 843			Mercian			
851						
c. 852	West Saxon					
867						
869						
871			Mercian & West Saxon			
877?						
886			West Saxon			
890				Viking		
					West Saxon	Viking

Note. During the late 880s and 890s, new mints under the West Saxons were also opened at Exeter, Gloucester and Oxford, and one in the north west.

is difficult, and there are problems in attributing coins of the Mercian kings of the mid ninth century as some of them are struck from Rochester-style dies and by Rochester moneyers. We are reasonably certain that London was operating a mint during Offa's earlier, light coinage, and it is possible that it was responsible for instituting the broad-penny reform under Offa. In the ninth century its output was intermittent and often small; no coins are known for a decade or more in the 830s and early 840s. There was then great activity for a few years, followed by a decade of exiguous output. In the 860s and early 870s the number of moneyers striking Burgred's coinage increased from two to about 25, and if they were all operating from London its output may for the first time have exceeded that of Canterbury. The city was held by the Vikings for a few years, before being liberated by Alfred in 886. Thereafter the mint grew in stature, becoming consistently the country's largest mint from the tenth century onwards.

A small number of coins were produced in Wessex in the late eighth century and again in the mid ninth century. The location of the mint, or mints, is uncertain, though it is perhaps more likely to have been at Southampton than Winchester. Winchester is named on the coinage in the 890s and rapidly became one of the most important mints in the south.

There were major changes in the currency and mint organization towards the end of the ninth century. Alfred, presumably as part of his major review of the administration and defence of the country which involved establishing a network of fortified towns (burhs), created a number of new mints, some of which are named on his coinage: Winchester, Exeter, Gloucester and Oxford. The policy was continued by his successors, so that by the second quarter of the tenth century there were more than 35 mints throughout England.

The establishment of Viking settlements in the north and east of the country also had a significant effect. Continental trade via the Channel ports was no longer the only major source of silver. The Vikings had acquired large quantities of bullion through plunder, tribute and trade, and they converted much of this into coin at their own mints. Their prosperity is also reflected in the emergence of a major English mint in north-west Mercia (Chester or Shrewsbury?) from the end of the ninth century, and the Danelaw mints retained their importance after the English reconquest. There was thus a radical change of axis in coin production from the south-east to the north, which left a permanent mark on the pattern of minting throughout the medieval period.

The dominance which south-east England had enjoyed over coin production – though not coin use – before the 890s is indicative of the importance of commercial factors in the organization of the coinage, notably the supply of bullion from Continental trade. The principal mints of Canterbury, Rochester, London and East Anglia were little affected by changes in political control – the output of London varied most with the changing fortunes of Mercia. The choice of coin legends and designs reflects a degree of political intervention, and restrictions on the right of minting and the exclusion of foreign money presumably had legal backing. Yet the remarkable continuity of moneyers which can be seen at each of these mints suggests that the actual mint organization was largely independent of the royal administration and was founded in the stable trading communities of each city. Thus there are moneyers spanning each of the eight changes of political control at Canterbury, the two changes at Rochester, the two at London and the six or so at the East Anglian mint before the Viking conquest.

In the first quarter of the ninth century Canterbury appears normally to have supported some six royal and one or two ecclesiastical moneyers, and Rochester two or three royal and one ecclesiastical moneyer (who is unnamed and may have been one of the royal moneyers). London employed up to six moneyers, and the East Anglian mint had as many as seven moneyers in the brief reign of Ceolwulf I, although usually it was less. By *c.* 870 the position had changed radically with perhaps 25 moneyers at Canterbury, 30–40 at London and six or seven in East Anglia. Greater political control is also evident from the mid ninth century in the standardizations of design between moneyers and also between certain mints, the designs changing periodically, and in the 860s and 870s there is evidence of an agreement between Wessex and Mercia on a form of monetary union. At the end of the century there were some 60 moneyers named on Alfred's last coinage, more than 70 on the St Edmund Memorial coinage of the Vikings of East Anglia and an unknown number participating in the Viking coinages of York and the Five Boroughs. These figures reflect an expansion in the mint organization during the ninth century, though they cannot be used as a measure of mint output since the function and status of the moneyer may well have differed from mint to mint and time to time.

(b) THE AGE OF OFFA: SOUTHERN COINAGES, *c.* 760–96

Literature

The standard reference for the coins of this period is Blunt 1961, which reviews and largely supersedes the earlier literature and illustrates all moneyers and types. Lockett 1920 remains useful for its plates. Subsequent articles have discussed chronology (Lyon 1967; Metcalf 1963a and 1974a), mint attributions (Metcalf 1963a; Stewart 1986), estimates of mint output and extent of circulation (a lengthy debate between Metcalf (1963a, 1963b, 1964b, 1965b) and Grierson (1963a, 1963b, 1967)), and imitations (Metcalf 1966c). North 1980 provides a descriptive classification based on Blunt, but a corpus of coins and a list of single-finds have yet to be published.

Historical background

The second half of the eighth century continued the period of Mercian domination. Much of its history remains obscure, for the annals of the *Anglo-Saxon Chronicle* written in ninth-century Wessex give only a summary record of events and much has to be pieced together from the indirect evidence of charters, ecclesiastical sources, and coins.

The history is dominated by the career of Offa (757–96), who after a brief succession dispute took the Mercian throne in 757 and was an even more ruthless and skilful ruler than his equally long-lived predecessor Æthelbald (716–57). For the first seven years of his reign he appears to have exercised little power outside Mercia. The charters then show him asserting direct control in Kent by making grants either alone or with Kentish kings. It has been suggested that these broke free from Mercian overlordship for a number of years following the battle of Otford (776), making grants without reference to Offa (Stenton 1971, 207; Brooks 1984, 113). It is unclear how long this situation lasted; he had certainly regained control by 785, possibly by

780, and an extended denial of access to the Canterbury mint would present problems for the chronology of his coinage. Elsewhere the ancient kingdoms of Sussex, Essex, East Anglia and Lindsey were treated virtually as Mercian provinces. Wessex, however, was not subdued, and Cynewulf (757–86) was even able to recover territory which had been taken by Æthelbald. But after Cynewulf's death Offa lent support to Beorhtric (786–802) by driving his rival, the young Egbert, into exile and in 789 Offa gave his daughter Eadburh in marriage to the new king.

By the end of his reign Offa had largely dominated England south of the Humber, and even in Northumbria he attempted to acquire a position of influence in 792 by marrying off another daughter to Æthelred I. On Offa's coins and in most of his charters he is styled *rex Merciorum* or simply *rex*. For a few years after 772 he may have used the title *Anglorum* or *rex totius Anglorum patriae*, but none of the charters in which this occurs survives in a contemporary manuscript (Brooks 1984, 113), and it is doubtful if a small group of coins which could be read *rex A* were intended to reflect a similar title (below, p. 279). He was firm in his dealings with the Church and in his Continental relations. He invited the pope to send a legation to review the state of the Church in England, and in 787 he succeeded in securing the establishment of a Mercian archbishopric at Lichfield, though it lapsed soon after his death. He had considerable respect for Charlemagne and was the only ruler in western Europe who could make a show of dealing on equal terms with him. When in 787 Offa had his only son, Ecgfrith, anointed king of the Mercians, apparently the first occasion in England on which a son was consecrated king during his father's lifetime, he was copying the anointing of Charlemagne's sons as kings by the pope in 781. When in about 789 Charlemagne proposed that his son, Charles, should marry one of Offa's daughters, Offa would only agree if Charlemagne's daughter, Bertha, could marry Ecgfrith. Charlemagne refused and broke off the correspondence, closing all Frankish ports to English traders, and only after protracted negotiations were relations restored and the ports reopened.

Coinage

The coinage of Offa's lifetime falls essentially into two phases, one of light pennies of medium flan comparable to those of the reign of Pepin and the first decades of that of Charlemagne in France, and another of heavier pennies struck on larger flans that date from Offa's last years and correspond in size to Charlemagne's *novus denarius* introduced in 793/4. But the sceat fabric survived in East Anglia under Beonna and until the mid ninth century in Northumbria, while the new-style coinages were not merely those of Offa, but were struck also by kings of East Anglia, Kent and Wessex, by two archbishops of Canterbury, and even in the name of Offa's queen, Cynethryth. By the mid eighth century the currency of southern England had become very debased and it is possible that minting had entirely ceased. In Northumbria sceattas were being issued in the name of Eadbert (738–58), some in conjunction with his brother, Archbishop Egbert.

The first attempt to restore a southern coinage appears to have been made in East Anglia, and its models were Northumbrian. The coins are of variable fineness (*c.* 50–80% silver) and are struck on a flan slightly larger than the earlier sceattas though comparable with the later Northumbrian coins; they include for the first time in the south a king's name, BEONNA REX in runic or in a mixture of runic and Roman letters. Beonna is one of the three kings who are recorded as having divided East Anglia between them on the death of Ælfwold in 749 and he was still reigning there at the time of Offa's accession in 757. His coins were extremely rare until the discovery in 1981/3 of some 50 in the Middle Harling hoard and of others in excavations at Barham and Burrow Hill in Suffolk. A full report of the hoard by Marion Archibald is in preparation.

Most of Beonna's coins follow the earlier East Anglian practice of including the name of the moneyer – there is only one type which does not (**1.1121A**) – and three moneyers are recorded, Efe, Werferth and Wilred. None of them is known from previous issues, but Wilred (**1.1121C**) later struck broad-flan pennies in Offa's name (*SCBI* Berlin 67). Efe's coins (**1.1121B**) have pellets in the reverse design, the number and position of which varies from die to die, and this has been seen as a deliberate system for differentiating the dies (Archibald 1983). The modified Standard design used on the reverses of Efe and Werferth harks back to the sceattas of Series R, which may have been produced at the same mint. Virtually all the coins from sources outside the Middle Harling hoard die-link with specimens in it, suggesting that coinage was limited in scale.

It is difficult to date Beonna's coins, for on the one hand the presence in the Middle Harling hoard of a number of base sceattas suggests that there was continuity of circulation with these, though not necessarily continuity of minting, while on the other the existence of a common moneyer with Offa's coinage points to a fairly late date. Unfortunately we know nothing of the circumstances in which Offa came to exercise control over East Anglia, or whether it antedates his assertion of supremacy in Kent. Beonna's coins should belong to the late 750s or early 760s, while Offa's East Anglian coinage may date from the late 760s, or early 770s, after the start of his coinage in Kent.

The much more successful and lasting currency reform in southern England was the introduction of the broader flan penny (*c.* 17mm), inspired by the fabric of Pepin's new Frankish coinage. The new pennies were struck to the old weight standard of 20gr. (1.3g), the same as that of the denier abroad, and were of good fineness (*c.* 96%; Metcalf, Merrick and Hamblin 1968, 39). But if in economic respects it was aligned with the Frankish currency, its design remained Anglo-Saxon. The placing of the king's name, accompanied by a Latin title and often in a circular legend, appears to have been copied from the East Anglian and Northumbrian coinages. The inclusion of the moneyer's name was also found on the East Anglian coinage, and its continued use marks a fundamental difference between English and Frankish mint practice which was to endure until the thirteenth century. Similarly the linking of the name of both king and archbishop on coins of Jaenberht and Æthelheard of Canterbury was inspired by the coinage of Archbishop Egbert of York.

Before a further reform in the early 790s there was no standardization of coin type, and many of the coins are of high artistic quality, far superior to anything produced by the Franks. Many have geometric designs incorporating cruciform patterns or decorated linear inscriptions, while a few include a serpent, coiled or in the form of a torque. Those with a portrait are among the most striking coins in the English series, and sufficiently original for few Roman or Byzantine models to be identified with assurance. The designs are often personal to particular moneyers and may be repeated on several pairs of dies. Their great diversity makes it difficult to order the coinage chronologically. There are no recorded English hoards of the new pennies deposited during Offa's reign to assist us, and even if the majority of the dies were cut by a small number of gifted die-cutters and one would expect identifiable developments in style and technique, attempts to arrange the coins satisfactorily on the basis of such criteria have not as yet met with much success. Blunt (1961) divided them into three classes, Classes I and II representing the medium coinage and Class III the later heavy coinage, but the distinction between Classes I and II seems an artificial one without chronological significance, since some coins of Class I with quite simple designs appear to be late in date (Lyon 1968).

The majority of the coins of this period are in the name of Offa. The most common form is OFFA REX, though on some the royal style is omitted while on others the title is expanded to OFFA REX MERCIORVM (**1.1124A**). A number of coins abbreviate the name and/or the title, the most contracted form being OF̲ R M. A few coins of the moneyer Alhmund appear to read OF̲ R A, but it is not clear whether the A belongs to the name OFFA, or is a contraction of *Anglorum* (Metcalf 1963a, 41). Some coins, as already indicated, bear the name of the archbishop, Jaenberht (765–92), with the title AREP, as well as that of Offa (**1.1133**); on these the moneyer's name is omitted. Jaenberht's coins all belong to the light coinage (Blunt and Dolley 1961). Some employ the three-line design, which was copied from the papal coinage of Adrian I (772–95) and later used by Offa as the standard design in his heavy coinage. Others have reverse designs based on an eight-pointed star, which was continued by his successor Æthelheard. The obverse on Jaenberht's coins normally has the king's name and title in two lines, similar to the regal coins of the moneyers Æthelnoth and Winoth. A die-link exists between a coin of Jaenberht and a regal coin of Æthelnoth (Blunt 1958), and it is possible that Æthelnoth was both a regal and an archiepiscopal moneyer, since some of his later coins have very similar designs to some of Æthelheard's (cf. Blunt 1961, nos. 100, 135–6).

A group of coins with the name Eadberht have been attributed to the bishop of London who held office between 772/82 and 787/9. Blunt hesitated over accepting the attribution since no other bishop of London appears to have enjoyed rights of coinage (Blunt 1961, 43–4), but the case is a strong one. On all the coins the name Eadberht is followed by a monogram apparently of EP (for *Episcopus*); although the monogram has the appearance of a variant of the letter M, it cannot stand for *moneta* as this title does not occur on the coins until *c.* 805 (the M on the reverse of late Offa coins of the moneyer Babba is probably ornamental, having been transposed with the three-line design from the obverse). Most of Eadberht's coins have the papal three-line reverse design which in the light coinage is only otherwise used on the archiepiscopal coins of Jaenberht. Since Offa was on bad terms with Jaenberht and endeavoured to diminish his authority over the Church in southern England, he might have granted the bishop of London coining rights and later withdrawn them when the see of Lichfield was established in 788.

On some quite exceptional coins, unparalleled in the rest of the English coinage, Queen Cynethryth's name replaces that of Offa (**1.1132**). These were probably suggested not by Roman prototypes, as has usually been thought, but by the example of the Byzantine empress Irene, who is shown on coins of her son Constantine VI from 780 onwards (*DOC* III.336–46). There is no direct copying of designs, and the Byzantine coins indeed may never even have reached England, but information regarding their existence would have been available to English pilgrims and other emissaries to Rome. The coins have REGINA around a central M for *Merciorum* and are usually combined with a portrait. All were struck by the moneyer Eoba, and some of the portraits are virtually identical with those on his coins of Offa, but others with an elaborate headdress were probably intended to depict the queen.

Coins were also struck in the name of two Kentish kings. A unique coin of Heabert is now in Mr Blunt's collection, and there are about a dozen coins known of Egbert (**1.1122**). Heabert was ruling in the mid 760s, for he subscribes charters of 764 and (with Egbert) of 765, but is not recorded thereafter, although he may have continued to rule as a joint king. Egbert is recorded in a number of documents until at least *c.* 779. The coin of Heabert and those of Egbert are related in design and must be of a similar date, but whether they head the Canterbury series, having been struck before Offa gained control of Kent in the mid 760s, or whether they belong to an interlude after Offa's authority lapsed, we cannot say (Lyon 1967). In favour of the later dating is the fact that two of the three moneyers who struck Egbert's coinage were still moneyers at the beginning of Coenwulf's reign (793–821). Against it is the fact that their coins are closer in design to the sceattas than are Offa's, suggesting that they come near to the head of the series (Blunt 1952a; cf. also Beonna's coins), and we know them to have been kings in the 760s. On general historical grounds Stenton favoured a date in the mid 760s for the introduction of Offa's coinage (Stenton 1958), and the occurrence at the East Anglian mint of a common moneyer with Beonna's coinage lends support to this view. If one accepted Metcalf's suggestion that a coin of Charlemagne's Class 1 of 768–*c.* 770 (P 6; MG 239) was copied from the design of a coin of Egbert by the moneyer Babba (Metcalf 1966c), one would have firm evidence in favour of the 760s, but the resemblance is not entirely convincing. Whether the new coinage was initiated by Offa, perhaps in a Mercian mint at London (Stewart 1986), or whether the credit belongs to one of the kings of Kent, must be left an open question.

Towards the end of Offa's reign the weight standard was increased from *c.* 20gr. (1.3g) to *c.* 22gr. (1.45g) and the moneyers at all mints adopted a standard obverse type of M/+OFFA/REX in three lines, based ultimately on papal coins and similar to the design which Jaenberht and Eadbert had employed in the light coinage. Some coins of the moneyer Babba form a minor exception, having the three-line design on the reverse and a circular obverse inscription. Variation was still possible in the reverse type; most moneyers adopted a design arranged in two or three lines, but some of the London (?) and East Anglian moneyers used cruciform designs. There are no heavy coins of Jaenberht or of Cynethryth, while all those of Archbishop Æthelheard appear to belong to this phase. Of the two titles accorded to Æthelheard, that of PONT(*ifex*) has been attributed to the period between his election following Jaenberht's death on 12 August 792 and his own receipt of the pallium in 793, and ARCEP(*iscopus*) to the following period. If this were correct the coinage reform could be dated to 792 or the early months of 793, but it is by no means certain that the differences in title have any significance at all.

In addition to its silver pennies, Offa's reign also saw some minting in gold. The only specifically royal coin is an imitation of an Abbasid dinar with OFFA REX forming a conspicuous part of the design. It was acquired by a collector in Rome and it presumably formed one of the 365 *mancuses* a year which the king promised to send annually as a gift to the pope. The other coins, whose function is unknown, were struck without royal attribution by the moneyers Pendred and Ciolheard, though the latter piece may belong to the early years of Coenwulf's reign. Some other Western imitations of late eighth-century Abbasid dinars may possibly be English, but a Frankish origin is just as likely. The coins, and the substantial literature to which they have given rise, are discussed in Appendix 1, pp. 328–9.

No coins of the late eighth century carry a mint-signature, and it was for long believed that all or nearly all of Offa's coins were struck at Canterbury. Current opinion would allow up to four possible mints: Canterbury, possibly Rochester, an unknown mint in East Anglia, and London. Moneyers can be ascribed to them as follows:

Canterbury. This would most naturally have been the mint for coins of the two archbishops, of the early Kentish kings Heabert and Egbert, and of the later kings Eadbert Præn (796–8), who seized control of Kent on Offa's death, and Cuthred (798–807), who was given the Kentish throne by Coenwulf. There is a die-link between Archbishop Æthelheard and Eadbert Præn (Dolley 1956). From their coins we can identify five moneyers (Babba, Ethelmod, Ethelnoth, Eoba and Udd) who operated at Canterbury in the eighth century and who struck coins for Offa and one (Eoba) those of Cynethryth as well.

Rochester. After *c.* 810 we know there was a mint at Rochester and this might have been operating earlier, although if so we cannot yet distinguish its products.

East Anglia. Here coins of the Mercian kings were punctuated by issues of local rulers – Beonna, Æthelbert (d. 794) and Eadwald (*c.* 796) – which allow us to identify four moneyers of Offa (Eadnoth, Lul, Wihtred and Wilred) as having minted in East Anglia, and the distinctive style of their dies and frequent use of runic letters associates three others (Botred, Hun. . .c and Oethelred) with them. Six of these moneyers struck the light and two the heavy coinage, but as several of them are represented by only one or two specimens our knowledge of the East Anglian mint is probably very incomplete.

London. Three moneyers (Diola, Ludoman and Wilhun) struck an early transitional type of Coenwulf (below, p. 292) which shows continuity with Offa's last coinage, and these must be attributed to some 'Mercian' mint because for the first year or two of his reign Coenwulf lost control of both Kent and East Anglia, and this can scarcely be anywhere but London. Two of these moneyers struck Offa's heavy coinage. Another moneyer, Ciolheard, was a productive London moneyer of Coenwulf and Ceolwulf I, and he also struck the heavy and light coinages for Offa.

It is thus possible to provide mint attributions for 15 of Offa's 34 moneyers. There remain 19 moneyers, 16 for the light and eight for the heavy coinage, and it has generally been assumed that they operated at Canterbury, the most active mint in the early ninth century, but Stewart favours a London attribution for most of them (Stewart 1986). However, the problems of classification and stylistic analysis are complex, and are not rendered less so by Stewart's suggestion that some dies may have been transferred between London and Canterbury, so while the possibility that London was a significant mint for the light coinage and may even have initiated it must be taken seriously, this cannot be regarded as assured.

In addition to these four mints there must have been a fifth in southern England, for Offa's son-in-law Beorhtric (786–802) minted briefly in Wessex, though probably not until after Offa's death (below, p. 294). Two moneyers are recorded, but the coins are so rare – only three are known – that it can have been only a small issue supplementary to the south eastern coinage already in circulation.

If Offa had by the end of his reign come to dominate most of England south of the Humber, it remains hard to say how much of this huge area made regular use of coin. Fewer than 500 coins of the period are known today and the great majority of these come from isolated finds, though since Offa's coins were already well known in the seventeenth and eighteenth centuries it is possible that there was an early hoard of which no record has survived. Several hoards deposited in the ninth century contain just one or two coins of Offa. On the Continent, the Ilanz hoard of the 790s (Jecklin 1906; above, p. 210) contained one coin of Egbert of Kent and two light coins of Offa, the Carolingian coins in it being spread over a long period and including nine of Pepin the Short (751–68). Italy, and in particular Rome, has produced a considerable number of coins of this period (Blunt 1986), presumably money spent by pilgrims or given to the Holy See.

Thirty years ago the known distribution of isolated finds of the late eighth and early ninth centuries was virtually restricted to an area of south-eastern England bounded by an arc from Southampton to the Wash (Dolley and Metcalf 1957), implying that the coins had more limited circulation than those of the earlier eighth century. Subsequent finds have filled in some gaps in the distribution to the north and the west, so that south of the Humber the distribution pattern has now a certain resemblance to that of the sceattas. It nonetheless remains a striking fact that no scholar has thought of ascribing any coins to Offa's capital, Lichfield, and there are certainly none of its sole archbishop, Hygebeorht. It has been argued that production and the use of the new penny grew only slowly following the collapse of the sceat coinage (Metcalf 1974a), but the absence of a systematic list of single-finds and problems of chronological arrangement make it difficult to test this theory. With the exception of Richborough in Kent (Rigold 1968) few sites have yielded broad pennies in numbers as large as the sceattas on some sites. Account has also to be taken of the fact that broad pennies of the eighth and later centuries, through indeed to the twelfth century, are generally less common as single-finds than are the sceattas, although it is not clear whether this is due to differences in the size of the coinages or the circumstances of use and loss (Hinton 1986). The extent to which isolated finds form a reliable measure of coin circulation when they are below a certain density has been a subject of debate (Metcalf 1963b, 1965b; Grierson 1963b), and conclusions drawn from such finds must be treated with reserve.

(c) THE RISE OF WESSEX: SOUTHERN COINAGES, 796–*c.* 850

Literature

Of the large post-war literature on these coinages, several articles give general reviews of particular periods or reigns. The coins of Mercia, Kent and the archbishops of Canterbury in the period 796–*c.* 840 are comprehensively discussed in Blunt, Lyon and Stewart 1963. The West Saxon kings Egbert and Æthelwulf are treated in Blunt 1957 and Dolley and Skaare 1961 respectively, though neither distinguishes the products of the Rochester mint, for which see Lyon 1968 and Pagan 1986, a survey of the southern coinages 796–874. Pagan 1982a studies the coins of the East Anglian kings *c.* 827–69.

Historical background

After Offa's death, his son Ecgfrith survived only five months and no coins of his are known. The Mercian throne then passed to a distant kinsman Coenwulf (796–821). Immediately he had to contend with a threatened break-up of the enlarged kingdom and dependencies created by Offa. Control of Kent was seized by Eadbert Præn, a former priest presumably of noble birth, and possibly the 'Odberht' who had been driven into exile in Charlemagne's court (Whitelock 1979, 848, no. 197). He struck a series of coins at Canterbury before being ousted by Coenwulf in 798. Similarly, in East Anglia the coins show that control of the region was temporarily lost to one Eadwald, although the event is not recorded in the documents.

Once these crises were contained Coenwulf's reign appears to have been relatively peaceful. He placed his brother Cuthred (798–807) on the throne of Kent. In Wessex, Beorhtric was succeeded by his rival Egbert (802–39), bringing to an end any sway Mercia had enjoyed over the kingdom. However, this was a period of reform in the Church, and Archbishop Wulfred (805–32) was determined to implement new policies. Measures adopted by the Synod of Chelsea in 816 restricting the alienation of Church property and the rights of lay lords to nominate heads of monastic houses led to a direct confrontation with the king, and Wulfred was suspended from office for some four years *c.* 817–21 (Brooks 1984, 175–206).

Coenwulf was succeeded by his brother Ceolwulf (821–3), of whose brief reign we know little, save that he led a successful campaign against the Welsh. In 823 he was deposed by Beornwulf (823–6), and at about the same time one Baldred assumed the Kentish throne. Beornwulf exercised authority in Essex, Middlesex and Kent and was presumably recognized as Baldred's overlord (Stenton 1971, 231). The circumstances in which Baldred gained the throne are unclear, but a series of anonymous coins interrupting both the royal and ecclesiastical series at Canterbury, though not Rochester, suggest that there was a period of uncertainty before his position was recognized.

In 825 Egbert seized the initiative for Wessex, when in a decisive battle at *Ellendun* (Wroughton, Wilts.) he defeated the Mercians and changed the course of Anglo-Saxon history. He sent an army into Kent to drive out Baldred, and received the submission of Kent, Essex, Surrey and Sussex. The East Angles appealed for his protection against the Mercians. Beornwulf was killed during the ensuing campaign (?826) and his successor Ludica in another shortly afterwards (?827) whereby East Anglia secured its independence again, though our sources do not agree as to the precise dates. The *Anglo-Saxon Chronicle* dates the expulsion of Baldred and the death of Beornwulf to 825, though charters show that Beornwulf was ruling until 826, the date Roger of Wendover gives for his death (Whitelock 1979, 185). It is more doubtful, however, whether Roger should be preferred in his attribution of the conquest of Kent to 827 and Ludica's death to 828. In 829 Egbert put all his weight behind a campaign against the Mercians, conquering the kingdom and all its dependencies, and he went on to secure the submission of the Northumbrians and the Welsh. He used the title *Rex M(erciorum)* on coins issued at London. Wessex had established its supremacy, which was to lead eventually to the unification of England, though Wiglaf (827–9, 830–*c.* 840) recovered Mercia in 830.

Egbert was succeeded as king of Wessex by his son Æthelwulf (839–58), who had been sub-king of Kent since the 820s, and Wiglaf as king of Mercia by Berhtwulf (*c.* 840–52). The sources for their reigns are preoccupied by the increasing menace of the Vikings. The earliest raiders in the late eighth century had been Norwegians, many of whom subsequently settled in the Northern and Western Isles and in Ireland. From the mid 830s attacks on England and the Continent were intensified, now by Danes interested only in plunder not settlement. Wessex and Kent appear to have borne the brunt of the attacks, though in 841 the Danes ravaged Lindsey and East Anglia, and in 842 they made 'great slaughter in London . . . and Rochester'. In 850 they wintered in England, in Thanet, for the first time, and the following year a large army stormed Canterbury and London, sending Berhtwulf and his men fleeing. They then turned south into Surrey, but they were intercepted by the West Saxon army and defeated, though the victory brought only a brief respite. The common threat of the Vikings may have served to bring Wessex and Mercia closer together, for an alliance evident from marriage and military arrangements in the early 850s may have had its origins in the 840s when, for example, the Rochester mint assisted Berhtwulf in re-establishing Mercian coinage (Keynes and Lapidge 1983, 12).

Coinage

The English coinage of the first half of the ninth century is difficult to interpret and arrange, for political control of the few mints changed frequently and few coins are mint-signed. The traditional method of cataloguing and describing the coinage under kingdoms obscures its general pattern and continuity. In the text and catalogue here an attempt is made to follow the activity of each mint, with some general trends being described first.

During the political upheaval immediately following Offa's death there was little change in the design and organization of the coinage at the three principal southern mints. Coenwulf at London, Eadbert Præn at Canterbury and Eadwald in East Anglia each used the three-line obverse design of Offa's late coinage (Table 23). Upon regaining control of Kent in 798, Coenwulf standardized the coin type at both Canterbury and London, attempting for the first time to impose uniformity in the reverse as well as the obverse design. This new 'tribrach' type was also struck by Archbishop Æthelheard and by Cuthred when he assumed minting rights at Canterbury in the early 800s, probably to the exclusion of Coenwulf.

In 805, or perhaps a little earlier, portrait coinages were introduced at all the southern mints. The initiative probably came from Canterbury, and the obverse of its cross-and-wedges type was soon copied at the London and East Anglian mints but with a variety of reverse types. The short period during the tribrach issue when Canterbury and London coins shared similar obverse and reverse types was thus brought to an end. Thereafter common influences in design can often be detected between mints, but there appears to have been no concerted effort to standardize coin types again until the late 840s when Canterbury and Rochester adopted the

Table 23. *Issues at southern English mints, 796–c. 830*

	Canterbury		Rochester		London	East Anglia
	regal	archiepiscopal	regal	episcopal	regal	regal
c. 796–*c.* 798	*Eadbert*: 3-line	—	—	—	*Coenwulf*: 3-line	*Eadwald*: 3-line
c. 798–*c.* 802	*Coenwulf*: tribrach	*Æthelheard w. Coenwulf*: tribach	—	—	*Coenwulf*: tribrach	Type continued?
c. 802–*c.* 804	*Cuthred*: tribach	Type continued?	—	—	Type continued	—
c. 804–*c.* 807	*Cuthred*: portrait (b)/cross-and-wedges	*Wulfred*: portrait/ *Dorovernia civitas* types	—	—	*Coenwulf*: portrait (b)/cross-crosslet etc.	*Coenwulf*: portrait (b)/ various
807–*c.* 810	*Coenwulf*: portrait (b)/cross-and-wedges	Type continued	*Coenwulf*: portrait (b)/cross-and-wedges	—	Type continued	Type continued
c. 810–21	*Coenwulf*: portrait (b)/ pincer cross, cross moline etc.	*Wulfred*: portrait (b)/*Dorovernia cv* monogram	*Coenwulf*: portrait (b)/ various	—	Type continued	Type continued
821–3	*Ceolwulf I*: portrait (b) and non-portrait/ various; and *Anonymous regal*: portrait (h)/mint-name-in-field	Type continued?, followed by *Anonymous archiep.*: portrait (h)/mint-name-in-field	*Ceolwulf I*: portrait (b and h)/ various	*Ceolwulf I*: portrait (h)/ *Dorobrebia cibitas* types	*Ceolwulf I*: portrait (b) and non-portrait/ various	*Ceolwulf I*: portrait (b)/ various
c. 823–5/6	*Baldred*: portrait (h)/*DrvrCits* and non-portrait/ various	*Wulfred*: portrait (h)/*DrvrCits*	*Baldred*: portrait (b)/various	—	*Beornwulf*: non-portrait/cross-crosslet?	*Beornwulf*: portrait (b)/ various
826–7				—	*Ludica*: portrait (b)/various	
827–9	SEE TABLE 24				*Wiglaf*: portrait (b and h) and non-portrait/ various	*Æthelstan*: portrait (b)/various, and ?ship/cross
829–				*Egbert*: non-portrait/cross-potent types	*Æthelstan*: non-portrait/various	

(b) = bust (h) = head

Dor⁻b⁻/Cant type. At London and the East Anglian mint, and from *c.* 810 at Rochester, the die-cutters were permitted considerable latitude in the selection of designs. A form of cross-crosslet is common, though not universal, on London coins and there is a great variety of portraits. During the second quarter of the ninth century, the designs of London coins were influenced more by issues of Rochester than Canterbury. In East Anglia the moneyers seem often to have adopted personal reverse designs which were repeated on a number of their dies, and this practice continued after *c.* 827 under the independent East Anglian kings. The Rochester die-cutter initially imitated Canterbury types, but attempts were later made to differentiate the Rochester coins. Thus Rochester did not adopt Canterbury's conspicuous mint-name-in-field reverse *c.* 822–5, and between *c.* 828 and *c.* 848 the mints used contrasting designs, each alternating between portrait and non-portrait types (Table 24). During the first half of the ninth century, such regulation of design as there was appears to have come from within the mints rather than been imposed upon them by any central authority.

The Mercian kings retained control of the four southern mints until the 820s. Canterbury and Rochester passed first to Baldred and then probably in 825 to Egbert, both mints thenceforth remaining in the control of Wessex. The East Anglian mint passed to independent rulers *c.* 827 and remained under them until the Viking conquest of the region in 869. London was thus the only mint retained by Mercia, and the sporadic and initially ephemeral nature of its activity may reflect a general decline in the kingdom's prosperity during the second quarter of the ninth century. The Mercian coinage was revived in the early 840s under Berhtwulf and it flourished for several years. But it suffered a setback, probably as a result of the Viking attack of 850/1, from which it took more than a decade to recover. The coinage of Wessex may also have been interrupted by this attack, but when it recommenced it was organized on a rather different basis, with uniformity of type being strictly imposed.

During the first half of the ninth century the coinages of the various kingdoms, except Northumbria, circulated freely in southern England, while Continental coins, which differed in weight from English coins, had since the late eighth century been largely excluded. Only two English hoards from this period are well recorded, London (Middle Temple) (dep. *c.* 840) and Sevington, Wilts. (dep. *c.* 850), but the later hoards from Dorking in Surrey (dep. *c.* 860) and Trewhiddle in Cornwall (dep. *c.* 868) include substantial elements from this period. These hoards contain a broad range of coins from Coenwulf's portrait coinage onwards, including East Anglian issues, suggesting that there had been no systematic reminting during the period. Nor does the virtual absence of earlier coins necessarily imply that a recoinage occurred at the end of the tribrach issue, for the Delgany hoard from Ireland, which seems to be essentially a parcel of 117 coins taken from circulation in southern England *c.* 828, contained 14 early coins dating from Offa's heavy coinage to the tribrach type (Pagan 1962).

The sequence of types at each of the mints is as follows:

Canterbury

After Offa's death, the Canterbury moneyers recognized the authority of Eadbert Præn (**1.1136**). His coins are similar to the last coins of Offa, but struck on slightly smaller flans. The dozen or so known specimens are by five moneyers, three of whom had worked for Offa and two

Table 24. *Issues of mints for Wessex*, c. *825–60*

Date[1]	Canterbury		Rochester		Winchester/Southampton
	regal	archiepiscopal	regal	episcopal	regal
Egbert (802–39)					
c. 825–*c.* 828	Portrait and non-portrait/various geometric	?Portrait/ *DrvrCits*	Portrait/various geometric	—	—
c. 828–39	Portrait/*DorbC* Monogram	Portrait/*DorbC* Monogram	Non-portrait: cross-potent	Portrait/*St Andrew*	Non-portrait: *Saxon* Monogram and *Saxoniorum* issues
Æthelwulf (839–58)					
839–*c.* 843	Non-portrait: cross-and-wedges/ *Saxoniorum*	Portrait/ *Dorovernia Ca* Monogram	Portrait/various geometric	Non-portrait: cross-and-wedges/ *Occidentalium Saxoniorum*	?Non-portrait: *Saxon* Monogram
c. 843–*c.* 848	New portrait/ various geometric	New portrait/ Christogram	Non-portrait: cross-and-wedges/various	—	—
c. 848–*c.* 851	Non-portrait: *Dor-b-/Cant*	Portrait/mint-name-in-field various	Non-portrait: *Dor-b-/Cant*	—	—
c. 852–58	Portrait/inscribed cross	Portrait/inscribed cross	Portrait/inscribed cross	—	—

1. The dates are those of the Canterbury regal issues. The issues indicated for the other series were roughly contemporary, although the type changes did not necessarily coincide.

subsequently struck for Coenwulf after Mercia resumed control of Kent in 798. Coenwulf's earliest Canterbury coins are of the tribrach type with the king's name and title around an M for *Merciorum* and on the reverse the moneyer's name in the angles of a tribrach (**1.1137–9**). Archbishop Æthelheard, who had abandoned his office during Eadbert's rule, struck coins of a comparable type in conjunction with the Mercian king (**1.1140**).

Coenwulf subsequently permitted Cuthred to strike coins at Canterbury, although probably not until the early 800s. Cuthred's first coins closely resemble those of Coenwulf with the central M replaced by a cross (**1.1141**); his title is simply *rex*. But variations on the basic tribrach design differentiate his subsequent coins and suggest that he had exclusive use of the mint rather than sharing it with his brother as has been suggested (Blunt, Lyon and Stewart 1963, but see Lyon 1968, 217). Tribrach coins of Coenwulf are two or three times more common than those of Cuthred. In the new portrait/cross-and-wedges type the position is reversed, coins of Cuthred (**1.1142–4**) being twice as common as those of Coenwulf (**1.1145–6**), and again there is some suggestion from the design that the issues were sequential rather than parallel. Two dies of Cuthred were subsequently recut with Coenwulf's name (Blackburn and Bonser 1984c, 66). The Canterbury die-cutter achieved much greater uniformity of style than existed elsewhere, and it is likely that he was responsible for initiating the new portrait type, which was also innovative in other respects. These were the first coins since the seventh century to include the description *moneta* often accompanied by the moneyer's name in the genitive, e.g. *Sigeberhti moneta* ('Sigeberht's coin'). Also for the first time Cuthred is accorded the title *rex Cant.* A date of *c.* 805 for the introduction of the type is suggested by the fact that the last coins of Archbishop Æthelheard (d. 805) belong to the tribrach issue and the first of Wulfred (acc. 805) to the new portrait coinage. Wulfred's coins do not carry a royal portrait, but a facing tonsured bust suggested by papal coins of Adrian I (cf. **1.1031–2**). They omit the king's name, initially replacing it with the mint name in the genitive, *Doroverniae civitatis*. Later the moneyer's name is placed in the legend, and the name of the mint forms a monogram in the centre.

In Coenwulf's later Canterbury coinage, struck from *c.* 810 on broader flans, a variety of reverse types was employed (**1.1147, 1149–50**). Some types were common to several moneyers and may have been sequential issues (e.g. 'pincer' cross, cross moline, 'crescent' cross) while others were only used by one moneyer (e.g. Dealla's cross-crosslet type). There are eight regal moneyers recorded in Coenwulf's later coinage and their coins can be broadly divided into early and late by the form of the bust. In contrast, only two Canterbury moneyers, Oba and Sigestef, struck coins in the name of Ceolwulf I; the other moneyers, and in due course these two as well, declined to recognize him, striking an anonymous coinage. However, Ceolwulf's early Canterbury coinage was not entirely transitory. Both moneyers used several pairs of dies and struck portrait and non-portrait coins. Oba's portrait coins employ a new reverse design, with his name and title in three lines, which is also found on coins of Rochester and East Anglia in this reign. The non-portrait coins are interesting, for similar types were struck at Canterbury under Baldred and Egbert (**1.1157**), and in each case they appear to have been issued in parallel with portrait coins (Blunt, Lyon and Stewart 1963, 16–18). They may have been intended to serve a different function, though they would have been too light for use in Continental trade and finds indicate that they circulated in England alongside the portrait coins. A non-portrait series was also issued at London under Ceolwulf, and one of Sigestef's non-portrait types copies the London type but with the Canterbury mint name added.

The greater proportion of coins issued at Canterbury during Ceolwulf I's reign were anonymous as to the issuing authority with just the moneyer's name on the obverse and the mint name (*Dorobernia civitas*) in three lines across the reverse, the latter presumably inspired by Class 2 coins of Louis the Pious (**1.763–89**). There are two forms of bust: the first, with hair shown as open parallel strokes, corresponds to that used by Ceolwulf and his predecessors, and the second, with hair contained within an outline, corresponds to that used on the coinage of Baldred and Egbert. There is a mule between an anonymous obverse and a Baldred reverse. In the archiepiscopal series there is a comparable group of anonymous coins with a facing bust (**1.1154–5**). It is tempting to associate these archiepiscopal coins with the period of Wulfred's dispute with Coenwulf *c.* 817–21, when he ceased to exercise his office (Brooks 1984, 135), but the similarity of reverse designs with those of the anonymous regal coinage indicates that they were contemporary and belong *c.* 822–3. Wulfred's earlier Monogram coinage (**1.1148**, **1152–3**) belongs to the period *c.* 810–22, but it may have been interrupted during the dispute.

The coinage of Baldred was struck by six moneyers, all of whom had worked for Coenwulf and were later to work for Egbert. The obverse inscription is *Baldred* (or *Beldred*) *rex Cant.* The reverse of the portrait coins retains the mint name in the field, but it is contracted to DR VR CITS in two lines in order to accommodate the moneyer's name (**1.1156**). There are parallel coins of Archbishop Wulfred with a similar reverse type. The non-portrait coins have a cross, a cross and pellets, or a cross-crosslet design on the obverse and reverse.

Egbert does not appear to have struck any coins before he acquired control of Kent *c.* 825. His earliest Canterbury coins continue the portrait and non-portrait series, but using geometric reverses for both (**1.1157**; Blunt 1957, groups 1 and 2). These issues were replaced, *c.* 828 on the evidence of the Delgany hoard, by a portrait type with a monogram of the letters DORB C on the reverse (**1.1158–60**; Blunt 1957, group 3), presumably inspired by papal issues with a ROMA monogram. Egbert made no further issue at Canterbury, and the *DorbC* monogram type probably continued until his death in 839, although there may have been an interruption in minting there towards the end of the reign (Lyon 1968, 223). The last archiepiscopal issue of Wulfred and the first of Ceolnoth from 833 have a similar *DorbC* monogram reverse type.

In Æthelwulf's reign four phases of coinages can be distinguished in both the regal and ecclesiastical coinages at Canterbury and a similar number in the regal coinage at Rochester, although the type changes did not necessarily coincide in each series (see Table 24). At the beginning of the reign the Canterbury moneyers reverted to a non-portrait type with *Saxoniorum* in three lines in the centre of the reverse. The same design had been used by Egbert on the obverse of his rare Winchester coins, representing a continuation of the obverse legend. Æthelwulf's *Saxoniorum* coins were among the latest in the London (Middle Temple) hoard deposited *c.* 840, possibly associated with the Viking raid on London in 842. This was soon replaced by a new portrait coinage employing several reverse designs: Christogram, cross-crosslet, star, etc. This portrait coinage can be divided into two groups, one in a crude style and another, probably later, of finer design and epigraphy (Pagan 1986). The third phase of Æthelwulf's coinage marked a first attempt to standardize the coin designs of Canterbury and

Rochester. A new non-portrait coinage was issued with DOR¯B¯, for either *Dorobernia* (Canterbury) or *Dorobrevia* (Rochester), in the obverse field and CANT (Kent) in the reverse (**1.1165**: a Rochester coin), but at Canterbury some portrait coins may also have been issued in parallel (Lyon 1968, 227). It is impossible to date the phases of Æthelwulf's coinage closely. Dolley and Skaare's suggested chronology – *Saxoniorum, c.* 839–43; new portrait, *c.* 843–8; *Dor¯b¯/Cant, c.* 848–51 – is largely based on an impression of the relative sizes of the issues and this is probably the best that one can do. The *Dor¯b¯/Cant* issue may have been brought to an end by the great Viking raids on Canterbury and London in 850/1. Only two of the eight Canterbury moneyers and two of the six Rochester moneyers of the *Dor¯b¯/Cant* type continued into the Inscribed Cross issue which followed. This is a lower survival rate than is usual between consecutive issues and there may have been some interruption in minting, though for how long we cannot be sure (Dolley and Skaare 1961, 73, and Pagan 1986 date the introduction of Inscribed Cross *c.* 855, while Lyon 1968 dates it *c.* 852).

In the archiepiscopal coinage, Ceolnoth's *DorbC* monogram issue of the 830s gave way *c.* 839 or a little earlier (Lyon 1968, 223–4) to a second Monogram issue (**1.1161**) harking back to earlier coins of Wulfred. Ceolnoth's third issue has a portrait and Christogram reverse (**1.1162**) similar to Æthelwulf's new portrait type of the mid 840s and presumably contemporary with it; the two styles of Æthelwulf's type are also evident in Ceolnoth's. This was followed by a variety of types with the name of the mint as well as the moneyer in the reverse legend. All are very rare and it is difficult to determine whether they precede or are contemporary with the regal *Dor¯b¯/Cant* type. Thereafter the archiepiscopal coins are uniform in type with the regal coinage, commencing with the Inscribed Cross issue. On Ceolnoth's first three issues the archbishop's name is spelt CIALNOTH, thereafter it is CEOLNOTH.

Rochester

The presence of a second substantial mint in Kent, active from *c.* 810 until the mid 850s or later, was recognized by Blunt, Lyon and Stewart (1963). They distinguished a sequence of moneyers whose coins are often of different types and in a different style from those of attested Canterbury moneyers, and which sometimes exhibit differences in the spelling of the king's name. The sequence of rulers controlling this mint is the same as at Canterbury, including Baldred, but there are no anonymous coins preceding his. The association with Rochester is virtually certain, although there is no direct link with the rare mint-signed coins of Ceolwulf I or with those of Egbert in the name of St Andrew, to whom the minster at Rochester was dedicated.

The first coins which have been attributed to this mint are somewhat crude versions of Coenwulf's portrait/cross-and-wedges type by the moneyer Ealhstan. One specimen is struck on a small flan and may be contemporary with the small-flan coins issued at Canterbury before *c.* 810. Ealhstan was joined by a second moneyer, Dun, and together they struck coins for Coenwulf that copy several of the reverse designs used at Canterbury. One pair of dies was probably supplied to Dun by the Canterbury die-cutter. By the end of the reign, the Rochester die-cutter had developed a style of his own, and this characterizes the products of the mint over the following decade or more.

The Rochester coins of Ceolwulf were struck by four moneyers and are more numerous than those from Canterbury. The king's name is spelt CIOL . . ., rather than the CEOL . . . of Canterbury portrait coins. Initially the portrait coins follow Coenwulf's with a bust breaking the inscription, but later coins have a head within a continuous inscription as on the anonymous Canterbury coinage. On two coins of the latter type associated with the bishop, the moneyer's name is replaced by that of the mint, *Dorobrebia cibi* with *tas* in field. Baldred's Rochester coins deliberately revert to a full bust type, and continue the tradition of using a variety of geometric reverse designs, rather than the contracted mint name in two lines of the Canterbury coinage. The king is given the title *rex* or *rex H* (for Hrofesceaster?), in contrast to *rex Cant* on the Canterbury coins. Under Egbert an early portrait issue with either a bust or a head (**1.1163**; Blunt 1957, group 4, 1–9) gave way to a series of non-portrait coins (**1.1164**; Blunt 1957, group 4, 10–21). The abandonment of a portrait type was probably intended to distinguish the coins from those of Canterbury, and a similar change was made at London and the East Anglian mint, although in the latter case the motive is more likely to have been to distinguish coins of the independent kingdom from their Mercian predecessors. The new Rochester coins mostly employ a cross-potent motif, and again there is a difference in spelling, normally ECGBEORHT, rather than Canterbury's ECGBEARHT or HECBEARHT. The rare episcopal coins with *Scs Andreas* or *Scs Andreas Apo(stolus* in field) have a portrait, but must belong to the end of the reign for there is a close resemblance in the bust to early coins of Æthelwulf.

Æthelwulf's Rochester coinage can be divided into four phases, as at Canterbury (see Table 24, p. 287 above). The first saw a change in design, the regal moneyers adopting a portrait coinage (the parallel Canterbury coinage was non-portrait) and the ecclesiastical issue taking a non-portrait design with *Occidentalium* around *Saxoniorum* in the reverse field. This is the last of the three ecclesiastical issues of Rochester which have been identified, all belonging to the term of Bishop Beornmod (803/5–842/4). The London (Middle Temple) hoard from early in Æthelwulf's reign contained 22 coins of his first Rochester type and two of his first Canterbury type, which has led Lyon (1968, 219–23) to suggest that some of the Rochester coins may have been struck before Egbert's death when Æthelwulf was sub-king of Kent. This might accord with other steps taken by Egbert to secure the succession for his son, such as the agreements with the churches of Canterbury and Winchester (Brooks 1984, 145–7). But as Pagan (1986) points out, the Rochester coins include several die-duplicates and it is probable that this portion of the hoard was drawn from a source rich in Rochester coins. The Rochester die-cutter provided Berhtwulf with dies of similar design and style to inaugurate the new Mercian coinage.

For Æthelwulf's second issue Rochester adopted a non-portrait design which served to distinguish it not only from the new portrait coinage at Canterbury, but also from Berhtwulf's coinage for which Rochester continued to supply the dies. The new type has a cross-and-wedges obverse similar to that used in the previous phase on both the Canterbury regal issue and the Rochester ecclesiastical coins, but the reverses differed, continuing to show a variety of geometric designs. Towards the end of the 840s, Rochester and Canterbury adopted the *Dor-b-/Cant* type, although their coins are stylistically distinct. The Danish army is not known to have attacked Rochester during its descent of 850/1, and there is no obvious reason why this coinage should not have continued until the introduction of the Inscribed Cross type.

London

The existence of a Mercian mint in the early ninth century can be deduced from the presence of a group of moneyers who apparently did not strike coins for kings of Kent or East Anglia and whose coins have no particular stylistic affinities with those of other mints (Blunt, Lyon and Stewart 1963, 30–6). Most if not all of these coins were presumably struck at London, although the mint is named only on the coinage of Egbert as king of Mercia in 829–30.

Three moneyers of Coenwulf struck coins attributed to London using a three-line obverse design similar to that of Offa's last coinage. These probably belong to the early years of the reign when Coenwulf had been ousted from Kent and East Anglia. One moneyer, Diola, used a form of tribrach reverse which is evidently the prototype for the main tribrach issue shortly to be introduced at London and Canterbury. The tribrach type was struck by between five and nine moneyers at London, though they were perhaps less productive than the Canterbury moneyers for their coins are scarcer. The dies are cut carefully to as high a standard as that of Canterbury, but the same is not true of the subsequent portrait coinages, which display much stylistic diversity. Most of them, down to the reign of Wiglaf, employ a cross-crosslet reverse design often omitting an inner circle. Ceolwulf I's three moneyers each issued both portrait and non-portrait coins as at Canterbury, the obverse of the latter having a Latin cross and CIOLVVLF REX MERCI, with ORṼ continuing the legend in the field. This design was also used at Canterbury, but is distinguished by the inclusion of the mint name in the legend.

Of Ceolwulf's immediate successors, there is only one fragmentary London coin which is perhaps to be attributed to Beornwulf (Blunt, Lyon and Stewart 1963, 35–6) and none of Ludica, although both struck coins at the East Anglian mint. Wiglaf's coins, although very rare, are known from three moneyers and there are portrait and non-portrait types. The non-portrait coins belong either immediately before or after the brief rule in Mercia (829–30) of Egbert, who struck coins of related style by the same moneyer (**1.1166**). However, for the obverse he adopted the cross-potent design of his new Rochester coinage, while on the reverse of some the mint name, + LVNDONIA CIVIT in three lines, proclaims his authority over the city. With the possible exception of the two non-portrait coins there are no coins attributable to Wiglaf's second reign, and no Mercian coinage was produced for a decade or more, until it recommenced under Berhtwulf in the early 840s.

The great majority of Berhtwulf's coins are portrait types which can be divided into two groups (North 1961). The earliest coins of Group I (**1.1167–8**; North's bust A) are so similar in style to Æthelwulf's first Rochester coinage that the dies were evidently cut by the same hand, and they are perhaps to be dated *c.* 841/2. The other coins of Group I (busts B–F) appear to be the work of the same Rochester die-cutter though a little later in date, contemporary with the non-portrait cross-and-wedges type at Rochester. The reverse designs are also similar to those found on Æthelwulf's first coinage and so for a short time – perhaps a year or two – Berhtwulf's coins were virtually indistinguishable from Æthelwulf's Rochester coins save in their inscriptions. This is strong evidence of co-operation between the kingdom's but whether some wider arrangement for a monetary union existed is doubtful. The Rochester moneyers soon adopted a non-portrait type, although the die-cutter continued to supply Berhtwulf's moneyers with portrait dies. A unique coin muling an official Berhtwulf obverse with a crudely imitative Æthelwulf cross-and-wedges *obverse* has been interpreted as some form of alliance issue, but it is more probable that an illiterate moneyer or forger produced a replacement reverse die by arbitrarily copying a coin of Æthelwulf.

Coins of Berhtwulf's Group II, introduced in the later 840s, are of quite a different style, the work of another die-cutter. This issue was probably brought to an end by the Viking attack of 850/1. The few non-portrait coins of Berhtwulf may belong to the very end of his reign before Burgred took the throne in 852. Two of Berhtwulf's eleven moneyers also worked for Æthelwulf at some stage in their careers, for Brid, a moneyer of Berhtwulf's early Group I, also struck the cross-and-wedges and *Dor̄b̄/Cant* issues at Rochester, and Liaba, a moneyer of late Group I and Group II, also struck the new portrait issue at Canterbury. From the sharing of a die cutter and of a moneyer, it has been suggested that Berhtwulf's coins were perhaps struck at Rochester (Lyon 1968, 228–9). But it is more likely that they were struck at London, and that the Rochester die-cutter was commissioned to supply the dies during the first few years (Pagan 1986). The moneyer Brid perhaps started at London and moved to Rochester at much the same time as Liaba moved from Canterbury to London – further evidence of friendly relations between the two kingdoms. Two other moneyers of the portrait series, and one found only on the non-portrait coins, continue as moneyers of Burgred, and there can be little doubt that his principal mint was in London.

The East Anglian mint to 869

Offa's East Anglian coinage was followed by one in the name of an otherwise unknown king Eadwald, who presumably seized control of at least part of the region following Offa's death in 796. Five coins of his are known struck by three moneyers, two of whom had struck for Offa and were subsequently to strike for Coenwulf. We have no idea how long Eadwald's usurpation lasted, but it may have been several years, for the first coins of Coenwulf are a portrait type probably struck after the introduction of Canterbury's portrait coinage in *c.* 805 or a little earlier. In view of the rarity of the later eighth-century East Anglian coinage, we cannot be sure that there was not an intermediate phase which has not survived. Coenwulf's earliest portrait coins, by the moneyer Lul, have a very crude bust, possibly modelled on coins of London rather than Canterbury, but the reverse is similar to the 'leaf' design used by the same moneyer on coins of Eadwald and Offa.

The East Anglian coinage of the 810s and 820s is much better represented in the surviving material owing largely to an ill-recorded nineteenth-century hoard from Suffolk (Blunt, Lyon and Stewart 1963, 43–4). The coins of the Mercian kings from Coenwulf to Ludica are without exception portrait types, and they employ a wide range of reverse designs which tend to be personal to particular moneyers rather than representing successive issues of the mint. A notable exception is Ceolwulf I's three-line reverse type used by three East Anglian moneyers (**1.1169–70**) as well as individual moneyers at Canterbury and Rochester. Under Beornwulf and Ludica the cross-crosslet design, typical of London, was used by several East Anglian moneyers. Runic letters, which had been common in the East Anglian coinage of the eighth century, occur occasionally down to the end of the series in 869.

The written sources do not record Mercia's loss of East Anglia. Ludica is the last Mercian king to strike coins there, and the coinage of an otherwise unrecorded King Æthelstan follows on directly. Four of his moneyers had struck coins for the Mercians and his earliest coins are of very similar designs to Ludica's (Pagan 1982a). The attribution to an Æthelstan of East Anglia rather than Æthelstan, sub-king of Kent (839–*c.* 850), is secured *inter alia* by a group of coins reading EDELSTAN/(rev.) REX ANG. The ethnic, *Anglia*, is otherwise only given on the earlier coins of Edmund which read + EADMVND REX AN, although the letter A is a common obverse design which may have had the dual meaning of *Anglia* and *alpha*, for *omega* occurs on some reverses.

An early unique coin of Æthelstan replaces the king's bust with a ship similar to that on Louis the Pious' coins of Dorestad. The style of lettering is closer to coins of the early 820s, and it has been suggested that it may have been struck during an earlier, abortive attempt to wrest control of East Anglia from the Mercians (Archibald 1982). Before long the East Anglian coinage, like that of Rochester and London, adopted non-portrait designs with various geometric or epigraphic types which were continued by Æthelstan's successors Æthelweard (**1.1173**) and Edmund (**1.1174–9**). Again, each moneyer had his own combination of types which distinguished his coins and dies. This has hindered any satisfactory chronological division of the coinage within the reigns, save that of Edmund where his later coins generally read + EADMUND REX, rather than + EADMUND REX AN, and most moneyers adopted a standard A/cross-and-pellets design (**1.1175–6**; Pagan 1982a, 49–50).

There are a few coins with the names of two kings Æthelred and Oswald, which bear a resemblance to the East Anglian coinage (Dolley 1962; North 1980, nos. 480, 487–8). The provenance of three of the coins, from the Cuerdale hoard, implies a date in the last three decades of the ninth century, and they were probably struck in East Anglia after the death of Edmund and before Guthrum's coinage of the later 880s (below, p. 318). The two coins with the name Æthelred (?copying that of Æthelred I) both have Continental temple-type obverses, and are struck by two moneyers Beornhae and Heahmod, the former possibly Edmund's moneyer of the same name. One of Oswald's coins is of the temple type by a moneyer Beor . . ., while the other, by an uncertain moneyer, has the common East Anglian design of an *alpha*.

The West Saxon mint (Winchester or Southampton?)

Between the mid eighth and the late ninth century Wessex appears to have possessed a mint only for two brief periods (Dolley 1970, with a virtual corpus of the coins). Beorhtric (786–802) struck coins of two types: one with A/cross-and-pellets by the moneyer Ecghard known from two specimens, and the other with *alpha*-and-*omega*/*omega* by the moneyer Peochthun known from just one coin. In their general appearance they most closely resemble the Mercian tribrach type and they probably belong to the very end of Beorhtric's reign.

The second phase of activity came in the 830s under Egbert and Æthelwulf. The attribution to a West Saxon mint is suggested by the use of the title *rex Saxoniorum* (although this was later used at Canterbury and Rochester) and by the absence of these moneyers from the Kentish series. There are two types of Egbert. One with a monogram of *Saxon* in the obverse field was struck by at least five moneyers, and the other and perhaps later type, with *Sax/onio/rum* in three lines in the field, is known for two moneyers. No more than a dozen coins in all exist.

Æthelwulf reverted to the *Saxon* monogram type, although only a single specimen survives.

It had been assumed that the mint was at Winchester, which from the late ninth century was one of the most important Anglo-Saxon mints. But this may have been a creation of Alfred, and a case has been argued for the commercial port of Southampton, where many of the Series H sceattas are thought to have been struck (Dolley 1970).

(d) NORTHUMBRIAN COINAGES, 758–867

Literature

A good deal was written on the Northumbrian coinage during the nineteenth century and the early part of this one, but it has been largely superseded by modern studies. The modern arrangement of the coinage was worked out essentially by Lyon (1956), with further observations in the first of his presidential addresses to the British Numismatic Society (1967) and in Pagan 1973a. The eighth-century coinages, which have been considerably swelled by recent finds, are the subject of a comprehensive study by Booth (1984). A radical revision of the chronology of the ninth-century kings and archbishops based on numismatic arguments has been proposed by Pagan (1969) but not generally accepted by historians. Two major programmes of metal analyses have been published in Metcalf *et al.* 1968 and Gilmore and Metcalf 1980.

There are no relevant hoards of the eighth century, but there are a number from the mid ninth century, most notably Hexham 1832, York (St Leonards Place) 1842, and Bolton Percy 1846 and 1967, each containing several thousand coins. A summary of all the hoards and single-finds is published in Pirie 1986. In addition to coins in *SCBI*, valuable comparative material will be found in the line drawings of nearly 1,000 of the Hexham coins in Adamson 1834–6 (plates reprinted in Ruding 1840), the catalogue of the Newcastle collection (Pirie 1982), and the report of the 1967 Bolton Percy hoard (Pagan 1973a). The rich collections at Leeds and York (including *c.* 3,000 coins from the St Leonards Place hoard) are being prepared for publication in *SCBI* by Pirie.

Historical background

Northumbria consisted originally of two kingdoms founded in the mid sixth century: Bernicia in the north, and Deira in the south-east, the region that is now Yorkshire. By the early seventh century both kingdoms were held under common, Bernician, rule and three of its kings, Edwin, Oswald and Oswiu, who ruled during the heyday of Northumbrian power which followed, were later acccorded the title of 'bretwalda' or chief overlord among the English kingdoms, indicating their considerable influence rather than a formal rank. The tradition of monastic learning in Northumbria which produced such outstanding scholars as Bede and Alcuin owed much to the patronage of King Aldfrith (685–704). Stenton (1971, 89) said of him that 'he stands beside Alfred of Wessex among the few Old English kings who combined skill in warfare with desire for knowledge'. It is no surprise that he was the first Anglo-Saxon king to issue a substantial coinage in his own name (above, p. 166).

Political decline is evident after Aldfrith's death, and although it was arrested during Eadbert's reign (738–58), subsequent Northumbrian history is punctuated by a succession of minor revolutions. Few kings of the second half of the eighth century or early ninth century retained the throne until their natural deaths, as members of the various Bernician royal lines vied for power against others whose origins are obscure. In 758 Eadbert retired into the Church, but within months his son and successor had been murdered and a noble named Æthelwald, with the cognomen 'Moll', had become king. However, Eadbert (d. 768) lived long enough to see Æthelwald deposed and his own kinsman, Alchred, take the throne in 765. We know that Alchred was in correspondence with the Franks and he was instrumental in despatching the mission of St Willehad, which led to the foundation of the archbishopric of Bremen. After nine years he was driven into exile by 'consent of all his people' and was replaced by Æthelred I, a son of Æthelwald 'Moll'. But the factional disputes continued. Æthelred was deposed in 779 by Ælfwald I, a grandson of Eadbert, and although he was reinstated in 790 for a second reign this ended with his murder six years later, a fate not altogether unjustified to judge from the chronicles. Coins are known of Alchred, Ælfwald I and Æthelred, but not of Eardwulf, the ealdorman who emerged as king in 796.

Events of the second half of the eighth century are comparatively well documented from sources which drew on a lost Northumbrian chronicle, but few Northumbrian documents of the mid-ninth century can have survived the Viking invasions. After 806, when this lost chronicle closes, virtually the only information we have of the kingdom are statements in the much later histories written by 'Simeon of Durham' and Roger of Wendover, who appear to have had access to a summary list of kings and bishops. The dates they give are in some respects inconsistent with the numismatic evidence and there may have been some corruption in the sources they were copying (below, pp. 301–3).

Eardwulf was deposed *c.* 806/8 by Ælfwald II, but was probably reinstated as the result of an intervention by Charlemagne (Stenton 1971, 94). On his death in *c.* 810 he was succeeded, according to 'Simeon', by his son Eanred, who ruled until *c.* 840 and struck a substantial coinage. Eanred was in turn succeeded by his son, Æthelred II, who is said by Roger of Wendover to have been ousted by one Redwulf in 844. But later in the same year Redwulf was killed in a battle against the Vikings and Æthelred regained the throne. This account is confirmed by a series of coins in the name of Redwulf which interrupts Æthelred's coinage. Æthelred is said to have ruled for four more years and been followed by Osbert, the king whom the Vikings killed when they captured York in 866/7. Before the Viking arrival there had been an uprising and a rival, Ælla, had been proclaimed king, but he too was killed at York. No coins are known of Ælla or of the nominal English kings that the Vikings established after 867.

Coinage

During the later eighth and ninth centuries, Northumbria was unique in Europe as the only kingdom not to adopt the broader, thinner flan for its coinage. The small sceat module continued to be used, although in the ninth century the coins became so base that numismatists since Thorsby in the seventeenth century have sought to distinguish them from their finer predecessors by using the term 'styca(s)'. It is the Northumbrian form of the OE word *stycce* ('piece', cognate with Germ. *Stück*) used in the Lindisfarne Gospel to translate the *duo minuta* ('two mites') offered by the poor widow in the Temple (Mark 12.42), though there is no evidence for its ever having been applied to these coins. However, the term is too well entrenched in the literature to be displaced. Even so its use has not been consistent; some writers have drawn the distinction between sceattas and stycas according to whether they lack or include the moneyer's name, while others make the division between the finer eighth-century and the baser ninth-century coins. The latter practice is followed here.

(i) *Sceattas*

Northumbria had a tradition of striking coins stretching back, albeit intermittently, to the mid seventh century, the date of the 'York' group of thrymsas. The remarkable regal coinages of Aldfrith and Eadbert and the archiepiscopal coinage of Egbert (*c.* 732–66) were each ahead of their age, and Eadbert had been the first to restore the fineness of the currency in the 740s against the declining standards of the south (**1.1180**). In contrast, the extreme conservatism of the later Northumbrian coinages is perhaps a reflection of the greater political instability of the kingdom. No coins are known from the brief reign of Oswulf (758) or, more surprisingly, that of the usurper Æthelwald 'Moll' (759–65). Two archiepiscopal coins, which have at times been attributed to Æthelwald (they were dismissed in Lyon 1956, 228, but restored in Lyon 1967, 216), have been shown to be coins of Alchred (765–74) with Egbert (Booth 1984, 81).

Alchred, on the other hand, ordered coins to be struck soon after taking the throne, perhaps to reinforce his claim to be descended, like Eadbert, from Ida (547–68), the first king of Bernicia. His regal coins are similar to Eadbert's though the beast is more stick-like and there is a cross between its legs (**1.1181**). Those issued with Archbishop Egbert belong to the very beginning of the reign and are the first non-pictorial coins from Northumbria, having inscriptions around a small cross on each side. The inscriptions on Alchred's coins are arranged in a variety of ways, some conventionally, some reading outwards or in two arcs, as on the specimen here. Booth records fifteen regal and seven archiepiscopal coins, with little die-linking among them.

Only one coin is known from Æthelred I's first reign (774–9), in this case with a triquetra between the beast's legs, a variety also found for Eadbert. When Ælfwald I (779–88) ousted Æthelred, he evidently produced a more substantial coinage of the walking beast type of which twelve specimens survive. There is considerable variation among them in the spelling and arrangement of the king's name and the symbols around the beast, and Booth (1984, 84–5) has suggested that they fall into a number of distinct classes which may have had significance for the issue of dies, as under Eadbert. There are two further coins in the name of Ælfwald which presumably belong to the end of his reign, for in place of the walking beast they have the name of a moneyer, Cuthheart, around a small cross. The unusual form of the king's name, FΓEVAΓDVƧ, is similar to that found on the most ornamented of his 'beast' coins and supports the attribution to Ælfwald I rather than Ælfwald II (*c.* 806–8).

Thereafter, all Northumbrian coins, regal and archiepiscopal, bear the name of the moneyer. There are no coins known from the brief reign of Osred (788–90). The next coins in the series belong to a King Æthelred. A few of his coins have a cross-and-triangle on the reverse with CVD/CLS OR CVD/CILS in two parts, probably for a moneyer Cuthgils. Others with a circular reverse inscription and a variety of central ornaments (cross, pellet, square, etc.) were struck by six moneyers, Ædilred, Ceolbald, Cuthheard, Eanbald, Hnifula and Tidwulf. They are distinguished from coins of Æthelred II by their much higher silver content, which is clear even from a visual inspection. Some of the coins have a monogram of Rx for *rex* in the centre of the obverse, presumably copying the early Kentish coins. Those with the name Eanbald could be an issue of Archbishop Eanbald I rather than a moneyer of that name, although one might have expected him to have been given the usual abbreviated title A or AR to make it clear that it was an archiepiscopal issue.

These coins, which are unrepresented here, are generally assigned to Æthelred I's second reign (790–6), followed by an interval of some 30 years before the next coins were produced for Eanred. However, Pagan (1969) has tentatively suggested that those with a circular inscription may belong to an otherwise unknown king Æthelred immediately before Eanred, he suggests in the 810s or 820s, the king's name having fallen out of the sequence owing to some dislocation in the record. But the customary attribution of these coins to Æthelred I is supported by the presence of the moneyer Cuthheart on coins of Ælfwald I.

A number of metal analyses of eighth-century Northumbrian coins have been published, but their interpretation is uncertain. Eadbert's coins vary between 90% and 50% silver, but when correlated with the typological classification they show no obvious progression or pattern (Booth 1984). Only one of the later 'beast' coins has been analysed, a coin of Ælfwald I containing *c.* 50% silver (Metcalf *et al.* 1968, 52). Six coins of Æthelred I's second reign had finenesses ranging from 92 to 62% (*ibid.* 52–3). More results are required before one can judge whether Æthelred raised the standard and then allowed it to fall, whether the fineness was highly erratic throughout the second half of the eighth century, or whether some of the analyses we have are simply unreliable.

(ii) *Stycas*

The ninth-century stycas are among the commonest and the least respected Anglo-Saxon coins as a result of the discovery of several large hoards, mostly deposited at the very end of the series. The coinage was substantial, but not as large as the volume of surviving material might imply, for there is a high degree of die-linking. The great majority of the coins have the same essential design as the earliest 'moneyer' coins of Ælfwald I and Æthelred I, most of the coin being taken up by the king's or archbishop's name on the obverse and the moneyer's on the reverse. There are various central motifs, crosses, pellets, stars, etc., which may be different on obverse and reverse, but they do not form discrete types with any obvious chronological or other significance. Some coins of Æthelred II's moneyer Leofthegn are quite distinctive, with unusual central motifs such as an *omega* and a quasi-swastika, and one reverse die has his name in three lines and a hound or other animal looking backwards, probably inspired by the 'beast' type of the eighth-century Northumbrian coinage (cf. **1.1487**, a cast).

Eanred's coins (**1.1182–1208**) fall into two phases, which were first distinguished on the basis of hoard evidence (Lyon 1956, 232–3). Both were reasonably well represented in the Hexham hoard, but by the time the other major hoards were deposited coins of the earlier phase had largely disappeared from circulation. Coins of Archbishop Eanbald II (**1.1276**) are contemporary with the first phase, those of Archbishop Wigmund with the later one. The earlier coins generally contain more silver (15–40%) than the later ones (5–15%), although this is not always apparent in their colour. There were largely different moneyers in each. In the first phase there were seven royal moneyers (Dægberht, Eadwini, Herreth, Hwætred, Tidwini, Wilheah and Wulfheard), as well as three archiepiscopal moneyers (Cunwulf, Eadwulf and Ethelweard) who also struck coins for the king. Variations in the style and fabric of these coins suggest that the first phase may have lasted some considerable time and it is unlikely that all ten moneyers were ever operating at once. Only one of the earlier moneyers, Ethelweard, continued during the later phase in which ten new regal moneyers are found (Aldates, Brother, Cuthheard, Folcnoth, Fordred, Gadutels, Monne, Odilo, Wintred and Wulfred). However, the division is not as neat as this implies for there is some overlap between the two groups; the earlier coins of Gadutels and Monne, for example, appear to be contemporary with the later coins of Dægberht and Herreth. In Eanred's coinage there is far less sharing of obverse dies between moneyers than has been found in later reigns, and it has been suggested that the form of the king's name was varied deliberately as between each moneyer to distinguish the dies issued to them (Pagan 1973a, 6).

The accession of Æthelred II caused no apparent interruption in minting. Seven moneyers of Eanred continued in office and a considerable number of die-links between reigns have been found (Lyon 1956, 236–7). In addition, fourteen new moneyers are recorded in Æthelred's coinage. The standard division of Æthelred's coins between his first and second reigns, interrupted by Redwulf's rule of a few months, is that proposed by Lyon (1956) on the evidence of die-links and hoards, and in particular the contrast between the Hexham and later hoards. The Hexham hoard contained some 8,000 coins of Æthelred I, Eanred, Æthelred II and Redwulf, and of Archbishops Eanbald II and Wigmund, but one of Osbert or Archbishop Wulfhere, so that it must have been deposited either in the reign of Redwulf or in the second reign of Æthelred II. Other documented hoards, which contain coins of Osbert or Archbishop Wulfhere, are all later. A substantial proportion (*c.* 25%) of the coins of Æthelred in these later hoards were struck by a single moneyer Eardwulf (**1.1259–65**), but there were relatively few of his coins present at Hexham. As he was not a moneyer of Redwulf, it is reasonable to attribute all his coins to Æthelred's second reign along with a few coins of other moneyers which are associated by die-links or style but not thought to be derivatives (e.g. **1.1266**). The remaining coins of Æthelred (**1.1209–53**) have been attributed to his first reign, on the assumption that Eardwulf's domination of the coinage began at the start of the second reign and that the Hexham hoard was deposited shortly thereafter. Convenient though this classification is, it is possible that many of the moneyers who struck coins for Redwulf, and who had before that struck under Æthelred, continued in office on his restoration and that Eardwulf's coinage belongs a little later. If so we have yet to distinguish early coins of the second reign from those of the first struck by the same moneyers. However, Lyon's classification, conveniently summarized in North 1980, is followed in the catalogue below.

There are twelve moneyers recorded on Redwulf's coinage (**1.1254–8**), nine of whom had probably struck coins during Æthelred's first reign. This gives us an indication of the normal complement of moneyers at this period, with never more than about ten regal and two archiepiscopal moneyers active at one time. The regal moneyers appear to have been working in close proximity to one another for there is considerable die-linking between their products, with three or more moneyers sometimes sharing the same obverse die. Arrangements for striking the archiepiscopal coinage may have been different, for although most of its moneyers also struck some regal coins, die-links between the two series are rare. The moneyers no longer had obverse dies with their own distinctive form of legend, and the variations seen in Æthelred's name – *Edel-*, *Edil-*, *Edfl-*, etc. – appear to reflect changes in die-cutting practice though their significance has yet to be worked out. Developments can also be seen in the legends on Archbishop Wigmund's coins (**1.1277–1301**), the earlier dies giving his title as AREP or APEP, and the later ones omitting it altogether. Since Wigmund's period of office spanned the reigns of Eanred, Æthelred and perhaps Redwulf, the order in which his four moneyers operated can be discerned from the regal coins which they also struck.

The regular coinage of Osbert (**1.1267–9**), the last independent English king of Northumbria, was smaller than those of his predecessors, but as with the coinage of Æthelred's second reign its interpretation is complicated by the existence of imitations or derivatives reproducing the names of earlier and contemporary moneyers (e.g. **1.1269**). Pagan (1973a, 10–11) has suggested that two moneyers, Eanwulf and Monne, who were operating at the end of Æthelred's reign continued under Osbert and that they were joined or replaced by three others, Ethelhelm, Winiberht and Wulfsigt. At much the same time Archbishop Wulfhere appears to have had only one moneyer Wulfred (**1.1303–4**), for those in the name of Eardwulf (**1.1302**) are probably derivatives. The fineness of the coinage had been further reduced from *c.* 5% silver at the start of Æthelred II's first reign to virtually pure brass with no appreciable silver content (Gilmore and Metcalf 1980).

An account of the Northumbrian coinage cannot ignore the very substantial number of contemporary imitations or derivatives which occur in the hoards and presumably circulated with the regular coins. They are typified by blundered legends, irregular styles, unexpected die-links between chronologically separate kings, archbishops or moneyers, combinations of two obverse or two reverse dies, and occasionally low weights and irregularly-shaped flans. Two distinct series have been identified; the earlier one (**1.1270**), well represented in Hexham, reproduces legends of coins down to Redwulf, while the later series (**1.1269, 1271–5, 1302**), found only in the later hoards, copies the whole range of stycas but particularly those of Æthelred's second reign and of Osbert. There are several large and complex die-chains, though many coins stand alone. It is often difficult to draw a satisfactory distinction between the regular and the irregular series, since a number of dies from the regular coinage were used to strike the derivatives. The status of these issues is thus far from clear. They are not apparently mere imitations competing fraudulently with the official coinage. They seem at least to have been tolerated by the authorities and to have had some connection with the mint(s) of the regular coinage, though we do not know whether they were actually struck by them during periods of political uncertainty, or were issued in parallel with the regular coinage by established though less well-disciplined workshops. It is clear that in general the regulation of the coinage broke down towards the end of the styca period, and that a large proportion of the coins issued towards the end of Æthelred's reign and under Osbert were effectively anonymous.

Two other coins should be mentioned, each unique and one certainly, the other possibly, of the Northumbrian kingdom. The first is the *Munus divinum* solidus in the name of Archbishop

Wigmund which is discussed in Appendix 1 (below, p. 330). The second coin, found in a hoard at Trewhiddle, Cornwall, is a silver penny of the broader southern module with EANRED REX around a bust and on the reverse D:ES MONETA ω ('coin of that [king]') around a cross device (North 1980, no.619). The dies appear to be southern cut, possibly at Rochester, and close affinities with Æthelwulf's Inscribed Cross issue indicate that it is likely to have been struck after c. 850 (Wilson and Blunt 1961, 113–16). The only recorded King Eanred to whom it might be attributed is that of Northumbria, but according to the traditional dating he died in 840 or 841, some ten years too early. If a substantial revision of the chronology such as that proposed by Pagan be accepted, Eanred would have been ruling in the early 850s and thus able to strike this coin, probably as a ceremonial issue rather than a serious attempt to introduce a broad-penny coinage in Northumbria. Otherwise the coin must remain attributed to an unknown ruler of a southern kingdom, unsatisfactory as this may be.

(iii) *Chronology*

The chronology of the ninth-century Northumbrian kings derived from Roger of Wendover and 'Simeon of Durham' presents a number of difficulties for the numismatist, besides that of the 'EANRED REX' silver penny just discussed. According to the written sources Osbert reigned for eighteen or thirteen years, yet his coinage and the associated irregular issues can scarcely have lasted so long. Another problem is that posed by Archbishop Wulfhere's coinage which must have commenced towards the end of Æthelred II's reign or at the beginning of Osbert's at the latest (Lyon 1956, 235), yet he is said to have taken the see of York c. 854, five years after Osbert's accession. Lyon concluded that the styca coinage could not have extended much beyond c. 855 and an even earlier terminus would be indicated if grounds could be found for moving Wulfhere's accession back by a few years. One implication of this was that the twenty or so hoards other than Hexham would have been the product of some unrecorded strife in the 850s rather than the Viking conquest of York in 866/7.

Pagan (1969) has taken a different approach, arguing that the end of the coinage and the deposit of these hoards are to be associated with the events of 866/7, but that Roger and Simeon were mistaken about the length of Osbert's reign. He points to various deficiencies in the accounts of this period and suggests that there had been a dislocation of some fourteen years in the chronology of the earlier kings back to Eanred, which may have been caused by a predecessor having slipped out of the record (Table 25). This would bring Eanred's death down to c. 854 and allow the silver penny to be attributed to him, but it also requires a number of arbitrary adjustments to be made to the archiepiscopal chronology.

Pagan's general approach seems justified and preferable to that of Lyon, but the choice of fourteen years for the period by which to retard the chronology arises from his estimate of five years as the likely length of Osbert's coinage and reign. This is a somewhat arbitrary figure, for the numismatic evidence cannot be interpreted so precisely in view of the reduction in the number of moneyers and the breakdown in mint control towards the end of Æthelred's reign. If a longer period were assigned to Osbert's reign no adjustment would be required to the dates of the archbishops, although an attribution of the silver penny to Eanred of Northumbria would be more difficult. It seems that there is a good case for attributing Osbert's coinage mainly

Table 25. *Kings and archbishops in Northumbria,* c. *810–67*

Dates derived from those in documentary sources compared with those proposed by Pagan (in italics). *e.* = earlier; *l.* = later

Kings	*Archbishops*
	Eanbald II 796–? (*796*–c. *840 or l.*)
Eanred c. 810–40 (c. *830 or e.*–c. *854*)	Wulfsige (*no coins*) ?–837 (c. *848 or e.*–c. *848 or l.*)
Æthelred II (1st reign) c. 840–4 (c. *854–8*)	Wigmund c. 837–54 (c. 848 *or e.*–c. *858 or l.*)
Redwulf c. 844 (c. *858*)	
Æthelred II (2nd reign) c. 844–8 (c. *852–62*)	
Osbert c. 848–67 (c. *862–7*)	Wulfhere 854–900? (c. *865–900?*)

to the 860s and Æthelred's second-reign coinage to the 850s, and this could be accounted for by some readjustment of the earlier chronology such as that proposed by Pagan, though a less radical one might satisfy both the numismatic and documentary evidence.

(e) THE EMERGENCE OF ENGLAND: SOUTHERN COINAGES, *c.* 850–924

Literature

General surveys of the coinage are Lyon 1968 and 1976 and, for the period to 874, Pagan 1986. Pagan 1965a provides a detailed though difficult study of the Lunette issue, somewhat clarified by Lyon 1968. A study of the chemical composition of the coins of this period is in preparation by Metcalf and Northover, who have kindly allowed us to cite their results for many of the coins in this collection in the catalogue below. Alfred's coinage is reviewed in Dolley and Blunt 1961, and the relevant hoards are described in Blunt and Dolley 1959. A corpus of the coins of Ceolwulf II is provided in Dolley 1963, supplemented by Pagan 1972, and of Archbishop Æthelred in Blunt 1962a. The periodic nature of the coinage *c.* 850–85 is considered in Lyon 1968 and Dolley 1983. A definitive study of Edward the Elder's coinage by Lyon will appear in a forthcoming volume on tenth-century coinage by Blunt, Lyon and Stewart.

Historical background

Æthelwulf had five sons, Æthelstan, Æthelbald, Æthelbert, Æthelred and Alfred, an example of the Germanic practice of name-giving whereby a common element frequently recurs within a family. Æthelwulf had appointed Æthelstan sub-king of Kent, as he himself had been during Egbert's reign, but Æthelstan died in the early 850s. In 853 Æthelwulf's daughter, Æthelswith, married the young Burgred, who had recently ascended the Mercian throne, cementing an alliance between the two kingdoms, which in the same year mounted a joint campaign against the Welsh. When Æthelwulf prepared for a pilgrimage to Rome with his youngest son Alfred in 855 he divided the kingdom between his two eldest surviving sons; Æthelbald was to rule Wessex proper in his absence, and Æthelbert, Kent, Surrey, Sussex and Essex.

On his return from Rome Æthelwulf visited Charles the Bald's court and took Charles' daughter, Judith, as his second wife. Æthelbald refused to relinquish control of Wessex, and until his death in 858 Æthelwulf was confined to the eastern provinces of Wessex. He was succeeded in the east by Æthelbert, but the division of Wessex was ended with Æthelbald's death in 860, and the kingdom was once again unified under Æthelbert. Thereafter the succession followed as Æthelwulf had intended, Æthelred becoming king in 865 and Alfred in 871.

Despite a defeat at *Aclea* in 851, the Viking raids gained increasing momentum through the 850s and 860s, their campaigns alternating between England and the Continent. Towards the end of 865 the *Anglo-Saxon Chronicle* ominously records the arrival of a 'great heathen army' which was to come within an ace of conquering the whole of England. The movement of this army and its reinforcements over the following two decades is recorded in detail, but only a summary is necessary here. After landing in East Anglia, it rode north to capture York in

Table 26. *Kings of Wessex, 802–955*

Dates are those of rulers as kings of Wessex unless otherwise indicated.

- EGBERT 802–39
  - ÆTHELWULF
k. of S.E. England, 825–39
k. of Wessex, 839–55
k. of S.E. England only, 855–8
    - ÆTHELSTAN
k. of S.E. England, 839–*c.* 851
    - ÆTHELBALD
855–60
    - ÆTHELBERT
k. of S.E. England, 855–65
k. of Wessex, 860–5
    - ÆTHELRED I
865–71
    - ALFRED
871–99
      - EDWARD THE ELDER
899–924
        - ÆTHELSTAN
924–39
        - EADMUND
939–46
          - *later kings*
        - EADRED
946–55
      - Æthelflæd 'Lady of the Mercians' = Æthelred, ealdorman of Mercia

866, killing the Northumbrian kings Osbert and Ælla and replacing them with their own puppet ruler. In autumn 869, after campaigning in Mercia, it returned to subdue East Anglia, putting King Edmund savagely to death. Thirty years later, as the coins show, he was to be venerated as a saint by the Viking settlers. During 870/1 the Vikings struck into central Wessex, where they met firm resistance. Reinforced by a second army, they occupied London and spent the following winter there. In 873/4 they defeated the Mercians at Repton, driving Burgred into exile and installing Ceolwulf II on the throne. The *Chronicle* is contemptuous of this 'foolish king's thegn' and implies that he was in the pocket of the Vikings, but he issued charters in his own name and a coinage in conjunction with Alfred. The Vikings then divided forces. The remnants of the original army of 865 led by Halfdan subdued Northumbria and ravaged the Scottish borders, while Guthrum and the reinforcements from the 871 campaign went to Cambridge (Keynes and Lapidge 1983, 212 n.13).

By 875 the Vikings had conquered the kingdoms of East Anglia, Mercia and Northumbria, and the principal phase of Scandinavian settlement then followed. Halfdan and his men settled in Northumbria in 876. In 877 Guthrum agreed with Ceolwulf II on a division of Mercia, Ceolwulf retaining the western half of the kingdom and part of Guthrum's army taking the eastern half, notably the region later known as the Five Boroughs (Leicester, Lincoln, Nottingham, Stamford and Derby) but also land to the south, possibly including London. The remainder of Guthrum's army settled in East Anglia in 880. The eastern and northern parts of England, known collectively as the Danelaw, thereby came under Viking rule, and their institutions, art and language were impressed to varying degrees with Scandinavian culture. Guthrum had not given up hope of the total conquest of England. In 875–7 he launched a second invasion of Wessex, although Alfred managed to negotiate a temporary peace. He returned early in 878, taking Alfred by surprise and driving him and his forces to a fortification at Athelney in the Somerset marches. But from there Alfred managed to rally sufficient support to achieve a decisive victory at Edington in Wiltshire. The Vikings soon capitulated, and a peace was settled at Wedmore. Guthrum was baptized, taking the name Æthelstan, with Alfred standing as sponsor, and the army returned to East Anglia.

Alfred had then to set about rebuilding his kingdom. By 883 Mercia was being governed by an ealdorman, Æthelred, who acknowledged Alfred's overlordship. In 886 Alfred captured London from the Vikings and in a ceremony which followed 'all the English people who were not under the subjection of the Danes submitted to him'. Alfred and Guthrum then entered into a treaty defining the border between 'English' Mercia and the Danelaw (Map 6), and providing penalties for injuries caused to each other's subjects. As part of the new scheme of defence, Alfred established a series of fortified burhs to be supported by men from their localities, and the project was continued by Edward the Elder. Many of these became thriving market centres and a law code of Æthelstan (924–39), possibly reflecting an earlier provision, gave every burh in Wessex the right to a mint. The increase in the number of mints towards the end of Alfred's reign and under Edward reflects this policy.

In 892 there was a renewal of trouble when two Viking armies that had been campaigning for many years on the Continent arrived in England. They first established themselves in Kent, but were subsequently driven across the Thames into the southern Danelaw. Between 893 and

Map 6 *England in the ninth century*

896 these armies, often operating independently and with the support of the East Anglian and Northumbrian settlers, roamed across Wessex and Mercia, once again stretching Alfred's defences to the limit. But the burghal system proved its worth, and in 896 the armies dispersed, some settling in the Danelaw and some returning to the Continent to plunder the Seine valley.

Alfred was succeeded by his son Edward the Elder in 899. Little headway was made against the Danes in his early years despite a number of encounters. But almost by chance his fortunes turned in 910 when a Northumbrian force returning from raids in western England was overtaken at Tettenhall in Staffordshire and annihilated with three of its kings. Although no land was reconquered as a direct consequence, the battle dealt such a severe blow to the Northumbrian Danes that when Edward started campaigning in the southern Danelaw they were unable to lend aid to their kinsmen. Indeed they were themselves being pressed and were eventually ousted by the more ruthless Norsemen of Dublin. Between 912 and 918 Edward and his sister Æthelflæd, 'Lady of the Mercians', gradually advanced the borders of Mercia in a masterly campaign, building new fortifications as they went to threaten the Danes and protect their gains. Slowly one Viking army after another submitted to them. East Anglia and Essex fell in 917 and the remainder of the East Midlands in the following year. The *Anglo-Saxon Chronicle* for 918 says of Edward that 'all the people who had settled in Mercia, both Danish and English, submitted to him' which would by implication include those at Lincoln and in Lindsey, but numismatic evidence suggests that these remained in Viking hands until the mid 920s (below, p. 323).

In 920 Edward turned his attention to the north, building new fortifications at Nottingham and in Derbyshire. In anticipation of a major campaign, Ragnald, the new Hiberno-Norse king of York, together with kings of Scotland, Strathclyde, and Bamburgh, came to Edward to acknowledge him as their overlord, gaining in return recognition of their authority in their own kingdoms. Edward died in 924, and in 927 his son Æthelstan gained direct control over Northumbria to become the first king of England.

Coinage

The third quarter of the ninth century saw a number of developments in the coinage of southern England, no doubt partly as a response to the Viking incursions. A standard design was adopted by all the West Saxon moneyers, royal and archiepiscopal, and from the 860s also by those of Mercia presumably as a result of some kind of monetary convention between the rulers concerned. The design was changed periodically, there being four main issues and a number of minor ones between *c.* 852 and *c.* 885 (Table 27). The hoard evidence suggests that after each main change of type the earlier issues were largely reminted, though we do not know whether this occurred through deliberate fiscal policy, or whether it resulted from general economic factors.

The concept of occasional *renovationes monetae* would have been known from the Franks, and its application would be consistent with the apparent aim of maintaining a currency of one standard type. But it seems unlikely that these were periodic coinages, with changes intended primarily as tax-raising events, as in the later tenth and eleventh centuries. Metcalf and Northover's as yet unpublished research has shown that towards the end of Æthelwulf's reign the

Table 27. *Issues of Wessex and Mercia, c.852–c.885*

Type	Issuer	Number of known moneyers	
Main issues			
Inscribed Cross (*c.* 852–62)	Wessex: Æthelwulf (**1.1305–9**)	14	59
	Æthelbert (**1.1310–14**)	49	
	Archiepiscopal: Ceolnoth (**1.1315**)	10	
Floriated Cross (*c.* 862–6)	Wessex: Æthelbert	7	8
	Archiepiscopal: Ceolnoth	1	
Lunette* (*c.* 866–75)	Wessex: Æthelbert?	1 ?(M)	40(C) 64(M)
	Æthelred I (**1.1342–4**)	19(C), 10(M)	
	Alfred (**1.1345–51**)	30(C), 12(M)	
	Mercia: Burgred (from *c.* 860; **1.1316–40**)	55(M)	
	Archiepiscopal: Ceolnoth	2(C)	
Cross-and-Lozenge (*c.* 878–85?)	Wessex: Alfred (**1.1352**)	18	22
	Mercia: Ceolwulf II	5	
	Archiepiscopal: Æthelred (**1.1353**)	2	
Minor issues			
Cross-crosslet and Pellets (*c.* 865?)	Archiepiscopal: Ceolnoth	1	
Four-line Lunette (866/7)	Wessex: Æthelred I (**1.1341**)	3	
Two Emperors (*c.* 875–8?)	Wessex: Alfred	1	2
	Mercia: Ceolwulf II	1	
Portrait/Quatrefoil (*c.* 875–8?)	Wessex: Alfred	1	1?
	Archiepiscopal: Æthelred	1	
Voided Cross/Quatrefoil (*c.* 875–8?)	Wessex: Alfred	1	
Name-in-field (*c.* 875–8?)	Mercia: Ceolwulf II	1	

*In the Lunette issue, C = moneyers using dies of Canterbury style; M = moneyers using dies of Mercian and other styles (including imitations).

coinage was significantly debased, and it became worse still under his successors. This alone could have been sufficient to drive the earlier, finer coins out of circulation without a formal recoinage, and it may have been one of a number of factors which prompted the changes in coin type between *c.* 850 and *c.* 885. There seems to have been a political motive underlying the adoption by Wessex of the Lunette design which established a common coinage in Wessex and Mercia, while the Cross-and-Lozenge type (and perhaps the Floriated Cross type of which we know so little) marked a restoration of a good silver standard. The issues of the later 870s are known from so few specimens that it is difficult to say anything about them, but they may also have had some political significance, as the London monogram type surely had a decade later.

This period also saw an increase in minting activity. There is no evidence that the number of mints increased, although we would not necessarily be able to recognize the products of new mints if their dies were supplied centrally from Canterbury or London. Rochester appears to have received its dies from Canterbury shortly after the beginning of the Inscribed Cross type, and we cannot tell for how long it continued to operate as a mint. But the number of moneyers striking the West Saxon coinage increased during Æthelbert's reign from about ten to perhaps as many as 40. It fell to less than 20 under Æthelred I, but rose again to 25 or 30 under Alfred. In Mercia there were virtually no coins struck during the 850s, and Burgred had only two moneyers working for him *c.* 860. But five years later he had six or eight, and by *c.* 870 the number of Mercian moneyers, presumably operating at London, had grown to 35 or 40. The scale of the coinage had likewise grown, though the coins themselves had become baser than at any time in England in the middle ages, the Northumbrian stycas excepted. In the later 870s and early 880s the coinage appears to have been much smaller, though as there are so few finds from this period no reliable comparison can be made.

The activity of the 'great army' in England is reflected in the incidence of coin hoards. There were some 40 hoards deposited *c.* 865–75, far more than in any other decade of the Anglo-Saxon period (Blackburn and Pagan 1986). Approximately half of these are Northumbrian finds, some of which may have resulted from civil strife rather than from the Viking incursions. But most of the hoards from south of the Humber may be taken to reflect Viking disturbances in some way, and in some cases they tie in with recorded historical events. The closely dated hoards from Croydon, Gravesend and London (Waterloo Bridge) were apparently deposited in 871/2 when the Vikings wintered in London; and the same may be true of the Barking and London (Westminster Bridge) hoards, though their contents are too poorly recorded for precise dating (Brooks and Graham-Campbell 1986). The hoard from Beeston Tor in Staffordshire probably dates from the winter of 873/4 when the Vikings defeated the Mercians at Repton, and the purse of five coins found among the remains of over 150 individuals in a charnel mound at Repton and another from a single grave there can be associated with that battle (Biddle *et al.* 1986).

Most of the Southumbrian hoards of this period contain exclusively coins of the Lunette issue with just the exceptional East Anglian coin. Some, such as the Croydon hoard, are more mixed including Carolingian and Islamic coins as well as silver ingots, indications that they were Viking treasures. A third group of hoards, represented by those from Dorking in Surrey (dep. *c.* 862) and Trewhiddle in Cornwall (dep. *c.* 868), contain coins stretching back to the first half of the century and were presumably drawn from savings rather than currency.

Inscribed Cross and Floriated Cross types

The Inscribed Cross type (**1.1305–15**) was Æthelwulf's last issue, and it was continued during the early years of Æthelbert's reign. On the reverse it has the moneyer's name and title written along the arms of a large voided cross and continued in the field. The archiepiscopal coins of Ceolnoth have the same reverse design (**1.1315**), but the obverse in this and the succeeding Floriated Cross type has a facing tonsured bust, rather than the right-facing bust of the regal coins. In later issues the regal and archiepiscopal coins have identical designs. The type was probably introduced in the early or mid 850s. Some early dies (**1.1305**) are in the same style as the Rochester *Dor‾b‾/Cant* issue and were presumably cut by the same hand, but before long they were all of the uniform Canterbury style, and products of the Rochester mint can no longer be distinguished stylistically. The two Rochester moneyers of the *Dor‾b‾/Cant* issue who also struck the Inscribed Cross type (Ethelhere and Manninc) continued into Æthelbert's reign using Canterbury-style dies, and while it is possible that the mint was closed down and these moneyers transferred to Canterbury, it is more likely that Canterbury supplied dies to the Rochester mint. As indicated above, the number of moneyers striking this type increased substantially during Æthelbert's reign, presumably in response to a greater demand for coinage. This demand may also be the reason for the decline in the silver standard, which had already begun under Æthelwulf. The main source of these coins is the Dorking hoard, deposited *c.* 860 or a little later, which contained approximately 350 Inscribed Cross coins, *c.* 100 of Æthelwulf and *c.* 250 of Æthelbert.

The Inscribed Cross type was succeeded in the early 860s by the Floriated Cross, which is not represented here. It was struck by Æthelbert and Archbishop Ceolnoth, and is very rare because we have no hoards deposited during its currency, so there were probably many more than the seven moneyers known for it today. The archbishop's coinage of this type is indeed known only from a single fragmentary specimen in the British Museum, but another unique coin, with the exceptional reverse design of a cross-crosslet and four pellets (*SCBI* Glasgow 403), may be an experimental issue of the same period.

Lunette type

Virtually no Mercian coinage was struck for a decade following the sack of London in 850/1. The Dorking hoard contained only a single coin of Burgred by the moneyer Tatel. It had the moneyer's name and title in three lines across the reverse, with the upper and lower lines enclosed in lunettes. This design had a Mercian tradition going back ultimately to the obverse of Offa's later coins, and it had been used as a reverse type by Ceolwulf I and Wiglaf. Tatel had been a moneyer of Berhtwulf, but whether he notionally held office throughout the 850s we do not know; if so it is perhaps surprising that the London mint did not respond more quickly to the increased demand reflected in the West Saxon coinage towards the end of the decade. In the early 860s Tatel was joined by a second moneyer, Dudecil, and then expansion was more rapid. By *c.* 865 there were perhaps a dozen moneyers, rising to almost 40 by the end of the reign, and the work of two principal and one subsidiary schools of die-cutting can be discerned.

Burgred's Lunette coinage has been the subject of a detailed study by Pagan (1965), who has proposed an arrangement which breaks away from the *BMC* classification based on reverse types. The *BMC* classification, however, remains useful for descriptive purposes and may be applied to the Lunette series as a whole. It is: *a*=closed lunettes; *b*=lunettes broken by curls in the centre of each arc; *c*=lunettes broken by curls at the ends of the horizontal lines; *d*=as *c* but arcs of lunettes omitted; *e*, added by Blunt 1958=as *d* with M above and below.

Pagan has distinguished three chronological groups. The Early group consists of coins of three distinct die-cutting styles, which Lyon (1968) has called B, F and G, and it runs until roughly the accession of Æthelred I. These coins are therefore contemporary with the Floriated Cross issue at Canterbury. Coins of the Early group (**1.1316–21**) typically have an initial cross in the obverse legend, while those of the later groups rarely do so. Within this group, the earliest coins are of type *a* and they are followed by coins of types *c* and *d*. In about 866 there were marked developments in the die-cutting styles B and F, and their successors, H (Pagan's 'Horizontal') and V (Pagan's 'Vertical') respectively, continued until the end of the coinage in 874. Style G (not represented here, but see *SCBI* Glasgow, 375 and 379) does not continue beyond the Early group. These developments occurred while reverse types *c* and *d* were still in use, so that the Middle group (**1.1322–4**) consists mainly of coins of style H or V with reverses of type *c* or *d*. The Middle group has been dated *c*. 866–8 on the evidence of the Trewhiddle hoard which contained substantial numbers of Burgred's Early and Middle coins and a few of Æthelred I's earliest Four-line variety. The Late group (**1.1325–39**), which is the largest, marks a reversion to the use of type *a*, often with a number of pellets in the corners of the lunettes. Coins of type *b* are much scarcer than the other types and mostly belong to the Late group. Type *e* is extremely rare and belongs to the Early group, style B. The majority of Burgred's coins appear to have been produced at one mint, for although there are two principal styles of die-cutting, they were employed indiscriminately by the moneyers of the time. This was probably at London, even if Rochester is accepted as the mint of Berhtwulf's coins (Lyon 1968, 233–4, 237). It is possible that Burgred also had mints elsewhere which struck coins for Ceolwulf II and Alfred in the late 870s and 880s.

When Æthelred I succeeded to Wessex in 866 a substantial Mercian coinage was already in circulation. He immediately introduced a new type for the West Saxon coinage (**1.1341**) with an obverse based on the Floriated Cross type and a four-line reverse partially inspired by Burgred's Lunette type *d*. These coins are rare, and the Canterbury mint soon adopted the standard Lunette type *a* for the coins of both Æthelred (**1.1342–4**) and Archbishop Ceolnoth, creating a single uniform coinage for both Wessex and Mercia. The Lunette type was continued by Alfred from 871 (**1.1345–51**), but it is not known for Archbishop Æthelred, who succeeded Ceolnoth in 870. The majority of the coins of Æthelred I and Alfred are from dies cut at Canterbury, exhibiting continuity in style with Canterbury dies of earlier issues. A small number, however, are in the V or H style, some sharing moneyers with Burgred. A number of these are imitations from late in the issue (**1.1345**; and specimens in the Repton finds, Biddle *et al.* 1986), but some in the name of Alfred appear to be official products suggesting that he may have enjoyed limited minting rights at London or some other shared mint. A unique Lunette coin in the name of Æthelbert of early V style (type *c*) could represent a striking under similar arrangements at the very end of his reign (Blunt 1952b).

Burgred's earliest coins were struck in fine silver, but the standard soon declined as it had in Wessex. Coins of Æthelred I were initially no better than 50% fine, and some of Alfred's and Burgred's later Lunette coins are less than 20% silver (information Metcalf and Northover). The debasement was most severe when the Viking attacks were greatest in the 870s. Yet the reduction had started much earlier and may have been caused by a general shortage of silver reflected most clearly in the Northumbrian coinage. There are no coins of Ceolwulf II of the

Lunette type and it is probable that Alfred did not continue striking it for long after Burgred's exile in 874.

*Cross-and-Lozenge and other types (*c. *875*–c. *885)*

For this period, the arrangement of the coinage is problematic. There is one substantial issue, Cross-and-Lozenge, and a number of extremely rare types whose positions and significance are not clear. The difficulties are largely owing to a lack of material. There is only one tiny hoard of four coins deposited during the period, and most of the surviving material comes from the early tenth-century Cuerdale hoard. The Cross-and-Lozenge issue (sometimes known as the 'Ceolwulf' type) was struck by Alfred, Ceolwulf and Archbishop Æthelred, and there is no doubt that it was much larger than the number of surviving specimens suggest. There are some 31 coins of Alfred (**1.1352**) struck by 21 moneyers, eight coins of Ceolwulf by five moneyers and two coins of the archbishop (**1.1353**) by two moneyers (Archibald 1978). There were at least two mints operating in this issue, Canterbury producing coins for Alfred and Archbishop Æthelred, and another used by both Ceolwulf and Alfred (Lyon 1968, 236). The location of the latter is uncertain. One of the moneyers, Liafwald, had operated for Burgred, which suggests that it might have been at London, but we do not know for how long London was in Viking hands before its recapture in 886 (Stenton 1971, 258–9) and it is unlikely that an official coinage would have been struck there in Alfred's name while under Viking control. A lead weight or trial piece bearing the imprints of a pair of Cross-and-Lozenge dies of the moneyer Ealdulf was found in the churchyard of St Paul's, London (Dolley 1953, 175–6), and may reflect minting activity in the City. The normal title for both kings in this issue is simply *rex*, but on a number of dies of anomalous style, possibly representing additional mints, Alfred is described as *rex Sax(oniorum)* and Ceolwulf as *rex M(erciorum)*.

With the Cross-and-Lozenge issue, the coinage was restored to fine silver and the base Lunette coins, to judge from their absence from later hoards, were reminted. It is unlikely that Alfred and Ceolwulf would have been in a position to effect a major coinage reform before the victory at Edington in 878, so this was presumably the main issue of the early 880s, with coins being issued exclusively in Alfred's name towards the end. Ceolwulf is not mentioned in historical sources after 877, and by 883 Mercia was ruled by ealdorman Æthelred under Alfred's overlordship. A Mercian regnal list assigns Ceolwulf a reign of five years, i.e. until 879, but the size of his coinage could suggest that he reigned longer.

The other types which belong to this period are all exceedingly rare. The remarkable 'Two Emperors' type with a reverse copied from a fourth-century solidus was perhaps intended to commemorate an alliance between Wessex and Mercia against the Danes. It is known only from a unique coin of Ceolwulf from the Cuerdale hoard, and from one of Alfred, a single-find from Croydon in Surrey. A coin in the name of a Viking king Halfdan is a later imitation (below, p. 319). The bust of the Ceolwulf coin is similar to that on his Cross-and-Lozenge issue, although with differently treated hair and an inner border, and the moneyer Eadwulf, who had also worked for Burgred, is the same as that of the lead piece from St Paul's churchyard. Alfred's coin is clearly from a different atelier, with a more delicate bust, although here again the moneyer had worked for Burgred. On this coin Alfred is given the unusual title of *rex*

Anglo, implying an uncharacteristic insensitivity to Mercian pride if, as it appears, this coin was issued during Ceolwulf's reign. A fragmentary coin from the Southampton excavations may be a mule between this and the Cross-and-Lozenge issue (Blunt 1950; Lyon 1968, 236).

Another type of this period has a portrait obverse and an ornamental quatrefoil on the reverse containing the moneyer's name. It is known from one coin of Archbishop Æthelred (hence it is sometimes known as the 'Æthelred' type) and a fragment of Alfred, both of unrecorded provenance. Both coins may have been struck by the same moneyer, Ethered, who had worked for Alfred in the Lunette issue. A third minor type of Alfred has a different form of Quatrefoil reverse and a non-portrait obverse made up of a voided cross with AELFRÆD REX inscribed on the arms and trefoils in the angles. The only known specimen is from the Cuerdale hoard, and again the mint is a problem since the moneyer, Luda, had struck for Burgred. Finally, the Cuerdale hoard contained a small fragment of a coin of Ceolwulf with a right-facing bust (?) within a beaded border, and on the reverse part of the moneyer's name . . . ANR . . . and a circular inner inscription of which only the letters . . . CO . . . are visible (Pagan 1972). If a mint name is intended, Lincoln is the only appropriate one which comes to mind, yet it is doubtful whether Ceolwulf would have been able to strike coins there even before the division of the kingdom in 877, which placed Lindsey firmly in Viking hands.

It has been suggested that the first three of these minor issues belong to the early or mid 880s after the Cross-and-Lozenges type (Dolley and Blunt 1961), but it is more likely that they were short-lived or experimental issues made before the Cross-and-Lozenge type had become established (Lyon 1968, 236). There are several arguments in favour of this arrangement. All the known moneyers of the minor issues are recorded on the Lunette coinage, whereas nine of the twenty-two Cross-and-Lozenge moneyers are new. Typologically they sit better there, since the three portrait types all have an inner border as on the Lunette coins but which is absent from Alfred's later portrait types, and some early Canterbury Cross-and-Lozenge coins have reverse borders apparently influenced by those on the two Quatrefoil types. The virtual absence of these coins from the Cuerdale hoard would imply an early date, and this arrangement avoids the necessity of either extending Ceolwulf's reign excessively or attributing very little coinage to the early and mid 880s, the period when Alfred's programme of reconstruction was beginning to take effect.

London Monogram and Two-line types

Alfred's later coins were struck to a revised weight standard, the median weight increasing from *c.* 20gr. (1.30g) to *c.* 24gr. (1.56g), and round halfpennies appear for the first time. Among the first coins struck to this heavy standard were a portrait issue with a large monogram of *Lundonia* on the reverse (**1.1354–8**), presumably celebrating Alfred's capture of London in 886. They break with the stylized form of portrait common since the early ninth century and copy directly a Roman prototype, the most faithful copy being a coin, unfortunately in bad condition, in this collection (**1.1354**). Some coins have a smaller monogram to allow room for the name of the moneyer, Tilewine (**1.1359**). Although the issue is reasonably plentiful today largely as a result of the London (Bucklersbury) and Cuerdale hoards, there is a high degree of die-linking and it was probably only short-lived. Within a few years it was being reminted in England (cf. **1.1363** and Banks and Purvey 1967; a West Mercian Two-line type and a coin of Plegmund overstruck on London Monogram coins), although a sufficient number remained in the Danelaw for it to become a popular type to imitate in the 890s. Four original halfpennies are known, others being Viking imitations.

The main coinage of Alfred's later years, which continued through much of the tenth century, was a non-portrait type with a small cross on the obverse and the moneyer's name in two lines on the reverse (**1.1360–8**). It must have commenced by 888 for one specimen is known in the name of Archbishop Æthelred who died on 30 June 888. A number of stylistic groups can be distinguished, the most important of which have been associated with London, Canterbury, the West Midlands and, towards the end of the reign, Winchester (Dolley and Blunt 1961, identifying the latter as a late London style; it is attributed to Winchester by Lyon in his forthcoming study of Edward the Elder's coinage). There are, in addition, many coins from the Danelaw, a few struck for Guthrum under his baptismal name of Æthelstan, but the majority merely copy Alfred's coins. Most coins have the obverse legend + EL FR ED RE(X) divided into four parts, but the Winchester group has AEL FRE DRE in three parts. Some of the Canterbury coins have a continuous legend with the mint name DORO inserted at the end (**1.1360**) and the counterpart in the archiepiscopal coinage of Plegmund has DO/RO in the field (**1.1369**). There is no continuity in style between Alfred's and Edward the Elder's coins of London and Canterbury, and it may be that they ceased operating for a period towards the end of the Alfred's reign. The suggestion that the Canterbury mint may have closed as early as 892, when the Vikings landed in Kent (Dolley and Blunt 1961, 86), cannot be sustained in the light of a discovery of a coin of Plegmund overstruck on a St Edmund Memorial penny dating from *c.* 895 (Banks and Purvey 1967).

A number of other mints are named for the first time on coins of this period. A unique coin of Gloucester from Cuerdale, with a portrait obverse and ÆT GLEA ƿ A ('at or from Gloucester') around a cross on the reverse, may be contemporary with the London monogram coins; there are affinities in its design with the Cross-and-Lozenge issue, but it is struck to the heavier standard. Almost as rare are the later non-portrait coins of Exeter and Winchester, which have + AELFRED REX SAXONVM in four lines on the obverse and EXA or ƿ IN vertically on the reverse. Two large silver pieces, almost seven times the weight of the average penny, with a similar obverse design and ELI/MŌ (for *Elimosina* = alms) on the reverse were presumably intended for charitable presentation. Another very rare group of coins with the name OHSNAFORDA are probably from Oxford (Lyon 1970, 196–7), their correct interpretation having for long been obscured by the existence of many Danelaw imitations (**1.1380–1**).

Most of Edward the Elder's coins are of a Two-line type with a small cross on the obverse similar to Alfred's, but a significant group has a left-facing bust (ninth-century portraits had been right facing) with the two-line reverse. There are other rare types with a geometric 'rose' design or, from West Mercia, a variety of pictorial reverses. The only mint-signed coins of the reign are those of Bath with BAÐ across the reverse, which were present in the Cuerdale hoard and hence very early. Lyon's study will greatly advance our understanding of the chronology and geographical arrangement of the coinage. Broadly it can be divided into three phases, Early (899–*c.* 910), Middle (*c.* 910–15) and Late (*c.* 915–24). From the beginning of the

Middle phase there is a marked and progressive increase in the flan size, from *c.* 20mm to *c.* 24mm by the Late phase, and similarly the diameter of the inner circle on non-portrait coins increases from *c.* 10mm to *c.* 14mm.

The four major groups identified in Alfred's Two-line issue (**1.1374–8**) can be traced through into Edward's reign. Initially London and Canterbury seem to have been virtually inactive, unless they were temporarily obtaining their dies from Winchester which had become the principal southern die-centre and mint. Four prolific moneyers of the Early period – Æthered, Athelulf, Wulfheard and Wulfred – can be associated with Winchester through die-links and mint-signed coins of Æthelstan, but other moneyers using dies of similar style may have operated elsewhere, e.g. at Oxford, with dies drawn from Winchester. Portrait coins (**1.1371–3**) were struck in the Early phase at Winchester, in West Mercia and occasionally at London, and in the Late phase at London and in East Anglia. When they occur, they seem to have been produced indiscriminately with non-portrait Two-line coins.

The 'rose' type was used at Canterbury for both Edward and Archbishop Plegmund and at Winchester at the transition from the Early to the Middle phase (Lyon 1983). At much the same time the pictorial series commenced in West Mercia. These include various floral designs decorating the moneyer's name. Others have a *Manus Dei* issuing from a cloud, while a third interesting group has architectural designs: a church or minster, a church tower (**1.1375A**), and probably a version of the fourth-century camp gate type. In the Late phase, West Mercian moneyers reverted to the Two-line type, and new styles are found representing mints established in the recently reconquered East Midlands. In East Anglia a large imitative coinage was produced mostly copying the Late London portrait coins, including the names of the moneyers blundered to varying degrees. The hoard from Morley St Peter in Norfolk, deposited at the beginning of Æthelstan's reign, included some 660 of these together with 41 blundered copies of the Two-line type (published and fully illustrated in *SCBI* East Anglian Museums). It is curious that a mint apparently within Edward's jurisdiction should have produced such a coinage, albeit short-lived, and it suggests that the region continued to enjoy a fair degree of autonomy. No coins were struck in East Anglia during the first nine years of Æthelstan's reign (Blunt 1974).

Archiepiscopal coins were issued only intermittently during Edward's reign. Apart from a unique coin of the 'rose' type, Plegmund's coins were of the Two-line type of the Middle and Late phases (Dolley 1974). These were the last coins to be issued in the name of a prelate; henceforth all ecclesiastical moneyers, whose existence is recorded in documents, used regal dies, usually without any distinguishing marks.

The expansion in the mint system commenced by Alfred was continued under Edward. The greatest increase appears to have come towards the end of his reign when the number of moneyers grew substantially. This was in part because of mints being established in the reconquered Danelaw, but new burhs in other parts of Mercia and in Wessex may also have opened mints. In some cases it is possible to attribute coins by tracing the moneyers back from mint-signed issues of Æthelstan, and it is likely that most of the 35 mints named on his coinage had been established before Edward's death. Moneyers appear to have been drawn from the Continent to set up these new mints, just as they were for the Viking mint in East Anglia. Continental Germanic names first appear among the moneyers of Alfred's Two-line type, and they represent some 20% of Edward's moneyers (Smart 1986). The proportion rises slightly during the second quarter of the tenth century, but then dwindles to a negligible level, either because they adopted English names for their children or because they were being replaced by native moneyers.

(f) ANGLO-VIKING COINAGES, *c.* 890–954

Literature

There are two major nineteenth-century surveys of the Viking coinage of Northumbria (Rashleigh 1869; Haigh 1876), and two modern general accounts (Dolley 1965a, 1978). Detailed studies have been published of the St Edmund Memorial coinage (Blunt 1969), the early Northumbrian series of Siefred and Cnut known mainly from the Cuerdale hoard (Lyon and Stewart 1961) and the coinages of Ragnald (Blunt and Stewart 1983), Sihtric Caoch (Dolley and Moore 1973; Stewart 1982), 'St Martin' of Lincoln (Stewart 1967) and the later Norse kings of York (Dolley 1958). The hoards relating to these coinages are conveniently summarized in Dolley 1958, 19–34.

Historical background

Some account has already been given (pp. 303–7) of the Viking conquest and settlement of the Danelaw during the second half of the ninth century and of the subsequent reconquest of those parts lying south of the Humber by Edward the Elder and Æthelflæd. The Viking kingdom of York was ruled initially by men of Danish origin, but from the early tenth century the Hiberno-Norsemen (Norwegians) of Dublin, having been temporarily driven out of Ireland, played an increasingly prominent role in Northumbrian affairs. Soon after the English victory at Tettenhall in 910, a Norse king Ragnald was campaigning in Northumbria and the Scottish Lowlands. He may have occupied York briefly *c.* 914, and he returned in *c.* 919 to be accepted as king, the first of a series of members of the Dublin royal house to rule there (Table 28). Ragnald was succeeded at York in 921 by the king of Dublin, a kinsman called Sihtric Caoch (the 'one eyed' or 'squinty'). In 926 Sihtric sought a treaty with Æthelstan, accepting Christianity and marrying the king's half-sister, but the following year he died and his brother Guthfrith, who had succeeded him at Dublin in 921, came to claim the York throne. Æthelstan seized the opportunity to invade Northumbria, and having expelled Guthfrith he succeeded for the first time in uniting England under one ruler.

The Vikings remained a threat since they were able to find ready support among the large Scandinavian population in Northumbria, and the English were to lose control of it on two subsequent occasions. In 937 at an epic battle at *Brunanburh*, Æthelstan successfully beat off a large invasion force of Norsemen, Scots and Strathclyde Britons led by the Dublin king, Anlaf Guthfrithsson, but Æthelstan's death two years later was seen as an opportunity to mount a second invasion. Within weeks Anlaf had entered York without resistance and had pressed on south of the Humber to raid Northampton, Tamworth and finally Leicester, where he was met by an army under the young King Edmund. A treaty was arranged between them, which left Anlaf in control of the region of the Five Boroughs as well as Northumbria, but this situation

Table 28. *Norse kings of York*, c. *919–54*

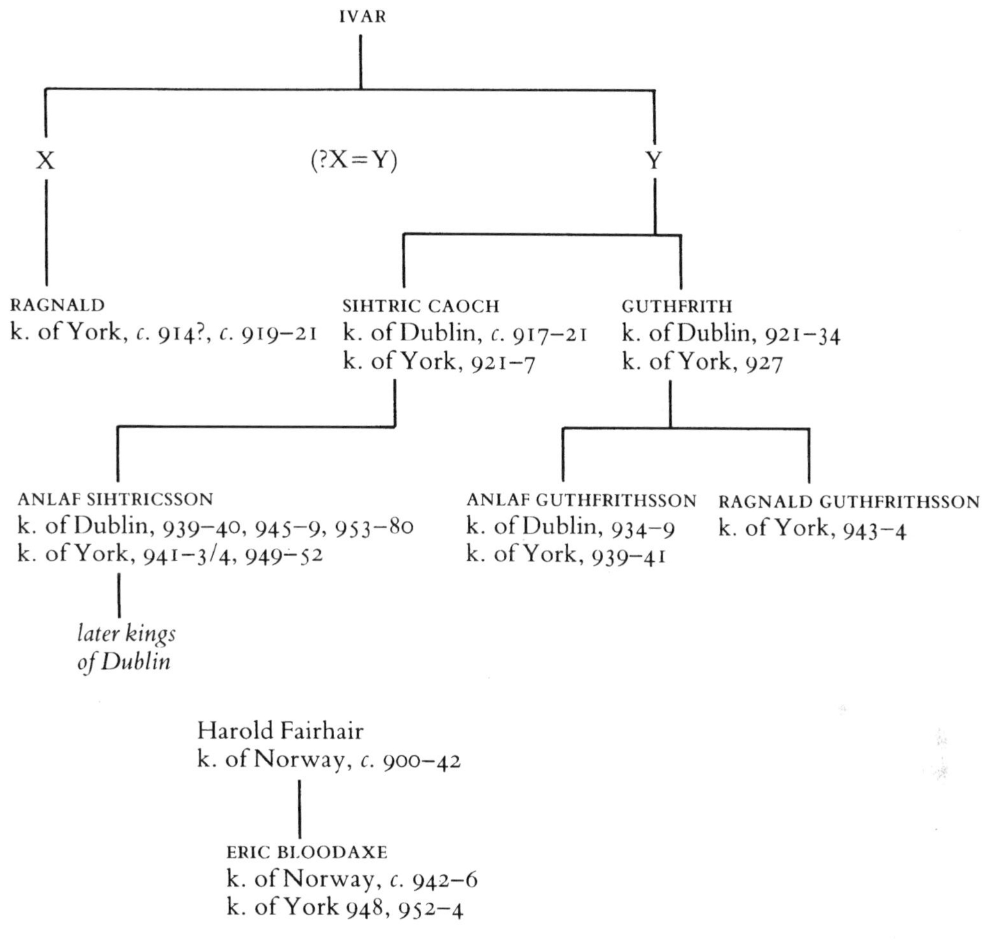

was not to last for long. Anlaf died in 941 and the kingdom was taken by another Anlaf (Sihtricsson), a son of Sihtric Caoch, who within a year had lost the lands south of the Humber and was expelled in 943 in favour of a cousin, Ragnald Guthfrithsson, though Anlaf may have continued to contest the throne. The name of yet another York king, Sihtric, is recorded on coins of this period, but his identity is uncertain (Dolley 1978, 28; Smyth 1975–9, II.124 n. 40). The rivalry at York was brought to an end when Edmund ousted the kings by force in 944 and once again restored the unity of England.

The final period of Scandinavian rule at York was brought about not by a Dubliner but by Eric Bloodaxe, a former king of Norway who had been expelled after a short but extremely violent reign. In 947 he appeared in Northumbria and was immediately accepted as king. Eadred led an army to regain the region and persuaded the people of York to abandon Eric, but Anlaf Sihtricsson came over from Dublin and was able to establish himself again as king of York. The events of these last years of Viking rule are obscure. Anlaf's second reign was apparently brought to an end by Eric's return in 952 and he held the throne for two more years. English control was re-established in 954 and successfully maintained thereafter.

Coinage

The Vikings who settled in Britain and Ireland were unfamiliar with the use of coin *per se*, for although they had received vast quantities of it in tribute from the Franks and the English and in trade across eastern Europe from Islam, this appears to have been treated as silver bullion. The only coinage of their own had been a small local one produced for the trading centre at Hedeby. The large, well-regulated coinages of pennies and halfpennies being struck in the Danelaw at the end of the ninth century suggest that in the main centres they soon established a monetary economy, although for a time elsewhere they clung to former habits. Thus some of the hoards from the Danelaw include cut pieces of ornamental silver and a mixture of Viking, English, Continental and Arabic coins of differing weights. The practice of testing the coins and silver objects by making nicks in them with a knife (known as 'peck-marks'), which was common in Scandinavia until the full establishment of national coinages in the mid eleventh century, was also used in the Danelaw. Peck-marks are found on many of the coins from the Cuerdale hoard (dep. *c.* 905), mainly on the Anglo-Saxon and Continental ones which had seen longer circulation, but also on the Viking issues (Archibald 1980, 120; cf. **1.881**, **941ff.**, **1364**, **1366**, **1379**, **1382**, **1389**, **1400**, **1407** and **1445**). It was also practised in the southern Danelaw, as shown by the recent hoard from Ashdon, Essex (dep. *c.* 895), and one unprovenanced coin in this collection (**1.1377**) suggests that it continued until at least *c.* 920.

(i) *Alfredian imitations and Guthrum's coinage*

As so often the case with an initial coinage, the earliest coins of the Vikings in England imitate those of the neighbouring states with which they were most familiar, i.e. Wessex and Mercia. They mainly copy Alfred's London Monogram, *Ohsnaforda* and Two-line types of the later 880s and 890s. This series has only received cursory attention (Dolley and Blunt 1961, 89–92, pl. 10), and most of the coins cannot be attributed to particular regions with confidence. The majority crudely reproduce the legends of their prototypes, but a series of Two-line coins were struck for Guthrum of East Anglia (880–90) in his baptismal name Æthelstan (**1.1387**). Some of Guthrum's coins carry names of moneyers who struck for Alfred, and a die-link between the coinages (Blunt 1952c) suggests that they may have shared a mint near the border with the Danelaw as part of the general accord reflected in the treaty they made after Alfred's recapture of London. Two-line coins imitating those of Alfred (and Guthrum?) were probably minted in East Anglia until the introduction of the St Edmund Memorial coinage *c.* 895.

Imitations of the Two-line type were also produced in the Five Boroughs, as both pennies and halfpennies (**1.1383–5**), if we are right in thinking that many of the coins in the Stamford hoard (Grueber 1903; Grierson 1957) are local products. A few of these and some derivatives of the London Monogram issue have the name or monogram of Lincoln, another has the inscription LICIRA CIVI, probably for Leicester. Three coins with the name of a king Halfdan (ALFDENE RX) – a penny muling the Two Emperors and London Monogram types, and two halfpennies of the Two-line type, one probably from the Stamford hoard – may, to judge from their style, also belong to this region. They must have been struck in the late 880s or early 890s and so cannot be attributed to either of the known kings of York of that name, Halfdan I (875–7) being too early and Halfdan II (902–10) too late unless he enjoyed earlier authority of which we are unaware. A fragmentary penny from the Ashdon hoard has on the obverse the name GVDEF . . ., possibly Guthfrith of York (*c.* 883–95), though the coin is related in style to the Halfdan and other halfpennies in the Stamford hoard and seems to have been struck in the Five Boroughs (Blackburn 1985). We do not know whether the large number of anonymous imitations of the London Monogram issue – some of which have a deliberately differenced, though enigmatic, monogram (**1.1379**) – come from this region or Northumbria, or both.

A number of imitations appear from their epigraphy and use of ornaments to precede or copy the Northumbrian coinage of Siefred and Cnut. These include the *Orsnaforda* coins (**1.1380–1**) which consistently misspell the Oxford mint-signature (*Ohsnaforda*), the Everat halfpenny (**1.1386**) and other coins with unintelligible inscriptions (e.g. **1.1382**). A Northumbrian origin has also been suggested for the substantial group of imitations of the Canterbury signed Two-line issue (*BMC* type xvii), many of which reproduce the same moneyer's name as that on the *Orsnaforda* coins (Dolley and Blunt 1961, 91). Two coins in the name of an Earl Sihtric (SITRIC COMES) copy the designs of the *Orsnaforda* type, but a southern Danelaw origin is suggested by the inclusion of a moneyer's name, GVNDIBERTVS, also found on St Edmund Memorial coins, and of a word SCELDFOR, which has been interpreted as a mint-name, Shelford either in Cambridgeshire or Nottinghamshire.

(ii) *St Edmund Memorial coinage (*c. *895–915)*

The East Anglian king Edmund, whom the Danes murdered in 869, was venerated as a saint by the next generation of Christianized Vikings. The large coinage which they struck in his name – SCE EADMVND REX ('O St Edmund the king!') but often blundered – was based on the *alpha*/cross designs of his original coins. Both pennies and halfpennies were struck, the latter being very rare presumably because of the preference for larger denominations in hoarding. The names of more than 70 moneyers are recorded, and what is remarkable is the high proportion that are of Continental Germanic origin. It would seem that the Vikings, determined to establish a substantial coinage, recruited a large number of men from the Continent (Smart 1985).

The earlier coins (**1.1388–1402**) are comparatively common owing to the presence of more than 1,800 specimens in the Cuerdale hoard. They include the coins of better style and longer, more literate legends, though some are very blundered; the legends are conveniently set out in Hawkins 1843, 25–36. The later coins (**1.1403**), represented in hoards such as Morley St Peter, are struck on smaller flans of lighter weight and have thicker lettering and shorter legends.

The moneyers represented in the post-Cuerdale group are listed in Blunt 1969, 247. On a handful of coins, struck from a single pair of dies, the moneyer's name is replaced by the legend + AEL-FRED REX DO (*BMC AS* II.38.2). They are of fine style and belong among the earliest St Edmund coins. They have been interpreted as evidence that the series was originated by Alfred at Canterbury (Blunt 1969, 242) or that an obverse die was captured during the Danish sack of Canterbury in 892 (Dolley 1965a, 17). But despite some similarities the obverse is not an official die of the Canterbury Two-line type (*BMC* type xvii), though it is no doubt based on it, and the coins are probably an early Viking experiment made before it was decided to place the name of the moneyer on the reverse, for they had been accustomed to producing good imitations with Alfred's name. Some coins have the St Edmund legend or the moneyer's name on both obverse and reverse, no doubt the result of careless die-cutting. Others have a reverse inscription +HEMNCXREXE, which appears to be a corruption of the attested moneyer's name Hamin (Smart 1985, 85), although Blunt (1969, 244) has tentatively revived an attribution to an unidentified King Hemming.

The St Edmund Memorial coins enjoyed wide circulation in the Danelaw. They were present in all the major Viking hoards of the earlier tenth century, but as single-finds they are concentrated in East Anglia and the East Midlands (Blackburn *et al.* 1983, 12, to which may be added two coins from excavations in Cambridge: **1.1395A–B**). It is generally assumed that they were minted in East Anglia; one coin has on the obverse NORDVICO (*SCBI* Midlands Museums 100) which has been interpeted as the mint-name Norwich, although it may be a personal name, Nordvic (Smart 1985, 86). In any event several mints are likely to have been involved, possibly including some in the Five Boroughs, though at present we lack evidence for firm attributions. A few coins have a blundered form of the York mint-signature *Eboraice civitas* (Blunt 1969, 245) and the presence of one in the hoard from Bossall near York (Pagan 1975) is suggestive of local minting, but they may be only chance copies of reverses of St Peter coins.

The coinage commenced *c.* 895, to judge from its absence from the Ashdon and Stamford hoards (dep. *c.* 893/5) and by the overstriking of a specimen by Archbishop Plegmund towards the end of Alfred's reign (Banks and Purvey 1967). It must have continued for a considerable time after the deposit of the Cuerdale hoard (*c.* 905), and may have lasted until the reconquest of East Anglia and eastern Mercia in 917/18.

(iii) *The Northumbrian coinage of Siefred and Cnut (*c. *900–5)*

This coinage would be known from a mere handful of coins today but for the discovery in 1840 of the great Cuerdale hoard (Hawkins 1843), the largest Viking-age hoard from the British Isles or Scandinavia, and only exceeded in Russia. It was found in a lead chest in the bank of the river Ribble in Lancashire, north-west England, and it has been suggested from the nature of the ingots and cut pieces of ornamental silver that the treasure was the property of a Hiberno-Norseman, rather than a Dane from York as had previously been supposed (Graham-Campbell 1976, 53–4). The 7,000 coins in the hoard, which represents only one-fifth of the total silver content, consisted of approximately 1,000 English coins of the period *c.* 875–*c.* 905 (Blunt and Dolley 1959, 240–7; Blunt 1983); 1,000 Frankish and Italian coins of the late ninth century, mainly of the mints of Melle, Limoges and Le Mans (Dolley and Morrison 1963, 80–1); 1 Byzantine coin; 36+Oriental dirhams (Lowick 1976); 3 semi-bracteates from Hedeby (Dolley and Talvio 1974; Archibald 1985) and some 5,000 Anglo-Viking coins, including 1,800 of the St Edmund Memorial issue and 3,000 of the Northumbrian coinage of Siefred and Cnut (Lyon and Stewart 1961). A deposit date of *c.* 903 has usually been assumed (*ibid.*, 98), the latest Continental coins being ones of Louis the Blind as emperor (901–2), but following his study of Edward the Elder's coinage Lyon now inclines to a slightly later date, *c.* 905.

The names of two kings commonly occur on the Northumbrian coinage, *Siefredus* (**1.1404–5, 1440**) or un-Latinized *Sievert* (**1.1442**) and *Cnut* (**1.1406–39, 1441, 1444–6**), both of whom are accorded the title *rex*. Most of Siefred's coins are earlier than those of Cnut, though there may have been a period when the kings were minting concurrently since there is close die-linking between certain of their coin types and some coins bear both their names. Others have the inscription *C Siefredus rex* in which the meaning of the initial C is unclear. Siefred is usually identified with Sigeferth *piraticus de Northhymbriorum* who according to Æthelweard harried the English coast in 893/4 (Stenton 1971, 263; Smyth 1975–9, I.33–7) and presumably became king of York sometime after Guthfrith's death in 895. The identity of Cnut has been something of a problem, for Haigh's (1876, 56–7) long-accepted attribution to Guthfrith is untenable (Lyon and Stewart 1961, 116), but the recent suggestion that he is the Cnut whom the sagas say was campaigning in Northumbria *c.* 900 seems probable (Smyth 1975–9, I.47–52). A third personal name, *Alvaldus*, is recorded on a few coins. He may be Æthelwold, the West Saxon prince who for a brief period *c.* 900 was accepted as king by the Northumbrians, notwithstanding doubts expressed by Lyon and Stewart (1961, 108, 113). Although the Siefred–Cnut coinage is plentiful today, it was struck from a limited number of dies with substantial die-linking and can have lasted only a few years. It is unlikely to have started much before the late 890s, and must have run its course within a short time of the burial of the Cuerdale hoard.

The coinage shows strong Christian and Frankish influences in the designs and legends, which include a cross-crosslet, a patriarchal cross, a cross-on-steps and a *Karolus* monogram, and the purely religious inscriptions *Dominus Deus rex* (abbreviated to DNS DS REX, **1.1442–3**), *Dominus Deus omnipotens rex* (abbreviated to DNS DS O REX), and *Mirabilia fecit* (**1.1444–6**). These legends are inspired by, though not copied from, the invocations on Frankish coins (above, p. 201), and they show that the coinage was designed by someone with learning and a precise knowledge of Latin, for errors rarely occur. The use of the Latin nominative for the king's name and the circular mint-signature *Ebraice civitas* on many coins also suggest influence from the Continent. The Danes may have taken advice from the clergy of York Minster, but it is probable that they invited Frankish moneyers to organize their mint, as their cousins in the southern Danelaw had done for the St Edmund Memorial coinage. A large number of Cnut's coins have the enigmatic word '*Cunnetti*', which does not look like a personal name and cannot be a mint name, since Lyon and Stewart's die-study shows that the whole coinage emanates from a single mint, York. The classification of the coinage is complicated because the various designs and inscriptions occur in a range of different combinations. Furthermore, while the lower (obverse) die invariably has a circular inscription and the upper (reverse) die a cruciform or two-line design, the king's name can occur on either face. The die-combinations seem always to be deliberately chosen, usually with the king's name on one face and either his title, the mint name or an invocation on the other, although about 7% of the coins lack any regal inscription, combining either an invocation and the mint name (**1.1443**) or two invocations. These must have been intended to be anonymous since the *Dns Ds o rex* and *Ebraice civitas* reverse dies are never used with Siefred or Cnut obverses, but they need not necessarily be regarded as ecclesiastical issues as has been suggested by some scholars (Lyon and Stewart 1961, 112).

The Cuerdale hoard also contained some 30 pennies and halfpennies crudely copying York coins of Cnut and Frankish coins of Quentovic (**1.1447**). Unlike the Northumbrian issues, die-links indicate that the side with the circular mint-signature is the reverse (Dolley and Morrison 1966, note to pl. 12). They do not belong to the main York series and have been regarded as a Viking issue of Quentovic. However, their weights conform to the English standard of *c.* 22gr. (1.42g) rather than the heavier Frankish one, and it is likely that they are composite imitations produced somewhere in the British Isles.

(iv) *The coinages of 'St Peter', Ragnald and Sihtric Caoch (*c. *905–27)*

The Northumbrian Viking coinages from the period after the deposit of the Cuerdale hoard until the English conquest of 927 consist of a major coinage in the name of St Peter, to whom York Minster was dedicated, interrupted by or struck concurrently with issues of Ragnald and Sihtric Caoch and a small anonymous group. The St Peter issue forms two distinct series, the coins without a sword in the design being earlier than those with a sword (Dolley 1957). The swordless St Peter coins have an inscription in two lines, SCI PETRI MO ('coin (or money) of St Peter') and occasionally there are additional symbols such as the Petrine key in the field (Bendixen 1982). The other side, which may technically be the obverse as in the preceding York issues, usually has a mint-signature spelt EBORACE CIV (cf. the earlier EBRAICE CIVITAS) around a small cross pattée (**1.1448**). There is a wide range of weights suggesting that the standard declined from *c.* 20gr. (1.30g) to *c.* 15gr. (0.97g) or less, possibly as a result of the Danes' defeat at Tettenhall in 910 or the subsequent raids by the Hiberno-Norse. Later York issues revert to standards approximating the higher of these. A variant of the Swordless St Peter type of heavy weight has the mint name spelt EBRAI CIT or similar around a *Karolus* monogram clearly copied from the coinage of Cnut, though stylistically it is more closely linked with that in the name of 'Raienalt' or 'Ragnold', which is generally attributed to Ragnald, the first Hiberno-Norse king of York.

Ragnald's coinage consists of three, apparently successive types, all struck to the heavier standard (Dolley 1955; Blunt and Stewart 1983). The first two have the mint-signature around a *Karolus* monogram, one combining it with a head looking left and the other with an open hand (**1.1450**) copied from coins of Edward the Elder and ultimately from the papal coinage of Benedict IV and Louis III (**1.1068**). The third type is innovative in its designs, having a *tau*-cross, presumably representing Thor's hammer, on one side and a bow and arrow on the other, though the legends are very blundered. The dating of Ragnald's coinage has been contentious. Some would associate it with his first campaigns in Northumbria *c.* 911 or *c.* 914 when he may have occupied York (Dolley 1957, 1978, 1982, the last written with knowledge of Blunt and Stewart's views; Smyth 1975–9, I, 105–7; 1978). But the better view would seem to be that advanced by Blunt and Stewart (1983) that the coins belong to his substantive reign of *c.* 919–21, interrupting the St Peter series. The *Karolus* monogram variety would stand at the end of the swordless St Peter issue.

The later St Peter coins were struck under Hiberno-Norse rule, and the sword which divides their two-line inscription has been interpreted as the 'sword of Carolus', a trophy known to have been prized by the Vikings of Dublin in the later tenth century (Haigh 1876, 69–71; Dolley 1982, 91). An iron die of this type has been found in excavations at York (Roesdahl *et al.* 1981, 130, no. YTC 26), showing that the side with the St Peter inscription was by now the obverse. These have been dated *c.* 921–7 on hoard evidence and a consideration of the three distinctive types of Sword St Peter coins (Stewart 1967; Dolley 1982) which are closely paralleled in the coinage of Sihtric Caoch (921–7) and in a rare issue of Lincoln in the name of St Martin. Attempts to revive an earlier dating in the 910s (Archibald 1980, 107–8) have not met with support. Numismatic evidence therefore suggests that Edward the Elder did not succeed in recapturing Lindsey in 918 as historians had assumed, but that Lincoln was still in Viking hands in the early and possibly the mid 920s. The three types have as their reverse designs (*a*) a *tau*-cross similar to that on Ragnald's coinage, (*b*) a hammer or mallet engraved in outline (**1.1449**), often flanked by three pellets, and (*c*) a cross pattée with pellets or crescents in each angle and an inverted Thor's hammer in the legend below the sword. The sequence of these types is uncertain, but it seems that the Sword St Peter and Sihtric coinages were issued more or less in parallel, though not necessarily from the same mint. None of Sihtric's coins, which are listed in Dolley and Moore 1973 (supplemented by Stewart 1982, 112–14), bears a recognizable York mint-signature. Some have names of moneyers, Adel. . .d, Are, Mana and Sibrant, while others have blundered inscriptions, although one might be read as a mint name, *Castra(e) Eort*, *Ort* or *Grt*. It has been suggested on stylistic grounds that some of Sihtric's coins may have been struck at a mint or mints in the Five Boroughs, possibly at Lincoln (Allen 1936; Dolley and Moore 1973, 53–6), but Stewart would go further and attribute them all to that region, as well as a small anonymous group of sword/*tau*-cross coins which partially copy the name of Edward the Elder (Stewart 1982).

The St Peter coinage has often been regarded as an ecclesiastical issue, but for some ten or fifteen years from *c.* 905 it seems to have been the only issue of the York mint, and after a brief interruption during Ragnald's reign it was the major if not the sole issue for the last five years before the English conquest of York in 927. It is unlikely that the Church would have monopolized the coinage of Viking York for almost two decades, but clerics may well have influenced the design and an inscription invoking their patron saint would have seemed appropriate in the early tenth century when the contemporary coinage of the southern Danelaw appealed to St Edmund.

(v) *The last Anglo-Norse coinages (939–44, 949–54)*

The last two phases of Norse rule in northern England each lasted some five years but spanned four and three reigns respectively. The modern arrangement of these coins is essentially that of Dolley (1958), although his account needs modifying in a number of important respects.

The re-establishment of an independent kingdom in Northumbria and the Five Boroughs in 939 caused little interruption to the coinage there. At Derby two of Æthelstan's moneyers continued striking the circumscription cross type in the name of a King Anlaf, one of them using an existing reverse die. There are also a number of blundered imitations from this region, including a coin which copies two obverses, one of Anlaf and the other of Æthelstan (retrograde). Other mints south of the Humber may have struck Two-line coins; one group by the moneyers Arnulf and Blaciager spells the king's name ONLOF and another by Bleseret, Hildulf, Nother and Rotbert spells it ANLAF or ANLEF (Dolley and Yvon 1971, 3–7). Most of these moneyers are known to have struck coins of north-eastern style for Æthelstan or Edmund or both, though the identity of the mint or mints is uncertain (Blunt 1974, 83, 87–8). These coins from mints south of the Humber are likely to have been struck for Anlaf Guthfrithsson or possibly for his cousin Anlaf Sihtricsson during the first months of his reign before he lost control of the region.

At York the moneyer Ragnald had enjoyed a virtual monopoly of minting under Æthelstan, but he did not continue under the Vikings. New moneyers were appointed in his place, several of whom continued under Edmund and survived into the final period of Norse rule. The designs of the York coins of the period 939–44 form a striking contrast with those that had gone before and their inscriptions are also distinctive, consistently employing the Old Norse title *Cununc* for 'king', also used on Anlaf's coins of Derby, and initially an Old Norse form *Minetr* for 'moneyer', although progressively the die-cutter moved back, via *Monetr* and *Monetra*, to the standard Latin *Moneta*. The earliest York coins of this period depict a raven with stretched wings and are normally attributed to Anlaf Guthfrithsson, though the type could have continued into Anlaf Sihtricsson's reign. The majority were struck by a moneyer Athelferth, but one coin of different style is by the moneyer Odeler and appears to come from a mint south of the Humber (Roesdahl *et al.* 1981, 135, no. YTC 43).

Three types can be attributed to Anlaf Sihtricsson's reign and the period when he shared or disputed the throne with Ragnald Guthfrithsson and a King Sihtric. Coins of all three rulers are known, although those of Ragnald and Sihtric survive in only a few specimens. One type with a simple cross and circular legend on both sides was struck for Anlaf and Sihtric, and there is a lead piece in the British Museum which has impressions of two reverse dies of this issue. Anlaf's main type has a triquetra device on the obverse and a triangular standard or banner on the reverse, but this was also struck for Sihtric and Ragnald. The third type, with a large cross moline on the obverse, was shared by Anlaf and Ragnald. The chronology of these issues is uncertain. Sihtric's coins appear to be contemporary with the earlier part of Anlaf's reign, but whether Anlaf continued to strike coins after Ragnald's assumption of the throne is not clear.

In the final period of Norse rule, 948–54, the York moneyers adhered to more conventional designs and used the common Latin style *rex*. For Eric's first reign they struck a Two-line type, and this was continued briefly under Anlaf Sihtricsson with his name spelt ONLAF, although Dolley (1958, 55, 75) attributed these coins by the moneyer Inglegar to Anlaf's earlier reign. The type was soon changed and most of Anlaf's remaining coins have a circular reverse inscription around a small cross. There is one other issue of an Anlaf which copies the Flower type of Edward the Elder and Edmund. These coins were struck by two York moneyers of Anlaf

Sihtricsson, and Dolley's attribution of them to Anlaf Guthfrithsson at Derby, postulating a transfer of the moneyers between the mints, is improbable. The obverse legends, which read ANLAF REX followed by A, EBR or TOD, would not fit well into Anlaf Sihtricsson's first York coinage, but they could belong to his second coinage, the final letters in the legends being paralleled by A, AL, EN, EFOR, etc., in Eric's Two-line issue and EC or EB in Edmund's York coinage by one of the same moneyers. The last Viking coins of York struck during Eric's second reign hark back to those of Sihtric I with a sword dividing the inscription of his name and title in two lines.

APPENDIX 1

GOLD PENNIES OF THE CAROLINGIAN AND EARLY FEUDAL PERIODS

The coins catalogued in this volume cover the transition from the use of gold to the use of silver in western Europe (above, p. 1, 3). The cessation of the minting of gold, which took place, according to the country involved, at various dates between the second half of the 7th and the middle of the 9th century, was followed by a period of from four to five centuries of what was virtually silver monometallism, ending in the mid 13th century in Italy and the mid 14th century in most countries north of the Alps. The only exceptions to it were those parts of Christendom recovered from the Muslims, where gold was regularly used, and areas close to these. There was some minting of gold at Barcelona in the early 11th century, and other Christian states in northern Spain followed suit in the late 12th and early 13th centuries; the minting of gold taris of Arab type was carried on uninterruptedly by the Normans in Sicily after their conquest of the island (1071), and similar coins were minted on the Italian mainland at Amalfi and Salerno; *besanti sarracenati* were struck by the Crusaders after their conquest of Syria and Palestine. But with these few exceptions the coinage of Latin Christendom was for many centuries essentially one of silver.

Yet the West remained acquainted with gold coin during this period. There was always the possibility of imports from these marginal lands and from the Muslim and Greek worlds, and occasionally there was some local minting of gold. The subject began to interest scholars over half a century ago (Monneret 1919–21; Bloch 1933). Monneret's conclusion that the alleged silver monometallism of the West was a myth, and that gold continued to be minted on a substantial scale, has not won general acceptance. Its documentation has also to be used with caution, partly because he relied on an edition of Anglo-Saxon documents by the French scholar Hubert Pierquin which failed to differentiate those that are authentic from the many that are false, and partly because he lacked any first-hand acquaintance with the numismatic evidence. But Bloch's article set off a lively discussion, with some scholars arguing in favour of large-scale Muslim imports (Lombard 1947; Bolin 1953), as indeed Monneret had done, and others doubting it, either on the testimony of the written documents or because of the lack of serious find evidence (Grierson 1954a; Himly 1955; Duplessy 1956). The latter view is now generally accepted. Gold in bullion form was often available (Latouche 1956) and sums of gold are not infrequently referred to in the documents, either for reasons of prestige or because they represented stable values in an era when the silver penny was often debased. Actual gold coins, however, were employed only marginally and essentially for ceremonial purposes. The *Liber Censuum* of the

Roman Church, for example, which dates from 1180 and lists the annual token payments promised to the Holy See by abbeys and other ecclesiastical establishments throughout Europe, often does so in terms of Muslim gold coins, but where returns are available we find them being paid in silver equivalents at whatever was the customary rate. But gold coin might be used for ceremonial payments where it was available. English financial records show Henry III of England (1216–72) regularly purchasing supplies of *oboli* and *denarii de musc'*, i.e. gold coins of Muslim Spain (Grierson 1951b, 1974b), in anticipation of each great festival of the Church, and even prior to the 13th century small supplies of gold coin, either imported or manufactured for the purpose, could be obtained in case of need (Blanchet 1955).

Imported gold coins need not be here discussed. This collection, however, is unusually rich in the rare ceremonial gold coins struck in western Europe during the denarial period, with a gold 'solidus' of Uzès (**1.734**), a gold denier of Melle (**1.965**), two solidi of Louis the Pious (**1.750–1**), and no fewer than five imitations of this last (**1.752–6**). These make it worth while to bring together references to other coins of the same kind, in order to put the phenomenon into perspective.

The coins form essentially three categories: (1) coins more or less based on ancient models or related to the silver coins of the day, (2) imitations of Arab coins, and (3) coins struck in gold from dies normally employed to strike silver pennies. In some cases it seems that no attempt was made to create coins of particular values, but since the relationship of gold to silver was in the region of 1:10 or 1:12 a gold coin only a little heavier than a normal penny would have formed the convenient multiple of a shilling. Others conformed to the weights of the bezant or the dinar, and others again had the value of a *mancus*, a unit of 30 pence (cf. Beltrán 1958b). The original meaning of this term, which first appears in Italy in the late 8th century and is common in Anglo-Saxon documents, has been much discussed. As *mancus* ('defective') it might seem a suitable description of the debased and light-weight solidi of Byzantine Italy, but *manqush* ('engraved') was an adjective sometimes used to characterize both dinars and dirhams in Arab records (Linder Welin 1965), and could easily have been interpreted by Westerners as the correct name of these coins (Longpérier 1842; *contra*, Allan 1914 and Grierson 1954a, both wrongly). As used in Frankish Italy in the first half of the 9th century, it meant either a dinar or its value in Carolingian currency, which was taken to be 30d. From Italy the term passed to England, initially meaning an Arab dinar and subsequently either a unit of 30d or the weight in gold (4.25g) of a dinar, in which sense it is commonly used in Anglo-Saxon wills when referring to bracelets and other gold objects. In 10th- and 11th-century Spain and in 11th- and 12th-century Italy it again came to be very widely applied to Arab coins, but these fall outside the chronological limits of this volume. In France its use was practically limited to the extreme south and the literature of the *chansons de geste*. The Bavarian 'long shilling' of 30 pence is described in Hebrew texts as a *mnku* as late as the 14th century (Toch 1982).

Coins based on ancient models, and on ones related to but not identical with current silver pennies, are practically limited to the last years of the 8th and the first of the 9th century, when coin designs were still fairly fluid and did not always conform to closely regulated patterns. They include, on the Frankish side, 'solidi' with the monogram or name of Charlemagne struck at Uzès, *Aurodis* and Dorestad (Grierson 1954c; Schramm 1954, 288–90), and solidi of Louis the Pious and coins derived from these. On the English side they consist of two gold mancuses bearing the names of moneyers and a mancus of Archbishop Wigmund of York, itself a derivative of those of Louis.

What were probably the earliest in date are the gold solidi minted at Uzès, a town in the Rhône valley 20km north of Nîmes. Four specimens are known (Grierson 1954c, corrected in the note to **1.734** here). They represent a variety of Class 2 of Charlemagne's deniers, with as reverse type the mint name VCE/CIA in two lines but on the obverse a roughly formed *Karolus* monogram and the letters REX (**1.734**). Since hoard evidence is lacking they could conceivably belong to the feudal period, to which Grierson was formerly prepared to assign them, but they have no precise Carolingian model – only denari of Treviso (**1.1498**) use a *Karolus* monogram, without REX, as obverse type – and it is difficult to imagine their design being devised at a much later date. It seems therefore better to place them early in Charlemagne's reign, despite the extraordinary blundering of their types and inscriptions, before the types of the coinage were so carefully regulated as they later became. The weights of surviving specimens are too variable (4.20g, 3.75g, 3.14g, 2.58g) for them to be regarded as corresponding to specific denominations, and one must assume that they were struck for some recurrent ceremonial purpose and with no care for their precise value.

A second gold coin (Grierson 1954c, 306–9) with a similar obverse type was minted at *Aurodis*, an unidentified locality perhaps identical with the *Ardis* of **1.722** in this collection and, like Uzès, in south-eastern France. The present whereabouts of the coin is unknown – it was in a private collection at Bordeaux in 1906 – and nothing can be said with certainty about it. A third coin (Dolley and Morrison 1966, no. 98; MG 643), with a profile bust of Charlemagne in an oval frame resembling an ancient gem, has been much discussed (Hävernick 1953; Grierson 1954b; Kent 1968; Pagan 1982b). The obverse inscription gives Charlemagne an unintelligently shortened version of the titles he bore prior to his recognition as emperor by Byzantium in 812 (CARLVS REX [FR] ET LAN ET [PAT] R), and the reverse one VICO DVRISTAT around an elaborate cross. Some scholars regard it as some sort of memorial issue of the mid 9th century – a mint name preceded by *in vico* is very characteristic of Lotharingian mints in the third quarter of the century – and as not having any specific monetary function, the more so since it is not clear whether the British Museum specimen is cast or struck. But a reference to Charlemagne's pre-imperial titles seems unlikely in the mid 9th century, and Dorestad is an improbable locality for a memorial coinage. It seems best, despite the blundered inscription, to regard it as an irregular gold coin of Charlemagne's own reign, particularly since it has no resemblance at all to the mid 9th-century 'Frisian' imitations of Louis the Pious' solidi. There is at Berlin a coin with the same reverse but a totally corrupt obverse inscription and the bust, without any frame, facing left instead of right (Berghaus 1959, pl. 4.20). Its weight (4.02g) would qualify it as a mancus.

The English counterparts of these Frankish coins begin with a gold 'penny' (3.74g = 58gr.) struck by Pendered, one of the moneyers of Offa's early coinage. It is copied from an aureus of Augustus with a profile head on the obverse and a standing figure on the reverse (Blunt and Dolley 1968), and Pendered's name appears on both sides as *Paendraed munitare* and *Pendred*. The second coin (Sutherland 1948, pl. 4.21; revised reading and attribution, Pagan 1965b), which weighs 4.12g, has for obverse type a profile bust copied from that of a late 4th-century solidus with the slightly blundered inscription CIOLHEARD. The reverse type is cross-on-steps copied from a 7th-century Byzantine solidus or, more probably, a contemporary Beneventan one. Ciolheard was a moneyer who worked on behalf of Offa and his successor Coenwulf (796–821) at London, and the weights of the two coins show them to represent mancuses of 30d in terms respectively of the light pennies of Offa and the heavier ones of Coenwulf's time (Lyon 1969, 208). Both coins are now in the British Museum.

More important than any of these early Frankish and English gold coins are the gold solidi of Louis the Pious (814–40), of which there are two specimens in the collection (**1.750–1**). They are basically Roman in design, with a laureate profile bust on the obverse and a cross-in-wreath surrounded by the inscription *Munus divinum* on the reverse (De Jonghe 1891; Grierson 1951a; Schramm 1954, 363–8; Schramm 1968–71, II. 63–7). About a dozen specimens are known, from four pairs of dies, two being much superior in style to the others. Since they gave rise to a large crop of imitations from Frisia, it seems clear that they originated in the extreme north of the Empire. It has been argued that they were minted at Dorestad (Hävernick 1953), and possibly this was the case for the poorer specimens, but the type is so strongly 'imperial' that the better ones are likely to have been minted at the court, and effectively at Aachen.

These coins were probably intended to have some ceremonial function, and since the profile bust also characterizes Class 1 of Louis' deniers it seems reasonable to associate them with his coronation by Pope Stephen V at Rheims in October 816. The inscription would have been intended to imply that the imperial crown – the Latin word *corona*, like the French *couronne*, means both 'wreath' and 'crown' – was a heavenly gift. On the other hand, it has been argued (Morrison 1961; *contra*, Grierson 1963c) that they were struck in 825 on the assumption that the phrase *Munus divinum* alludes not to the wreath but to the cross, and a synod at Paris in 825 condemned any dishonour shown to this. They weigh *c.* 4.40g and thus correspond to the old Roman and contemporary Byzantine solidus, not to the lighter *mancus*. There is in the Bibliothèque Nationale (P 1070) a heavier coin (7.04g) of exceptionally fine workmanship on which the emperor's bust faces left instead of right. It is presumably a sesquisolidus made for some particular purpose, or perhaps intended for someone of higher rank than the intended recipients of the others. What was presumably a similar multiple in honour of Lothar, and perhaps struck for his coronation in 817, appears to have existed at one time, but it is known only in the form of a derivative with blundered inscriptions at Berlin that has for reverse type a striding warrior holding a spear (Morrison 1961).

The *Munus divinum* solidi were widely imitated in Frisia (Grierson 1951a; further material listed in Boersma 1977), either by the Frisians themselves or by the Northmen who were in occupation of much of the country in the middle decades of the 9th century. The copies are often of poor quality gold and crude workmanship, with the bust roughly rendered and the inscriptions reduced to little more than a series of upright strokes and circles. They sometimes even reproduce, as an element in the design, a crack which developed on the reverse die used for one group of Louis' coins and very apparent in its products. Several of these imitations are in this collection (**1.752–6**), one of them from the Delfzijl hoard of twenty specimens all from the same pair of dies. The imitations have been found over a wide area extending from

Norway to Brittany (Hävernick 1953; Hatz 1970), and it is possible that one group originated in England (see note to **1.753**).

In addition to the copies, the *Munus divinum* solidus provided the inspiration for a few other 9th-century derivatives with more elaborate obverse or reverse designs, some probably intended as ornaments from the first but others apparently intended as coin, albeit of a ceremonial character (Grierson 1951a; Berghaus 1959). The best known of these derivatives is one in the British Museum (Blunt 1960, iv–vii; Stewart 1978, A.123) struck in the name of Archbishop Wigmund of York (837–54?). It retains Louis' reverse type but has on the obverse the archbishop's name and title (VIGMVND Λ̄RE P) and his facing bust copied from that of the archbishops of Canterbury on their pennies. Its design and superior style are totally different from those of the stycas which in Wigmund's time were the staple products of the mint of York, and the coin may have been struck at Canterbury or some other south-eastern mint in honour of the archbishop. The coin weighs 4.16g (64¼gr.), rather less than the coins of Louis, and was presumably intended as a mancus. The derivatives are not always in gold: one, with a seated figure on the reverse, is in lead (Chalon 1859).

The ceremonial gold coins which took the form of imitations of Muslim dinars date from the late 8th century and are quite distinct from the later ones of Spain, south Italy and the Crusader lands that were intended for commercial purposes. The best known is that of Offa of Mercia, who promised the pope in 786 to send him an annual gift of 365 mancuses. Papal letters of thanks in 797 and 802 make it clear that the subvention was paid, though possibly at the reduced rate of 120 mancuses, i.e., ten a month instead of one for every day in the year. Such an undertaking, if it was to be carried out, would have required the manufacture of home-made dinars. One such takes the form of a coin (4.28g) with a slightly blundered inscription but a legible date (A.H. 157=773/4) which has the words OFFA REX in two lines as part of the inscription but inserted upside down in relation to the Cufic text, which the English die-sinker naturally could not read (Carlyon-Britton 1908; Allan 1914). This mancus, acquired in Rome sometime before 1841 and now in the British Museum, is unique, but there are other imitations without a royal name which bear dates of the second half of the 8th century, and sometimes have crosses in the field (Linder Welin 1964; Lowick 1973). They are likely to have been minted in England or France, though the absence of any comparable inscription makes it impossible to say precisely who was responsible for them.

There are, finally, the 'strikes' in gold from ordinary penny dies, at regular mints, that were made for special purposes which we cannot usually identify. The 2,000 mancuses for whose making the West Saxon king Eadred (d. 955) left gold in his will, and which were to be given in alms to various bishoprics, would have taken such a form, as would the gold penny to be struck at Louvain (*aureum denarium . . . Lovaniensis monetae*) which the abbot of Vlierbeek in Brabant undertook in 1173 to pay annually to the abbey of Affligem *in testimonium subjectionis* (Grierson 1954c, 304, other references in Wauters 1882–4). The best-known surviving examples of such gold pennies are three English ones. The earliest is one of Edward the Elder (899–925) struck by the moneyer Deorwald, which was found in Switzerland in 1909 and is now in the

Cantonal Museum at Lausanne (Molin 1913; Blunt 1948a; Stewart 1978, A.125). It weighs 4.8g (=74gr.). The second in date is one of Æthelred II (978–1016) in the British Museum. It is of the Helmet type struck by the moneyer Leofwine at the mint of Lewes (Evans 1879; Stewart 1978, A.126) and weighs 3.34g (=51½gr.). The third (Stewart 1978, A.126) is of Edward the Confessor (1042–66) of the Expanding Cross type struck by Leofinc at the mint of Warwick (Allen 1948). The authenticity of these pieces was regarded by many scholars as doubtful until that of the second was confirmed by the discovery of a silver penny sharing with it the same reverse die. The coin of Edward the Elder also shares an obverse die with a penny in the British Museum. Although the weights of the three coins are very different they are in each case about three times that of the current silver penny – an Ely document of the 10th century refers to the purchase of some land for *centum tripondii auri*, i.e. with coins weighing 3d (Stewart 1978, 161 n. 92) – and so would have represented *mancuses* of 30d (Lyon 1969, 207–8). The rarity of such coins is partly explained by the fact that they normally ended up in the hands of ecclesiastical authorities, who turned them to other purposes. The Abingdon Chronicle has preserved the metrical inscription on a reliquary in the abbey's possession, recording how it was made at the orders of King Cnut and Queen Aelfgifu from 230 gold mancuses 'refined by fire' and two pounds of silver (*Chron. monasterii de Abingdon* I.433).

Similar gold pennies have been recorded for a number of Continental series – e.g. in those of Utrecht and Cologne, in the names of Bishop Bernwold (1027–59) and Archbishop Hermann III (1089–99) respectively – and there is in this collection one of the mint of Melle that dates from the late 9th or early 10th century (**1.965**). It came to light in the 1840s, probably from a local find in Poitou, and what little is known of its early history will be found in the note on it. Its weight of 1.64g points to its having been intended as a sou.

APPENDIX 2

FORGERIES OF EARLY MEDIEVAL COINS

This volume concludes with three plates of modern forgeries in the period it covers. It does not include a few poor quality casts, since their reproduction would be of no value to scholars. But the more dangerous forgeries are worthy of publication. The bulk of those in the Grierson collection were either gifts from dealers or were acquired at nominal prices as forgeries, partly to remove them from the market and partly to have a record of their style and other features. Others were bought in the belief that they were authentic, or because they were given the benefit of the doubt. No satisfactory guide to the recognition of forgeries can be given, though in recent years the elaboration of methods of non-destructive analysis has proved a welcome addition to the resources of the harassed collector (Merrick and Metcalf 1969; Pirie 1982).

The series involved are as follows:

OSTROGOTHIC AND RELATED COINAGES

Forgeries in these series are unusual in their being mainly small AR and Æ, i.e. types which are rarely forged because of their small intrinsic value. Some are casts, easily detected by their blurred details and rounded contours, but others are struck. The principal contributor to the stock of Ostrogothic forgeries, as indeed to those in other north Italian series, was Luigi Cigoi (1811–75), a native of Udine and a tanner by profession, who had dies cut by workmen in a number of localities and used his technical knowledge of chemical processes to give his products a suitable patina and air of antiquity. His personal collection, including a large number of his forgeries, is now in the Museo Civico at Udine, and forms the basis of the only modern study (Brunetti 1966). He specialized in providing north Italian mints with types or varieties known only for mints elsewhere, and his products are often very dangerous. In *BMC Vand*, pls. 5.8–9 (nummi of Odovacar, sharing the same dies), 10.4 (small AR of Witigis), and 10.11 (small AR of Justinian ascribed to Matasuntha) are all the work of Cigoi. **1.1452** in this collection is one of a silver coin of Odovacar, which can be compared with a genuine coin of this ruler on Plate 3, and there are a few Cigoiana or probable Cigoiana in other series (**1.1514, 1518**).

LOMBARD AND BENEVENTAN COINAGE

Forgeries of pseudo-imperial Lombard coins, as well as those of several later kings (especially Desiderius) and the municipal coinages of the Tuscan cities, have been made since the 18th century (Bernareggi 1980, but modified by Bernareggi 1983b). A supposed coin of Aripert II in association with a Duke Iffo has given rise to some discussion because of its constitutional implications (Laffranchi 1934; Grierson 1956b). This all turns out to have been pointless, since the coin is now recognized as false (Bernareggi 1965a). In some cases, notably that of the municipal coinage of Lucca, it is virtually impossible to distinguish stylistically between genuine and false coins, and here studies of fineness can be of help. Some doubtful pieces of Beneventan gold and silver began to come on the market in the 1970s, and the collection of the late Prof. F. P. Tinozzi of Pavia is known to have included large numbers of Lombard and Beneventan forgeries, in some cases probably made to satisfy the acquisitiveness of this wealthy but uncritical collector. The relatively few coins of these series in this collection, however, all appear to be authentic, with the possible exception of **1.1100**.

VISIGOTHIC COINS

These have been imitated since the 17th century. An invented tremissis of Reccared, of the mint of Marseille, was already in the French royal collection before 1690. By the 19th century forgeries had become so numerous, and until the publication of the photographic illustrations in Miles' monograph (1952) so difficult to detect, that some dealers virtually refused to handle the series. Forgeries masquerading as genuine pieces regularly appear in sale catalogues of the first half of this century, and occasionally still do so. The catalogue of the Glendining sale in 1945 of the great Shore collection of Portuguese gold coins, which was prepared by Leonard Forrer, one of the most experienced numismatists of his generation, illustrates three forgeries of Visigothic coins as authentic (lots 616, 618, 624).

The three main series of forgeries were produced respectively by the celebrated coin forger Carl Wilhelm Becker (1772–1830), by some unidentified person in Spain in the middle of the 19th century, and (according to Reinhart) by someone active in Valencia and Seville early in the present one. Becker's notebooks and dies still survive, and reproductions of all his coins have been published (Hill 1925). He was mainly interested in ancient coinage, and strayed into the Visigothic field only through having been for a time in charge of the coin cabinet of Prince Carl von Isenburg, a Napoleonic general who had served in Spain and there acquired the coins that served as Becker's models. His own products are struck, and are of excellent style, but are usually too heavy (cf. **1.1465**, **1467**, weighing 1.72g and 1.79g, as against *c.* 1.5g), for they were made at a time when little attention was paid to metrology and weights were often not recorded. They tend to have rough, broken edges, which explains why they have not always been identified from the well-rounded casts used for Hill's illustrations. There is much muling of dies, since Becker often used one reverse die, with a mint name, for several rulers often quite widely separated in date. Some of Becker's strikes are in silver (**1.1457**), which misled Lelewel and some other 19th-century scholars into supposing that the Visigoths had a coinage in that metal. Becker was also responsible for a few forgeries of Merovingian coins (**1.1476**), as well as of some Carolingian and early German ones (**1.1501**).

The other Visigothic forgeries are much inferior to those of Becker, being poorly designed, with lettering and type cut in very low relief without the help of punches, so that their appearance is quite different from that of genuine coins. There is again much muling between different rulers and mints, and Grierson once saw 36 specimens from the same pair of dies. Occasional errors (cf. **1.1464**) show the designs to have been taken usually from the illustrations in the first systematic study of the Visigothic series, Henrique Florez's monograph of 1773 on Spanish coins, which suggests that they originated before the publication of Alois Heiss' monograph of 1872. These forgeries have been much studied (Mateu y Llopis 1936, 395–410 and pls. A–I; Reinhart 1937b and 1939b; most fully, Beltrán 1948), but it is not usually necessary to go behind the lists and illustrations provided by Miles in his monograph on Visigothic coinage (Miles 1952, 447–98 and pls. A–F). The illustrations on Plate 63 show two Beckers and twelve other forgeries. One of these (**1.1462**) is not in Miles, and its authenticity was not suspected until a specific gravity test by Oddy showed it to be of pure gold. Many of the forgeries, however, are of base gold, either because this was cheaper or because one of the forgers realized that Visigothic regal coins were always debased.

MEROVINGIAN AND RELATED COINAGES

Forgeries in these series are commoner than is generally believed. Early 19th-century collectors had an unfortunate propensity for making reproductions of their rarities as gifts for their friends or for scholarly purposes or even for sale, and when these were of the appropriate metal – they were often of silver instead of gold – they might sometimes be subsequently taken as 'originals'. They seem to have been more frequent in the pseudo-imperial series, especially perhaps that of the Burgundians, and in those likely to interest collectors in more than one country. A Merovingian coin of Trier with an unusually precise legend (B 4403: TREVERIS CIVITATE) is known to have been treated very early in this manner (Saulcy 1837b; cf. Lecointre-Dupont 1840c). The great interest in very early Merovingian coins in the 1830s and 1840s coincided with the invention of electrotyping by the German chemist M. H. von Jacobi in the late 1830s – 'le procédé Jacobi', it was first called – and already in the 1840s Renier Chalon was lamenting the proliferation of Merovingian electrotypes whose lead interiors ensured their being the correct weight (*RBN* 1845, 411–12). The practice is far from extinct; in the last decades several forgeries of a tremissis of the mint of Aosta (B 570) have appeared on the market. The style of Merovingian coins is so lacking in uniformity that the forgeries are not always easy to recognize, and several of those in this collection (**1.1472–5**) were discovered only when it came to be catalogued.

CAROLINGIAN COINS

Carolingian forgeries, which are probably also more numerous than is supposed, have not been systematically studied. The varying designs of the earliest deniers was an open invitation to both the confection of new types and the imitation of those whose existence was attested by hoard evidence. Find provenance is in some groups the only satisfactory guarantee of authenticity, but as coins pass from one collector or dealer to another the thread is easily lost. Three exceptionally well-preserved specimens in this collection have been given the benefit of the doubt (**1.720**, **1.722–3**). The presence of mint names on later and, in general, commoner coins likewise tended to promote the production of pieces of local interest: the Catalan and Flemish markets were, one suspects, ultimately responsible for the forged deniers of Barcelona (**1.1500**) and Bruges (**1.1506**) respectively. Others are the casual products for collectors that appear in every coin series. Two groups require special mention, the products of the Italian forger Tardani and those of the elusive French forger Louis Farrigault of Châtellerault, both of them mainly active in the early decades of this century.

Tardani seems to have worked in Rome from the 1890s to about the time of the First World War. His main interest was in medieval Italian coins, where his forgeries of papal *antiquiores* are extremely dangerous, but he also produced some in the Carolingian field (Grierson 1958). They are of high quality, copied with exceptional fidelity from illustrations in standard works of reference, and may have deceived many collectors. Over a thousand of his coin dies were acquired in 1919, after his death, by the Museo Nazionale Romano. Sir George Hill, when preparing his monograph on Becker's forgeries in the early 1920s, made an effort to secure their publication, but without success. They in any case form only a fraction of the dies he used.

Tardani's Carolingian coins are mainly of Italian mints, either real or supposed, but he was also responsible for a series of imitations of coins struck at Metz, Toul and Verdun. These may have been made to deceive the well-known Paris dealer Jules Florange (d. 1937), who came from Lorraine and was an ardent collector of the coins of his homeland. Tardani's designs for these go back to the sale catalogue of the Robert collection (Rollin & Feuardent 27.3.1886), which is still a standard work of reference and in which many rare or unique pieces of the region are illustrated. Three of them in this collection are reproduced on Plate 64 (**1.1502–4**). They were acquired in 1951, in company with a fragment of a papal coin (**1.1522**) that has also turned out to be a forgery of Tardani, from the Paris firm of Ciani, though Grierson does not doubt that Pierre Ciani, a grandson of Tardani and its then director, was as ignorant as he was of their fraudulent character.

Tardani's slightly later French counterpart Farrigault is more elusive, and little can be said about him (cf. Lafaurie 1970, 135–6). His name appears occasionally in the Procès-Verbaux of the Société française de numismatique as having furnished Adolphe Dieudonné (d. 1947), Conservateur-en-chef of the Cabinet des Médailles from 1924 to 1937 and one of the greatest names in French numismatics, with information or coins. He seems to have performed the same services to Charles Prieur, a distinguished private collector (d. 1932), and it is to be feared that many of the Merovingian, Carolingian and early Capetian rarities which this scholar exhibited at meetings of the Société française de numismatique were products of Farrigault's workshop. Any unusual coins in these series that are known to have first appeared in the decade after 1915 must in fact be examined with care. A study of Henri Rolland's sumptuous catalogue (1932) of the Motte collection, which was put together by a wealthy industrialist at Roubaix, shows that out of fifteen coins illustrated on plate 7 no fewer than six early Capetian deniers and obols are false. Their divergence from the fabric of genuine coins of the period, which often seems to us now fairly apparent, passed unnoticed at the time, and Dieudonné, in reviewing the catalogue and commenting on the many extraordinary rarities in the collection, was rash enough to use the phrase 'pas une pièce suspecte' (*RN* 1932, 258). Several late Carolingian coins in this collection which were bought as authentic are probably confections of Farrigault (**1.1508–9**; perhaps also **1.992**).

EARLY PAPAL COINS

The anomalous copper 'coins' bearing the names of Pope Gregory III (731–41) and his successor Pope Zachary (741–52) have been imitated since the 18th century, and dies for making both types are known (see note to **1.1513**). At the other end of the early papal series an equally anomalous coin, a small bracteate of Pope Paschal II (1099–1118), is so out of keeping with other coins of the time that it must be dismissed as an 18th-century invention (see note on **1.1529**). In between these there is a small number of miscellaneous forgeries, some the work of Cigoi (Maldura 1880) and detectable because of anomalies in their metal, fabric or design, and there is the formidable mass of Tardani forgeries which invaded Italian collections on a substantial scale in the first three decades of this century. The coin tickets accompanying the forgeries in the royal collection, most of them bought between 1900 and 1904, show them to have come on the market mainly through the agency of the dealers Ortensio Vitalini (like **1.1519** here) and Pietro Stettiner, and it was probably from these also that such collectors as Martinori, Giardini, and Ruchat acquired the forgeries that were subsequently to appear in their sale catalogues.

Tardani's masterpiece, which has never been adequately studied, was the invention of an entire coin hoard, alleged to have been found at Bolsena, north of Viterbo, which was sold in large part to the Vatican in 1909 by an individual calling himself Alessio Gilli (or Gigli). Still more reached the same cabinet with the acquisition of the Celati collection in 1921. An encrusted mass of coins from Celati convinced Camillo Serafini, curator of the Vatican collection and a fine numismatist, of their authenticity (Serafini 1910–28, IV.389 n. 9), despite the fact that the supposed hoard contained over 31 different papal coin types ranging in date from the early 9th to the mid 11th century and absolutely uniform in fabric and condition (Grierson 1958, 1965a). The initial series of plates in Serafini's great catalogue of papal coins is almost completely free from forgeries, but his supplementary plate 46, produced after he had acquired the hoard, contains ten of Tardani's products (nos. 3, 4, 5, 6, 7, 8, 11, 12, 13, 14) or possibly even eleven, for no. 2 may also not be authentic.

Tardani's products are never worn, but they are often artificially corroded or encrusted together by immersion in a bath of acid. He took as his general model some coin of the late 9th century, and his coins of popes of about this date are extremely difficult to separate from those that are genuine. But he did not know that the style and still more the fabric of papal *antiquiores* changed over the years, so that his forgeries of coins of much earlier and later popes are not too hard to recognize. The designs themselves are mainly taken from the line illustrations in the monograph of Domenico Promis, *Le monete dei papi avanti il mille* (Turin, 1858), but he sometimes used subsequently discovered material and meticulously reproduced any errors he found in his sources (see **1.1523**). Seven of his early papal forgeries are reproduced on Plate 65.

ANGLO-SAXON COINS

The earliest forgeries of Anglo-Saxon coins seem to be of the 17th century, but the great majority belong to the second half of the 18th or to the 19th (cf. note on **1.1479**). Those of sceattas are exceptional, and in the later series some rulers – Offa, Cynethryth, Coenwulf – have received more than their fair share of attention. The quality of the forgeries is variable. Casts can usually be identified without much difficulty, and many coins can be condemned on stylistic grounds, as can those late Anglo-Saxon coins which have sometimes been struck over commoner Anglo-Norman ones, a procedure that got round the difficulty of providing modern strikes with satisfactorily worn edges. But some forgeries, notably those for which the mid 19th-century forger Edward Emery was responsible, are of such high quality that they long passed unrecognized by collectors. Improbable die-linkages have here provided many essential clues, but such linkages are difficult to detect when the dies have been partially recut and other explanations seem possible. L. A. Lawrence, one of the best English numismatists of his day, defended in the 1890s the authenticity of three coins of Æthelbald of Wessex (855–60), struck with a recut die of his predecessor Æthelwulf (839–58), on the ground that such recutting would have been natural to a 9th-century moneyer, but would have required greater knowledge and skill than a modern forger was likely to possess. The subsequent discovery that the phenomenon was more widespread forced him to abandon this position and agree that the coins are false, as they are now accepted as being (Lawrence 1893 and 1905, 407–9). Die-links that one would not expect are in any case easy to overlook. In the Fitzwilliam Museum *Sylloge* Grierson condemned, on the advice of Mr Blunt, a coin of Ecgberht (no. 991) but failed to notice that it shared a reverse die with no. 527 of Æthelwulf, which was treated as genuine but must now be regarded as a forgery too (Pagan 1971, 155, nos. 6, 7). They are **1.1494** and **1.1495** in this catalogue, and the products of Emery.

The earliest important publication on the subject (Lawrence 1905) did little more than publish a series of photographic illustrations of the forgeries that had come its author's way, with a few related originals for purposes of comparison. Later studies have added alarmingly to Lawrence's list and eventually identified the forgers of the most dangerous coins. One mid 18th-century purveyor of forgeries was a London hatter, John White, who was a dealer on the side and whose speciality was tooled coins. His collection was sold in 1788 after his death and his activities were known even to his contemporaries, though his products, where they can be identified, would scarcely deceive anyone today (Blunt and Thompson 1955–7). Another early forger, who seems to have produced mainly cast coins, was a person who appears variously under the name of 'Singleton', alias 'James', alias 'Dr Edwards', and whose period of activity has been dated to *c.* 1825–40. Much more dangerous than either of these was a certain Edward Emery, professionally a London manufacturer of plate-glass, whose activities as a coin forger were exposed in 1842, when many of his dies were seized and destroyed, and who died at Hastings in 1851 (Pagan 1971, with detailed list of his products amplified from Blunt and Thompson 1955–7). There is some reason to believe that, like Cigoi, he did not make his dies himself, but relied on the skill of W. J. Taylor (1802–85), a medallist of somewhat dubious reputation who worked in London from the 1830s onwards. Emery's products begin to appear in public auctions in the 1850s and became common in the great sales of the 1880s, when his activities had presumably been forgotten by a younger generation of collectors. The fact that many of his coins have passed unquestioned through a sequence of famous collections, and have sometimes been used to illustrate standard works of reference, makes it extremely difficult to remove them from the accepted corpus of Anglo-Saxon coins.

Virtually distinct from the forgeries of southern England are those of Northumbria, which did not greatly interest Lawrence and are not covered by his article of 1905. Already in the 18th century a specimen of the 'York' thrymsa had given rise to a forgery which is in the present collection (**1.1481**), and doubt has even been cast on the authenticity of the thrymsas themselves (Metcalf 1961, 102–3), though without justification (Grierson 1962b, and see note on **1.1481**). More serious are the forgeries in the sceatta and styca series. The discovery in 1808 of a substantial hoard of over 500 coins at Kirkoswald in Cumbria (Thompson no. 225) created a lively interest in stycas, and prior to the finding of the huge Hexham and York hoards (Thompson nos. 188, 391) in 1832 and 1842 respectively many coins now regarded as fairly common fetched high prices and were extensively forged, either with the help of false dies or by casting from genuine specimens. Sometimes there is the same inappropriate muling of 'dies' as has been already noted amongst the Visigothic forgeries: e.g. a reverse of the (royal) moneyer Monne used for the three kings Eanred, Æthelred II and Redwulf being linked with an obverse of Archbishop Eanbald (Lyon 1956, 234). The cast forgeries are usually much too heavy (cf. **1.1482** ff.), and analysis shows that they are sometimes made from Rose's metal, an alloy of lead, tin, and bismuth first known in the 19th century which has a melting point under the boiling point of water (cf. Pirie and Warren 1983, and note on Plate 64).

The most serious numismatic consequence of forgery in these series arose out of the concoction of what now appears to have been a completely spurious 'hoard' alleged to have been found in 1813 in a grave at Heworth (Thompson no. 187) which contained the only known coins (North 175) bearing the name of the Northumbrian king Ecgfrith (670–85), all struck from the same pair of dies. It is possible that it was originally a hoax intended to deceive the Rev. John Hodgson, who had an interest in maintaining the antiquity of the church at Heworth of which he was the incumbent, but its contents deceived scholars for a century and a half. Doubts were cast on the attribution of the coins in 1956, since while perfectly acceptable in the early 19th century, when little was known of Northumbrian coinage, they had ceased to fit the pattern that had emerged through subsequent discoveries (Lyon 1956, 229), and chemical analysis has now shown them to be false. The impurities in their alloy differ completely from those occurring in other coins of the time but correspond exactly to those of George III halfpennies, which evidently provided the metal from which they were made (Pirie 1982, 3–4, 19).

Nine Northumbrian forgeries are illustrated on Plate 64.

BIBLIOGRAPHY

ABBREVIATIONS OF PERIODICALS AND SERIALS

Annales ESC	*Annales: Economies, Sociétés, Civilisations*
ASFN	*Annuaire de la Société française de numismatique*
BAR	British Archaeological Reports
BCEN	*Bulletin du Centre d'Etudes numismatiques* (Brussels)
BMF	*Blätter für Münzfreunde*
BMNA	*Bulletin mensuel de numismatique et d'archéologie*
BNJ	*British Numismatic Journal*
BSFN	*Bulletin de la Société française de numismatique*
DAN	Grierson 1979a (*Dark Age Numismatics*)
DJBN	*Deutsches Jahrbuch für Numismatik*
HBN	*Hambürger Beiträge zur Numismatik*
JESHO	*Journal of the Economic and Social History of the Orient*
JMP	*Jaarboek voor Munt- en Penningkunde*
JNG	*Jahrbuch für Numismatik und Geldgeschichte*
LMN	Grierson 1979b (*Later Medieval Numismatics*)
MBNG	*Mitteilungen der Bayerischen Numismatischen Gesellschaft*
MN	*Museum Notes* (American Numismatic Society)
NC	*Numismatic Chronicle*
NCirc	(Spink's) *Numismatic Circular*
NNÅ	*Nordisk Numismatisk Årsskrift*
NNM	Numismatic Notes and Monographs (American Numismatic Society)
NNUM	*Nordisk Numismatisk Unions Medlemsblad*
NZ	*Numismatische Zeitschrift*
QT	*Quaderni ticinesi (di) numismatica e antichità classiche*
RBN	*Revue belge de numismatique*
RIN	*Rivista italiana di numismatica*
RN	*Revue numismatique*
RSN	*Revue suisse de numismatique (Schweizerische Numismatische Rundschau)*
SCMB	*Seaby's Coin and Medal Bulletin*
SM	*Schweizerische Münzblätter*
TMP	*Tijdschrift voor Munt- en Penningkunde*
ZfN	*Zeitschrift für Numismatik*

ADAMSON 1834/6 J. Adamson, 'An account of the discovery at Hexham, in Northumberland, of a brass vessel, containing a number of Anglo-Saxon coins called stycas', *Archaeologia* 25 (1834), 279–310; 26 (1836), 346–8; reprinted in *Archæologia Æliana* 3.2 (1840), 77–111.

ADDYMAN and HILL 1968 P. Addyman and D. H. Hill, 'Saxon Southampton: a review of the evidence', *Proc. Hampshire Field Club* 25 (1968), 61–93.

ADELSON 1957 H. L. Adelson, 'A note on the miliarense from Constantine to Heraclius', *MN* 7 (1957), 125–35.

ADELSON 1958 — 'Silver currency and values in the early Byzantine Empire', in *Centennial Publication of the American Numismatic Society*, ed. H. Ingholt (New York, 1958), 1–26.

ADELSON 1967 — 'The monetary deterioration in the fifth century', in *The Patterns of Monetary Development in Palestine and Phoenicia in Antiquity*, ed. A. Kindler (Tel Aviv, 1967), 262–82.

ADELSON and KUSTAS 1960 H. L. Adelson and G. L. Kustas, 'A bronze hoard of the period of Leo I', *MN* 9 (1960), 139–88.

ADELSON and KUSTAS 1962 — *A Bronze Hoard of the Period of Zeno I* (NNM 148; New York, 1962).

ADELSON and KUSTAS 1964 —'A sixth century hoard of minimi from the western Peloponnese', *MN* 11 (1964), 159–205.

ADHÉMAR 1934 J. Adhémar, 'Le trésor d'argenterie donné par Saint Didier aux églises d'Auxerre (VIIe siècle)', *Revue archéologique*[6] 4 (1934), 44–54.

AEBISCHER 1965 P. Aebischer, 'Roland, mythe ou personnage historique?', *Revue belge de philologie et d'histoire* 43 (1965), 849–901.

AKERMAN 1842 J. Y. Akerman, 'Rude coins discovered in England', *NC*[1] 5 (1842), 30–4

AKERMAN 1844 — 'Description of some Merovingian, and other gold coins, discovered in the parish of Crondale, in Hampshire, in the year 1828', *NC*[1] 6 (1843–4), 171–82.

ALBRECHT 1957 C. Albrecht, *Dortmunder Fund römischer Goldmünzen* (Dortmund, 1957).

ALFÖLDI 1968 M. R. Alföldi, 'Le trésor de Wiesbaden-Kastel (IVe–Ve siècles)', *BCEN* 5 (1968), 95–102.

ALFÖLDI 1978 — 'Il medaglione d'oro di Teodorico', *RIN* 80 (1978), 133–41.

ALLAN 1914 J. Allan, 'Offa's imitation of an Arab dinar', *NC*[4] 14 (1914), 77–89.

ALLARA 1898 T. Allara, 'Ancora sui titoli di Teodorico', *RIN* 11 (1898), 67–74.

ALLARD 1907 P. Allard, 'Une grande fortune romaine au cinquième siècle' *Revue des questions historiques* 81 (1907), 5–30.

ALLEN 1936 D. F. Allen, 'Northumbrian pennies of the tenth century', *BNJ* 22 (1935–6), 175–86.

ALLEN 1948 — 'Edward the Confessor's gold penny', *BNJ* 25 (1948), 259–76.

ALLEN and TEIXEIRA 1865 E. A. Allen and H. N. Teixeira, 'Monnaies d'or suevo-lusitaniennes', *RN*[2] 10 (1865), 235–68.

ALVIN 1914 F. Alvin, 'Triens mérovingien inédit', *RBN* 70 (1914), 5–9.

AMARDEL 1898a G. Amardel, 'Les monnaies d'Anastase, de Justin et de Justinien frappées à Narbonne', *Bull. de la Comm. arch. de Narbonne* 5 (1898), 133–53.

AMARDEL 1898b — 'Les plus anciennes monnaies wisigothes de Narbonne', *Bull. de la Comm. arch. de Narbonne* 5 (1898), 389–401.

AMARDEL 1899 — 'Le denier mérovingien de Narbonne', *Bull. de la Comm. arch. de Narbonne* 5 (1899), 403–11.

AMARDEL 1900 — 'La première monnaie de Milon', *Bull. de la Comm. arch. de Narbonne* 6 (1900), 381–90.

AMARDEL 1901 — 'Numismatique de Narbonne au VIIIe siècle', *RN*[4] 5 (1901), 201–24, 348–62.

AMARDEL 1902a — 'Le comte Milon', *Bull. de la Comm. arch. de Narbonne* 7 (1902), 47–76.

AMARDEL 1902b — 'Les marques monétaires de l'atelier de Narbonne au VIe siècle', *Bull. de la Comm. arch. de Narbonne* 7 (1902), 119–62.

AMARDEL 1904 — 'Le T cursif dans les inscriptions monétaires carolingiennes', *Bull. de la Comm. arch. de Narbonne* 8 (1904), 1–25.

AMARDEL 1907 — 'Trois monnaies mérovingiennes inédites', *RN*[4] 11 (1907), 66–78 (early AR).

AMÉCOURT 1864 G. de Ponton d'Amécourt, *Essai sur la numismatique mérovingienne comparée à la géographie de Grégoire de Tours* (Paris, 1864).

AMÉCOURT 1866a — 'Excursion numismatique dans la Bourgogne du VIIe siècle sur les frontières de l'Austrasie', *ASFN* 1 (1866), 110–73.

AMÉCOURT 1866b — 'Bibliographie générale des monnaies mérovingiennes', *ASFN* 1 (1866), 383–93.

AMÉCOURT 1868a — 'Recherches sur les monnaies mérovingiennes de Touraine', *ASFN* 3 (1868–72), 86–134.

AMÉCOURT 1868b — 'Le monétaire Abbon', *ASFN* 3 (1868–72), 299–305.

AMÉCOURT 1868c —'Recherches sur l'origine et la filiation des types des premières monnaies carlovingiennes', *ASFN* 3 (1868–72), 306–25.

AMÉCOURT 1870 — 'Les monnaies mérovingiennes qui portent au revers les lettres CG–VII', *Comptes-rendus de la Soc. franç. de numism.* 2 (1870), 390–4.

AMÉCOURT 1872 — 'Farther notes on the gold coins discovered in 1828 at Crondal, Hants.', *NC*[2] 12 (1872), 72–82.

AMÉCOURT 1873 — 'Description raisonnée des monnaies mérovingiennes de Chalon-sur-Saône', *ASFN* 4 (1873–6), 37–152.

AMÉCOURT 1875 — 'Remarques sur un certain nombre de légendes de monnaies mérovingiennes', *Comptes-rendus de la Soc. franç. de numism.* 6 (1875), 173–82.

AMÉCOURT 1877a — 'Notes sur les monnaies au type de la boucle perdue', *ASFN* 5 (1877–81), 34–45.

AMÉCOURT 1877b — 'Type de l'orant sur les monnaies mérovingiennes', *ASFN* 5 (1877–81), 175–7.

AMÉCOURT 1881–3 — 'Recherche des monnaies mérovingiennes de Cenomannicum', *Rev. hist. et arch. du Maine* 10 (1881), 281–324; 11 (1882), 29–79, 129–80, 281–318; 12 (1883), 5–36, 121–57, 229–62.

AMÉCOURT 1882 — 'Les monétaires francs. Encore Abbon et Saint-Eloi' *ASFN* 6 (1882), 71–83.

AMÉCOURT 1883a — 'Monnaies mérovingiennes de Gévaudan', *ASFN* 7 (1883), 30–64, 128–54, 182–213, 263–300.

AMÉCOURT 1883b — 'Monnaies de l'Heptarchie anglo-saxonne. Un triens de Winchester (royaume de Wessex)', *ASFN* 7 (1883), 326–43.

AMÉCOURT 1885 — 'Monnaies de l'Ecole palatine', *ASFN* 9 (1885), 258–81.

AMORÓS 1952 J. Amorós and A. Mata Berruezo, *Catalogo de las monedas visigodas del Gabinete Numismatico de Cataluña* (Barcelona, 1952).

ANDREWS and METCALF 1984 P. Andrews and D. M. Metcalf, 'A coinage for King Cynewulf of Wessex?', in Hill and Metcalf 1984, 175–9.

ARBOIS DE JUBAINVILLE 1900 H. d'Arbois de Jubainville, *Etudes sur la langue des Francs à l'époque mérovingienne* (Paris, 1900).

ARCHÉOLOGIE 54 *Archéologie* no. 54 (June 1981; this issue of a lavishly illustrated French periodical is entirely devoted to Roman silverware).

ARCHIBALD 1978 M. M. Archibald, 'An Alfred penny from Rochester', *Archaeologia Cantiana* 94 (1978), 55–9 (Cross-and-Lozenge type).

ARCHIBALD 1980 — 'Coins and currency', in *Viking Artefacts*, ed. J. Graham-Campbell (London, 1980), 103–22.

ARCHIBALD 1982 — 'A Ship type of Athelstan I of East Anglia', *BNJ* 52 (1982), 34–40.

ARCHIBALD 1983 — 'Cash credentials of King Beonna', *Brit. Mus. Soc. Bull.* no. 42 (March 1983), 34.

ARCHIBALD 1985 — 'A Scandinavian coin of Carolingian type from the Cuerdale hoard', *Hikuin* 11 (1985), 79–82.

ARCHIBALD *et al.* 1979 M. M. Archibald, D. M. Metcalf and S. E. Rigold, 'The coins, counters and a token', in *St Peter's Street, Northampton: Excavations 1973–1976*, ed. J. H. Williams (Northampton, 1979), 243–7.

ARDANT 1851 M. Ardant and cte de Gourgue, 'Monnaies rares du Limousin', *RN* 1851, 253–62.

ARNALDI 1957 G. Arnaldi, 'Profilo di Alberico di Roma', *Atti dell'Accademia de Scienze morali e politiche della Società Nazionale di Scienze, Lettere ed Arti di Napoli* 68 (1957), 138–58.

ARNALDI 1967 — 'Berengario I', in *Dizionario biografico degli Italiani* IX (Rome, 1967), 1–26.

ARSLAN 1978 E. A. Arslan, *Le monete di Ostrogoti, Longobardi e Vandali. Catalogo delle Civiche Raccolte Numismatiche di Milano* (Milan, 1978).

ARSLAN 1983 —'Goti, Bizantini e Vandali: a proposito di ripostigli enei di VI secolo in Italia centrale', *QT* 12 (1983), 213–28.

ASHTOR 1970 E. Ashtor, 'Quelques observations d'un orientaliste sur le thèse de Pirenne', *JESHO* 13 (1970), 166–94.

AUTUN 1977 *Numismatique Autonoise (Musée Rolin). Exposition temporaire à l'occasion des 'journées' de la Société française de numisatique, 4 et 5 juin 1977* (mimeographed catalogue, photographic plates).

AUZIAS 1937 L. Auzias, *L'Aquitaine carolingienne (778–987)* (Toulouse-Paris, 1937).

BABELON 1901 E. Babelon, 'La silique romaine, le sou, et le denier de la loi des Francs saliens', RN^4 5 (1901), 325–47.

BABELON 1955 J. Babelon, 'Les monnaies de Jumièges', in *Jumièges. Congrès scientifique du XIIIe centenaire* I (Rouen, 1955), 479–82.

BALAGUER 1980 A. M. Balaguer, 'Descoperta d'un nou exemplar de las rares siliques de Màxim Tirà, atribuides a la seca de Barcelona. Corpus de les emisions de Màxim', *Numisma* 30, nos. 165–7 (1980), 141–54.

BALAGUER 1983 — 'El problema de la localización de la Roda visigoda', *Acta Numismatica* 13 (1983), 109–18.

BANKS and PURVEY 1967 F. Banks and F. Purvey, 'Two overstruck pennies of Archbishop Plegmund', *BNJ* 36 (1967), 189–90.

BARATTE 1975 F. Baratte, 'Les ateliers d'argenterie au Bas-Empire', *Journal des Savants* 1975, 193–212.

BARATTE 1976 — 'Quelques remarques à propos des lingots d'or et d'argent du Bas-Empire', in *Frappes et ateliers monétaires dans l'Antiquité et Moyen Age* (Belgrade, 1976), 63–71.

BARATTE 1978 — 'Lingots d'or et d'argent en rapport avec l'atelier de Sirmium', in *Sirmium* VIII (Rome-Belgrade, 1978), 99–109.

BARCELÓ 1974 M. Barceló, 'Las monedas suevas del British Museum', *Acta Numismatica* 4 (1974), 165–71.

BARCELÓ 1977 — 'Monedas visigodas de Hispania: un estado de la cuestión y algunas problemas de metrología y organización de las emisiones monetarias', *Numisma* 27 (1977), 55–80.

BARCELÓ 1978 — 'El rei Akhila i els fills de Wititzas encara un altra recerca', *Miscellanea Barcinonensia* 17 (1978), 59–77.

BARRAL 1975 X. Barral y Altet, 'Trésor de monnaies d'or des Ve et VIe siècles, trouvé à Seville', *BSFN* 30 (1975), 749–52.

BARRAL 1976 — *La circulation des monnaies suèves et visigothiques. Contribution à l'histoire économique du royaume visigot* (*Francia*, Beiheft 4; Munich, 1976).

BARRAL 1980 — 'Monnaies suèves contremarquées à la pointe', in *Lafaurie* 1980a, 167–9.

BARTHÉLEMY 1851 A. Barthélemy, 'Les concessions du droit de frapper monnaie faites par les Carlovingiens au prélats', *RN* 1851, 27–35.

BARTHÉLEMY 1861 — 'Numismatique mérovingienne. Etude sur les monnayers, les noms de lieux et de la fabrication de la monnaie', *Revue archéologique*[2] 11 (1865), 1–20.

BARTHÉLEMY 1877 — 'Les monnaies de Charlemagne', in A. Vetault, *Charlemagne* (Tours, 1877), 515–28.

BASTIEN 1972 P. Bastien, 'Les multiples d'or de l'avènement de Dioclétien à la mort de Constantin: essai de classement chronologique', *RN*[6] 14 (1972), 49–82.

BATAULT 1868 M. Batault, 'Trouvaille d'Issy-l'Evêque', *ASFN* 3 (1868), 402.

BATTELY 1745 O. Battely, *Antiquitates Rutupinae* (Oxford, 1745).

BAUER 1951 H.-U. Bauer, 'Der Triens de Rauchomaros', *SM* 2 (1951), 96–102.

BÉCHADE 1906 J. L. Béchade, 'Une trouvaille de monnaies carolingiennes', *RN*[4] 10 (1906), 302–5 (at Lauzès, nr Cahors).

BEHRENS 1939 G. Behrens, 'Merowingische Gewichte und Waagen', *Mainzer Zeitschrift* 34 (1939), 17–22.

BEHRENS 1947 — *Merowingerzeit: Original-Altertümer des Römisch-Germanischen Zentralmuseums im Mainz* (Katalog 13; Mainz, 1947) (w. plate of 5th/6th-century silver coins from Schwarzrheindorf).

BELFORT 1892–5 A. de Belfort, *Description générale des monnaies mérovingiennes*, 5 vols. (Paris, 1892–5).

BELFORT 1894 'Des tiers-de-sol d'or avec la légende TRIECTVM', *TMP* 2 (1894), 31–7, 142–53.

BELLINGER and BERLINCOURT 1962 A. R. Bellinger and M. A. Berlincourt, *Victory as a coin type* (NNM 199; New York, 1962).

BELLONI 1974 G. G. Belloni, 'La zecca di Lucca dalle origini a Carlo Magno', in *Le zecche minori toscane fino al XIV secolo: Convegno a Pistoia, 16–19 sett. 1967* (Pistoia, 1974), 91–111.

BELTING 1962 H. Belting, 'Studien zum beneventanischen Hof im 8. Jahrhundert', *Dumbarton Oaks Papers* 16 (1962), 141–93.

BELTRÁN 1941 P. Beltrán Villagrasa, 'Judila e Sunifredo, reyes godos (estudio numismático)', *Ampurias* 3 (1941), 97–104 (repr. in Beltrán 1972, 158–69).

BELTRÁN 1948 — 'Rectificaciones y falsificaciones en las monedas visigodas', *Cronica del III Congreso Arqueologico del Sudeste Español, Murcia, 1947* (Cartagena, 1948), 385–449 (repr. in Beltrán 1972, II. 97–157).

BELTRÁN 1953 — 'Monedas de Leovigildo en el tesorillo de Zorita de los Canes (año 1945)', *Numario Hispanico* 2/3 (1953), 19–54 (repr. in Beltrán 1972, II. 177–212).

BELTRÁN 1957 — 'Las primeras monedas suevas', *Caesaraugusta. Publicaciones del Seminario de Arqueologia y Numismatica Aragonesas* 7/8 (1957), 115–29.

BELTRÁN 1958a — 'Interpretaciones de algunas monedas suevas', *Nummus* 5 (1958–9), 81–90.

BELTRÁN 1958b — 'Introduccion del "Mancuso" en la economia carolingia', in *Centennial Publication of the American Numismatic Society*, ed. H. Ingholt (New York, 1958), 83–8.

BELTRÁN 1972 — *Obra completa* II; *Numismatica de la edad media y dos reyes catolicos* (Saragossa, 1972).

BENDIXEN 1972 K. Bendixen, Mønterne fra Dankirke', *Nationalmuseets Arbejdsmark* 1972, 61–6.

BENDIXEN 1974 — 'The first Merovingian coin-treasure from Denmark', *Mediaeval Scandinavia* 7 (1974), 85–101.

BENDIXEN 1981 — 'Sceattas and other coin finds', in *Ribe Excavations 1970–76* I, ed. M. Bencard (Esbjerg, 1981), 63–101.

BENDIXEN 1982 — 'Ny St. Peters-mønt fra Vikingetidens York', *NNUM* 1982, 2–6.

BENDIXEN 1984 — 'Finds of sceattas from Scandinavia', in Hill and Metcalf 1984, 151–7.

BENINGER 1940 F. Beninger, *Die Quaden* (Leipzig-Berlin, 1940).

BERGES 1954 W. Berges, 'Das Monogramm der Berner Gemme', in Schramm 1954, 222–6.

BERGHAUS 1958 P. Berghaus, 'Die ost-friesischen Münzfunde', *Friesisches Jahrbuch* 1958, 9–73.

BERGHAUS 1959 — 'Ein karolingischer Münzring von Herbrum (Kreis Aschendorf-Hümmling)', *Die Kunde*[2] 10 (1959), 90–7 (important for *Munus divinum* derivatives).

BERGHAUS 1973 — 'Karolingische Münzen in Westfalen', *Westfalen* 51 (1973), 22–32.

BERGHAUS and SCHNEIDER 1967 P. Berghaus and K. Schneider, *Anglo-Friesische Runensolidi im Lichte des Neufundes von Schweindorf (Ostfriesland)* (Cologne-Opladen, 1967) (but see reviews by R. I. Page in *NC*[7] 7 (1967), 304–6, and S. E. Rigold in *BNJ* 37 (1968), 199–201).

BERGMANN 1838 J. Bergmann, 'Zur Münzkunde des neunten Jahrhunderts', in *Der Oesterreichische Geschichtsforscher* I, ed. J. Chmel (1838), 217–25 (the Briosco hoard).

BERNAREGGI 1960 E. Bernareggi, *Il sistema economico e la monetazione dei Longobardi nell'Italia superiore* (Milan, 1960).

BERNAREGGI 1963 — 'Le monete dei Longobardi nell'Italia Padana e nella Tuscia', *RIN* 65 (1963), 35–142.

BERNAREGGI 1965a — 'Problemi di numismatica longobarda. Il tremisse di Ariperto con Iffo', *RIN* 67 (1965), 105–17.

BERNAREGGI 1965b — 'Problemi di numismatica longobarda. Le cosidette "Silique de Pertarito"', *Annali dell'Istituto italiano di numismatica* 12–14 (1965–7), 119–30.

BERNAREGGI 1968 — 'Problemi di numismatica longobarda. La monetazione di Re Aistolfo a Ravenna', *Annali dell'Istituto italiano di numismatica* 15 (1968), 63–9.

BERNAREGGI 1969 — 'Il medaglione d'oro di Teoderico', *RIN* 71 (1969), 89–106.

BERNAREGGI 1970 — 'Attività economiche e circolazione monetaria in età longobarda nella testimonianza delle "chartae"', *RIN* 72 (1970), 117–37.

BERNAREGGI 1971 — 'Conclusioni sulle diverse fasi della monetazione longobarda', *RIN* 73 (1971), 135–53.

BERNAREGGI 1972 — 'Un tremisse inedito di Desiderio, re dei Longobardi', *SM* 22 (1972), 14–17.

BERNAREGGI 1976 — 'Struttura economica e monetazione del regno longobardo', *QT* 5 (1976), 331–76.

BERNAREGGI 1977 — 'I tremissi longobardi e carolingi del ripostiglio di Ilanz, nei Grigioni', *QT* 6 (1977), 341–64.

BERNAREGGI 1980 — 'I falsi nella seria monetale dei Longobardi in Italia', in *Lafaurie* 1980a, 175–9.

BERNAREGGI 1983a — 'Carolingian gold coins from the Ilanz hoard', in *Grierson* 1983a, 127–35.

BERNAREGGI 1983b — *Moneta Langobardorum* (Milan, 1983).

BERTOLINI 1920 P. Bertolini, 'La data dell'ingresso dei Longobardi in Italia', *Bollettino della Società pavese di storia patria* 20 (1920), 11–70 (repr. in *Scritti scelti di storia medioevale*, ed. O. Banti (Leghorn, 1968), 19–61).

BERTOLINI 1941 O. Bertolini, *Roma di fronte a Bisanzio e ai Longobardi* (Storia di Roma 9; Bologna, 1941).

BERTOLINI 1952–5 — 'I papi e le relazioni politiche con i ducati longobardi di Spoleto e di Benevento', *Rivista di storia della Chiesa in Italia* 6 (1952), 1–46; 8 (1954), 1–22; 9 (1955), 1–57.

BERTOLINI 1962 P. Bertolini, 'Arechi II', in *Dizionario biografico degli Italiani* IV (Rome, 1962), 71–8.

BERTOLINI 1965 O. Bertolini, 'Carlomagno e Benevento', in *Karl der Grosse* I, ed. H. Beumann (Düsseldorf, 1965), 609–71.

BERTOLINI 1978 P. Bertolini, *Figura velut qua Christus designatur. La persistenza del simbolo della croce nell'iconografia numismatica durante il periodo iconoclasta: Constantinopoli e Benevento* (Istituto storico italiano per il medio evo. Studi storici 90; Rome, 1978).

BESSON 1910 M. Besson, *Antiquités du Valais (Ve–Xe siècles)* (Fribourg, 1910).

BEYERLE 1962 F. Beyerle, *Leges Langobardorum 643–866* (2nd edn; Witzenhausen, 1962).

BIDDLE 1984 M. Biddle, 'London on the Strand', *Popular Archaeology* 6.1 (July 1984), 23–7.

BIDDLE *et al.* 1986 M. Biddle *et al.*, 'Coins of the Anglo-Saxon period from Repton, Derbyshire', in *Dolley* 1986.

BIRCH 1885–93 W. de G. Birch, *Cartularium Saxonicum*, 3 vols. (London, 1885–93).

BIRKHAN 1971 J. Birkhan, 'Pfennig', *NZ* 86 (1971), 59–65.

BIRÓNÉ SEY 1976 K. Bíróné Sey, 'A szikáncsi V. századi solidus lelet', *Numizmatikai Közlöny* 74–5 (1975–6), 7–9 ('The fifth-century hoard of Szikáncs').

BISSON 1979 T. N. Bisson, *Conservation of Coinage. Monetary Exploitation and its Restraint in France, Catalonia, and Aragon (c. A.D. 1000–c. 1225)* (Oxford, 1979).

BLACKBURN 1983 M. A. S. Blackburn, 'A penny of Coenwulf and a small hoard of Cnut from Bottisham, Cambridgeshire', *BNJ* 53 (1983), 176–7.

BLACKBURN 1984 — 'A chronology for the sceattas', in Hill and Metcalf 1984, 165–74.

BLACKBURN 1985 — 'A preliminary account of the 9th-century coins in the Ashdon (Steventon End) hoard 1984', *NCirc* 1985, 43–4.

BLACKBURN and BONSER 1984a M. A. S. Blackburn and M. J. Bonser, 'A derivative of the *Ver* group of intermediate sceattas found at Springfield, Essex', in Hill and Metcalf 1984, 229–31.

BLACKBURN and BONSER 1984b — 'Sceattas, a styca, and other coin finds from a site in north-east Lincolnshire', in Hill and Metcalf 1984, 233–9.

BLACKBURN and BONSER 1984c — 'Single finds of Anglo-Saxon and Norman coins – I', *BNJ* 54 (1984), 63–72.

BLACKBURN and PAGAN 1986 M. A. S. Blackburn and H. E. Pagan, 'A revised listing of coin hoards from the British Isles AD 500–1100', in *Dolley* 1986.

BLACKBURN and SORENSON 1984 M. A. S. Blackburn and D. Sorenson, 'Sceattas from an unidentified site near Cambridge', in Hill and Metcalf 1984, 223–7.

BLACKBURN *et al.* 1983 M. Blackburn, C. Colyer and M. Dolley, *Early Medieval Coins from Lincoln and its Shire* c. *770–1100* (The Archeology of Lincoln VI–1; London, 1983).

BLAKE 1962 E. O. Blake (ed.), *Liber Eliensis* (London, 1962) (with foreword by D. Whitelock).

BLANCARD 1884–5 L. Blancard, 'La question Gondovald. Essai critique sur les mémoires de M. Deloche et M. Ch. Robert, membres de l'Institut, rélatifs à cette question', *Mém. de l'Acad. des sciences, belles-lettres et arts de Marseille* 1884–5, 409–42.

BLANCHET 1900 A. Blanchet, *Les trésors de monnaies romaines et les invasions germaniques en Gaule* (Paris, 1900).

BLANCHET 1908 — 'Le monnayage de l'empire romain après la mort de Théodose Ier', *Comptes-rendus de l'Académie des Inscriptions* 1908, 77–82.

BLANCHET 1910 — 'Les "sous gaulois" du Ve siècle', *Le Moyen Age*^{2} 14 (1910), 45–8.

BLANCHET 1912 — *Manuel de numismatique française* I: *Monnaies frappées en Gaule depuis les origines jusqu'à Hugues Capet* (Paris, 1912).

BLANCHET 1914 — 'Attila dans la numismatique', *RN*^{4} 18 (1914), 297–328.

BLANCHET 1955 — 'Le denier et l'obole d'or: redevances médiévales', in *Recueil des travaux offerts à M. Clovis Brunel* I (Paris, 1955), 147–51.

BLOCH 1933 M. Bloch, 'Le problème de l'or au moyen-âge', *Annales d'histoire économique et sociale* 5 (1933), 1–34 (repr. in his *Mélanges historiques* II (Paris, 1963), 839–67).

BLOCKMANS 1973 W. Blockmans, 'Le poids des deniers carolingiens', *RBN* 119 (1973), 179–81.

BLUNT 1948a C. E. Blunt, 'A gold penny of Edward the Elder', *BNJ* 25 (1945–8), 277–81.

BLUNT 1948b — 'Four Italian coins imitating Anglo-Saxon types', *BNJ* 25 (1945–8), 282–5.

BLUNT 1950 — 'A new type for Alfred', *BNJ* 26 (1949–51), 213–15.

BLUNT 1952a — 'A coin of Heahberht, king of Kent. Lord Grantley's attribution vindicated', *BNJ* 27 (1952–4), 52–4.

BLUNT 1952b — 'A Burgred-type coin with, apparently, the name of King Æthelbearht of Wessex', *BNJ* 27 (1952–4), 54–6.

BLUNT 1952c — 'A die-identity between a coin of Alfred and one of Æthelstan II of East Anglia', *BNJ* 27 (1952–4), 56–7.

BLUNT 1954 — 'Saxon coins from Southampton and Bangor', *BNJ* 27 (1952–4), 256–62.

BLUNT 1957 — 'The coinage of Ecgbeorht, king of Wessex 802–39', *BNJ* 28 (1955–7), 467–76.

BLUNT 1958 — 'An Offa-Iaenberht die-link', *BNJ* 29 (1958–9), 8–9.

BLUNT 1960 — 'Ecclesiastical coinage in England. Part I, to the Norman Conquest', NC^6 20 (1960), Proceedings, i–xvii.

BLUNT 1961 — 'The coinage of Offa', in *Stenton* 1961, 39–62.

BLUNT 1962a — 'The coinage of Æthelred, archbishop of Canterbury, 870–89', *BNJ* 31 (1962), 43–4.

BLUNT 1962b — 'Tenth-century half-pennies and C. Roach Smith's plate of coins found in London', *BNJ* 31 (1962), 44–8.

BLUNT 1969 — 'The St Edmund memorial coinage', *Proc. Suffolk Institute of Archaeology* 31 (1969), 234–55.

BLUNT 1974 — 'The coinage of Athelstan, 924–939. A survey', *BNJ* 42 (special vol., 1974), 35–158.

BLUNT 1979 — 'The Hougham hoard of sceattas *c.* 1870', NC^7 19 (1979), 108–10.

BLUNT 1983 — 'The composition of the Cuerdale hoard', *BNJ* 53 (1983), 1–6.

BLUNT 1986 — 'Anglo-Saxon coins found in Italy', in *Dolley* 1986.

BLUNT and DOLLEY 1959 C. E. Blunt and R. H. M. Dolley, 'The hoard evidence for the coins of Alfred', *BNJ* 29 (1958–9), 220–47.

BLUNT and DOLLEY 1961 — 'Coins at Nostell Priory, Yorkshire', *BNJ* 30 (1960–61), 360–1.

BLUNT and DOLLEY 1967 — 'On an alleged penny of Ludica, king of Mercia 815–17' *BNJ* 36 (1967), 28–31 (19th-century forgery in the Glasgow Museum).

BLUNT and DOLLEY 1968 — 'A gold coin of the time of Offa', NC^7 8 (1968), 151–60 (coin of the moneyer Pendred).

BLUNT, LYON and STEWART 1963 C. E. Blunt, C. S. S. Lyon and B. H. I. H. Stewart, 'The coinage of southern England, 796–840', *BNJ* 32 (1963), 1–74.

BLUNT and STEWART 1983 C. E. Blunt and B. H. I. H. Stewart, 'The coinage of Regnald I of York and the Bossall hoard', *NC* 1983, 146–63.

BLUNT and THOMPSON 1955–7 C. E. Blunt and J. D. A. Thompson, 'Forgery in the Anglo-Saxon series', *BNJ* 28 (1955–7), 18–25 (in part superseded by Pagan 1971, who carries the investigation much further).

BÖHNER 1958 K. Böhner, 'Münzen', in *Die fränkischen Altertümer des Trierer Landes* (Berlin, 1958), I.206–13 and II, pls. 58–9.

BOELES 1915 P. C. J. A. Boeles, 'Les trouvailles de monnaies carolingiennes dans les Pays-Bas, spécialement celles des trois provinces septentrionales', *JMP* 2 (1915), 1–98.

BOELES 1947 — 'Merovingische munten van het type Dronrijp en de vondst van Nietap', in *Gedenkboek A. E. van Giffen* (Meppel, 1947), 369–84.

BOELES 1951 — *Friesland tot de elfde eeuw* (2nd edn; The Hague, 1951) (index by H. T. Obreen as a separate brochure; Leeuwarden, 1962).

BOELES 1954 — 'De handel van Groter-Friesland met Frankrijk in de merovingische tijd', *Bijdragen voor de geschiedenis der Nederlanden* 8 (1954), 237–50.

BOERSMA 1977 J. W. Boersma, 'Een imitatie-solidus van het type *Munus divinum* uit de omgeving van Ten Post (Gr.) en sortegelijke in Noord Nederland gevonden exemplaren', *Groninger Oudheden* 13 (1976–7), 161–82 (brings together material found since Grierson 1951a).

BOGNETTI 1944 G. P. Bognetti, 'Il problema monetario dell'economia longobarda e il "panis" e "scutella di cambio"', *Archivio storico lombardo*[2] 9 (1944), 112–20.

BOLIN 1953 S. Bolin, 'Mohammed, Charlemagne and Ruric', *Scandinavian Economic History Review* 1 (1953), 5–39 (repr. in Hübinger 1968b).

BOMPOIS 1871 F. Bompois, *Notice sur un dépot de monnaies carlovingiennes découvert en juin 1871 aux environs du Veuillin* (Paris, 1871).

BÓNA 1964 I. Bóna, 'Die Pannonischen Grundlagen der langobardischen Kultur im Licht der neuesten Forschungen', in *Problemi della civiltà e dell'economia longobarda. Scritti in memoria di G. P. Bognetti* (Milan, 1964), 71–99.

BONAMY 1746 P. N. Bonamy, 'Histoire de Gondevald, prétendu fils de Clotaire Ier, pour servir d'explication à des médailles frappées à Arles et à Marseille au coin de l'empereur Maurice', *Mémoires de l'Académie des Inscriptions*[1] 20 (1746), 184–210.

BONNET 1909 E. Bonnet, 'Boson, roi de Provence et l'atelier monétaire d'Arles', *RN*[4] 13 (1909), 229–42.

BOONE 1954 W. J. de Boone, *De Franken van hun eerst optreden tot de dood van Childerik* (Amsterdam, 1954).

BOONE 1979 — 'De oudste afbeeldingen van "sceattas"', *Westerheem* 28 (1979), 159–67.

BOONE 1981 — 'Cannegieter, Domburg, trienten en sceattas', *Westerheem* 30 (1981), 72–81.

BOOTH 1984 J. Booth, 'Sceattas in Northumbria', in Hill and Metcalf 1984, 71–111.

BORDEAUX 1893 P. Bordeaux, 'Les monnaies de Trèves pendant la période carolingienne', *RBN* 49 (1893), 279–343, 431–58.

BORDEAUX 1907 — 'Un trésor de monnaies carolingiennes au musée de Coire', *RBN* 63 (1907), 5–18.

BORDEAUX 1908 — 'Essai d'interprétation du mot *Flavia* figurant sur les triens des rois lombards Aistaulf, Didier et Charlemagne', *RIN* 21 (1908), 97–112.

BORGIA 1763–9 S. Borgia, *Memorie istoriche della Pontificia Città di Benevento dal sec. VIII al sec. XIII*, 3 vols. (Rome, 1763–9).

BOSWORTH and TOLLER 1898 J. Bosworth and T. N. Toller, *An Anglo-Saxon Dictionary* (Oxford, 1898); *Supplement* by T. N. Toller (Oxford, 1921).

BOUTIN 1983 S. Boutin, *Monnaies des empires de Byzance. Collection N. K.* (= N. Kapamadji) (Maastricht, 1983).

BRAMBILLA 1867 C. Brambilla, 'Altro tremisse di re Astolfo battuto a Ravenna', in his *Alcune annotazioni numismatiche* (Pavia, 1867), 12–17.

BRAMBILLA 1883 — *Le monete di Pavia* (Pavia, 1883).

BRATIANU 1938 G. I. Bratianu, 'La distribution de l'or et les raisons économiques de la division de l'Empire romain', in his *Etudes byzantines d'histoire économique et sociale* (Paris, 1938), 57–91.

BREILLAT 1935 P. Breillat, *La langue des inscriptions monétaires mérovingiennes* (Ecole nationale des Chartes, Positions des thèses; Paris, 1935).

BRENOT 1976 C. Brenot, 'Rapport préliminaire sur les monnaies des fouilles de Marseille (quartier de la Bourse)', *Actes du 8e Congrès international de numismatique, New York–Washington 1973* (Paris–Basel, 1976), 217–26.

BRENOT 1980 — 'Monnaies en cuivre du VIe siècle frappées à Marseille', in *Lafaurie* 1980a, 181–8.

BRENOT and MORRISSON 1983 C. Brenot and C. Morrisson, 'La circulation du bronze en Césarienne occidentale à la fin du V siècle: la trouvaille de Rabelais–Aïn Merane', *QT* 12 (1983), 191–211.

BREUILLAC 1909 E. Breuillac, 'Un coin monétaire de l'atelier de Melle', *Procès-verbaux et mém. de la Soc. hist. et scientifique de Sèvres* 5 (1909), 359–61.

BREZZI 1947 P. Brezzi, *Roma e l'impero medioevale* (Storia di Roma 10; Rome, 1947).

BROGAN 1936 O. Brogan, 'Trade between the Roman empire and the free Germans', *Journal of Roman Studies* 26 (1936), 195–222.

BROOKE 1922–5 G. C. Brooke, 'Anglo-Saxon acquisitions of the British Museum. I. Thrymsa and sceatta series; Mercia', *NC*[5] 2 (1922), 214–44; 'II. Kent; archbishops of Canterbury; East Anglia', *NC*[5] 3 (1923), 243–59; 'III. Northumbria', *NC*[5] 4 (1924), 86–95; 'IV. Wessex; Ecgberht to Æthelred I', *NC*[5] 4 (1924), 239–53, 'V. Alfred to Eadwig', *NC*[5] 5 (1925), 343–65 (additions to *BMC AS*, often abbreviated as 'BMA'; not continued).

BROOKE 1950 — *English Coins* (3rd edn; London, 1950).

BROOKE 1963 C. N. L. Brooke, *The Saxon and Norman Kings* (London, 1963).

BROOKS 1984 N. P. Brooks, *The Early History of the Church at Canterbury* (Leicester, 1984).

BROOKS and GRAHAM-CAMPBELL 1986 N. P. Brooks and J. A. Graham-Campbell, 'Reflections on the Viking-age silver hoard from Croydon, Surrey', in *Dolley* 1986.

BROWN 1981 D. Brown, 'The dating of the Sutton Hoo coins', in *Anglo-Saxon Studies in Archaeology and History* 2 (BAR British Series 92; Oxford 1981), 71–86.

BRUCE-MITFORD 1975 R. L. S. Bruce-Mitford (ed.), *The Sutton Hoo Ship-burial* I (London, 1975) (Ch. 9 deals with the coins: see Kent 1975 and Rigold 1975).

BRUNETTI 1966 L. Brunetti, *Opus monetale Cigoi* (n.p. (Trieste?), 1966).

BRUNNER 1906 H. Brunner, *Deutsche Rechtsgeschichte* I (2nd edn; Leipzig, 1906).

BRUNNER 1908 — 'Über das Alter der *Lex Salica* und des *Pactus pro tenore pacis*', *Zeitschrift der Savigny-Stiftung für Rechtsgeschichte* 29, *Germanistische Abteilung* (1908), 136–79.

BRUNŠMID 1924 J. Brunšmid, 'Die Münzen des Gepidenkönigs Kunimund', *NZ* 57 (1924), 1–5.

BUCHNER 1933 R. Buchner, *Die Provence in merowingischer Zeit. Verfassung – Wirtschaft – Kultur* (Arbeiten zur deutschen Rechts- und Verfassungsgeschichte IX; Stuttgart, 1933).

BUHOT 1884 A. Buhot de Kersers, 'Bulletin de numismatique (No. 11)', *Mémoires de la Société des Antiquaires du Centre* 11 (1884), 277–317 (the section 'Mérovingiennes' on pp. 280–98 is his account of the Saint-Pierre-les-Etieux hoard).

BURNS 1980 T. S. Burns, *The Ostrogoths: Kingship and Society* (Wiesbaden, 1980).

BURY 1923 J. B. Bury, *History of the Later Roman Empire from the Death of Theodosius I to the Death of Justinian (A.D. 395 to A.D. 565)*, 2 vols. (London, 1923).

CABRÉ AGUILÓ 1946 J. Cabré Aguiló, *El tesorillo visigodo de trientes de las excavaciones del Plan Nacional de 1944–45 en Zorita de los Canes (Guadalajara)* (Madrid, 1946).

CAGIATI 1916–17 M. Cagiati, *La zecca di Benevento* (Milan, 1916–17) (repr., with the addition of a 21-page bibl., from a series of articles in *RIN* 28 (1915) 287–312; 29 (1916), 83–120, 335–66, 471–96).

CAGIATI 1925 — *I tipi monetali della zecca di Salerno: Atlante-Prezzario* (Caserta, 1925).

CAHEN 1965 C. Cahen, 'Quelques problèmes concernant l'expansion économique musulmane au haut moyen âge', *L'Occidente e l'Islam nell'alto medioevo* (Settimane di Studio del Centro italiano di studi sull'alto medioevo XII; Spoleto, 1965), 391–432, w. discussion on 487–515.

CAHN 1930 J. Cahn, 'Ein Goldmünzenfund des frühen 7. Jahrhunderts aus dem Grabfeld von Munningen', *Germania* 14 (1930), 161–5 (repr. in *Frankfurter Münzzeitung*[2] 1 (1931), 325–8).

CAHN 1938 H. A. Cahn, 'Münzfunde, Kleinhünigen', *RSN* 26 (1938), 425–34.

CAHN 1956 — 'Münzfund bei Tarasp (Graubunden)', *SM* 6 (1956), 70–1.

CALICÓ 1960 F. X. Calicó, 'En torno a una posible moneda barcelonesa del siglo IV', *Cuaderno de Arqueologia e Historia de la Ciudad (de Barcelona)* 1 (1960), 95–105.

CALLMER 1984 J. Callmer, *Sceatta Problems in the Light of the Åhus Finds* (Kungliga humanistiska vetenskabssamfundet i Lund. Scripta minora 1983–4: 2; Lund, 1984).

CALLU 1980 J.-P. Callu, 'PAX ET LIBERTAS: une légende monétaire de Théodebert Ier', in *Lafaurie* 1980a, 189–99.

CALMETTE 1901 J. Calmette, *La diplomatie carolingienne du traité de Verdun à la mort de Charles le Chauve (843–877)* (Bibl. de l'Ecole des Hautes Etudes, fasc. 135; Paris, 1901).

Cambridge Economic History of Europe *The Cambridge Economic History of Europe* I– (Cambridge 1941–).

Cambridge Medieval History *The Cambridge Medieval History*, 8 vols. (Cambridge, 1911–36). Abbreviated as '*CMH*'.

CAPOBIANCHI 1892 V. Capobianchi, 'Pesi proporzionali desunti dai documenti della Libra Romana, Merovingia e di Carlo Magno', *RIN* 5 (1892), 79–114.

CAPOBIANCHI 1900 — 'Les *Caroli pondus* conservés en Italie', *Mélanges d'archéologie et d'histoire* (Ecole francaise de Rome) 20 (1900), 43–77.

CAPPELLI 1972 R. Cappelli, *Studio sulle monete della zecca di Salerno* (Rome, 1972).

CARLES-TOLRÁ 1936 *Catálogo de la colección numismatica Emilio Carles-Tolrá* (Barcelona, 1936).

CARLYON-BRITTON 1908 P. W. P. Carlyon-Britton, 'The gold mancus of Offa, king of Mercia', *BNJ* 5 (1908), 55–72.

CARPENTIN 1861 A. Carpentin, 'Pièces gallo-grecques de Marseille', *RN*[2] 6 (1861), 397–406 (no. 10, on pp. 404–6, is a Merovingian denier of Marseille).

CARPENTIN 1864 — 'Marseille. Monnaies des patrices', *RN*[2] 9 (1864), 118–30.

CARSON 1950 R. A. G. Carson, 'A Roman imperial mint at Narbonne?', *NC*[6] 10 (1950), 144–8.

CARSON 1981 — *Principal Coins of the Romans* III: *The Dominate, A.D. 294–498* (London, 1981).

CARTIER 1839 E. J. B. Cartier, 'Lettres sur l'histoire monétaire de France. VII. Nouvelles considérations sur les monnaies mérovingiennes', *RN* 1839, 417–40.

CARTIER 1846 — 'Appendice aux mémoires sur les monnaies bléso-chartraines antérieures au Xe siècle', *RN* 1846, 107–33.

CARTIER 1853 — 'Des monnaies de Charlemagne et particulièrement de celles qui portent, avec son monogramme, la légende CARLVS REX FR', *RN* 1853, 348–410.

CASTELLANE 1900 H. de Castellane, 'Denier de Corbie au type de Louis le Bègue', *RN*[4] 4 (1900), 435–8.

CASTELLANE 1916 — 'Observations sur le monnayage de Corbie au IX siècle', *RN*[4] 20 (1916), 193–213.

CATEMARIO 1953 E. Catemario di Quadri, 'Considerazioni sulle monete di Benevento', *Boll. del Circolo numismatico Napoletano* 38 (1953), 3–7.

CAUCICH 1867 A. R. Caucich, 'Di due conii falsi recentamente scoperti in Roma', *Bull. di num. italiana* 1 (1867), 44–5.

CEREXHE 1886–7 M. Cerexhe, *Les monnaies de Charlemagne*, 2 parts (Ghent, 1886–7).

CESANO 1913 L. Cesano, 'Della moneta enea corrente in Italia nell'ultima età imperiale romana e sotto i re Ostrogoti', *RIN* 26 (1913), 511–51.

CHABOUILLET 1890 — A. Chabouillet, *Catalogue raisonné de la collection des deniers mérovingiens des VIIe et VIIIe siècles de la trouvaille de Cimiez* (Paris, 1890).

CHALON 1852 R. Chalon, 'Attribution d'un denier carlovingien à Mons (*Castrilocus*)', *RBN*[2] 2 (1852), 134–8.

CHALON 1859 — 'Un singulier plomb trouvé à Gand', *RBN*[3] 3 (1859), 545.

CHALON 1870 — 'Curiosités numismatiques. Pièces rares ou inédites (16e article)', *RBN*[5] 2 (1870), 494–507 (includes the Merovingian *Cornilio* coin).

CHARVET 1870 J. Charvet, 'Monnaies découvertes à Glisy', *RBN*[5] 2 (1870), 417–39 (the summary by E. Gariel in *ASFN* 2 (1867), 349–58, notes the collectors who acquired each of the coins).

CHASTAGNOL 1966 A. Chastagnol, *Le Sénat romain sous le règne d'Odoacre. Recherches sur l'épigraphie du Colisée au Ve siècle* (Bonn, 1966).

CHENU 1932 P. Chenu, 'Un dépot de monnaies carolingiennes dans le département du Cher', *Mém. de la Soc. historique, littéraire et scientifique du Cher*[4] 39 (1932), 103–26 (hoard of Chaumoux-Marcilly).

CHIFLET 1655 J. J. Chiflet, *Anastasis Childerici I Francorum regis, sive Thesaurus sepulchralis Tornaci Nerviorum effossus et commentario illustratus* (Antwerp, 1655).

CHIJS 1866 P. O. Van der Chijs, *De munten der frankische- en deutsch-nederlandsche Vorsten* (De munten der Nederlanden van de vroogste tijd tot aan de Pacificatie van Gend, 1576. Vol. IX; Haarlem, 1866).

CIPOLLA 1962 C. Cipolla, 'Sans Mahomet Charlemagne est inconcevable', *Annales ESC* 17 (1962), 130–6.

CLAUDE 1961a D. Claude, *Adel, Kirche und Königtum in Westgotenreich* (Sigmaringen, 1961).

CLAUDE 1961b — 'Zu Fragen der merowingischen Geldgeschichte?', *Vierteljahrschrift für Sozial- und Geldgeschichte* 48 (1961), 236–50.

CLOVER 1978 F. M. Clover, 'Carthage in the age of Augustine', in Humphrey 1976–, IV (Ann Arbor, 1978), 1–15.

CLOVER 1982a —'Carthage and the Vandals', in Humphrey 1976–, VII (Ann Arbor, 1982), 1–22.

CLOVER 1982b — 'Emperor worship in Vandal Africa', in *Romanitas-Christianitas. Untersuchungen zur Geschichte und Literatur der römischen Kaiserzeit Johannes Straub zum 70. Geburtstag gewidmet* (Berlin–New York, 1982), 661–74.

CLOVER forthcoming — 'Relations between North Africa and Italy A.D. 476–500; some numismatic evidence', in *Aufstieg und Niedergang der römischen Welt* II. *Principat*, ed. H. Temporini and W. Haase (Berlin, 1974–).

COCHET 1852 D. Cochet, 'Note sur cinq monnaies d'or trouvées dans le cimetière mérovingien de Lucy près Neufchâtel en 1851', *Revue archéologique* 8 (1851–2), 747–52.

COHEN 1880–92 H. Cohen, *Description historique des monnaies frappées sous l'empire romain*, 8 vols. (2nd edn; Paris, 1880–92).

COLIN 1868 J. Colin, 'Bibliographie générale des monnaies carlovingiennes', *ASFN* 3 (1868), 469–89.

CONBROUSE 1839 G. Conbrouse, *Catalogue raisonné des monnaies nationales de France* I: *Mérovingiennes* (Paris, 1839). (The author's name is usually spelled Co*m*brouse, but it is Co*n*brouse on the title-page of this work. The pagination is in total confusion.)

CONBROUSE 1840–1 — *Atlas des monnaies nationales de France*, 2 vols. (Paris, 1840–1).

CONRAT 1908 M. Conrat (Cohn), 'Ein Traktat über romanisch-fränkisches Ämterwesen', *Zeitschrift der Savigny-Stiftung für Rechtsgeschichte* 29, *Germanistische Abteilung* (1908), 239–60.

CORDERO 1834 G. Cordero di San Quintino, 'Sulla moneta dei Longobardi in Italia', *Il Progresso delle Scienze, delle Lettere e delle Arti* 7 (1834), 216–35.

CORDERO 1860 — *Della zecca e delle monete di Lucca nei secoli di mezzo* (Memorie e documenti per servire alla storia di Lucca XI.1; Lucca, 1860).

Corpus Nummorum Italicorum *Corpus Nummorum Italicorum*, 20 vols. (Rome, 1910–70) (repr. 1970).

COTHENET and LAFAURIE 1969 A. Cothenet and J. Lafaurie, 'Trésor de monnaies d'or de Valentinien III trouvé à Arçay (Cher)', *BSFN* 24 (1969), 443–4.

COURCELLE 1964 P. Courcelle, *Histoire littéraire des grandes invasions germaniques* (3rd edn; Paris, 1964).

COURTOIS 1954 C. Courtois, 'Les monnaies de Gildo', *RN*[5] 16 (1954), 71–7.

COURTOIS 1955 — *Les Vandales et l'Afrique* (Paris, 1955).

COURTOIS *et al.* 1952 C. Courtois and others (ed.), *Tablettes Albertini. Actes privés de l'époque vandale (fin du Ve siècle)* (Paris, 1952).

CREMASCHI 1955 L. Cremaschi, 'Circa il ritrovamento monetale in Pavia, 1934', *Bollettino della Società pavese di storia patria* 1955, 91–2.

CRUSAFONT 1980 M. Crusafont i Sabater, 'Nou tipus carolingi de Barcelona de Carles el Calb. El diner de Barcelona fins a R. Berenguer I', *II Simposi Numismàtic de Barcelona* (Barcelona, 1980), 47–56.

CRUSAFONT 1982 — *Numismatica de la Corono Catalano-Aragonesa medieval (785–1516)* (Madrid, 1982).

CRUSAFONT, BALAGUER and PUIG 1979 M. Crusafont i Sabater, A. M. Balaguer and I. Puig, 'Els Comtats catalans: les seves encunyacions i àrees d'influència. I Corpus', *Symposium Numismatic de Barcelona* I (Barcelona, 1979), 377–503.

CUMONT 1890 G. Cumont, 'Monnaies franques découvertes dans les cimetières francs d'Eprave (province de Namur)', *RBN* 46 (1890), 212–69.

CUMONT 1893 — 'Monnaies découvertes dans les cimetières francs de Corbois près Rochefort et *Sur-le-Mont*, à Eprave', *RBN* 49 (1893), 423–30.

CUMONT 1894 — 'Des tiers de sou d'or à la légende TRIECTVM', *TMP* 2 (1894), 63–76, 190–8.

DANNENBERG 1876 and 1894 H. Dannenberg, *Die deutschen Münzen der sächsischen und fränkischen Kaiserzeit* vols. I and II (Berlin, 1876 and 1894).

DE CLERCQ 1936 C. de Clercq, *La législation réligieuse franque de Clovis à Charlemagne* (Louvain–Paris, 1936).

DE COSTER 1852 L. de Coster, 'Restitution de quelques monnaies à Charlemagne', *RBN*[2] 2 (1852), 369–403.

DE COSTER 1853 — 'Renseignements pour servir à la numismatique de la seconde race', *RBN*[2] 3 (1853), 357–69.

DE COSTER 1855 — 'Nouvelles considérations sur les monnaies restituées à Charlemagne', *RBN*[2] 5 (1855), 1–21.

DE COSTER 1857 — 'Explications faisant suite aux précédentes notices sur l'attribution à Charlemagne de quelques types monétaires', *RBN*[3] 1 (1857), 30–54.

DE COSTER 1862 — 'Lettre à M. Hoffmann', *Le Numismate* 1862–4, 57–60 (Eekeren hoard).

DEER 1957 J. Deér, 'Die Vorrechte des Kaisers in Rom (772–800)', *Schweizer Beiträge zur Allgemeinen Geschichte* 15 (1957), 5–63.

DE HAAN 1866 F. de Haan, *Angelsaksische munten, in 1866 gevonden in Friesland, bescheven en historisch toegelicht* (Leeuwarden, 1866) (the Hallum hoard, with a commentary by W. Eekhoff).

DE JONGHE 1891 B. de Jonghe, 'De la frappe de l'or sous les Carolingiens et spécialement sous Louis-le-Debonnaire', *Congrès international de numismatique, Bruxelles 1891. Procès-Verbaux et Mémoires*, ed. G. Cumont and A. de Witte (Brussels, 1891), 209–23.

DE JONGHE 1896 — 'Un denier inédit de Pépin le Bref', *RBN* 52 (1896), 261–4.

DE JONGHE 1897 — 'Un denier frappé à Mayence par l'empereur Lothaire avant le traité de Verdun (843)', *RBN* 53 (1897), 249–62.

DELOCHE 1863 M. Deloche, *Description des monnaies mérovingiennes du Limousin* (Paris, 1863) (reprint of 11 articles in the *RN* 1857–62.)

DELOCHE 1879 — 'Dissertation sur une médaille d'or mérovingienne portant à la fois le nom gallo-romain et le nom plus récent d'une ville gauloise. Observations sur le changement de noms de ville dans la Gaule du IIIe au VIIe siècle', *Mémoires de l'Académie des Inscriptions* 29/2 (1879), 331–46 (repr. in Deloche 1890a, 236–53).

DELOCHE 1880 — 'Explication d'une formule inscrite sur plusieurs monnaies mérovingiennes', *Revue archéologique*[2] 40 (1880), 171–6 (repr. in Deloche 1890a, 227–35).

DELOCHE 1883a — 'Le monnayage en Gaule au nom de l'empereur Maurice Tibère. Ses rapports avec l'expédition du prétendant Gondovald (an 583–585)', *Mémoires de l'Académie des Inscriptions* 30/2 (1883), 375–95, and in *Revue archéologique*[2] 43 (1882), 301–15 (repr. in Deloche 1890a, 176–96).

DELOCHE 1883b — 'Deuxième mémoire sur le monnayage en Gaule au nom de l'empereur Maurice Tibère', *Mémoires de l'Académie des Inscriptions* 30/2 (1883), 439–64 (repr. in Deloche 1890a, 197–226).

DELOCHE 1886a — 'Des monnaies d'or au nom de Théodebert Ier', *Mémoires de l'Académie des Inscriptions* 32/1 (1886), 425–39 (repr. in Deloche 1890a, 48–65).

DELOCHE 1886b — 'Monnaies mérovingiennes inédites. X.', *RN*[3] 4 (1886), 27–32 (solidus attributed to Bonn; repr. in Deloche 1890a, 66–71).

DELOCHE 1886c — 'Considérations générales sur les monnaies d'or du roi Théodebert Ier, des causes de leur abondance, de leur titre élevée et de la substitution sur ces monnaies de la légende royale à la légende impériale', *RN*[3] 4 (1886), 372–86 (repr. in Deloche 1890a, 72–86).

DELOCHE 1888 — 'Réponse aux observations présentées par M. P.-Ch. Robert sur son second mémoire concernant les monnaies frappées au nom de Théodebert Ier, roi d'Austrasie', *Mémoires de l'Académie des Inscriptions* 32/2 (1888), 93–117.

DELOCHE 1890a — *Etudes de numismatique mérovingienne* (Paris, 1890) (reprint of a selection of articles).

DELOCHE 1890b — 'De l'organisation de la fabrication des monnaies dans l'Austrasie proprement dite, sous le règne de Théodebert Ier', in Deloche 1890a, 144–75.

DELOGU 1964 P. Delogu, '*Consors regni*: un problema carolingio', *Bullettino dell'Istituto storico italiano per il Medio Evo* 76 (1964), 47–98 (pp. 90–5 on the Empress Angilberga).

DELOGU 1977 — *Mito di una città meridionale: Salerno secoli VIII–XI* (Naples, 1977).

DE MAN 1894 M. G. A. de Man, 'Sou d'or barbare trouvé en Frise', *RBN* 50 (1894), 305–27.

DE MAN 1895 — 'Sceattas anglo-saxons inédits ou peu connus', *TMP* (1895), 117–46.

DE MAN 1899 — 'Que sait-on de la plage de Dombourg?', *TMP* 7 (1899), 1–61, 85–116, 153–73.

DE MAN 1907 — *Catalogus der Numismatische verzameling van het Zeeuws Genootschap der Wetenschappen* (Middelburg, 1907).

DE MAN 1925 — 'Over eenige te Domburg gevonden merkwaardige munten', *JMP* 12 (1925), 1–25.

DEMOUGEOT 1979 E. Demougeot, *La formation de l'Europe et les invasions barbares* II: *De l'avènement de Dioclétien (284) à l'occupation germanique de l'Empire romain d'Occident (début du VIe siècle)* (Paris, 1979).

DEMOUGEOT 1983 — 'A propos des *Solidi gallici* du Ve siècle après J.-C.', *Revue historique* 270 (1983), 3–30.

DENARO 1955 V. F. Denaro, 'The mint of Malta', *NC*[6] 15 (1955), 173–87.

DENNETT 1948 D. C. Dennett, 'Pirenne and Muhammad', *Speculum* 23 (1948), 165–90 (repr. in Hübinger 1968b).

DESCHAMPS 1839 L. Deschamps, 'Quelques monnoies des empereurs de la race carlovingienne frappées en Italie', *RN* 1839, 371–91.

DESSÌ 1908 V. Dessì, 'I tremissi longobardi a proposito di un piccolo ripostiglio di monete d'oro di Liutprando, rinvenuto presso il villaggio di Ossi (Sassari)', *RIN* 21 (1908), 295–311 (repr. in his *Gli scritti di numismatica* (Sassari, 1970), 225–44).

DE VITA 1754–64 G. De Vita, *Thesaurus antiquitatum Beneventanarum*, 2 vols. (Rome, 1754–64).

DHÉNIN 1970 R. and M. Dhénin, 'Trouvailles de monnaies d'or byzantines ou pseudo-byzantines dans les départements du Nord et du Pas-de-Calais', *Septentrion* 1 (1970), 147–50.

DHÉNIN 1980a M. Dhénin, 'Découverte d'un denier mérovingien à Pontault-Combault (Seine-et-Marne)', *BSFN* 35 (1980), 663–4 (denier of Metz).

DHÉNIN 1980b — 'Monnaies des Ve–VIe siècles des nécropoles de Vron (Somme) et de Hordain (Nord)', in *Lafaurie* 1980a, 201–7.

DHONDT 1962 J. Dhondt, 'Les problèmes de Quentovic', in *Studi in onore di Amintore Fanfani* I (Milan, 1962), 182–248.

DHONDT 1976 — *Le haut moyen âge (VIIIe–XIe siècles)* (Paris, 1976) (Fr. transl. by M. Rouche; revised version of the original Germ. edn of 1968, with particular attention to economic factors).

DÍAZ 1960 M. C. Díaz y Díaz, 'La legenda *Regi a Deo vita* de una moneda de Ermenegildo', *Analecta sacra Tarraconensia* 31 (1960), 261–9 (see comment in Vives 1960).

DICKIE and PARROTT 1950 D. P. Dickie and R. D. Parrott, 'Merovingian coins in the collection of the American Numismatic Society', *MN* 4 (1950), 91–6.

DIEPENBACH 1950 W. Diepenbach, 'Die Münzprägungen am Mittelrhein im Zeitalter der Merowinger', *Mainzer Zeitschrift* 44–5 (1949–50), 141–52.

DIESNER 1965 H. J. Diesner, 'Vandalen', in A. F. von Pauly and G. Wissowa, *Real-Encyclopädie der classischen Altertums-Wissenschaft*, Supplementband X (1965), 957–92.

DIEUDONNÉ 1908 A. Dieudonné, 'Récentes acquisitions du Cabinet des Médailles. I. Monnaies mérovingiennes', *RN*^{4} 12 (1908), 490–8.

DIEUDONNÉ 1915 — 'Acquisitions du Cabinet des Médailles: monnaies carolingiennes', *RN*^{4} 19 (1915), 211–42.

DIEUDONNÉ 1920a — 'Les poids du moyen âge et la numismatique d'après une étude [de Guilhiermoz] publiée en 1906', *Le Moyen Age* 31 (1920), 157–78.

DIEUDONNÉ 1920b — 'Quelques hypothèses sur le sou de 40 deniers et le sou de 12 deniers', *RBN* 72 (1920), 11–26.

DIEUDONNÉ 1923 — 'Métrologie du Bas-Empire et des Mérovingiens. A propos d'un article récent', *RBN* 75 (1923), 121–7 (discussion of Naville 1922).

DIEUDONNÉ 1926 — 'Le sou de 12 deniers: considérations additionnelles', *RBN* 78 (1926), 7–10.

DIEUDONNÉ 1939 — Le denier de la Loi salique', *RN*^{5} 3 (1939), P.-V., xi–xviii.

DIEUDONNÉ 1942 — 'Les monétaires mérovingiens', *Bibl. de l'Ecole des Chartes* 103 (1942), 20–51.

DIEUDONNÉ 1943 — 'Le denier de la Loi salique', *RN*^{5} 7 (1943), 159–61 (supplement to Dieudonné 1939).

DIRKS 1863 J. Dirks, 'Monnaies anciennes trouvées en Frise', *RBN*^{4} 1 (1863), 393–9.

DIRKS 1869 — 'La trouvaille de Pingjum (Frise) en juin 1868', *RBN*^{5} 1 (1869), 199–205.

DIRKS 1870 — 'Les Anglo-Saxons et leurs petits deniers, dits sceattas. Essai historique et numismatique', *RBN*^{5} 2 (1870), 81–128, 269–320, 387–409, 521–41.

DIRKS 1887 — *De vondst van gouden voorwerfen en merovingische munten te Dronrijp* (Leeuwarden, 1887).

DOEHAERD 1949 R. Doehaerd, 'La richesse des Mérovingiens', in *Studi in onore di Gino Luzzatto* (Milan, 1949), 30–46.

DOEHAERD 1952 — 'Les réformes monétaires carolingiennes', *Annales ESC* 7 (1952), 13–20.

DOEHAERD 1971 — *Le haut moyen âge occidental. Economies et sociétés* (Paris, 1971).

DOLLEY 1953 R. H. M. Dolley, 'A piedfort lead-trial piece of Edward the Confessor', *BNJ* 27 (1952–4), 175–8.

DOLLEY 1955 — 'A neglected but vital Yorkshire hoard', *BNJ* 28 (1955–7), 11–17 (Bossall/Flaxton hoard).

DOLLEY 1956 — 'A new type and moneyer for Eadbearht "Præn"', *BNJ* 28 (1955–7), 243–8.

DOLLEY 1957 —'An unpublished Irish hoard of "St Peter" pence', *NC*[6] 17 (1957), 123–32.

DOLLEY 1958 — 'The post-Brunanburh Viking coinage of York, with some remarks on the Viking coinages which preceded the same', *NNÅ* 1957/58, 13–85.

DOLLEY 1962 — 'Some Temple-type coins found in Great Britain', *HBN* 5/16 (1962), 321–4.

DOLLEY 1963 — 'An unpublished hoard-provenance for a penny of Ceolwulf II of Mercia', *BNJ* 32 (1963), 88–90.

DOLLEY 1964 — *Anglo-Saxon Pennies* (London, 1964).

DOLLEY 1965a — *Viking Coins of the Danelaw and Dublin* (London, 1965).

DOLLEY 1965b —'New light on the pre-1760 Coney Street (York) find of coins from the Duurstede mint', *JMP* 52–3 (1965–6), 1–7.

DOLLEY 1966 — *The Hiberno-Norse Coins in the British Museum* (*SCBI* 8; London, 1966).

DOLLEY 1970 — 'The location of the pre-Ælfredian mint(s) of Wessex', *Proc. Hampshire Field Club* 27 (1970), 57–61.

DOLLEY 1974 — 'Towards a revision of the internal chronology of the coinages of Edward the Elder and Plegmund', *Anglo-Saxon England* 3 (1974), 175–7.

DOLLEY 1978 — 'The Anglo-Danish and Anglo-Norse coinages of York', in *Viking Age York and the North*, ed. R. A. Hall (CBA Res. Rep. 27; London, 1978), 26–31.

DOLLEY 1982 — 'Dateringen af de seneste St. Petersmønter fra York', *NNUM* 1982, 82–92 (a reply to Bendixen 1982).

DOLLEY 1983 — 'Ælfred the Great's abandonment of the concept of periodic recoinage', in *Grierson* 1983a, 153–60.

DOLLEY 1986 *Anglo-Saxon Monetary History. Essays in Memory of Michael Dolley*, ed. M. A. S. Blackburn (Leicester, 1986).

DOLLEY and BLUNT 1961 R. H. M. Dolley and C. E. Blunt, 'The chronology of the coins of Ælfred the Great, 871–99', in *Stenton* 1961, 77–95.

DOLLEY and METCALF 1957 R. H. M. Dolley and D. M. Metcalf, 'Two stray finds from St Albans of coins of Offa and of Charlemagne', *BNJ* 28 (1955–7), 459–66.

DOLLEY and MOORE 1973 M. Dolley and C. N. Moore, 'Some reflections on the English coinages of Sihtric Caoch, king of Dublin and York', *BNJ* 43 (1973), 45–59.

DOLLEY and MORRISON 1962 R. H. M. Dolley and K. F. Morrison, 'A note on four "type immobilisé" coins of Melle from British finds', *NC*[7] 2 (1962), 157–60.

DOLLEY and MORRISON 1963 — 'Finds of Carolingian coins from Great Britain and Ireland', *BNJ* 32 (1963), 75–87.

DOLLEY and MORRISON 1966 — *The Carolingian Coins in the British Museum* (London, 1966).

DOLLEY and SÁRKÁNY 1972 M. Dolley and T. Sárkány, 'Four Carolingian coins found at Wijk-bij-Duurstede and now in the Royal Cabinet at Stockholm', *JMP* 58–9 (1971–2), 5–9.

DOLLEY and SKAARE 1961 R. H. M. Dolley and K. Skaare, 'The coinage of Æthelwulf, king of the West Saxons 839–58', in *Stenton* 1961, 63–76.

DOLLEY and STRUDWICK 1955 R. H. M. Dolley and J. S. Strudwick, 'The provenances of the Anglo-Saxon coins recorded in the two volumes of the British Museum catalogue', *BNJ* 28 (1955–7), 25–9.

DOLLEY and TALVIO 1974 M. Dolley and T. Talvio, 'An unpublished hoard-provenance for the ninth-century coinage of Hedeby', *NC*[7] 14 (1974), 190–2.

DOLLEY and YVON 1971 M. Dolley and J. Yvon, 'A group of tenth-century coins found at Mont-Saint-Michel', *BNJ* 40 (1971), 1–16.

DOPPELFELD 1960 O. Doppelfeld, 'Das fränkische Frauengrab unter dem Chor des Kölner Domes', *Germania* 38 (1960), 87–113.

DOPSCH 1927 A. Dopsch, *The Economic and Social Foundations of European Civilization* (London, 1927) (transl. of a slightly condensed version of the 2nd edn of his *Wirtschaftliche und soziale Grundlagen der Europäischen Kulturentwicklung aus der Zeit von Caesar bis auf Karl den Grossen*, 2 vols. (Vienna, 1923–4)).

DOPSCH 1930 — *Naturalwirtschaft und Geldwirtschaft in der Weltgeschichte* (Vienna, 1930).

DOPSCH 1962 — *Die Wirtschaftsentwickelung der Karolingerzeit, vornehmlich in Deutschland*, 2 vols. (3rd edn; Cologne, 1962).

DOUCET 1882 L. Doucet, 'Notice sur des monnaies carlovingiennes trouvées à Juaye-Mondaye, en 1870', *Mém. de la Soc. d'agriculture, science, arts, et belles-lettres de Bayeux* 9 (1879–82), 215–58.

DOUCET 1883 — *Recherches sur l'emplacement de l'atelier où ont été frappées les monnaies carolingiennes portant la légende* I CVRTI SASONIEN (Bayeux, 1883) (brochure of 13 pages; also summary of his lecture on the same subject in *Bull. du Comité des travaux historiques et scientifiques: archéologie* 1883, 15–16).

DUBOIS 1980 J. Dubois, 'Numismatique mérovingienne et hagiographie', in *Lafaurie* 1980a, 209–13.

DUBY 1974 G. Duby, *The Early Growth of the European Economy: Warriors and Peasants from the Seventh to the Twelfth Century*, transl. H. B. Clark (London, 1974).

DUCHALAIS 1852 A. Duchalais, 'Observations sur quelques monnaies mérovingiennes publiées en Belgique et en Russie', *RN* 1852, 237–56.

DUCHALAIS 1854 — 'Triens de la Frise', *RN* 1854, 51–60.

DUCHESNE 1886–92 L. Duchesne (ed.), *Liber Pontificalis*, 2 vols. (Paris, 1886 and 1892) (the reprint of 1955–7 adds an index, which was absent in the original edn).

DUCHESNE 1904 — *Les premiers temps de l'Etat Pontifical* (2nd edn; Paris, 1904) (this is preferable to the Eng. transl.).

DUCHESNE 1907–15 — *Fastes épiscopaux de l'ancienne Gaule*, 3 vols. (2nd edn; Paris, 1907–15).

DUHAMEL 1897 V. Duhamel, 'Denier mérovingien d'argent frappé à Orléans, vers le milieu du VIIIe siècle', *Bull. de numismatique* 4 (1897), 117–19.

DUMAS 1971 F. Dumas-Dubourg, *Le trésor de Fécamp et le monnayage en Francie Occidentale pendant la seconde moitié du Xe siècle* (Paris, 1971).

DUMAS 1973 — 'Le début de l'époque féodale en France d'après les monnaies', *BCEN* 10 (1973), 65–77.

DUMAS 1975 — 'Le tombeau de Childéric: les monnaies', in *Dans la Normandie souterraine* (Musée départemental des Antiquités, Rouen, Exposition, 3 juillet–2 novembre 1975), 26–9.

DUMAS 1976 — 'Emma Regina', in *Actes du 8e Congrès international de numismatique, New York-Washington 1973* (Paris-Basel, 1976), 405–13.

DUMAS 1977 — 'Un denier de Pépin le Bref trouvé à Bibracte', *BSFN* 32 (1977), 223–6.

DUMAS 1978 — 'Chartres et Château-Landon – deniers de Raoul au monogramme carolin', *BSFN* 33 (1978), 290–1.

DUMAS 1980 — 'Les monnaies de Raoul, roi de France (923–936)', in *Lafaurie* 1980a, 215–22.

DUMAS 1981 — 'Un complément au monnayage de Raoul, roi de France, grace aux découvertes de Cakajovice (Slovaquie)', *RN*[6] 23 (1981), 101–6.

DUMAS and LA PERRIÈRE 1977 F. Dumas and P. de La Perrière, 'Un denier inédit du roi Lothaire pour Chinon', *RN*[6] 19 (1977), 152–61.

DUMAS and TEMPLE 1974 F. Dumas and A. Temple, 'De quelques monnaies carolingiennes d'Uzès, inédites', *BSFN* 29 (1974), 576–8.

DUMBARTON OAKS CATALOGUE *Catalogue of the Byzantine Coins in the Dumbarton Oaks Collection and in the Whittemore Collection*, ed. A. R. Bellinger and P. Grierson (Washington, 1966–73) (publ. vols. cover the periods: I, 491–602; II, 602–717; III, 717–1081. Vols. IV (1081–1261) and V (1261–1453) are in preparation). Abbreviated as '*DOC*'.

DÜMMLER 1887–8 E. Dümmler, *Geschichte des ostfrankischen Reiches*, 3 vols. (2nd edn; Leipzig, 1887–8).

DUPARC 1951 P. Duparc, 'Les *cluses* et la frontière des Alpes', *Bibl. de l'Ecole des Chartes* 109 (1951), 5–31.

DUPLESSY 1956 J. Duplessy, 'La circulation des monnaies arabes en Europe occidentale du VIIIe au XIIIe siècle', *RN*[5] 18 (1956), 101–64.

DUPLESSY 1977 — 'Denier inédit de Raoul (923–936) frappé à Beaugency', *BSFN* 32 (1977), 274.

DUPLESSY 1978a — 'Numismatique de Pépin II, roi d'Aquitaine (839–864)', *RBN* 124 (1978), 217.

DUPLESSY 1978b — 'Le monnayage de Dreux au Xe siècle (à propos d'un denier inédit de Raoul)', *BSFN* 33 (1978), 291–3.

DUPLESSY 1978c — 'Aschères (Loiret), atelier monétaire inédit de Raoul (923–936)', *BSFN* 33 (1978), 307.

DUPLESSY 1978d — 'Les oboles carolingiennes d'Aquitaine au nom de Louis, roi (Louis le Jeune, 854?)', *BSFN* 33 (1978), 407–8.

DUPLESSY 1978e — 'Denier d'Etampes (inédit)', *BSFN* 33 (1978), 333–4.

DUPLESSY 1978f — 'Le monnayage du roi Raoul (923–936) en Orléanais', *Bull. de la Soc. archéol. et hist. de l'Orléanais* 49 (1978), 115–24.

DUPLESSY 1979 — 'Variété d'un denier de Raoul émis à Château-Landon', *BSFN* 34 (1979), 502–3.

DUPLESSY 1981 — 'Obole inédite d'Orléans (fin du Xe ou début du XIe siècle)', *BSFN* 36 (1981), 36.

DUPRAZ 1948 L. Dupraz, *Contribution à l'histoire du Regnum Francorum pendant le troisième quart du VIIe siècle (656–680)* (Fribourg, 1948).

DUPRAZ 1952 — 'Essai sur une chronologie nouvelle des règnes de Clotaire III – 657–73 – et de Childéric II – 662–675', *Revue suisse d'histoire* 2 (1952), 525–68.

DUROCHER 1905–6 L. D(urocher), 'Notice sur quelques deniers mérovingiens provenant de la trouvaille de Bais (Ille-et-Vilaine) et de quelques autres trouvailles', *Bull. de numismatique* 12 (1905), 107–12; 13 (1906), 1–3.

DUVAL 1959 N. Duval, 'Recherches sur la datation des inscriptions chrétiennes d'Afrique en dehors de la Mauritanie', *Atti del Terzo Congresso internazionale de Epigrafia greca e latina (Roma, 4–8 settembre 1957)* (Rome, 1959), 245–62.

ECKEL 1899 A. Eckel, *Charles le Simple* (Bibl. de l'Ecole des Hautes Etudes, fasc. 124; Paris, 1899).

ECKHARDT 1951 K. A. Eckhardt, 'Zur Entstehungszeit der Lex Salica', in *Festschrift zur Feier des Zweihundertjährigen Bestehens der Akademie der Wissenschaften in Göttingen* II (Berlin-Göttingen-Heidelberg, 1951), 1–31.

ECKHARDT 1954 — (ed.), *Pactus Legis Salicae* I (Göttingen, 1954).

ECKHARDT 1982 K. A. Eckhardt and A. Eckhardt (ed.), *Lex Frisionum (*MGH, Fontes Iuris Germanici Antiqui 12; Hanover, 1982).

EITEN 1907 G. Eiten, *Das Unterkönigtum im Reiche der Merowinger und Karolinger* (Heidelberg, 1907).

ENGEL and SERRURE 1887–9 A. Engel and R. Serrure, *Répertoire des sources imprimées de la numismatique française*, 2 vols. and supplement (Paris, 1887–9).

ENGEL and SERRURE 1891–1905 — *Traité de numismatique du moyen âge*, 3 vols. (Paris, 1891–1905; repr. Bologna, 1964).

ENSSLIN 1959 W. Ensslin, *Theoderich der Grosse* (2nd edn; Munich, 1959).

ERCOLANI COCCHI 1983 E. Ercolani Cocchi, *Imperi romano e bizantino, regni barbarici in Italia, attraverso le monete del Museo di Ravenna* (Ravenna, 1983) (exhibition catalogue of exceptional quality).

EVANS 1879 J. Evans, 'On gold coins struck in later Saxon times', *NC*[2] 19 (1879), 62–5 (those of Æthelred and Edward the Confessor).

EVANS 1882 — 'On a hoard of early Anglo-Saxon coins found in Ireland', *NC*[3] 2 (1882), 61–86.

EVANS 1894 — 'On a small hoard of Saxon sceattas found near Cambridge', *NC*[3] 14 (1894), 1–11.

EVANS 1942 A. Evans, 'Notes on early Anglo-Saxon gold coins', *NC*[6] 2 (1942), 19–41.

EWIG 1952 E. Ewig, 'Die fränkischen Teilungen und Teilreiche (511–613)', *Abhandlungen d. Geistes- und Sozialwissenschaftlichen Klasse. Akademie der Wissenschaften und der Literatur* 1952 (Mainz-Wiesbaden), no. 9, 649–715 (repr. in Ewig 1976, 114–71).

EWIG 1953 — 'Die fränkischen Teilreiche im 7. Jahrhundert (613–714)', *Trierer Zeitschrift* 22 (1953), 85–144 (repr. in Ewig 1976, 172–250).

EWIG 1963 — 'Résidence et capitale pendant le haut moyen âge', *Revue historique* 230 (1963), 25–72 (repr. in Ewig 1976, 362–408).

EWIG 1964 — 'Beobachtungen zur politisch-geographischen Terminologie des fränkischen Grossreiches und der Teilreiche des 9. Jahrhunderts', in *Spiegel der Geschichte: Festschrift Max Braubach* (Münster, 1964), 99–140 (repr. in Ewig 1976, 323–61).

EWIG 1976 — *Spätantikes und fränkisches Gallien* I (Beihefte der Francia 3.1; Munich, 1976) (reprints many of his papers).

FAGERLIE 1967 J. M. Fagerlie, *Late Roman and Byzantine Solidi found in Sweden and Denmark* (NNM 157; New York, 1967).

FALCE 1930 A. Falce, *La formazione della marca di Tuscia (secc. VIII–IX)* (Florence, 1930).

FALLON 1958 H. C. Fallon, 'Imperial symbolism on two Carolingian coins', *MN* 8 (1958), 119–31.

FARCINET 1892 C. Farcinet, 'Etude sur les monnaies mérovingiennes attribuées à la Vendée', *ASFN* 16 (1892), 153–70.

FARCINET 1893 — 'Les identifications géographiques des monnaies mérovingiennes et le *Catalogue de la Bibliothèque Nationale*', *ASFN* 17 (1893), 37–49.

FASOLI 1945 G. Fasoli, *Le incursioni ungare in Europa nel secolo X* (Florence, 1945).

FASOLI 1958 — 'Aspetti di vita economica e sociale nell'Italia del secolo VII', in *Caratteri del secolo VII in Occidente* I (Settimane di Studio del Centro italiano di studi sull'alto medioevo V; Spoleto, 1958), 103–59.

FASOLI 1962 — *I rè d'Italia 888–962* (Florence, 1962).

FAVRE 1893 E. Favre, *Eudes, comte de Paris et roi de France (882–898)* (Bibl. de l'Ecole des Hautes Etudes, fasc. 99; Paris, 1893).

FELDER 1970 E. Felder, 'Zu den merowingischen Münzmeisternamen Charecaucius und Gaucemare', *Beiträge zur Namenforschung*[2] 5 (1970), 14–22.

FELDER 1978 — *Germanische Personnamen auf merowingischen Münzen. Studien zum Vokalismus* (Beiträge zur Namenforschung, N.F. Beiheft 14; Heidelberg, 1978).

FELDER 1980a — 'Beiträge zur merowingischen Numismatik I, II', *JNG* 30 (1980), 33–6; 31–2 (1981–2), 77–101.

FELDER 1980b — 'Zur Münzprägung der merowingischen Könige in Marseille', in *Lafaurie* 1980a, 222–9.

FENGLER 1907 O. Fengler, 'Quentovic, seine maritime Bedeutung unter Merowingern und Karolingern', *Hansische Geschichtsblätter* 13 (1907), 91–107.

FÉVRIER 1966 P. A. Février, 'Inscriptions de basse époque récemment découvertes et chronologie vandale', *Bull. de la Soc. nationale des antiquaires de France* 1966, 93–5 (with comments by N. Duval).

FILLON 1845 B. Fillon, 'Monnaies royales inédites', *RN*[1] 10 (1845), 345–59.

FILLON 1851 — *Considérations historiques et artistiques sur les monnaies de France* (Fontenay-Vendée, 1851).

FILLON 1853 — *Lettres à M. Ch. Dugast-Matifeux sur quelques monnaies françaises inédites* (Paris, 1853).

FILLON 1856 — *Etudes numismatiques* (Paris, 1856).

FILLON and ROCHEBRUNE 1865 B. Fillon and O. de Rochebrune, *Poitou et Vendée. Le trésor mérovingien de la Bogisère* (Fontenay, 1865).

FIORAVANTI 1734 B. Fioravanti, *Antiquiores pontificum Romanorum denarii* (Rome, 1734) (revised reprint of G. Vignoli's work with the same title, publ. in 1709).

FISHER 1973 D. J. V. Fisher, *The Anglo-Saxon Age* c. *400–1042* (London, 1973).

FLOREZ 1793 H. Florez, *Medallas de las Colonias, Municipios y Pueblos antiguos de España hasta hoy no publicadas, con las de los Reyes Godas* (Madrid, 1773).

FOCKEMA 1949 S. J. Fockema Andreae, 'Friesland van de vifde tot de tiende eeuw', in *Algemene Geschiedenis der Nederlanden* I (Utrecht, 1949), Ch. 5 (pp. 386–406; bibl. on pp. 427–9).

FÖRSTEMANN 1900 E. Förstemann, *Altdeutsches Namenbuch* I: *Personennamen* (2nd edn; Bonn, 1900).

FOUGÈRES and CARTIER 1839 F. Fougères and E. Cartier, 'Monnoies inédites de la seconde race', *RN* 1839, 94–106.

FRÈRE 1971 H. Frère, 'Anthisnes, atelier monétaire carolingien?', *BCEN* 8 (1971), 21–30.

FRÈRE 1977a — 'Les noms de lieux sur les monnaies carolingiennes de "Belgique"', *RBN* 123 (1977), 133–48.

FRÈRE 1977b — *Le denier carolingien, spécialement en Belgique* (Louvain-la-Neuve, 1977).

FRÈRE 1980 — 'Le denier carolingien', *RBN* 126 (1980), 109–27 (supplement to preceding work).

FRIEDLAENDER 1844 J. Friedlaender, *Die Münzen der Ostgothen* (Berlin, 1844).

FRIEDLAENDER 1849 — *Die Münzen der Vandalen, Nachträge zu den Münzen der Ostgothen* (Berlin, 1849).

FUCHS 1944 S. Fuchs, *Kunst der Ostgotenzeit* (Berlin, 1944).

GAETTENS 1932 R. Gaettens, 'Prägungen Ludwig des Blindes in Oberitalien', *BMF* 77 (1932), 529–32.

GAETTENS 1950 — 'Münzen Karls d. Gr. sowie der Päpste Hadrian I. und Leo III. von historischer, staatsrechtlicher und währungsgeschichtlicher Bedeutung', *JNG* 2 (1950–1), 47–67.

GAETTENS 1955 — 'Hatten wir im Karolingerreich Naturalwirtschaft oder Geldwirtschaft?', *BMF* 79 (1955), 290–305.

GALSTER 1959 G. Galster, 'Carolingian coins found in Denmark', in his *Coins and History* (Aarhus, 1959), 65–78.

GANSHOF 1938 F. L. Ganshof, 'Notes sur les ports de Provence du VIIIe au Xe siècle', *Revue historique* 183 (1938), 28–37.

GANSHOF 1957 — 'Note sur le *Praeceptum Negotiatorum* de Louis le Pieux', in *Studi in onore di Armando Sapori* I (Milan, 1957), 103–12.

GANSHOF 1960 — 'Les bureaux de tonlieu de Marseille et de Fos. Contribution à l'histoire des institutions financières de la monarchie franque', in *Etudes historiques à la mémoire de Noël Didier* (Paris, 1960), 125–33.

GANSHOF 1966 — 'Note sur l'*Inquisitio de theloneis Raffelstettensis*', *Le Moyen Age* 72 (1966), 197–224.

GARIEL 1883–4 E. Gariel, *Les monnaies royales sous la race carolingienne*, 2 vols. (Strasbourg, 1883–4; repr. New York, 1974). Abbreviated as 'G'.

GARNIER 1975 J. P. Garnier, 'Une obole et deux deniers inédits de Raoul frappés à Châlons-sur-Marne (923–936)', *BSFN* 30 (1975), 752–3.

GASPARRI 1978 S. Gasparri, *I duchi longobardi* (Istituto storico italiano per il Medio Evo. Studi storici 109; Rome, 1978).

GAVAZZI 1890 G. Gavazzi, 'Congetture sull'attribuzione di alcuni tremissi longobardi', *RIN* 3 (1890), 207–16.

GAY 1904 J. Gay, *L'Italie méridionale et l'empire byzantin depuis l'avènement de Basile Ier jusqu'à la prise de Bari par les Normands (867–1071)* (Bibl. des Ecoles françaises d'Athènes et de Rome, fasc. 90; Paris, 1904).

GEDAI 1972 I. Gedai, 'A Kiskunfélegyházi X. századi sírlalet érmei' ('Coins from the tenth-century tomb-find at Kiskunfélegyhaza'), *Cumania* 1 (1972), 169–75.

GEIGER 1977 H. U. Geiger, 'Quelques problèmes du monnayage mérovingien en Valais', *BSFN* 9 (1977), 258–61.

GEIGER 1979a — 'Die merowingischen Münzen in der Schweiz', *RSN* 58 (1979), 83–178.

GEIGER 1979b — 'Münzwesen, Wirtschaft und Handel', in *Ur- und frühgeschichtliche Archäologie der Schweiz* VI (Basel, 1979), 185–202.

GEIGER 1980 — 'Ein kleiner frühmittelalterlicher Münzschatz vom Wittnauer Horn', *Archäologie der Schweiz* 3 (1980), 55–9.

GEISS 1931 H. Geiss, *Geld- und naturwirtschaftliche Erscheinungsformen im staatlichen Aufbau Italiens während der Gotenzeit* (Vierteljahrschrift f. Sozial- und Wirtschaftsgeschichte, Beiheft 27; Stuttgart, 1931).

GENDRE and DHÉNIN 1974 P. Gendre and M. Dhénin, 'Denier inédit de Lothaire (954–986), frappé à Laon', *BSFN* 29 (1974), 557–61.

GENTILI 1890 T. Gentili di Rovelone, 'Le monete dei pontificie romani Leone VIII (ritenuto antipapa) e Giovanni XIII, anni dell'era cristiana 963–972', *RIN* 3 (1890), 52–89.

GIANNOCCARO and ORLANDONI 1978 F. Giannoccaro and M. Orlandoni, 'Una moneta inedita ed unica di Ildibado re dei Goti', *QT* 7 (1978), 261–6.

GIL FARRÉS 1955 O. Gil Farrés, 'Algunos aspectos de la numismatica visigoda. Consideraciones acerca del "tipo tercero" de Leovigildo', *Numisma* 17 (1955), 25–61 (on grouping of types and mints).

GIL FARRÉS 1980 — 'La moneda sueva y visigoda', in R. Menéndez Pidal, *Historia de España III* (4th edn; Madrid, 1980), 177–91.

GILLES 1982 K.-J. Gilles, *Die Trierer Münzprägung im frühen Mittelalters* (Koblenz, 1982).

GILMORE and METCALF 1980 G. R. Gilmore and D. M. Metcalf, 'The alloy of the Northumbrian coinage of the mid-ninth century', *Metallurgy in Numismatics* 1 (1980), 83–98.

GNECCHI 1895 F. Gnecchi, 'Medaglione d'oro di Teoderico re', *RIN* 8 (1895), 149–65.

GNECCHI 1897 — 'Un ripostiglio miserabile', *RIN* 10 (1897), 19–22.

GNECCHI 1912 — *I medaglioni romani*, 3 vols. (Milan, 1912).

GOFFART 1957 W. Goffart, 'Byzantine policy in the West under Tiberius II and Maurice: the pretenders Hermengild and Gundovald', *Traditio* 13 (1957), 73–118.

GOUBERT 1942 P. Goubert, 'L'aventure de Gondovald et les monnaies franques de l'empereur Maurice', *Echos d'Orient* 39 (1941–2), 414–57.

GOUBERT 1955 — *Byzance avant l'Islam* II (Paris, 1955).

GRAHAM-CAMPBELL 1976 J. A. Graham-Campbell, 'The Viking-age silver hoards of Ireland', *Proc. of the Seventh Viking Congress, Dublin 15–21 August 1973*, ed. B. Almqvist and D. Greene (Dublin, 1976), 39–74.

GREGOROVIUS 1885 F. Gregorovius, 'Die Münzen Alberichs, des Fürsten und Senators der Römer (932–954)', *Sitzungsberichte der philosophisch-philologischen und historischen Classe der k.b. Akademie der Wissenschaften zu München* 1885, 27–45 (repr. in his *Kleine Schriften für Geschichte und Kultur* I (Leipzig, 1887), 155–79).

GRELU 1984 J. Grelu, 'La découverte monétaire de la rue Dinet à Mâcon, *BSFN* 39 (1984), 488–90.

GRICOURT 1960 J. Gricourt, 'Trésor du VIe siècle de Houdain-lès-Bavai (Nord)', *RN*[6] 2 (1959–60), 131–52.

GRIERSON 1941 P. Grierson, 'The relations between England and Flanders before the Norman Conquest', *Transactions of the Royal Historical Society*[4] 23 (1941), 71–112.

GRIERSON 1951a — 'The gold solidus of Louis the Pious and its imitations', *JMP* 38 (1951), 1–41 (repr. w. additions and corrections in *DAN*, no. XXII).

GRIERSON 1951b — 'Oboli de musc', *English Historical Review* 66 (1951), 75–81 (repr. in *LMN*, no. VII).

GRIERSON 1952a — 'The dating of the Sutton Hoo coins', *Antiquity* 26 (1952), 83–6.

GRIERSON 1952b — 'The coronation of Charlemagne and the coinage of Pope Leo III', *Revue belge de philologie et'd'histoire* 30 (1952), 825–33 (repr. w. additional note in *DAN*, no. XX).

GRIERSON 1952c — 'The Canterbury (St Martin's) hoard of Frankish and Anglo-Saxon coin-ornaments', *BNJ* 27 (1952–4) 39–51 (repr. in *DAN*, no. VI).

GRIERSON 1953a — 'La trouvaille monétaire d'Ilanz', *Gazette numismatique suisse* 4 (1953), 46–8 (repr. in *DAN*, no. XVI).

GRIERSON 1953b — 'Visigothic metrology', *NC*[6] 13 (1953), 74–87 (repr. in *DAN*, no. XII).

GRIERSON 1953c — 'A new Anglo-Saxon solidus', *NC*[6] 13 (1953), 88–91 (repr. in DAN, no. VII).

GRIERSON 1953d — 'A stray from the Crondall hoard', *NC*[6] 13 (1953), 148–9 (a Merovingian coin).

GRIERSON 1954a — 'Carolingian Europe and the Arabs: the myth of the mancus', *Revue belge de philologie et d'histoire* 32 (1954), 1059–74 (repr. with corrections and additions in *DAN*, no. III).

GRIERSON 1954b — 'Cronologia delle riforme monetarie di Carlo Magno', *RIN* 56 (1954), 65–79 (repr. in *DAN*, no. XVII).

GRIERSON 1954c — 'Le sou d'or d'Uzès', *Le Moyen Age* 60 (1954), 293–309 (repr. in *DAN*, no. XXIV).

GRIERSON 1954d — 'Zum Ursprung der karolingischen Goldprägung in Nordwest-Europa', *HBN* 8 (1954), 199–206 (repr. in *DAN*, no. XXI).

GRIERSON 1954e — 'Problemi monetari dell'Alto Medio Evo', *Bollettino della Società pavese di storia patria* 54 (1954), 67–82 (repr. in *DAN*, no. I).

GRIERSON 1955 — 'Una ceca bizantina en España', *Numario Hispanica* 4 (1955), 305–14.

GRIERSON 1956a — 'The Salernitan coinage of Gisulf II (1052–1077) and Robert Guiscard (1077–85)', *Papers of the British School at Rome* 24 (1956), 37–59 (repr. in *LMN*, no. II).

GRIERSON 1956b — 'The silver coinage of the Lombards', *Archivio storico lombardo*[8] 6 (1956), 130–47 (repr. w. corrections in *DAN*, no. XIV).

GRIERSON 1957 — 'Halfpennies and third-pennies of King Alfred', *BNJ* 28 (1955–7), 477–93.

GRIERSON 1958 — 'Some modern forgeries of Carolingian coins', in *Centennial Publication of the American Numismatic Society*, ed. H. Ingholt (New York, 1958), 303–15 (repr. in *DAN*, no. XXVIII).

GRIERSON 1959a — 'The *Tablettes Albertini* and the value of the *solidus* in the fifth and sixth centuries', *Journal of Roman Studies* 49 (1959), 73–80 (repr. in *DAN*, no. IV).

GRIERSON 1959b — 'Commerce in the Dark Ages: a critique of the evidence', *Transactions of the Royal Historical Society*[5] 9 (1959), 123–40 (repr. in *DAN*, no. II).

GRIERSON 1959c — '*The Patrimonium Patri in illis partibus* and the pseudo-imperial coinage in Frankish Gaul', *RBN* 105 (1959), 95–111.

GRIERSON 1959d — 'Matasuntha or Mastinas? A reattribution', *NC*[6] 19 (1959), 119–30.

GRIERSON 1960a — 'The monetary reforms of 'Abd al-Malik: their metrological basis and their financial repercussions', *JESHO* 3 (1960), 241–64 (repr. in *DAN*, no. XV).

GRIERSON 1960b — 'Una moneta d'argento inedita di Teodorico il Grande', *Numismatica*[2] 1 (1960), 113–15 (repr. in *DAN*, no. V).

GRIERSON 1961 — 'La fonction sociale de la monnaie en Angleterre aux VIIe–VIIIe siècles', in *Moneta e scambi nell'alto medioevo* (Spoleto, 1961), 341–85 (repr. in *DAN*, no. XI).

GRIERSON 1962a — 'A tremissis of the Suevic king Audeca (584–5)', *Estudos de Castello Branco* II/6 (1962), 27–32 (repr. in *DAN*, no. XIII).

GRIERSON 1962b — 'The authenticity of the York "thrymsas"', *BNJ* 31 (1962), 8–10 (repr. in *DAN*, no. VIII, with an additional note publishing **1.1481** which had come to light since the original article).

GRIERSON 1963a — 'Mint output in the time of Offa', *NCirc* 71 (1963), 114–15 (repr. in *DAN*, no. XXV).

GRIERSON 1963b — 'Some aspects of the coinage of Offa', *NCirc* 71 (1963), 223–5 (repr. in *DAN*, no. XXVI).

GRIERSON 1963c — 'La date des monnaies d'or de Louis le Pieux', *Le Moyen Age* 69 (1963), 67–74 (repr. in *DAN*, no. XXIII).

GRIERSON 1963d — 'A new triens of Reccared (586–601) of the mint of Calapa', *NC*[7] 3 (1963), 81–2.

GRIERSON 1964 — 'Weight and coinage', *NC*[7] 5 (1964), Proceedings, iii–xvii (repr. in *LMN*, no. XX).

GRIERSON 1965a — '"HENRICVS IMP or ALBRICVS PRINCIPS". A note on the supposed denaro of Pope Leo IX (1049–54) and Henry III', *Numismatika Meddelanden* 30 (1965), 51–6 (repr. in *DAN*, no. XXIX).

GRIERSON 1965b — 'Money and coinage under Charlemagne', in *Karl der Grosse* I, ed. W. Braunfels (Düsseldorf, 1965), 501–36 (repr. in *DAN*, no. XVIII).

GRIERSON 1967 — 'The volume of Anglo-Saxon coinage', *Economic History Review*[2] 20 (1967), 153–60 (repr. in *DAN*, no. XXVII).

GRIERSON 1970 — 'The purpose of the Sutton Hoo coins', *Antiquity* 44 (1970), 14–18 (repr. in *DAN*, no. IX).

GRIERSON 1972 — 'La cronologia della monetazione salernitana nel secolo XI', *RIN* 74 (1972), 153–65 (repr. in *LMN*, no. III).

GRIERSON 1974a. — 'A new *Audulfus Frisia* triens', *JMP* 60 (1973–4), 153–5.

GRIERSON 1974b — 'Muslim coins in thirteenth-century England', in *Near Eastern Numismatics . . . Studies in Honor of George C. Miles*, ed. D. K. Kouymjian (Beirut, 1974), 387–91 (repr. in *LMN*, no. VIII).

GRIERSON 1974c — 'The Sutton Hoo coins again', *Antiquity* 48 (1974), 139–40 (repr. in *DAN*, no. X).

GRIERSON 1975 — 'Une trouvaille imaginaire: le trésor de Cuenca', *BSFN* 30 (1975), 810–12.

GRIERSON 1976a — *Monnaies du Moyen Age* (Fribourg, 1976); Germ. edn: *Münzen des Mittelalters* (Fribourg, 1976).

GRIERSON 1976b — 'Symbolism in early medieval charters and coins', in *Simboli e simbologia nell'alto medioevo* (Settimane di Studio del Centro italiano di studi sull'alto medioevo XXIII; Spoleto, 1976), 601–30, w. discussion on 631–40.

GRIERSON 1977 — 'Un denier carolingien de Saint-Bavon de Gand', *BCEN* 14 (1977) 59–61.

GRIERSON 1978 — 'Un denier de l'empereur Arnoul frappé à Milan en mars 896', *BSFN* 33 (1978), 286–9.

GRIERSON 1979a — *Dark Age Numismatics* (London, 1979) (reprint of 29 articles w. notes of additions and corrections). Abbreviated as '*DAN*'.

GRIERSON 1979b — *Later Medieval Numismatics (11th–16th Centuries)* (London, 1979) (reprint of 22 articles w. notes of additions and corrections). Abbreviated as '*LMN*'.

GRIERSON 1981 — 'The *Gratia Dei rex* coinage of Charles the Bald', in *Charles the Bald: Court and Kingdom*, ed. M. Gibson and J. Nelson (BAR Int. ser. 101; Oxford, 1981), 39–51.

GRIERSON 1983a *Studies in Numismatic Method presented to Philip Grierson*, ed. C. N. L. Brooke *et al.* (Cambridge, 1983).

GRIERSON 1983b — 'A rediscovered siliqua of Valentinian III (425–55)', *NC* 143 (1983), 217–18.

GRIERSON 1985 — 'The date of the gold medallion of Theoderic the Great', *Hikuin* 11 (a *Festschrift* for Brita Malmer, 1985), 19–26.

GROTE 1862 H. Grote, 'Die Solidi und Denarii der Merowinger', in his *Münzstudien* II (Leipzig, 1862), 789–858.

GRUAZ 1922 J. Gruaz, 'Le trésor d'Hermenches et les temps carolingiens', *Revue historique vaudoise* 30 (1922), 193–212.

GRUEBER 1903 H. A. Grueber, 'A find of coins of Alfred the Great at Stamford', *NC*[4] 3 (1903), 347–55.

GRUNTHAL 1958 H. Grunthal, 'Medieval and modern coins acquired by the American Numismatic Society, 1954–1958', *MN* 8 (1958), 133–8.

GRUNTHAL 1965 — 'Tentative attributions of some hitherto uncertain Carolingian coins', *Dona Numismatica Walter Hävernick zum 23. Januar 1965 dargebracht*, ed. P. Berghaus and G. Hatz (Hamburg, 1965), 51–4 (few of them are acceptable).

GUADAN 1958 A. M. de Guadan, 'Las copias suevas de los solidos de Honorio', *Nummus* 5 (1958), 11–23.

GUALAZZINI 1961 H. Gualazzini, 'Aspetti giuridici dei problemi monetari in Italia durante l'alto medioevo', in *Moneta e scambi nell'alto medioevo* (Spoleto, 1961), 89–122.

GUÉRARD 1844 B. Guérard (ed.), *Polyptique de l'abbé Irminon*, 2 vols. (Paris, 1844).

GUEY 1965 J. Guey, 'Encore le SOLIDUS et le FOLLIS des "Tablettes Albertini": 1,400 folles (ou seulement 350?) au solidus?', *BSFN* 20 (1965), 455–6.

GUILHIERMOZ 1906 P. Guilhiermoz, 'Note sur les poids du moyen-âge', *Bibl. de l'Ecole des Chartes* 67 (1906), 161–233, 402–50.

GYSSELING 1960 M. Gysseling, *Toponomisch Woordenboek van België, Luxemburg, Noord-Frankrijk en West-Duitsland (voor 1226)*, 2 vols. (Brussels, 1960).

HAHN 1922 E. Hahn, 'Ritrovamenti di monete medioevali dell'Italia superiore nel Canton Grigioni', *RIN* 35 (1922), 28–56.

HAHN 1973–81 W. Hahn, *Moneta Imperii Byzantini*, 3 vols. (Vienna, 1973–81) (the vols. cover the periods: I, 491–565; II, 565–610; III, 610–720). Abbreviated as '*MIB*'.

HAHN 1979a — 'Die östliche Gold- und Silberprägung unter Theodosius II', *Litterae numismaticae Vindobonenses Roberto Goebl dedicatae* (Vienna, 1979), 103–28.

HAHN 1979b — 'Monetine italiane di Giustiniano I', *Felix Ravenna* 117 (1979), 57–67.

HAIGH 1845 D. H. Haigh, *Essay on the Numismatic History of the Ancient Kingdom of the East Angles* (Leeds, 1845).

HAIGH 1869 — 'Miscellaneous notes on the Old English coinage', *NC*[2] 9 (1869), 171–96.

HAIGH 1870 — 'Coins of Ælfred the Great', *NC*[2] 10 (1870), 19–39.

HAIGH 1876 — 'The coins of the Danish kings of Northumberland', *Archaeologia Æliana*[2] 7 (1876), 21–77.

HALBERTSMA 1966 H. Halbertsma, 'The Frisian kingdom', *Berichte van de Rijksdienst voor het Oudheidkundig Bodemonderzoek* 15–16 (1965–6), 69–108.

HALL 1774 C. Hall, *Saxon Coins of the Heptarchy* (London, 1774).

HALL and METCALF 1972 E. T. Hall and D. M. Metcalf (ed.), *Methods of Chemical and Metallurgical Investigation of Ancient Coinage* (RNS Special Publication 8; London, 1972).

HARMER 1952 F. E. Harmer, *Anglo-Saxon Writs* (Manchester, 1952).

HARTMANN 1900–23 L. M. Hartmann, *Geschichte Italiens im Mittelalter*, 4 vols. (Gotha, 1900–23).

HÁSKOVÁ 1982 J. Hásková, 'Emma Regina in numismatic and historical sources', *Proceedings of the Ninth International Congress of Numismatics. Berne, Sept. 1979* II (Louvain-la-Neuve and Luxemburg, 1982), 793–7.

HATZ 1959 G. Hatz, 'Fund eines Sceattas in Maschen, Kreis Harburg', *HBN* 12–13 (1958–9), 249–53.

HATZ 1970 — 'Munus-divinum-Nachahmungen aus Haithabu', *Berichte über die Ausgrabungen aus Haithabu*, IV (Neumünster, 1970), 24–6.

HATZ 1983 — 'Finds of English medieval coins in Schleswig-Holstein', in *Grierson* 1983a, 205–24.

HÄVERNICK 1929 W. Hävernick, 'Münzen der Merowingerzeit aus rheinischen Gräberfeldern (Schwarzrheindorf, Ober-Olm, Dietersheim)', *Mainzer Zeitschrift* 24–5 (1929–30), 100–4.

HÄVERNICK 1935 — *Die Münzen von Köln* I: *Vom Beginn der Prägung bis 1304* (Cologne, 1935).

HÄVERNICK 1947 — 'Hamburg als karolingische Münzstätte', *HBN* 1 (1947), 9–13.

HÄVERNICK 1953 — 'Die Anfänge der karolingischen Goldprägung in Nordwesteuropa', *HBN* 6–7 (1952–3), 55–60.

HÄVERNICK 1954 — 'Die karolingischen Münzreformen. Ende der alten Zustände oder Beginn einer neuen Entwicklung?', *Vieteljahrschrift f. Sozial- und Wirtschaftsgeschichte* 41 (1954), 146–7.

HÄVERNICK 1961 — 'Zur Münzgeschichte der Karolingerzeit und des 10./11. Jahrhunderts', *HBN* 15 (1961), 5–12.

HAWKES *et al.* 1966 S. C. Hawkes, J. M. Merrick and D. M. Metcalf, 'X-ray fluorescent analysis of some Dark Ages coins and jewellery', *Archaeometry* 9 (1966), 98–138.

HAWKINS 1843 E. Hawkins, 'An account of coins and treasure found at Cuerdale', *NC*[1] 5 (1842–3), 1–48, 53–104.

HAWKINS 1887 — *The Silver Coins of England* (3rd edn by R. L. Kenyon; London, 1887).

HEIDRICH 1974 I. Heidrich, 'Die merowingische Münzprägung im Gebiet von oberer Maas, Mosel und Seille', *Rheinische Vierteljahrsblätter* 38 (1974), 78–91.

HEISS 1872 A. Heiss, *Description générale des monnaies des rois wisigoths d'Espagne* (Paris, 1872).

HEISS 1891 — 'Essai sur le monnayage des Sueves', *RN*[3] 9 (1891), 146–63.

HENDY 1985 M. F. Hendy, *Studies in the Byzantine Monetary Economy c. 300–1450* (Cambridge, 1985).

HESS 1962 W. Hess, 'Geldwirtschaft am Mittelrhein in karolingischer Zeit', *Blätter f. deutsche Landesgeschichte* 98 (1962), 26–63.

HILL 1925 G. F. Hill, *Becker the Counterfeiter*, 2 parts (London, 1925).

HILL 1949 P. V. Hill, 'The coinage of Britain in the Dark Ages', *BNJ* 26 (1949–51), 1–28.

HILL 1950 — 'Saxon sceattas and their problems', *BNJ* 26 (1949–51), 129–55.

HILL 1951 — 'The "Standard" and "London" series of Anglo-Saxon sceattas', *BNJ* 26 (1949–51), 251–79.

HILL 1952 — 'The animal, "Anglo-Merovingian", and miscellaneous series of Anglo-Saxon sceattas', *BNJ* 27 (1952–4), 1–38.

HILL 1953 — 'Uncatalogued sceattas in the national and other collections', *NC*[6] 13 (1953), 92–114.

HILL 1954 — 'Anglo-Saxon and Frisian sceattas in the light of Frisian hoards and site-finds', *JMP* 41 (1954), 11–17.

HILL 1955 — 'Two hoards of sceattas from the province of Groningen', *JMP* 42 (1955), 104–5 (both part of the same hoard from Lutje-Saaksum).

HILL 1958 — 'Anglo-Frisian trade in the light of eighth-century coins', *Trans. London and Middlesex Archaeol. Soc.* 19 (1958), 1–9.

HILL 1977a D. H. Hill, 'Die-adjustment in the Wodan-Monster series of sceattas', *NC*[7] 17 (1977), 171–2.

HILL 1977b — 'The "Hanover" hoard of porcupine sceattas', *NC*[7] 17 (1977), 173–4.

HILL 1981 — *An Atlas of Anglo-Saxon England* (Oxford, 1981).

HILL and METCALF 1984 D. H. Hill and D. M. Metcalf (ed.), *Sceattas in England and on the Continent* (BAR British Series 128, Oxford, 1984).

HILL and SHARPLES 1974 D. H. Hill and J. Sharples, 'The Lutje-Saaksum hoard: a correction', *JMP* 60–1 (1973–4), 156–7.

HILL *et al.* 1960 P. V. Hill, J. P. C. Kent and R. A. G. Carson, *Late Roman Bronze Coinage A.D. 324–498* (London, 1960). Abbreviated as '*LRBC*'.

HILLGARTH 1961 J. N. Hillgarth, 'La conversion de los Visigodas: notas críticas', *Analecta sacra Tarraconensia* 34 (1961), 21–46.

HILLGARTH 1966 — 'Coins and chronicles: propaganda in sixth-century Spain and the Byzantine background', *Historia* 15 (1966), 483–508.

HILLIGER 1903 B. Hilliger, 'Der Schilling der Volksrechte und das Wergeld', *Historische Vierteljahrschrift* 1903, 175–220, 453–502.

HILLIGER 1907 — 'Der Denar der *Lex Salica*', *Historische Vierteljahrschrift* 1907, 1–56, 60.

HILLIGER 1909 — 'Alter und Münzrechnung der *Lex Salica*', *Historische Vierteljahrschrift* 1909, 161–211.

HIMLY 1955 F. Himly, 'Y a-t-il eu emprise musulmane sur l'économie des Etats européens du VIIe au Xe siècle?', *Revue suisse d'histoire* 5 (1955), 31–81 (repr. in Hübinger 1968b).

HINTON 1986 D. A. Hinton, 'Coins and commercial centres in Anglo-Saxon England', in *Dolley* 1986.

HIRSCH and SCHIPA 1968 F. Hirsch and M. Schipa, *La Langobardia meridionale (570–1077)* (Rome, 1968) (reprint w. updated bibl. and index of Schipa's transl. (publ. Turin, 1890) of Hirsch's work, *Das Herzogthum Benevent bis zum Untergange des langobardischen Reiches (*Leipzig, 1871), and of Schipa 1887).

HLAWITSCHKA 1960 E. Hlawitschka, *Franken, Alemannen, Bayern und Burgunder in Oberitalien (774–962)* (Forschungen zur oberrheinischen Landesgeschichte VIII; Freiburg im Breisgau, 1960).

HOC 1970 M. Hoc, *Histoire monétaire de Tournai* (Brussels, 1970).

HODGES 1982 R. Hodges, *Dark Age Economics. The Origins of Towns and Trade A.D. 600–1000* (London, 1982).

HODGES and WHITEHOUSE 1983 R. Hodges and D. Whitehouse, *Mohammed, Charlemagne and the Origins of Europe* (London, 1983).

HODGKIN 1880–99 T. Hodgkin, *Italy and her Invaders*, 8 vols. (Oxford, 1880–99).

HOFMEISTER 1906 A. Hofmeister, *Markgrafen und Markgrafschaften im Italienischen Königreich in der Zeit von Karl dem Grossen bis auf Otto den Grossen* (Mitteilungen des Instituts für Oesterreichischen Geschichtsforschung 7. Ergänzungsband; Vienna, 1906).

HOLST 1931 H. Holst, *On the coins of the Hon find* (Minor Publications of the Norwegian Numismatic Society no. 4; Oslo 1931), 1–18.

HOLST 1951 — 'Nye bidrag til belysning av Honfunnets mynter', *NNÅ* 1951, 17–27.

HOLUM 1977 K. G. Holum, 'Pulcheria's crusade of A.D. 421–22 and the ideology of Imperial Victory', *Greek, Roman and Byzantine Studies* 18 (1977), 153–72.

HOLWERDA 1930 J. H. Holwerda, 'Opgravingen van Dorestad', *Oudheidkundige Mededeelingen van het Rijksmuseum van Oudheden te Leiden* 9 (1930), 32–93.

HORSTMANN 1966 H. Horstmann, 'Der Adler Karls des Grossen', *Archivum Heraldicum* 1966, 18–21.

HÜBINGER 1968a P. E. Hübinger (ed.), *Kulturbruch oder Kulturkontinuität in Ubergang von der Antike zum Mittelalter* (Darmstadt, 1968) (repr. of studies by various authors on the 'Pirenne thesis').

HÜBINGER 1968b — *Bedeutung und Rolle des Islam beim Ubergang vom Altertum zum Mittelalter* (Darmstadt, 1968) (repr. of studies by various authors on the economic aspects of the 'Pirenne thesis').

HUMPHREY 1976– J. Humphrey (ed.), *Excavations at Carthage conducted by the University of Michigan* I– (Ann Arbor, 1976–) (these contain detailed lists of Vandal and other coins found).

HUNTER-BLAIR 1977 P. Hunter-Blair, *An Introduction to Anglo-Saxon England* (2nd edn; Cambridge, 1977).

HUSZÁR 1955 L. Huszár, *Das Münzmaterial in den Funden der Völkerwanderungszeit im mittleren Donaubecken* (Acta Archaeologica Academiae Scientiarum Hungaricae 5; Budapest, 1955).

ILIESCU 1965 O. Iliescu, 'Nouvelles informations relatives aux lingots romains d'or, trouvées en Transylvanie', *Revue des études sud-est européennes* 3 (1965), 269–81.

JAHN 1874 A. Jahn, *Die Geschichte der Burgundionen und Burgundiens bis zum Ende der I. Dynastie* (Halle, 1874).

JAMES 1980 E. James (ed.), *Visigothic Spain. New Approaches* (Oxford, 1980).

JANSEN 1866 L. J. F. Jansen, 'Der merowingische Goldschmuck aus Wieuwerd', *Jahrbücher des Vereins von Alterthumsfreunden im Rheinlande* 41 (1866), 57–91.

JECKLIN 1906 F. Jecklin, 'Der Langobardisch-karolingische Münzfund bei Ilanz', *MBNG* 25 (1906–7), 28–79.

JELLEMA 1955 D. Jellema, 'Frisian trade in the Dark Ages', *Speculum* 30 (1955), 15–36.

JELOČNIK 1967 A. Jeločnik, 'Les multiples d'or de Magnence découverts à Emona', *RN*[6] 9 (1967), 209–35.

JESSE 1921 W. Jesse, 'Zum ältesten hamburgischen Münzgeschichte', *Zweite Veröffentlichung des Hamburger Vereins der Münzenfreunde* (Hamburg, 1921), 3–28.

JESSE 1955 — 'Wik-Orte und Münzprägung', *Hansische Geschichtsblätter* 73 (1955), 106–16.

JESSE 1956 — 'Noch einmal der Denar der *Lex Salica*', *HBN* 9–10 (1955–6), 11–21.

JONES 1962 A. H. M. Jones, 'The constitutional position of Odoacer and Theoderic', *Journal of Roman Studies* 52 (1962), 126–30.

JONES 1964 — *The Later Roman Empire 284–602. A Social, Economic and Administrative Survey*, 3 vols. and maps (Oxford, 1964).

JULLIAN 1890 C. Jullian, *Inscriptions romaines de Bordeaux* II (Bordeaux, 1890) (Merovingian coin inscription on pp. 67–101).

KAISER 1976a R. Kaiser, 'Münzprivilegien und bischöfliche Münzprägung in Frankreich, Deutschland und Burgund im 9.–12. Jahrundert', *Vierteljahrschrift f. Sozial- und Wirtschaftsgeschichte* 63 (1976), 289–338.

KAISER 1976b — 'Karl des Kahlen Münzprivileg für Besançon vom 1. November 871', *RSN* 55 (1976), 179–201.

KEARY 1879 C. F. Keary, *The Coinages of Western Europe from the Fall of the Roman Empire under Honorius to its Reconstruction under Charles the Great* (London, 1879) (repr. from *NC*[2] 18 (1878), 49–72, 132–65, 216–58; 19 (1879), 23–61).

KENNER 1888 F. Kenner, 'Römische Goldbarren mit Stempeln', *NZ* 20 (1888), 19–46.

KENT 1956 J. P. C. Kent, 'Gold coinage in the late Roman Empire', in *Essays in Roman Coinage presented to Harold Mattingly*, ed. R. A. G. Carson and C. H. V. Sutherland (Oxford, 1956), 190–204.

KENT 1959 — 'Zeno and Leo, the Most Noble Caesars', *NC*[6] 19 (1959), 93–8.

KENT 1960 — '*Auream monetam . . . cum signo crucis*', *NC*[2] 20 (1960), 129–32.

KENT 1961 — 'From Roman Britain to Saxon England', in *Stenton* 1961, 1–22.

KENT 1966 — 'Julius Nepos and the fall of the Western Empire', in *Corolla memoriae Erich Swoboda dedicata* (Graz, 1966), 146–50.

KENT 1967 — 'Problems of chronology in the seventh-century Merovingian coinage', *Cunobelin* 13 (1967), 24–30.

KENT 1968 — 'Charles the Great or Charles the Bald', *NC*[7] 8 (1968), 173–6.

KENT 1971 — 'The coinage of Theodoric in the names of Anastasius and Justin I', in *Mints, Dies and Currency. Essays dedicated to the Memory of Albert Baldwin*, ed. R. A. G. Carson (London, 1971), 67–74.

KENT 1972a — 'Gold standards of the Merovingian coinage, A.D. 580–700', in Hall and Metcalf 1972, 69–74.

KENT 1972b — 'The Aston Rowant treasure trove', *Oxoniensia* 37 (1972), 243–4.

KENT 1974 — 'Un monnayage irrégulier du début du Ve siècle de notre ère', *BCEN* 11 (1974), 23–8.

KENT 1975 — 'The date of the Sutton Hoo hoard' and 'Catalogue of the Sutton Hoo coins, blanks and billets', in Bruce-Mitford 1975, 588–647.

KENT 1978 — *Roman Coins* (London, 1978).

KENT 1982 — 'The Italian silver coinage of Justinian I and his successors', in *Studia Paulo Naster oblata* I, ed. S. Scheers (= Orientalia Lovaniensia Analecta 12; Louvain, 1982), 275–82.

KENT and PAINTER 1977 J. P. C. Kent and K. S. Painter, *Wealth of the Roman World. A.D. 300–700* (London, 1977).

KEYNES and LAPIDGE 1983 S. D. Keynes and M. Lapidge, *Alfred the Great* (Harmondsworth, 1983).

KIENER 1900 F. Kiener, *Verfassungsgeschichte der Provence seit der Ostgotenherrschaft bis zur Errichtung der Konsulate (510–1200)* (Leipzig, 1900).

KING 1972 P. D. King, *Law and Society in the Visigothic Kingdom* (Cambridge, 1972).

KLOSS 1929 F. Kloss, *Goldvorrat und Geldverkehr im Merowingerreich* (Veröffentlichungen des Seminars für Wirtschafts- und Kulturgeschichte an der Universität in Wien 5; Vienna, 1929).

KLUGE 1967 F. Kluge, *Etymologisches Wörterbuch der deutschen Sprache* (20th edn by W. Mitzka; Berlin, 1967).

KOS 1981 P. Kos, 'Neue langobardische Viertelsiliquien', *Germania* 59 (1981), 97–103.

KRAUS 1928 F. F. Kraus, *Die Münzen Odovacars und des Ostgotenreiches in Italien* (Halle, 1928).

KRICHELDORF 1958 H. Kricheldorf, 'Eine Ganzsiliqua Theodorichs', *SM* 8 (1958), 25–7.

KRUSCH 1882 B. Krusch, 'Zur Chronologie der merowingischen Könige', *Forschungen zur deutschen Geschichte* 22 (1882), 449–90.

KUBITSCHEK 1913 W. Kubitschek, 'Gold und Silber in IV. Jahrhundert n. Chr.', *NZ* 46 (1913), 161–70.

LABRUZZI 1912 F. Labruzzi, 'Di una moneta di Alberico Principe e Senatore dei Romani', *Archivio della R. Società Romana di Storia patria* 35 (1912), 133–49.

LACAM 1974 G. Lacam, *Civilisation et monnaies byzantines* (Paris, 1974).

LACAM 1983 — *La fin de l'empire romain et le monnayage or en Italie 455–493*, 2 vols. (Lucerne, 1983).

LADÉ 1890 A. Ladé, 'Les deniers mauriçois', *Bull. Soc. suisse de numismatique* 9 (1890), 238–56.

LADNER 1935 G. Ladner, 'Die Papstbildnesse auf den Münzen des 8. und 10. Jahrhunderts', *NZ* 68 (1935), 46–50.

LADNER 1941 — *I ritratti dei Papi nell'Antichità e nel Medioevo* I: *Dalle origini fino alla lotta per le investiture* (Pontificio Istituto di archeologia cristiana. Monumenti di antichità cristiana[2] IV; Vatican City, 1941).

LAFAURIE 1951 J. Lafaurie, 'Denier de Louis l'Aveugle pour Lyon', *BSFN* 6 (1951), 12.

LAFAURIE 1952a — 'Le trésor monétaire du Puy', *RN*[5] 14 (1952), 59–169.

LAFAURIE 1952b — 'A propos de la trouvaille de Bordeaux', *RN*[5] 14 (1952), 229–35.

LAFAURIE 1955 — 'Denier de Bourges au nom de Louis le Pieux', *BSFN* 10 (1955), 324–5.

LAFAURIE 1958a — 'Trésor de monnaies carolingiennes découvert dans le Jura', in *Centennial Publication of the American Numismatic Society*, ed. H. Ingholt (New York, 1958), 407–15.

LAFAURIE 1958b — 'Le trésor de Gourdon (Saône-et-Loire)', *Bull. de la Soc. nationale des antiquaires de France* 1958, 61–76.

LAFAURIE 1959 — 'Le trésor d'Alésia', *BSFN* 14 (1959), 262–4.

LAFAURIE 1960a — 'Le trésor d'Escharen (Pays-Bas)', *RN*[6] 2 (1959–60), 153–210.

LAFAURIE 1960b — 'Trésor de monnaies de cuivre trouvé à Sidi-Aïch (Tunisie)', *RN*[6] 2 (1960), 113–30.

LAFAURIE 1961 — 'Les routes commerciales indiquées par les trésors et trouvailles monétaires mérovingiens', in *Moneta e scambi nell'alto medioevo* (Spoleto, 1961), 231–78, discussion 313–37.

LAFAURIE 1963a — 'Trésor de deniers mérovingiens trouvé à Savonnières (Indre-et-Loire)', *RN*[6] 5 (1963), 65–81.

LAFAURIE 1963b — 'La monnaie bordelaise du haut moyen âge', in C. Higounet, *Bordeaux pendant le haut moyen âge* (Bordeaux, 1963), 295–325.

LAFAURIE 1964a — 'Les monnaies des Burgondes au VIe siècle', *BSFN* 19 (1964), 368–70.

LAFAURIE 1964b — 'Monnaie en argent trouvée à Fleury-sur-Orne. Essaie sur le monnayage d'argent Franc des Ve et VIe siècles', *Annales de Normandie* 14 (1964), 173–222 (incl. a detailed list and analysis of finds).

LAFAURIE 1964c — 'Triens mérovingien avec représentation de monétaire', *BSFN* 19 (1964), 342–3.

LAFAURIE 1965a — 'Deux trésors monétaires carolingiens: Saumeray (Eure-et-Loir), Rennes (Ille-et-Vilaine)', *RN*[6] 7 (1965), 262–305.

LAFAURIE 1965b — 'Denier de Childéric II trouvé à Onzain (Loir-et-Cher)', *BSFN* 20 (1965), 512–14.

LAFAURIE 1966a — 'Trésor monétaire du VIe siècle trouvé à Alise-Sainte-Reine en 1804', in *Connaissance d'Alésia* (Dijon, 1966), 99–111.

LAFAURIE 1966b — 'Monnaies franques en argent trouvées à Ouerre (Eure-et-Loir)', *Bull. des Sociétés archéologiques d'Eure-et-Loir* 1966, 49–54.

LAFAURIE 1967a — 'Un denier le Limoges de Louis le Pieux, roi d'Aquitaine', *BSFN* 22 (1967), 184–5.

LAFAURIE 1967b — 'Monnaies de Charles le Chauve et Charles le Simple', *Annuaire de l'Ecole Pratique des Hautes Etudes (IVe Section)* 1966–7, 241–3.

LAFAURIE 1967c — 'Trésor de monnaies lombardes trouvé à Linguizetta (Corse)', *BSFN* 22 (1967), 123–5.

LAFAURIE 1967d — 'Découvertes nouvelles de trémisses de Dorestate', *BSFN* 22 (1967), 197–8.

LAFAURIE 1967e — 'Panorama de la numismatique mérovingienne', *BCEN* 4 (1967), 41–51.

LAFAURIE 1968a — 'Observations sur les monnaies d'or attribuables à Thierry Ier, fils de Clovis', *Bull. de la Soc. nationale des antiquaires de France* 1968, 30–9.

LAFAURIE 1968b — 'Triens mérovingiens de Solignac et de Blond (Haute-Vienne)', *BSFN* 23 (1968), 268–9.

LAFAURIE 1968c — 'L'Article XII de l'édit de Pîtres du 25 juin 864', *BSFN* 23 (1968), 324–6.

LAFAURIE 1969a — 'Monnaies d'argent mérovingiennes des VIIe et VIIIe siècles: les trésors de Saint-Pierre-les-Etieux (Cher), Plassac (Gironde) et Nohanent (Puy-de-Dôme)', *RN*[6] 11 (1969), 98–219.

LAFAURIE 1969b — 'Les trouvailles de monnaies mérovingiennes et carolingiennes d'Amiens', *BSFN* 24 (1969), 404–7.

LAFAURIE 1969c — 'Inventaire sommaire du trésor de Pilligerheck', *Annuaire de l'Ecole Pratique des Hautes Etudes (IVe Section)* 1969–70, 323–6.

LAFAURIE 1969d — 'Tiers de sou mérovingien inédit frappé à Toulouse', *BSFN* 24 (1969), 357–8.

LAFAURIE 1970 — 'Des Carolingiens aux Capétiens', *Cahiers de civilisation médiévale* 13 (1970), 117–37.

LAFAURIE 1971a — 'Chronologie des émissions de deniers carolingiens au IXe siècle', *Annuaire de l'Ecole Pratique des Hautes Etudes (IVe Section)* 1970–1, 341–6.

LAFAURIE 1971b — 'Un tremissis mérovingien trouve à Bordeaux', *BSFN* 26 (1971), 85–8.

LAFAURIE 1971c — 'Les trouvailles des monnaies des Visigots en Gaule', *Actes du 94e Congrès national des Sociétés savantes, Pau 1969* (Section d'Archéologie) (Paris, 1971), 111–28.

LAFAURIE 1971d — 'Catalogue des monnaies trouvées au cours des fouilles au necropole d'Hérouvillette', *Archéologie médiévale* 1 (1971), 174–87.

LAFAURIE 1971e — 'Deux monnaies mérovingiennes trouvées à Reculver (Kent)', *Bull. de la Soc. nationale des antiquaires de France* 1971, 209–19 (**1.437** and **465** in this collection).

LAFAURIE 1972a — 'Le trésor carolingien de Sarzana-Luni', in *Les monnaies et médailles racontent l'histoire de France* (Paris, 1972), 23–38, and in *Le zecche minori toscane fino al XIV secolo* (Pistoia, 1974), 43–55.

LAFAURIE 1972b — 'Les monnaies frappées à Lyon au VIe siècle', *Mélanges de travaux offerts à Maître J. Tricou* (Lyon, 1972), 193–205.

LAFAURIE 1972c — 'Trouvailles de monnaies des VIe–VIIe siècles de l'Empire d'Orient en Gaule mérovingienne', *BSFN* 27 (1972), 206–9.

LAFAURIE 1972d — 'Monnaies mérovingiennes du Puy-de-Dôme', *BSFN* 27 (1972), 228–32.

LAFAURIE 1973a — 'Deniers de Charles le Chauve trouvés à Clairoix', *Revue archéologique de l'Oise* 4 (1973), 23–6 (w. observations on the GDR coinage).

LAFAURIE 1973b — 'Numismatique romaine et médievale (rapports des conférences)', *Annuaire de l'Ecole Pratique des Hautes Etudes (IVe Section)* 1972–3, 326–9.

LAFAURIE 1973c — 'Monnaies mérovingiennes de Nantes du VIe siècle', *BSFN* 28 (1973), 391–4.

LAFAURIE 1973d — 'Monnaies de bronze marseillaises du VIe siècle', *BSFN* 28 (1973), 480–2.

LAFAURIE 1973e — 'Monnaies mérovingiennes du Gévaudan', in *Le Club de la Médaille* 41 (1973), 126–33.

LAFAURIE 1974a — 'Des Mérovingiens aux Carolingiens. Les monnaies de Pépin le Bref', *Francia* 2 (1974), 26–48.

LAFAURIE 1974b — 'Les animaux dans la numismatique mérovingienne', in *Le bestiaire des monnaies, des sceaux et de médailles* (Hôtel de la Monnaie exhibition; Paris, 1974), 137–50.

LAFAURIE 1975a — 'Le troisième trésor de monnaies carolingiennes trouvé à Cosne-sur-Loire', *Les Annales des Pays nivernais* 10–11 (1975), 51–6.

LAFAURIE 1975b — 'Monnaies mérovingiennes de Limoges', in *Journées numismatiques. Musée municipal, Limoges* 1975, 59–60, 63.

LAFAURIE 1975c — 'Monnaies épiscopales de Limoges aux VIIe–VIIIe siècles', *BSFN* 30 (1975), 778–82.

LAFAURIE 1975d — 'Trésors et trouvailles monétaires mérovingiens aux Pays-Bas', in *Festoen opgedragen aan A. N. Zadoks-Josephus Jitta bij haar zeventigste verjaardag* (Groningen-Bussum, 1975), 383–91.

LAFAURIE 1976a — 'Trésor de monnaies du Xe siècle trouvé à Fresnes (Val-de-Marne)', *BSFN* 31 (1976), 4–7.

LAFAURIE 1976b — 'La chronologie typologique des monnaies de Charles le Chauve et le trésor de Cosne (Nièvre)', *Annuaire de l'École Pratique des Hautes Etudes (IVe Section)* 1975–6, 444–7.

LAFAURIE 1976c — 'Moneta Palatina', *Francia* 4 (1976), 59–87.

LAFAURIE 1976d — 'Monnaies décriées dans la seconde appendice de la *Lex Burgundionum*', *BSFN* 31 (1976), 73–5.

LAFAURIE 1977a — 'Eligius Monetarius', *RN*[6] 19 (1977), 111–51.

LAFAURIE 1977b — 'Nouvelles recherches sur le trésor de Chissey-en-Morvan (Saône-et-Loire) l. d. Buis', *BSFN* 32 (1977), 211–16.

LAFAURIE 1978a — 'Les monnaies impériales de Charlemagne', *Comptes-rendus de l'Académie des Inscriptions et Belles-Lettres* 1978, 154–72.

LAFAURIE 1978b — 'La surveillance des ateliers monétaires au IXe siècle', in *Histoire comparée de l'administration (IVe–XVIIIe siècles)* (*Francia*, Beiheft 9, 1980), 486–96.

LAFAURIE 1978c — 'Deniers du VIIIe siècle de Saint-Ouen de Rouen', *BSFN* 33 (1978), 368–72 (repr. in *Histoire et numismatique en Haute Normandie*, ed. N. Gauthier (Caen, 1980), 111–15).

LAFAURIE 1978d — 'Monnaies d'argent franques trouvées à Envermeu (Seine-Maritime)', in *Actes du colloque Abbé Cochet* (Rouen, 1978), 421–8.

LAFAURIE 1978e — 'Trésor monétaire mérovingien de Lucy (Seine-Maritime)', in *Actes du colloque Abbé Cochet* (Rouen, 1978), 429–39.

LAFAURIE 1980a *Mélanges de numismatique, d'archéologie et d'histoire offerts à Jean Lafaurie*, ed. P. Bastien *et al.* (Paris, 1980).

LAFAURIE 1980b — 'Réattribution de quelques monnaies mérovingiennes au type de la croix à huit rais', *BSFN* 35 (1980), 647–51.

LAFAURIE 1980c — 'Deux trouvailles de monnaies du Ve siècle à Châtelaillon, près La Rochelle', *BSFN* 35 (1980), 715–16.

LAFAURIE 1981a — 'Une initiative avortée d'individualisation de la monnaie du royaume d'Aquitaine en 622', *BSFN* 36 (1981), 14–17.

LAFAURIE 1981b — 'Trémisses mérovingiens aux légendes ANTRO VICO et PETRAFICTO VICO', *BSFN* 36 (1981), 47–9.

LAFAURIE 1981c — 'Les monnaies de Marseille du VIe au VIIIe siècle', *BSFN* 36 (1981), 68–73.

LAFAURIE 1981d — (ed.), *Catalogue des deniers mérovingiens de la trouvaille de Bais (Ille-et-Vilaine)*, by M. Prou and E. Bougenot (Paris, 1981) (reprint, with important introduction, of Prou and Bougenot 1907).

LAFAURIE 1981e — 'L'article XI de l'Edit de Pîtres du 25 juin 864', *Lagom, Festschrift für Peter Berghaus zum 60. Geburtstag*, ed. T. Fischer and P. Ilisch (Münster, 1981), 113–17.

LAFAURIE 1981f — 'Les monnaies mérovingiennes en région parisienne', in *Le haut moyen âge en Ile-de-France* (*Mémoires de la Fédération des Sociétés historiques et archéologiques de Paris et de l'Ile-de-France* 32 (1981)), 161–84.

LAFAURIE 1982a — 'Monnaies du Ve au VIIIe siècles découvertes dans le département du Maine-et-Loire', *BSFN* 37 (1982), 192–4.

LAFAURIE 1982b — 'A propos de deux monnaies d'or de Sévère III trouvées en Anjou', *BSFN* 37 (1982), 194–6.

LAFAURIE 1982c — 'Nouvelles découvertes de deniers mérovingiens à Fécamp (Seine-Maritime)', *BSFN* 37 (1982), 134–7.

LAFAURIE 1983a — 'Deux monnaies en argent du VIe siècle trouvées à Saint-Blaise, com. de Saint-Mitre-les-Remparts (Bouches-du-Rhône)', *BSFN* 38 (1983), 411–13.

LAFAURIE 1983b — 'Quelques monnaies du VIe siècle conservées au Musée de Saint-Omer', *BSFN* 38 (1983), 345–7.

LAFAURIE 1983c — 'The *novi denarii* and forgery in the ninth century', in *Grierson* 1983a, 137–45.

LAFAURIE 1983d — 'Trésor de monnaies du VIe siècle découvert à Alise-Sainte-Reine en 1804', *RN*[6] 25 (1983), 101–38.

LAFAURIE *et al.* 1961 J. Lafaurie, B. Jansen and A. N. Zadoks-Josephus Jitta, 'Le trésor de Wieuwerd', *Oudheidkundige Mededelingen uit het Rijksmuseum van Oudheden te Leiden* 42 (1961), 78–107.

LAFAURIE and DHÉNIN 1981 J. Lafaurie and M. Dhénin, 'Quatre monnaies mérovingiennes trouvées à Saint-Denis (Seine-Saint-Denis)', *BSFN* 35 (1980), 122–5.

LAFAURIE and DUPLESSY 1962 J. Lafaurie and J. Duplessy, 'Numismatique de Corbie', *Bull. trimestriel de la Société des Antiquaires de Picardie* 1962, 15–43.

LAFAURIE and ZADOKS-JITTA 1958 J. Lafaurie and A. N. Zadoks-Jitta, 'Deux trésors monétaires du 6e siècle trouvés aux Pays-Bas', in *La Monnaie, trésor d'art et d'histoire* (exhibition catalogue, Musée monétaire, May–July 1958) (Paris, 1958), 73–6.

LAFFRANCHI 1933 L. Laffranchi, 'Lodovico II, III e V imperatori e re d'Italia nella monetazione pavese o milanese di tipo carolingio', *Rassegna numismatica* 30 (1933), 5–10.

LAFFRANCHI 1934 — 'Il tremisse di Ariperto con Iffo e le prime monete beneventane', *Rassegna numismatica* 31 (1934), 31–6.

LAGOY 1843 Marquis de Lagoy, *Explication de quelques médailles à monogramme des roi goths d'Italie* (Aix, 1843).

LAGOY 1856 — *Recherches sur l'explication des monogrammes de quelques médailles inédites. Des derniers temps de l'empire d'Occident et de l'époque mérovingienne* (Aix, 1856).

LA GRANGE 1851 L. de la Grange, 'Monnaies mérovingiennes d'argent', *RN* 1851, 19–26 (summary account of the Plassac hoard; superseded by Lafaurie 1969a).

LALLEMAND 1964 J. Lallemand, 'Sou d'or de Zénon frappé à Thessalonique', *BCEN* 1 (1964), 49–51.

LALLEMAND 1965 — 'Vedrin: sous d'or de Magnus Maximus à Anastase', in *Études numismatiques* (Bibl. royale de Belgique, Cabinet des Médailles) 3 (1965), 109–44.

LALLEMAND 1967 — 'Trésor de monnaies romaines en bronze: Constance II à Zénon', in *Ordona* II (Brussels, 1967), 19–30.

LA MOTTE-COLLAS 1957 M. de La Motte-Collas, 'Les possessions territoriales de l'abbaye de Saint-Germain-des-Prés du début du IXe au début du XIIe siècle', *Revue de l'histoire de l'église de France* 43 (1957), 49–80.

LANGLOIS 1849 V. Langlois, 'Quelques monnaies monogrammatiques de cuivre d'Eraric, roi des Ostrogoths', *Revue archéologique* 6.1 (1849), 389–92.

LATOUCHE 1956 R. Latouche, 'Sainte Foy de Conques et le problème de l'or aux temps carolingiens', *Annales du Midi* 68 (1956), 209–15.

LATOUCHE 1967 — *The Birth of Western Economy. Economic Aspects of the Dark Ages* (2nd edn; London, 1967) (transl. of *Les origines de l'économie occidentale* (Paris, 1956); the 2nd edn slightly updates the bibl. in the 1st, of 1961).

LAUER 1900 P. Lauer, *Le règne de Louis IV d'Outre-Mer* (Bibl. de l'Ecole des Hautes Etudes, fasc. 127; Paris, 1900).

LAUER 1910 — *Robert Ier et Raoul, rois de France* (Bibl. de l'Ecole des Hautes Etudes, fasc. 188; Paris, 1910).

LAURENT 1851 J. Laurent, 'Catalogue des monnaies et médailles . . . du Musée départemental des Vosges. 2e supplément', *Annales de la Soc. d'Emulation des Vosges* 7 (1851), 3–34.

LAWRENCE 1893 L. A. Lawrence, 'The coinage of Aethelbald', *NC*³ 13 (1893), 40–5.

LAWRENCE 1905–7 — 'Forgery in relation to numismatics', *BNJ* 2 (1905), 397–409; 3 (1906), 281–90; 4 (1907), 311–16.

LEBECQ 1978 S. Lebecq, 'Francs contre Frisons (VIe–VIIIe siècles)', *Actes du 101e Congrès national des Sociétés savantes, Lille, 1976* (Paris, 1978), 53–71.

LEBECQ 1983 — *Marchands et navigateurs frisons du haut moyen âge*, 2 vols. (Lille, 1983).

LEBLANC 1690 F. Leblanc, *Traité historique des monnoyes de France* (Paris, 1690).

LECOINTRE-DUPONT 1836 G. Lecointre-Dupont, 'Des anciens noms de la ville de Melle', *RN* 1836, 99–108.

LECOINTRE-DUPONT 1839 — 'Notice sur un denier de l'empereur Lothaire', *RN* 1839, 344–51.

LECOINTRE-DUPONT 1840a — *Essai sur les monnaies frappées en Poitou, et sur l'histoire monétaire de cette province* (Poitiers, 1840) (repr. of 2 articles publ. in the *Mém. de la Soc. des Antiquaires de l'Ouest* 6 (1839), 263–376; 7 (1840), 203–48).

LECOINTRE-DUPONT 1840b — 'Dissertation sur les monnoies portant les noms de Charles roi et de la ville de Melle, vulgairement attribuées à Charles-le-Simple. Origine du mot *maille*', *RN* 1840, 39–66.

LECOINTRE-DUPONT 1840c — 'Notice sur trois tiers de sol d'or mérovingiens. Contrefaçon moderne de l'une de ces pièces', *RN* 1840, 314–23.

LECOINTRE-DUPONT 1846 — *Lettres sur l'histoire monétaire de la Normandie et du Perche* (Paris, 1846) (revised text of articles publ. in *RN* 1842–5).

LECOMTE 1895 M. Lecomte, 'Ateliers monétaires mérovingiens: identifications et observations', *RN*[3] 13 (1895), 177–85.

LEDERER 1934 P. Lederer, 'La zecca di "Ticinum" Pavia sotto Odoacro', *Atti e Memorie dell'Istituto italiano di numismatica* 8 (1934), 145–51.

LEFROY 1870 J. H. Lefroy, 'Further notice of gold coins discovered in 1828, by the late C. E. Lefroy, Esq.', *NC*[2] 10 (1870), 164–76.

LE GENTILHOMME 1936 P. Le Gentilhomme, 'Trouvaille de monnaies d'or des Mérovingiens et des Wisigoths faite à Bordeaux en 1803', *RN*[4] 39 (1936), 87–133 (repr. in Le Gentilhomme 1940a, 5–51).

LE GENTILHOMME 1937 — 'Notes de numismatique mérovingienne', *RN*[5] 1 (1937), 71–83 (repr. in Le Gentilhomme 1940a, 53–65).

LE GENTILHOMME 1938a — 'La circulation des sceattas dans la Gaule mérovingienne', *RN*[5] 2 (1938), 23–49 (repr. in Le Gentilhomme 1940a, 67–93; Engl. transl. as 'The circulation of sceats in Merovingian Gaul', *BNJ* 24 (1943–4), 195–210).

LE GENTILHOMME 1938b — 'Les monnaies mérovingiennes de la trouvaille de Buis', *RN*[5] 2 (1938), 133–68 (repr. in Le Gentilhomme 1940a, 95–130).

LE GENTILHOMME 1940a — *Mélanges de numismatique mérovingienne* (Paris, 1940) (reprint of 5 articles).

LE GENTILHOMME 1940b — 'Aperçus sur quelques aspects du monnayage des peuples barbares', *RN*[5] 4 (1940), 134–47 (repr. in Le Gentilhomme 1940a, 131–47).

LE GENTILHOMME 1943–4 — 'Le monnayage et la circulation monétaire dans les royaumes barbares en Occident (Ve–VIIIe siècle)', *RN*[5] 7 (1943), 46–112; 8 (1944), 13–59.

LE GENTILHOMME 1947 — 'Trouvaille de Barbuise (Aube)', *RN*[5] 9 (1947), P.-V. xi–xii.

LEGRAND 1916 M. Legrand, 'Deux trouvailles en une seule: trouvaille d'Etampes', *RN*[4] 20 (1916), 173–80.

LELEWEL 1835 J. Lelewel, *Numismatique du moyen-âge, considérée sous le rapport de type*, 3 vols. and plates (Paris, 1835).

LENORMANT 1848–54 C. Lenormant, 'Lettres à M. de Saulcy sur les plus anciens monuments numismatiques de la série mérovingienne', *RN* 1848, 106–31, 181–212; 1849, 17–39, 99–139; 1853, 277–316; 1854, 257–74, 305–46.

LENZI 1913 F. Lenzi, 'Della numismatica di Odoacro', *Rassegna numismatica* 10 (1913), 36–49.

LE PRÉVOST 1840 A. Le Prévost, 'Anciennes divisions territoriales de la Normandie', *Mémoires de la Société des Antiquaires de Normandie*[2] 1 (1840), 1–59.

LESNE 1910–43 E. Lesne, *Histoire de la propriété ecclésiastique en France* (Mémoires et travaux publiés par les professeurs des Facultés catholiques de Lille, fasc. 6, 19, 30, 34, 44, 46, 50, 53; 8 vols. in 6; Lille, 1910–43).

LEVI 1919 A. Levi, 'Sessa Aurunca: tesoretto di monetine di bronzo bizantine (follari o nummi)', *Notizie degli Scavi di Antichità* 1919, 356–8.

LEVILLAIN 1913 L. Levillain, 'La succession d'Austrasie au VIIe siècle', *Revue historique* 112 (1913), 62–93.

LEVILLAIN 1926 — *Recueil des actes de Pépin Ier et de Pépin II rois d'Aquitaine (814–848)* (Paris, 1926).

LIEBERMANN 1903–16 F. Liebermann, *Die Gesetze der Angelsachsen*, 3 vols. (Halle, 1903–16).

LINDER WELIN 1964 U. S. Linder Welin, 'Elias Brenners arabiska guldpenning och andra dinarer funna i Sverige', *NNÅ* 1964, 1–25.

LINDER WELIN 1965 — 'Some rare Samanid dirhams and the origin of the word "mancusus" ', in *Congresso internazionale de numismatica, Roma 1961* II: *Atti* (Rome, 1965), 499–508.

LINDSAY 1842 J. Lindsay, *A View of the Coinage of the Heptarchy* (Cork, 1842).

LLEWELLYN 1971 P. Llewellyn, *Rome in the Dark Ages* (London, 1971).

LOCKETT 1920 R. C. Lockett, 'The coinage of Offa', *NC*⁴ 20 (1920), 57–89.

LOMBARD 1947 M. Lombard, 'Les bases monétaires d'une suprématie économique: l'or musulman du VIIe au XIIe siècle', *Annales ESC* 2 (1947), 143–60 (repr. in his *Espaces et réseaux du haut moyen âge* (Paris, 1972), 7–29).

LONGNON 1878 A. Longnon, *Géographie de la Gaule au VIe siècle* (Paris, 1878).

LONGNON 1885 — *Atlas historique de la France* (Paris, 1885).

LONGPÉRIER 1842 A. de Longpérier, 'The gold mancus', *NC* 5 (1842–3), 122–4 (repr. in his *Oeuvres* IV (Paris, 1883), 112–14).

LONGPÉRIER 1847 — *Notice des monnaies françaises composant la collection de M. J. Rousseau* (Paris, 1847).

LONGPÉRIER 1856 — 'Quelques deniers de Pépin, de Carloman et de Charlemagne', *RN*² 1 (1856), 180–9 (Bel-Air find, w. some others; repr. in his *Oeuvres* IV (Paris, 1883), 337–45).

LONGPÉRIER 1858 — 'Cent deniers de Pépin, de Carloman et de Charlemagne, découvert près d'Imphy en Nivernais', *RN*² (1858), 202–62 (repr. in his *Oeuvres* V (Paris, 1883), 1–53).

LONGUET 1930 H. Longuet, 'Les triens mérovingiens au buste de face', *RN*⁴ 33 (1930), 173–90.

LONGUET 1939 — 'Apropos du monnayage mérovingien', *RN*⁵ 3 (1939), 43–64.

LOPEZ 1943a R. S. Lopez, 'Byzantine law in the seventh century and its reception by the Germans and Arabs', *Byzantion* 16 (1942–3), 445–61.

LOPEZ 1943b — 'Mohammed and Charlemagne: a revision', *Speculum* 18 (1943), 14–38 (repr. in Hübinger 1968b).

LOPEZ 1949 — 'Continuità e adattamento nel medio evo: un millennio di storia delle associazoni di monetieri nell'Europa occidentale', in *Studi in onore di Gino Luzzatto* (Milan, 1949), 74–117.

LOPEZ 1953 — 'An aristocracy of money in the early middle ages', *Speculum* 28 (1953), 1–43.

LOT 1891 F. Lot, *Les derniers carolingiens: Lothaire, Louis V, Charles de Lorraine (954–991)* (Bibl. de l'Ecole des Hautes Etudes, fasc. 87; Paris, 1891).

LOT 1921 — 'Un grand domaine à l'époque franque; Ardin en Poitou. Contribution à l'étude de l'impôt', *Bibl. de l'Ecole des Hautes Etudes, sciences, hist. et phil.*, fasc. 230 (Cinquentenaire de l'Ecole des Hautes Etudes, 1921), 109–29 (repr. in *Recueil des travaux historiques de Ferdinand Lot* II (Geneva, 1970), 191–211).

LOT, PFISTER and GANSHOF 1941 F. Lot, C. Pfister and F. L. Ganshof, *Histoire du moyen âge* I: *Les destinées de l'Empire en Occident, 395–888* (2nd edn; Paris, 1940–1).

LOWICK 1973 N. M. Lowick, 'A new type of *solidus mancus*', *NC*[7] 13 (1973), 173–82.

LOWICK 1976 — 'The Kufic coins from Cuerdale', *BNJ* 46 (1976), 19–28.

LOYN 1968 H. R. Loyn, *Anglo-Saxon England and the Norman Conquest*, (2nd edn; London, 1968).

LOYN 1977 — *The Vikings in England* (London, 1977).

LOYN 1984 — *The Governance of Anglo-Saxon England 500–1087* (London, 1984).

LUSCHIN 1908a A. Luschin von Ebengreuth, 'Beiträge zur Münzgeschichte im Frankenreich. I. Der Münzfund von Ilanz', *Neues Archiv der Gesellschaft für ältere deutsche Geschichtskunde* 33 (1908), 435–59.

LUSCHIN 1908b — 'Il sistema monetario degli aurei italiani di Carlomagno', *RIN* 21 (1908), 89–96.

LUSCHIN 1910a — *Der Denar der Lex Salica* (*Sitzungsberichte d. Kaiserliche Akademie d. Wissenschaften in Wien, Philos.-Hist. Klasse*, Band 163, Abhandl. 4; Vienna, 1910).

LUSCHIN 1910b — 'Zur Geschichte des Denars der *Lex Salica*', in *Historische Aufsätze Karl Zeumer zum 66. Geburtstage als Festgabe dargebracht* (Weimar, 1910), 201–7.

LUSCHIN 1926 — *Allgemeine Münzkunde und Geldgeschichte des Mittelalters und der neueren Zeit* (Munich-Berlin, 1926).

LUSUARDI SIENA 1973 S. Lusuardi Siena, 'Eligio, orafo e monetiere', *Contributi dell'Istituto di archeologia (Milano)* IV (Milan, 1973), 132–221.

LYON 1956 C. S. S. Lyon, 'A reappraisal of the sceatta and styca coinage of Northumbria', *BNJ* 28 (1955–7), 227–42.

LYON 1967 — 'Historical problems of Anglo-Saxon coinage (1)', *BNJ* 36 (1967), 215–21.

LYON 1968 — 'Historical problems of Anglo-Saxon coinage (2), the ninth century – Offa to Alfred', *BNJ* 37 (1968), 216–38.

LYON 1969 — 'Historical problems of Anglo-Saxon coinage (3), denominations and weights', *BNJ* 38 (1969), 204–22.

LYON 1970 — 'Historical problems of Anglo-Saxon coinage (4), the Viking Age', *BNJ* 39 (1970), 193–204.

LYON 1976 — 'Some problems in interpreting Anglo-Saxon coinage', *Anglo-Saxon England* 5 (1976), 173–224.

LYON 1983 — 'A significant "Winchester" die-link in the reign of Edward the Elder (899–924)', *NCirc* 1983, 261–2.

LYON and STEWART 1961 C. S. S. Lyon and B. H. I. H. Stewart, 'The Northumbrian Viking coinage in the Cuerdale hoard', in *Stenton* 1961, 96–121.

LYON and STEWART 1964 — 'The classification of Northumbrian Viking coins in the Cuerdale hoard', *NC*[7] 4 (1964), 281–2.

MAHIEU 1924 A. M[ahieu], 'Monnaies pseudo-impériales', *RBN* 76 (1924), 187–9.

MALDURA 1880 L. Maldura, *Due parole di una nuova monetina papale, avanti il mille* (Rome, 1880) (a forgery by Cigoi of a denaro of Paul I, 757–67).

MALLINSON 1936 A. Mallinson, 'Historical British coins', *Trans. Internat. Numismatic Congress, London 1936*, ed. J. Allan *et al.* (London, 1938), 372–82.

MALLINSON 1982 — *The Leaning Tower or Out of the Perpendicular* (Oxford, 1982).

MANN 1902 H. K. Mann, *The Lives of the Popes in the Early Middle Ages* I (London, 1902).

MANTEYER 1942 G. de Manteyer, *La Monnaie. Poids des grains de céréales, aloi de métal et cours des prix* I: *De l'Egypt à la France mérovingienne* (Gap, privately printed, 1942).

MARCHANT 1851 *Lettres du Baron Marchant sur la numismatique et l'histoire* (Paris, 1851).

MARTIN 1966 C. Martin, 'Un ripostiglio di monete italiane del IX° secolo', in *Atti del I° Convegno internazionale di studi sull'alto medioevo. Orta, 15–18 sett. 1963* (Novara, 1966), 87–91.

MARTIN 1977 — 'Denier de Charlemagne frappé à Genève', *SM* 27 (1977), 68–9.

MARTIN 1980 — 'Le trésor de Riaz: monnaies d'argent du VIe siècle', in *Lafaurie* 1980a, 231–7.

MARTIN 1982 P. H. Martin, 'Neue Münzanhänger und Schmuckscheiben aus einem Grab des 5. Jahrhunderts in Baden', in *Proceedings of the Ninth International Congress of Numismatics. Berne, Sept. 1979* II (Louvain-la-Neuve and Luxemburg, 1982), 715–30.

MASSAGLI 1861 D. Massagli, 'Dissertation sur les monnaies frappées à Lucques pendant la domination des francs aux VIIIe et IXe siècles', *RN*² 6 (1861), 429–50.

MASSAGLI 1870 — *Introduzione alla storia della zecca e delle monete lucchesi* (Memorie e documenti per servire alla storia di Lucca XI. 2; Lucca, 1870) (repr. w. introduction by F. Panvini Rosati (Lucca, 1976)).

MATEU Y LLOPIS 1936 F. Mateu y Llopis, *Catálogo de las monedas previsigodas y visigodas del Gabinete numismático del Museo arqueológico nacional* (Madrid, 1936).

MATEU Y LLOPIS 1941 — 'Las fórmulas y los simbolos cristianos en los tipos monetales visigodos', *Analecta sacra Tarraconensia* 14 (1941), 75–96.

MATEU Y LLOPIS 1942 — 'Inscripciones cristianas en monedas visigodas', in J. Vives, *Inscripciones cristianas de la España romana y visigoda* (Barcelona, 1942), 147–60 (repr. without change in the 2nd edn of 1969).

MATEU Y LLOPIS 1972 *Bibliografia de Felipe Mateu y Llopis reunida en su LXX aniversario MCMLXXI* (Barcelona, 1972).

MATTINGLY 1925 H. Mattingly, 'Graf Salis und seine numismatische Methode', *NZ* 58 (1925), 121–6.

MAXE-WERLY 1862 L. Maxe-Werly, *Essai sur la numismatique rémoise* (Paris, 1862).

MAXE-WERLY 1867 — 'Numismatique rémoise', *RN*² 12 (1867), 201–14.

MAXE-WERLY 1879 — 'Numismatique de Remiremont et de Saint-Dié', *Mém. de la Soc. d'archéologie lorraine*³ 7 (1879), 204–82.

MAXE-WERLY 1888–9 — 'Etat actuel de la numismatique rémoise: II, III', *RBN* 44 (1888), 542–65; 45 (1889), 57–87.

MAXE-WERLY 1889–90 — 'Etudes numismatiques à l'époque mérovingienne', *RBN* 45 (1899), 509–29; 46 (1890), 5–33.

MAXE-WERLY 1890 — 'Monnaies mérovingiennes. Trouvaille de Saint-Aubin (Meuse)', *RN*³ 8 (1890), 12–53.

MAZEL 1836 – Mazel, 'Notes sur quelques monnaies du moyen âge, inédites ou peu connues', *Bull. de la Soc. archéologique de Béziers* 1 (1836), 225–32.

MCKITTERICK 1983 R. McKitterick, *The Frankish Kingdoms under the Carolingians 751–987* (London-New York, 1983).

MEERT 1960 C. Meert, 'Les monnaies mérovingiennes de l'atelier de Dinant', *RBN* 106 (1960), 267–84.

MEIXNER 1968 I. Meixner, 'Tri nepoznata novca kralja Teodorika', *Numizmaticke Vijesti* 15 (1968), 53–5.

MENADIER 1911 J. Menadier, 'Karolingerdenare', *Amtliche Berichte aus den Königl. Kunstsammlungen* 32 (1911), 263–82.

MENÉNDEZ PIDAL 1980 R. Menéndez Pidal (ed.), *España visigoda* (vol. III of his *Historia de España*) (4th edn; Madrid, 1980).

MERRICK and METCALF 1969 J. M. Merrick and D. M. Metcalf, 'Milliprobe analyses of some problematic Burgundian and other gold coins of the early middle ages', *Archaeometry* 11 (1969), 61–5.

METCALF 1961 D. M. Metcalf, 'Some finds of medieval coins from Scotland and the north of England', *BNJ* 30 (1960–1), 88–123.

METCALF 1963a — 'Offa's pence reconsidered', *Cunobelin* 9 (1963), 37–52.

METCALF 1963b — 'English monetary history in the time of Offa: a reply', *NCirc* 1963, 165–7.

METCALF 1964a — 'Coins of Charlemagne reading DMAG.C.S.', *HBN* 18/19 (1964–5), 13–20.

METCALF 1964b — 'Evidence relating to die-output in the time of Offa', *NCirc* 1964, 23.

METCALF 1965a — 'Coins of Pepin minted at Saint-Denis?', *Cunobelin* 11 (1965), 19–29, 54.

METCALF 1965b — 'How large was the Anglo-Saxon currency?', *Economic History Review*² 18 (1965), 475–82.

METCALF 1966a — 'A stylistic analysis of "porcupine" sceattas', *NC*⁷ 6 (1966), 179–205.

METCALF 1966b — 'A coinage for Mercia under Æthelbald', *Cunobelin* 1966, 26–39.

METCALF 1966c — 'Artistic borrowing, imitation and forgery in the eighth century', *HBN* 20 (1966), 379–92.

METCALF 1967 — 'The prosperity of western Europe in the eighth and ninth centuries', *Economic History Review*² 20 (1967), 344–57.

METCALF 1968 — 'Pre-reform coins of Charlemagne from the grave-find at Breuvery', *NCirc* 76 (1968), 150–4.

METCALF 1969a — *The Origins of the Anastasian Currency Reform* (Amsterdam, 1969).

METCALF 1969b — 'A hoard of "porcupine" sceattas', *MN* 15 (1969), 101–18.

METCALF 1970 — 'An early Carolingian mint: *Bona* – Tiel', *RBN* 116 (1970), 141–52.

METCALF 1971 — 'A coin of Offa from Deddington Castle, Oxon.', *BNJ* 40 (1971), 171–2.

METCALF 1972a — 'The "Bird and Branch" sceattas in the light of a find from Abingdon', *Oxoniensia* 37 (1972), 51–65.

METCALF 1972b — 'Analyses of the metal contents of medieval coins', in Hall and Metcalf 1972, 383–434.

METCALF 1974a — 'Monetary expansion and recession: interpreting the distribution patterns of seventh- and eighth-century coins', in *Coins and the Archaeologist*, ed. J. Casey and R. Reece (BAR British Series 4; Oxford, 1974), 206–23.

METCALF 1974b — 'Sceattas found at the Iron-Age hill fort of Walbury Camp, Berkshire', *BNJ* 44 (1974), 1–12.

METCALF 1976a — 'Twelve notes on sceatta finds', *BNJ* 46 (1976), 1–18.

METCALF 1976b — 'Sceattas from the territory of the Hwicce', *NC*⁷ 16 (1976), 64–74.

METCALF 1977 — 'Monetary affairs in Mercia in the time of Æthelbald', in *Mercian Studies*, ed. A. Dornier (Leicester, 1977), 87–106.

METCALF 1978 — 'Chemical analysis of English sceattas', *BNJ* 48 (1978), 12–19.

METCALF 1979 — 'La traversée de la Manche (VIIIe–IXe siècles)', *BSFN* 34 (1979), 511–14.

METCALF 1981 — 'A sketch of the currency in the time of Charles the Bald', in *Charles the Bald: Court and Kingdom*, ed. M. Gibson and J. Nelson (BAR International Series 101; Oxford, 1981), 53–84.

METCALF 1983a — 'Interpreting the alloy of the Merovingian silver coinage', in *Grierson* 1983a, 113–25.

METCALF 1983b — 'An eighth-century archer', *The Ashmolean* 2 (1983), 12–13.

METCALF 1984a — 'Monetary circulation in southern England in the first half of the eighth century', in Hill and Metcalf 1984, 27–69.

METCALF 1984b — 'Twenty-five notes on sceatta finds', in Hill and Metcalf 1984, 193–205.

METCALF 1984c — 'A note on sceattas as a measure of international trade, and on the earliest Danish coinage', in Hill and Metcalf 1984, 159–64.

METCALF and HAMBLIN 1968 D. M. Metcalf and L. K. Hamblin, 'The composition of some Frisian sceattas', *JMP* 55 (1968), 28–45.

METCALF *et al.* 1968 D. M. Metcalf, J. M. Merrick and L. K. Hamblin, *Studies in the Composition of Early Medieval Coins* (Newcastle, 1968).

METCALF and MISKIMIN 1968 D. M. Metcalf and H. A. Miskimin, 'The Carolingian pound: a discussion', *NCirc* 76 (1968), 296–8, 333–4.

METCALF and SCHWEIZER 1970 D. M. Metcalf and F. Schweizer, 'Milliprobe analyses of some Visigothic, Suevic and other gold coins of the early middle ages', *Archaeometry* 12 (1970), 173–88.

METCALF and STÓS-GALE 1982 D. M. Metcalf and Z. Stós-Gale, 'Chemical analyses of some sceattas from the Southampton excavations', *NC* 142 (1982), 142–8.

METCALF and WALKER 1967 D. M. Metcalf and D. R. Walker, 'The "wolf" sceattas', *BNJ* 36 (1967), 11–28.

METCALF and WALKER 1976 — 'Tin as a minor constituent in two sceattas from the Shakenoak excavations', *NC*[7] 16 (1976), 228–9.

MICKWITZ 1932 G. Mickwitz, *Geld und Wirtschaft im romischen Reich des vierten Jahrhunderts n. Chr.* (Societas Scientiarum Fennica. Commentationes Humanarum Litterarum IV.2; Helsinki, 1932).

MICKWITZ 1933 — *Die Systeme des römischen Silbergeldes im IV. Jhdt. n. Ch.* (Societas Scientiarum Fennica. Commentationes Humanarum Litterarum VI.2; Helsinki, 1933).

MICKWITZ 1934 — 'Le problème de l'or dans le monde antique', *Annales d'histoire économique et sociale* 6 (1934), 235–47.

MILES 1952 G. C. Miles, *The Coinage of the Visigoths of Spain: Leovigild to Achila II* (New York, 1952).

MILES 1955 — 'Notes on the Visigothic coins in the Gabinete Numismático de Cataluña', *Numisma* 5.16 (1955), 57–62.

MILNE 1926 J. G. Milne, 'The currency of Egypt in the fifth century', *NC*[5] 6 (1926), 43–92.

MISKIMIN 1967 H. A. Miskimin, 'Two reforms of Charlemagne? Weights and measures in the middle ages', *Economic History Review*[2] 20 (1967), 35–52.

MITARD 1978 P. H. Mitard, 'Monnaies des Ve/VIe et VIIe siècles découvertes à Genainville (Val-d'Oise)', *RN*[6] 20 (1978), 117–30 (supersedes a preliminary publ. of 1969).

MÓCSY 1964 A. Mócsy, 'Der Name Flavius als Rangbezeichnung in der Spätantike', *Akte des IV. Internationalen Kongresses f. griechische und lateinische Epigraphik, Wien 17-22. Sept. 1962* (Vienna, 1964), 257–63.

MOLA 1974 M. Mola, 'Le monnayage de bronze des Vandales', *Cahiers numismatiques* 11 (1974), 19–28.

MOLIN 1913 A. de Molin, 'La penny d'or de Lutry', *RSN* 19 (1913), 315–28 (gold penny of Edward the Elder).

MOMMSEN 1888 T. Mommsen, 'Goldbarren aus Sirmium', *ZfN* 16 (1888), 351–8.

MOMMSEN 1910 — 'Das römisch-germanische Herrscherjahr', in his *Gesammelte Schriften* VI (Berlin, 1910), 343–58.

MONNERET 1919–21 U. Monneret de Villard, 'La monetazione nell'Italia barbarica', *RIN* 32 (1919), 22–38, 73–112, 125–38; 33 (1920), 169–232; 34 (1921), 192–218.

MONTPELLIER 1974 *Monnaies d'or et d'argent de la Société archéologique de Montpellier. Journées numismatiques, 1974* (Mimeographed exhibition catalogue, photographic plates.)

MOR 1952 C. G. Mor, *L'età feudale* (Milan, 1952).

MORCALDI *et al.* 1873–83 Morcaldi *et al.* (ed.), *Codex diplomaticus Cavensis*, 8 vols. (Naples-Milan, 1873–83).

MOREHART 1970 M. J. Morehart, 'Some dangers of dating sceattas by typological sequences', *BNJ* 39 (1970), 1–5.

MOREHART 1984 — 'Ango-Saxon art and the "archer" sceat', in Hill and Metcalf 1984, 181–92.

MOREL-FATIO 1871 A. Morel-Fatio, 'Ferreyres. Description de quelques monnaies du XIIe siècle trouvées dans cette localité', *Revue savoisienne* 12 (1871), 33–8 (immobilized temple-type coins w. name of Louis the Pious).

MORLET 1968–72 M.-T. Morlet, *Les noms de personne sur le territoire de l'ancienne Gaule du VIe au XIIe siècle*, 2 vols. (Paris, 1968–72).

MORRISON 1961 K. F. Morrison, 'The gold medallions of Louis the Pious and Lothaire I and the Synod of Paris (825)', *Speculum* 36 (1961), 592–9.

MORRISON 1963 — 'Numismatics and Carolingian trade: a critique of the evidence', *Speculum* 38 (1963), 403–32.

MORRISON and GRUNTHAL 1967 K. F. Morrison and H. Grunthal, *Carolingian Coinage* (NNM 158; New York, 1967). Abbreviated as 'MG.'

MORRISSON 1976 C. Morrisson, 'Les origines du monnayage vandale', in *Actes du 8e Congrès international de numismatique, New York–Washington 1973* (Paris-Basel, 1976), 461–72.

MORRISSON 1980 — 'La trouvaille d'Aïn Kelba et la circulation des *minimi* en Afrique au début du VIe siècle', in *Lafaurie* 1980a, 239–48.

MORRISSON 1983 — 'The re-use of obsolete coins: the case of Roman imperial bronzes revived in the late fifth century', in *Grierson* 1983a, 95–111.

MORRISSON and SCHWARTZ 1982 C. Morrisson and J. H. Schwartz, 'Vandal silver coinage in the name of Honorius', *MN* 27 (1982), 149–79.

MÜLLER 1860 J. H. Müller, *Deutsche Münzgeschichte bis zu der Ottonenzeit* (Leipzig, 1860).

MÜLLER-KARPE 1954 H. Müller-Karpe, 'Das Hammelburger Kriegergrab der Völkerwanderungszeit', *Mainzfränkisches Jahrbuch* 6 (1954), 203–16 (with note by H. J. Kellner on two AR found).

MUNTONI 1972–4 F. Muntoni, *Le monete dei Papi e degli Stati pontifici*, 4 vols. (Rome, 1972–4).

MURATORI 1967 S. Muratori, *Delle monete anonime ravennate che recano la leggenda 'Felix Ravenna'* (Ravenna, 1967) (reprint of 2 articles in *Felix Ravenna* 1 (1911)).

MURPHY 1952 F. X. Murphy, 'Julian of Toledo and the fall of the Visigothic kingdom in Spain', *Speculum* 27 (1952), 1–27.

MUSSET 1965 L. Musset, *Les invasions: les vagues germaniques* (Paris, 1965; the Eng. transl., *The Germanic Invasions* (London, 1975), has a slightly updated bibl.).

MUSSET 1971 — *Les invasions: le second assaut contre l'Europe chrétienne (VIIe–XIe siècles)* (Paris, 1971).

NAHUYS 1868 M. Nahuys, 'Considérations sur quelques monnaies anglo-saxonnes', *RBN*[4] 6 (1868), 65–74 (on the coins found at Hallum).

NAHUYS 1888 — 'Considérations sur les deniers flamands au nom de Baudouin et explication d'un emblème figurant sur quelques-unes de ces monnaies', *RBN* 44 (1888), 447–70 (pp. 459ff. discusses a rev. type of some Merovingian and early Carolingian AR).

NASTER 1950 P. Naster, 'Trouvaille de monnaies carolingiennes à Zelzate (1949)', *RBN* 96 (1950), 208–24.

NAU 1966 E. Nau, 'Die Rübenbacher Argenteus, die Münzenanhänge aus dem Frauengrab Heilbronn-Böckingen und die Silbermünzen des Dortmunder Schatzes', *SM* 16 (1966), 23–33.

NAU 1982 — 'Ein angelsächsischer Sceatta und das Goldblattkreuz von Ulm-Ermingen', *Fundberichte aus Baden-Württemberg* 7 (1982), 475–9.

NAVILLE 1920 L. Naville, 'Fragments de métrologie antique', *RSN* 22 (1920), 42–60.

NAVILLE 1922 — 'La livre romaine et le denier de la loi salique', *RSN* 22 (1920–2), 257–63.

NEWELL 1933 E. T. Newell, *Two Hoards from Minturno* (NNM 60; New York, 1933).

NÖBBE 1936a E. Nöbbe, 'Münzfunde vom Stadtplatz Haithabu 1905–31', in *Festschrift zur Hundertjahrfeier des Museums vorgeschichtlicher Altertümer in Kiel* (Neumünster i.H., 1936), 131–5.

NÖBBE 1936b — 'Der karolingische Münzschatz vom Krinkberg', in *ibid.* 136–60.

NOGUE 1966 M. Nogue, 'Un trésor du IXc siècle, découvert à Arzens, près Carcassonne', *BSFN* 21 (1966), 30–2.

NORTH 1961 J. J. North, 'The coinage of Berhtwulf of Mercia (840–852)', *NCirc* 1961, 213–15.

NORTH 1980 — *English Hammered Coinage* I (2nd edn; London, 1980).

NOVÝ 1967 R. Nový, 'Die Münz- und Wahrungsreform Karls des Grossen', *Historica* 14 (1967), 3–32.

ODDY 1972a W. A. Oddy, 'The analysis of four hoards of Merovingian gold coins', in Hall and Metcalf 1972, 111–25.

ODDY 1972b — 'Analyses of Lombardic tremisses by the specific-gravity method', *NC*[7] 12 (1972), 193–215.

ODDY 1974 — 'Analysis of the gold coinage of Beneventum', *NC*[7] 19 (1974), 78–109.

ODDY 1978 — 'Specific gravity analyses of selected coins', in Stewart 1978, 171–2.

ODDY 1980 — 'The *Moneta Genavensis* of the *Lex Burgondionum*', *RN*[6] 22 (1980), 131–7 (incl. comments by Lafaurie).

ODDY *et al.* 1972 W. A. Oddy *et al.*, 'Analyses of the Sutton Hoo gold coins and of other Merovingian gold coins in the British Museum', in Hall and Metcalf 1972, 96–107.

ODEGAARD 1951 C. Odegaard, 'The empress Engelberge', *Speculum* 26 (1951), 77–103.

O'DONOVAN 1972–3 M. A. O'Donovan, 'An interim revision of episcopal dates for the province of Canterbury, 850–950', *Anglo-Saxon England* 1 (1972), 23–44; 2 (1973), 91–113.

OP DEN VELDE 1982 W. Op den Velde, 'De in Nederland voorkomende sceattas', *De Beeldenaar* 6 (1982), 40–52, 83–96.

OP DEN VELDE *et al.* 1984 W. Op den Velde, W. J. de Boone and A. Pol, 'A survey of sceatta finds from the Low Countries', in Hill and Metcalf 1984, 117–45.

ORLANDONI 1975 M. Orlandoni, 'Una moneta inedita di Baduela rinvenuta in Valle d'Aosta', *QT* 4 (1975), 281–2.

ORLANDONI 1982 — 'Le monete altomedioevali del Museo del Gran San Bernardo nelle vicende archeologiche del Plan de Jupiter', *SM* 32 (1982), 43–9.

PAGAN 1962 H. E. Pagan, 'Anglo-Saxon coins in the Westminster School collection', *BNJ* 31 (1962), 11–22.

PAGAN 1965a — 'Coinage in the age of Burgred', *BNJ* 34 (1965), 11–27.

PAGAN 1965b — 'A third gold coin of Mercia', *BNJ* 34 (1965), 8–10.

PAGAN 1968 — 'A new type for Beonna', *BNJ* 37 (1968), 10–15.

PAGAN 1969 — 'Northumbrian numismatic chronology in the ninth century', *BNJ* 38 (1969), 1–15.

PAGAN 1971 — 'Mr Emery's mint', *BNJ* 40 (1971), 139–70.

PAGAN 1972 — 'An unpublished fragment of a coin of Ceolwulf II', *BNJ* 41 (1972), 14–20.

PAGAN 1973a — 'The Bolton Percy hoard of 1967', *BNJ* 43 (1973), 1–44.

PAGAN 1973b — 'A cross-Channel view of the Fécamp hoard', *NCirc* 81 (1973), 96–7.

PAGAN 1975 — 'A halfpenny of St Eadmund essaying the York mint-signature', *NC*[7] 15 (1975), 191–4.

PAGAN 1982a — 'The coinage of the East Anglian kingdom from 825 to 870', *BNJ* 52 (1982), 41–83.

PAGAN 1982b — 'M. Lecarpentier's gold coin of Dorestad', *NC* 142 (1982), 151–5.

PAGAN 1986 — 'Coinage in southern England, 796–874', in *Dolley* 1986.

PAGE 1973 R. I. Page, *An Introduction to English Runes* (London, 1973).

PAINTER 1972 K. S. Painter, 'A late Roman silver ingot from Kent', *Antiquaries Journal* 52 (1972), 84–92.

PALLMANN 1863–4 R. Pallmann, *Die Geschichte der Völkerwanderung nach den Quellen*, 2 vols. (Gotha, 1863; Weimar, 1864).

PANVINI 1976 F. Panvini Rosati, 'Note di numismatica pisana', *RIN* 78 (1976), 209–19.

PAPADOPOLI 1893 N. Papadopoli, *Le monete di Venezia* I (Venice, 1893).

PARISOT 1899 R. Parisot, *Le royaume de Lorraine sous les Carolingiens (843–923)* (Paris, 1899).

PARTNER 1972 P. Partner, *The Lands of St Peter. The Papal States in the Middle Ages and the Early Renaissance* (London, 1972).

PATTERSON 1972 C. C. Patterson, 'Silver stocks and losses in ancient and medieval times', *Economic History Review*^{2} 25 (1972), 205–35.

PELLEGRINO 1966 E. Pellegrino, 'La monetazione longobarda nel Novarese', in *Atti del I° Convegno internazionale di studi sull'alto medioevo. Orta, 15–18 sett. 1963* (Novara, 1966), 129–41.

PERINI 1902 Q. Perini, *Le monete di Verona* (Rovereto, 1902).

PERPIGNAN 1979 *Monnaies de Catalogne et du Roussillon. Journées numismatiques. Perpignan 1979* (mimeographed catalogue of gold coins of the 5th–7th centuries in the Musée numismatique Joseph Puig of the city).

PERROY 1954 E. Perroy, 'Encore Mahomet et Charlemagne', *Revue historique* 202 (1954), 232–8 (repr. in Hübinger 1968b).

PETRIE 1958 F. Petrie, 'Merowingerzeitliche Voraussetzungen für die Entwicklung des Städtewesens zwischen Maas und Nordsee', *Bonner Jahrbücher* 158 (1958), 233–45.

PFLUGK-HARTTUNG 1903 J. von Pflugk-Harttung, 'Uber Münzen und Siegeln der älteren Päpste', *Quellen und Forschungen aus italienischen Archiven* 5 (1903), 1–18.

PFLUGK-HARTTUNG 1904 — 'Das Hoheitsrecht über Rom auf Münzen und Urkunden bis zur Mitte des 11. Jahrhunderts', *Historiches Jahrbuch* 25 (1904), 34–61, 465–84.

PICQUÉ 1888 C. Picqué, 'Note sur quelques acquisitions faites en 1887 par le Cabinet de Numismatique de l'Etat, à Bruxelles', *ASFN* 12 (1888), 337–44.

PIERFITTE 1933 G. Pierfitte, 'Numismatique toulousaine: les monnaies de Charlemagne et de Charles le Chauve', *RN*^{4} 36 (1933), 149–54.

PIGANIOL 1945 A. Piganiol, 'Le problème de l'or au IVe siècle', *Annales d'histoire sociale* 7 (1945), 47–53 (repr. in his *Scripta varia* III (= *Latomus* 133; Brussels, 1973), 306–15).

PINDER and FRIEDLAENDER 1843 M. Pinder and J. Friedlaender, *Die Münzen Justinians* (Berlin, 1843) (Ostrogothic coins on pp. 58–67).

PINETTE 1897 P. Pinette, 'Le trésor de Bourgneuf', *Gazette numismatique française* 1 (1897), 43–53.

PIOT 1848 C. Piot, 'Recherches sur les ateliers monétaires des Mérovingiens, Carolingiens et empereurs d'Allemagne en Belgique', *RBN* 4 (1848), 322–72 (a useful work ignored by Prou and Belfort).

PIRENNE 1923 H. Pirenne, 'Un contraste économique. Mérovingiens et Carolingiens', *Revue belge de philologie et d'histoire* 2 (1923), 223–35 (repr. in Hübinger 1968b).

PIRENNE 1937 — *Mahomet et Charlemagne* (Paris–Brussels, 1937; Engl. transl. as *Mohammed and Charlemagne* (London, 1939).

PIRIE 1982 E. J. E. Pirie, *Catalogue of the Early Northumbrian Coins in the Museum of Antiquities, Newcastle upon Tyne* (Newcastle upon Tyne, 1982).

PIRIE 1986 — 'Finds of sceattas and stycas of Northumbria', in *Dolley* 1986.

PIRIE and WARREN 1983 E. J. E. Pirie and S. E. Warren, 'Bismuth alloy forgeries of early Northumbrian coins', *Proc. of the 22nd Symposium on Archaeometry, University of Bradford*, ed. A. Aspinall and S. E. Warren (Bradford, 1983), 254–60.

POEY D'AVANT 1858–62 F. Poey d'Avant, *Monnaies féodales de France*, 3 vols. (Paris, 1858, 1860, 1862).

POL 1977 A. Pol, 'De 7e-eeuwse muntvondst Nietap', *JMP* 62–4 (1975–7), 23–62.

POL 1978 — 'De verspreidingsgebieden van in Nederland geslagen Merovingische gouden munten der 7e eeuw', *Westerheem* 27 (1978), 145–55.

POUPARDIN 1901 R. Poupardin, 'Etude sur la diplomatique des princes lombards de Bénévent, de Capoue et de Salerne', *Mélanges d'archéologie et d'histoire* (Ecole française de Rome) 21 (1901), 117–80.

POUPARDIN 1906 — 'Etudes sur l'histoire des principautés lombards de l'Italie méridionale et de leurs rapports avec l'empire franc', *Le Moyen Age*[2] 10 (1906), 1–26, 245–74; 11 (1907), 1–25.

POUPARDIN 1907 — *Les institutions politiques et administratives des principautés lombardes de l'Italie méridionale (IX–XI s.)* (Paris, 1907).

POWICKE and FRYDE 1961 F. M. Powicke and E. B. Fryde, *Handbook of British Chronology* (2nd edn; London, 1961).

PREVITÉ-ORTON 1917 C. W. Previté-Orton, 'Italy and Provence, 900–950', *English Historical Review* 32 (1917), 335–47.

PRIEUR 1927 P. Prieur, 'Oboles de Pépin II, roi d'Aquitaine', *RN*[4] 30 (1927), P.-V. xlii.

PROMIS 1858 D. Promis, *Monete dei romani pontefici avanti il Mille* (Turin, 1858).

PROU 1886 M. Prou, 'Tiers de sou d'or mérovingiens de Tidiriciacum', *RN*[3] 4 (1886), 203–17.

PROU 1888a — 'Catalogue des monnaies mérovingiennes d'Autun', *Mémoires de la Société éduenne* 16 (1888), 1–20.

PROU 1888b — 'Notes sur des tiers de sou mérovingiens du Musée britannique', *RN*[3] 6 (1888), 69–77.

PROU 1888c — 'Les ateliers monétaires mérovingiens', *RN*[3] 6 (1888), 542–50.

PROU 1889 — 'Deux tiers de sou du roi Gontran (561–592)', *RN*[3] 7 (1889), 539–55.

PROU 1890 — 'Inventaire sommaire des monnaies mérovingiennes de la collection d'Amécourt acquises par la Bibliothèque Nationale', *RN*[3] 8 (1890), 145–240, 273–357.

PROU 1891 — 'Monnaies barbares d'argent trouvées dans le cimetière mérovingien d'Herpes', *RN*[3] 9 (1891), 134–45.

PROU 1892a — *Les monnaies mérovingiennes* (*Catalogue des monnaies françaises de la Bibliothèque Nationale*) (Paris, 1892). Abbreviated as 'P'.

PROU 1892b — 'Le monogramme du Christ et la croix sur les monnaies mérovingiennes', in *Mélanges G.B. de Rossi. Suppl. aux Mélanges d'archéologie et d'histoire publiés par l'Ecole française de Rome* 12 (Paris-Rome, 1892), 207–19.

PROU 1893 — 'Recueil de dessins de monnaies mérovingiennes donné à la Bibliothèque Nationale par M. A. de Barthélemy', *RN*[3] 11 (1893), 459–73.

PROU 1895 — 'La livre dite de Charlemagne', *Mémoires de la Société nationale des antiquaires de France*[6] 4 (1895), 244–63.

PROU 1896a — *Les monnaies carolingiennes (Catalogue des monnaies françaises de la Bibliotheque Nationale)* (Paris, 1896). Abbreviated as 'P'.

PROU 1896b — 'Monnaies mérovingiennes acquises par la Bibliothèque Nationale de 1893 à 1896', *RN*[3] 14 (1896), 425–46.

PROU 1897 — 'Notes sur quelques monnaies mérovingiennes', *Gazette numismatique française* 1 (1897), 413–22.

PROU 1898 — 'Note sur le titre de quelques deniers des IXe et XIe siècles essayés à la Monnaie', *Gazette numismatique française* 2 (1898), 227–32.

PROU 1904 — 'Une monnaie de Childebert II', *RN*[4] 8 (1904), 215–21.

PROU 1909 — 'Notes sur le latin des monnaies mérovingiennes', in *Mélanges offerts à M. Maurice Wilmotte* (Paris, 1909), 523–40.

PROU 1910 — 'Le denier de la loi salique', *RN*[4] 14 (1910), 100–4 (repr. from *Le Moyen Age* 1910).

PROU and BOUGENOT 1907 M. Prou and S. Bougenot, 'Catalogue des deniers mérovingiens de la trouvaille de Bais', *RN*[4] 11 (1907), 184–228, 362–96, 481–514 (repr. in Lafaurie 1981d).

QUADRAS Y RAMÓN 1892 *Catálogo de la Collección de monedas y medallas de Manuel Vidal Quadras y Ramón de Barcelona*, 3 vols. (Barcelona, 1892; repr. 1975).

RASHLEIGH 1869 J. Rashleigh, 'Remarks on the coins of the Anglo-Saxon and Danish kings of Northumberland', *NC*[2] 9 (1869), 54–105.

REGLER 1954 H. Regler, 'Ein unbekanntes Gepräge des letzten Vandalenkönigs Gelimer', *Berliner Numismatische Zeitschrift* 16 (1954), 75–7 (a Cigoi forgery, Brunetti 503).

REGLING 1908 K. Regling, *Dortmunder Fund römischer Goldmünzen* (Dortmund, 1908).

REINHART 1937a W. Reinhart, 'Die Münzen des Swebenreiches', *MBNG* 55 (1937), 151–90.

REINHART 1937b — 'Neuerliche Falschungen westgotischer Münzen', *Deutsche Münzblätter* 57 (1937), 225–32.

REINHART 1938 —'Die Münzen des tolosanischen Reiches der Westgoten', *DJBN* 1 (1938), 107–35.

REINHART 1939a — 'Die früheste Münzprägung im Reiche der Merowinger', *DJBN* 2 (1939), 37–56.

REINHART 1939b — 'Über einige weitere Fälschungen westgotischer Münzen', *Deutsche Münzblätter* 59 (1939), 389–91.

REINHART 1940 — 'Die Münzen des westgotischen Reiches von Toledo', *DJBN* 3–4 (1940–41), 69–101 (survey from 507 onwards).

REINHART 1941 — 'Die swebischen und westgotischen Münzen als kulturhistorische Denkmäler', *Germania* 25 (1941), 188–93.

REINHART 1942 — 'El reino hispanico de los Suevos y sus monedas', *Archivo Español de Arqueologia* 15 (1942), 308–28.

REINHART 1944 — 'Los sueldos "gallecanos" – monedas gallegas', *Cuadernos de Estudios Gallegos* 2 (1944), 177–84.

REINHART 1945 — 'Nuevas aportaciones a la numismatica visigoda', *Archivo Español de Arqueologia* 18 (1945), 212–35 (on 5th/6th-century pre-regal coinage).

REINHART 1952 — *Historia general del reino hispanico de los Suevos* (Madrid, 1952).

REIS 1959 P. Batalha Reis, 'Elissabona Felicitas Ivlia. Nova oficina monetária dos Visigodos', *Nummus* 5 (1959), 131–41.

RETHAAN MACARÉ 1838 C. A. Rethaan Macaré, *Verhandeling over de bij Domburg gevondene romeinsche, frankische, britannische, noordsche en andere munten* (Middelburg, 1838).

RETHAAN MACARÉ 1856 — *Tweede verhandeling over de bij Domburg gevonden romeinsche, frankische, britannische en andere munten* (Middelburg, 1856).

RETHAAN MACARÉ 1858 — 'Denier de Pepin', *RN*[2] 3 (1858), 457–8.

RICHARD 1893 A. Richard, 'Observations sur les mines d'argent et l'atelier monétaire de Melle sous les Carolingiens', *RN*[3] 11 (1893), 194–225.

RICHÉ 1974 P. Riché, 'Le renouveau culturel à la cour de Pépin III', *Francia* 2 (1974), 59–70.

RIDGEWAY 1892 W. Ridgeway, *The Origin of Metallic Currency and Weight Standards* (Cambridge, 1892).

RIGOLD 1954 S. E. Rigold, 'An imperial coinage in southern Gaul in the sixth and seventh centuries?', *NC*[6] 14 (1954), 93–133.

RIGOLD 1960 — 'The two primary series of sceattas', *BNJ* 30 (1960–1), 6–53.

RIGOLD 1966 — 'The two primary series of sceattas: addenda and corrigenda', *BNJ* 35 (1966), 1–6.

RIGOLD 1968 — 'The post-Roman coins', in J. P. Bushe-Fox, *Report on the Excavation of the Roman Fort at Richborough* V (London, 1968), 217–23.

RIGOLD 1974 — 'Coins found in Anglo-Saxon burials', in *Coins and the Archaeologist*, ed. R. Reece and J. Casey (Oxford, 1974), 201–5.

RIGOLD 1975 — 'The Sutton Hoo coins in the light of the contemporary background of coinage in England', in Bruce-Mitford 1975, 653–77 (w. list of 6th–7th century gold coins found in England).

RIGOLD 1977a — 'The principal series of English sceattas', *BNJ* 47 (1977), 21–30.

RIGOLD 1977b — 'A group of three sceattas from excavations at Mucking, Essex', *BNJ* 47 (1977), 126–7 (all of Series Bx).

RIGOLD and METCALF 1977 S. E. Rigold and D. M. Metcalf, 'A check-list of English finds of sceattas', *BNJ* 47 (1977), 31–52 (list superseded by Rigold and Metcalf 1984, but illustrations of finds remain useful).

RIGOLD and METCALF 1984 — 'A revised check-list of English finds of sceattas', in Hill and Metcalf 1984, 245–68.

RIISING 1952 A. Riising, 'The fate of Henri Pirenne's theses on the consequences of the Islamic expansion', *Classica et Mediaevalia* 13 (1952), 87–130 (repr. in Hübinger 1968b).

ROACH SMITH 1845 C. Roach Smith, 'Merovingian coins, &c., discovered at St Martin's, near Canterbury', *NC*¹ 7 (1845), 187–91.

ROACH SMITH 1850 — *The Antiquities of Richborough, Reculver, and Lympne* (London, 1850).

ROACH SMITH 1860 — 'On Anglo-Saxon remains recently discovered in various places in Kent', *Archaeologia Cantiana* 3 (1860), 35–46.

ROBERT 1842 P. C. Robert, 'Tiers de sou frappé en 558 au nom de Childebert Ier et de son neveu Chramne', *RN* 1842, 340–3.

ROBERT 1851a — *Monnaies mérovingiennes de la Collection de feu M. Renault* (Metz, 1851).

ROBERT 1851b — *Considérations sur la monnaie à l'époque romaine et description de quelques triens mérovingiens* (Metz, 1851) (reprint of his opening address to the meeting of the Congrès archéologique at Metz in 1846).

ROBERT 1852 — *Etudes numismatiques sur une partie du nord-est de la France* (Metz, 1852).

ROBERT 1863a — 'Sceau et monnaies de Zuentibold, roi de Lorraine; monnaie de son successeur Louis', *Mém. de la Soc. d'archéologie et d'histoire de la Moselle* 1863, 273–6.

ROBERT 1863b — 'Monnaies mérovingiennes. Agaune, Auxerre, Orléans, Famars, Metz, Bellange, Toul, Mayence, Beaucé, Lieuvillers, Jubleins', *RN*² 8 (1863), 342–9.

ROBERT 1866 — 'Mélanges de numismatique. II. Monnaies de Trèves, de Metz et de Verdun', *RN*² 11 (1866), 165–71.

ROBERT 1867 — 'Mélanges de numismatique. III. Tiers de sou d'or austrasiens', *RN*² 12 (1867), 435–45.

ROBERT 1868 — 'Etat actuel de la numismatique de Toul', *RN*² 13 (1868), 453–66.

ROBERT 1879 — 'Numismatique de la province de Languedoc. II. Période wisigothe et franque. III. Période carolingienne', in C. Devic and J. Vaissette, *Histoire générale de Languedoc* VII (2nd edn; Toulouse, 1879), 295–388.

ROBERT 1882a — 'Trésor de Chinon', *ASFN* 6 (1882), 164–78.

ROBERT 1882b — 'Tiers de sou d'or de Marsal, de Vic, de Novéant et de Naix. Observations sur les monnaies mérovingiennes', *Mélanges de numismatique* 3 (1882), 382–400.

ROBERT 1883 — 'Sur la prétendue restauration de Maurice Tibère dans la Province et sur les monnaies qui en seraient la preuve', *Mém. de l'Académie des Inscriptions* 30.2 (1883), 397–433.

ROBERT 1887 — 'Observations sur la deuxième mémoire de M. Deloche relatif aux monnaies d'or frappées sous le roi d'Austrasie Théodebert Ier (539–548)', *Comptes-rendus de l'Académie des Inscriptions*⁴ 15 (1887), 471–80.

ROBERTS 1964 P. C. Roberts, 'The Pirenne thesis', *Classica et Mediaevalia* 25 (1964), 297–315.

ROBINSON 1980 P. H. Robinson, 'A Merovingian tremissis from Norton, Wilts.', *Wiltshire Archaeological Magazine* 74–5 (1979–80), 188–9.

ROEHRICH 1944 A. Roehrich, 'Les monnaies mérovingiennes frappées sur le territoire de la Suisse', *RSN* 31 (1944), 6–24.

ROESDAHL *et al.* 1981 E. Roesdahl *et al.* (ed.), *The Vikings in England and in their Danish Homelands* (London, 1981) (catalogue for an exhibition shown at Copenhagen, Aarhus and York, 1981–2).

ROGER 1905 F. Roger, 'Le trésor d'Huriel', *Mém. de la Soc. des Antiquaires du Centre* 29 (1905), 89–95.

ROLLAND 1932 H. Rolland, *Monnaies françaises. Etude d'après le cabinet numismatique de M. Georges Motte de Roubaix* (Mâcon, 1932).

ROLLAND 1949 — 'Deux deniers merovingiens trouvés à Saint-Rémy', *RN*[5] 11 (1949), 161–2 (of Marseille and Arles).

ROLLAND 1961 — 'Monnaie de Gontran, roi de Bourgogna', *BSFN* 16 (1961), 3–5.

Roman Imperial Coinage *Roman Imperial Coinage*, ed. H. Mattingly and others, 9 vols. (London, 1923–81). Abbreviated as '*RIC*'.

ROMANO and SOLMI 1940 G. Romano and A. Solmi, *Le dominazioni barbariche in Italia 395–888* (3rd edn; Milan, 1940).

RONDIER 1863 – Rondier, 'Remarques sur des monnaies frappées à Melle', *RN*[2] 8 (1863), 131–3.

ROOSENS 1950 H. Roosens, 'Trouvaille de monnaies carolingiennes à Muizen-lez-Malines (1906)', *RBN* 96 (1950), 203–8.

ROSSI 1884 G. B. de Rossi, 'Il tesoro della Casa delle Vestale', *Atti della R. Accademia dei Lincei* 281 (1883–4). Serie terza. *Mém. della Classe di Scienze morali, storiche e filologiche* 13 (1884), 107–34.

ROUCHE 1979 M. Rouche, *L'Aquitaine des Wisigoths aux Arabes 418–781. Naissance d'une région* (Paris, 1979) (but see W. Goffart's review in *Speculum* 56 (1981), 652–6).

ROUEN 1978 *Musée départemental des Antiquités, Rouen. Monnaies, médailles et jetons* (exhibition catalogue produced on the occasion of the visit of the Société française de numismatique, 3–4 June 1978).

RUDING 1840 R. Ruding, *Annals of the Coinage*, 3 vols. (3rd edn; London, 1840).

RUGGERO 1908 G. Ruggero, 'Annotazioni numismatiche italiane. XVII. Un tremisse di Rachis', *RIN* 21 (1908), 137–8.

RUGGINI 1961 L. Ruggini, *Economia e società nell'Italia Annonaria. Rapporti fra agricoltura e commercio dal IV al VI secolo d. C.* (Milan, 1961).

SABATIER 1862 J. Sabatier, *Description générale des monnaies byzantines*, 2 vols. (Paris, 1862).

SAINT-OMER 1983 *Musée de Saint-Omer. Catalogue des monnaies d'or* (Arras, 1983) (special number of the Bull. de la Commission Départementale d'Histoire et d'Archéologie du Pas-de-Calais issued on the occasion of the visit of the Société française de numismatique to Saint-Omer, 4–5 June 1983).

SALOMONSON 1961 J. W. Salomonson, 'Zwei spätrömische Geschenk-Silberbarren mit eingestempelten Inschriften in Leiden', *Oudheidkundige Mededeelingen uit het Rijksmuseum van Oudheden te Leiden* 42 (1961), 63–77.

SAMBON 1898 A. Sambon, 'Monnaies italiennes inédites ou incertaines', *RN*[4] 2 (1898), 293–312.

SAMBON 1902 — 'Le sou d'or italique et le sou de comte de douze deniers', *RN*[4] 6 (1902), 115–21.

SAMBON 1912 G. Sambon, *Repertorio generale delle monete coniate in Italia e da Italiani al estero dal secolo V al XX.* I: *Periodo dal 476 al 1266* (Paris, 1912).

SAMBON 1919 A. Sambon, *Recueil des monnaies du sud de l'Italie avant le domination des Normands* (Paris, 1919) (apart from the preface (pp. i–xvii) and the index, this reproduces articles in *Le Musée* for 1908, published early enough to be used by Wroth).

SAULCY 1837a F. de Saulcy, 'Deniers carlovingiens, déterrés à Belvezet, près d'Usez (Gard)', *RN* 1837, 347–59, 376.

SAULCY 1837b — 'Triens mérovingiens de coin moderne', *RN* 1837, 299–301 (of the mint of Trier).

SAULCY 1838 — 'Monnaies mérovingiennes inédites', *RN* 1838, 266–75.

SAUVAIRE 1882 J. Sauvaire, *Matériaux pour servir à l'histoire de la numismatique et de la métrologie musulmanes* (Paris, 1882).

SAWYER 1968 P. H. Sawyer, *Anglo-Saxon Charters: An Annotated List and Bibliography* (London, 1968).

SCHÄRLI 1983 B. Schärli, 'Ein Basler denar Ludwigs IV. des Kindes (900–11) aus der Ajoie (1982)', *SM* 33 (1983), 16–20.

SCHIAPARELLI 1929–33 L. Schiaparelli (ed.), *Codice diplomatico longobardo* (Fonti per la Storia d'Italia 62, 64), 2 vols. (Rome, 1929–33); supplementary vol., ed. C.-R. Brühl (Rome, 1973).

SCHIEDER 1976 T. Schieder (ed.), *Handbuch der europäischen Geschichte* I (Stuttgart, 1976).

SCHIPA 1887 M. Schipa, 'Storia del principato longobardo di Salerno', *Archivo storico delle provincie napoletane* 12 (1887), 79–137, 209–64, 513–88, 740–77 (repr. in Hirsch and Schipa 1968).

SCHMIDT 1910–18 L. Schmidt, *Geschichte der deutschen Stämme bis zum Ausgange der Völkerwanderung*, 2 vols. (Berlin, 1910–18).

SCHMIDT 1942 — *Geschichte der Wandalen* (2nd edn; Munich, 1942).

SCHMIT 1920 E. Schmit, 'Contribution à l'étude de la numismatique carolingienne. Découverte à Breuvery, canton d'Ecury-sur-Coole (Marne)', *Compte-rendu de la 44e session de l'Association française pour l'avancement des sciences, Strasbourg* 1920, 596–603.

SCHNEIDEMÜLLER 1979 B. Schneidemüller, *Karolingische Tradition und frühes französisches Königtum: Untersuchungen zur Herrschaftslegitimationen der westfränkisch-französischen Monarchie im 10. Jahrhundert* (Wiesbaden, 1979).

SCHOLTEN 1945 C. Scholten, 'Der Munten in de Lex Frisionum', *JMP* 30–2 (1943–5), 1–68.

SCHRAMM 1954 P. E. Schramm, *Herrschaftszeichen und Staatssymbolik* I (=Schriften der Monumenta Germaniae Historica 13.1; Stuttgart, 1954).

SCHRAMM 1968–71 — *Kaiser, Könige und Päpste. Gesammelte Aufsätze zur Geschichte des Mittelalters*, 4 vols. (Stuttgart, 1968–71) (discussion of *Munus divinum* formula in II.63–7).

SCHRÖDER 1904 E. Schröder, 'Saiga', *ZfN* 24 (1904), 339–46.

SEEBOHM 1903 F. Seebohm, 'On the currencies of the German tribes', *Vierteljahrschrift für Sozial- und Wirtschaftsgeschichte* 1 (1903), 171–95.

SEEGER 1976 J. A. Seeger, 'A hoard of late Roman bronze coins', *Coin Hoards* 2 (1976), no. 187, pp. 55–60.

SEGRÈ 1931 A. Segrè, 'La circolazione monetaria del regno dei Franchi', *Rivista storica italiana* 48 (1931), 465–98.

SENCKLER 1850 A. Senckler, 'Übersicht der Münzgeschichte des Rheinlandes bis zur Mitte des achten Jahrhunderts', *Jahrbücher des Vereins von Alterthumsfreunden im Rheinlande* 15 (1850), 143–72.

SERAFINI 1910–28 C. Serafini, *Le monete e le bolle plumbee pontificie del Medagliere Vaticano*, 4 vols. (Milan, 1910–28).

SERRURE 1880 C. P. Serrure, *Notice sur le cabinet monétaire de S.A. le prince de Ligne, d'Amblise et d'Epinoy* . . . (2nd edn; Ghent, 1880).

SERRURE 1882 R. Serrure, 'Numismatique mérovingienne', *BMNA* 2 (1882–3), 155–6 (discussion of a brochure of 1713).

SERRURE 1885 C. A. Serrure, 'Dorestad et Wijk-bij-Duurstede', *BMNA* 4 (1884–5), 37–48.

SERRURE 1892 R. Serrure, 'Jelsum', *Bull. de numismatique* 1 (1891–2), 146.

SICKEL 1902 W. Sickel, 'Alberich II und das Kirchenstaat', *Mittheilungen des Instituts f. Oesterreichischen Geschichte* 23 (1902), 50–126.

SIEMS 1980 H. Siems, *Studien zur Lex Frisionum* (Ebelsbach, 1980).

SIMONETT 1978 C. Simonett, 'Die für Chur geprägte Goldmünze Karls des Grossen', *QT* 7 (1978), 275–8.

SIMSON 1874–6 B. Simson, *Jahrbücher des fränkischen Reiches unter Ludwig dem Frommen*, 2 vols. (Leipzig, 1874–6).

SKAARE 1966 K. Skaare, 'Die karolingischen Münzfunde in Skandinavien und der Schatzfund von Hon', *HBN* 20 (1966), 395–408.

SMART 1985 V. J. Smart, 'The moneyers of St. Edmund', *Hikuin* 11 (1985), 83–90.

SMART 1986 — 'Scandinavians, Celts and Germans in Anglo-Saxon England: the evidence of moneyers' names', in *Dolley* 1986.

SMYTH 1975–9 A. P. Smyth, *Scandinavian York and Dublin*, 2 vols. (Dublin and New Jersey, 1975/79).

SMYTH 1978 — 'The chronology of Northumbrian history in the ninth and tenth centuries', in *Viking Age York and the North*, ed. R. A. Hall (CBA Research Reports 27; London, 1978), 8–10.

SOETBEER 1862–6 A. Soetbeer, 'Beiträge zur Geschichte des Geld- und Münzwesens in Deutschland', *Forschungen zur deutschen Geschichte* 1 (1862), 205–300, 543–636; 2 (1862), 293–383; 4 (1864), 241–354; 6 (1866), 1–112.

SPUFFORD 1961 P. Spufford, 'Some hoard evidence from a nineteenth-century collection', *BNJ* 30 (1961), 213–16.

STAHL 1976 A. M. Stahl, 'The Merovingian CA coinage of Austrasia', *MN* 21 (1976), 129–51.

STAHL 1982 — *The Merovingian Coinage of the Region of Metz* (Numismatica Lovaniensia 5; Louvain-la-Neuve, 1982).

STEFAN 1925 F. Stefan, 'Die Münzstatte Sirmium unter den Ostgoten und Gepiden', *BMF* 16 (1925), 231–9, 250–69 (and as a separate brochure, Halle/Saale, 1925).

STEFAN 1957 — 'Münze der Rugenkönige aus der ehemaligen Rugenlande Oesterreichs', *Congrès international de numismatique, Paris, 1953* II: *Actes* (Paris, 1957), 443-51.

STEIN 1947 S. Stein, 'Lex Salica I, II', *Speculum* 22 (1947), 113–34, 395–418.

STEIN 1959/1949 E. Stein, *Histoire du Bas-Empire*, Fr. edn by J.-R. Palanque, 2 vols. (Paris, 1959 and 1949).

STEINBÜCHEL 1826 A. Steinbüchel, *Notice sur les médallions romains en or du Musée impérial et royal de Vienne trouvés en Hongrie dans les années MDCCXCVII et MDCCCV* (Vienna, 1826).

STEINMEYER and SIEVERS 1879–1922 E. von Steinmeyer and E. Sievers, *Die althochdeutschen Glossen*, 5 vols. (Berlin, 1879–1922).

STENTON 1958 F. M. Stenton, 'The Anglo-Saxon coinage and the historian', in his *Preparatory to Anglo-Saxon England* (1970), 371–82 (a lecture delivered to the British Numismatic Society in 1958).

STENTON 1961 *Anglo-Saxon Coins. Studies Presented to F. M. Stenton on the Occasion of his 80th Birthday*, ed. R. H. M. Dolley (London, 1961).

STENTON 1971 — *Anglo-Saxon England* (3rd edn; Oxford, 1971).

STEPHENS 1866–1901 G. Stephens, *The Old-Northern Runic Monuments of Scandinavia and England*, 4 vols. (London, 1866–1901).

STEWART 1967 B. H. I. H. Stewart, 'The St Martin coins of Lincoln', *BNJ* 36 (1967), 46–54.

STEWART 1978 — 'Anglo-Saxon gold coins', in *Scripta Nummaria Romana, Essays Presented to Humphrey Sutherland*, ed. R. A. G. Carson and C. M. Kraay (London, 1978), 143–72 (with appendix by W. A. Oddy).

STEWART 1982 — 'The anonymous Anglo-Viking issue with Sword and Hammer types and the coinage of Sihtric I', *BNJ* 52 (1982), 108–16.

STEWART 1984 — 'The early English denarial coinage, *c.* 680–*c.* 750', in Hill and Metcalf 1984, 5–26.

STEWART 1986 — 'The London mint and the coinage of Offa', in *Dolley* 1986.

STEYERT 1897 A. Steyert, *Nouvelle histoire de Lyon* II (Lyon, 1897).

STIENNON 1960 J. Stiennon, 'Le denier de Charlemagne au nom de Roland', *Cahiers de civilisation mediévale* 3 (1960), 90–5.

STORCH 1971 R. H. Storch, 'The trophy and the cross; pagan and Christian symbolism in the fourth and fifth centuries', *Byzantion* 40 (1971), 105–17.

STÜCKELBERG 1898 E. A. Stückelberg, 'Les titres de Théoderic', *RIN* 11 (1898), 63–6.

SUCHODOLSKI 1965 S. Suchodolski, 'Les poids des monnaies de Charlemagne émises après la réforme', in *Dona Numismatica Walter Hävernick zum 23. Januar 1965 dargebracht*, ed. P. Berghaus and G. Hatz (Hamburg, 1965), 43–50.

SUCHODOLSKI 1974 — 'Karolińskie wolywy na mennictvo europejskie w X i XI w.', *Wiadomosci Numizmatycny* 18/1 (1974), 17–23 (influence of Carolingian coinage; Eng. summary).

SUCHODOLSKI 1976 — 'Les influences carolingiennes sur le monnayage européen aux Xe et XIe siècles', in *Actes du 8e Congrès international de numismatique. New York–Washington 1973* (Paris–Basel, 1976), 477–85.

SUCHODOLSKI 1980 — 'Les livres carolingiennes', in *II Simposi Numismatic de Barcelona* (Barcelona, 1980), 43–6.

SUCHODOLSKI 1981a — 'Vom Gold zum Silber', in *Lagom. Festschrift für Peter Berghaus*, ed. T. Fischer and P. Ilisch (Münster, 1981), 97–104.

SUCHODOLSKI 1981b — 'La date de la grande réforme monétaire de Charlemagne', *QT* 10 (1981), 399–409.

SUCHODOLSKI 1982 — *Moneta i obrót pieniężny w Europie zachodniej ('Coinage and monetary circulation in Western Europe')* (Wrocław (etc.), 1982).

SUCHODOLSKI 1983 — 'On the rejection of good coin in Carolingian Europe', in *Grierson* 1983a, 147–52.

SUHLE 1929 A. Suhle, 'Die Münzprägung der Franken unter den merowingischen Königen', *Trierer Zeitschrift* 4 (1929), 9–17.

SUNDWALL 1915 J. Sundwall, *Weströmische Studien* (Berlin, 1915).

SUNDWALL 1919 — *Abhandlungen zur Geschichte des ausgehenden Römertums* (Helsinki, 1919).

SUTHERLAND 1942 C. H. V. Sutherland, 'Anglo-Saxon sceattas in England: their origin, chronology and distribution', NC^6 2 (1942), 42–70.

SUTHERLAND 1948 — *Anglo-Saxon Gold Coinage in the Light of the Crondall Hoard* (Oxford, 1948).

SUTHERLAND 1973 — *English Coinage 600–1900* (London, 1973) (see the detailed review by C. S. S. Lyon, *BNJ* 44 (1974), 84–8).

TAGLIAFERRI 1964 A. Tagliaferri, 'Le diverse fasi dell'economia longobarda con particolare riguardo al commercio internazionale', in *Problemi della civiltà e dell'economia longobarda. Scritti in memoria di G. P. Bognetti* (Milan, 1964), 227–88.

TAYLOR 1970 H. M. Taylor, 'The origin, purpose, and date of pilaster-strips in Anglo-Saxon architecture', *North Staffs. Journal of Field Studies* 10 (1970), 21–47 (inc. an appendix by M. Dolley on the 'Church tower' coins of Edward the Elder at pp. 42–3).

TELLENBACH 1957 G. Tellenbach, 'Der grossfrankische Adel und die Regierung Italiens in der Blütezeit des Karolingerreiches', in *Studien und Vorarbeiten zur Geschichte des Grossfränkischen und Frühdeutschen Adels*, ed. G. Tellenbach (Freiburg im Br., 1957), pp. 40–70.

TESSIER 1964 G. Tessier, *Le baptême de Clovis* ('Trente journées qui ont fait la France. 3'; Paris, 1964).

TESTART 1907 G. Testart, 'Les anciennes fouilles de Mont-Auxois', *Pro Alésia* 1907–8, 260–8, 293.

THOMPSON 1915 J. W. Thompson, 'The commerce of France in the ninth century', *Journal of Political Economy* 23 (1915), 857–87.

THOMPSON 1954 M. Thompson, *Coins, from the Roman through the Venetian Period* (The Athenian Agora II; Princeton, 1954).

THOMPSON 1956 J. D. A. Thompson, *Inventory of British Coin Hoards AD 600–1500* (RNS Special Publication 1; London, 1956).

THOMPSON, M., 1966 M. Thompson, 'The monogram of Charlemagne in Greek', *MN* 12 (1966), 125–7 (repr. in *DAN*, no. XIX).

THOMPSON, E. A., 1966 E. A. Thompson, *The Visigoths in the Time of Ulfila* (Oxford, 1966).

THOMPSON 1969 — *The Visigoths in Spain* (Oxford, 1969).

THOMSEN 1873–6 *Catalogue de la collection de monnaies de feu Christian Jürgensen Thomsen. 2e partie. Les monnaies du moyen-âge*, 3 vols. (Copenhagen, 1873–6) (coll. acq. by the National Museum of Denmark).

THORPE 1840 [B. Thorpe (ed.)], *Ancient Laws and Institutes of England*, 2 vols. (London, 1840).

TOCH 1982 M. Toch, 'Der Mankus – eine spätmittelalterliche Auferstehung', *JNG* 31–2 (1981–2), 127–32.

TOLSTOI 1912–14 J. Tolstoi, *Monnaies byzantines*, 9 fasc. (unfinished) (St Petersburg, 1912–14; repr. Amsterdam, 1968).

TOMASINI 1964 W. H. Tomasini, *The Barbaric Tremissis in Spain and Southern France, Anastasius to Leovigild* (NNM 152; New York, 1964).

TONINI 1863 P. Tonini, 'Denier de Charlemagne portant la légende FLORENT', *RN*[2] 8 (1863), 124–30.

TOURNEUR 1923 V. Tourneur, 'Le sou de douze deniers de la loi des Francs Ripuaires', *Revue belge de philologie et d'histoire* 2 (1923), 215–22.

TOYNBEE 1944 J. M. C. Toynbee, *Roman Medallions* (New York, 1944).

TOYNBEE 1947, 1951 — 'Roma and Constantinopolis in Late-Antique art from 312 to 365', *Journal of Roman Studies* 37 (1947), 135–44; continued from 365 to 578 in *Studies Presented to David Moore Robinson*, ed. G. E. Mylonas (St Louis, 1951), II, 261–77.

TRAVAGLINI 1974 E. Travaglini, *Thesaurus Massafrensis* (Brindisi, 1974).

TRAVER 1938 E. Traver, *Histoire de Melle* (Melle, 1938).

TRICOU 1965 J. Tricou, 'Légendes et symboles chrétiens des monnaies burgondes', *Studi di Antichità cristiana* 26 (1965), 551–5 (w. bibl. of Burgundian coinage).

TROUSSEL 1950 M. Troussel, 'Les monnaies vandales d'Afrique: découvertes de Bou-Lilate et du Hamma', *Recueil des Notices et Mémoires de la Société archéologique de Constantine* 67 (1950), 147–94.

TURCAN 1961 R. Turcan, 'Trésors monétaires à Tipasa: la circulation de bronze en Afrique romaine et vandale aux Ve et VIe siècles ap. J.-C.', *Libyca: Archéologie-Epigraphie* 9 (1961), 201–57.

TURCAN 1972 — 'Une trouvaille monétaire à Announa (Algérie)', *Latomus* 31 (1972), 130–45.

ULLMANN 1970 W. Ullmann, *The Growth of Papal Government in the Middle Ages* (3rd edn; London, 1970).

ULRICH-BANSA 1949 O. Ulrich-Bansa, *Moneta Mediolanensis (352–498)* (Venice, 1949).

VACANDARD 1896 E. Vacandard, 'Le règne de Thierry III et la chronologie des moines de Fontenelle', *Revue des questions historiques* 59 (1896), 491–506.

VALDEAVELLANO 1961 L. G. de Valdeavellano, 'La moneda y la economia de cambio en la peninsula iberica desde el siglo VI hasta mediados del siglo XI', in *Moneta e scambi nell' alto medioevo* (Spoleto, 1961), 203–30.

VANDERKINDERE 1872 L. Vanderkindere, 'La signification de CLUSAS', *Comptes-rendus de la Commission royale d'histoire* (Académie royale de Belgique)[3] 14 (1872), 241–5.

VAN ES 1969 W. A. van Es, 'Excavations at Dorestad; a preliminary report: 1967–68', *Berichten van de Rijksdienst voor het Oudheidkundig Bodemonderzoek* 19 (1969), 183–207.

VAN ES *et al.* 1980 W. A. van Es *et al.*, *Excavations at Dorestad* I: *The Harbour, Hoogstraat I* (The Hague, 1980).

VAN GELDER 1961 H. E. van Gelder, 'De karolingische muntslag te Duurstede', *JMP* 48 (1961), 15–42.

VAN GELDER 1965 — 'Le trésor carolingien d'Ide', *RN*[6] 7 (1965), 241–61.

VAN GELDER 1969 — 'Muntvondst Roermond', *De Geuzenpenning* 19 (1969), 25–7 (preliminary summary).

VAN GELDER 1980 — 'Coins from Dorestad, Hoogstraat I', in Van Es *et al.* 1980, 212–24.

VANHOUDT 1982 H. Vanhoudt, 'De merovingische munten in het Penningkabinet van de Koninklijke Bibliotheek te Brussel. Een katalogus van de hedendaagse verzameling', *RBN* 128 (1982), 95–194.

VAN HOUTTE *et al.* 1949 J. D. van Houtte *et al.* (ed.), *Algemene geschiedensis der Nederlanden* I: *Oudheid en vroege middeleeuwen tot het jaar 925* (Utrecht, 1949).

VANNAIRE 1867 V. Vannaire, 'Monnaies carlovingiennes découvertes à Gannat (Allier)', *RN*[2] 12 (1867), 316–18.

VANNÉRUS 1947 J. Vannérus, 'Où chercher dans nos contrées les ateliers monétaires mérovingiens?', *RBN* 93 (1947), 41–56.

VANNÉRUS 1948 — 'Les deniers de Charles le Chauve (840–877) aux légendes DE ou IN FISCO ...', *RBN* 94 (1948), 77–100.

VAN REY 1972 M. van Rey, 'Die Münzprägung Karls des Kahlen und die westfränkische Königslandschaft', in *Die Stadt in der europäischen Geschichte. Festschrift Edith Ennen* (Bonn, 1972), 153–84.

VASILIEV 1950 A. A. Vasiliev, *Justin the First* (Dumbarton Oaks Studies I; Washington, 1950).

VASSY 1928 A. Vassy, 'Note sur la trouvaille de monnaies d'or de Viviers', in *Rhodania. Congrès d'Aubenas et de Val-les-Bains (1927) de l'Association des préhistoriens, des archéologues et des numismates du Bassin du Rhône* (Vienne, 1928), 120–8.

VELAZQUEZ 1759 L. J. Velazquez, *Congeturas sobre las medallas de los reyes Godos y Suevos de España* (Malaga, 1759).

VERCAUTEREN 1934a F. Vercauteren, *Etude sur les civitates de la Belgique seconde* (Brussels, 1934).

VERCAUTEREN 1934b — 'L'interprétation économique d'une trouvaille de monnaies carolingiennes faite près d'Amiens en 1865', *Revue belge de philologie et d'histoire* 13 (1934), 752–8.

VERCAUTEREN 1961 — 'Monnaie et circulation monétaire en Belgique et dans le nord de la France du VIe au XIe siècle', in *Moneta e scambi nell'alto medioevo* (Spoleto, 1961), 279–340.

VERMEULE 1958 C. C. Vermeule, *Aspects of Victoria on Coins, Gems and in Monumental Art* (London, 1958).

VIAN 1929 C. Vian, 'Le trésor de Viviers', *RN*[4] 32 (1929), 109–10, 249.

VIERCK 1974 H. Vierck, 'Werke des Eligius', in *Studien zur vor- und frühgeschichtlichen Archäologie. Festschrift für Joachim Werner zum 65. Geburtstag* II (Munich, 1974), 309–85.

VINCENT 1927 A. Vincent, *Les noms de lieux en Belgique* (Brussels, 1927).

VINCENT 1937 — *Toponomie de la France* (Brussels, 1937).

VISCONTI 1921 A Visconti, '"Aurum figurare, monetam configere" (a proposito del c.242 di Rotari)', *Rendiconti del Reale Istituto Lombardo di scienze e lettere*[2] 54 (1921), 286–94.

VIVES 1960 J. Vives, 'Sobre la leyenda "A Deo vita" de Hermenegildo', *Analecta sacra Tarraconensia* 32 (1960), 31–4 (comment on Díaz 1960).

VOILLEMIER 1840 J.-B. Voillemier, 'Notice sur un sol d'or mérovingien', *RN* 1840, 29–38.

VOILLEMIER 1841 — 'Des premières monnoies d'or mérovingiennes, et spécialement de quelques-unes de Théodebert Ier', *RN* 1841, 91–123.

VÖLCKERS 1952 H. H. Völckers, 'Die *Christiana Religio* Gepräge. Ein Beitrag zur Karolingerforschung', *HBN* 6–7 (1952–3), 9–54.

VÖLCKERS 1965 — *Karolingische Münzfunde der Frühzeit (751–800)* (Abhandlungen der Akademie der Wissenschaften in Göttingen, Philologisch-Historische Klasse[3] 61; Göttingen, 1965).

VOLZ 1971 P. Volz, 'Königliche Münzhoheit und Münzprivilegien im Karolingischen Reich und die Entwicklung in der sächsischen und fränkischen Zeit. I. Die karolingische Zeit', *JNG* 21 (1971), 157–86.

WAITZ 1860 G. Waitz, 'Uber die Münzverhältnisse in den älteren Rechtsbüchern des fränkischen Reichs', *Abhandlungen der k. Gesellschaft der Wissenschaften zu Göttingen, Hist.- Philol. Classe* 9 (1860), 221–59.

WALLACE-HADRILL 1952 J. M. Wallace-Hadrill, 'Archbishop Hincmar and the authorship of *Lex Salica*', *Revue d'histoire du droit* 20 (1952) (repr. in Wallace-Hadrill 1962, 95–120).

WALLACE-HADRILL 1962 — *The Long-Haired Kings and other Studies in Frankish History* (London, 1962).

WAUTERS 1882–4 A. Wauters, 'Le monnayage de l'or en Belgique au XIIe et au XIIIe siècle', *BMNA* 2 (1882–3), 122–7; 3 (1883–4), 95–6.

WELLS 1972 C. Wells, 'An orthographic approach to early Frankish personal names', *Trans. of the Philological Society* 1972, 101–64.

WERNER 1935 J. Werner, *Münzdatierte Austrasische Grabfunde* (Berlin, 1935).

WERNER 1954 — *Waage und Geld in der Merowingerzeit* (Sitzungsberichte der Bayerischen Akademie der Wissenchaften 1954. 1; Munich, 1954).

WERNER 1961 — 'Fernhandel und Naturalwirtschaft im östlichen Merowingerreich nach archäologischen und numismatischen Zeugnissen', in *Moneta e scambi nell'alto medioevo* (Spoleto, 1961), 557–618, 687–97 (repr. in *Berichte der Römisch-Germanischen Kommission* 42 (1961), 307–46).

WERNER 1971 — 'Neue Analyse des Childerichgrabes von Tournai', *Rheinische Vierteljahrsblätter* 35 (1971), 43–6.

WERNER 1976 K. F. Werner, 'Westfranken-Frankreich unter den Spätkarolinger und frühen Kapetingern (880–1060)', in Schieder 1976, 731–83.

WHITELOCK 1930 D. Whitelock, *Anglo-Saxon Wills* (Oxford, 1930).

WHITELOCK 1979 — *English Historical Documents* I: *c. 500–1042* (2nd edn; London–New York, 1979).

WICKHAM 1980 C. Wickham, 'Economic and social institutions in northern Tuscany in the 8th century', in C. Wickham *et al.*, *Istituzioni ecclesiastiche della Toscana medioevale* (Galatina, 1980), 7–34.

WICKHAM 1981 — *Early Medieval Italy. Central Power and Local Society 400–1000* (Manchester, 1981).

WIELANDT 1939a F. Wielandt, 'Die Monetarmünzen der oberrheinischen merowinger Münzstätten', *DJBN* 2 (1939), 57–84.

WIELANDT 1939b — 'Bodman und Zürich, zwei bisher unbekannte merowinger Münzstätten im Alemannenland', *Zeitschrift f. d. Geschichte des Oberrheins*[2] 52 (1939), 424–43.

WIELANDT 1941 — 'Zur Frage der merowingischen Prägung in Zürich', *Zeitschrift f. d. Geschichte des Oberrheins*[2] 54 (1941), 456–67.

WIELANDT 1951 — 'Zum Münzwesen der Merowinger in Baden', *Zeitschrift f. d. Geschichte des Oberrheins* 99 (1951), 613–16 (AR from Rheinsheim graves).

WIELANDT 1967 — 'Die Fundmünzen aus dem Fränkischen Gräberfeld Klepsau, Krs. Buchen', *HBN* 7 (1967), 11–20.

WIELANDT 1971 — *Die Basler Münzprägung von der Merowingerzeit bis zur Verpfändung der bischöflichen Münze an die Stadt im Jahr 1373* (Bern, 1971).

WIGERSMA 1902 S. Wigersma, 'Muntvondst te Oudwoude', *De Vrije Fries*[4] 20 (1902), 65–82.

WILDE and DOMPIERRE DE CHAUFEPIÉ 1898 C. Wilde and H. J. de Dompierre de Chaufepié, 'La trouvaille d'Escharen', *RBN* 54 (1898), 253–72.

WILLERS 1898 H. Willers, 'Römische Silberbarren mit Stempeln', *NZ* 30 (1898), 211–35.

WILSON and BLUNT 1961 D. M. Wilson and C. E. Blunt, 'The Trewhiddle hoard', *Archaeologia* 98 (1961), 75–120.

WIT 1980 G. W. de Wit, 'Zur Datierung spätkarolingischer Münzen', *SM* 30 (1980), 10–13.

WOLFF 1965 P. Wolff, 'L'Aquitaine et ses marges', in *Karl der Grosse* I, ed. W. Braunfels (Düsseldorf, 1965), 269–306 (repr. in his *Regards sur le Midi médiéval* (Toulouse, 1978), 20–67).

WOLFRAM 1980 H. Wolfram, *Geschichte der Goten, von den Anfängen bis zur Mitte des sechsten Jahrhunderts* (2nd edn; Munich, 1980).

WOOD 1983 I. N. Wood, *The Merovingian North Sea* (Occasional Papers in Medieval Topics 1; Alingsås, 1983).

WORSAAE 1851 J. J. A. Worsaae, *Minder om de Danske og Nordmaendene i England, Skotland og Irland* (Copenhagen, 1851).

YPEY 1959 J. Ypey, 'De verspreiding van vroegmiddeleeuwsche vondsten in Nederland', *Berichten van de Rijksdienst voor het Oudheidkundig Bodemonderzoek* 9 (1959), 98–118.

YVON 1953 J. Yvon, 'Note sur deux groupes de monnaies mérovingiennes du nord-est de la Gaule', *RN*^{5} 15 (1953), 67–77.

ZADOKS-JOSEPHUS JITTA 1949 A. N. Zadoks-Josephus Jitta, 'Vroeg-Karolingische munten van Dorestad', *JMP* 36 (1949), 96–8.

ZADOKS-JOSEPHUS JITTA 1959a — 'Problemen van de merovingische muntslag in Nederland', *De Geuzenpenning* 9 (1959), 13–17.

ZADOKS-JOSEPHUS JITTA 1959b — 'Muntsieraden', in *Honderd eeuw en Nederland (= Antiquity and Survival* II, 1959), 168–77.

ZADOKS-JOSEPHUS JITTA 1960 — 'Midlum (Fr.) 1925', *JMP* 47 (1960), 94–6.

ZADOKS-JOSEPHUS JITTA 1961 — 'De eerste muntslag te Duurstede', *JMP* 48 (1961), 1–14.

ZEDELIUS 1980 V. Zedelius, 'Neue Sceattas aus dem Rheinland–Bonn und Xanten', *Zeitschrift f. Archäologie des Mittelalters* 8 (1980), 139–52.

ZÖLLNER 1970 E. Zöllner, *Geschichte der Franken bis zur Mitte des sechsten Jahrhundert* (Munich, 1970).

CATALOGUE

FORMATION OF THE COLLECTIONS

A summary list of previous owners referred to in the catalogue is provided on pp. 399–414. A consolidated list, expanded to include some account of their interests and periods of activity where these are known, is reserved for the final volume. But some account must be given here of the Fitzwilliam Museum collection, the Grierson collection, and the collections of the colleges. That of the second has been expanded to include the Grantley collection, partly because this was the source of a substantial proportion of the Grierson coins and partly because Lord Grantley's death during the Second World War meant that neither his collecting activities nor the fate of his great collection could receive the attention that was their due.

(i) THE FITZWILLIAM MUSEUM COLLECTION

The nucleus of the Fitzwilliam Museum collection is formed by the Old University Collection, originally kept in the University Library and transferred in two cabinets to the Fitzwilliam Museum by a Grace of 30 April 1856.

The University Collection started through the bequest in 1589 by Andrew Perne, Master of Peterhouse, of his 'greatest black book of antiquities of gold and silver coins of emperors and consuls of Rome and other antiquities'. An inventory, printed as a broadside, was kept with the coins until the early eighteenth century, but no copy is known to survive. Other collections were bequeathed to the University in 1686 by Owen Mayfield, Mayor of Cambridge, and in 1774 by Roger Gale, Fellow of Trinity. Gale's collection consisted only of Roman coins and was kept separate from the others, which had fallen into disorder by the early eighteenth century. A manuscript catalogue prepared later in the century of the University's general collection (excluding Gale's which was separately catalogued) shows that it contained more than 400 Roman coins, with some 30 Greek, 60 medieval English, and 100 Continental coins of the sixteenth and seventeenth centuries. Most of the Roman coins presumably came from Perne and the Continental coins from Mayfield, but we cannot ascribe provenances to the coins more specifically.

The Museum's own collection of medieval European coins, excluding those on loan from the colleges, today numbers over three thousand, about three-quarters of them being English, Scottish or Irish. Only rarely can provenances be ascribed to coins acquired in the second half of the nineteenth century and the first years of the twentieth, since it was not thought necessary at the time to keep a precise record. Detailed accession registers date from 1909.

Such medieval coins as came to the Museum in the half-century after 1856 were mainly English and formed parts of more substantial gifts. The most important of these were the collection of the Cambridge Antiquarian Society in 1886, which included significant material from the Cuerdale hoard and of which a catalogue had been published in 1847 (see *SCBI* Cambridge, p. x), and those given in the 1860s by Churchill Babington (1821–89), Disney Professor of Archaeology, a scholar with varied interests in botany, ornithology, classics and medieval history; by A. A. Vansittart (1824–82) of Trinity, who gave two cabinets of English and foreign coins, said to include some very fine pieces, in 1864 and a further series in 1877; and by Dr G. M. Bacon (d. 1883) of Fulbourn, who bequeathed a cabinet of English and foreign coins. A major addition was made by the Rev. W. G. Searle (1829–1913), who interested himself in the well-being of the Museum's collection from the 1850s onwards: he served on the Syndicate as early as 1856 and was Honorary Keeper 1909–13. In 1899 he presented his whole collection of some 12,000 ancient, medieval and modern coins. Searle was a scholar with wide antiquarian interests – his many publications include an *Onomasticon Anglo-Saxonicum* (1897) and *Anglo-Saxon Bishops, Kings and Nobles* (1899), the first a list of Anglo-Saxon personal names from the seventh century to the time of King John, the second a guide to episcopal successions and lay pedigrees – and two large MS volumes left to the Museum suggest that in the 1860s he was planning a detailed work on European medieval and modern coinage. Although now completely superseded, it reveals a surprising depth of knowledge for one still in his mid-30s.

Apart from these early gifts and bequests, from the college loans, and from occasional gifts and purchases, most of the Museum's holdings of medieval coins came as almost incidental elements in the gifts or legacies of four major benefactors between 1920 and 1936:

(1) F. W. Hasluck (1878–1920), a Fellow of King's, who spent a number of years in Greece and Turkey as an archaeologist and became an expert on Greek ethnology and folklore. His bequest of 1,500 coins includes over 200 coins of the Crusader period collected in the Aegean area, but his interests were wide and a number of Anglo-Saxon coins from his collection are included in this volume.

(2) T. C. G. Duncanson (1873–1933), of Emmanuel College, was a wealthy country gentleman who inherited the collection built up by an uncle, Frank G. Smart (*c.* 1846–1913), of Caius, and presented it to the Museum in 1930. Smart himself was a doctor with an interest in botanical research and large private means who had been a generous benefactor of both his college and the University. His collection of nearly 1,000 coins was built up over the three decades 1879–1909, and its contents, almost entirely English, Scottish or Irish and a fifth of them medieval, were mainly bought from dealers, not at sales, and only occasionally do we know from where they came. Although he was not a numismatic scholar in the technical sense he showed great taste and judgement in his acquisitions, and many of the Museum's rarities are from his collection.

(3) James Stuart Henderson (d. 1933) left the Museum a collection of over 3,000 coins and medals, as well as a splendid collection of armour and many books and manuscripts. The coins had mainly been acquired at sales of the late nineteenth and early twentieth centuries, apparently between 1885 and 1916. The main strength of his collection is in the field of English, Scottish and Irish coins – over 2,700, a third of them medieval and nearly 90 of the Anglo-Saxon period.

(4) Arthur W. Young (1852–1936), a member of Trinity College, was a wealthy collector

on a grand scale, almost universal in his interests, who two years before his death presented over 300 incunabula and early printed books to the University Library and left to the Museum a collection of paintings and over 4,500 coins. These had seemingly been chosen on the basis of their historical or aesthetic interest. Many were acquired from dealers from the 1880s onwards, and some from his brother Charles E. B. Young (1850–1928), a wealthy and public-spirited lawyer, but he bought extensively at a few sales, notably at the first and second Carlyon-Britton sales in 1913 and 1916 respectively. Over 1,000 are coins of the British Isles, a third of them medieval, but there are also a number of French and Italian coins that will figure in later volumes of this catalogue.

In addition to these greater benefactions the Coin Room has made many acquisitions from Museum funds over the years, with the help of money contributed by the Friends of the Fitzwilliam Museum, the National Art-Collections Fund, the Pilgrim Trust, and other bodies. Coins found locally and of scholarly interest have been acquired where possible, and special attention has been paid to building up the Museum's collection of coins of the Cambridge mint. A more detailed account of the history of the Coin Room was contributed by Graham Pollard to the 26th Compte-Rendu (1979) of the International Numismatic Commission (pp. 41–51), with some description of the way in which the other parts of the collection were formed, in particular its outstanding series of Greek coins.

(ii) THE GRIERSON AND GRANTLEY COLLECTIONS

The Grierson collection was begun by chance in 1945, when Grierson, then an assistant lecturer in medieval history, happened to acquire what he subsequently learned was a copper half-follis of the Byzantine emperor Phocas. It was identified for him by Charles Seltman and gave him the idea of acquiring a few medieval European coins to show to students. There were at that particular time great numbers of such coins, mostly from the Grantley collection, on the London market. He consequently became interested in numismatics as a field of research and began to build up a collection that would supplement that in the Fitzwilliam Museum, whose medieval holdings were mainly coins of the British Isles.

In its early stages the collection, like most large collections, grew very quickly, since it was easy to find coins not already represented in it. Nearly half of its coins had been acquired by 1950, most of them in London. The revival of the international coin market was hampered by the long retention, in Britain and elsewhere, of exchange restrictions. From 1947 onwards, however, it was possible to travel abroad with a fair degree of ease. Grierson's position was aided by the fact that his pre-war field of research in early Flemish history had made him many friends in Belgium, where his new interests resulted in his adding to his Cambridge post the chair in numismatics and the history of money at the Université libre de Bruxelles, which was vacated in 1948 by the retirement of Victor Tourneur (1878–1967). This post, which he held till his own retirement in 1981, made him for over thirty years a regular visitor to Belgium, while participation in historical congresses and symposia, and many friendships with Continental scholars, took him frequently to France and Italy. The list of provenances in this and later volumes of this catalogue will show how often he bought coins in Brussels and Paris, Milan and Rome,

Basel and Amsterdam, besides participating, sometimes in person but more often through the agency of London dealers, at many of the great international coin sales of the past three decades.

These same references, however, show how much his collection owes to its much larger and more prestigious predecessor, that of Lord Grantley.

The fifth Lord Grantley (1855–1943) was an eccentric and extremely wealthy landowner whose numismatic interests, if his son's account can be trusted, were partly engendered by the need for a hobby as a result of the social ostracism he experienced after his involvement in a divorce scandal in 1879. His knowledge of numismatics, aided by an exceptional command of languages, was phenomenal, though he published virtually nothing and some at least of the pleasure he derived from his coins came from the bargaining in which their acquisition had involved him. His collection of some 50,000 coins ultimately became one of the largest ever formed by a single person, and it was certainly one of the finest. Unlike the Grierson collection it was universal in its scope, including ancient, modern and oriental coins as well as medieval ones. The medieval European section, however, was exceptionally rich, for its owner was interested in genealogy and enjoyed following up the minutiae of the *Art de vérifier les dates* and the *Trésor de chronologie*, for coins could be found to illustrate the minting rights of almost every petty dynasty of the Holy Roman Empire. Many of the coins were acquired in their countries of origin, as Lord Grantley was an inveterate traveller and haunted antique shops, but he also bought extensively at many important sales over the five decades of his collecting career. His Merovingian, Carolingian and Anglo-Saxon series were of exceptional quality, including as they did the entire Crondall hoard, now in the Ashmolean Museum; he was indeed rumoured in the 1890s to be preparing a study of Frankish coinage. He regularly noted the provenances of his coins (but not the dates of acquisition) on his coin tickets. Unfortunately these were not always preserved by the dealers who eventually bought the coins and, since in large lots the tickets could not subsequently be precisely matched with the coins, the earlier history of Grantley material cannot always be traced.

The end of the collection came in 1943–5. Lord Grantley had sold off several groups of unwanted coins during his lifetime. Miscellaneous duplicates and hoard material were sold in Amsterdam (Schulman 10.5.1912), some classical coins, more hoard material and decorations in London (Sotheby 3.2.1914), and his very large and important Indian collection in Amsterdam after the end of the First World War (Schulman 12.12.1921). A further batch of duplicates was sold anonymously as lots 151–65 at a Glendining sale of 10.5.1943, lots 151–4 consisting of over 900 French medieval coins and the remaining lots being unidentified and sold by weight. (A number of coins from these are now in the Grierson collection, having been acquired from Christopher Blunt in 1948.) In March 1943, however, at the age of 87, Lord Grantley found himself again co-respondent in a divorce case. When he died the following August his son had no alternative but to sell the whole collection, partly to pay death duties and partly to provide the £10,000 which his father had left to the lady involved and whom, but for his untimely death, he would have married. The coins were disposed of in eleven huge sales at Glendining's spread over the next eighteen months. The catalogues, prepared in great haste by Leonard Forrer of Spink's, are very summary and because of war conditions very inadequately illustrated, so that they quite fail to do justice to the magnificence of the collection. Nor were the sales a financial success, for the absence of Continental competition meant that a high proportion of lots were bought, often at derisory prices, by London dealers. Many of the medieval coins, however, were acquired subsequently by Grierson, either directly from the dealers or by way of the third Lockett sale in 1956, so probably at least half Lord Grantley's medieval holdings of Continental coins, which with his Anglo-Saxon and Anglo-Norman coins formed the most important part of his collection from the scholarly point of view, are now in the Fitzwilliam Museum.

(iii) THE COLLEGE COLLECTIONS

A number of the colleges acquired small collections by gift or bequest in the course of the eighteenth century, and individual Fellows sometimes tried to develop them systematically, presumably with a view to their use for study or teaching purposes. A catalogue of the collection at Gonville and Caius College was even published in 1845. But the college librarians who were normally responsible for such collections were usually only too conscious that they did not possess the necessary qualifications for their proper custody, and there was an ever-present danger of inadvertent loss or theft.

The creation of a central and well-housed collection in the Fitzwilliam Museum offered the possibility of making these coins more accessible to scholars, and in 1937 the Museum Syndicate, at the prompting of the Honorary Keeper S. W. Grose, who in the 1920s had produced a magnificent catalogue of the McClean Greek collection, asked the colleges if they would be willing to deposit their coins in the Museum on indefinite loan. Six of the eleven colleges with collections agreed to do so. The great majority of the coins that thus reached the Museum were Greek or Roman, and their contents do not concern the present publication. Only the Trinity collection included a substantial holding of medieval coins, for the most part English, and Emmanuel is the owner of one Anglo-Saxon coin of outstanding interest (**1.665**), which was retained by the college in 1937 but deposited later. Corpus Christi and Queens', however, which retained their collections in 1937, have kindly allowed the medieval coins in these to be included in this publication, so that as many as possible of those in Cambridge collections may be made available to students. The Museum of Archaeology and Anthropology also has a small group of Anglo-Saxon coins which were overlooked in 1958, when *SCBI* Cambridge was published, but are included here.

The Trinity College loan (1937) is an important collection of over 6,000 coins and medals. Although the medieval series represents only a small proportion of the total, the Anglo-Saxon, Anglo-Gallic, and later medieval English gold coins are particularly fine.

The nucleus of its Anglo-Saxon series was a collection of antiquities made in Kent by Archdeacon John Battely (1646–1708) and presented to the college by his nephew, another John, in the middle of the eighteenth century. It included a number of Anglo-Saxon and three Merovingian coins, two gold and one silver, which had been found at various times at Reculver and are all identifiable from the illustrations on pls. 6 and 7 of the second edition of the archdeacon's *Antiquitates Rutupinae* (Battely 1745). Other Anglo-Saxon coins were included in a collection left to the college by the Norfolk antiquary Beaupré Bell (1704–41), identifications being here possible through a MS catalogue of the Trinity collection compiled by a Dr Mason and now on indefinite loan to the Coin Room. The author was probably Charles Mason (1699–1771), Fellow of Trinity and Professor of Geology 1734–62. Subsequent additions in the medieval field, traceable through a three-volume accession register covering the years 1869–1925, were made from time to time. The last Trinity scholar to interest himself seriously in the collection, however, was the Rev. C. W. King (1818–88), for many years Senior Fellow, and in the twenty years prior to the transfer of the coins to the Fitzwilliam Museum only one gift of coins is recorded. Further information on the history of the collection can be found in *SCBI* Cambridge, xii–xiii.

The Corpus Christi College collection differs completely from that of Trinity, since instead of being built up from gifts and bequests over two centuries it was the creation of a single individual. Samuel Savage Lewis (1836–91), the son of a surgeon at Croydon, was a wealthy collector of wide interests who became a Fellow of the College in 1869 and its Librarian a year later. He was an inveterate traveller in Europe and the Near East, and despite extremely defective eyesight built up a collection of Greek gems, vases and other antiques and works of art that turned his College rooms into a virtual museum. His collection of Greek coins, which is of exceptional quality, is now in process of publication in the *Sylloge Nummorum Graecorum* (1972–). His medieval series, of which a MS catalogue was prepared by Dr Peter Spufford in the 1960s, is smaller and less important, but although it runs to only some 200 coins, or 250 if the Byzantine series be included, it contains a number of spectacular rarities and coins of high artistic quality: a solidus of Theodebert (**1.389**), a *denier à la reine* and a *petit royal* of Philip IV, two *anges d'or* of Philip VI, an augustale of Frederick II, Milanese and French testoons of Louis XII. Lewis's coin tickets show that the collection was formed between about 1872 and the date of his marriage in December 1887. Some coins came as gifts from friends or by exchange, but most were bought at antique shops on his travels – at Rouen on several occasions, at Nevers in 1880 – or from dealers in Paris and London, these including some fine coins from the Saulcy sale of 1881 and the Gariel sale of 1885.

There are two other college collections with substantial medieval series. That of Peterhouse was given to the College in 1934 by W. E. Barnes (1859–1939), Hulsean Professor of Divinity, and deposited with the Museum in 1960. It consists of 414 coins and tokens, principally English and Irish but with some Roman and modern foreign coins as well. Only one coin is relevant to this volume (**1.1373**), but a further 69 will be included in the later British ones. The Queens' College collection contains some 175 medieval coins, mostly English silver post-1180 but with a few earlier English and Continental, five of these being Carolingian. There seems to be no record of their earlier ownership or provenance, but a note on one ticket suggests that the collection was formed around the turn of this century.

COLLECTORS, DEALERS AND DONORS

This list is primarily intended as an index and key to the provenances recorded in the catalogue. Even when these fall short of disclosing when and where a coin was found, a knowledge of previous owners sometimes makes it possible to identify existing specimens with ones described in the literature or to establish their authenticity.

The scholars, collectors and dealers of each generation generally know each other but are unable to identify their predecessors. Some explanatory matter has therefore been inserted where this is available, but, as already stated, a consolidated and much expanded list is envisaged for Vol. 13. The use of the word 'scholar' to describe individuals indicates that these have published work on numismatics; it does not imply that other collectors may not have been scholars also.

When a sale extended over several days, only that of the opening date is given. Individual purchases from dealers or made at sales of miscellaneous material are not indexed except for those local to Cambridge.

ADDINGTON, Samuel. A London merchant whose collection of English coins was acquired *en bloc* by MONTAGU in 1883. **1308**.

AES RUDE SA. Coin auctioneers at Chiasso (Switzerland) from 1978. **1022**.

AMÉCOURT, Gustave, vicomte de Ponton d' (1825–88). Scholar and collector (mainly of Roman and French, esp. Merovingian, coins). A large part of his collection of the last (1,131 coins) went to the BN; the remainder were sold by Rollin & Feuardent (9.6.1890). **392, 395, 397, 412–13, 432, 434–5, 439–42A, 445, 448, 452, 456, 460–1, 464, 476, 486–7, 502, 523, 603, 613, 626, 670–1, 1479**.

AMERICAN NUMISMATIC SOCIETY ('ANS'). Duplicates acquired from. **205, 220, 224, 229, 232, 261, 996**.

ANDERSON, Mrs E. M. Coin given to the Museum by. **197**.

ARS ET NUMMUS. See NASCIA, G.

'ASTRONOMER'. See MCCLEAN, Frank.

AUSSANT, J. (1805–72), Rennes. Scholar (Breton coins) and collector. Collection sold by Rollin & Feuardent 20.4.1864. **452**.

BABINGTON, Rev. Churchill (1821–89). 19th-century benefactor of the Coin Room (see p. 394). **682, 1280, 1306, 1336, 1362, 1483–6**.

BAGEHOT. British collector (1956), untraced. **43**.

BALDWIN, MESSRS A. H. & SONS. One of the leading London coin dealers since the 1890s.

BANK LEU (Zurich). Since the late 1940s one of the chief coin dealers and auctioneers (often in assoc. w. ADOLPH HESS NACHF., Lucerne) in Switzerland.

BARANOWSKY, Michele (d. 1968). Coin dealer and auctioneer at Milan (and subsequently Rome) from the late 1920s onwards. The firm continues under his daughter.

BARNES, Prof. William Emery (1859–1939). Donor of a general coin collection to Peterhouse (see p. 398). **1373**.

BASCOM, George Jonathan. Sotheby sale, 15.6.1914. **1369**.

BATTELY, Archd. John (1646–1708). Antiquarian whose collection of coins was given by his nephew, another John Battely, to Trinity College *c.* 1740 (see p. 397). For a list of coins received, see 'Reculver' in the index of find-spots.

BEAUFOY, Henry Benjamin Hanbury (1786–1851). Collector of English coins which were dispersed in a Christie sale of 18.6.1909. **1134, 1493**.

BELL, Beaupré (1704–41). Norfolk antiquary who bequeathed his coins to Trinity College (see p. 397). **1136**.

BELLENBERG. German collector. **541, 595**.

BERGHAUS, Peter (1919–). Scholar, one of the most eminent numismatists of this century. **21, 233, 235, 541, 595**.

BERGNE, John Brodribb (1800–73). Collection sold by Sotheby 20.5.1873. **1146–7, 1308, 1379, 1494**.

BIRKLER & WADDELL. Coin dealers and auctioneers at Washington (D.C.) in the 1970s. See also WADDELL.

BLISS, Thomas (d. 1913). Collection sold by Sotheby 22.3.1916. **1128, 1143, 1153, 1158, 1450**.

BLOM, Christian. Coin dealer in Arlington, Virginia, since the 1950s.

BLUNT, Christopher Evelyn (1904–). Scholar and collector. A number of coins in the Grierson collection came from him, notably the Grantley duplicates (above, p. 396) though not these alone. **39, 796, 804, 806, 917, 936, 943–4, 950–1, 955–6, 967, 975, 1513**.

BONHAM-VECCHI. See VECCHI.

BORDEAUX, Paul (1846–1925). Scholar and collector. Collection dispersed in three sales by Feuardent, the Merovingian and Carolingian series being in the first sale on 26.4.1926. **721, 760**.

BORGHESI, Bartolommeo (1781–1860). Scholar and collector. Collection dispersed in four sales by G. Sambon (Rome) in 1879–81. One coin from the fourth sale (31.5.1881) is now here. **63**.

BORRELL, Maximilian John. London coin dealer in the mid 19th century. **148**.

BOULTON, Sir Samuel (1830–1918). Business man, philanthropist, and collector. His collection, especially important for Italian coins acquired in the decade before 1914, was bought from his heirs by Spink in 1943 and provided Grierson with many coins in 1945–6. **151, 158, 312, 1008, 1011, 1013, 1015, 1018, 1021, 1023**(?), **1026, 1031, 1034, 1039, 1045–6, 1048, 1050, 1052–3, 1055, 1057, 1060, 1067, 1069, 1074, 1077, 1082, 1115, 1514**.

BOURGEY, Etienne (1865–1942). Succeeded by his son Emile, one of the chief Paris coin dealers and auctioneers from the 1890s onwards.

BOUTIN, Serge. Coin dealer in Paris.

BRICE, William (*c.* 1812–87). Collector. His collection was acquired *en bloc* by MONTAGU in 1887. The MS catalogue of it is now in the Fitzwilliam Museum, ex Montagu (V) 724, as are a number of his coins. **1123, 1132, 1146–7, 1155–6, 1177, 1309–10, 1341, 1372, 1494**.

BUNN, Charles John (d. 1948). A London newsagent whose large collection, mainly of Byzantine copper coins, was presented to the Museum by his heirs in 1950. A few non-Byzantine coins are here. **56, 100, 105, 108, 113, 130, 137, 160–1, 296**.

BURKITT, Miles Crawford (1890–1971). Lecturer in archaeology in Cambridge University 1926–58. One coin is amongst those presented by his widow. **69**.

BUTE, John Crichton-Stuart, Marquess of (1881–1947). Vendor of an important collection formed mainly by his ancestor the second Earl of Bute (1713–92) but added to by the earl's successors down to the second Marquess (1793–1848). The Visigothic coins, of which three are here, were included on 7.5.1951 in the first of the three Sotheby sales in which the collection was dispersed. **221, 223, 273**.

BUTTON, Elisabeth (d. 1962). Frankfurt coin dealer and auctioneer who took over the great firm of A. E. Cahn in 1936 and carried it on under the name of Frankfurter Münzhandlung, though her fixed-price lists appear under her own name. After her death it was carried on by her widower R. G. Wolf.

BUVIGNIER, Amand (1823–*c*. 1880), of Verdun. Scholar and collector. **450**.

CAHN, Adolph E. (Frankfurt-am-Main). Coin dealers and auctioneers. One of the major coin firms in Europe from the 1870s to 1936, when it was taken over by Julius Cahn's secretary, Elisabeth BUTTON, as the Frankfurter Münzhandlung. The traditions of the firm were carried on in Switzerland by Münzhandlung Basel, later MÜNZEN UND MEDAILLEN A. G. BASEL.

CAMBRIDGE ANTIQUARIAN SOCIETY. Collection deposited in the Museum in 1886 (above, p. 394). **1129, 1408, 1412–14, 1416, 1419, 1421, 1423–7, 1430–5, 1437, 1439, 1483–9**.

CANESSA, C. and E. Coin and antique dealers and auctioneers during the first three decades of this century. The firm was based in Naples but had branches in Paris and New York.

CARBERY EVANS, John (1835–93). Cambridgeshire country gentleman, whose collections of objets d'art included a few coins (Christie 30.11.1893). **380, 532**.

CARLES-TOLRÁ, Emilio. Collector. His collection of Spanish coins, a catalogue of which was published in 1936, disappeared in the Spanish Civil War. Coins from it began to come on the market in the 1950s, and eventually the heirs waived their claims in return for an indemnity. **230**.

CARLYON-BRITTON, Philip William Poole (1863–1938). Scholar and collector. Most of his Anglo-Saxon coins were included in the first (Sotheby 17.11.1913) of the three sales in which his collection was dispersed, and references are to this unless one of the others is specifically indicated. **373, 636, 677–80, 685, 691–3, 717, 751, 1122–4, 1126, 1135, 1141, 1146–7, 1150, 1154, 1156–7, 1162, 1165, 1168, 1171, 1175, 1177, 1179, 1182–4, 1186, 1189, 1191, 1195–7, 1200–1, 1218, 1221, 1224, 1230, 1233, 1235, 1238, 1244–8, 1254–6, 1261–2, 1264–5, 1272, 1282, 1285–7, 1289, 1292–3, 1298, 1302, 1307, 1315–16, 1324, 1326, 1329, 1331, 1339, 1341, 1353, 1357, 1359, 1370, 1378, 1380, 1383–6, 1391, 1394, 1399, 1401, 1409–10, 1415, 1417, 1428, 1440, 1446, 1495**. Second sale (20.11.1916): **1145, 1358, 1361**. Third sale (11.11.1918): **1352**.

CARTIER, Etienne (1779–1859). An immensely prolific scholar, one of the founders of numismatic studies in France, but only casually a collector. **603**.

CELATI, Luigi Agenore. Lawyer at Rome, collector of papal coins. His collection was bought by the Vatican in 1921 (Serafini 1923), duplicates being subsequently disposed of, mainly to Carlo GAVAZZI, though he had disposed of others in his lifetime to RUCHAT and others. **1037, 1049, 1051, 1064–5, 1070, 1075, 1078, 1084, 1528–9**.

CHAPPÉE, Julien. French collector and scholar, mid 20th century. **769, 780**.

CHARVET, Jean (1824–64). Dealer, scholar and collector. Ponton D'AMÉCOURT had the pick of his Merovingian coins after his death, the remainder of the coins and miscellaneous objets d'art being sold by Hoffman 5.5.1883. **403, 413**.

CHIERICI, R. Doctor, collector (at Suvereto, nr Leghorn), owner of the Montelibretti hoard. **77, 78**.

CHIGI, Prince Mario. Collector of papal coins. **1037, 1051, 1070, 1078, 1084, 1528**.

CHIJS, Pieter Otto van der (1802–67). Scholar and collector, Director of the Coin Cabinet of the University of Leyden. His large general collection was sold by Bom (Amsterdam 13.6.1870). **360, 371**.

CHILVERS, C. A. Collector at Snettisham, Norfolk. **712, 1164, 1370, 1382**.

CHRISTIE & Sons (London). General auctioneers since the 18th century.

CIANI, Giorgio. Collection sold by Ratto (Milan) 28.10.1910. See **1048, 1074**.

CIANI, Louis (1884–1929). Scholar, dealer and auctioneer in Paris from the early 1920s. The firm continued until 1957, when his brother Pierre died. See p. 335.

CLARKE, Louis C. G. (1881–1961). Archaeologist and art collector, Director of the Fitzwilliam Museum 1937–46, a frequent benefactor to the coin collection. **59**.

'COLLECTION D . . .', untraced. **834**.

'COLLECTION D'UN AMATEUR SUISSE'. See DOLIVO, D.

'COLLECTION F.H.', untraced. **630**.

'COLLECTION H . . .', untraced (Paris, 31.1.1912). **907**.

'COLLECTION MÉROVINGIENNE'. A collection of undisclosed (allegedly Spanish) origin which, apart from a single silver coin (**594**) that reached Santamaria, was acquired by MMAG Basel from Calico in the late 1940s. It was the largest collection of Merovingian coins to come on the market since the dispersal of the Amécourt collection in 1890. Much of it, impeccably catalogued, was included in MMAG Basel Auction 8 of 8.12.1949 (lots 305–463), with an overflow in Auction 9 of 21.6.1951 (lots 132–45). Some of the unsold lots, in company with a large number of mainly unidentified coins that had appeared in neither sale, were bought by Grierson in 1952. **392, 394, 396, 398, 410, 412–13, 422, 427–8, 432, 434–5, 438–50, 452–4, 456–7, 462, 464, 467, 470–1, 474–5, 477–85, 494, 498, 594**.

COLLINS & CLARK, Cambridge. Antique dealers. See WYATT, J.

COLONNA, Prince Ferdinando (1837–?). Archaeologist, scholar and collector. Collection sold by Canessa (Naples) 3.5.1909. **1076**.

CONYBEARE, Rev. Edward (1843–1931), of Trinity College. While vicar of Barrington, Cambs. (1871–98), he made a large collection of coins found locally. It passed to his daughter and ultimately to her niece, Miss F. M. MCCORMICK, who donated it to the Museum in 1975. **648, 662, 1368A**.

CORPUS CHRISTI COLLEGE. See LEWIS, S. S.

CORSI, avv. Collector of papal coins. **1525**.

CRIPPA, Carlo. Coin dealer at Milan from the 1960s onwards.

CROMPTON ROBERTS, Charles Montagu (1865–1931). Collection formed in the 1880s and 1890s and purchased by Spink *c.* 1920. **1164**.

CROWTHER, Rev. George Francis. Sotheby 10.11.1904. **1307**.

CUFF, James Dodsley (1780–1853). Banker and collector, esp. of Anglo-Saxon coins. The sale (Sotheby 8.6.1854) was spread over a record period of 18 days. **1156, 1172, 1179**(?), **1307–8**.

CURETON, Harry Osborn (*c.* 1795–1858). London coin dealer. **1418**.

DASSY, M. Mid 19th-century collector at Meaux. The detailed commentaries by Longpérier in the sale catalogue of his collection (Rollin & Feuardent 3.5.1869) make this volume an important contribution to scholarship. **484**.

DAVIES, Major. Collector. **658**.

DAWSON, Very Rev. Henry Richard (1792–1840), Dean of St Patrick's Cathedral, Dublin. Collector (English and Irish coins). Sotheby 30.6.1842 ('Dean of St Patricks'). **1144**.

'DEAN OF ST PATRICKS' sale. See DAWSON, H. R.

DE FALCO, Giuseppe. Coin dealer at Naples.

DE NICOLA, Luigi. Coin dealer in Rome, late 1940s to late 1960s.

DERRIMAN, J. P. Collector in the late 1940s who acquired some of his coins while serving in North Africa during Second World War. **9, 31–2**.

DEVONSHIRE, William, 2nd Duke of (d. 1729). Collection preserved in family till sold anonymously by Christie on behalf of the 6th duke in 2 parts: (I) 18.3.1844, Greek and Roman; (II) 28.3.1844, Anglo-Saxon, English. **1149**.

DEWICK, Rev. Edward Samuel (1844–1917), of St John's College. A distinguished antiquary and donor of a large collection of coins to the Museum in 1918. **95, 125, 152, 1438**.

DILLEN, Joseph ('Jeff'), Brussels. Coin dealer 1938–*c.* 1943, when he died in a German concentration camp. The firm was carried on by his widow down to her death in 1955.

DOLIVO, Dimitri (1891–1961). Swiss scholar and collector. His important collection of medieval coins was sold anonymously, as 'Collection d'un amateur suisse', by MMAG Basel in four sales between 1962 and 1965. **390, 749**.

DONAUESCHINGEN. See FÜRSTENBERG.

DOROTHEUM (Vienna). Auctioneering firm since the 18th century.

DU LAC, Jules (1824–1909). Scholar and collector. Two sales by Rollin & Feuardent: (I) 12.5.1910, Roman, Byzantine; (II) 6.6.1910, French. **760**.

DUMBARTON OAKS ('DO'), Center of Byzantine Studies founded in 1940 in Georgetown, a suburb of Washington (D.C.). A number of its duplicates and non-Byzantine coins were sold in the late 1950s. **48, 167, 176, 186, 192, 222, 241, 263, 348, 377, 425, 747, 840, 844, 1019, 1111, 1470**.

DUNCANSON, T. J. G. (1873–1933), of Emmanuel College. Presented to the Fitzwilliam Museum in 1930 the coin collection inherited from his uncle F. G. SMART (see p. 394).

DUPRIEZ, Charles (d. 1952), Brussels. Coin dealer and auctioneer. Succeeded by B. FRANCESCHI.

DYMOCK, Rev. Thomas Frederick (*c.* 1807–58). Collection sold by Sotheby 1.6.1858. **1155, 1307**.

EASTWOOD, George (*c.* 1819–66). London coin dealer. **1377**.

EMMANUEL COLLEGE, CAMBRIDGE. Its coin collection is deposited on indefinite loan to the Museum (see p. 397). **665, 1130**.

ERSKINE, Hon. Robert William Hervey (1930–), of King's College. Collector and dealer in prints and objets d'art. **712**.

EVANS, Sir John (1823–1908). One of the most eminent numismatists of his day. His English collection was bought *en bloc* by Pierpont Morgan and eventually acquired by the BM, but some came on the market. **708, 1331**.

EVENS, P. L. Finder of coin at Bottisham, Cambs. **1139**.

FALCO, G. De. See DE FALCO, G.

FARMER, Miss M. Donor of coin in 1928. **468**.

FEUARDENT FRÈRES. See ROLLIN & FEUARDENT.

FITZWILLIAM, Earl. Christie sale (30.5.1949) of a collection of Roman Imperial Æ formed in the mid eighteenth century by Charles Watson-Wentworth, 2nd Marquess of Rockingham (1730–82). **70**.

FLORANGE, Jules (1862–1936). Coin dealer, auctioneer (1892 onwards) and scholar. The firm was inherited by his sons Charles (who had opened a separate firm in 1928) and Jules, effectively the latter, on whose death it passed to Nadia KAPAMADJI, for many years his assistant.

'FOREIGN AMBASSADOR' sale, Glendining 7.3.1957. **301**.

FORRER, Leonard Steyning (d. 1968). Son of L. Forrer of Spink, for which firm he initially worked. He set up independently in London as a coin dealer after 1945, but his firm closed in 1955 and he joined Schulman's in Amsterdam.

FRANCESCHI, Bartolommeo (Brussels). Coin dealer in succession to DUPRIEZ.

FRANKFURTER MÜNZHANDLUNG, See BUTTON, E.

FRERE, Mrs P. H. (d. 1870). Widow of Philip Howard Frere (1813–68; Trinity), bursar of Downing College and author of several works on agriculture. She gave a miscellaneous collection of 73 coins to Trinity College. **1312, 1403**.

FRIENDS OF THE FITZWILLIAM MUSEUM. Benefactors of the Coin Room. **669, 1123, 1124A, 1132, 1140–1**.

FULLER. Owner of collection bought by Spink in 1938. **107**.

FÜRSTENBERG, Prinz von, at Donaueschingen (Baden). A great collection formed in the nineteenth century mainly by Prinz Karl Egon II (1804–54), and dispersed in 14 sales by Adolph E. Cahn (Frankfurt-am-Main) and Otto Helbing Nachf. (Munich). The sales that concern this volume are Cahn 79 (14.12.1932), which contained the Merovingian and Carolingian coins (**390**, **1478**) and Helbing 73 (27.10.1933), with the Italian ones (**1068**).

GAETTENS, Richard (1886–1965). German scholar, dealer and collector. **1000**.

GALERANDE. Mid nineteenth-century collector at Clermont (Oise). **530**.

GANS, Edward (1887–1979). One of the leading coin dealers in the United States (New York 1938–53, subsequently Berkeley, California) under the name of Numismatic Fine Arts.

GARIEL, Ernest (d. 1884). Business man, scholar and collector. His coins, which included the most important Carolingian series ever to come on the market, were sold by Hoffman 27.5.1885. **347**, **389**, **414**.

GAVAZZI, Carlo (d. 1947). Collection of Italian coins divided between his heirs, many of them going to ULRICH-BANSA and a number being here. **63**, **323**, **325**, **1035–8**, **1040–4**, **1047**, **1049**, **1051**, **1054**, **1058–9**, **1061–2**, **1064–6**, **1070**, **1073**, **1075–6**, **1078**, **1080–1**, **1083–4**, **1517**, **1519**, **1525**, **1527–9**.

GAVAZZI, Giuseppe (1831–1913). Scholar and collector (Italian coins), whose coins were sold by Ratto (Milan) 24.4.1911. **1011**, **1013**, **1021**, **1050**, **1055**, **1077**.

GAVET, Gabriel. Bourgey sale, 29.3.1897. **617**.

GENT, E. Nineteenth-century collector. **719**.

GIBBS, James (1825–86). Collector, whose coins were bought by Spink after his death. **1370**.

GLENDINING & CO. The leading firm of coin auctioneers in London since the early 1920s.

GOFF, Sir Edward. Collector. Christie 13.12.1948. **340**, **343**.

GRANTA STAMP AND COIN SHOP, Cambridge. **699**, **701**, **710**, **711**, **713**.

GRANTLEY, Lord (1855–1943). See above, pp. 396–7 and concordance, below pp. 647–8.

GRIERSON, Philip. Coins presented to the Museum. **60**, **70**, **313**, **666**, **696**, **700**, **708**, **712**, **1134A**, **1364**, **1375A**.

GROSE, Sidney William (1886–1980). Classical scholar and Fellow of Christ's, Honorary Keeper of the Coins at the Fitzwilliam Museum 1922–8, 1936–49. His teaching collection of 72 Greek and Roman coins was presented to the Museum by his daughter and son-in-law, Mr and Mrs A. H. Laurie. One of the coins is Ostrogothic. **155**.

GROVER, Brian. Occasional dealer (London). **208**.

GUTTERIDGE, Harold Cooke (1876–1953), of Trinity Hall. Professor of Comparative Law at Cambridge University. Donor of a small collection of coins to the Museum in 1939. **51**, **162**, **1455**.

HAEX, Albert Clément (1878–1949). Dutch business man (Maastricht), whose specialized collection of coins relating to Limburg was bought by Schulman in 1949. Most of it was included (anonymously) in a sale of 30.3.1949. **360**, **371**, **497**.

HAINES, Geoffrey Colton (1899–1981). Scholar and collector. His collection of Roman coins was presented to the Barber Institute of Fine Arts in the University of Birmingham, but there is one coin, a gift to Grierson, in this collection. **204**.

HALL, W. H. Bullock. Finder of coin at Fréjus. **195**.

HALLIDAY, John Edmund. Collector. Sotheby 8.7.1902. **676**.

HAMBURGER, L. and L. Coin dealers and auctioneers at Frankfurt-am-Main, from the 1860s to 1929, under the cousins Leo (1846–1929) and Leopold (1836–1910). Succeeded by NUSSBAUM.

HANSEN, Franz Johan. Danish Consul General in London. Collection purchased by B. A. Seaby *c.* 1946. **7**, **141**, **144**.

HARQUART. Curé at Naix (Meuse), former owner of **502**.

HASLUCK, Frederick William (1878–1920), of King's College. Classical scholar and archaeologist who bequeathed to the Museum his collection of 1,600 coins, mainly acquired in the Near East but including some others. **947, 952–3, 1193, 1227–8, 1295, 1334, 1388–9, 1392.**

HAUËT, M. Sale (Mme Serrure) 20.2.1908. **410, 457, 477.**

HAY, Maj. William Edward (1805–80). Sale (Sotheby) 8.4.1880. See note on **1150** in catalogue.

HAZLITT, William Carew (1834–1913). Man of letters and collector, his collection being sold by Sotheby 5.7.1909. **1053.**

HELBING, Otto. Coin auctioneer at Munich. Succeeded by KRESS.

HENDERSON, James Stewart (d. 1933). Collector of antiquities on a lavish scale who bequeathed his collection of over 3,000 coins and medals to the Museum (see p. 394). **647, 654, 656, 658, 661, 664, 673, 683, 1187, 1209, 1213, 1281, 1301, 1308–10, 1343, 1354–5, 1363, 1372, 1397–8, 1406, 1429, 1494, 1496.**

HERZFELDER, Hubert (1911–63). Scholar and dealer (Paris). **43, 1479.**

HESS, Adolph (Frankfurt-am-Main). A major firm of coin dealers and auctioneers from the 1870s to 1931. At Frankfurt it was taken over by PEUS, but a successor to it was set up at Lucerne under Hermann Rosenberg (1896–1970) under the name ADOLPH HESS NACHF. It conducted important auctions through the 1930s and, in association with BANK LEU, from 1954 onwards.

HILL, Elizabeth (1900–). Professor of Slavonic Studies at Cambridge 1948–68. **351.**

HILL, Philip Victor (1917–). Scholar and collector, specialist on Roman imperial and early Anglo-Saxon coinage. **707.**

HIRSCH, Gerhard (1903–82). Prolific author, coin dealer and auctioneer who worked initially (1922–35) in the firm of Helbing Nach., then managed by his uncle Heinrich Hirsch, and who, after surviving Theresienstadt and Auschwitz, settled in Munich and presided over the Münzhandlung Gerhard Hirsch from 1953 till his death.

HIRSCH MYNTHANDEL (Stockholm). Coin dealers. Founded by M. C. Hirsch in 1893 as antique dealers. Trading in coins since 1930s.

HOFFMANN, Henri (1823–97). Coin dealer, auctioneer and scholar, author of what was for long the standard work on French royal coinage. Parts of his own collection were sold in 1886–7, the remainder after his death (Rollin & Feuardent 2.5.1898). Three coins in the Lewis collection are from the first sale of his French coins (Hoffmann 2.3.1887): **598, 764, 1475,** and another from his sale of 3.5.1890: **429.**

HOLLSCHEK, Karl (1859–1941). Austrian collector who acquired (amongst others) the WINDISCH-GRÄTZ collection. His collection of *c.* 200,000 coins, the largest ever made by a single individual, was dispersed in 20 Dorotheum sales over the years 1956–64. A few coins are here, **328** from Auktion VII (21.5.1958) and **22** from Auktion XII (18.10.1960).

HOLZER, Hans (1920–). American author (born in Vienna) who in the 1940s made an important collection of countermarked coins now mainly in the ANS Museum. In 1953 he allowed Grierson to buy 30 of the 31 countermarked early imperial bronze coins that he possessed, on the understanding that he would pass on five each to the ANS and to the Yale University collection. The remaining 20 are here. No further provenances for them are known; Mr Holzer had acquired them over the years from Spink in London and from dealers in New York. It is likely that some of them were found together, but the varying degree of cleaning they have undergone would make it hazardous to try and ascertain which ones. **66–8, 72–6, 79–91.**

HUGHES, Thomas McKenny (1853–1917), of Trinity College. Professor of Geology, donor to Trinity College of a coin found at Haslingfield (Cambs). **1151.**

HUMPHRY, Isabel L. Wife of Dr Laurence Humphry (1856–1920), of Trinity College. In 1915 she and her brother, Sir Arthur STOKES, gave to the Museum a collection of 76 Roman, medieval and modern

European coins, which may once have belonged to their father, Prof. Sir George Gabriel Stokes (1819–1903), Master of Pembroke College. **1214**, **1222**.

HUTH, Reginald (1853–1926). Collector. The third of the three sales in which his collection was dispersed (Sotheby 14.6.1927) included an unusual Visigothic series, one coin from it being here. **244**.

JAMES, John Henry (1825–1904). London solicitor, classical scholar, and collector of English coins which he sold on retirement (Sotheby 7.8.1888). **1363**.

JENKINSON, F. J. Hilary (1853–1923), of Trinity College. University Librarian (1889–1923), who early in his career had interested himself in numismatics and bequeathed to the Museum a collection of over 300 coins and medals formed in the 1880s. **924**, **1095**.

KAPAMADJI, Nadia (1901–78). Dealer and collector. In 1950 she took over the firm of FLORANGE, in which she had worked since the late 1930s, and continued to run it under the name of Florange down to her death.

KEIM. Paris coin dealer, early twentieth century. **586**, **631**.

KENYON, Joseph. An attorney's clerk and subsequently a schoolmaster at Preston (Lancs.) who collected coins and apparently had access to coins in the Cuerdale hoard before the inquest. **1386**.

KING, Rev. Charles William (1818–88). An expert on antique gems, his collection of which is now in the Metropolitan Museum of Art in New York. He was for many years a Senior Fellow of Trinity College and a generous benefactor to its collection. **1333**, **1411**, **1443–4**.

KIRCHERIANO, MUSEO (Rome). A collection founded by the great seventeenth century polymath P. Atanasio Kircher (1601–80). When the possessions of the Jesuits were secularized by the Italian government after 1870, many coins and other objects were entrusted to friendly hands to save them from sequestration and came ultimately on the market. **1529**.

KRAUS, Franz Ferdinand. Coin dealer at Brunswick during the 1920s, author of a standard work on Ostrogothic coins. Stock bought by Spink in 1931. **121**, **1452**.

KRESS, Karl (1892–1969). Coin dealer and auctioneer at Munich from 1938 onwards in succession to Otto HELBING Nachf.

KRICHELDORF, Hans Hellmuth (1909–80). Coin dealer, auctioneer, and numismatic publisher, working successively in the firms of MMAG BASEL and Freiburger Münzhandlung Helga Frey (later Blaser-Frey) before setting up under his own name at Stuttgart in 1955.

KRÜGER. German collector, untraced. **21**, **233**, **235**.

KUNST UND MÜNZEN AG. Coin dealers and auctioneers, at Lugano.

LA GRANGE, Lelièvre, Marquis de (1796–1876). Scholar and collector, whose coins, including the Plassac hoard, were sold 19.2.1877 by Rollin & Feuardent ('collection de feu M. le Marquis de L.'). **586**, **589**, **594**, **615**, **618–19**.

LAURIE, Mr and Mrs A. H. See GROSE, S. W.

LAWRENCE, Laurie Asher (1857–1949). London ophthalmic surgeon, scholar and collector. Author of many important papers on English coinage. Some of his English coins were sold by Sotheby, 24.2.1903; his main collection of English and Roman coins were sold in six sales by Glendining, 1950–1. A few coins here (**700**, **712**) are from the second of the sales of English coins (14.3.1951), and two others had belonged to him (**372**, **981**).

LECOINTRE-DUPONT, Gabriel (1809–88). Scholar and collector. Collection sold privately, several coins from it being here. **454**, **965**.

LEU, BANK, (Zurich). See BANK LEU.

LEWIS, Rev. Samuel Savage (1836–91). Scholar and collector. Bequeathed his fine collection of coins and other objects to Corpus Christi College, of which he was Fellow and Librarian. See p. 398 above.

148, 389, 403, 414, 429, 598, 764, 776, 916, 920–1, 942, 1176, 1198, 1211, 1320, 1322, 1332, 1340, 1346–9, 1351, 1456, 1475.

LIGNE, Eugène Lamoral, Prince de (1804–80). Belgian politician and art connoisseur, grandson of the great eighteenth-century soldier and statesman. Selective catalogue, interrupted by the death of Ligne, published by Serrure (1880). Collection largely dispersed in two Sotheby sales, (I) 26.6.1968 and (II) 17.6.1976. Three coins from the first sale occur in this volume: **342, 374, 496.**

LINCOLN, W. S. & Son (London). Dealers, mid nineteenth century – 1920s.

LINDSAY, John (1784–1870). Dublin barrister and author of a number of important works, including what was for long the standard book on Irish coinage. Collection sold by Sotheby 14.8.1867. **1379.**

LITCHFIELD, Edward (*c.* 1787–1864). A fruiterer in Cambridge who founded his own small museum of antiquities. Most of his coins were sold by Sotheby 6.3.1865, but he gave a few, mostly false, to the Cambridge Antiquarian Soc. in 1847. **1483–9.**

LOCKETT, Richard Cyril (1873–1950). Scholar and collector, whose magnificent collection, especially strong in Ancient Greek coins (published in *SNG*) and English coins, was sold by Glendining in 13 parts. The parts relevant to this volume are as follows:

I (English 1: 6.6.1955), **669, 1122–4, 1132, 1140–1, 1155, 1181, 1369.**

III (Continental: 29.2.1956), **262, 388, 391, 423, 455, 518, 530, 534–5, 543–4, 546–7, 549, 551–3, 556, 558, 564, 566–7, 570, 577–8, 580–1, 583–8, 590–1, 593, 596–7, 599–600, 602, 605–6, 608, 611–12, 615–17, 619–20, 624, 626–8, 630–1, 633–4, 636–7, 720, 746, 760, 768, 822, 824, 842, 851, 888, 935, 978, 1005–6, 1008, 1015, 1103, 1478.**

X (English 4: 27.4.1960), **1352.**

LONGUET, Henry (1887–1963). Doctor, scholar and collector at Mulhouse (Alsace). Collection, mainly Byzantine, acquired by KAPAMADJI and the bulk of it subsequently sold at auction (Platt 17.3.1970). **10, 12, 13, 27–9, 54–5, 163, 165, 324.**

MACK, Richard Paston (1901–74). Collector and scholar, author of standard works on the coinages of ancient Britain and of the reign of Stephen. There were two Glendining sales of his main collection, (I) 18.11.1975 and (II) 23.3.1977, while other coins were bought by Spink. **696, 700, 707, 716, 1134A.**

MAINGUY, A. J. D. Owner of a collection acquired by Seaby *ante* 1950. **836, 889.**

MALLINSON, Rev. Arnold (1896–1985). Vicar of St Frideswide's, Osney, Oxford, and collector. Collection sold in Spink sale 39 (6.12.1984). **1124A.**

MALTER, Joel L., & Co. Coin dealers at Encino, California.

MANDER, Gerald Poynton (1885–1951). Collection acquired by Spink. **302.**

MANN, A. Collection of English coins sold by Sotheby 29.10.1917. **1124.**

MARMOD, son-in-law of NOCAS. Former owner of **502.**

MARSHAM, Hon. Robert (1834–1914). Sotheby 19.11.1888 (English coins). **1162, 1171, 1352.**

MARTIN, Rev. Joseph William (*c.* 1776–1858). Sotheby 23.5.1859 (English coins). **1305, 1494.**

MARTINETTI, M. Canessa (Naples) 28.11.1907. **1018.**

MARTINORI, Edoardo (d. 1935). Scholar and collector, specializing in the coins of Rome and the Papacy. The sale catalogue of his collection (Santamaria 24.11.1913) is one of the most useful general reference works on Italian coinage. **1034, 1039, 1046, 1052, 1065, 1067.**

MATTHEWS, Rev. Douglas Gilbert. MA (Cantab.) 1913; rector of Southover, Lewes, 1931–63. Collector. His collection, sold to Spinks in the 1960s, included a number of rare but damaged coins. **1375A.**

MAZARD, Jean. Scholar and collector, author of standard works on the coinage of ancient Mauritania and the French colonies. One important coin here comes from his collection. **734.**

MAZEL, M. Magistrate at Pézenas (nr Béziers) in the 1830s. Collector of coins found locally. **734.**

MCCLEAN, Frank (1837–1904). Wealthy engineer and astronomer, who collected a great variety of objets d'art. His illuminated MSS, ivories, etc., were left to the Fitzwilliam Museum, but his English and Roman coins were sold anonymously by Sotheby in two sales on 11 and 13.6.1906 as the 'Collection of an Astronomer Recently Deceased'. His son J. R. McClean (1872–1913) ranks as one of the major benefactors of the Museum, but in the field of Greek and not medieval coins. **1135, 1147, 1155–6, 1168, 1341.**

MCCORMICK, Miss F. M. See CONYBEARE, E.

MMAG BASEL. See MÜNZEN UND MEDAILLEN A.G. BASEL.

'MONNAIES BYZANTINES' sale. R. Ratto (Lugano) 5.12.1930. **609.**

'MONNAIES DES PAPES' sale, Bourgey 15.6.1914. The papal coins from the VIDAL QUADRAS collection. **1031, 1045, 1062, 1069, 1082, 1514.**

MONNIER, Auguste (1802–64). Specialist in the coinage of Lorraine. Collection sold by Rollin & Feuardent, 7.4.1874. **410.**

MONTAGU, Hyman (1846–95). A wealthy London solicitor who in the course of two decades put together an immensely valuable collection of classical and English coins and medals. Unless the contrary is indicated, coins here are from the first of the English sales (Sotheby 18.11.1895): **612, 1123–4, 1128, 1132, 1135, 1146–7, 1155–6, 1162–3, 1164(?), 1168, 1171, 1177, 1179, 1305, 1308–10, 1341, 1352, 1370, 1372, 1374, 1494, 1496.** One coin is from the fifth sale (Sotheby 16.11.1897): **1153.**

MONTCARRA, M. de. See VIRY, Pierre, comte de.

MONTENUOVO, Wilhelm Albrecht, Fürst von (1821–95). Illegitimate son of the Empress Marie Louise, duchess of Parma and widow of Napoleon I, by Count von Neipperg (= Neu-Berg = Montenuovo). A general in the Austro-Hungarian army and creator of a great collection sold by Hess in a series of dealers' lists and sales between 1880 and 1886. **1062.**

MOORE, Major General William Yorke (1806–90). Sotheby 1.3.1889. **152.**

MORÉ DE PRÉVIALA, Emile de (b. 1827), of Serverette (Lozère). Specialist on the Merovingian coinage of the Gévaudan. **428.**

MOTTE, Georges. Industrialist at Roubaix. His important collection of (mainly) French coins, of which a sumptuous catalogue was published by Rolland (1932), was sold by Bourgey 11.12.1951. See **473, 750, 752, 754, 756, 965,** and p. 335 for a note on some of the forgeries it contained.

MÜNZEN UND MEDAILLEN A.G. BASEL ('MMAG Basel'). Coin dealers and auctioneers. The firm, one of the most important in Europe, was founded in 1933 by the brothers Erich (1913–) and Herbert (1915–) Cahn, sons of Ludwig Cahn and grandsons of Adolph E. CAHN, under the name of Münzhandlung Basel. The name was changed to the present one in 1942.

MURCHISON, Capt. Roderick Maingey (d. 1873). Collector. His ancient British and Anglo-Saxon coins formed the Sotheby sale of 28.5.1866, his later English ones having been sold already on 27.6.1864. The Coin Room possesses a scrap-book of coin illustrations made by Murchison (HENDERSON bequest, ex MONTAGU (V) 644), but not all of them represent coins in his own collection. **1135, 1155, 1305, 1371.**

MURDOCH, John Gloag (d. 1902). Collector. His huge collection of coins and medals of the British Isles was dispersed by Sotheby in eight sales over 1903–4, those in this volume being from the first sale on 31.3.1903. **1305, 1352–3, 1496.**

MUSEUM OF ARCHAEOLOGY AND ANTHROPOLOGY ('MAA'), CAMBRIDGE. Coins belonging to. **98A, 649, 657, 1297, 1368, 1395A–B.**

NASCIA, Giuseppe (d. 1982). Coin dealer at Milan, trading as ARS ET NUMMUS, from the 1960s to 1982.

NELIGAN, Rev. William Chadwick. Irish collector (Shandon, Co. Cork). Sotheby 10.11.1881. **808.**

NEVILLE, Latimer (1853–1904), Master of Magdalene College. **753.**

NOCAS (Ligny). Collector. **502**.

NORBLIN, Louis Pierre Martin (1781–1854). Important collection catalogued by F. Poey d'Avant and sold by Rollin 2.7.1855. **1479**.

NUMISMATIC FINE ARTS. See GANS, E.

NUNN, J. J. Sotheby 27.11.1896. **1171**.

O'HAGAN, Henry Osborne. Two Sotheby sales, I (English coins) 16.12.1907; II (Continental and others) 27.4.1908. **1101**.

OLD UNIVERSITY COLLECTION. See p. 393. **1131**.

PALMER, Rev. W. Rector of Eynesbury (Hunts.). Donor to the CAMBRIDGE ANTIQUARIAN SOCIETY in 1845. **1129**.

PATRIZI, Marchese Filippo. Important collection of Italian coins begun by Filippo's father, Giovanni, in 1863. The medieval portion was acquired by CELATI in 1914, who resold part to RUCHAT. **1049, 1064**.

PEIRCE, Hayford (1883–1946). Byzantine scholar, art historian, and collector. His collection, mainly of Byzantine coins and formed in the 1920s and 1930s, was acquired *en bloc* by DUMBARTON OAKS in 1948. Many duplicates and non-Byzantine coins in it were subsequently sold, and a number are here. **167, 176, 186, 192, 196, 222, 241, 263, 348, 377, 747, 840, 844, 1019, 1470**.

PEMBROKE, Thomas Herbert, 8th earl of (1656–1733). Eighteenth-century politician and connoisseur, a great collector of what a contemporary airily described as 'statues, dirty gods, and coins' (*DNB*). Illustrations of the last were published in 1746, and the collection finally sold by Sotheby 31.7.1848. **1146**.

PERCEVAL, Spencer G. (1858–1922), of Trinity Hall. A generous benefactor of the Museum, who in addition to a substantial legacy gave it in his lifetime many objets d'art including (in 1920) a miscellaneous collection of over 500 coins. Nine of them are in this volume, five from a single hoard (**1159, 1327–8, 1335, 1337**) and the others being **1240, 1250, 1253, 1279**.

PERRET, R. A French collector whose coins were published in 1958 by BOURGEY and subsequently sold by the latter, but individually and not by auction. **336**.

PETERHOUSE. Coin in the collection on loan from (see p. 398). **1373**.

PEUS, Busso (1902–83). Coin dealer, auctioneer, and scholar, one of the leading figures in the German numismatic world in the middle years of this century. He entered the firm of Adolph HESS Nachf. in 1924, became its director in 1934, and changed its name to Busso Peus & Co., in 1940. He retired in 1967, and the firm continues as Busso Peus Nachf.

PHILIPSEN, Gustav (1853–1925). Danish collector of Greek and Roman coins. His main collection was dispersed by Jacob Hirsch in his Auktionen 26 (29.11.1909) and 32 (14.11.1912), but other coins were acquired for stock by Spink. **199**.

PILGRIM TRUST. Contributor to the purchase of **1122, 1352**.

PLATT, Maison. Firm of Paris coin dealers and auctioneers founded by Clément Platt (1874–1952) in 1906. He moved into the old business premises of Serrure in 1919, and in due course was succeeded by his son Marcel in association with René Kampmann (d. 1977).

POSWICK, untraced collection. **725**.

PRICE, Lake. Sotheby 27.5.1880. **1155, 1305**.

QUEENS' COLLEGE. Collection of (see p. 398). **855, 867, 874, 878, 904, 1338, 1395, 1490–2**.

RASHLEIGH, Evelyn W. Owner of a great family collection started by Philip Rashleigh (1729–1811) in the late eighteenth century and enormously expanded by Philip's great-nephew Jonathan (1820–1905), Evelyn's father, in the second half of the nineteenth. Sold by Sotheby 21.6.1909. **716, 1144, 1152, 1157, 1167**(?), **1170**(?), **1172, 1258, 1275, 1379, 1386**.

RATTO, Mario. Coin dealer and auctioneer, initially in Paris – where he bought out H. Rolland in 1928 and where he was succeeded by VINCHON – and subsequently, in succession to his father Rodolfo, at Milan.

RATTO, Rodolfo (1864–1949), Milan and Lugano. Founder in 1900 of one of the major European firms of coin dealers and auctioneers.

RÉCAMIER, Etienne (1834–93). Collector at Lyon, basically of Roman coins but with an important specialized collection of Lyon sold by Bourgey 2.3.1925. **393**.

REINHART, Wilhelm (1880–1953). An Austrian engineer who settled in Spain in 1913 and became a leading expert on Visigothic and Suevic coins. Many of his coins are in this collection. They were acquired either directly, or through dealers, or as duplicates from the ANS, which bought what remained of his collection from his heirs in 1956. **191, 194, 205, 210, 214, 217, 220, 224, 227, 229, 230–2, 246, 261, 265–6, 267, 278, 280, 347**.

REMEDI, Marchese Angelo (d. 1889). Scholar and collector at Luni (N. of Pisa). The sale catalogue of his collection (Sambon, Milan, 5.1.1885) is important as containing the Sarzana hoard (Longpérier 1858; Lafaurie 1972a). **1064**.

RENAULT (d. *c*. 1850). Collector at Vaucouleurs (on the Meuse W. of Toul) whose Merovingian coins were described by Robert (1851a) before being sold. **440**.

RICH, William Bennett. Coins sold anonymously by Sotheby 7.7.1828. **1305**.

RIDGEWAY, Sir William (1853–1926). Disney Professor of Archaeology at Cambridge and author of a fundamental work on the origins of weight systems and metallic currency. His legacy to the MUSEUM OF ARCHAEOLOGY AND ANTHROPOLOGY included a few coins. **649, 1297**.

RITCHIE, Jean Margaret (d. 1963). Bequeathed to the Museum some 600 coins collected by her grandfather, the Hebrew scholar C. D. Ginsburg (d. 1915), of which 173 were selected for retention and the remainder, as she had wished, were sold to provide a fund for future purchases. **127, 153**.

ROBERT, Charles (1812–87). One of the leading French numismatists of the nineteenth century. The sale catalogue of his main collection (Rollin & Feuardent 29.3.1886) remains a standard reference work for the coinage of Lorraine and the Three Bishoprics. His Merovingian coins were sold privately during his lifetime to AMÉCOURT. **392, 442A, 456, 476, 486**.

ROBINSON, Thomas William Usherwood (*c*. 1826–88). A Durham collector. Sotheby sale 1.5.1891. **669, 1450**.

ROLLIN & FEUARDENT. Paris coin dealers, auctioneers, publishers and scholars. The firm was founded in 1834 by Charles Louis Rollin (1777–1853), who was initially a money changer but after the first decade of the century interested himself more and more in coins and from 1834 onwards dealt in them exclusively. The firm was carried on by his son Camille (1813–83) and grandson, another Camille (d. 1906), but in 1860 it had been joined by Felix Feuardent (1819–1907), a bookseller and printer from Cherbourg with strong numismatic interests. For many years Rollin & Feuardent had a branch in London and for over half a century they played a leading role in the French numismatic world. After the death of the younger Camille Rollin the firm carried on as FEUARDENT FRÈRES.

ROSSI, Giancarlo (1818–98). Wealthy collector who formed in succession two great collections of Italian coins, the first sold by Sambon 6.12.1880 and the second by Vitalini 22.4.1895. First sale: **1062**.

ROTH, Bernard (1852–1915). A leading London surgeon who interested himself in numismatics during the last two decades of his life and published important studies on Celtic and Hiberno-Norse coins. His collection was dispersed in two Sotheby sales (I) 19.7.1917 and (II) 14.10.1918. First sale: **490**.

ROTHSCHILD, untraced collection. **392**.

ROUCY, Albert de. Scholar and collector at Compiègne, mid nineteenth century. **424**.

ROUX. Coin dealer at Bordeaux and subsequently at Nice in the late nineteenth and early twentieth century. A source of some of Grantley's coins.

RUCHAT, Carlo (1848–1919). Collector of Italian coins (esp. Tuscan and papal). The collection, formed between 1913 and 1919, was dispersed in four sales by Santamaria in 1921–3. Several of the papal coins in this collection passed through the third sale (29.5.1922). **1037, 1049, 1051, 1062, 1064–5, 1070, 1072, 1525.**

RYAN, Valentine John Eustace (1882–1947). Collector of Greek, Roman, English and Scottish coins. The Anglo-Saxon series was included in the second (Glendining 22.1.1952) of the five sales in which this immensely rich collection was dispersed. **1164, 1370, 1382.**

SADD, Alfred Henry (1852–1915). The third and last of three generations of antique dealers on King's Parade, Cambridge. His letterhead describes him as 'Numismatist, Antiquary, Jeweller, Silversmith, etc. Established 1815'. Coins found locally often passed through his hands. **949, 1345, 1367, 1393, 1442.**

ST LOUIS STAMP AND COIN COMPANY (St Louis, Missouri), a firm set up in 1904 by Burdette G. Johnson (d. 1947) and the source of a number of Peirce's coins in the 1920s and 1930s.

ST NEOTS URBAN DISTRICT COUNCIL. Donor of coin from local excavations. **655.**

SAMBON, Jules or Giulio (1836–1921). Dealer, auctioneer, scholar and collector. Sambon was French by nationality but born in Naples, and throughout his life did business in France and Italy (Rome, later Florence) indifferently. From 1899 onwards his son Arthur or Arturo (1886–1947), a prolific writer on medieval Italian coinage, did business in Paris, the firms being formally separate but father and son working in close association together.

'SAMMLUNG EINES RHEINISCHEN GELEHRTEN'. See VERWORN, Max.

SANTAMARIA, P. and P. (Rome). Coin dealers, auctioneers and publishers over the past century, the firm having been founded in 1898 by the cousins Pietro (1863–1930) and Pio (1881–1947) and carried on by their descendants.

SCHULMAN, Jacques (1849–1914). Founder in Amersfoort in the 1880s of a firm of coin dealers which transferred to Amsterdam in 1902 and which since that time, under his sons Maurits ('Max': 1876–1943) and André (1877–1936) and André's son Jacques (1906–), has remained one of the most important in Europe.

SCHULMAN, Hans M. F. (1913–). Son of Max Schulman, emigrated to New York in 1938 and set up a firm which flourished in the decades after 1945.

SEABY, B. A. One of the leading firms of coin dealers and numismatic publishers in London since 1926, founded by Herbert ('Bert') Seaby (1898–1979).

SEARLE, Rev. William George (1829–1913). Fellow of Queens' College, vicar of Oakington (Cambs.), scholar, collector and benefactor of the Museum; see above, p. 394. Only a few of the many coins he is known to have given can be identified and only one is in this volume. **949.**

SELTMAN, Charles Theodore (1886–1957). Fellow and Librarian of Queens' College and lecturer in Classics in the University, with a special interest in Greek art and numismatics. His father, Ernest John Seltman, had been an antique dealer and collected Greek coins. The younger Seltman did not collect coins very seriously himself, and disposed of the few he had to Spink's in the 1940s. One in this vol. was acquired by Grierson. **96.**

SERRURE, Raymond (1862–99). Scholar and coin dealer, the last of three generations of distinguished numismatists. His firm (Paris) was carried on by his widow down to 1913.

SHEPHERD, Rev. Edward John (*c.* 1801–74). Rector of Trottersclifie (Kent) from 1827 to his death. A number of Anglo-Saxon coins are from the sale of his coin collection (Sotheby 22.7.1885). **1135, 1137, 1168, 1192, 1199, 1217, 1225, 1231, 1257, 1269, 1271, 1296, 1304, 1307, 1365, 1496.**

SHERBORN, Charles Davies (1861–1942). Professionally a specialist in nomenclature on the staff of the Natural History Museum in South Kensington, Sherborn started collecting Byzantine Æ in 1914 and in 1939 gave his large collection (over 1,800 coins) to the Fitzwilliam Museum apart from some already presented to the BM. A few related coins in his collection are catalogued in this volume: **25, 40, 94, 129, 143, 150, 159**.

SHORE, Robert Alexander (d. 1939). A British businessman who lived in Portugal and whose important collection of Portuguese and Brazilian gold coins was sold by Glendining 16.7.1945. Most of his Visigothic coins are in this collection: **203, 218, 238, 249, 260, 270, 279, 281–2, 1458, 1465–7, 1471**.

SHORTHOUSE, E. Ludlow, Roberts & Weller 29.2.1886. **1496**.

SIGNORELLI, Angelo (d. 1952). An eminent Rome doctor who collected objets d'art ranging from Greek vases to modern Italian paintings. His important coin collection was dispersed by Santamaria in six sales over the years 1951–5, one of the *antiquiores* now in this collection being from the fourth sale (25.1.54). **1086**.

SIVARD DE BEAULIEU, Pierre-Louis Antoine (1767–1826). French politician, Administrateur-Général of the Paris mint 1799–1826 and a collector of coins and medals which were bought by Rollin from his heirs in 1854. References in Belfort (3300ff.) show that he at some time acquired an important hoard of sceattas and Merovingian deniers. **670–1**.

SMART, Francis Gray (1846–1913). A doctor with scientific interests and large private means who built up an important coin collection, especially rich in the Anglo-Saxon field. It was inherited by his nephew T. J. G. DUNCANSON, who gave it to the Fitzwilliam Museum in 1930. **651, 668, 1134, 1144, 1149, 1152, 1160–1, 1167, 1170, 1172–3, 1178, 1180, 1194, 1258–9, 1267, 1275, 1278, 1303, 1305, 1313, 1325, 1344, 1350, 1356, 1366, 1371, 1374, 1396, 1405, 1407, 1422, 1441, 1449, 1451, 1493** (See p. 394).

SMITH, A. Donor of two coins to the Museum in 1942. **1207, 1390**.

SMITH, Aquil(l)a (1806–90). Dublin doctor and antiquary, a copious writer on Irish archaeology and coinage. His collection of Irish coins and tokens was bought after his death by the Royal Irish Academy and is now in the National Museum at Dublin; other coins were sold privately. **1379**.

SORENSON, David. American research student at Queens' College in 1982–6, who gave to the Museum several Anglo-Saxon coins found locally. **699, 701, 710–11**.

SOTHEBY, Wilkinson and Hodge (London). General auctioneers since the eighteenth century and displaced by GLENDINING's as the chief London firm of coin auctioneers only in the 1920s.

SOUTHEY, R. G. Glendining 21.7.1948. **1088**.

'SPANISH COLLECTION'. A large group of Visigothic coins, of undisclosed ownership, included in a Christie sale of 16.6.1959. **169, 178, 193, 215–16, 226, 236, 240, 248, 250, 252, 253, 255, 257, 271–2, 274–5, 277, 284, 287**.

SPINK & SONS (London). A major firm of antique dealers since the 18th century. Their eminence as coin dealers and numismatic publishers dates from the 1890s, after Leonard FORRER (1869–1953) joined the firm (in 1887).

STERNBERG, Frank. Coin dealer and auctioneer at Zurich from the 1940s onwards.

STEWART, Ian Halley (1935–). Scholar and collector. **1498**.

STOKES, Sir Arthur (1858–1916), of King's College. See Isabel L. HUMPHRY.

TAIT, A. R. Wine merchant at Oporto, owner of a few coins occasionally acquired in Portugal by his father or himself. **206, 213, 283, 1094, 1459, 1469**.

THIEME, C. G. A German firm of coin dealers and numismatic publishers at Leipzig (1863–1900) and Dresden (1900–late 1920s). **146**.

THÉRY, L. Important collection in part sold by Vinchon: (I) 22.10.1963 and (II) 20.3.1964. **409**.

THORBURN, Philip (1900–64). Coin collector and scholar. **557, 1354–5**.

TINCHANT, Paul (1893–1981). Coin dealer at Brussels from the early 1930s to his retirement in 1964.

TINOZZI, Francesco Paolo (1894–1973). A distinguished Pavese surgeon who collected coins and antiquities extensively if not always wisely, since, when his collection gradually came on the market after his death, a large proportion of his acquisitions turned out to be far from competent modern forgeries. Others, however, were genuine. **1033, 1056, 1071–2, 1079, 1100**.

TODERI, Giuseppe. Coin dealer at Florence, mid 20th century.

TRINITY COLLEGE. Collection deposited on indefinite loan in the Fitzwilliam Museum in 1937. See above, pp. 397–8. **112, 116, 134, 437, 465, 625, 640, 646, 650, 652–3, 660, 667, 681, 684, 686, 694–5, 697–8, 702–6, 718, 1136, 1151, 1202, 1223, 1312, 1333, 1403, 1411, 1443–4**. One relevant coin came to the Museum in a 1957 gift of miscellaneous items: **706A**.

TRINKS, Wilhelm (1841–1907). Collector and subsequently dealer in Prague and (from 1893) Vienna. One of Grantley's sources.

TROTTMANN, H. French collector, untraced. **734**.

ULRICH-BANSA, Barone Oscar (1892–1982). Italian scholar and collector, specialist in late Roman numismatics. His medieval coins, coming mainly from his relative C. GAVAZZI, were disposed of during his lifetime. **63, 175, 300, 323, 325, 327, 366, 368, 1035–8, 1040–4, 1047, 1049, 1051, 1054, 1058–9, 1061–2, 1064–6, 1070, 1073, 1075, 1120**.

VACCARI, Emanuele (d. 1918). A doctor at Ferrara who formed an outstanding collection of Italian coins sold by Santamaria, (I) 5.12.1924, (II) 3.6.1925. **1054**.

VAN DER CHIJS, P. O. See CHIJS, P. O. van der.

VAQUER. Untraced French collector. **597**.

VECCHI, V.C. & Sons. London coin dealers and auctioneers, usually jointly with some other firm: Bonham-Vecchi (**5, 742**), Vecchi-Schwer (**748**).

VERITY, James (1845–1910). A Leeds businessman who collected coins and was for a time (*c.* 1870 onwards) a dealer at Dewsbury (Yorks.). The residue of his stock was bought after his death by Spink. **1123**.

VERWORN, Max (1863–1921). Professor of Physiology at the University of Bonn and collector of Celtic coins and those of the German migration period. They were sold anonymously by CAHN (Auction 49: 11.12.1922) under the title 'SAMMLUNG EINES RHEINISCHEN GELEHRTEN'. **735**.

VIDAL QUADRAS y Ramon, Manuel (1818–94). A Barcelona collector whose huge collection of (mainly) Spanish coins was published in 4 vols. in 1892 and acquired by the Paris dealer Bourgey. Only the papal section has subsequently come on the market: see 'MONNAIES DES PAPES' sale.

VINCHON, Jean. Paris dealer and auctioneer in succession to Mario RATTO.

VIRY, Pierre, comte de. Owner of an eighteenth-century collection formed at Grenoble by F. S. de Bally de MONTCAR(R)A (1691–1767) and sold by Sotheby 24.2.1909. **899–900, 906**.

VITALINI, Ortensio (1842–1919). Italian coin dealer and numismatic publisher, initially at Camerino and subsequently at Rome. See p. 336. **1521**.

WADDELL, Edward J. Coin dealer at Washington, D.C., at first in association with BIRKLER but (after 1981) independently.

WARNE, Charles (1801–81). Dorset antiquarian. Sotheby sale 24.5.1889. **1163**.

WEBB, Henry (1809–94). London solicitor, collector of English coins. Two Sotheby sales, 9.7.1894 and 25.7.1895. **605**.

WEBB, untraced collector or dealer. **1374**.

WEBER, F. Parkes (1863–1962). A London doctor, son of Sir Hermann WEBER (see next entry), writer on a wide variety of subjects and donor of coins to the Museum on a number of occasions early in this century. **103, 954**.

WEBER, Sir Hermann (1823–1918), an eminent London physician now best remembered for his collection of Greek coins, the great catalogue of which by Forrer remains a standard work of reference. Some of his English coins, sold anonymously by Sotheby 16.6.1885, were bought by Young and are now here. **954, 1174, 1311, 1317–19, 1321, 1400, 1402, 1436, 1445**.

WEBSTER, William (1821–85). Coin dealer in succession to his uncle William Till. Stock sold in 2 parts by Sotheby, 18.2.1886 and 22.12.1886. **1132**.

WHITBOURN, Richard (*c.* 1811–68). Sotheby sale 2.2.1869. **1386**.

WHITE, J. D. Assistant Librarian at Trinity College and donor of a number of coins to the College collection. **1202, 1223**.

WHITE, William Archibald Armstrong (1776–1847). Sotheby sale 27.11.1848. **1144**.

WHITTON, Cuthbert Alexander (d. 1950). English schoolmaster, scholar and collector. His collection was disposed of privately via Seaby after his death. **893**.

WIDRANGES, Hippolyte, comte de (1800–80). Scholar and collector. His collection, which included some important Merovingian coins, was sold by Rollin & Feuardent 4.6.1884 (name spelled 'Videranges' on title-page). **487**.

WIGAN, Edward (1823–71). An extremely wealthy collector of Greek and Roman coins. The pick of them went to the British Museum, but the bulk of the collection was bought in 1872 by Rollin & Feuardent and in due course dispersed. Three coins here once belonged to his English collection, which was inherited from his uncle John Alfred Wigan (1787–1869) and had been formed from the 1830s onwards. **1156, 1352, 1495**.

WIGERSMA, Servaas (1857–1912). Dutch scholar and collector, whose collection was sold by F. Muller (Amsterdam) 1.12.1913. **360, 371**.

WINDISCH-GRÄTZ, Ernst Prinz zu. Creator of an immense general collection of which a detailed catalogue (7 vols. in 5) was published by E. Fiala and others (Prague and Vienna, 1895–1912). Part of the Greek and Roman series was sold by Cahn (Sale 47: 17.5.1922), but the bulk was acquired by HOLLSCHEK. **328**.

WOLFE, Charles Henry. Coin dealer at Lakeside, Ohio, U.S.A.

WYATT, James (1816–78). Treasurer to Bedford Borough Council, who in the 1860s and 1870s put together a small collection of coins, mainly of local interest. A few of them, found long after his death in furniture that had belonged to him, were acquired by the Museum in 1974 through the good offices of the Cambridge antique dealers Messrs Collins & Clarke. **1206, 1212, 1216, 1232, 1263, 1375**.

YOUNG, Arthur William (1852–1936). One of the major benefactors of the Museum collection (above, pp. 394–5), the coins in this volume included in his bequest being **373, 672, 674–5, 677–80, 685, 691–3, 925–32, 1126, 1128, 1135, 1137, 1143, 1145–7, 1150, 1153–4, 1156–8, 1162, 1165, 1168, 1171, 1174–5, 1177, 1179, 1182–4, 1186, 1189, 1191–2, 1195–7, 1199–1201, 1215, 1217–18, 1221, 1224–6, 1230–1, 1233–5, 1237–8, 1243–9, 1254–7, 1261–2, 1264–5, 1269, 1271–2, 1274, 1276–7, 1282, 1285–7, 1289–93, 1296, 1298–9, 1302, 1304, 1307, 1311, 1315–19, 1321, 1324, 1326, 1329, 1331, 1339, 1341, 1353, 1357–9, 1361, 1365, 1378, 1380, 1383–6, 1391, 1394, 1399, 1400–2, 1409–10, 1415, 1417, 1428, 1436, 1440, 1445–7, 1450, 1495**.

YOUNG, C. E. B. Brother of A. W. YOUNG; see p. 395. **925–32**.

YOUNG, James Halliburton. Sotheby sale 7.4.1881. **1495**.

YOUNG, Matthew (1771–1837). The main London coin dealer of his day. His stock was disposed of in nine sales (Sotheby 1839–42). **1156**.

ARRANGEMENT OF THE CATALOGUE

NUMBERING. The coins are numbered separately in each volume. Cross-references between volumes use these numbers preceded by that of the volume and a full-stop (e.g. **1.1318** means no. 1318 in Vol. 1).

LEGENDS AND DESCRIPTION. These are generally only given where they may not be clear from the illustration, although in some series the full legends have been set out as a matter of course. For Anglo-Saxon coins, following *SCBI* practice, the moneyer's name is given as it appears on the coin, followed in brackets by the normalized West-Saxon form as used in *SCBI* 28 (the Index to Vols. 1–20) where this seems desirable.

IDENTIFICATIONS AND REFERENCES. The standard works on each coin series are listed before each section, and references are given to these; see also the 'Literature' sections to each chapter of the 'Introduction'. The degree of precision varies according to the amount of work that has been done on each particular series, so that sometimes no more than a type identification is possible.

WEIGHTS. These are given in grams (abbreviated g), but grains (abbreviated gr.) are given as well for English coins, since there is good reason to believe that the modern weight corresponds to that used by the moneyers of the time. 1gr. = 0.0648g; 1g = 15.432gr.

METAL. The customary symbols for gold (AV), silver (AR) and copper (Æ) are used. Where the coins on one plate are predominantly of one metal this is indicated at the top of the page.

Virtually all the gold coins in this volume have been analysed by Mr W. A. Oddy in the British Museum Research Laboratory using the specific gravity method described in Oddy *et al.* 1972. Most were made as part of a major programme of analysis of Dark-Age coinages in the early 1970s intended to facilitate Dr Kent's work on Sutton Hoo. Subsequent acquisitions, and certain Museum coins originally omitted, were analysed in 1983. The Lombard and Beneventan results were published in Oddy 1972 and 1974 respectively, and references to them are cited in the catalogue. For the other coins the specific gravity is given and the fineness calculated using Table II in Oddy *et al.* 1972. Metcalf has analysed the Merovingian silver deniers and some of the Frisian sceattas using an X-ray fluorescence spectrometer. The results, including the proportions of various trace elements, are published in Metcalf 1983, but only the silver fineness is given in this volume. Metcalf and Northover have analysed a number of the ninth-century English pennies by electron-probe micro-analysis (below, p. 598). Both gold and silver finenesses are given to the nearest 1%, since the inaccuracies in early medieval minting techniques and the experimental margin of error in the analyses make greater precision irrelevant.

DIE-AXES. Die-axes have been measured to the nearest 10° using a converted protractor as described in *NCirc* 1981, p. 364 (↑=0°, →=90°, ↓=180°, ←=270°). The tops of the obverse and reverse designs have been taken on the same alignment as the illustration on the plate. Where the design has no feature by which to align it, the die-axis has been omitted. Late Roman and Byzantine coins are normally 180°, but are sometimes 0° or at Carthage 90°. Only a few medieval series have regular die-axis, though in some series coins from a single pair of dies may bear one of four 90° relationships (normally 0°, 90°, 180° and 270°, but occasionally positions between them, e.g. 20°, 110°, 200° and 290°). An irregular die-axis in a series where it is normally regular may suggest that a coin is imitative.

SIZE. Only in the case of certain Italian coins where it is relevant to their attribution are the diameters of the flans (and the reverse die faces) given. For the other coins their sizes can be judged from the illustrations, which are of natural size save where enlargements × 2 (indicated by an asterisk) have been added.

NOTES ON THE COINS. Discussions which are too long for the catalogue entries form a separate section, 'Notes on the Coins' (pp. 631–46 below).

PROVENANCES. The first letters indicate which collection the coin is in:

- FM Fitzwilliam Museum
- PG Grierson collection (deposited in the Fitzwilliam Museum)
- CCC Corpus Christi College (Lewis collection)
- MAA Museum of Archaeology and Anthropolgy
- QC Queens' College

Information about these collections and the individuals, firms, and sales referred to in the provenances will be found in the sections 'Formation of the Collections' (pp. 393–8 above) and 'Collectors, Dealers and Donors' (pp. 399–414 above). A series of dots (. . .) in a provenance indicates that there is a break in continuity of known ownership, and there may be others elsewhere of which there is no record.

PLATES

VANDALS (1)

All regular coins are of the Carthage mint. Principal references are: *BMC Vand* and *MIB*.

PSEUDO-IMPERIAL COINAGE, *c.* 440–*c.* 490

With the name of Honorius (393–423)
For attribution to the Vandals, see p. 20 above.

1 *Siliqua.* Obv. **DNHONORI: VSPFΛ[VG]** Rev. **[V]RBS ROIIΛ, [R]VPS** (for *Ravenna pusulatum*). AR 1.74g 330°. *BMC Vand* 2.6–9; *MIB* –. The prototype is a siliqua of Ravenna, Cohen VIII, 188.70.

2 *As last.* Obv. **DNHONORI[** Rev. **VRB[ ]OIIΛ, RVPS.** AR 1.64g 320°. Ref. as last.

3 *As last.* Obv. **]IVSPEΛVC** Rev. **VRBS ROII[** , ex. off flan. AR 1.53g 190°. Ref. as last. Much cruder style than preceding coins.

4 *Half-siliqua.* Obv. **]NHONORI VSPEΛ[** Rev. **VICTOR[, RV** (for *Ravenna*). AR 0.72g 220°. *BMC Vand* –; *MIB* –. The prototype is a half-siliqua of Ravenna, Cohen VIII, 184.38.

5 *As last.* Obv. **ΓhONO[** Rev. **]AVCI, RV.** AR 0.70g 10°. Ref. as last.

REGAL COINAGE, *c.* 490–533

GUNTHAMUND, 484–96

6 *100 denarii.* Obv. **DNREXGV[ ]HAMVNDV** Rev. **DN** w. **C** below (for 100 denarii). AR 1.87g 60°. *BMC Vand* 8.1–2; *MIB* I, pl. 42.2.

7 *As last.* Obv. **DNREXG[ ]HAMVNDV.** AR 2.01g 160°. Ref. as last.

8 *50 denarii.* Obv. **DNRXG[ ]NTHA** Rev. **DN** (for 500 nummi = 50 denarii?). AR 1.08g chipped 20°. *BMC Vand* 8–9.3–7; *MIB* I, pl. 42.3. For interpretation of the mark of value, see p. 19.

9 *As last.* Obv. **]NTHA.** AR 0.95g chipped and broken 150°. Ref. as last.

10 *As last.* Obv. **DNRX[ ]NTHA.** AR 0.76g 160°. Ref. as last.

11 *25 denarii.* Obv. **DNR[** Rev. **DN XXV** (for 25 denarii). AR 0.52g 310°. *BMC Vand* 9.8; *MIB* I, pl. 42.4. The attribution to Gunthamund rather than Thrasamund is based on the style of portrait and epigraphy.

12 *As last.* Obv. **]HA**? AR 0·54g chipped and corroded 10°. Ref. as last. Possibly a coin of Thrasamund.

13 *Nummus.* Obv. bust r. Rev. **D** in wreath. Æ 0.78g 100°. *BMC Vand* 35.150–1; *MIB* II, pl. 40.N14. For the attribution to Gunthamund, see p. 22.

14 *As last.* Æ 0.98g 280°. Ref. as last.

THRASAMUND, 496–523

Class 1, distinguished by finer style of bust, wreath and epigraphy.

15 *50 denarii.* Obv. **DNRGTHR ASAMVDS.** AR 1.06g chipped 120°. *BMC Vand* 12.11; *MIB* I, pl. 42.5b.

16 *25 denarii.* Obv. **]RGTH ASA[** . AR 0.46g chipped 120°. *BMC Vand* –; *MIB* I, pl. 42.7.

Class 2, with more stylized bust and wreath, the 50-denarius pieces with the mark of value **L** on the rev.

17 *50 denarii.* Obv. **DNR[ ]SAMVNDS.** AR 0.94g 310°. *BMC Vand* 12.12; *MIB* I, pl. 42.6a.

18 *As last.* Obv. **]SAMVNDS.** AR 1.00g 140°. Ref. as last.

19 *Nummus.* Obv. **DNRC[** , bust r. Rev. Victory l. Æ 0.64g 160°. *BMC Vand* 21.32–6; *MIB* I, pl. 42.16.

20 *As last.* Obv. **DNRC[** Æ 0.94g 110°. Ref. as last.

For imitations of these nummi, see **31–2**.

HILDERIC, 523–30

21 *50 denarii.* Obv. **DNHILDI RIXREX** Rev. **FELIX KARTG,** Carthago standing. AR 1.12g pierced 110°. *BMC Vand* 13.3; *MIB* I, pl. 42.8.

22 *As last.* Legends as last. AR 1.17g pierced 70°. Ref. as last.

23 *25 denarii.* Obv. **D[NHILD] RIXREX.** AR 0.56g chipped 270°. *BMC Vand* 14.8; *MIB* I, pl. 42.10 (this coin).

24 *Nummus.* Obv. **HILD [REX].** Æ 0.80g 70°. *BMC Vand* 14.9; *MIB* I, pl. 42.21.

25 *As last.* Obv. obliterated. Æ 0.89g. Ref. as last.

1. PG: Spink 12.2.1945; ex Grantley 2772; acq. in Paris.
2. PG: Dillen 29.3.1949.
3. PG: Baldwin 27.5.1948; from Glendining 12.5.1948, lot 217.
4, 17. PG: M. Ratto 30.5.1971.
5. PG: Bonham-Vecchi sale 7 (29.3.1982), lot 482; from a Tunisian hoard, see *Coin Hoards* 2 (1976), 322 (part only) and Morrisson and Schwartz 1982.
6, 18. PG: Seaby 17.10.1945; ex Grantley 2774 (**18** incorrectly identified in cat.).
7. PG: Seaby 8.1.1947; ex Hansen; ex Sotheby 2.6.1924, lot 161.
8. PG: Seaby 17.10.1945; ex Grantley 2774; from Schulman.
9. PG: Baldwin 26.5.1949; ex Derriman; acq. in Carthage 1944.
10, 12, 13. PG: Kapamadji 1.10.1964; ex Longuet.
11. PG: Kapamadji 21.10.1960.
14. PG: Baldwin 8.10.1952.
15, 23. PG: MMAG Basel 22.1.1970 (list 308, nos. 30 and 32).
16. PG: Kricheldorf sale 8 (2.11.1960), lot 272.
19. PG: Kunst und Münzen 24.2.1983 (list 50, no. 450).
20. PG: Spink 1.12.1981 (*NCirc* Dec. 1981, no. 8386).
21. PG: Berghaus 15.11.1952; ex Krüger.
22. PG: Hollschek XII 943.
24. PG: Seaby 17.10.1945; ex Grantley 2775.
25. FM: Sherborn 1939.

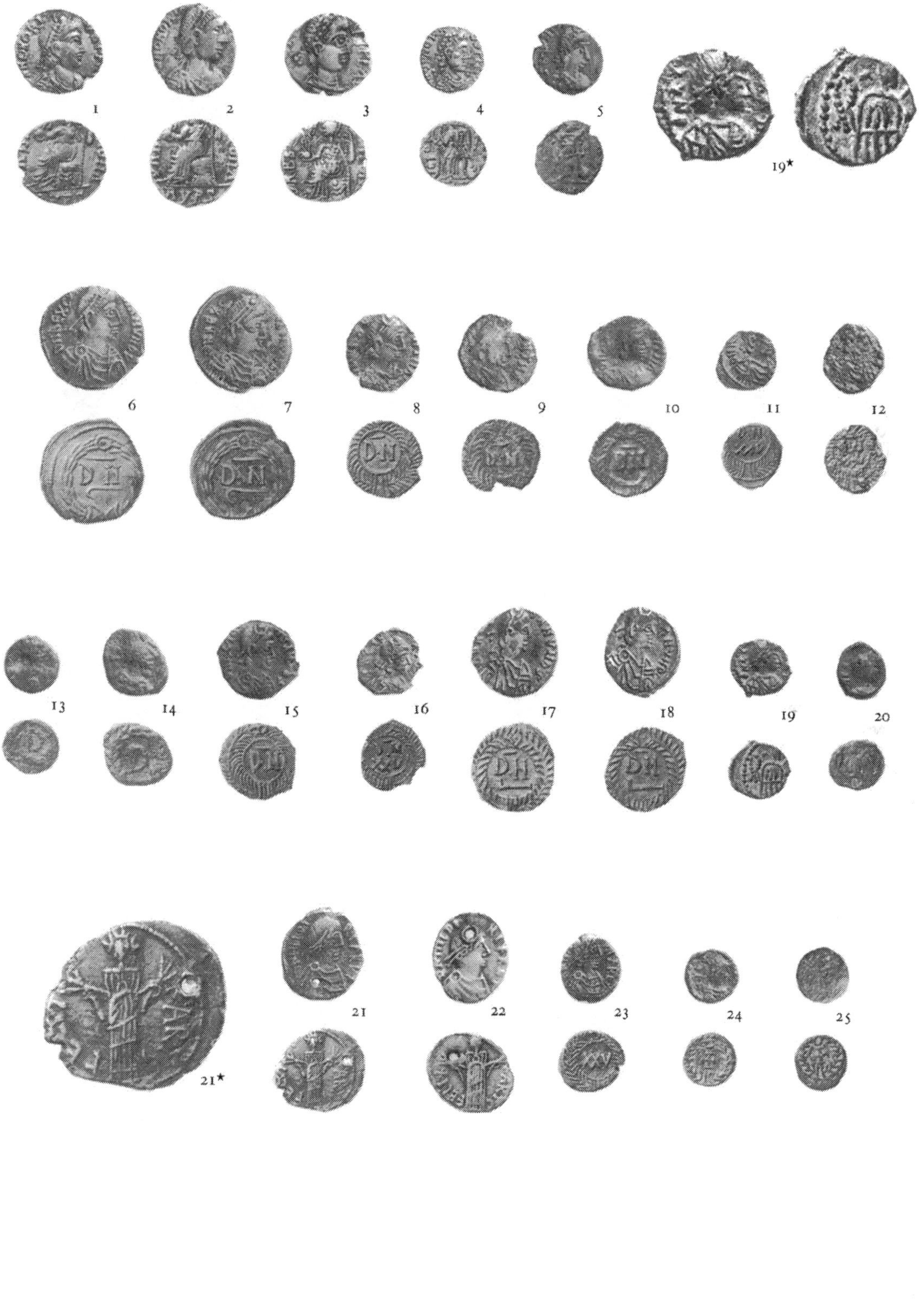
1 2 3 4 5
19*
6 7 8 9 10 11 12
13 14 15 16 17 18 19 20
21 22 23 24 25
21*

VANDALS (2)

REGAL COINAGE (*cont.*)

GELIMER, 530–4

26 *50 denarii*. Obv. **DNRE[XG]EIIAMIR**. AR 1.20g 180°. *BMC Vand* 15.2; *MIB* I, pl. 42.12.

27 *25 denarii*. Legend indistinct. AR 0.38g 90°. *BMC Vand* –; *MIB* I, pl. 42.90 (as Hilderic); *MIB* II, pl. 40.N12 (re-attributed to Gelimer).

28 *Nummus*. Obv. **GEIL[** , bust r. Rev. monogram of *Gelimer*. Æ 0.62g 190°. *BMC Vand* 16.4; *MIB* I, pl. 42.25.

29 *As last*. Obv. **GEIL[** . Æ 0.94g 180°. Ref. as last.

30 *As last*. Obv. **]AMIR**. Æ 0.69g 300°. Ref. as last, but var. of legend.

VANDALIC IMITATIONS (NUMMI)

The majority of the small bronze coins tentatively attributed by Wroth to the Vandals (*BMC Vand* 17–42) are either not African or post-date Justinian's re-establishment of imperial rule in 534. The Vandals did, however, produce unofficial, tiny bronze coins in large quantity, the commonest being imitations of Thrasamund's Victory nummi (**19–20**), which have been found in quantity at Carthage and in such hoards as those of Sidi Aïch (Lafaurie 1960b) and Aïn Kelba (Morrisson 1980). See pp. 17, 23 above.

31 Obv. bust l.(?) Rev. Victory l. Æ 0.21g 150°. *BMC Vand* 22.40 var.; Morrisson 1980, nos. 389ff. Imitation of a nummus of Thrasamund (**19–20**).

32 Obv. bust r. Rev. Victory (only robe visible). Æ 0.47g 40°. *BMC Vand* 22.40; Morrisson 1980, nos. 752ff.

33 Obv. bust r. in thick border. Rev. Christogram(?) in circle and wreath. Æ 0.35g. *BMC Vand* –. Possibly a Vandalic imitation of a nummus of Gunthamund with a Christogram (as *MIB* I, pl. 42.15).

SEMI-AUTONOMOUS COPPER COINAGE OF CARTHAGE, *c.* 480–533

Class 1, c. 480–*c.* 523. Heavy series. Obv. Carthago standing, crowned w. corn wreath and holding ears of corn, within laurel wreath. Rev. mark of value within laurel wreath.

42 nummi ($\frac{1}{12}$th-siliqua).

Var. a. Pellet in wreath-ornament. *BMC Vand* 6.3; *MIB* I, pl. 42.17a.

34 12.47g 0°.
35 11.66g worn 200°.
36 10.75g 220°.
37 9.78g very worn 200°.
38 10.39g worn 20°.

Var. b. Cross in wreath-ornament. *BMC Vand* 6.7: *MIB* I, pl. 42.17b.

39 11.70g worn 340°.
40 10.83g scraped 330°.

21 nummi ($\frac{1}{24}$th-siliqua). *BMC Vand* 6.8; *MIB* I, pl. 42.18.

41 9.84g 340°.

12 nummi ($\frac{1}{1000}$th-solidus). *BMC Vand* 7.8–11; *MIB* I, pl. 42.19.

42 4.69g 100°.

26. PG: Seaby 17.10.1945; ex Grantley 2776.
27–9. PG: Kapamadji 1.10.1964; ex Longuet.
30. PG: Seaby 17.10.1945; ex Grantley 2777.
31–2. PG: Derriman 1946; found at Carthage 1944.
33. PG: Spink 18.10.1961.
34. PG: Baldwin 30.5.1947; ex Grantley 2773.
35. FM: provenance unrecorded.
36. PG: C. Blom 1.8.1968.
37. PG: Vinchon sale 25.4.1960, lot 728.
38. PG: Wolfe 19.7.1969.
39. PG: Blunt 10.1.1951; found at Tunis.
40. FM: Sherborn 1939.
41. PG: Birkler & Waddell 16.7.1981 (list 2, no. 66).
42. PG: Kapamadji 21.10.1960.

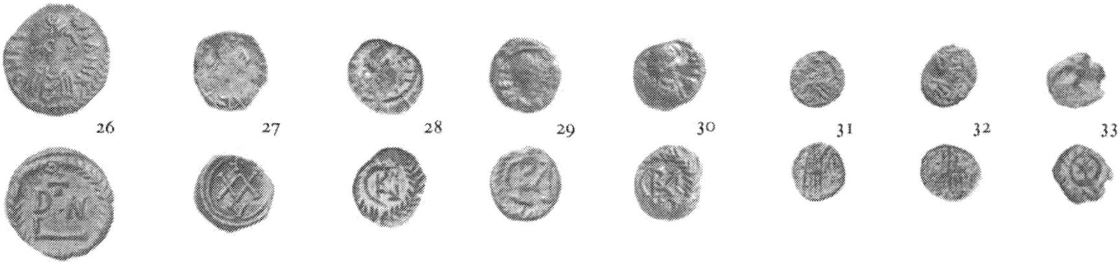

26 27 28 29 30 31 32 33

34 35 36 37 38

39 40 41 42

VANDALS (3)

SEMI-AUTONOMOUS COPPER COINAGE OF CARTHAGE (*cont.*)

Class 2 (*c.* 523–33). Light series. Obv. **KART HAGO**, soldier standing Rev. horse's head above mark of value.

42 nummi. BMC Vand 3.10–13; *MIB* I, pl. 42.22.

43 9.48g 80°.
44 8.68g 200°.

21 nummi. BMC Vand 4.14–17; *MIB* I, pl. 42.23.

45 8.17g 300°. Illus. *MIB* I, pl. 42.23.
46 6.64g 270°.
47 7.80g 260°.

12 nummi. BMC Vand 4.18–22; *MIB* I, pl. 42.24.

48 5.38g 230°.
49 4.63g 250°.
50 5.15g 40°.

4 nummi ($\frac{1}{1000}$th-tremissis). Obv. bust l. holding palm Rev. $\overline{\textbf{N}}$ above IIII. *BMC Vand* 7.12–14; *MIB* I, pl. 42.20.

51 1.09g 90°.
52 0.91g 130°.
53 1.07g 20°.
54 1·04g 300°.
55 1.24g 60°.
56 0.98g 70°.

ITALY: ODOVACAR, 476–93

References are: *BMC Vand* and Kraus = Kraus 1928.

With the name of Zeno (474–91)

57 *Tremissis.* Milan. Obv. **DNΣENO PERPAVG** Rev. **COMOB**. *A/* 1.40g (SG 18.87: 97% Au) 180°. *BMC Vand* 45.14 var.; Kraus 54.15 var. The attribution to Milan is based on the style of the bust and the character of the wreath.

58 *As last.* Obv. **DNZENO PERPΛVG** (**ΛV** ligatured) Rev. **COMOB**. *A/* 1.38g (SG 17.11: 84% Au) 180°. Ref. as last.

59 *As last.* Obv. **DNZENO PERPΛVG** (**ΛV** ligatured) Rev. **COMOB**. *A/* 1.45 g (SG 18.23: 93% Au) 180°. Ref. as last.

60 *As last.* Obv. **DNZENO PERPΛVC** (**ΛV** ligatured) Rev. **COMOB**. *A/* 1.44g (SG 18.82: 97% Au) 190°. Ref. as last.

61 *Half-siliqua.* Milan? Obv. **DNZENO PERPΛVG** Rev. eagle. *Æ* 0.96g 310°. *BMC Vand* –; Kraus 55.22.

62 *Half-siliqua.* Milan. Obv. **DNZENO PERPΛVC** (**ΛV** ligatured) Rev. standing figure wearing mural crown and holding staff and cornucopia, w. **MD** (for *Mediolanum*) in field. *Æ* 0.92g 0°. *BMC Vand* –; Kraus 55.20.

Follis, see **92**.

With the name or monogram of Odovacar

63 *Half-siliqua.* Ravenna. Obv. **]L[ ]OVΛC** (for FL*avius* ODOVAC*ar*) Rev. monogram of **ODOVA**, w. **RV** (for *Ravenna*) below. *Æ* 0.86g 170°. *BMC Vand* 44.9; Kraus 25; Friedlaender 1844, pl. 2.2 (this coin).

Half-siliqua, w. the name of Anastasius. For a modern forgery, see **1452**.

64 *Nummus.* Ravenna? Obv. bust r. w. **]Λ[** Rev. monogram of **ODOVA**. *Æ* 0.78g (pierced) 100°. *BMC Vand* 45.10–11 (false); Kraus 36, 36a (false).

43. PG: Herzfelder 21.2.1956; ex Bagehot.
44. PG: Spink 17.1.1961.
45. PG: MMAG Basel 10.12.1968 (list 295, no. 1).
46, 53. PG: Vinchon sale 25.4.1960, lot 728.
47. PG: Spink 22.4.1954.
48. PG: DO 1958.
49. PG: Kapamadji 21.10.1960.
50. FM: W. S. Lincoln, Feb. 1902.
51. FM: Gutteridge 1939.
52. PG: Baldwin 30.5.1947; ex Grantley 2773.
54–5. PG: Kapamadji 1.10.1964; ex Longuet.
56. FM: Bunn 1950.
57. PG: Dillen 12.7.1949.
58. PG: Baldwin 2.10.1948.
59. FM: Clarke 1959; from Spink (*NCirc* Oct. 1959, no. 16458).
60. FM: Grierson 1968; from Santamaria 3.9.1948.
61. PG: Spink 1.12.1981 (*NCirc* Dec. 1981, no. 8391).
62. PG: Spink sale 25 (24.11.1982), lot 317.
63. PG: MMAG Basel 8.6.1971; ex Ulrich-Bansa; ex C. Gavazzi; ex Borghesi IV 1471; acq. by Borghesi from the peasant who had found it near Savignano, between Ravenna and Rimini, in or before 1835.
64. PG: Ars et Nummus 7.1.1977 (list Nov. 1976, no. 455 bis).

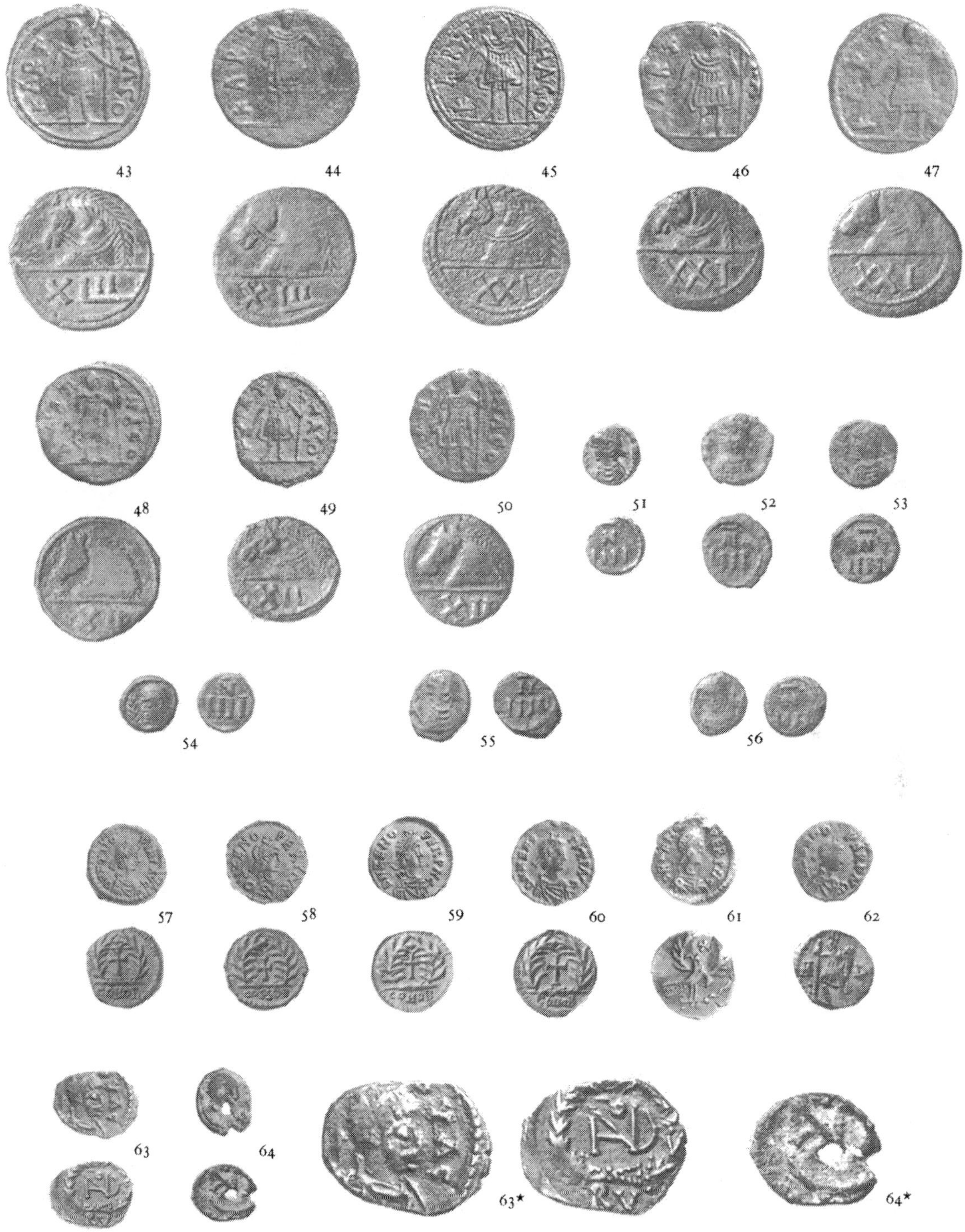

43 44 45 46 47

48 49 50 51 52 53

54 55 56

57 58 59 60 61 62

63 64 63* 64*

COUNTERMARKED EARLY IMPERIAL BRONZE COINS (1)

The coins are asses unless otherwise indicated. In each case, where the type is identifiable, the original mint is Rome, and on all except **84** the countermark is on the obverse. References are: *BMC RE* and *RIC* for the underlying coin types, and Morrisson = Morrisson 1983 for such of the coins as are there illustrated. It is argued above (pp. 29–30) that the countermarking took place in Italy, so that the coins are effectively Ostrogothic, but Hahn follows tradition in regarding them as Vandalic, the double follis and follis being *MIB* I, pl. 42.13 and 14 respectively.

Double follis (cmk LXXXIII)

65 Vespasian, for Titus (A.D. 72/3). *Sestertius*. 26.37g 200°. Cmk upwards in bottom r. field. Obv. **[TCAESAR] VESPASIANIMPIIIIPONTR[POTIICOSII]** Rev. **IVD[EAC]APTA**, soldier and Jewish captive standing w. palm tree between. *BMC RE*–; *RIC* –; same type and from same rev. die as Ryan V (Glendining 2.4.1952), lot 2382. Morrisson 1; also illus. (as 'recently in Dr Cahn's trays', but seemingly in error) in Metcalf 1969a, pl. 1.4, and obv. in *MIB* I, pl. 42.13.

Follis (cmk XLII)

66 Claudius (A.D. 41–54). Cmk downwards on l. Obv. **]SARAVG[ ]PP** Rev. standing figure (Minerva?). 10.03g 230°. ?*BMC RE* I, 185.149; *RIC* I, 129.66; Morrisson 3.

67 Claudius (A.D. 41–54). Cmk upwards on l. Coin unidentifiable through wear. 10.75g. Morrisson 17.

68 Nero (A.D. 54–6). Cmk (imperfect, **XI**...) downwards on r. Obv. **]ARA[** . Coin unidentifiable through wear. 8.74g.

69 Galba (A.D. 68–9). Cmk upwards on r. Obv. **]ERSVLP GALBACAE[** Rev. **LIBERTAS[** , Libertas standing l. 10.49g 160°. *BMC RE* I, 333.144; *RIC* I, 205.60.

70 Vespasian (A.D. 70). *Dupondius*. Cmk upwards on r. Obv. **IMPCAESVESPASIANA[VGC]O[SII]** Rev. **TVTELA AVGVSTI**, female seated l. w. children. 13.18g 180°. *BMC RE* II, 112.527; *RIC* II, 63.398.

71 Vespasian (A.D. 71). Cmk upwards on r. Obv. **IMPCAES VESPASIANAVGCOSIII** Rev. no inscription, eagle on globe. 9.06g 180°. *BMC RE* II, 132.612; *RIC* II, 74.497; Morrisson 7.

72 Vespasian (A.D. 71 or 72/3). Cmk upwards on r. Obv. **]VESPASIANAV[** Rev. no inscription, eagle on globe. 9.36g 180°. *BMC RE* II, 132.612 or 138; *RIC* II, 74.497 or 77.528; Morrisson 25.

73 Vespasian, for Titus (A.D. 72). Cmk upwards on r. Obv. **TCAESVESPASIANIMPPTR[** Rev. **PAX AVGVST**, Pax standing l. 11.40g 180°. *BMC RE* –, cf. II, 142–3; *RIC* –, cf. II, 87–8; Morrisson 24.

74 Vespasian (A.D. 72–6?). Cmk downwards on r. Obv. **]VESPAVG[** Rev. **VICTORIA[** , Victory r. 10.76g 180°. *BMC RE* II, 138.625b, etc.; *RIC* II, 77.529, etc.; Morrisson 16.

75 Vespasian, for Domitian (A.D. 73). Cmk downwards on l. Obv. **CAESARAVGFDOMITIANCOS[** Rev. **]AVGVST**, Pax standing. 10.75g 180°. *BMC RE* II, 157.682; *RIC* II, 97.695b.

76 Vespasian (A.D. 73–8?). Cmk upwards on r. Obv. inscription illegible, Spes advancing l. 8.82g 180°. Cf. *BMC RE* II, 151.663, etc.; *RIC* II, 79.545, etc.

All coins are in the Grierson collection and ex Holzer 10.10.1953 with the following exceptions:

65. PG: Glendining 25.11.1953, lot 157.

69. FM: Mrs Miles Burkitt 2.12.1976.

70. FM: Grierson 13.6.1949; ex Earl Fitzwilliam 488.

71. PG: Ars et Nummus 13.7.1960 (list July–Aug. 1960, no. 193); found near Bergamo.

65

66 67 68 69 70

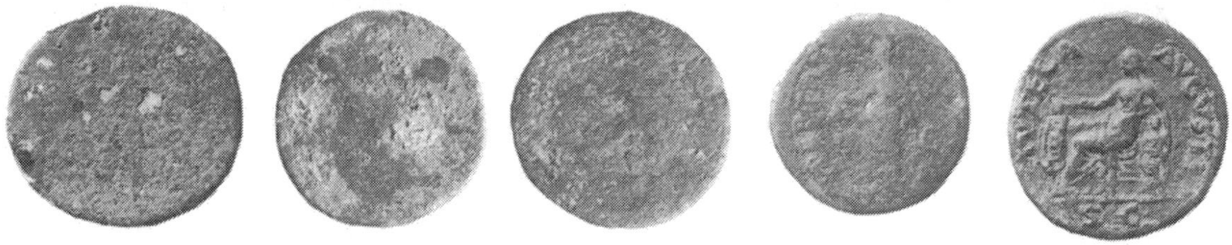

71 72 73 74 75

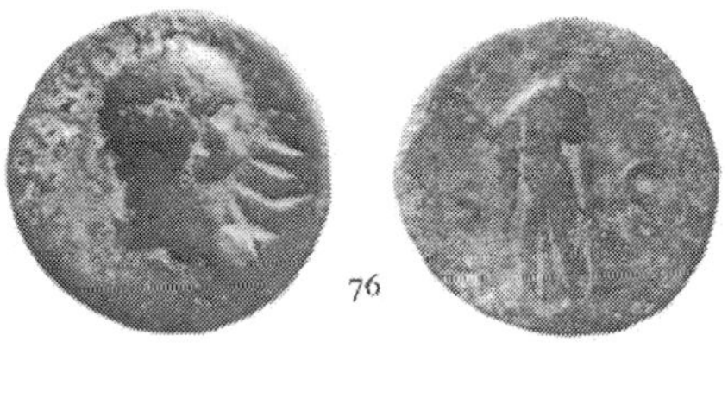

76

COUNTERMARKED EARLY IMPERIAL BRONZE COINS (2)

Descriptions and references as on Plate 1

77 Vespasian (A.D. 74). Cmk downwards on l. Obv. **IMP CAESARVE[ ]ENS** Rev. **AEQVITAS AVG[** , Aequitas w. scales and measuring rod. 9.71g 160°. *BMC RE* II, 161.702; *RIC* II, 80.557b.

78 Vespasian (A.D. 74–8?). Cmk upwards on r. Obv. **IMP CAESAR[** Rev. no inscription, Spes advancing l. 10.85g 180°. *BMC RE* II, 161.703, 169.725–6 or 174.738; *RIC* II, 80.560a, 83.583a or 84.598.

79 Vespasian, for Domitian (A.D. 77/8). Cmk upwards on r. Obv. **CAE[SA]RAV[G]FDOMITIA[NC]OSV** Rev. **VICTORIA[** , Victory r. 10.64g 180°. *BMC RE* II, 177.745c; *RIC* II, 99.725.

80 Vespasian (A.D. 77/8 or 79). Cmk downwards on l. Obv. **IM[ ]VESPASIANCOSVIII** or **VIIII** (outwards and counter-clockwise) Rev. **]GVST**, Victory r. 8.32g 180°. *BMC RE* II, 174.740 or 178.746; *RIC* II, 85.600 or 604.

81 Vespasian (A.D. 77/8 or 79). Cmk downwards on l. Obv. **]PASIAN[** (outwards and counter-clockwise) Rev. **]AVGVST**, Victory r. 8.80g 180°. Ref. as last.

82 Titus (A.D. 80/1). Cmk (blundered, **X+**) upwards on l. Obv. **]TCAESVESPAVGPMTRPCOSVIII** Rev. inscription illegible, Aeternitas standing. 7.99g 160°. *BMC RE* II, 265.206; *RIC* II, 130.122–3; Morrisson 27.

83 Titus, for Germanicus (A.D. 80/1). Cmk upwards on r. Obv. **]AVGVSCAESARTIAV[** Rev. obscure. 9.94g. *BMC RE* II, 288.293 var. (footnote); *RIC* II, 145.226–7.

84 Titus, for Germanicus (A.D. 80/1). Cmk on rev. Obv. **GER[ ]ICVSCAESARTIAVG[** Rev. obscure. 8.66g. Ref. as last. Morrisson 10.

85 Domitian (A.D. 86 or 88/9). Cmk (blundered, **VII**?) downwards on r. Obv. **]GERM COS[** Rev. inscr. illegible, Fides standing r. 8.61g 180°. *BMC RE* II, 383.385 or 391.415a; *RIC* II, 195.332 or 200.370; Morrisson 5.

86 Domitian (A.D. 87). Cmk upwards on r. Obv. **]ITAVG GERMCOSXIIICENSPERPP** Rev. **]GVST[** , Virtus standing r. 8.70g 180°. *BMC RE* II, 388.404; *RIC* II, 198.356.

87 Aelius? (A.D. 136–9). Cmk upwards on r. Too worn for identification. 6.74g.

88 Antoninus Pius, for Faustina (after A.D. 141). Cmk downwards on r. Obv. **DIVA FAVSTINA** Rev. **AE[ ]NITAS** Pietas standing l. 8.42g 310°. *BMC RE* IV, 249.1558; *RIC* III, 166.1161; Morrisson 14.

89 Commodus, for Marcus Aurelius (A.D. 180). Cmk downwards on r. Obv. **DIVVSMAN[ ]PIVS** Rev. **]SEC[ ]O**, eagle on pyre. 8.89g 0°. *BMC RE* IV, 764.405; *RIC* III, 441.664; Morrisson 13.

90 Commodus (A.D. 181–4?) *Sestertius*. Cmk downwards on r. Inscriptions illegible. Rev. Annona standing. 20.55g 0°. *BMC RE* IV, 770.442, etc.; *RIC* III, 403.307, etc.; Morrisson 9.

91 *Uncertain* (Claudius?). Cmk downwards on l. Too worn for identification. 7.77g.

All coins are in the Grierson collection and ex Holzer 10.10.1953 save for **77** and **78**, both from R. Chierici (via Santamaria) 20.11.1953 and from the Montelibretti hoard of *c.* 1952.

77 78 79 80 81

82 83 84 85 86

87 88 89 90 91

OSTROGOTHS (1), 493–553

Principal references are: *BMC Vand*, *MIB* and Kraus = Kraus 1928.

MUNICIPAL BRONZE COINAGES OF ROME

Class 1. With the name of Zeno (474–91), period of Odovacar

92 *Follis* (*40 nummi*). Obv. **IMPZENOFELIC[ISS]IM[O] SENAVG** (outwardly), **IIII** Rev. **IMVICT A ROMA**, w. **SC** in field and **XL** (for value) in ex. Æ 16.13g 0°. *BMC Vand* 100–1.1–4; Kraus 57.28–31 (as Odovacar). On the date (477/8?), see p. 31 above.

Class 2. Heavy series

93 *Follis* (*40 nummi*). Obv. **IMVICT AROMA** Rev. wolf and twins, w. **XL** above and **·IIII·** in ex. Æ 14.08g 0°. *BMC Vand* 105.26; *MIB* I, pl. 40.70; Kraus 219.21.

94 *As last.* Inscriptions as last. Æ 13.32g 40°. Ref. as last.

95 *As last.* Inscriptions as last. Æ 13.25g 20°. Ref. as last.

96 *As last.* Obv. **IMVIC TAROMA** Rev. type as last but ex. illegible. Æ 13.58g 20°. *BMC Vand* 105.29; *MIB* I, pl. 40.70; Kraus 219.24.

97 *Half-follis* (*20 nummi*). Obv. **IM[ ] TAROMA** Rev. wolf and twins, w. **I** above and **XX** (for value) in ex. Æ 7.69g 0°. *BMC Vand* 105.30; *MIB* I, pl. 40.71b; Kraus 220.29.

98 *As last.* Obv. **]TAROMA** Rev. as last. Æ 8.39g 20°. Ref. as last.

98A *As last.* Obv. **IM[ ]OM[** Rev. as last. Æ 6.97g 10°. Ref. as last.

99 *As last.* Obv. **INVIC TAROMA** Rev. as last but Christogram above. Æ 8.39g 170°. *BMC Vand* 105.33; *MIB* I, pl. 40.71c; Kraus 221.30.

Class 3. Light series

100 *Follis* (*40 nummi*). Obv. **INVICT [ ] ROMA** Rev. **XL** before eagle w. **·II·** in ex. Æ 9.11g 0°. *BMC Vand* 103.11; *MIB* I, pl. 40.74a; Kraus 218.11.

101 *As last.* Obv. **IMVICT· AROMA** Rev. as last but **·Δ·** in ex. Æ 13.04g 0°. *BMC Vand* 103.14 var.; *MIB* I, pl. 40.74a; Kraus 218.13.

102 *As last.* Obv. **INVIC TAROMA** Rev. as last but **·Є·** in ex. Æ 9.91g 20°. *BMC Vand* 103.18; *MIB* I, pl. 40.74a; Kraus 218.14.

103 *As last.* Inscriptions as last. Æ 8.05g 20°. Ref. as last.

92. PG: Birkler & Waddell 1.6.1981 (list 2, March 1981, no. 48).
93. PG: Santamaria 29.6.1947.
94. FM: Sherborn 1939.
95. FM: Dewick 1918.
96. PG: Spink 2.5.1945; ex Seltman.
97. PG: Glendining 3.5.1951, lots 110–12.
98. FM: from same unidentified coll. as **104** and **147**; . . . from Sambon 1888.
98A. MAA: provenance unrecorded.
99. PG: MMAG Basel 19.3.1951.
100. FM: Bunn 1950.
101. PG: Baldwin 22.6.1983.
102. PG: Franceschi 19.3.1969.
103. FM: Parkes Weber, Jan. 1907.

92*

92 93 94

95 96 97 98 98A

99 100 101 102 103

OSTROGOTHS (2)

References as on Plate 6.

MUNICIPAL BRONZE COINAGES OF ROME (*cont.*)

Class 3 (cont.)

104 *Follis (40 nummi)*. Inscriptions as last. Æ 8.67g 0°. Ref. as last.

105 *As last*. Obv. **INVIC TA[** Rev. as last. Æ 9.45g 0°. Ref. as last.

106 *As last*. Obv. **INVICT AROMA** Rev. as last. Æ 9.39g 20°. *BMC Vand* 103.15; *MIB* I, pl. 40.74a; Kraus 218.14.

107 *As last*. Obv. **IMVICTAROMA** Rev. as last but •Э• in ex. Æ 8.51g 20°. *BMC Vand* 103.17; *MIB* I, pl. 40.74a; Kraus 218.15.

108 *As last*. Obv. **]MVICT A ROMA** Rev. as last but value and ex. off-flan. Æ 9.47g 20°. *BMC Vand* 102.6f.; *MIB* I, pl. 40.74a; Kraus 217.5f.

109 *As last*. Inscriptions illegible or off-flan. Æ 4.02g 0°. Ref. as last.

110 *Half-follis (20 nummi)*. Obv. **IMVICT A ROMA** Rev. **•XX•** in ex. Æ 8.63g 30°. *BMC Vand* 103.19; *MIB* I, pl. 40.75; Kraus 220.25.

111 *As last*. Obv. **]ROM[** Rev. as last. Æ 5.21g 340°. Ref. as last.

PSEUDO-IMPERIAL AND REGAL COINAGES

THEODERIC, 493–526

With the name of Anastasius (491–518). For the mint identifications, see pp. 35–6.

112 *Solidus*. Rome. Obv. **DNANASTA SIVSPFAVG** Rev. **VICTORI AAVCCCA, COMOB**. AV 4.43g (SG 19.25: 99% Au) 180°. *BMC Vand* 55.61; *MIB* I, pl. 36.9; Kraus 83.5; Kent 1971, 6.

113 *Solidus*. Rome? Obv. **DNANASTA SIVSPFAVG** Rev. **VICTORI AAVCCC** (Christogram). AV 4.36g (SG 19.01: 98% Au) 180°. *BMC Vand* 55.62; *MIB* I, pl. 36.5 var.; Kraus 83.6; Kent 1971, pl. 9.11.

114 *Tremissis*. Rome. Obv. **DNANASTA SIVSPFAVC** Rev. **VICTORIA AVCVSTOROM, COMOB**. AV 1.43g (SG 18.91: 97% Au) 150°. *BMC Vand* 56.67 var.; *MIB* I, pl. 36.10; Kraus 86.20 var.; Kent 1971, 11.

115 *As last*. Obv. **DNANASTA SIVSPFAVC** Rev. **VIC TORIAAVCVSTORVM, COMOB**. AV 1.46g (SG 19.05: 98% Au) 180°. Ref. as last.

116 *Tremissis*. Milan (derivative?). Obv. **DNANASTA SIVSPAVG** (**G** inverted), star above head Rev. **VICTORIAAVCVSTOROM, COIIOB**. AV 1.45g (SG 19.12: 98% Au) 170°. *BMC Vand* 47.6 var., cf. 84.5, 85.8 (Baduila); *MIB* I, pl. 37.23; Kraus 85.14 var.; Kent 1971, 8 var.

117 *Half-siliqua*. Rome. Obv. **DNANAST ASIVSAVC**. AR 1.31g 170°. *BMC Vand* 49.20; *MIB* I, pl. 38.37b; Kraus 88.35; Kent 1971, 22.

118 *Quarter-siliqua*. Rome. Obv. **DN[ ]SIVSAVG** Rev. monogram of **THEODORICVS**, w. cross above. AR 0.66g 180°. *BMC Vand* 50.24; *MIB* I, pl. 38.39b; Kraus 89.38; Kent 1971, 23.

119 *Quarter-siliqua*. Milan. Obv. **DNANASTA SVSPPAVG** (retrograde outwardly), w. **OIIO** below bust Rev. **INVIC TAROMA**, w. cross above and star below monogram. AR 0.77g 160°. *BMC Vand* 58.79 var.; *MIB* I, pl. 38.44a; Kraus 92.54 var.; Kent 1971, 17.

120 *Quarter-siliqua*. Milan. Obv. **]ANAS TASIVSP** (retrograde outwardly) Rev. **]TAROMA**, w. cross above and star below monogram. AR 0.72g 190°. *BMC Vand* 58.78 var.; *MIB* I, pl. 38.44b; Kraus 92.53 var.; Kent 1971, 19 var.

With the name of Justin I (518–27)

121 *Quarter-siliqua*. Rome. Obv. **DNIVSTA NVSPAVC** (**AV** ligatured). AR 0.73g 170°. *BMC Vand* 51.31 var.; *MIB* I, pl. 38.49; Kraus 94.68 var.; Kent 1971, 26. This coin may have been struck during the reign of Athalaric, see p. 36 above.

104. FM: from same coll. as **98** and **147**; . . . bt *c*. 1882.
105, 108, 113. FM: Bunn 1950.
106. FM: W. S. Lincoln, Feb. 1902.
107. PG: Spink 16.6.1945; ex Fuller, Sept. 1938.
109. PG: acq. in Venice 16.9.1947.
110. PG: Baldwin 27.9.1945; ex Grantley 2789.
111. FM: provenance unrecorded.
112, 116. FM: Trinity College 1937.
114. PG: Sotheby 7.8.1947, lot 82.
115. PG: M. Ratto 21.9.1967.
117. PG: Baldwin 15.4.1947.
118–19. PG: Baldwin 13.3.1948.
120. FM: provenance unrecorded.
121. PG: Spink 6.12.1945; ex Kraus 1931.

104 105 106 107

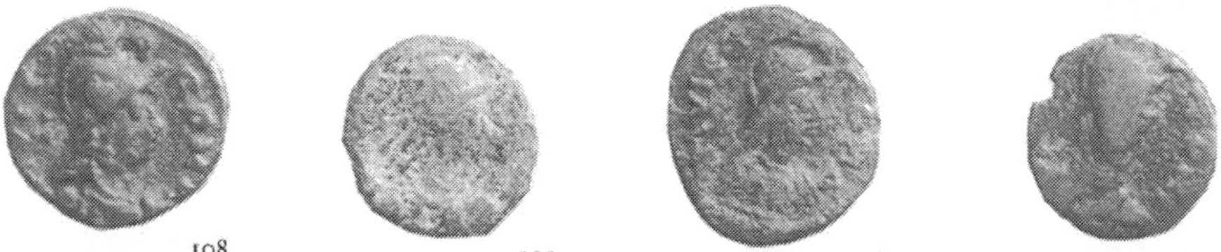

108 109 110 111

112 113 114 115 116

115*

119*

117 118 119 120 121

OSTROGOTHS (3)

References as on Plate 6.

PSEUDO-IMPERIAL AND REGAL COINAGES (*cont.*)

ATHALARIC, 526–34

With the name of Justinian I (527–65)

Nos. **122–4** may have been struck under Athalaric's immediate successors, see p. 36 above.

122 *Solidus.* Rome. Obv. **DNIVSTINI ANVSPΓAVC** (**AV** ligatured) Rev. **VICTORI AAVCCCA, COMOB**, w. star in field l. Ꜿ 4.40g (SG 19.09: 99% Au) 180°. *BMC Vand* 60.1 (as Ravenna); *MIB* I, pl. 37.28; Kraus 110.1 (as Ravenna).

123 *Tremissis.* Rome. Obv. **DNIVSTINI ANVSPΓAVC** (**AV** ligatured) Rev. **VICTORIAAVCVSTORVM, COMOB**(?), w. star in field r. Ꜿ 1.43g (SG 19.09: 99% Au) 180°. *BMC Vand* 61.10 (as Ravenna); *MIB* I, pl. 37.29a; Kraus 111.10 (as Ravenna).

124 *As last.* Legends as last, but obv. **PP**; no star in rev. field. Ꜿ 1.45g (SG 18.98: 97% Au) 170°. *BMC Vand* 62.17 (as Ravenna); *MIB* I, pl. 37.29a var.; Kraus 112.16 (as Ravenna).

125 *Half-siliqua.* Rome. Obv. **DNIVSTI NIANAVC** Rev. monogram of *Athalaricus*, w. cross above, star below and **DN** in field. Ꜵ 1.45g 170°. *BMC Vand* 64.32 (as Ravenna); *MIB* I, pl. 39.53a; Kraus 116.42 (as Ravenna).

126 *Half-siliqua.* Rome. Obv. **DNIVSTINI ANVSPAVC** Rev. as last. Ꜵ 1.40g 150°. *BMC Vand* 64.30 (as Ravenna); *MIB* I, pl. 39.53a; Kraus 116.40 (as Ravenna).

Half-siliqua. For a modern forgery, see **1453**.

127 *Quarter-siliqua.* Rome. Obv. **DNIVSTI NIANAVC** Rev. **DN/ATHAL/ARICVS/RIX**. Ꜵ 0.66g 180°. *BMC Vand* 64.35 (as Ravenna); *MIB* I, pl. 39.54; Kraus 116.46 (as Ravenna).

128 *As last.* Obv. **DNI[ ]NIA[** Rev. as last. Ꜵ 0.67g 180°. Ref. as last.

129 *As last.* Obv. **DNIVSTI NIA[** Rev. as last. Ꜵ 0.72g 170°. Ref. as last.

130 *As last.* Obv. **DNIVSTI NI[** Rev. as last. Ꜵ 0.59g 170°. Ref. as last.

131 *As last.* Obv. **DN[ ]TI[** Rev. w. **REX**. Ꜵ 0.68g 140°. Ref. as last.

132 *Decanummium.* Rome. Obv. **INVIC TAROMA** Rev. **DNATHAL RICVS**, w. **SC** (for *Senatus consulto*) and **X** (for the value) in field. Æ 2.49g 190°. *BMC Vand* 69.71; *MIB* I, pl. 40.77; Kraus 122.82.

133 *As last.* Obv. **]CT AROMA** Rev. **DN/ATHAL/ARICVS/REX**. Æ 4.25g 170°. *BMC Vand* 67.57; *MIB* I, pl. 40.78; Kraus 119.64.

134 *As last.* Obv. **INVICT[** Rev. as last. Æ 2.90g worn 180°. Ref. as last.

135 *Nummus.* Rome. Obv. **IVSTI NIANI** Rev. monogram of *Athalaricus*. Æ 1.04g 180°. *BMC Vand* 66.49 (as Ravenna); *MIB* I, pl. 40.80 (as $2\frac{1}{2}$-nummus piece); Kraus 124.93 (as Ravenna).

136 *As last.* Obv. **IVSTI[** Rev. as last. Æ 1.04g 190°. Ref. as last.

137 *As last.* Obv. inscription illegible Rev. as last. Æ 0.97g 180°. Ref. as last.

AMALASUNTHA, 534–5

With the name of Justinian I (527–65) and monogram of Theoderic

138 *Quarter-siliqua.* Ravenna. Obv. **DN[ ]VS˙[ ]IIIAIIAVC**. Ꜵ 0.70g 170°. *BMC Vand* 78.9 (as Witigis); *MIB* I, pl. 39.59 (as Witigis); Kraus 170.3 (as Hildebad). For the attribution, see p. 137 above.

THEODAHAD, 534–6

With the name of Justinian I (527–65)

Half-siliqua. For forgeries, see **1454–5**.

139 *Quarter-siliqua.* Rome. Obv. **DNIVSTI NIANAVC** Rev. **DN/THEODA/HATHVS/REX**. Ꜵ 0.63g 170°. *BMC Vand* 73.4 var. (as Ravenna); *MIB* I, pl. 39.56; Kraus 142.9 (as Ravenna).

140 *As last.* Obv. **DNIVS[ ]NIANAVC** Rev. as last, but **RIX**. Ꜵ 0.68g 170°. *BMC Vand* 73.7 (as Ravenna); *MIB* I, pl. 39.56; Kraus 142.10 (as Ravenna).

141 *Follis (40 nummi).* Rome. Obv. **DNTHE[ ]AHATVSREX** Rev. **VICTORIA PRIИCIPV**, w. **SC** in field. Æ 8.89g 180°. *BMC Vand* 76.24 var.; *MIB* I, pl. 39.81; Kraus 147.36 var. Same obv. die as next and Kraus 147.36–7.

142 *As last.* Obv. **DNTHEOD AHATVSREX** Rev. **VIC TORIA PRINCIPVM**, w. **ƧC** in field. Æ 9.23g 180°. Ref. as last. Same obv. die as last and Kraus 147.36–7.

143 *As last.* Obv. **DNTHEODA HATVSREX** Rev. **VIC TORIA PRINCIPVM**, w. **SC** in field. Æ 9.92g pierced 180°. *BMC Vand* 75.19 var.; *MIB* I, pl. 41.81; Kraus 146.29. Same dies as Kraus 146.29 and same obv. die as *BMC Vand* 75.19–20.

144 *Decanummium.* Rome. Obv. **INVICT[** Rev. **DN/THEODA/HATHVS/REX**. Æ 3.32g 160°. *BMC Vand* 74.16 (as Ravenna); *MIB* I, pl. 41.82; Kraus 145.23 (as Ravenna).

122. PG: Glendining 20.10.1948, lot 149.
123. PG: Baldwin 14.6.1947.
124. PG: Seaby 20.3.1945; ex Grantley 2785; bt in Vienna.
125. FM: Dewick 1918.
126. PG: Spink 8.2.1945.
127. FM: Ritchie 1963.
128, 131, 140. FM: provenance unrecorded.
129. FM: Sherborn 1939.
130. FM: Bunn 1950.
132. PG: Spink 9.4.1945; ex Grantley 2786.
133, 138. PG: Baldwin 30.5.1947.
134. FM: Trinity College 1937.
135. PG: Spink 19.4.1945.
136. PG: MMAG Basel 22.1.1970 (list 308, no. 40).
137. FM: Bunn 1950.
139. PG: Baldwin 13.3.1948.
141, 144. PG: Seaby 4.1.1947; ex Hansen.
142. PG: Baldwin 18.12.1947.
143. FM: Sherborn 1939.

122
123
124
125
126
127
128
129
130
131
132
132*
133
134
135
136
137
138
139
140
141
142
142*
143
144

OSTROGOTHS (4)

References as on Plate 6.

MUNICIPAL BRONZE COINAGE OF RAVENNA, 536–54

Decanummium: (a) Without cross above monogram

145 Obv. **FELIXR AVENNA** Rev. monogram of Ravenna. Æ 2.77g 110°. *BMC Vand* 107.37; *MIB* I, pl. 40.72a (as Rome); Kraus 222.3.

146 Inscription as last. Æ 3.03g 170°. Ref. as last.

147 Obv. **FELIXR[** . Æ 2.78g 170°. Ref. as last.

148 Obv. **]AVENNA**. Æ 3.10g 180°. Ref. as last.

149 Obv. inscription illegible. Æ 2.72g 180°. Ref. as last. For a forgery see **1456**.

(b) With cross above monogram

150 Obv. **FELIXR[** . Æ 2.27g 170°. *BMC Vand* 107.40; *MIB* I, pl. 40.72b (as Rome); Kraus 223.5.

REGAL COINAGE, 536–54

WITIGIS, 536–40

With the name of Justinian I (527–65)

151 *Half-siliqua*. Ravenna. Obv. **DNIVSTI NIANAVC** Rev. **DN/VVIT/ICES/REX**. AR 1.30g 180°. *BMC Vand* 77.3; *MIB* I, pl. 39.57; Kraus 158.8.

152 *As last*. Inscriptions as last, but **RIX**. AR 1.28g 190°. Ref. as last.

BADUILA, 541–52

With the name of Anastasius I (491–518)

153 *Half-siliqua*. Pavia (*Ticinum*). Obv. **DNANASTA[** Rev. **DN/BADV/ILA/RIX**. AR 1.40g 180°. *BMC Vand* 86.14 (same obv. die); *MIB* I, pl. 39.63; Kraus 188.17.

154 *As last*. Obv. **DNAN[** Rev. as last. AR 1.26g 180°. Ref. as last.

155 *As last*. Obv. **DNANAST ASIVSPIAV** Rev. **DN/BADV/ILA/REX**. AR 1.30g 180°. *BMC Vand* 87.15 var.; *MIB* I, pl. 39.63; Kraus 189.27 var.

156 *Quarter-siliqua*. Pavia. Obv. **DANASTA SIVSPPAVG** (**AV** ligatured) Rev. as last. AR 0.67g. 180°. *BMC Vand* 88.20 var.; *MIB* I, pl. 39.64; Kraus 190.33 var.

157 *Decanummium*. Rome. Obv. **ƆИBADV IL AREX** Rev. **DNB/ADV/ILA/REX** in wreath. Æ 6.43g 0°. *BMC Vand* 91.38 (as Pavia); *MIB* I, pl. 41.89a; Kraus 193.52 (as Pavia).

158 *As last*. Obv. **]BA[** Rev. **DNB/ADV/ELA/REX**. Æ 5.32g 40°. *BMC Vand* 92.41 (as Pavia); *MIB* I, pl. 41.89a; Kraus 194.55 (as Pavia).

159 *As last*. Obv. inscription illegible Rev. as last. Æ 4.86g 0°. Ref. as last.

160 *As last*. Obv. inscription illegible Rev. as last. Æ 5.31g 200°. Ref. as last.

161 *As last*. Obv. inscription illegible Rev. as last. Æ 5.31g 30°. Ref. as last.

162 *Decanummium*. Obv. **]VILAREX** Rev. **FLOREAS SEMPER**, standing figure w. **X** in field. Æ 4.42g 180°. *BMC Vand* 94.49 var.; *MIB* I, pl. 41.90b; Kraus 196.65.

163 *Nummus*. Pavia? Obv. **]NO**, bust r. Rev. monogram of *Baduila*(?), w. **S** above and **O** beneath. Æ 0.79g 190°. *BMC Vand* –, cf. 89.24–7; *MIB* I –, cf. pl. 41.87 (as 2½-nummus piece); Kraus –.

164 *Nummus*. Pavia. Obv. **DNA[** Rev. **DN̄ RE/B**. Æ 0.86g 20°. *BMC Vand* 90.30; *MIB* I, pl. 41.88 (as 2½-nummus piece); Kraus 197.73.

165 *As last*. Obv. **DN[** Rev. as last. Æ 0.57g 40°. Ref. as last.

145–6. FM: provenance unrecorded.
147. FM: from same coll. as **98** and **104**; from Thieme (Leipzig) 1888.
148. CCC (*Catalogue* no. 55): Lewis 1891; ex Borrell.
149. PG: Seaby 17.10.1945.
150, 159. FM: Sherborn 1939.
151, 158. PG: Spink 12.2.1945; ex Boulton.
152. FM: Dewick 1918; ex Yorke Moore 1142.
153. FM: Ritchie 1963.
154. FM: provenance unrecorded.
155. FM: Mr and Mrs A. H. Laurie 1980; ex Grose.
156. PG: Toderi 12.12.1975 (list 1975: 3, no. 291).
157. PG: Baldwin 11.10.1947.
160–1. FM: Bunn 1950.
162. FM: Gutteridge 1939.
163, 165. PG: Kapamadji 1.10.1964; ex Longuet.
164. PG: Baldwin 27.9.1945; ex Grantley 2789; from Spink.

145 146 147 148 149 150

151 152 153 154 155 156

162* 157 158 159

160 161 162 163 164 165 163*

VISIGOTHS (1): PSEUDO-IMPERIAL SERIES

In Gaul, 417–507; in Spain, 507–*c.* 580

The principal references are to various papers of Reinhart, Tomasini = Tomasini 1964 and, for Roman imperial prototypes, Cohen = Cohen 1880–92. Attributions are discussed on pp. 46, 48–9 above. The coins are all gold and unless otherwise indicated are tremisses.

With the name of Honorius (393–423)

166 *Solidus.* Obv. **DNHONORI VSPFAVC** Rev. **VICTORI AAVCCC, COMOB,** w. **RV** (for *Ravenna*) in field. 4.45g (SG 19.00: 98% Au) 170°. Reinhart 1938, no. 2; Kent 1974, fig. 1. The prototype is a solidus of Ravenna (Cohen VIII, 185.44).

With the name of Valentinian III (423–55)

167 *Solidus.* Obv. **DNPLAVALENTI NIANVSPIAVC** Rev. **VICTORI AAVCCC, COMOB,** w. **RV** in field. 4.38g (SG 18.51: 95% Au) 160°. Reinhart 1938, no. 11. The prototype is a solidus of Ravenna (Cohen VIII, 212.19).

168 *Solidus.* Obv. **DNPLAVALENTI NIANVSPFAVC** Rev. as last. 4.38g (SG 18.96: 98% Au) 160°. Reinhart 1938, no. 8.

169 *Solidus.* Legends as last. 3.67g pierced (SG 18.98: 98% Au) 150°. Ref. as last.

170 *Solidus.* Legends as last, but each surrounded by a bold wreath, and star to l. of head on rev. Die cracks apparent on rev. 4.34g (SG 18.76: 96% Au) 160°. Reinhart 1938, no. 11 var.

171 Obv. **DNPLAVALENTINIANVSPF** Ref. **COIIOB.** 1.42g (SG 18.24: 93% Au) 180°. Reinhart 1938, no. 42 var.; *BMC Vand* 2.5 (as Vandalic). The prototype is a tremissis of Ravenna or Rome (Cohen VIII, 216.49).

172 Obv. **DNPLAVALENTINVSPFAVC** Rev. **CONOB.** 1.39g (SG 17.82: 90% Au) 0°. Reinhart 1938, no. 48 var.

173 Obv. **ƆNVALENTINIANVSPFAVC** Rev. **VICTORI AAVCCC, COMOB.** 1.44g (SG 17.64: 89% Au) 180°. Reinhart 1938, no. 55. Similar in style of bust and epigraphy to the next two coins. The prototype of the rev. is a solidus with the type of Cohen VIII, 212.17.

With the name of Severus III (461–6)

174 *Solidus.* Obv. **DNIIBIVSSEVE RVSPFAVC** Rev. **VIC TORI AAVGGG, COMOB,** w. **RA** in field. 4.31g (SG 18.44: 94% Au) 170°. Reinhart 1938, no. 72 (found at Narbonne). The prototype is a solidus of Ravenna w. **RV** (Cohen VIII, 227.8).

175 *Solidus.* Legends as last, but obv. commences **DNIB.** 4.32g (SG 18.20: 93% Au) 160°. Reinhart 1938, no. 72 var.

176 *Solidus.* Obv. **ƆNIIBIVSSEVI RVƧPFAVC** Rev. **VIC TORI AAVCCC, COMOB,** w. **RA** in field. 4.32g (SG 16.89: 83% Au) 160°. Ref. as last.

With the name of Anastasius I (491–518). Some of the tremisses are possibly Merovingian, see p. 48 above.

177 *Solidus.* Obv. **DNANASTA∽ IVSPTAVC** Rev. **VIC TORI AAVCCCA, CONOB.** 4.41 g (SG 19.15: 99% Au) 180°. Reinhart 1938, no. 132 var. = Reinhart 1940, pl. 7.2 var. Copied from a type (Victory holding long-headed cross surmounted by Christogram) introduced by Anastasius at Constantinople probably in 507 (*DOC* I, 7.7). There was a coin of the same type and style, but in the name of Justin I, in the Chinon hoard (B 5152 = Robert 1882a, pl. 4.24).

178 Obv. **DNANASIA SIVSPΓAVC** Rev. **VICTORIA AVCVSTORVH, CONOƆ.** 1.46g (SG 18.85: 97% Au) 130°. Tomasini 3 (same dies, this coin noted), group A1 (as Toulouse or Narbonne).

179 Obv. **DNANASTA ƧIVSPPAVG** Rev. **]TORIA AVGCSTORVM, COIIOB.** 1.48g (SG 16.72: 81% Au) 150°. Reinhart 1938, no. 134 var. (as Toulouse); Tomasini 16 var., group A1 (as Toulouse or Narbonne).

180 Obv. **DNANAST ASIVSPAC** Rev. **CTOPIA[ ] VSTOPVI, COHOB,** w. **C** in field l. 1.47g (SG 18.71: 96% Au) 190°. Tomasini 643 (this coin), unclassed sub-group of A1.

181 Obv. **DNANASTA SIVSPPAVC** Rev. **VICTORIA AVCVSTORVI, COHOB.** 1.46g (SG 16.50: 79% Au) 170°. Reinhart 1938, no. 133 (as Toulouse); Tomasini 47 (same dies; ex Alesia hoard), group A2a (as Narbonne or Ostrogothic from Arles?).

182 Obv. **DANASTA SIVSPAVC** Rev. **VICTORIA AVCSTORV, DON.** 1.44g (SG 19.10: 99% Au) 180°. Tomasini 47 var., group A2a (as Narbonne or Ostrogothic from Arles?).

183 Obv. **DNANASTA SIVSPPAVC,** w. large pellet before face Rev. **IICIOPAI CYSЯOƆII, ƆOIIOƆ,** w. **V** in field l. and pellet r. 1.39g (SG 18.83: 97% Au) 170°. Tomasini 641 (this coin), anomalous cf. group A2c. Struck from rusty dies.

184 Obv. **ƆИAИSTA SISPPAVC** Rev. **VICTORIA [ ]CVSTOIA, CONOB.** 1.46g (SG 18.64: 96% Au) 190°. Reinhart 1939a, pl. 4.7 (as Merovingian); Tomasini 69 (this cited), 72–3 (same obv. die), group A3 (as Narbonne).

185 Obv. **ƆNANAƧT IVSPPAI** Rev. **IVCTOAA[ ]VOSN, COИOB.** 1.41g (SG 18.53: 95% Au) 180°. Tomasini 638 (this coin), anomalous. Struck from rusty dies.

166. PG: Glendining 29.7.1947, lot 8.
167. PG: DO 20.10.1958; ex Peirce 1948; from Schulman Nov. 1928.
168. PG: Vinchon 24.9.70.
169. PG: Christie 16.6.1959 ('Spanish collection'), lot 35.
170. PG: G. Hirsch sale 11 (10.12.1956), lot 994.
171. PG: Baldwin 15.10.1949.
172. PG: Franceschi 26.3.1965.
173. PG: Platt 1.9.1950.
174. PG: Spink 7.11.1950.
175. PG: Ulrich-Bansa 18.11.1950.
176. PG: DO 20.10.1958; ex Peirce 1948; bt in Budapest 1924.
177. PG: Malter 1.4.1968.
178. PG: Christie 16.6.1959 ('Spanish collection'), lot 33.
179. PG: Bourgey 14.7.1967.
180. PG: Spink 10.1.1947: ex Grantley 2782; from W. S. Lincoln, Dec. 1906.
181. PG: Spink 21.1.1954.
182. PG: Spink 15.10.1970.
183. PG: Baldwin 16.10.1945.
184. PG: Seaby 19.11.1946.
185. PG: Spink 12.2.1945.

166

167

168

169

170

171

172

173

174

175

176

173*

177

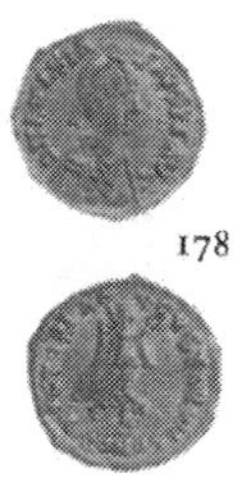
178

179

180

181

182

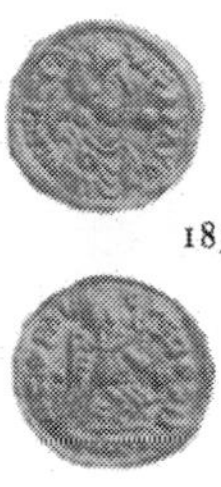
183

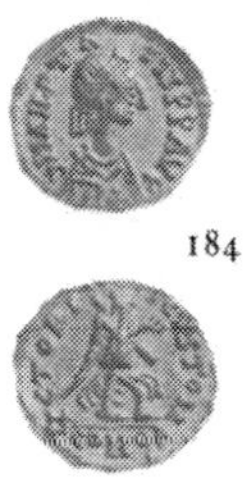
184

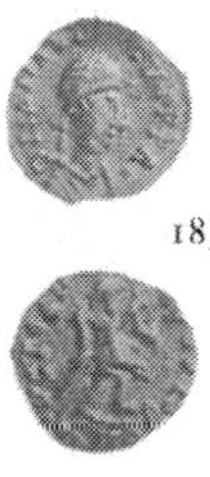
185

178*

VISIGOTHS (2): PSEUDO-IMPERIAL SERIES

References as on Plate 10. The coins are all gold and unless otherwise indicated are tremisses.

With the name of Justin I (518–27)

186 Obv. **ƆNVSTIN VSFPAVIC** Rev. **VICTORVA AVCV2TORVAI, COИOB.** 1.45g (SG 18.43: 94% Au) 170°. Reinhart 1939a, pl. 3.19 var. (as Merovingian), but cf. Reinhart 1940, pl. 9.1 (as Narbonne or Barcelona); Tomasini 140 (this coin), group J1 (as Narbonne).

187 Obv. **ƆNIVSIIN VSPFAV·T·C** Rev. **VICTORIA AGVSTORVAI8, COИOB.** 1.43g (SG 18.72: 96% Au) 160°. Reinhart 1940, pl. 9.3 var. (as Narbonne or Barcelona); Tomasini 197 var., group J12 (as Narbonne or Ostrogothic from Arles?). The ·T·, that also occurs on other coins of this group, might justify an attribution to the Frankish king Thierry I (511–34) (Lafaurie 1968a).

188 Obv. **ƆNIVSTI NVSPPAVC** Rev. **VICTORA AVCVSTOA, CONOB.** 1.44g (SG 18.97: 98% Au) 160°. Reinhart 1939a, pl. 3.29–30 var. (as Merovingian); Tomasini 180 (this cited), group JI2 (as Narbonne or Ostrogothic from Arles?).

189 Obv. **DNIVSTINVSPPAVCC** Rev. **VICTORIA ACVSTORV, COIIOD.** 1.37g (SG 18.61: 95% Au) 180°. Reinhart 1939a, pl. 3.16 var. (as Merovingian); Reinhart 1940, pl. 10.20 var.; Tomasini 220 (this coin), group JI3b (as Merovingian?).

With the name of Justinian I (527–65)

190 *Solidus.* Obv. **IV2TI NNANI** Rev. **VICTORI AAVCCCN, CONOB.** 4.41g (SG 19.13: 99% Au) 180°. Reinhart 1940, pl. 8.2 (same dies).

191 *Solidus.* Obv. **DNIV2T ININANI** Rev. **VICTOFI AAVCCCИ, COИOD.** 4.38g (SG 19.05: 98% Au) 170°. Reinhart 1940, pl. 8.4 (this coin).

192 Obv. **ƆNIVSTNI IANPPAVC** Rev. **VICTORIA CVSTORVA, CONOB.** 1.46g (SG 18.87: 97% Au) 180°. Tomasini 213 (this coin), group JI3 (as Narbonne).

193 Obv. **ƆIVITII· ·IAIIVIC** Rev. **VICT· ·AAII:, C·И·Ɔ.** 1.42g (SG 17.80: 90% Au) 170°. Reinhart 1940, pl. 9.12 var. (as Narbonne or Barcelona); Tomasini 646 (this coin), group JAN 1? (as Narbonne?).

194 Obv. **DNIVITINI ANVSddI** Rev. **VICTOIVI VTONAVI, CONOƆ.** 1.28g (SG 18.66: 96% Au) 180°. Reinhart 1940, pl. 9.8 (this coin, as Narbonne or Barcelona); Tomasini 253 (this coin), group JAN 2 (as Barcelona).

195 Obv. **DNATI· ·ITANT:C** Rev. **·ƆVII ·ITAIIV, CONOƆ.** 1.26g (SG 17.91: 90% Au) 160°. Reinhart 1940, pl. 9.15 var. (as Narbonne or Barcelona); Tomasini 275 var., group JAN 2 (as Barcelona).

196 Obv. **ƆIVIT· ·IVITIC** Rev. **VITIOI ·IVIOI, COIIOƆ,** pellet between legs of Victory. 1.44g (SG 17.91: 91% Au) 170°. Reinhart 1940, pl. 9.13 var. (as Narbonne or Barcelona); Tomasini 281 (this coin), group JAN 2a (as Barcelona).

197 Obv. **ƆIVITIII INTVII** Rev. **VΓTOAI IIOTIAVI, CONOƆ.** 1.23g (SG 18.50: 94% Au) 180°. Reinhart 1940, pl. 9.8 var. (as Narbonne or Barcelona); Tomasini 283 var., group JAN 2a (as Barcelona).

198 Obv. **ƆNIVSINI AИVSPPAVC** Rev. **VICTORN ·AVCTITOЯI, COIIOB.** 1.45g (SG 18.71: 96% Au) 170°. Reinhart 1939a, pl. 3.34 var. (as Merovingian); Tomasini 299 (this cited), group JAN 3 (as Andalusian?, an attribution supported by the presence of several specimens in the 1972 Seville hoard (Barral 1976, 78–80 and pls. 2–3)).

199 Obv. **ƆNIVSTИI ANVSPPAC** Rev. **VICTORIA AVCVSTORO, CONOB.** 1.45g (SG 18.55: 95% Au) 180°. Reinhart 1939a, pl. 3.33 var. (as Merovingian); Tomasini 299 (this cited), group JAN 3 (as Andalusian?).

200 Obv. **INIVNI ANVIPAC** Rev. **VICTRI AVCVAI, CMND.** 1.44g (SG 18.56: 95% Au) 180°. Reinhart 1940, pl. 10.7 var. (as Mérida?); Tomasini 645 (this coin), anomalous group JAN 3?

201 Obv. **NIVSTINI ANVSPPAC** Rev. **VICTORIA AVSIORVN, CONOB,** w. cross in field l. 1.16g (SG 15.89: 74% Au) 170°. Reinhart 1940, pl. 11.1 var. (as Toledo?); Tomasini 333 (this coin), group JAN 4b (as irregular, possibly a later derivative of Mérida coins). The low weight and fineness support Tomasini's view, based on style, that the piece is irregular, though not a modern forgery.

202 Obv. **IIVDVIII IIIИIIIИI** Rev. **IIIII-CVI IIPINVIV, OIIIIO.** 1.21g (SG 17.42: 87% Au) 170°. Reinhart –; Tomasini –. Possibly an imitation of Tomasini's group JAN 8, attributed to Toledo.

186. PG: DO 20.10.1958; ex Peirce 1948; from Schulman, March 1931.
187. PG: Franceschi 9.4.1962.
188. PG: Seaby 20.3.1945.
189. PG: L. S. Forrer 28.9.1950.
190. PG: MMAG Basel 16.5.1960 (list 199, no. 43).
191. PG: Reinhart 5.2.1951.
192. PG: DO 20.10.1958; ex Peirce 1948; from St Louis Coin Co., Dec. 1930.
193. PG: Christie 16.6.1959 ('Spanish collection'), lot 39.
194. PG: Reinhart 30.9.1951.
195. FM: Mrs W. H. Bullock Hall and Mr A. Hall 1905; found in the Amphitheatre at Fréjus (Var) by W. H. Bullock Hall.
196. PG: DO 20.10.1958; ex Peirce 1948; from St Louis Coin Co., July 1930.
197. FM: Mrs E. M. Anderson 30.11.1938.
198, 200. PG: Seaby 19.11.1946.
199. PG: Spink 6.1.1953; ex Philipsen.
201. PG: Kress sale 107 (10.3.1958), lot 619.
202. PG: Baldwin 15.3.1946; ex Grantley 2794; bt in Vienna.

[*continued overleaf*]

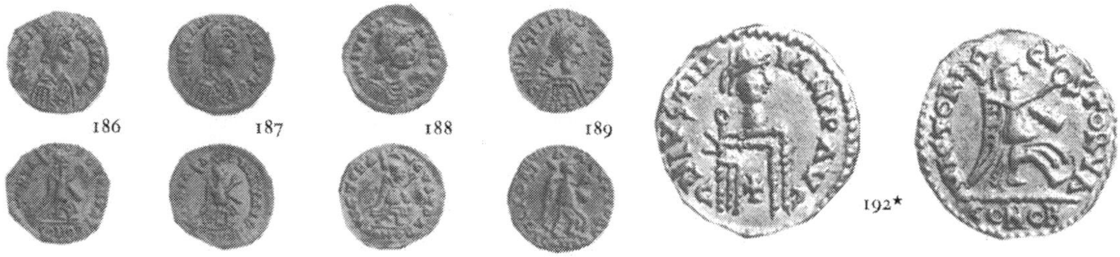

186 187 188 189 192*

190 191 192 193 194 195

196 197 198 199 200 201 202

203 204 205 206 207 208

PLATE 11 *(cont.)*

With the name of Justin II (565–78) or contemporary blundered coins

203 Obv. **IVIVIVIVIVIVIVIVI** Rev. **IVIVV IVIVIVI, OИO**. 1.43g (SG 18.19: 93% Au) 160°. Reinhart 1940, pl. 10.13 (this coin, as Mérida?); Tomasini 484 (this coin), group JII4 (as Mérida). Cf. the profile bust on Leovigild's earliest mint-signed coins of Mérida (Miles 1952, pl. 3.8).

204 Obv.]**VITAIIIIVFPVICVVC** Rev. **IVIIII**[ ]+**VIIIVI, COIIO**. 1.36g pierced (SG 18.61: 95% Au) 180°. Tomasini 660 (this coin), anomalous, possibly group JII4a (derivative of Mérida).

205 Obv. **IIIVƧTI IIIΛVΛ** Rev. **VIƆTVΛ ITORVΛΦ, COIIO**. 1.47g (SG 18.67: 96% Au) 160°. Reinhart 1940, pl. 10.3 var. (as Andalusian?); Tomasini 503, group JII5 (as Narbonne). Cf. **209** below, probably from the same mint (Toledo).

206 Obv. **ƆNVƧII NPΛVC** Rev. **IVIRI ICNOVI, CONOD**. 1.43g (SG 17.53: 88% Au) 150°. Reinhart 1940, pl. 9.27 (as Andalusian?); Tomasini 535 var., group JII7 (as Evora?).

With the inscription 'Curru'

207 Obv. **ƆVRRΛTINIIVЯЯVC** Rev. **VVRRTIИΛVЯЯV, OИO**, w. pellet between legs of Victory. 1.40g (SG 18.59: 95% Au) 180°. Reinhart 1940, pl. 11.9 (as Toledo); Tomasini 573 (this cited), group C3 (as Toledo).

208 Obv. **ƆVRVΛVI -ИVЯVC** Rev. **VVIPTИIVЯVƆ, OИO**. 1.30g (SG 18.21: 93% Au) 180°. Tomasini 599 var., group C5 (as Mérida?).

203. PG: Shore 612.
204. PG: Haines 3.9.1946.
205. PG: ANS 23.8.1959; ex Reinhart.
206. PG: A. R. Tait 26.5.1962; ex W. C. Tait (grandfather); bt at Oporto, May 1908.
207. PG: L. S. Forrer 28.9.1950.
208. PG: Spink 29.6.1965; from Grover 1965.

VISIGOTHS (3): REGAL SERIES

The principal reference is: Miles = Miles 1952. The coins are all gold tremisses, and types are only described when they are not clear from the illustrations. For the location of the mints, see map on p. 47. Modern place-names are normally used when the identifications are certain, the Latin forms that are not obvious being *Caesaraugusta* (Saragossa), *Elvora* (Evora), *Eminio* or *Iminio* (Coimbra), *Emerita* (Mérida), *Ispali* (Seville), *Mentesa* (La Guardia), and *Tucci* (Martos). The name of *Eliberri*, probably the village of Atarfe near Granada, is preserved in that of the district, the Sierra de Elvira.

LEOVIGILD, sole ruler 572–86

Class 1. Victory type (c. 580–3). Light coins.

209 *Mint unspecified (Toledo).* Obv. **IIIV?TI IIIAVA** Rev. **CLIVVIGILDIREGIS**. 1.30g (SG 17.37: 86% Au) 170°. Miles 1(b).

Class 2. Cross-on-steps type (c. 584). Light coins.

210 *Evora* (southern Portugal). Obv. **DNLIVVICILDVS** Rev. **RE+ ELVOR+A**, w. **ONO** beneath steps. 1.28g (SG 15.58: 71% Au) 330°. Miles 36(a) 3 (this coin). Illus. Reinhart 1940, pl. 11.17; Reinhart 1941, pl. 33.7–8.

Class 3. Two facing busts type (c. 585–6). Heavy coins.

Cordova. For a forgery, see **1458**.

211 *Evora.* Obv. **+LEOVIGILDVS RE+** Rev. **IVS+ TOSELVORA**. 1.52g (SG 15.47: 70% Au) 180°. Miles 38(a).

Mérida. For a forgery, see **1459**.

212 *Toledo.* Obv. **+LEOVIGILDVSREX** Rev. **+TOLETO IVSTV∽**. 1.52g (SG 16.20: 77% Au) 160°. Miles 29(a)13 (this coin).

RECCARED I, 586–601

213 *Calabor* (north-western Spain, prov. Zamora). Obv. **+RECCARIDVSRE:** Rev. **+CALAPATIAPIV∽**. 1.50g (SG 15.63: 71% Au) 180°. Miles – (cf. 104 w. *Calabacia Victor* inscription). This unique specimen publ. Grierson 1963d. For the mint identification, see Miles, p. 130.

214 *Coimbra* (central Portugal). Obv. **+RECCARIDVSRE** Rev. **+IMINIOPIVS**. 1.48g (SG 15.44: 70% Au) 180°. Miles 96(d)1 (this coin).

215 *Cordova.* Obv. **+RECCAREDVCREX** Rev. **+COR DODAPV∽**. 1.50g (SG 15.96: 74% Au) 200°. Miles 82(k) var.

216 *Eliberri* (near Granada). Obv. **+RECCAREDVSRE+** Rev. **+ELIBERRIPIV∽**. 1.47g (SG 15.19: 67% Au) 160°. Miles 83(a).

217 *Evora.* Obv. **+RECCAREDVSRE+** Rev. **ELVORAIVS+ TOS**. 1.51g (SG 15.89: 74% Au) 200°. Miles 90(b)6 (this coin).

218 *Evora.* Obv. **+RECCAREDVSREX** Rev. **+ERBO:RA: PIVS**. 1.45g. (SG 14.45: 59% Au) 190°. Miles 91.1 (this coin). Illus. Reinhart 1941, pl. 33.9–10. Miles (pp. 222–3) regarded its authenticity as doubtful as the spelling *Erbora* is otherwise unattested, and the poor style and low fineness show it to be a contemporary forgery (Grierson 1953b, 84–6, no. 9).

219 *Mérida.* Obv. **+RECCAREDVSRE** Rev. **+EMERITA PIV∽**. 1.49g (SG 16.03: 75% Au) 190°. Miles 94(d)2 (this coin).

220 *Mérida.* Obv. **+RECCAREDVSREX** Rev. **+EMERITA VICTOR**. 1.46g (SG 16.14: 76% Au) 160°. Miles 93(a)4 (this coin). Illus. Reinhart 1937a, pl. 37.25; Reinhart 1940, pl. 12.10. On the unusual *Victor* in the inscription, see p. 52 above.

221 *Seville.* Obv. **+RECCAREDVSRE·** Rev. **+PIVSISPALI**. 1.55g (SG 16.06: 75% Au) 180°. Miles 86(e)4 (this coin).

222 *Seville.* Obv. **+RECCAREDVSRE** Rev. **+ISPALIPIVS·**. 1.46g (SG 15.67: 72% Au) 190°. Miles 85(e)1 (this coin).

223 *Toledo.* Obv. **+RECCAREDVSREX** Rev. **+TOLETO PIV∽**. 1.53g (SG 15.94: 74% Au) 180°. Miles 81(c)27 (this coin).

LIUVA II, 601–3

224 *Mérida.* Obv. **+DNLIVVAREX** Rev. **+EMERETAPIV∽**. 1.43g (SG 15.86: 74% Au) 190°. Miles 12(a)3 (this coin).

225 *Seville.* Obv. **+DNLIVVARE+** Rev. **+PIVSISPALI**. 1.48g (SG 16.17: 76% Au) 180°. Miles 120(b)3 (this coin).

Seville. For a forgery, see **1460**.

209. PG: Baldwin 6.6.1961.
210, 217. PG: Reinhart 30.9.1951.
211. PG: Baldwin 10.10.1952.
212. PG: Seaby 17.12.1950.
213. PG: A. R. Tait 26.5.1962; ex W. C. Tait (grandfather); bt at Monção, April 1908.
214. PG: Reinhart 5.2.1951.
215–16. PG: Christie 16.6.1959 ('Spanish collection'), lots 41 and 42 respectively.
218. PG: Shore 613.
219. PG: Seaby 17.11.1950.
220, 224, 229, 232. PG: ANS 10.8.1956; ex Reinhart.
221, 223. PG: Bute I 118 and 117 respectively.
222. PG: DO 11.5.1958; ex Peirce 1948; from St Louis Coin Co. 1930.
225. PG: Baldwin 27.7.1949; from Glendining 21.6.1949, lot. 148.

[continued overleaf]

209* 209 210 211 212 213

214 215 216 217 218

219 220 221 222 223 224 225

226 227 228 229 230 231 232

WITTERIC, 603–9

226 *Eliberri*. Obv. +**VVITTIRICVSRE** Rev. +**PIVS ELIBERRI**. 1.44g (SG 15.10: 66% Au) 190°. Miles 139(a).

227 *Mérida*. Obv. +**VVITTERICVSREX** Rev. +**EMERITA PIV∽**. 1.51g (SG 15.71: 72% Au) 180°. Miles 143(g)1 (this coin).

228 *Seville*. Obv. +**VVITTERICVSRE'** Rev. +**PIVSISPALI**. 1.50g (SG 15.58: 71% Au) 180°. Miles 140(c).

229 *Toledo*. Obv. +**VVITTIRICVSREX** Rev. +**TOLETO PIV∽**. 1.50g (SG 15.71: 75% Au) 180°. Miles 137(a)5 (this coin).

GUNDEMAR, 609–12

230 *Eliberri*. Obv. +**GVNDEMARVSRE** Rev. +**PIVS ELIBERRI**. 1.45g (SG 15.14: 67% Au) 190°. Miles 168(b)2 (this coin).

Seville and *Tarragona*. For forgeries, see **1461–2** respectively.

SISEBUT, 612–21

231 *Mérida*. Obv. +**SISEBVTVSREX** Rev. +**EMERITA PIVS✱**. 1.45g (SG 15.40: 69% Au) 190°. Miles 192(b)5 (this coin).

Oporto (Portocale). For a forgery, see **1463**.

232 *Seville*. Obv. +**SISEBVTVSRE** Rev. **✠ISPALIPIVS**. 1.48g (SG 15.54: 71% Au) 190°. Miles (187(c)4 (this coin). Illus. Reinhart 1940, pl. 12.9, and 1944, pl. 1.5.

226. PG: Christie 16.6.1959 ('Spanish collection'), lot 49.

227, 231. PG: Reinhart 30.9.1951.

228. PG: Bank Leu 27.6.1958.

230. PG: MMAG Basel 5.12.1950; ex Reinhart; ex Carles-Tolrá (cat. no. 1008).

VISIGOTHS (4): REGAL SERIES

References as on Plate 12. The coins are all gold tremisses.

SISEBUT, 612–21 (*cont.*)

233 *Tarragona*. Obv. +**SISEBVTVSRE**+ Rev. **TARR.**+ **COIV:TO** (for *Tarraco iustos*). 1.43g (SG 14.65: 62% Au) 180°. Miles 178(b).

Tarragona. For a forgery, see **1464**.

234 *Toledo*. Obv. +**SISEBVTVSREX** Rev. +**TOLETOPIV∽**. 1.42g (SG 14.95: 65% Au) 140°. Miles 183(a).

SWINTHILA, 621–31

235 *Barbi*. Obv. +**SVIИTHILRE** Rev. +**PIVSBARBI**. 1.44g (SG 14.81: 63% Au) 180°. Miles 224(c). The location of *Barbi* is uncertain, but it was probably the ancient *Municipium Barbitanus*, near *Tucci*, i.e. the modern Martos south-west of Jaén in southern Spain (Miles 1952, 104).

236 *Cordova*. Obv. **✱SVINTHIL˙REX** Rev. +**CORAOBA PIVƧ**. 1.28g (SG 13.72: 51% Au) 200°. Miles 226(c)var.

237 *Eliberri*. Obv. +**SVINTIIAR** Rev. +**PIVSEIIBER**. 1.36g (SG 14.43: 59% Au) 180°. Miles 227(b).

Eliberri. For a forgery, see **1465**.

238 *Mérida*. Obv. +**SVINTHILAREX** Rev. +**EMERITA PIVS**. 1.43g (SG 14.89: 64% Au) 180°. Miles 235(a)35 (this coin).

239 *Mérida*. Obv. +**SVINTHILARE** Rev. +**EMERITA PIVS**·. 1.40g (SG 15.06: 66% Au) 170°. Miles 23(i)2 (this coin).

240 *Seville*. Obv. +**SVINTIHL.ARE** Rev. +**ISPALIPIVS**. 1.47g (SG 15.26: 68% Au) 170°. Miles 228(c).

241 *Tarragona*. Obv. +**SVIИTHILARE** Rev. **TARR.**+ **COPIV**· (for *Tarraco pius*). 1.35g (SG 14.29: 58% Au) 170°. Miles 215(h)1 (this coin).

242 *Toledo*. Obv. +**SVINTHIL˙AREX** Rev. +**TOLETO PIV∽** (the **O** solid). 1.42g (SG 14.73: 62% Au) 180°. Miles 223(a).

243 *Tucci* (modern Martos, near Jaén in southern Spain: see Miles, p. 113). Obv. +**SVINTIIARE:** Rev. +**IVSTVS TVCI**. 1.19g (SG 14.30: 58% Au) 190°. Miles 229(i)2 (this coin).

SISENAND, 631–6

244 *Cordova*. Obv. +**SISENAN:VSRE** Rev. +**CORDOBA PIVƧ✱**. 1.25g (SG 13.99: 54% Au) 200°. Miles 267(d)3 (this coin).

245 *Cordova*. Obv. +**ƧIƧENA.NDVƧRE·:** (**NA** ligatured) Rev. +**CORΔOBAPIVƧ✱**. 1.46g (SG 14.04: 55% Au) 170°. Miles 267(j)1 (same dies).

246 *Mentesa* (modern La Guardia, near Jaén in southern Spain; see Miles, p. 95). Obv. +**SISENAN·IV·R** Rev. **|PIVS MENTE·A**. 1.12g chipped (SG 13.63: 49% Au) 190°. Miles 262(a)1 (this coin, wrongly described; it has bust of Type 5f on *both* sides).

247 *Mérida*. Obv. +**SISENANDVSRE✱** Rev. +**EMERITA PIVS**. 1.50g (SG 13.80: 52% Au) 190°. Miles 273(f)3 (this coin, but wrongly classified, the star after obv. inscription putting it into his 273(g) group).

CHINTILA, 636–9

248 *Eliberri*. Obv. +**CHINTILAR** Rev. +**PIVSI·IIBIRI**. 1.12g (SG 13.30: 45% Au) 180°. Miles 290 var.

249 *Mérida*. Obv. +**CINTNILAREX˙** Rev. +**EMERITA PIVS**. 1.41g (SG 13.96: 54% Au) 160°. Miles 293(b)2 (this coin).

Mérida. For a forgery, see **1466**.

250 *Seville*. Obv. +**CHI˙NTIL˙ARE** Rev. +**ISPAL˙IPI˙VS**. 1.41g (SG 13.95: 54% Au) 190°. Miles 291(b).

251 *Toledo*. Obv. +**CHINTILAREX** Rev. +**TOLETOPIV∽** (flower). 1.49g (SG 15.67: 72% Au) 150°. Miles 285(d)5 (this coin).

TULGA, 639–42

252 *Saragossa*. Obv. +**TVLC.ANREX** Rev. **XCE:AR: CO:TA∵** (for *Cesaracosta*, i.e. *Caesaraugusta*). 1.40g (SG 13.68: 50% Au) 140°. Miles 301 var.

CHINDASWINTH, 642–53

Alone (*642–9*)

253 *Cordova*. Obv. +**C⁝N[ ]TVƧRE** Rev. **]RDOBAPIVS[** 1.01g fragment (SG 13.69: 50% Au) 180°. Miles 319.

254 *Mérida*. Obv. +**CHINDASVINΘVSR̷** (**HINDA** as a monogram) Rev. +**EMERITAPIVS**. 1.27g (SG 14.06: 55% Au) 200°. Miles 330(a)7 (this coin).

Narbonne. For a forgery, see **1467**.

255 *Seville*. Obv. +**CINDASVNTSR** Rev. +**ISPALIPIVS**. 1.44g (SG 13.38: 46% Au) 170°. Miles 324 var.

256 *Toledo*. Obv. +**CHINDASVĪΘVSR̷** (**HINDA** as a monogram) Rev. +**TOLETOPIVS**. 1.48g (SG 14.84: 63% Au) 170°. Miles 318(c).

With Recceswinth (*649–53*)

257 *Mérida*. Obv. +**CHINDASVINΘVSR̷** around monogram of **EMRA** (i.e. *Emerita*) Rev. +**RECCESVINΘVSR̷**. 1.49g (SG 15.19: 67% Au) 190°. Miles 350(a) var.

233, 235. PG: Berghaus 7.8.1952; ex Krüger.
234. PG: G. Hirsch 14.10.1958.
236, 240. PG: Christie 16.6.1959 ('Spanish collection'), lots 56 and 58 respectively.
237. PG: Gans 28.8.1954.
238, 249. PG: Shore 615 and 617 respectively.
239. PG: Spink 9.11.1950.
241. PG: DO 11.5.1958; ex Peirce 1948 (acquired by him in 1928).
242. PG: G. Hirsch 14.10.1958.
243. PG: MMAG Basel 7.8.1951.
244. PG: Baldwin 16.10.1945; ex Huth III 233.
245. PG: G. Hirsch sale 11 (10.12.1956), lot 997.
246. PG: Baldwin 25.2.1962; ex Reinhart.
247. PG: Reinhart 30.9.1951.
248, 250, 252. PG: Christie 16.6.1959 ('Spanish collection'), lots 62, 63 and 64 respectively.
251. PG: Seaby 17.11.1950.
253, 255, 257. PG: Christie 16.6.1959 ('Spanish collection'), lots 67, 68 and 69 respectively.
254. PG: Franceschi 7.7.1949.
256. PG: Bank Leu 27.6.1958.

233 234 235 236 237 238

239 240 241 242 243 244

245 246 247 248 249 250

251 252 253 254 255 256 257

VISIGOTHS (5): REGAL SERIES

References as on Plate 12. The coins are all gold tremisses.

RECCESWINTH, alone 653–72

Class 1. Varied types (653). See p. 51. Coins of this class, which lasted only a short time, are very rare. The first of those below is unique and only three specimens are recorded of the second.

(a) Profile bust and monogram

258 *Seville.* Obv. +**RECCESVINTVSRE** (**VINTV** as a monogram) Rev. +**ISPALIPIVS**, monogram of **SPAL** (i.e. *Ispali*). 1.45g (SG 15.60: 71% Au) 180°. Miles 366.1 (this coin).

(b) Two facing busts (Cordova and Toledo only)

259 *Toledo.* Obv. +**RECCESVINΘVSRE** Rev. +**TOLETO PIVS**. 1.58g plugged (SG 15.88: 74% Au, but figure distorted by plugging) 180°. Miles 339.3 (this coin).

Class 2. Profile bust and cross-on-steps (653–72)

260 *Cordova.* Obv. +**RECESSVINΘVSR** Rev. +**CORDOBA PATR·CIA**. 1.40g (SG 15.31: 68% Au) 180°. Miles 364(f)3 (this coin). On the legend, see p. 52 above.

261 *Mérida.* Obv. +**RECCESVINΘVSR℞** Rev. +**EMERITA PIVS**. 1.50g (SG 15.83: 73% Au) 160°. Miles 374(e) var. (of bust).

262 *Seville.* Obv. +**RECCESVINTVSR** Rev. +**ISPALIPIVS**. 1.50g (SG 15.06: 66% Au) 170°. Miles 369(a).

263 *Toledo.* Obv. +**RECCESVINΘVSR℞** Rev. +·**TOLETO PIVS**·. 1.46g (SG 15.10: 66% Au) 170°. Miles 360(c)4 (this coin).

WAMBA, 672–80

Hereafter, the obv. legend commences w. *In Dei nomine*, abbreviated.

264 *Mérida.* Obv. +**I·D·IN·M·EVVAMBA℞** (**MB** ligatured) Rev. +**EMERITAPIVS**. 1.50g (SG 14.29: 58% Au) 160°. Miles 394(a)8 (this coin).

265 *Mérida.* Obv. +**I·D·IN·M·EVVAMBA℞** Rev. +**EMERI TAPIVS**. 1.38g (SG 14.76: 63% Au) 160°. Miles 394(b)1 (this coin).

Mérida. For a forgery, see **1468**.

266 *Toledo.* Obv. +**I·D·N·M·N·VVAMBA℞** Rev. +**TOLETOPIVS**. 1.59g (SG 14.27: 57% Au) 180°. Miles 386(b)11 (this coin).

ERWIC, 680–7

267 *Mérida.* Obv. +**I·D·IN·M·N·ERVIGIVSR℞** (around head of Christ superimposed on cross on base) Rev. +**EMERITAPIVS**. 1.46g (SG 14.41: 59% Au) 0°. Miles 415(a)23 = Reinhart 1940, pl. 12.18 (this coin).

268 *Seville.* Obv. +**I·Δ·INMERVIGIVSR℞** Rev. +**✱ISPALI PIVS**. 1.47g (SG 14.22: 57% Au) 0°. Miles 409(b)2 (this coin).

269 *Seville.* Obv. +**I·Δ·INMERVIGIVSR℞** Rev. +**✱ISPALI PIVS**. 1.46g (SG 13.87: 53% Au) 0°. Miles 410(a)4 (this coin).

270 *Toledo.* Obv. +**I·D·NMNERVIGIVSR℞** Rev. +**TOLETO PIVS**. 1.43g pierced (SG 14.36: 57% Au) 40°. Miles 399(a)14 (this coin).

271 *Tucci* (see **243**). Obv. +**I·D·IN·M·ERVIGIVSRX** Rev. +**TVCCI**|flower|**PIVS**|pierced star. 1.49g (SG 14.06: 55% Au) 20°. Miles 412(a) var.

EGICA, 687–702

Alone (687–95)

272 *Gerona* (north-eastern Spain). Obv. +**IND·N·M·N·EGICA℞** (**IND** ligatured) Rev. +**GERVNΘPIVS**. 1.23g cracked (SG 12.91: 40% Au) 200°. Miles 424(c).

273 *Mérida.* Obv. +**INDIN·H·NEEGICA℞** (**ND** and **NE** ligatured) Rev. +**EMERITAPIVS**. 1.37g (SG 13.93: 53% Au) 170°. Miles 448(a)1 (this coin).

274 *Mérida.* Obv. +**I·D·N·M·N·EGICA℞** Rev. +**EMERI TAPIVS**. 1.43g cracked (SG 13.94: 53% Au) 180°. Miles 449(a).

Narbonne. For a forgery, see **1469**.

275 *Tarragona.* Obv. +**I·D[ ]N·EGICA℞** Rev. +**TAR RACO[ ]S**. 1.17g broken and segment missing (SG 13.44: 47% Au) 330°. Miles 426(c)?

Tarragona. For a forgery, see **1470**.

276 *Toledo.* Obv. +**N+PN·M·EGICA℞** (**N+PN·M·** for *In Christi nomine*) Rev. +**TOLETOPIVS**. 1.49g (SG 13.08: 42% Au) 290°. Miles 436(i)2 (this coin).

277 *Toledo.* Obv. +**N+PINONN·EGICANVC·R** (for *In Christi nomine Egica rex victor*, the **N** after *Egica* being an error for **℞**) Rev. +**TOLETOPIVS**. 1.48g (SG 14.31: 58% Au) 110°. Miles 437(b) var.

258. PG: Seaby 17.11.1950.
259. PG: MMAG Basel 15.1.1951.
260, 270. PG: Shore 619 and 620 respectively.
261. PG: ANS 16.8.1956; ex Reinhart.
262. PG: Lockett III 273.
263. PG: DO 11.5.1958; ex Peirce 1948.
264. PG: Baranowsky 27.3.1951.
265–6. PG: Reinhart 30.9.1951.
267. PG: Baldwin 25.5.1962; ex Reinhart.
268. PG: Baldwin 16.10.1945; ex Grantley 2799.
269. PG: Baldwin 15.4.1946; ex Grantley 2800.
271–2. PG: Christie 16.6.1959 ('Spanish collection'), lots 75 and 78 respectively.
273. PG: Bute I 119 (as Chindaswinth).
274–5, 277. PG: Christie 16.6.1959 ('Spanish collection'), lots 76, 79 and 81 respectively.
276. PG: Platt 1.10.1950.

[*continued overleaf*]

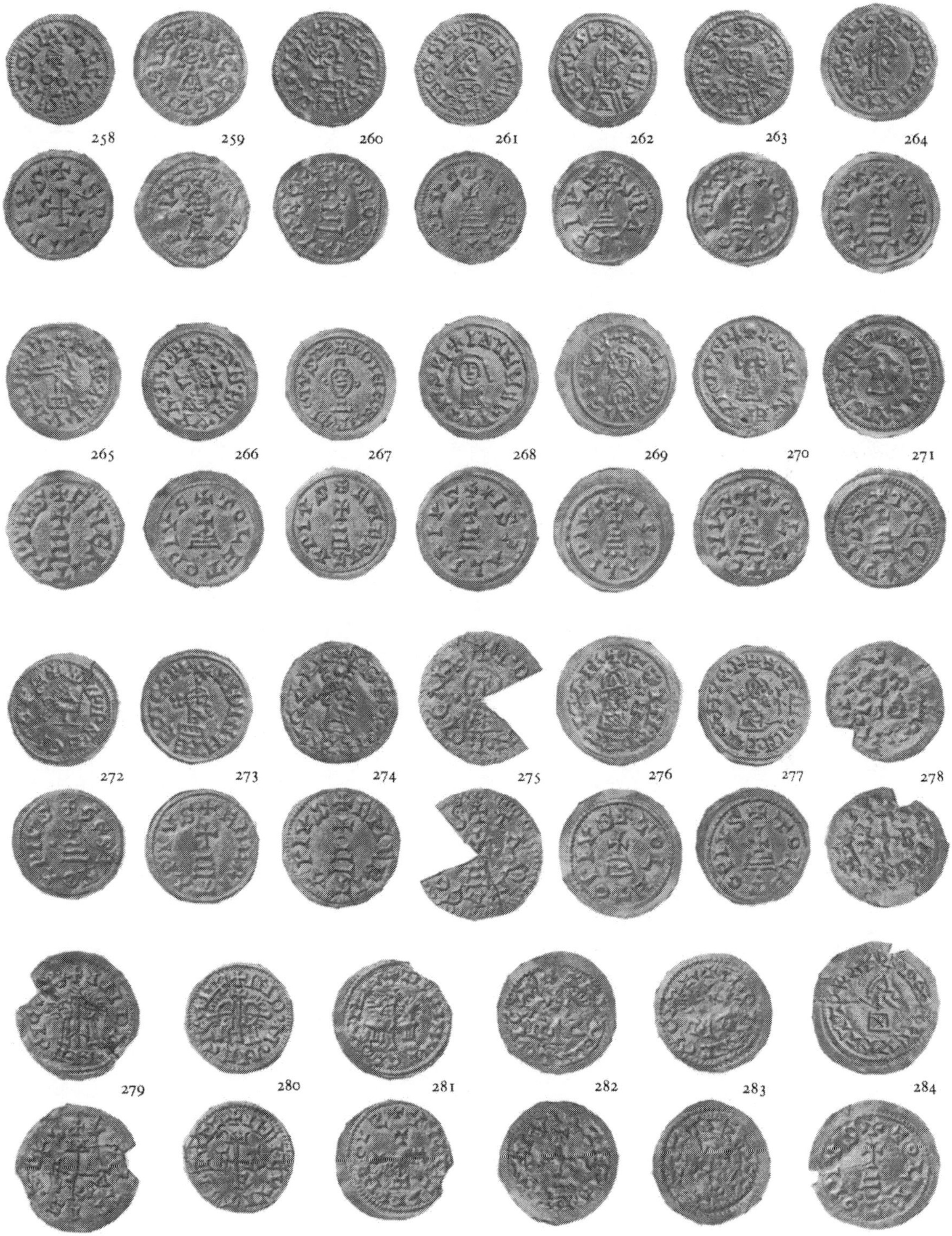

258 259 260 261 262 263 264

265 266 267 268 269 270 271

272 273 274 275 276 277 278

279 280 281 282 283 284

PLATE 14 (*cont.*)

With Wittiza (695–702)

Types are two confronting busts (w. cross-sceptre between) and monogram of mint name on arms of cross.

278 *Evora.* Obv. +**INDINMNEGICAR** Rev. +**VVITTIZAR REGIS**, monogram of **ELBOA** (i.e. *Elbora*). 1.09g chipped and cracked (SG 12.72: 37% Au) 20°. Miles 485(c)1 (this coin, but inscriptions misread and weight incorrect).

279 *Mérida.* Obv. +**INDN·M·EGICAR** Rev. +**VVIT TIZARS**, monogram of **EMERITA**, w. 2 flowers in field. 1.37g chipped and trace of mount on obv. (SG 12.67: 37% Au; chemical analysis gave 36.9% Au and 57.5% Ag: Grierson 1953b, 85, no. 41) 340°. Miles 486(k)1 (this coin).

280 *Mérida.* Obv. +**IND·N·MEGICAR** Rev. +**INEMEVVIT TIZAR** (**NE** and **ME** ligatured), same monogram. 1.20g (SG 12.26: 31% Au) 180°. Miles 486(h)1 (this coin).

281 *Toledo.* Obv. +**INDINNEGICAR** Rev. +**VVITIZAR REGIS**, monogram of **TOLETO**. 1.47g broken, repaired and gilded 220°. Miles 468(d)1 (this coin).

282 *Toledo.* Obv. +**INDINNEGICAR** Rev. +**VVIT TIZAR**, monogram of **TOLETO**. 1.50g (SG 13.62: 49% Au) 160°. Miles 468(j) var.

283 *Toledo.* Obv. +**INDINNEGICAR** Rev. +**VVIT TIZAR**. 1.40g (SG 13.53: 48% Au) 290°. Miles 468(j) var.

WITTIZA, alone 702–10

284 *Toledo.* Obv. +**INDINEVVITTIZR** (**ND** and **NE** ligatured) Rev. **TOLETOPIVS**. Pale AV 1.52g chipped, broken and mended 90°. Miles 498 var.

RODERICK, 710–11

Toledo. For a forgery, see **1471**.

278. PG: Baldwin 25.5.1962; ex Reinhart.

279, 281. PG: Shore 623 and 621 respectively.

280. PG: Reinhart 5.2.1951.

282. PG: Baldwin 16.7.1956; ex Shore 622.

283. PG: A. R. Tait 26.5.1962; fd at Guimarães in 19th c.

284. PG: Christie 16.6.1959 ('Spanish collection'), lot 83.

SUEVI, *c.* 435–585

The principal reference is: R = Reinhart 1937a. All coins are gold. For the basis of the attributions to this series, see p. 79 above. The lettering can be only approximately rendered, especially that of the later coins. **285–7** are probably mid 5th century, **288–91** mid 6th century and **292–3** of the 580s.

Solidus. Imitation of Honorius (393–423).

285 Obv. **DHHOHORI VSPFΔVG** Rev. **VICTORI ΛΛVCCC, COИOB**, w. **ИD** (for MD = *Mediolanum*, Milan) in field. 4.22g (SG 16.50: 79% Au) 0°. Reinhart 1942, fig. 1.3 (same obv. die).

Tremisses

Class 1. Imitations of Valentinian III (425–55), w. his name blundered.

(a) Normal bust of emperor

286 Obv. **DIIIIИIINITIHILI·VMIVC** Rev. **COIIOB**. 1.33g (SG 17.15: 85% Au) 0°. R26 (same dies). Note test scratches or graffiti on rev.: horizontal scratches to l. and r. of wreath and small V to r. of legend.

287 Obv. **ƆNPIVΛIINIΓΛNVSPΛC** Rev. **COIIOB**. 1.38g (SG 16.62: 80% Au) 0°. R33 (same obv. die).

(b) With spear-head breaking obv. inscription

288 **I HVΛLEИTINFI IIVSΠI** Rev. **CONOB** (retrograde). 1.40g (SG 16.28: 77% Au) 330°. R46 (this specimen noted). Note test scratches or graffiti on rev.: + above and X to either side of wreath.

289 Obv. **ƆNVΛLEИTIИΛV VƧVIV** Rev. **COIIOB**. 1.30g (SG 14.65: 62% Au) 330°. R47 (same obv. die, very rusty; this specimen noted). Same obv. die as next.

290 Obv. **ƆNVΛLEИT[** Rev. **ƆOIIOB**. 1.42g (SG 16.52: 80% Au) 30°. R47 (same obv. die). Same obv. die as last. Overstruck on another Suevic tremissis with **CONOB** and star at top of rev. (cf. R36).

(c) With totally corrupt inscriptions and letters or symbols in the field

291 Obv. **BOVΛIVIVVIIVVΛIΛIEI**, w. **Π** in field Rev. **OIIO**, w. star above and inverted **L** to l. (for León?). 1.27g (SG 17.27: 86% Au) 330°. R70–3 var.

292 Obv. **OΛΛΛSDΛVDOMI·TMNTOI** Rev. **OIIO**, w. **O** above, **C** to l., and pellet to r. 0.86g broken and repaired 150°. R –. The **C** may possibly stand for *Conimbriga* (Condeixa a Velha, 12km south of Coimbra).

Class 2. With mint name in inscription.

293 *León*. Obv. **LEIOIΛ COTIS MVNITΛ**, w. 3 pellets before face Rev. **IONIOƆ**, w. inverted **L** to r. and **I** to l. 1.22g chipped (SG 14.40: 59% Au) 170°. R61 **COTIS** presumably implies that this was struck immediately after the Visigothic conquest.

LOMBARDS, 568–774

References are: Arslan = Arslan 1978, *BMC Vand* and Bernareggi = Bernareggi 1960. Analyses of most of the coins were published by Oddy (1972b, nos. SG291–379); for unpublished analyses, also by him, the specific gravity is given. The coins are gold tremisses unless otherwise indicated.

LOMBARDY: Pseudo-imperial coinage, *c.* 568–*c.* 690

With the name of Justinian I (527–65)

294 Obv. **DNIVSTINI ANVSPPAVI** Rev. **VICTORIA AVIVTORVM, CONOB**. 1.41g (Oddy no. SG291; 97% Au) 170°. Arslan 1 var.; *BMC Vand* –. Cf. *DOC* I, 75.19.2 as possible model.

295 *Half-siliqua*. Obv. **DNIVSTIII ΛƧIΛVC**. Ꜷ 0.65g 180°. Arslan –; *BMC Vand* 124.4. Cf. *DOC* I, 183.339 for model.

296 *As last*. Obv. **DNIVSTINI ΛNVSP[** . Ꜷ 0.55g 340°. Arslan –; *BMC Vand* 124.6.

297 *As last*. Inscription obscure. Ꜷ 0.61g 180°. Arslan –; *BMC Vand* 124.5.

With the name of Justin II (565–78)

298 Obv. **DNIVSTI NVSPPAVC** Rev. **VICTORIA ΛVCUSTORVM, CONOB**. 1.44g (Oddy no. SG292; 97% Au) 180°. Arslan 2; *BMC Vand* 123 var. For prototype, see *DOC* I, 260.212.

299 Obv. **IIVΠIIU ΛIIVSVIII** Rev. **VƆTOIINIVΛVCVC TORVH, COIIO**. 1.46g (SG 18.65: 96% Au) 180°. Arslan –; *BMC Vand* –.

285. PG: MMAG Basel 2.11.1960.
286. PG: L. S. Forrer 8.11.1950.
287. PG: Christie 16.6.1959 ('Spanish collection'), lot 37.
288–9. PG: Spink 19.3.1945; ex Grantley 2804 and 2805 respectively.
290. PG: H. Schulman 27.11.1969.
291–2. PG: Christie 17.3.1981, lot 284.
293. PG: Sotheby 6.6.1973, lot 83.
294. PG: Santamaria 20.7.1955.
295. PG: Spink 28.5.1945; ex Grantley 2786.
296. FM: Bunn 1950.
297. FM: provenance unrecorded.
298. PG: Spink 6.12.1945; ex Grantley 2808.
299. PG: Spink 6.12.1945; ex Grantley 2807; bt in Vienna.

[*continued overleaf*]

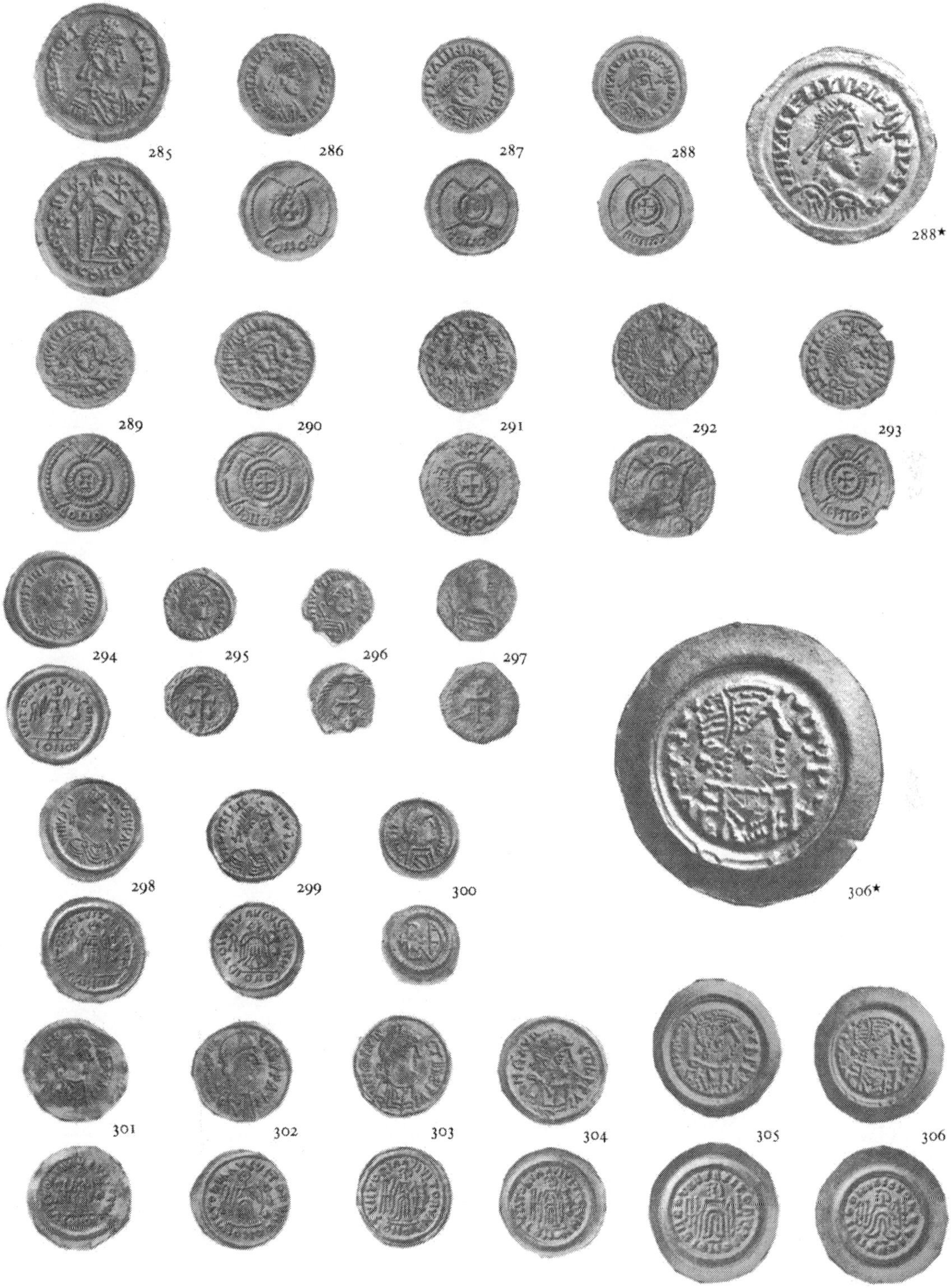

285 286 287 288 288*

289 290 291 292 293

294 295 296 297

298 299 300 306*

301 302 303 304 305 306

PLATE 15 (*cont.*)

With the name of Tiberius II (578–82)

300 *Half-siliqua of Duke Farwald of Spoleto, minted at Classis 579(?)–c. 590.* Obv. **DNIOIT IINVID** (for *DNConstantinus PPA*) Rev. monogram of **+FARVALD DX** (or **RX**?) in inverted wreath. AR 0.48g 0°. Arslan –; *BMC Vand* 144.4 var. (as Liutprand). For discussion of the attribution and monogram, see note on coin.

With the name of Maurice Tiberius (582–602)

(a) Normal size flan, design and epigraphy of fairly good style

301 Obv. **DNMARC TIbPPAVC** Rev. **VICTORIAAVCVS TORVN, CONOB**, no star in field. 1.47g (Oddy no. SG296; 96% Au) 180°. Arslan –; *BMC Vand* –; cf. *DOC* I, 370.287.

302 Obv. **DNMAVRC TIbPPAVC** Rev. **VICTORIA AVCVSTORVN, IONOΔ**. 1.49g (SG 18.08: 92% Au) 160°. Arslan 4 var.; *BMC Vand* 128.22 var.

303 Obv. **DNMAVR CTIbPPVI** Rev. **VICTORIAAVIVI TORVN, CONOR**. 1.41g (Oddy no. SG296, wrongly as in BM; 97% Au) 170°. Arslan 4; *BMC Vand* 128.22.

304 Obv. **DNMAVR CTIbPPVI** Rev. **VIITORIAAVIVI TORVN, CONOR**. 1.46g (Oddy no. SG299; 95% Au) 170°. Ref. as last.

(b) Larger flan, stylized Victory and epigraphy

305 Obv. **DNMA[ ]TIbPP[** (partially obliterated by incuse border) Rev. **IITOИIIIITOLAI, IONOI**, no star in field. 1.27g (SG 15.87: 74% Au) 60°. Arslan 19; *BMC Vand* –; Bernareggi 1.

306 *Obv.* **DИMVRI**(?) **ITbPPVC** Rev. **ꓘHROTAIVIV-TORИꓤ, IOIIOI**. 1.43g (SG 16.36: 78% Au) 180°. Arslan 18 var.; *BMC Vand* –; Bernareggi 1. Note the almost symmetrical reverse inscription.

300. PG: Ulrich-Bansa 17.10.1948; ex 'A. Sambon 490'.
301. PG: 'Foreign Ambassador' 540.
302. PG: Spink 7.1.1954; ex G. P. Mander; from Spink.
303. PG: Kricheldorf 5.2.1962 (list 59, no. 12).
304. PG: Spink 19.3.1945 (bt Oct. 1940).
305. PG: Bank Leu sale 24 (18.10.1979), lot 4.
306. PG: Toderi 7.5.1983.

LOMBARDS (2)

References as on Plate 15. The coins are gold tremisses unless otherwise indicated.

TUSCANY: Pseudo-imperial coinage, *c.* 620–*c.* 700

With the name of Heraclius (610–41)

307 Obv. **DNHERAC LIVSPPAVC** Rev. **VICTORIA AVIVSTORVM, CONOB.** 1.29g (Oddy no. SG318; 97% Au) 160°. Arslan –; *BMC Vand* 131.34 var. The prototype is a tremissis of Ravenna (*DOC* II, 368.276).

308 Obv. **ONHERAIII VIPPAVI** Rev. **VNTOAIVAVIVI TOAVH, IONOB.** 1.51g (Oddy no. SG315; 93% Au) 170°. Arslan –; *BMC Vand* 131.32 var.

309 Obv. **DNCRAC LIVƧPPAV** (**AV** ligatured) Rev. **VIITORIAAXIVITOAV, CONOB.** 1.49g (Oddy no. SG322; 93% Au) 180°. Arslan –; *BMC Vand* 131.33 var.

310 Obv. **ON[ ]AC L[ ]PAVC,** w. cross above head Rev. **VIITORAAVIPITCV, IONOI.** 1.45g (Oddy no. SG330: 77% Au) 180°. Arslan –; *BMC Vand* 131.38 var.

With the name of Constans II (641–68)

311 Obv. **DNIOITA NTIIIVI** Rev. **VICTIRIAAVIVITI, IOIIOA.** 1.45g pierced and plugged (Oddy no. SG337; 81% Au but plugged) 0°. Arslan –; *BMC Vand* 133.44 (same dies). The prototype is a tremissis of Ravenna (*DOC* II, 507.202).

312 Obv. **OIИIORV[ ]IIINTVI,** w. cross on breast Rev. **VIOITIVIOAИVAOT, NOИOI.** 1.50g pierced and plugged (Oddy no. SG336; 85% Au but plugged) 30°. Arslan –; *BMC Vand* 133.44 var.

With completely blundered inscriptions

313 Obv. **VNOIV VHOИV** Rev. **ΠIOHVAVHOIH, ANA.** 1.44g (Oddy no. SG347; 79% Au) 300°. Arslan 80–2 var.; *BMC Vand* 135.12 var.; Rigold 1975, no. 26 (this coin).

314 Obv. **INVNV VIOHVI** Rev. **MIOHVIVHOIM, AИA.** 1.46g (Oddy no. SG346; 79% Au) 150°. Arslan 80–2 var.; *BMC Vand* 135.12 (same dies).

315 Obv. **AVIVO TИVNTA** (**TИ** ligatured) Rev. **AVIIO IIIVIИIVIIIOIVV.** 1.44 g (Oddy no. SG349; 74% Au) 290°. Arslan 82 var.; *BMC Vand* –.

316 Obv. **IVNV- -VHOVI,** w. **B** before face Rev. **ΠIOH VAVHTOΠ, AИA.** 1.47g (Oddy no. SG354; 81% Au) 270°. Arslan –; *BMC Vand* 134.1.

317 Obv. **TИT- -VI-ИT,** w. **B** before face Rev. **-VVOVIV VNOVИ.** 1.33g (Oddy no. SG357; 66% Au) 100°. Arslan –; *BMC Vand* 135.6 var. This coin appears to have been struck to a reduced weight standard of *c.* 1.35g.

TUSCANY: Autonomous municipal coinage, *c.* 700–*c.* 749

318 *Lucca.* Obv. monogram of **LVCA,** w. ᵯ above Rev. cross potent surrounded by pseudo-inscription of **VAVA** etc. 1.28g (Oddy no. SG365; 51% Au) 30°. Arslan 84 var.; *BMC Vand* 151.4 var.; Bernareggi 200.

319 Obv. **+FLAVIALVCA,** flower Rev. **✱VIVIVIV✱ VIVIVIV.** 1.34g broken and repaired (Oddy no. SG370, wrongly as in BM; 35% Au but soldered) 40°. Arslan –; *BMC Vand* 150.1 var.; Bernareggi 206.

LOMBARDY AND TUSCANY:
Regal coinage, 688–774
(in Tuscany from 749)

The tremisses below all have a diademed bust r. w. letter before face and St Michael standing l. w. cross; types w. a facing bust or monogram on the obv. or a Victory rev. are not represented.

CUNINCPERT, 688–700

320 Obv. **DNCVN ИICPER,** w. **M** before face Rev. **SCSMI HAHIL.** 1.33g (Oddy no. SG307; 94% Au) 0°. Arslan 43 var.; *BMC Vand* 138.2 var.; Bernareggi 22.

ARIPERT II, 700–12

321 Obv. **DNAR IPER,** w. **G** before face Rev. **SCSMI HAHIL.** 1.32g (Oddy no. SG309; 97% Au) 240°. Arslan 46 var.; *BMC Vand* 141.1 var.; Bernareggi 51 var.

LIUTPRAND, 712–44

322 Obv. **DNLIV PRAИR** (**NL** ligatured; first half partially obscured by incuse border), w. **L∵** before face Rev. **SCS MHIL.** 1.23g (SG 14.32: 58% Au) 140°. Arslan 47 var.; *BMC Vand* 143.1 var.; Bernareggi 74.

307. PG: Spink 12.2.1945; ex Grantley 2810.
308. PG: Baldwin 6.10.1948.
309. PG: provenance unrecorded (acq. before 1972).
310. PG: Spink 26.5.1949; from H. Schulman.
311. PG: Spink 10.1.1947.
312. PG: Spink 19.3.1945; ex Boulton; from 'Ratto 297'.
313. FM: Grierson 17.11.1966; acq. from a man whose father had found it while digging an allotment near Sheffield during the First World War.
314–17. PG: Spink 18.7.1956.
318. PG: M. Ratto 22.7.1967.
319. PG: M. Ratto 2.4.1953.
320. PG: MMAG Basel sale 6 (6.12.1946), lot 909.
321. PG: Kunst und Münzen sale 7.12.1967, lot 420.
322. PG: Seaby 28.3.1978 (*SCMB* April 1978, no. A357).

[*continued overleaf*]

307 308 309 310 311 312

313 314 315 316 317 318 319

320 321 322 323 324 324*

328*

325 326 327 328 329 330 331

AISTULF, 749–56

323 *Lucca.* **D·NAI2TVL·F·REX** and **+·F·L·AVIA·LVCA.** 1.15g (Oddy no. SG373; 56% Au) 220°. Arslan 86 var.; *BMC Vand* 148.1 var.; Bernareggi 217. The tremisses of Aistulf and Desiderius follow the practice of the Tuscan municipal coinages in making the mint name technically the obverse inscription, the royal name and titles thus becoming the reverse.

324 *Follis. Ravenna (751–6).* Obv. **[ΩNAIS TVLF]℞**, bearded bust facing Rev. **M**, w. cross above, **ANNO** to r. and **R[** (for the mint name) below. The year is off the flan to the r. Æ 1.67g 190°. Arslan –; *BMC Vand* –; Bernareggi –. Illus. *RN*[5] 2 (1938), pl. 1.6 (as Byzantine). For this coinage, see p. 65 above.

DESIDERIUS, 757–74

325 *Lucca.* **D-NDESIDE℞** and **+FL·AVIALVCA.** 1.04g (Oddy no. SG375; 41% Au) 180°. Arslan –; *BMC Vand* 149.1 var.; Bernareggi 229 var.

326 *Castelnovate* (Varese). **+DNDESI[** (**ND** ligatured) and **+[ ]OVAT:ARI.** 0.58g fragment (Oddy no. SG379; 28% Au) 0°. Arslan 64–6 var.; *BMC Vand* –; Bernareggi 198 (this coin). For the attribution, see note on coin.

327 *Piacenza.* **]ESIDE℞ R[** and **]L:AVIA PLA[** . 0.56g fragment, broken and mended (Oddy no. SG378, wrongly as in BM: 43% Au but soldered) 40°. Arslan –; *BMC Vand* 149.3; Bernareggi 172 bis (this coin).

SILVER COINAGE

With imperial bust and monogram of PER (for Perctarit, 672–88)
This coinage starts as biface, having on the obverse an imperial bust without inscription, but later issues, which continue into the second quarter of the 8th century, are uniface and have only the monogram. They are discussed above, pp. 65–6.

Class a. With bust and wreath

328 Obv. bust r. w. 3 pellets before face and 6 or more behind head, in a beaded border Rev. **P℞** (tail of **℞** as 3 pellets) in a wreath, w. 3 pellets between and to l. of letters. AR 0.23g chipped 160°. Arslan 23 var.; *BMC Vand* 136.15 var.; Bernareggi 1968, 9.

Class b. With bust and no wreath

329 Obv. traces of bust, w. pellets behind head Rev. monogram of **PE℞** in plain border, w. 4 pellets above, below and to l. of letters, and 2 to r. AR 0.20g 180°. Arslan 23 var.; *BMC Vand* 136.15 var.; Bernareggi 1968, 14 var.

330 Obv. traces of design in pelleted border Rev. monogram of **PE℞** (tail of **℞** as 3 pellets) in plain border, w. 3 pellets above, and to l. of letters. AR 0.18g Arslan 23 and 30 var.; *BMC Vand* 136.15 and 17 var.; Bernareggi 1968, 47 var.

Class c. With reverse type only

331 Rev. monogram of **PE℞** (tail of **℞** as 3 pellets) in plain border, w. 3 pellets above. AR 0.18g Arslan 28–9; *BMC Vand* 136.16 var.; Bernareggi 1968, 41.

323, 325. PG: Ratto 10.12.1966; ex Ulrich-Bansa 1949; ex C. Gavazzi.
324. PG: Longuet 494.
326. PG: Ratto 25.3.1963 (= sale 20.1.1956, lot 415 = sale 24.11.1960, lot 128).
327. PG: Ratto 10.12.1966; ex Ulrich-Bansa 1949.
328. PG: Hollschek VII 770; ex Windisch-Grätz (cat. no. 7871).
329. PG: Ars et Nummus 17.4.1967.
330. PG: Seaby 22.2.1945.
331. PG: Spink 18.7.1956.

UNATTRIBUTED GERMANIC, BURGUNDIAN AND MEROVINGIAN COINS

Principal references are: B = Belfort 1892–5, P = Prou 1892a and, for tremisses, Tomasini = Tomasini 1964. The coins are gold unless otherwise indicated.

UNATTRIBUTED GERMANIC COINS

The following four pseudo-imperial coins, ranging in date from the late 4th to the late 6th century, cannot at present be closely attributed.

332 *Imitation of late 4th-century siliqua.* Obv. **IIIIIIII IVIΠI[** Rev. blundering of **VOTA**, numeral and mint-mark in deformed wreath. Æ 1.05g chipped 180°. Grierson 1976a, 19, no. 4, 5 (this coin). See note on coin.

333 *Tremissis, with the blundered name of Valentinian III (425–55).* Obv. **OIIΛVTIII IIIΛIIVΛC** Rev. **OOIIOↃ, OOIIO8.** 1.49g (SG 17.27: 86% Au) 10°. B –. A type imitated by the Visigoths in the mid 5th century, but the extreme blundering of the emperor's name and the repetition of **CONOB** above and below the wreath show that it cannot be an official Visigothic issue.

334 *Solidus, with the name of Anthemius (467–72).* Obv. **]NANTHE MIVƧPIΛVC** Rev. **VΛIVQVEI PΓICVE** (for *Salus rei publicae*), **ΓM** (for **RM** = Rome) between soldiers, ex. illegible. 3.99g pierced and worn 0°. Imitation of Cohen VIII, 231.6. Perhaps struck in Frisia; specimens of the original are not likely to have reached England.

335 *Solidus, with the name of Zeno (474–91).* ?Sardinia, under Odovacar or the Vandals. Obv. **DNZEN PERPΛVC** Rev. **VICTORI ΛΛVCCCS, CONOB.** 4.28g (SG 16.45: 79% Au) 180°. Grierson 1976a, no. 2, 3 (this coin). See note on coin.

BURGUNDIANS

GUNDOBALD, 473–516

With the name of Anastasius I (491–518). GVB monogram in field.

336 *Solidus.* Obv. **DNΛNΛSTΛ SIVSPRΛVC** Rev. **VIC TORI ΛΛVCCCRVM** (**RVM** ligatured), **CONOB.** 4.41g (SG 18.84: 97% Au) 180°. B 2241, 2245; Amécourt 1866a, no. 1.

337 *Tremissis.* Obv. **DNΛNΛSTΛ SIVSPRΛVC** (**ΛV** ligatured) Rev. **IVCTORIΛ ΛVCVTOVИ, CONOB.** 1.47g (SG 19.01: 98% Au) 160°. B 2250; Amécourt 1866a, no. 2; Tomasini 103–12.

338 *Tremissis.* Obv. as last Rev. **IVICTORIΛΛ VCVTOVM, CONOB.** 1.42g (SG 18.91: 97% Au) 170°. Ref. as last.

339 *Nummus.* No obv. inscription, bust r. Rev. **GVB** monogram above **LD** (for *Lugdunum*, Lyon). Æ 0.43g 180°. B 2248; Amécourt 1866a, no. 5.

SIGISMUND, 516–24

With the name of Justin I (518–27). S ending rev. legend

340 *Solidus.* Obv. **DNIVSTI NVSPPΛVC** Rev. **VICTOR I ΛΛVCCCIS, CONOB.** 4.45g (SG 18.88: 97% Au) 180°. B 5154; Amécourt 1866a, –. There were 20 specimens in the Gourdon hoard (Lafaurie 1958b) from the same pair of dies. The style, coupled with the fact that an **S** follows the mechanically copied officina letter **I**, excludes it from the imperial series.

GUNDOMAR II, 524–32

With the name of Justin I (518–27)

341 *Tremissis.* Obv. **DNIVSTINVSPPΛVC** Rev. **VICTORI ΛΛ VCCCΛ, COMOB,** w. **MAR** monogram in field. 1.43g (SG 18.28: 93% Au) 170°. B 5215 (as Amalaric); Amécourt 1866a, –; Tomasini 227–31.

342 *Tremissis.* Obv. **DИIVSTINVSPΛV** Rev. **VICTORI ΛΛVCCC, COИOB.** 1.42g (SG 18.05: 92% Au) 350°. B –; Amécourt 1866a, –. The style, weight and fineness are very similar to the preceding coin, but the absence of a **G** or **MAR** monogram suggests that this may have been struck by the Franks when they briefly occupied much of Burgundy in 523–4.

For later Merovingian coins copying tremisses of Gundomar II, see **360–1**.

332. PG: Spink 20.2.1962.
333. PG: Spink 20.10.1948.
334. PG: Baldwin 2.7.1977; found at Piercebridge, Co. Durham, *c.* 1955.
335. PG: Seaby 20.3.1945.
336. PG: Bourgey 17.4.1959; ex Perret.
337. PG: Spink 19.3.1945; ex Grantley.
338. FM: provenance unrecorded.
339. PG: MMAG Basel 22.1.1970 (list 308, no. 49).
340. PG: Goff 34; no doubt ultimately from the Gourdon hoard.
341. PG: Spink 19.3.1945; ex Grantley 2793; from Rollin.
342. PG: Prince de Ligne I 106.

[*continued overleaf*]

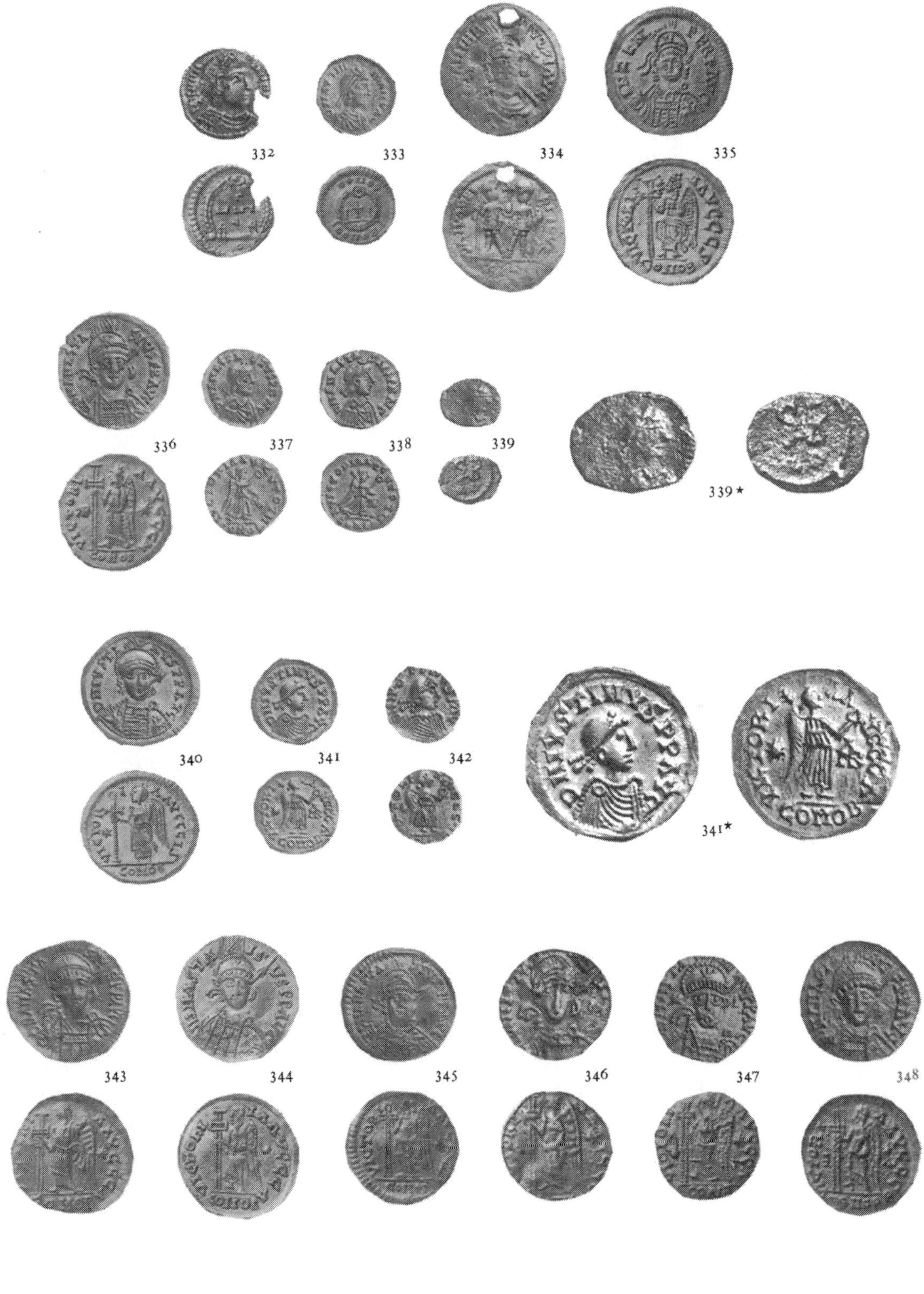

332 333 334 335

336 337 338 339 339*

340 341 342 341*

343 344 345 346 347 348

MEROVINGIANS (1): PSEUDO-IMPERIAL COINAGE, *c.* 500–*c.* 580

With the name of Anastasius I (491–518)
Solidi. With Victory holding long voided cross and star in r. field. The prototypes were Ostrogothic solidi (cf. **112**). **343**, **347** and **348** are shown by the provenance of closely related specimens to be Frankish, the others are probably so.

343 Obv. **DNANASTA SIVSPPAVC** Rev. **VICT[O]RI AAVCCCA, COMOB**. 4.47g (SG 18.76: 97% Au) 180°. B 5035 (Chinon hoard); Reinhart 1938, no. 125 var. (as Visigothic). Cf. Dhénin 1980b, pl. 20.E (coin from very similar obv. die, w. **L** in the rev. field, found in a grave at Houdain, dép. Nord).

344 Obv. **NANASTA ISVSPPAVC** Rev. **VICTORI IAAVCCCA, CONOB**. 4.38g (SG 18.94: 98% Au) 180°. Cf. B 5035. Note graffito, a cross lightly incised on rev. above star.

345 Obv. **ƆNANASTA SIVSPFAVC** Rev. **VICTORI AAVCCCA, CONOB**. 4.04g (SG 18.39: 94% Au) 170°. B 5038 var.

346 Obv. **DNIIL[ ]TA SIVSIA[** Rev. **]TORI AA[ ]CC[** , ex. off-flan. 4.23g (SG 18.85: 97% Au) 170°. B –.

347 Obv. **DNASTA SICPPAVC**, w. star and **L** in field. Rev. **VIOTORI AAVCCCA, COAIB**, w. **A** and **I**(?) in field. 4.21g (SG 19.18: 99% Au) 180°. Reinhart 1940, pl. 7.3 = Robert 1882a, pl. 4.13 (this coin, Chinon hoard). Reinhart wrongly supposed his specimen to be from an imaginary *Cuenca* hoard (Grierson 1975). There is a curious knob on the coin below the **A** on l. of rev., the die surface having apparently been holed at this point.

348 Obv. **DNANASTA[ ]VCPPAVC** Rev. **VICTORI AAVCCCΘ, COIIOB**, w. reversed **E** and **N** (or **A**?) in field. 4.32g (SG 18.89: 97% Au) 170°. B –. Struck from worn dies.

343. PG: Goff 34.
344. PG: Christie 16.6.1959, lot 35.
345. PG: Spink 19.5.1965.
346. PG: Seaby 7.7.1972 (*SCMB* July 1972, no. 1206).
347. PG: Reinhart 30.9.1951; . . . ex Gariel 317; from Chinon hoard.
348. PG: DO 20.10.1958; ex Peirce 1948; acq. in Paris.

MEROVINGIANS (2): PSEUDO-IMPERIAL COINAGE, *c.* 500–*c.* 580

References as on Plate 17. The coins are all gold tremisses.

With the name of Anastasius I (491–518) (cont.)
Victory with palm and wreath type
This type was also issued by the Visigoths (**178–85**) and Burgundians (**337–8**). The division between the Merovingian and Visigothic issues is not always clear.

349 Obv. **ƆNANASTA SIVSPPAVC** Rev. **VICTORIA AVCVSTORVA, CONOB**. 1.47g (SG 16.94: 83% Au) 170°. Tomasini 57, group A2b (as Merovingian?).

350 Obv. **ƆИAИASII SIVSPPNC** Rev. **]TIPIAIAUCISTOR I**, ex. off-flan. 1.36g (SG 18.55: 95% Au) 180°. Reinhart –; Tomasini –. Apparently a crude (Merovingian?) derivative of the Burgundian coinage of Lyon (Tomasini group A5).

Facing Victory type (copied from Ostrogothic coins)

351 Obv. **ƆNANAƧTA + SIVSPAVC** Rev. **VICTORIA AVCVSTORVИ, COMOB**, w. 2 stars in field. 1.42g (SG 16.67: 81% Au) 180°. B –.

352 Obv. **ƆNANASTA SIVSPFAVC** Rev. **VICTORIA ACVSTORVM, COMOB**. 1.40g (SG 18.93: 93% Au) 160°. B 5083 var.

353 Obv. **NANASTOTVSPPANC** Rev. **VICTORIA AVCVSTORVN, OИCB** (inverted). 1.47g (SG 18.78: 96% Au) 170°. B –.

354 Obv. **DNANASTA SIVSPPAVC** Rev. **VICTORIA AVCVITOIIV, CONOB**. 1.44g (SG 18.22: 93% Au) 180°. B –.

With the name of Justin I (518–27)
Facing Victory type

355 Obv. **ƆNIVƧTIII IIVSPΓNC** Rev. **VITORIAAVCVƧ TORVNC, COИO**. 1.40g (SG 17.96: 91% Au) 170°. B –.

With the name of Justinian I (527–65)
Facing Victory type

356 Obv. **DNIVSTINI ANVSPFAVC** (tiny letters, w. cross strokes weakly formed) Rev. **VICTORIAAVCVS TORV, C·N·**. 1.32g chipped? (SG 17.29: 86% Au) 150°. B 5283 var. A close (Merovingian?) copy of an Ostrogothic tremissis of Athalaric (cf. **123–4**).

357 Obv. **DNIVSTIN IANVSPΓNC** Rev. **VICTORIA AVCVSTORVM, CONOD**. 1.27g (SG 17.71: 89% Au) 170°. B 5285 var.

358 Obv. **DNIV[ ]VC** Rev. **VICTVRIAAVCVƧ[** , ex. off-flan and position of star, wreath and cross interchanged from l. to r. 1.43g (SG 17.43: 87% Au) 180°. B –. Die flaw before face.

359 Obv. **DIIIVSTIIVIVIVIAIIVSPPAV** Rev. **VICTOATA ACIIVCIIOAI, CON**. 1.47g (SG 16.80: 82% Au) 180°. Cf. Wielandt 1967, no. 8 (grave-find from Klepsau, Krs Buchen).

With the name of Justin I (518–27), but not contemporary
Victory with palm and wreath type

360 Obv. **·IIIVIII NVSCO** Rev. **OVƆV AITV, ···** in ex. 1.31g (SG 14.71: 62% Au) 180°. Chijs 1866, pl. 22.3 (this coin). This and the next coin are partly derived from Burgundian coins of Gundomar II (**341**).

361 Obv. **·IIIV·II NVVC·**, w. **R** before face Rev. **VDV ƆVITV, ···** in ex. 1.41g (SG 14.97: 65% Au) 160°. B 3717 (as Rennes, probably this coin), 5872 (same dies); Werner 1935, M122 (same dies, found at Kümmern, Krs Saarburg).

With the name of Justin II? (565–78)
Facing Victory type

362 *North Burgundy* (mint or moneyer **ELA**?). Obv. **IVƧT IИVƧPƧ** Rev. **DNVICTO RIAELA, COИO**. 1.36g (SG 14.72: 62% Au) 180°. B 5864 (this coin, in Robert coll.). For the attribution, see note on coin. The bust on this and the following coins with a detached loop behind the diadem is known in French as 'à la boucle perdue'.

363 *As last.* Obv. **ELADVIAIVƆTIC** Rev. **VICTVRI AVCOƧTV, COИO**. 1.36g (SG 13.45: 47% Au) 180°. B –. See note on **362**.

364 Obv. **IVSTI NVVPPAVC** Rev. **TORVAVCVƆI TIOANHO, COM**. 1.40g (SG 15.10: 66% Au) 170°. Chijs 1866, pl. 23.2 var.

Cross-on-steps type

365 Obv. **HIVSTI NVꟼIAI** Rev. **IVHOV VOIΓST**(?) 1.43g (SG 14.14: 56% Au) 250°. B –. The cross-on-steps design was first used in the imperial coinage on solidi of Tiberius II (578–82) and not again until the reign of Heraclius (610–41). The design of this coin was inspired by the former.

349–50, 352, 356–7. PG: Dillen 12.7.1949.
351. PG: E. Hill 10.6.1957; acq. in Yugoslavia.
353. PG: Baldwin 22.5.1971; ex Grantley, uncertain lot.
354. PG: M. Ratto 21.9.1967.
355. PG: Seaby 20.3.1945.
358. PG: Baldwin 22.5.1971; ex Grantley 667.
359. PG: Spink 25.7.1946.
360. PG: J. Schulman sale 30.3.1949, lot 752 (Haex coll.); ex Wigersma 387; ex Chijs 1914; found in the Netherlands (see Chijs 1866, 360).
361. PG: Bourgey 14.9.1967 . . . probably ex Amécourt (uncertain lot no.).
362. PG: Bank Leu 2.6.1959.
363. PG: Baldwin 22.5.1971; ex Grantley 650; from Schulman.
364. PG: Bourgey 27.9.1946.
365. PG: Spink 7.5.1964; ex Grantley 669; from Schulman 1897.

[*continued overleaf*]

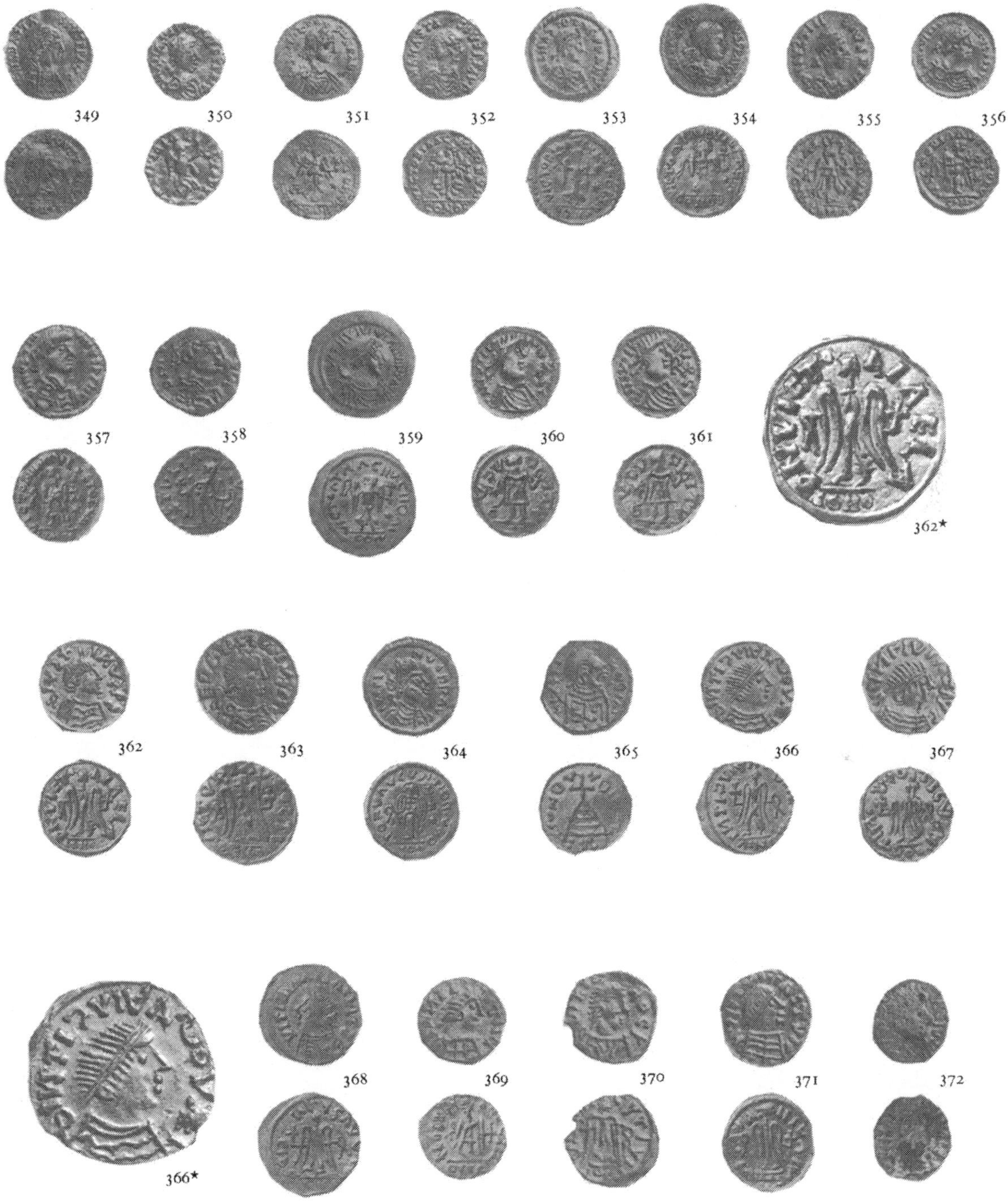

349 350 351 352 353 354 355 356

357 358 359 360 361 362★

362 363 364 365 366 367

366★ 368 369 370 371 372

PLATE 18 (*cont.*)

With blundered legends
Facing Victory type

366 *Lausanne.* Obv. **IVA~OVNEI IИTIↃV** (commencing above head) Rev. **IVA[ ]И ΓИTIↃV** (commencing above cross), w. **AIN** in ex. 1.39g (SG 15.85: 73% Au) 170°. Cf. B 2115 (as Lausanne), 5392 = P 16 (as Lausanne?). For the attribution, see note on coin.

367 *Burgundy region.* Obv. **IVVИΓIVIΛTIVT** Rev. **TIИ. VPOITICVИI, ↃOI.** 1.32g (SG 14.29: 58% Au) 160°. B 5873 var. Overstruck on coin of uncertain type. The style is typical of mint-signed coins of the Burgundy region.

368 *Lyon region.* Obv. **VITNIVVΛIIΛIIΛT** Rev. **VOIↃИI TSΛVVTV, O[** . 1.35g (SG 14.51: 60% Au) 190°. B –. The style suggests a mint in the Lyonnais.

369 Obv. **IIIИI[ ]TIIN** Rev. **IIOIIΛIIΛICIIII,•II•.** 1.37g (SG 15.40: 69% Au) 180°. B 5416 var.

370 Obv. **VIKVИ ROCY** Rev. **VI[ ]CYTIVI, IOH.** 1.25g chipped (SG 14.09: 55% Au) 180°. B –.

371 Obv. **NVIITVIIIΛITVIC** Rev. **VITIVΛ: IIIVΛIV, NO.** 1.14g (SG 12.12: 29% Au) 160°. B 5339 = Chijs 1866, 14, no. 18 and pl. 1.18 (this coin).

372 *Contemporary plated imitation.* Obv. **NVV[ ]IIINII** Rev. **IIIIIИIIIIIIVIIII, +.** Æ plated w. AV 0.51g 100°. B –. Copy of a coin from the Burgundy region. Grantley's ticket shows that he regarded it as a plated burial piece.

366, 368. PG: Ulrich-Bansa 18.11.1950.
367, 369–70. PG: Baldwin 22.5.1971; ex Grantley 666; from Trinks 1899.
371. PG: J. Schulman sale 30.3.1949, lot 753 (Haex coll.); ex Wigersma 386; ex Chijs 1910; fd in Utrecht or Gelderland (see Chijs 1866, 14).
372. PG: Baldwin 22.5.1971; ex Grantley 656; gift of L. A. Lawrence.

MEROVINGIANS (3): PSEUDO-IMPERIAL COINAGE, *c.* 500–*c.* 580

References as on Plate 17. The coins are gold tremisses, unless otherwise indicated.

With blundered legends (cont.)
Facing Victory type (cont.)

373 *Lower Rhineland.* Obv. **VTSRИT TRИRSTV** Rev. **TSV8HR C ƆИT 8VSVT, ∞Ɔ∝.** 1.29g (SG 14.78: 63% Au) 190°. B 5385–6, 5408, 5429 = Chijs 1866, pl. 1.4–7 (all found in Frisia); Werner 1935, M84 (grave-find from Erle, Krs Recklinghausen); Rigold 1975, no. 32 (this coin, as Burgundy region).

374 *As last.* Obv. **TIVR NT TR H[** Rev. **RΠRΠИO OΛHVR, ƆOR OC.** 1.28g (SG 13.35: 46% Au) 160°. Ref. as last.

375 *As last.* Obv. **]RHT[ ]V∽R[** Rev. **]ΛVRT∽Ꞁ,]RΛ.** 1.16g (SG 13.13: 43% Au, but very pale appearance) 210°. Ref. as last.

376 *Germanic.* Obv. **DNAOVDC ᗡI٩ИZV٩Ꞁ** Rev. **VITOIIIUV–VCTOCVN, ONO.** 1.37g (SG 16.07: 75% Au) 170°. B –. A specimen from the same dies, but gold plated on copper and weighing only 0.66g, was found in a grave at Cobern, Krs Koblenz (Werner 1935, M85).

377 *Alamannic?* Obv. **ꞀHVIƆSIIIƆΘIISΘꞀ٩II** Rev. **NTOIVИPIVΛCVSTOISVN, CCNOI.** 1.49g (SG 17.85: 90% Au) 180°. B –; cf. Reinhart 1939a, fig. 7.6 (as Germanic).

378 *As last.* Obv. **-OCCTΛCTCIOCTCHⵔO** Rev. **IƆTOTIIƆƆIIƆTƆHOTVI, III.** 1.41g (SG 17.45: 87% Au) 180°. B –; Reinhart 1939a, fig. 7.10 (as Germanic); Werner 1935, M44, cf. M45–6, M200–2 (all w. German or presumed German find-spots); Vanhoudt 1982, no. 36.

379 *As last.* Obv. **ΘƆᗡIIIIΘT ИVIIII** Rev. **ΘIIIV CIIIIIV, ΘIIΘ.** 1.32g (SG 12.07: 28% Au) 180°. Ref. as last.

380 *As last.* Obv. **WO ∽O** Rev. **O OUVUΛ LH, IΛ.** 1.36g (SG 15.83: 73% Au) 180°. Wielandt 1967, nos. 4–5 (grave finds from Klepsau, Krs Buchen, as East Frisian); cf. Reinhart 1939a, fig. 7.7–9 (as Germanic).

381 Obv. degenerate head l., w. ribbed hair and cross? Rev. degenerate Victory. 1.26g (SG 17.45: 87% Au) 110°. B –.

382 Obv. **+NU O**, degenerate bust r. Rev. degenerate Victory(?), w. cross in field r. 1.33g (SG 16.32: 78% Au) 10°. B –.

Victory with palm and wreath type

383 Obv. **]ΛIV I– –·ΛT**, crude bust r. Rev. **VITOR IΛIV,]ONO[.** 1.49g (SG 18.08: 92% Au) 160°. B –.

Two soldiers and standard type

384 *Alamannic?* Obv. **ƆDIPƧIL·ΠΓSΛƧIIO** Rev. **]NCTOIOV XV·IOTƆNƆIVI, ΛONOΛ.** 1.29g (SG 13.63: 50% Au) 180°. B 5442 var. (found at Domburg); *SCBI* Merseyside 7 (from St Martin's, Canterbury); Werner 1935, M57 var. (grave-find from Soest). The prototype is a Constantinian bronze coin of the 4th century. Sir Arthur Evans (1942, 38–40) considered these coins English, but the find distribution of these and other coins w. comparable helmeted busts suggests that they come from east of the Rhine, possibly Swabia (Grierson 1952c, 43–4).

Cross-potent type

385 *Germanic.* **-ΛΓ·Γ VIIIVII** Rev. **VIT·ꜰΛΛVIVTOVVO, CICIΛ.** 1.28g (SG 17.04: 84% Au) 340°. Cf. B 5363 ('Heraclius'). The cross potent was first used on the imperial coinage by Tiberius II (578–82), but the style and fabric of this coin place it in the 7th century.

386 Obv. **OΛOTΛIΛ⁻ΛIOIΛΛO**, fantastic head w. cross potent beneath Rev. **VOTΛOCOVTΛHVO.** 1.19g (SG 17.26: 86% Au) 150°. B –; cf. Cahn sale 79, 14.12.1932, lot 949 (Fürstenberg coll.).

Cross-on-globule type

387 *Middle Rhineland?* Obv. **– –ΛIΓ-**, uncertain design, head l. or possibly 2 confronting busts? Rev. **III[ ]IIIIII, IIHI.** 0.83g (SG 18.46: 94% Au) 0°. B –; cf. Böhner 1958, M40 (Rheinisches Landesmuseum, Trier, without provenance). The prototype is probably a late 6th-century coin of Provence.

373. FM: Young 1936; ex Carlyon-Britton I 134; found at Canterbury.
374. PG: Prince de Ligne I 163 (not listed in Serrure 1880, which is very selective).
375. PG: Spink 19.3.1945; ex Grantley 667; acq. in Vienna.
376. PG: Spink 7.5.1946; ex Grantley 669; acq. in Vienna 1899.
377. PG: DO 20.10.1958; ex Peirce 1948.
378. PG: Baldwin 15.10.1946; ex Grantley 4219; from Trinks 1899.
379. PG: Baldwin 22.5.1971; ex Grantley 667.
380. PG: Spink 7.5.1946; ex Grantley 675; ex Carbery Evans.
381. PG: L. S. Forrer 20.4.1949.
382. PG: Baldwin 22.5.1971; ex Grantley 658; from Trinks.
383. PG: Baldwin 22.5.1971; ex Grantley 669; from Roux 1903.
384. PG: Baldwin 22.5.1971; ex Grantley, uncertain lot.
385. PG: Baldwin 22.5.1971; ex Grantley 673; from Trinks 1899.
386. PG: Baldwin 22.5.1971; ex Grantley 662; from Rollin 1899.
387. PG: Baldwin 22.5.1971; Grantley (662?); from Rollin 1899.

[*continued overleaf*]

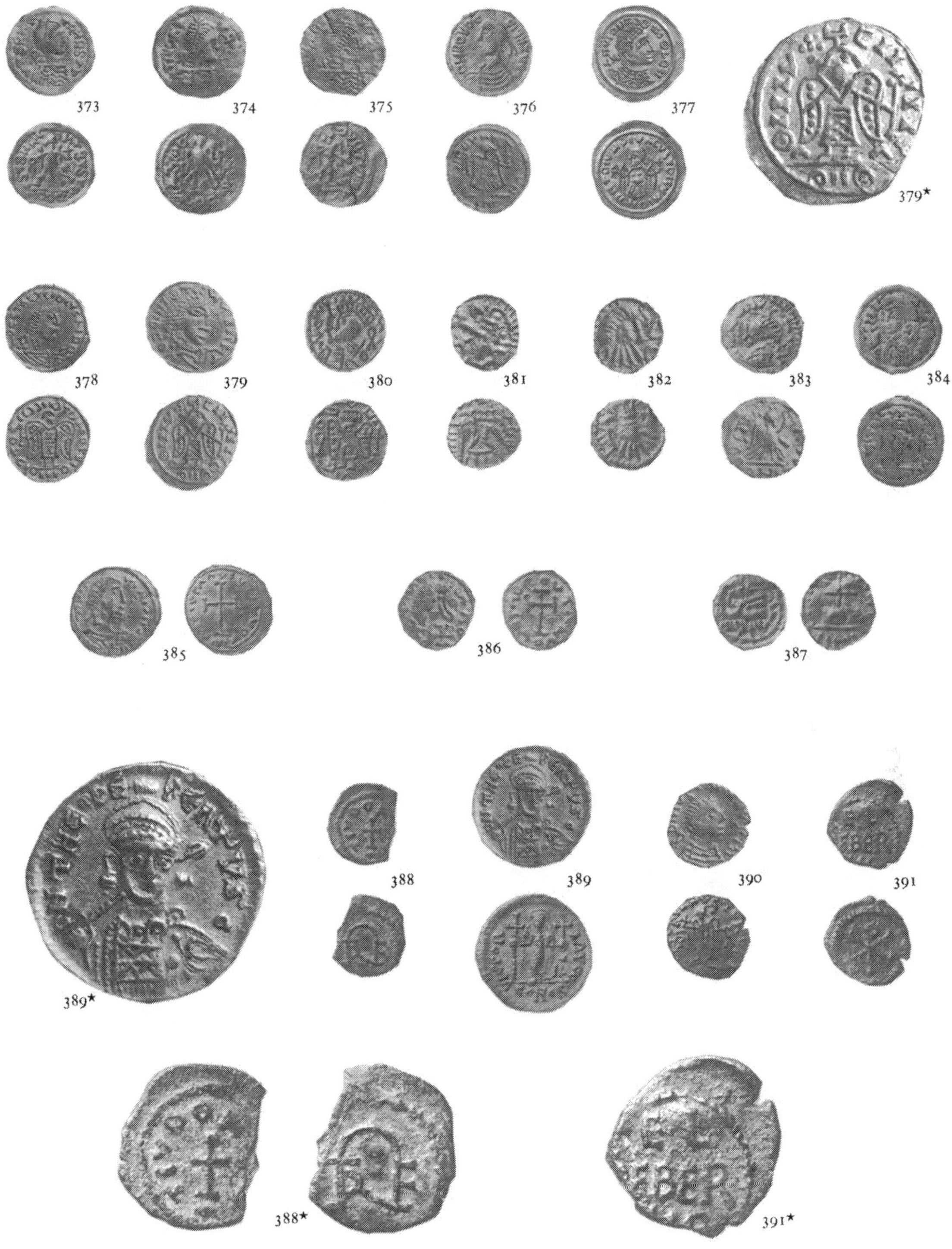

373 374 375 376 377 379*

378 379 380 381 382 383 384

385 386 387

389* 388 389 390 391

388* 391*

REGAL COINS WITHOUT MINT NAMES

THIERRY I

'King of Metz', 511–34

Tremissis. For a coin, possibly of Thierry I, see **187**.

388 *Nummus.* Obv. **TEVDOR[ICI]**, cross on base above step Rev. monogram of **TEVDRE** (for *TEVDERicus REx*) in wreath. Æ 0.41 fragment 340°. B 5452 (this coin); P 32 var.; Lafaurie 1968a, 37, no. 10 (this coin). Probably minted in Provence.

THEODEBERT I

'King of Metz', 534–48

389 *Solidus.* Obv. **DNTHEOD BERTVS.** Rev. **VICTOR ΛΛVCCC, CONOB**, w. **M** in field. *AV* 4.40g 180°. B 2896 (this coin, as Metz); P 44. For the significance of the letter in rev. field, see p. 117 above.

CHILDEBERT I

'King of Paris', 511–58

390 *Tremissis. Lyon.* Obv. **DNIVSTINIΛNVSIPΛ** Rev. **]TVRIΛΛVSTOROFI**, ex. illegible, monogram in field l. 1.39g (SG 16.47: 79% Au) 200°. B 2286 var.; P –. Probably posthumous; see Lafaurie 1972b, 203–4, who also queries the traditional attribution of the monogram to Childebert, and would make it rather one of **LVGDVNI**.

391 *Nummus. Marseille.* Obv. **EL / DEBER / TIR** in wreath Rev. Christogram. Æ 1.11g fragment 190°. B 5455 (this coin); P 36; Brenot 1980, 188, no. III.4 (this coin). For attribution and dating, see Brenot 1976 and 1980. Two of the five recorded specimens were found in excavations in the region of the Bourse at Marseille.

388. PG: Lockett III 307; ex Grantley; from Rollin.

389. CCC (*Catalogue* no. 58): Lewis 1891; ex Gariel 339. Prou inferred that the BN specimen (P 44), bought from Feuardent in 1889, was that in the Gariel sale, but wrongly, as Lewis' ticket and his marked copy of the sale catalogue show.

390. PG: MMAG Basel sale 29 (27.11.1964), lot 2 (Dolivo coll.); ex Fürstenberg (Cahn sale 79 (14.12.1932), lot 1050).

391. PG: Lockett III 307; ex Grantley; from Rollin.

MEROVINGIANS (4): GOLD COINAGE, NATIONAL SERIES

Principal references are: B = Belfort 1892–5 and P = Prou 1892a. Coins are gold tremisses unless otherwise indicated.

BURGUNDY AND PROVENCE

392 *Albens* (*Savoie*), moneyer *Maximus*. Obv. **ALBINNO FI[T]** (outwardly) Rev. +**MAXVM[VS MONE]TA** (outwardly). 1.20g (SG 17.07: 84% Au) 330°. B 74 (this coin); P 1336.

393 *Autun*, moneyer *Teudulfus*. Obv. **AVGVV∾TEDVИO FI** Rev. +**TEVDVLFO M** (**L** and **F** inverted), w. **AC** (for *Augustodunum*, Autun) in field. 1.23g (SG 15.69: 72% Au) 190°. B 460 var.; P 139 var. Struck from rusty dies.

394 *As last*. Obv. corroded (by heat?) Rev. **TEVDVLFO MONET[A]**, w. **AC** in field. 1.26g (SG 16.49: 79% Au). B 456; P 137.

395 *Besançon*, moneyer *Gennardus*. Obv. **GE|NNARΔVS +ERO** Rev. +**VESVNCIONE DE SELEQVS**, w. **VII** in field. 1.18g (SG 17.32: 86% Au) 150°. B 4791 (this coin, wrongly equated w. P 1248); P 1248 var. Illus. Amécourt 1866a, pl. 8.61. The +**ERO** in the obv. inscription is probably a blundering of *monetario* derived from coins w. **MN** in the field and an inscription ending +*aerio*; cf. B 4784–8, P 1248, 1251–3. The **DE SELEQVS** and **VII** refers to the reduced weight (see p. 107 above).

396 *Chalon-sur-Saône*, moneyers *Baudomeris* and *Rignoaldus*. Obv. **CAVILO|NO FIT** Rev. +**BA[VDOMERE ET] RIGNOALDO M**, w. **CA** (for mint name *Cabilonnum*) in field. 1.28g (SG 17.45: 87% Au) 180°. B 1135 = P 173 (same dies).

397 *As last*. Obv. **CAVILON|NO FIT**, bust r. w. branch before face Rev. +**BAVDOM[ERE E]T R[IGNO]ALDO M**, w. **CA** in field. 1.24g (SG 16.81: 82% Au) 170°. B 1136 (this coin); P –. Illus. Amécourt 1873, pl. 1.27.

398 *Chalon-sur-Saône?*, uncertain moneyer. Obv. inscription off flan Rev.]**VER**[, w. **CA** in field. 1.24g (SG 15.42: 69% Au) 0°. Cf. B 1125–51; P 172–5, etc. This may be from a mint other than Chalon, since this type w. **CA** in the field was widely copied elsewhere. The letters visible on the rev. do not correspond w. those on any known coins of Chalon and the form of the wreath (a zig-zag w. pellets) is unusual.

399 *Chalon-sur-Saône*, moneyers *Wintrio* and *Duccio*. Obv. **CABILO[ ]O FIT** Rev.]**RIO ET DVCC**[, w. **CA** in field. 1.17g (SG 13.93: 53% Au) 190°. B –; P –.

400 *Chalon-sur-Saône*, moneyer *Bonefacius*. Obv. **CABIL ONNO FIT** Rev.]**FACIO M˜O**, w. **CA** in field. 1.22g (SG 13.63: 49% Au) 170°. B 1197 var.; P –.

401 *Chalon-sur-Saône*, moneyer *Mummolus*. Obv. **CABL ONNO** Rev. **MVMMOVS** (**MV** ligatured), w. **CA** in field. 1.30g (SG 12.93: 40% Au) 160°. B 1210–13; P 195.

402 *Mâcon*, moneyer *Joseph*. Obv. **MATASCONE FIIT** Rev. +**IVSEF MONCTARIVS FICT**, w. **VII** in field. 1.25g (SG 17.68: 89% Au) 170°. B 2776 (same dies?); P 239 var.

403 *Marseille*, solidus, with the name of Maurice (582–602). Obv. **DNMAV· ·CRPPAVC** Rev. **VICTORI· ·AAVCCV, CONOB**, w. **M** (for *Massilia*) and **XXI** (i.e. 21 siliquae) in field. 3.61g 170°. B 2454 = P 1378; Rigold 1954, no. 58.

404 *Marseille*, with the name of Maurice (582–602). Obv. **ƆNMAVRC|IIVƧ PPU** Rev. **VICVORI AVTOVA, CONOB**, w. **MA** and **VII** (i.e. 7 siliquae) in field. 1.08g (SG 17.65: 89% Au) 340°. B 2439 var.; P 1373 var.; Rigold 1954, no. 36b (this coin).

405 *Marseille*, contemporary plated forgery of solidus of Dagobert I (629–39). Obv. **ACIИV∽ƆƎ+** Rev. +**AAƆLIƎSAITOI'VVƆИ**, w. **MA** and + + (for **XX**, i.e. 20 siliquae) in field. Æ gilt 1.98g 60°. Cf. B 2497; P 1393.

406 *Marseille*, solidus of Sigebert III (639–56). Obv. **ƧIII|RTVS R**(?), w. **C** before face Rev. **V[ ]RIA**, w. **MA** and **XXI** in field. 3.67g pierced (SG 12.40: 33% Au) 180°. B 2522 = P 1403.

407 *Marseille*, Sigebert III. Obv. **M[ ]IΓIA** (for *Massilia*), bust w. diadem terminating in 3 pellets Rev. **∽LΩIBER[ ]IX**, w. **MA** in field. 0.78g fragment (SG 13.19: 44% Au) 130°. B 2540 (this coin); P 1411 var.

Marseille, Sigebert III. For a forgery, see **1473**.

408 *Marseille*, solidus of Childeric II (662–75). Obv. **CHID-LRI|ICVS R**[, w. pellet in field Rev. **MASILI C[ ]ITATI**, w. 3 pellets to l. and 2 pellets to r. of base, and **MA** in field. 3.80g (SG 12.21: 30% Au) 180°. B 2546; P 1414 var.

392. PG: MMAG Basel 1.4.1952 (= sale 8 (8.12.1949), lot 336—'Collection mérovingienne'); ex Rothschild; ex Amécourt (not in sale); ex Robert.

393. PG: Spink 26.11.1946; ex Récamier (not in sale catalogue).

394, 396, 398. PG: MMAG Basel 1.4.1952 ('Collection mérovingienne').

395. PG: Peus sale 105 (18.9.1961), lot 1; ex Amécourt 299.

397. PG: Forrer 12.11.1946 . . . ex Amécourt 51.

399. PG: Baldwin 9.2.1952.

400. PG: Seaby 10.11.1950.

401. PG: Florange 17.4.1959.

402. PG: Glendining 30.5.1961, lot 258.

403. CCC (*Catalogue* no. 57): Lewis 1891; ex Charvet 240.

404. PG: Vinchon 7.9.1950.

405. PG: Baldwin 15.9.1946.

406. FM: provenance unrecorded.

407. PG: Baldwin 9.2.1952; ex Grantley 187; from Rollin.

408. PG: Vinchon sale 28.2.1972, lot 230.

[*continued overleaf*]

392 393 394 395 396 397 398 399 400

401 402 403

408*

404 405 406 407 408 409 410

411 412 413

409*

409 *As last.* Obv. **MA22|ILIA**, bust r. in arcade Rev. +**HILΔERICA~ REX**, w. **MA** in field. 3.73g (SG 11.72: 23% Au) 350°. B 2561; P 1417.

410 *Meuvy* (*Haute-Marne*), moneyer *Marculfus*. Obv. +**MOωA VICO** Rev. +**MARCVLFO MOИ**. 1.20g (SG 16.44: 79% Au) 180°. B 3067 (this coin), 3066 = P 161 (same dies). The coin slipped in the die, doubling the second letter in the obv. legend.

411 *Moutiers-en-Tarentaise* (*Savoie*), moneyer *Optatus*. Obv. **DA RANTA2** (**NT** ligatured) Rev. **O+TATVω MOИITARIV[** . 1.20g (SG 17.01: 84% Au) 80°. B 1697 var.; P –.

412 *Moutiers-en-Tarentaise*, moneyer *Rinchinus*? Obv. **DARA TAωIA F** Rev. **]NA~ MVNI[** . 1.25g (SG 13.32: 45% Au) 340°. B 1714 (this coin); P 1281 var.

413 *Moutiers-en-Tarentaise*, uncertain moneyer. Obv. **DARAИT|ASIA F** Rev. +[**]ONITARIVωI**. 1.29g (SG 13.61: 49% Au) 120°. B 1701 = 1715 (this coin); P 1280 var.

409. PG: purchased 1970s . . . Théry (Vinchon, 22.10.1963), lot 343.

410. PG: MMAG Basel 1.4.1954 (= sale 8 (8.12.1949), lot 415—'Collection mérovingienne'); ex Hauët 234; ex Monnier 31.

411. PG: Seaby 7.6.1966 (*SCMB* May 1966, no. G1046); found near Diss, Norfolk.

412. PG: MMAG Basel 1.4.1952 (= sale 8 (8.12.1949), lot 311—'Collection mérovingienne'); ex Amécourt 311.

413. PG: MMAG Basel 1.4.1952 (= sale 8 (8.12.1949), lot 399—'Collection mérovingienne'); ex Amécourt 309; ex Charvet (not in sale).

MEROVINGIANS (5): GOLD COINAGE, NATIONAL SERIES

References as on Plate 20. The coins are gold tremisses.

BURGUNDY AND PROVENCE (cont.)

414 *Saint-Maurice d'Agaune*, Dagobert I (629–39), moneyer *Romanus*. Obv. **DA[GO]BERTOS R** Rev. **ROMANOS MV·ACAVNI[NSIS]** (mint name *Acavno*), w. **VII** in field. 1.22g 0°. B 19; P 1296 (same dies). The mint is discussed in Geiger 1979a, 135ff.

415 *Sisteron* (Alpes-de-Haute-Provence). Pseudo-imperial type w. blundered legends. Obv. **VAVIA VVSIAV·** Rev. **VICTORI AVCVSTOA, CONOB**, w. **SE** in field. 1.35g (SG 18.75: 96% Au) 180°. Unpublished type. **SE** could stand for *Sedelocum*, i.e. Saulieu in the Côte-d'Or (B 4048 = P 149), but the type is Provençal, and Sisteron (*civitas Segusteriorum*) is in this case preferable. Cf. Lafaurie 1960a, 199–200.

416 *Troyes*, moneyer *Audolenus*. Obv. **+TREC|AS ΓIT** (outwardly) Rev. **+AVDOL[ ]S MΩ** (outwardly), w. **AƆ** in field (in imitation of Chalon coins). 1.26g (SG 16.64: 81% Au) 10°. B 4380–3; P 598.

417 *Troyes*, moneyer *Mummolenus*. Obv. **TRE|CAS+** Rev. **]MOLIMИA∾ ƎIƆI** (outwardly, for *Mummolenus fici*). 1.27g (SG 16.67: 81% Au) 190°. B 4385 = P 604 (same dies?).

418 *Viviers* (Ardèche). With the blundered name of Maurice (582–602). Obv. **ƆN[ ]AVI IAd PAV** Rev. **VICAORI AV[ ], ICNB, VIVA** (for *Vivarios*) and **VII** in field. 1.17g (SG 16.98: 83% Au) 160°. Cf. B 4919, 6499–500; P 1345–6; cf. Rigold 1954, nos. 78 and 83 (which he dates *c.* 612 and *c.* 615).

419 *Uncertain mint* (**CORNA**?), moneyer *Launomundus?* Obv. **OO[ ]LIAOI**(?) Rev. **+LAVN[ ]V∽ ΕI⅃** (**AV** ligatured), w. **A** in field l. 1.19g (SG 15.02: 65% Au) 160°. B 3298; cf. B 1646–7, 3214, 5529, 5904; P 2599. The obv. legend is doubtful; related coins of Launomund read **COANA VI** or **CORNV CASTRO**, an unidentified mint in the Burgundy region.

420 *Uncertain mint* (Autun region), moneyer *Imaurino*. Obv. **]ANVVI** Rev. **+IMAVRINO**. 1.14g chipped (SG 13.61: 50% Au) 350°. B –; P –.

AQUITAINE

421 *Banassac* (Lozère). Obv. **GAVALORVM**, bust r. Rev. monogram of **BANA** in wreath. 1.24g (SG 16.29: 77% Au) 180°. B 628; P 2067. Banassac is in the region of Javols (*Gavalorum*). On the mint and type, see p. 133 above.

422 *Banassac*, moneyer *Elafius*. Obv. without inscription, head r. in wreath, 3 pellets before face Rev. **ELAFIU∽ MONET**, chalice. 1.29g (SG 16.35: 78% Au) 180°. B 650; P 2075.

423 *As last*. Obv. as last but branch before face Rev. **TELAFIV∾ MONETA**. 1.26g (SG 15.72: 72% Au) 180°. B 653; P 2073–4. The (olive) branch, a symbol of peace, replaces the word **PAX** found on other coins of Elafius (B 654–6). The first **T** in the rev. inscription is the remains of an initial cross.

424 *Banassac*, Charibert II (629–32). Obv. **NTARIBERTVS RΣX** Rev. **BANNIAΣIACO FIIT**. 1.28g (SG 15.03: 65% Au) 180°. B 6014 (this coin), 685 = P 2057.

425 *Banassac*, moneyer *Maximinus*. Obv. **MAXIMIN|VS MO** Rev. **+BANNAACIACO FII**. 1.24g (SG 14.09: 55% Au) 170°. B 689–92; P 2070.

426 *Banassac*. Obv. without inscription, bust r. between 2 palms surmounted by crosses Rev. **GAVALETANO F** (**VA** ligatured), **BAH** in ex. 1.28g (SG 14.29: 57% Au) 20°. B 710; P 2080.

427 *As last*. Type and inscription as last. 1.27g (SG 14.06: 55% Au) 180°. Ref. as last.

428 *As last*. Obv. as last Rev. **G[ ]ETANO, [B]AH** in ex. 1.26g (SG 13.64: 50% Au) 180°. B 754 (this coin); P 2080 var.

429 *As last*. Obv. **+BAH** Rev. **GAVALЄTANO F** (**VA** ligatured), branch above chalice. 1.22g 180°. B 724 var.; P 2084 var.

430 *Banassac*, contemporary Æ forgery. Obv. **+BH** Rev. **GAVALETAIO, IIΓ** in ex. Æ 0.70g corroded 340°. Cf. B 714, 6023 = P 2088.

430A *Banassac*, contemporary forgery. Obv. **++** Rev. **GAV[ ]ETANO, BAN** in ex. Æ gilt 0.99g 90°. B 765; P 2104.

431 *Bordeaux*, moneyer *Teodericus* (or *Leopetricus*?). Obv. **+BVRDEƆALA F** Rev. **]EOPERICVS**. 1.21g (SG 16.35: 78% Au) 60°. B 1067 = P 2123. For the moneyer's name, see note on coin.

Bourges. For a forgery, see **1472**.

432 *Brive-la-Gaillarde* (Corrèze?), moneyer *Saricus*, contemporary plated forgery. Obv. **+[BRI?]VA FITO**

414. CCC (*Catalogue* no. 59): Lewis 1891; ex Gariel 343.

415. PG: Seaby 10.11.1950.

416–17. PG: Spink 19.5.1970.

418. FM: provenance unrecorded.

419. PG: Baldwin 22.5.1971; ex Grantley 608; from Roux 1903. From Buis (Chissey-en-Morvan) hoard, noted in the Barthélémy MS albums (no. 3473) in the BN (Lafaurie 1977b, 212 and fig.).

420. PG: Baldwin 22.5.1971; ex Grantley (uncertain lot).

421. PG: MMAG Basel 10.12.1968 (list 295, no. 33).

422. PG: MMAG Basel 1.4.1952 ('Collection mérovingienne').

423. PG: Lockett III 64; ex Glendining 27.7.1942, lot 16.

424. PG: Spink 25.7.1946 . . . ex Roucy.

425. PG: DO 20.10.1958.

426. PG: Forrer 23.4.1952.

427, 430A. PG: MMAG Basel 1.4.1952 ('Collection mérovingienne').

428. PG: MMAG Basel 1.4.1952 ('Collection mérovingienne') . . . ex de Moré.

429. CCC (*Catalogue* no. 61): Lewis 1891: ex Hoffmann 3.5.1890; found at Banassac.

430. PG: MMAG Basel 27.9.1948 ('Collection mérovingienne').

431. PG: Seaby 10.11.1950.

432. PG: MMAG Basel 1.4.1952 ('Collection mérovingienne'); ex Amécourt (not in sale).

[*continued overleaf*]

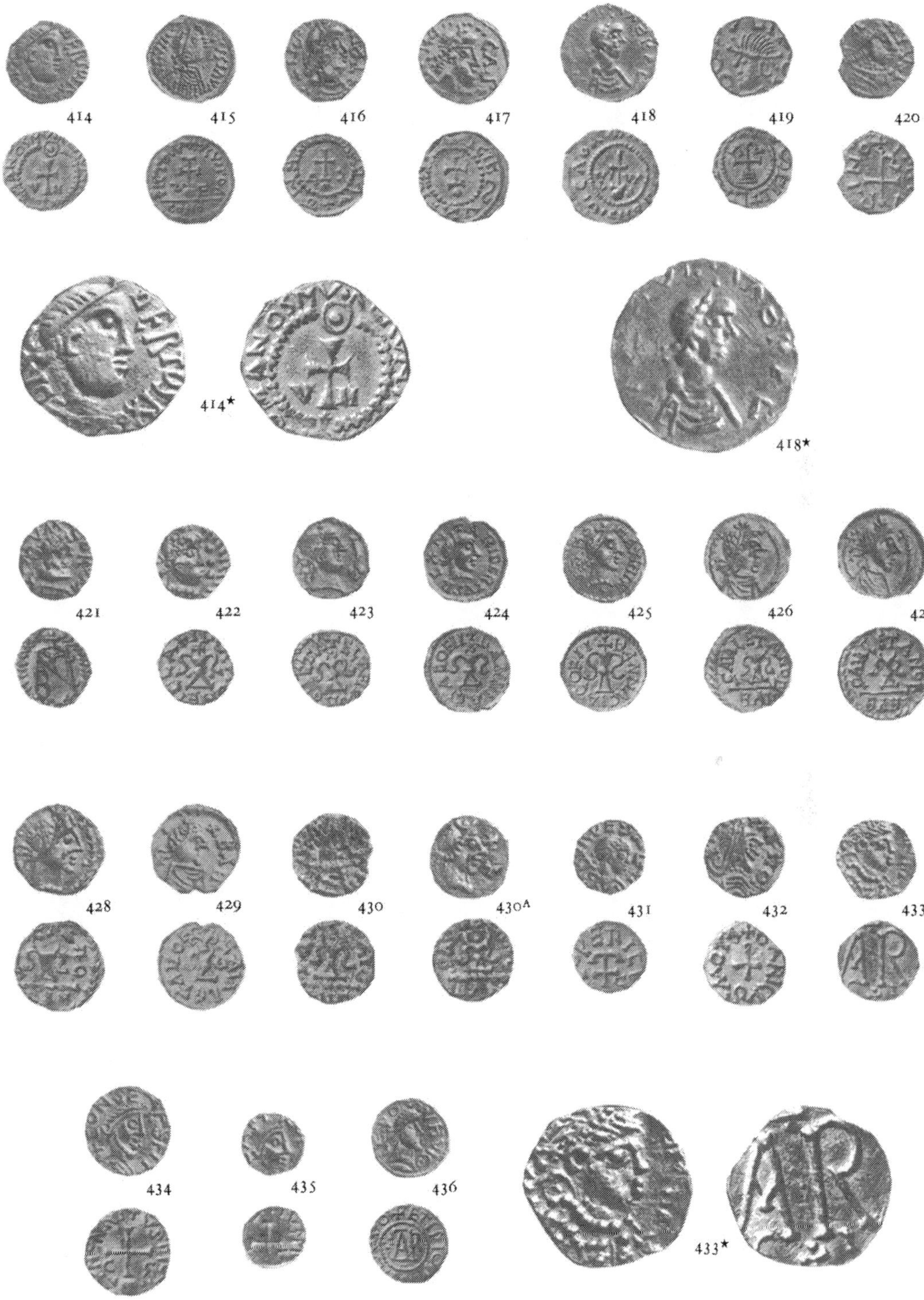

414 415 416 417 418 419 420

414* 418*

421 422 423 424 425 426 427

428 429 430 430A 431 432 433

434 435 436 433*

Rev. **SARICVS MOTA**. Æ gilt 0.89g 160°. B 995 (this coin); P –.

433 *Clermont-Ferrand*, Childebert II (575–95). Obv. **]BORE** Rev. **AR**, w. cross above and below and **CI** in field for AR*verno* CI*vitas*. 1.22g SG 18.21: 93% Au) 170°. Cf. B 335–8; P 1714 (as Childebert, son of Grimoald, 656–73; but the good quality of the gold precludes this).

434 *Comminges, Saint-Bertrand-de* (Haute-Garonne), moneyer *Nonnitus*. Obv. **+CONBENAS FIT** Rev. **+NONNITVS MO¯**, **CG** and **VII** in field. 1.44g (SG 19.00: 98% Au) 160°. B 1617 (this coin); P 2428. Illus. Amécourt 1881–3 (vol. 12) 243. **CG** probably stands for *celegae*, i.e. *siliquae*, to be read in conjunction with the **VII**, despite the high weight of this coin (cf. Deloche 1890, 4–7). It also occurs on coins of nearby Foix (**435**) and Cieutat (Hautes-Pyrénées) (B 811) of similar style, evidently the work of the same die-cutter.

435 *Foix*, moneyer *Redemptus*. Obv. [+]**CASTRO F[VC¯]** Rev. [+**RED]EMTVS MO**, cross-on-globule, w. **CG** and **VII** (off-flan) in field. 1.40g (SG 18.21: 93% Au) 0°. B 1449 (this coin, but illustration belongs to 1448), 1448 = P 2456 (same dies).

436 *Lezoux* (Puy-de-Dôme), moneyer *Elidius*. Obv. **LEDO ∽VM VICO** Rev. **+ETIDIO MOIIEARIO**, w. **AR** in field. 1.16g (SG 13.68: 50% Au) 330°. B 6219; P 1836 var. Lezoux is situated near Clermont-Ferrand from which the letters **AR** derive.

433. PG: MMAG Basel 10.12.1968 (list 295, no. 32).

434. PG: MMAG Basel 1.4.1952 (= sale 8 (8.12.1949), lot 323—'Collection mérovingienne'); ex Amécourt 475.

435. PG: MMAG Basel 1.4.1952 (= sale 8 (8.12.1949), lot 319—'Collection mérovingienne'); ex Amécourt 477.

436. PG: Vinchon 27.9.1970.

MEROVINGIANS (6): GOLD COINAGE, NATIONAL SERIES

References as on Plate 20. The coins are gold tremisses.

AQUITAINE (cont.)

437 *Marcilly-en-Gault* (Loir-et-Cher), Clovis II (639–57), moneyer *Dendus*. Obv. **+HLODOVIVƧ Я** Rev. **DƎHDV∾ M+ITA**. 1.26g (SG 12.11: 29% Au) 70°. B –; P –; Lafaurie 1971e, 210, no. 2 (this coin); Rigold 1975, no. 83 (this coin); cf. B 2394; P 651. Unique. For the mint attribution, see note on coin.

438 *Neuvic-d'Ussel* (Corrèze), moneyer *Betto*. Obv. **+NOVO VICO** Rev. **+BETTO MON**. 1.33g (SG 13.04: 42% Au) 70°. B –; P –. For the mint attribution, see note on coin.

Poitiers, moneyer *Fridircus*. For a cast in silver, see **1475**.

439 *Rodez*, moneyer *Tuo*...? Obv. without inscription, bust in wreath. Rev. **TV◆[ ]M◆** or **MVTV◆[** ? around monogram of **RVTENISX**. 1.26g (SG 17.07: 84% Au) 0°. B 3878 (this coin); P –. The significance of the **X** in this and some of the following monograms is unclear.

440 *Rodez*, moneyer *Vendemius*. Obv. as last, but extra pellet before forehead Rev. **+VENDIMIV∽** (retrograde). 1.28g (SG 16.28: 77% Au) 280°. B 3882 (this coin); P –. Illus. Robert 1851a, pl. 1.1.

441 *Rodez*, uncertain moneyer. Obv. **=VUIVΓΛ**(?), rude bust r. Rev. without inscription, monogram. 1.19g (SG 15.13: 67% Au) 270°. B 3874 (this coin); cf. P 1871.

442 *Rodez*, moneyer *Vendemius*. Obv. without inscription, bust in hatched border Rev. **+VENEMIV∾· MNE** (**NE** ligatured). 1.26g (SG 15.28: 68% Au) 350°. B 3885 (this coin); P –.

442A *As last*. Design as last but **+VENE[ ]MNE** (**NE** ligatured). 0.86g (SG 14.16: 56% Au) 240°. B 3886 (this coin); P –.

443 *As last*. Obv. bust w. ◆ before face Rev. **+VEИŒMIVS ‾MИET** (**Œ** and **ИE** ligatured). 1.24g (SG 14.64: 61% Au) 260°. B 3896–7 var.; P 1879–80 var.

444 *As last*. Obv. **NETIΛ** (**NET** ligatured) continuation of rev. legend Rev. **+ENŒMIV∽ M‾** (**Œ** ligatured). 1.15g (SG 14.54: 60% Au) 180°. B 3906 (this coin); P 1883 var.

445 *Rodez*, moneyer *Rosolus*. Obv. **NETTIΛ** (**NET** ligatured) continuation of rev. legend Rev. **+RO∽OΓV∽ MN**. 1.22g (SG 12.26: 31% Au) 300°. B 3916 (this coin); P –.

446 *As last*. Obv. bust w. branch before face (degeneration of the **NET** ligature of the previous coin?) Rev. **+RO∽OIV∽ M‾N**. 1.20g (SG 12.31: 32% Au) 120°. B 3921 = P 1888.

447 *As last*. Obv. bust w. palm surmounted by cross before face Rev. **+RO∽OXVS M‾**. 1.22g chipped (SG 13.12: 43% Au) 10°. B 3924-7 var.; P 1890 var.

Saint-Bertrand-de-Comminges (Haute-Garonne), see *Comminges*.

448 *Toulouse*, moneyer *Loppus*. Obv. **ꞆOLOSΛ FIIꞆ**, head r. Rev. **LOPPVS MO**. 0.94g (SG 13.14: 43% Au) 0°. B 1608 (this coin; as 'Colosa'); P –. The attribution to Toulouse was suggested by H. A. Cahn in the catalogue entry for the piece in MMAG Basel sale 8.12.1949.

449 *Trizay-sur-le-Lay* (Vendée), moneyer *Ginsulfus*. Obv. **+TIDIRICIA‾** Rev. **+CIИ∾VLFVƧ‾**. 0.99g (SG 15.62: 71% Au) 200°. B 4289 var.; P 2359 var. For a forgery of this mint, see **1476**.

450 *Uncertain mint* ('*Ianate*'), moneyer *Fedomeris*. Obv. **+IANATE**, degenerate bust w. drapery typical of coins of Poitiers region Rev. **+FEDOMERIƧ**, cross pattée on globule? 1.33g (SG 16.33: 78% Au) 30°. B 1931 (this coin); P –.

NEUSTRIA

451 *Angers*, moneyer *Aunardus*. Obv. **+ANDEꞆΛVIS** Rev. **+VVNXARDV∾**, Victory l. 1.40g (SG 17.74: 89% Au) 180°. B 159 var., 5905 var.; P 508–9 var.

452 *Beaufay* (Sarthe), moneyer *Fredomundus*. Obv. **+BELLO FAETOI** Rev. **+FREDOMVND**. 1.03g (SG 14.55: 60% Au) 270°. B 834 = 836 (this coin); P 437 var.

453 *Blois*, moneyer *Dommio*. Obv. **BΓEXO[** Rev. **DOM-[M]IONE**. 1.01g (SG 14.22: 57% Au) 0°. B 876 = P 575.

454 *Corbon* (Orne), moneyer *Godobodes*. Obv. **CVRBNΛ CVNΛO** Rev. **+GODOBODE MONE**, cross w. **CE** in field. 1.18g (SG 14.19: 56% Au) 90°. B 1672 (this coin); P –. Illus. Lecointre-Dupont 1840c, 317; Cartier 1846, pl. 7.11; Amécourt 1881–3 (vol. 12), 252. Apparently the only recorded coin of this mint. The **CE** stands for *Cenomannis* (Le Mans), in the region of which Corbon lies.

437. FM: Trinity College 1937; ex J. Battely *c.* 1740; ex Archd. Battely 1708; found at Reculver, Kent. Illus. Battely 1745, pl. 7, and from this in Roach Smith 1850, pl. 7.9.

438. PG: MMAG Basel 1.4.1952 (= sale 9 (22.6.1951), lot 144—'Collection mérovingienne').

439. PG: MMAG Basel 1.4.1952 ('Collection mérovingienne'); ex Amécourt 380.

440. PG: MMAG Basel 1.4.1952 ('Collection mérovingienne'); ex Amécourt 382; ex Renault.

441. PG: MMAG Basel 1.4.1952 ('Collection mérovingienne'); ex Amécourt 378.

442. PG: MMAG Basel 1.4.1952 ('Collection mérovingienne'); ex Amécourt 383; ex Feuardent sale 7.6.1886, lot 148.

442A. PG: MMAG Basel 1.4.1952 ('Collection mérovingienne'); ex Amécourt 379? (description inexact, but same light weight); ex Robert.

443, 446-7. PG: MMAG Basel 1.4.1952 ('Collection mérovingienne').

444. PG: MMAG Basel 1.4.1952 ('Collection mérovingienne'); ex Rollin.

445. PG: MMAG Basel 1.4.1952 ('Collection mérovingienne'); ex Amécourt 390; ex Rollin.

448. PG: MMAG Basel 1.4.1952 (= sale 8 (8.12.1949), lot 322—'Collection mérovingienne'); ex Amécourt 124.

449. PG: MMAG Basel 1.4.1952 (= sale 9 (21.6.1951), lot 139—'Collection mérovingienne').

450. PG: MMAG Basel 1.4.1952 ('Collection mérovingienne') . . . ex Buvignier.

451. PG: Spink 18.3.1981 (*NCirc* March 1981, no. 2261).

452. PG: MMAG Basel 1.4.1952 (= sale 8 (8.12.1949), lot 438—'Collection mérovingienne'); ex Amécourt 121; ex Aussant.

453. PG: MMAG Basel 1.4.1952 (= sale 8 (8.12.1949), lot 388—'Collection mérovingienne').

454. PG: MMAG Basel 1.4.1952 ('Collection mérovingienne') . . . ex Lecointre-Dupont, ex Boilleau.

[*continued overleaf*]

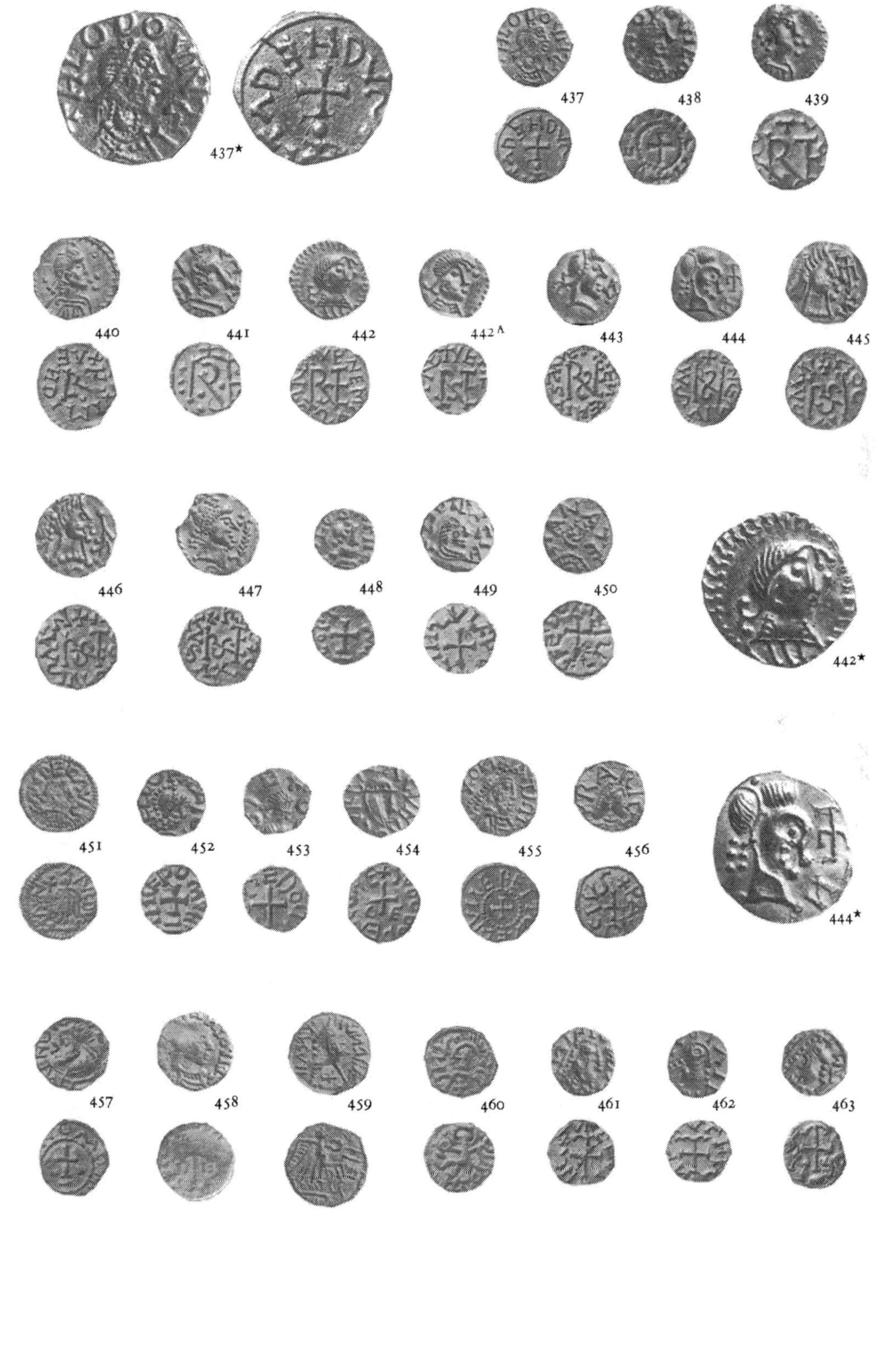
437★
437
438
439
440
441
442
442A
443
444
445
446
447
448
449
450
442★
451
452
453
454
455
456
444★
457
458
459
460
461
462
463

455 *Essonnes* (Essonne, com. Corbeil-Essonne), moneyer *Betto*. Obv. **XOИ|A TICIT** (for *Exona fecit*) Rev. **BETTOИE WVИE**. 1.27g (SG 13.65: 50% Au) 0°. B 1911–14 var.; P 842 var.

456 *Evrecy* (Calvados), moneyer *Patricius*. Obv. **+APRA RICA** Rev. **+PATRICIVS**. 1.18g (SG 17.94: 91% Au) 90°. B 236 (this coin); P 290.

457 *Ménouville* (Val-d'Oise), moneyer *Silvanus*? Obv. **MEN OIO[V]IL[A]**, bust l. Rev. **]NO MONIT**, w. **UV** in field. 1.09g (SG 15.51: 70% Au) 90°. B 6275 = P 2567 var.

458 *Moussy* (Seine-et-Marne), moneyer *Wandelegiselus*. Obv. **]ИƆO VIƆ+** bust r. Rev. **VV[AN]DELEGIƧEIO M**, cross on globule, w. **IƆƎ** in field. 1.16g (SG 11.74: 23% Au) 340°. B 1640; P 882 (possibly same dies). See note on coin.

459 *Nantes*, moneyer *Gen*... Obv. **NAИT IVИΛΓL**, bust l., w. cross on shoulder Rev. **GEN** (outwardly and upwards), w. **И** in ex., Victory r. 1.40g (SG 17.42: 87% Au) 200°. Cf. B 3092–6; P 534–6; Tomasini 1964, no. 644 (this coin, as Visigothic). For a discussion of the Victory type at Nantes, imitating Visigothic tremisses, see Lafaurie 1973c.

460 *Nantes*. Obv. **ИV|II** (= **NAM** retrograde outwardly?), bust l. Rev. **IVIO**, w. **И** in ex., Victory l. 1.35g (SG 17.88: 90% Ag) 170°. B 3094 (this coin). Cf. last coin and refs.

461 *Orléans*, moneyer *Angiulfus*. **ΛVILIΛNI**ᔕ (outwardly, **ΛV** ligatured, for *Aurelianis*), head r. Rev. **NG+VLFV ∩**, cross ancrée. 1.28g (SG 18.11: 92% Au) 90°. B 531 (this coin), 530 = P 636. Crack in rev. die.

462 *As last*. Obv. **ΛVRILIAN** (outwardly, **ΛV** ligatured) Rev. **ИͰ+VΓͰVS** (cf. inscription of last coin). 1.23g (SG 17.48: 87% Au) 270°. B 534; P 636 var.

463 *As last, derivative*. Obv. **Λ[ ]ΓIΛИI** (outwardly) Rev. **NG|VV ∩**. 1.12g (SG 15.27: 68% Au) 310°. B 532 var., 5983 = P 641 var.

455. PG: Lockett III 66; ex Grantley 617.

456. PG: MMAG Basel 1.4.1952 (= sale 8 (8.12.1949), lot 445—'Collection mérovingienne'); ex Amécourt 494; ex Robert.

457. PG: MMAG Basel 1.4.1952 (= sale 8 (8.12.1949), lot 424—'Collection mérovingienne'); ex Hauët 249.

458. PG: Platt 1.9.1950.

459. PG: Spink 19.6.1945; ex Grantley 2791; ex Rollin 1899.

460. PG: Baldwin 22.5.1971; ex Grantley 627; ex Amécourt (uncertain lot).

461. PG: Spink 12.2.1945 . . . ex Amécourt 147.

462. PG: MMAG Basel 1.4.1952 (= sale 9 (21.6.1951), lot 141—'Collection mérovingienne').

463. PG: Spink 7.5.1946; ex Grantley 660; acq. in Vienna.

MEROVINGIANS (7): GOLD COINAGE, NATIONAL SERIES

References as on Plate 20. The coins are gold tremisses.

NEUSTRIA (cont.)

464 *Palace* (*Paris*), moneyer *Ingomarus*. Obv. **IN D~ACIO I** (for *In palacio fecit*, blundered) Rev. **INGOMARO MOT**. 1.12g (SG 13.81: 52% Au) 0°. B 3510 = 6519 (this coin); P 696 *bis* (p. 581) var.

465 *Palaiseau* (Essonne), moneyer *Domnolenus*. Obv. **+PALACIOLOI** Rev. **+DOMOLEHO**. 1.21g sheared (SG 14.86: 64% Au) 20°. B 6302 = P 866 (same dies); B 3325 = P 867 (same obv. die); Lafaurie 1971e, 210, no. 1 (this coin); Rigold 1975, no. 90 (this coin).

466 *Palaiseau*, moneyer *Domegiselus*. Obv. **PALACIOL**[Rev. **DOMEGISELO MONE**, cross pattée on circle, w. crescent above. 1.07g chipped (SG 12.78: 39% Au) 170°. B 3322; P 924 var. (as Pfalzel, near Trier). For the attribution to Palaiseau, see Stahl 1982, 35–6 and refs. there cited.

467 *Paris*, moneyer *Vitalis*. Obv. **PARISVS FIT**, head r. Rev. **VITAL~ MONI**, cross ancrée on globule. 1.25g (SG 17.85: 90% Au) 180°. B 3397; P 728.

468 *Paris*, moneyer *Arnoaldus*. Obv. **PARISIVS** Rev. **+ARNOA**[, globule beneath cross ancrée obscured by piercing. 1.16g pierced (SG 13.15: 48% Au) 180°. B 3373 = P 720–1.

469 *As last*. Obv. **IVIIVIOVIV** (*Parisius* blundered) Rev. **+ARИOALV**[. 1.10g (SG 14.01: 54% Au) 10°. B 3372–8 var.; P 718–22 var.

470 *Pennery?* (Loiret), moneyer *Modericus*. Obv. [**M**]**ODE-RI**[**CV**], head r. Rev. **PEИOB**[**RI**]. 1.15g (SG 16.68: 81% Au) 0°. B 3642 = P 2614. The attribution to Pennery was proposed by Engel and Serrure (1891–1905, vol. I, 139).

471 *Quentovic* (Pas-de-Calais), moneyer *Aldinus*. Obv. **+AL૧IИO**[**IИOИIT**] Rev. **VVIC**[**VS**] **FIT**. 1.24g (SG 13.54: 48% Au) 180°. B 4983 = P 1137; Vanhoudt 1982, no. 246 (same dies). Alvin's proposed transfer of all coins with *Wicus* to Wijk-bij-Maastricht (Alvin 1914) is unacceptable, despite the typological rapprochements he establishes with neighbouring mints, since there is no likelihood of the existence of the place at so early a date.

472 *Quentovic*, moneyer *Ela*. Obv. **+ELA MOИIT** Rev. **VVICVS FIT**. 1.27g (SG 13.54: 48% Au) 190°. B 4984–6; P 1138–9.

473 *Quentovic*, moneyer *Dutta*, derivative. Obv. **XIX** [**VV**]**ICO~+** Rev. **+DVTTA MONET**. 1.32g (SG 13.60: 49% Au) 200°. B 2198 var. = P 1141 var.

474 *As last*. Obv. **XIX VVICO~+** Obv. **+OVTTA MONET** (**NE** ligatured). 1.33g (SG 12.49: 34% Au) 320°. Ref. as last.

475 *Rouen*, moneyer *Mertus*. Obv. **+PTOT**[**OM**] **CIVIT PT**, bust r. Rev. **+MEЯ / TO M**, monstrance(?) 1.28g worn, by water? (SG 17.16: 85% Au) 160°. B 3814 var.; P 261 var.

476 *Rouen*, moneyer *Cr* (or *Er*) . . . *ido?* Obv. **RODOMO CI**, degenerate head l. Rev. **+CR**[ ]**LDO·**(?). 1.17g chipped (SG 12.19: 30% Au) 290°. B 3829 (this coin); P –.

477 *Ruan* (Loir-et-Cher), moneyer *Arivaldus* (= Charivaldus). Obv. **+RIOMO**, bust r. Rev. **+ARIVALDO**. 1.21g (SG 15.63: 71% Au) 240°. B 3798 var. = P 579 var.

478 *Serillac* (Sarthe), moneyer *Launomundus*. Obv. **CI RIALACO** Rev. **+LAVNOMVND**. 1.07 g (SG 16.00: 75% Au) 70°. B 1564 = P 443.

479 *Sully-sur-Loire* (Loiret), moneyer *Mallebodus*. Obv. **+~OLIACO VICI**, head r. Rev. **+MΔLLEBOPS**. 1.23g (SG 16.24: 77% Au) 180°. B 4164 var.; P 669–70 var.

480 *As last*. Obv. [**Λ**]**LEBODV2** Rev. **2ΛVL**[ ]**O+**. 1.07g (SG 16.37: 78% Au) 90°. B 4168 = P 664.

481 *Vendôme*, moneyer *Agrigisilus*. Obv. **+**[**VID**]**OGINO** Rev. **+AGRIGI~ILO**. 1.24g (SG 16.04: 75% Au) 170°. B 4883 = P 583.

482 *Veuves* (Loir-et-Cher), moneyer *Francobodus*. Obv. **VIDVΛ VICO FIT** Rev. **FRANC·+·OBODO M**. 1.12g (SG 12.07: 28% Au) 340°. B 4805 (this coin); P 406 var.

483 *Le Vimeu* (Somme), moneyer *Pipero*. Obv. **XVIMI+NAO** Rev. **PIPERONE**, 2 crosses on globules w. star between, mounted on 3 steps. 1.36g (SG 17.98: 90% Au) 160°. B 4870 = P 1118 (same rev. die). *Viminao* = Le Vimeu, the region south of the Somme estuary. Lafaurie has suggested (*per litteram*) that this coin may have been struck at Saint-Valéry-sur-Somme in Le Vimeu.

484 *Uncertain mint* (NIGROLOTO), moneyer *Gennobaudus*. Obv. **+NIGRQCQTQ** Rev. **+GENNQAVDI**. 1.21g (SG 16.69: 81% Au) 0°. B 6291 (this coin?); P 2600.

485 *Uncertain mint* (ODIGINO?), moneyer *Ar*...? Obv. **ODIGINO**, crude bust r. Rev. **+AR**[ ]**ON**. 1.07g (SG 15.40: 69% Au) 350°. B 317 (as Aron); P 2611.

464. PG: MMAG Basel 1.4.1952 (= sale 8 (8.12.1949), lot 312—'Collection mérovingienne'); ex Amécourt 170.

465. FM: Trinity College 1937; ex J. Battely *c.* 1740; ex Archd. Battely 1708; found at Reculver, Kent. Illus. Battely 1745, pl. 7, and from this in Roach Smith 1850, pl. 7.

466. PG: Baldwin 22.5.1971; ex Grantley 634.

467. PG: MMAG Basel 1.4.1952 (= sale 9 (21.6.1951), lot 143—'Collection mérovingienne').

468. FM: Miss M. Farmer 27.6.1928.

469. PG: Baldwin 22.5.1971; ex Grantley 646; from Roux 1903.

470. PG: MMAG Basel 1.4.1952 (= sale 8 (8.12.1949), lot 394—'Collection mérovingienne').

471, 475, 478–80, 482, 485. PG: MMAG Basel 1.4.1952 ('Collection mérovingienne').

472. PG: Vinchon 4.4.1952.

473. PG: Motte 93 (= Rolland 1932, no. 100).

474. PG: MMAG Basel 1.4.1952 (= sale 8 (8.12.1949), lot 446—'Collection mérovingienne').

476. PG: Franceschi 19.3.1949 . . . ex Amécourt 91; ex Robert.

477. PG: MMAG Basel 1.4.1952 (= sale 8 (8.12.1949), lot 440—'Collection mérovingienne'); ex Hauët 258.

481. PG: MMAG Basel 1.4.1952 (= sale 8 (8.12.1949), lot 396—'Collection mérovingienne').

483. PG: MMAG Basel 1.4.1952 (= sale 8 (8.12.1949), lot 450—'Collection mérovingienne').

484. PG: MMAG Basel 1.4.1952 ('Collection mérovingienne') . . . possibly ex Dassy 308.

[*continued overleaf*]

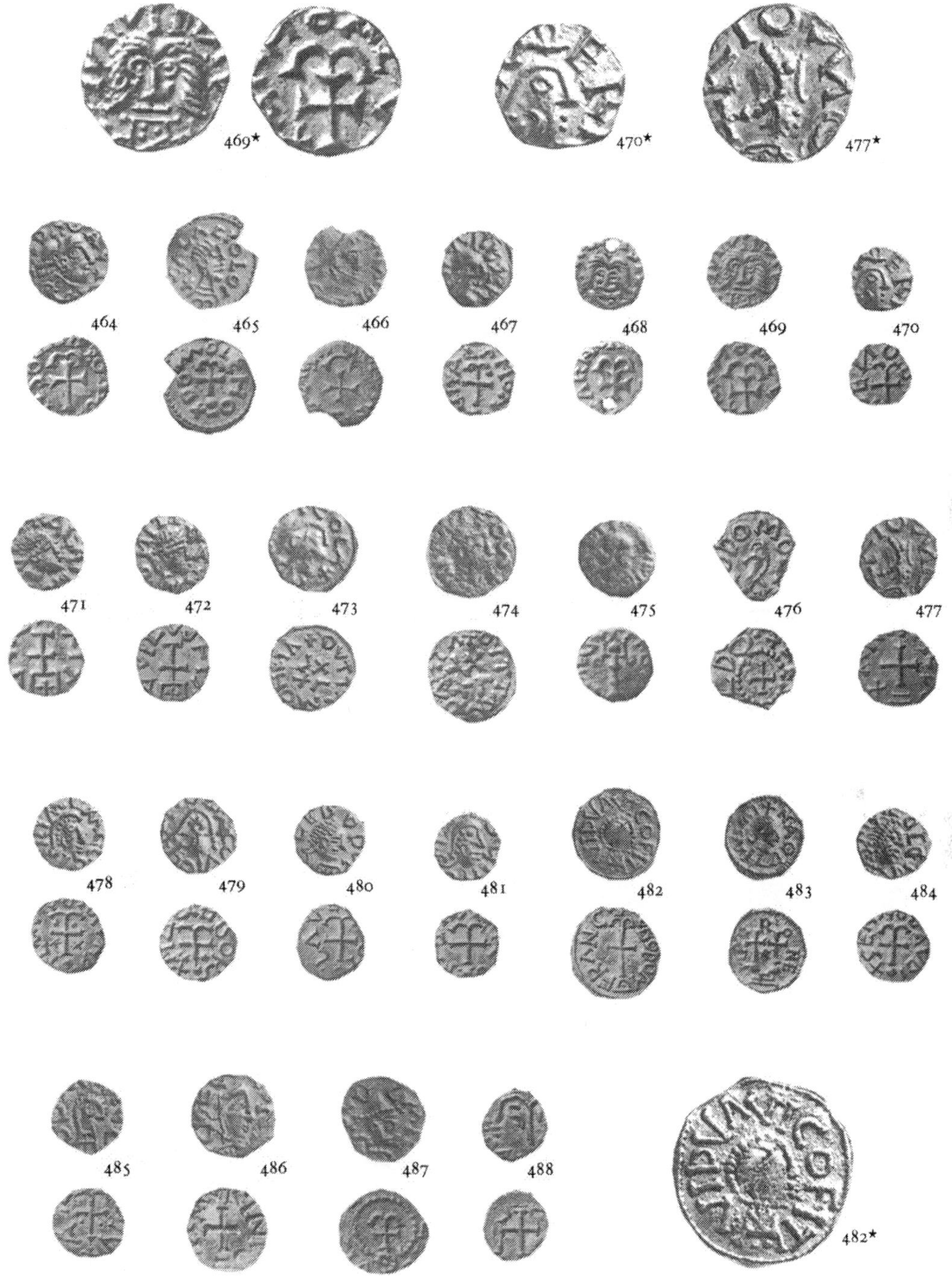

469* 470* 477*

464 465 466 467 468 469 470

471 472 473 474 475 476 477

478 479 480 481 482 483 484

485 486 487 488 482*

486 *Uncertain mint* (CAEL...N), moneyer ...*nmurinus*? Obv. **CAEL[ ]N** Rev. **]ИMVRINVS**. 1.16g (SG 13.26: 45% Au) 90°. B 6545 (this coin); P –. The design is similar to coins of the Tours region; cf. B 4529, P 363.

487 *Uncertain mint*. Obv. **]DEOCMN**?, bust r. Rev. **VIM[ ]LIO**? 1.30g (SG 13.58: 49% Au) 310°. B 4060 (this coin) = ?4866; P –. Illus *RN*³ 8 (1890), pl. 2.21. The circle and pellet breaking the inner border of the rev. is found on coins of Lieusaint (Seine-et-Marne); cf. B 2202f., P 850f.

488 *Uncertain mint*. Obv. **]VII[** , crude head l. Rev. **]V -V- -[** . 1.19g (SG 16.34: 78% Au) 310°. B –; P –. This is a derivative of Neustrian coins of the early 7th century w. a bust having the *appendice perlé*.

486. PG: Spink 7.5.1946; ex Grantley 642; ex Amécourt 509; ex Robert.

487. PG: Baldwin 22.5.1971; ex Grantley 656; from Roux 1903; ex Amécourt 552; ex Widranges 195; from Sommières hoard.

488. PG: Spink 7.5.1946; ex Grantley 660.

MEROVINGIANS (8): GOLD COINAGE, NATIONAL SERIES

References as on Plate 20. The coins are gold tremisses.

AUSTRASIA

489 *Binson* (Marne), moneyer *Airulfus*. Obv. **+BAINISSONE** Rev. **+AIRVLFO MON**. 1.16g (SG 18.01: 91% Au) 180°. B 599 var = P 1062 var.

490 *Brieulles-sur-Meuse* (Meuse), moneyer *Audomlus*? Obv. **]IVNLII?**, bust r. Rev. **AVDOMLV∽[ ]A?**, w. **BRIO** (for *Briodorum*) in quarters of cross. 1.27g (SG 13.45: 47% Au) 180°. B –; P –; Rigold 1975, no. 67a (this coin).

491 *Cologne*, derivative. Inscriptions illegible, obv. bust r.; rev. barbarous Victory w. cross l.? 1.31g (Oddy 1972a, no. SG 207; 92% Au) 180°. Cf. B 1602 = P 1169. Lafaurie 1960a, 201, no. 15 (this coin).

492 *Dieuze* (Moselle), moneyer *Bocceghildus*. Obv. **VO∽O AICOI+ PATC** (for *Doso vico facit*) Rev. **+BOC-CINIIVO MONITA**. 1.12g (SG 13.15: 43% Au) 0°. B 6165; P 955; Stahl 1982, G1e (this coin).

493 *Dorestad* (Netherlands), moneyer *Madelinus*. Obv. **ΔORESTATI FIT** Rev. **MAΔELINVS M**. 1.25g (SG 13.64: 50% Au) 90°. B 1773 var.; P 1224 var.

494 *As last*, but immobilization or imitation. Obv. **Δ:R:E∽TAT FIT**, bust r. Rev. **HAVEL+HVS H**. 1.26g (SG 13.05: 42% Au) 320°. B 1792 var.; P –.

495 *As last*. Obv. **Δ:OR∵E∽TAT FIT**, bust r. Rev. **NAVELINV∽ H**. 1.23g (SG 12.90: 40% Au) 350°. B 1781; P 1227 var. For a denier of similar design, see **633**.

496 *Maastricht*, moneyer '*Hainondes*'? Obv. **TRICECT[ ]FIT** (for *Triectu fit*), bust r. Rev. **··HAINOIIDESS· MO**, cross-on-step and globule. 1.27g (SG 17.62: 88% Au) 190°. B –; P –; cf. B 4417; P 1183. The dies are worn and the inscriptions may possibly have been recut, introducing blunderings into them. The first letter of the rev. legend may be an **M** rather than **H**, and the second **S** may be the product of double striking. The bust, based on that of coins of Magnentius, belongs to the group studied by Bauer (1951) and Yvon (1953).

497 *Maastricht*, derivative. Obv. **+TƎIƆƆTOS** (for *Triecto f*) Rev. **TSTI∽TƆHƆTNVO**. 1.32g (SG 16.75: 82% Au) 180°. B 4184; P 1192–3; Pol 1977, nos. 18–19 (Nietap hoard; same dies). For prototype cf. B 446–51; P 1178.

Metz. For a modern forgery, see **1474**.

498 *Mouzon* (Ardennes), moneyer *Caiobodes*. Obv. **M[O]∽OMO FIET** Rev. **CAI[O]BODEƧ MO**. 1.16g pierced (SG 16.48: 79% Au) 180°. B 3072; P –.

499 '*Saxsebacio*' (unidentified mint in Toul neighbourhood), moneyer *Civncelus*. Obv. **SAXSEBACIO** Rev. **CIVN CELVS**. 1.29g (SG 16.99: 83% Au) 180°. Cf. B 4003 = P 1015.

500 *Strasbourg* or derivative? Obv. traces of inscription, rude head l. in border Rev. no inscription visible, figure moving l. w. raised arms. 1.16g (SG 11.74: 23% Au) 320°. Cf. B 304–9; P 1158–62.

501 *Tiel* or *Nijmegen* (Netherlands). Obv. **TЄLЄV[AИV∽]** Rev. **+ЧIOMΔ**, [**GO** in ex.] (all retrograde), w. **ЯA** in field. 1.26g (SG 17.78: 90% Au) 0°. B 4235 = P 1366; Lafaurie 1960a, 202, nos. 31–4 (same dies and this coin cited). The rev. is interpreted by Lafaurie as 'Niomago', i.e. Nijmegen close to Tiel.

Void (Meuse). For a possible contemporary imitation in silver, see **613**.

502 *Yvoy*, now *Carignan* (Ardennes), moneyer *Mannus* or derivative. Obv. **EOP[ ]·ΓICTI** (retrograde, for *Epocio fecit*) Rev. **+MANNO MET** (retrograde), w. **TT** (degeneration of **CA**) in upper quarters of cross. 1.24g (SG 13.65: 50% Au) 230°. B 1889 = 5522 (this coin); Stahl 1982, H2h (this coin); cf. B 27, 1894, 6174 = P 911–14. The modern name Carignan (from Italian *Carignano*) dates from the 17th century, when Louis XIV created Yvoy a duchy for a member of the house of Savoy.

503 *Zülpich* (Germany, east of Aachen), moneyer *Chuno*? Obv. **CHA / NO M** (retrograde) Rev. **TVLBIAO +CH[ ]O**. 1.27g (SG 13.21: 45% Au) 0°. B 3802 = P 1222 (as 'Rittudiaco'); cf. B 4475–7; P 1173–4.

504 *Uncertain mint* (Upper Moselle valley). Obv. **MASƎIΓ ΓIVIΓO** Rev. **+[ ]IVS MON, VA** (for **CA**) in lower quarters of cross. 1.10g (SG 12.09: 28% Au) 110°. B–; P–. The style is typical of mints in the Moselle valley above Metz, although the execution is crude. The most probable mint is Marsal (Meuse), w. the obv. legend a corruption of *Marsallo vico*; cf. B 2410f., P959f.

505 *Uncertain mint* (Mainz region). Obv. **ΟENEꞒAVꞒIIA**, bust l. Rev. **ONAREꞒAV·CIV∾IIOIꞒ**, cross on globule w. **IIA** (for value **VII**) in field. 1.31g (SG 16.36: 78% Au) 190°. B 2019 = Vanhoudt 1982, no. 166 (same dies); B 2020 = P 1165 (same dies, but before development of die cracks and minor recutting of inscription). Prou read the mint name as ... *enegavgiia* and the moneyer as *Charecavcius*, but the inscriptions are more probably meaningless.

489. PG: Bourgey 27.9.1946.

490. PG: Spink 16.3.1970 . . . from Spink (*NCirc* Jan. 1920; no. 77784); ex Roth I 45; found at Bourton-on-the-Water, Glos., 1850.

491. PG: Baldwin 22.8.1971; ex Grantley 650; from Schulman; ex Escharen hoard.

492–3. PG: Seaby 20.3.1945; ex Grantley 616 and 615 respectively.

494, 498. PG: MMAG Basel 1.4.1952 ('Collection mérovingienne').

495. PG: Baldwin 9.2.1952.

496. PG: Prince de Ligne I 108.

497. PG: J. Schulman 30.8.1950; ex Haex.

499. PG: Baldwin 12.10.1960.

500. PG: Baldwin 22.5.1971; ex Grantley 633; from Rollin 1898.

501. PG: Baldwin 22.5.1971; ex Grantley 632; ex Escharen hoard.

502. PG: Seaby 16.6.1947; ex Grantley 611; ex Amécourt 511; ex Marmod (son-in-law of Nocas); ex Nocas (of Ligny); ex Harquart *curé* at Naix; found near Naix (Meuse). See *RN*[3] 8 (1890), 51–2 and pl. 2.28.

503. PG: Franceschi 1.4.1977.

504. PG: Spink 7.5.1946; ex Grantley 660; from Rollin.

505. PG: Baldwin 22.5.1971; ex Grantley 647; ex Rollin 1898.

[*continued overleaf*]

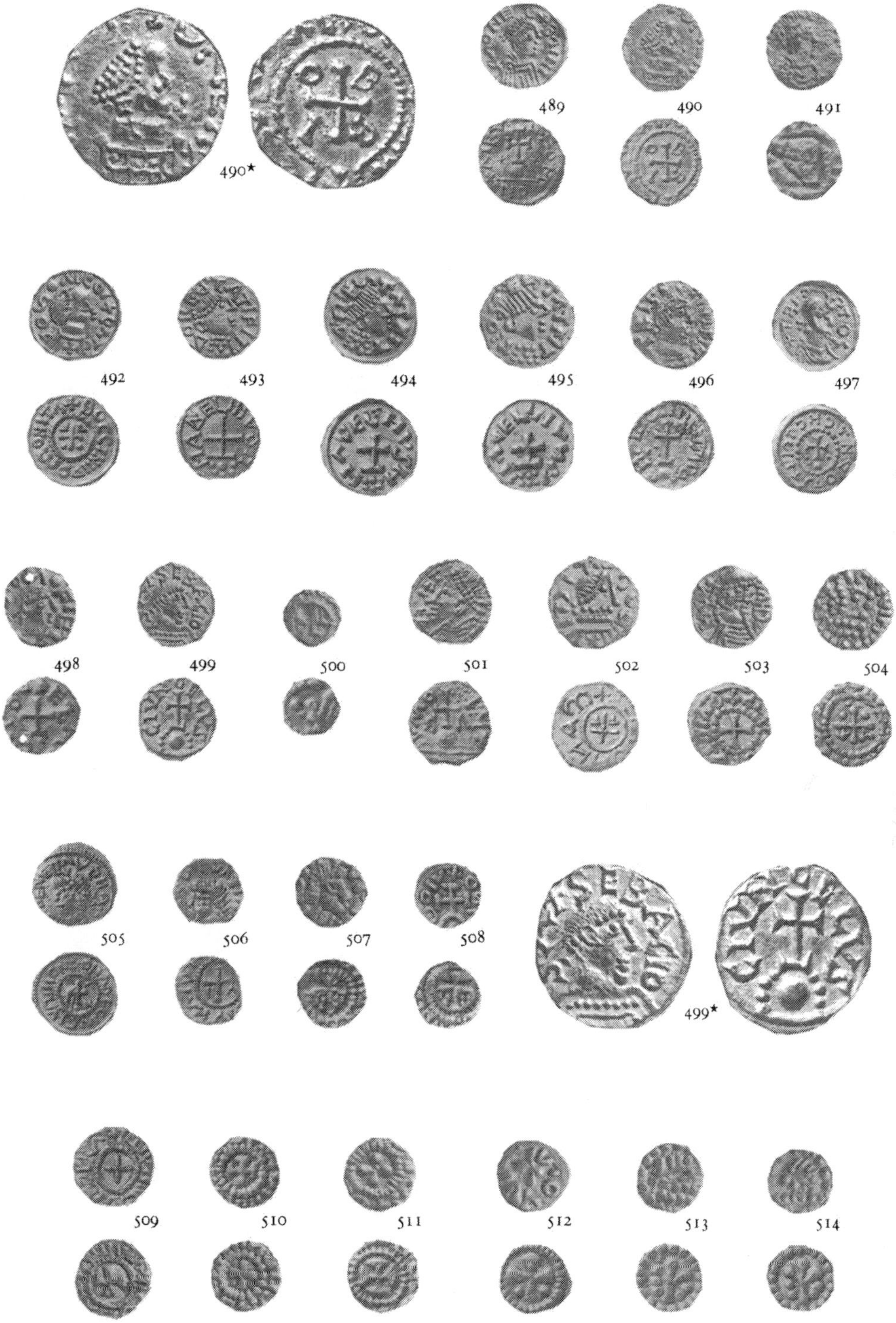
490★
489
490
491
492
493
494
495
496
497
498
499
500
501
502
503
504
505
506
507
508
499★
509
510
511
512
513
514

506 *As last.* Obv.]VIVATIΛ[, head l. Rev.]IVHΛI◊I[, design as last. 1.23g (SG 16.33: 78% Au) 110°. B 4938 (this coin); P –. Illus. Conbrouse 1840–1, pl. 48.34.

507 *As last.* Obv. inscription illegible. Rev. •+•[ ]O MOИ? w. VII in lower quarters of cross. 1.20g (SG 12.76: 38% Au) 0°. Cf. B 3003–9; P 1152–4; Werner 1935, no. M140 (same dies, ex Fessenheim hoard). Derivative of a coin of Mainz, moneyer *Garoaldus.*

508 *As last.* Obv. OOIV+OИI Rev.]N[, w. VII in lower quarters of cross. 1.25g (SG 13.29: 45% Au) 180°. B 3015; P –.

509 *As last.* Blundered inscriptions. 1.26g (SG 13.04: 42% Au). B 3016, 3030–2 (Dronrijp hoard), 5586–7 = P 1244–5.

510 *As last.* 1.18g (SG 12.04: 28% Au). Cf. ref. for last.

511 *As last.* 1.25g (SG 12.46: 34% Au). Werner 1935, no. M145 (ex Fessenheim hoard).

512 *Uncertain mint* (Middle Rhineland). Obv. V•OUVΛ•, cross. 1.18g (SG 13.35: 46% Au); Werner 1935, nos. M143–4 (grave-finds from Dietersheim and Meisenheim), M207–8 (without provenance).

513 *Uncertain mint* (Middle Rhineland?). Obv. rude head r.? Rev. branch or tree w. 4 pellets in field. 1.06g (SG 11.43: 18% Au) 160°. B –; P –.

514 *As last*, but head l.? 1.09g (SG 11.64: 21% Au) 180°. B –; P –.

506. PG: Baldwin 22.5.1971; ex Grantley 674; from Roux 1903.

507–8, 510–11. PG: Baldwin 22.5.1971; ex Grantley 654.

509. PG: Baldwin 22.5.1971; ex Grantley 624; from Rollin 1892.

512–13. PG: Baldwin 22.5.1971; ex Grantley 654; from Rollin 1890 and 1899 respectively.

514. PG: Baldwin 22.5.1971; ex Grantley 654; from Trinks.

MEROVINGIANS (9): GOLD COINAGE, NATIONAL SERIES

References as on Plate 20. The coins are gold tremisses.

AUSTRASIA (cont.)

515 *Uncertain mint* (Frisia or Lower Rhineland?). Obv. **NIZI**?, horse (or dragon) r., w. head turned l., mane standing on end Rev. pseudo-inscription of Is, cross-potent on globule, w. 3 pellets and a **T**(?) in field. 1.26g (Oddy 1972a, no. SG245; 85% Au) 0°. B –; P –; Lafaurie 1960a, 205, nos. 46–59 (same dies and this coin cited). There were 14 die-duplicates of this in the hoard from Escharen on the Lower Maas, and Lafaurie suggests that they were struck in that locality.

516 *Same dies as last.* 1.27g (Oddy no. SG243; 88% Au) 0°. Ref. as last. Two further specimens from the Escharen hoard struck from the same dies which were formerly in the Grierson collection (also ex Grantley: Oddy 1972a, no. 242, 1.28g 0°, and no. SG244, 1.29g 340°) were disposed of in 1984 to the BM and Ashmolean Museum.

517 *Uncertain mint* (Frisia). Obv. **EA+ / NR+**, bust l. Rev. **+OΓИ+VΛ+Γ+⊥A**, w. **LU** flanking cross-on-step and pellet. 1.23g (SG 16.59: 80% Au) 220°. B 2332–4, P 1239; Boeles 1947, type B. This and the next 4 coins belong to a group of coins known as the 'Dronrijp' type, which was struck in Frisia, although the design is probably derived from coins of Chalon. They occurred in the Dronrijp and Nietap hoards from Frisia, and have been classified by Boeles (1947). There was a specimen similar to this one in the Crondall hoard (Sutherland 1948, 12, no. 20).

518 *As last.* Obv. degeneration of legend of last coin, but bust r. Rev. **VNϽNXV+NCN**, design as last. 1.23g (SG 16.34: 78% Au) 210°. B –; P –. Boeles 1947, type C.

519 *As last.* Obv. **ΛΛϽ/–LIC–**, bust l. Rev. **VΛVVΛ ΛVΛOΛ**, design as last. 1.29g (SG 16.29: 78% Au) 200°. B 2343 (same dies); P 1240 (same dies); Boeles 1947, type D.

520 *Same dies as last.* 1.27g (SG 16.69: 81% Au) 210°. Ref. as last.

521 *Uncertain mint* (Frisia?). Obv. **OΛOTH:∽Ͻ[ ]ET**, bust r. Rev. **ΛVΛVΛVΛVΛOΛVΛV**, design as last. 1.19g (SG 16.22: 77% Au) 170°. B 2345, 2347; P –; Boeles 1947, nos. 36–7 (the first found at Franeker). The obv. is of superior style to the foregoing, but the rev. closely resembles that of the last two coins. Boeles attributed them to the Middle Rhineland, although the nexus with the 'Dronrijp' type makes a Frisian origin preferable.

522 *Uncertain mint* (N. Gaul or Frisia?). Obv. **ΛIIOVΛƎIⅢ**, head r. Rev. **ΓϽNII∽VLOΠIϽZΛI**, cross w. one limb bent (degenerate cross chrismée?), and wedges in 3 quarters projecting from inner border. 1.25g (SG 16.81: 82% Au) 0°. B 3025–6, 3036 (as Mainz; all ex Dronrijp † hoard); P –; Werner 1935, no. M210 (same dies).

UNCERTAIN MINT AND REGION

523 *Uncertain mint.* Obv. **O[ ]AX** Rev. **SCVSΛ⅃OREΓΛI** (retrograde). 1.21g (SG 18.63: 96% Au) 90°. B 4046 (this coin); P –.

524 *Uncertain mint.* Obv. traces of an inscription, bust r. w. 5 pellets before face Rev. **IIMELMON[** , broad cross pattée on step w. 4 pellets in each quarter. 1.47g (SG 18.55: 95% Au) 150°. B –; P –. While the obv. is a reasonably good rendering of a Provençal bust, the rev. is very crude and quite untypical of that region.

525 *Uncertain mint.* Obv. **OA**, bust r. Rev. **OΓIISΛ⅃ΛV**. 1.31g (SG 17.20: 85% Au) 350°. B –; P –.

526 *Uncertain mint.* Obv. **DICUIΛ[** ?, head r. Rev. **+OTD∽ [ ]ΛI–**. 1.18g (SG 17.38: 87% Au) 270°. B –; P –.

527 *Uncertain mint.* Obv. **ИIIIOИ** –, bust r. Rev. **FVNI∽IV**. 1.21g (SG 17.21: 85% Au) 0°. B –; P –.

528 *Uncertain mint.* Obv. **TASINIO**? (outwardly retrograde) Rev. **SΛᗡ[ ]I⊥I⅃**, voided patriarchal cross, w. indistinct letters in field. 1.44g (SG 13.87: 53% Au) 340°. B –; P –. For a coin w. a related bust from the Limoges region, see P 1962.

529 *Uncertain mint.* Obv. **HM / IVO**, bust r. Rev. inscription of **N**s and curls. 1.25g (SG 15.62: 71% Au) 270°. B –; P –.

530 *Uncertain mint.* Obv. **IOϽC+[ ]O[ ]IV** Rev. **ШIIIHIИ IIIΛVΓO+IIϽ**. 1.25g (SG 13.27: 45% Au) 120°. B 6591 (this coin); P –.

531 *Uncertain mint.* Obv. **VΛΘI**, crude bust l.(?) Rev. **ΘIIIΘCИ[** . 1.28g (SG 14.26: 57% Au) 340°. B –; P –.

532 *Uncertain mint.* Obv. **HVE+VƎFƎ**, bust r. Rev. figure seated(?) between 2 crosses, w. **ШШ** in field and **A** below. 1.40g (SG 16.11: 75% Au) 0°. B 6524 (this coin); P –; Ardant 1851, 253, no. 8 and pl. 14.7 (this coin); cf. B 5563 (found at Domburg).

533 *Uncertain mint.* Obv. **CU./VNO∽**(?), bust l. Rev. **M·A·M·R**(?). 1.23g (SG 13.68: 50% Au) 110°. B –; P –. Cf. a denier, **622** below.

515–16. PG: Baldwin 22.5.1971; ex Grantley (uncertain lot); from Escharen hoard.

517. PG: Baldwin 22.5.1971; ex Grantley 671; from Rollin 1893.

518. PG: Lockett III 90; ex Grantley 661.

519. PG: Baldwin 22.5.1971; ex Grantley 671; from Roux 1903.

520. PG: Baldwin 22.5.1971; ex Grantley 671; from Rollin 1898.

521. PG: Seaby 16.6.1947; ex Grantley 621.

522. PG: Baldwin 22.5.1971; ex Grantley 655; from Rollin 1897.

523. PG: Baldwin 22.5.1971; ex Grantley 651; from Rollin 1899; ex Amécourt 584.

524. PG: Baldwin 22.5.1971; ex Grantley 648; from Rollin 1899.

525–6. PG: Baldwin 22.5.1971; ex Grantley (uncertain lot); from Rollin 1892 and 1899 respectively.

527. PG: Baldwin 22.5.1971; ex Grantley 658; from Roux 1903.

528. PG: Baldwin 22.5.1971; ex Grantley 649; from Rollin 1899.

529. PG: Baldwin 22.5.1971; ex Grantley 656; from Rollin 1899.

530. PG: Lockett III 88; ex Grantley 643; from Schulman 1897; ex Galerande.

531. PG: Baldwin 22.5.1971; ex Grantley 650; from Rollin 1899.

532. PG: Spink 7.5.1946; ex Grantley 675; ex Carbery Evans; from Feuardent.

533. PG. Baldwin 22.5.1971; ex Grantley 662; from Spink 1903.

[*continued overleaf*]

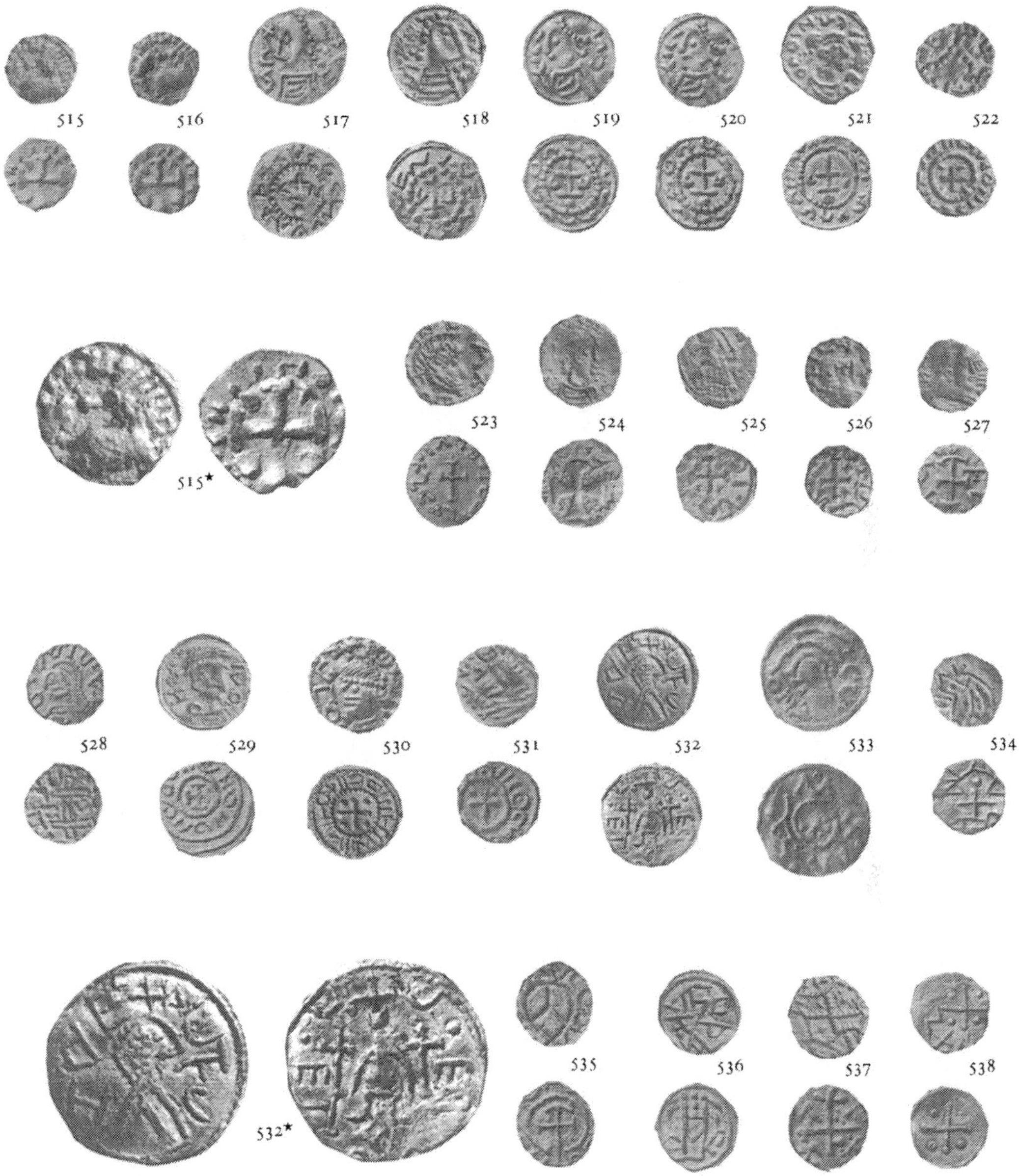

515 516 517 518 519 520 521 522

515* 523 524 525 526 527

528 529 530 531 532 533 534

532* 535 536 537 538

534 *Uncertain mint.* Obv. head l.? Rev. cross-on-step w. pellet above, in border w. 4 protruding triangles. 1.04g (SG 15.78: 75% Au) 10°. B –; P –.

535 *Uncertain mint.* Obv.]**AVCUDV**, tribrach in looped border Rev. inscription off flan, cross-potent ancrée w. lower arm breaking inner border. 0.95g (SG 12.68: 37% Au) 350°. B –; P –.

536 *Uncertain mint.* Obv. uncertain design, w. **V◇ÞA+** in field Rev. tower flanked by **S**s (double struck). 1.40g (SG 14.33: 58% Au) 270°. B –; P –.

537 *Uncertain mint.* Obv. distorted cross fourchée? Rev. no inscription, crude cross fleury, w. **T**s or **L**s in 3 quarters. 1.20g (SG 17.66: 89% Au). B –; P –.

538 *Uncertain mint.* Obv.]**VXZ**[Rev. no inscription. 1.28g (SG 15.43: 70% Au). B –; P –.

534. PG: Lockett III 83; bt in London.

535. Lockett III 82; ex Grantley 644; from Rollin 1899.

536. PG: Baldwin 22.5.1971; ex Grantley 664.

537. Baldwin 22.5.1971; ex Grantley 664; from Rollin 1899; found in the River Saône.

538. PG: Baldwin 22.5.1971; ex Grantley 655.

MEROVINGIANS (10): SILVER DENIERS, *c.* 670–*c.* 750

Principal references are: B = Belfort 1892–5 and P = Prou 1892a. Hoard references are:

Bais	Lafaurie 1981d	Plassac	Lafaurie 1969a, 184–213
Cimiez	Chabouillet 1890 (text nos.)	Saint-Pierre-les-Etieux	Lafaurie 1969a, 157–83
Nohanent	Lafaurie 1969a, 214–19	Savonnières	Lafaurie 1963a

Most of the coins have been analysed for Metcalf using an X-ray fluorescence spectrometer, and the full results, including the figures for trace elements, are published in Metcalf 1983a. Only the silver contents, rounded to the nearest 1%, are given here.

BURGUNDY AND PROVENCE

539 *Chalon-sur-Saône*, moneyer *Inportunus*. Obv. [+]**NPOR TV[NO MO]**, Christogram in border Rev. **CAB [LO]NNO+** (for *Cabilonnum*). 1.29g (Metcalf 3; 92% Ag) 270°. B 1260 = P 211; Plassac 1; Bais 3; Amécourt 1873, pl. 7.139–40. For the moneyer, see p. 145 above.

540 *As last*, uncertain moneyer. Obv. +**A** (or **R**)**VII**, helmeted bust r. Rev.]**VIΟAL**[. 1.02g (Metcalf 4; 92% Ag) 260°. B –; P –; Nohanent 6 (this coin).

541 *Lyon*, See of. Obv. **LV** (for *Lugduno*) Rev. **EPS** in the quarters of a cross chrismée turned l. 1.15g (Metcalf 1; 93% Ag) 220°. B 2363 = P 109 = Cimiez 138. The obv. design is similar to the rev. of Lyon coins of Pepin, Carloman, and the early years of Charlemagne (Amécourt 1868c, 324–5).

542 *Marseille*. Obv. **M**, w. pellet above, 2 pellets to either side, and line above and below Rev. lozenge design w. pellet in field. 1.24g (Metcalf 75; 91% Ag) 160°. B 6261 = Saint-Pierre-les-Etieux 73 (this coin); Cimiez 93 var.; Bais 112 var. The attribution to Marseille is supported by isolated finds from the locality (Lafaurie 1969a, 175).

543 *Marseille*, patrician *Ansedert*. Obv. bust l., w. **A** before face Rev. +**ANSEDER** around **T**. B 2691 = P 1478 = Cimiez 8. 1.00g (Metcalf 47; 84% Ag) 140°. For a discussion of the persons named on the coins of Marseille, see pp. 146–8 above.

544 *As last*. Obv. bust r., w. [**H** or **M**] before face Rev. +**A**[**NSE**]**DERT** around **M**. 1.25g (Metcalf 48; 87% Ag) 140°. B 2692 = P 1465 = Cimiez 9; B 2707.

545 *As last*. Obv. bust l., w. cross(?) before face Rev. **AN∽[ED]ERT** around retrograde **S** in border. 1.21g (Metcalf 49; 89% Ag) 180°. B 2710; P 1472 = Cimiez 13.

546 *As last*. Type as last, rev. +[**ANS**]**EDERT**. 1.01g (Metcalf 50; 89% Ag) 60°. Ref. as last.

547 *Marseille*, patrician *Nemfidius*. Obv. bust l., w. **N**(?) before face Rev. +[**M**]**FIDIU∽** around **NE** ligatured. 1.16g (Metcalf 51; 90% Ag) 40°. B 2608; P 1482 = Cimiez 27.

548 *As last*. Obv. head r. Rev. +**II·FDIVS** cross. 1.16g (Metcalf 52; 88% Ag) 90°. B 2593, 2595; P 1502 = Cimiez 36.

549 *As last*. Type as last Rev. +**HI·FIDIVS**. 0.86g (Metcalf 54; 83% Ag) 70°. B 2594; P 1499 (same dies as this); Cimiez 34.

550 *As last*. Obv. as last Rev. **ИI·ᑕIDVS**, fleur. 1.09g (Metcalf 53; 85% Ag) 140°. B 2589 var.; P 1508; Cimiez 38.

551 *As last*. Obv. head l., w. cross before face Rev. **ИEW FI[DIVS]**. 1.14g (Metcalf 55; 86% Ag) 90°. B 2602 = P 1529 = Cimiez 48 (as pl.).

552 *As last*. Type as last, rev. **И[EMFI]ƆIՈ∾**. 1.14g (Metcalf 56; 87% Ag) 140°. Ref. as last.

553 *As last*. Obv. head r., w. cross before face Rev.]**mS**–[. 1.15g (Metcalf 57; 85% Ag) 330°. B 2615; P 1542 (same dies); Cimiez 51.

554 *As last*. Obv. trace of head(?) Rev.]**UIOII**] . 1.12g (Metcalf 58; 86% Ag). Ref. as last.

555 *As last*. Obv. bust r. between 2 crosses Rev. letters **NFDS** (for **N***em***F***i***D***iu***S**) in cruciform monogram. 1.13g (Metcalf 59; 70% Ag) 0°. B 2634 = P 1546 = Cimiez 53.

556 *As last*. Obv. head r., w. cross below Rev. +**ND** w. **I** below and **S** above (for **N***emf* **ID***iu***S**). 1.10g (Metcalf 60; 71% Ag) 290°. B 2652 = P 1559 = Cimiez 57.

557 *As last*. Obv. bust r., w. cross behind Rev. **HEF** (**HE** ligatured, for **NE***m***F***idius*) w. cross above and below. 1.18g (91% Ag; Metcalf analysis and illus. 64, but description and weight 61) 100°. B 2649 = P 1556; Cimiez 59.

558 *As last*. Type as last, but **NEF** (**NE** ligatured). 1.01g (61% Ag; Metcalf analysis and illus. 65, but description and weight 62) 140°. Ref. as last.

559 *As last*. Obv. bust r. w. cross l. and flower(?) r. Rev. **N** surrounded by 4 crosses and 4 pellets. 1.08g (65% Ag; Metcalf analysis and illus. 61, but description and weight 63) 340°. B 2656 = P 1576 (same dies) = Cimiez 64.

539. PG: Grantley 4559; from Rollin.

540. PG: Grantley 4559; from Rollin; ex Nohanent hoard.

541. PG: Berghaus 12.3.1953; ex Bellenberg.

542. PG: Seaby 21.7.1948; ex Glendining 7.7.1948, lot 107; ex Grantley 625; ex Saint-Pierre-les-Etieux hoard.

Most, if not all, of **543–59** must come from the Cimiez hoard, although the provenance is not specifically recorded.

543–4, 546. PG: Lockett III 308; ex Grantley 623; from Rollin.

545. PG: Baldwin 8.10.1968; ex Grantley 623.

547, 549, 551–3, 556, 558. PG: Lockett III 308; ex Grantley 622; from Rollin.

548, 555. PG: Baldwin 23.11.1946.

550. PG: Baldwin 10.5.1947.

554, 559. PG: Baldwin 8.10.1968; ex Grantley 622.

557. PG: Thorburn 9.11.1950.

539 540 541 541*

542 543 544 545 546 547 548

549 550 551 552 558*

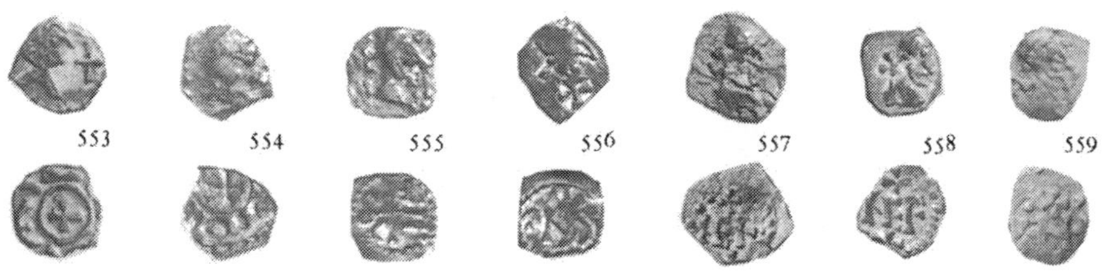

553 554 555 556 557 558 559

MEROVINGIANS (11): SILVER DENIERS

References as on Plate 26.

BURGUNDY AND PROVENCE (cont.)

560 *Marseille*, patrician *Nemfidius*. Same dies as last. 1.12g (93% Ag; Metcalf analysis and illus. 62, but description and weight 64) 70°. Ref. as last. Rev. double struck.

561 *As last*. Same dies. 1.05g (86% Ag; Metcalf analysis and illus. 63, but description and weight 65) 200°. Ref. as last.

562 *As last*. Obv. bust r., w. cross before face Rev. monogram of **NEM** in border. 1.15g (Metcalf 66; 88% Ag) 180°. B 2664, 2767; P 1586 = Cimiez 67.

563 *As last*. Obv. crude bust l., w. cross before face Rev. degenerate monogram of **NEMF**. 0.95g (Metcalf 67; 66% Ag) 200°. B 2667 = P 1519 = Cimiez 70 (pl. 4.83).

564 *As last*. Type as last, variant monogram. 0.96g (Metcalf 68; 80% Ag) 160°. B 2669 = P 1596 = Cimiez 70 (pl. 4.85).

565 *As last*. Type as last, but bust very degenerate, no cross, and similar monogram. 1.08g (Metcalf 69; 77% Ag) 300°. B 2670 = P 1598 = Cimiez 71.

566 *As last*. Type as last, but another monogram variant, pellet above. 1.17g (Metcalf 70; 83% Ag) 270°. Ref. as last.

567 *Marseille*, patrician *Antenor II*(?) Obv. monogram of **ANT** (for ANT*enor*?) Rev. monogram of **ARD**. 0.93g (Metcalf 78; 82% Ag) 130°. B 291 (as Arles); P 2827 (same dies, as uncertain mint); Cimiez 110.

568 *As last*. Same dies. 0.94g (Metcalf 79; 54% Ag) 110°. Ref. as last.

569 *As last*. Same obv. die as last two. Rev. **SM** w. cross above. 1.01g (Metcalf 80; 71% Ag) 240°. B 6263 = P 2832 = Cimiez 111.

570 *Marseille?*, *Ran*... Obv. bust r., w. cross behind Rev. monogram of **RAN** (**AN** ligatured). 1.19g (Metcalf 76; 54% Ag) 200°. B 3189 (as Nîmes) = P 1637 = Cimiez 98. For attribution, see p. 149 above.

571 *Marseille?*, *Pal*... Obv. bust r., w. cross before face Rev. **PAL** (**AL** ligatured, last letter as **V**), w. pellet above and 3 pellets below. 1.15g (Metcalf 77; 58% Ag) 190°. B 3196 (as Nîmes) = Cimiez 103. For attribution, see p. 149 above.

572 *Marseille*. Obv. **M**, w. 2 pellets below (one visible on this specimen) and cross above Rev. **OCΛS** in angles of cross. 1.18g (Metcalf 71; 82% Ag) 60°. B 2756; P 1602 (same dies); Cimiez 87. On the inscription **OCΛS**, see p. 148 above.

573 *As last*. Same dies. 1.14g (Metcalf 72; 77% Ag) 60°. Ref. as last.

574 *As last*. Same dies as last two. 1.09g (Metcalf 73; 75% Ag) 20°. Ref. as last.

575 *As last*. Same obv. die as last three. Rev. **OCA** in 3 angles of cross. 1.02g (Metcalf 74; 75% Ag) 90°. B 2755 = P 1606 = Cimiez 88.

576 *Marseille region*? Obv. bust r., w. cross before face Rev. **VII** in lower quarters of cross ancrée. 1.25g (Metcalf 44; 92% Ag) 340°. B 3051 (as Mainz) = Saint-Pierre-les-Etieux 74; P –; Nohanent 11 (this coin); Bais 320. For attribution, see p. 149 above.

577 *As last*. Type as last, but very degenerate bust l. 1.11g (Metcalf 45; 92% Ag) 180°. B 3045 (as Mainz) = Cimiez 107 (pl. 7.113); P –.

578 *As last*. Type as last, but bust r. 0.91g (Metcalf 46; 70% Ag) 90°. B 3042 (as Mainz) = Cimiez 107 (pl. 6.110); P –.

AQUITAINE

579 *Bourges region*. Uncertain mint and moneyer. Obv.]**OAL**[, head r. Rev.]**ΛCIUΛ**[. 1.04g (Metcalf 15; 93% Ag) 350°. Cf. B 853 = P 1674 (Bourges); Saint-Pierre-les-Etieux 46. For the attribution of this and the next 10 coins to the Bourges region, see note on coin.

580 *As last*. Obv. **Λ**[ ]**ᔕO**, bust r. Rev. +**X**[ ]**DᔕO**. 1.06g (Metcalf 16; 93% Ag) 90°. Cf B 5633–40; P 2258–65.

581 *As last*. Obv. legend indecipherable, helmeted bust r., w. 4 pellets before and 3 pellets behind Rev.]**LAC**[or]**CAL**[? 1.33g (Metcalf 19; 91% Ag) 310°. Ref. as last.

582 *As last*. **VIVΛIIIVCVVIIV**, crude head r. Rev. legend indecipherable. 1.15g (Metcalf 24; 91% Ag) 150°. B –; P –.

583 *As last*. Obv. +**BVPV**[ ]**⊥VD**(?), bust l., w. cross before face Rev. +**Rᔕ**[ ]**IM** (outwardly). 1.13g (Metcalf 14; 93% Ag) 160°. Cf. B 5634; P 2246 and 2411; Plassac 52.

Most, if not all, of **560–75, 577–8** must come from the Cimiez hoard, although the provenance is not specifically recorded.

560, 572. PG: Tinchant 14.4.1947.

561. PG: Baldwin 14.4.1952.

562. PG: Tinchant 22.4.1947.

563, 574. PG: Baldwin 14.4.1952.

564. PG: Lockett III 308; ex Grantley 622; from Rollin.

565. PG: Platt 1.9.1950.

566. PG: Lockett III 315; ex Grantley 622.

567. PG: Lockett III 307; ex Grantley 623; from Rollin.

568. PG: Peus 18.9.1961 (list 105, no. 9).

569, 575. PG: Seaby 21.7.1948; ex Glendining 7.7.1948, lot 107; ex Grantley 625.

570. PG: Lockett III 312; ex Grantley 630; from Rollin.

571. PG: Baldwin 8.10.1968; ex Grantley 626; from Rollin.

573. PG: Baldwin 23.11.1946.

576. PG: Seaby 21.7.1948; ex Glendining 7.7.1948; ex Grantley 625; ex Nohanent hoard.

577–8. PG: Lockett III 309; ex Grantley 623.

579, 582. PG: Baldwin 8.10.1968; ex Grantley 731.

580–1, 583. PG: Lockett III 314; ex Grantley 678.

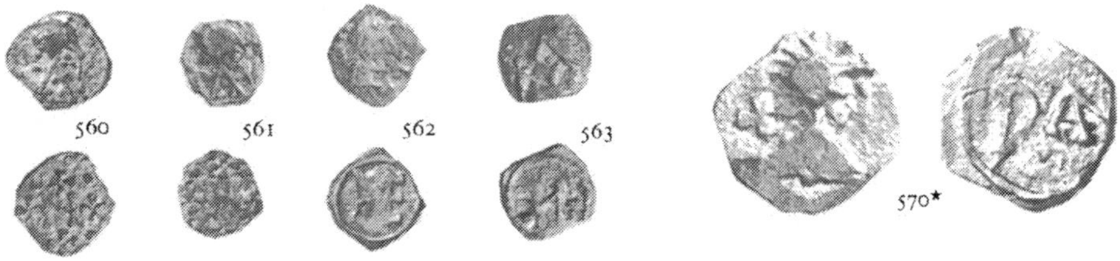

560 561 562 563 570*

564 565 566 567 568 569 570 571

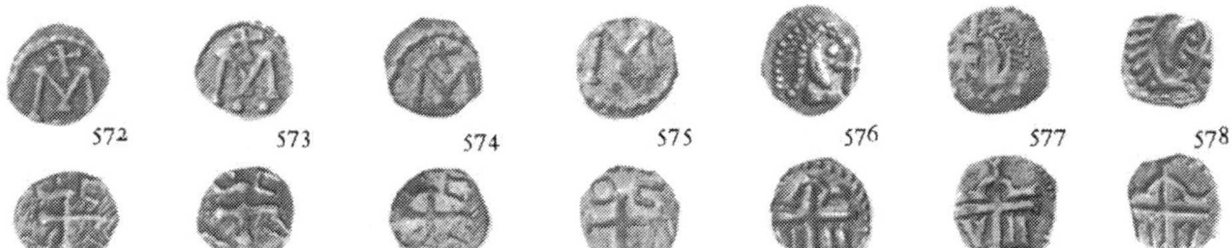

572 573 574 575 576 577 578

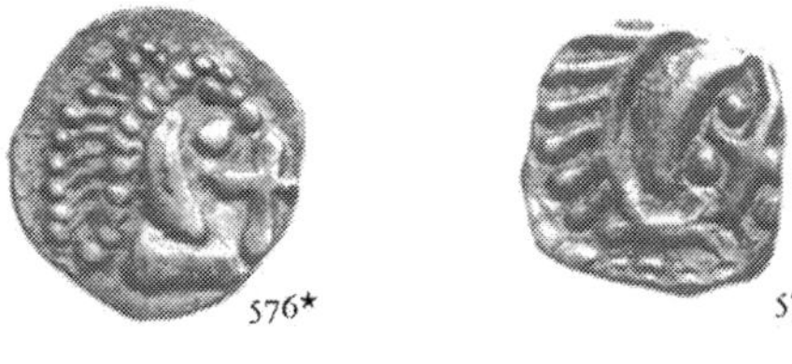

576* 578*

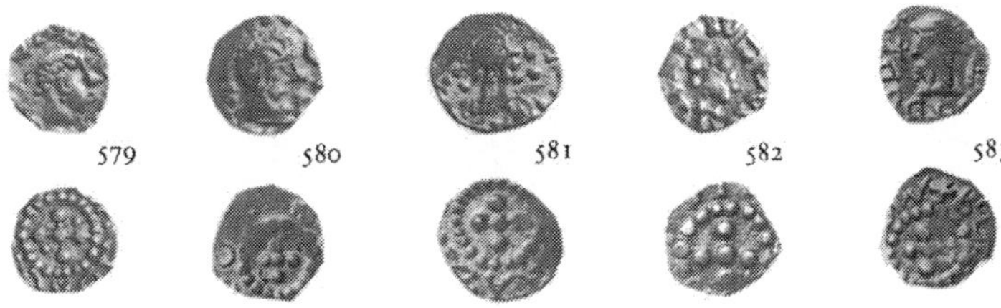

579 580 581 582 583

MEROVINGIANS (12): SILVER DENIERS

References as on Plate 26.

AQUITAINE (cont.)

584 *Bourges region*. Obv. +**~**[ ]**XƎOΛ**, bust r., w. deformed nose Rev. +**ИI**[, w. small pellets around central globule of cross. 0.95 chipped (Metcalf 18; 92% Ag) 90°. B –; P –. See note on coin.

585 *As last*. Obv. +**V~IIVII**[ ]**~**, deformed radiate bust r., w. cross behind Rev. legend indecipherable. 1.09g (Metcalf 22; 91% Ag) 70°. B 6381 var.; P 2251 var.; same dies as Bais 196A and Plassac 66.

586 *As last*. Obv. +**OⲈ**[ ]**LΛTΛⲈ**, fantastic radiate head r. on top of another inverted Rev.]**RIⲈHI~**[. 1.14g (Metcalf 21; 90%) 140°. Plassac 67 (this coin); B 6387 = P 2242 = Cimiez 264 (said to be the same obv. die as this: Lafaurie 1969a, 194); B 438 = 6378 = 6388 = Saint-Pierre-les-Etieux 50. Ancient cut in edge, to test silver? For discussion of the type, see note on coin.

587 *As last*. Obv. legend indecipherable, deformed radiate bust r. w. standing figure before face and **L**(?) behind Rev. +**V**[, additional pellet in each quarter of cross. 1.01g (Metcalf 23; 87% Ag) 350°. B –; P –.

588 *As last*. Obv. +**VXNVΛIIΛIV**, deformed bust r., w. long hair and inverted standing figure(?) in place of face Rev. [**VIIV**]**OVIIMV**[**II~·**]. 1.27g (Metcalf 20; 89% Ag) 0°. Same dies as B 5641 = P 2255 = Plassac 70 and Bais 128; same rev. die as Bais 127 and 127a.

589 *As last*. Two rev. types: **∴OHVIOⲈΛII⁚**, cross of 5 pellets; without inscription, copy of rev. of 'porcupine' sceat. 1.20g (Metcalf 17; 93% Ag) 340°. B –; P –; Plassac 72 (probably this coin). For localization, see note on coin.

Bourges region. For a forgery, see **1477**.

590 *Gournay?* (Indre). Moneyer uncertain. Obv. [+**C**]**OR NA**[**CVS**], nimbate figure of Christ l. on an ass Rev. **PE**[...**LW**]**NO**. 1.13g (Metcalf 13; 93% Ag) 100°. B 5711 = Plassac 40 (this coin); same dies as B 3749 = P 2204 = Plassac 42 and B 5762 = Plassac 41. For the attribution to Gournay near Bourges, see Lafaurie 1969a, 167. For the type, see p. 145 above.

591 *Limoges(?)*, See of, moneyer *Theodoal(d)*. Obv. **ER** (for *Racio ecclesie*) w. cross and 5 pellets in field Rev. +**THEODOAL**. 1.31g (Metcalf 25; 92% Ag) 90°. B 1867 = 3560 = P 826; Bais 134; Plassac no. 76. Ancient cut in edge, to test silver? For attribution, see p. 145 above.

592 *As last*. Type as last, but only two pellets in obv. field? Rev. +**THEO**[. 1.03g chipped (Metcalf 26; 90% Ag) 340°. Ref. as last.

593 *Poitiers*, moneyer *Audolenus*. Obv. +**PEⲈTA** (for *Pectavis*) Rev. +**ΛVDOLN** (**ΛV** ligatured). 1.06g (Metcalf 86; 93%) 110°. B 3616–18; P 2210–13.

594 *Poitiers*, moneyer *Godolaicus*. Obv. +**DECTAVI**[ ] **CIVET** (for *Pectavis civitas*) Rev. **GOCO**[ ]**OMN** (for *Godolaico moneta*), Latin cross with 2 pellets by side and upper arms. 1.09g chipped (Metcalf 27; 89% Ag) 270°. B 3604 var.; P 2197 var.; Plassac 89 (this coin)

595 *Poitiers region*. Uncertain mint and moneyer. Obv. +**PIIIIΛ**[ ]**T~IIII** (partly off flan) Rev. **IIIIIIIIIII**[. Types as last, but head l. 1.02g (Metcalf 28; 61% Ag) 350°. B –; P –. The meaningless legends and poor quality silver suggest that this is a contemporary imitation.

AUSTRASIA AND NEUSTRIA

596 *Metz*. Obv. **ME** (ligatured for *Mettis*) Rev. **D** (for *denarius*) over line. 1.40g (Metcalf 29; 92% Ag) 20°. B 2971 = Saint-Pierre-les-Etieux 66 (this coin); P 2839. The attribution is supported by 3 stray finds from Metz or its environs (Lafaurie 1969a, 173).

597 *Paris*, moneyer uncertain. Obv. +**PARI**[, bust r. Rev.]**CHVGVSI**[cross ancrée w. ends of cross-arms turned down and pellet in each quarter. 0.96g (Metcalf 12; 58% Ag) 110°. B 6308 (this coin); P –.

598 *Paris*. Obv. **PARI~IV~O**, bust r. Rev. cross as last coin, in border broken by small cross and 3 pelleted annulets. 1.02g 230°. B 3426 = P 736 (same dies).

599 *Paris(?)*; *Palace mint*. Obv. [**IN PAL**]**IⲈIO**. 1.25 g (Metcalf 9: 92% Ag). B 3534, 6346 (both same dies as this?); P 697–8; Plassac 47 (same dies as this?); Saint-Pierre-les-Etieux 28 (probably this coin).

600 *Paris region*. Obv. +[ ]**OI**[ ]**O**, diademed bust r. sculptured in dots Rev. as **598**. 1.12g (Metcalf 8: 91% Ag) 330°. B 3428-9, 3445; P 752 = Cimiez 217; Saint-Pierre-les-Etieux 23.

601 *As last*. Obv. head r., w. cross before face Rev. **M**, w. cross above, **E** to l., and **A** to r. 0.99g (Metcalf 85: 46% Ag) 90°. Cf. B 3473–4 = P 897–9 = Cimiez 205–6.

584. PG: Lockett III 314; ex Grantley 678; from Baldwin.

585, 587. PG: Lockett III 312; ex Grantley 678.

586. PG: Lockett III 312; ex Grantley 630; from Keim 1905; ex Lagrange 231; ex Plassac hoard.

588. PG: Lockett III 314; ex Grantley 677; from Rollin 1892.

589. PG: Baldwin 8.10.1968; ex Grantley 736; probably ex Lagrange 378; ex Plassac hoard.

590. PG: Lockett III 314; ex Grantley 677; from Spink 1900.

591, 602. PG: Lockett III 311; ex Grantley 629; from Rollin 1891.

592. PG: Vinchon 17.4.1959.

593. PG: Lockett III 315; ex Grantley 678.

594. PG: Santamaria 8.4.1953 ('Collection mérovingienne'); ex Lagrange 209; ex Plassac hoard.

595. PG: Berghaus 12.3.1953; ex Bellenberg.

596. PG: Lockett III 309; ex Grantley 623; ex Saint-Pierre-les-Etieux hoard.

597. PG: Lockett III 310; ex Grantley 629; from Rollin; ex Vaquer.

598. CCC (*Catalogue* no. 60): Lewis 1891; from Hoffmann sale 2.3.1887, lot 189.

599. PG: Lockett III 311; ex Grantley 629; probably ex Saint-Pierre-les-Etieux hoard. The coin recorded by Belfort (B 3534) from Fillon 1853, pl. 5.4, communicated to him by Lelewel, is almost certainly that from the Fürstenberg collection (Cahn sale 79 (14.12.1932), lot 1175), but *pace* Lafaurie (1969a, 164) that is a different specimen from this, although probably from the same dies.

600. PG: Lockett III 310; ex Grantley 629; from Rollin.

601. PG: Baldwin 8.10.1968; ex Grantley 629.

[*continued overleaf*]

584* 586* 587* 588*

584 585 586 587 588 589 590

591 592 593 594 595 590*

596 597 598 599 600 601

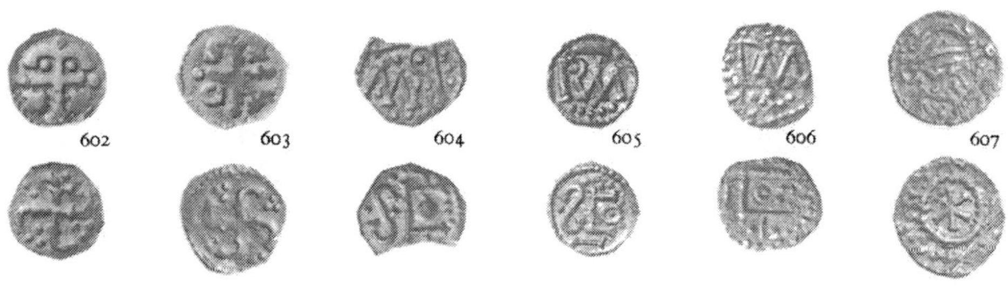

602 603 604 605 606 607

602 *As last.* Obv. cross ancrée w. pellets in upper and saltires in lower quarters. 1.31g (Metcalf 10: 91% Ag). B 3542; P 793; Saint-Pierre-les-Etieux 26; Bais 95.

603 *As last.* Obv. cross ancrée, w. **O** and **A** in lower quarters. 1.14g (Metcalf 11: 92% Ag). B 3540 (this coin?); P 791; Bais 94.

604 *Rheims(?).* Obv. **RM** retrograde Rev. monogram of **SCO** (meaning obscure), w. cross above and pellets in field. 0.85g fragment (Metcalf 32; 88% Ag) 0°. B 3789 var.; P 2852; Cimiez 298. See note on coin.

605 *As last.* Type as last, but rev. retrograde w. bar above and obv. not retrograde. 1.19g (Metcalf 31; 82% Ag) 300°. B 1870 = 3786, 3791; P 2851; Cimiez 299.

606 *As last.* Type as last: crude contemporary forgery in copper. Æ 0.79g (Metcalf 33; 100% Cu) 280°. B –; P –.

607 *Rheims region.* Obv. helmeted bust r. w. confused letter(?) in front Rev. Christogram in wreath surrounded by 4 crosses alternating w. groups of 3 pellets. 1.26g broken and repaired (Metcalf 2; 93% Ag) 180°. B 1278 (as Chalon); P –; Amécourt 1873, pl. 5.151 (found at Buxy, near Chalon). For the attribution, see note on coin.

603. PG: Spink 12.2.1945 . . . possibly ex Amécourt 174; ex Cartier.

604. PG: Franceschi 21.3.1952.

605. PG: Lockett III 315; ex Grantley 742; ex Webb 1895.

606. PG: Lockett III 313; ex Grantley (uncertain lot).

607. PG: Grantley 4559; from Rollin.

MEROVINGIANS (13): SILVER DENIERS

References as on Plate 26.

AUSTRASIA AND NEUSTRIA (cont.)

608 *Tours, abbey of Saint-Martin*, moneyer *Unicter*. Obv. **+SCI MARTIN**, head r. Rev. **+VNICTER**. 1.10g (Metcalf 5; 93% Ag) 270°. B 4573, 6466; P 339; Savonnières 13 (this coin).

609 *Tours?* Obv. deformed monogram of **[T]VRONES** Rev. **]IIVIIVII[** , around barred **S** in border. 0.89g (Metcalf 6; 89% Ag) 50°. B –; P –; Bais 289 var. The designs are related to those found on coins of Tours (cf. obv. Bais 28–30; rev. B 4574 = P 338). This coin has blundered legends and may be a derivative struck elsewhere.

610 *Tours region*. Obv. **]VNI** w. branch or arm in front of head Rev. deformed monogram of Tours. 0.86g chipped (Metcalf 84; 93% Ag) 270°. B 5680, 5661 var. = P 2860 var. The legends of this and the specimens cited could be read as **TNV C**, possibly for *Turonus civi*.

611 *Tours region*. Type as last, no legend visible. 0.92g (Metcalf 88; 89% Ag) 0°. Ref. as last.

612 *Tours/Poitiers region*. Obv. **+HODA~**, large globule surrounded by circle of pellets Rev. pentalpha, w. 6 pellets. 0.96g (Metcalf 7; 92% Ag). Cf. B 3698 = P 2216 = Savonnières 32; Savonnières 31, 37–9. Coins of this design w. legible mint names are known from Chinon, Châteaudun and Poitiers (Lafaurie 1963a, 68–71). The design of a globule in a circle of pellets surrounded by a legend is also found on coins of Saint-Martin of Tours of Pepin and early coins of Charlemagne (MG nos. 19–20 and 150).

613 *Void* (*Meuse*), moneyer *Meferamnus*. Obv. **ИOV[ ] WAIC·** (for *Noventum Vico*) Rev. **+WEFERAMИI**, w. 2 pellets and 2 **V**s in quarters of cross. 1.16g (Metcalf 30; 90% Ag, 2% Au) 70°. B 3228 (this coin), cf. 3222; P –. For the identification with Void (Meuse), called in the Merovingian and Carolingian periods *Novientum super Vidum*, see Duchalais 1852, 239–42. The fabric and general appearance of this coin suggest that it is struck from tremissis dies, perhaps a contemporary forgery, and not a true denier.

UNCERTAIN MINT AND REGION

614 *Uncertain ecclesiastical mint* (?Senlis). Obv. **ECL** (for *Ecclesia*), w. pellets in field Rev. confused letters. 1.20g (Metcalf 82; 62% Ag) 270°. B 4561 = P 2805 = Cimiez 112; Bais 275 var. (rev. **ID EPS**). For suggested attributions, see note on coin.

615 *Uncertain ecclesiastical mint*. Obv. **+RACLO ECLIS**, w. **I** and **ω** in field Rev. cross pattée, w. pellet in one quarter. 1.22g (Metcalf 81; 93% Ag). B 4550 = P 345 (same dies); B 3706 = Plassac 128 (this coin). Lafaurie has suggested, on grounds of epigraphy, that this coin belongs to a mint in the Poitiers region (Lafaurie 1969a, 203).

616 *Uncertain mint*, moneyer *Apalsar*. Rev. **+APALSAR** (retrograde). 0.84g (Metcalf 92; 88% Ag) 120°. B 5753 (this coin); P –. The design of a globule in a circle of pellets is known on coins from the Tours/Poitiers region (see **612** above).

617 *Uncertain mint* (*Cudin*...?), moneyer *Hedelmaric*. Obv. **+HEDELMARIC** Rev. **+CVDIN[ ]VT**. 1.19g (Metcalf 83; 88% Ag) 80°. B 2105 (as Laon rev. **+CVDINV[ ]VI**), 6359–60 (as Poitiers); P 2240–1 (as Poitiers); Cimiez 265.

618 *Uncertain mint*. Obv. +[**]AINL**, crude bust r. Rev. **]OИMVC** cross on forked base, w. 2 pellets at ends of other arms. 0.88g (Metcalf 97; 92% Ag) 290°. B –; P –; Plassac 129 (this coin). The rev. has affinities w. coins of the Poitiers region (cf. **594**) and Rennes (Ille-et-Vilaine) (Bais 46).

619 *Uncertain mint*. Obv. **~ECI·T·IIGC>** (outwards counter-clockwise), degenerate bust r. Rev. **]MAMONE[** (outwards counter-clockwise). 1.31g (Metcalf 95; 90% Ag) 130°. B –; P –; Plassac 141 (this coin).

620 *Uncertain mint*. Obv. legend illegible, bust r., w. annulet below, pearls under and surrounding shoulders, and annulet before face Rev. **+N∵IIO[ ]T**. 1.01g (Metcalf 96; 93% Ag) 180°. B –; P –.

621 *Uncertain mint*. Obv. **]R[ ]S[** Rev. **+M[ ]M**, w. **Λ**(?) to l. of cross. 0.90g (Metcalf 100; 95% Ag) 0°. B –; P –.

622 *Uncertain mint*. Obv. **]AIAII:II[** , facing head Rev. **IA⁝E[ ]A⁝E** systematically around cross pattée w. pellet in each quarter. 1.10g (Metcalf 99; 91% Ag) 80°. Cf. B 62 = 6628 (found at Blois); P –.

623 *Uncertain mint*. Obv. **RIPΠIOƧA** (outwards), facing head? Rev. **RAΓIVI OƆ** (outwards counter-clockwise). 1.07g (92% Ag; see note on coin) 0°. B –; P –.

624 *Uncertain mint*. Obv. **A**, w. annulet below surrounded by pellets and pellets in field Rev. **S**, w. **Ɔ** to l. and **T** to r. 1.13g (Metcalf 89; 82% Ag) 200°. B 5692 var. = P 2789 var.; Bais 274, 274a; Le Gentilhomme 1937, no. 13; cf. B 4585 = P 343 (as Tours?).

608. PG: Lockett III 313; ex Grantley 634; from Rollin; ex Savonnières hoard.

609. PG: Spink 12.2.1945; from Bourgey; ex Ratto sale 9.12.1930, lot 2456.

610. PG: MMAG Basel 30.6.1959.

611. PG: Lockett III 315; ex Grantley 678.

612. PG: Lockett III 312; ex Grantley 630; ex Montagu 385; found at 'Eck', presumably Eck-en-Wiel, close to Tiel in modern Gelderland on the lower Rhine.

613. PG: Baldwin 8.10.1968; ex Grantley 626; from Rollin; ex Amécourt 216.

614. PG: Vinchon 17.1.1959.

615. PG: Lockett III 313; ex Grantley 634; from Rollin; ex Lagrange 287; ex Plassac hoard.

616. PG: Lockett III 314; ex Grantley 677; from Rollin 1892.

617. PG: Lockett III 312; ex Grantley 630; from Gavet sale.

618. PG: Baldwin 8.10.1968; ex Grantley 740; ex Lagrange 339; ex Plassac hoard.

619. PG: Lockett III 314; ex Grantley 678; ex Lagrange 332; ex Plassac hoard.

620. PG: Lockett III 318; ex Grantley 678.

621, 623. PG: Baldwin 8.10.1968; ex Grantley 731.

622. PG: MMAG Basel 15.11.1950.

624. PG: Lockett III 313; ex Grantley 678.

[*continued overleaf*]

608 609 610 611 612 613

608★

614 615 616 617

618 619 620 621 622 623 624

625 626 627 628 629 630 631 632

616★

631★

625 *Uncertain mint.* Obv. **A**, w. 3 pellets above and to l., and one or more below and to r. Rev. globule w. protruding rays (degenerate head?), cross above and pellets in field. 0.79g fragment 90°. Cf. B 5697.

626 *Uncertain mint.* Obv. **A** w 2 pellets to l. and 3 to r. Rev. **ꟺ** and **Λ** beneath inverted anchor? 1.29g (Metcalf 90; 91% Ag) 190°. B 5698 (this coin); P –; Bais no. 272; cf. B 5705 = P 2787. Illus. Amécourt 1868c, 308, no. 3.

627 *Uncertain mint.* Obv. **NH·V[ ]ᔓƆ**, degenerate monogram? Rev. cross w. **A** and **M** to l. and r. and small cross above. 0.99g (Metcalf 91; 92% Ag) 190°. Cf. B 5716, 5690 (found at Domburg); P –. The Domburg find appears to be the most literate specimen and reads **TROMOSC**.

628 *Uncertain mint.* Obv. **C̄Ā** Rev. **m̄** or **IE**. 1.30g (Metcalf 87; 92% Ag) 190°. Cf. Nohanent 17; Bais 131–2, 279?

629 *Uncertain mint.* Obv.]**MOꟷΛ**[Rev. +**ADOᔓII**. 0.87g (Metcalf 98; 94% Ag) 0°. B –; P –.

630 *Uncertain mint.* Obv. cross w. 2 pellets at each end giving the appearance of bones Rev. woven design and 5 pellets. 1.27g (Metcalf 93; 92% Ag). B 6692 (this coin); P –.

631 *Uncertain mint.* Obv. bird l. in torque Rev. cross ancrée with 2 cross-bars and pellets in field. 1.23g (Metcalf 94; 74% Ag) 200°. B 6697 = P 2902 = Cimiez 242; cf. B 5677. The obv. is a close copy of an Anglo-Saxon sceat (*BMC* type 38; Rigold 1977a, Series O) and the rev. has the Parisian cross ancrée. The coin must be from northern Francia or Frisia.

632 *Uncertain mint.* Obv. bust l. in pelleted border Rev.]**EVOΓ**] , cross pattée and pellets. 0.62g (Metcalf 40; *c.* 25% Ag) 350°. B –; P –. Possibly a derivative of the Continental Runic sceattas (**639–45**).

625. FM: Trinity College 1937; ex J. Battely *c.* 1740; ex Archd. J. Battely 1708; found at Reculver, Kent. Illus. Battely 1745, pl. 6.

626. PG: Lockett III 314; ex Grantley 677; from Schulman 1899; ex Amécourt (uncertain lot).

627. PG: Lockett III 314; ex Grantley 746.

628. PG: Lockett III 314; ex Grantley 678.

629. PG: Seaby 21.7.1948; from Glendining 7.7.1948, lot 107; ex Grantley 625.

630. PG: Lockett III 315; ex Grantley 677; from Florange; ex 'Collection F.H.'.

631. PG: Lockett III 314; ex Grantley 629; from Keim 1903.

632. PG: Baldwin 8.10.1968; ex Grantley 731.

FRISIA: SILVER DENIERS OR 'SCEATTAS'

Principal references are as on Plate 26, but Brooke = Brooke 1950; North = North 1980; and *SCBI* = *SCBI* Cambridge. Reference is also made to particular coins in hoards: Franeker = Dirks 1870, pls. A–C; Hallum = Dirks 1870, pls. C–D; 'Franceschi' hoard = Metcalf 1969b. All coins are silver. They are conventionally referred to as 'sceattas', although this was not their true name (above, p. 149). Their attributions and chronology are discussed above (pp. 151–4).

'Madelinus' type (B –; cf. B 1794ff.)
A continuation in silver of the immobilized coins in the name of the Dorestad moneyer Madelinus (**494–5**). Last quarter of 7th century.

633 Obv. **VOEVAATII** (retrograde), bust l. Rev. **IᔕIAIVI**. 1.02g 10°.

Interlace type (B 5990–9; P 2885, 2888–9)
Find distribution suggests a mint in the Lower Rhineland, rather than the traditional Maastricht (see note on coin). Probably struck *c.* 710–50.

634 0.83g (Metcalf 34; 86% Ag). Franeker 37; Hallum 16.
635 0.90g (Metcalf 35; 42% Ag). Ref. as last.

Star of David type (B 5737–43, 5746–7; P 2876–7)
Find distribution suggests a mint in the Lower Rhineland or central Frisia, not the traditional Herstal. Contemporary with the Interlace type.

636 0.93g (Metcalf 42; 79% Ag). Franeker 28; Hallum 22.
637 1.15g (Metcalf 43, but wrong description; 81% Ag). Ref. as last.
638 *Intersecting As and petal type.* 1.28 g (Metcalf 41; 92% Ag). B 5704 = P 2878–9 = Plassac 159–60 (same dies); cf. B 5687–9, 6656; P 2880–1. Lafaurie (1969a, 208) has suggested that this may be the forerunner of the Star of David type, although none is recorded from Frisia.

Continental Runic type (Rigold Series D; *BMC AS* 2c, 8, 10, 50; Brooke 9; North 50, 163, 168–9, 172)
These coins, struck *c.* 700–10, copy the obverse of the English Series C, some retaining the runic inscription *Apa* and the **A** behind the bust, but they are distinguished by their cross-and-pellets reverse design. Their find distribution suggests an origin on or south of the Lower Rhine. The legends are often meaningless and their reproduction can only be approximate.

639 **NW**. 1.27g (Metcalf 36; 92% Ag) 90°. *SCBI* –.
640 **ΓᛚΓ**(?). 1.25g 210°. *SCBI* 231.
641 **]IИ**. 1.05g (Metcalf 37; 92% Ag) 40°. *SCBI* –.
642 **[a]pa** (runes). 0.73g (Metcalf 39; 90% Ag) 290°. *SCBI* –.
643 **WΛ**. 0.83g (Metcalf 38; 92% Ag) 270°. *SCBI* –.
644 Inscription off flan. 0.46g 0°.
645 Degraded bust, w. large eye in lozenge? 0.54g 150°. *SCBI* –; cf. Hill 1953, pl. 6.1.

For a possible derivative of this type, see **632**.

'Porcupine' types (Rigold Series E; *BMC AS* 4–6: Brooke 7–8; North 45–9, 155–6)
The most common 'sceattas' in Frisian and Frankish hoards and they often occur in English finds. The classification is that of Metcalf 1966a, which defines the nine main classes present in the Aston Rowant, Hallum and Franeker hoards, but not the many contemporary derivatives which borrow elements from one or more of these. The earliest varieties, those represented in the Aston Rowant hoard, were probably struck *c.* 690/700–710.

Aston Rowant varieties

646 *Class G.* 1.27g/19.6gr. 60°. *SCBI* 241; Saint-Pierre-les-Etieux 95; Bais 309A.
647 *As last.* 1.13g/17.4gr. 120°. *SCBI* 243; other ref. as last.
648 *As last.* 0.68g/10.5gr. worn 160°. *SCBI* –; other ref. as last. Illus. Metcalf 1966a, pl. 16.39.
649 *As last.* 1.26g/19.4gr. 270°. *SCBI* –; other ref. as last.
650 *VICO type.* 1.20g/18.5gr. 0°. *SCBI* 238; Saint-Pierre-les-Etieux 98; Bais 309e.
651 *As last.* 1.12g/17.3gr. 230°. *SCBI* 242; other ref. as last.
652 *Derivative of VICO type?* 1.03g/15.6gr. chipped. *SCBI* 239; cf. *BMC AS* 8.60 (= Metcalf 1966a, pl. 15.9). The obv. also has affinities w. Class A, cf. Hallum 6, 'Franceschi' hoard 1–4.
653 *Class J, 'plumed bird' type.* 1.17g/18.1gr. 90°. *SCBI* 246; Cimiez 323 (= Le Gentilhomme 1938a, pl. 4.60).
654 *As last.* 1.16g/17.9gr. 270°. *SCBI* 247; other ref. as last.
655 *As last.* 1.22g/18.8gr. corroded 240°. *SCBI* –; other ref. as last. Illus. Rigold and Metcalf 1977, pl. 1.12.

633. PG: Lockett III 315.
634. PG: Lockett III 315; ex Grantley (uncertain lot).
635. PG: Baldwin 22.5.1971; ex Grantley (uncertain lot).
636. PG: Lockett III 314: ex Carlyon-Britton I 160.
637. PG: Lockett III 314; ex Grantley 738.
638. PG: Franceschi 10.1.1957.
639, 641–2. PG: Baldwin 8.10.1968; ex Grantley 731.
640, 646, 650, 652–3, 660. FM: Trinity College 1937; ex J. Battely *c.* 1740; ex Archd. J. Battely 1708; found at Reculver, Kent. Illus. Battely 1745, pls. 6–7.
643. PG: Platt 1.9.1950.
644. PG: Baldwin 14.4.1952.
645. PG: Baldwin 8.10.1968; ex Grantley (uncertain lot).
647. FM: Henderson 1933.
648, 662. FM: Miss F. M. McCormick 1975; ex Miss D. F. Conybeare; ex Revd. E. Conybeare; found near Barrington, Cambs.
649. FM: MAA; ex Ridgeway 1926.
651. FM: Duncanson 1930; ex Smart.
654. FM: Henderson 1933; from Spink *c.* 1888.
655. FM: St Neots U.D.C. 1965; St Neots Priory (Hunts.) excavations 1963 (*Proc. Camb. Antiq. Soc.* 59 (1966), p. 41).

[*continued overleaf*]

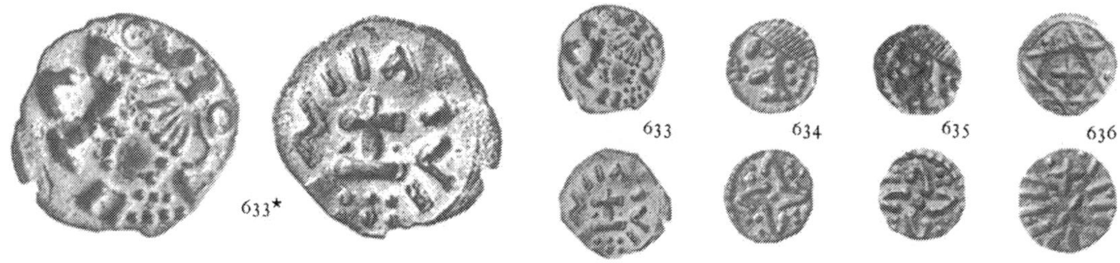

633★ 633 634 635 636

637 638 639 640 641 634★

642 643 644 645 646 647 648 649 650

650★ 651 652 653 654 655

656 657 658 659 660 661 662 663 664

PLATE 30 (*cont.*)

Hallum varieties

656 *Class A.* 1.08g/16.7gr. 320°. *SCBI* 244; Hallum 8.

657 *As last.* 1.13g/17.4gr. 160°. *SCBI* –; other ref. as last.

658 *Derivative of Class C.* 1.17g/18.0gr. 300° *SCBI* 245; Hallum 1.

659 *Derivative of Class E.* 1.44g/22.3gr. 220°. *SCBI* 240; cf. Hallum 10; 'Franceschi' hoard 18–19; *SCBI* Glasgow 30 (same rev. die, but obv. derivative of Class A).

Franeker varieties

660 *Class F.* 0.60g/9.2gr. broken. *SCBI* 983 (as a plated forgery, but subsequent analysis by the BM Conservation Laboratory shows it to have a silver core); Franeker 15.

661 *Derivative of Class B?* 0.86g/13.2gr. *SCBI* 237; cf. Franeker 5 and 10; rev. of Cimiez 322 (= Le Gentilhomme 1938a, pl. 4.60).

Other varieties

662 0.76g/11.7gr. *SCBI* –; Cimiez 322 (= Le Gentilhomme 1938a, pl. 4.51); 'Franceschi' hoard 28–9; Metcalf 1966a, pl. 16.34–8 (38 = this coin).

663 0.90g/13.9gr. (87% Ag: see note on coin). *SCBI* –; ref. as last.

'*Woden/monster*' *type* (Rigold Series X; *BMC AS* 31; Brooke 27; North 16–17)
Found in large numbers in the Hallum and Terwispel hoards from central Frisia and prominent in Danish finds. Probably struck from *c.* 715.

664 1.02g/15.7gr. 90°. *SCBI* 261; Hallum 29; Cimiez 327 (= Le Gentilhomme 1938a, pl. 4.74 var.).

656, 661. FM: Henderson 1933; from Spink 1.10.1888.

657. FM: MAA; purchased 1936.

658. FM: Henderson 1936; ex 'Major Davies collection'.

659. FM: provenance unrecorded.

663. PG: Tinchant 15.12.1952.

664. FM: Henderson 1936; from Spink *c.* 1888.

ANGLO-SAXONS (1)

Principal references are: *BMC AS* (ref. to types, not coin numbers), *BMC AS* (*Hill*) = Hill 1953 (continuing the *BMC AS* numbering of types), Rigold = Rigold 1960, *SCBI* = *SCBI* Cambridge, and Sutherland = Sutherland 1948.

EARLY GOLD COINS, *c.* 590–*c.* 675

665 is a solidus and **666–9** are commonly called 'thrymsas' but probably correspond to the shillings of the law codes. For a forgery of a late 6th-century 'thrymsa', see **1479**.

665 *Solidus*, mid 7th century. Obv. **ƆИAT TAVC** Rev. **ITORT TA[ ]G, COШOƆ**. 4.14g/63.9gr. pierced and part of mount adhering (SG 13.46: 47% Au) 270°. *SCBI* 217; Grierson 1953c; Stewart 1978, no. A93 (this coin). Probably intended as an ornamental piece. The obv. is copied from an imperial solidus of the late 4th century, and the rev. from a solidus of Heraclius (610–41).

666 *Wuneetton type*. Rev. **N[ ]V□W**. 1.30g/20.1gr (SG 18.86: 97% Au) 90°. *SCBI* –; Sutherland, class IV iii; Stewart 1978, no. A97 (this coin). This type was not represented in the Crondall hoard, unlike the *Witmen* type from which it is probably derived. The coin is of unusually fine gold.

667 *Two Emperors type*. 1.27g/19.6gr. (SG 13.00: 41% Au) 300°. *SCBI* 218; Sutherland, class II v; Stewart 1978, no. A99. Coins of this type are less fine than those in the Crondall hoard and were probably struck *c.* 750–70. The prototypes are imperial coins of the late 4th century. *York type*. For two forgeries based on 'thrymsas' of this type, see **1480–1**.

Transitional pale gold shillings (*c.* 660–*c.* 675)

668 *Pada* (in runes in rev. field). Obv. **ITIIC** Rev. **MIZƆTOT TATM**. Pale *A/* 1.29g/19.9gr. (SG 11.46: 18% Au) 300°. *SCBI* 219; Sutherland –; Rigold P IIA.1; Stewart 1978, no. A111 (this coin). The prototype is probably Constantinian, the obv. legend representing a degeneration of a final . . . **IVNNC** (Rigold, p. 14).

669 *Pada* (in runes inserted into rev. legend). Obv. **ƆNCA VNAVC** Rev. **NOI pada ANVSPFAV**. Pale *A/* 1.25g/19.2gr. (SG 11.02: 10% Au) 0°. *SCBI* 220; Sutherland, class VI iii; Rigold P III.2; Stewart 1978, no. A113. The prototype is probably a late 4th-century coin of Valentinian I or Gratian (Rigold, p. 14).

EARLY SILVER PENNIES OR 'SCEATTAS', *c.* 675–*c.* 750

The classification by series is that of Rigold 1960 and 1977a, and is set out on pp. 170–9 above.

PRIMARY AND INTERMEDIATE SERIES, *c.* 675–*c.* 710

Series Va

Early transitional series, with degeneration of *Varimundus mone*, derived from a Merovingian issue. **671** may be a pale gold shilling.

670 Obv. **O∽ AV∽** Rev. **+TMV∾ИMC**. Æ 1.24g/19.1gr. (SG 10.17: 0% Au) 0°. *SCBI* –; Belfort 3303 (this coin); Sutherland –; Rigold VB8 (this coin).

671 Obv. **OTV AV∽** Rev. **MII∽VMI∽V**. Pale *A/*/Æ 1.04g/16.0gr. worn (SG 10.59: 1.5% Au; Isoprobe analysis: 8% Au, Metcalf 1978, no. G101) 0°. *SCBI* –; Belfort 3305 (this coin); Sutherland –; Rigold VB9 (this coin).

Series A

Obv. **TIC** before and **A** behind a radiate bust r. Rev. **TT/O/II** on standard w. fantail above and cross below. The coins (all *BMC AS* 2a) have been divided by Rigold (1960) into early (A1 and A2) and later (A3) on grounds of style and weight. A2 was present in large numbers in the Hougham (Kent) hoard *c.* 1780, which may be the ultimate source of some of those here.

672 1.30g/20.1gr. 340°. *SCBI* 223; Rigold A2.4.
673 1.29g/19.9gr. 180°. *SCBI* 228; Rigold A2.6.
674 1.27g/19.5gr. 180°. *SCBI* 227; Rigold A2.7.
675 1.27g/19.5gr. 240°. *SCBI* 222; Rigold A2.10.
676 1.29g/19.9gr. 180°. *SCBI* 224; Rigold A2.11.
677 1.15g/17.7gr. 0°. *SCBI* 225; Rigold A2.12.
678 1.27g/19.5gr. 190°. *SCBI* 229; Rigold A2.19.
679 1.02g/15.7gr. chipped 270°. *SCBI* 230; Rigold A2.21.
680 1.27g/19.6gr. 240°. *SCBI* 221; Rigold A3.1.
681 1.11g/17.1gr. worn 0°. *SCBI* 226; Rigold A3.6.

665. FM: Emmanuel College 1957.

666. FM: Grierson and University Purchase Fund 1982; from Sotheby 22.7.1982, lot 212; from Seaby (*SCMB* Feb. 1976, no. G135).

667, 681, 684, 686. FM: Trinity College 1937; ex J. Battely *c.* 1740; ex Archd. J. Battely 1708; found at Reculver, Kent. Illus. Battely 1745, pls. 6–7, and from this in Roach Smith 1850, pl. 7.

668. FM: Duncanson 1930; ex Smart.

669. FM: Friends 1955; ex Lockett I 207; ex Grantley 748; ex Robinson 180.

670. PG: Baldwin 2.7.1968; ex Grantley 741; ex Amécourt 201; ex Sivard.

671. PG: Baldwin 8.10.1968; ex Grantley 741; ex Amécourt (not identified in sale); ex Sivard.

672, 674–5. FM: Young 1936.

673. FM: Henderson 1933.

676. FM: Spink *c.* 1902; ex Halliday 183.

677. FM: Young 1936; ex Carlyon-Britton I 152.

678–80. FM: Young 1936; ex Carlyon-Britton I 141.

[*continued overleaf*]

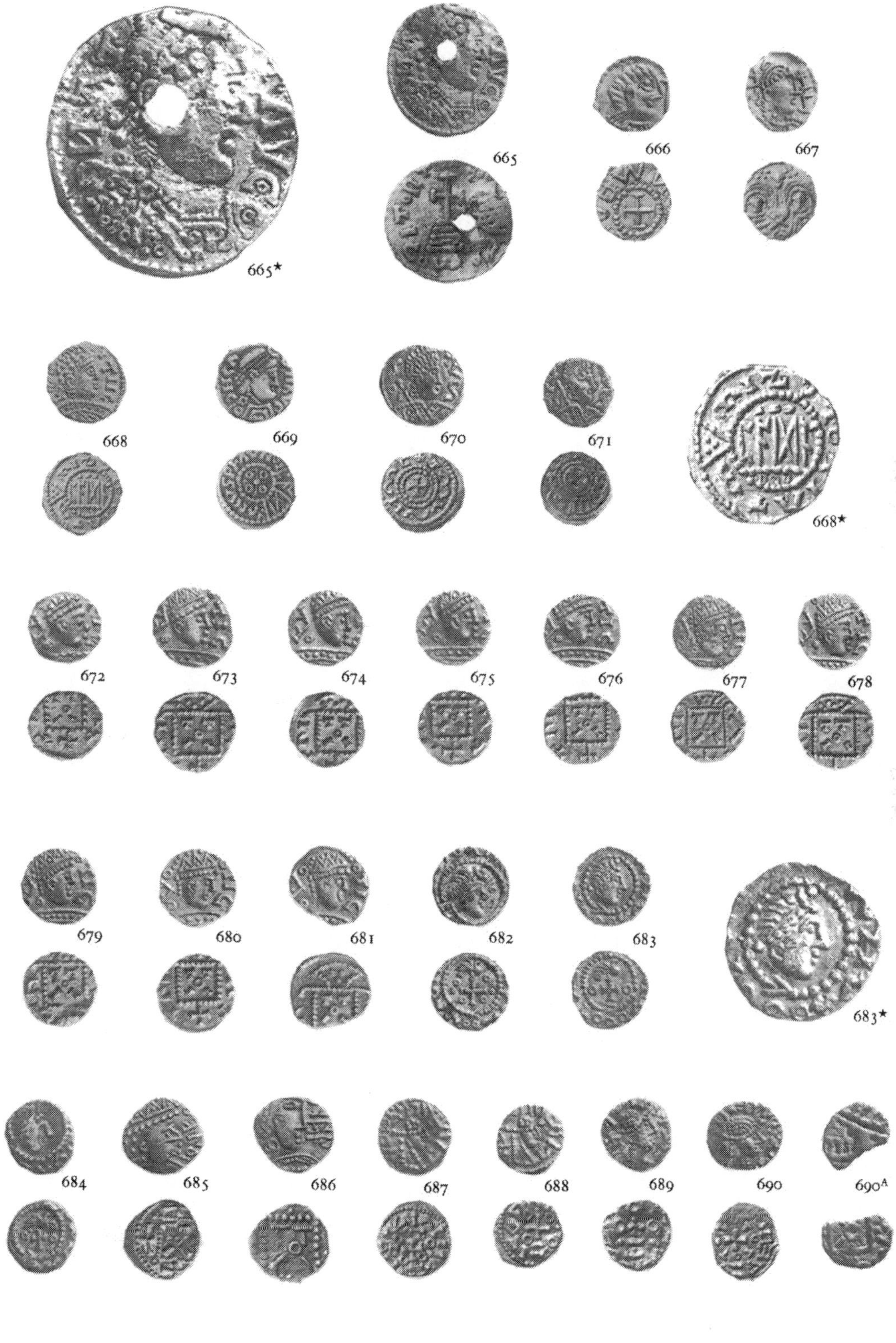

665★ 665 666 667

668 669 670 671 668★

672 673 674 675 676 677 678

679 680 681 682 683 683★

684 685 686 687 688 689 690 690A

Series B

Obv. diademed head or bust Rev. bird on cross (occasionally cross on steps) with combination of pellets, annulets and crosses. The inner ring on obv. and rev. is a torque of pellets w. a triangular terminal.

682 Obv. **[TAV]~AM[VHVA–]** Rev. **ooVA~[VAM VAII]VAo**. 1.12g/17.3gr. 270°. *SCBI* 250; *BMC AS* 27b; Rigold BIB.2b.

683 Obv. **oTA[V–V]AHVAoo** Rev. **OTA( )AVoo**. 1.07g/16.5gr. 90°. *SCBI* 249; *BMC AS* 27b; Rigold BIc.5.

684 Both legends a series of **A**s and **V**s. 1.21g/18.7gr. worn and part of mount(?) adhering 0°. *SCBI* 251; *BMC AS* 27b; Rigold BII.10.

Series C

Similar to Series A but with runic inscriptions on the obv., probably representing the names of moneyers. The type is divided between two series, C and R.

685 *As*(?) 1.17g/18.1gr. 90°. *SCBI* 232; *BMC AS* 2 'runic'; Rigold R1y or 1z.

686 *Epa*. 1.28g/19.8gr. 180°. *SCBI* 233; *BMC AS* 2 'runic'; Rigold R1z.

Series D. Continental Runic series. Frisian, see **639–45**.

Series E. 'Porcupine' series. Frisian, see **646–63**.

Series F

Obv. diademed bust r., w. pellets for hair and drapery Rev. cross-on-steps w. annulets, and on later coins **TT/II** added from standard type of Series A.

687 Pale *AV* 1.15g/17.7gr. (Isoprobe analysis: 9/11% Au and 85% Ag, Metcalf 1978, no. G102) 0°. *SCBI* –; *BMC AS* 24a.

688 1.12g/17.3gr. (Isoprobe analysis: 92% Ag, Metcalf 1978, no. G103) 270°. *SCBI* –; *BMC AS* 24a.

689 1.10g/17.0gr. (Isoprobe analysis: 93% Ag, Metcalf 1978, no. G105) 0°. *SCBI* –; *BMC AS* 24a.

690 With **T** in each quarter of rev. 1.07g/16.5gr. (Isoprobe analysis: 92% Ag, Metcalf 1978, no. G104) 90°. *SCBI* –; *BMC AS* 24b.

Series –

690A *Degraded 'Ver' type*. Obv. **VE[** (retrograde), stylized bust l. Rev. standard w. fantail r. 0.78g/12.0gr. fragment 220°. *BMC AS* (*Hill*) pl. 6.2; *SCBI* –; Blackburn and Bonser 1984a.

682. FM (*Catalogue 1867*, no. 12): Babington 1866.

683. FM: Henderson 1933; acq. *c*. 1885(?).

685. FM: Young 1936; ex Carlyon-Britton I 152; found near Cambridge.

687. PG: Spink 18.1.1959.

688–90. PG: Baldwin 8.10.1968; ex Grantley 736, 742 and 742 respectively.

690A. PG: J. Basham (finder) 1984; found at Springfield, near Chelmsford, Essex, June 1982. See Blackburn and Bonser 1984a.

ANGLO-SAXONS (2)

References as on Plate 31.

EARLY SILVER PENNIES OR 'SCEATTAS', *c.* 680–*c.* 750 (cont.)

SECONDARY SERIES, *c.* 710–*c.* 750

Series H ('Hamwic' series)

The coins here are all of *BMC AS* 49, with a face surrounded by bosses and a fantastic bird walking r. The series was probably struck at Southampton (*Hamwic*) where large numbers have been found in excavations (see p. 169 above).

691 0.93g/14.4gr. 40°. *SCBI* 258.
692 0.98g/15.1gr. 160°. *SCBI* 259.
693 0.94g/14.5gr. 340°. *SCBI* 260.

Series J

694 *Diademed bust/bird-on-cross.* 0.93g/14.35gr. 90°. *SCBI* 253; *BMC AS* 27a; Rigold BIIIA.3. Possibly a contemporary copy of the Primary series B; the Aston Rowant hoard contained some coins of the BIIIA (Kent 1972b).
695 *As last.* 0.98g/15.1gr. chipped 90°. *SCBI* 252; *BMC AS* 27; Rigold BIIIB.7.
696 *Confronting busts/array of 4 flying birds.* 0.91g/14.04gr. *SCBI* Mack 321 (this coin); *BMC AS* 37. The rev. design has parallels in contemporary ornamental metalwork (Morehart 1970).

Series K

The coins here are all of *BMC AS* 32a, with on the obverse a diademed bust holding a cross and on the reverse a wolf-whorl. The 'wolf' types have been the subject of a stylistic analysis (Metcalf and Walker 1967) and tentatively associated with mints in Kent and in the S. Midlands (Metcalf 1984a, 38).

697 *Wolf-whorl r., with two legs.* 0.95g/14.7gr. 0°. *SCBI* 254; Metcalf and Walker 1967, no. 9(b) (group AB = Kentish?).
698 *Wolf-whorl l., no legs.* 1.07g/16.5gr. 270°. *SCBI* 255; Metcalf and Walker 1967, no. 31(a) (indeterminate group = S. Midlands copy of Kentish style?).
699 *As last* but around wolf a linear torque terminating in a small head above wolf's head. 1.00g/15.4gr. 270°. *SCBI* –; cf. Metcalf and Walker 1967, no. 36 (imitation? of group EF).

Series L ('London' series)

700 *Bust r., facing figure in boat(?) holding two long crosses.* **LƆNDONIΛ**. 0.92g/14.1gr. 200°. *SCBI* Mack 339 (this coin); *BMC AS* 12.
701 *As last.* **ՈNIOIU** (blundered *Lundonia*). 0.87g/13.4gr. *SCBI* –; *BMC AS* 12. Same rev. and probably same obv. die as *BMC AS* no. 91 (Metcalf's 'Hwiccian' style, but see pp. 182–3 above).

Series M

702 *Hound/spiral branch* (counter-clockwise). 1.12g/17.3gr. 0°. *SCBI* 257; *BMC AS* 45.
703 *As last,* but branch clockwise. 0.69g/10.6 gr. chipped 0°. *SCBI* 257; *BMC AS* 45.

Series N

Obv. two standing figures with a cross Rev. mythical beast r., possibly a griffin, looking backwards. Metcalf has identified two principal styles, which he suggests might represent two mints (Metcalf 1972a).

704 *Figures confronting.* 1.02g/15.7gr. 270°. *SCBI* 263; *BMC AS* 41a; Metcalf 1977, pl. 1.C.
705 *Figures facing, w. heads turned towards one another.* 1.10g/17.0gr. 320°. *SCBI* 264; *BMC AS* 41b/a; Metcalf 1977, pl. 1.D.
706 *As last?,* but beast l. 0.97g/15.0gr. worn 340°. *SCBI* 265; *BMC AS* 41b/a?; Metcalf 1977, pl. 1.E.

Series O

706A *Face l. in wreath and pelleted border/facing figure w. moustache, in boat(?) holding two long crosses.* 0.30g/4.6gr. fragment 160°. *SCBI* –; *BMC AS* 21. Same dies as *BMC AS* no. 108.

Series Q

707 *Bust w. blundered runic inscription* (**eu**?)/*beast walking r., w. trifurcate tail.* 0.68g/10.5gr. 40°. *SCBI* Mack 327 (this coin); *BMC AS (Hill)* 73; Ruding 1840, pl. 2.15. This coin combines the angular variety of Series Q with an obv. copied from Series R.

Series R

Type as Series C, but cruder design, the runic legends often blundered and the silver much debased (Rigold 1960, 17). Its distribution is essentially East Anglian. They are all *BMC AS* 2 'runic'.

691. FM: Young 1936; ex Carlyon-Britton I 171; found at Dorchester, Dorset.

692–3. FM: Young 1936; ex Carlyon-Britton I 171.

694–5, 697–8, 702–6, 718. FM: Trinity College 1937; ex J. Battely *c.* 1740; ex Archd. J. Battely 1708; found at Reculver, Kent. Illus. Battely 1745, pls. 6–7, and from this in Roach Smith 1850, pl. 7.

696. FM: Grierson 1983; from Spink 22.7.1983 (*NCirc* June 1983, no. 3887); ex Mack (not in sales); from Spink 2.7.1947.

699, 701, 710–11. FM: Sorenson 1983; from Granta Stamp and Coin Shop, Feb. 1983; found near Cambridge. See Blackburn and Sorenson 1984.

700. FM: Grierson 1983; from Spink 22.7.1983 (*NCirc* June 1983, no. 3871); ex Mack (not in sales); ex Lawrence II 191.

706A. FM: Trinity College 1957; ex J. Battely *c.* 1740; ex Archd. J. Battely 1708; found at Reculver, Kent. Illus. Battely 1745, pl. 7, then a larger fragment. Described from this erroneously as a type 38/40 mule (Rigold and Metcalf 1984).

707. FM: Mack I 9; ex Hill. Illus. Hill 1952, pl. 4.14, and Hill 1953, pl. 7.26.

[*continued overleaf*]

691 692 693 694 695 696

691★ 700★

697 698 699 700 701

702 703 704 705 706 706A 707 708

709 710 711 712 713 714 715

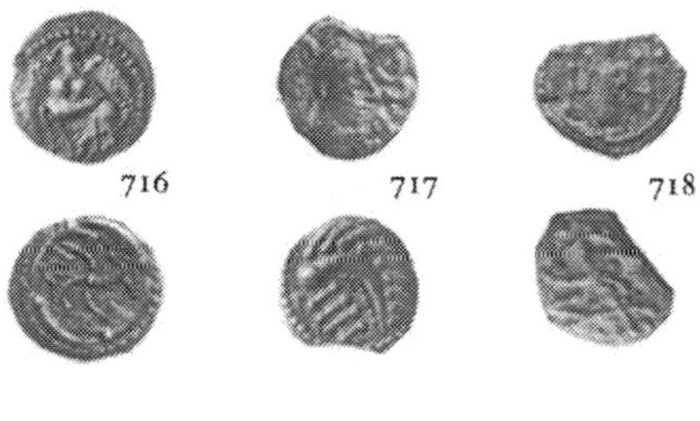

716 717 718

713★ 705★

708 *Ep*. 0.81g/12.5gr. 180°. *SCBI* –; Rigold, normal R2.
709 *Epa*. 0.71g/11.0gr. 90°. *SCBI* 234; Rigold, early R2.
710 *Epa*. Contemporary plated forgery. Æ on Æ. 0.85g/13.1gr. *SCBI* –.
711 Inscription uncertain, possibly *Epa*. 1.13g/17.4gr. *SCBI* –.
712 *Spi*. 0.87g/13.4gr. 0°. *SCBI* –; Rigold, normal R2; Hill 1953, 106 (this coin).
713 *Tilberlt* (= Tilbert?). Four **T**s in rev. standard. 0.59g/9.1gr. chipped. *SCBI* –. New moneyer, first noted by Miss M. M. Archibald from a specimen in the Middle Harling hoard 1981/3. The coin is thin and very base.
714 *Wigrd* (= Wigræd). 0.84g/13.0gr. 90°. *SCBI* 235; Rigold, normal R2.
715 *Wigrd* (retrograde). Bust l. 0.86g/13.3gr. 290°. *SCBI* 236; Rigold, normal R2.

Series S

716 Obv. sphinx standing l. looking backwards Rev. whorl of wolves' heads, their tongues meeting at the centre. 0.88g/13.6gr. slightly chipped. *SCBI* Mack 362 (this coin); *BMC AS* 47.

Series T

717 **LEV** or **LEL** (outwardly). 0.90g/13.9gr. 210°. *SCBI* 248; *BMC AS* 9.

Series U

Metcalf has distinguished two stylistic groups which he attributes to mints in Kent and in the S. Midlands (Metcalf 1984a, 36).

718 *Standing figure w. head l. in boat(?)/bird r. in branch*. 0.64g/9.9gr. chipped 330°. *SCBI* 262; *BMC AS* 23b; Metcalf 1972a, 56 and pl. 6.6 (Kentish group).

Series X. Woden/monster series. Frisian, see **664**.

Series Y. Regal series of Northumbria, see **1180**.

708. FM: Grierson 1970; from Baldwin 8.10.1968; ex Grantley 754; ex Evans; from hoard found 'in or near Cambridge'. Illus. Evans 1894, pl. 2.5.

709, 714–15. FM: provenance unrecorded.

712. FM: Grierson 1967; ex Chilvers; ex R. W. H. Erskine; ex Lawrence II 193(b); found at Woodbridge, Suffolk (before 1934).

713. FM: Granta Stamp and Coin Shop 1983; found at Middle Harling, Norfolk, Jan. 1983. Possibly a stray from the Middle Harling hoard.

716. FM: Grierson 1983; from Spink 22.7.1983 (*NCirc* June 1983, no. 3883); ex Mack (not in sales); ex Grantley 685; ex Rashleigh 29.

717. FM: Young 1936; ex Carlyon-Britton I 152; found at Stamford, Lincs.

CAROLINGIANS (1): FRANKISH KINGDOM

Principal references on Plates 33–45 are: *CNI*, G = Gariel 1883–4 (refs. to plates in vol. II), MG = Morrison and Grunthal 1967, P = Prou 1896a and PA = Poey d'Avant 1858–62. All coins on this plate are silver deniers except **734**, which is a gold solidus.

PEPIN THE SHORT

Mayor of the Palace, 741–51; King of the Franks, 751–68

All Pepin's coins date to his period as king.

719 *Unspecified mint (probably Dorestad)*. Obv. **ЧPIPI** Rev. **RP** (for *rex Pipinus*) with **T** above. 1.15g corroded 90°. P –; G I 14; MG 27. Mint discussed in note on coin.

720 *Uncertain mint (?Antrain, Ille-et-Vilaine)*. Obv. **RP** Rev. **ΔNT / TRΔ– / NO** (**ΔN** ligatured). 1.17g 80°. P 2; G I 2; MG 47. Mint discussed in note on coin.

CHARLES THE GREAT (Charlemagne)

King of the Franks, 768–814; of the Lombards, 774–814; emperor, 800–14

Classes 1 and 2 are light deniers of *c.* 1.3g, and Classes 3 and 4 are heavy deniers of *c.* 1.7g. The dating is discussed above, pp. 207–9. For a forgery of Narbonne (Count Milo), corresponding to period of Classes 1–2 but without royal name, see **1497**.

Class 1 (768–71). Irregular forms of royal name on obv.; normally mint name on rev. Frankish mints only.

721 *Chartres* (**CARNOTIS** around **S**, for *Senonum*?). 0.67g corroded and chipped 130°. P 488; G VI 25; MG 153. Belongs to Class 1 because the **A** and **R** in *Carlus* are separate letters and there is no **O**. Chartres was situated in the *Provincia Senonia*, as the *Provincia Lugdunensis quarta* was commonly called.

Class 2 (771–93/4). Regular form of royal name, **CARO / LVS**, the **AR** being ligatured.

Frankish series

722 *Arles?* (**ΛRDIS**). 1.75g 320°. P 890 var.; G V 13 var.; MG 238. Mint attribution uncertain. The identification of **ARDIS** as Arles (*Arelatensis*) is improbable, especially as there is sometimes an abbreviation mark between **A** and **R**, but the unusual type of large central cross occurs also at Marseille (MG 199–201) and points to a Provençal mint.

723 '*Clusas*' (**CLS**). 1.09g chipped 60°. P 934 var.; G VI 33; MG 249. For the mint identity, see note on coin.

724 *Dorestad* (**DOR / STAT**, the **D**, **R** and **A** deformed). 1.25g 90°. P 59; G VI 46; MG 699. The axe on the rev. is a feature of the mint, and for coins of Charlemagne with similar deformed letters see Nöbbe 1936b, nos. 41ff., and Van Gelder 1961.

725 *Limoges* (**LEM** for *Lemovicas*, cross beneath). 0.81g corroded and chipped 40°. P 773; G VII 65; MG 260.

726 *Lyon* (**LVG / DVN**). 1.05g chipped 340°. P 628 var.; G VII 69 var.; MG 165.

727 *Melle* (**MEDOLVS**, **L** in form of hook). 0.94g 320°. P 681–2; G VIII 91; MG 268.

728 *Melle* (**METOLO**, with **&** for **ET**, **L** in form of hook and **b** for **O**). 1.26g 0°. P 683; G VIII 87 var.; MG 268.

729 *Uncertain mint*. 0.46g fragment 0°. P –; G –; MG –. Rev. otherwise unknown, and from this fragment difficult to interpret. It appears to read **ΛN.. / VN..** or **CN.. / VN..**, but turned the other way up it could be read **..NΛ / ..HV**.

730 *Unspecified mint*. **℞F** for *rex Francorum* on rev. 1.32g 10°. P 891; G V 2; MG 226.

731 *As last*. 1.03g fragment 10°. Ref. as last.

Italian series (from 781)

732 *Milan* (**MED** in monogram, for *Mediolanum*, to l. of the **℞F**). 1.19g 220°. *CNI* V, 6.34 var.; P 895; G XI 161–3; MG –.

733 *As last*, with 4 pellets below **R**. 1.92g including modern protective mount 70°. Ref. as last.

Treviso. For what is probably a forgery, see **1498**.

719. PG: Spink 22.2.1945 (*NCirc* May 1943, no. 19684); probably the specimen in the E. Gent coll. and found at Richborough, Kent in 1880 or earlier (Metcalf 1966c, 384–7).

720. PG: ex Lockett III 218; ex Grantley 2843.

721. PG: Spink 19.4.1945; ex Bordeaux I 167; from Hoffmann 1889.

722. PG: Spink 5.3.1945; ex Grantley 2845; from Baldwin.

723. PG: Vinchon 7.9.1950.

724. PG: Spink 8.11.1945 (*NCirc* Jan. 1945, no. 28431); ex Grantley 2846.

725. PG: Franceschi 10.7.1955; ex Poswick.

726. PG: Spink 15.7.1983.

727. PG: Baldwin 15.5.1957.

728. PG: Seaby 27.8.1946; ex Grantley 2848.

729. Ciani 4.4.1952. Lafaurie has pointed out (*per litteram*) that this is the coin from a small hoard found before 1872 (Völckers 1965, no. XXI.3) at Chézy-l'Abbaye (Aisne, arr. Château-Thierry, cant. Charly) of which we had a description but no illustration.

730. PG: Spink 5.3.1945.

731. PG: Knobloch 19.7.1969.

732. PG: MMAG Basel sale 6 (6.12.1946), lot 304.

733. PG: Seaby 1.3.1946; ex Grantley 2851.

[*continued overleaf*]

719* 719 720 721 722

723 724 725 726 727 728

729 730 731 732 733 734

735 736 737 738 739 740

PLATE 33 (*cont.*)

Gold solidus

The rev. type associates this coin with the Class 2 deniers, though the obv. type is different. For these coins in general, see Appendix 1 (pp. 326–31) and the note on this specimen.

734 *Uzès* (**VCE/CIA** boustrophedon in two lines separated by a bar w. hooked ends). Obv. crude *Karolus* monogram w. **RE**, **F**, and pellets and crescent (for **X** and **R**) in the field. AV 3.72g (SG 16.68: 81% Au) 180°. P –; G XI 140 (this coin); MG –; Grierson 1954c, 294.A (this coin). See note on coin.

Class 3 (793/4–812). Karolus monogram and mint-signature on obv. and (usually) cross and **CARLVS REX FR** on rev. Obv. and rev. inscriptions occasionally interchanged.

Frankish series

735 *Agen* (**AGINNO**). **RX** for **REX**. 1.57g 20°. P 793; G XXII 26 var.; MG 178.

736 *Agen* (**AGINNO**). 1.24g 50°. P 794; G XXII 26; MG 179. Possibly Charles the Bald.

737 *Arles* (**AR:ELATO**). **CAR·LVS**. 1.53g 200°. P 854; G XII 186–7, XXII 32–3; MG 192–7.

738 *Arles* (**AR·E·LATO**). **CAR·LVS R·EX FR**. 1.67g 340°. Ref. as last.

739 *Bourges* (**BITVRICAS**). **R** for **FR**. 1.76g 70°. P 728 var.; G XXII 30 var.; MG 173.

740 *Bourges* (**BITVRICA∽**). Crescent in each rev. quarter. 1.63g 20°. P 729; G XXII 43; MG 174.

734. PG: Kapamadji 2.2.1961; ex J. Mazard; ex H. Trottmann; ex private coll. at Libourne (Gironde) in 1923. In collection of M. Mazel (of Pézénas, north-east of Béziers) in 1834, and probably found locally.

735. PG: Spink 12.11.1945; ex Grantley 2849; ex Verworn 497; from Biebrich hoard (Völckers 1965, no. XLII.1 (this coin)).

736. PG: Kress sale 116 (28.9.1960), lot 1429.

737. PG: Tinchant 29.3.1949.

738–9. PG: Vinchon 7.9.1950.

740. PG: Baldwin 1.2.1946; ex Grantley 2866; ex Schulman sale 9.4.1912, lot 1468.

CAROLINGIANS (2): KINGDOM AND EMPIRE

References as on Plate 33. The coins are silver deniers except **750–6**, which are gold solidi.

CHARLES THE GREAT, 768–814 (cont.)

Class 3 (793/4–812) (cont.)

Frankish series (cont.)

741 *Mainz* (**MOGONTIA**). 1.70g 120°. P 32; G XIII 206; MG 92.

742 *Mainz* (**MOGONTIΛ**). Rev. cross above three steps. 1.74g 160°. P 30–1; G XIII 204 var.; MG 91.

Melle (**METVLLO**). For a coin that may be of Charlemagne, see **923**.

Italian series (with **C** instead of **K** in monogram)

743 *Milan* (**MEDIOL**, with contraction mark through the **L**). 1.72g 310°. *CNI* V, 5.24; P 905–6; G XII 178; MG 212.

744 *Pavia* (**P˙APIA**, w. wedge between **P** and **A**). 1.54g 30°. *CNI* IV, 467.10 var.; P 897 var.; G XII 179 var.; MG 208 var.

745 *Pavia* (**PAPIA˙**). 1.60g 180°. *CNI* IV, 468.22; P 897 var.; G XII 179 var.; MG 208.

Ravenna. For a forgery of the abnormal issue with Charles' monogram in Greek, see **1499**.

746 *Treviso* (**.TARVI∽**). 1.73g 120°. *CNI* VI, 228.15–24; P 912; G XII 182; MG 220.

747 *Treviso* (**TΛRVI∽**). **R** of *Carlvs* retrograde. 1.68g 160°. Ref. as last.

Class 4 (812–14), as emperor. On obv. profile bust and imperial inscription (variously worded); and on rev. some symbolic object and either a mint name or **+XPICTIANA RELIGIO** (for *Christiana religio*).

Frankish series

748 *Arles* (**[A]RELATO**, gateway). **CARLVS IMP AV[G]**. 0.84g badly corroded 130°. P –; G –; MG –; Grierson 1965b, pl. 2.34 var. This variety, with **CARLVS** instead of **KAROLVS** and a gateway design shared with Lyon, is unrecorded.

749 *Quentovic* (**QVENTVVV[IC]**, ship with bird at masthead). **KAROLVS IMP ΛVG**. 1.65g 90°. P –; G –; MG 121a. Unique. It probably formed the prototype for the similar portrait coin of Dorestad, though this has a cross at the masthead. The bird on the mast is discussed by Horstmann (1966).

LOUIS THE PIOUS

King of Aquitaine, 781–813; co-emperor, 813–14; emperor, 814–40

Solidi (816–19?). See p. 213 above, and Appendix 1, pp. 329–30. The solidi and imitations are classified according to Grierson 1951a.

750 *Unspecified mint* (Aachen?). AV 5.65g including mount (SG 16.92, w. mount: 83% Au) 320°. Grierson 2. For other imitation coins with similar but more elaborate mounts of the period, see Zadoks-Josephus Jitta (1959b) and the exhibition catalogue *Karl der Grosse* (Aachen, 1965), pl. 32.

751 *Unspecified mint.* AV 4.32g (SG 17.25: 86% Au) 0°. Grierson 10.

Frisian imitations of solidi (c. *830–50*)

752 AV 4.37g (SG 15.08: 66% Au) 0°. Grierson IV(a). The obv. legend **DHIHNVVDOVSHHAVC** is recognizably derived from that of the prototype. The rev. legend and the legends of the following specimens are very degenerate.

753 AV 4.30g (SG 16.07: 76% Au) 0°. Grierson XVI(c); Stewart 1978, no. A124b. Scratch (test mark?) on rev. Perhaps minted in England: see note on coin.

754 AV 4.09g (SG 12.57: 35% Au) 70°. Grierson XXII(a).

755 AV 4.06g (SG 13.42: 47% Au) 90°. Grierson XXII, dies O1 R2. Scratched cross (test mark?) on obv.

756 AV 4.18g (SG 14.03: 54% Au) 315°. Grierson XXIV(a).

741. PG: Seaby 1.1.1946; ex Grantley 2851; bt in London.

742. PG: Bonham-Vecchi sale 6 (14.9.1981), lot 787.

743. PG: Spink 10.10.1945; ex Grantley 3192; ex Schulman sale 9.4.1912, lot 1453.

744. PG: Spink 17.1.1946.

745. FM: provenance unrecorded.

746. PG: Lockett III 324.

747. PG: ex DO 12.5.1958; ex Peirce 1948.

748. PG: Vecchi-Schwer sale 1 (13.5.1983), lot 633; from a Swiss coll.

749. PG: MMAG Basel sale 29 (27.11.1964), lot 5 (Dolivo coll.).

750. PG: ex Motte 109 (= Rolland 1932, no. 116).

751. PG: Baldwin 29.9.1945; ex Grantley 189; ex Carlyon-Britton I 270.

752. PG: ex Motte 110 (= Rolland 1932, no. 117); ex Delfzijl hoard 1906 (see Grierson 1951a, 29–30).

753. FM: Neville before 1904; found in the River Cam near Magdalene Bridge, Cambridge.

754. PG: ex Motte 112 (= Rolland 1932, no. 119).

755. PG: Bourgey sale 17.3.1952, lot 25.

756. PG: ex Motte 111 (= Rolland 1932, no. 118).

[*continued overleaf*]

741 742 743 744 745 746 747 748 749 749* 750 751 752 753 754 755 756 757 758 759 760 761

Deniers

Class 1 (*814–19*). A continuation of Charlemagne's Class 4, obv. type a laureate bust surrounded by **HLVDOVVICVS IMP AVG**, on rev. mint name or **XPISTIANA RELIGIO** around symbolic object.

Frankish series

757 *Dorestad* (**DORE[S]TATAS**, with inverted **V** and ship with cross at masthead). 1.16g pierced and worn 190°. P 63; G XVI 59–60; MG 330. Double struck.

758 *Melle* (**METALLVM** and minting tools: dies and two hammers). 1.69g 140°. P 712; G XVI 73, XVII 74–5; MG 396.

759 *Orléans* (**AVRELIANIS** and city gate). 1.71g 120°. P 507; G XVII 89; MG 372.

760 *Unspecified mint* (**XPISTIANA RELIGIO** and temple). 1.69g 45°. P 984–6; G XLIII 1–2; MG 984–6.

Italian series

761 *Uncertain mint* (**PAPIIALI**? and temple). 1.26g 340°. P –; G –; MG –. Probably a contemporary imitation. The legend seems to derive from **PAPIA**, although Pavese coins normally have a city gate and not a temple. The portraiture and epigraphy, although crude, are not dissimilar to those of Italian issues.

757. PG: Button sale 96 (24.1.1957), lot 429.

758. PG: MMAG Basel 8.3.1957 (list 165, no. 175).

759. PG: Spink 22.2.1945; from Hamburger 1928.

760. PG: Lockett III 325; ex Bordeaux I 234; ex Du Lac II 479.

761. PG: Ratto 25.4.1977.

CAROLINGIANS (3): EMPIRE

References as on Plate 33. The coins are silver, and are deniers unless otherwise indicated.

LOUIS THE PIOUS, 814–40 (cont.)

Class 2 (var.) (c. *819?*). Cross on obv. and rev. For a suggested explanation, and the date proposed, see p. 215 above.

762 *Melle* (**METALLVM**). **HLVDOVVICVS IMP**. 1.49g 290°. P 722; G XVI 70; MG 400.

Class 2 (819–22). Mint name in the rev. field. The obv. inscription is +**HLVDOVVICVS IMP**.

Frankish series

763 '*Aquitaine*' (**AQVI/TANIA**). Cross above and below mint name. 1.69g 270°. P 657; G XIV 18 var.; MG 389.

764 *As last*. 1.67g chipped 70°. Ref. as last.

765 *Arles* (**AREL/ATVM**). W. **ƧS** in obv. legend. 1.61g chipped 270°. P 859 var.; G XIV 22 var.; MG 439.

Barcelona. For a modern forgery, see **1500**.

766 *Bourges* (**BITV/RIGES**). 1.61g 200°. P 734; G XV 40; MG 410.

767 *As last*. 1.58g chipped 50°. Ref. as last.

768 *Cambrai* (**CAMA/RACVS**). 1.69g 320°. P 114; G XV 43; MG 342.

769 *Chalon-sur-Saône* (**CAVIL/ONVM**). 1.57g 190°. P –; G XV 44 var.; MG 378.

770 *Dorestad* (**D▾OR/ESTA/▾TVS▾**). Wedge in first and second quarters of obv. 1.76g 110°. P 65–7 var.; G XVI 54 var.; MG 332 var.

771 *Dorestad* (**DOR/ESTA/TVS**). Two pellets in second and third quarters of obv. 1.62g 200°. P 65–7 var.; G XVI 56 var.; MG 332 var.

772 *Lyon* (**LVGD/VNVM**). 1.76g 310°. P 630–1; G XVI 64; MG 379.

773 *Marseille* (**MASS/ILIA**). 1.62g 150°. P 886; G XVI 65; MG 444.

774 *Melle* (**META/LLVM**). 1.80g 270°. P 715–19; G XVI 68; MG 398.

775 *As last*. 1.76g 150°. Ref. as last.

776 *As last*. 1.55g 200°. Ref. as last.

777 *Melle* (**METALLVM**). *Obol*. 0.57g worn 110°. P 709; G XIV 5; MG 394.

778 *Melle* (**METIILLVH**). *Obol*. Three pellets in centre of obv. and pellet in each quarter of rev. 0.72g 90°. P 709–10 var.; G XIV 5 var.; MG 393.

779 *Narbonne* (**NAR/BONA**). Pellet in 2nd quarter. 1.60g 220°. P 836 var.; G XVII 85 var.; MG 430 var.

780 '*Palace*' (**PALA/TINA MO/NETA**). 1.78g 30°. P 8; G XVII 91; MG 320.

781 *Paris* (**PARISII**). 1.73g 340°. P 317–18; G VIII 32–3; MG 361.

782 *Rheims* (**REMIS/CIVIS**). 1.83g 340°. P 294–5; G XVIII 106; MG 357.

783 *Sens* (**SENO/NES˙**). 1.97g 40°. P 566–7 var.; G XVIII 117; MG 376. Ghosting of obv. cross on rev.

784 *Toulouse* (**·T·OIO/SΛ CIVI/TΛƧ·**). *Obol*. **HIVDOVV·CVS IP**, pellet in each quarter of obv. 0.41g 60°. P –; G XIX 127 var.; MG 423.

785 *Tours* (**TVRO/NES**). 1.58g 270°. P 447; G XIX 131; MG 371.

786 *Verdun* (**VIRID/VNVM**). Pellet before and wedge after obv. legend. 1.62g chipped 130°. P 145–6; G XIX 144; MG 347.

762. PG: Glendining 28.1.1946, lot 218; ex Grantley 2856.
763. PG: Kapamadji 6.10.1962.
764. CCC (*Catalogue* no. 63): Lewis 1891; from Hoffmann sale 2.3.1887, lot 244.
765. PG: Vinchon 7.9.1950.
766. PG: Seaby 1.1.1946; ex Grantley 2852; from Rollin.
767. PG: Seaby 1.1.1946; ex Grantley 2852.
768. PG: ex Lockett III 329.
769. PG: Kapamadji 15.12.1966; ex J. Chappée coll., and said to be from a hoard found in 1919 at Saint-Julien near Angers.
770. PG: Spink 12.2.1945 (*NCirc* Jan. 1945, no. 28435); ex Grantley 2853.
771. PG: Baldwin 27.12.1971.
772. PG: Spink 20.3.1947 (*NCirc* Jan. 1945, no. 28434); ex Grantley 2855; ex Schulman sale 9.4.1912, lot 1455.
773. PG: Vinchon 14.7.1967.
774. FM: provenance unrecorded.
775, 777. PG: Glendining 28.1.1946, lot 218; ex Grantley 2856.
776. CCC (*Catalogue* no. 64): Lewis 1891.
778, 784. PG: Vinchon 7.9.1950.
779. PG: Gans 17.6.1957 (list 27, no. 5225).
780. PG: Kapamadji 15.12.1966; ex J. Chappée coll., and said to be from a hoard found at Saint-Denis.
781. PG: MMAG Basel 8.3.1957 (list 165, no. 178).
782–3, 786. PG: Kress sale 116 (28.9.1960), lots 1401, 1405, and 1409 respectively.
785. PG: MMAG Basel 8.3.1957 (list 165, no. 180).

762 763 764 765 766 767

768 769 770 771 772 773

774 775 776 777 778 779 780

781 782 783 784 785 786

CAROLINGIANS (4): EMPIRE

References as on Plate 33. The coins are silver and are deniers unless otherwise indicated.

LOUIS THE PIOUS, 814–40 (cont.)

Class 2 (*819–22*) (cont.)

Italian series

787 *Milan* (**MEDIO/LANVM**). Pellet in **C** of obv. legend. 1.71g 270°. *CNI* V, 9.12–25 var.; P 909; G XVII 80; MG 451.

788 *Pavia* (**PAPIA**). 1.73g 90°. *CNI* IV, 469.5; P 902; G XVII 95; MG 447.

789 *Venice* (+**VEN/ECIAS**). 1.50g 10°. *CNI* VII, 4.18; P 918; G XIX 140; MG 456.

790 *Venice* (+**VEN/ECIAS**), contemporary forgery. +**LVDO-VVICVS IMP**. Æ plated w. AR 1.27g corroded 180°. Type as last.

Class 3 (*822–40*). Obv. same legend and design as last, but pellet in each quarter of cross and the letters **IMP** sometimes ligatured Rev. **XPISTIANA RELIGIO** around temple (i.e. the normal reverse of Charlemagne's Class 4 but with **XPIS** instead of **XPIC**). Mints are not specified but a few can be identified by peculiarities of style or other features found on earlier or later mint-signed coinages. References, unless more specifically indicated, are: P 987ff.; G XLI–XLIV; MG 472.

791 *Unspecified mint* (*Milan*). Pellet in **O** and **C** of obv. legend. **XPSTIANA**. 1.73g 30°. The forms of the letters and splayed ends of the obv. cross and the presence of pellets in the letters of the obv. legend are typical of Milan coins (cf. **787** above, and p. 217), justifying the attribution.

792 *Unspecified mint* (*Pavia*?). 1.56g 20°. Lettering and form of cross very similar to last, but lacks the pellets in the letters that characterize Milanese coins of this period.

793 1.82g 240°.

794 1.48g 170°.

795 1.45g 90°.

796 1.56g 0°.

797 Ligatured **HL**. 1.41g 260°. The forms of the letters and of the cross and temple are similar to those of **798** and **799**, as well as to P 998 and Dolley and Morrison 1966, nos. 90–1 (Lothar I). All appear to be the work of the same die-cutter and thus probably of the same mint.

798 *As last*. 1.13g very thin flan 170°. See note to **797**.

799 Annulet below and pellet either side of temple. 1.22g cracked 170°. P 998; G XLIII 19; MG 490. See note to **797**.

800 1.79g 225°.

801 **HI** for **HL**, **PILIGIO**. 1.26g chipped 60°.

802 1.58g 320°.

803 1.69g 80°.

804 **HI** for **HL**. 1.36g chipped 40°.

805 1.10g chipped 230°.

806 Three pellets to left of temple. 1.45g 180°. P –; G XLIII 10 var.; MG 501. Groups of pellets in the reverse field were used later on mint-signed temple-type coins of Huy (MG 541–2) and Quentovic (MG 715).

807 Pellet to left of gable. 1.47g pierced 210°. P –; G –; MG –.

808 **IILVDOVVICVS IMP**, w. ligatured **MP** and blundered ending to rev. (**REL•**...). 1.37g 90°. P 987 var.; G XLIV 37 var.; MG 472 var.

809 Obol. 0.76g 340°. P 1005; G XLIV 43 var.; MG 473.

810 Contemporary forgery. Retrograde rev. legend starting w. ✱ instead of **X**. Æ 1.46g chipped 40°.

787. PG: Baldwin 1.2.1946; ex Grantley 2861; ex Schulman sale 9.4.1912, lot 1456.

788. PG: Baldwin 1.2.1946; ex Grantley 2861; ex Cahn 218 (in untraced list or sale).

789. PG: Seaby 6.11.1945.

790. PG: Tinchant 4.1.1951.

791. PG: *Ars et Nummus* 5.3.1981 (1980, list 4, no. 461).

792. PG: Baldwin 1.2.1946; ex Grantley 2884.

793. PG: Baldwin 28.8.1946.

794. PG: Spink 8.2.1945; ex Grantley 3193.

795. FM: provenance unrecorded.

796, 804, 806. PG: ex Blunt 17.3.1948; ex Grantley duplicates.

797. PG: Baldwin 1.2.1946; ex Grantley 2884.

798–800. FM: provenance unrecorded.

801–3. PG: Baldwin 1.2.1946; ex Grantley 2884.

805, 807. FM: provenance unrecorded.

808. FM: ... ex Neligan 718.

809. PG: Vinchon 7.9.1950.

810. PG: Sotheby 28.7.1947, lot 91.

787 788 789 790 791 792

793 794 795 796 797 798

799 800 801 802 803 804

805 806 807 808 809 810

CAROLINGIANS (5): AQUITAINE, THE MIDDLE KINGDOM AND GERMANY

References as on Plate 33. The coins are silver and are deniers unless otherwise indicated.

AQUITAINE

PEPIN II, 839–52

For attribution and chronology, see pp. 218–19 above. The deniers have as legends **PIPINVS REX**, often followed by **EQ**(*uitaniorum*) or, at Toulouse, by **F**(*rancorum*), and either *Christiana religio* or *Aquitaniorum* or the mint name of Bourges, Limoges, Melle, Poitiers, Toulouse, or Dax.

811 *'Aquitaine'* (**AQVITANIORVM**). Temple type. 1.71g 170°. P –; G XX 4; MG 599. The grey, slightly pitted surface of this coin puts its genuineness in question, but the defect may be no more than a consequence of the way in which it has been cleaned.

812 *'Aquitaine'* (**AQVI/TAINA**). Obol. Two-line type. **PIPPINVS REX**. 0.59g 90°. P 664 var.; G XX 1 var.

813 *'Aquitaine'* (**AQVI/TANIA**). Obol. Two-line type. **PIPPIИVS RE+**. 0.83g 50°. P 659 var.; G XX 2; MG 601.

814 *Melle* (**METVLLO**). Monogram type. 1.72g 70°. P 689; G XXXVII 2; MG 606.

815 *Melle* (**METVLLO**). Obol. Monogram type. 0.82g 40°. P 691; G XXXVII 4; MG 608.

816 *Toulouse* (**TOLOSA CIVI**). Monogram type. **PIPPHVS REX F**. Monogram with limb of **N** in 1st instead of 3rd quarter of rev. 1.63g 200°. P 809 var.; G XXXVII 6; MG 618.

817 *Toulouse* (**TOLOSA CIVI**). Obol. **PIPPINVS REX F**. Monogram type with **N** and **S** in monogram interchanged and **I** in 3rd instead of 4th quarter of rev. 0.66g 0°. P –; G XXXVII 8; MG 619.

THE MIDDLE KINGDOM

LOTHAR I

Emperor, 840–55

For types and chronology, see p. 223 above.

Lotharingia

818 *Dorestad* (**DOR/ESTA/TVS**). **HLOTHARIVƧ MPIERA**, w. **TH** ligatured. Three-line type. 1.51g 350°. P 69; G LIX 15; MG 521.

819 *Dorestad, Frisian imitation(?)* (**DORESTATVS MOII**). **IOTAMVSIPIEIPAT**. Temple type. 1.57g 180°. P 74; G LIX 17 var.; MG 525.

820 *Dorestad, Frisian imitation* (**DOR/ESTA/TVS**). **IIIOTIA-IIVSIIA**. Three-line type. 1.73g 0°. P 73; G LIX 16; MG 524.

Germany

Strasbourg. For a forgery, see **1501**.

Italy

821 *Milan* (**MEDIOL**, w. **ME** ligatured and contraction mark) **HLOTHARIVS IMP**, w. **HL** ligatured and **A** having form **N**. 1.42g 270°. *CNI* V, 9.2; P 910; G LIX 21; MG 558.

822 *Pavia* (**PAPIA**). **HIOTHARIVS IMP AV**, w. **TH** ligatured. 1.70g 200°. *CNI* IV, 470.3; P 904; G LIX 24; MG 556.

LOTHAR II

King, 855–69

Lotharingia

Metz. For a forgery, see **1502**.

LOUIS THE BLIND

King of Provence, 890–928; of Italy, 900–1; emperor from 901

Class 1 (*890–901*). With **LVDOVVICVS** and no further title. The coins have a *Karolus* monogram modified into a *Ludovicus* one.

823 *Arles* (**ARELA CIVIS**). 1.47g 50°. P 882; G XXXVII 2 (as Louis the Stammerer); MG 1653.

824 *As last*. 1.52g 330°. Ref. as last.

Class 2 (*901–28*). With **LVDVVICVS MPR** (for *imper*) and across field **T[ ]R**, uncertain letter above, **:C:** below.

825 *Vienne* (**VIENNA CIVIS**). 1.41g 190°. P 848 (same dies); G LXIII 2; MG 1573 (same dies as coin illus.). This coin looks much later in date (11th/12th century), but does not differ in fabric from, for example, the Limoges series in the Cuerdale hoard which ante-date 905.

811, 814. PG: Kricheldorf sale 8 (2.11.1960), lots 315 and 316 respectively.
812. PG: Vinchon 7.9.1950.
813. PG: Tinchant 27.4.1947.
815, 817. PG: Kapamadji 6.10.1962.
816. PG: Kapamadji 1.9.1952.
818. PG: Schulman sale 275 (27.9.1982), lot 246.
819. PG: Tinchant 9.4.1948.
820. PG: Schulman sale 206 (30.1.1956), lot 263.
821. PG: Spink 12.2.1945; ex Grantley 3194; from Rollin.
822. PG: Lockett III 336.
823. PG: Platt 10.1.1969.
824. PG: Lockett III 353; ex Grantley 2879; from Rollin.
825. PG: Spink 16.6.1945; acq. in France 1939.

[*continued overleaf*]

811 812 813 814 815* 815 816 817 818 819 820 821 822 823 824 825 826 827 828 829 830 831

GERMANY

ARNULF OF CARINTHIA

King of Germany, 887–99; of Italy, 895–6; titular emperor from 896

His name is spelled *Arnvlfus* or, at Mainz, *Arnoldus*.

826 *Mainz* (+**WO[ ]CIVIT**). **]DV~ RE**. Temple type. 1.49g 90°. P 36–7; G LXII 1; MG 1532–3.

827 *Mainz* (+**WOGOИCIΛE CIVIT**). **ΛRИOIDV~ RE**. Temple type. 1.40g 10°. Ref. as last.

Toul. For a forgery, see **1504**.

LOUIS THE CHILD

King of Germany, 899–911; with Lotharingia from 900

The obverse inscription is normally +**(H)LVDOVVICVS REX**, but at Strasbourg **REX** is replaced by **PIVS**.

828 *Cologne* (**S/COLONIA/A**, for *Sancta Colonia Agrippina*). 1.84g 60°. P 80–1; G LXIV 18–20; MG 1557–60.

829 *Mainz* (**WOↃ[ ]IΛE CIΛT**). **]IDOIΛΛ[ ]ΛSE[** . 1.58g 10°. P 38–9; G LXIV 4–6; MG 1546, 1548.

830 *Strasbourg* (**ΛRGEИTI/HΛ CVHVƧ**, for *Argentina civitas*). 1.34g 50°. P 48–51; G LXI 6–8 (as Emp. Louis II); MG 1550–5.

831 *Strasbourg* (**ΛRGEИTI/ИΛ CVИΛS**). 1.33g 30°. Refs. as last.

Cologne and *Strasbourg*. For coins struck for Charles the Simple after 911, see **999–1000**.

826. PG: Spink *c.* 1966.
827. PG: Seaby 5.3.1946.
828. PG: Kress sale 116 (28.9.1960), lot 1506.
829. PG: MMAG Basel 4.5.1958.
830. PG: Hess (Lucerne) 2.4.1958.
831. PG: Bourgey 10.4.1956 (list March 1956, no. 323).

CAROLINGIANS (6): WEST FRANKISH KINGDOM

References as on Plate 33. The coins are silver and are deniers unless otherwise indicated. For arrangement and dating, see pp. 230–5 above.

CHARLES THE BALD

King of the West Franks, 840–75; emperor, 875–7

Class 1 (840–64)

Anomalous early types

(a) With cross and mint name in field

Deniers known are for the mints of Meaux, Paris and Sens. Obols, forming a different group to the deniers but equally dating from the early 840s, are known only for 'Aquitaine' and Barcelona.

832 *Meaux* (**MEL/DIS**). 1.60g 230°. P –; G I 41; MG 849.

833 *Paris* (**PARI/SII**). **CAR·LVS R·EX·**. 1.64g 180°. P 322; G LI 55 var.; MG 825.

834 *'Aquitaine'* (**AQVI/TANIA**). Obol. 0.62g 50°. P 672; G XXII 30; MG 1053. Probably continued after 864.

(b) With bust and mint name in field (Bourges only). Not represented

(c) With cross and city gate in field (Orléans and Chartres only)

835 *Orléans* (**AVRE/LI/ANIS**). 1.56g 90°. P 511; G XII 11; MG 944.

836 *Orléans* (**AVRE/LI/ANNIS**, w. **NN** ligatured). 1.53g 320°. P 511 var.; G XXI 11 var.; MG 944.

837 *Orléans* (**AVRE/LI/ANI**). With pellet in centre and either side of city gate. 1.37g chipped 220°. Ref. as last.

(d) With cross and monogram

Mainly mints in Aquitaine, where the type continued after 864. Coins of Melle are treated separately, see Plates 42–3. The obv. inscription is **CARLVS REX** unless otherwise indicated.

Agen. For a possible coin of Charles the Bald, see **736**.

Beauvais. For a coin of similar type but contemporary w. Class 2, see **909**.

838 *Bourges* (**BITVRICES CIVI**). 1.78g 320°. P 379; G XXII 39; MG 1071.

839 *As last*. Obol. 0.79g 340°. P 741; G XXII 41; MG 1072.

840 *Palace* (**PALATINA MONETA**). **CAROLVS REX**. Pellet in each rev. quarter. 1.58g 315°. P 12; G LI 53; MG 625. The hoard evidence shows that these continued to be struck during Class 2, but perhaps only in Aquitaine, since there are *Palatina moneta* coins elsewhere with the 'GDR' inscription (**884**).

841 *Toulouse* (**TOLOSA CIVI**). Monogram badly formed, w. **L** retrograde in form ⅃. 1.50g 0°. P 819; G XXIII 68 var.; MG 1097.

Cross and temple type. The main type struck 840–64, carrying on from Class 3 of Louis the Pious but with **CARLVS REX FR** (normally) and usually a mint name substituted for **XPISTIANA RELIGIO**.

842 *Auxerre* (**AVTISIODIRO CA**, retrograde). **CAROLVS REA FR** (**F** inverted). 1.59g 160°. P 583 var.; G XX 1 var.; MG 988.

843 *Paris* (**PARISII CIVITAS**). 1.50g chipped 90°. P 323; G XXI 12; MG 827.

844 *Sens* (**SENONES CIVITAS**). 1.61g 310°. P 574; G XXI 20; MG 982.

845 *Tours, St Martin's* (**SCI MARTIN MONETA**). **CARLVS REX**. Temple design on obv., pellet in 3 rev. quarters. 1.55g 350°. P 441 var.; G XXI 18; MG 920.

846 *Without mint name*. **XPISTIANA RELIGIO**. 1.67g 320°. P 1062; G XXI 22; MG 1159.

847 *As last*. 1.62g 190°. Ref. as last.

848 *As last*. 1.53g 200°. Ref. as last.

849 *As last*. 1.48g 340°. Ref. as last.

832. PG: Kricheldorf sale 8 (2.11.1960), lot 309.

833. PG: Spink 1.3.1973 (*NCirc* March 1973, no. 2770); ex Grantley 2889; from Rollin.

834. PG: Seaby 9.7.1945; ex Grantley 2878; ex 'Collection B...' 308.

835. PG: Baldwin 1.2.1946; ex Grantley 2872.

836. PG: Seaby 30.5.1950; ex A. J. D. Mainguy.

837. PG: Vinchon 16.6.1958 (list 14, no. 418).

838. PG: Kress sale 116 (28.9.1960), lot 1434.

839. PG: Baldwin 1.2.1946; ex Grantley 2866.

840, 844. PG: DO 12.5.1958; ex Peirce 1948.

841. PG: Vinchon 7.9.1950.

842. PG: Lockett III 341; ex Grantley 2865.

843. PG: Bourgey 10.4.1956 (list March 1956, no. 293).

845. PG: Baldwin 1.2.1946; ex Grantley 2875; from Bourgey.

846–8. PG: Baldwin 1.2.1946; ex Grantley 2884.

849. PG: Baldwin 24.2.1950.

832 833 834 835 836 837

838 839 840 841 835*

842 843 844 845

846 847 848 849

CAROLINGIANS (7): WEST FRANKISH KINGDOM

References as on Plate 33. The coins are all silver deniers.

CHARLES THE BALD, 840–77 (cont.)

Class 2 (864–77 and later). Characterized by the *Gratia D-i rex* ('GDR') legend around a royal monogram on the obv. and the mint name round a cross on the rev.

850 *Amiens* (**AMBIANIS CIVIT**). 1.63g 150°. P 231 var.; G XXV 3; MG 751.

851 *Angers* (**ANDEGAVIS CIVITAS**). 1.50g 30°. P 429; G XLVI 2 var.; MG 912, 1407.

852 *Arras* (**ATREB·ATIS CIVIT·A·S**). 1.43g 200°. P 216; G XXV 11; MG 738. The light weight suggests that this may be a coin of Charles the Simple, but the presence of specimens in the Glisy hoard (dep. *c.* 880, MG hoard 75) with similar punctuation of the rev. legend is in favour of Charles the Bald.

853 *Auxerre* (**AVTISIODER CIVI**). **RE** for **REX**. 1.78g 130°. P 585 var.; G XXV 22 var.; MG 997 var.

854 *Bayeux* (**HBAIOCAS CIVITAS**, w. **HB** ligatured). 1.69g 220°. P 404; G XXVI 45; MG 887.

Bayeux. For a forgery, see **1505**.

855 *Blois* (**BLESIANIS CASTRO**). 1.70g 250°. P 471; G XXVII 52; MG 923.

856 *Blois* (**BLESIANIS CASTRO**, w. limb of **L** bisecting upright). 1.75g 10°. P 474; G XXVII 52 var.; MG 927 var.

857 *Blois* (**BIESIANIS CASTRO**). 1.71g 330°. P 473; G XXVII 52 var.; MG 928.

858 *Châlons-sur-Marne* (**CATAIAVNIS CI**). 1.51g 80°. P 311 var.; G XXVII 65 var.; MG 822 var.

859 *Chartres* (**CARNOTIS CIVITĀ**). 1.74g 230°. P 492; G XXVII 72; MG 936. A lighter coin of different style with a related monogram is placed under Raoul, **1001**.

860 *Courcessin* (**HCVRTISASONIEN**, w. **HC** ligatured). 1.69g 240°. P 411; G XXVIII 94; MG 895. On the identity of the mint, see note on this coin. The type was struck at this mint under Charles the Bald and Charles the Simple and their issues cannot be satisfactorily distinguished, so for convenience all are placed here.

861 *As last*. 1.69g 290°. Ref. as last.

862 *As last*. 1.52g 20°. Ref. as last.

863 *As last*. 1.48g 40°. Ref. as last.

864 *As last*. 1.35g 250°. Ref. as last.

865 *As last*, but obv. w. wedge in **C**. 1.58g 90°. P 411 var.; G XXVIII 94 var.; MG 895.

866 *As last*, but **GRATA** for **GRATIA**. 1.46g 350°. P 413 var.; G XXVIII 94 var.; MG 898 var.

867 *As last*, but w. pellet to left of monogram. 1.54g 170°. P 411 var.; G XXVIII 94 var.; MG 895 var.

868 *Evreux* (**EBROCAS CIVITAS**). 1.61g 110°. P 399; G XXIX 107; MG 883.

869 *Laon* (**LVGDVNI CLAVATI**). 1.70g 300°. P 270; G XXX 125; MG 794.

870 *Laon* (**LVGDVNI CL·AVATI**). Pellet in each quarter of rev. 1.77g 290°. P –; G –; MG –.

871 *Lisieux* (**LICSOVINI CIVIIT**). 1.66g 240°. P 401; G XXX 133; MG 886 var.

872 *Le Mans* (**CINOMANIS CIVITAS**). 1.70g 0°. P 420; G XXX 129; MG 905. For coins of this type attributed to Charles the Simple, see **993–5**.

873 *As last*. 1.69g 270°. Ref. as last.

850, 852, 854. PG: Kapamadji 6.10.1962.
851. PG: Lockett III 341.
853, 858–9. PG: Vinchon 7.9.1950.
855, 867. QC: provenance unrecorded.
856–7. PG: Baldwin 1.2.1946; ex Grantley 2866.
860. FM: provenance unrecorded.
861–5. PG: Baldwin 1.2.1946; ex Grantley 2868.
866. PG: Sotheby 28.7.1947, lot 91.
868–70. PG: Vinchon 7.9.1950.
871. PG: Kress sale 116 (28.9.1960), lot 1449.
872. PG: Spink 8.2.1945; ex Grantley 2869.
873. PG: Sotheby 28.7.1947, lot 81.

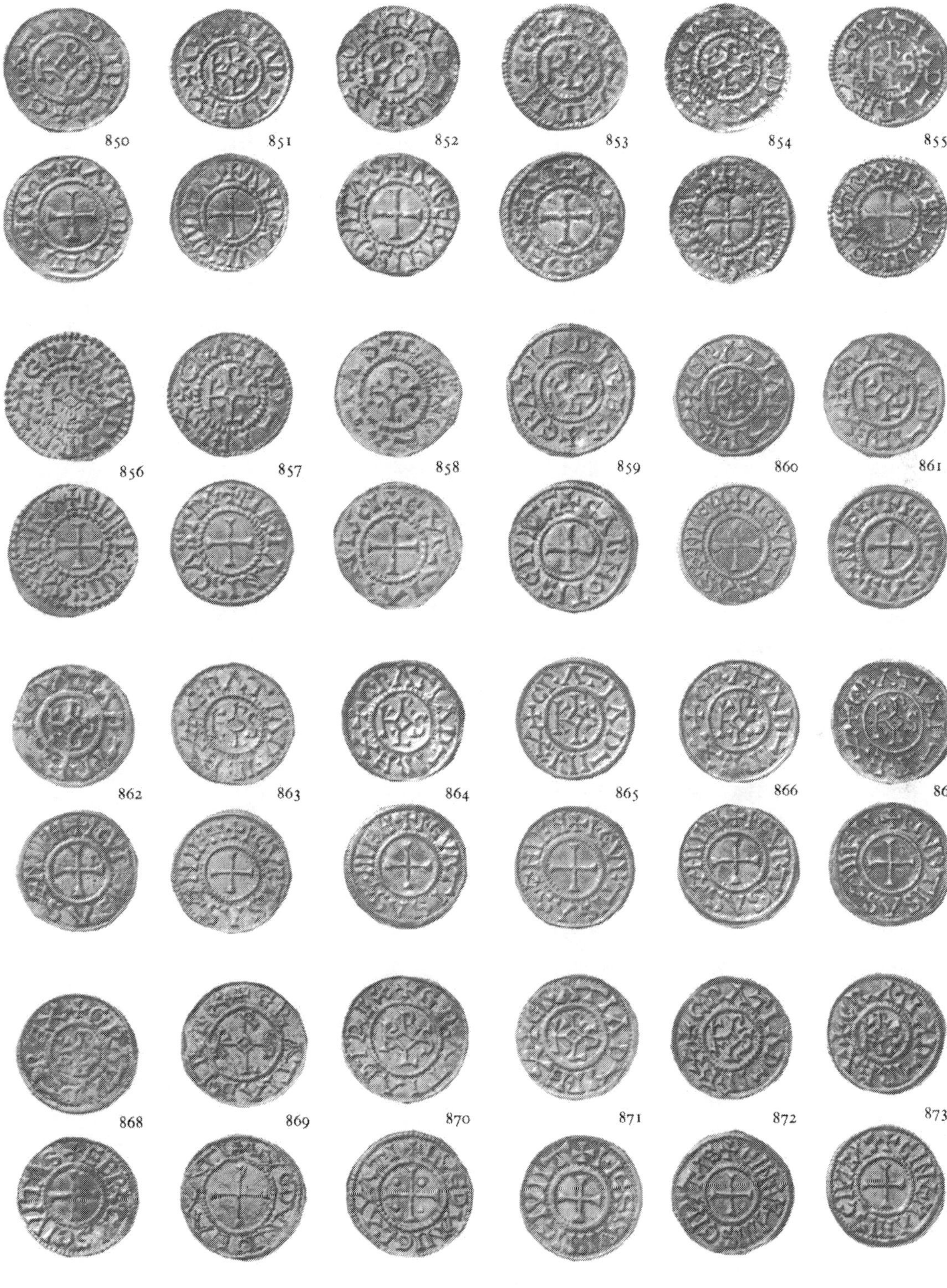

850 851 852 853 854 855

856 857 858 859 860 861

862 863 864 865 866 867

868 869 870 871 872 873

CAROLINGIANS (8): WEST FRANKISH KINGDOM

References as on Plate 33. The coins are silver and are deniers unless otherwise indicated.

CHARLES THE BALD, 840–77 (cont.)

Class 2 (864–77 and later) (cont.)

874 *Le Mans* (**CINOMANIS CIVITAS**). 1.71g 0°. Ref. as **872**. From same obv. die as coin in Saumeray hoard (Lafaurie 1965a, pl. 24.10).

875 *Meaux* (**·MEL·DIS·CI·VI·TAS·**). **GRATI·A·D¯I·REX**. 1.79g 150°. P 364 var.; G XXXI 145 var.; MG 854.

876 *Melun* (**CASTELLO MILED**). **L** in monogram retrograde. 1.61g 90°. P 371; G XXXI 147; MG 864.

877 *Orléans* (**AVRELIANIS CIVITAS**). 1.79g 70°. P 516; G XXXI 164; MG 948.

878 *As last*. 1.71g 30°. Ref. as last.

879 *As last*. 1.80g 0°. Ref. as last.

880 *As last*. 1.22g chipped 200°. Ref. as last.

881 *Orléans* (**AVRELIAINS CIVITAS**). 1.77g 230°. P 516 var.; G XXXI 165 var.; MG 948 var. Two peck-marks on rev. Perhaps of Charles the Simple. The coin is struck off-centre and shows a pellet on the outer flange of the obv. die. Four pellets of this type were present on the two dies and on the three trial plates of the early 10th century found in recent excavations at York (to be published by Pirie). There are no similar pellets on the Carolingian die of Melle (p. 235 above), but its surface is in poor condition. They probably assisted the engraver to plan the design, although on this die the one visible pellet does not bear a simple 90° relationship to the coin type.

882 *Orléans* (**AVRELIANIS CIVITAS**). Pellet in each rev. quarter. 1.78g 90°. P 516 var.; G XXXI 165 var.; MG 948 var.

883 *Orléans* (**AVRELIANIS CIVITAS**). Obol. 0.85g 160°. P 519; G XXXI 166 var.; MG 949.

884 *Palace* (**PALATINA MONET**). 1.70g 350°. P 21 var.; G XXXI 168 var.; MG 631.

885 *Paris* (**PARISII CIVITAS**). **GRATI** for **GRATIA**. 1.63g 280°. P 328; G XXXII 182 var.; MG 832.

886 *Quentovic* (**QVVENTOVVICI**). Pellet in 1st and 4th quarter of rev. 1.80g 210°. P 191; G XXXII 187; MG 716.

887 *Quentovic* (**QVVENTOVICI**). Pellet in 1st and 4th quarters of rev. 1.59g 110°. P 191 var.; G XXXII 187 var.; MG 716.

888 *Quentovic* (**QVENTOVICI**). Obol. **D¯RE** for **D¯I REX**. 0.60g 220°. P 196; G XXXII 190 var.; MG 720.

889 *Rennes* (**HREDONIS CIVITS**). 1.24g 20°. P 652 var.; G XXXII 199 var.; MG 1045. This coin and the next, despite their light weight, probably belong to Charles the Bald rather than Charles the Simple, since coins of the latter have the mint name **REDONIS** (cf. Rennes hoard, MG hoard 102). Some 900 coins of this mint of Charles the Bald were found in the Bourgneuf hoard (MG hoard 71).

890 *Rennes* (**HREDONIS CIVITAS**). 1.47g 260°. P 652; G XXXIII 199; MG 1045.

891 *Rheims* (**REMIS CIVITAS**). **RE** for **REX**. 1.65g 270°. P 299; G XXXIII 193 var.; MG 815.

892 *Rheims* (**REMIS CIVITAS**). **GRACIA** for **GRATIA**, monogram retrograde. 1.45g 0°. P 302; G XXXIII 194 var.; MG 1389 var. This variety occurred in the Glisy hoard (MG hoard 75).

893 *Rouen* (**ROTVM·ACVS CIVII**). 1.63g 0°. P 378; G XXXIII 205 var.; MG 878.

894 *Rouen* (**ROTVMACVS CIVII**). Retrograde **S** in monogram. 1.50g chipped 180°. P 378 var.; G XXXIII 205 var.; MG 878.

895 *Rouen* (**ROTVMACVS CIVII**). Obol. Monogram retrograde. 0.53g 20°. P 385 var.; G XXXIII 210 var.; MG 878 var.

896 *Rouen* (**ROTVIIACVS II**). Obol. **GRTIA RI REX**, pellet instead of cross-bar in **A**. Monogram retrograde. 0.81g 220°. P 389 var.; G XXXIII 210 var.; MG 873 var.

897 *Saint-Denis* (**SCI ΔIONVSII M**). 1.61g 270°. P 344; G XXXIV 219; M 843.

874, 878. QC: provenance unrecorded.

875. PG: Baldwin 1.2.1946; ex Grantley 2871 (not noted in catalogue).

876. PG: Kapamadji 6.10.1962.

877, 880, 882. PG: Baldwin 1.2.1946; ex Grantley 2872.

879. FM: provenance unrecorded.

881. PG: Baldwin 15.5.1957; ?ex Cuerdale hoard, suggested by the peck-marks.

883. PG: Vinchon 16.6.1958 (list 14, no. 429).

884. PG: Vinchon 7.9.1950.

885, 890, 892. PG: Platt 1.9.1950.

886. PG: Tinchant 27.3.1950.

887. PG: Tinchant 22.4.1950.

888. PG: Lockett III 352; ex Grantley 2876.

889. PG: Seaby 30.5.1950; ex Mainguy.

891. PG: MMAG Basel 8.3.1957 (list 165, no. 185).

893. PG: Seaby 30.5.1950; ex Whitton.

894–6. PG: Vinchon 7.9.1950.

897. PG: Baldwin 1.2.1946; ex Grantley 2875; from Schulman sale 9.4.1912, lot 1487.

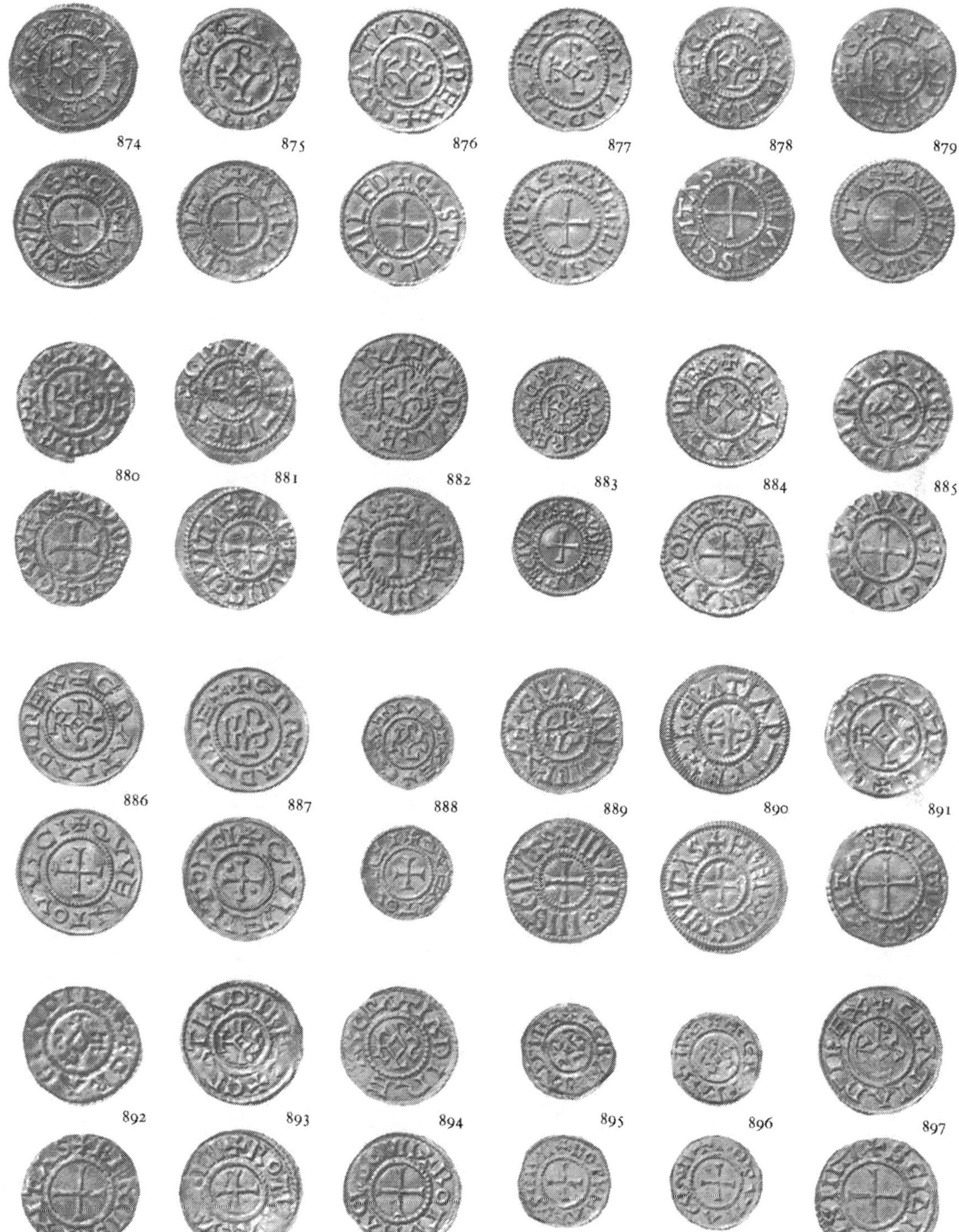

874 875 876 877 878 879

880 881 882 883 884 885

886 887 888 889 890 891

892 893 894 895 896 897

CAROLINGIANS (9): WEST FRANKISH KINGDOM

References as on Plate 33. The coins are silver and are deniers unless otherwise indicated.

CHARLES THE BALD, 840–77 (cont.)

Class 2 (864–77 and later) (cont.)

898 *Saint-Denis* (**SCI ΔIONVSII M**). Obol. 0.74g 270°. P 347 var.; G XXXIV 122 var.; MG 844.

899 *Saint-Quentin* (**:SC̄I QVINTINI MO:**). **GRIATIA D̄I RIX**. 1.63g 0°. P 253; G XXXIV 236 var.; MG 772.

900 *Sens* (**SENONES CIVITAS**). 1.73g 210°. P 577; G XXXV 243 var.; MG 984.

901 *Soissons* (**SVESSIO CIVITAS**). 1.69g 290°. P 278; G XXXV 248; MG 805.

902 *Soissons, Saint-Sébastien* (**S̄CI SEBASTIANI M̄**). 1.80g 260°. P –; G XXXIV 240; MG 1145.

903 *Tours* (**TVR◇NES CIVITAS**). 1.76g 140°. P 450; G XXXVI 267; MG 916.

904 *Tours* (**HTVR◇NES CIVITAS**). 1.58g 10°. P 450; G –; MG 915.

905 *Troyes* (**TRECAS CIVITAS**). **D** in obv. legend retrograde. 1.55g 250°. P 547 var.; G XXXVI 271 var.; MG 956 var.

906 *Valenciennes* (**VALENCIANIS PORT**). 1.70g 10°. P 208; G XXXVI 277; MG 730.

Class 2 var. With **KARL CTD** inscription and **℞** in the field, i.e. KARL*us* Gra*T*ia *D*ei Re*X*, a version of the GDR formula used only at Autun. The Issy-l'Évêque hoard (MG hoard 76) shows the coins to be of Charles the Bald.

907 *Autun, Saint-Nazaire* (**MONT S NAΣ**). 1.69g 260°. P 603; G XXXIX 16; MG 1419; PA 5643 var.

908 *As last*, but retrograde **℞** monogram. 1.32g 270°. P 603 var.; G XXXIX 16 var.; MG 1419; PA 5643 var.

Anomalous type contemporary with Class 2

909 *Beauvais* (**BELGEVAGVS CIVI**). **CAROLVS REX FRAN**. Monogram with lower arm of **K** missing and **L** and **S** transposed. 1.48g 0°. P 256 var.; G XLII 42; MG 1375. These are the earliest Carolingian coins of Beauvais, and the Arras and ANS hoards (MG hoards 67 and 84) show them to be contemporary with Class 2.

Class 3 (876–7), imperial coinage. With **CARLVS IMPERAT** or **CARLVS IMP AVG** or derivative around cross on obv. and mint name around monogram on rev. On the distinction between coins of Charles the Bald and Charles the Fat as emperor, see pp. 233, 235 above. The type and legend were immobilized, however, and some of those here may be later issues. For an Italian coin of Charles the Bald as emperor, see **1009**.

910 *Arles* (**ARELA CIVIS X**). **IMPERAT**. 1.22g 150°. P 869 var.; G XL 10; MG 1496.

911 *Arles* (**ARELA CIVIS +**). **NPEART**. Monogram retrograde. 1.42g 160°. P 880; G XL 10 var.; MG 1514.

912 *Arles* (**ARELA CIVIS +**). **NREART**. 1.52g 40°. P 879; G XL 10 var.; MG 1509.

913 *Bourges* (**BITVRICES CIVITA**). **IM̄P AVC**. 1.59g 0°. P 747; G XLII 45 var.; MG 1480 var.

914 *Bourges* (**BITVRICES CIVIT**). **IM̄P AV̄C**. 1.67g 190°. P 743; G XLII 45 var.; MG 1479.

915 *Bourges* (**BITVRICES CIVIT**). **IM̄P AVC**. 1.50g 130°. P 743 var.; G XLII 45 var.; MG 1480.

916 *As last*. 1.57g 40°. Ref. as last.

917 *Bourges* (**BITVRICES CIVI**). **IMP AV̄C**. 1.76g 180°. P 747 var.; G XLII 44; MG 1485.

918 *Bourges* (**BITVRCES CIVT**). Obol. **IM̄P AVG**. Monogram retrograde. 0.77g 220°. P 746 var.; G XXIV 88 var.; MG 1487.

919 *Nevers* (**NEVERNIS CIVIT**, w. inverted **U** for **N**). **IM̄P AVC**. 1.65g 220°. P 596; G XXIV 91; MG 1464. The Issy-l'Évêque hoard of *c.* 880 (MG hoard 76) shows that these belong to Charles the Bald.

920 *As last*. 1.63g 100°. Ref. as last.

921 *As last*. Obol. **IM̄P AVC**. 0.80g 290°. P 598; G –; MG 1467.

922 *Toulouse* (**TOLOSA x CIVI**). **IMPR̄**. With letters **CA/RL** in centre of rev. 1.41g 320°. P 821; G XLII 57; MG 1488. The **X** in the reverse legend is reminiscent of that found on many coins of 'Melle', see Plates 42–3.

898, 901. PG: Vinchon 7.9.1950.

899–900. PG: Seaby 16.7.1945; ex Grantley 2877; ex Viry 331.

902. PG: Boutin 6.10.1962.

903. PG: Seaby 16.7.1945; ex Grantley 2877.

904. QC: provenance unrecorded.

905. PG: Seaby 16.7.1945; ex Grantley 2877 (not noted in catalogue).

906. PG: Seaby 16.7.1945; ex Grantley 2878; ex Viry 333.

907. PG: Baldwin 1.2.1946; ex Grantley 3032; ex Coll. H... (Paris 31.1.1912) 99.

908. PG: Bourgey 17.4.1959.

909. PG: Baldwin 18.4.1946.

910. PG: Wolfe 25.5.1970.

911. PG: MMAG Basel 30.9.1946.

912. PG: Baldwin 15.5.1947.

913. PG: Spink 22.2.1945.

914. PG: Baldwin 1.2.1946; ex Grantley 2866.

915. FM: provenance unrecorded.

916, 920–1. CCC (*Catalogue* nos. 66–8): Lewis 1891; bought at Nevers 21.9.1880 and said to have been found at Veuillin (Cher), but there was perhaps a confusion with the Veuillin hoard of Louis the Pious' reign (MG hoard no. 15). Perhaps from the Issy-l'Évêque hoard (MG hoard 76).

917. PG: ex Blunt 17.3.1948; ex Grantley duplicates.

918. PG: Platt 1.9.1950.

919. PG: Spink 4.1.1967.

922. PG: Baldwin 21.7.1946.

898 899 900 901 902 903

904 905 906 907 908 909

910 911 912 913 914 915

916 917 918 919 920 921 922

CAROLINGIANS (10): COINS OF 'MELLE' WITH *KAROLVS* MONOGRAM

This plate and the next include all deniers of 'Melle' having as types a *Karolus* monogram and a cross and the legends **CARLVS REX FR** and **METVLLO** or **METxVLLO**, together with the corresponding obols. It seems reasonable to group them together, since those of Charlemagne cannot be distinguished with certainty from those struck early in Charles the Bald's reign, or those of Charles the Bald's later years from those struck subsequently, as an immobilized type, during the last quarter of the 9th century and continuing possibly down to the mid 10th century. See above, pp. 238–9, where it is also argued that the inscription **METxVLLO** – which started in Charles the Bald's reign and was used concurrently with, and eventually much more frequently than, the original **METVLLO** – was intended to differentiate coins struck at Poitiers from those of Melle itself.

References as on Plate 33. The coins are silver.

A. *Coins without* **X** *in inscription or field*

(a) Deniers with **METVLLO**

923 was probably struck under Charlemagne and **924–33** probably under Charles the Bald. All have a chevron in the centre of the monogram. References are P 688, 692–8; G XII 209, XXIII 58; MG 172, 1063; PA 2347.

923 1.66g 190°.
924 1.73g 270°. Obv. double struck.
925 1.65g 220°.
926 1.72g 0°. Chevron indistinct.
927 1.65g 220°.
928 1.67g 40°.
929 1.77g 280°.
930 1.65g 60°.
931 1.64g 300°.
932 1.77g 210°.
933 1.53g 110°.

(b) Obol, monogram without **X** in field

934 With chevron in centre of monogram. 0.65g chipped 110°. P 703; G XXIV 76; MG 1060; PA 2349.

B. *Coins with* **X** *in inscription or field*

(a) Early deniers with **METxVLLO**, some probably struck under Charles the Bald

All are without a chevron in the monogram. References are: P 699; G XXIII 59; MG 1064; PA 2357.

935 1.58g 60°.
936 1.65g 160°.
937 1.69g 70°.
938 1.57g 160°.
939 Retrograde **S** in monogram. 1.70g 90°.

(b) Later deniers with **METxVLLO**, of cruder style (late 9th/early 10th centuries)

All are without a chevron in the monogram. References are: P 701; G –; MG 1064; PA 2357ff. Those with Viking peck-marks are probably from the Cuerdale hoard (dep. *c.* 905), although this provenance is documented in only a few cases.

940 1.56g 220°.
941 1.76g 320°. Peck-mark on rev.
942 1.60g 320°.
943 1.61g 220°. One peck-mark on obv., 2 on rev.
944 1.57g 340°.
945 1.63g 0°.
946 Retrograde **S** in monogram. 1.67g 0°.

923. PG: Baldwin 28.8.1946.
924. FM: Jenkinson 1923.
925–32. FM: Young 1936; ex C. E. B. Young (his brother); ex Sotheby 8.4.1880, lot 292. These coins share the same dark sandy deposit on their surfaces and, together with 5 coins of a similar type in the next lot at the Sotheby sale, are evidently a parcel from a hoard, possibly Bonnevaux 1854 (MG hoard 70).
933. PG: Baldwin 1.2.1946; ex Grantley 3072.
934, 938. PG: Baldwin 1.2.1946; ex Grantley 2871.
935. PG: Lockett III 363; ex Spink.
936. PG: Blunt 17.3.1948; ex Grantley duplicate.
937. PG: Baldwin 29.8.1946.
939. PG: Sotheby 28.3.1947, lot 91.
940. FM: provenance unrecorded.
941. FM: provenance unrecorded; ?ex Cuerdale hoard, suggested by peck-mark.
942. CCC (*Catalogue* no. 65): Lewis 1891.
943. PG: Blunt 17.3.1948; ex Grantley duplicate; ?ex Cuerdale hoard, suggested by peck-marks.
944. PG: Blunt 17.3.1948; ex Grantley duplicate.
945. PG: Baldwin 1.2.1946; ex Grantley 3072.
946. FM: provenance unrecorded.

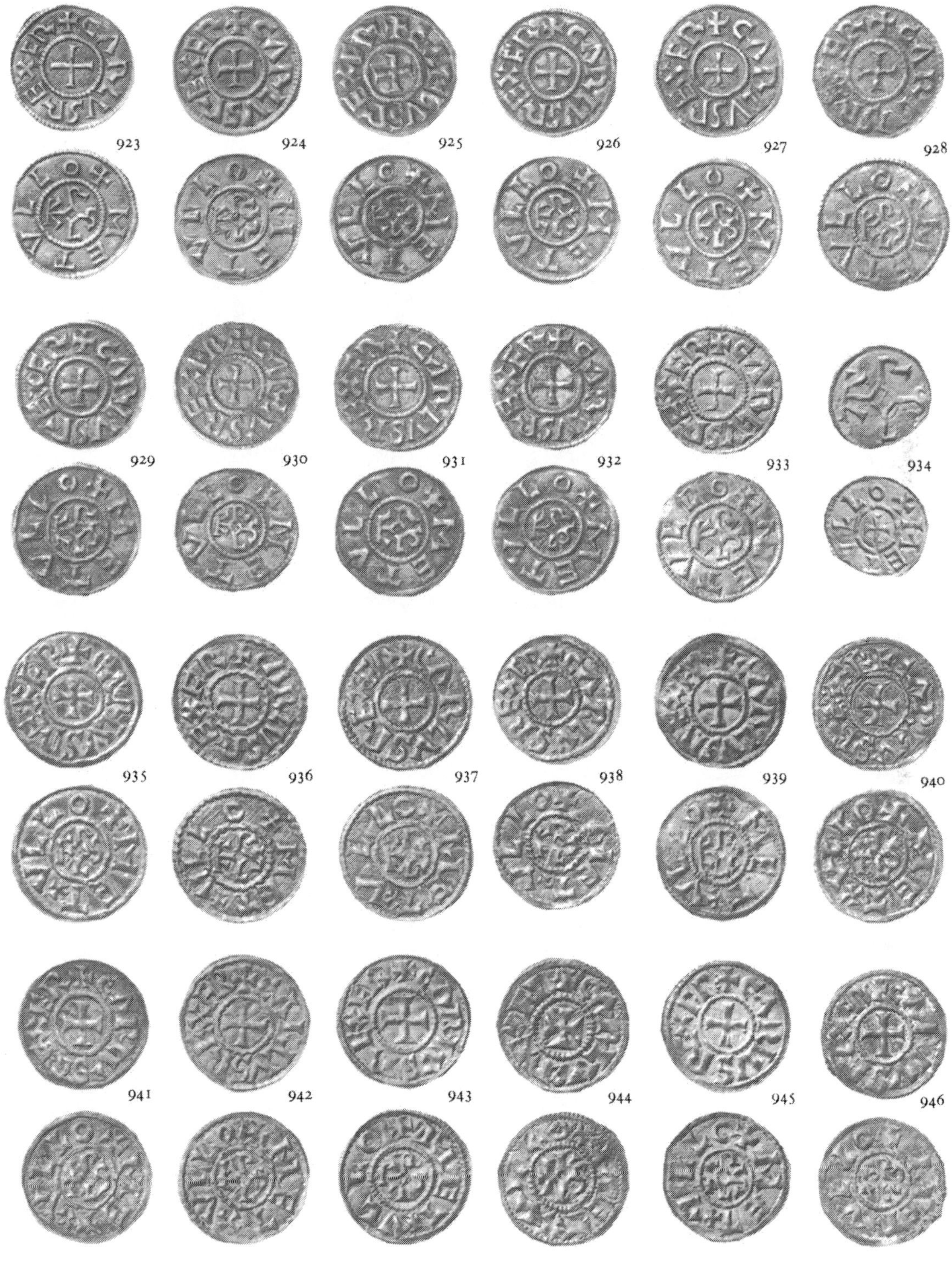

923 924 925 926 927 928

929 930 931 932 933 934

935 936 937 938 939 940

941 942 943 944 945 946

CAROLINGIANS (11): COINS OF 'MELLE' WITH *KAROLVS* MONOGRAM

References as on Plate 33. The coins are silver, except **965** which is gold. Those with Viking peck-marks are probably from the Cuerdale hoard (dep. *c.* 905), although this provenance is only documented in a few cases.

B. *Coins with* **X** *in inscription or field* (cont.)

(b) Later deniers with **METxVLLO**, of cruder style (late 9th/early 10th centuries) (cont.)

947 **CARLV REX FR**. 1.51g 180°. 2 peck-marks on obv.
948 *As last.* 1.64g 330°.
949 **CARLV2 REX FR**, retrograde **S** in monogram. 1.62g 160°. Peck-mark on obv.
950 *As last.* 1.53g 130°.
951 *As last.* 1.63g 20°. Peck-mark on rev.
952 **CARLVS REX F**. 1.65g 60°.
953 *As last.* 1.52g 80°. One peck-mark on obv., one on rev.
954 *As last.* 1.40g 140°. 2 peck-marks on obv., 2 on rev.
955 *As last.* 1.60g 160°.
956 *As last.* 1.64g 290°. Peck-mark on obv. and 'nick' on rev.
957 *As last.* 1.64g 30°. Peck-mark on obv.
958 *As last.* 1.59g 70°.
959 **CARLV2 REX F**, retrograde **S** in monogram. 1.71g 180°. 2 peck-marks on obv.
960 **CARLVS REX R**. 1.64g 220°.
961 *As last.* 1.57g 230°. 2 peck-marks on obv., one on rev.

(c) Obols, monogram with **X** in lower left field
All are without a chevron in the monogram.

962 0.76g 0°. P 706; G XXIV 77; MG 1061; PA 2361.
963 0.46g chipped 300°. Ref. as last.
964 Retrograde **S** in monogram. 0.74g 320°. P 706 var.; G XXIV 78; MG 1061; PA 2361 var.

(d) Gold denier with **METxVLLO**

965 **CARLVS REX R**. 1.64g (SG 15.66: 72% Au) 270°. MG 1062 = PA 2364 (this coin). See note on coin and Appendix 1.

947. FM: Hasluck 1920; ex Cuerdale hoard.
948. PG: Baldwin 1.2.1946; ex Grantley 3072.
949. FM: Searle? (ticket in his hand); ex Sadd; ex Cuerdale hoard, suggested by peck-mark.
950, 955. PG: Blunt 17.3.1948; ex Grantley duplicate.
951, 956. PG: Blunt 17.3.1948; ex Grantley duplicate; ?ex Cuerdale hoard, suggested by peck-marks.
952–3. FM: Hasluck 1920; ex Cuerdale hoard.
954. FM: Parkes Weber, Jan. 1907; 'from H.W., 1885' (i.e. Sir Hermann Weber); ?ex Cuerdale hoard, suggested by peck-marks.
957. PG: Baldwin 1.2.1946; ex Grantley 3072; ?ex Cuerdale hoard, suggested by peck-mark.
958. PG: Baldwin 18.4.1946.
959. PG: Spink 12.2.1945; ex Cuerdale hoard.
960. FM: provenance unrecorded.
961. PG: Baldwin 1.2.1946; ex Grantley 3072; ?ex Cuerdale hoard, suggested by peck-marks.
962. FM: provenance unrecorded.
963–4. PG: Baldwin 1.2.1946; ex Grantley 2871.
965. PG: Bourgey sale 6.6.1955, lot 297; ex Motte coll. (= Rolland 1932, no. 131; but not in Motte sale) . . . ex Lecointre-Dupont.

947 948 949 950 951 952

953 954 955 956 957 958

959 960 961 962 963 964

965

CAROLINGIANS (12): WEST FRANKISH KINGDOM

References as on Plate 33. The coins are silver and are deniers unless otherwise indicated.

LOUIS II (THE STAMMERER)

King of Aquitaine, 867–77; of the West Franks, 877–9

or

LOUIS III

Joint king of the West Franks, 879–82

966 *Toulouse* (**TOLOSA CIVI**). **LVDOVICVS REX. LV/DO** in centre of rev. 1.61g 350°. The design with **LV/DO** on the rev. is found only at Toulouse and is similar to the **CA/RL** used under Charles the Bald (see **922**).

967 *Tours* (**TVR◇NES CIVITAS**). **MISERICORDIA D¯I REX** around *Hludovicus* monogram. 1.55g 190°. P 453; G XXXVIII 13; MG 1255.

CARLOMAN

Joint king of the West Franks, 879–82; sole king, 882–4

968 *Substantion* (**ƧVƧTANCONE**). **CARLAMAN RE.** With **KSLM** monogram. 1.53g 120°. P 841 var.; G XXXIV 19 var.; MG 1206.

CHARLES THE FAT

King of the West Franks, 884–7; emperor, 881–7; d. 888

969 *Cambrai, Saint-Géry* (**SCI GAVGERICI MON**). **IMPERA TOR A·CVST** around *Carolus* monogram with retrograde **S**. 1.38g 140°. P 125 = G XLII 56; MG 1445. For the attribution to Charles the Fat rather than Charles the Bald, see p. 235 above.

For an Italian coin of Charles the Fat as emperor, see **1012**, and for a forgery of a coin of his from the Middle Kingdom, Verdun, see **1503**.

ODO (Eudes)

King of the West Franks, 888–97

Odo's coin types and inscriptions were often immobilized (or in some cases re-adopted) in the 10th century, and not all the following coins belong to Odo's reign. But the distinction is difficult, for the Cuerdale hoard shows that coins which appear to be late because of their spread fabric and coarse lettering can in fact be of the late 9th century.

Gratia Dei rex types

With some form of the name **ODO** in the field surrounded by **GRATIA D¯I REX** on the obverse and the mint name around a cross on the reverse.

970 *Angers* (**ANDEGAVIS CIVITAS**). **+◇DO** around pellet. 1.75g 240°. P 432; G XLIV 4; MG 1291.

971 *As last*, but **D¯REX**. 1.02g chipped and corroded 180°. P 432 var.; G XLIV 4 var.; MG 1291.

972 *Chartres* (**CARN◇TIS CIVITASI**). **◇D◇**, w. + above and below, 4 radiating strokes, and 2 pellets to left. 1.80g 120°. P 497; G XLVI 19 var.; MG 1315.

973 *Limoges* (**LIM◇VICS CIVIS**). **◇D◇**, w. + above and below. **RE** for **REX**. 1.77g 10°. P 783; G XLVII 28; MG 1332.

974 *As last*, but **CIVIƧ**. 1.76g 310°. P 782; G XLVII 28 var.; MG 1332.

975 *As last*. 1.75g 230°. Ref. as last.

976 *As* **973**, but **CIVI**. 1.44g 90°. P 799 var.; G XLVII 26 var.; MG 1333.

977 *Limoges* (**LIM◇VICA∽**). Obol. Obv. **+◇D◇ REX E**, around **◇**. 0.56g worn 200°. P 787; G XLVII 28; MG 1336.

978 *Orléans* (**AVRELIANIS CIVITA**). Obv. **GRATIA¯II**, around **◇D◇ RƎX** disposed in field. 1.65g chipped 340°. P 523 var.; G XLVII 32; MG 1324.

979 *Soissons* (**SVESSIO CIVITAS**). **OD◇** and 2 crosses in field. 1.67g chipped 30°. P 286; G XLVIII 50; MG 1279. Same dies as P 286 and MG, pl. 40.1279.

Misericordia Dei types

With monogram **◇DO RX** in the field surrounded by **MISERI CORDIA D¯I** or derivative on the obverse and the mint name around a cross on the reverse.

980 *Blois* (**BLESIANIS CASTR◇**). **DE¯I**. 1.65g 220°. P 482; G XLVI 9; MG 1311.

981 *As last*. 1.60g 220°. Ref. as last.

982 *Tours* (**HTVR◇NES CIVITAS**). 1.65g 270°. P 461; G XLVIII 57; MG 1295.

983 *As last*, but w. **DH** for **D¯I** and monogram retrograde. 1.68g 270°. P 465; G XLVIII 58 var.; MG 1304.

966. PG: Kapamadji 6.10.1962.
967, 975. PG: Blunt 17.3.1948; ex Grantley duplicate.
968. PG: Boutin 5.10.1951.
969. PG: Bourgey sale 14.6.1966, lot 373.
970. PG: Vinchon 7.9.1950.
971. PG: Kapamadji 1.9.1950.
972, 979. PG: Kress sale 116 (28.9.1960), lots 1495 and 1500 respectively.
973. PG: Sotheby 28.7.1947, lot 91.
974. PG: Spink 12.2.1945; ex Grantley 2886.
976, 982. FM: provenance unrecorded.
977. PG: Platt 1.9.1950.
978. PG: Lockett III 363.
980. PG: Spink 8.2.1945; ex Grantley 2886.
981. PG: Baldwin 10.10.1952; ex Lawrence.
983. Vinchon 7.9.1950.

[*continued overleaf*]

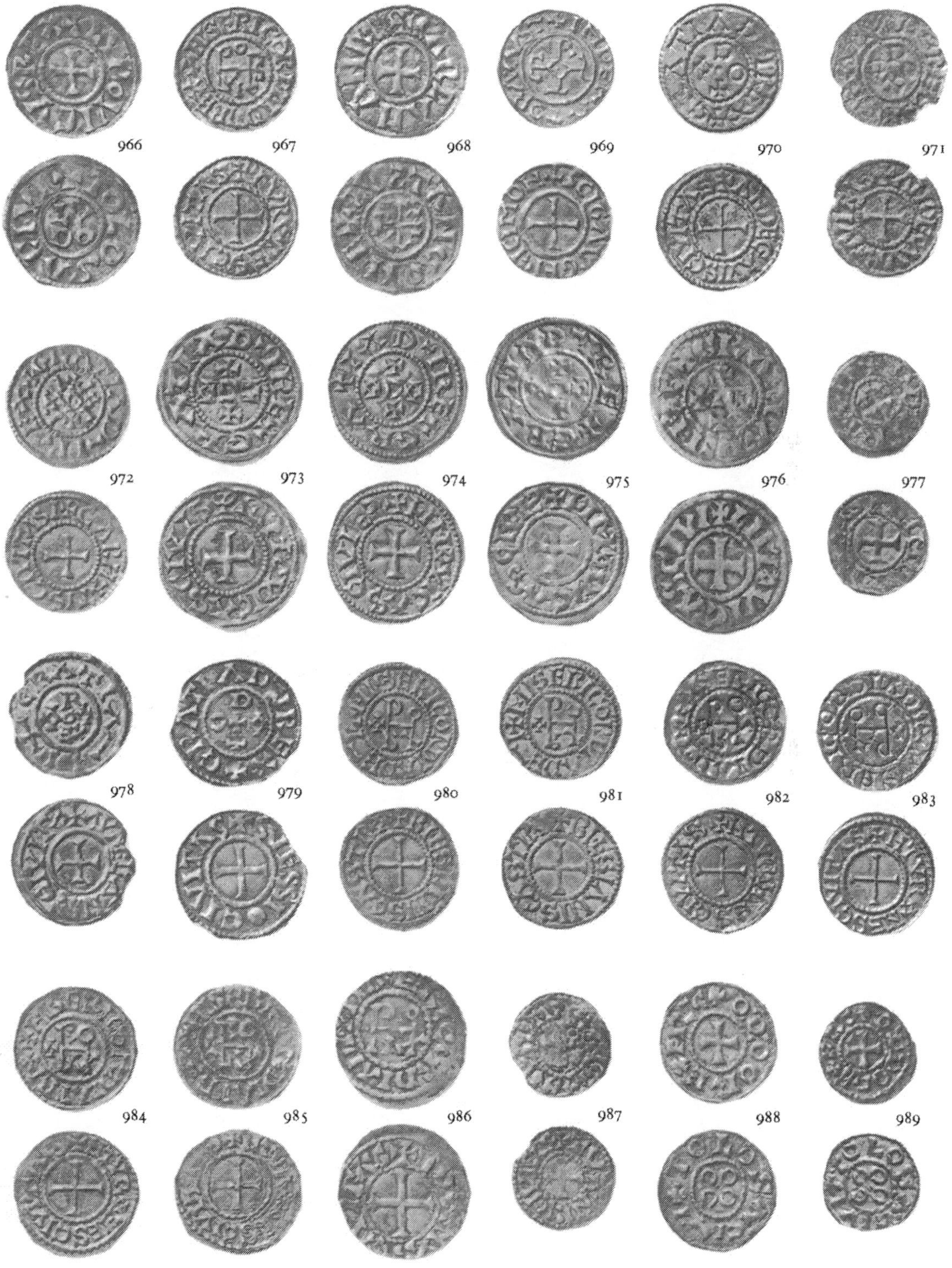

966 967 968 969 970 971

972 973 974 975 976 977

978 979 980 981 982 983

984 985 986 987 988 989

984 *As* **982**, but w. **IRI** for **D‾I** and **R** for **D** in monogram. 1.68g 90°. P 464 var.; G XLVIII 58 var.; MG 1304 var.
985 *As* **982**, but w. **IRD** for **R‾I** and **R** for **D** in monogram. 1.64g 0°. Ref. as last.
986 *Tours* (**TVR◆NVS CIVITAS**). **DI** for **D‾I**. 1.43g 210°. P 469 var.; G XLVIII 4 (Robert I); MG 1301; PA 1616. This is of crude style and is probably a posthumous copy of the foregoing coins. Lafaurie attributes coins of this type to Raoul (Lafaurie 1965a, 286).
987 *Tours* (**TV◆NIS CIVITAS**). Obol. +**GRATIA DI REX**. With a monogram **S**, **O** and **X**? 0.65g corroded 180°. P –; G XLVIII 59; MG 1249; PA 1617.

Oddo rex Francorum types

With the obv. legend **ODDO REX FR** or derivative. A form of this legend was used on coins of Amiens, Corbie, Limoges (obols only, cf. **977**) and Toulouse, although the coin design differed in each case.

988 *Toulouse* (**TOLOSA: CIVI**). +**O:D:DO REX FR‾C**. With **ODDO** in field of rev. 1.38g 140°. P 823 var.; G XLVIII 54; MG 1340.
989 *Toulouse* (**TOLOSA· CIVI**). Obol. +**O:D:DO REX FR‾C**. With **OOOO** in field of rev. 0.63g 120°. P 825 var.; G XLVIII 55 var.; MG 1339.

984. PG: Platt 1.9.1950. 985. PG: Spink 20.3.1947. 986. PG: Baldwin 21.12.1971. 987–9. Vinchon 7.9.1950.

CAROLINGIANS (13): WEST FRANKISH KINGDOM

References as on Plate 33. The coins are silver and are deniers unless otherwise indicated.

CHARLES THE SIMPLE

King of the West Franks, 897–922 (nominally from 893; dep. 922; d. 929)

Although most of Charles the Simple's coins follow the GDR type of Charles the Bald, so that it is sometimes difficult to distinguish between the coins of the two rulers, some mints, like Paris, adopted different designs.

990 *Arras* (**ATREB·A2 CIV**). **DVTI:I RE+** retrograde; a deformation of *Gratia Dei rex*. Crescent or **C** in 1st and 4th quarters of rev. 1.54g 70°. P 226; G –; MG 746. No hoard provenances for coins of this type are known, but their absence from the Fécamp and Le Puy hoards suggests that they belong to the first half of the 10th century.

Arras. For another possible coin of Charles the Simple, see **852**.

991 *Beauvais* (**BELGEVACVS CIVI**). Monogram with lower arm of **K** missing and **L** and **S** transposed. 1.81g 200°. P 261 var. (as Raoul immobilization); G XLIX 8 var.; MG 1577 (as Raoul). This type has been attributed by some to Raoul because of the form of the monogram, but the same monogram is found on coins of Charles the Bald (cf. **909**), and the form of the mint name, the weights, and the absence of these coins from the Fécamp hoard suggest that they belong to Charles the Simple. True coins of Raoul of Beauvais are MG 1578–9.

992 *Brive* (**BRIVIO VICI**). *Obol*. **CAILVS REX**. 0.84g 160°. P –; G –; MG 1430 (this coin). See note on coin for the mint identification. This coin is supposedly unique, but its authenticity is not certain.

Bruges. For a forgery, see **1506**.

Courcessin. For possible coins of Charles the Simple, see **860–7**.

993 *Le Mans* (**CINOMANIS CIVITAS**). 1.74g 150°. P 426; G –; MG 909. This and the following two coins belong to the first series distinguished by Mme Dumas in her Fécamp publication (Dumas 1971, 228). The weights of these specimens, compared with the weights of those in the Rennes and Fécamp hoards, suggests that they belong early in Charles the Simple's reign.

994 *Le Mans* (**CINOM:ANIS CIVITAS**). 1.71g 70°. P 426 var.; G –; MG 909.

995 *Le Mans* (**CINOMANIS CIVITAS**). **GRATI"A" D:I REX**. 1.67g 50°. Ref. as last.

996 *Paris* (**PARISI/CIVITA**). **DI** for **D̄I**. Mint name in rev. field. 1.68g 20°. P 334; G LI 57 var.; MG 1391.

997 *As last*. 1.23g chipped, broken and repaired. 310°. Ref. as last. Struck from pitted dies.

Provins. For a forgery, see **1507**.

998 *Quentovic* (**QVVENTOVVIC**). Pellet in each rev. quarter. 1.35g 290°. P 200 var.; G LI 60; MG 718. The type became immobilized during the second half of the 10th century; such a specimen will be published in Vol. 5.

Rennes. For a possible coin of Charles the Simple, see **889–90**.

German issues (after 911). With mint name in field.

999 *Cologne* (**S/COLONIA/A**, for *Sancta Colonia Agrippina*). Obv. **KVROLVS REX**, cross with pellet in each quarter. 1.51g 0°. P 82; G XL 1; MG 1352; Hävernick 1935, 23b var.

1000 *Strasbourg* (**ARGEIITI/IIA C̄VIT** for *Argentina civitas*). **IWIROLVS PIVS REX**. 1.02g chipped 40°. P 55 var.; G LI 72 var.; MG 1351.

RAOUL

King of France, 923–36

Gratia Dei rex type

1001 *Chartres* (**CARNOTIS CIVITAS**). Blundered *Rudolfus* monogram in *Karolus* form. 1.30g 315°. P 498 (as Charles the Simple); G –; MG –. Probably Raoul. The left hand letter in the monogram has vertical rather than horizontal wedges suggesting that the letter **R** is intended, although it lacks the central wedge on the lower letter to form an **F** as is usual on coins of Raoul of this type (Dumas 1980, no. 20). The two coins of Chartres of Charles the Simple in the Rennes hoard (Lafaurie 1965a, nos. 25–6) are of a rather different style and have horizontal wedges to the letter **C**.

1002 *Orléans* (**AVRELIANIS CIVITAS**). *Rudolfus* monogram in *Karolus* form. 1.36g 120°. P 529 var.; G LIV 34; MG 1595 var.

Courcessin and *Rheims*. For modern forgeries, see **1508–9**.

Posthumous issue

1003 *Orléans* (**AVRELIANIS CIVITA**). Rudolfus monogram of Odo type. 1.33g 210°. P 525 var.; G LIV 31 var.; MG 1598. Coins with this monogram form post-date those with the *Karolus* form and were probably introduced after Raoul's death at mints in the region where Hugh the Great exercised authority (Dumas 1980, 219). This type was immobilized until the end of the century.

990. PG: Baldwin 1.2.1946; ex Grantley 3031.
991. PG: Baldwin 1.2.1946; ex Grantley 2866.
992. PG: MMAG Basel sale 7 (3.12.1948), lot 163.
993. PG: Spink 18.10.1961.
994. PG: Baldwin 28.1.1946.
995. FM: provenance unrecorded.
996. PG: ANS (duplicate) 1.9.1961.
997. PG: Baldwin 28.11.1947; ex Grantley 2889; bt in London.
998. PG: Seaby 8.6.1946.
999. PG: Kress sale 116 (28.9.1960), lot 1569.
1000. PG: Gaettens sale 22 (18.11.1966), lot 53 (Gaettens coll.).
1001. PG: Platt 1.9.1950.
1002. PG: Platt 6.2.1982.
1003. PG: Platt 29.10.1970.

[*continued overleaf*]

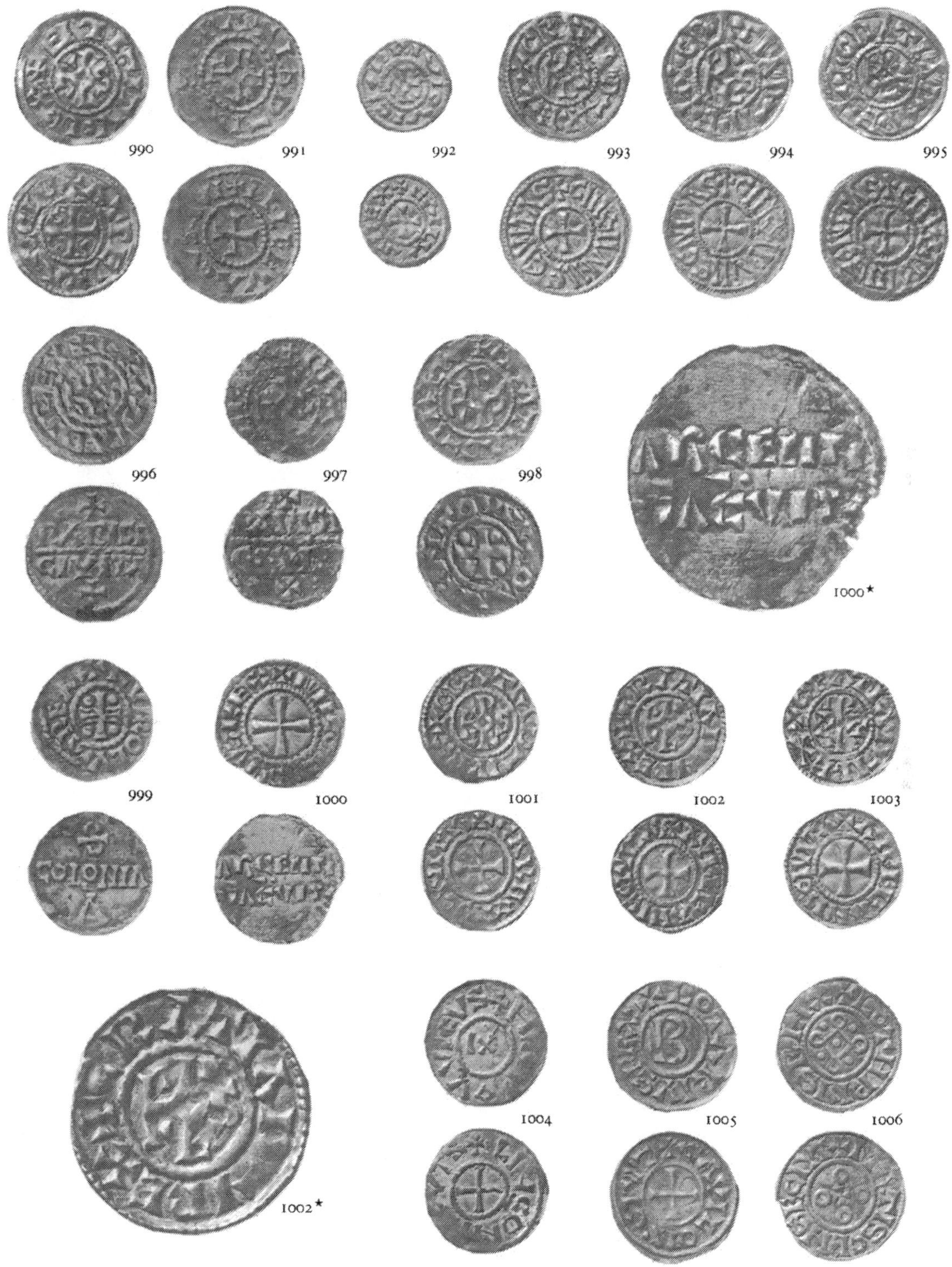

990 991 992 993 994 995

996 997 998 1000*

999 1000 1001 1002 1003

1002* 1004 1005 1006

PLATE 45 (*cont.*)

LOUIS IV

King of France, 936–54

Rx in field type

1004 *Langres* (**LINGONIS CVTS**). **HLVD◊VVICVS**. With **IX** (deformed ℞) in field. 1.14g 20°. P 611 var.; G LV 10 var.; MG 1636. The type became immobilized during the second half of the 10th century (Dumas 1971, 174–5), and this specimen may well have been struck after Louis' death.

LOTHAIRE

King of France, 954–86

1005 *Chalon-sur-Saône* (**CAVILON.CIVT**). **LOTARIVS REX**, w. **B** (for *Burgundia*) in field. 1.24g 270°. P 622 var.; G LVII 12; MG 1663.

1006 *Mâcon* (**MATISCENSE CIVT**). **LOTHRIVS REIX**. Rev. design of four **O**s around a cross derived from an Odo monogram. 1.11g chipped 90°. P 624 var.; G LVII 17 var.; MG 1664 var.

Bourges. The four coins in the collection with **LOTERIVS REX**, monogram and temple, are reserved for Vol. 5, since they are 11th century in date.

1004. PG: Seaby 6.3.1945; ex Grantley 2893.
1005. PG: Lockett III 364; ex Grantley 2891; from Rollin.
1006. PG: Lockett III 364; ex Grantley 2892.

ITALY, 855–961

Principal references are: *CNI* and Sambon = Sambon 1912. All the coins are silver denari. Most of those on the plate are of *Christiana religio* type, without any formal indication of mint, and attributions depend partly on letter-forms, partly on the form of the cross and partly on module. For detailed explanations, see pp. 252 ff. above. Since the size of the coins are in some cases relevant for their identification, the diameters of both the flan and the reverse die-face are given. Most of the coins from **1008** onwards are slightly saucer-shaped (*scodellato*). For Italian coins of Charlemagne, Louis the Pious and Lothar I, see Plates 33–7.

LOUIS II

Emperor, 855–75

(a) Small module

1007 *Unspecified mint* (*Milan*). Obv. **+HLVDOVVICVS IMP** Rev. **XRISTIANA REIICIO**. 1.70g 20/22mm 320°. *CNI* V, 18.27. The letter forms, especially the **S**, the barred **A**, and the **I** for **L** in *religio*, are typical of Milanese coins of Louis II and his successors. This appears to be an early issue of Louis II, struck on a similar module to coins of his predecessor Lothar (see **821–2**).

(b) Larger module

1008 *Unspecified mint* (*Milan*). Obv. **+HLVDOVVICVS IMP** Rev. **XPISTIANA REIICIO**. 1.76g 25/21mm 160°. Sambon 592 (as Louis I); *CNI* V, 16.2.

For Louis II's coins minted at Benevento, see **1116–18**.

CHARLES THE BALD

Emperor, 875–7

1009 *Unspecified mint* (*Milan*). Obv. **+HCAROLVS IMPER** Rev. **XPISTIANA REIICIO**. 1.54g chipped 25/22mm 90°. Sambon 626; *CNI* V, 22.3 var.

CARLOMAN

King of Italy, 877–9

1010 *Unspecified mint* (*Milan*). Obv. **+CARLOMAN REX** Rev. **XPISTIANA REIICIO**. 1.76g 27/23mm 190°. Sambon 627; *CNI* V, 23.1.

1011 *Unspecified mint* (*Pavia*). Obv. **+HCARLEMANNVS RE** Rev. **XDISTIANA RELICIO**. 1.72g 26/23mm 110°. Sambon 628 var.; *CNI* V, 24.8 (as Milan). The coin has typical Pavese features: the **A**s unbarred, the **E**s ending in spikes, the **S**s almost straight, the **P** formed virtually as a **D**, and an **L** in *religio*.

CHARLES THE FAT

Emperor, 881–7

1012 *Unspecified mint* (*Milan*). Obv. **+CAROLVS IMP** Rev. **XRISTIANA REIICIO**. 1.72g 30/24mm 310°. Sambon 630; *CNI* V, 25.6 var.

BERENGAR I

King of Italy 888–915; emperor, 915–24

First coinage, as king (888–9)

1013 *Unspecified mint* (*Pavia*). Obv. **+DERENGARIVS REX** Rev. **XDIITIANA RELIGIO**. 1.50g 30/26mm 70°. Sambon 645; *CNI* V, 31.35 (as Milan). In addition to the Pavese features referred to above, the **D** for **B** and **XDII** in *Christiana* are typical of the mint.

GUY OF SPOLETO

Emperor, 891–4

1014 *Unspecified mint* (*Pavia*). Obv. **+VVIDO IMPERATOR** (**MP** ligatured) Rev. **XDIITIANA RELIGIO**. 1.57g 33/27mm 230°. Sambon 633; *CNI* V, 26.7 var.

LAMBERT OF SPOLETO

Emperor, 894–8

First coinage (894)

1015 *Unspecified mint* (*Pavia*). Obv. **+LAMDERTVS IMPE** Rev. **XDIITIANA RELIGIO**, obscured by ghosting. 1.42g 31/26mm 90°. Sambon 635; *CNI* V, 27.2.

1007. PG: de Falco 16.5.1983.

1008. PG: Franceschi 10.4.1956; ex Lockett III 340; ex Boulton; ex Ratto sale 24.2.1913, lot 7.

1009. PG: Spink 12.2.1945; ex Grantley 2884; from Schulman.

1010. PG: Bank Leu 10.6.1983.

1011. PG: Spink 21.9.1945; ex Boulton; ex G. Gavazzi 426.

1012. PG: Spink 21.9.1945 (*NCirc* Feb. 1945, no. 29148); ex Grantley 3196.

1013. PG: Spink 21.9.1945; ex Boulton; ex G. Gavazzi 12.

1014. PG: Spink 9.7.1945; ex Grantley 3409; from Schulman.

1015. PG: Lockett III 482; ex Boulton; ex Ratto sale 21.4.1914, lot 146.

[*continued overleaf*]

1007 1008 1009 1010 1011

1012 1013 1014 1015

1016 1017 1018 1019 1020

BERENGAR I (cont.)

Second coinage, as king (898–900)

1016 *Unspecified mint* (*Milan*). Obv. +**BERENCARIVI PE** Rev. **XPISTIANIA RELCIO**, cross w. pointed ends. 1.51g 23/20mm 270°. *CNI* V, 29.17 var.

Third coinage, as king (901–15)

1017 *Milan*. Obv. +**BERENGARIVI REX** Rev. **XPISTIANA REIICIO, MEDI/C/OLA** (the letters are so compressed, and the upright strokes so thick, that horizontal strokes are barely visible). 1.73g 22/19mm 10°. Sambon 644; *CNI* V, 28.2.

1018 *Unspecified mint* (*Venice*). Obv. +**BERENCARIVS RE**, cross w. pointed ends Rev. **XPI-IANI-PIO**. 1.41g 21/15mm 310°. Sambon 647 var.; *CNI* V, 29.17 (as Milan). The obv. die is larger than the rev. and the obv. inscription not entirely struck up. This coinage probably started at Venice as early as 898.

Fourth coinage, as emperor (915–24)

1019 *Pavia*. Obv. +**BERENGARIVS IMP** Rev. **XPIITANA RELI, PA/PIA/CI**. 1.83g 21/17mm (flattened) 230°. Sambon 652; *CNI* IV, 473.10 var. The high weight and unusually good state of preservation of this coin raise doubts about its authenticity, but the surface quality is that of a genuine piece and it is unlikely that a modern forger would have been able to imitate Pavese letter-forms this accurately.

1020 *Unspecified mint* (*Venice*). Obv. +**BERENCAR IVMP** (**MP** ligatured), cross w. pointed ends Rev. **XPITIAIIA RGIO**. 1.27g 22/17mm 210°. Sambon 651; *CNI* V, 33.53 (as Milan).

1016. PG: Spink 17.1.1946.
1017. PG: Spink 21.9.1945 (*NCirc* Feb. 1945, no. 29149); ex Grantley 3197.
1018. PG: Spink 17.1.1946; ex Boulton; ex Martinetti 200.
1019. PG: DO 12.5.1958; ex Peirce 1948.
1020. PG: Toderi 27.5.1982.

ITALY (2)

References as on Plate 46. The coins are silver denari.

RUDOLF (II) OF BURGUNDY

King of Italy, 922–6; d. 937

1021 *Milan*. Obv. **+RODVLFO PIVS RE** Rev. **+XPIITIAИΛ PCIO** around **MDI/OLA**. 1.31g 20/16mm 130°. Sambon 655; *CNI* V, 34.1.

1022 *As last*. 1.24g 20/15mm 140°. Ref. as last.

1023 *Pavia*. Class 2. Obv. **+RODVLFVS RX** Rev. **+XPII-TIΛNΛ RE** around **PΛ/PIΛ**. 1.73g 20/15mm 120°. Sambon 657; *CNI* IV, 474.2. Brambilla 1883, pl. 3.5.

HUGH OF ARLES

King of Italy, 926–47

Alone (926–31)

1024 *Unspecified mint, perhaps Venice*. Obv. **+VIVI PIVI RE+** (blundered from *Ugo pius rex*) Rev. **+XPI-IΛNΛ I-IIO**, around temple. 1.21g 21/15mm 0°. Sambon 659 (as Verona or Pavia); *CNI* –. Coins of this mint are not scodellati, but have a broad outer border. They probably continued to be struck throughout the reign.

With Lothaire II (931–47)

1025 *Pavia*. Obv. **+VGO LOHTΛRIV**, around monogram of **HVGO** Rev. **+XPIITIΛNΛ RE**, around **PΛ/PIΛ**. 1.41g 20/18mm 330°. Sambon 665; *CNI* IV, 474.1, Brambilla 1883, pl. 3.9.

1026 *As last*. 1.45g 19/18mm 270°. Ref. as last. *Pavia*. For a modern forgery, see **1512**.

LOTHAIRE II

Sole king, 946–50

Lothaire's coins retain the **HVGO** monogram.

1027 *Pavia*. **+HLOH[ ]RIV R** and **+XPIITIΛNΛ RE**, around **PΛ/PIΛ**. 1.48g 19/18mm 40°. Sambon 669; *CNI* IV, 476.2; Brambilla 1883, pl. 3.12.

1028 *As last*, but obv. **+[ ]OHTΛRIV RE**. 1.56g 19/18mm 160°. Ref. as last.

BERENGAR II AND ADALBERT

Joint kings, 950–61

Coins of Milan and Pavia, which are not represented here, bear the names of both sovereigns, but those of Verona have that of Berengar only.

1029 *Verona*. **+BERENCΛRIVS PE** and **VE/RO/NΛ**. 1.20g 21/16mm 40°. Sambon 676; *CNI* VI, 252.2; Perini 1902, 4b. Patination suggests the coin has been in a fire.

PAPAL AND PAPAL-IMPERIAL COINAGE, 731–983

Principal references are: *CNI*; Promis = Promis 1858; Muntoni = Muntoni 1972–4, vol. I; and Serafini = Serafini 1910–28, vol. I. The coins are all silver and from **1031** onwards are denari. The mint was Rome.

GREGORY III, 731–41

1030 *Quarter-siliqua(?)* Obv. bust of Emperor Leo III between 2 stars Rev. cross and letters **GROE** (for GREGOR*ius*). 0.30g chipped 170°. *BMC Vand* 159.2, 3 (as Duke Gregory of Benevento 732–9, but doubtfully); *DOC* III, 278.92 (as Emperor Leo III in assoc. w. Pope Gregory III). Attribution discussed in note on coin.

ZACHARY, 741–51

Æ exagium. For a forgery, see **1513**.

ADRIAN I, 772–95

Class 2 (781–95)

1031 Obv. **ƆN ΛƆRI· ·ΛNVS PΛ**, w. **IB** (of uncertain meaning) in field Rev. **VICTOR IΛDNN:˙, CONOB**, w. **RM** (for *Roma*) in field. 1.20g 100°. Promis pl. 1.7; *CNI* XV, 63.10 var.; Serafini 4.1; Muntoni 3.1. For dating and comments on type, see note on coin.

1032 *As last*, but obv. inscr. ends **PΛPΛ**. 1.22g 90°. Promis pl. 1.9; *CNI* XV, 63.11 var.; Serafini 4.1 var.; Muntoni 3.1.

1021. PG: Spink 17.1.1946; ex Boulton; ex G. Gavazzi 16.
1022. PG: *Aes Rude* sale 6.4.1979, lot 944.
1023. PG: Spink 17.1.1946; ex Boulton(?).
1024. PG: Toderi 27.5.1982.
1025. PG: Ratto 3.10.1946.
1026. PG: Spink 17.1.1946; ex Boulton; ex Ratto sale 25.2.1913, lot 365.
1027–8. PG: Baldwin 1.2.1947.
1029. PG: Kunst und Münzen 15.11.1977 (list 34, no. 624).
1030. PG: Spink 10.1.1947; ex Grantley 2821.
1031. PG: Spink 23.9.1945; ex Boulton; ex 'Monnaies des papes' sale, lot 1 (= Vidal Quadras coll., no. 11,778).
1032. PG: Crippa 28.4.1969.

[*continued overleaf*]

1021 1022 1023 1024 1025

1026 1027 1028 1029

1030 1031 1032 1033 1033*

1034 1035 1036 1037 1038 1039

LEO III, 795–816

Alone (796–800)

1033 Obv. **S̄C̄S PETRVS** Rev. **D̄N̄·/·LEONI·/PAPE.** 1.07g broken 90°. Promis pl. 9.1; *CNI* XV, 95.6; Serafini IV, 11.4; Muntoni 21.3 (all as Leo VIII). For the attribution, see note on coin. The horizontal lines on the rev. caused a weakness in the flan; the BM specimen, from different dies, is broken in the same place.

With Charlemagne (801–14). For a forgery, see **1514**.

With Louis the Pious (814–16). Not represented.

GREGORY IV, 827–44

With Louis the Pious (827–40)

1034 Obv. **✱SCS·PETRVS,** around **+/GRE/II** Rev. **+LVDOVVICVS IMP** (**MP** ligatured), around **PIVS** monogram. 1.49g pierced 200°. Promis pl. 2.11; *CNI* XV, 69.3; Serafini 7.2; Muntoni 6.2.

1035 *As last*, but rev. ends **MP** (ligatured) for **IMP**. 1.48g 270°. Promis pl. 3.1; *CNI* XV, 69.4; Serafini 7.3; Muntoni 6.2. Double struck.

1036 *As last*. 1.33g 260°. Ref. as last.

1037 *As last*. 1.37g cracked 180°. Ref. as last.

1038 Legends as last, but w. **PP** (for *perpetuus*) in place of cross in obv. field and **PP** at end of rev. legend. 1.75g 190°. Promis pl. 2.12; *CNI* XV, 69.9; Serafini 7.8; Muntoni 6.3. The terminal **PP** is confused with the initial cross of the inscription owing to double-striking.

With Lothar I (840–4)

1039 Obv. as last Rev. **+HLOTHARIV∽ MP,** around **PIVS** monogram. 1.44g 110°. Promis pl. 3.3; *CNI* XV, 70.12; Serafini 7.12 var.; Muntoni 6.4.

1033. PG: MMAG Basel sale 50 (27.3.1975), lot 692; ex Tinozzi.

1034. PG: Spink 23.9.1945; ex Boulton; ex Martinori 2834.

1035, 1038. PG: Ratto 15.6.1955; ex Ulrich-Bansa; ex C. Gavazzi.

1036. PG: Ratto 15.6.1955; ex Ulrich-Bansa; ex C. Gavazzi; from Baranowsky list II/III (1929), no. 2266.

1037. PG: Ratto 15.6.1955; ex Ulrich-Bansa; ex C. Gavazzi; ex Ruchat III 8; ex Celati; ex Chigi.

1039. PG: Spink 21.9.1945; ex Boulton; ex Martinori 2836.

PAPAL-IMPERIAL COINAGE (2)

References as on Plate 47. The coins are silver denari.

SERGIUS II, 844–7

With Lothar I (844–7)

1040 Obv. +∽C∽ **PETRV∽**, around ··/**SER**/·**P**· Rev. +**HLOTHARIV∽ MP** (ligatured), around **PIVS** monogram. 1.60g chipped 290°. Promis pl. 3.46; *CNI* XV, 71.7; Serafini 8.1; Muntoni 6.1.

1041 *As last.* 1.47g 90°. Ref. as last.

LEO IV, 847–55

With Lothar I (847–55)

Class 1. With monogram of **PIVS**. Not represented.

Class 2. With monogram of **IMP**.

1042 Obv. +·∽C∽· **PETRV∽**, around **LO PA** monogram Rev. +**HLOTHARIV∽**, around **IMP** monogram, w. 1 pellet above and 2 beneath. 1.39g 130°. Promis pl. 3.9–10; *CNI* XV, 72.1; Serafini 8.3; Muntoni 7.3 var. II.

1043 *As last.* 1.41g 140°. Ref. as last.

1044 *As last,* but w. 2 pellets above monogram and 2 beneath. 1.02g 300°. Promis pl. 3.8; *CNI* XV, 72.2; Serafini 8.1; Muntoni 7.3 var. I.

1045 *As last.* 1.29g 80°. Ref. as last.

BENEDICT III, 855–8

With Lothar I (855). Not represented.

With Louis II (855–8)

1046 Obv. +∽C∽ **PETRV∽**, around ·**B**·/**NED**/·**PA**· (**PA** ligatured) Rev. ✱**LVDOVVICVS MP** (ligatured), around **PIVS** monogram. 1.32g 260°. Promis pl. 4.1; *CNI* XV, 73.7; Serafini 10.6; Muntoni 8.4.

1047 *As last.* 0.98g 330°. Ref. as last. There is no obvious explanation for the low weight. The coin is slightly chipped at one place on the edge, but not enough to account for it. There is no reason to doubt its authenticity.

NICHOLAS I, 858–67

With Louis II (858–67)

1048 Obv. +∽C∽ **PETRV∽**, around **NICOLAVS** monogram Rev. +**LVDOVVICV∽ MP** (ligatured), around **ROMA** monogram. 1.42g 150°. Promis pl. 4.4; *CNI* XV, 74.1; Serafini 10.1; Muntoni 8.1.

1049 *As last,* but w. pellet to l. of papal monogram. 1.30g 340°. Promis pl. 4.5; *CNI* XV, 74.2; Serafini 11.8; Muntoni 8.1 var.

For two forgeries, see **1515–16**.

ADRIAN II, 867–72

With Louis II (867–72)

1050 Obv. +∽C∽ **PETRVS**, around **ADR** monogram Rev. +**LVDOVVICV∽ MP** (ligatured), around **ROMA** monogram. 0.95g chipped 180°. Promis pl. 4.6; *CNI* XV, 74.1; Serafini 11.2; Muntoni 8.1.

1051 *As last,* but monogram of +**ADRIAN**. 1.18g 90°. Promis pl. 4.7; *CNI* XV, 74.4; Serafini 11.3; Muntoni 9.2.

JOHN VIII, 872–82

With Louis II (872–5)

1052 Legends as last, but **IOHANS** monogram. 1.15g 160°. Promis pl. 4.8; *CNI* XV, 75.1; Serafini 12.1; Muntoni 9.1.

With Charles the Bald (875–7) and Charles the Fat (881–2)

1053 Obv. **SCS**/**PETRVS**, bust of St Peter Rev. +**KAROLV∽ MP** (ligatured), around **IOHANS** monogram. 1.24g 40°. Promis pl. 4.11; *CNI* XV, 75.5; Serafini 12.4; Muntoni 9.1. This type was probably also struck over the four years 877–81, Charles the Bald's name being continued on the coins without change.

For forgeries of denari struck at Capua in John VIII's name, see **1510–11**.

ADRIAN III, 884–5

With Charles the Fat (884–5). For a forgery, see **1517**.

1040–4, 1047. PG: Ratto 15.6.1955; ex Ulrich-Bansa; ex C. Gavazzi.

1045. PG: Spink 21.9.1945; ex Boulton; ex 'Monnaies des papes' sale, lot 5 (= Vidal Quadras coll., no. 11782).

1046, 1052. PG: Spink 21.9.1945; ex Boulton; ex Martinori 2839 and 2841 respectively.

1048. PG: Spink 21.9.1945; ex Boulton; ex G. Ciani 994.

1049. PG: Ratto 15.6.1955; ex Ulrich-Bansa; ex C. Gavazzi; ex Ruchat III 17; ex Celati; ex Patrizi.

1050, 1055. PG: Spink 21.9.1945; ex Boulton; ex G. Gavazzi 1180 and 1182 respectively.

1051. PG: Ratto 15.6.1945; ex Ulrich-Bansa; ex C. Gavazzi; ex Ruchat III 19; ex Celati; ex Chigi.

1053. PG: Spink 21.9.1945; ex Boulton; ex Hazlitt 527.

[*continued overleaf*]

1040 1041 1042 1043 1044

1045 1046 1047 1048 1049 1050

1051 1052 1053 1053*

1054 1055 1056 1057 1058 1059

STEPHEN V, 885–91

With Charles the Fat (885–8) and later, to 891

1054 +ꟿCꟿ **PETRVS**, around cruciform monogram of **SEPHAN** Rev. +**CAROLVꟿ MP** (ligatured), around **ROMA** monogram. 1.38g 120°. Promis pl. 5.3; *CNI* XV, 77.3; Serafini 14.3; Muntoni 11.3.

1055 *As last.* 1.27g 0°. Ref. as last.

1056 Legends as last, but w. obv. monogram of **SEPNM**(?) and rev. monogram of **IPA** (for *Imperator*). 0.79g chipped 40°. Promis pl. 5.5; *CNI* XV, 77.5; Serafini –; Muntoni 10.1. Attribution doubtful, see note on coin.

With Guy of Spoleto (891). Not represented.

FORMOSUS, 891–6

With Guy of Spoleto (891–4)

1057 Obv. **FORMOꟿ IP.**, bust w. **SP** in field Rev. +**VVIDO MP·:·** (**MP** ligatured), around **ROMA** monogram. 1.39g 10°. Promis pl. 5.8; *CNI* XV, 79.4; Serafini 14.4; Muntoni 11.1.

1058 *As last*, but end of obv. legend obscure. 1.13g 50°. There is no key in the saint's hand (as with *CNI* XV, 79.2).

1059 Obv. +ꟿCꟿ **PETRVꟿ**, around **FOR/MO/·S·** Rev. +**VVIDO MP·** (**MP** ligatured), around **RO/MA**. 1.12g 60°. Promis pl. 5.9; *CNI* XV, 74.9; Serafini 15.7; Muntoni 11.2.

With Arnulf (894). Not represented.

1054. PG: Ratto 25.6.1955; ex Ulrich-Bansa; ex C. Gavazzi; ex Vaccari II 9.

1056. PG: MMAG Basel sale 50 (27.3.1975), lot 679; ex Tinozzi.

1057. PG: Spink 21.9.1945; ex Boulton; ex G. Gavazzi 1183.

1058–9. PG: Ratto 15.6.1955; ex Ulrich-Bansa; ex C. Gavazzi.

PAPAL-IMPERIAL COINAGE (3)

References as on Plate 47. The coins are silver denari.

STEPHEN VI, 896–7

With Arnulf (896)

1060 Obv. +∽C∽· **PETRV∽**, around **STEPHAN** monogram, w. pellet below Rev. +**ARNULFV IMP** (ligatured), around **ROMA** monogram, w. pellet above. 1.14g 80°. Promis pl. 5.10; *CNI* XV, 80.2; Serafini 15.6; Muntoni 12.1.

1061 *As last*, but no pellet in obv. legend. 1.34g 340°. Promis pl. 5.10 var.; *CNI* XV, 80.2; Serafini 15.1; Muntoni 12.1. For two forgeries, see **1518–19**.

With Lambert (897). Not represented.

ROMANUS, 897

With Lambert (897)

1062 Obv. +∽C∽ **PETRV∽**, around **ROMANVS** monogram, w. pellet below Rev. +**LAMVERTO MP** (ligatured), around **ROMA** monogram. 1.31g 340°. Promis pl. 5.12; *CNI* XV, 81.1; Serafini 16.1; Muntoni 12.1.

JOHN IX, 898–900

With Lambert (898) and later, to 900

1063 Obv. **SCS/PETRVS**, bust of St Peter Rev. +**LANTVERT MP** (ligatured), around **IOHANS** monogram. 0.86g 90°. Promis pl. 6.2–3; *CNI* XV, 82.1; Serafini 16.1; Muntoni 13.1.

1064 *As last*. 1.06g 230°. Ref. as last. For a forgery, see **1520**.

BENEDICT IV, 900–3

Alone (900–1)

1065 Obv. +∽C∽ **PETRV∽**, around **BENEDICT** monogram Rev. +∽C∽ **PAVLV∽**, around **ROMA** monogram. 1.00g 30°. Promis pl. 6.4; *CNI* XV, 83.1; Serafini 17.1; Muntoni 13.1.

With Louis III (901–3)

1066 Obv. +∽C∽ **PETRVS**, around **BENDT** monogram, w. pellet above and below Rev. +**LVVDOICV∽ MP** (ligatured), around **ROMA** monogram. 1.22g 230°. Promis pl. 6.8; *CNI* XV, 83.3; Serafini 17.3; Muntoni 14.2.

1067 *As last*. 1.09g 20°. Ref. as last.

1068 Obv. +**BENEDICT P**, bust of St Peter, w. **SP** in field Rev. +**LODOVVICV∽ MP** (ligatured), **RO** and open hand (making *Ro-manus*) in field. 1.29g 230°. Promis pl. 65; *CNI* XV, 84.7; Serafini 17.6; Muntoni 14.3.

CHRISTOPHER (Antipope, 903–4)

With Louis III (903–4). For a forgery, see **1521**.

SERGIUS III, 904–11

With Louis III (904–5). Not represented.

Alone (905–11). Order of issues uncertain.

1069 Obv. ∽**ER+GI**ᵛ**PP**˙, bust of St Peter Rev. +∽C∽ **PETRVS**, around **RO/MA**. 1.02g 180°. Promis pl. 6.10; *CNI* XV, 85.5; Serafini 18.2 var.; Muntoni 15.3.

1070 Obv. bust of St Peter w. key and $\overline{\textbf{SP}}$ in field Rev. +**RO∴MA**, around **SERG** monogram. 0.90g 90°. Promis pl. 7.3; *CNI* XV, 86.11; Serafini 18.4; Muntoni 15.5.

1071 Obv. +∽**ALV∽ PATRIE**, around **SERG** monogram Rev. +∽C∽ **PETRV∽**, around **ROMA** monogram. 1.27g 90°. Promis pl. 7.4; *CNI* XV, 86.14; Serafini 19.7; Muntoni 14.2.

1060. PG: Spink 21.9.1945; ex Boulton; ex Ratto 25.9.1913, lot 1567.

1061, 1066, 1073. PG: Ratto 15.6.1955; ex Ulrich-Bansa; ex C. Gavazzi.

1062. PG: Ratto 15.6.1955; ex Ulrich-Bansa; ex C. Gavazzi; ex Ruchat III 32; ex 'Monnaies des papes' sale, lot 14 (= Vidal Quadras coll., no. 11,791); ex Rossi I 3737; ex Montenuovo.

1063. PG: Spink 12.2.1945; ex Grantley 3267; from Rollin.

1064. PG: Ratto 15.6.1955; ex Ulrich-Bansa; ex C. Gavazzi; ex Ruchat III 31; ex Celati; ex Patrizi; ex Remedi.

1065. PG: Ratto 15.6.1955; ex Ulrich-Bansa; ex C. Gavazzi; ex Ruchat III 34; ex Celati (1916); ex Martinori 2833.

1067. PG: Spink 21.9.1945; ex Boulton; ex Martinori 2854.

1068. PG: Santamaria 10.6.1955; ex Fürstenberg (Helbing sale 73 (27.10.1933), lot 1651).

1069. PG: Spink 21.9.1945; ex Boulton; ex 'Monnaies des papes' sale 18 (= Vidal Quadras coll., no. 11,795).

1070. PG: Ratto 15.6.1955; ex Ulrich-Bansa; ex C. Gavazzi; ex Ruchat III 36; ex Celati (1917); ex Chigi.

1071. PG: MMAG Basel sale 50 (27.3.1975), lot 686; ex Tinozzi.

[*continued overleaf*]

1068* 1060 1061 1062

1063 1064 1065 1066 1067

1068 1069 1070 1071 1072

1073 1074 1075 1072*

JOHN X, 914–28

Alone (*914–15*). For a forgery, see **1522**.

With Berengar I (*915–24*) *and ?later*

1072 Obv. **IOH/S PETRVS**, papal bust Rev. +**BERNEGARIV MP** (ligatured), **ROMA** around cross in field. 0.80g slightly chipped 80°. Promis pl. 7.7; *CNI* XV, 88.1; Serafini 19.1; Muntoni 16.5. The bust on the obv. is sometimes described as that of St Peter, and the inscription is ambiguous, but the costume (w. pallium) is that of a pope and no key is shown. There is no reason to doubt the authenticity of this specimen, despite the low weight.

1073 Obv. +**BERNEGARIV IMP** (ligatured), around monogram of **IOHANS PA** Rev. +**∽C∽ PETRV∽**, around **ROMA** monogram in square border. 1.04g 26/20 mm scodellato 150°. Promis pl. 7.8; *CNI* XV, 88.4; Serafini 20.4; Muntoni 16.3.

1074 *As last.* 1.14g broken and repaired 26/20mm scodellato 210°. Ref. as last.

JOHN XI, 931–5

With Alberic (*932–5*). For two forgeries, see **1523–4**.

LEO VII, 936–9

With Alberic (*936–9*)

1075 Obv. +**∽[C∽ PETRV]∽**, around **LE/OP** in square border Rev. [+**ALBRCV**] **PRIC**[, around **ROM/ANO/RV**. 0.62g fragment 110°. Promis pl. 10.1; *CNI* XV, 99.1 (both as Leo IX w. Henry III); Serafini –; Muntoni 18.1. For the attribution, see note on coin.

1072. PG: MMAG Basel sale 50 (27.3.1975), lot 689; ex Tinozzi; ex Ruchat III 38.

1074. PG: Spink 17.1.1946; ex Boulton; ex G. Ciani 998.

1075. PG: Ratto 15.6.1955; ex Ulrich-Bansa; ex C. Gavazzi; ex Celati.

PAPAL-IMPERIAL COINAGE (4)

References as on Plate 47. The coins are silver denari.

ALBERIC

Senator and patrician, 932–54

For the ascription of these coins to Alberic alone, see note on **1076–7**.

1076 Obv. +**S[CS] PETRVS**, bust of St Peter w. cross Rev. +**ALBERICVS PR** (ligatured), around monogram of **PACVS** (for *pacificus*?). 1.67g 110°. Promis pl. 8.2 var.; *CNI* XV, 91.1; Serafini 21.1 var.; Muntoni 19.1 (all as Agapitus II with Alberic).

1077 *As last*, but end of rev. legend obscure. 1.39g 20°. Ref. as last.

For a forgery, see **1525**.

JOHN XII, 955–63 (dep.; d. 964)

For a forgery of John XII, supposedly struck under the name of Octavian before his election, see **1526**.

Alone (*955–62*). Not represented.

With Otto I (*962–3*)

1078 Obv. +**DOM IOANES**, around **PAPA** monogram Rev. +**OTTO IMPE[R]ATO**, head of emperor. 1.51g 60°. Promis pl. 8.7–8; *CNI* XV, 93.9; Serafini 21.6; Muntoni 20.3. The attribution of this coin to John XII with Otto I is customary, but it could equally well be one of John XIII with Otto I (965–72).

LEO VIII, 963–5

For a coin wrongly attributed to this pope, see **1033**.

JOHN XIII, 965–72

With Otto I (*965–72*)

The attribution to John XIII of the three following types is customary, but one of them may belong to the overlap of a few days between John XIV and Otto II in Nov./Dec. 983. John XV (985–96) is impossible, since Otto II had died before this pope's accession and Otto III was not crowned till after his death.

1079 Obv. **IOS**(?)/**PAPA/OTTO** Rev. +**S[CS] PETRVS**, around **PA/O** (for APO*stolus*). 1.34g 110°. Promis pl. 9.2; *CNI* XV, 96.1; Serafini 22.1; Muntoni 22.2. The pope's name is normally rendered **IOHS**, but apparently not on this specimen. Overstruck, but under-type not clear.

1080 Obv. +**IO[ANNE]S PAP**, around **OTTO** monogram Rev. +**SCS PETRV[S]**, around **ROMA** monogram. 1.44g chipped 240°. Promis pl. 9.3; *CNI* XV, 96.2; Serafini 22.4; Muntoni 22.3.

1081 Obv. +**SCS PETRVS [RO]**, around **·P·/IOH/·P·** Rev. +**[OTTO]NI IMPER**, cross. 1.17g chipped 290°. Promis pl. 9.4; *CNI* XV, 96.6; Serafini 22.6; Muntoni 22.1.

For a forgery of this last type, see **1527**.

BENEDICT VI with OTTO I (973) or

BENEDICT VI with OTTO II (973–4) or

BENEDICT VII with OTTO II (974–83)

One or more of the five types bearing the names of Benedict and Otto probably belong to the year and a half (19 January 973–June 974) of Benedict VI's pontificate, but no satisfactory distinction has been made between his coins and those of Benedict VII.

1082 Obv. +**BENE/PAP**, papal bust Rev. +**SCS PETR· OTTO**, around **R·O/MA**. 1.30g 180°. Promis pl. 9.7; *CNI* XV, 97.3; Serafini 23.1 var.; Muntoni 23.2.

1083 *As last*, but **BEN** to l. of bust. 1.11g 270°. Promis pl. 9.7 var.; *CNI* XV, 97.1 var.; Serafini 23.1; Muntoni 23.2.

1084 Obv. +**SCS PE[TRVS· AP]**, around **BEN P** monogram Rev. +**O[TTO IMPER R]OMA** (**MA** ligatured), building. 1.43g 340°. Promis pl. 9.9; *CNI* XV, 98.5; Serafini 23.1; Muntoni 23.6.

Leo IX with Henry III (*1049–54*) *and Paschal II* (*1099–1118*). For supposed coins (forgeries), see **1528–9**.

1076. PG: Ratto 15.6.1955; ex C. Gavazzi; ex Colonna 595.
1077. PG: Spink 21.9.1945; ex Boulton; ex G. Gavazzi 1190.
1078, 1084. PG: Ratto 14.4.1955; ex C. Gavazzi; ex Celati; ex Chigi.
1079. PG: MMAG Basel sale 50 (27.3.1975), lot 694; ex Tinozzi.
1080–1, 1083. PG: Ratto 14.4.1955; ex C. Gavazzi.
1082. PG: Spink 11.1.1947; ex Boulton; ex 'Monnaies des papes' sale, lot 21 (= Vidal Quadras coll., no. 11,789).

[*continued overleaf*]

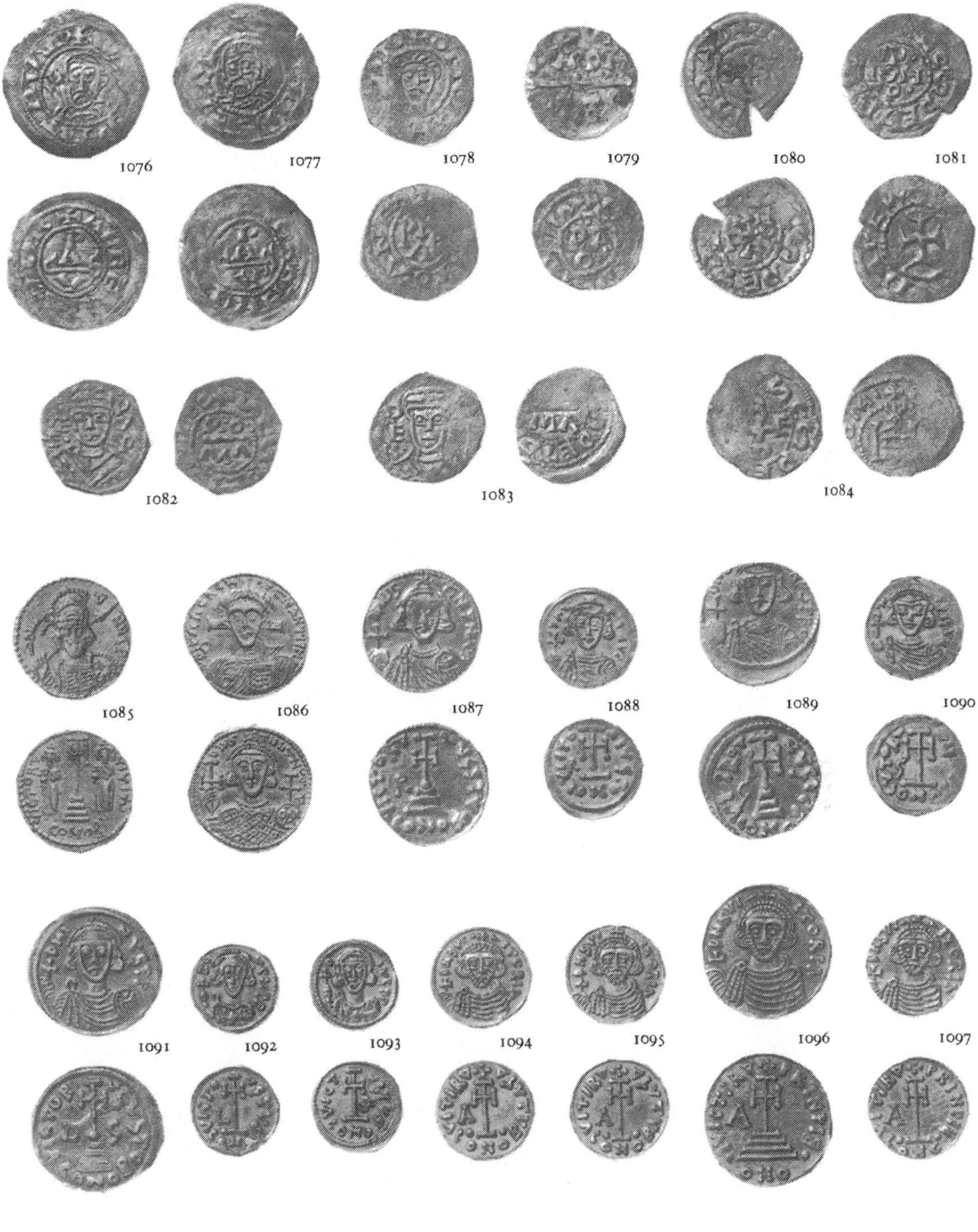

1076 1077 1078 1079 1080 1081

1082 1083 1084

1085 1086 1087 1088 1089 1090

1091 1092 1093 1094 1095 1096 1097

BENEVENTO, *c.* 680–870

The principal references are: *BMC Vand* and Sambon = Sambon 1912. Specific gravity analyses of many of the coins in this collection have been published by Oddy (1974).

EARLY ANONYMOUS COINAGE

1085 *Solidus.* Imitation of Constantine IV (668–85). Obv. **ON VRVGP** Rev. **VICTORV VIVI+U, CONOB.** AV 4.36g (SG 17.56: 88% Au) 190°. Cf. *DOC* II, 560.70b (uncertain Italian mint). Possibly Beneventan. The prototype is to be dated 674–81.

GISULF I, 689–706

1086 *Solidus.* With the name of Justinian II (2nd reign, 705–11). Obv. **DNI hSChSREX REGNANTIЧM**, w. **G** in field l. Rev. **DIVS TINIVNVS V**, w. **PAX** on orb. AV 4.02g (Oddy no. SG381; 77% Au) 180°. *BMC Byz* 343.60 var. (as Justinian II).

ROMOALD II, 706–31

1087 *Solidus.* With the name of Justinian II. Obv. **DNIUS TINVNVPP** Rev. **VICTORV VVGSTV˙, CONOB**, w. **R** in field l. AV 3.77g (Oddy no. SG394; 72% Au) 200°. *BMC Vand* 156.3–6 var.

1088 *Tremissis.* Obv. **DVΛI· ·TИVS** Rev. **VICTO ЯIVG, CONOB.** AV 1.32g (Oddy no. SG399; 66% Au) 210°. *BMC Vand* 157.11–15 var.

GREGORY, 732–9

It is not certain how coins with **G** (**1089–90**) or **DG** (**1091**) in the field should be distributed between Gregory, Gottschalk and Gisulf II (731, 742–51).

1089 *Solidus.* Obv. **DNU[ ]NSPPC** Rev. **VVILOT VVGUS, CONOB**, w. **G** in field l. AV 3.97g (Oddy no. SG402; 54% Au) 200°. *BMC Vand* –; Sambon 388 var.

1090 *Tremissis.* Obv. **D˙N PPЧGVS** Rev. **VTOΗT TIGIT, ƆONOI**, w. **G** in field l. AV 1.36g 190°. *BMC Vand* 159.1 var.; Sambon 392 var.

GOTTSCHALK, 739–42

1091 *Solidus.* With the name of Justinian II. Obv. **DNI NVSPP** Rev. **VICTOR VSVSTO, CONOB**, w. **D** and **G** in field. AV 3.87g (Oddy no. SG406; 52% Au) 170°. *BMC Vand* –; Sambon 395 var.

LIUTPRAND, 751–8

Liutprand's earliest coinage in association with his mother Scauniperga (751–5), with **L** and **S** in the reverse field, is not represented.

(a) With **L** in rev. field

1092 *Tremissis.* Obv. **DI VCNPP** Rev. **VICTO VGTV, CONOB.** AV 1.31g (Oddy no. SG418; 63% Au) 190°. *BMC Vand* 165.5 var.; Sambon 403 var.

(b) With monogram of **DVX** (sometimes wrongly read as **L DVX**) in rev. field

1093 *Tremissis.* Obv. **D IVGPP** Rev. **VICT VSTV, CONOB.** AV 1.34g (Oddy no. SG421; 66% Au) 180°. *BMC Vand* 166.7 var.; Sambon 405 var.

ARICHIS II, 758–87

Class 1 (758–65), as *Dux*. Facing bust holding cross and akakia; w. **A** in rev. field. Not represented.

Class 2 (765–74), as *Dux*. Facing bust holding orb; rev. similar to Class 1. For the date, and the inscription *Dns victoria*, see p. 70 above.

1094 *Tremissis.* Obv. **DNSVI CTORIΛ** Rev. **VITIRV VGVTV, CONOB.** AV 1.30g (Oddy no. SG435; 49% Au) 180°. *BMC Vand* 168.6; Sambon 414.

1095 *Tremissis.* Inscriptions as last, but lacks wedges above head. AV 1.32g (SG 13.65: 50% Au) 190°. *BMC Vand* 168.8 var.; Sambon 414.

Class 3 (774–87), as *Princeps*. As Class 2, but **PRINPI** replaces **AVGVSTI** in rev. inscription.

1096 *Solidus.* Obv. **DNSVI CTORIΛ** Rev. **VICTIRV PRINPI, CONOB.** AV 3.82g (Oddy no. SG441; 48% Au) 180°. *BMC Vand* 169.10; Sambon 415.

1097 *Tremissis.* Obv. **DNSVI CTORIΛ** Rev. **VITIRV PRINPI, CONOB.** AV 1.25g (Oddy no. SG437; 50% Au) 170°. *BMC Vand* 169.11; Sambon 416.

1085. PG: Baldwin 14.5.1970.
1086. PG: M. Ratto 11.3.1960; ex Signorelli IV 1049.
1087. PG: Spink 23.4.1945 (*NCirc* July 1944, no. 25982); ex Santamaria (list Jan. 1929, no. 271).
1088. PG: Southey 130.
1089. PG: Ars et Nummus 8.12.1966.
1090. PG: M. Ratto 14.5.1983.
1091. PG: Spink 10.1.1947.
1092. PG: M. Ratto 28.4.1969.
1093. PG: MMAG Basel 10.12.1968 (list 295, no. 26).
1094. PG: A. R. Tait 26.5 1962.
1095. FM: Jenkinson 1923; bt 31.1.1882.
1096. PG: M. Ratto 10.12.1966.
1097. PG: Ratto (Milan) 3.10.1946.

BENEVENTO (2)

References as on Plate 50.

GRIMOALD III, 788–806

As Dux *with Charlemagne (788–92)*

1098 *Tremissis.* Obv. **GRIM|VALD** Rev. **DOMS CAR˙R̷, VICV.**, w. **G** and **R** in field. *AV* 1.25g (Oddy no. SG444; 48% Au) 190°. *BMC Vand* 171.7; Sambon 422.

Alone as Princeps *(792–806)*

Class 1. Gold w. rev. cross on steps (solidi) or on base (tremisses). Also denari.

1099 *Tremissis.* Obv. **GRIM|VALD** Rev. **VITORΔ PRINCIP, CONO**, w. **G** and **R** in field. *AV* 1.33g (Oddy no. SG453; 57% Au, wrongly described as in BM) 180°. Sambon 427; *BMC Vand* 172.14 var.

1100 *Denaro.* Obv. monogram of *Grimoaldus* Rev. **BENE|BENTV**, w. **A** and **ω** in field. *AR* 1.47g chipped 190°. Sambon 428; *BMC Vand* 173.18 var. Authenticity doubtful; the surface is of an unusual texture, and the provenance (ex Tinozzi coll.) is not reassuring.

Class 2. Rev. cross on globule and steps, or on globule and base.

1101 *Solidus.* Obv. **GRIM|VALD** Rev. **VICTORV PRINCIP, CONOB** w. **G** and **R** in field. *AV* 3.84g (Oddy no. SG461; 44% Au) 160°. *BMC Vand* 157.11 var.

GRIMOALD IV, 806–17

No gold coins are known for Grimoald IV.

1102 *Denaro.* Obv. **GRIMOALD FILIVS ERMENRIH** Rev. **ARCHANGELVS MICHAEL**. *AR* 1.43g 350°. *BMC Vand* 175.2.

SICO, 817–32

1103 *Solidus.* Obv. **SICO P|RINCES** Rev. **ARCHANGELV MIHAEL, ONO**. *AV* 3.77g (Oddy no. SG467; 37% Au) 340°. *BMC Vand* 176.2 var.

1104 *Tremissis.* Obv. **SICO PRINCES** Rev. **ARCHANGELVS MICHAEL**, w. **Ɔ** and **Ƨ** in field. *AV* 1.28g (Oddy no. SG470; 38% Au) 160°. *BMC Vand* 177.6.

1105 *Denaro.* Obv. +**PRIHCES BEHEBEHTI**, monogram of **SICO** Rev. **ARCHANGELVS MICHAEL·**. *AR* 1.06g chipped 160°. *BMC Vand* 177.7 var.

1106 *Denaro.* Obv. +**PRINCES BENEBENTI**, monogram of **SICO** w. pellet in each quarter. Rev. **˙A˙RCHANGELVS MIHAEL**, w. wedge in field l. and r. *AR* 1.09g 340°. *BMC Vand* 177.10 var.

1107 *Denaro.* Obv. +**PRIHCES BENEBEHTI·**, monogram of **SICO** w. star in 4th heraldic quarter Rev. **ARCHANGELVS MICHAEL·**. *AR* 1.17g chipped 340°. *BMC Vand* 178.14.

SICARD, 832–9

1108 *Solidus.* Obv. **SIC|ARDV·** w. wedge in field r. Rev. **VICTOR·PRINCI, CONOB**, w. **S** and **I** in field and wedge in field l. and r. *AV* 3.72g (Oddy no. SG481; 28% Au) 340°. *BMC Vand* 179.3.

1109 *Tremissis.* Obv. **SIC|ARDV·** w. wedge in field r. Rev. **VICTOR˙PRINCI, CONO** , w. **S** and **I** in field. *AV* 1.21g chipped (Oddy no. SG473; 38% Au) 30°. *BMC Vand* 179.7.

1110 *As last.* *AV* 1.22g slightly chipped (Oddy no. SG478; 31% Au, wrongly described as in BM) 0°. Ref. as last.

1111 *Denaro.* Obv. +**PRINCE BENEBEИTI**, monogram of **SICARD** (**D** retrograde) Rev. **˙A˙RCHANGELV MIHAE**, w. wedge and pellet in field. *AR* 1.10g 50°. *BMC Vand* 180.8 var.

1112 *Denaro.* Obv. +**PRINCE BENEBENTI**, monogram of **SICARD** Rev. **ARCHANGE[ ]MIHAEL**. *AR* 1.00g chipped 20°. *BMC Vand* 180.8 var.

ADELCHIS, 853–78

Alone (853–67)

1113 *Denaro.* Obv. **ADELCHIS PRIN** Rev. **S˙C˙A M|ARIA**. *AR* 1.18g 280°. *BMC Vand* –; Sambon 450.

1114 *Denaro.* Obv. **ADELCHIS PRN** Rev. **ᔕ˙C˙A M|ARIA**. *AR* 0.84g slightly chipped and small piece of another coin adhering 10°. Ref. as last.

1115 *Denaro.* Obv. monogram of **ADELCHIS**, w. **V** above, Latin cross to l. and star on stalk to r. Rev. **BENE|BENTV˙** around cross-on-steps, w. **M** and **H** (for *Michael*) in field. *AR* 0.86g chipped 50°. *BMC Vand* 185.3; Sambon 445.

With Louis II (866–71). Not represented.

LOUIS II AND ANGILBERGA (his wife), 866–71

1116 *Denaro.* Obv. +**LVDOVVICVS INP** Rev. +**ANGIL BERGA NP**. *AR* 0.87g slightly chipped 220°. *BMC Vand* –; Sambon 460.

1098. PG: Spink 28.5.1945.
1099. PG: Spink 12.2.1945.
1100. PG: MMAG Basel 4.7.1976 (list 376, no. 36; ex Tinozzi.
1101. PG: Seaby 4.10.1946; ex O'Hagan II 226.
1102. PG: Seaby 18.7.1945; ex Grantley 2827.
1103. PG: Lockett III 169.
1104. PG: Baldwin 30.5.1947.
1105. PG: Spink 1.3.1945.
1106. PG: Spink 17.1.1946.
1107. PG: Ars et Nummus 27.10.1966 (list, Sept. 1966, no. 513).
1108. PG: Spink 11.1.1947; ex Grantley 2829.
1109. PG: Spink 10.1.1947.
1110. PG: Seaby 8.1.1947; ex Grantley 2830; from Ratto.
1111. PG: DO 1958.
1112. PG: Seaby 16.7.1945; ex Grantley 2830; ex Seltman (senior).
1113–14, 1117. PG: Santamaria 26.6.1947.
1115. PG: Spink 10.1.1947; ex Boulton; from Ratto sale 1913, lot 206.
1116. PG: Spink 17.1.1946.

[*continued overleaf*]

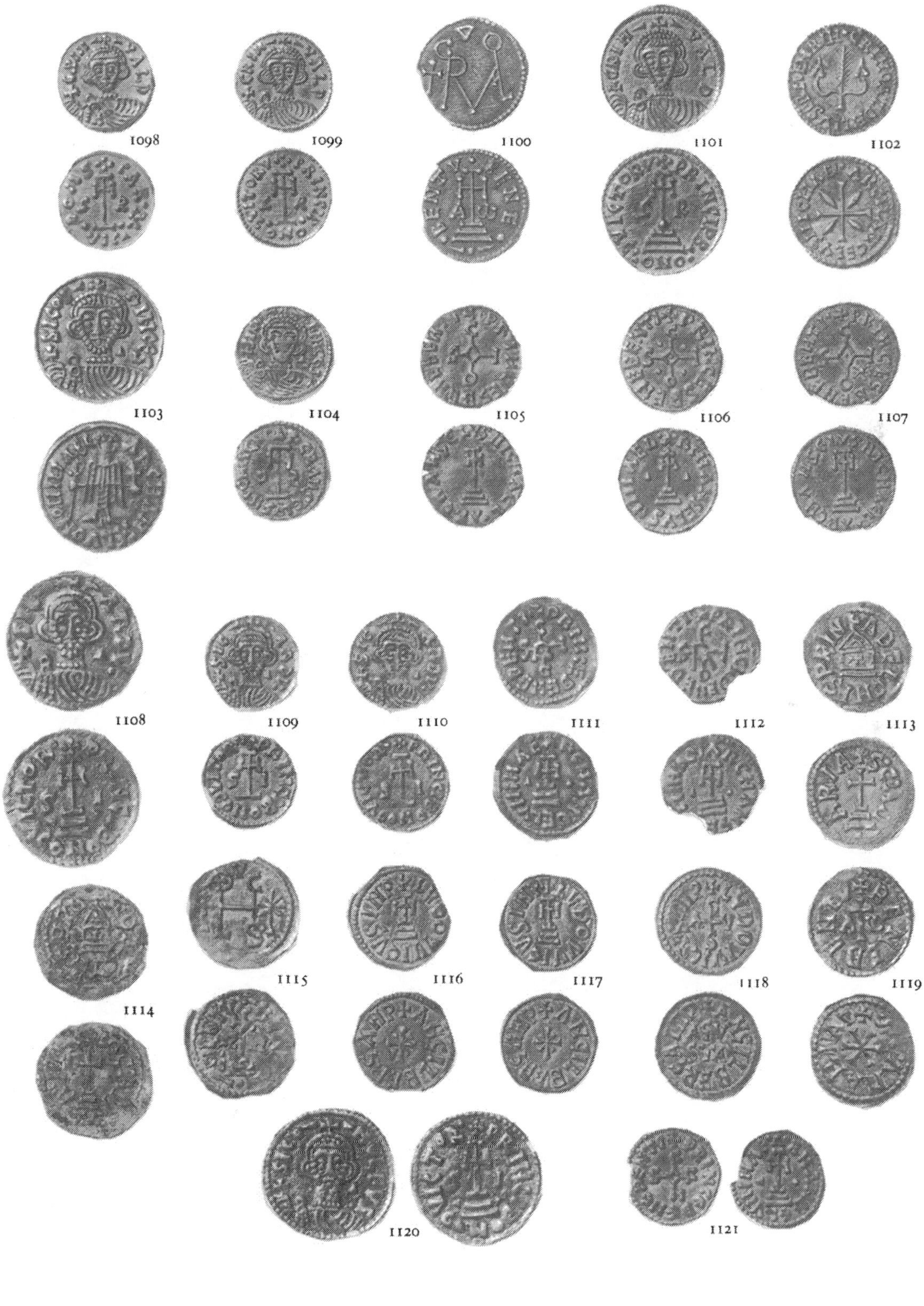
1098
1099
1100
1101
1102
1103
1104
1105
1106
1107
1108
1109
1110
1111
1112
1113
1114
1115
1116
1117
1118
1119
1120
1121

1117 *As last.* Æ 0.88g 90°. Ref. as last.

1118 *Denaro.* Obv. **+LVDOVVICVS IIIP** around monogram of **AGVS** (for *Augustus*) Rev. **+ANGILBERGA IMP** around **AGV/STA**. Æ 0.97g 120°. *BMC Vand* –; Sambon 461.

ANONYMOUS ISSUE, uncertain date

1119 *Denaro.* Obv. **+BENEBENTV**, w. **A** and **ω** to l. and r. of cross Rev. **+ω·C·A MARIAV**. Æ 1.06g 340°. *BMC Vand* –; Sambon 466. The common attribution to the regency of Bishop Peter (897) is unlikely.

SALERNO

SICONULF, 839–49

1120 *Solidus.* Obv. **SICO|NOLFVS** Rev. **VICTOR· PRINCI, CONOB**, w. **S** and **I** in field. Pale AV 3.50g chipped (Oddy no. SG487; 10% Au) 140°. *BMC Vand* –; Sambon 494.

1121 *Denaro.* Obv. **+PRINCE BENEBENTI** around monogram of **SCONF** (for *Siconulf*) Rev. **·A·RHANGELV MIHAE**, w. wedge and pellet in field. Æ 0.99g chipped 170°. *BMC Vand* –; Sambon 497.

1118. PG: Spink 1.3.1945; ex Grantley 3195.
1119. PG: de Falco 9.9.1948.
1120. PG: Ulrich-Bansa 17.12.1947.
1121. PG: Seaby 8.1.1947; ex Grantley 2828; from Canessa.

ANGLO-SAXONS (3)

Principal references are: Blunt = Blunt 1961, BLS = Blunt, Lyon and Stewart 1963, North = North 1980 and *SCBI* = *SCBI* Cambridge. The coins are silver pennies.

SOUTHERN COINAGES, *c.* 760–96

The first coins on this plate are reformed sceattas (pennies) of Beonna, of enhanced fineness and bearing his name. These are followed by the broader thinner flan coins of Offa and the kings of Kent. Offa's coins were struck by at least three mints: Canterbury, London and one in East Anglia.

Reformed sceattas (*c.* 760?)

BEONNA, King of East Anglia (749–57 or later)

1121A No moneyer. Interlace type. **beonna rex** (runic). 0.91g (54% Ag, information M. M. Archibald and M. R. Cowell) 290°. *BMC AS* –; North 430/1; Pagan 1968. Full analytical details of this and 1121C (1121B was considered unsuitable for analysis), including trace elements, will be published by Miss Archibald.

1121B *Efe*. **bEOnna rEx** (mixed runic and Roman). 1.04g 300°. *BMC AS* 83.1; North 430. The complex arrangement of pellets on the rev. of the coins of Efe varies on each of the known dies and is probably a system to control the issues of dies.

1121C *Wilred* (runic). **benna rx** (runic). 0.95g (50% Ag; information M. M. Archibald and M. R. Cowell) 0°. *BMC AS* –; North –. The last letter of the obv. inscription is a runic symbol otherwise unknown. Professor R. I. Page suggests that it is a ligature of R and X for *rex*. Wilred is also a moneyer of Offa's light coinage.

Light penny coinage (*c.* 765?–*c.* 792)

EGBERT II, King of Kent, *c.* 765–*c.* 780 or later

1122 *Udd*. Canterbury. **EGCBERHT**. 1.89g/18.1gr. 300°. *SCBI* 428; Blunt 4.

OFFA, King of Mercia, 757–96

The obv. legend is **OFFA REX** unless otherwise indicated.

1123 *Alhmund* (= Ealhmund). Canterbury or London? 1.18g/18.2gr. 90°. *SCBI* 386; Blunt 42.

1124 *Alhmund*. Canterbury or London? **OF R M**. 1.19g/18.4gr. corroded 0°. *SCBI* 387; Blunt 40.

1124A *Dud*. Canterbury or London? **+OFFA REX MERCIORUM**. 1.30g 150°. *SCBI* –; Blunt 27. Die-duplicate of *BMC AS* 26.13.

1125 *Dud*. Canterbury or London? 1.01g/15.6gr. worn 0°. *SCBI* 388; Blunt 25.

1126 *Eadhun*. Canterbury or London? 1.19g/18.3gr. 90°. *SCBI* 389; Blunt 39.

1127 *Eoba*. Canterbury. **O F R M**. 1.21g/18.7gr. 0°. *SCBI* 390; Blunt 17.

1128 *Ethilvald* (= Æthelweald). Canterbury or London? 1.26g/19.47gr. 240°. *SCBI* 391; Blunt 58.

Ibba. For a forgery, see Pl. 64.

1129 *Lulla*. Canterbury or London? 1.16g/17.9gr. 90°. *SCBI* 392; Blunt 67.

1130 *Osmod*. Canterbury or London? 1.13g/17.5gr. 280°. *SCBI* 393; Blunt 19.

1131 *Vinoth* (= Winenoth?). Canterbury or London? 1.23g/19.0gr. 180°. *SCBI* 394; Blunt 83.

CYNETHRYTH, wife of OFFA

1132 *Eoba*. Canterbury. **CYNEðRYð REGINA** around **M** (for *Merciorum*). 1.21g/18.77 gr. 0°. *SCBI* 396; Blunt 120. The authenticity of this piece has been questioned because of its unusual style (Metcalf 1966c, 392).

JAENBERHT, Archbishop of Canterbury (765–92), with OFFA

1133 No moneyer. **IENBERHT AREP**. 1.13g/17.4gr. pierced 90°. *SCBI* 435; Blunt 127.

1121A–C. FM: University Purchase Fund 1984; ex Middle Harling hoard 1981/3.

1122. FM: Pilgrim Trust 1955; ex Lockett I 324; ex Carlyon-Britton I 292; found at Stamford Hill, Middlesex, 1906.

1123. FM: Friends 1955; ex Lockett I 348; ex Carlyon-Britton I 272; ex Verity; ex Montagu 192; ex Brice; ex Sotheby 11.8.1879, lot 327; found at Stilton, Hunts.

1124. FM: Lockett Executors 1955; ex Lockett I 354; ex Mann 134; ex Carlyon-Britton I 274; ex Montagu 221.

1124A. FM: Friends 28.1.1985; bt Baldwin; ex Mallinson 71; bt at King's Sutton, Northants., before 1936; discovered 'in a little bowl used for odd buttons, pins, etc., in an old lady's cottage', possibly a local find. Mallinson 1936, 373–5; 1982, 55.

1125. FM (*Catalogue c. 1886*): provenance unrecorded.

1126. FM: Young 1936; ex Carlyon-Britton I 271; found at Deddington Castle, Oxon., *c.* 1866. See Metcalf 1971.

1127. FM: provenance unrecorded (post 1886).

1128. FM: Young 1936; ex Bliss 35; ex Montagu 175; found in 'the City' (of London).

1129. FM: Cambridge Antiquarian Soc. 1886 (*CAS Catalogue 1847*, p. 28, no. 3); ex Rev. W. Palmer 1845.

1130. FM: Emmanuel College 1937.

1131. FM (*Catalogue 1867*, no. 13): Old University Collection.

1132. FM: Friends 1955; ex Lockett I 361; ex Montagu 224; ex Brice; ex Webster; found in Hampshire *c.* 1877. Brice MS (in FM) states: 'Bought by me in June 1877 of Mr Webster, who told me it had lately been found in Hampshire.'

1133. FM: provenance unrecorded (post 1886).

[*continued overleaf*]

1121A 1121B 1121C 1121A★ 1122 1123

1124 1124A 1125 1126 1127 1128 1129

1128★ 1130 1131 1132 1133 1134 1135

1136 1137 1138 1139 1140 1141

Heavy penny coinage (*c.* 792–6)

OFFA, King of Mercia (cont.)

1134 *Babba*. Canterbury. **OFFA REX M̄**. 1.19g/18.4gr. broken and repaired 130°. *SCBI* 395; Blunt 85.

1134A [*Vi*]*htred* (= Wihtræd). East Anglian mint. **+OFFA REX M̄**. 1.12g/17.3gr. fragment, small piece of solder adhering 270°. *SCBI* Mack 574; Blunt 115. The moneyer Wihtræd struck coins in East Anglia from Offa's light coinage until Ceolwulf I, that of Eadwald of East Anglia (*c.* 796) being of very similar design to this specimen.

ÆTHELHEARD, Archbishop of Canterbury (793–805), with OFFA

1135 No moneyer. **AEDILHEARD ARCEPI** and **OFFA REX M̄**. 1.43g/22.0gr. 160°. *SCBI* 436; Blunt 136.

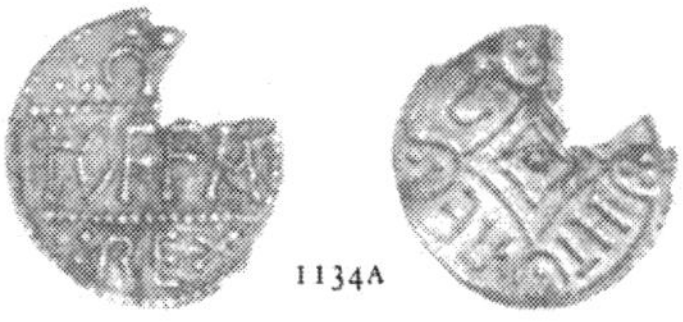

1134A

SOUTH-EASTERN COINAGES, 796–*c.* 851

There were four principal mints in southern England during the first half of the 9th century – Canterbury, Rochester, London and one in East Anglia – and at different times they fell under the control of various issuers, kings of Mercia, Wessex, Kent and East Anglia and archbishops of Canterbury. Winchester/Southampton operated briefly as a mint in the late 830s, but its coins are very rare and there are none in the collection.

The catalogue here is arranged by mints, rather than in the traditional fashion by rulers, in order to show the sequence of issues and demonstrate the essential continuity at each mint notwithstanding changes in authority.

CANTERBURY, 796–*c.* 851

Period I (796–*c.* 805). Non-portrait types.

EADBERT PRÆN, King of Kent, 796–8

1136 *Babba*. Three-line type. 1.20g/18.4gr. 90°. *SCBI* 429; BLS Ep 1(c); North 202. The moneyer Babba also struck coins for Egbert of Kent, Offa (**1134**) and Coenwulf, apparently representing the work of one man over some 20–30 years.

COENWULF, King of Mercia, 796–821 (controlled Kent from 798)

1137 *Dudda*. Tribrach type. 1.28g/19.8gr. 0°. *SCBI* 397; BLS Cn 7(a); North 342.

1138 *Eaba*. Tribrach type. 1.25g/19.3gr. pierced 340°. *SCBI* 990 (as false); BLS Cn 8; North 342. Possibly same moneyer as Eoba (**1127, 1132**). This coin was described in *SCBI* as a tooled cast, however the only other recorded specimen (in BM) is from different dies and on reflection we now think that it may be authentic. The smooth appearance, which is most marked on the part farthest from the piercing, may be because the coin was worn as an ornament.

1139 *Seberht*. Tribrach type. 1.27g/19.6gr. corroded and chipped 350°. *SCBI* –; BLS Cn 12; North 342.

ÆTHELHEARD, Archbishop of Canterbury (793–805), with COENWULF

1140 No moneyer. Tribrach type. **AEDILHEARD AR** around **C̄P** and **COENVVLF REX** around **M̄** (for *Merciorum*). 1.37g/21.2gr. 0°. *SCBI* 437; BLS Æ 2(f); North 232.

CUTHRED, King of Kent, 798–807 (coinage from *c.* 800)

1141 *Sigeberht*. Tribrach type. **CVÐ/RED/REX**. 1.39g/21.5gr. 130°. *SCBI* 430; BLS Cd 11(b); North 210/2.

1134. FM: Duncanson 1930; ex Smart; ex Beaufoy 43.

1134A. FM: Grierson 1985; from Spink 2.9.1985 (*NCirc* Sept. 1985, no. 5726); ex Mack (not in sales); from Spink 1919 (*NCirc* Sept./Oct. 1919, no. 74699).

1135. FM: Young 1936; ex Carlyon-Britton I 297; ex 'Astronomer' 123; ex Montagu 300; ex Shepherd 49; ex Murchison 77.

1136. FM: Trinity College 1937; ex Beaupré Bell 1741.

1137. FM: Young 1936; ex Shepherd 22.

1138. FM (*Catalogue c. 1886*): provenance unrecorded.

1139. FM: P. L. Evens of Bottisham (finder) 1983; found at Bottisham, Cambs. 5.4.1983. See Blackburn 1983.

1140. FM: Friends 1955; ex Lockett I 333; from Spink 1916 (*NCirc* May–June 1916, no. 41526); found near Cissbury, Sussex.

1141. FM: Friends 1955; ex Lockett I 329; ex Carlyon-Britton I 294.

ANGLO-SAXONS (4): SOUTH-EASTERN MINTS, 796–c. 852

References as on Plate 52. The coins are silver pennies.

CANTERBURY (cont.)

Period II (c. 805–c. 810). Portrait/Cross-and-wedge types

CUTHRED, King of Kent (cont.)

The obv. legend reads **CVÐRED REX CANT**.

1142 *Duda.* 1.26g/19.5gr. 90°. *SCBI* 431; BLS Cd 15(d); North 211.

1143 *Sigeberhti* (genitive form). 1.26g/19.5gr. 150°. *SCBI* 432; BLS Cd 20(b); North 211.

1144 *Verheardi* (= Wærheard, genitive form). 1.21g/18.7gr. pierced and worn 270°. *SCBI* 433; BLS Cd 22(b); North 211.

COENWULF, King of Mercia (cont.)

1145 *Seberht.* 1.23g/19.0gr. 0°. *SCBI* 401; BLS Cn 27; North 344.

1146 *Verheardi* (= Wærheard, genitive form). 1.34g/20.6gr. 0°. *SCBI* 403; BLS Cn 30(d); North 344.

Period III (c. 810–c.815). Portrait coins struck on larger flans; first bust

COENWULF, King of Mercia (cont.)

1147 *Della.* Cross-crosslet type. 1.35g/20.8gr. 160°. *SCBI* 398; BLS Cn 43; North 356.

WULFRED, Archbishop of Canterbury, 805–32

1148 *Saeberht. Dorobernia civitas* monogram. **VVLFREDI ARCHIEPISCOPI**. 1.34g/20.6gr. 0°. *SCBI* 438; BLS Wu 3(b); North 240. This is an early variety of Wulfred's First Monogram type. Note the genitive form of his name.

Period IV (c. 815–c. 823). Portrait coins struck on larger flans: second bust

COENWULF, King of Mercia (cont.)

1149 *Tidebearht.* Pincer-Cross type. 1.43g/22.1gr. 270°. *SCBI* 402; BLS Cn 45(g); North 347.

1150 *Oba.* Cross Moline type. 1.39g/21.5gr. 10°. *SCBI* 399; BLS Cn 65(c); North 352.

1151 *As last.* 1.14g/17.5gr. chipped and pierced 50°. *SCBI* 400; BLS Cn 65(d); North 352.

WULFRED, Archbishop of Canterbury (cont.)

1152 *Saeberht. Dorobernia civitas* monogram. **VVLFRED ARCHIEPI**. 0.89g/13.8gr. corroded 90°. *SCBI* 439; BLS Wu 6(d); North 240/1. The regular First Monogram type of this and the next coin is contemporary with the regal coins of Period IV, but it is likely that the archiepiscopal coinage was interrupted for a time during Wulfred's quarrel with the king between 817 and 821.

1153 *Swefherd.* Monogram and obv. legend as last. 1.51g/23.3gr. 270°. *SCBI* 440; BLS Wu 7A; North 240/1.

CEOLWULF I, King of Mercia, 821–3.

Canterbury coins not represented.

ANONYMOUS ARCHIEPISCOPAL COINAGE, c. 822–3

Towards the end of Ceolwulf's reign and in the period which followed before their recognition of Baldred, the Canterbury moneyers issued two series of anonymous coins, one with a regal bust (not represented) and one with an archiepiscopal bust.

1154 *Luning.* **DOROBERNIA CIVITAS**. 1.36g/21.0gr. 0°. *SCBI* 441; BLS Wu 13(a); North 238.

1155 *As last.* 1.37g/21.2gr. 180°. *SCBI* 442; BLS Wu 13(b); North 238.

Period V (c. 823–c. 828)

BALDRED, King of Kent, c. 823–5

1156 *Tidebearht.* **DRVR CITS**. 1.38g/21.3gr. 0°. *SCBI* 434; BLS Ba 6; North 220.

EGBERT, King of Wessex, 803–39 (controlled Kent from c. 825)

1157 *Oba.* Non-portrait type. 1.40g/21.7gr. 270°. *SCBI* 523; Blunt 1957, group 2, no. 9; North 566. Described by Kenyon in 3rd edn of Hawkins (1887, 113, no. 16) from this coin. This is one of a variety of portrait and non-portrait types issued at Canterbury c. 825–8.

For a forgery of a portrait coin, see **1494**.

1142. FM: Provenance unrecorded (post 1886).

1143. FM: Young 1936; ex Bliss 45.

1144. FM: Duncanson 1930; ex Smart; ex Rashleigh 83; ex White (1848); ex 'Dean of St Patrick's' 105.

1145. FM: Young 1936; ex Carlyon-Britton II 878.

1146. FM: Young 1936; ex Carlyon-Britton I 276; ex Montagu 246; ex Brice; ex Bergne 61; ex Pembroke 17.

1147. FM: Young 1936; ex Carlyon-Britton I 278; ex 'Astronomer' 93; ex Montagu 233; ex Brice; ex Bergne 59.

1148. FM: provenance unrecorded.

1149. FM: Duncanson 1930; ex Smart; ex Devonshire 18.

1150. FM: Young 1936; ex Carlyon-Britton I 279; ex Hay (so Carlyon-Britton catalogue, but not in Hay sale).

1151. FM: Trinity College 1937; ex Prof. T. M. Hughes 1876; found at Haslingfield (Cambs.) 'in the coprolite diggings'.

1152. FM: Duncanson 1930; ex Smart; ex Rashleigh 93.

1153. FM: Young 1936; ex Bliss 46; ex Montagu V 3.

1154. FM: Young 1936: ex Carlyon-Britton I 299.

1155. FM: Lockett Executors 1955; ex Lockett I 337; from Spink 1907 (*NCirc* Nov. 1907, no. 46875); ex 'Astronomer' 131; ex Montagu 309; ex Brice; ex Lake Price 20; ex Murchison 91; ex Dymock 42.

1156. FM: Young 1936; ex Carlyon-Britton I 295; ex 'Astronomer' 80; ex Montagu 292; ex Brice; ex Wigan; ex Cuff 260; from Mathew Young; from a Suffolk hoard, probably before 1829 (Blunt, Lyon and Stewart 1963, 43–4).

1157. FM: Young 1936; ex Carlyon-Britton I 322; ex Rashleigh 200; from Trewhiddle hoard 1774.

[*continued overleaf*]

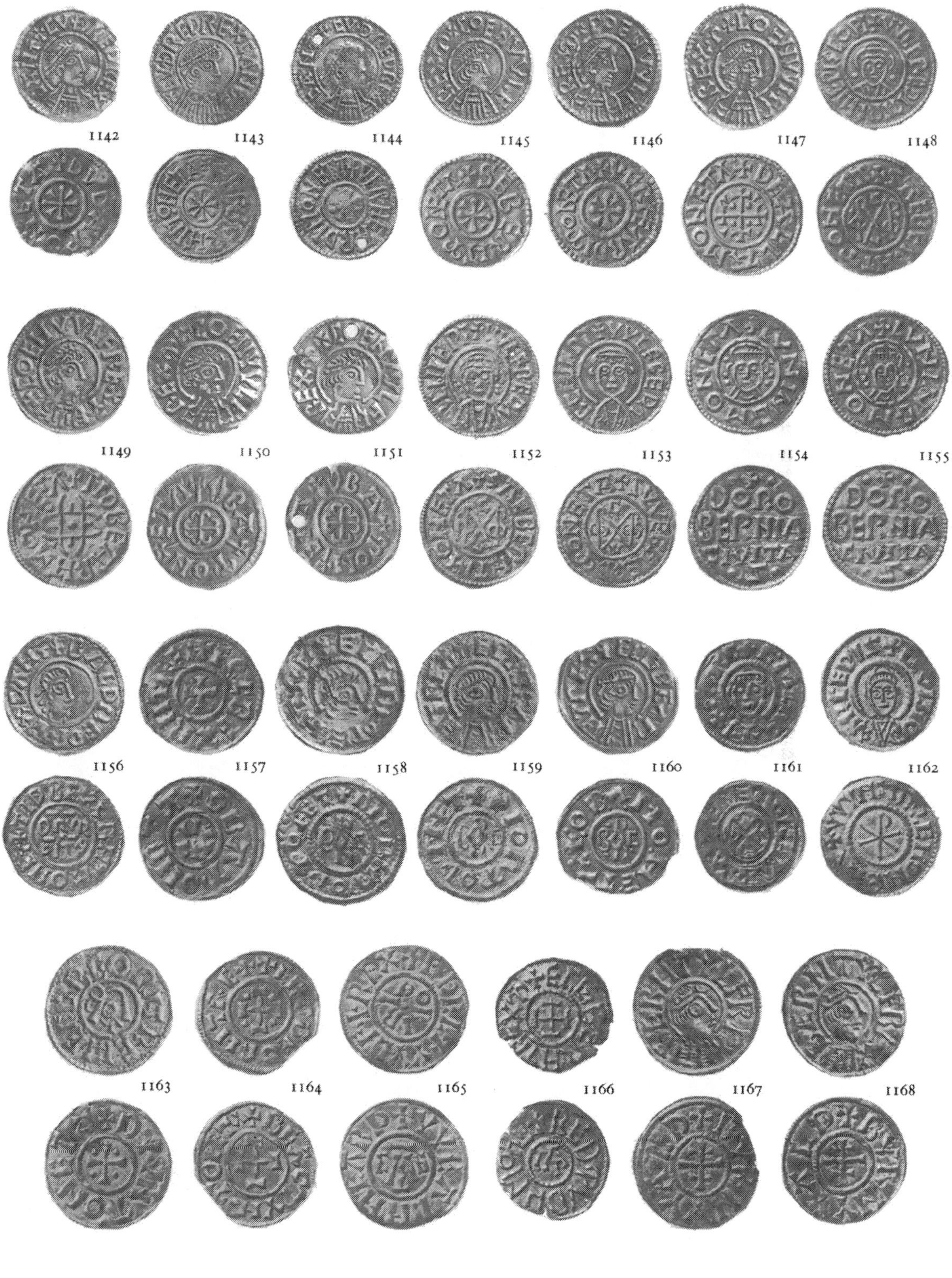

1142 1143 1144 1145 1146 1147 1148

1149 1150 1151 1152 1153 1154 1155

1156 1157 1158 1159 1160 1161 1162

1163 1164 1165 1166 1167 1168

Period VI (*c.* 828–*c.* 843)

EGBERT, King of Wessex (cont.)

Portrait/DORB C Monogram type (North 573)

1158 *Biornmod.* 1.40g/21.6gr. 170°. *SCBI* 520.
1159 *Diormod.* 1.44g/22.1gr. 270°. *SCBI* 521.
1160 *Oba.* 1.26g/19.5gr. chipped 180°. *SCBI* 522.

ÆTHELWULF, King of Wessex, 839–58

Non-portrait *Saxoniorum* coins of Canterbury, not represented.

CEOLNOTH, Archbishop of Canterbury, 833–70

1161 *Where* or *Wnere* (= Wynhere). **DOROVERNIA CA**(?) monogram. **CIALNOD ARC**. 1.29g/20.0gr. 320°. *SCBI* 444; North 241. This type is contemporary with Æthelwulf's *Saxoniorum* issue (*c.* 839–*c.* 843).

Period VII (*c.* 843–*c.* 848)

For a forgery of Æthelwulf's Canterbury portrait series, see **1495**.

CEOLNOTH, Archbishop of Canterbury (cont.)

1162 *Wynhere.* **CIALNOD ARCEPIS**. 1.25g/19.2gr. 90°. *SCBI* 445; North 242. This new portrait/Christogram issue was struck *c.* 843–*c.* 848.
For a later coin of Ceolnoth, see **1315**.

ROCHESTER *c.* 810–*c.* 851

For the mint attribution, see pp. 290–1.

Period V (*c.* 823–*c.* 828)

EGBERT, King of Wessex (cont.)

1163 *Duun.* **ECGBEORHT RE**. 1.34g/20.7gr. 260°. *SCBI* 525; Blunt 1957, group 4, no. 2; North 575.

Period VI (*c.* 828–*c.* 840)

EGBERT, King of Wessex (cont.)

1164 *Beagmund.* **ECGBEORHT**, square in each angle of obv. cross. 1.29g/19.9gr. 0°. *SCBI* –; Blunt 1957, Group 4, no. 16; North 580.

Period VIII (*c.* 848–*c.* 851). *Doribi/Cant* type

ÆTHELWULF, King of Wessex (cont.)

1165 *Wealhheard.* **EDELVVLF REX**. 1.35g/20.8gr. 0°. *SCBI* 526; North 614.
For later coins of Æthelwulf, see **1305–9**.

LONDON 796–*c.* 851

For the mint attribution, see pp. 292–3.

Period VI (*c.* 828–*c.* 840)

EGBERT of Wessex, as King of Mercia, 829–30

1166 *Redmudn* (= Rædmund). **ECGBERHT REX M** (for *Merciorum*). 1.25g/19.2gr. chipped 270°. *SCBI* 524; Blunt 1957, 472–3; North 584. Rædmund also struck coins for Wiglaf of Mercia.

Period VII (*c.* 843–*c.* 848)

BERHTWULF, King of Mercia, 840–52

1167 *Burnwald.* 1.18g/18.2gr. chipped 280°. *SCBI* 406; North 407 (bust A). Probably of the London mint, although the dies of this and the next were engraved by the Rochester die-cutter *c.* 842/3 (see p. 292).
1168 *As last.* 1.29g/19.9gr. 0°. *SCBI* 407; North 407 (bust A).

1158. FM: Young 1936; ex Bliss 62; from Croydon Palace hoard, before 1907 (see *NC* 1907, 341).

1159 FM: Perceval 1920. The discoloration on this coin shows it to be from the same hoard as **1327–8**, **1335**, **1337** (all ex Perceval), but probably not from Trewhiddle 1774, as suggested in *SCBI*, as this hoard is not now thought to have contained late coins of Burgred or coins of Alfred (Pagan 1965a, 19).

1160–1. FM: Duncanson 1930; ex Smart.

1162. FM: Young 1936; ex Carlyon-Britton I 302; ex Montagu 319; ex Marsham 114.

1163. FM: Henderson 1933; ex Montagu 464; ex Warne 172.

1164. FM: Chilvers 1967; ex Ryan II 688; ex Compton-Roberts; ?ex Montagu 467.

1165. FM: Young 1936; ex Carlyon-Britton I 328.

1166. FM: provenance unrecorded.

1167. FM: Duncanson 1930; Smart; ?ex Rashleigh 64.

1168. FM: Young 1936; ex Carlyon-Britton I 283; ex 'Astronomer' 102; ex Montagu 271; ex Shepherd 27.

ANGLO-SAXONS (5): EAST ANGLIA 796–869 and NORTHUMBRIA 738–867

References as on Plate 52, and Pagan – Pagan 1982a.

EAST ANGLIAN MINT, 796–869

The operation of an East Anglian mint, probably located in Suffolk, can be traced, via a continuity of moneyers, from the coinage of Beonna (**1121A–C**), through a period of Mercian domination, to a coinage of local rulers which ended with the Viking conquest of 879. The coins are silver pennies.

CEOLWULF I, King of Mercia, 821–3

1169 *Hereberht*. 1.34g/20.8gr. 60°. *SCBI* 404; BLS Cl 28(f); North 392.

1170 *Woddel*. 1.33g/20.5gr. 240°. *SCBI* 405; BLS Cl 32(h); North 392.

ÆTHELSTAN, King of East Anglia, *c*. 825–*c*. 845

1171 *Mon*. **AEÐILSTAN R**. 1.34g/20.7gr. 0°. *SCBI* 448; North 446; Pagan 60.III.1.

1172 *Mon*. **AEDILSTAN R**. 1.36g/21.0gr. 0°. *SCBI* 449; North 445; Pagan 62.I.1.

ÆTHELWEARD, King of East Anglia, *c*. 845–55

1173 *Aethelhelm*. **EDECPARD REX**. 1.32g/20.3gr. 310°. *SCBI* 450; North 452; Pagan 67.III.1.

EDMUND, King of East Anglia, 855–69

No clear chronology has been worked out for the coinage of Edmund, although Pagan (1982a) points out that coins reading **EADMVND REX** are generally later than those reading **EADMVND REX AN** (**1178** is an exception, reading **REX** but belonging earlier in the reign).

1174 *Beornferth*. **EADMVND REX AN**. 1.36g/21.0gr. 340°. *SCBI* 451; North 459; Pagan 72.III.2.

1175 *Beornferd*. **EADMVND REX**. 1.42g/21.9gr. 90°. *SCBI* 452; North 459; Pagan 74.I.2.

1176 *Beornhæh*. **EADMVND REX**. 1.30g/20.0gr. 270°. *SCBI* –; North 456; Pagan 74.III.1.

1177 *Eadmund*. **EADMVND REX AN**. 1.29g/19.9gr. 180°. *SCBI* 453; North 456; Pagan 75.VI.1.

1178 *Eadmund*. **EADMVND REX**. 1.36g/21.0gr. 280°. *SCBI* 454; North 456; Pagan 76.V.1.

1179 *Twigca*. **EADMVND REX AN** around cross-on-*omega*. 1.17g/18.0gr. 270°. *SCBI* 455; North 462; Pagan 80.II.1.

KINGS OF NORTHUMBRIA, 738–867

In Northumbria, coins of a similar module and weight to the sceattas were struck intermittently from the early 8th century until the Vikings seized York in 866/7. The 8th-century coins are conventionally known as 'sceattas' and the much baser 9th-century coins as 'stycas', though neither is likely to have been an original name. There is some uncertainty about the dates of the 9th-century kings and archbishops (see pp. 301–3 above). Below we give the traditional dating and, in parentheses, an alternative chronology proposed by Pagan (1969).

EADBERT, 738–58

1180 **EΛDBERHTVΓ** (last symbol representing **S**). 1.04g/16.0gr. 0°. *SCBI* 266; Rigold 1977a, Series Y; Booth 1984, A 10.

ALCHRED, 765–74

1181 **ALCHRED**. 1.01g/15.6gr. 320°. *SCBI* 267; Booth 1984, no. 9.

EANRED, *c*. 810–*c*. 840 (*c*. 830 or earlier–*c*. 854)

The earliest coins are of base silver (40–15%) and are contemporary with those of Archbishop Eanbald II. The latest coins are very base, 15–5% silver. The king's name is spelt **EANRED**, unless otherwise indicated.

(i) *Earlier phase, base silver*

1182 *Cvnwlf* (= Cynewulf). 1.17g/18.1gr. 260°. *SCBI* 271. Same obv. die as next.

1183 *As last*. 1.21g/18.7gr. 0°. *SCBI* 272. Same obv. die as last.

1184 *Cynavlf* ('v' inverted A). 1.32g/20.4gr. 110°. *SCBI* 273. Same rev. die as next.

1185 *As last*. 1.22g/18.8gr. 220°. *SCBI* 274. Same rev. die as last.

1186 *Cvwhlf* (with letters abnormal, inverted, or ligatured). 1.22g/18.8gr. 270°. *SCBI* 275.

1169. FM: provenance unrecorded.

1170. FM: Duncanson 1930; ex Smart; ?ex Rashleigh 53.

1171. FM: Young 1936; ex Carlyon-Britton I 307; ex Nunn 59; ex Montagu 347; ex Marsham 96.

1172. FM: Duncanson 1930; ex Smart; ex Rashleigh 111; ex Cuff 343.

1173, 1178, 1180. FM: Duncanson 1930; ex Smart.

1174. FM: Young 1936; ex H. Weber 7.

1175. FM: Young 1936: ex Carlyon-Britton I 311.

1176. CCC (*Catalogue* no. 146); Lewis 1891; bt at Tunbridge Wells 2.7.1872; from Croydon hoard 1862 (Spufford 1961, 214).

1177. FM: Young 1936; ex Carlyon-Britton I 310; ex Montagu 359; ex Brice.

1179. FM: Young 1936; ex Carlyon-Britton I 312; ex Montagu 363; said in the Carlyon-Britton catalogue to be ex Cuff, but Cuff 335 is now in the Blunt collection (see Pagan 1982a, 80).

1181. FM: Lockett Executors 1955; ex Lockett I 266.

1182–4, 1186, 1200–1. FM: Young 1936; ex Carlyon-Britton I 188.

1185, 1188, 1190, 1203. FM: provenance unrecorded.

[*continued overleaf*]

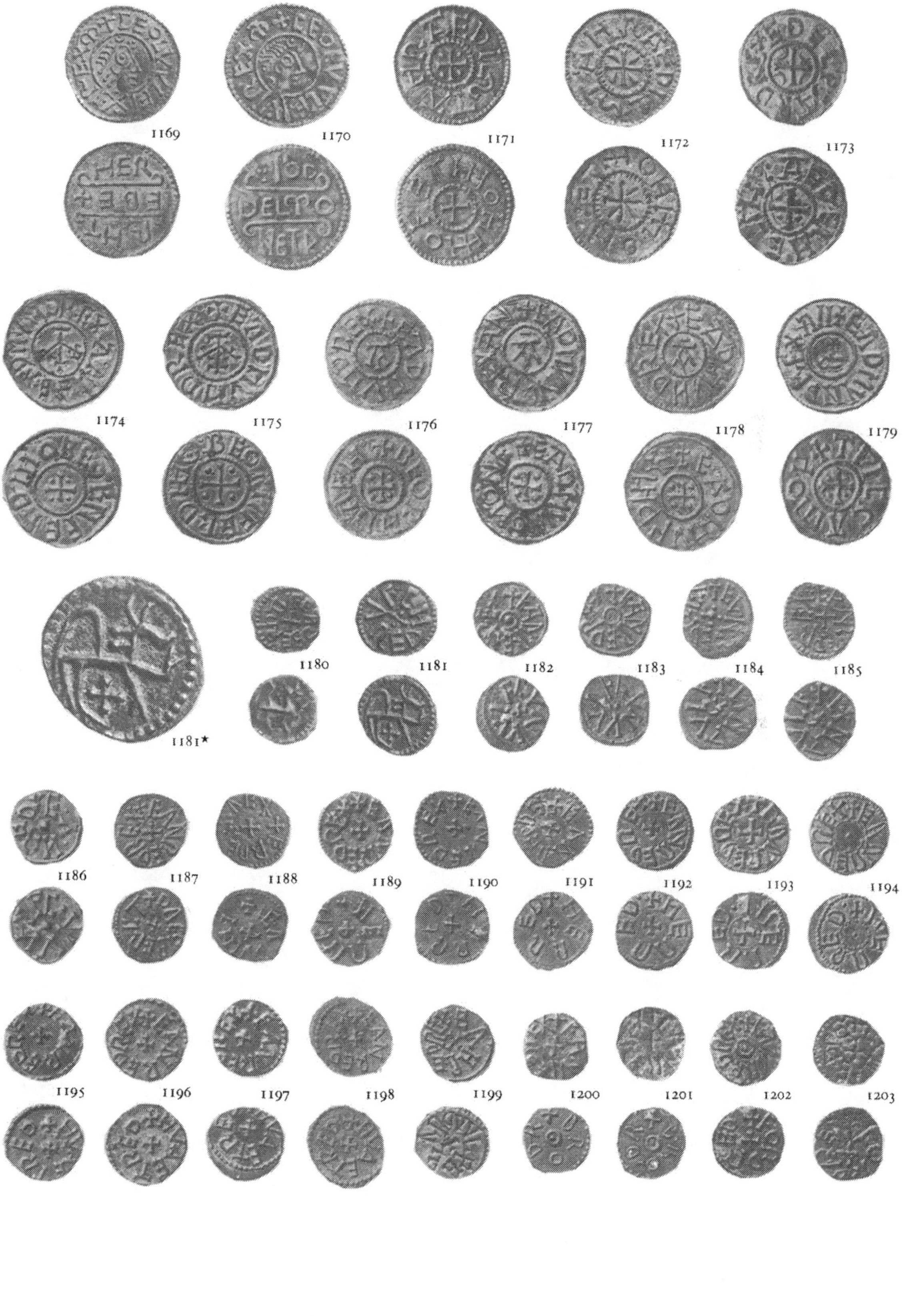

1169 1170 1171 1172 1173

1174 1175 1176 1177 1178 1179

1180 1181 1182 1183 1184 1185

1181*

1186 1187 1188 1189 1190 1191 1192 1193 1194

1195 1196 1197 1198 1199 1200 1201 1202 1203

1187 *Daegberct* (= Dægbeorht). 1.36g/21.0gr. 270°. *SCBI* 276.
1188 *Eadvini* (= Eadwine). King's name retrograde. 1.34g/20.7gr. 180°. *SCBI* 277.
1189 *Herred* (= Hereræd). 1.19g/18.4gr. 270°. *SCBI* 283.
1190 *As last*. 1.21g/18.7gr. 180°. *SCBI* 285.
1191 *As last*. 1.22g/18.8gr. 90°. *SCBI* 286.
1192 *As last*. 1.10g/16.9gr. 90°. *SCBI* 284.
1193 *As last*. 1.24g/19.1gr. 0°. *SCBI* 288.
1194 *As last*. 1.24g/19.1gr. 90°. *SCBI* 287.
1195 *Hvaetred* (= Hwætræd). 1.23g/19.1gr. 0°. *SCBI* 289.
1196 *As last*. 1.26g/19.4gr. 90°. *SCBI* 290.
1197 *As last*. 1.12g/17.3gr. 110°. *SCBI* 291.
1198 *As last*. 1.24g/19.0gr. 90°. *SCBI* –.
Wilheah. For forgeries, see **1483–4**.
1199 *Vulfheard* (= Wulfheard). 1.10g/17.0gr. 110°. *SCBI* 278.

(ii) *Later phase, very base silver*

1200 *Brodr* (= Brother). 1.15g/17.7gr. 270°. *SCBI* 268. Same dies as next.
1201 *As last*. 1.23g/19.0gr. 0°. *SCBI* 269. Same dies as last.
Brother. For a forgery, see **1482**.
1202 *Fordred*. 1.23g/19.0gr. 120°. *SCBI* 282.
1203 *As last*. 1.24g/19.1gr. 270°. *SCBI* 279.

1187. FM: Henderson 1933.

1189, 1191, 1195–7. FM: Young 1936; ex Carlyon-Britton I 196.

1192, 1199. FM: Young 1936; ex Shepherd 38.

1193. FM: Hasluck 1920.

1194. FM: Duncanson 1930; ex Smart.

1198. CCC (*Catalogue* no. 140): Lewis 1891; bt in Newcastle 11.6.1877; ex Hexham hoard (Spufford 1961, 214, no. i).

1202. FM: Trinity College 1937; ex J. D. White (Assistant Librarian) 1876; found with **1223** in a tumulus near Carlisle, Sept. 1876.

ANGLO-SAXONS (6): NORTHUMBRIA, 738–867

References as on Plate 52. The coins are base stycas.

KINGS OF NORTHUMBRIA (cont.)

EANRED (cont.)

(ii) *Later phase, very base silver* (cont.)

1204 *Fordred*. King's name retrograde. 1.32g/20.4gr. 270°. *SCBI* 281.
1205 *As last*. 0.84g/13.0gr. worn 280°. *SCBI* 280. Very poor metal, possibly a later imitation.
1206 *Gaduteis* (= Gadutels). 1.05g/16.2gr. 270°. *SCBI* –.
1207 *Monne*. 1.26g/19.4gr. 0°. *SCBI* 293.
1208 *As last*, but initial **E** of king's name reversed. 1.05g/16.2gr. 180°. *SCBI* 292.

ÆTHELRED II, first reign *c*. 840–*c*. 844 (*c*. 854–*c*. 858)

The coins are divided between Æthelred's first and second reigns according to the arrangement of Lyon 1956. The king's name is spelt so variously on the coins that it is given in each case.

1209 *Alghere*. **AEDILRED**. 1.25g/19.3gr. 180°. *SCBI* 296.
1210 *As last*. 1.05g/16.2gr. 20°. *SCBI* 297.
1211 *Brother*. **EÐFLAED**. 1.19g/18.3gr. *SCBI* –.
1212 *Brother*. **EDILRED**. 1.32g/20.3gr. 180°. *SCBI* –.
1213 *Eanred*. **EÐFLRED**. 1.09g/16.8gr. 0°. *SCBI* 305. Double struck.
1214 *As last*. 1.24g/19.1gr. chipped 20°. *SCBI* 303. Same obv. die as next.
1215 *As last*. 1.11g/17.1gr. 90°. *SCBI* 304. Same obv. die as last.
1216 *As last*. 1.28g/19.8gr. 180°. *SCBI* –.
1217 *Eanred*. **AEILRED**. 1.43g/22.1gr. 0°. *SCBI* 298. Same obv. die as next two coins.
1218 *As last*. 1.20g/18.5gr. 260°. *SCBI* 299. Same obv. die as last and same dies as next.
1219 *As last*. 1.05g/16.2gr. 0°. *SCBI* 300. Same dies as last.
1220 *As last*. 1.26g/19.4gr. 270°. *SCBI* 301.
1221 *Eanred*. **EDILRED**. 1.18g/18.2gr. 90°. *SCBI* 308.
1222 *Eanred*. **EDILRED** (**L** inverted). 1.30g/20.1gr. 260°. *SCBI* 302.
1223 *As last*. 1.43g/22.1gr. 90°. *SCBI* 310.
1224 *As last*. 1.17g/18.1gr. 90°. *SCBI* 306.
1225 *As last*. 1.34g/20.7gr. 0°. *SCBI* 307.
1226 *As last*. 1.25g/19.3gr. 90°. *SCBI* 309.
1227 *Fordred*. **EÐFLRED**. 1.30g/20.1gr. 90°. *SCBI* 311.
1228 *Forthred*. **EÐELREP**. 1.14g/17.6gr. 90°. *SCBI* 312.
1229 *Leofdegn* (= Leofthegn). **AEdELREd**. 1.36g/28.5gr. chipped 0°. *SCBI* 318. Same obv. die as next.
1230 *As last*. 0.84g/13.0gr. chipped 0°. *SCBI* 319. Same obv. die as last. Poor metal, silver-plated?
1231 *Leofdegn*. **EDELRED**. 1.19g/18.4gr. 90°. *SCBI* 320.
1232 *As last*. 1.36g/21.0gr. 90°. *SCBI* –.
1233 *As last*. 1.30g/20.0gr. 180°. *SCBI* 317.
1234 *As last*. 0.94g/14.5gr. 60°. *SCBI* 313. Same obv. die as **1243** (Odilo).
1235 *Leofdegn*. **EDILRED**. 1.06g/16.4gr. 90°. *SCBI* 316.
1236 *Leofdegn* ('*n*' runic). **EDILRED** (**L** inverted). 1.34g/20.7gr. 180°. *SCBI* 314.
1237 *Leofdegn*. **EDILRED** (**L** inverted). 1.15g/17.7gr. 90°. *SCBI* 315.
1238 *As last*. 1.18g/18.2gr. 90°. *SCBI* 321.
Leofdegn. For forgeries, see **1485–7**.
1239 *Monne*. **AEDELRED**. 1.27g/19.6gr. 90°. *SCBI* 324.
1240 *Monne*. **EDELRED**. 1.16g/17.9gr. 80°. *SCBI* 323.
1241 *Monne*. **AEDILRED**. 0.96g/14.8gr. 180°. *SCBI* 325.
1242 *Monne*. **EDLIRED**. 1.44g/22.2gr. 90°. *SCBI* 322.
1243 *Odilo Mo*. **EDELRED**. 1.11g/17.1gr. 0°. *SCBI* 326. Same obv. die as **1234** (Leofthegn). Some dies read *Odilo Mon*, and the last element may be either a second name or *moneta*.
1244 *Vendelberht* (= Wendelbeorht). **EDILRED**. 1.20g/18.5gr. 220°. *SCBI* 329.
1245 *As last*. 1.23g/19.0gr. 200°. *SCBI* 330.
1246 *Vendelberht*. **EDILRED** (retrograde). 1.23g/19.0gr. 90°. *SCBI* 332.
1247 *As last*. 1.19g/18.4gr. 320°. *SCBI* 333.
1248 *Vendelberht*. **EILRED**. 1.13g/17.4gr. 140°. *SCBI* 331.
1249 *Vendelberht*. **EDILRED**? 1.13g/17.4gr. 0°. *SCBI* 328. Same rev. die as next.
1250 *Vendelberht*. **EDILRED** (**L** inverted). 1.25g/19.3gr. 20°. *SCBI* 327. Same rev. die as last.
1251 *Wihtrd* (= Wihtræd). **EDILRED**. 1.22g/18.8gr. 0°. *SCBI* 356.
1252 *Vulfred* (= Wulfræd). **EDILRED**. 1.20g/18.5gr. 70°. *SCBI* 334.
1253 *Vulfsic* (= Wulfsige, read outwardly). **EDLIRED**. 1.18g/18.2gr. 180°. *SCBI* 335.

1204–5, 1208, 1210, 1219–20, 1222, 1229, 1236, 1239, 1241–2, 1251–2. FM: provenance unrecorded.
1206. FM: Collins & Clark 1974; ex Wyatt.
1207. FM: A. Smith 1942.
1209, 1213. FM: Henderson 1933.
1211. CCC (*Catalogue* no. 141): Lewis 1891; bt at Newcastle 11.6.1877; ex Hexham hoard (Spufford 1961, 214, no. ii).
1212, 1216, 1232. FM: Collins & Clark 1974; ex Wyatt.
1214, 1222. FM: Mrs Laurence Humphry and Sir Arthur Stokes 1915.
1215, 1226, 1234, 1237, 1243, 1249. FM: Young 1936.
1217. FM: Young 1936; ex Shepherd 38.
1218, 1221. FM: Young 1936; ex Carlyon-Britton I 207.
1223. FM: Trinity College 1937; ex J. D. White 1876; found w. **1202** in a tumulus near Carlisle, Sept. 1876.
1224. FM: Young 1936; ex Carlyon-Britton I 196.
1225, 1231. FM: Young: ex Shepherd 39.
1227–8. FM: Hasluck 1920.
1230, 1233, 1235, 1238. FM: Young 1936; ex Carlyon-Britton I 213.
1240, 1250, 1253. FM: Perceval 1922.
1244–8. FM: Young 1936; ex Carlyon-Britton I 218.

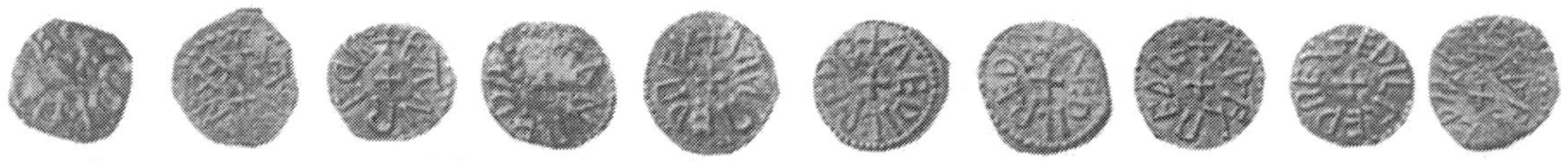

1204 1205 1206 1207 1208 1209 1210 1211 1212 1213

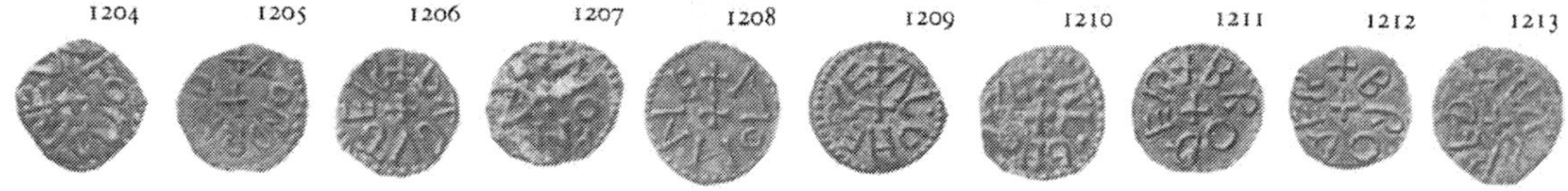

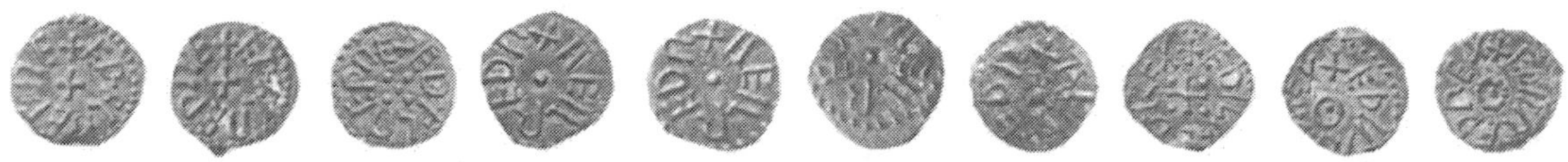

1214 1215 1216 1217 1218 1219 1220 1221 1222 1223

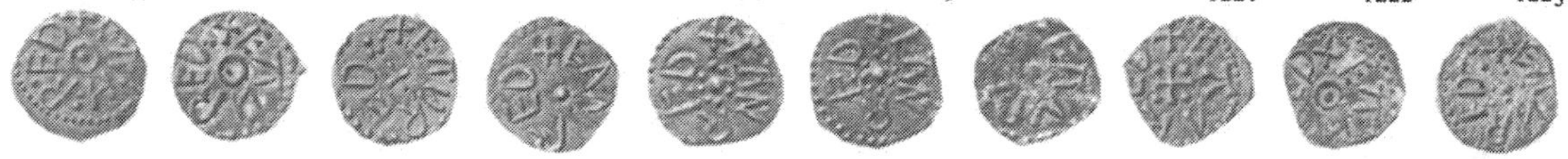

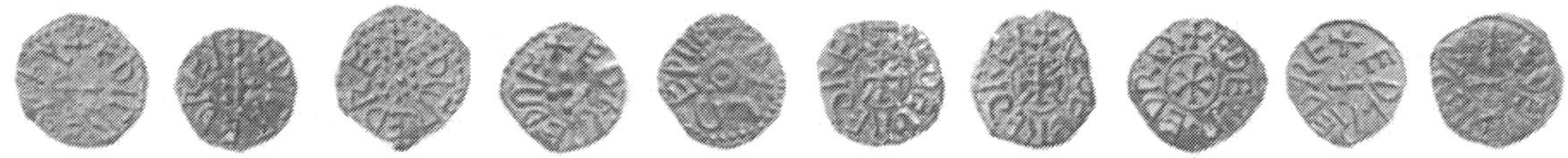

1224 1225 1226 1227 1228 1229 1230 1231 1232 1233

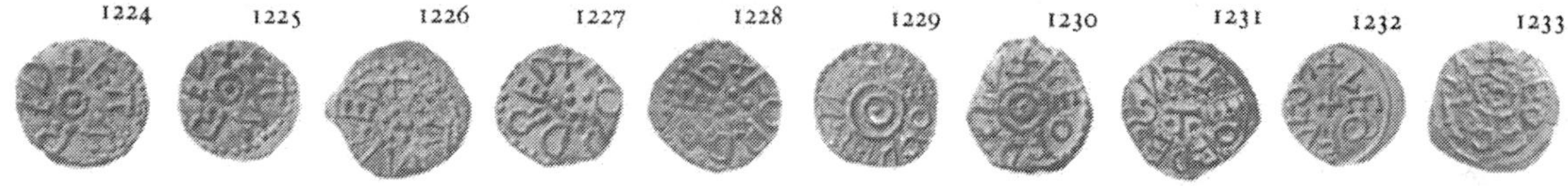

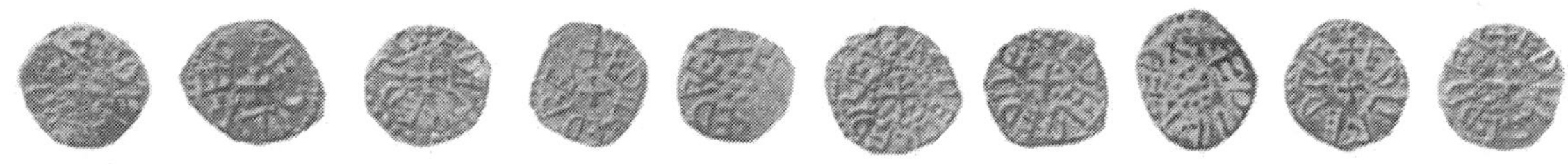

1234 1235 1236 1237 1238 1239 1240 1241 1242 1243

1244 1245 1246 1247 1248 1249 1250 1251 1252 1253

ANGLO-SAXONS (7): NORTHUMBRIA, 738–867

References as on Plate 52. The coins are base stycas.

KINGS OF NORTHUMBRIA (cont.)

REDWULF *c.* 844 (*c.* 858)

The king's name is spelt **REDVLF**, unless otherwise indicated.

1254 *Cudbereht* (= Cuthbeorht). 1.40g/21.6gr. 0°. *SCBI* 336.
Eardwulf. For an irregular coin, see **1272**.

1255 *Eordred* (= Fordræd). 1.31g/20.2gr. 0°. *SCBI* 337.

1256 *As last.* 1.11g/17.1gr. 90°. *SCBI* 338.

1257 *Mnne* (retrograde; = Monne). 1.24g/19.1gr. 350°. *SCBI* 339.

1258 *Vendelberht.* **REVDDLF**. 0.82g/12.7gr. 270°. *SCBI* 340.

ÆTHELRED II, second reign, *c.* 844–*c.* 848 (*c.* 858–*c.* 862)

The king's name is spelt **EDILRED** throughout.

1259 *Eardvulf* (= Eardwulf). 1.00g/15.4gr. 270°. *SCBI* 341.

1260 *As last.* 1.52g/23.5gr. 180°. *SCBI* 342.

1261 *As last.* 1.04g/16.0gr. 0°. *SCBI* 343.

1262 *As last.* 1.24g/19.1gr. 170°. *SCBI* 345.

1263 *As last.* 1.45g/22.4gr. 170°. *SCBI* –.

1264 *Eardvule.* 0.96g/14.8gr. chipped 90°. *SCBI* 344.

1265 *Eradvvlde* (= Eardwulf?) 0.98g/15.1gr. 290°. *SCBI* 347. Miss Pirie has supplied the rev. reading from a die-duplicate in the Yorkshire Museum.
Eardwulf. For irregular coins, see **1271–3, 1302**.

1266 *Fordred* (retrograde). 1.25g/19.3gr. 90°. *SCBI* 348.
Odilo. For an irregular coin, see **1274**.

OSBERT, *c.* 848–67 (*c.* 862–7)

1267 *Mnne* (retrograde; = Monne). **OSBERCHT**. 1.34g/20.7gr. 320°. *SCBI* 349.

1268 *Viniberht* (= Winebeorht). **OSBERCHT** (both legends read outwards). 1.10g/17.0gr. 90°. *SCBI* 350.

1269 Blundered name (**VOLRNF**). **OSBERCHL** (retrograde). 1.10g/17.0gr. 270°. *SCBI* 351. An irregular rev. die, though Miss Pirie informs us that the obv. die was used by the moneyers Eanwulf and Monne.

IRREGULAR COINS

(a) Earlier (Hexham) group

1270 **ROÐER** and **FORDRED** (both retrograde). 1.18g/18.3gr. 160°. *SCBI* 353. Miss Pirie informs us that this is die-linked to coins by the moneyer Monne (reading **EÐELRED**) attributed to Æthelred's first reign.

(b) Later group

1271 **EARDVÆI**(?) and **EARDVVLF** (both retrograde). 1.23g/19.0gr. 290°. *SCBI* 354.

1272 **REDVF[** and **EARDVVL** (both retrograde). 1.06g/16.4gr. 50°. *SCBI* 355.

1273 **EDILRED REX** and **EARDVVLF** (both retrograde). 1.10g/17.0gr. 290°. *SCBI* 346. Miss Pirie informs us that this and the next two coins belong to a vast die-chain which connects with coins attributed to Æthelred's second reign.

1274 **EDIEDEDX** and **ODILO** (both retrograde). 1.13g/17.4gr. 240°. *SCBI* 352.

1275 **EHDEVOL** (retrograde) and **BEOMRE**. 0.99g/15.3gr. 320°. *SCBI* 357. For the erroneous attributions of this coin to Beonna of East Anglia, see note in *SCBI*.
See also **1269** and **1302**.

ARCHBISHOPS OF YORK

EANBALD II, 796–unspecified date (796–*c.* 840 or later)

The coins are base silver and contemporary with those of the earlier phase of Eanred's coinage.

1276 *Edilvard* (= Æthelweard). **ANBALD ARCE**. 0.99g/15.2gr. 180°. *SCBI* 358.
For forgeries, see **1488** (Eadwine), **1489** (Æthelweard) and **1490** (Cynewulf).

WIGMUND, *c.* 837–*c.* 854 (*c.* 848 or earlier–*c.* 858 or later)

The coins date from the later years of Eanred's reign until possibly the second reign of Æthelred II. The archbishop's name is spelt **VIGMVND**. Where it is accompanied by the archiepiscopal title, this is indicated below. Miss Pirie points out that those dies with **AREP** or **APEP** appear to be the earliest and those without title the latest. The order in which the moneyers operated (Æthelweard, Coenræd/Hunlaf, Æthelhelm) is confirmed by their participation in the regal coinage.

1277 *Edelhelm* (= Æthelhelm). 1.15g/17.7gr. 180°. *SCBI* 359. Same obv. die as next.

1278 *As last.* 1.21g/18.7gr. 270°. *SCBI* 360. Same obv. die as last.

1279 *As last.* 1.15g/17.7gr. 270°. *SCBI* 361.

1280 *As last.* 1.28g/19.8gr. 90°. *SCBI* 362.

1281 *As last.* 1.17g/18.1gr. 0°. *SCBI* 363.

1282 *Edilveard* (= Æthelweard). **APEP** (for archbishop). 1.26g/19.5gr. 270°. *SCBI* 364. Same obv. die as next.

1254–6, 1272. FM: Young 1936; ex Carlyon-Britton I 222.

1257, 1269, 1271. FM: Young 1936; ex Shepherd 39.

1258. FM: Duncanson 1930; ex Smart; from Baldwin; ex Rashleigh 142.

1259, 1267, 1278, 1303. FM: Duncanson 1930; ex Smart.

1260, 1266, 1268, 1273. FM: provenance unrecorded.

1261–2, 1264–5. FM: Young 1936; ex Carlyon-Britton I 207.

1263. FM: Collins & Clark 1974; ex Wyatt.

1270. FM (*Catalogue c. 1886*): provenance unrecorded.

1274, 1276–7, 1290–1, 1299. FM: Young 1936.

1275. FM: Duncanson 1930; ex Smart; ex Rashleigh 106.

1279. FM: Perceval 1922.

1280. FM (*Catalogue 1867*, no. 17): Babington 1866.

1281, 1301. FM: Henderson 1933.

1282, 1292–3, 1298. FM: Young 1936; ex Carlyon-Britton I 237.

[*continued overleaf*]

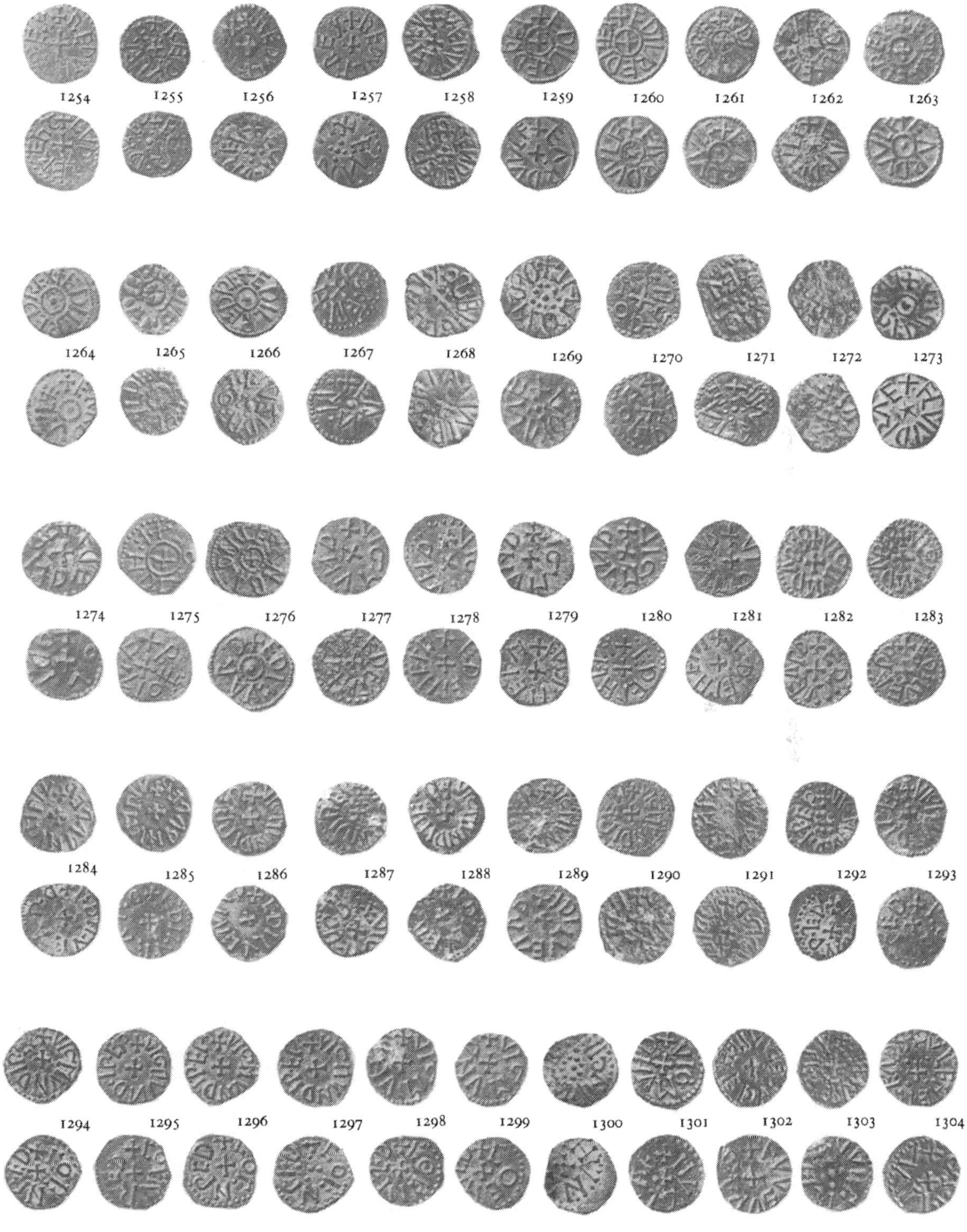

1254 1255 1256 1257 1258 1259 1260 1261 1262 1263

1264 1265 1266 1267 1268 1269 1270 1271 1272 1273

1274 1275 1276 1277 1278 1279 1280 1281 1282 1283

1284 1285 1286 1287 1288 1289 1290 1291 1292 1293

1294 1295 1296 1297 1298 1299 1300 1301 1302 1303 1304

1283 *As last.* 1.15g/17.8gr. 270°. *SCBI* 365. Same obv. die as last.

1284 *Edilveard.* **VIGMVND AREP** (retrograde). 1.15g/17.8gr. 90°. *SCBI* 371. Same dies as next.

1285 *As last.* 1.20g/18.5gr. 0°. *SCBI* 372. Same dies as last.

1286 *Edilveard.* **IRER** (for abp). 1.08g/16.6gr. 0°. *SCBI* 368.

1287 *Edilveard.* **IPEP** (for abp). 1.44g/22.2gr. 280°. *SCBI* 370.

1288 *As last.* 1.19g/18.4gr. 240°. *SCBI* 369.

1289 *As last.* 1.33g/20.4gr. 90°. *SCBI* 367. Same obv. die as last.

1290 *Edilveaid* (retrograde). **IPER** (for abp). 1.19g/18.4gr. 270° *SCBI* 366. Same obv. die as last.

1291 *Edilveard.* **VIGMVND IPEP** (both legends retrograde). 0.98g/15.1gr. 0°. *SCBI* 373. Double struck.

1292 *Coenred.* **AREP**? (for abp). 1.11g/17.1gr. 90°. *SCBI* 377.

1293 *Coenred.* **IREP** (for abp). 1.06g/16.4gr. 0°. *SCBI* 376.

1294 *As last.* 1.15g/17.8gr. 90°. *SCBI* 378.

1295 *As last.* 1.19g/18.4gr. 180°. *SCBI* 379.

1296 *As last.* 1.26g/19.4gr. 10°. *SCBI* 380.

1297 *As last.* 1.10g/17.0gr. 90°. *SCBI* –.

1298 *Coenred.* 1.39g/21.5gr. 270°. *SCBI* 374. Same obv. die as next.

1299 *As last.* 1.18g/18.2gr. 0°. *SCBI* 375. Same obv. die as last.
Coenred. For a forgery, see **1491**.

1300 *Hunlaf.* **IPE**? (for abp). 0.79g/12.3gr. worn 90°. *SCBI* 382.

1301 *Hunlaf.* 1.13g/17.4gr. 180°. *SCBI* 381.
Hunlaf. For a forgery, see **1492**.

WULFHERE, *c.* 854–900? (*c.* 865 or earlier–900?)

The coins are contemporary with those of Æthelred II's second reign and that of Osbert.

1302 *Eardevvf* (= Eardwulf). **VVLFHED AREP** (both legends retrograde). 1.06g/16.3gr. 0°. *SCBI* 383. Probably a derivative; this coin die-links into the irregular die-chain referred to under **1273**.

1303 *Vulfred* (= Wulfræd). **VLFHERE ABED** (retrograde). 1.22g/18.9gr. 0°. *SCBI* 384.

1304 *Vulfred* (retrograde). **VVLFHERE ABD**. 1.12g/17.3gr. 0°. *SCBI* 385.

1283–4, 1288, 1294, 1300. FM: provenance unrecorded. The Museum bought 2 coins of Wigmund in 1908.

1285–7, 1289. FM: Young 1936; ex Carlyon-Britton I 239.

1295. FM: Hasluck 1920.

1296, 1304. FM: Young 1936; Shepherd 57.

1297. FM: MAA; ex Ridgeway 1926.

1302. FM: Young 1936; ex Carlyon-Britton I 244.

ANGLO-SAXONS (8): SOUTH-EASTERN MINTS, *c.* 852–*c.* 885

In Wessex, the regal and archiepiscopal coinages were standardized on a common design. In the mid 860s a monetary convention seems to have been established with Mercia, Wessex adopting the Mercian design, and thereafter they changed their coin types together.

References as on Plate 52. The coins are silver pennies. The silver contents of many of the coins measured by electron-probe micro-analysis (EPMA) have kindly been made available by Metcalf and Northover in advance of their study to be published in *NC*. Details of the trace elements will be given in their paper.

Inscribed Cross type (*c.* 852–*c.* 862) (North 618, 620, 245)

Issued by Æthelwulf and Æthelbert of Wessex and Archbishop Ceolnoth. Initially the coins were struck at both Canterbury and Rochester, but die production was soon centralized at Canterbury and we cannot tell whether Rochester continued to operate thereafter.

ÆTHELWULF, King of Wessex, 839–58

For an earlier coin of Æthelwulf, see **1165**. Unless otherwise indicated, the obv. legend is **AEÐELVVLF REX** and the dies are of Canterbury style.

1305 *Ethelere* (= Æthelhere). 1.32g/20.4gr. (46% Ag; EPMA) 0°. *SCBI* 529. Rochester style. Æthelhere was a Rochester moneyer in previous issues.

1306 *Ethelnoth* (= Æthelnoth). 1.30g/20.0gr. broken and repaired 0°. *SCBI* 528.

1307 *Manna*. 1.35g/20.8gr. (52% Ag; EPMA) 0°. *SCBI* 530.

1308 *Tirvald* (= Tirweald). **AEÐLVLF REX**. 1.18g/18.3gr. (31% Ag; EPMA) 180°. *SCBI* 531. Anomalous style; the coin has a low silver and high tin content and is perhaps a contemporary imitation.

1309 *Torhtulf*. 1.31g/20.2gr. (41% Ag; EPMA) 180°. *SCBI* 532.

ÆTHELBERT, King of Kent, 858–65; of Wessex, 860–5 (coins from 858)

The obv. legend is **ÆÐELBEARHT REX**.

1310 *Beahmund*. 1.06g/11.4gr. (28% Ag; EPMA) 180°. *SCBI* 533.

1311 *Degbearht* (= Dægbeorht). 1.31g/20.2gr. (41% Ag; EPMA) 90°. *SCBI* 534.

1312 *As last*. 1.05g/16.1gr. chipped (30% Ag; EPMA) 270°. *SCBI* 535.

1313 *Hunred*. 1.34g/20.7gr. (31% Ag; EPMA) 270°. *SCBI* 536.

1314 *Vilnoth* (= Wilnoth). 0.88g/13.6gr. chipped 270°. *SCBI* 537.

CEOLNOTH, Archbishop of Canterbury, 833–70

For earlier coins of Ceolnoth, see **1161–2**.

1315 *Hebeca*. **CEOLNOÐ ARCHIEP¯**. 1.27g/19.7gr. (45% Ag; EPMA) 90°. *SCBI* 443.

Floriated Cross type (*c.* 862–5) (North 621, 247)

Issued by Æthelbert of Wessex and Archbishop Ceolnoth. Very rare; not represented in this collection.

Lunette type (Mercia, *c.* 860?–74; Wessex, *c.* 865–75) (North 423–7, 622–3, 248–9)

Issued by Burgred of Mercia, Æthelred I and Alfred of Wessex, and Archbishop Ceolnoth. The classification of Burgred's main coinage (the very early coins of Tatel and Dudecil are not represented) into *Early*, *Middle*, and *Late* groups follows Pagan 1965 and Lyon 1968. For an explanation of the reverse types and die-cutting style referred to, see pp. 310–11 above.

BURGRED, King of Mercia, 852–74

The mint is probably London, see p. 311 above.

Early group (c. *863–5*)

1316 *Cenred* (= Coenræd). Type *c*, style F. 1.23g/19.1gr. (72% Ag; EPMA) 0°. *SCBI* 422.

1317 *Cenred*. Type *d*, style B. 0.75g/14.7gr. fragments 270°. *SCBI* 425.

1318 *Dudecil*. Type *c*, style B. 1.37g/21.1gr. (66% Ag; EPMA) 0°. *SCBI* 423.

1305. FM: Duncanson 1930; ex Smart; ex Murdoch 63; ex Montagu 486; ex Lake Price 22; ex Murchison 164; ex Martin 6 (illus. Lindsay 1842, pl. 4.90 as Martin's); ex Rich 38; ex Dorking hoard 1817 (MS note by J. D. Cuff in his copy of Rich catalogue).

1306. FM (*Catalogue 1867*, no. 18): Babington 1866.

1307. FM: Young 1936; ex Carlyon-Britton I 325; probably ex Crowther 13; ex Shepherd 61; ex Dymock; ex Cuff 424 (illus. Ruding 1840, pl. D.26 as Cuff's).

1308. FM: Henderson 1933; ex Montagu 487; ex Addington; ex Bergne 144; ex Cuff 429 (illus. Ruding 1840, pl. D.25 as Cuff's).

1309. FM: Henderson 1933; ex Montagu 484; ex Brice.

1310. FM: Henderson 1933; ex Montagu 499; ex Brice.

1311. FM: Young 1936; ex H. Weber 14.

1312. FM: Trinity College 1937; ex Mrs P. H. Frere 4.5.1870.

1313, 1325. FM: Duncanson 1930; ex Smart.

1314. FM: Baldwin 1908.

1315. FM: Young 1936; ex Carlyon-Britton I 301.

1316, 1326. FM: Young 1936; ex Carlyon-Britton I 286; from the London (Waterloo Bridge) hoard, before 1884 (illus. *BNJ* 3 (1906), 59–66, pl., nos. 9 and 13 respectively).

1317. FM: Young 1936; ex H. Weber 37. This and **1318–19, 1321** (ex H. Weber) are all of Burgred's early group and probably derive from a common hoard.

1318–19, 1321. FM: Young 1936; ex H. Weber 5. See note on provenance of **1317**.

[*continued overleaf*]

1305 1306 1307 1308 1309 1309*

1310 1311 1312 1313 1314 1315

1316 1317 1318 1319 1320 1321*

1321 1322 1323 1324 1325 1326

PLATE 57 (*cont.*)

1319 *Eanred*. Type *a*, style F. 1.29g/20.0gr. (63% Ag; EPMA) 270°. *SCBI* 415.

1320 *Etheluff* (= Æthelwulf). Type *c*, style B. 1.21g/18.7gr. 0°. *SCBI* –.

1321 *Wine*. Type *c*, style F. 1.12g/17.3gr. (76% Ag; EPMA) 90°. *SCBI* 424.

Middle group (c. *865–8*)

1322 *Diarulf* (= Deorwulf). Type *c*, style F. 1.22g/18.8gr. 180°. *SCBI* –.

1323 *Hungered*. Type *d*, style H. 1.38g/21.4gr. (59% Ag; EPMA) 90°. *SCBI* 426.

1324 *Vulfeard* (= Wulfheard). Type *d*, style H. 1.39g/21.4gr. (51% Ag; EPMA) 270°. *SCBI* 427.

Late group (c. *868–74*)

1325 *Beagstan*. Type *a*, style V. 1.27g/19.5gr. (45% Ag; EPMA) 90°. *SCBI* 408.

1326 *As last*. 1.34g/20.6gr. (41% Ag; EPMA) 90°. *SCBI* 409.

1320, 1322. CCC (*Catalogue* nos. 144 and 143): Lewis 1891; bt at Tunbridge Wells 2.7.1872; from Croydon hoard 1862 (Spufford 1961, 214, nos. 63 and 60 respectively).

1323. FM (*Catalogue c. 1886*): provenance unrecorded.

1324. FM: Young 1936; ex Carlyon-Britton I 291.

ANGLO-SAXONS (9): SOUTH-EASTERN MINTS, *c.* 852–*c.* 885

References as on Plates 52 and 57. The coins are silver pennies.

Lunette type (cont.)

BURGRED, King of Mercia (cont.)

Late group (cont.)

1327 *Berheah* (= Beornheah?). **BVRGR+ED REX** Type *a*, style V. 1.17g/18.1gr. 90°. *SCBI* 410.

1328 *Berheah*. Type *a*, style V. 1.03g/15.9gr. 340°. *SCBI* 411.

1329 *Cenred* (= Coenræd). **REMX** Type *a*, style H. 1.11g/17.2gr. (68% Ag; EPMA) 270°. *SCBI* 412.

1330 *Cunehl* (= Cynehelm). Type *a*, style V. 1.30g/20.0gr. (31% Ag; EPMA) 180°. *SCBI* 413.

1331 *Diarulf* (= Deorwulf). Type *b*, style V. 1.30g/20.1gr. (58% Ag; EPMA) 270°. *SCBI* 420.

1332 *Diga*. Type *a*, style V. 0.88g/13.6gr. chipped 270°. *SCBI* –.

1333 *Dudwine*. Type *a*, style V. 1.38g/21.2gr. (47% Ag; EPMA) 90°. *SCBI* 414.

1334 *Heavulf*. Type *a*, style H. 1.16g/17.8gr. 270°. *SCBI* 416.

1335 *Heavulf*. Type *a*, style V. 1.25g/19.3gr. chipped and encrusted (27% Ag; EPMA) 270°. *SCBI* 417.

1336 *Osmund*. Type *a*, style H. 1.26g/19.5gr. (53% Ag; EPMA) 90°. *SCBI* 418. This coin has features which suggest that it is transitional between the Middle and Late groups, namely the obv. initial cross typical of Middle coins and the rev. type *a* of the Late coins.

1337 *Vulferd* (= Wulfheard). Type *a*, style V. 0.97g/15.0gr. worn and chipped 90°. *SCBI* 419.

1338 *Vulfeard*. Type *a*, style H. 1.19g/18.4gr. 90°. *SCBI* –.

1339 *Vulfheard*. Type *b*, style V. 1.24g/19.1gr. (23% Ag; EPMA) 270°. *SCBI* 421.

1340 *Uncertain moneyer*. Burgred? Type *a*, style H?; London mint? 0.48g/7.4gr. encrusted and broken fragment 90°.

ÆTHELRED I, King of Wessex, 865–71

Four-line lunette reverse (865/7)

Early transitional type; Canterbury only.

1341 *Biarnmod* (= Beornmod). 1.28g/19.7gr. (42% Ag; EPMA) 270°. *SCBI* 541.

Normal lunette reverse (c. *867–871*)

Mostly Canterbury, but some struck w. his name posthumously at Burgred's mint (see p. 311 above). The following specimens are all from the Canterbury mint.

1342 *Bearhea* (= Beornheah?). Type *a*, style C. 1.14g/17.6gr. (29% Ag; EPMA) 0°. *SCBI* 538.

1343 *Elbere* (= Ælfhere). Type *a*, style C. 1.21g/18.6gr. (31% Ag; EPMA) 0°. *SCBI* 539.

1344 *Mann*. Type *a*, style C. 1.32g/20.3gr. (23% Ag; EPMA) 180°. *SCBI* 540.

ALFRED (the Great), King of Wessex, 871–99

Alfred's coins were struck at Canterbury and a mint shared with Burgred, probably London. The obverse legend reads **ΛELBRED REX**, unless otherwise indicated. The reverse types are as described for Burgred, not the *BMC AS* types.

1345 *Dduda*. **ΛELBRD** Type *c*, barbarous work; contemporary imitation? 0.87g/13.4gr. chipped 270°. *SCBI* 542.

1346 *Dudin* (= Duding). Type *a*, style H; London mint. 1.03g/15.9gr. chipped 0°. *SCBI* –.

1347 *Ealhere*. Type *a*, style C; Canterbury mint. 1.04g/16.0gr. chipped 180°. *SCBI* –.

1348 *Ethered*. Type *a*, style C; Canterbury mint. 1.32g/20.3gr. 90°. *SCBI* –.

1349 *Luhinc*. Type *a*, style C; Canterbury mint. 0.68g/10.5gr. chipped and broken 220°. *SCBI* –.

1350 *Sefreth* (= Seaferth). Type *a*, style C; Canterbury mint. 1.19g/18.3gr. (20% Ag; EPMA). *SCBI* 543.

Tata. For a forgery, see **1496**.

1350A ...*mund*. Obv. **+ΛELBRE[ ]EX** Rev. **]MV/[ ]D MO/NET∴** (**NE** ligatured). Type *d*, style ? 0.40g/6.2gr. fragments 270°. *SCBI* –. A moneyer ...mund is not recorded for this type, which belongs to the very end of the Lunette issue. It may be Denemund, Ethelmund or Torhtmund who are known for type *a* of Alfred, or possibly Deigmund although he is recorded only from one irregular coin of type *a* (Pagan 1965a, 18). It may, however, be a new moneyer since our knowledge of these later types is so sparse.

1327–8, 1335, 1337. FM: Perceval 1920. Part of a hoard?; see note on provenance of **1159**.

1329. FM: Young 1936; ex Carlyon-Britton I 286.

1330. FM: provenance unrecorded.

1331. FM: Young 1936; ex Carlyon-Britton I 286; ex Evans.

1332, 1346–9. CCC (*Catalogue* nos. 142, 147–50): Lewis 1891; bt at Tunbridge Wells 2.7.1872; from Croydon hoard 1862 (Spufford 1961, 214–15, nos. 22, 152, 155, 159, 169).

1333. FM: Trinity College 1937; ex King 11.11.1876.

1334. FM: Hasluck 1920.

1336. FM (*Catalogue 1867*, no. 14): Babington 1866.

1338. QC: provenance unrecorded.

1339. FM: Young 1936; ex Carlyon-Britton I 291; from London (Waterloo Bridge) hoard, before 1884 (illus. *BNJ* 3 (1906), 59–66, pl., no. 22).

1340, 1351. CCC (*Catalogue* nos. 145, 151): Lewis 1891; provenance unrecorded, but the brown staining and fragile condition suggest that, like the only other 9th-century Anglo-Saxon coins in this collection (**1320**, **1322**, **1332**, **1346–9**), they were bought at Tunbridge Wells 2.7.1872 and were from the Croydon hoard 1862 (Spufford 1961, 214–15).

1341. FM: Young 1936; ex Carlyon-Britton I 335; ex 'Astronomer' 150; ex Montagu 504; ex Brice.

1342. FM: W. S. Lincoln, Aug. 1899.

1343. FM: Henderson 1933; from Spink 'Xmas 1895'.

1344, 1350. FM: Duncanson 1930; ex Smart.

1345. FM: Sadd.

1350A. MAA: excavations at Fenston Farm, Great Shelford, Cambs., 1980 (unpublished).

[*continued overleaf*]

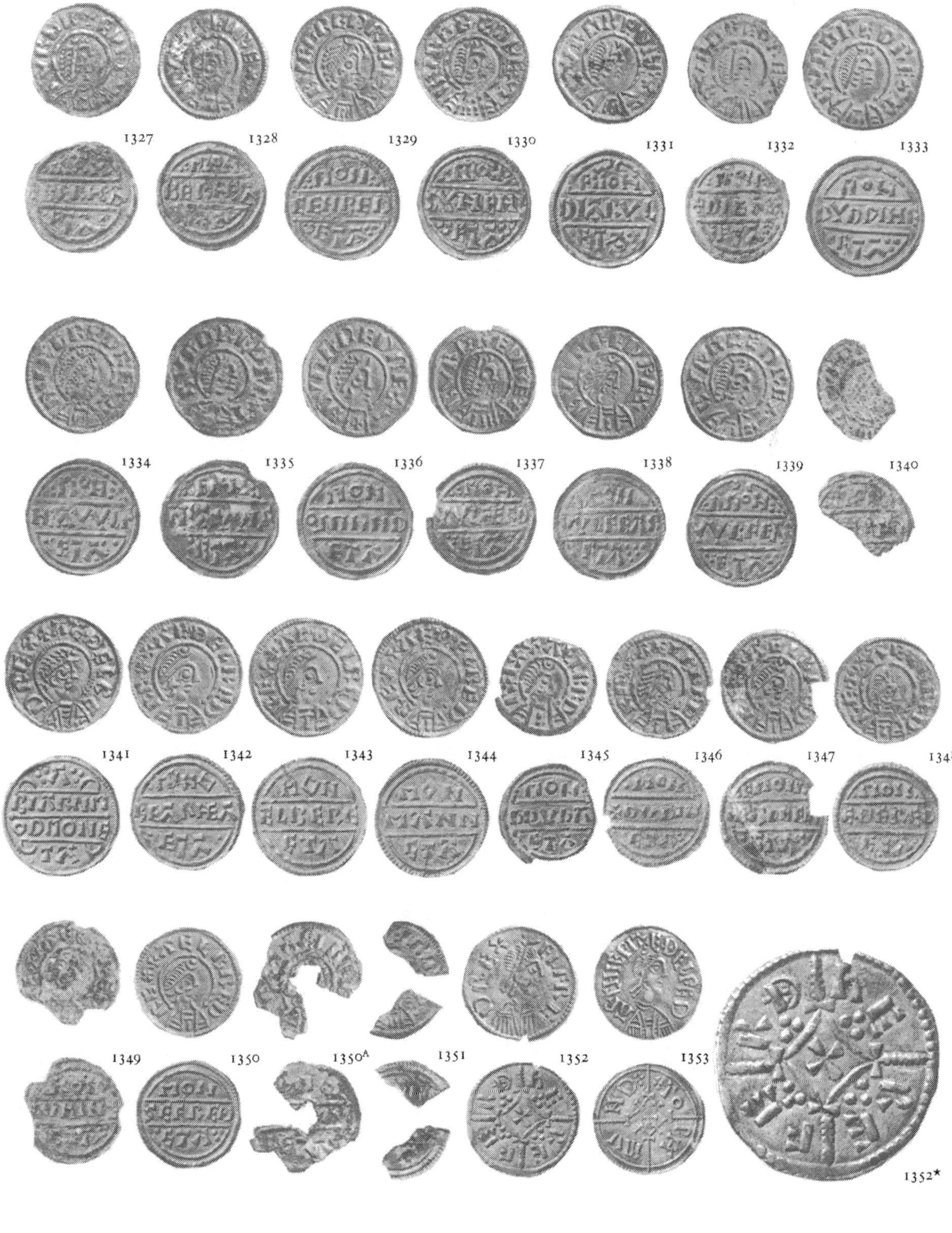

1327 1328 1329 1330 1331 1332 1333

1334 1335 1336 1337 1338 1339 1340

1341 1342 1343 1344 1345 1346 1347 1348

1349 1350 1350A 1351 1352 1353

1352*

1351 *Uncertain moneyer. Obv.* **]ELBR[ ]D∴[** Rev. **]ON [/ /]TA˙[** . Type *a*, style H; London mint. 0.36g/5.5gr. fragments, possibly of two coins. *SCBI* –. For similar groups of three pellets in the obverse legend, see Brooke 1925, nos. 454 and 473.

Cross-and-lozenge type (*c.* 878–*c.* 885)

The type was issued at Canterbury for Alfred and Archbishop Æthelred, and at London for Alfred and Ceolnoth of Mercia. The mint attributions are those of Lyon (1968, 236).

ALFRED, King of Wessex (cont.)

1352 *Hereferth*. 'Mercian' style. 1.26g/19.4gr. (92% Ag; EPMA) 180°. Chipped. *SCBI* –.

ARCHBISHOP ÆTHELRED, 870–88

1353 *Torhtmund*. Canterbury style. **ETHELRED ARCHIEPI⁻**. 1.33g/20.5gr. 270°. *SCBI* 446. Only four coins of Archbishop Æthelred survive, of which two are of this type (Blunt 1962a).

1352. FM: Pilgrim Trust 1960; ex Lockett X 3632; ex Carlyon-Britton III 1649; ex Murdoch 82; ex Montagu 557; ex Marsham 155; ex Wigan; from the Cuerdale hoard.

1353. FM: Young 1936; ex Carlyon-Britton I 303; ex Murdoch 44; found near Tetbury, Glos.

ANGLO-SAXONS (10): WESSEX *c.* 885–924

Outside the Danelaw, coins were now being struck only by the kings of Wessex and the archbishops of Canterbury. The period saw an expansion in the number of mints, commenced by Alfred and continued by Edward the Elder. The coins remained current until Edgar's reform, *c.* 973. References as on Plate 52. The coins are silver pennies.

ALFRED THE GREAT, 871–99 (cont.)

London Monogram type (886/7) (*BMC AS* vi; North 644)

The type has plausibly been associated with Alfred's recapture of London in 886. Other mint-signed types were issued from Canterbury (**1360**), Winchester, Exeter, Oxford, Gloucester and, under Edward, Bath, all but the first being extremely rare.

The obverse legend is **AELFRED REX** unless otherwise indicated. All but **1359** are without moneyer's name.

1354 1.38g/21.4gr. fragments 180°. *SCBI* 548. Black patination, as next. Bust of exceptionally fine style, copied directly from a coin of Valens or some other emperor of his time.

1355 1.66g/25.6gr. 340°. *SCBI* 544. Black patination, as last.

1356 1.50g/23.2gr. chipped 90°. *SCBI* 546. Same dies as next.

1357 1.55g/23.9gr. 180°. *SCBI* 547. Same dies as last.

1358 1.56g/24.1gr. 0°. **AELFRD REX** (**L** and **F** inverted). *SCBI* 545. Unusual drapery, blundered legend, and five pellets in place of cross above monogram. However, die-linked specimens suggest that it is official work; same rev. as *SCBI* Glasgow 577, which is from same obv. as *SCBI* Norweb 142, which in turn shares a rev. w. Carlyon-Britton I 341.

1359 *Tilevine.* 1.60g/24.7gr. 270°. *SCBI* 549; *BMC AS* ix; North 646.

For a Viking imitation of this type, see **1379**.

Two-line type (c. *885–99*)

This type, also known as the 'Guthrum' type, was struck by at least four mints, distinguished by the style of their dies; London, Canterbury, Winchester and an unidentified Mercian centre.

With mint name (*BMC AS* xvii; North 638)

1360 Canterbury (**DORO**), *Diarvald.* **ELFRED REX.** 1.54g/23.8gr. 250°. *SCBI* 560. Double struck.

Without mint name (*BMC AS* xv; North 635–6, 638)

1361 *Athelulf.* Winchester style. 1.59g/24.5gr. 0°. *SCBI* 559. Æthelwulf was a prolific moneyer of Edward the Elder (**1376**) and Athelstan, striking mint-signed coins of Winchester for the latter.

1362 *Byrnelm.* Winchester style. 1.70g/26.2gr. 270°. *SCBI* 551.

1363 *Cudberht.* **ELFRED RE.** West Mercian style. 1.57g/24.2gr. 180°. *SCBI* 552. The coin is overstruck on a *London Monogram* coin.

1364 *Cuthberht.* West Mercian style. 1.45g/22.4gr. 180°. *SCBI* –. Peck-mark on obv.

1365 *Eadwald.* West Mercian style, **ELFRED RE.** 1.58g/24.5gr. 0°. *SCBI* 553.

1366 *As last.* West Mercian style (crude). 1.44g/22.3gr. 0°. *SCBI* 554. Two peck-marks on obv. and one on rev.

1367 *Simun* (**SIMVN ME FEC***it*). East Mercian or East Anglian? **ELFRED RE.** 1.34g/20.7gr. 200°. *SCBI* 556.

1368 *Vulfred* (= Wulfræd). Winchester style. 1.53g/23.6gr. rev. corroded by adhesive 50°. *SCBI* –. Wulfred, one of Alfred's most prolific late moneyers, is also found on early coins of Edward the Elder (**1373**) which Lyon (1983) has shown are of the Winchester mint. Cross on obv. incuse.

1368A *As last.* 1.56g/24.1gr. broken and fragmentary 250°. *SCBI* –.

ARCHBISHOP PLEGMUND, 890–923

The obv. legend is **PLEGMUND ARCHIEP**.

Class 1 (c. *890–5*)

1369 Canterbury (**DORO**), *Hunfreth.* 1.34g/20.6gr. 180°. *SCBI* 447; North 253.

Class 2 (*after* c. *910*)

1370 *Eicmund.* 1.55g/23.9gr. *SCBI* –; North 256. Same dies as *SCBI* Norweb 90 and *SCBI* Mack 672 (ex Vatican hoard).

1354–5. FM: Henderson 1933; ex Thorburn 2 and 3, respectively; possibly from the Erith hoard (see Grierson 1957, 480–1).

1356. FM: Duncanson 1930; ex Smart.

1357–9. FM: Young 1936; ex Carlyon-Britton I 343, II 930 and I 340, respectively.

1360. FM: provenance unrecorded.

1361. FM: Young 1936; ex Carlyon-Britton II 937.

1362. FM (*Catalogue 1867*, no. 19): Babington 1866.

1363. FM: Henderson 1933; ex James 8.

1364. FM: Grierson 1959; from MMAG Basel 1959; ?ex Cuerdale hoard, suggested by peck-mark.

1365. FM: Young 1936; ex Shepherd 74.

1366. FM: Duncanson 1930; ex Smart; ?ex Cuerdale hoard, suggested by peck-marks.

1367. FM: Grantley 1017; from Sadd; 'found Cambridge'.

1368. MAA; bt 1936.

1368A. FM: Miss F. M. McCormick 1975; ex Miss D. F. Conybeare; ex Rev. E. Conybeare; found near Barrington, Cambs.?

1369. FM: Lockett Executors 1955; ex Lockett I 344; ex Bascom 22.

1370. FM: Chilvers 1967; ex Ryan 654; ex Carlyon-Britton I 305; ex Montagu 336; ex Gibbs.

[*continued overleaf*]

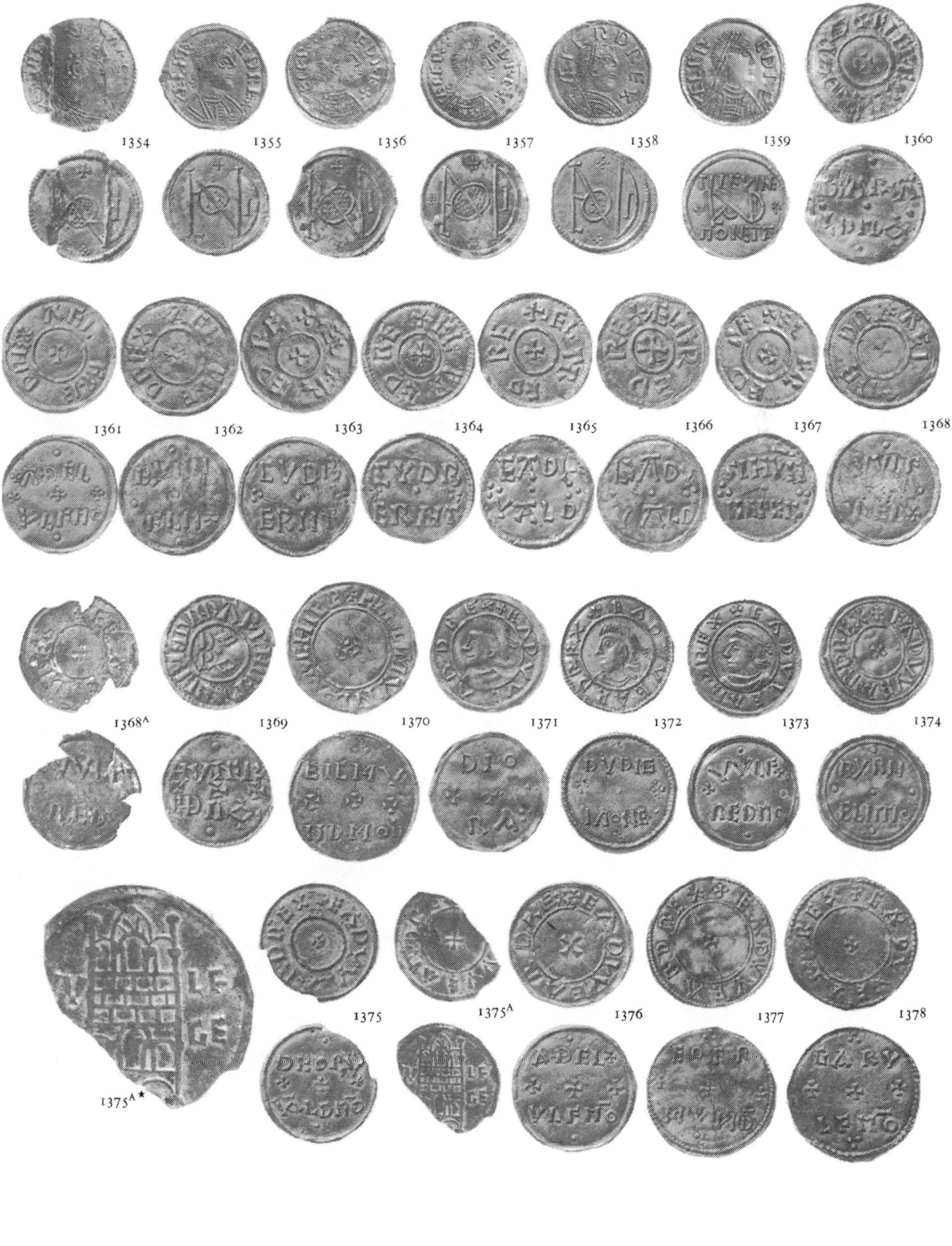

1354 1355 1356 1357 1358 1359 1360

1361 1362 1363 1364 1365 1366 1367 1368

1368A 1369 1370 1371 1372 1373 1374

1375 1375A 1376 1377 1378

1375A★

EDWARD THE ELDER, 899–924

(a) Early issues, small flan

Portrait type (*BMC AS* iii; North 651)

1371 *Diora*. **BEX** for **REX**. Unusual style, London? 1.65g/25.5gr. 90°. *SCBI* 568.
1372 *Dudig*. West Mercian style. 1.61g/24.9gr. 200°. *SCBI* 569.
1373 *Vulfred* (= Wulfræd). Winchester style. 1.58g/24.4gr. 0°. *SCBI* –. From same dies as coin in Lord Clitheroe's collection, ex Cuerdale hoard (information C. S. S. Lyon). For a coin of Alfred by this moneyer, see **1368**.

Two-line type (*BMC AS* ii; North 649)

1374 *Byrneli* (= Burhhelm). London style. 1.54g/23.7gr. 270°. *SCBI* 565. From same dies as *BMC AS* 89.26, ex Cuerdale hoard (information C. S. S. Lyon).
1375 *Deorwald*. Canterbury style. 1.45g/22.4gr. chipped 90°. *SCBI* –.

Pictorial types

1375A *Vulf...ge* (= Wulfsige). Church tower, West Mercian. 1.11g/17.1gr. fragment 90°. *SCBI* –; *BMC AS* xii; North 666. This depicts a stone tower with three stages of blind arcading on pilaster-strips, the upper two divided by a stage of ashlar, and probably surmounted by a spire which is more developed on other dies. The use of pilaster-strips was common in Mercia and Wessex from the 9th century (Taylor 1970).

(b) Later issues, larger flan

Two-line type (*BMC AS* ii; North 651)

1376 *Athelulf*. Winchester style. 1.54g/23.7gr. 170°. *SCBI* 564. For a coin of Alfred by this moneyer, see **1361**.
1377 *Eofrmund*. Shrewsbury? West Mercian style. 1.55g/23.9gr. cracked 20°. *SCBI* 566. Eoformund also struck one of the 'Flower' types for Edward and was a moneyer of Æthelstan, striking mint-signed coins of Shrewsbury. The coin has a peck-mark on the obv., but is too late to be from the Cuerdale hoard.
1378 *Garulf*. London style. 1.57g/24.3gr. 200°. *SCBI* 567.

1371. FM: Duncanson 1930; ex Smart; ex Murchison 235 (illus. Murchison MS in Fitzwilliam Museum).
1372. FM: Henderson 1933; ex Montagu 573; ex Brice.
1373. FM: Peterhouse 1960; ex Barnes 1934.
1374. FM: Duncanson 1930; ex Smart; ex Webb (purchaser at Montagu sale); ex Montagu 585.
1375. FM: Collins & Clarke 1974; ex Wyatt.
1375A. FM: Grierson 1985; bt Spink 5.12.1984; ex Matthews.
1376. FM: Spink 1910.
1377. FM: . . . Eastwood. Presumably the London dealer G. Eastwood (d. 1866).
1378. FM: Young 1936; ex Carlyon-Britton I 366.

ANGLO-VIKING COINAGES (1), *c.* 890–954

Three areas produced coins under the Vikings: East Anglia, the Five Boroughs (i.e. Lincolnshire and the East Midlands) and Northumbria (at York). The earliest coins are imitations of Alfred's coinage of the late 880s. Within the Danelaw, coins seem to have mixed rapidly and it is difficult to attribute these imitations to particular regions. Coins bearing the name of Guthrum of East Anglia or a Lincoln monogram are exceptions. In the 890s substantial series were commenced in East Anglia and at York, but production in the Five Boroughs appears to have been intermittent and for the most part took the form of anonymous imitations.

References as on Plate 52. The coins are silver pennies, except for **1383–6** which are halfpennies.

IMITATIONS OF ALFRED'S COINAGE

London Monogram type

1379 *Uncertain monogram* (of letters **R**(or **P**)**OISENG**, not necessarily in that order), *Aetheluf.* 1.51g/23.4gr. 100°. *SCBI* 550; North 467. One peck-mark on rev. Overstruck. See note on coin.

Two-line type

With mint name

1380 '*Oxford*' (**ORSNAFORDA**), *Bernvald.* **ELFRED.** 1.31g/20.2gr. 0°. *SCBI* 561; North 472. This and the next coin are probably Viking imitations of coins of Oxford reading **OHSNAFORDA** (Lyon 1970, 196–7). Other imitations of this type have a cross-on-steps design, which also occurs on the 'Cunnetti' coinage, suggesting that they belong to the Northumbrian series.

1381 '*Oxford*' (**ORSNAFORDA**), *Bernafid* (retrograde, blundering of Bernwald). **ÆLFRED** 1.46g/22.6gr. 180°. *SCBI* 562; North 472.

Without mint name

1382 Enigmatic rev. legend. Obv. **ÆLFRED RE.** 1.48g/22.9gr. 90°. *SCBI* –. One peck-mark on rev. There are four known specimens, two from the same dies as this (*BMC AS* 453 and Lockett II 498) and the third from different dies (*SCBI* Merseyside 145). No satisfactory explanation of the rev. legend has been offered, but the style suggests that it belongs to the Northumbrian series (Dolley and Blunt 1961, 92).

1383 *Rafing.* Halfpenny. **ELFRDI RE.** 1.41g/21.7gr. 0°. *SCBI* 555; Grierson 1957, 488, no. 36. This and the next two coins, which Grierson erroneously regarded as third-pennies, belong to a group of light-weight imitations with small epigraphy which is known only from the Stamford hoard. They are of similar style to a unique halfpenny with a Lincoln monogram (*SCBI* Lincolnshire 4), and were probably all struck in the Five Boroughs.

1384 *Tilvvvin* (for Tilewine). Halfpenny. **ELFRED RE.** 0.47g/7.3gr. 70°. *SCBI* 558; Grierson 1957, 488, no. 32.

1385 *Tilvvvn* (for Tilewine). Halfpenny. **ELFRED RE.** *Alpha* and *omega* rev. 0.50g/7.6gr. 200°. *SCBI* 557; Grierson 1957, 488, no. 46.

1386 *Everat.* Halfpenny. Rev. **ME FECIT** ('made me'). 0.61g/9.4gr. 90° *SCBI* 563; North 478; Grierson 1957, 487, no. 26; Haigh 1870, 38 and pl. 6.6. The high weight and the cross-on-steps design, which also occurs on the 'Cunnetti' coinage, suggests that the coin belongs to the Northumbrian series.

VIKINGS OF EAST ANGLIA

GUTHRUM (Æthelstan), 880–90

Guthrum was baptised as Æthelstan at 'Aller' in 878, and settled with his army in East Anglia in 880. His coins date from after *c.* 885, and some may be posthumous imitations.

1387 *Abenel.* **EDELIA RE** (for *Æthelstan rex*). 1.35g/20.9gr. 300°. *SCBI* 456; North 479.

ST EDMUND MEMORIAL COINAGE, *c.* 895–915

The division between Early and Late is somewhat arbitrarily, but conveniently, based on types present in, or absent from, the Cuerdale hoard (dep. *c.* 905). An extensive and extremely useful listing of the legends on the coins from Cuerdale can be found in Hawkins 1843, 25–36. The much rarer post-Cuerdale types have

1379. FM: Grantley 1010; ex Rashleigh 219; ex Bergne 156; ex Lindsay 46; ex Aquilla Smith (illus. Lindsay 1842, pl. 4.93 as Dr Smith's). Hawkins (1843, 101–2) records three specimens, two ex Cuerdale hoard (*BMC AS* II, 54.155 and Assheton coll.) and this coin from Lindsay, which may be a stray from the hoard. It had been offered to J. W. Martin before Aquilla Smith (*BNJ* 54 (1984), 55–6).

1380. FM: Young 1936; ex Carlyon-Britton I 345.

1381, 1387. FM: provenance unrecorded.

1382. FM: Chilvers 1963; from Seaby 1957 (*SCMB* April 1957, no. 4335); ex Ryan II 723; from Cuerdale hoard. Hawkins records only 3 specimens of this type in the Cuerdale hoard (Hawkins 1843, 13, no. 25), although 4 are known today, one probably being a stray from the hoard which was not shown to Hawkins.

1383–5. FM: Young 1936; ex Carlyon-Britton I 356, 355 and 354, respectively; probably from Stamford hoard 1902.

1386. FM: Young 1936; ex Carlyon-Britton I 358; ex Rashleigh 231; ex Whitbourn 86; ex J. Kenyon; from Cuerdale hoard (not in Hawkins 1843; see Blunt 1983).

[*continued overleaf*]

1379 1380 1381 1382 1383 1384 1385 1386

1387 1388 1389 1390 1391 1392

1393 1394 1395 1395 A 1395 B 1396 1397

1398 1399 1400 1401 1402 1403

larger, thicker lettering, and thus shorter legends, and were struck on progressively smaller flans. The attribution and origin of the names is based on Smart's *SCBI* Index to vols. 1–20 (OE = Old English; CG = Continental Germanic).

(*a*) *Early phase*, c. *890–c. 905*

1388 **ADALBERT NE** (CG Adalbert). **SC EADMVND RE**. Obv. with one pellet on each side of **Λ**. 1.40g/21.6gr. 180° *SCBI* 462.

1389 **AOLBRT NIIME** (CG Adalbert). **SC EADMVNI.E** Type as last. 1.28g/19.8gr. 160°. *SCBI* 463. Two peck-marks on rev.

1390 **AOLBRA IIIME** (CG Adalbert). **SC EADMVNR**. Type as last. 1.32g/20.3gr. 170°. *SCBI* 461.

1391 **ADRADVS MOT** (CG Adrad). **SC EADMVNDI RE**. Obv. with 2 pellets on each side and 2 dots above **Λ**. 1.21g/18.6gr. 210°. *SCBI* 464.

1392 **ANSIER HONTA** (CG Ansigar). **SCE CADMVHDE**. Obv. without additional pellets. 1.28g/19.8gr. 340°. *SCBI* 457.

1393 **CVRNETIE** (obscure name, possibly includes blundering of *moneta*). **CI EADMIVE**. Type as last. 0.91g/14.0gr. 270°. *SCBI* 459.

1394 **DAIEMOND MOI** (OE Dægmund). **SCE EADMVNDE**. Obv. with 3 pellets on each side of **Λ**. 1.33g/20.6gr. 180°. *SCBI* 465.

1395 **DAIEMOND MOA**. **SCE EADMVNDE R**. Types as last. 1.35g/20.8gr. 90°. *SCBI* –.

1395A **DEGEMVИD MONETΛ. SC EDMVИ RE**. Obv. without additional pellets. 0.64g/9.9gr. chipped and corroded 0°. *SCBI* –; *BMC AS* I, 111.320 (ex Cuerdale hoard; same dies).

1395B **ƎRDHVC[II]EVSII** (name obscure, OE Eard—?). **ƎCΛDMV[M]D RIE** (retrograde). Type as last. 0.63g/9.7gr. corroded fragments 340°. *SCBI* –; *BMC AS* I, 116.389 (ex Cuerdale hoard; similar legends, but not same dies).

1396 **ERSALT MON** (CG? Ersal). **CDRENIDANAC** (commencing at 5 o'clock position). Obv. with 1 dot above, 1 to each side and 2 below **Λ**. 1.50g/23.1gr. 190°. *SCBI* 470.

1397 *At last*, same dies. 1.52g/23.5gr. 10° (i.e. 180° difference from last). *SCBI* 471.

1398 **REART VIODH** (Reart, origin obscure). **SC EAIDMVNDE**. Obv. without additional pellets. 1.33g/20.5gr. 180°. *SCBI* 460.

1399 **VVINER MONE** (CG or OE? Winegar). **SCE EADMVND**. Obv. with three pellets above **Λ**. 1.39g/21.4gr. 170°. *SCBI* 469.

1400 **VVINER MONETAI. SCE EADMVND RI**. Type as last. 1.43g/22.0gr. 160°. *SCBI* 466. One peck-mark on obv.

1401 **VVINEIR MOMXE. SCE EADMVN**. Type as last. 1.34g/20.7gr. 350°. *SCBI* 467.

1402 *As last*, same dies. 1.53g/23.6gr. 170° (i.e. 180° difference from last). *SCBI* 468.

(*b*) *Late phase*, c. *905–15*

1403 **BADI+MO** (CG Bado). **SC EADIV** Obv. without additional pellets. 1.35g/20.8gr. 280°. *SCBI* 458.

1388, 1392. FM: Hasluck 1920.
1389. FM: Hasluck 1920.
1390. FM: A. Smith 1942.
1391, 1394, 1399, 1401. FM: Young 1936; ex Carlyon-Britton I 318.
1393. FM: Sadd.
1395. QC: provenance unrecorded.
1395A–B. MAA: two associated coins found in excavations on Castle Hill, Cambridge 1968.
1396. FM: Duncanson 1930; ex Smart.
1397. FM: Henderson 1933; acq. March 1890.
1398. FM: Henderson 1933.
1400. FM: Young 1936; ex H. Weber 7.
1402. FM: Young 1936; ex H. Weber 7.
1403. FM: Trinity College 1937; ex Mrs P. H. Frere 14.5.1870.

ANGLO-VIKING COINAGES (2)

VIKINGS OF NORTHUMBRIA, *c.* 895–954

COINAGE OF YORK *c.* 900–5

References as on Plate 52. The arrangement follows the classification discussed in Lyon and Stewart 1961, and the numbering set out in Lyon and Stewart 1964. Their die analysis has shown that the die with the royal name is usually the reverse. The coins are silver pennies, except for **1407** which is a halfpenny. For the identity of *Siefrid* and *Cnut*, see p. 321 above.

Group I. With obv. EBRAICE CIVITAS or similar

I(a). Obv. small cross without pellets, no stops Rev. **C SIEFREDVS REX** in two lines.

1404 Obv. **EDRAICE CIVI** Rev. **C SIEFREDIIS E**. 1.22g/18.8gr. 90°. *SCBI* 507.

I(h). Obv. small cross with pellets in angles, no stops Rev. **SIEFREDVS REX** around cross-crosslet.

1405 Obv. **EBIAICE CIVI**. 1.45g/23.0gr. 200°. *SCBI* 506.

I(s). Obv. small cross with pellets in angles, with stops Rev. **CNVT REX** disposed around inverted patriarchal cross.

1406 Obv. **EBIAIICE I**. 1.26g/19.4gr. 70°. *SCBI* 504.

I(u). Obv. *Carolus* monogram, no stops Rev. **CNVT REX** around inverted patriarchal cross.

1407 *Halfpenny*. Obv. **EDIAI CIVI**. Monogram retrograde. 0.57g/8.8gr. 10°. *SCBI* 505. Peck-mark on rev.

Group II. With obv. CVNNETTI or similar

The obv. reads **CVNNETTI** unless otherwise indicated.

II(d). Obv. small cross with pellets in angles Rev. **CNVT REX** around plain cross.

1408 1.32g/20.4gr. 270°. *SCBI* 472.
1409 **CVNNETI**. 1.33g/20.5gr. 70°. *SCBI* 473.
1410 1.31g/20.2gr. 50°. *SCBI* 474.

II(e) Obv. small cross with pellets in angles Rev. **CNVT REX** around inverted patriarchal cross.

1411 **CVNNTI**. 1.44g/22.3gr. 200°. *SCBI* 475.
1412 **CVNNETT**. 1.19g/18.4gr. 50°. *SCBI* 476.
1413 1.25g/19.3gr. 50°. *SCBI* 477.
1414 1.36g/20.9gr. 130° *SCBI* 478.
1415 **CVNNETITI**. 1.29g/19.9gr. 310°. *SCBI* 479.
1416 1.16g/17.8gr. chipped 0°. *SCBI* 480.
1417 1.28g/19.7gr. 300°. *SCBI* 481. Same dies as next and same obv. as **1429**.
1418 1.31g/20.2gr. 120°. *SCBI* 482. Same dies as last (die-axis 180° different) and same obv. die as **1429**.
1419 1.38g/21.2gr. 320°. (Wts of this and next confused in *SCBI*.) *SCBI* 483. Same dies as next.
1420 1.26g/19.4gr. 230°. *SCBI* 484. Same dies as last, die-axis 90° different.
1421 1.36g/21.0gr. 40°. *SCBI* 485.
1422 1.36g/21.0gr. 240°. *SCBI* 486.
1423 1.43g/22.1gr. 270°. *SCBI* 487.
1424 1.17g/18.1gr. 200°. *SCBI* 488. Same obv. die as **1427**.
1425 1.35g/20.9gr. 240°. *SCBI* 489.
1426 1.22g/18.9gr. 180°. *SCBI* 490.
1427 1.43g/22.0gr. 110°. *SCBI* 491. Same obv. die as **1424**.

All the coins on this plate are probably from the Cuerdale hoard, but it is documented only in certain cases.

1404. FM: provenance unrecorded.

1405, 1422. FM: Duncanson 1930; ex Smart.

1406. FM: Henderson 1933.

1407. FM: Duncanson 1930; ex Smart.

1408, 1412–14, 1416, 1419, 1421, 1423–7. FM: Cambridge Antiquarian Soc. 1886 (*CAS Catalogue 1847*, 28, no. 4); presented by the Chancellor of the Duchy of Lancaster, July 1844; from Cuerdale hoard of 1840. The 20 Northumbrian Viking coins presented by the Duchy, together with 12 silver ingots from the hoard, can be distinguished in the trays by a number (1–20) in indian ink, or a trace of one, written on the surface of the coins.

1409. FM: Young 1936; ex Carlyon-Britton I 250*d*; from Cuerdale hoard.

1410. FM: Young 1936; ex Carlyon-Britton I 250*e*.

1411. FM: Trinity College 1937; ex King 1876; from Cuerdale hoard.

1415. FM: Young 1936; ex Carlyon-Britton I 250*c*.

1417. FM: Young 1936; ex Carlyon-Britton I 250*b*.

1418. FM: ... from Cureton (dealer d. 1858).

1420. FM: provenance unrecorded (in *SCBI* wrongly as ex Cambridge Antiquarian Soc.).

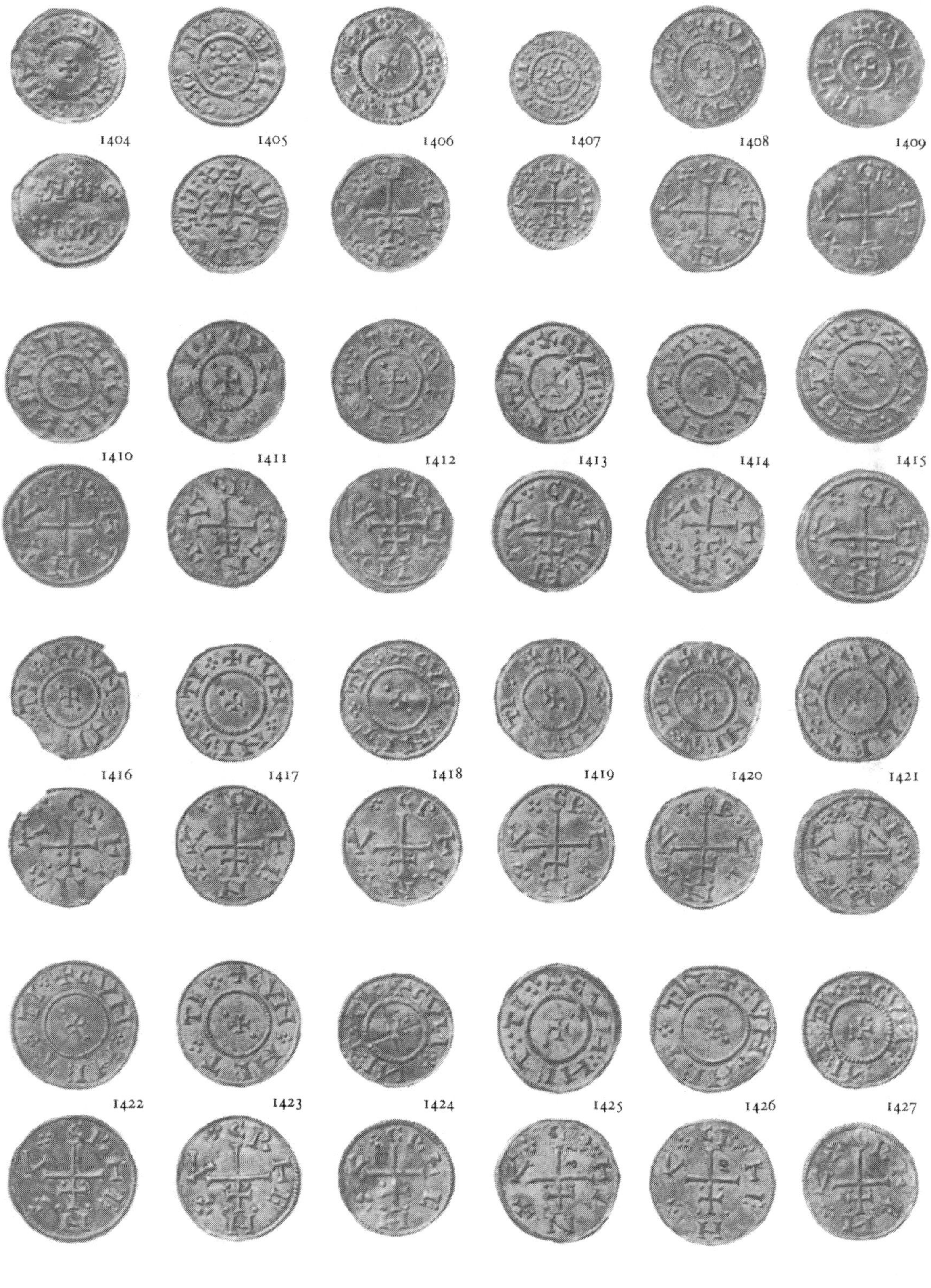

1404 1405 1406 1407 1408 1409

1410 1411 1412 1413 1414 1415

1416 1417 1418 1419 1420 1421

1422 1423 1424 1425 1426 1427

ANGLO-VIKING COINAGES (3)

Descriptions and references as on Plate 61. The coins are silver pennies, except for **1439** which is a halfpenny.

VIKINGS OF NORTHUMBRIA (cont.)

COINAGE OF YORK *c.* 900–5 (cont.)

Group II. With obv. CUNNETTI or similar (cont.)

II(e) (cont.). Obv. small cross with pellet in angles Rev **CNVT REX** around inverted patriarchal cross. The obv. reads **CVNNETTI** unless otherwise indicated.

1428 1.32g/20.3gr. 0°. *SCBI* 492.

1429 1.22g/18.8gr. 300°. *SCBI* 493. Same obv. die as **1417–18**.

1430 **CVNNITTI**. 1.26g/19.5gr. 60°. *SCBI* 495.

1431 **CVNNETI**. 1.35g/20.8gr. 300°. *SCBI* 496.

1432 1.42g/21.9gr. 50°. *SCBI* 497.

1433 1.33g/20.5gr. 170°. *SCBI* 498.

1434 1.41g/21.8gr. 180°. *SCBI* 499.

1435 1.42g/21.9gr. 350°. *SCBI* 500. Same dies as next.

1436 1.29g/19.8gr. 200°. *SCBI* 501. Same dies as last.

1437 **CVNNELTI**. 1.38g/21.4gr. *SCBI* 502.

1438 Obv. legend retrograde Rev. cross with two limbs crosslet. Imitation? 1.19g/18.3gr. 310°. *SCBI* 503.

1439 *Halfpenny*. **CVNNCLTI**. 0.48g/7.4gr. chipped 90°. *SCBI* 494.

Group III. With obv. SIEFREDVS.

III(a). Obv. small cross with pellets in angles Rev. **REX** around cross-crosslet.

1440 1.39g/21.5gr. 320°. *SCBI* 509.

III(d). Obv. small cross with pellet in two angles Rev. **CNVT REX** around inverted patriarchal cross.

1441 1.28g/19.8gr. 140°. *SCBI* 508.

Group V. Obv. DNS DS REX for Dominus Deus rex.

V(a). Obv. small cross with pellet in two angles Rev. **SIEVERT REX** around patriarchal cross.

1442 **SICURT RE**. 1.33g/20.6gr. 10°. *SCBI* 513.

V(b). Obv. small cross with pellet in two angles Rev. **EBRAICE CIVITAS** around patriarchal cross.

1443 **EBRAICE C**. 1.27g/19.6gr. 350°. *SCBI* 514.

Group VI. Obv. MIRABILIA FECIT or similar.

VI(d). Obv. small cross with pellets in two angles Rev. **CNVT REX** around inverted patriarchal cross.

1444 **MIRABILA FECIT**. 1.36g/21.0gr. 220°. *SCBI* 510. Same obv. die as next.

1445 **MIRABILA FECIT**. 1.24g/19.2gr. 0°. *SCBI* 511. One peck-mark on obv. Same obv. die as last.

1446 **MIRABILIA FEI**. 1.31g/20.3gr. *SCBI* 512.

Group VIII. Obv. **QVENTOVICI** around small cross Rev. **CNVT REX** with additional strokes around small cross pattée with limbs extended and pellet in each angle.

This series is known only from the Cuerdale hoard. The reverses crudely copy legends on the York coins, but the quality of die-cutting and lack of die-links suggests that it does not belong to that series, although it is most unlikely that they were actually issued by Vikings in Quentovic.

1447 **QVENTOIVICI**. 1.37g/21.2gr. 310°. *SCBI* 515.

ST PETER COINAGES

Anonymous issues of York, *c.* 905–27

Issue without sword, c. *905–20*

1448 **SCI PETRI M[** and **EBORACE C**. 0.76g/11.8gr. chipped 90°. *SCBI* 517. The light weight suggests that this coin belongs to the latter part of the issue.

Issue with sword, c. *920–7*

Thor's hammer type

1449 **SCI IECII IIO** and **REVITII** 1.29g/19.9gr. 270°. *SCBI* 518.

NORSE KINGS OF YORK

RAGNALD, *c.* 914?, *c.* 919–20

The coins reading **RAIENALT** or **RAGNOLT** are probably attributable to this Ragnald, but see pp. 322–3 above for consideration of their date.

1450 **RACIIOLT** around *Manus Dei* and **R[X]EACICIT** (retrograde, a blundering of *Eborace civit(as)*) around a retrograde *Carolus* monogram. 1.22g/18.9gr. 10°. *SCBI* 516. The side with the king's name and hand of God is technically the reverse.

ANLAF GUTHFRITHSSON, 939–41

Raven/Small Cross type

1451 *Athelferd*. **ANLAF CVNVNCIΓ**. 1.15g/17.7gr. chipped 270°. *SCBI* 519. *Cununc* is the Old Norse for 'king' and *Minetr* is the form usually used in this series for 'moneyer'.

1428. FM: Young 1936; ex Carlyon-Britton I 250*a*.

1429. FM: Henderson 1933.

1430–5, 1437, 1439. FM: Cambridge Antiquarian Soc. 1886 (*CAS Catalogue 1847*, 28, no. 4); presented by the Chancellor of the Duchy of Lancaster July 1844; from Cuerdale hoard. See also Pl. 61.

1436. FM: Young 1936; ex Weber 18.

1438. FM: Dewick 1918.

1440. FM: Young 1936; ex Carlyon-Britton I 255; from Cuerdale hoard.

1441, 1449, 1451. FM: Duncanson 1930; ex Smart.

1442. FM: Sadd.

1443–4. FM: Trinity College 1937; ex King 1876; from Cuerdale hoard.

1445. FM: Young 1936; ex Weber 18.

1446. FM: Young 1936; ex Carlyon-Britton I 248; from Cuerdale hoard.

1447. FM: Young 1936.

1448. FM: provenance unrecorded.

1450. FM: Young 1936; ex Bliss 59; ex Robinson 29.

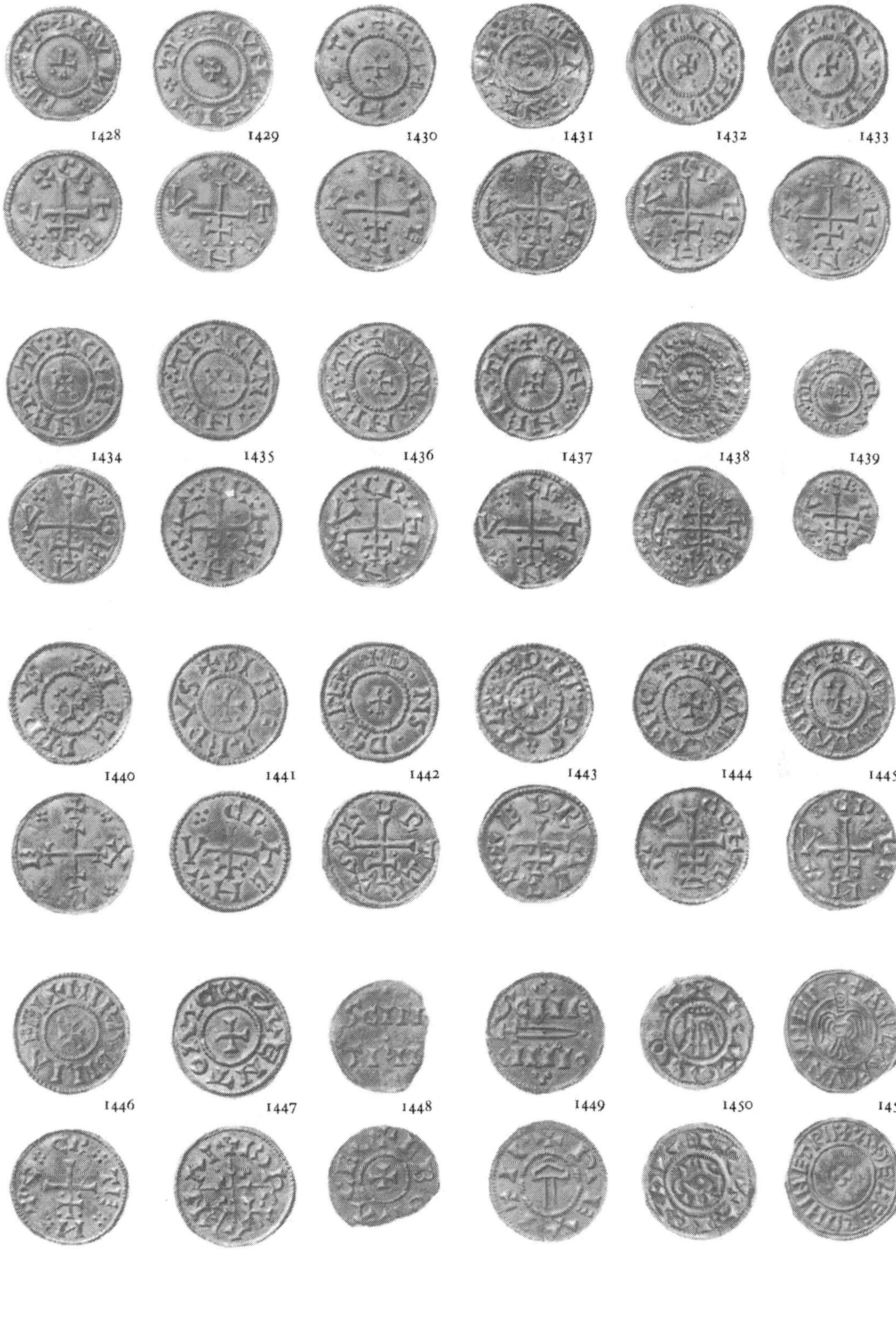

1428 1429 1430 1431 1432 1433

1434 1435 1436 1437 1438 1439

1440 1441 1442 1443 1444 1445

1446 1447 1448 1449 1450 1451

FORGERIES (1)

OSTROGOTHIC AND RELATED COINAGES

1452 *Odovacar* (476–93), after 491. Quarter-siliqua. Obv. **DNANASTASIVSAVC** Rev. monogram of **DN ODOAC P**. AR 0.57g 180°. (As Lagoy 1843, pl. 1.3, etc.) Brunetti 1966, no. 461 (same dies). Struck forgery of Cigoi: for attribution and history, see note on coin.

1453 *Athalaric* (526–34). Half-siliqua. Rome. Obv. **DNIVSTINI ANVS[** Rev. monogram. AR 1.17g 150°. Cast forgery. See **125–6**.

1454 *Theodahad* (534–6). Half-siliqua. Rome. Obv. **DNIVSTI NIANAVG** Rev. monogram. AR 1.29g 170°. *BMC Vand* 72. 1–3; *MIB* I, pl. 39.55. Electrotype.

1455 *As last*, cast from same moulds. AR plated 1.34g corroded 170°. Not illustrated.

1456 *Ravenna, municipal coinage*. Decanummium. Æ 4.30g 0°. Electrotype. See **144–9**.

VISIGOTHS

References are to Velazques (1759) and Florez (1773) for models, to Hill (1925) for Becker's forgeries, and to the list of forgeries in Miles (1952, 450ff.), where in some cases the existence of up to a dozen or more specimens of each is noted. All are gold except **1457**, which is silver.

Pseudo-Imperial Coinage

1457 *Mint unspecified*. Obv. **IIIVƧTI ILIAV** Rev. **ᔕTVA TOOVAO**, w. **CONO** beneath. AR 1.71g 170°. Hill 275. Becker forgery.

Regal coinage

1458 *Leovigild* (573–86). *Cordova*. Obv. +**LEOVIGILDVSREX** Rev. +**CORDOBABISOPTINVIT**. AV 1.34g (SG 15.01: 65% Au) 0°. Miles 11(b) 17 (this coin); from Florez 181. The *Bis optinuit* inscription, referring to Leovigild's recovery of Cordova after Hermenegild's rebellion, made this a highly attractive coin to collectors.

1459 *Same ruler*. *Mérida*. Obv. +**DNLEOVIGILDVSREX** Rev. +**PIVƧEMERITAVICTOR**. AV 1.19g (SG 14.63: 61% Au) 20°. Miles 14 (same dies); from Florez 182.

1460 *Liuva II* (601–3). *Seville*. Obv. +**DNLIVVAREX** Rev. +**PIVSISPALI**. AV 1.31g pierced (SG 15.07; 66% Au) 0°. Miles 32(b), 12 (this coin); from Florez 216.

1461 *Gondemar* (610–12). *Seville*. Obv. +**GVNDEMARVƧRE·** Rev. +**IƧPALIPIVƧ:**. AV 1.28g (SG 13.40: 46% Au) 0°. Miles 37.13 (this coin); from Florez 225.

1462 *Same ruler*. *Tarragona*. Obv. +**C·ON:OMARVSRE** Rev. +**TARRACO:AIV:O:** (for *Tarracona Iusto*). AV 1.33g (SG 19.23: 100% Au) 160°. Miles 164(c). Not in Miles' list of forgeries and acquired as authentic, since its style and fabric are above suspicion, but its gold content is impossible for a genuine coin.

1463 *Sisebut* (612–21). *Oporto* Obv. +**SISIBVTVSREX** Rev. +**PORTOCALEPIV**. AV 1.14g (SG 14.84: 63% Au) 0°. Miles 46(a), 14 (this coin); from Florez 233.

1464 *Same ruler*. *Tarragona*. Obv. +**SISEBVTVSRE**+ Rev. **TARR.**+**COIVSTC** (for *Tarraco Iusto*). AV 1.30g (SG 14.48: 60% Au) 0°. Miles 39.13 (this coin); from Florez 234, and reproducing the erroneous **C** (for **O**) of Florez's illustration. Same rev. die as that of **1470**.

1465 *Swinthila* (621–31). *Eliberri*. Obv. +**SVINTILARE** Rev. +**PIVSELIBER**. AV 1.72g (SG 16.01: 75% Au) 220°. Miles 50.1 (this coin); mule of Hill 281 (Swinthila–*Toledo*) and 278 (Witteric–*Eliberri*). Becker forgery.

1466 *Chintila* (636–9). *Mérida*. Obv. +**CINTHILAREX** Rev. +**EMERITAPIVS**. AV 1.35g (SG 15.08: 66% Au) 340°. Miles 60(a), 12 (this coin); from Florez 248. The second specimen Miles records as being in this collection, also from Shore 625, was given to the Ashmolean in 1952.

1467 *Chindaswinth* (642–53). *Narbonne*. Obv. +**CHIND: SVID.RE** Rev. +**NARB[ON]AP:S**. AV 1.79g (SG 16.24: 77% Au) 0°. Miles 63(a) (this coin); Hill 285. Becker used the same rev. die for coins of Sisebut and Sisenand.

1468 *Wamba* (672–80). *Mérida*. Obv. +**I·D·IN·M·E-VVAMBAR** (**MB** ligatured) Rev. +**EMERITAPIVS**. AV 1.39g (SG 14.64: 61% Au) 0°. Miles 81(d), 8 (this coin); from Florez 268.

1469 *Egica* (687–702). *Narbonne*. Obv. +**I·I·IINMEGICAR** Rev. +**NARBONAPIVS**. AV 1.35g (SG 15.41: 69% Au) 10°. Miles 88(d) (same dies); the obv. is copied from Velazquez no. 125, the rev. from Florez 280.

1470 *Same ruler*. *Tarragona*. Obv. +**IND:IN:M:EEGICAPX** Rev. **TARR.**+**COIVSTC**. AV 1.30g (SG 14.07: 55% Au) 0°. Miles 89(b) 1 (this coin). This is a mule of an obv. die of Egica–*Cordova* (from Florez 277) and the rev. die used for Sisebut–*Tarragona* (**1464** above).

1471 *Roderick* (709–11). *Toledo*. Obv. +**IИDNERVDERICVSR** (**ИD** and **NE** ligatured) Rev. +**TOLETOPIᔕ:**. AV 1.35g (SG 14.66: 62% Au) 10°. Miles 105(b), 7 (this coin); no genuine prototype.

1452. PG: Spink 12.2.1945; ex Grantley 2781; from Spink; ex Kraus.
1453. FM: provenance unrecorded.
1454. PG: Spink 12.2.1945; ex Grantley 2787.
1455. FM: Gutteridge 1939.
1456. CCC (*Catalogue* no. 56): Lewis 1891.
1457. PG: Kapamadji 9.1.1970.
1458, 1466. PG: Shore 625.
1459, 1469. PG: A. R. Tait 25.6.1962.
1460. PG: Seaby 3.8.1945.
1461, 1463. PG: Santamaria 26.9.1947.
1462. PG: Ars et Nummus 10.10.1962 (list, Sept. 1962, no. 14).
1464. PG: Baldwin 27. 9.1945.
1465. PG: Shore 616.
1467. PG: Spink 25.7.1946; ex Shore 618.
1468. PG: Seaby 3.8.1945.
1470. PG: DO 11.5.1958; ex Peirce 1948.
1471. PG: Spink 25.7.1946; ex Shore 624.

[*continued overleaf*]

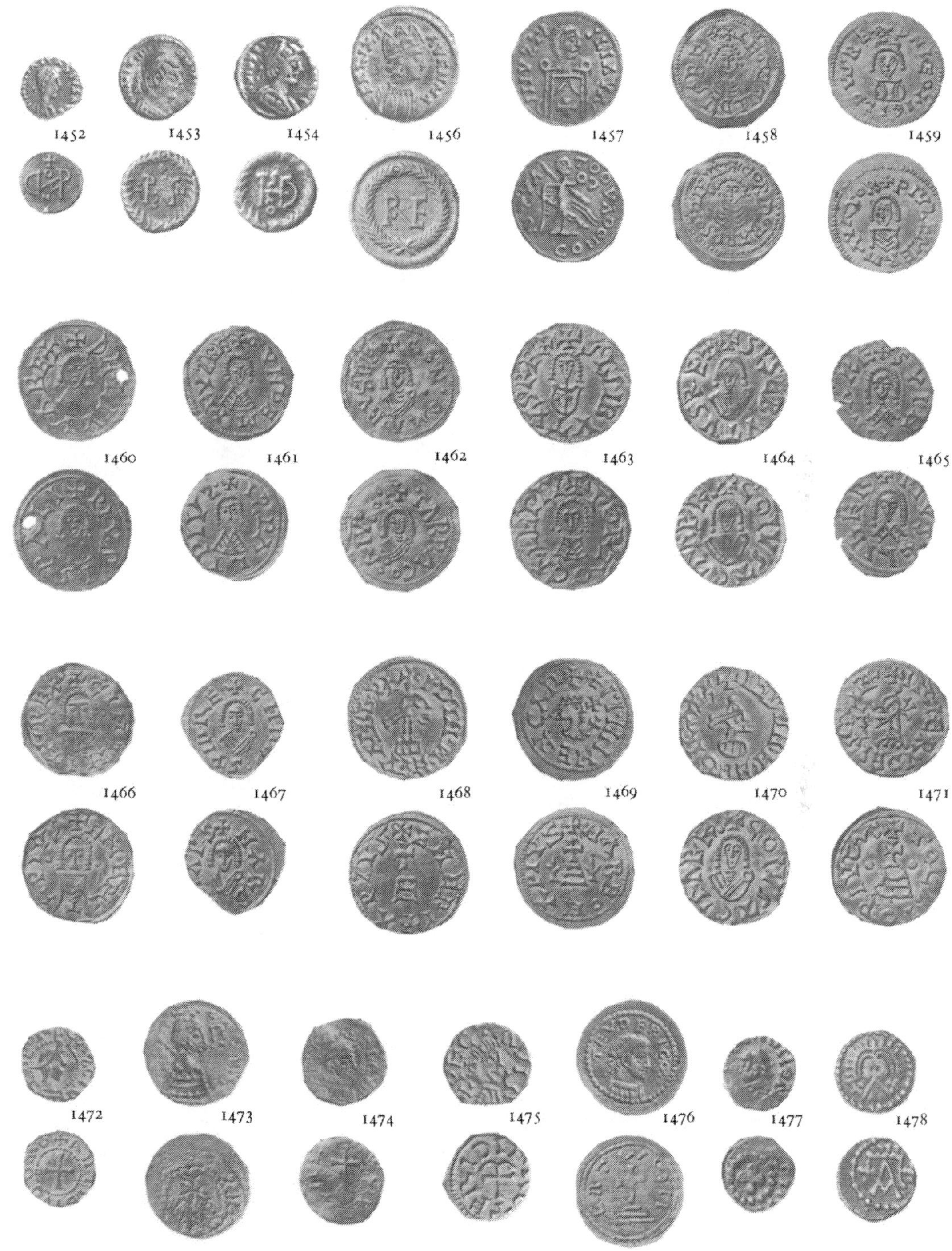

1452 1453 1454 1456 1457 1458 1459

1460 1461 1462 1463 1464 1465

1466 1467 1468 1469 1470 1471

1472 1473 1474 1475 1476 1477 1478

PLATE 63 (*cont.*)

MEROVINGIANS

References: B = Belfort 1892–5, P = Prou 1892a.

Tremisses

1472 *Bourges* (Cher), moneyer *Antidiusus*. Obv. +**BEOREGA2 CIV** Rev. +**ANTIDIVSO MO**. 1.19g (SG 19.29: 99.9% Au) 90°. B 852 = P 1670 (same dies). Struck forgery, early 19th century, the fineness being impossible for a coin of this period. There are two other specimens, apparently from the same dies and presumably also false, one in the BN (ex Dassy 3.5.1869, lot 214) and the other in Cahn 79 (14.12.1932), lot 992 (Fürstenberg coll., ex Saulcy; publ. Saulcy 1838, 268 and pl. 10.2).

1473 *Marseille*, Sigebert III (639–56). Solidus. Obv. [ ]**ЄRTVS** Rev. **VIC**[ ]**A**, w. **MA** and **VII** in field. 0.87g (SG 8.19: gilded base metal) 190°. B 2525 (the coin, now in the BM, from which this is cast).

1474 *Metz* (Moselle), moneyer *Chuldericus*. Obv. **CHVLD+RICVS** (**VL** ligatured) Rev. +**ME**[ ]**SCIV**. AV 1.57g (SG 17.52: 88% Au) 180°. B 2906–7 (as Childeric II, 660–73); P –; Stahl 1982, A4b (this coin, as probably false). Struck forgery. The relief is abnormally flat and weight and fineness are both too high for coins from this region.

1475 *Poitiers* (Vienne), moneyer *Fredericus*. Obv. +**PECTAVIS** Rev. +**FRIDIRICO**. AR 1.02g 220°. B 3621 (this coin). Cast in silver of a tremissis (B 3586 = P 2188).

1476 *Trizay-sur-le-Lay* (Vendée). Obv. **TEVDERIC** Rev. **ERTWᔕM** AR 1.52g 340°. Hill 1925, no. 302. Becker forgery struck in silver. The obv. is copied from a tremissis illustrated by Leblanc 1690, 19 (= B 4287 = P 2646), but with a varied rev. type and meaningless rev. legend. The original was formerly attributed to Thierry I (511–34) or II (596–613), but the inscription is better interpreted as the place-name *Teudericiacum* (Prou 1886).

Deniers

1477 *Bourges region*. Obv.]**OMONI**[Rev.]**ᔕIIV**[. 1.57g. B 6629 (Barthélemy album, no. 3604, from former Voillemier coll.). Either the Voillemier coin or a cast of it. The weight is impossible, and an unpublished analysis by Metcalf shows it to be an alloy of lead and bismuth, w. some tin.

1478 *Uncertain mint*, possibly Frisian. Obv. stylized facing bust Rev. monogram formed around letter **Ā**. 1.34g 90°. B 6655 (this cited). P –. Electrotype. Unpublished analysis by Metcalf shows it to be of lead.

1472. PG: Spink 26.1.1946.
1473. PG: Grantley 3255.
1474. PG: Baldwin 16.10.1945.
1475. CCC (*Catalogue* no. 62): Lewis 1891; ex Hoffmann sale, 2.3.1887, lot 195.
1476. FM: provenance unrecorded.
1477. PG: Spink 18.1.1959.
1478. PG: Lockett III 315; ex Grantley 678; ex Fürstenberg (Cahn sale 79 (14.12.1932), lot 1173).

FORGERIES (2)

ANGLO-SAXONS

References: *SCBI* = *SCBI* Cambridge.

Thrymsa series

1479 Copy of a late 6th-century thrymsa based on a Merovingian coin, but with *Aniwulufu* in runes inserted in the obv. legend. This forgery reads: Obv. **+CADAINΔI+ILIO** Rev. **VENTA INI** (**NT** ligatured). *AV* 1.41g/21.8gr. (SG 18.45: 94% Au) 0°. Belfort 4731 (this coin); *SCBI* – For a discussion of the prototypes and the history of this forgery, see note on coin.

1480 '*York' type*. Æ 1.01g/15.6gr. 270° *SCBI* –. Cast of the specimen in the Ashmolean Museum, Oxford (ex Lockett 205: illus. Sutherland 1948, pl. 4.19). Unpublished analysis by Metcalf indicates a significant lead content.

1481 Fabrication based on type of preceding coin, but with the fictitious legend **+EADBALD·R·CA**, i.e. *rex Cant.* Æ 1.00g/15.4gr. 270°. *SCBI* –. Illus. (with added border) by Hall 1774, with attribution to Eadbald of Kent (616–40). Struck forgery. Unpublished analysis by Metcalf indicates that it is virtually pure silver. See note on coin.

Northumbrian series

1482 *Eanred* (*c.* 810–*c.* 840). *Brother* ('other' in runes). Æ 1.78g/27.5gr. 260°. *SCBI* 270. Cast, recognized as such by Miss Pirie.

1483 *Same ruler. Vilheah* (= Wilheah). Æ 1.36g/21.0gr. 100°. *SCBI* 294. A skilful copper-plated cast from the same moulds as the next. Both coins have been analysed using X-ray spectroscopy by Dr J. A. Charles of the Dept. of Metallurgy and Materials Science, Cambridge. The surface patination makes accurate quantification impossible, but values obtained for the core suggest that the ternary eutectic (32% Pb, 15.5% Sn, 52.5% Bi) with a melting point of 96° C was being aimed at.

1484 *As last.* Æ 1.48g/22.9gr. 100°. *SCBI* 295. From same moulds as last. See comment on last. Not illustrated.

1485 *Æthelred II, 1st reign* (*c.* 840–*c.* 844) *Leofdegn.* Æ 2.54g/39.3gr. 160°. *SCBI* 984. Cast from the same moulds as next.

1486 *As last.* Æ 2.35g/36.2gr. 160°. *SCBI* 985. From same moulds as last. Not illustrated.

1487 *Same ruler and moneyer*, but hound type. Æ 2.95g/45.5gr. 200°. *SCBI* 986. Cast.

1488 *Eanbald II*, archbishop of York (796–830s). *Eadvine.* Æ 1.50g/23.2gr. 170°. *SCBI* 987. Cast.

1489 *Same archbishop. Edilvard* (= Æthelweard). Æ 2.43g/37.5gr. 180°. *SCBI* 988. Cast.

1490 *Same archbishop. Cyrnw . . .*, (= Cynewulf?). Æ 2.44g/37.6gr. 350°. *SCBI* –. A very crude, oversized and heavy cast of similar work to the next two.

1491 *Wigmund*, archbishop of York (*c.* 837–*c.* 854). *Coenred.* Obv. legend retrograde. Æ 2.66g/41.0gr. 270°. *SCBI* –. Same fabric as last.

1492 *Same archbishop. Hunlaf.* Æ 1.53g/23.6gr. 0°. *SCBI* –. Same fabric as last.

1493 *Offa of Mercia* (757–96). *Ibba.* Light issue (pre-792). Æ 1.72g/26.6gr. pierced 20°. *SCBI* 989; cf. Blunt 1961, no. 64. Cast; for another from the same moulds, see *SCBI* (4) Copenhagen i, 829.

1494 *Egbert of Wessex* (802–39). *Osmund.* Canterbury, early portrait issue (*c.* 825–8). Æ 1.17g/18.0gr. 180°. *SCBI* 991. Struck. Emery forgery, from the same rev. die as the next (Pagan 1971, 155, no. 6a = this coin). Osmund was not a moneyer of this issue.

1495 *Æthelwulf of Wessex* (839–58). *Osmund.* Canterbury, portrait issue (*c.* 842–8). Æ 1.35g/20.9gr. 160°. *SCBI* 527 (wrongly as authentic). Struck. Emery forgery, sharing same rev. die as last (Pagan 1971, 155, no. 7a = this coin).

1496 *Alfred of Wessex* (871–99). *Tata.* 'Lunette' type (a) (871–*c.* 875). Æ 1.16g/17.9gr. 0°. *SCBI* 992. Emery forgery (Pagan 1971, 156, no. 15a = this coin).

CAROLINGIANS

References: G = Gariel 1883–4 (ref. to plates in vol. II); MG = Morrison and Grunthal 1967; P = Prou 1896a.

1497 *Milo, Count of Narbonne*, c. *780*. Obv. **MIL◇** Rev. **NRB◇**. Æ 1.08g 90°. P 834; G –; MG –. See note on coin.

1498 *Charlemagne* (768–814). *Treviso* (**TARVISIO**). Æ 0.64g corroded and chipped 135°. *CNI* VI, 227.8, 9, 12; P –; G XII 183; MG 216. Its low weight and flat relief make it unlikely to be authentic, even taking its poor condition into account, though it might be a contemporary forgery. Coins of Treviso of Charlemagne's Class 2 (781/93 in Italy) are abnormal in having a monogram as obv. type.

1499 *Same ruler. Ravenna* **CARLVS REX FR** and **ET LANCACPATROM**, w. monogram of **RAVE**. Æ 1.31g 270°. Struck mid 19th-century forgery (pre-1859), w. misunderstood monogram. See note on coin.

1479. PG: Herzfelder 5.7.1953 . . . ex Amécourt; ex Norblin (not in sale catalogue).

1480–1. PG: Baldwin 2.7.1968; ex Grantley 746.

1482. FM (*Catalogue c. 1886*): provenance unrecorded (the 'Hexham hoard' provenance of *SCBI* is an error).

1483–4. FM: one of these coins = *Catalogue 1867*, no. 15, ex Babington 1866; the other = Cambridge Antiquarian Society 1886 (*CAS Catalogue 1847*, 28, no. 5, as forgery), ex Litchfield 1847.

1485–6. FM: one of these coins = *Catalogue 1867*, no. 16, ex Babington 1866; the other = Cambridge Antiquarian Society 1886 (*CAS Catalogue 1847*, 28, no. 5, as forgery), ex Litchfield 1847.

1487–9. FM: Cambridge Antiquarian Society 1886 (*CAS Catalogue 1847*, 28, no. 5, as forgery); ex Litchfield 1847.

1490–2. QC: no provenance.

1493. FM: Duncanson 1930; ex Smart; ex Beaufoy.

1494. FM: Henderson 1933; ex Montagu 463; ex Brice; ex Bergne 130; ex Martin 3.

1495. FM: Young 1936; ex Carlyon-Britton I 323; ex J. H. Young 11; ex Wigan.

1496. FM: Henderson 1933; ex Murdoch 83; ex Montagu 548; ex Shorthouse 94; ex Shepherd 69.

1497. PG: Kapamadji 17.4.1959, from an alleged hoard of 10+ specimens said to have been found in the 19th c.

1498. PG: ex I. H. Stewart 8.11.1964; from Platt 21.9.1962.

1499. PG: Kapamadji 9.1.1970.

[*continued overleaf*]

1479 1480 1481 1482 1483 1485

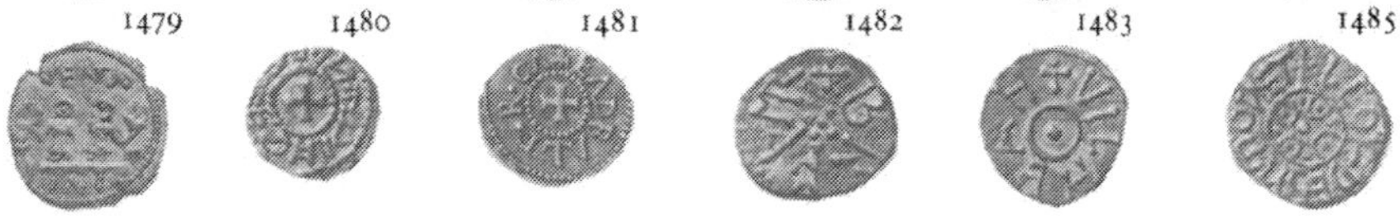

1487 1488 1489 1490 1491 1492

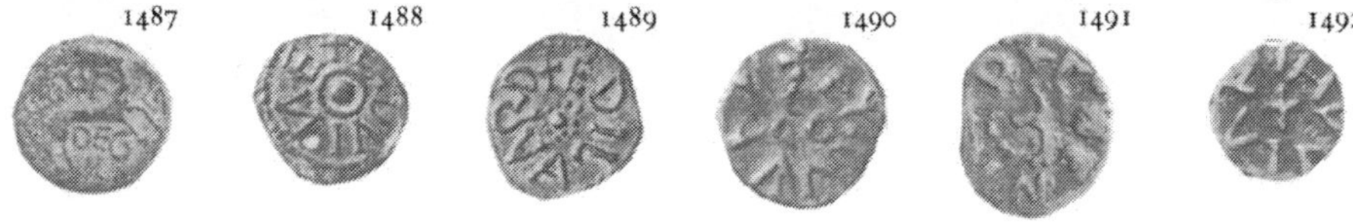

1493 1494 1495 1496 1497 1498

1499 1500 1501 1502 1503 1504

1500 *Louis the Pious* (814–40). *Barcelona* (**BVRCINONA**). Æ 1.43g 180°. P 832; G XV 36; MG 428; Botet 1918 (I) 4. Struck forgery in very low relief. Botet cites two specimens reading BVR instead of BAR, (a) BN = P 832, (b) Vidal Quadras no. 526. The specimen here looks identical with the latter coin, and is either it or copied from it. Cf. Crusafont, Balaguer and Puig 1979, 387–8 var.

MIDDLE KINGDOM AND GERMANY

1501 *Lothar I* (840–55). *Strasbourg* (**STRAƧB/CIVITA**). Æ 2.47g. Struck. Becker forgery (Hill 310).

1502 *Lothar II* (855–69). *Metz* (**METTIS CIVITAS**). **HLOTHARIVS REX**. Æ 1.56g 160°. P –; G LX 1; MG 1186. Struck. Tardani forgery, copied from illustration in Robert catalogue, lot 395. Three others recorded from same dies. Publ. Grierson 1958, pl. 19.7(c).

1503 *Charles the Fat* (880–7). *Verdun* (**VIRDVNVM CVI**). **REX INPERATOR**. Æ 1.29g 180°. P 154; G XLII 59; MG 1457. Struck. Tardani forgery, copied from Robert catalogue, lot 1045. Rev. die in the Museo Nazionale at Rome. One other known from same dies. Publ. Grierson 1958, pl. 19.9(b).

1504 *Arnulf* (888–99). *Toul* ( ]**VLLO CIVIT**[ ). Rev.]**VLFVS RE**[. Æ 0.50g fragment P 136; G –; MG 1535. Struck. Tardani forgery, copied from Robert catalogue, lot 943. Three other specimens recorded, including one in the Vatican making part of an encrusted block of the supposed 'Bolsena' hoard. Noted but not illus. in Grierson 1958, 314, no. 10d (the coin illus. on pl. 19 is really 10c, not 10d).

1500. PG: Tinchant 4.6.1952. 1501. PG: provenance unrecorded. 1502–4. PG: Ciani 23.5.1951.

FORGERIES (3)

CAROLINGIANS (cont.)

References as on Plate 64. The coins are silver.

WEST FRANKISH KINGDOM

1505 *Charles the Bald* (840–77). *Bayeux* (**HBAIOCAS CIVITAS**). 1.29g 270°. P 404; G XXVI 45; MG 887. Weight and fabric are equally unsatisfactory.

1506 *Charles the Simple* (898–923). *Bruges* (**BRVCCIAMO**). **CRATAƆ-RX**, monogram retrograde. 1.81g 90°. P 174 var.; G XXVII 55 var. (as Charles the Bald); MG 699 (as Charles the Bald). Struck. The high weight and general aspect are against its being authentic, though genuine coins exist, there being 139 specimens in the Assebrouck hoard 1858 (MG hoard 60, misdated *c.* 870; rectè *c.* 900).

1507 *Same ruler. Provins* (**CASTIS PRVVINS**). 1.44g 120°. P –; G –; MG –. Struck. Poor lettering and appearance. The type exists for Louis II/III, with a *Ludovicus* monogram (MG 1254).

1508 *Raoul* (923–36). *Courcessin* (**CVRTISASONIEN**). 1.01g 140°. P 418; G –; MG 1590 (monogram on specimen illustrated wrongly read). Struck. Lettering, etc., quite incorrect. P 418 is also false, but from different dies, and there are no genuine coins of Raoul of this mint (Dumas 1980, 222). Probably the work of Farrigault.

1509 *Same ruler. Rheims* (**REMIS CIVITAS**). *Obol.* Obv. **GRATIA DI RIX**. w. **RD/VLF** in field. 0.78g 0°. P –; G –; MG –. Struck; lettering and general appearance unconvincing. Probably the work of Farrigault. No genuine coins are known of Raoul for Rheims.

ITALY

1510 *Pope John VIII* (879). *Capua*. 1.30g 20°. *CNI* XVIII, 239.1. Struck Tardani forgery, as is the coin illus. in the *CNI* XVIII, pl. 12.16. The only possible authentic specimen is that in the former Italian royal collection, ex Tafuri coll., which is illus. in the sale catalogue of the latter (Sambon-Dura, 12.4.1880, lot 206). The chronicler Erchempert records the minting of coins in Pope John VIII's name when he visited Capua in 879 (*in cuius vocamine et chartae et nummi figurati sunt*).

1511 *As last*, same dies. 1.44g 190°. Not illustrated.

1512 *Hugh and Lothaire* (931–47). *Pavia*. Obv. **VGO LOHTARIV[** Rev. **XPIITIANA RE**. 1.58g 70°. *CNI* IV, 474.1 var. Cast. For genuine specimens, see **1025–6**.

PAPAL AND PAPAL-IMPERIAL COINAGE

References as on Plate 47. The coins are silver denari save for **1513**.

1513 *Zachary* (741–52). Obv. **+/ZAC/CHAR/IAE** Rev. **+/PA/PAЄ**. Copper exagium. 1.54g slightly concave; chipped, broken and repaired 0°. As Promis pl. 1.3; Serafini 3.1; *CNI* XV, 61.3; Muntoni –. Nature and authenticity discussed in note on coin.

1514 *Leo III with Charlemagne* (800–14). Monograms of **LEO PAPA** and **+IPA** (for *imperator*). 1.49g 260°. As Promis pl. 1.11 var.; Serafini 5.1–2; *CNI* XV, 65.1 var.; Muntoni 4.1. Struck, with letters engraved on the die in very low relief instead of being built up with small punches, as is normal with genuine coins of the time. Mid 19th-century forgery, probably by Cigoi (Brunetti 1966, no. 716: specimen at Udine, though not from Cigoi's coll.).

1515 *Nicholas I with Louis II* (858–67). Monograms of **NICOLAVS** and **+ROMA**. 1.05g chipped 270°. As Promis pl. 4.5; Serafini 11.8; *CNI* XV, 74.2; Muntoni 8.1 var. Tardani forgery. Three others known from same dies.

1516 *As last*, same dies. 0.95g chipped 270°. Not illustrated.

John VIII (872–82). See **1510–11**.

1517 *Adrian III with Charles the Fat* (884–5). Monograms of **ADRIANI** and **+ROMA**. 1.35g 180°. As Promis pl. 5.9; Serafini 13.1–2; *CNI* XV, 76.1; Muntoni 10.1. Neither the letter forms nor the surface are satisfactory, and it is probably a 19th-century forgery.

1518 *Stephen VII with Arnulf* (896–7). Monograms of **STEF ANVS** and **ROMA** 1.32g 200°. Struck. Forgery of Cigoi (Brunetti 1966, no. 724). Fabric differs completely from that of Stephen's genuine coins, whose coins w. Arnulf have a different *Roma* monogram (**1060–1**). There is a specimen amongst Cigoi's coins in the Museo Civico at Udine.

1519 *As last*, same dies. 1.34g 90°. Not illustrated.

1520 *John IX with Lambert* (898). Types as **1063–4**. 1.84g 260°. Electrotype on thick flan.

1521 *Christopher (antipope) and Louis III* (903–4). **CTOFRS** and monogram of **ROMA**. 1.18g 240°. As Promis pl. 4.9; Serafini 18.1–3; Muntoni IV, 143.1. Tardani fogery; other specimens from the same dies in the former Italian royal collection (*CNI* XV, pl. 5.22, acquired from Vitalini in 1900) and in the Papadopoli coll., no. 16515.

1522 *John X* (913–28). Alone 913–15. Obv. **ᔕCᔕ[** and upper part of monogram Rev. upper part of church. 0.33g fragment. As Promis pl. 7.11; Serafini 319–20.6–8 (forgeries); *CNI* XV, 89.9 (forgeries); Muntoni –. Two others from the same dies, both acquired from 'Gilli' and in the Vatican, are illustrated in Serafini pl. 46.4–5.

1523 *John XI with Alberic* (932–5). **PIOE**. i.e. P(*apa*) IO(*ann*)E(*s*) and **EI/ERI/IV**, error for **FIERI IV**(*ssit*), continuing the **ALBRIC PRICIP** of the inscr. 1.37g 20°. As Serafini pl. 5.8 (genuine) = *CNI* XV, 90.2 = Muntoni 17.4. Tardani forgery. Three others known from same dies (one in the Vatican illus. as genuine by Serafini pl. 46.7 = *CNI* XV, 90.2). The sole genuine specimen of this coin, found in the Tiber, was illus. in the Rossi sale catalogue, lot 3476, but the significance of the legend was not understood and it

1505. PG: Platt 1.9.1950.
1506. PG: Franceschi 25.3.1947.
1507–8. PG: Kapamadji 6.10.1962.
1509. PG: Kapamadji 10.1.1969.
1510–11. PG: Kapamadji 9.1.1970.
1512. PG: MMAG Basel 30.9.1946.
1513. PG: Blunt 10.8.1955; acq. in Paris 1947.
1514. PG: Spink 21.9.1945; ex Boulton; ex 'Monnaies des papes' sale, lot 2 (= Vidal Quadras coll., no. 11,779); ex Sambon sale, Rome 8.7.1883, lot 876. Withdrawn at the 'Monnaies des papes' sale but acq. subsequently for Boulton by L. Forrer (of Spink), who believed it to be authentic.
1515–16, 1518. PG: Kapamadji 9.1.1970.
1517, 1519. PG: Ratto 15.6.1955; ex C. Gavazzi.
1520. PG: Sternberg 27.6.1958.
1521. PG: Baldwin 27.9.1945; ex Grantley 3268 (no. missing in catalogue); from Vitalini.
1522. PG: Ciani 23.5.1951.
1523–4. PG: Kapamadji 9.1.1970.

[*continued overleaf*]

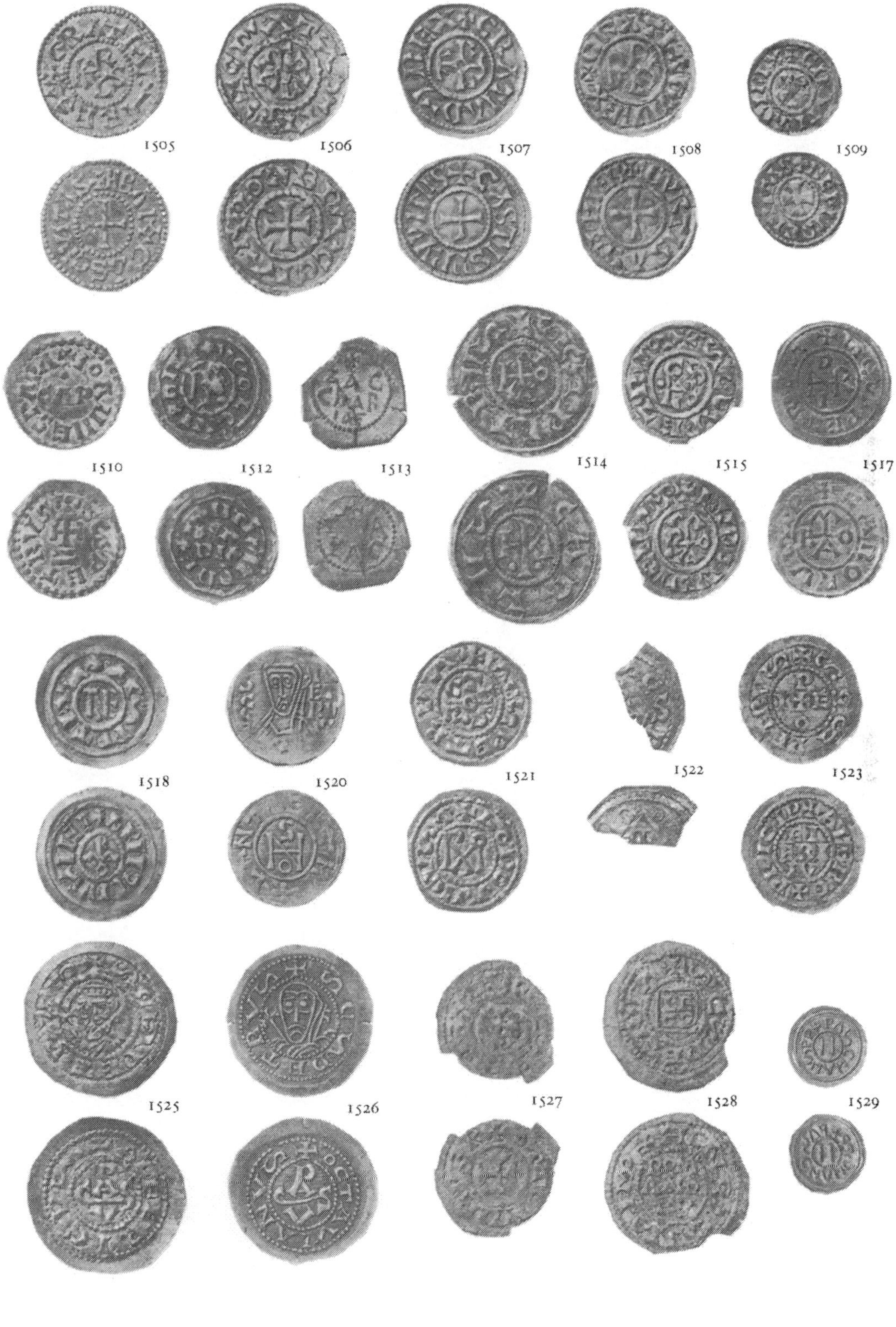

1505 1506 1507 1508 1509

1510 1512 1513 1514 1515 1517

1518 1520 1521 1522 1523

1525 1526 1527 1528 1529

was reproduced in the catalogue as **EI/ERI/IV**, an error copied on Tardani's die.

1524 *As last*, same dies. 1.18g broken 10°. Not illustrated.

1525 *Alberic* (932–54), *alone*. **PACVS**, (for *pacificus*?) in field. 1.34g 40°. As Promis pl. 8.2; Serafini 21.1; *CNI* XV, 92.4; Muntoni 19.1. Tardani forgery, copied from Promis and reproducing an error in the illus. which substitutes a pellet for the **R** (for **PR**, i.e. *princeps*) after Alberic's name. Others from same dies in Cahn sale 31.3.1913, lot 33, and in the Martinori sale, lot 2861.

1526 *Octavian* (Senator 954–5), *later Pope John XII* (955–64). **OCTAVIANVS**, and **PACVS** in the field. 1.35g A grotesque forgery, based on the design of the preceding coin and perhaps encouraged by Promis's conjecture (p. 88) that such a coin was likely to exist. The forgery probably originated in N. Italy; there are specimens in private collections at Milan and Verona.

1527 *John XIII with Otto I* (965–72). Obv. **.P./IOH/.P.** in field. Rev. **OTTON IMPER**. 0.80g corroded and chipped 180°. As Promis pl. 9.4; Serafini 22.6–9; *CNI* XV, 96.4; Muntoni 22.1. Tardani forgery; the corroded edges and surface are very typical of how he sometimes overdid the treatment with acid to 'age' his products. Six others from the same dies are known: one in the Vatican (ex Celati, ex 'Bolsena') is illustrated by Serafini pl. 218.7. The fabric is quite different from that of the genuine coin (**1081**).

1528 '*Leo IX* (1049–54)' *with* '*Henry III*'. +**HENRICVꟅ IM** and **ROM/ANO/RV** in the field. 1.04g corroded and chipped. Promis pl. 10.1; Serafini 321.1–2; *CNI* XV, 99.2; Muntoni –. Tardani forgery; there are at least eight others from the same dies, four of them in the Vatican (cf. Serafini pl. 46.13–14). See note on coin.

1529 *Paschal II* (1099–1118). Uniface. +**PAꟅCHALIꟅ PP**,w. **II** in field. 0.27g. Promis pl. 10.2. See note on coin.

1525. PG: Ratto 14.4.1955; ex Gavazzi; ex Ruchat III 40; ex Avv. Corsi 1912.
1526. PG: Ratto 15.6.1955.
1527. PG: Ratto 15.6.1955; ex C. Gavazzi.
1528. PG: Ratto 14.4.1955; ex C. Gavazzi; ex Celati duplicates; ex Chigi.
1529. PG: Ratto 15.6.1955; ex C. Gavazzi; ex Celati duplicates; ex Kircheriano.

NOTES ON THE COINS

300 This coin was hesitantly attributed by Wroth (*BMC Vand* 144 n. 2), following de Salis, to King Liutprand (712–44). Sambon followed suit, stating incorrectly that there were specimens in the Luni hoard (Sambon 1912, no. 338). Its style and fabric are those of the 6th and early 7th centuries, quite different from those of coins of the 8th, and the legend is blundered from the *Constantinus* of a Ravennate silver coin of Tiberius II (578–82). This prompted an attribution to Adalwald (615–24), since although he lived forty years after Tiberius II he was the first Lombard king to whom the letters of the monogram could apply (Grierson 1956b). It was subsequently pointed out (*DAN*, no. XIV addenda), that since the monogram includes the letters FARVLDX and no others an altogether more satisfactory candidate was Duke Farwald of Spoleto, who captured Classis, the port of Ravenna, in *c.* 579 and held it for ten years (Paul the Deacon, *Historia Langobardorum* III.13). Farwald, *primus Spolitanorum dux*, was one of the thirty-five dukes who, unable to agree on a successor to King Cleph in 574, maintained a ten-year interregnum until the election, *communi consilio*, of King Authari in 584. Classis was recovered for the Empire by a certain Droctulf, a feat recorded in the latter's epitaph (*Hist. Lang.* III.19).

326 Another specimen, complete and from different dies, reads + FL·A·NOVATARI (Bernareggi 1972). The mint (Castelnovate, Varese), 2km from Vizzola Ticino, is close to the other minor mints of Pombia and Castel Seprio. Such a locality is preferable to Novate Milanese, 9km north-west of Milan (Bernareggi 1972) or Novara (Pellegrino 1966).

332 The broad bust shows the model to have been a siliqua of Valentinian I (364–75) or a colleague; cf. *RIC* IX, pl. 4.7. It is related to, though not identical with, the many pseudo-imperial AR of this period, often mounted, from the Dortmund hoard and graves at Heilbronn and elsewhere (cf. Regling 1908; Albrecht 1957, 15–17; Nau 1966; Alföldi 1968; Martin 1982).

335 The unusual style of portrait and Victory is found in no other series. Specimens from the same dies, one in the Lacam collection (Lacam 1974, pl. 107.B1) and another in Mme Kapamadji's collection (Boutin 1983, no. 994), both acquired in Sardinia, suggest that the final S of the reverse legend may allude to a mint on that island while under occupation by Odovacar or by the Vandals.

362 This coin and the next (identical in type and style and linked by an ELA which in one case finishes the legend of the reverse and in the other starts that of the obverse) must both have been struck in the same mint and by the same moneyer at a time (*c.* 580) when the pseudo-imperial coinage was drawing to an end and moneyers were beginning to insert their names or those of their mints somewhere in the legends but had not yet eliminated the pseudo-imperial elements in these. The anomalous DN preceding VICTORIA in the rev. legend of **362** occurs on coins of identical style (P 896) struck at Brinon-les-Allemands (*Briunnone*), dép. Nièvre, and a coin (P 902) of the

neighbouring mint of Decize (dép. Nièvre), also with a 'Justin' obv. and of similar style, has the mint-signature in the rev. legend following VICTORIA. It is therefore reasonable to attribute **362** and **363** to northern Burgundy. *Elu* may stand for a mint, but is more likely to represent a moneyer. It could be short for *Elafius* or some such name, but the fact of its appearing in the same form in two different positions suggests that it is complete, and *Ela* does appear as a complete name on some coins of Quentovic (B 4984–6 = P 1138–9: *Ela monit*). The Quentovic moneyer, however, must be a different person, for his coins, struck in another part of France, are much later in date.

366 The style is similar to two coins of Lausanne with rev. legends LANSONNA CIVETATE PER (B 2114–15; Geiger 1979a, nos. 11, 11a). The obv. and rev. legends of this coin virtually repeat each other and are very close to the obv. legend of B 2115, itself perhaps a blundering of *Lausonna civitas*. The attribution of this coin to Lausanne or to some neighbouring mint seems assured.

431 The moneyer's name was read as *Teodericus* by Belfort (B 1067) and Jullian (1890, 99, no. 936), both following Amécourt (1864, 189), but as *Leodericus* by Prou (P 2123) and *Leopetricus* by Lafaurie (1963b, 298). The first letter is in fact illegible on the few known specimens, the fourth could be either D or P, and on a specimen at Berlin the loop of the R projects to the left of the vertical stroke, as if to form a monogram of TR, whence Lafaurie's *Leopetricus*. But the specimen here has only a simple R, and the traditional reading seems preferable.

437 The mint attribution, that of Lafaurie (1971e), is based on the occurrence of the moneyer Dendus on coins with the mint name *Marciliac*, Prou's identification of which with Marcilly-en-Gault is justified by their style and type. Lafaurie dates the coin to the early 640s.

438 *Novo Vico* could apply to many localities (cf. P 392–3, 464–8, 1994–8, 2332–3), but since the bust is Limousin in style Lafaurie (*per litteram*) favours Neuvic-d'Ussel. Neither this moneyer nor type is known for any other *Novo Vico* coin.

458 Other coins of this moneyer and type have an obverse inscription MVNCI[ACO] VICOV for Moussy (B 3556 = MMAG Basel sale 8 (8.10.1949), lot 425), or the variant EMVNLIACO (B 1357, 1887 = 2171 = 6173; P 878–9). The style is Parisian and the letters in the reverse field are copied from coins of Paris with ELIGI (*us*).

579–90 In the catalogues of Belfort and Prou, coins of this basic reverse type (a cross of five pellets in a pearl border) and without mint names were mostly attributed (B 6363–70; P 2264–5) to the region of Poitiers. In his account of the Bais hoard, Prou revised the attributions of many of them, assigning them to the Bourges region on the analogy of mint-signed coins of the locality (Prou and Bougenot 1907, note to no. 116). This attribution was accepted and further justified by Lafaurie 1969a, 167–9.

584 The neatly rounded head, which looks as if it were wearing a closely fitting cap turned up in front and behind, copies that on coins of Paris (B 3415–30, P 787, 839, etc.), but it is also found on coins of the Bourges region (B 6331 = P 788; Plassac 54; attributed to Jailly, dép. Nièvre, near Bourges in Lafaurie 1969a, 192). The rev., with its additional inner circle of small pellets, also occurs on coins with a horse on the obv. attributed to the mint of Bourges (B 3614 = P 2203 = Saint-Pierre-les-Etieux no. 34; for attribution see Lafaurie 1969a, note on this last).

586 The form of radiate bust with the band of the crown having the appearance of a pair of scissors is probably derived from coins of Poitiers (B 3599–610, P 2194–201) or possibly Orléans (B 545–54, P 642–6), but the coins are probably to be attributed to the Bourges region (Lafaurie 1969a, 169). This and the three following coins well illustrate its bizarre treatment. Although specimens

occurred in the Cimiez, Bais, Saint-Pierre-les-Etieux and Plassac hoards, the series is not extensive and there is much die-duplication; coins of northern Aquitaine were in any case strongly represented in these hoards. The specimen cited as comparable with this coin suggests that the rev. legend should be restored + MARCHISILO, but there seems to be nothing in the association suggested by Prou with coins reading HEDE . . . MARIC (B 2105, P 2240–1).

589 This coin combines what are normally two reverse types, one the cross of large globules typical of the Bourges region and the other a 'standard' presumably copied from that of a 'porcupine' sceat of Class G, specimens of which occurred in the hoards from Bais (nos. 309–10), Saint-Pierre-les-Etieux (nos. 95–8), and Nohanent (nos. 20–3). Unlike the true 'porcupine' reverses, however, this has an outer border of pellets and no letters or symbols surrounding the 'standard'. This combination is not recorded from English or Frisian finds and an attribution to northern Aquitaine is in any case suggested by the occurrence of a specimen in the Plassac hoard (no. 72), illustrated by Lafaurie from Maxe-Werly's tinfoil impression in the museum of Bar-le-Duc and to all appearances this coin (and consequently ex La Grange sale, lot 378).

604–5 Coins of this type, with RM in the obverse field, are absent from all hoards save that of Cimiez (Cimiez 296–9 = B 1870, 3786–91 = P 2848–53). An isolated specimen was found at Domburg (Rethaan Macaré 1856, pl. 3.6), and another with SCO replaced by two facing heads (Rethaan Macaré 1838, pl. 3.57). Morel-Fatio and Prou treated their mint as uncertain; Belfort gave them doubtfully to Rheims. Apart from the RM there is no evidence in favour of this, and the presence of five specimens in Cimiez suggests a mint further south, though the fabric is not Provençal. The two facing heads on one of the Domburg specimens perhaps links them to coins of a similar type in the Savonnières hoard (nos. 33–6) which Lafaurie, reading their inscription as SAP . . ., doubtfully ascribes to Savonnières (*Saponaria*) itself (Lafaurie 1963a, 71–2), in which case the heads would be those of SS Gervase and Protasius, to whom the local church was dedicated.

607 This anonymous coin is traditionally but incorrectly attributed to Chalon-sur-Saône. A specimen in the Cartier collection was originally published without any mint attribution (Cartier 1839, p. 421, pl. 17.8). Amécourt (1868b, 301; 1873, nos. 150–1) ascribed it to Chalon, since a specimen in the museum of this town had been found in the immediate neighbourhood at Buxy and a simplified Christogram occurs on Chalon deniers. But these coins differ in all other respects from those of Chalon, notably in fabric and in their anonymity (see **1.539–40**), and the helmeted bust does not occur in the Chalon series. Maxe-Werly (1888–9, 558) attributed them to the neighbourhood of Rheims, on the double ground that specimens had been found in north-eastern France and that a similar helmeted bust occurs on Rheims tremisses of the moneyers Garibertus and Betto. He gives no details of the findings to which he refers, but a coin of this type, and eight others combining the same reverse with a different obverse, made up a hoard (Le Gentilhomme 1947) found at Barbuise, only 35 miles south-west of Rheims in the Seine valley. The relationship of the bust on this coin to that of the tremisses cited by Maxe-Werly thus justifies the removal of this coin from Chalon to some unknown mint in north-eastern France, probably in the neighbourhood of Rheims.

614 Belfort followed Chabouillet in attributing coins of this type to Uzès (Gard), reading the letters on the reverse as VCECA, but Prou regarded the mint as uncertain and pointed to the more literate reverse of a coin in the Bais hoard (ID EPS) as evidence against the Uzès attribution. Lafaurie (1978c, 369; 1981d, vii) suggested that the legend might refer to an Idoinus of Senlis (Oise), the only bishop listed in the index to Duchesne's *Fastes épiscopaux* whose name begins *Id-* and who could be dated to the first half of the 8th century. But *Idoinus* occurs only in a

list of the late 10th century in which the names are sometimes corrupt, and Duchesne regarded its form as doubtful. The matter must therefore be left in suspense, for it is possible that only the I is a personal initial and the D an epithet.

623 The coin was analysed by Metcalf at the same time and using the same procedures as those published in Metcalf 1983a, but the results were not included in this article. They were: Ag 92.14%; Cu 5.88%; Au 0.92%; Pb 0.94%; Sn —; Zn —; Ni —; Bi 0.12%; 'silver' 94.12%.

634–5 This type, with crude head and an interlace design, has been much discussed, not least because it bridges the latest Merovingian and the earliest Carolingian coinages (Amécourt 1868c). The reverse type, which in slightly varying forms is also found as a decorative element on Frankish buckles and jewellery, has sometimes been described as a rosette or quatrefoil, but when properly formed consists of two intersecting rings seen from an angle (Nahuys 1888, 459–70), though any reference to ring-money is improbable. In the Carolingian period it occurs on two of Pepin's deniers in the Imphy hoard (G II 38, 39) and on a coin of Charlemagne's second type (G VII 70). The traditional attribution to Maastricht is based partly on the presence of an apparent TR – the first letter is doubtful – on the obverse of one of the Imphy coins and partly on a fancied resemblance of the design to a star which formed part of the medieval arms of this city. It is accepted for the Carolingian coins by Gariel (1883–4, II, 60–2) and Völckers (1965, 123, no. I.16), but Morrison and Grunthal (MG 33 and 230) treat them as indeterminate. A recent study of the find-spots of the Merovingian ones points to them being Frisian (Zedelius 1980, 148–52), but the further suggestion that they might have originated in Dorestad is contradicted by the finding of three specimens in company with Dorestad deniers of blundered 'Madelinus' type (cf. **1.633**) at Wittnauer Horn in the Jura (Geiger 1980) and by the existence of Dorestad deniers of quite different type under Pepin and Charlemagne.

663 The coin was analysed by Metcalf as **623** above. The results were: Ag 86.60%; Cu 8.56%; Au 0.64%; Pb 0.86%; Sn 3.30%; Zn —; Ni —; Bi 0.04%; 'silver' 88.14%.

719 The battle-axe (*francisca*, a pun on the name of Frank) commonly occurs on early coins of Charlemagne with the mint name of Dorestad, though also on the much rarer coins of Bonn (MG 107–8; the alternative attribution to Tiel (Metcalf 1970) seems fanciful), Saint-Bavon at Ghent (MG 241; on the mint see Grierson 1977), and Condé-sur-l'Escaut (MG 113). The fact that the abbreviation mark between the R and P on the reverse is neither a simple horizontal stroke nor a cross but has the form of a T has led some scholars to regard it as standing for *Traiectum*, i.e. either Utrecht (Chijs 1866, 95 and pl. 9.2; Metcalf 1966c, 385–7) or Maastricht (Bordeaux 1893, 309–11), or as a piece of incompetent workmanship showing the coin to be a Frisian imitation (Dumas 1977, 226). But most of the coins with a battle-axe and without mint name are undoubtedly of Dorestad – there were 23 specimens in the Dorestad (Hoogstraat I) hoard found in 1972 (Van Gelder 1980) – and a straightforward Dorestad attribution seems preferable.

720 The significance of the rev. inscription, which occurs in varying degrees of degeneration and carries on into Charlemagne's Class 2 (MG 234), is uncertain. Longpérier, publishing the Imphy hoard, suggested a moneyer Auttramnus (Longpérier 1858, 226–9), but Gariel (1883–4, II 42–4) preferred an attribution to a mint at Antrain (Ille-et-Vilaine, arr. Fougères), not far from Imphy, although the occurrence of seven specimens in the Ilanz hoard shows this not to be conclusive. Metcalf has suggested Saint-Denis, interpreting it as ANT(*istitio*) R(*egio*) D(*io*)N(*usiac*)O (Metcalf 1965a), but although his article brings together much useful material such an interpretation must be dismissed as wholly fanciful in the context of Carolingian coin inscriptions (Grierson 1965b, 512 n. 59).

723 Various interpretations for CLS have been proposed, such as *Clusis* for Sluys (Longpérier 1847, 104–5), *Castrilocus* for Mons (Chalon 1852), *Colonia Sancta* for Cologne (Serrure 1892). The form of the ligatured AR in *Carolus* locates the coin, which is one of the commoner types of Charles' early years, to the Netherlands (cf. **1.724**), and a charter of Charles of December 775 to Bishop Eddo of Strasbourg links *Sclusis* (*Clusis* in later confirmations) with Quentovic and Dorestad as one of three ports at which tolls are regularly paid. Changes in the coastline of Flanders makes the correspondence of this place with that of the modern Sluys (Fr. L'Ecluse), on the Dutch frontier 16km north-east of Bruges and best remembered as the scene of Edward III's naval victory over the French in 1340, somewhat doubtful, but there seems little doubt that a Carolingian 'Sluys' was where the coin was minted. Since there are no later Carolingian coins of *Clusas* the place presumably did not survive the 8th century, being replaced by Bruges in the same way as Dorestad was later to be replaced by Tiel and Quentovic by Boulogne. The later Sluys only appears under this name in the 14th century, but the use of *clusas* in the sense of a narrow waterway (Fr. *écluse*, Eng. *sluice*), as distinct from a mountain pass, is well attested in the Carolingian period (Vanderkindere 1872; Duparc 1951).

734 References to the significance of the gold coins of Uzès – the incautious suggestion made by Grierson (1965b, 531–2) that the mint might be Vicenza (*Ucetia*) in Italy is disproved by the evidence of findspots, all recorded ones being in the Midi – will be found in Appendix 1, but a note is required on the history of this specimen. In Grierson 1954c, 294–5, two specimens of it were noted, one in the Archaeological Museum at Montpellier (Médailler Ricard), which could not be found when he enquired about it in 1949, and the other in the Mazard collection. He had in fact wrongly assumed that Adolphe Ricard, who supplied a drawing of the coin in the 1870s to Charles Robert for the study on the Carolingian coinage in southern France which he contributed to vol. VII (1879) of the new edition of Devic and Vaissette's *Histoire générale de Languedoc* (p. 366, no. 4; pl. 11) was its owner, and that the coin must subsequently have passed in 1893 with the rest of his collection to the Société archéologique de Montpellier. Ricard in fact never claimed to own the coin, and the only known specimen of the class is the one here. It was first published (Mazel 1836) by M. Mazel, a lawyer at Pézenas near Béziers, in company with a few other rarities in his collection that clearly represent local finds.

753 Two dies are know for coins of Group XVI, one represented by a single coin acquired (in England?) by A. W. Franks in the 19th century and now in the BM, the other by three specimens, of which this one and one in the Ashmolean were certainly and a third (in the BM) was probably found in this country. It is possible that one of these may have been the specimen found at Portchester (Hants.) and described as reading NIIVVDOVIIN.NAV which was in the William Hoare sale (Sotheby 25.3.1850, lot 247) but whose existence was unknown to Grierson in 1951. One may conjecture that a specimen was brought to England from Frisia in the 9th century and the others are copies made here at the time (Grierson 1951a, 11 and 34).

860ff There is a large and not very satisfactory literature on the identity of the mint represented by the inscription H(or I)CVRTISASONIEN, i.e. *Curti(s) Sasonien(sis)* preceded by what is more probably an intrusive aspirate (above, p. 197) than the *in* preferred by some scholars. It was a small hamlet now called Courcessin, 3km east of Corbon (Orne, arr. Alençon, cant. Mortagne) in the Hiémois, close to the border between Normandy and Perche. The name that occurs on modern maps has been shortened from the 19th-century Court-Sessin (Le Prévost 1840, 53) and the earlier variant Courtisson (Leblanc 1690, 128). In the 9th century the estate belonged to the Parisian abbey of Saint-Germain-des-Prés, whose polyptych gives the position of the *villa quae dicitur*

Curtis Saxone with satisfactory precision as being *in pago Oximense in centena Corbonensi* (Guérard 1844, II. 126–7), *Oximense* being the Hiémois, the *pays* of Exmes, and Corbon a village whose name has survived unchanged to the present day. This 9th-century text, which provided an identification found satisfactory by such 19th-century scholars as Lecointre-Dupont (1846, 98) and Longpérier (1847, 167–8), renders it unnecessary to discuss the various alternative identifications that have from time to time been put forward – Saosnes (Doucet 1882, 1883; Dieudonné, *RN* 1920, p. xxxix), Courtisols, Auxonne, Courson-Monteloup (Lafaurie 1965a, 277–9, but with the reservation that its antiquity requires confirmation), an unidentified locality in Calvados (Blanchet 1912, 386 n. 2), etc.

The name of the place, which means '*curtis* of the Saxons', requires explanation. It commemorates one of the small groups of Saxon settlements in this part of northern Gaul which date to the 5th and 6th centuries. The presence of these *Saxones Bajocassini* in the Bessin is referred to by Gregory of Tours (*Hist. Franc.* V 19; X 9), the main region where they settled having apparently become largely Saxon in speech and called in consequence the *Otlingua Saxonum*, a term found in a charter of Charles the Bald of 843 and in the Capitulary of Servais (853). It corresponded to the eastern part of the diocese of Bayeux (Longnon 1885, 98–9), but since the capitulary of Servais makes it clear that the *pagus* of Exmes, in the diocese of Séez, did not form part of it we must assume that the *curtis Saxone* near Corbon took its name from an isolated settlement of Saxons a few miles further inland. The name could not indeed have identified the place very satisfactorily if the *curtis* had been situated in an area that was anyway largely Saxon-speaking.

The Courcessin identification accords well with the hoard evidence for the localization of the coins. Although these occur in many north French hoards of the late 860s and 870s there are three in which they preponderate, one the hoard (MG hoard 101; Doucet 1882) found at Juaye-Mondaye near Bayeux (*c.* 700 coins out of 800+) and the others found far from this, one 'near Autun' in 1852 (MG hoards —; Charvet 1870, 423–4: *c.* 500 coins out of *c.* 1,500) and the other *ante* 1868 at Issy-l'Evêque (MG hoard 76: 40+ out of 70+). The Issy-l'Evêque hoard, however, is unhelpful, for the presence in it of coins from Rennes and Lisieux shows part at least of its contents coming from western Gaul, probably through some refugee from Northmen ravages, and the Courcessin coins could have come with these. The same explanation applies to the coins in the 1852 hoard, also from the Autun region, if indeed the two hoards are not in reality one and the same. But the other contents of the Juaye-Mondaye hoard show it to represent the circulating medium in some part of the region between Paris, the Breton frontier, and the Channel. Since it contained only 21 coins of Bayeux, it was presumably formed much further inland than its find-spot. Le Mans was after Courcessin the next-best represented mint in it, with 88 coins, and these are the kind of figures one would expect from a hoard put together in the southern part of the Calvados. Apart from Bayeux itself, it would have been the only mint between Le Mans and the Channel.

The mint of Courcessin must have been open for some four decades, since coins are known of Charles the Bald, of Odo (MG 1289), and Charles the Simple (e.g. those of the Saumeray hoard: Lafaurie 1965a). Much later ones attributed to Raoul are either misread or false (see **1.1508**), and the absence of any of Louis II/III is common to many mints and explicable by continued striking in the name of Charles the Bald. The limiting dates are the introduction of the GDR type in 864 and probably the cession of Normandy to Rollo in 911. It is at first sight surprising that coins of a locality of such obscurity should occur in so many hoards, and be among the commonest of the Carolingian period. The explanation is probably the fact that Courcessin was a possession of Saint-Germain-des-Prés. The abbey, though one of the wealthiest in France, had no mint in Paris itself, and there was none at Séez, the diocese in which Courcessin was situated; Séez is indeed the only episcopal see in northern France which played no part in the GDR coinage. A mint at Courcessin would have made it possible for the rents of the large group of abbatial estates in the region (see La Motte-Collas 1957, map) to be turned into coin on the spot, and go far to explaining the commonness of these coins today.

965 This coin can be traced back to the 1840s, but this by itself is no guarantee of authenticity; see note on **1.1479**. In general appearance, however, it can in no way be differentiated from the silver deniers of Melle of the late 9th century, and, given the well-documented existence of 'pennies' occasionally struck in gold (see Appendix 1), there seems every reason to regard it as genuine.

The coin was first illustrated by Fillon in his *Etudes numismatiques* (Fillon 1856, 39) and reproduced from this by Poey d'Avant (1858–62, II, no. 2364, pl. 52.20). Its existence is mentioned by Fillon in his *Considerations historiques* (Fillon 1851, 116), the preface to which is dated 1850, as belonging to Lecointre-Dupont, and must have been acquired by the latter in the 1840s, since it is not mentioned in his essay on the coinage of Poitou (Lecointre-Dupont 1840a). Nothing seems to be known of its history between the break-up of the Lecointre-Dupont collection sometime after its owner's death (1888), presumably by private sale, and its reappearance in Rolland's catalogue of the Motte collection in 1932. It was not included in the Motte sale of 1951 because the cataloguer, unaware of the literary evidence for the existence of gold pennies, assumed that such a coin must necessarily be false, and when, at Grierson's urging, it was finally offered for sale four years later no guarantee of authenticity was given.

992 The general appearance of this coin is too similar to that of some of Farrigault's forgeries (see pp. 335–6 and **1.1509**) to be reassuring, but the existence of corresponding deniers of unimpeachable authenticity (MG 1429) justifies its being given the benefit of the doubt. The identification of the mint is a problem, for *briva* meant 'river' in Gaulish and occurs in many French place-names, either alone (Brives, Brie, etc.) or in combination with a river name (Brissarthe, Chabris, etc.). The type and the absence of FR in the royal title point to a locality in Aquitaine. The most obvious candidate is Brive (dèp. Corrèze) in the Limousin, where the route from Limoges to Toulouse crosses the Corrèze. This was a town going back to Roman times; it was where the pretender Gondovald had been proclaimed king of Aquitaine in 584. An alternative locality is a former *vicus* in the vicinity of Bourges whose memory is perpetuated in a rue de Brives in the city (Longnon 1878, 465) and which appears in 6th-century sources. Identification with it is favoured by the finding of two deniers of Brive in a grave at Tiszaeslár in Hungary (MG hoard 285 = Huszár 1955, no. CCXXXII) in company with two much earlier deniers of Louis the Pious of the mint of Bourges, more especially since the great Magyar invasion of 937, which provided the Frankish coins for many Hungarian grave-finds, penetrated as far as Berry (Lauer 1900, 21, 23), but not beyond. But it is not likely that a small hamlet so close to Bourges would have been the site of a mint, and Brive in the Limousin seems more likely. The attribution to Charles the Simple and not Charles the Bald is justified by the fabric of the coins and their slightly blundered inscriptions, together with their absence from late 9th-century hoards and the presence of two in a Hungarian grave-find of the second quarter of the 10th century.

1030 This coin, from Muratori onwards, has generally been attributed (cf. *BMC Vand.*, 160) to Duke Gregory of Benevento (732–9), a nephew of King Liutprand. Style and fabric place it in the first half of the 8th century, and exclude other possibilities of the 7th or late 9th century, but the style is not that of Benevento, where a silver coinage was introduced only in the 790s and then on the Frankish model. Giulio Sambon, without giving any reasons, attributed it to Pope Gregory III (731–41), who is in fact the most likely claimant (Sambon 1912, no. 681). The attribution of this coin to a pope is confirmed by the presence of a specimen in a small hoard of about twenty Byzantine silver coins mostly with RM reverses and found in the Tiber at or near Rome which is unpublished at the time of writing. The style is that of the solidi and tremisses of the Roman mint in the second quarter of the 8th century and the portrait is that of the emperor Leo III towards the end of his reign (741) on the same coinage (*DOC* III. 238). The coin is thus technically imperial, and the use of a papal monogram on the reverse an expression of papal claims. But Rome was from the early 730s effectively under papal control, and one may compare this coin with those of the Ostrogothic period, when Theoderic and his successors placed their names or monograms on the silver but not on the gold. The hoard alluded to above also contained coins attributable to Zachary and other popes prior to Pope Adrian.

1031 Adrian I's coins are of two types. The first, of which only three specimens seem to be recorded, has on the obverse a cross-on-steps with HADR|IANVS|PAPA across it, and on the reverse SCI|PET|RI in three lines. The design is an adaptation of that of the contemporary Byzantine silver miliaresion, but the coin is half its size and weight (1.14g, i.e. a *scripulum*). Despite the absence of any reference to the emperor, it is still part of the traditional Roman-Byzantine monetary system and can best be dated 772–81.

Adrian's second coinage is that represented here. The weight (*c.* 1.3g) now corresponds to that of the Frankish denari introduced into Italy in 781. The type is that of the solidus as struck in Rome during much of the 8th century. Late in the reign of Constantine V (741–75) there had even been coins which, like this, had RM (for *Roma*) in the reverse field (*DOC* III, pl. 11.9). The obverse legend retains the DN (*Dominus noster*) of imperial coins, but no satisfactory explanation has been offered for the large I B in the obverse field. As a Greek numeral it is 12, and similar letters in the field were often used in the Byzantine period for indictional or regnal dates, either real or immobilized. Indiction 12 occurred under Adrian I only in 773/4 and 788/9, the first too early and the second too late, and Adrian's twelfth regnal year (783/4) would only be possible if it be taken as immobilized, for no other letters occur. Another possibility is that the letters represent the initials Ἰησοῦς Βασιλεύς ('King Jesus'), for Adrian referred to the 'rule' of Christ, in conjunction with his own pontifical year and the indiction, in dating documents (*DOC* III.90).

1033 This extremely rare coin was attributed to Leo VIII (963–5) by Promis (1858, 91) on the assumption that this pope, intruded into the papacy by Otto I in December 963 and expelled from Rome by John XII in 964, might have caused it to be struck somewhere in the Patrimony and not in Rome itself. This could explain its anomalies in style and fabric if it were indeed of the mid 10th century – the coin is broad and thin, in contrast to the small module and thick fabric of other *antiquiores* of the 960s – but it would not account for the unusual DN preceding LEONI or the omission of Otto's name, which occurs on Leo VIII's other denari and which, since Otto was his main source of support, would not have been omitted wherever his coins were struck. The attribution to Leo VIII though argued at length by Gentili (1890) is in fact unwarranted. Evans pointed out in 1882 that the coin must be one of Leo III struck prior to the coronation of Charlemagne in 800, since there was a specimen in a small hoard of Anglo-Saxon coins found at Delgany, Ireland, and datable to *c.* 830 (Evans 1882; Grierson 1952b; Pagan 1962). This attribution was subsequently confirmed by the presence of three specimens in the Biebrich hoard of 1922 (Völckers 1965, 186, nos. XLII.45–7), whose other contents were coins of Charlemagne and an Arab dirham dated 790/1 and which must date from *c.* 800.

1056 Conventionally attributed to Stephen V and Charles the Fat, though all scholars admit this to be unsatisfactory since the monogram contains neither T nor H, which *Stephanus* should have, and has instead an M that should not be there. But the only pope contemporary with Charlemagne as emperor (800–14) was Leo III, and those of the years covered by Charles the Bald (875–7) and Charles the Fat (881–8) as emperors were John VIII (872–82), Marinus I (882–4), Adrian III (884–5), and Stephen V (885–91). There is no correspondence at all with *Leo* or *Adrianus*, and *Marinus* should not contain an E; even adding *papa* in the genitive (*Marini pape*) would not help matters, for it would eliminate the S that is certainly there. Possibly the monogram stands for an earlier name of one or other of these popes, although the practice of an ecclesiastic changing his name on election as pope is usually believed to have begun only in the 10th century and no previous name for any of them is recorded in the *Liber Pontificalis*. In the absence of any better solution the traditional attribution of the coin to Stephen V is retained here.

1075 This coin is now known only from two fragments, this and a larger one in the former royal collection at Rome (*CNI* XV.99.1), which between them allow the almost complete reading of the rev. inscription as + ALBRCVPRIC . . ., only the final two or three letters (EPS?) being missing. The inscription on a now untraceable third specimen, misread as + HENRICVSIMP, provided the model for a large number of Tardani forgeries. See note on **1.1528**.

1076–7 Scholars have differed as to whether this coin is one of Alberic alone or one of Alberic and Agapitus II, the monogram in the first case being read as PA(*tri*)C(*i*)VS and in the second as AGAP(*it*)VS or, since it seems to begin with a P, as PAPA AGAP(*it*)VS (cf. Gregorovius 1885; Labruzzi 1912). The latter attribution is that of most modern authorities (Serafini, the *CNI*, Muntoni), but the former seems preferable. The letter to the left in the monogram is a C, not a G; an A hidden in the middle of a monogram is unlikely to represent the initial letter of anyone's name; and another type of denaro of Alberic and Agapitus exists with Agapitus' name in full and a monogram of ALBR (Promis 1858, pl. 7.3).

It is possible, however, that *patricius*, though a title applied to Alberic by some contemporaries, may not be the correct interpretation of the monogram, for this seems to imply a word ending in CVS, not CIVS – the suspension stroke between C and V should stand for more than an I – and there is no T or R. A possible reading of PAC-VS should be *pacificus*, qualifying the R (for PR*inceps*) of Alberic's title in the inscription in exactly the same way as a monogram of PIVS had qualified the MP ligatured (for IMP*erator*) that had followed the emperor's name on many earlier coins.

For the dating of these coins to the whole period of Alberic's rule (932–54), and their relationship to his rare joint issues with successive popes, see above p. 265.

1379 Many interpretations of the monogram on this coin have been made, the most commonly adopted being that of Haigh (1870, 31) to Castle Rising, Norfolk, but its attribution must be considered an open question. The reverse shows signs of having been overstruck, with . . . E . . ED . . . of the underlying type visible. This appears from the size of the letters to be the obverse legend of either a 'Two-line' type or an imitative 'London monogram' type. It may even be a second impression from these dies, the coins having been turned over during striking.

1452 A coin of this type was found near Saint-Rémy in Provence in or about the 1830s and attributed by Lagoy, an extremely competent numismatist, to Odovacar, the monogram being read as DN ODOVAC P(*atricius*) or something similar (Lagoy 1843, 7–9, pl. 1.3). Such an attribution is not on the surface very likely. Odovacar's copper and late silver coins have a different monogram (**1.63–4**) and Anastasius came to the throne only in January 491, by which date Odovacar was blockaded by Theoderic in Ravenna. But varying monograms appear on the coins of other rulers of this period, and since Anastasius was ill-disposed towards Theoderic at the opening of his reign – he did not recognize him until 497 – Odovacar might well have tried to curry favour with the emperor by ordering the minting of coins in his name. Certainly the letters in the monogram, especially if the letter on the right of the monogram was an R and not a P – Lagoy's damaged specimen is defective at this point – fit Odovacar's name better than they do that of any other contemporary ruler, or of the later Ostrogothic kings Totila and Theia who reverted to the use of Anastasius' name on their coins. In any event, the coin was reproduced without question in most of the subsequent literature (Friedlaender 1844, 8; Marchant 1851, 140 and pl. 13.3; Sabatier 1862, I.195–6, no. 1, and pl. 18.1; Engel and Serrure 1891–1905, I.24; Sambon 1912, no. 14 and pl. 1.14; *CNI* X, 640, no. 1 and pl. 42.16; Kraus 1928, 57, no. 27 and 60 n. 8), though some scholars were clearly unhappy about the identification (Wroth in *BMC Vand.*, 44 n. 2). Unfortunately the subsequent fate of Lagoy's unique specimen and its present whereabouts are both unknown.

It was presumably in the 1850s or 1860s that it became the basis of Cigoi's forgery. The period in which the existence of the coin became generally known was precisely that at which he was most active, and as a small denomination of the late Empire it was exactly the type of coin he delighted to imitate. He completed the obverse inscription – only DNANA was legible on Lagoy's damaged specimen – though not very intelligently, for there is no PF before AVG, and he also eliminated the exergual line beneath the monogram on the reverse. The Cigoian origin of this specimen, which Grantley believed to be authentic and which Grierson acquired as such, is shown by the presence of two further ones from the same dies in the Museo Civico at Udine (Brunetti 1966, no. 461). The coin here, according to Lord Grantley's coin ticket, came from Kraus, but Kraus does not mention it in his monograph of 1928 and presumably acquired it at some later date.

1479 This coin was acquired as genuine, despite its strange design, dubious appearance, and the doubts expressed by many scholars (e.g. B 4731), very largely because it had a pedigree taking it back by way of the Amécourt and Norblin collections to the 1830s. It is, in fact, false, and can only be understood in the light of two other coins of identical type, one with a normal Latin legend (+ CORNILIO), the other with a partly runic one.

1 2 3

(1) THE CORNILIO COIN

This coin, now in the Hague, has a looped mount and a design similar to **1.1479** but with the legend + CORNILIO on the obverse and + TENESN (T inverted) on the reverse. It weighs 1.40g, including the mount. It was first published by Chalon (1870, 507 and pl. 10.13), who proposed to identify *Cornilio* with Corneillan (Gers), a few miles north of Pau in the northern foothills of the Pyrenees, and interpreted the reverse as *Tenes M(onetarius)*. It was subsequently discussed by Stephens (1866–1901, III, 241–3), who wrongly regarded it as a derivative of the runic coin instead of the other way about, but it was missed by Belfort. There is some confusion about its earlier provenance. Chalon describes it as being in the Leyden cabinet, but it is not listed amongst the coins transferred to The Hague from the Leyden collection in 1881 and 1893, and the coin ticket says that it was bought from S. L. Kuijt on 23 May 1867 (Inventory 17364). Since Kuijt is not otherwise known as a dealer or collector, Dr Zadoks-Jitta told Grierson in 1952, when he examined the coin at The Hague, that it was probably brought in by someone who had found it in Holland. The inventory gives it to Corrèze, in which département there is in fact a locality named Cornil (arr. and cant. Tulle) to which coins of a different type (B 1648 = P 1975), with the inscription CORNILIO CAS, are customarily assigned.

The unusual reverse design must be derived, as de Salis noted, from a late Roman coin showing two emperors or two soldiers, and the somewhat enlarged hands are reminiscent of the greatly enlarged head of the Victory on a late 6th-century coin of Agen (B 3570, misread) of which there was a specimen in the Canterbury (St Martin's) hoard (Grierson 1952c, no. 6). Since unusual coin types are very characteristic of mints in south-western Gaul during the transition from the pseudo-imperial to the 'national' Frankish coinage, Chalon's attribution of the coin to Corneillan is preferable to Cornil, which is near Limoges in central France. The letters on the reverse, though legible, do not form a sensible legend and may be merely decorative, as was sometimes the case with coins of the transitional period before the use of moneyers' names had become firmly established. The coin can be dated to *c.* 580. The loop, the mint location, and the date suggest a link with the Canterbury hoard, which contained a number of looped coins from the same region, and of the same period. The possibility of its being a stray from this hoard cannot be excluded, but the gap of over twenty years between 1844 and 1867 is against it. In any case, the coin is a normal Frankish one of the Merovingian period.

(2) THE RUNIC (ANIWULUFU) COIN

This coin, whose present whereabouts is unknown, was exhibited on 9 November 1732 at a meeting of the Spalding Gentlemen's Society, the oldest antiquarian society in Britain – Spalding is a town in south Lincolnshire – by the Rev. Mr Ray, with the information that it had been found at Folkestone and was 'very thin'. It was again exhibited, by Maurice Johnson (1688–1755), founder and for many years secretary of the Spalding Gentlemen's Society and an excellent numismatist, at a meeting of the Society of Antiquaries on 24 February 1737 (Minute Book). The Spalding Society minute book contains a careful drawing of the coin, and its accuracy is confirmed by various casts that date from the late 18th or early 19th century. There are two in silver in the Ashmolean (Sutherland 1948, 49 n. 4) and one in gold in the British Museum (illus. Sutherland 1942, pl. 2, from a cast furnished earlier to Evans). A silver one in the Timm collection at Copenhagen, which was acquired by the Saxon collector von Römer and passed from him to the Dresden cabinet, was very fully described by C. J. Thomsen in the sale catalogue of the third part of the Timm sale of 27 October 1834 (*Fortegnelse over Georg Friderich Timms udmaerkede mynt- og medaillesamling*, 72, no. 21) and was subsequently illustrated by Worsaae (1851, 419) from an impression made by C. F. Herbst before the coin left Copenhagen. The British Museum one was presented by Count de Salis in 1856, and purported to have been found in England earlier in the century. Although originally believed to be authentic it is now recognized as a cast, which presumably explains its omission from Keary's catalogue in 1887.

There is every reason, however, to accept the authenticity of the lost Spalding specimen; it was indeed confirmed by the discovery of the *Cornilio* coin, for this showed how the runic version came about. Some 6th-century English die-cutter reproduced the details of a *Cornilio* coin with substantial accuracy, though the cloak of the figure on the obverse was transmuted into scale armour, the raised hands of the figures on the reverse were further exaggerated, and the heads of the same figures were grotesquely enlarged and made to look upwards, each being provided with a single huge eye. The lettering on the reverse was miscopied in minor respects – the upper N was reversed, an A was intruded after it, and the NS in the reverse was made I ∽ I. But the obverse inscription was much more drastically altered, for while its beginning and end (+C and ILIO) were retained the intervening ORN was replaced by a runic inscription. This is retrograde, as is often the case with runic coin inscriptions, the die-sinker having cut the letters on the die from left to right as he was accustomed to do (e.g. Sutherland 1948, no. 27). Similar runic intrusions into Latin inscriptions occur occasionally on coins of the late 6th and the 7th centuries, though usually only when the name is too short to make up a full inscription. A comparable case, for the 7th century, is the Pada thrymsa (**1.668–9**).

The attempts of Thomsen and Worsaae to amalgamate the Latin and runic letters on the Timm specimen to read *Cunit i Diefli*, with consequent ascription to an imaginary king Cnut at Dublin, are best forgotten. Haigh read the British Museum coins as ANIWULUFU, assuming that the penultimate letter should have had a second branch (making it F instead of L), an acceptable early form of Anglo-Saxon *Eanwulf* followed by the unexplained final *u* that occurs also on the *Scanomodu* coin in the British Museum (Haigh 1869, 172–4). Stephens preferred to make the penultimate letter a runic K and read ANIWULU KU(*nung*), i.e. 'Anwulf king' (Stephens 1866–91, III, 236–41), but R. I. Page is of the view (*per litteram*) that, if the letters are really runic and not blundered Roman ones, the first reading is preferable. In fact, although the ᚢ (*ur*) could be a badly formed Λ and the ᚫ (*aesc*) an F, the ᚹ (*wynn*) and the ᛚ (*lagu*) can scarcely be anything but runic. We have of course no idea of who Anwulf may have been, or where in southern England the coin was struck, or how far the piece, which must be more or less contemporary with the Liudhard medalet, was intended as a coin. If it was, it is the earliest true Anglo-Saxon coin that we know to have been minted. Although the model for the reverse type was Roman, Haigh and Stephens may well have been correct in believing that the maker of the runic version took the reverse type to represent the traditional ceremony of oath-taking on a ring held jointly by the parties concerned.

(3) THE CADAINDI FORGERY

This coin (B 4731), which was exhibited at a meeting of the British Numismatic Society in 1962 with some account of its history (*BNJ* 31 (1962), 171–2), was acquired from the dealer Hubert Herzfelder in Paris in 1953. Its type is almost identical with that of the runic coin, but the obverse inscription reads + CΛDΛINΔI + ILIO) and on the reverse the inverted T has become a V, the N a ligatured NT, the A has a straight bar rather than a chevron and the exergual letters are INI. In the early 1830s it belonged to Louis Norblin (1781–1854), a landed proprietor at Connantre near Epernay (Marne) who was one of the great collectors of the day. Lelewel described it at the time (Lelewel 1835, I.38) as '(une pièce) de Cadaindilgilio à Vence, (qui) offre deux personnes se tenant par la main (communiquée par M. Norblin)'. Four years later Conbrouse described it again ('VENTA. Profil. *Rev*. CADAM GILGILIO. Croix.'), attributing it doubtfully to Vence? or *Venta Icenorum* ? and characteristically making a muddle of the types (Conbrouse 1839, 53 no. 849). It was not in the Norblin sale (Rollin 2.7.1855) but was at some date prior to 1875 acquired by Amécourt, who read the essential element of the reverse legend as *Venta* and published the coin twice, attributing it on the first occasion to Vannes (*Veneta*) in Britanny (Amécourt

1875, 176) and on the second to Winchester (Amécourt 1883b, 335–41). The second article is accompanied by a meticulous drawing that makes clear the identity of the coin in this collection with the Norblin–Amécourt one, though nothing is known of its history between the dispersal of the Amécourt collection after its owner's death in 1888 and its acquisition by Grierson in 1953.

Although the weight of the coin (1.41g) and its fineness (SG 18.45 : 94% Au) would be acceptable for a triens of the late 6th century, and the coin is struck and not cast, its general aspect arouses suspicion – the 'modern' treatment of the face and eye, the way in which the initial cross of the legend links up with the linear border, the broken, granular edge. But it is the meaningless obverse inscription that mainly condemns it, for it has clearly been reproduced by a die-cutter of the early 19th century who had seen a cast, or more probably a drawing, of the *Aniwulufu* coin and, not realizing that some of the letters were runes, turned them into their nearest acceptable equivalents. ᚢ (*ur*) thus became Λ, the second ᛚ (*lagu*) was given a complete loop to become a D or a P, the ᚹ (*wynn*) became a Δ (*delta*), the ᚾ (*nyd*) a cross, and the ᚫ (*aesc*) an F. The coin is a forgery, and the interpretation of the obverse inscription, together with the localization of VENTA, need no longer trouble scholars.

1481 This forgery combines the obverse design of the 'York' thrymsas (Sutherland 1948, no. 75) with a reverse that has replaced the meaningless inscription of the original with the name of King Eadbald of Kent (616–40). It was first published in a plate of coins, without explanatory text, by Hall (1774, pl. 1.3), and reproduced from this by J. Strutt, *The Chronicle of England* I (London,

1779), pl. 17.2. It has played a role in the dispute over the authenticity of the 'York' thrymsas (*contra:* Metcalf 1961, 102–3; *pro:* Grierson 1962b; the reprint in *DAN*, Addenda, 5–6, publishes this coin). The authenticity of the thrymsas has been subsequently confirmed by metal analysis (Metcalf, Merrick and Hamblin 1968) and by the discovery of a closely related coin, incorporating the same egg-shaped 'head', that was sold by Sotheby 9.10.1979, lot 119, and is now in the BM.

1497 Deniers of the early Carolingian period bearing the name of Milo are of two types, a smaller and presumably earlier one having on the reverse the letters TRE, the T reversed and having the appearance of a P (cf. Prou 1896a, 115–16), the others (P 834) having NRBO in the quarters of a cross. There is no doubt that NRBO stands for *Narbo*, i.e. Narbonne. Since a count Milo was a party to a dispute over some landed property with the archbishop of Narbonne in 782, and was also co-founder of the abbey of Caunes near Carcassonne in *c.* 790, it is reasonable to identify him with the Milo of the coins. One of the Caunes documents shows him to have died before 5 December 791. The TRE of the earlier coin has been doubtfully identified with *Trencianum*, the modern Trausse (Aude, arr. Carcassonne, cant. Peyriac-Minervois), an estate in the neighbourhood of Caunes that belonged to the abbey in the 9th century. The two coins are of exceptional interest as bearing the name of a private person instead of that of Charlemagne, though the late conquest of Septimania from the Muslims (759) and its remoteness from the centre of Carolingian power make the phenomenon easy to understand. The large 19th-century literature on the subject is summed up, albeit discursively, by Amardel (1900, 1902a, 1904).

Forgeries of the coin with NRBO already existed in the 19th century (Morel-Fatio in *RBN* 1867, 379). The specimen in this collection seems to be one, the low relief and weight and the style of lettering being highly suspicious. It was one of a group of ten specimens, ranging in weight from 1.10g to 1.70g, which Grierson was shown by Mme Kapamadji in 1959, and although they were from several different dies, and at the time Grierson believed them to be genuine, he would now find it difficult to accept their authenticity.

1499 The monogram on the rare Ravenna denaro of Charlemagne (P 896; G XII 184; MG 308) of which this is a copy was only explained in 1966. The obverse is of the normal Frankish type introduced in 793/4, with a *Karolus* monogram and Charles' name and Frankish royal title. This is continued on the reverse with his Lombard title and that of Patrician of the Romans (*et Lang' ac Pat' Rom'*) accompanied by the monogram of Charles' name in Greek, ΚΑΡω (sometimes υ) ΛΟC (M. Thompson 1966). The Lombard title points to a mint in Italy and the use of Greek narrows it down to Ravenna, which had been the capital of the Exarchate down to 751 and where Greek was still widely known. Ravenna was formally in papal territory, and it is possible that the coin was struck by Adrian I or Leo III in Charles' honour between 794 and 801. But jurisdiction in the papal state was very uncertain, and it is better to regard it as a royal issue. It would probably have ended in 801, when the papal-imperial coinage started in Rome, for the title of *patricius Romanorum* would have been anomalous after that year.

The forgeries of the coin, of which this is one, are easy to recognize. Quite apart from the poor quality of the silver, the flat surface and shallow relief, and the too-regular pellets in the border, the forger has misunderstood the monogram as one of the mint name RAVE(*nna*), turning the rounded *omega* into a square E and the rounded *sigma* into a right-angled V. The forgery is north Italian in origin and must date from before 1859, when Promis published a specimen in the royal collection at Turin (*CNI* X, 681.1, pl. 43.17) that is from the same dies as this one (Promis 1858, 103–4).

1513 This is one of a group of copper 'coins' of similar design bearing the name in the genitive case of either Pope Gregory III (731–41) or Pope Zachary (741–51), those of Gregory having +/GREII/PAPE on the obverse and +/SCI/PTR on the reverse. They have been known for three centuries, one of Gregory having been published by Papenbroch in 1685 and one of Zachary by Mabillon in 1687, though they only became widely known through their reproduction in Francesco Ficoroni's classic work on ancient seals, *De plumbeis antiquorum numismatibus tam sacris quam profanis* (Rome, 1750). Their simple designs, interesting associations, and enigmatic nature led to their being repeatedly forged. Dies for making both were acquired in 1866 by a collector of papal medals, Luigi Pizzamiglio, in an antique shop at Rome (Caucich 1867) and although these are now safely in the Vatican (Serafini 1910–28, I.323) Pizzamiglio added to a later generation's troubles by using them to make 'strikes' as curiosities for his friends. The imitations are of all sizes – recorded weights range from 0.87g to 11.48g – and may be in lead, silver, or even gold as well as copper, though only copper ones in the 1.5g weight range are dangerous to scholars.

These copper pieces were thought by the earliest writers to have been actual coins, comparable with Byzantine copper folles and their fractions, but later writers have tended to believe that they served as tokens connected with papal charities and refer to them as *tesserae*, a convenient blanket term applicable to any piece of struck metal whose purpose is unknown. A more likely hypothesis, adopted at Grierson's suggestion by Muntoni (1972–4, I.3), is that they were coin-weights (*exagia*). These, in the Byzantine empire, normally bore the names or monograms of eparchs or other magistrates, so that it would have been natural for those made in Rome in the 730s and 740s to bear some papal mark of authorization. The fact of their being known only for Gregory III and Zachary is also easily understandable, for the mint of Rome was quite unprecedentedly active in issuing solidi and tremisses at precisely this period (*DOC* III.87–8, 272–8). Such an explanation falls into line with the fact that several of the better attested specimens weigh about 4.0/4.5g or *c.* 1.5g and would have served for weighing solidi and tremisses respectively.

The proliferation of forgeries and the simplicity of the designs of these *exagia* makes it difficult to determine the authenticity of individual specimens. The one here weighs 1.54g and has lost a chip at its edge that cannot have weighed less than 0.3g, giving it an original weight unacceptably above that of a tremissis. It is possibly a product of Pizzamiglio's dies, but although it corresponds very closely to Serafini's illustration this is not clear enough for one to be sure.

1528 This Tardani forgery, one of at least nine from the same dies that are known, requires explanation, for no genuine coins of Leo IX and Henry III exist (Grierson 1965a). It arose out of an error in Fioravanti's publication of a genuine but poorly preserved specimen of Leo VII and Alberic (936–9), a coin now known only from the fragmentary specimens in this collection (**1.1075**) and in the former royal collection now in the Museo Nazionale at Rome (*CNI* XV, 99.1, pl. 6.38). The obverse was reproduced quite accurately, but the reverse inscription, of which presumably all that was clearly legible was . . .RICV . . ., was reconstructed as +HENRICVS IMP (S sideways and IMP ligatured) instead of +ALBRICVSPRIC. Promis, misled by Fioravanti, reproduced (Promis 1858, pl. 10.1) essentially the same reading from the specimen now at Rome, though what is really legible on this is +ALBRICVP. . . But the erroneous Fioravanti–Promis reading was sufficient to provide Tardani with a model and many major collections with specimens of his forgeries, for there are four in the Vatican, one each in the Berlin, Papadopoli, and Zoppola collections, one here, and several others that have passed through the sale room but whose present whereabouts is unknown. The supposed existence of coins of Leo IX and Henry III has played a role in discussions of papal administrative history (Pflugk–Harttung 1904).

1529 This strange coin, unrelated in fabric and appearance to any others of the period, exists in two forms. One, that represented here, is a thin bracteate struck on only one face while the obverse design appears incuse on the reverse. The other is an ordinary biface coin with the same design in relief on both sides. The two are almost certainly false, and no coins of Paschal II exist. This was the view of Muntoni, who follows the *CNI* in simply omitting them, but since Serafini accepted them and there is no relevant literature such a condemnation has to be justified.

The coin was unknown to Vignoli (1709) and Scilla (1715), the earliest writers on papal coinage. A uniface specimen was first published by Fioravanti, from one in his own collection, in his revised edition of Vignoli (Fioravanti 1734, 98–9). Promis (1858, pl. 10.2) published what seems to be the same specimen, then in the collection of Prince Chigi. This was subsequently acquired by Celati, passed in 1921 to the Vatican, and in 1924 was disposed of by Serafini to Gavazzi either as a duplicate or a forgery. If this pedigree is correct the coin here is identical with Fioravanti's and so presumably unique, but there may well be others. The coin was attributed to the mint of Benevento (Promis 1858, 99) because of the existence of a very similar uniface Beneventan coin having the legend +BENEBENTVS and a monogrammatic design variously interpreted as two keys or as the letters PR linked at the bottom. If the coins were genuine the attribution of Paschal's one to a mint at Benevento would not be unreasonable, for in 1101 the pope, with the help of Roger Borsa, managed to expel its *rector* Anso, who was trying to make himself independent, and thereafter paid repeated visits to the city, often staying for several months at a time.

Uniface coins of this kind can come into existence through faulty striking, for if a coin adheres to the upper die its obverse type becomes a 'reverse' for the next coin to be struck. But the existence of the Beneventan coins shows that the fabric was intentional. Both Paschal's coin and those of Benevento, however, were produced at a moment when German bracteates were first becoming widely known through recent publications by Leuckfeld and Seeländer. These are indeed cited by Fioravanti in 1734 as providing parallels to his coin. Its Beneventan counterparts were not published till thirty years later, in two large works on local Beneventan history (De Vita 1754–64, II. 233–4, 285–6; Borgia 1763–9, II. 285, III. ix note, lvii), but both had been long in preparation and the coins were alleged to have come from a hoard found in 1735. Since this hoard is said to have also contained some north Italian coins of the 10th/11th centuries, some Arab dirhams, and some unidentified coins which the illustration shows to be north German bracteates of the 13/14th centuries, it had, if it ever existed, clearly been 'salted' with extraneous matter. One need not hesitate to follow Sambon in regarding both groups of uniface coins as forgeries (Sambon 1912, nos. 469–70, 772). Both go back to the 1720s or early 1730s and were suggested, like Seeländer's own forgeries in the German series, by the discovery of two major bracteate hoards in the first decades of the 18th century.

The biface coins require less consideration. The 19th-century forger copied the design in Fioravanti, but he did not read the accompanying text carefully enough to understand that the reverse inscription was incuse and in consequence produced a reverse inscription in relief. A number of specimens are known, all from the same dies. One was in the Vidal Quadras collection (no. 11,802), but when offered for sale at the Monnaies des Papes sale (1914), lot 25, it was withdrawn as false. One of the two in the Vatican (Serafini 1910, I.25, nos. 1, 2) reached it in bad company, as part of a hoard alleged to have been found near Ancona which also contained a denaro of Leo IV, four of Nicholas I, and one of Marinus I (Serafini 1910–28, I. lxxvii n. 10). The impossibility of a hoard so extended in time is obvious, and since the coin of Marinus is false one can only assume that the hoard was invented to pass two rare but spurious coins into circulation under the protection of several genuine but relatively common ones of Leo IV and Nicholas I.

CONCORDANCES

I. GRANTLEY COLLECTION WITH *MEC* I

The Grantley coins in this volume came mainly from the second and eighth of the sales of his collection. Lots were numbered continuously (1–4636) through the eleven sales, with varying numbers of coins in each lot. Since Grierson bought the coins subsequently from dealers or at Lockett sale III, and with the exception of a few in the eleventh sale not at the Grantley sales themselves, there is sometimes no exact correspondence between the number of coins in a lot and those in *MEC*, since individual items had already been sold to other collectors. A few coins are known to have come from the Grantley collection but from lots that cannot be precisely identified owing to their having been inadequately described.

The left hand column in the table is that of the Grantley lots, the figures in parentheses giving the number of relevant coins (i.e. those falling within the scope of *MEC* I) that each contained.

lot	*MEC*
1st sale (29.11.1943)	
187 (1)	407
189 (1)	751
2nd sale (27.1.1944)	
608 (1)	419
611 (1)	502
615 (1)	493
616 (1)	492
617 (1)	455
621 (1)	521
622 (14)	547, 549, 551–4, 556, 558–9, 564, 566
623 (12)	543–4, 545–6, 577–8
624 (2)	509
625 (6)	542, 569, 575–6, 629
626 (2)	571, 613
627 (2)	460
629 (7)	591, 600–2, 631
630 (4)	570, 586, 612, 617
632 (1)	501
633 (2)	500
634 (3)	466, 608, 615
642 (1)	486
643 (1)	530
644 (1)	535
646 (1)	469
647 (1)	505
648 (2)	524
649 (3)	528
650 (3)	363, 491, 531
651 (3)	523
654 (7)	507–8, 510–11, 512–14
653 (3)	522
655 (3)	538
656 (3)	372, 487, 529
658 (3)	382, 527
660 (3)	463, 488, 504
661 (2)	518
662 (3)	386–7, 533
664 (2)	536–7
666 (3)	367, 369–70
667 (3)	358, 375, 379
669 (3)	365, 376, 383
671 (3)	517, 519, 520
673 (2)	385
674 (2)	506
675 (2)	380, 532
Uncertain Merovingian lots, 353, 384, 388, 391, 420, 515–16, 525–6, 566, 606, 634–5	
677 (13)	588, 590, 616, 630
678 (21)	580–1, 583–5, 587, 593, 611, 619–20, 624, 628, 1478
685 (3)	716
731 (9)	579, 582, 621, 623, 632, 639, 641–2, 689
736 (3)	589, 688

lot	*MEC*
736 (3)	637
740 (1)	618
741 (2)	670–1
742 (2)	689–90
745 (2)	605
746 (6)	627, 1480–1
748 (1)	669
754 (1)	708
Uncertain AS lot 645	
7th sale (25.7.1944)	
2772 (3)	1
2773 (5)	34, 52
2774 (4)	6, 8, 18
2775 (2)	24
2776 (1)	26
2777 (20)	30
2781 (1)	1452
2782 (1)	180
2785 (3)	124
2786 (12)	132, 295
2787 (4)	1454
2789 (7)	110, 164
2791 (2)	459
2793 (1)	341
2794 (1)	202
2799 (1)	268
2800 (1)	269
2804 (1)	288
2805 (1)	289
2807 (1)	299
2808 (1)	298
2810 (1)	307
2821 (1)	1030
2827 (1)	1102
2828 (4)	1121
2829 (1)	1108
2830 (2)	1110, 1112
8th sale (25.10.1944)	
2843 (1)	720
2845 (1)	722
2846 (1)	724
2848 (3)	728
2849 (1)	735
2851 (2)	733, 741
2852 (2)	766–7
2853 (1)	770
2855 (1)	772
2856 (3)	762, 775, 777
2861 (2)	787–8
2865 (1)	842
2866 (6)	740, 839, 856–7, 914, 991
2868 (7)	861–5
2869 (5)	872
2871 (7)	875, 934, 938, 963–4
2872 (4)	835, 877, 880, 882
2875 (2)	845, 897
2876 (4)	888
2877 (5)	899–900, 903, 905
2878 (3)	834, 906
2879 (2)	824
2884 (9)	792, 797, 801–3, 846–8
2886 (5)	974, 980
2889 (2)	833, 997
2891 (1)	1005
2892 (1)	1006
2893 (1)	1004
3031 (9)	990
3032 (10)	907
3072 (*c.* 10)	933, 945, 948, 957, 961
3192 (1)	743
3193 (6)	794
3194 (1)	821
3195 (7)	1118
3196 (1)	1012
3197 (1)	1017
3255 (1)	1473
3267 (1)	1063
3268 (1)	1521
9th sale (8.12.1944)	
3409 (1)	1014
10th sale (7.2.1945)	
4219 (1)	378
11th sale (26.4.1945)	
4559 (3)	539–40, 607

2. *SCBI* CAMBRIDGE WITH *MEC* 1

This does not include the Ancient British (Celtic) coins in *SCBI* Cambridge, since these do not fall within the scope of *MEC*. Coins in *SCBI* from Athelstan (924–39) onwards will come in *MEC* 8.

SCBI	*MEC*
217	665
218	667
219	668
220	669
221	680
222	675
223	672
224	676
225	677
226	681
227	674
228	673

SCBI	MEC	SCBI	MEC	SCBI	MEC
229	678	272	1183	315	1237
230	679	273	1184	316	1235
231	640	274	1185	317	1233
232	685	275	1186	318	1229
233	686	276	1187	319	1230
234	709	277	1188	320	1231
235	714	278	1199	321	1238
236	715	279	1203	322	1242
237	661	280	1205	323	1240
238	650	281	1204	324	1239
239	652	282	1202	325	1241
240	659	283	1189	326	1243
241	646	284	1192	327	1250
242	651	285	1190	328	1249
243	647	286	1191	329	1244
244	656	287	1194	330	1245
245	658	288	1193	331	1248
246	653	289	1195	332	1246
247	654	290	1196	333	1247
248	717	291	1197	334	1252
249	683	292	1208	335	1253
250	682	293	1207	336	1254
251	684	294	1483	337	1255
252	695	295	1484	338	1256
253	694	296	1209	339	1257
254	697	297	1210	340	1258
255	698	298	1217	341	1259
256	702	299	1218	342	1260
257	703	300	1219	343	1261
258	691	301	1220	344	1264
259	692	302	1222	345	1262
260	693	303	1214	346	1273
261	664	304	1215	347	1265
262	718	305	1213	348	1266
263	704	306	1224	349	1267
264	705	307	1225	350	1268
265	706	308	1221	351	1269
266	1180	309	1226	352	1274
267	1181	310	1223	353	1270
268	1200	311	1227	354	1271
269	1201	312	1228	355	1272
270	1482	313	1234	356	1251
271	1182	314	1236	357	1275

SCBI	MEC
358	1276
359	1277
360	1278
361	1279
362	1280
363	1281
364	1282
365	1283
366	1290
367	1289
368	1286
369	1288
370	1287
371	1284
372	1285
373	1291
374	1298
375	1299
376	1293
377	1292
378	1294
379	1295
380	1296
381	1301
382	1300
383	1302
384	1303
385	1304
386	1123
387	1124
388	1125
389	1126
390	1127
391	1128
392	1129
393	1130
394	1131
395	1134
396	1132
397	1137
398	1147
399	1150
400	1151

SCBI	MEC
401	1145
402	1149
403	1146
404	1169
405	1170
406	1167
407	1168
408	1325
409	1326
410	1327
411	1328
412	1329
413	1330
414	1333
415	1319
416	1334
417	1335
418	1336
419	1337
420	1331
421	1339
422	1316
423	1318
424	1321
425	1317
426	1323
427	1324
428	1122
429	1136
430	1141
431	1142
432	1143
433	1144
434	1156
435	1133
436	1135
437	1140
438	1148
439	1152
440	1153
441	1154
442	1155
443	1315

SCBI	MEC
444	1161
445	1162
446	1353
447	1369
448	1171
449	1172
450	1173
451	1174
452	1175
453	1177
454	1178
455	1179
456	1387
457	1392
458	1403
459	1393
460	1398
461	1390
462	1388
463	1389
464	1391
465	1394
466	1400
467	1401
468	1402
469	1399
470	1396
471	1397
472	1408
473	1409
474	1410
475	1411
476	1412
477	1413
478	1414
479	1415
480	1416
481	1417
482	1418
483	1419
484	1420
485	1421
486	1422

SCBI	MEC
487	1423
488	1424
489	1425
490	1426
491	1427
492	1428
493	1429
494	1439
495	1430
496	1431
497	1432
498	1433
499	1434
500	1435
501	1436
502	1437
503	1438
504	1406
505	1407
506	1405
507	1404
508	1441
509	1440
510	1444
511	1445
512	1446
513	1442
514	1443
515	1447
516	1450
517	1448
518	1449
519	1451
520	1158

SCBI	MEC
521	1159
522	1160
523	1157
524	1166
525	1163
526	1165
527	1495
528	1306
529	1305
530	1307
531	1308
532	1309
533	1310
534	1311
535	1312
536	1313
537	1314
538	1342
539	1343
540	1344
541	1341
542	1345
543	1350
544	1355
545	1358
546	1356
547	1357
548	1354
549	1359
550	1379
551	1362
552	1363
553	1365
554	1366

SCBI	MEC
555	1383
556	1367
557	1385
558	1384
559	1361
560	1360
561	1380
562	1381
563	1386
564	1376
565	1374
566	1377
567	1378
568	1371
569	1372
983	660
984	1485
985	1486
986	1487
987	1488
988	1489
989	1493
990	1138
991	1494
992	1496

There are five coins which were included in *SCBI* (20) R. P. Mack Collection:

SCBI	MEC
321	696
339	700
327	707
362	716
574	1134A

INDEXES

Ordinary type indicates pages, bold type catalogue entries.

Additional abbreviations used in indexes:

abp	archbishop	comm.	commune
arr.	arrondissement	dép.	département
bp	bishop	nr	near
cant.	canton	prov.	province

MONEYERS REPRESENTED IN THE CATALOGUE

The names are indexed in the nominative form, but otherwise they have been normalized only where they are seriously blundered. Variants of the same name are gathered under one entry. Where the form on the coin differs from the main entry this is shown in parentheses.

HOARDS AND SINGLE-FINDS REPRESENTED IN THE CATALOGUE

References are to coin numbers in the catalogue. Entries in this index represent single-finds unless specifically described as a hoard. For finds cited in the text, see the General index.

GENERAL INDEX

This index covers mainly personal names, place-names and names of peoples. These are given in the forms and spellings most familiar in English, with cross-references where the Latin or other forms used at the time, or those current today, diverge appreciably from these.

Denominations, legends, types and other features are indexed only when they are exceptional (e.g obols, DN DS REX, graffiti, peck-marks). Only approximate localizations are given for familiar place-names easily found in any map or gazetteer, but for smaller localities more detailed indications are provided. Names of moneyers and find-spots are included only where these appear in the text; for those in the catalogue of coins, see the separate indices. Entries in the section Collectors, Dealers and Donors are not indexed.

Made in the USA
Monee, IL
14 September 2026

63198304R00387